Cour Permanente de Justice Internationale.

COMITÉ CONSULTATIF DE JURISTES.

Permanent Court of International Justice.

ADVISORY COMMITTEE OF JURISTS.

PROCÈS-VERBAUX

DES

SÉANCES DU COMITÉ

16 JUIN—24 JUILLET 1920

AVEC

ANNEXES.

PROCÈS-VERBAUX

OF THE

PROCEEDINGS OF THE COMMITTEE

JUNE 16TH—JULY 24TH 1920

WITH

ANNEXES.

With a new introduction by Jörg Kammerhofer

THE LAWBOOK EXCHANGE, LTD.
Clark, New Jersey

ISBN 978-1-58477-693-2

Lawbook Exchange edition 2006, 2017

The quality of this reprint is equivalent to the quality of the original work.

The Lawbook Exchange, Ltd.
33 Terminal Avenue
Clark, New Jersey 07066-1321

Please see our website for a selection of our other publications and fine facsimile reprints of classic works of legal history:
www.lawbookexchange.com

Library of Congress Cataloging-in-Publication Data

League of Nations. Advisory Committee of Jurists for the Establishment of a Permanent Court of International Justice.
Procès-verbaux of the proceedings of the Committee, June 16th-July 24th 1920, with annexes = Procès-verbaux des séances du Comité, 16 juin-24 juillet 1920, avec annexes / introduction by Jorg Kammerhofer.
p. cm.
Originally published: The Hague : Van Langenhuysen Brothers, 1920.
Includes bibliographical references and index.
ISBN-13: 978-1-58477-693-2 (alk. paper)
ISBN-10: 1-58477-693-5 (alk. paper)
1. Permanent Court of International Justice--History--Sources. 2. International Court of Justice--History--Sources. 3. International Courts--History. I. Title. II. Title: Procès-verbaux des séances du Comité, 16 juin-24 juillet 1920, avec annexes.

KZ6260.L43 2005
341.5'52--dc22 2006002453

Printed in the United States of America on acid-free paper

INTRODUCTION

Jörg Kammerhofer*

Between 16 June and 24 July 1920 ten highly respected men held 35 meetings in the Peace Palace in The Hague to draft a statute for a Permanent Court of International Justice (PCIJ). The present work is a reprint of the *procès-verbaux* of these sessions, including annexes. This introduction aims to demonstrate how very important these proceedings are for our understanding of the Statute of the PCIJ and its successor, the International Court of Justice (ICJ). After a short historical overview I shall tackle the following questions: In what ways can the *procès-verbaux* be useful for today's international lawyer interpreting the ICJ Statute? What can they teach us about the state of international legal scholarship in 1920? How did these ten men influence the perception of international law in later generations? What are the limitations of the *procès-verbaux* in our quest to cognise positive international law? I will also ask what they can*not* tell us.

1. The History of the Court's Statute[1]

Article 14 of the Covenant of the League of Nations provided that "The Council shall formulate and submit to the Members of the League for adoption plans for the establishment of a Permanent Court of International Justice." Accordingly, on 12 February 1920 the Council of the League decided to invite twelve individuals[2] to form a committee to prepare plans and to report to the Council. The ten men[3] who finally met at The Hague on 15 June 1920[4] were statesmen, scholars and diplomats; sev-

---

* Mag. iur. (Vienna), LL.M. (Cantab). I would like to thank Christian Tams and Wolfram Karl for their generous support.

1 Antonio Sánchez de Bustamante y Sirvén, La Cour Permanente de Justice Internationale (1925) 96-113; Alexander P. Fachiri, The Permanent Court of International Justice. Its constitution, procedure and work, (2nd ed. 1932) 1-10; Manley O. Hudson, The Permanent Court of International Justice 1920-1942. A treatise (1943) 113-129.

2 Six of these declined the opportunity. Later four others were invited to serve.

3 *Infra* at III.

4 Ole Spiermann, 'Who attempts too much does nothing well': The 1920 Advisory Committee of Jurists and the Statute of the Permanent Court of International Justice, 73 British Yearbook of International Law 2002 (2003) 187-260 at 192-193.

eral had participated in the Hague Conferences of 1899 and 1907, where the Permanent Court of Arbitration was created and modified and at whose seat in the Peace Palace they convened. Other members had participated in the many private plans to draft a statute for such a court.

The Legal Section of the Permanent Secretariat of the League had prepared a memorandum detailing the various questions that were likely to come up and answers to the various schemes already proposed.[5] It also contained an appendix with an interpretation of Articles 12-15 of the Covenant,[6] a very important task for deciding the nature and competence of the new court, bound as it was to the authorising provisions of the Covenant.

The Advisory Committee of Jurists, as it was now known, took less than six weeks to come up with a draft. The 35 official meetings (and a small number of unofficial meetings, which were not recorded)[7] were spent in a most curious way that is likely to baffle the modern reader familiar with the contemporary questions of ICJ-Statute interpretation. The table infra demonstrates how the Committee's time was spent.

Wednesday, 16 June 1920	1st meeting	Public opening
Thursday, 17 June 1920	2nd meeting	General discussion: organisation of the work, nature of the Court
Friday, 18 June 1920	3rd meeting	
Saturday, 19 June 1920	4th meeting	Organisation of the Court: mode of election of judges
Monday, 21 June 1920	5th meeting	
Tuesday, 22 June 1920	6th meeting	
Wednesday, 23 June 1920	7th meeting	
Thursday, 24 June 1920	8th meeting	
Friday, 25 June 1920	9th meeting	

[5] Advisory Committee of Jurists, Documents presented to the Committee relating to existing plans for the establishment of a Permanent Court of International Justice (1920) 1-120. The schemes themselves had been attached as annexes to the memorandum.

Friday, 25 June 1920 Saturday, 26 June 1920 Tuesday, 29 June 1920 Wednesday, 30 June 1920 Thursday, 1 July 1920	9th meeting 10th meeting 11th meeting 12th meeting 13th meeting	Competence of the Court: jurisdiction
Thursday, 1 July 1920 Friday, 2 July 1920 Saturday, 3 July 1920	13th meeting 14th meeting 15th meeting	Competence of the Court: law to be applied *qua* sources of law
Saturday, 3 July 1920	15th meeting	Procedure of the Court
Monday, 5 July 1920 Tuesday, 6 July 1920 Wednesday, 7 July 1920 Thursday, 8 July 1920 Friday, 9 July 1920 Saturday, 10 July 1920 Monday, 12 July 1920 Tuesday, 13 July 1920 Wednesday, 14 July 1920	16th meeting 17th meeting 18th meeting 19th meeting 20th meeting 21st meeting 22nd meeting 23rd meeting 24th meeting	Organisation of the Court: general discussion (again mostly mode of election of judges)
Wednesday, 14 July 1920	24th meeting	Competence of the Court: general discussion
Monday, 19 July 1920	25th meeting 26th meet-	First reading: organisation of the Court

[6] Documents I (1920) *supra* note 5 at 112-119.

	ing	
Monday, 19 July 1920	27th meeting	First reading: competence of the Court
Tuesday, 20 July 1920	28th meeting	First reading: procedure of the Court
Tuesday, 20 July 1920 Wednesday, 21 July 1920	29th meeting 30th meeting	First reading: reserved articles
Thursday, 22 July 1920	31st meeting	Second reading
Friday, 23 July 1920	32nd meeting	Signing of the *avant-projet*
Friday, 23 July 1920 Saturday, 24 July 1920	32nd meeting 33rd meeting 34th meeting	Reading of de Lapradelle's report on the *avant-projet*
Saturday, 24 July 1920	35th meeting	Public termination of work

The importance of the four substantive topics has changed between 1920 and 2006: (1) The Committee spent a vast amount of time resolving the question of the election of judges, while in contemporary practice electing the ICJ's judges is not problematic. The reason for the Committee's attention to this question is that in 1907 the Draft Convention on the Court of Arbitral Justice had failed largely because the nomination procedure could not be resolved.[8] The ingenious solution – attributed to Elihu Root – that transpired in the Statute of the PCIJ in part allows this process to be so unproblematic today. The Committee by its efforts seemed to have contributed to defusing one of the core problems of a permanent tribunal. (2) The Courts' jurisdiction, on the other hand, remains a thorny issue, but the emphasis has changed (Section 3.1). (3) The discussion on Article 38[9] (Article 35 of the *avant-projet* produced by the Committee) has also shifted from the law the Court ought to apply in finding its judgments to the abstract level of what sources there are in international law

[7] *Infra* at 331.

[8] Spiermann (2003) *supra* note 4 at 201-202.

[9] Articles without source refer to the Statute of the International Court of Justice as valid today.

(Section 3.2). (4) The procedure the Court ought to follow, on the other hand, was hardly discussed at all in the meetings of the Committee. The text they arrived at in the *avant-projet* was largely identical with Chapter IV (Articles 29-51 of the Draft) of the so-called "Five Powers project"[10] which, in turn, is based largely on the 1907 Draft Convention mentioned *supra*:

> The PRESIDENT [Baron Descamps] opened the discussion on the rules of procedure. He said that it had been proposed to take the project of the Five Powers as the basis for the discussion. ... He pointed out that as a matter of fact the text of the project of the Five Powers, only reproduced, with some modifications, the rules of procedure of the Convention of 1907.[11]

Today, however, scholarly debate on the Statute centres primarily on issues of procedure, e.g. the nature of provisional measures (Article 41), Section 3.3, or the intervention of third parties (Article 62).

After the Committee had transmitted its *avant-projet* and de Lapradelle's report to the Council of the League, it went through a series of modifications, first by the Council at its Brussels session in October 1920, then by the Assembly. The Third Committee of the League Assembly formed a sub-committee and both it and this sub-committee considered and modified the *avant-projet inter alia* in the light of responses by member states.[12] The text was presented as a Protocol of Signature on 16 December 1920 and entered into force on 1 September 1921.[13]

2. The Relevance of the *Procès-Verbaux* Today

The *procès-verbaux* of the Advisory Committee of Jurists are by far the single most important document on the establishment of either the PCIJ or the ICJ. Furthermore, since "the establishment of the Permanent Court has been seen by many as a watershed",[14] one cannot but agree with Ole

[10] Documents I (1920) *supra* note 5 at 312-321.
[11] *Infra* at 338-339; for a synoptical comparison of the procedural provisions by Elihu Root see *infra* at 347-350.
[12] League of Nations, Documents concerning the action taken by the Council of the League of Nations under Article 14 of the Covenant and the adoption by the Assembly of the Statute of the Permanent Court (not including material collected for, or the minutes of, the Advisory Committee of Jurists) (1921); Hudson (1943) *supra* note 1 at 118-129.
[13] Hudson (1943) *supra* note 1 at 128.
[14] Spiermann (2003) *supra* note 4 at 189.

Spiermann that "the proceedings of the Advisory Committee [are] a critical point in the development of international dispute settlement."[15] This section will deal with the present-day relevance and limits of the *procès-verbaux* by raising several issues.

First, there are limits to what a *procès-verbal* can tell us. As a category, such a form of record is limited because it is only a summary of what the speaker said. Since it is not a verbatim record many nuances may elude us, not only because of the condensed format, but also because of its digested nature. Another person (from the Secretariat) interprets what the speaker said and we are left with that interpretation, rather than the original speech. The usual practice of allowing speakers to alter their part of the *procès-verbal* after the session is also prone to abuse. Despite the President's restriction "to slight alterations",[16] Åke Hammarskjöld, the Deputy Secretary-General of the Committee, wrote "that members of a committee, when they see in the *procès-verbaux* what they have said, wish that they had said something else, write down this something and have it inserted".[17]

There is also no denying that this form of summary and corrected record presents a somewhat idealised form of the debates in the Committee and fails to tell us about its internal wrangling and politics. In a 2003 paper in the *British Yearbook of International Law*, Spiermann attempted to enrich the idealised picture one gets when reading the *procès-verbaux* by referring to confidential and frank reports made by Hammarsjköld. While of immense importance, such an attempt, basing itself, as it does, on one man's personal opinion, will not be able to present a balanced picture and thus has to be taken as much *cum grano salis* as the *procès-verbaux* itself.

Second, the *procès-verbaux* are not the only *travaux préparatoires* of the statutes of the PCIJ and ICJ and one has to query its status within the various documents. The published *travaux préparatoires* of the PCIJ Statute consist of three volumes, of which the *procès-verbaux* are the second. The first volume contains the Memorandum presented to the members of the Committee by the Legal Section of the Permanent Secretariat of the League, which, as mentioned *supra*, also contains the various proposals drafted by states, organisations and private individuals.[18] The third vol-

---

[15] Spiermann (2003) *supra* note 4 at 189.

[16] *Infra* at 117.

[17] Spiermann (2003) *supra* note 4 at 191, who is to be commended for having published, if only fragmentarily, the once confidential reports made by Hammarskjöld to the Permanent Secretariat of the League of Nations on the progress of the Committee's work.

[18] Documents I (1920) *supra* note 5.

ume is a collection of documents relating to the Committee's *avant-projet* after it had left the Committee's hands. It contains the Council and the Assembly's deliberations on the *avant-projet*. It shows how the *avant-projet* became the PCIJ Statute.[19] In a wider context the *travaux préparatoires* of the 1899 and 1907 Hague Conferences, the 1929 amendment to the PCIJ Statute and the Conference of San Francisco 1945 are also relevant.

What status do the *procès-verbaux* have? They are arguably the single most important document of those mentioned above. As I have noted *supra*, the Committee lacked the political clout of the League Council and Assembly. Indeed, its deliberations and de Lapradelle's report seem a bit like an International Law Commission (ILC) report in relation to the *travaux préparatoires* of the diplomatic conference to draft the convention the ILC had been working on before. And its expert opinion at times seems "spoiled" by the diplomatic wrangling, by the "package deals" and the *dilatorische Formelkompromisse* (dilatory compromise formulas), to use Carl Schmitt's terminology. On first glance it seems that the opinions of these ten men do not matter much in relation to the "true" diplomatic *travaux préparatoires*. But this impression is quickly dispelled once one compares the results of the Committee's deliberations and of the Statute in its various manifestations.

Third, despite these fundamental reservations it can be argued that the *procès-verbaux* truly are the premier document for historical interpretation of either Statute.[20] If one compares the *avant-projet* and the Statute(s) article by article, one will find that the Committee's text is often only *linguistically*–but not *substantially*–removed from the current text: "it remains the basis and contains, broadly speaking, the system of the Court as actually set up."[21] The League deliberations and the San Francisco Conference for the most part effected only drafting changes. Again, most provisions of the *avant-projet* are *substantially identical to the Statute of the International Court of Justice;* a number is wholly identical.[22]

Despite being thrice removed from the current ICJ Statute, a close inspection of the texts compels one to agree with Spiermann:

---

[19] Documents II (1921) *supra* note 12.

[20] We shall leave aside the question of the value of historical interpretation within the 'canon of interpretation' in international law (cf. Article 32 Vienna Convention on the Law of Treaties 1969).

[21] Fachiri (1932) *supra* note 1 at 3.

[22] Articles 6, 11, 15, 44, 48, 52, 56, 58, 60 and 64.

> Its draft-scheme has remained the backbone of the Statute of ... the International Court of Justice. A study of the work of the Advisory Committee ... may produce insights relevant to the International Court of Justice and the interpretation of its present Statute.[23]

The issue, then, in evaluating the usefulness of the *procès-verbaux* is not whether the *avant-projet* and the ICJ Statute match in form, but whether the process of getting to the *avant-projet* is helpful for understanding the various statutes of the two courts. And here is the major advantage of the *procès-verbaux*: only here can we find a scholarly debate on the draft *by the people who drafted it*. Nearly all earlier or later commentary is either scholarly but un-authoritative, or authoritative but merely diplomatic and political, or neither. There are exceptions of course, primarily the *procès-verbaux* of the sub-committee of the Third Committee of the Assembly[24] – where five of the ten members of the Committee again served[25] – but the Advisory Committee's work surpasses theirs by being the author of the draft that was discussed later. Again, the Committee found itself in a similar position to the ILC by drafting a convention and, just as its deliberations and commentary are accorded special importance amongst the *travaux préparatoires* today, we should regard the Committee's deliberations in a similar manner.

3. The Varying Usefulness of the *Procès-Verbaux*: Articles 36, 38 and 41 Contrasted

An example of the care one needs to take in using the *procès-verbaux* – despite their importance – may be furnished by a comparison of the drafting histories of Article 36, on jurisdiction, Article 38, on the applicable law, and Article 41, on provisional measures.

3.1 Article 36 – Important Change Amid Weighty Consideration

The Committee discussed the matter of the Court's jurisdiction at length.[26] The basis of its discussion was the relation between Article 14 of the Covenant, which reads in part, "[t]he Court shall be competent to

---

23 Spiermann (2003) *supra* note 4 at 190; Ole Spiermann, Historical introduction, in: Andreas Zimmermann *et al.* (eds), The statute of the International Court of Justice. A commentary (2006) at MN 50.

24 Documents II (1921) *supra* note 12 at 82-203.

25 Hudson (1943) *supra* note 1 at 119.

26 *Infra* at 204-293.

hear and determine any dispute of an international character which the parties thereto submit to it." and Article 13(2):

> Disputes as to the interpretation of a treaty, as to any question of international law, as to the existence of any fact which if established would constitute a breach of any international obligation, or as to the extent and nature of the reparation to be made for any such breach, are declared to be among those which are generally suitable for submission to arbitration or judicial settlement.

It is not important to discuss the course of the Committee's deliberations in detail; it is enough to note the result: Article 34 of the *avant-projet* gave the Court compulsory jurisdiction. Any member of the League of Nations could bring a case against another concerning the questions in *lit. a-e* of the article[27] without either party having to consent to the Court's jurisdiction other than by being a member of the League. Arturo Ricci-Busatti and Mineichiro Adatci, on the other hand, wanted to follow the traditional scheme of arbitration with a *compromis*, or at least individual consent to jurisdiction for every dispute.[28] Not only was this a dispute about the interpretation of Article 14 of the Covenant, but also one on how well compulsory jurisdiction would be received by states (presumably not well).

The stroke of genius, the compromise that is now Article 36, was achieved during the deliberations of the Assembly's Third Committee. Raoul Fernandes, who had already been a member of the Advisory Committee, had re-introduced an idea for the "optional clause"[29] that now allows states to agree to accept the jurisdiction of the Court in general without consenting to specific disputes, but with the possibility of putting in reservations to their declaration. Thus, while the *procès-verbaux* remain important, the matter is regulated differently in the Statutes than in the *avant-projet*, and the weight of the discussion of the Court's jurisdiction has shifted to the optional clauses.[30]

3.2 Article 38 – Little Change and Important Deliberations

---

[27] *Lit. a-d* were mentioned in Article 13(2) of the Covenant.

[28] Spiermann (2003) *supra* note 4; *infra* at 541-543.

[29] Spiermann (2003) *supra* note 4 at 250; Hudson (1943) *supra* note 1 at 192-193; Institut für ausländisches öffentliches Recht und Völkerrecht (ed.), Statut et règlement de la Cour Permanente de Justice Internationale. Éléments d'interprétation (1934) 253-255.

[30] John Collier, Vaughan Lowe, The settlement of disputes in international law: institutions and procedures (1999) 140-155.

In contrast, the Committee's ideas for what is now Article 38 remain valid. Indeed, the article has changed little over the years. Nearly three sessions were devoted to discussing the applicable law for the proposed court[31] and, despite some confusion with the issue of the Court's jurisdiction, the *procès-verbaux* contains as thorough a debate as is possible in this format. The debate shows us (*a*) that the issue was to define the applicable law for the Court, not to enumerate the sources of positive international law, as this article is often thought to.[32] The Committee's explicit admission of rules other than positive law to be applied by the Court shows that the enumeration in Article 38 is not meant to be a list of sources of positive law. (*b*) The result of the Commission's labours on this point is a highly positivistic construct that, paradoxically, emerged from openly natural-lawyerly discourse. Natural law positivised is positive law,[33] yet the Commission thought there was more to international law than positive rules.[34] (*c*) The 'general principles of law recognised by civilised nations' in Article 35(3) of the *avant-projet* were intended not as source of positive law, but as gap-filler to avoid the dreaded *non liquet*. The Commission as a whole thought that the Court was prohibited from

---

[31] *Infra* at 293-338, 584.

[32] R. S. Pathak calls it the '*repository* of those sources'. R.S. Pathak, The general theory of the sources of contemporary international law, 19 Indian Journal of International Law (1979) 483-495 at 484 (emphasis mine); Gennady M. Danilenko, The theory of international customary law, 31 German Yearbook of International Law (1988) 9-47 at 17 ('is at present incorporated into treaty law by Art. 38'); Rudolf Bernhardt, Ungeschriebenes Völkerrecht, 36 Zeitschrift für ausländisches öffentliches Recht und Völkerrecht (1976) 50-76 at 64; Antonio Cassese, International law (2001) 149; Jonathan Charney, International lawmaking – article 38 of the ICJ statute reconsidered, in: Jost Delbrück (ed.), New trends in international lawmaking – international 'legislation' in the public interest (1997) 171-191 at 174; Ulrich Fastenrath, Lücken im Völkerrecht. Zu Rechtscharakter, Quellen, Systemzusammenhang (1991) 88-89; Peter Fischer, Heribert Franz Köck, Allgemeines Völkerrecht (4th ed. 1994) 35; Gerald G. Fitzmaurice, Some problems regarding the formal sources of international law, in: F.M. van Asbeck *et al.* (eds), Symbolae Verzijl. Présentées au Prof. J.H.W. Verzijl á l'occasion de son LXX-ième anniversaire (1958) 153-176 at 173; Malcolm N. Shaw, International law (4th ed. 1997) 55; Hugh Thirlway, International Customary Law and Codification (1972) 36; Michel Virally, The sources of international law, in: Max Sørensen (ed.), Manual of public international law (1968) 116-174 at 122.

[33] Hans Kelsen, Naturrecht und positives Recht. Eine Untersuchung ihres gegenseitigen Verhältnisses, 2 Internationale Zeitschrift für Theorie des Rechts (1927) 71-94, in: Hans Klecatsky, René Marcić, Herbert Schambeck (eds), Die Wiener rechtstheoretische Schule. Ausgewählte Schriften von Hans Kelsen, Adolf Julius Merkl, Alfred Verdross (1968) 215-244.

[34] Spiermann (2006) *supra* note 23 at MN 14.

pronouncing a *non liquet* for lack of law,[35] which they held to be a distinct possibility if only treaties and custom were consulted by the Court. Dissent only came from Ricci-Bussati, who held that *non liquet* could be avoided by declaring "that one party has no right against the other, that the conduct of the accused State was not contrary to any admitted rule."[36] The Commission's debates are thus highly relevant, and highly topical, today.

3.3 Article 41 – Little Change, But Ominous Silence

The article empowering the Court to "suggest" provisional measures, in contrast, was not seriously debated in the official meetings of the Committee. ("Suggest" was later replaced with "indicate"; the French version uses "*indiquer*" throughout.) The few references to "provisional measures" in the *procès-verbaux*[37] indicate that the clause was apparently included in the text of Chapter III submitted to the Advisory Committee by its Drafting Committee on 19 July 1920,[38] but they do not relate to how that provision came to be inserted. Apparently the members of the Committee had discussed this at an unofficial meeting. Fernandes proposed a slight amendment on 20 July 1920, which did refer to the so-called Bryan treaties as the origin of his proposal, and which was closer to the original in the treaties mentioned,[39] but the amendment was not adopted. De Lapradelle's report also mentions the Bryan treaties as the genesis of the provisions,[40] but it is doubtful whether – due to the different nature of the "protective measures" there – that one can usefully refer to the *travaux préparatoires* of these treaties for a historical interpretation on this point.

The issue of the binding nature *vel non* of provisional measures came up for decision in the recent *LaGrand* case before the International Court of Justice. In that case, the present Court did "not consider it necessary to resort to the preparatory work in order to determine the meaning of that Article".[41] In 1920 de Lapradelle was convinced that "[t]there is no ques-

---

[35] *Infra* at 311 (per Loder), 312 (per de Lapradelle).

[36] *Infra* at 314; Hans Kelsen, Reine Rechtslehre (2nd ed. 1960) 252.

[37] *Infra* at 588, 608-609, 567-568, 637-638, 735-736, 754; Documents II (1921) *supra* note 12 at 134.

[38] *Infra* at 551, 567-568.

[39] *Infra* at 588, 608-609.

[40] *Infra* at 735; IaöRV (1934) *supra* note 29 at 309. Manley Hudson also mentions Article 18 of the 1907 Convention creating the Central American Court of Justice (Hudson (1943) *supra* note 1 at 198).

[41] *LaGrand (Germany* v. *United States of America)*, Judgment of 27 June 2001, ICJ Reports (2001) 466 at 503 (§ 104).

tion here of a definite [i.e. binding] order, even of a temporary nature, which must be carried out at once",[42] while 81 years later the Court was equally convinced that these measures were binding, even after looking at the *procès-verbaux* and the other *travaux préparatoires*.[43] The paucity of materials on Chapter III of the *avant-projet* in the *procès-verbaux* severely limits their usefulness for ICJ Statute interpretation of matters of procedural law. Discussion of such issues as the nature of Article 41 will thus have to do without *travaux préparatoires*.[44] At best, their being mentioned in the 1907 Draft Arbitration Treaty – provisional measures were not mentioned[45] – leads to the use of the 1907 *travaux préparatoires*.

4. Conclusion

What, then, is the value of the *procès-verbaux* today? They are, first, a fascinating historical record of how international law worked in the early 20th century. They show that this type of committee always operates in the same fashion, whether in 1920 or in 2006. The international lawyer reading this volume is reminded repeatedly of how much we "modern" international lawyers still think in the same categories as our predecessors 86 years ago. Where our predispositions, prejudices or theories differ, our otherwise identical frame of mind highlights the differences. Second, however, because of their outstanding importance within the other *travaux préparatoires* and the substantial identity between the Commission's *avant-projet* and the ICJ Statute, and because the International Court of Justice of 2006 is still very much the same animal as the brain-child of these ten men, international lawyers interpreting the Statute today – even if they happen to be judges of the ICJ – would be negligent if they did not at least consult the *procès-verbaux* before they decided on an issue.

April 5, 2006

---

42 *Infra* at 735.

43 *LaGrand* (2001) *supra* note 41 at 506 (§ 109).

44 In interpreting Article 41 in a recent paper, I have deliberately abstained from consulting the *travaux préparatoires* (Jörg Kammerhofer The binding nature of provisional measures of the International Court of Justice: The 'settlement' of the issue in the *LaGrand* case, 16 Leiden Journal of International Law (2003) 67-83 at 76). The Court's rather short treatment of the history (*LaGrand* (2001) *supra* note 41 at 503-504 (§§ 104-107)) is testament to the paucity of the material.

45 IaöRV (1934) *supra* note 29 at 309.

Cour Permanente de Justice Internationale.

COMITÉ CONSULTATIF DE JURISTES.

PROCÈS-VERBAUX

DES

SÉANCES DU COMITÉ

16 JUIN—24 JUILLET 1920

AVEC

ANNEXES.

LA HAYE — VAN LANGENHUYSEN FRÈRES — 1920.

Permanent Court of International Justice.

ADVISORY COMMITTEE OF JURISTS.

PROCÈS-VERBAUX

OF THE

PROCEEDINGS OF THE COMMITTEE

JUNE 16TH—JULY 24TH 1920

WITH

ANNEXES.

THE HAGUE — VAN LANGENHUYSEN BROTHERS — 1920.

PREFACE.

Lors de sa deuxième session, à Londres, en Février 1920, le Conseil de la Société des Nations, sur le rapport de M. LÉON BOURGEOIS, décida de constituer un Comité, chargé de préparer un projet pour l'établissement de la Cour Permanente de Justice Internationale, visée à l'Article 14 du Pacte, et de présenter un rapport au Conseil.

Ce Comité fut, en définitive, composé comme suit :

M. MINEICHIRO ADATCI, Envoyé Extraordinaire et Ministre Plénipotentiaire de S. M. L'Empereur du Japon à Bruxelles;

M. RAFAEL ALTAMIRA, Sénateur, Professeur à la Faculté de Droit de l'Université de Madrid;

M. CLOVIS BEVILAQUA, Conseiller juridique au Ministère des Affaires Etrangères du Brésil ;

M. LE BARON DESCAMPS, Sénateur, Ministre d'Etat de Belgique ;

M. FRANCIS HAGERUP, Envoyé Extraordinaire et Ministre Plénipotentiaire de S. M. le Roi de Norvège à Stockholm;

M. ALBERT DE LAPRADELLE, Professeur à la Faculté de Droit de Paris ;

M. LE DOCTEUR LODER, Membre de la Cour de Cassation des Pays-Bas;

LORD PHILLIMORE, Membre du Conseil privé de S. M. le Roi d'Angleterre ;

M. ARTURO RICCI-BUSATTI, Ministre Plénipotentiaire de S. M. le Roi d'Italie ; Conseiller Juridique au Ministère des Affaires Etrangères d'Italie ;

Mr. ELIHU ROOT, Ancien Secrétaire d'Etat des Etats-Unis d'Amérique.

M. RAOUL FERNANDES, ancien délégué brésilien à la Conférence de Paris, a d'abord assisté aux séances du Comité avec voix consultative, comme conseiller de M. BEVILAQUA, empêché; au cours des travaux du Comité il a été nommé membre du Comité en remplacement de celui-ci.

PREFACE.

At its second meeting, in London, in February 1920, the Council of the League of Nations. after hearing the report of M. LÉON BOURGEOIS, decided to appoint a Committee for the purpose of preparing plans for the establishment of the Permanent Court of International Justice provided for in Article 14 of the Covenant, and of presenting a report to the Council.

The membership of the Committee, as finally settled, was as follows:

M. MINEICHIRO ADATCI, Envoy Extraordinary and Minister Plenipotentiary of His Majesty the Emperor of Japan, at Brussels;

M. RAFAEL ALTAMIRA, Senator, Professor of the Faculty of Law of the University of Madrid;

M. CLOVIS BEVILAQUA, Legal Adviser to the Ministry of Foreign Affairs of Brazil;

BARON DESCAMPS, Senator, Belgian Minister of State;

M. FRANCIS HAGERUP, Envoy Extraordinary and Minister Plenipotentiary of His Majesty the King of Norway, at Stockholm;

M. ALBERT DE LAPRADELLE, Professor of the Faculty of Law of the University of Paris;

Dr. LODER, Member of the Supreme Court of the Netherlands;

LORD PHILLIMORE, Member of the Privy Council of His Majesty the King of England;

M. ARTURO RICCI-BUSATTI, Minister Plenipotentiary of His Majesty the King of Italy, Legal Adviser to the Ministry of Foreign Affairs of Italy;

Mr. ELIHU ROOT, Former Secretary of State of the United States of America.

M. RAOUL FERNANDES, former Brazilian delegate to the Paris Conference, was present at the meetings of the Committee, at first in a consultative capacity, as adviser to M. BEVILAQUA, who was prevented from attending; but in the course of the Committee's work he was ap-

Le Docteur JAMES BROWN SCOTT a assisté aux séances en qualité de conseiller juridique de Mr. ROOT.

Les membres du Comité, acceptant la gracieuse invitation du Gouvernement de S. M. la Reine des Pays-Bas, décidèrent de siéger au Palais de la Paix, à La Haye. C'est là que se tinrent les séances du 16 juin au 24 juillet 1920.

Le présent volume contient les procès-verbaux du Comité, avec leurs annexes. Les annexes remises au cours d'une séance ont été imprimées immédiatement après le procès-verbal de cette séance. Un double index chronologique et systématique, des procès-verbaux et des annexes facilitera les références.

Tous les membres du Comité, à l'exception de Mr. ELIHU ROOT, s'étant exprimés en français, c'est le texte anglais des procès-verbaux qu'il convient de considérer comme une traduction, sauf pour les discours et remarques de Mr. ROOT.

LONDRES, septembre 1920.

Le Secrétariat du Comité
Consultatif de Juristes.

pointed a member of the Comittee to replace the latter. Dr. JAMES BROWN SCOTT was present at the meetings as legal adviser to Mr. ROOT.

The members of the Committee, accepting the gracious invitation of the Government of Her Majesty the Queen of the Netherlands, decided to meet at the Peace Palace at the Hague. It was there that the meetings were held from June 16th to July 24th 1920.

The present volume contains the Procès-Verbaux of the Committee together with their annexes. The annexes are printed immediately after the Procès-Verbal of the Meeting at which they were presented. A double index, according to the chronology and subject-matter of the Procès-Verbaux and annexes, will facilitate references.

As all the members of the Committee, with the exception of Mr. ELIHU ROOT, spoke in the French language, the English text of the Procès-Verbaux is to be looked upon as a translation, except in so far as concerns the speeches and remarks of Mr. ROOT.

LONDON, September 1920.

The Secretariat of the Advisory
Committee of Jurists.

PREMIÈRE SÉANCE (publique),
tenue au Palais de la Paix, à La Haye, le 16 juin 1920, à 4 heures.

Présidence de M. le BARON DESCAMPS. [1])

Sont présents: M. Léon Bourgeois, Membre du Conseil de la Société des Nations; M. le Jonkheer H. A. van Karnebeek, Ministre des Affaires Etrangères des Pays-Bas; tous les membres du Comité, excepté M. Bevilaqua; le Secrétaire Général et les Secrétaires.

Dès l'ouverture de la séance, M. le JONKHEER VAN KARNEBEEK prononce un discours pour souhaiter la bienvenue de la part du Gouvernement Néerlandais au représentant du Conseil de la Société des Nations et aux membres du Comité. (Voir annexe 1).

M. LÉON BOURGEOIS salue, au nom du Conseil de la Société des Nations, les membres du Comité et exprime la gratitude du Conseil envers le Gouvernement Néerlandais pour l'hospitalité qu'il a offerte au Comité. (Voir annexe 2).

Le PRESIDENT remercie, de la part des membres du Comité, M. le Jonkheer van Karnebeek et M. Léon Bourgeois. (Voir annexe 3).

La séance est levée à 5 heures.

Le Président:
(signé) Brn. DESCAMPS.

Le Secrétaire-Général:
(signé) D. ANZILOTTI.

1) Lors d'une séance secrète, à laquelle étaient présents tous les membres du Comité, sauf M. Bevilaqua, et qui s'est tenue immédiatement avant la séance publique, le Comité a élu comme Président M. le Baron Descamps et comme Vice-Président M. Loder.

Il a été communiqué au Comité que le Secrétaire Général de la Société des Nations, a désigné comme Secrétaire Général du Comité M. le Commandeur Anzilotti, sous-Secrétaire Général de la Société des Nations; et pour le remplacer en cas d'empêchement M. Hammarskjöld, Secrétaire de Légation, membre du Secrétariat Permanent de la Société des Nations.

FIRST MEETING (Public),
held at the Peace Palace, the Hague, on June 16th 1920, at 4 p. m.

BARON DESCAMPS in the chair. [1])

Present: M. Léon Bourgeois, Member of the Council of the League of Nations; M. le Jonkheer H. A. van Karnebeek, Minister of Foreign Affairs for the Netherlands; all the members of the Committee, except M. Bevilaqua; the Secretary General and the Secretaries.

At the opening of the meeting, M. le JONKHEER VAN KARNEBEEK delivered a speech of welcome on behalf of the Dutch Government to the Representative of the Council of the League of Nations and to the members of the Committee. (See Annex 1).

M. LÉON BOURGEOIS welcomed, in the name of the Council of the League of Nations, the Members of the Committee, and expressed the gratitude of the Council to the Dutch Government for the hospitality which it had offered to the Committee. (See Annex 2).

The PRESIDENT thanked, on behalf of the members of the Committee, M. le Jonkheer van Karnebeek and M. Léon Bourgeois. (See Annex 3).

The meeting closed at 5 p.m.

The President:
(signed) Brn. DESCAMPS.

The Secretary-General:
(signed) D. ANZILOTTI.

1) During a secret meeting at which there were present all the members of the Committee, except M. Bevilaqua, and which was held immediately before the public meeting, the Committee elected as President Baron Descamps, and as Vice-President M. Loder.

It was announced to the Committee that the Secretary General of the League of Nations had named as Secretary General of the Committee Commendatore Anzilotti, under-Secretary General of the League of Nations, and to replace him in case of impediment, M. Hammarskjöld, Secretary of Legation, and member of the Permanent Secretariat of the League of Nations.

ANNEXE No. 1.

Discours prononcé par M. le Jonkheer van Karnebeek.

Mesdames et Messieurs,

Avant qu'il soit procédé à l'installation de la Commission nommée par le Conseil de la Société des Nations en vertu de l'article 14 du Pacte pour préparer le projet d'une Cour Permanente de Justice Internationale, je voudrais, au nom du Gouvernement de Sa Majesté la Reine, vous saluer et vous adresser quelques paroles de bienvenue.

Je saisis cette occasion pour saluer tout d'abord Son Excellence Monsieur Léon Bourgeois, l'éminent représentant de la Société des Nations à cette réunion. Qu'il soit le bienvenu sur le sol néerlandais. Je salue en sa personne l'homme d'Etat qui a présidé aux travaux de la grande commission dans chacune des deux Conférences de La Haye et auquel les services rendus à la cause de la justice internationale ont valu des titres d'autorité et de mérite impérissables et universellement reconnus.

En adhérant à la grande institution internationale qui marque une étape nouvelle dans l'histoire de l'humanité, les Pays-Bas se sont promis de contribuer dans la mesure de leurs forces à la réalisation des hautes idées éthiques qui ont présidé à sa création. Heureux de mettre, dans l'avenir comme dans le passé, leurs ressources à la disposition de l'organisation du droit et de la justice internationale, le Gouvernement et le peuple néerlandais apprécient hautement l'accueil qui fut fait au témoignage de sympathie qu'ils éprouvaient le besoin de donner à l'œuvre que la Société se propose d'entreprendre ici, et ils la remercient d'avoir accepté l'offre d'hospitalité que, dans un esprit d'estime et de collaboration, ils ont été amené à lui faire.

En m'adressant plus particulièrement à vous, Messieurs les membres du Comité, je rends hommage à la haute autorité juridique et morale que vos noms représentent. Le problème de la communauté internationale et des moyens de résoudre pacifiquement les conflits entre Etats, a été, notamment dans les dernières décades, la préoccupation constante des esprits les plus élevés et des hommes d'état les plus éclairés. La

ANNEX No. 1.

Speech delivered by M. le Jonkheer van Karnebeek.

Ladies and Gentlemen,

Before the launching of the Committee appointed by the Council of the League of Nations in accordance with Article 14 of the Covenant to prepare a plan for a Permanent Court of International Justice, may I on behalf of the Government of Her Majesty the Queen bid you welcome.

I seize the opportunity to greet, first of all, His Excellency M. Léon Bourgeois, the eminent representative of the League of Nations at this gathering. May he be welcome to Dutch soil! In him I greet the statesman who has presided over the labours of the chief Committee of each of the two Hague Conferences and whose services to the cause of international justice have entitled him to a position of authority and imperishable merits which are universally recognised.

In joining the great international institution which marks a new stage in the history of mankind, the Netherlands intend to aid to the utmost of their ability in the realisation of the high moral ideas which have led to its formation. The Dutch Government and people are always glad, in the future as in the past, to put their resources at the disposal of the movement destined to organise justice and international law. They highly appreciate the reception accorded to their expression of sympathy with the work which the League is to undertake here and beg to thank the League for having accepted the offer of hospitality which they have made wishing to collaborate and to show their respect for the work to be undertaken.

Addressing myself now in particular to you, Gentlemen, members of the Committee, I wish to pay homage to the high judicial and moral authority associated with your names. The problem of international community and the methods of peaceful solution of disputes between States has, especially in the last few decades, been the constant thought of the most distinguished minds and the most far-seeing statesmen. The First Hague Conference, the work of which is often-

Première Conférence de la Haye, dont l'œuvre souvent méconnue s'arrêta aux limites des possibilités pratiques, créa, à la suite d'une proposition de l'éminent délégué britannique Lord Pauncefote of Preston, à la veille du siècle actuel, l'appareil ingénieux destiné à faciliter et à favoriser — comme l'exposa dans son admirable rapport il y a plus de vingt ans le Baron Descamps ici présent — le recours à l'arbitrage reconnu par les Puissances à cette époque comme le moyen le plus équitable de régler les litiges qui n'ont pas été résolus par la voie diplomatique. Depuis lors s'accentua le mouvement qui tendait à l'introduction dans les rapports internationaux d'une instance permanente, de nature essentiellement juridique, appelée à résoudre par l'application des règles du droit les différends qui pourraient surgir entre les Etats. Ce mouvement, s'inspirant d'une remarquable initiative américaine, à laquelle se rattachent les noms bien connus de Messrs. Elihu Root et James Brown Scott, que nous avons également l'honneur de voir parmi nous, — ce mouvement prit forme à la Seconde Conférence et aurait abouti si l'accord sur le choix des juges et la constitution de la Cour avait pu s'établir. Le sort échu ensuite à la Cour des Prises eut raison des efforts qui furent encore faits par certaines Puissances en 1910 pour achever l'œuvre que la Conférence de 1907 n'avait pas terminée.

Messieurs! Les événements n'ont pu arrêter la marche progressive des idées. La Société des Nations a repris le fil qui semblait abandonné pour longtemps, et vous a confié la mission de l'éclairer en vue des décisions importantes à prendre dans un avenir prochain. La grandeur de cette tâche se révèle, quand on aperçoit au-dessus de la lutte des intérêts et des passions, la clarté de l'idée puissante de régler l'avenir de l'humanité par le droit. Dans un monde qui a passé par une des plus grandes épreuves que l'histoire ait jamais connue, dans une communauté internationale chancelante et presqu'à bout de ressources, l'œuvre, consacrée à la justice, qui va se poursuivre dans ce Palais destiné à cette fin, apparaît comme un réveil, comme une promesse de reconstruction morale, comme le message d'un avenir meilleur, digne de la Société des Nations.

Il ne m'appartient pas d'approfondir les problèmes que soulève l'examen auquel vous allez vous livrer. Ces problèmes sont difficiles et multiples; mais les difficultés se dissiperont devant l'expérience de jurisconsultes consommés, qui, hommes d'état à la fois, n'ignorent pas combien l'Etat, personne juridique sensible et complexe,

underrated, went as far as was practicable at the time, and created on the eve of the present century, on the proposal of the eminent British delegate, Lord Pauncefote of Preston, the ingenious machinery destined to facilitate and to encourage recourse to arbitration which was recognised by the Powers, at that time, as the most equitable means of adjusting disputes not capable of solution by diplomatic means. This was most ably explained by Baron Descamps in his report, more than 20 years ago. Since then there has been a decided impetus to the movement which tended to the introduction in international relations of a permanent tribunal, with a purely judicial basis, and empowered to resolve by rules of law disputes which might arise between States. This movement, gaining new inspiration from a remarkable American initiative with which is associated the well known names of Elihu Root and James Brown Scott, whom we likewise have the honour to see amongst us, took form at the Second Hague Conference and would have been successful, if it had been possible to reach agreement on the method of choosing Judges and on the constitution of the Court. Later the fate met with by the Prize Court proved too strong for the efforts made by certain Powers in 1910 to complete the work which the Conference of 1907 had not finished.

Gentlemen, events have not been able to arrest the onward march of ideas. The League of Nations has taken up again the thread which for a long time seemed abandoned, and has entrusted to you the task of assisting it, by your advice, to formulate the important decisions to be taken in the near future. The grandeur of this task is apparent when, above the conflict of interests and passions of mankind, is seen the guiding star of the noble idea of governing the future by the laws of justice. In a world which has passed through one of the greatest trials which history has ever known, in an international society shaken to its fundations, and almost at the end of its rescurces, the work of justice which is to be carried on in this Palace appears like an awakening, like a promise of moral reconstruction, like the message of a better future worthy of the League of Nations.

It does not fall to me to examine in details the problems which the work to which you are to devote yourself will raise. These problems are difficult and multiple, but they will be dissipated before the experience of jurists versed in international law who, being also statesmen, fully realise how much the State, as a delicate and complex legal organism, differs from an indi-

essentiellement différente de la personne naturelle, se soumet difficilement à tout système qui ne tient pas compte de son caractère et de ses besoins spéciaux.

Messieurs! Permettez-moi de rappeler à cette occasion les paroles de M. Léon Bourgeois, qui résumait sa pensée en disant: „L'obligation de résoudre par un règlement pacifique les conflits internationaux est la loi première de la Société humaine".

C'est là l'idée élevée à laquelle le Palais, où nous sommes réunis et où vos travaux vont se poursuivre, à été consacré. Soyez — en convaincus que les sympathies du peuple néerlandais vous entourent et que nous formons le vœu sincère que le grand effort que vous ferez pour enrichir l'humanité d'une institution de justice qui aura la confiance de toutes les nations, soit couronné de succès.

vidual and who know with what difficulty the State submits itself to any system which does not take account of its special character and needs.

Gentlemen, permit me to recall on this occasion the words of M. Léon Bourgeois, who summarized his viewpoint in the following words: "The obligation of settling international conflicts by pacific means is the first law of human Society".

It is to this lofty ideal that the Palace where we are gathered and where your meetings are to be held is consecrated. Rest assured that the sympathies of the Dutch people surround you and that we cherish the sincere wish that the great effort which you are to make to enrich humanity with a institution of Justice, which shall have the confidence of all the Nations, may be crowned with success.

ANNEXE No. 2.

Discours prononcé par M. Léon Bourgeois.

C'est un grand honneur pour moi d'avoir été délégué par le Conseil de la Société des Nations pour ouvrir les travaux du Comité des juristes chargé de préparer le statut de la Cour Permanente de Justice Internationale.

L'autorité personnelle des membres de votre Comité assure le succès de vos travaux. Elle est le présage et le gage du respect qui entourera dans l'avenir l'institution suprême dont les décisions devront établir dant le monde la souveraineté du droit.

Je salue ici MM. Adatci, Altamira, Bevilaqua, Descamps, Hagerup, de Lapradelle, Loder, Lord Phillimore, M. Ricci-Busatti et, particulièrement, Mr. Elihu Root, le grand jurisconsulte et l'éminent homme d'état américain dont la présence nous permet d'affirmer que, dans l'œuvre qui nous rassemble, l'ancien et le nouveau monde ne sauraient, malgré des difficultés passagères, être séparés par une barrière durable. Ces deux mots d'ancien et de nouveau monde ne peuvent plus signifier que monde du passé et monde de l'avenir. C'est bien l'humanité toute entière qui formera demain le monde nouveau.

ANNEX No. 2.

Speech delivered by M. Léon Bourgeois.

It is a great honour for me to have been delegated by the Council of the League of Nations to open the meetings of the Committee of Jurists charged with the duty of preparing the constitution of the Permanent Court of International Justice.

The personal authority of the members of your Committee assures the success of your labours. That authority at once presages and guarantees the respect which will surround in the future that supreme institution whose decisions must establish the sovereignty of law in all the world.

I welcome here Messrs. Adatci, Altamira, Bevilaqua, Descamps, Hagerup, de Lapradelle, Loder, Lord Phillimore, Ricci-Busatti and particularly Mr. Elihu Root, the great jurist and eminent American statesman, whose presence permits us to affirm that in the work which has called us together the old world and the new world, in spite of passing difficulties, cannot be separated by a durable barrier, and that indeed the two words „old world" and „new world" can now have no other meaning than the world of the past and the world of the future. For it is nothing less than humanity as a whole which will form the new world of to-morrow.

Il est juste que La Haye ait été désignée pour la réunion de votre Comité. Le souvenir des Conférences de 1899 et de 1907 ne peut s'effacer de la mémoire de ceux qui ont eu l'honneur — il en est parmi vous — d'y participer. Il serait injuste d'oublier ces premiers essais de l'organisation de la justice et de la paix. Certes, les ouvriers d'alors n'ont pas eu le pouvoir et n'ont même jamais rêvé d'établir d'un seul coup, dans un même temps, la puissance souveraine du droit. Ils savaient que la force des intérêts et des passions demeure et demeurera toujours redoutable. Il a fallu trois siècles au christianisme pour établir son empire sur le monde, et nul ne pouvait imaginer qu'une convention internationale suffirait, quelle qu'en fût la solennité, pour réaliser ce qui n'était rien de moins qu'une révolution universelle.

L'œuvre, cependant, est loin d'avoir été inutile.

It is fitting that The Hague has been designated for the meetings of your Committee. The recollection of the Conferences of 1899 and 1907 can never pass from the memory of those who had the honour, — and there are some of them amongst you — to take part in them. It would be unjust to allow these first steps in the organisation of justice and peace to be forgotten. It is true that the artisans of these times had not the power and did not even dream of establishing at a single blow and at once the sovereign power of right. They knew that the force of special interests and of passion remains and will remain always formidable. It took three centuries for Christianity to establish its empire in the world, and no one could have imagined that an international convention, however solemn, could suffice to realise what must be nothing less than a universal revolution.

Les chemins ont été ouverts. Les méthodes ont été déterminées. L'idée généreuse qui, depuis Henri IV, grâce aux travaux des philosophes du 18ème et du 19ème siècles, avait pu gagner les esprits supérieurs, avait pris pour la première fois, à La Haye, une forme concrète dans une série d'actes internationaux qu'avaient contresignés les représentants de plus de quarante nations.

Et l'importance des résultats pratiques ne peut être méconnue.

Est-ce dans le Palais de la Haye qu'on peut oublier les arbitrages et les enquêtes qui, notamment dans les affaires du Dogger Bank, de Casablanca, du „Carthage" et du „Manouba" ont, à plusieurs reprises, écarté des risques de conflits graves et peut-être des guerres entre plusieurs grandes Puissances?

Mais il fallait sans doute qu'une terrible leçon de choses fût donnée au monde pour que la semence germât, pour que pénétrât dans la pensée, non seulement des Gouvernements mais des peuples, cette vérité essentielle que ce n'est pas dans les conflits de la force qu'on pourra jamais découvrir les fondements de la paix entre les Etats, pas plus que ceux de la paix entre les hommes.

Hélas, il a fallu les horreurs de ces quatre années de guerre, les ruines accumulées, les millions de morts, les crimes inexpiables pour ouvrir les yeux du plus grand nombre, et si, dans certains pays, la folle ambition des politiques peut encore admettre le retour de semblables catastrophes, elle soulèvera désormais dans l'âme des simples innombrables la révolte ouverte du sentiment et de la conscience.

Une autre condition s'est réalisée. La victoire des soldats de la civilisation et de la liberté a permis de réparer les plus graves des injustices de l'histoire, d'abolir les plus cruelles des servitudes du passé. Les peuples conquis ont été libérés, les droits des nations à se constituer elles-mêmes ont été reconnus. Il est possible maintenant d'envisager l'heure où l'état de fait ne sera plus contraire aux règles du droit.

Un tribunal dont les sentences doivent garantir le maintien de la paix n'a d'autorité que si cette paix est fondée sur le droit lui-même. La paix, avons-nous déjà dit, c'est la durée du droit. Dans toute la mesure où le droit aura été assuré par la victoire, vous pourrez, Messieurs, travailler librement à son triomphe définitif.

The work, however, is far from having been useless. Roads were opened. Methods were laid down. That generous idea which, since the time of Henry IV, thanks to the labours of the philosophers of the eighteenth and nineteenth centuries, has succeeded in winning the support of all superior intelligences, took for the first time at The Hague a concrete form in a series of international acts which were countersigned by the representatives of more than forty nations.

Nor should the importance of the practical results be disregarded.

It is not here, in this Palace of The Hague, that we should forget the arbitrations and the inquiries which, notably in the affairs of the Dogger Bank, of Casablanca, of the "Carthage" and of the "Manouba", on several occasions warded off the risk of serious conflicts and perhaps even of war between several great Powers.

It needed, however, without doubt that a terrible object-lesson should be given to the world in order that into the minds not only of governments but of peoples there might sink the essential truth that it is not in the conflicts of force that one can ever discover the foundations of peace between States any more than between individuals.

It has, alas, needed the horrors of four years of War, of accumulated ruins, of millions of dead and of crimes which are inexpiable, to open the eyes of the greater number of men, and if in some countries the mad ambition of politicians can still contemplate a return to similar catastrophes, it would arouse immediately in the soul of innumerable simple people the open revolt both of feeling and of conscience.

And another condition has been realised. The victory of the soldiers of civilisation and of liberty enabled reparation to be made for some of the most serious injustices of history and the abolition of some of the most cruel servitudes of the past. The conquered peoples have been freed and the rights of nations to constitute themselves have been recognised. It is possible now to contemplate the hour when the world *de facto* will not be contrary to the world *de jure*.

A tribunal whose sentences should guarantee the maintenance of peace has only authority if that peace is founded on public right itself. Peace, as we have already said, is simply the stable existence of right, and in all that measure in which right has been assured by the victory, you will be able, Gentlemen, to work in freedom towards its final triumph.

Je suis venu ici, Messieurs, au nom du Conseil de la Société des Nations. C'est, en effet, ce Conseil qui a, par application de l'article 14 du Pacte de Versailles, été chargé de l'organisation de la Justice internationale. Un mémorandum du Secrétaire Général a posé devant vous, avec une interprétation aussi exacte que possible du Pacte, les questions principales que vous aurez à résoudre. Ces questions, j'en rappelais moi-même quelques-unes dans mon rapport à la session du Conseil tenu à Londres au mois de février dernier:

Comment la Cour Permanente sera-t-elle organisée?

Comment ses membres seront-ils nommés?

Quel sera leur nombre et leur situation?

En quel pays, en quelle ville son siège sera-t-il fixé?

Quelles seront ses règles de procédure, aussi bien en ce qui concerne l'instruction que le jugement des litiges?

Quelles seront, enfin, les limites de sa compétence? Sur ce dernier point, le Pacte lui-même et les divers traités qui viennent d'être signés ne vous donnent pas seulement un certain nombre d'indications, mais vous apportent des décisions précises, et si quelques dispositions de ces traités et du Pacte vous semblent impliquer des restrictions regrettables, il ne faut pas oublier que, sans même envisager aucun amendement au Pacte, le Conseil et l'Assemblée, inspirés par vos travaux, peuvent, en vertu des art. 12 et 15, accroître considérablement le champ d'action de la Cour.

Dès maintenant, certains points vous paraîtront sûrement acquis. La Cour de Justice doit être une véritable Cour Permanente. Ce n'est pas simplement à des arbitres choisis éventuellement en cas de conflit par les parties intéressées, c'est à un petit nombre de juges siégeant constamment, recevant un mandat dont la durée permettra l'établissement d'une véritable jurisprudence, qu'il appartiendra de dire le droit. Cette permanence est un symbole. C'est un siège élevé au milieu des nations, où toujours sont présents les juges, vers qui puisse toujours se porter l'appel des faibles et se dresser la protestation du droit violé. Choisis non en considération de l'Etat auquel ils appartiennent mais à raison de leur autorité personnelle, de leur passé, du respect qui s'attache à leur nom connu du monde entier, ces juges représenteront le véritable esprit international, qui n'est nullement, comme on l'a pré-

I have come here, Gentlemen, in the name of the Council of the League of Nations. That Council, by the application of Article 14 of the Covenant of Versailles, was charged with the organisation of international justice. A Memorandum by the Secretary-General has set out for you, with as exact as possible an interpretation of the Covenant, the principal questions which you will have to resolve. These questions I summed up myself to a certain degree in my report to the session of the Council held in London in February last:

How should the Permenant Court be organised?

How should its members be appointed?

What will be their number and status?

In what country and in what town will the seat of the Court be fixed?

What will be its rules of procedure, both in the matter of preliminary pleadings and of judgment?

What will be, finally, the limits of its competence?

On this last point the Covenant itself and the different treaties which have been lately signed not only give you a certain number of indications, but bring you precise decisions, and if some of the dispositions of these treaties and of the Covenant appear to you to imply regrettable restrictions, it must not be forgotten that without necessarily envisaging any amendment of the Covenant, the Council and the Assembly, inspired by your labours and in virtue of Articles 12 and 15, can considerably increase the field of activity of the Court.

From the start, however, some points will appear to you to be already certainly obtained. The Court of Justice must be a true Permanent Court. It is not simply a question of arbitrators chosen on a particular occasion, in the case of conflict, by the interested parties; it is a small number of judges sitting constantly and receiving a mandate the duration of which will enable the establishment of a real jurisprudence, who will administer justice. This permanence is a symbol. It will be a seat raised in the midst of the nations, where judges are always present, to whom can always be brought the appeal of the weak and to whom protests against the violation of right can be addressed. Chosen not by reason of the State of which they are citizens, but by reason of their personal authority, of their past career, of the respect which attaches to their names known over the whole world, these judges will represent a truly international spirit which

tendu, la négation des légitimes intérêts de chaque nation, mais qui est, au contraire, la sauvegarde de ces intérêts, dans la limite même de leur légitimité.

Cette Cour Permanente ne sera pas, nous l'avons dit, une Cour d'arbitrage, mais une Cour de justice. La Cour d'Arbitrage dont nous avons rappelé les éminents services, ne cessera point de fonctionner, dans tous les cas pour lesquels elle a été créée. Mais elle a ses caractères propres, son domaine déterminé. Il y a, entre la sentence arbitrale et l'arrêt d'un tribunal, une différence essentielle, différence aussi profonde que celle qui existe entre l'équité et la justice.

L'arbitrage peut tenir compte de mille éléments de fait, de mille contingences, souvent de certaines nécessités d'ordre politique. L'arrêt de justice ne tient compte que de la règle définie et fixée par la loi. On peut dire que, dans chaque Etat, le domaine de la justice proprement dite s'est étendu peu à peu à mesure que les législations, s'étendant elles-mêmes et pénétrant plus profondément dans le jeu des relations individuelles, précisaient pour chacune de ces relations les droits et les obligations de chacun des citoyens.

Certes, la définition juridique des droits et des obligations n'atteindra jamais la totalité des rapports entre les hommes, mais on peut dire que le progrès de la vie normale, à l'intérieur des Etats, a toujours suivi l'accroissement du domaine de l'autorité judiciaire, et c'est pourquoi l'indépendance de l'autorité judiciaire vis à vis des pouvoirs politiques semble, de plus en plus, l'une des garanties essentielles de la liberté et de la paix intérieure.

Messieurs, nous pouvons donc prévoir qu'il en sera de même pour les Etats. Ils n'ont encore, les uns vis à vis des autres, que des rapports incertains, dont la nature est mal définie, dont les règles sont livrées encore aux contestations sans fin, au hasard, à l'arbitraire, ainsi qu'il en était entre les citoyens de chaque Etat aux premiers âges de la civilisation.

Ce que la Société des Nations se propose précisément de créer, c'est cette définition nouvelle et plus complète du nombre le plus grand possible des relations entre les Etats, de façon à donner une compétence toujours plus étendue au pouvoir suprême de la justice.

Je sais que, pour certains esprits, ce qui devrait être organisé avant tout, c'est la justice internationale. Il n'y a pas d'opposants contre le projet de constitution de la Cour de Justice, mais plusieurs juristes éminents voudraient réserver, jusqu'à nouvel ordre, l'organisation proprement dite de la Société des Nations.

is by no means, as some people pretend, a negation of the legitimate interests of each nation, but which is, on the contrary, the safeguard of these interests, within the very limits of their legitimacy.

This Permanent Court will not be, as I have said, a Court of arbitration, but a Court of justice. The Court of Arbitration, whose eminent services we all remember, will certainly not cease to function in all the cases for which it was set up. But it has a special character and its range of action is already determined. There is between the sentence in an arbitration and the judgment of a tribunal an essential difference, a difference as profound as that which exists between equity and justice. Arbitration can take account of a thousand elements of fact and a thousand contingencies, and often of certain necessities of a political kind. The decrees of justice take account only of a rule defined and fixed by law. In every State the domain of justice properly so-called has spread step by step as the body of legislation, extending itself and penetrating more deeply into the interplay of individual relations, defined for each one of these relations the rights and obligations of every citizen.

Certainly the juridical definition of these rights and obligations will never reach the sum of the points of contact between people, but it is fair to say that progress in normal life, in the interior of States, has always followed an enlargement of the domain of judicial authority, and it is for that reason that the independence of the judicial authority vis-à-vis the political power appears more and more one of the essential guarantees of liberty and internal peace.

Gentlemen, we can foresee then that it will be the same in the case of States themselves. They have up to now one towards another uncertain modes of contact, the nature of which is badly defined, the laws of which are still at the mercy of endless differences of opinion, or of arbitrary chance, just as it was between the citizens of each country in the first ages of civilisation.

The precise object of the League of Nations is just this new and more complete definition of the largest possible number of relations between States, in such a way as to give an always-increasing competence to the supreme power of justice.

I know that, in the minds of certain people, the view is that what must be organised before everything is international justice itself. There are no real opponents of the project of setting up a Court of Justice, but there are certain eminent jurists who would prefer to reserve, until some fresh

Me sera-t-il permis de dire pourquoi le Conseil de la Société des Nations a considéré les deux institutions comme complémentaires l'une de l'autre, comme devant être organisées en même temps, comme ne pouvant, si elles doivent vivre, se passer l'une de l'autre?

Essayons de nous rendre compte de la puissance d'action d'une institution de justice internationale.

Quelle sera la matière offerte à ses décisions?

Quel sera son pouvoir de pénétration dans les faits?

Quelle sera la garantie d'une exécution exacte de ses arrêts?

La justice suit nécessairement l'organisation de la vie elle même. Dans l'intérieur d'un Etat, les tribunaux ne peuvent véritablement et utilement statuer que si des lois précises ont déterminé les rapports entre les hommes, fixant, par conséquent, les droits et les obligations, et offrant aux représentants du droit le moyen de confronter les faits avec le droit ainsi défini et d'en réprimer les violations.

En d'autres termes, la vie précède le droit. Tant qu'elle est inorganisée, tant que le fonctionnement de ses différentes formes politiques, sociales ou économiques n'ont pas été déterminées, une action d'équité peut s'exercer entre les tendances et les forces contraires, mais l'action véritable du droit n'est pas née.

Entre les Etats, il ne peut en être autrement. La vie internationale tend à se développer chaque jour avec une intensité que nul, il y a un siècle, n'aurait pu prévoir et n'aurait osé mesurer. L'interdépendance des phenomènes de tout ordre, politiques, économiques, financiers, sociaux, fait retentir jusqu'aux extrémités du monde la répercussion des besoins et des activités de chacun.

La création d'organes internationaux où se réglera, dans un intérêt supérieur, le flux et le reflux de toutes ces forces est indispensable à la paix et à la prospérité de chacun et de tous. Le Conseil de la Société des Nations s'est donné pour tâche de créer aussi rapidement que possible ces organes de la vie internationale: organisation de la statistique universelle, organisation du travail, organisation de l'hygiène, organisation de la liberté du transit; tels sont les principaux objets auxquels il a consacré sa dernière session de Rome.

L'institution d'un organisme économique et financier n'a pu être enterprise dès cette session; la situation générale du monde, profondément troublée par les conséquences de la guerre, ne peut être d'ailleurs déterminée tant que la si-

arrangement, the organisation of the League of Nations specially so-called.

May I be permitted to say why the Council of the League of Nations consider the two institutions as complementary the one to the other, as of necessity being organised at the same time and as being unable, as long as they wish to preserve their existence, to do without each other?

Let us try now to estimate the scope of action of an institution of international justice.

What will be the material offered for its decisions?

What will be its power of exploring facts?

What will be the guarantee of an exact execution of its decisions?

Justice follows necessarily the organisation of life itself. In the interior of a State the Courts can only give decisions in any real and useful sense, if precise laws have already determined the relations between men, fixing in consequence their rights and obligations and offering to the representatives of law the means of confronting the facts with the law so defined and of repressing the violations of it.

In other words life precedes law. In so far as it is unorganised, in so far as the functioning of its different forms, political, social or economic, have not been determined, the action of equity can be exercised between conflicting forces and tendencies, but the true action of law has not yet been born.

Between States it cannot be otherwise. International life tends to develop every day with an intensity which no one a century ago could have foreseen or dared to estimate. The interdependence of matters of every order, political, economic, financial, social, makes felt at the very extremities of the world the repercussion of the needs and activities of everyone. The creation of an international organ through which, in the higher interest of all, the flux and reflux of all these forces shall be regulated, is indispensable to the peace and prosperity of each and all. The Council of the League of Nations has undertaken the task of creating as rapidly as possible these organs of international life: the organisation of universal statistics, the organisation of labour, of health, of the freedom of transit: these are the chief objects with which it dealt at its last session in Rome.

At that session, the institution of an economic and financial organisation could not be undertaken. The general situation of the world, profoundly troubled as it is by the consequences of the war, cannot be determined until the special

tuation spéciale des signataires du Traité de Paix n'aura pas elle-même été définie par les Etats directement intéressés. Mais, dès maintenant, le Conseil a arrêté le programme des travaux de la Conférence universelle à laquelle seront confiées les études préliminaires, qui permettront de jeter les bases de cette mutualité financière qui donnera une forme stable au crédit international.

Comment l'ensemble de ces organismes pourrait-il être protégé contre les conflits de chaque jour si l'institution judiciaire n'était point toujours présente et toujours prête à les éviter ou à les résoudre?

Mais comment, en retour, l'organisation judiciaire internationale, qui doit avoir pour tâche de garantir le respect des droits et l'exécution des obligations entre toutes les nations pourrait-elle suffire à sa tâche si le fonctionnement régulier de tous ces organes de la vie internationale n'avait pas été d'abord préalablement assuré?

Enfin, il est un dernier point de vue auquel il faut se placer pour envisager les rapports nécessaires de la Société des Nations et de la Justice Internationale, et l'étroite solidarité qui existe et qui existera toujours davantage entre leurs deux actions.

J'aborde ici nettement le problème décisif des sanctions.

Quelle serait l'efficacité, quelle serait la réalité d'une sentence de justice, si elle ne trouvait pas dans une forte organisation des institutions internationales ce qu'on appelle en termes techniques l'exécutive de ses décisions?

Le Pacte prévoit plusieurs degrés de sanctions: sanctions juridiques, sanctions diplomatiques, sanctions économiques; en dernier lieu, et dans des limites très spécialement déterminées, sanctions militaires.

Il est souhaitable qu'on ne soit pas obligé d'y avoir recours, mais il est impossible de penser que toutes tentatives de violence disparaîtront de ce monde et que, par conséquent, l'opposition de la force du droit à la force de la violence ne soit pas, hélas, encore bien longtemps nécessaire.

Le Pacte a prévu, dans son art. 9, la constitution d'une commission militaire, navale et aérienne, chargée de donner son avis sur l'exécution des dispositions des articles 1 et 8 et, d'une façon générale, sur les questions militaires navales et aériennes.

Le Conseil de la Société a, dès sa session à Rome, fixé le statut de cette commission militaire, qui, dès maintenant, peut se mettre à l'œuvre.

Ainsi, peu à peu, va se former le cycle com-

situation of the signatories of the Treaty of Peace has itself been defined by the States directly interested. But already the Council has drawn up the programme of work for the universal Conference to which shall be entrusted the preliminary investigations which will enable the foundation to be laid of that financial co-operation which will give stability to international credit.

How is this collection of organisations to be protected against the conflicts of everyday, if the judicial institution is not always present and always ready to ward off a conflict or to settle it?

But how on the other hand, can the international judicial organisation which must have for its task to guarantee respect for the rights and the execution of the obligations between all the nations, be sufficiently strong for its task, if the regular functioning of all these other organisations of international life has not been assured beforehand?

Finally, there is a last point of view, which we must take in order to envisage the necessary relations between the League of Nations and the International Court of Justice, and the close solidarity which exists and which will always exist to an increasing degree between their two actions.

I approach here briefly the decisive problem of sanctions.

What would be the efficacy, what would be the reality of a sentence of justice, if it did not find in a strong organisation of international institutions what one calls in a technical term the executory of these decisions?

The Covenant foresees several degrees of sanction, juridical sanction, diplomatic sanction, economic sanction, and as a last resort and, within limits very closely confined, military sanction.

It is much to be desired that we should not be obliged to have recourse to that, but it is impossible to think that all tendencies towards violence will disappear from the world and that in consequence the opposition of the force of right to the force of violence will not be, alas, still for a long time necessary.

The Covenant has provided in Article 9 the constitution of a military, naval and air Commission, charged with advising on the execution of the dispositions of Articles 1 and 8, and in a general way to advise on military, naval and air questions.

The Council of the League at its session in Rome laid down the terms of reference for this Commission, which can now get to work.

So little by little there will be a complete cycle of international life. The organisations whose co-ordination is necessary for the development

plet de la vie internationale. Les organes dont la coordination est nécessaire au développement de cette vie vont pouvoir entrer en action. Les obligations précises qui résulteront, pour chacun des Etats, de leur intégration dans cette existence commune, pourront être définies successivement. Le réseau du droit se resserrera entre ces personnes morales dont le développement particulier dépendra chaque jour davantage du développement de la vie commune. Et les conditions juridiques auxquelles seront soumis, en vertu des mêmes principes de droit, les actes de chacun et les actes de tous, offriront à la justice internationale la matière toujours plus riche, plus abondante de ses décisions.

Messieurs, les jurisconsultes qui sont assemblés à La Haye me pardonneront d'avoir semblé devancer les avis que nous sollicitons de leur science et de leur expérience.

Je suis loin, croyez-le, d'avoir eu une telle pensée. Parlant au nom du Conseil de la Société des Nations, j'ai voulu simplement montrer quelle grande place, à nos yeux, doit prendre la Cour de Justice dans l'organisation internationale du monde. Nous la voulons armée de la plus haute puissance morale, organisée pour une pénétration aussi profonde que possible dans les rapports de la vie des nations.

Nous sommes prêts à assurer aussi complètement que possible et l'étendue de sa compétence et l'exécution de ses arrêts, et c'est en raison même de la confiance que nous mettons en son action bienfaisante que nous devons établir entre les pouvoirs généraux du Conseil et de l'Assemblée et les pouvoirs propres de la Cour la solidarité la plus étroite et l'harmonie la plus parfaite.

Vous allez, Messieurs, donner la vie au pouvoir judiciaire de l'humanité. Les philosophes et les historiens nous ont dit les lois de la grandeur et de la décadence des Empires; nous attendons de vous, Messieurs, les lois qui assurent la perpétuité du seul empire qui ne peut connaître de décadence; l'empire de la Justice, expression de l'éternelle Vérité.

of this life will be able to begin to work. The precise obligations which will result for each State from their integration in this common existence will be one after another defined. The network of law will be drawn more tightly between these legal personalities whose individual development will become daily more and more dependent upon the development of their relations one with another. The acts of one and all will be subject to the same legal standards, judged according to the same principles of justice, and consequently a continually increasing abundance of material will be furnished upon which the decisions of international justice may be based.

Gentlemen, the jurists who are assembled at The Hague will pardon me for having appeared to forestall the advice which we solicit from their knowledge and their experience.

I am far, you must believe, from having had any such thought. Speaking in the name of the Council of the League of Nations I have wished simply to show what a large place in our eyes the Court of Justice must take in the international organisation of the world. We wish to see it armed with the highest moral power and organised for a penetration as deep as possible into all the points of contact in the life of nations.

We are ready to assure as completely as possible the extent of its competence and the execution of its judgements, and it is just because of the confidence that we place in its beneficent action that we wish to establish between the general powers of the Council and the Assembly and the special powers of the Court the closest solidarity and the most profound harmony.

You are about, Gentlemen, to give life to the judicial power of humanity. Philosophers and historians have told us of the laws of the growth and decadence of Empires. We look to you, Gentlemen, for laws which will assure the perpetuity of the only empire which can show no decadence, the empire of justice, which is the expression of eternal truth.

ANNEXE No. 3.

Discours prononcé par le Baron Descamps.

Ma première parole comme Président du Comité des Jurisconsultes chargé de rédiger un projet de Cour Permanente de Justice Internationale, sera une demande à M. le Ministre des Affaires Etrangères de vouloir bien transmettre à Sa Majesté la Reine des Pays-Bas, avec l'expression de notre profond respect, les vœux que nous formons pour Son auguste personne, pour la Famille Royale et pour le peuple néerlandais.

Je remercie M. le Ministre des Affaires Etrangères et M. le Délégué du Conseil de la Société des Nations qui ont bien voulu nous apporter, avec leur souhaits de bienvenue, l'appui de leurs paroles autorisées. Il y a des souvenirs qui sont plus qu'une joie, qui sont une force pour l'âme. Celui que nous emporterons des discours de Leurs Excellences M. le Jonkheer van Karnebeek et M. Léon Bourgeois sera de ce nombre. Il demeurera pour nous un puissant réconfort et le meilleur des encouragements au moment où nous allons nous efforcer de remplir une mission difficile entre toutes.

Le Conseil de la Société des Nations a constitué un Comité de jurisconsultes chargé de lui présenter un projet d'organisation de la Cour Permanente de Justice Internationale, visée par l'article 14 du Traité de Versailles du 28 juin 1919. La première tâche qui s'impose naturellement à ce Comité est de constater l'état actuel du droit international.

Trois conférences de la Paix, les deux premières tenues à La Haye, la troisième tenue à Paris, se sont occupées, dans des conditions différentes, de l'organisation de la justice internationale. Il importe, en vue d'une solution lumineuse du problème posé, de caractériser l'intervention de chacune d'elles.

C'est à la Conférence de la Paix de 1899 que revient l'honneur d'avoir créé pour la première fois une Cour mondiale de justice internationale sur la base de l'arbitrage.

Le rapport à la Conférence s'exprime sur ce point dans les termes suivants: „L'établissement d'une Cour Permanente d'Arbitrage répond aux aspirations les plus profondes des peuples civilisés, aux progrès réalisés dans les relations des Etats, au développement moderne du conten-

ANNEX No. 3.

Speech delivered by Baron Descamps.

My first words as President of the Committee of Jurists entrusted with drawing up a plan for a Permanent Court of International Justice, will be to request the Minister for Foreign Affairs to be good enough to convey to Her Majesty the Queen of the Netherlands the expression of our profoundest respect and our good wishes for Herself, the Royal Family and the Dutch people.

I beg to tender my thanks to the Minister for Foreign Affairs and to the Delegate from the Council of the League of Nations who have welcomed us and are giving us the support of their authority. There are memories which are more than joys — memories which strengthen the soul. The recollection of the speeches of Their Excellencies M. le Jonkheer van Karnebeek and M. Léon Bourgeois will be one of these. It will be a powerful encouragement to us in the eminently difficult mission we are about to undertake.

The Council of the League of Nations has established a Committee of Jurists, to formulate and submit to it for adoption a plan for the establishment of the Permanent Court of International Justice, provided for in Article 14 of the Treaty of Versailles dated June 28th, 1919. The first task with which this Committee is confronted is clearly to ascertain the present state of international law.

Three Peace Conferences, the first two held at the Hague, the third at Paris, have under different circumstances, dealt with the organisation of international justice. In order to throw light on the problem before us, it is important that we should define what each of these has accomplished.

The honour of having created for the first time an international Court of Justice based on arbitration belongs to the Peace Conference of 1899.

The Report on this question laid before the Conference reads as follows: „The establishment of a Permanent Court of Arbitration is in response to the highest aspirations of civilised peoples, to those ideas of progress which have been realised in international relations, to the

tieux international, au besoin qui pousse les nations de nos jours à rechercher une justice plus accessible dans une paix moins précaire. Cette grande institution peut être un puissant auxiliaire pour l'affermissement du sentiment du droit dans le monde."

Les traits caractéristiques de la nouvelle institution, au point de vue de son organisation, étaient les suivants:

I. Désignation par chacune des Puissances signataires d'un nombre égal d'arbitres inscrits sur une liste générale au titre de membres de la Cour.

II. Libre choix, fait dans cette liste, des arbitres appelés à former le tribunal en exercice dans les divers cas de recours à l'arbitrage.

III. Institution à La Haye d'un Bureau international servant de greffe à la Cour et pourvoyant aux services administratifs.

IV. Institution d'un Conseil Permanent d'administration et de haut contrôle, composé des représentants diplomatiques des Puissances accrédités à La Haye, sous la présidence de M. le Ministre des Affaires Etrangères des Pays-Bas.

Au point de vue de la compétence, la Convention pour le règlement pacifique des conflits internationaux, après avoir traité des bons offices et de la médiation ainsi que des commissions internationales d'enquête, donnait de l'arbitrage, à l'article 15, la définition suivante: „L'Arbitrage international a pour objet le règlement de litiges entre les Etats par des juges de leur choix et sur la base du respect du droit."

Précisant la portée de cet article, le rapport à la Conférence s'exprimait comme suit: „Dire que l'arbitre est juge et qu'il statue en droit, c'est dire que l'arbitrage ne s'applique pas à toute espèce de différends entre Etats.

L'article 16 déterminait ensuite la nature des questions litigieuses qui sont du ressort propre de l'arbitrage.

L'article 16 n'allait pas toutefois au delà de cette reconnaissance générale. Sous l'empire de cet article, chaque Etat décidait souverainement, à ce point de vue, si tel ou tel cas serait soumis à l'arbitrage, sous la réserve des obligations qu'il pouvait avoir contractées par d'autres traités.

Touchant ce dernier point, l'article 19 renfermait la disposition suivante: „Indépendamment des Traités généraux ou particuliers qui stipulent actuellement l'obligation du recours à l'arbitrage pour les Puissances signataires, ces Puissances se réservent de conclure, soit avant la ratification du présent acte, soit postérieurement, des

modern development of international litigation, to the need which urges nations in our day to seek a more accessible justice in a less uncertain peace. This great institution can be a powerful auxiliary for the strengthening of the feeling of justice in the world".

The characteristic features of the new institution, from the point of view of organisation, were the following:

I. The appointment by each of the signatory Powers of an equal number of arbitrators, entered in a general list as members of the Court.

II. The free choice, from this list, of arbitrators who would be chosen to form the tribunal for each case which may arise for arbitration.

III. The establishment, at the Hague, of an International Office which would serve as registry to the Court and provide for the administrative services.

IV. The establishment of a Permanent administrative Council, to exercise supreme control, composed of the diplomatic representatives of the Powers accredited to The Hague, with the Dutch Minister for Foreign Affairs as President.

With regard to the competence of the Court, the Convention for the pacific settlement of international disputes, after referring to "good offices" and to mediation, and also to international commissions of enquiry, gives under Article 15 the following definition of arbitration: "International arbitration has for its object the settlement of differences between States by judges of their own choice, and on the basis of respect for law".

The Report submitted to this Conference defines the meaning of this Article more accurately in the following terms: „To say that the arbitrator is judge and acts according to law, is to say that arbitration is not applicable to every variety of dispute between States".

Article 16 further defines the nature of litigious questions which come under the competence of arbitration proper.

Article 16 did not, however, go beyond this general recognition. Under the present Convention, each State decided absolutely, from this point of view, whether such a case should be submitted to arbitration, saving always obligations it might have contracted by other treaties.

On this last point, Article 19 embodied the following regulation: „Independently of general or private Treaties expressly stipulating recourse to arbitration as obligatory on the signatory Powers, these Powers reserve to themselves the right of concluding, either before the ratification

accords nouveaux, généraux ou particuliers, en vue d'étendre l'arbitrage obligatoire à tous les cas qu'elles jugeront possible de lui soumettre."

C'est en application de cette disposition que s'est formé un réseau extrêmement remarquable de conventions arbitrales dans le monde des Etats.

L'article 21 de la convention stipulait que „la Cour Permanente sera compétente pour tous les cas d'arbitrages à moins qu'il n'y ait entente entre les parties pour l'établissement d'une juridiction spéciale".

En ce qui concerne la procédure arbitrale, il n'existait pas, avant la Conférence de 1899, de règles juridiques générales acceptées de concert par les Etats. Un projet de règlement concernant cette matière avait été élaboré par l'Institut de Droit International, et complété par d'autres travaux de jurisconsultes éminents. L'œuvre à laquelle s'était adonné l'Institut avait été fécondée par la pratique de nombreux arbitrages internationaux. C'est en puisant à la double source de la Science et de l'Expérience que la Conférence de 1899 a consacré un des chapitres les plus intéressants de son œuvre à l'élaboration d'un Code de procédure arbitrale comprenant les points fondamentaux de cette procédure, appelé à servir de règlement type, à combler les lacunes des compromis, et à constituer un ensemble de règles que la volonté des parties peut sans doute dominer et modifier, mais qui sont particulièrement précieuses pour les cas et dans la mesure où les Etats ne disposent point autrement.

Telle a été dans ses grandes lignes l'œuvre imparfaite sans doute, mais remarquable de la Conférence de 1899.

On a fait à cette œuvre divers reproches dont les uns sont sans doute fondés à certains égards, mais dont les autres ne paraissent pas toujours justifiés.

On s'est plaint du nombre peu considérable de litiges déférés à la Cour Permanente de La Haye. Le rapport du Secrétaire général atteste que durant la période qui s'est écoulée depuis l'entrée en action de la Cour de La Haye, une vingtaine de litiges ont été soumis à cette Cour. Il y a quelque rigueur, ce semble, à demander à la jeunesse les fruits de l'âge mûr, et il n'est peut être pas juste de reprocher à une institution ce qui est imputable, dans une large mesure, à la volonté défaillante des Etats. Il convient seulement de reconnaître que certaines conditions du fonctionnement de cette institution ne sont pas de nature à donner toujours une impulsion

of the present act or later, new agreements, general or private, with a view to extending obligatory arbitration to all cases which they may consider it possible to submit to it."

The application of this disposition has given rise to an extremely remarkable system of arbitral conventions between the members of the family of nations.

Article 21 of the Convention laid down that „the Permanent Court shall be competent for all arbitration cases, unless the parties agree to institute a special tribunal."

As regards the procedure of arbitration, there was, prior to the 1899 Conference, no general judicial regulation in existence which had the endorsement of all the States. A draft-scheme, designed to regulate this matter, had been formulated by the "Institut de Droit International" and had been supplemented by other works of eminent jurists. The work to which the Institut devoted itself had borne fruit in numerous cases of international arbitration. Thus the 1899 Conference, under the twofold inspiration of Science and Experience, devoted one of the most interesting chapters of its work to the elaboration of a Code of Procedure in Arbitration which, since it contained the governing principles of this Procedure, was intended to serve as a standard body of rules to fill the gaps of compromises and to establish a compendium of rules which the parties can, no doubt, overrule and modify, but which are of particular value in cases where the Governments do not make other arrangements.

Such, in broad outline, was the work of the 1899 Conference, imperfect no doubt, but nevertheless remarkable.

Its work has met with diverse criticisms, some of which are undoubtedly legitimate in certain respects, while others do not always appear to be justified.

It has been made a ground of complaint that so little litigation is brought before the Permanent Court of The Hague. The report of the Secretary-General shows that from the time the Hague Court first entered upon its duties, some twenty cases have been referred to it. It would appear somewhat exacting to demand of youth the experience of a ripe age, and it is scarcely just to reproach the institution with inactivity, when this is in a large measure due to the lack of response on the part of Governments. We must admit however, that the working of this institution is, under certain conditions, not always calculated to give a real stimulus to the

efficace à une telle volonté, et à faire éclore et mûrir les fruits que l'on peut attendre d'une organisation développée de la justice internationale.

Fonctionnement trop coûteux pour de multiples affaires contentieuses, a-t-on remarqué, et d'où sont trop absentes les garanties de permanence vraie et de professionnalité de la judicature, telles que nous les voyons assurées dans les juridictions nationales, au grand avantage du développement d'une jurisprudence ferme, continue et progressive. Il y a peut être quelque méprise à vouloir calquer l'organisation de la juridiction internationale sur le type des juridictions nationales. Il convient de ne jamais perdre de vue ce que les jurisconsultes, dans leur langage parfois un peu rude, mais expressif, entendent dire lorsqu'ils affirment que „le siège de la matière" n'est pas précisément le même, les sociétés nationales étant, par essence, des sociétés de subordination des individus à un gouvernement souverain à leur égard, et la société internationale étant, par excellence, une société de coordination entre Etats jouissant d'une égale souveraineté. Mais sans admettre ici une assimilation complète, il est à coup sûr expédient de rechercher comment des résultats favorables dans l'ordre national peuvent être atteints, en une large mesure, tout au moins, par des moyens appropriés, à une situation distincte dans l'ordre international.

C'est sans doute en se plaçant à ce point de vue que le programme de la Seconde Conférence de La Haye portait: „Améliorations à apporter aux dispositions de la Convention relative au règlement pacifique des conflits internationaux en ce qui regarde la Cour d'Arbitrage".

Observons maintenant comment la nouvelle Conférence a dirigé ses travaux dans cette voie.

Un effort très remarquable a été fait en 1907 par la Seconde Conférence de la Paix en vue de réaliser le progrès de la justice internationale dans deux sphères d'importance primordiale: celle de l'organisation et celle de la compétence des juridictions.

Au premier point de vue, la Conférence, en même temps qu'elle revisait la Convention pour le règlement des conflits internationaux, et formulait notamment des règles nouvelles concernant la pratique en matière de commissions internationales d'enquête, et de procédure sommaire arbitrale, la Conférence a consacré une bonne part de son activité à l'élaboration d'un „Projet de Convention relative à l'établissement d'une Cour de justice arbitrale" appelée à fonctionner „à côté" — suivant une expression souvent reproduite — de la Cour existante, et destinée, même dans l'opinion des principaux protagonistes

goodwill of the Governments and to bring to maturity the fruits which might be expected to result from a completely organised system of international justice.

It has been said that this is too costly an organ for the multitudious matters which are in dispute, and one which lacks the guarantees of a truly permanent and professional judicature, such as we know to be assured in national jurisdiction, to the great advantage of a firm, continuous and progressive jurisprudence. There may possibly be a mistaken idea underlying this desire to model the organism of international jurisdiction upon the prototype of national jurisdiction. It would be well never to lose sight of what jurists mean, when, in their somewhat crude but expressive language, they assert that the "subject-matter" is not precisely the same, as in national communities; the individuals are subordinated to the sovereign Government, while the international community is eminently one in which the States are coordinated and enjoy equal sovereignty. Without, however, admitting in this case complete assimilation, it is unquestionably expedient to ascertain in what manner results favourable in the national order, can be attained, to a high degree at any rate, by means which are appropriate to a clearly defined international situation.

It was, no doubt, from this point of view that the following words were contained in the programme of the Second Hague Conference: "Improvements to be made in the provisions of the Convention relative to the pacific settlement of international disputes as regards the Court of Arbitration".

Let us now consider what the new Conference has done in this direction.

A very remarkable effort was made in 1907 by the Second Peace Conference with a view to assuring the progress of international justice in two spheres of the greatest importance: its organisation and its judicial competence.

In the first instance, while revising the Convention for the pacific settlement of international disputes and formulating fresh regulations governing the practice of international Commissions of Enquiry and of summary procedure in arbitration, the Conference devoted a good deal of its time to the elaboration of a "Draft Convention relative to the creation of a Court of Arbitral Justice", called upon — according to a much-used term — to act "side by side" with the existing Court and intended by the principal advocates of the new institution to take the place of the former organisation at a relatively early date.

de l'organisme nouveau, à se substituer, à une date plus ou moins rapprochée, à l'organisme antérieur.

Les premiers articles de ce projet sont ainsi conçus:

„Art. 1. Dans le but de faire progresser la cause de l'arbitrage, les Puissances contractantes conviennent d'organiser, sans porter atteinte à la Cour permanente d'arbitrage, une Cour de justice arbitrale, d'un accès libre et facile, réunissant des juges représentant les divers systèmes juridiques du monde et capable d'assurer la continuité de la jurisprudence arbitrale.

Art. 2. La Cour de justice arbitrale se compose de juges et de juges suppléants choisis parmi les personnes jouissant de la plus haute considération morale et qui tous devront remplir les conditions requises, dans leurs pays respectifs, pour l'admission dans la haute magistrature, ou être des jurisconsultes d'une compétence notoire en matière de droit international.

Les juges et les juges suppléants de la Cour sont choisis, autant que possible, parmi les membres de la Cour permanente d'arbitrage. Le choix sera fait dans les six mois qui suivront la ratification de la présente Convention."

Mais quant au mode de composition de la Cour, il a dû être omis dans le projet, tous les efforts faits et toutes les combinaisons présentées pour concilier le principe de l'égalité des Etats avec l'établissement d'un nombre nécessairement restreint de juges, ayant finalement échoué.

Cette lacune demeurant ouverte, le projet admet dans son article 6 que la Cour en perspective désignera annuellement trois juges effectifs avec trois suppléants, appelés à former une délégation spéciale répondant à des exigences pratiques souvent signalées.

Remarquons encore, au point de vue du fonctionnement de la délégation spéciale, qu'aux termes de l'article 20: „Chacune des parties a le droit de désigner un juge de la Cour pour prendre part, avec voix délibérative, à l'examen de l'affaire soumise à la délégation. Si la délégation fonctionne en qualité de Commission d'enquête, ce mandat peut être confié à des personnes prises en dehors des juges de la Cour".

L'essai d'établissement d'une nouvelle Cour de justice arbitrale à côté de la Cour existante est demeuré à l'état de desideratum. La Conférence a dû se borner à consigner parmi les vœux émis par elle la recommandation suivante:

„La Conférence recommande aux Puissances signataires l'adoption du projet ci-annexé de

The first articles of this Draft are thus conceived:

„Art. 1. With a view to promoting the cause of arbitration, the contracting Powers agree to constitute, without altering the status of the Permanent Court of Arbitration, a Court of Arbitral Justice, of free and easy access, composed of judges representing the various juridical systems of the world and capable of ensuring continuity in jurisprudence of arbitration.

Art. 2. The Court of Arbitral Justice is composed of judges and deputy judges chosen from persons of the highest moral reputation, and all fulfilling conditions qualifying them, in their respective countries, to occupy high legal posts, or be jurists of recognised competence in matters of international law.

The judges and deputy judges of the Court are appointed, as far as possible, from the members of the Permanent Court of Arbitration. The appointment shall be made within the six months following the ratification of the present Convention".

But the way of constituting the Court had to be omitted in the Draft, all the efforts made and all the combinations suggested for conciliating the principle of the equality of States with the fixation of a necessarily limited number of judges having finally failed.

This point remaining undecided, the Draft lays down, in Article 6, that the proposed Court shall annually designate three acting judges and three supplementary judges to form a special delegation answering to practical requirements as often indicated.

It is also to be noted, with regard to the working of the special delegation, that under Article 20: "each of the parties concerned may nominate a judge of the Court to take part, with power to vote, in the examination of the case submitted to the delegation. If the delegation acts as a Commission of Inquiry, this task may be entrusted to persons other than the judges of the Court."

The attempt to establish a new Court of Arbitral Justice, in addition to the existing Court, has not advanced beyond the stage of a desideratum. The Conference was obliged to limit itself to including among the resolutions issued the following recommendation:

"The Conference recommends to the signatory Powers the adoption of the herewith annexed

convention pour l'établissement d'une Cour de justice arbitrale, et sa mise en vigueur dès qu'un accord sera intervenu sur le choix des juges et la constitution de la Cour."

Sur un autre point, qui tient à la compétence des cours d'arbitrage, la Conférence n'a pas été beaucoup plus heureuse: il s'agit de l'arbitrage obligatoire. Après des tentatives multiples et d'admirables joutes en vue d'arriver à une entente concernant un traité mondial d'arbitrage, soit sans réserves, soit accompagné de réserves avec indication toutefois de certaines catégories de litiges où l'arbitrage serait en tout cas obligatoire, la Conférence a fini par résumer de la manière suivante les points sur lesquels l'accord s'est trouvé acquis:

„La Conférence est unanime:

1. à reconnaître le principe de l'arbitrage obligatoire;

2. à déclarer que certains différends et notamment ceux relatifs à l'interprétation et à l'application des stipulations conventionnelles internationales, sont susceptibles d'être soumis à l'arbitrage obligatoire sans aucune restriction."

C'est dans l'état rappelé à grands traits par les observations précédentes que la Conférence de Paris trouva l'organisation de la justice internationale lorsqu'après une guerre sans précédent dans les annales de l'humanité, son attention se porta sur les exigences futures de l'établissement et du fonctionnement des institutions organiques de la justice du monde.

La Conférence, pressée sans doute par des travaux estimés plus urgents, ne crût pas devoir aborder une tâche qui, à tant de titres, paraissait s'imposer à elle. Elle s'est bornée à consigner dans le Traité de Versailles un article 14 ainsi conçu: „Le Conseil (de la Société des Nations) est chargé de préparer un projet de Cour permanente de justice internationale et de le soumettre aux membres de la Société. Cette Cour connaîtra de tous différends d'un caractère international que les Parties lui soumettront. Elle donnera aussi des avis consultatifs sur tout différend ou tout point, dont la saisira le Conseil ou l'Assemblée."

Ce n'est pas que le Pacte de Versailles ait omis de parler de l'arbitrage comme instrument propre à terminer les différends internationaux. Dans l'ordre des moyens de résoudre les conflits susceptibles d'amener une rupture des relations pacifiques, il a, au contraire, divisé nettement les contestations en litiges arbitrables et en litiges qui ne le sont pas. „Tous les membres de la Société", dit l'article 12, „conviennent que s'il

Draft Convention for the establishment of a Court of Arbitral Justice, and of bringing it into force as soon as an agreement has been reached respecting the selection of the judges and the constitution of the Court."

On another point, bearing on the competence of the courts of arbitration, the Conference was not much more successful: the question of obligatory arbitration. After numerous and admirable attempts to arrive at an understanding in the matter of a worldwide Treaty of Arbitration, either without exceptions or recognising exceptions but indicating certain categories of disputes in which arbitration would always be obligatory, the Conference ended by summing up in the following manner the points upon which agreement had been reached:

"The Conference is unanimous:

1. in admitting the principle of compulsory arbitration;

2. in declaring that certain disputes, in particular those relating to the interpretation and application of the provisions of international agreements, may be submitted to compulsory arbitration without any restriction."

It was in the conditions broadly summed up by the preceding observations that the Paris Conference found the organisation of International Justice, when, after a war unprecedented in the annals of humanity, it directed its attention to the need, in future, of the establishment and activity of the organic institutions for the world's justice.

The Conference, doubtless under the pressure of seemingly more urgent work, thought it should not enter upon a task, which had seemed to claim its attention on so many grounds. It confined itself to including in the Treaty of Versailles an Article 14 to this effect: „The Council (of the League of Nations) shall formulate and submit to the Members of the League for adoption plans for the establishment of a Permanent Court of International Justice. The Court shall be competent to hear and determine any dispute of an international character which the parties thereto submit to it. The Court may also give an advisory opinion upon any dispute or question referred to it by the Council or by the Assembly."

The Covenant of Versailles did not fail to refer to arbitration as the proper instrument for terminating international disputes. On the contrary, among the means of settling conflicts which might lead to a rupture of pacific relations, the Covenant makes a clear-cut division into differences which are arbitrable and those which are

s'élève entre eux un différend susceptible d'entraîner une rupture, ils le soumettront soit à la procédure de l'arbitrage, soit à l'examen du Conseil." Mais réduisant à ses limites extrêmes la sphère des litiges arbitrables, il n'a admis la première des procédures prévues par lui qu'à l'égard des différends entre Puissances, qui sont susceptibles, à leur avis, d'une solution arbitrale. Et il s'est contenté, en formule dernière, d'ajouter que „parmi les litiges qui sont généralement susceptibles de solution arbitrale, on déclare tels les différends relatifs à l'interprétation d'un traité, à tout point de droit international, à la réalité de tout fait qui, s'il était établi, constituerait la rupture d'un engagement international, ou à l'étendue, ou à la nature de la réparation dûe pour une telle rupture".

L'énumération des litiges généralement susceptibles de solution arbitrale était textuellement la même que l'énumération consignée dans une lettre adressée le 29 mars 1919 par l'honorable Elihu Root au président du Comité national républicain. Mais la portée des deux énumérations est toute différente grâce à l'addition du terme „généralement".

Le Comité des jurisconsultes, chargé de préparer un projet de Cour permanente de justice internationale, ne peut se dissimuler les difficultés grandes d'une tâche où tant d'hommes d'état et de juristes ont échoué lors de la Conférence de 1907. Mais, pénétré de la nécessité et de la grandeur de l'œuvre à accomplir, il se met à l'œuvre, estimant qu'il faut s'efforcer de tirer des obstacles rencontrés il y a quelques années et dont beaucoup n'ont pas disparu aujourd'hui, non un motif de douter d'une heureuse solution, mais une méthode sûre pour atteindre celle-ci.

Les questions de procédure relatives au fonctionnement de la justice internationale ne présentent pas actuellement de bien graves difficultés. Résolues une première fois, dans les points fondamentaux auxquels il convient de se limiter, par la Conférence de 1899, elles ont été reprises et élucidées à nouveau par la Conférence de 1907, et l'entente a pu assez facilement s'établir à leur égard. C'est sur les points relatifs à l'organisation et à la compétence des juridictions internationales, à l'obligation de recourir éventuellement à ces juridictions, et aux règles que doivent suivre les juges dans l'appréciation des faits qui leur sont soumis, qu'il importe de faire la lumière et d'arriver à de satisfaisantes solutions.

Quoiqu'il en soit, nous nous efforcerons d'examiner en jurisconsultes profondément dévoués à l'œuvre qui nous rassemble les nombreuses

not. "All the Members of the League", says Article 12, "agree that if there should arise between them any dispute likely to lead to a rupture, they will submit the matter either to arbitration or to inquiry by the Council." But reducing the sphere of arbitral suits to its extreme limits, the Covenant admits the first of the procedures provided for, only in the case of such differences between Powers as in their opinion are susceptible of settlement by arbitration. And it contents itself with adding as a concluding formula that "disputes as to the interpretation of a treaty, as to any question of international law, as to the existence of any fact which if established would constitute a breach of any international obligation, or as to the extent and nature of the reparation to be made for any such breach, are declared to be among those which are generally suitable for submission to arbitration."

The list of cases which can generally be considered susceptible to settlement by arbitration was identically the same as that mentioned in a letter dated March 29th, 1919, addressed by the Honourable Elihu Root to the President of the National Republican Committee. But the tendency of the two lists is entirely different owing to the addition of the word "generally."

The Committee of Jurists, entrusted with the preparation of a plan for a Permanent Court of International Justice, fully realises the great difficulties which are attached to a task in the accomplishment of which numbers of statesmen and jurists have failed since the Conference of 1907. Inspired, however, by the urgency and grandeur of the work to be accomplished, it will undertake the task, hoping to profit by the obstacles experienced in the past many of which have not yet disappeared, and to see in them, not a reason to doubt an ultimate successful solution but a method of reaching it.

The questions of procedure relating to the operation of international justice do not actually present great difficulties. They were resolved in the first instance — on fundamental principles by which it is necessary to be guided — at the Conference of 1899, and have been reconsidered and revised by the Conference of 1907, and it was comparatively easy for the agreement to be reached on the subject. It is the clauses relating to the organisation and the competence of international jurisdiction, to the obligation of having recourse to this jurisdiction, and to the rules and regulations which the judges will have to follow in considering and dealing with the facts submitted to them, which will need elucidating and solving in a satisfactory manner.

questions qui sollicitent notre attention et j'ai la profonde conviction qu'une réunion composée d'hommes comme les Loder, les Lord Phillimore, les Elihu Root, les Adatci, les de Lapradelle, les Ricci-Busatti, les Hagerup et les Altamira, ne se séparera pas sans avoir jeté quelque lumière sur les grands problèmes dont elle est appelée à s'occuper et sans concourir, pour sa part, au progrès de la justice internationale et de la civilisation mondiale.

As far as we are concerned, we will endeavour, as jurists profoundly devoted to the task which has brought us together, to examine the numerous questions which require our attention, and I am thoroughly convinced that an assembly composed of men like M. Loder, Lord Phillimore, Mr. Elihu Root, MM. Adatci, de Lapradelle, Ricci-Busatti, Hagerup and Altamira, will not separate before having thrown some light on the important problems set before them, and before having contributed to the progress of international justice and universal civilisation.

2IÈME SÉANCE (non-publique), tenue au Palais de la Paix, à La Haye, le 17 juin 1920.

Présidence de M. le BARON DESCAMPS.

Sont présents: tous les membres du Comité (excepté M. Bevilaqua); Mr. James Brown Scott; les secrétaires particuliers de M. le Baron Descamps et de M. Adatci; les membres du Secrétariat.

La séance est ouverte à 9.30 h. du matin.

Le PRESIDENT ouvre la discussion sur le projet de règles de procédure soumis au Comité par le Secrétariat. (Annexe 1).

Les articles 1, 2 et 3 du projet sont adoptés sans discussion.

M. ALTAMIRA demande que le mot (langues) „officielles" soit biffé de l'article 4; autrement il serait obligé de demander l'addition de l'espagnol.

M. HAGERUP demande que le texte du plan qui doit être rédigé par le Comité, soit rédigé en français seulement, en raison des difficultés qui surgissent lorsqu'il s'agit d'interpréter un document rédigé en deux langues, quand les deux textes doivent avoir un caractère authentique. Si cette proposition était adoptée, les membres conserveraient, bien entendu, le droit de parler français ou anglais pendant les travaux du Comité, selon leurs préférences.

Après une discussion, à laquelle prennent part Lord Phillimore (qui exprime le désir que le document final dans lequel seront incorporées les décisions du Comité soit rédigé en français et en anglais), Messieurs de Lapradelle, Loder et le Secrétaire général du Comité, M. Anzilotti, le PRESIDENT constate la décision du Comité de laisser de côté des règles de procédure l'article 4 et de remettre à plus tard la question de la langue dans laquelle les décisions du Comité seront rédigées. Toutefois, le Comité admet que les membres du Comité ont le droit de se servir de la langue française ou anglaise et de demander qu'un résumé soit fait, en français ou en an-

2ND MEETING (Private), held at the Peace Palace, the Hague, on June 17th, 1920.

BARON DESCAMPS in the chair.

Present: all members of the Committee (with the exception of M. Bevilaqua); Mr. James Brown Scott; the private secretaries of Baron Descamps and of M. Adatci; the members of the Secretariat.

The meeting was opened at 9.30 a.m.

The PRESIDENT proceeded to the discussion of the proposed rules of procedure submitted to the Committee by the Secretariat. (Annex 1).

Articles 1, 2 and 3 of the draft were adopted without discussion.

M. ALTAMIRA proposed that in article 4 the word "official" (languages) be omitted; if not he would have to request that the Spanish be added.

M. HAGERUP proposed that the text of the plan to be drafted by the Committee should be made out only in French because of the difficulties connected with the interpretation of a document drafted in two languages, when both of the texts were to be authentic. He suggested that, if his proposal be accepted, the members would continue to have the right of exercising their choice between speaking French or English in the Committee.

After a discussion in which the following members took part: Lord Phillimore (who expressed the desire that the final document embodying the decisions of the Committee be made out in French and in English), Messrs. de Lapradelle, Loder, and the Secretary-General of the Committee, M. Anzilotti; the PRESIDENT stated that the Committee had agreed to omit Article 4 from the rules of procedure and to defer until a later time the question of the language in which the decisions of the Committee were to be drafted. The Committee, however, agreed that the members would have the right to use the French or the English langu-

glais, d'un discours prononcé dans l'une ou l'autre langue par l'un des membres.

L'article 5 est adopté, à l'exception des mots: „si un membre en exprime le désir". On convient aussi que le procès-verbal de chaque séance sera mis à la disposition des membres du Comité au moins une heure avant l'ouverture de la séance suivante.

L'article 6 est adopté sans discussion.

Le premier paragraphe de l'article 7 est également adopté sauf quelques légères modifications à la rédaction du texte français. Quant au 2e paragraphe, LORD PHILLIMORE fait remarquer que, en sa qualité de représentant de la Grande Bretagne, il ne saurait considérer comme définitives des décisions prises à la simple majorité des voix. De telles décisions ne peuvent être que provisoires.

Le PRESIDENT fait observer que le Comité ne peut pas invalider d'avance ses propres décisions.

M. LODER estime qu'il y a là un malentendu. Les décisions doivent être prises à la majorité des voix. Tout membre dissident peut exposer librement les motifs de sa décision contraire, et ces motifs seront consignés au procès-verbal. Toutefois, M. Loder pense que l'on pourrait donner satisfaction à Lord Phillimore en stipulant qu'il y aura une seconde lecture des décisions adoptées. Si l'on se mettait d'accord sur cet amendement, les premières décisions prises à la majorité des voix seraient toujours provisoires jusqu'au vote définitif.

LORD PHILLIMORE ne pense pas que le moyen proposé par M. Loder satisfasse complètement à son objection. Sans doute certaines décisions d'une importance secondaire pourraient être prises à la majorité des voix, mais pour des questions d'une importance réelle, l'unanimité s'impose. Il estime qu'il ne lui est pas possible, personnellement, de se lier par des décisions qui causeraient un mécontentement plus ou moins vif dans son pays.

M. HAGERUP fait remarquer que les membres du Comité ne sont pas les représentants de tel ou tel pays, mais bien des juristes indépendants: leurs différents pays auront toute liberté de décision quant à la proposition qui sera le résultat du travail du Comité. Le Comité n'est pas une conférence diplomatique. S'il présentait ce caractère, il serait en effet nécessaire que ses

age, and to ask that a résumé be made in French or English of a speech made in English or French by one of the members.

Article 5 was adopted, except the words: "should a member so desire". It was further agreed that the procès-verbal of one sitting should be placed at the disposition of the members of the Committee at least one hour before the beginning of the next meeting.

Article 6 was adopted without discussion.

The first paragraph of Article 7 was also adopted after some slight modifications in the draft of the French text. Concerning the second paragraph, LORD PHILLIMORE made it clear that, as a representative of Great Britain, he was unable to agree to any decisions being taken by a simple majority vote. He wanted it to be understood that such decisions could only be provisional.

The PRESIDENT remarked that the Committee cannot invalidate its own decisions beforehand.

M. LODER thought there was a misunderstanding. The decisions must be taken by majority votes; an objecting member could always have his divergent opinion noted in the procès-verbal. M. Loder thought that the objection of Lord Phillimore could be met by stipulating that there should be a second reading. If this amendment were adopted, the first decisions taken by majority vote would always be provisional until the final vote.

LORD PHILLIMORE remarked that he did not think that his objection could be entirely met in the way proposed by M. Loder. No doubt in some matters of minor importance, it would be possible to accept majority decisions, but matters of real importance would have to be decided unanimously. He stated that it would be impossible for him to consider himself as bound by decisions which would give rise to more or less keen dissatisfaction in his own country.

M. HAGERUP pointed out that the members of the Committee were not representatives of individual countries: they were independent jurists; their countries had complete liberty of decision on the proposal which would be the outcome of the work of the Committee. The Committee was not a diplomatic conference. If it were, unanimous decisions would be necessary.

décisions fussent prises à l'unanimité. Mais tel n'est pas le cas. D'autre part, il faut que les travaux du Comité aboutissent à un résultat tangible, c'est à dire au projet qui sera soumis à l'Assemblée. Ce projet devra forcément faire l'objet d'un vote final et s'il n'obtient pas l'adhésion de la totalité des membres du Comité, celle de la majorité suffira.

Such was not the case. On the other hand it was necessary that the efforts of the Committee produce tangible results, namely a plan to submit to the Assembly. This plan must come to a final vote, and if it did not obtain unanimous support, a majority vote would suffice.

M. ADATCI estime que l'opinion de M. Hagerup est la plus logique et que celle de Lord Phillimore est la plus humaine. Il pense que les opinions divergentes qui sont exprimées au sein du Comité, pourraient et devraient être conciliées, grâce aux efforts du Président en vue d'obtenir l'unanimité.

M. ADATCI submitted that the opinion of M. Hagerup was the more logical one and that of Lord Phillimore the more human. He thought that the divergent opinions expressed in the Committee might be reconciled and that this should be done by the efforts of the President in order to obtain unanimity.

Le PRESIDENT promet de s'efforcer de concilier les différentes opinions. Il propose la procédure suivante: il y aura d'abord un vote en première lecture, puis une seconde lecture. Si l'unanimité ne peut être obtenue à la seconde lecture, mention sera faite au procès-verbal des opinions divergentes des membres opposants et des motifs sur lesquels ces opinions sont fondées. Le Président rédigera, d'accord avec Lord Phillimore, un texte en ce sens, qui formera un nouvel article des règles de procédure.

The PRESIDENT gave assurance that he would use every effort to conciliate the different opinions. He proposed the following procedure. There should be: first a provisional vote, then a second reading. If a unanimous decision is not reached after the second reading, the divergent opinions of dissident members together with the grounds on which differences are based should be recorded in the procès-verbal. The President would draft, in agreement with Lord Phillimore, a text on these lines, which would form a new Article of the rules of procedure.

M. ALTAMIRA insiste sur ce point que les raisons données à l'appui d'une opinion divergente ne pourront être que des raisons ayant un caractère juridique.

M. ALTAMIRA emphasized that the grounds employed in support of a divergent opinion could only be of a juridical nature.

Le PRESIDENT passe ensuite à l'examen de la question de la méthode de travail que devra suivre le Comité. Il pense que le projet d'ordre du jour soumis par le Secrétariat (annexe 2) contient des questions à la fois trop nombreuses et trop détaillées pour une première délibération. A son avis, le Comité devrait commencer par étudier un nombre restreint de points importants nettement définis.

The PRESIDENT proceeded to the consideration of the method of work to be followed by the Committee. He thought that the draft agenda submitted by the Secretariat (annex 2) contains too many and too detailed questions for a preliminary discussion. In his opinion the Committee should start by considering a limited number of clearly defined important points.

Mr. ROOT présente un projet de résolution à l'adoption du Comité. (Voir annexe 3).

Il dit qu'il est tout à fait d'accord avec les remarques du Président. Le Comité devrait prendre pour point de départ les travaux qui ont déjà été faits. Le monde sait qu'on est en train de reprendre le travail pour la réalisation du principe de la justice dans les relations internationales. Dans le monde entier, il existe un respect profond pour les travaux qui ont été faits à La Haye, lors des Conférences de 1899 et de 1907. Le Comité devrait commencer par fixer les relations qui existent entre ses travaux et ce qui a été fait lors des Conférences de la Haye. L'opinion publique

Mr. ROOT presented a resolution for adoption by the Committee. (See Annex 3).

He said that he was in entire harmony with the views expressed by the President. The Committee should take as its starting point the work which already has been accomplished. The world knows that we are about to resume the task of making possible the application of the principle of justice in international relations. Throughout the entire world there is much respect for the work done at the Hague in the Conferences of 1899 and 1907. The Committee should start by making clear the relations which exist between its work and that accomplished at the

dans les divers pays serait reconnaissante de savoir que le Comité commence ses travaux dans cet esprit. Mr. Root sait que ce sera le cas surtout en Amérique. Les membres du Comité ont reçu du Secrétariat de la Société des Nations des projets pour l'établissement d'une Cour Permanente de Justice Internationale. Mr. Root mentionne les projets établis par des juristes de la Norvège, du Danemark, de la Suède, de la Hollande et de la Suisse; il mentionne également les projets communiqués par l'Allemagne et par l'Autriche. Mr. Root exprime le désir que le Comité témoigne sa reconnaissance et exprime son respect pour tous ces travaux.

Le premier objet de la résolution est le suivant: il ne serait pas heureux de choisir un seul plan, parmi ceux qui existent, et d'en faire la base des discussions du Comité, si ce n'était pas les travaux de la seconde Conférence de La Haye qu'on prenait comme point de départ. Il ne faut pas oublier que les membres présents ne représentent que dix pays. Il faut prendre en considération, dans les travaux du Comité, les sentiments de tous les autres peuples qui ne sont pas représentés au Comité. A cet effet, il serait même désirable, dans l'opinion de Mr. Root, d'adopter une résolution qui impliquât la prise en considération de tous les projets communiqués aux membres. Il faut que tous les pays se sentent représentés au sein du Comité par leurs travaux préparatoires. En se plaçant à un point de vue pratique, on peut dire que l'adoption de cette résolution aurait le même effet que la proposition du Président: on devrait soumettre d'abord aux discussions du Comité des questions de principe. Mr. Root prend un exemple. Si l'on commençait par traiter de l'organisation de la Cour, on prendrait comme point de départ les dispositions du plan provisoire de 1907; puis on lirait les dispositions du projet des Cinq Etats, puis celles de l'Autriche, et ainsi de suite. Puis, on discuterait.

Toutefois, l'effet de la résolution serait moins d'influencer la méthode de travail du Comité que de lui fournir un point de départ pour ses délibérations.

Le PRESIDENT remercie Mr. Root dont les principes sont très analogues aux siens. Il exprime le vœu que les membres qui le désirent soumettent au Comité leurs opinions sur les problèmes généraux à résoudre. C'est du reste ce que lui-même a l'intention de faire plus tard, au cours de la séance.

M. HAGERUP demande à Mr. Root s'il désire que le Comité s'adresse, en premier lieu,

Hague Conferences. Public opinion in the various countries would be grateful to know that the Committee was beginning its work in this spirit. Mr. Root knew that it would be so in America. The members of the Committee had received from the Secretariat of the League of Nations plans for the establishment of a Court of International Justice. Mr. Root mentioned the plan drawn up by jurists of Norway, Denmark, Sweden, Holland and Switzerland, also the plans sent by Germany and Austria. Mr. Root expressed the desire that the Committee should indicate its recognition and respect for all these efforts.

The first purpose of the resolution is the following: it might not be timely to select one single plan from among those in existence and to adopt it as the basis of the Committee's discussions, if it was not the results of the Second Hague Conference that were adopted as a starting point. It must not be forgotten that the members present represented only ten countries. In all the work of the Committee, the sentiments of all the other peoples not represented on the Committee must be taken into consideration. For this purpose, Mr. Root thought that it would be desirable to adopt a resolution which involved the consideration of all the plans communicated to the members. All countries must feel that they are represented on the Committee by their preparatory efforts. From a practical standpoint, it could be said that the adoption of this resolution would have the same effect as the adoption of the President's plan: questions of principle should first be discussed by the Committee. Mr. Root cited an example. If one begins by considering the Court's organisation, the provisions of the tentative plan of 1907 would be taken as a starting point; then the provisions of the plan submitted by the Five Powers would be read, then those of Austria, and so on. Then there would be a discussion.

In any case, the effect of the resolution would not be so much to affect the order of the Committee's work as it would be to furnish a starting point for its deliberations.

The PRESIDENT conveyed his thanks to Mr. Root whose principles very much coincided with the opinions of the President. The President expressed the desire that the members who so wished might explain their viewpoints on the general problem before the Committee. He intended to do so himself later in the session.

M. HAGERUP asked Mr. Root if he desired to have the Committee address itself directly to

à l'opinion publique du monde. Dans l'affirmative, pense-t-il que la résolution doive être publiée afin de donner au monde l'assurance que le Comité prendra en considération les travaux des conférences de La Haye et les divers plans gouvernementaux et autres qui ont été mis à sa disposition? M. Hagerup pense qu'il ne serait pas nécessaire de faire mention de cette intention, parce que le mandat des membres du Comité comprend la prise en considération desdits projets.

En ce qui concerne la méthode de travail, M. Hagerup propose qu'on discute d'abord quelques principes fondamentaux, tels que les principes mentionnés par M. Bourgeois dans le discours prononcé par lui à la séance solennelle.

M. LODER s'élève contre la publication de la résolution. Si des communications doivent être faites, il faut qu'elles fournissent des renseignements exacts sur des points déterminés et non seulement de vagues déclarations ou des vœux.

M. DE LAPRADELLE émet quelques observations sur les deux points visés par la proposition de Mr. Root. Premièrement Mr. Root désire rendre hommage aux travaux qui ont déjà été faits en vue de la solution du problème devant lequel le Comité se trouve actuellement placé. Cet hommage peut sans inconvénient être consigné dans le procès-verbal, dont on pouvait faire parvenir un extrait à la presse. En second lieu Mr. Root désire, dans l'opinion de M. de Lapradelle, choisir un des projets existants pour servir de base aux travaux du Comité. Ce projet devrait, selon Mr. Root, être celui de 1907. M. de Lapradelle pense, cependant, qu'il serait imprudent de se lier à un projet déterminé. Il vaudrait mieux étudier tous les projets mis à la disposition du Comité, les oublier, et puis se mettre au travail.

M. de Lapradelle propose l'adoption de la partie de la résolution de Mr. Root qui vise le premier point; quant à l'autre partie de la résolution, il propose qu'elle soit réservée.

M. ADATCI et M. HAGERUP déclarent se rallier au point de vue émis par M. de Lapradelle. M. Hagerup est d'avis que si le Comité commençait par rendre hommage de la façon proposée par M. de Lapradelle, cela ferait un excellent effet; mais il préférerait que cet hommage fût rendu d'une manière générale et sans nommer spécialement chacun de ceux auxquels il s'adresse.

public opinion in the world. If so, was Mr. Root of the opinion that the resolution should be published in order to give to the world the assurance that the Committee was going to take into account the works of the Hague conferences and the different governmental or private schemes which have been placed at its disposition? M. Hagerup thought that it was not necessary to mention this intention, for the reason that the mandate to the members of the Committee gave instructions to consider the schemes in question.

With regard to the method of work, M. Hagerup moved that some fundamental principles should, first of all, be discussed, such for instance as the principles mentioned by M. Bourgeois during his speech at the formal opening meeting.

M. LODER was opposed to publication of the resolution. If something was to be published, it ought to be some definite points and not vague expressions of opinion, or vœux.

M. DE LAPRADELLE contributed various observations on the two points referred to in Mr. Root's proposition. First Mr. Root desired to pay homage to the work which has already been accomplished for the solution of the problem before the Committee. This homage might well be made in the procès-verbal, and an extract from it communicated to the press. Secondly Mr. Root wished, as M. de Lapradelle understood him, to select one of the existing schemes as a basis for the work of the Committee. This scheme should be, according to Mr. Root, the 1907 scheme. M. de Lapradelle believed however that it would be imprudent to identify oneself with a given plan. It would be better to study all the schemes placed at the disposition of the Committee, then to forget them, and finally to set to work.

M. de Lapradelle moved the adoption of the first part of Mr. Root's resolution and the postponement of a decision on the second part.

M. ADATCI and M. HAGERUP declared that their points of view coincided with that of M. de Lapradelle. M. Hagerup was of the opinion that it would make a favorable impression if the Committee started by paying homage in the way proposed by M. de Lapradelle, but he would prefer to have that homage expressed in a general way rather than by enumerating individually each one to whom the resolution was addressed.

Mr. ROOT, par l'organe de Mr. Brown Scott, fait ressortir que la proposition de M. de Lapradelle n'est pas identique à la sienne. Mr. Root désire que les travaux de La Haye forment le point de départ des travaux du Comité.

M. DE LAPRADELLE, de son côté, fait observer qu'il est opposé à l'idée de prendre le projet élaboré à La Haye en 1907 comme base des travaux du Comité. Ces travaux doivent être absolument indépendants. Il désire également attirer l'attention de ses collègues sur ce fait qu'il y a un grand nombre de plans: il mentionne spécialement le projet de l'Union Juridique Internationale, qui va être distribué aux membres du Comité par les soins du Secrétariat.

Le PRESIDENT désire savoir si Mr. Root consentirait à ce qu'on adoptât la première partie de la proposition qu'il a faite et à ce qu'on en réservât la seconde partie.

Personnellement, le Président ne désire pas se prononcer sur la question de savoir quel plan on choisirait pour servir de base aux travaux du Comité.

LORD PHILLIMORE désire qu'hommage soit rendu au projet de La Haye de 1907, mais ce doit être seulement un hommage; il désire que l'on rende également hommage au plan élaboré par la Conférence des Neutres, au mois de février 1920.

Mr. ROOT dit que la résolution qu'il a proposée peut parfaitement se scinder en deux. Il serait très satisfait si la première partie pouvait être prise en considération immédiate. Cette partie est celle aux termes de laquelle le résultat des travaux de la Conférence de La Haye serait pris comme point de départ pour les travaux du Comité.

Le PRESIDENT fait remarquer qu'en 1907 deux points importants ne purent être résolus. Pour cette raison, il pense qu'il ne serait peut-être pas expédient d'adopter le projet de 1907 comme base de la discussion. Il exprime le désir que Mr. Root n'insiste pas sur la proposition et qu'il se contente de voir rendre hommage aux travaux de La Haye.

M. RICCI-BUSATTI est d'avis qu'il serait préférable de faire ressortir seulement d'une façon générale, les liens qui rattachent les travaux du Comité à ceux de la Conférence de la Haye, plutôt que de se servir de ces derniers comme base pour l'accomplissement de la tâche du Comité.

Mr. ROOT pointed out, through Mr. Brown Scott, that M. de Lapradelle's proposal was not identical with that of Mr. Root, whose wish was that the work of the Hague should be made the starting point of the Committee's work.

M. DE LAPRADELLE, on his side, pointed out that he was opposed to the idea of taking the scheme worked out at the Hague in 1907 as the basis of the work of the Committee. Its work ought to be absolutely independent. He desired also to draw the attention of his colleagues to the fact that a great number of schemes exists; he especially mentioned the scheme of the Union Juridique Internationale, which is to be supplied to the Committee by the Secretariat.

The PRESIDENT wanted to know if Mr. Root would agree to having the first part of his proposal adopted and to defer action on the second part.

Personally, the President did not desire to decide on the question which scheme ought to be chosen as the basis for the work of the Committee.

LORD PHILLIMORE desired that respect be paid to the Hague scheme of 1907, but that nothing further be implied. He desired also to render homage to the scheme elaborated by the conference of the Neutral Powers in February 1920.

Mr. ROOT said that the resolution proposed by him might perfectly well be divided into two parts. He would be quite satisfied if the first part only were given immediate consideration. According to the terms of this part of his resolution, the results of the work of the Hague Conference should be taken as starting point for the work of the Committee.

The PRESIDENT remarked that in 1907 two important points could not be agreed upon. For this reason, he thought it would not be advisable to adopt the 1907 scheme as the basis of the discussion. He expressed the desire that Mr. Root would not press the point, but be content in having homage paid to the work of the Hague.

M. RICCI-BUSATTI was of opinion that it would be better to point out only in a general way the connection between the work of the Committee and the work of the Hague Conference, rather than to adopt this work as basis for the work of the Committee.

Le PRESIDENT rappelle le fait qu'à côté du projet de 1907, il existe un grand nombre de plans d'origine privée. Il ne serait pas possible d'en faire une énumération complète.

LORD PHILLIMORE fait remarquer qu'il est maintenant parfaitement clair que la proposition de M. de Lapradelle est différente de celle de Mr. Root. Il demande que la proposition de Mr. Root soit réservée et que l'on ne prenne de décision qu'après avoir consulté tous les membres.

M. DE LAPRADELLE est d'accord avec cette proposition, quant au fond, mais il s'agit de se mettre aussi d'accord sur les termes. Il demande la permission de lire le projet de communiqué à la presse qu'il vient de rédiger. (Voir annexe 4).

Mr. ROOT fait remarquer que, sous sa forme actuelle, le communiqué tend à rabaisser le travail de la Conférence au même niveau que les autres travaux, œuvres de commissions particulières ou de juristes isolés. Il rend hommage à tout le monde également et sans distinction.

M. LODER est d'avis que des remerciements et des louanges vagues ne sont point nécessaires et pourraient même produire une impression défavorable sur l'opinion publique. Toutefois il ne s'oppose pas à cette communication, mais il voudrait qu'on fît une déclaration précise quant à la base des travaux du Comité.

M. DE LAPRADELLE répond aux objections de fond de Mr. Root, et à celles de M. Loder, qui sont des objections d'opportunité. Il ne croit pas l'objection de Mr. Root justifiée. Les travaux de la Conférence de La Haye sont placés en tête de l'énumération. En mentionnant d'autres travaux à la suite de ceux de La Haye, il indique seulement que le Comité entend puiser libéralement à toutes les sources. On pourrait, avec avantage, diviser cette énumération en deux parties et les traiter dans deux alinéas différents. Le Comité veut faire une œuvre juridique scientifique. Quant à l'objection de M. Loder, M. de Lapradelle pense que son texte indique clairement que le Comité tiendra compte de tous les projets provenant des différents pays, et que, de cette façon, l'opinion publique sera satisfaite.

Le PRESIDENT, sur une remarque de Mr. Root, propose de viser dans deux alinéas séparés, les travaux de La Haye, et les documents et projets particuliers.

The PRESIDENT called the members' attention to the fact that a great number of schemes of private origin existed in addition to the scheme of 1907, and that it would be impossible to make a complete enumeration of them.

LORD PHILLIMORE pointed out that it was now quite evident that the proposal of M. de Lapradelle was different from that of Mr. Root. He suggested that Mr. Root's proposal should be reserved, and that no decision should be taken until all the members should have been consulted.

M. DE LAPRADELLE agreed in principle with this suggestion, but desired to arrive at an agreement on details. He asked permission to read a proposed press communiqué which he had prepared. (See Annex 4).

Mr. ROOT pointed out that in its present form the communiqué tended to reduce the work of the Conference to the same level as other work undertaken by special committees or individual jurists. It pays homage to all equally and without distinction.

M. LODER considered that expressions of thanks and praise were quite unnecessary, and that they might even create an unfavorable impression on public opinion. However, he would not oppose this communication, but wished that a definite announcement be made concerning the basis of the work of the Committee.

M. DE LAPRADELLE answered Mr. Root's objections founded on principle and those of M. Loder founded on expediency. He did not consider that Mr. Root's objection was justified. The work of the Hague Conference was placed at the beginning of the list. In mentioning other works in addition to those undertaken at the Hague, he only intended to show that the Conference meant to draw upon all possible sources of information. It might be advantageous to divide the list into two parts and to treat them under two separate headings. The Committee aims to produce a scientific legal structure. Regarding M. Loder's objection, M. de Lapradelle considered that his text clearly showed that the Committee would take into consideration all schemes from various countries, and that this should satisfy public opinion.

The PRESIDENT, following a remark made by Mr. Root, proposed that the works undertaken at the Hague, and private documents and schemes, should be dealt with in separate paragraphs.

M. HAGERUP se rallie à cette proposition.

Le PRESIDENT donne lecture d'un exposé qu'il a rédigé après étude des divers documents soumis au Comité. Cet exposé fait suite au discours prononcé par lui la veille. (Voir annexe 6).

Après avoir donné lecture de son exposé, le Baron Descamps l'explique et le résume en ces termes:

Il est nécessaire, tout au moins à l'origine, que tous les Etats prennent part, dans une certaine mesure, au choix des jurisconsultes, mais il faut essayer de concilier le principe de l'égalité juridique des Etats avec certaines garanties qu'il conviendrait de donner aux grands Etats.

Il faut donner initialement aux grands Etats le droit de nommer leurs arbitres, et comme ceux-ci seront, sans nul doute, les jurisconsultes les plus éminents de chaque Etat, on pourra leur laisser en pleine confiance le soin de nommer ensuite les membres de la partie permanente de la Cour de Justice, soit 9 juges et 6 juges suppléants. Ce sera ensuite la Cour qui établira son règlement d'ordre intérieur, en vue, par exemple, de se scinder en chambre de procédure sommaire et en chambre de justice ordinaire. Comme garantie, on soumettrait ce règlement à l'approbation du Conseil ou de l'Assemblée de la Société des Nations.

Rappelant ensuite la part importante que Lord Pauncefote a prise à l'établissement de la Cour d'Arbitrage, le Baron Descamps remarque que le résultat des travaux de cette Cour est fort honorable: elle a examiné un nombre assez considérable de cas, à la satisfaction générale.

Ainsi la totalité des membres nommés par chaque Etat à la Cour d'Arbitrage, à raison de quatre arbitres par Etat, formeront un collège qui devra choisir les juges destinés à composer la partie permanente de la nouvelle Cour.

En procédant à ce choix, les membres du collège ne devront pas perdre de vue que les grands systèmes juridiques du monde doivent être représentés à la Cour Permanente.

M. ADATCI exprime d'abord sa sympathie pour les efforts du Baron Descamps de concilier toutes les susceptibilités. Il constate que l'opinion courante est celle de l'adoption du principe de l'égalité des Etats.

Ce principe est admis depuis longtemps, mais il est parfois fictif, et il faut, avant tout, songer à la viabilité de la Cour. M. Adatci est d'avis qu'il faut traiter cette grave question, à la manière de jurisconsultes sociologues plutôt qu'à celle de jurisconsultes formalistes.

M. HAGERUP agreed with this proposal.

The PRESIDENT then read a report which he had composed after considering the documents submitted to the Committee. This report was complementary to the speech delivered by him the day before. (See Annex 6).

After having read his report, Baron Descamps explained and summarised it as follows:

It is essential, especially at the outset, that all States take part, to a certain extent, in the selection of jurisconsults, but an attempt must be made to reconcile the principle of juridical equality of States with certain guarantees which should be given to the great Powers.

States originally must have the right to nominate their arbitrators, and as these will doubtless be the most distinguished jurisconsults of each State, they may safely be entrusted with the task of nominating subsequently the members of the permanent part of the Court of Justice, namely nine judges and six deputy judges. The Court itself would define its own rules of procedure. It might for instance divide itself into a court of summary procedure, and an ordinary court of justice. As a precaution, such administrative arrangements would be subject to the approval of the Council or Assembly of the League of Nations.

After recalling the important part which Lord Pauncefote has taken in establishing the Court of Arbitration, Baron Descamps pointed out that the results achieved by this Court were very creditable; it has examined a considerable number of cases to the satisfaction of all concerned.

Thus all the members chosen by each State for the Court of Arbitration, four being selected by each State, will form an electoral college to choose the judges who will constitute the permanent section of the new Court.

In making their selections, it is incumbent on the electoral college not to lose sight of the fact that the great systems of jurisprudence of the world ought to be represented in the permanent Court.

M. ADATCI expressed first his sympathy for the efforts made by Baron Descamps to put at ease all susceptibilities. He considered that general opinion was in favour of the adoption of the principle of equality amongst States.

This principle has long been recognised, but is often more apparent than real. The viability of the Court must be primarily considered. In the opinion of M. Adatci, this vital question must be treated from the standpoint of sociological rather than formalistic jurisprudence.

L'adoption de Monaco comme Membre de la Société des Nations a été proposée. En droit formel, les droits de Monaco sont égaux à ceux des Etats-Unis. Mais cette solution serait-elle satisfaisante pour la conscience publique? M. Adatci fait appel à l'expérience de ses collègues qui admettront que la question est pour le moins douteuse.

La base de la paix mondiale, dit-il, c'est la réalité vivante de l'existence des principales Puissances et des autres Etats. D'ailleurs, à tous les points de vue: population, territoire, richesse, mouvement économique, commercial et financier, histoire, races, systèmes de civilisation et de jurisprudence, intérêts vitaux, régionaux etc., en un mot en ce qui regarde tous les éléments de l'activité humaine, il est indispensable que lesdites Puissances soient représentées au sein de la Cour qu'il s'agit de créer; quel que soit l'aspect sous lequel on envisage la question, on arrive à ce résultat final qu'il faut que les cinq grandes Puissances soient représentées à la Cour.

M. Adatci insiste sur la justesse de la distinction qu'il y a lieu de faire entre les affaires judiciaires intérieures et les affaires internationales. Il est profondément convaincu que l'exclusion éventuelle de la Cour d'une ou de plusieurs personnes ressortissants desdites Puissances, la rendrait nécessairement non-viable. C'est là une vérité éclatante que personne ne peut nier. Pourquoi donc ne pas l'admettre franchement, sans aucune ambiguité? Il faut, dit-il, que nous ayons tous ici le courage juridique et la tournure d'esprit réaliste sans lesquels on ne saurait créer une personne juridique viable. Quoique, naturellement, on fasse abstraction de la nationalité des juges dans l'exercice de leurs fonctions à la Cour internationale en question, il faut tenir compte du sentiment intuitif des peuples, fluide délicat, violent et irrésistible.

M. Adatci passe ensuite à la question relative au nombre des juges. Les juges permanents seraient, selon le Baron Descamps, au nombre de 9 et les suppléants de 6. M. Adatci pense qu'un total de 13 serait préférable: 5 juges que les grandes Puissances seraient invitées à désigner et 8 qui seraient nommés par les autres Etats lesquels seront bientôt au nombre de 50 environ. Cette organisation nécessiterait la nomination d'un juge ad hoc par les Puissances, parties aux litiges, qui n'auraient pas de représentant, ce qui pourrait, le cas échéant, porter momentanément à 15 le nombre des juges; il en serait de même au cas où une des colonies anglaises, „self governing dominions", par exemple le Canada ou l'Australie, serait mêlée à l'affaire. Il fait aussi

Monaco was proposed as a member of the League of Nations. According to strict law, the rights of Monaco are equal to those of the United States. But would such a solution of the problem satisfy public sense of justice? He felt sure that his colleagues would, from their own experience, admit the doubtfulness of the question.

The real basis of world-peace, he declared, was the co-existence of the principal Powers and the other states. Furthermore, from all points of view: population, territory, wealth, trade and commerce, finance, history, race, systems of civilisation and jurisprudence, vital interests, regional interests, etc., in brief with regard to every human activity it was imperative that the named Powers be represented on the Court in process of formation. From whatever points of view the question was considered, the conclusion was reached that the five great Powers must be represented on the Court.

M. Adatci insisted on the accuracy of distinguishing between internal judicial questions and those of international character. He was decidedly of the opinion that the possible exclusion from the Court of one or more persons representing the named Powers would render the Court impracticable. That fact was undeniable. Why not admit it frankly, without any ambiguity? Here we must all, he declared, possess the juridical courage and a sense of realities, lacking which we shall be unable to create a living juridical organism. Although naturally the nationality of judges in the discharge of their duties on the international Court in question may be disregarded, it is necessary to consider the intuitive sensibilities of peoples, a delicate quality, violent and irresistible.

He (M. Adatci) then turned to the question of the number of judges. According to Baron Descamps there should be 9 permanent judges and 6 supplementary judges. M. Adatci believed that a total of 13 would be preferable: 5 judges which the principal Powers should be asked to designate, and, 8 who should be named by the other Powers; those Powers will soon number approximately 50. This organisation would entail the selection of a judge *ad hoc* by those parties who, being parties to any law suit, possess no representative on the court. This might, should the situation arise, increase temporarily the number of judges to 15. The same procedure would be followed if one of the English self-governing colonies, for example Canada or Australia, were concerned in a case. He noted also that according to his scheme the principal Powers should be always in the minority, a cir-

remarquer que, d'après son plan, les principales Puissances seront toujours en minorité, ce qui pourra donner pleine garantie aux autres Etats.

M. HAGERUP propose une motion d'ordre. Il est prématuré, d'après lui, de discuter déjà les détails des problèmes. Il propose un échange de vues sur les points suivants:

1⁰. Organisation de la Cour;

2⁰. Juridiction de la Cour;

3⁰. Règlementation de la procédure;

4⁰. Siège de la Cour.

Mr. ROOT demande, qu'avant de prendre une décision sur la proposition de M. Hagerup, on procède à un vote sur le projet de résolution soumis par M. de Lapradelle. (Annexe 5).

Après lecture, le projet est adopté à l'unanimité.

On soulève alors la question de savoir si la résolution doit être communiquée à la presse. Mr. ROOT désire qu'on procède à cette communication. Les autres membres ne s'y opposant pas, la proposition de Mr. Root est adoptée. Le Secrétariat est chargé d'assurer l'exécution de la décision.

La discussion sur l'ordre du jour de la séance suivante est reprise. On adopte la proposition de M. Hagerup dans ce sens que l'on décide que la discussion sera limitée à l'organisation de la Cour.

Sur la proposition de LORD PHILLIMORE, il est entendu que chaque membre sera libre de donner son avis sans être lié par un questionnaire.

Sur la proposition de M. DE LAPRADELLE, le Secrétariat est chargé de préparer un tableau synoptique des différentes dispositions des projets existants relatifs à l'organisation de la Cour. (Voir annexe 7). Le Secrétariat est également chargé de faire imprimer pour la séance prochaine le discours du Président.

La séance est levée à 12 h. 30 de l'après-midi.

Le Président:

(signé) Brn. DESCAMPS.

Le Secrétaire-Général:

(signé) D. ANZILOTTI.

cumstance giving full guarantees to the other Powers.

M. HAGERUP raised a point of order. He thought it premature to discuss the details of the problems at this stage. He suggested an exchange of views on the following points:

1. Organisation of the Court;
2. Jurisdiction of the Court;
3. Rules of Procedure;
4. Seat of the Court.

Mr. ROOT requested that before coming to a decision concerning M. Hagerup's proposal, a vote should be taken on the draft resolution submitted by M. de Lapradelle. (Annex 5).

After being read, the draft was adopted unanimously.

The question was raised as to whether this resolution should be communicated to the press. Mr. ROOT wished that this should be done. The other members had no objection, and Mr. Root's proposal was carried. The Secretariat was instructed to carry out this decision.

The discussion of the agenda for the next meeting was reopened. The proposal of M. Hagerup was adopted with the understanding that only the question of the Court's organisation should be discussed.

On the suggestion of LORD PHILLIMORE, it was agreed that each member might express his opinion freely without being subjected to a "questionnaire".

In consequence of a proposal made by M. DE LAPRADELLE, the Secretariat was entrusted with the preparation of a tabular synopsis of the different existing schemes concerning the organisation of the Court. (See Annex 7). The secretariat was also instructed to have the President's speech printed for the next meeting.

The meeting closed at 12.30 p.m.

The President:

(signed) Brn. DESCAMPS.

The Secretary-General:

(signed) D. ANZILOTTI.

ANNEXE No. 1.

Projet de règles de Procédure pour le Comité Consultatif de Juristes.

1. Les séances du Comité ne sont pas publiques; toutefois, dérogation pourra être faite à cette règle dans des cas déterminés et par décisions spéciales. Les délibérations sont confidentielles; cependant, le Secrétariat est autorisé à fournir au public des résumés succincts des questions traitées dans chaque séance et du progrès qui a été fait.

2. Les membres du Comité ont seuls le droit de prendre part aux discussions. Le secrétaire du Comité a le droit de fournir lui-même des explications et de charger des membres du Secrétariat d'en fournir.

3. Les conseillers et les secrétaires privés des membres ont le droit d'accompagner les membres aux séances. Avec le consentement du Comité un membre pourra dans des cas déterminés, charger ses conseillers de fournir des explications.

4. Le Français et l'Anglais sont reconnus comme les langues officielles du Comité et de ses travaux. Si un membre du Comité en exprime le désir, un discours prononcé dans l'une de ces langues sera résumé oralement dans l'autre, par les soins du Secrétariat.

5. Les procès-verbaux des séances contiendront un résumé succinct des délibérations et, in extenso, les décisions du Comité, ainsi que les déclarations, les projets et amendements déposés par ce membre. Un projet ronéographié de procès-verbal de chaque séance sera présenté aux membres au commencement de la séance suivante. Ces procès-verbaux ne seront pas lus à la séance.

6. Tous les projets et tous les amendements soumis à la décision du Comité seront dans la mesure du possible présentés par écrit au Président.

Si un projet ou un amendement n'a pas été distribué avant le commencement de la séance, l'ajournement de la séance sera prononcé si un membre en exprime le désir.

7. A la fin de chaque séance, le Président soumettra au Comité l'ordre du jour de la séance

ANNEX No. 1.

Draft of rules of Procedure for the Advisory Committee of Jurists.

1. The sittings of the Committee are, unless otherwise decided in special cases, not public. The deliberations are confidential. However, the Secretariat is authorised to furnish short public statements of the questions treated and of the progress made at the sittings.

2. Only the members of the Committee have the right to take part in the discussions. The Secretary of the Committee has the right to give himself, and to ask members of the Secretariat to give, explanations.

3. The counsellors and private secretaries of the members are entitled to accompany the members to the sittings. With the consent of the Committee, a member may, in special cases ask his counsellors to furnish explanations.

4. French and English are recognised as the official languages of the Committee and of the documents pertaining to its work. A speech pronounced in one of these languages shall, at the request of any member of the Committee, be analysed verbally in the other by the Secretariat.

5. The procès-verbaux of the sittings shall contain a brief analysis of the deliberations, and, *in extenso,* points adopted by the Committee and declarations, proposals or amendments that may have been made by any member should he so desire. A draft procès-verbal of each sitting shall be presented to the members (in roneographed copies) at the beginning of the next. These procès-verbaux shall not be read.

6. All proposals and all amendments to be discussed by the Committee shall, if possible, be presented to the President in writing.

Should a proposal or amendment not have been distributed before the sitting, the adjournment shall be pronounced at the request of any member.

7. At the end of each sitting, the President shall submit to the Committee the agenda of the next.

prochaine. L'ordre du jour une fois adopté, ne pourra être modifié que par une décision du Comité.

Les décisions du Comité sont prises à la majorité des voix. Les opinions divergentes seront consignées dans les procès-verbaux des séances et, à la requête des membres directement intéressés, il en sera fait mention dans le protocole final constatant les résultats des travaux du Comité.

The agenda once having been adopted can be modified only by a decision of the Committee.

The decisions of the Committee are taken by a majority of votes. Divergent opinions shall be rendered in the procès-verbaux of the sittings, and at the request of the members concerned, be noted in the final protocol containing the results arrived at by the Committee.

ANNEXE No. 2.

Projet d'agenda général.

a. Questions préliminaires.

I. Quelle forme devra être donnée aux résultats du travail du Comité?

Rapport avec, comme annexe, projet complet de convention?

Exposé des motifs à côté du rapport?

Le document à présenter au Conseil de la Société des Nations?

b. Principes généraux.

II. Quels traits devront distinguer une Cour permanente de justice internationale?

Permanence réelle: comment la définir?

Les juges ne devront pas être choisis par les parties à chaque litige spécial.

La juridiction de la Cour sera obligatoire.

La Cour se laissera guider exclusivement par des principes de droit.

Les principes à appliquer devront être les mêmes dans tous les cas. Les jugements antérieurs de la Cour seront pris en considération comme précédents, en vue de l'établissement d'une jurisprudence permanente.

III. Les traits ci-dessus sont ils compatibles avec des fonctions arbitrales?

Si oui, la nouvelle Cour devra-t-elle être en même temps une Cour de Justice et une Cour d'Arbitrage?

Dans l'affirmative, la Cour d'Arbitrage de La Haye devra-t-elle subsister? Si non, la nouvelle Cour devra-t-elle être complètement exclue des fonctions arbitrales ou peut-on laisser aux parties à un litige la faculté de demander à la Cour ou à ses membres de faire fonction d'arbitre?

IV. Quelle importance doit être accordée aux dispositions des articles 12 et 14 du Pacte de la Société des Nations pour la réponse à donner aux questions de principe ci-dessus?

V. Le projet de convention à proposer par le Comité doit-il contenir, dans un préambule, les principes qui inspireront les réponses aux questions ci-dessus?

c. Compétence de la Cour.

VI. La Cour devra-t-elle avoir compétence pour connaître de tout litige soumis à elle par les parties, ou la compétence de la Cour devra-t-elle être limitée? Dans ce dernier cas, la Cour

ANNEX No. 2.

Draft of general agenda.

a. Preliminary questions.

I. What form should be given to the outcome of the work of the Committee:

Report with complete draft convention as an annex?

Exposé des motifs apart from report?

Document to be presented to Council of the League of Nations?

b. General principles.

II. What features should distinguish a permanent Court of International Justice?

Real permanency: how to define?

Judges not to be chosen by the parties in each special case.

Jurisdiction of Court compulsory.

Court to be guided exclusively by principles of law.

The principles to be followed not to vary from case to case. Earlier judgments of Court to be taken into consideration as precedents for establishing a permanent practice.

III. Can above features be conciliated with arbitral functions?

If so, shall new Court be, at the same time, Court of Justice and of Arbitration?

If affirmative, shall Hague Arbitration Court subsist? If not, is new Court to be wholly excluded from arbitral functions, or can it be left open to the parties to a dispute to ask the Court or its members to act as arbiter?

IV. What should be the influence on the answers to the above questions of principle of the provisions of the Covenant of the League of Nations Artt. 12 to 14?

V. Should the draft convention to be proposed by the Court contain, in a preamble, the principles which will form the answers to the above questions?

c. Competency of the Court.

VI. Shall the Court be competent to hear and determine all cases brought before it by the parties, or shall the competency of the Court be limited in some way? In the latter case, shall the

devra-t elle décider elle-même si elle est compétente ou non dans un cas donné (conformément à des règles à formuler)?

Si la Cour est compétente dans tous les cas qui lui seront soumis, se prononcera-t-elle sur le litige tout entier ou seulement sur les questions de droit impliquées dans chaque cas?

Si la compétence doit être limitée, comment faut-il tirer les lignes de démarcation? La compétence doit-elle être restreinte à des conflits de nature juridique? à des questions qui peuvent être résolues sur la base de principes de droit?

Quid, au sujet des réserves habituelles concernant l'indépendance, l'honneur et les intérêts vitaux? Interprétation du passage de l'article 13 du Pacte concernant les questions généralement susceptibles d'une solution arbitrale; ce passage est-il applicable à la Cour à créer en conformité de l'article 14? Si oui, quelle est la portée du passage: devra-t-il être considéré comme une série d'exemples de questions de droit, ou comme une énumération de questions spéciales susceptibles d'être résolues par l'arbitrage?

VII. La Cour (conformément aux principes résultant des réponses aux questions ci-dessus) n'est-elle compétente que pour connaître de litiges entre les Membres de la Société, ou bien est-elle également compétente pour connaître des litiges entre des Membres et des Etats qui ne sont pas Membres, ou entre deux ou plusieurs Etats qui ne sont pas Membres?

VIII. La Cour Permanente aura-t-elle compétence pour connaître seulement de litiges entre Etats ou bien aussi de litiges entre des Etats et des particuliers ou entre deux ou plusieurs particuliers ressortissants de différents Etats?

Si un particulier peut être partie à un litige soumis à la Cour, quelles sont les conditions dans lesquelles cette possibilité pourra être reconnue: le particulier doit-il être supporté par son gouvernement? Des „litiges touchant à des intérêts internationaux?"

En cas de doute, qui décide sur la compétence de la Cour?

IX. La Cour aura-t-elle seulement compétence pour connaître de litiges portés devant elle par accord entre les parties, ou aussi de litiges dont elle aura été saisie par une des parties seulement?

Si la réponse à la seconde partie de la question précédente est affirmative, la Cour aura-t-elle le droit d'appeler devant elle l'autre partie, et aura-t-elle le droit d'instituer une procedure ordinaire ou devra-t-elle se restreindre à instruire le cas?

X. Les règles générales de la compétence de la Cour Permanente une fois fixées, la Cour

Court itself decide whether it is competent or not in a special case (according to rules to be laid down)?

If the Court is competent in all cases brought before it, shall it give a decision on the whole case or only on the legal points involved in the case?

If competency be limited, how are the limits to be drawn: Competency restricted to conflicts of a juridical nature? to questions that can be resolved according to principles of law?

What about the customary reservations for independence, honour and vital interests? Interpretation of expression in covenant, Art. 13, about questions generally suitable for arbitral solution: is that passage applicable to the Court set up according to Article 14; if so, what is its scope: should it be considered as a series of examples of juridical questions or as an enumeration of special questions suitable for arbitration?

VII. Is the Court competent to hear and determine disputes (according to principles resulting from answers to above questions) only between Members of the League of Nations or also between Members and non-members and between two or more non-members?

VIII. Shall the Permanent Court be competent to hear and determine disputes only between States or disputes also between States and private citizens or between two or more private citizens of different States?

If a private citizen is permitted to be a party to a dispute before the Court, what are the conditions: is the private citizen's case to be supported by his State? "Disputes interesting international relations".

Who is to decide on the competency in doubtful cases?

IX. Shall the Court be competent to hear and determine only such disputes as are brought before it by agreement between the parties or also such disputes as are brought to its notice by one party only?

If the latter part of the question be answered in the affirmative, shall the Court have the right to summon the other party and start an ordinary procedure or shall it restrict itself to an investigation of the facts of the case?

X. The general rules of competency of the Permanent Court once having been laid down, shall

devra-t-elle, en dehors de ces principes, avoir compétence pour connaître de litiges définis spécialement, par exemple, dans le Traité de Paix?

Interprétation de l'expression „juridiction instituée par la Société des Nations" dans le Traité de Versailles etc.

XI. La compétence de la Cour en conformité de l'article 14 du Pacte pour donner des opinions légales sur des questions de droit.

Ce droit devra-t-il être entouré de garanties visant l'exclusion de la possibilité pour la Cour de donner des opinions légales sur des points qui pourront plus tard être portés devant elle pour former l'objet d'un jugement?

XII. Le problème de la nouvelle Cour, ou d'une section de la nouvelle Cour, comme cour d'appel dans des procès de droit international privé, ou des procès de prises.

d. Siège de la Cour.

XIII. La nouvelle Cour devra-t-elle être établie au siège de la Société des Nations?

Si non, quel endroit doit être considéré comme le lieu le mieux adopté pour servir de siège à la Còur Permanente?

Points de vue: tradition, conditions locales.

e. Composition de la Cour.

XIV. Quelles conditions devront être remplies par les membres de la Cour?

(1) Conditions à remplir à l'époque de l'élection ou de la nomination.

Tous les membres de la Cour devront-ils avoir une haute compétence juridique? (cette question devra être considérée en même temps que celle de la compétence de la Cour: compétence pour toutes les questions soumises à la Cour; pour des questions de droit international privé; pour des questions de prise).

Comment constater l'existence de connaissances juridiques dans les cas où ces connaissances sont requises? (nécessité d'avoir rempli les conditions requises pour être nommé aux hautes fonctions judiciaires dans son propre pays? nécessité d'avoir exercé pareilles fonctions? autorité reconnue en matière de droit international?)

Qui sera compétent pour décider dans des cas douteux si les conditions requises ont été remplies ou non?

(2) Faits entraînant la révocation, la suspension ou l'exclusion des juges.

Les fonctions de juge à la Cour Permanente seront-elles compatibles avec d'autres fonctions publiques?

Des fonctions internationales? des fonctions

the Court, apart, from such principles, be competent in specially determined cases resulting, for instance, from the Peace Treaty.

Interpretation of the term „jurisdiction set up by the League of Nations" in the Versailles, etc. Treaty.

XI. The competency of the Court according to Art. 14 to give advisory opinion on legal points.

Should this right be surrounded by certain guarantees intended to exclude the possibility of the Court giving legal opinions in cases which may later come before it for judgment?

XII. Problem of new Court, or section of new Court, as Court of Appeal for cases of private international law and for prize cases.

d. Seat of the Court.

XIII. Shall the new Court be established at seat of the League of Nations?

If not, what place should be considered as best fitted to serve as the seat of the Permanent Court of Justice.

Viewpoints: tradition; premises.

e. Composition of the Court.

XIV. What qualifications should be fulfilled by the members of the Court?

(1) Conditions to be fulfilled at time of election or appointment.

Shall high juridical competency be required from all members of the Court (this question to be considered in connection with question of competency of the Court: competency for all questions submitted to the Court; for private international law questions; for prize questions)?

Where juridical knowledge is required, how shall the existence of such knowledge be stated (fulfilment of conditions for an appointment to high judicial functions in own country? actual exercise of such functions? recognised authority in matters of international law?

Who is finally to decide in doubtful cases whether conditions fulfilled or not?

(2) Facts that entail revocation, suspension or exclusion of judges.

Can other public offices be held at the same time as office of judge on Permanent Court?

International offices? offices either in own or other countries? Private positions?

dans son propre pays ou ailleurs? des positions privées?

Les juges auront-ils le droit de recevoir d'autres appointements que ceux qui leur sont attribués en leur qualité de juges?

Autres raisons de révocation: p. ex. incapacité notoire de remplir ces fonctions.

Qui devra en décider: la Cour elle-même? Le corps ayant élu ou nommé la personne en question? Le corps ayant présenté la personne en question?

(3) Un juge qui vient d'être nommé, doit-il prêter serment d'impartialité ou faire une déclaration solennelle au même effet mais sous une autre forme?

XV. La méthode d'élire ou de nommer les juges.

Principes: il faut qu'il soit impossible de mettre en doute l'impartialité de la Cour. Il faut que le principe de l'égalité des Etats soit sauvegardé. Il faut que la Cour ne soit pas trop nombreuse pour pouvoir travailler efficacement.

Nomination directe? Par les gouvernements. Par d'autres corps. Système de roulement.

Election par les gouvernements par scrutin de liste mais sans composition préalable d'une liste générale, et sans désignation préalable.

Composition d'une liste générale par désignation par les gouvernements. Election par les gouvernements parmi les candidats figurant sur la liste.

Désignation par un corps; nomination par un autre.

Division des états en groupes: chaque groupe fera un certain nombre de désignations et un certain nombre d'élections parmi les personnes désignées par les autres groupes.

Désignation par les gouvernements. Election par un collège électoral spécial: les membres de la Cour d'Arbitrage de La Haye? L'Assemblée de la Société des Nations?

Si le système de désignation par les gouvernements est adopté, combien de candidats seront désignés par chaque gouvernement? Combien de candidats choisis parmi les ressortissants et combien choisis parmi les étrangers?

Dans la même hypothèse, la liberté de choix des gouvernements doit-elle être limitée, p. ex. par l'obligation de tenir compte de propositions faites par des corps spéciaux, des universités, etc.

Dans toute hypothèse, combien de juges seront choisis ou nommés? Combien pourront être des ressortissants du même Etat? Les élections se feront-elles individuellement ou par scrutin de liste?

Can money be drawn from other sources (except private fortune) during office as judge on Permanent Court?

Other grounds: examples, notorious incapacity to fill office.

Who is to make decision: Court itself? Body having elected or appointed person in question? Body having nominated person in question?

(3) Shall an oath or other solemn declaration as to intended impartiality, etc. be taken from newly-appointed judge?

XV. Method of electing or appointing judges of Court.

Principles: it should be impossible to question the impartiality of the Court; the principle of equality of States should be safeguarded; the Court should not be so large that it cannot carry on efficient work.

Direct appointments? By governments. By other bodies. Rotation system.

Voting by governments, by lists, without foregoing composition of general list, and without nominations?

Composition of general list by nomination by governments. Election by governments from general list.

Nomination by one body; appointment by another.

Division of states into groups: each group to make a certain number of nominations, and a certain number of elections from among the persons nominated by the other groups.

Nomination by governments. Election by special electoral body: Hague Arbitration Court panel? Assembly of the League of Nations?

If system of nomination by governments is adopted, how many candidates shall be nominated by each government? How many of own and of foreign nationality?

In same case, shall certain restrictions be put on the liberty of nomination of the governments; shall they, for instance, take into account proposals made by special bodies such as universities, etc.?

In any case, how many judges shall be elected or appointed? How many judges may be citizens of the same state? Shall the elections be made individually or by block vote?

If elections are made by states shall each state have the same number of votes?

Length of judges' terms of office.

Si les élections sont faites par les Etats, tous les Etats auront-ils le même nombre de voix?

Durée du mandat des juges.

Comment remplir les vacances: Election ou nomination de juges suppléants, dans l'affirmatif, comment régler leur entrée en fonctions? Doit-on procéder à une nouvelle élection? Le juge suppléant doit-il être nommé par le corps ayant désigné son prédécesseur?

f. Organisation de la Cour.

XVI. Le Président de la Cour, comment doit-il être élu: par la Cour elle-même, par un corps autre que la Cour? (Société des Nations).

XVII. La Cour doit-elle siéger in pleno ou doit-elle se diviser en plusieurs chambres? Dans ce dernier cas, doit-on laisser à la Cour le soin de décider si pareille division est nécessaire ou non?

Chambres spéciales pour des procès de droit international privé; pour des procès de prise; pour remplir les fonctions d'un tribunal de requête; pour les questions de travail etc.

Quorum *in pleno* et dans les chambres.

XVIII. Les parties au litige doivent-elles avoir le droit d'influencer la composition de la chambre de la Cour qui connaîtra du litige en question?

Droit de récusation: d'office; par l'intermédiaire de la Cour; par les parties sans donner d'explications; par les parties et par la Cour pour des raisons d'intérêt spécial touchant l'objet du litige.

XIX. Doit-il être permis à un juge ressortissant d'un des états partie au litige de prendre part à l'instruction et au jugement de ce litige? Dans l'affirmative, ce droit doit-il être absolu ou conditionnel (réciprocité)?

Le juge doit-il avoir le droit de refuser de siéger à la Cour pendant la considération d'un litige spécial? Dans l'affirmative, ce droit doit-il être absolu?

XX. Vacances, traitements, allocations, immunités et privilèges des juges.

Domicile des juges.

XXI. Secrétariat de la Cour. Greffe de la Cour. L'organisation de ces institutions doit-elle être réglée laissée à la Cour elle-même, ou doit-elle être réglée par exemple dans le document établissant la Cour?

How to provide for vacancies: shall deputy judges be elected (appointed) and, if so, according to what rules shall they take office; or shall new elections be held; or shall the deputy judge be appointed by the body which nominated the judge whose seat has become vacant?

f. Organisation of Court.

XVI. How is the president of the Court to be elected: by the Court itself? By a body other than the Court? (League of Nations).

XVII. Shall the Court sit *in pleno* or shall it be divided into several chambers? In the latter case, shall it be left to the Court to decide whether such division is necessary or not?

Special chamber for private international lawsuits, for prize cases, to act as Court of Claims, etc.?

Quorum in full Court and in chambers.

XVIII. Shall the parties to a dispute have the right of influencing the composition of the committee of the Court that is to hear and determine the dispute in question?

Right to challenge: by office, through the Court, by the parties without giving reasons; by the parties and through the Court for reasons of interest in the subject-matter of the case.

XIX. Shall a citizen of one of the parties be allowed to take part in the hearing and determination of the case to which his state is a party? If so, shall the right be absolute or conditional (reciprocity)?

Shall a judge have the right to refuse to sit in the Court during the consideration of a special dispute? If so, shall this right be unconditional?

XX. Holidays, treatment, allowances, immunities, and privileges for judges.

Domicile of judges.

XXI. Registry and Secretariat of Court.

Shall the organisation of these bodies be left to the Court itself, or, for instance, be made in the document establishing the Court?

g. Droit matériel à appliquer par la Cour.

(Comparer *b* ci-dessus).

XXII. Les principes de droit à appliquer par la Cour, doivent-ils être formulés seulement d'une façon générale ou bien en détail?

Dans ce dernier cas, quelles seront les règles à appliquer? L'adoption d'un système avec des règles détaillées, rendra-t-elle nécessaire une codification extensive du droit international?

Dans le premier cas, comment faudrait-il définir les principes de droit à appliquer?

Quelle importance devra être donnée au fait que la Cour doit établir une jurisprudence continue?

La Cour elle-même doit-elle être seul juge sur l'interprétation des principes formulés pour servir de base à son activité?

Comment faut-il remplir les lacunes du droit international actuel, et des principes mêmes de ce droit?

h. De la chose jugée.

XXIII. Le jugement doit-il prendre ses effets seulement pour ce qui concerne le litige lui-même et les parties à ce litige, ou doit-il avoir une portée plus étendue?

Quid, au sujet de jugements impliquant l'interprétation de traités généraux?

Jusqu'à quel degré le droit d'intervention doit-il être accordé à des parties tierces, et quel sera l'effet du jugement sur les tierces parties?

XXIV. La solution du conflit par la Cour doit-elle être considérée comme finale?

Droit d'appel? Possibilité d'une révision?

Conditions à remplir pour une action en révision?

i. Exécution du jugement.

XXV. Dans quel délai les jugements doivent-ils être exécutés? Est-ce que des règles générales doivent être formulées à cet égard? ou vaut-il mieux laisser à la Cour le soin de décider dans chaque cas spécial?

XXVI. Doit-il y avoir des sanctions ou garanties pour l'exécution de bonne foi des jugements de la Cour?

Le dernier alinéa de l'article 13 du Pacte de la Société des Nations, est-il applicable à la présente question; si oui, comment faut-il interpréter ce passage?

g. Material law to be applied by the Court.

(Compare *b.* above.)

XXII. Shall the principles of law to be applied by the Court be laid down only in a general way or in detail?

In the latter case, what body of law shall be applied? Would the adoption of a system of detailed rules necessitate very extensive codifications of international law?

In the former case, how should the principles of law to apply be described?

What importance should be given to the practice to be established by the Court?

Should the Court itself be sole judge over the interpretation of the principles laid down as base for its authority?

How should existing gaps in international law and in principles of such law, be filled?

h. Res judicata.

XXIII. Is the judgment to take effect with regard only to the present dispute and the present parties, or shall it have a wider scope?

What about judgments involving interpretation of general treaties?

To what extent should a right of intervention be granted third parties, and what will be the effect of judgments on intervening third parties?

XXIV. Shall the decision of the dispute by the Court be considered as final?

Right of appeal? Possibility of revision?

Conditions for revision.

i. Enforcement of judgments.

XXV. Within what period of time shall a judgment of the Court be carried out? Shall there be general rules in this respect, or shall the decision be left to the Court in each special case?

XXVI. Are there to be any sanctions or guarantees for the proper carrying out of the sentences of the Court?

Is the last paragraph of Art. 13 of the Covenant of the League of Nations applicable to the present question; if so, how is that paragraph to be interpreted?

XXVII. Quelle solution faudra-t-il adopter dans certains cas où l'exécution d'un jugement de la Cour serait en conflit avec le droit constitutionnel des pays en question?

k. Procédure.

XXVIII. Les règles de procédure de la Cour doivent-elles être fixées dans le Statut constitutionnel de la Cour, ou doit-on laisser à la Cour elle-même le soin de formuler ses propres règles de procédure?

XXIX. Supposons que la première solution soit adoptée; dans ce cas:

(1) Quelles règles doivent-être formulées pour la soumission d'un litige à la Cour?
Compromis.
Quasi-compromis.
Accord présumé entre les parties (cette solution rendra nécessaire une indication en genre ou en espèce, dans le Statut constitutionnel de la Cour, des matières concernant lesquelles pareil accord doit être considéré comme existant).
Quid, dans les cas où des litiges sont portés devant la Cour par une des parties seulement?

(2) Procédure ordinaire.

a. Publique ou secrète? Si le point n'est pas règlé dans le Statut constitutionnel, qui doit prendre la décision dans le cas spécial?
b. Langues: le droit de décision doit-il être laissé à la Cour, aux parties?
c. Procédure écrite ou orale?
d. Agents, avocats.
e. Témoins et experts.
f. La Cour doit-elle pouvoir recueillir des dépositions en dehors des locaux de la Cour?
g. Communication des documents par les parties, à la Cour et aux parties adverses; droit de la Cour de demander la production des documents.
h. Délais.
i. Décisions de la Cour:

aa. Les décisions doivent-elles être prises à l'unanimité ou à la majorité des voix? Dans le dernier cas les opinions divergentes doivent-elles être notées?
bb. Délai dans lequel la Cour doit donner sa décision.
cc. Jugement:
au nom de qui le prononcer; comment l'authentiquer; comment le communiquer et éventuellement le publier et le conserver; mention des opinions divergentes; jugement à être interprêté par

XXVII. How to proceed in cases where the execution of a sentence will be in conflict with the constitutional law of the respective countries?

k. Procedure.

XXVIII. Shall the rules of procedure of the Court be embodied in the Constituent statute of the Court, or shall it be left to the Court itself to lay down its own rules of procedure?

XXIX. Assuming the first course to be adopted:

(1) What rules shall be laid down for the bringing of a dispute before the Court.
Compromise.
Quasi-compromise.
Presumed agreement between the parties (this solution will make necessary an indication ***in genere*** or ***in specie*** in the constituent statute of the Court, of matters concerning which such agreement shall be considered to exist).
Quid in case of disputes brought before the Court by one party only?

(2) Ordinary procedure.

a. Publicity or secrecy? — if point left open in constituent statute, who is to decide in the special case?
b. Languages: — shall liberty of decision be given to the Court? — to the parties?
c. Written or oral procedure.
d. Agents, Counsel.
e. Witnesses and experts.
f. Collecting of evidence by the Court outside the premises of the Court.
g. Communication of documents by parties to Court and to other parties; right of Court to request production of documents.
h. Times.
i. Decisions of the Court:

aa. Decisions to be taken unanimously or by majority vote? In the latter case, shall divergent opinions be noted?
bb. Times for giving decisions.
cc. Award:
In whose name to be given? How authenticate? How communicate, publish and preserve? Divergent opinions to be noted? Judgments to be interpreted by Court? Draft of judgment to

la Cour; projet de jugement à être communiqué préalablement aux agents des parties afin de permettre à ceux-ci de proposer une meilleure rédaction des passages jugés ambigus.

k. Frais.

XXX. Un *locus standi* spécial doit-il être donné à la Société des Nations ou à ses organes (Bureau de travail) etc. devant la Cour; dans l'affirmative quel doit-être ce *locus standi*?

XXXI. S'il est considéré comme désirable d'adopter le système d'une procédure sommaire, comment faudra-t-il l'organiser? Procédure écrite seulement, en vue de la limitation des délais?

be communicated to parties' agents beforehand in order to have them suggest re-drafting of passages which seem to them not to be clear.

k. Expenses.

XXX. Shall a special *locus standi* be given to the League of Nations before the Court: if so, what shall this *locus standi* be?

XXXI. If summary procedure is adopted, how should it be organised? Written procedure only, for shortening of times?

ANNEXE No. 3.

Projet de Résolution présenté par Mr. Root.

Il est proposé:

Que le Comité adopte comme base de ses délibérations sur la matière qui lui a été soumise, les actes et résolutions de la seconde Conférence de la Paix de 1907.

Que les divers plans pour l'établissement d'une Cour permanente de Justice qui ont déjà été préparés par des juristes au nom de

la Suède,
du Danemark,
de la Norvège,
des Pays-Bas,
de la Suisse,
de l'Allemagne,
de l'Autriche,

soient soumis au Comité et que les matières dont ils traitent respectivement soient prises en considération par lui.

ANNEX No. 3.

Draft Resolution submitted by Mr. Root.

Resolved:

That the Committee adopts as the basis for consideration of the subject referred to it the Acts and Resolutions of the 2nd Peace Conference at the Hague in the year 1907.

That the provisions of the several plans for an International Court of Justice already elaborated by Representative Jurists of

Sweden,
Denmark,
Norway,
Holland,
Switzerland,
Germany,
Austria,

be laid before the Committee and considered as the subjects to which they respectively relate are taken up for consideration.

ANNEXE No. 4.

Projet de Résolution présenté par M. de Lapradelle.

La Commission commence ses délibérations en rendant hommage aux travaux des deux Conférences de La Haye, des Gouvernements, des Associations Scientifiques Internationales et des Jurisconsultes de toute nationalité dont les études ont précédé la sienne; elle tiendra compte de toutes les sources d'information qui sont maintenant à sa disposition, pour répondre à la confiance de la Société des Nations.

ANNEX No. 4.

Draft Resolution submitted by M. de Lapradelle.

The Commission starts its deliberation by paying homage to the work performed at the two Hague Conferences, by the several Governments and by the scientific Associations and the jurists of all nationalities, the work of which have preceded the works of the Committee and which will guide the Committee in its efforts to fulfil the object for which it has been summoned by the League of Nations.

ANNEXE No. 5.

Résolution adopté par le Comité.

La Commission commence ses délibérations en rendant tout d'abord hommage aux travaux des deux Conférences de La Haye qui ont déjà préparé, avec une exceptionnelle autorité, la solution du problème de l'organisation d'une Cour de Justice Internationale.

Prête à considérer encore les projets émanés des Gouvernements, des Conférences d'initiative Gouvernementale, des Associations Scientifiques Internationales et des Jurisconsultes de toute nationalité dont les études ont précédé la sienne, elle tiendra compte de toutes les sources d'informations qui sont maintenant à sa disposition pour répondre à la confiance de la Société des Nations.

ANNEX No. 5.

Resolution adopted by the Committee.

The Committee starts its déliberations by paying homage to the work of the two Hague Conferences which have already prepared, with an outstanding authority, the solution of the problem of the organisation of the Court of International Justice.

The Committee is prepared to take into consideration also the schemes emanating from several governments, from conferences summoned at the initiation of governments, from international scientific organisations and from jurists of all nationalities, the works of which have preceded those of the Committee. The Committee will avail itself of all the sources of information which are, at the present moment, at its disposal in order thus to fulfil the object for which it has been summoned by the League of Nations.

ANNEXE No. 6.

Exposé lu par le Baron Descamps.

Les difficultés du problème soumis au Comité des Jurisconsultes. — La méthode appropriée à la solution de ces difficultés.

Le Comité des jurisconsultes, chargé de préparer un projet de Cour permanente de Justice internationale, ne peut se dissimuler les difficultés grandes d'une tâche où tant d'hommes d'état et de juristes ont échoué lors de la Conférence de 1907. Mais, pénétré de la nécessité et de la grandeur de l'œuvre à accomplir, il s'est mis à l'œuvre, estimant que ce qu'il faut s'efforcer de tirer des obstacles rencontrés il y a quelques années et dont beaucoup n'ont pas disparu aujourd'hui, ce n'est pas un motif de douter d'une heureuse solution, mais une méthode sûre pour atteindre celle-ci.

Les questions de procédure relatives au fonctionnement de la justice internationale ne présentent pas actuellement de bien graves difficultés. Résolues une première fois, dans les points fondamentaux auxquels il convient de se limiter, par la Conférence de 1899, elles ont été reprises et élucidées à nouveau par la Conférence de 1907, et l'entente a pu assez facilement s'établir à leur égard. C'est sur les points relatifs à l'organisation et à la compétence des juridictions internationales, à l'obligation de recourir éventuellement à ces juridictions, et aux règles que doivent suivre les juges dans l'appréciation des faits qui leur sont soumis, qu'il importe de faire la lumière et d'arriver à de satisfaisantes solutions.

Un fait est constant à ce point de vue: autant l'œuvre réalisée par la première conférence de la Paix a été féconde et a fini par recueillir, dans la conscience générale d'un grand progrès réalisé, un assentiment unanime et enthousiaste, autant l'œuvre entreprise par la seconde conférence de la Paix a été en butte à d'irréductibles oppositions et a été finalement compromise en partie dans sa réalisation.

D'aucuns ont signalé comme cause de ce résultat le manque de préparation suffisante qui a nui sur plus d'un terrain aux délibérations de la Haute Assemblée. Et il semble bien que la conférence a reconnu elle-même le bien-fondé, à certains égards, de ce fait, lorsqu'en prévision d'une réunion ultérieure, elle a cru devoir appeler précisément l'attention des Puissances „sur la né-

ANNEX No. 6.

Note read by Baron Descamps.

About the difficulties of the problem submitted to the Jurists Committee and a proper method for solving these difficulties.

The Jurists Committee, which has been entrusted with the preparation of a plan for a Permanent Court of International Justice, cannot forget the great difficulties of a task which so many statesmen and jurists have failed to achieve at the 1907 Conference. Convinced, however, of the necessity and of the greatness of the work to be accomplished, the members of that Committee have set to work, considering that the remembrance of the obstacles which had to be overcome a few years ago, and of which a few have not yet disappeared, ought to provide them with the means of finding the true method which will enable them to reach a satisfactory solution, rather than lead them to doubt the possibility of reaching that solution.

The questions of procedure concerning the working of international justice do not present any really serious difficulties now. They were already solved, at least in their essential points, to the discussion of which the Committee ought to limit its activity, at the 1899 Conference; they were discussed again and elucidated at the 1907 Conference and it was then easy to come to an agreement. There remain now to discuss and make clear, so that satisfactory solutions may be reached, the questions concerning the organisation and the competence of international jurisdictions, the obligation of having eventually to accept them, and the rules which the judges will have to follow in their appreciation of the facts which may be submitted to them.

It may be observed that whereas the work of the first Conference was rich in successful results and met in the end with a unanimous and enthusiastic approval, the work undertaken by the second Conference met with unbreakable opposition and its results were partly a failure.

The want of sufficient preparation, which was a handicap to the progress of the deliberations of the Conference on several questions, was pointed out as a cause of that failure; and it seems that the Assembly itself recognised the truth of that fact when, in anticipation of a subsequent meeting, it precisely called the

cessité de préparer les travaux de cette troisième conférence assez longtemps d'avance, pour que ses délibérations se poursuivent avec l'autorité et la rapidité indispensables". Mais les sources des embarras survenus sont en réalité plus objectives et plus profondes, et il n'est pas sans importance de les relever dans les sphères diverses où elles se sont accusées.

Dans la sphère de l'organisation des juridictions internationales, le dualisme des deux Cours appelées à constituer ces juridictions a paru trop accentué à beaucoup d'Etats qui au lieu de nouvelles institutions campées en face de l'institution existante, destinées à lui faire concurrence et, dans l'intention de plusieurs, à la supplanter définitivement, auraient préféré l'adoption dans l'espèce, d'une méthode moins radicale et plus harmonique. C'est en se plaçant à ce point de vue qu'un éminent jurisconsulte de la Délégation Suisse, M. Carlin, avait instamment demandé „qu'on reste sur le terrain de l'œuvre de 1899, c'est à dire conserver à la Cour permanente son caractère et sa composition actuelle et chercher dans ses limites les améliorations dont pouvait être susceptible le fonctionnement de cette institution".

D'autre part, le système de classification des Etats au point de vue de la part attribuée à chacun dans le fonctionnement pratique de la nouvelle Cour, a prêté le flanc à trop de critiques pour qu'on pût se promettre un résultat universellement adopté. Et certes, la distinction entre la jouissance d'un droit et son exercice, l'une présentée comme sauvegardant foncièrement l'égalité juridique des Etats, l'autre représentée comme pouvant porter de multiples atteintes à cette même égalité, n'était pas de nature à donner à tous, tout apaisement.

Dans la sphère de la compétence, soit virtuelle, soit effectivement rendue obligatoire, la diversité de nature des différends internationaux, dont les uns sont d'ordre juridique et les autres d'ordre politique, la difficulté de trouver entre ces deux ordres une ligne de démarcation toujours nette, le caractère mixte attribué à certains litiges considérés comme se référant à la fois au droit et à la politique, et surtout, la crainte manifestée par divers Etats, ombrageux à toute perspective de limitation de leur souveraineté, d'être entraînés dans la voie des procédures juridictionnelles obligatoires à abandonner d'avance et sans réserve des droits estimés, à tort ou à raison, inaliénables, semblaient détourner les esprits pratiques de l'adoption de règles impliquant une astreinte commune et uniforme.

D'autres points encore comme celui des sources auxquelles doivent puiser les juges pour so-

attention of the Powers to the necessity of "preparing, long beforehand, the work which would have to be accomplished by the third Conference so that the deliberations might progress with the necessary speed and authority". But those difficulties are in fact derived from deeper and more objective causes and it is not useless to search for them and hold them to light.

In the domain of the organisation of international jurisdictions, the dualism of the two Courts which are going to form those jurisdictions has seemed too strongly marked to several States. They would have preferred a less thorough and more conciliating method which would have avoided all antagonism between the already existing institution and the new one, bound to compete with, and supposed to supplant it altogether. The eminent jurist of the Swiss Delegation, M. Carlin, adopted the former point of view and therefore instantly asked that the next conference should remain within the limits of the work of the 1899 Conference, id est: should preserve the character and the actual composition of the Permanent Court and try and find, within the limits of that institution, the improvements which might be brought to it.

On the other hand the system which consists in establishing an order among the States to determine the share which each of them ought to have in the practical working of the new Court has incurred too many criticisms to enable one to expect a universally adopted result. As a matter of fact, the distinction between the possession of a right and the exercise of it, the one being considered as safeguarding completely the legal equality of States, and the other as involving numerous attacks upon it, was not of a nature to give satisfaction to all.

With regard to competence, either potential, or made efficiently obligatory, the variety of international differences, — some of which are of a legal order while the others are political, — the difficulty of finding a clear line of demarcation between those two classes, the mixed character of certain differences which are considered as proceeding at the same time from law and from politics, and above all, the fear of various States that a limitation might be imposed on their sovereignty, that they might have to submit to obligatory jurisdiction, and sacrifice beforehand and altogether certain rights considered as inalienable, were as many reasons capable of preventing practical men from accepting rules which implied a common obligation, identical for all.

Other points, such as the sources from which the judges might borrow in order to solve

lutionner les différends internationaux, ne laissaient pas de susciter certaines appréhensions.

Les difficultés graves, à coup sûr, que nous venons de signaler, ne paraissent pas dans l'ordre de l'organisation de la justice internationale, insurmontables, à condition de chercher le progrès en donnant le pas à une méthode unitaire et évolutive sur une méthode peut-être trop radicalement dualiste, et de trouver un terrain de conciliation plus heureux que celui où l'on s'est trop cantonné, entre les exigences légitimes de l'égalité des Etats et les nécessités d'une composition éclectique du personnel des juridictions internationales.

Et dans l'ordre de la compétence effective de ces juridictions, il ne paraît nullement impossible d'adopter des mesures sérieusement et loyalement obligationnelles, sans faire litière d'une part de certaines appréhensions persistantes avec lesquelles il faut compter, sans donner d'autre part aux règles adoptées un caractère purement potestatif et sans livrer tout engagement à des faux-fuyants qui l'annulent, en le subordonnant, ou peu s'en faut, à cette condition où s'accuse trop la vieille conception absolutiste de la souveraineté: „si tel est le bon plaisir individuel des engagés".

En tout cas, il ne paraît pas que la solution des difficultés pendantes doive être cherchée dans ce que l'on a appelé la séparation complète et méthodique des conceptions d'arbitrage et de justice. Insistons un instant sur ce point pour dissiper tout équivoque.

S'il s'agissait simplement d'observer que la juridiction d'arbitres se caractérise par le choix des juges appelés à statuer, sans faire appel à des magistrats permanents et professionnels de carrière, tandis que dans la juridiction que l'on peut appeler magistraturale pour la distinguer de la juridiction arbitrale, le juge est nommé une fois pour toutes dans des conditions indépendantes du choix des parties, on constaterait un fait incontestable.

Si l'on ajoutait que dans la juridiction arbitrale les normes à suivre pour rendre la justice, peuvent dépendre à leur tour plus ou moins du choix des parties, tandis que dans la juridiction magistraturale, l'interprétation et l'application des règles de droit sont soumises à des normes plus stables et universellement reconnues, on constaterait encore un fait général constant.

Si l'on faisait en outre remarquer que la juridiction arbitrale est ordinairement, à la différence de la juridiction magistraturale, une juridiction de concert, qui revêt le plus souvent à ce titre un caractère volontaire des deux parts et ne permet pas, comme la juridiction magistra-

international differences, were the cause of some apprehension.

It does not seem impossible to overcome those difficulties as far as the organisation of international justice is concerned, if we are determined to achieve progress by using a unitary and progressive method, rather than an absolutely dualist one, and to find a more appropriate ground for conciliation than the one on which we have stood up to now, between the legitimate demands of the equality of States and the eclectic composition of the staff of international tribunals.

With regard to the effective competence of those tribunals, it does not seem at all impossible to adopt certain measures which would be seriously and loyally obligatory, which would reassure at the same time certain persisting fears, on the other hand it would be necessary to avoid that those rules, when accepted, had a merely potential character, that conventions could be rendered useless by possible subterfuges: which would be the case if the competence of those jurisdictions was practically subordinated to the condition: "if such is the will of the parties concerned", which is but an expression of the ancient absolutist conception of sovereignty.

In any case, it does not appear that the solution of those difficulties ought to be found in what has been called the complete and methodical separation of the concepts of arbitration and of justice. Let us consider this point one moment in order to avoid all mistake.

If it was only a question of making it clear that the jurisdiction of arbitrators is characterised by the possibility for the parties of choosing their judges without choosing necessarily professional and permanent judges, whereas in the judiciary jurisdiction, the judge is nominated once for all under conditions which exclude a choice by the parties, there would be no difficulty whatever. It would suffice to state this recognised fact.

If one added that, in the arbitral tribunal, the rules to be followed may depend more or less on the choice of the parties, whereas in the judicial tribunal those rules are to be applied and interpreted according to more stable and indeed universally recognised principles, it would still be stating a recognised fact.

If one stated also that the arbitral jurisdiction is ordinarily a jurisdiction of conciliation, which affects in most cases a voluntary character on both sides and which does not allow the unilateral exercise of a legal action, and that all those points constitute as many differences

turale, l'exercice unilatéral, au moins généralement, d'une action en justice, on constaterait un fait non moins général et non moins constant.

Mais si l'on part de ces observations pour placer le criterium de distinction entre les deux juridictions, dans ce fait que l'une aurait pour objet propre et essentiel de dire le droit tandis qu'il n'en serait pas de même de l'autre, il semble bien que l'on commet une véritable méprise. L'objet propre de l'arbitrage n'est pas en soi différent de l'objet propre de la fonction magistraturale. La première conférence de la Paix l'a rappelé en donnant de l'arbitrage à l'article 15 de la Convention pour le réglement pacifique des Conflits internationaux, cette définition demeurée classique: „l'arbitrage international a pour objet le règlement de litiges entre Etats par des juges de leur choix et sur la base du respect du droit". Déterminant ensuite la nature des questions litigieuses qui sont du ressort propre de la juridiction arbitrale, l'article 16 signale expressément les questions d'ordre juridique.

Sans doute il est possible, que l'arbitre soit, de par la volonté des parties, investi d'un pouvoir appréciateur qui lui permette d'adopter des solutions conciliatrices au lieu de rendre strictement à chacun ce qui lui est dû en droit. Mais une telle prérogative qui n'est pas d'ailleurs toujours et nécessairement étrangère au fonctionnement de la juridiction magistraturale, constitue une attribution exceptionnelle, adventice, qui n'est pas liée de soi à la fonction arbitrale et qui n'empêche pas que l'arbitrage demeure de sa nature un pouvoir de dire le droit, *jus-dicere*.

On a reproché, il est vrai, aux arbitres de La Haye, par une interprétation large de leurs pouvoirs, alors qu'ils n'en avaient pas reçu l'autorisation formelle, d'avoir, dans certains de leurs jugements fait œuvre de pacification plutôt qu'œuvre de justice, et dans d'autres cas d'avoir préféré l'équité au strict droit. De tels reproches qui, pour avoir quelque valeur, devraient être précisés davantage, n'ont en tout cas qu'une portée accidentelle. Et si le premier, au cas où il serait justifié, constituerait un abandon peu explicable de la véritable mission des arbitres, il importe, pour apprécier le second, de se rendre bien compte du rôle que peut légitimement remplir l'équité dans l'application du droit international.

Au point de vue de la fonction jurisprudentielle comme auxiliaire du développement et de l'illustration du droit, il est possible sans doute que toutes les décisions arbitrales rendues à La Haye n'aient pas le même mérite. Mais en examinant les solutions intervenues, il convient peut être de

between the two jurisdictions, one would bring no new element into discussion.

But if one deduces from these facts that the essential object of one of those tribunals is to state the law whilst the object of the other is something different, one makes a real mistake. The proper object of arbitration is not in itself different from the proper object of the judiciary function. The first Peace Conference made that clear in clause 15 of the Convention for the pacific settlement of international conflicts, which contains a definition which has become classical: "The object of international arbitration is the settlement of conflicts between States by judges of their choice and on the basis of the respect of the law." In article 16 which defines the nature of the litigious questions which are of the competence of the arbitral jurisdiction, legal questions are expressly mentioned.

It is no doubt possible for the arbitrator to be given, if such is the will of the parties, a power of appreciation which enables him to render conciliatory awards instead of determining what is strictly owed to each party by law, but such a prerogative, which moreover may also belong to the judicial tribunal, is only exceptional and adventitious; it is not, in itself, bound to the arbitral function and it does not divert the arbitration from its essential nature, which is that of stating the law: *jus dicere*.

It has been alleged against the arbitrators at the Hague that, in virtue of a broad interpretation of their powers, and without having received any formal authorisation to do so, they had, in some of their judgments, aimed at pacification rather than justice and that, in others, they had preferred equity to strict law. Such reproaches ought to be more precise to be taken into consideration. At any rate, they are but accidentally justified; it is true that the first criticism, were it justified, could be considered as an unexplainable forgetfulness of their true task on the part of the arbitrators, but to appreciate the value of the second criticism it would be necessary to arrive at a clear conception of the part which equity may be legitimately allowed to play in the application of international law.

If we consider the rôle of jurisprudence as an auxiliary in the development of law, we may no doubt find that the arbitral decisions rendered at the Hague have not all the same value. But, when we examine those various solutions, we must remember that the combinations of facts which are amenable to law are infinitely varied; that the various cases do not give the judge an equal opportunity of rendering those judgments

se rappeler que la combinaison des faits qui donnent lieu à l'application pratique du droit, varie à l'infini; que tous les cas ne donnent pas également l'occasion de rédiger ces arrêts de principe qui illuminent de brillantes clartés le domaine juridique; que le fait de s'attacher à quelque point particulier pertinent et relevant, au lieu de viser à résoudre toutes les questions de droit qui se trouvent plus ou moins engagées dans une espèce, est un phénomène qui n'est pas étranger au fonctionnement des plus hautes Cours nationales de justice dans les divers pays; qu'enfin, si en face d'une règle de droit positive et claire, le devoir de celui qui est appelé à exercer une juridiction, est de l'appliquer, l'équité est en droit international, comme d'ailleurs en tout droit national, le complément indispensable du droit positif. Car le juge, ayant le devoir inéluctable de statuer, est souvent, par la force des choses, constitué ministre d'équité chargé de suppléer par les lumières de sa conscience et de la raison, à l'obscurité, à l'insuffisance ou au silence du droit positif. Et certes, les lacunes et l'imperfection du droit des gens ne sont pas de nature à diminuer l'importance de cette tâche.

founded on principles, which seem to enlighten the whole juridical domain; that the fact of taking into consideration some well established point instead of attempting to solve all the legal questions which are more or less involved in a case, is a phenomenon which one may observe in the working of the highest national courts of justice in the various States; that if it is the duty of the judge to apply the law, where it exists, we must not forget that equity is, in international as well as in national law, a necessary complement of positive law. The first duty of the judge is to render a sentence and he is often obliged by circumstances to render a sentence based on equity and to use the suggestions of his own conscience and of his reason in order to supply the deficiency of positive law; and the many gaps and imperfections in the law of nations are not of a nature to lessen the difficulties of our task.

La solution harmonique et intégrale du problème des Juridictions Internationales.

En vue d'arriver à une solution harmonique et intégrale du problème des juridictions internationales, essayons de nous élever, si possible, à la conception d'un vaste organisme unitaire, ayant pour point de départ une égale délégation faite par les Etats, s'appuyant sur les institutions existantes pour réaliser le progrès, possédant à suffisance les éléments de permanence et de professionnalité, se développant sur la base du procédé de la cooptation pratiquée par d'éminents jurisconsultes, et où satisfaction se trouve donnée d'une manière pratique, selon la nature des affaires, à l'ensemble des desiderata concernant la distribution de la justice entre Nations.

Considéré sous cet aspect, l'office général de la justice internationale envisagé en toute son ampleur englobera les organismes suivants:

1°. Il comprendra d'abord la Cour d'Arbitrage actuellement existante qui pour dissiper toute équivoque entre la permanence d'une liste d'arbitres et la permanence juridictionnelle, et pour mieux répondre à la réalité, prendra, si l'on veut, le nom de Cour des Arbitres Internationaux.

Sa compétence s'étendra virtuellement à tous les cas que les parties s'engageront de lui sou-

About the "harmonious" and "integral" solution of the problem of International Jurisdictions.

With a view to arriving at a harmonious and integral solution of the problem of international jurisdictions, one ought to try and rise to the conception of a vast, homogeneous structure — at the basis of that structure are the delegations sent by the States, all equal. On the other hand, existing institutions, with sufficient guarantees of permanence and professionality, would also be taken as the foundations from which the new institution would develop by means of a co-optation among eminent jurisconsults. The whole of the desiderata concerning the distribution of justice between nations would thus receive a satisfactory solution.

If we consider it in that way, the general office of international justice considered in all its magnitude will contain the following organisms:

1°. It will include the Court of Arbitration, actually existing. In order to avoid any misunderstanding regarding the permanence of a list of arbiters and jurisdictional permanence, and in order to correspond more closely to facts, the Court of Arbitration might take the name of Court of International Arbitrators.

Its competence will extend virtually to all the

mettre, sous réserve de leur libre entente pour établir des juridictions en dehors de l'office général de justice internationale, ou d'une dévolution à d'autres juridictions ayant droit de cité dans cet office.

2⁰. Elle comprendra secondement une Haute Cour de Justice internationale, également non permanente dans son fonctionnement, composée d'un conseiller par Etat, coopté par le Collège des délégués de chaque Etat à la Cour des Arbitres internationaux.

Cette Haute Cour de justice internationale sera compétente pour juger les affaires qu'à raison de leur gravité exceptionnelle au point de vue de l'ordre public international — comme lorsqu'il s'agit de crimes contre le droit des gens universel — l'Assemblée de la Société des Nations ou le Conseil de cette Société lui déféreront.

3⁰. L'office général de la justice internationale comprendra en troisième lieu un Tribunal permanent de justice internationale composé de neuf juges avec six suppléants cooptés par les membres de la Haute Cour de justice internationale, de manière que les principaux systèmes juridiques du monde soient représentés dans ce Tribunal.

Sa compétence virtuelle s'étendra à tous les litiges que les parties peuvent être engagées à lui soumettre, réserve faite encore naturellement ici des cas où les parties s'entendront pour établir une juridiction en dehors de l'office général de justice internationale ou pour déférer le cas à une autre juridiction au sein de cette Cour.

Pour l'expédition des affaires, le Tribunal permanent de justice internationale se répartira conformément à un règlement d'ordre intérieur, dans les offices suivants: 1⁰. une première Chambre dite des vacations ordinaires composée de cinq juges effectifs avec trois suppléants; 2⁰. une seconde Chambre dite des procédures sommaires composée de trois juges et de deux suppléants et à laquelle pourra être déférée en outre les litiges pour lesquels les parties estimeront qu'une juridiction de trois juges est suffisante; 3⁰. un juge unique avec un suppléant, compétent pour les cas où les parties, à raison de la nature de l'affaire, estimeront pouvoir lui soumettre de préférence leurs litiges.

Le tribunal permanent de justice internationale peut, dans les conditions déterminées par son règlement d'ordre intérieur, fonctionner comme commission internationale d'enquête, soit à la demande des parties, soit en vertu d'une décision de l'Assemblée de la Société des Nations ou du Conseil de cette Société.

cases which the parties will agree to submit to it, under reservation of their decision to recognise jurisdictions outside the general office of international justice, or of a devolution to some other jurisdiction having a sort of right of citizenship within that office.

2⁰. It will include a High Court of international Justice, not permanent, which will be composed of one councillor for each State, chosen by the delegates of the States at the Court of Arbitration, by means of co-optation.

This High Court of international justice will be competent to judge certain cases which the Assembly or Council of the League of Nations will submit to it by reason of their exceptional gravity with regard to international public order, as would be for instance crimes against the universal law of nations.

3⁰. The general office of international justice will include a Permanent Tribunal of international justice composed of nine judges and six deputy-judges, who will be chosen by the members of the High Court by means of co-optation, and in such a manner that the chief juridical systems of the world will be represented on that tribunal.

The potential competence of this tribunal will extend to all the differences which the parties may have agreed to submit to it, excepting, of course, such cases as the parties have agreed to submit to a jurisdiction outside the general office of international justice, or to another jurisdiction within the Court.

For despatching cases, the tribunal will be divided, according to internal regulations, into the following offices: 1⁰. a first chamber, called "ordinary sessions Court" which will be composed of five judges and three deputy-judges; 2⁰. a second chamber called "summary procedure Court", which will be composed of three judges and two deputy-judges and to which will be submitted also all differences for which the parties consider a tribunal of three judges sufficient; 3⁰. one judge and one deputy-judge, who will be competent in all cases which the parties decide to submit to him in consideration of the nature of the affair.

The Permanent tribunal of international justice can, under the conditions fixed by its internal regulations, sit as an international Committee of inquiry in virtue of a decision of the Assembly or of the Council of the League of Nations, or of a demand of the parties to that effect.

Il peut, en outre, dans les mêmes conditions, être chargé par l'Assemblée ou par le Conseil de donner des avis consultatifs sur tout différend ou tout point dont ils estimeront devoir le saisir.

Le réglement d'ordre intérieur par lequel le tribunal permanent de justice internationale exerce ses attributions, doit être soumis à l'approbation du Conseil et à celle de l'Assemblée de la Société des Nations.

The Tribunal can also, under the same conditions, be required by the Assembly or the Council to give advisory opinions about any difference or any point which they think proper to submit to it.

The internal regulations which the Permanent tribunal will apply in the performance of its work must be submitted to the approval of the Council and of the Assembly of the League of Nations.

ANNEXE No. 7.

ANNEX No. 7.

TABLEAU SYNOPTIQUE.

SYNOPSIS.

TABLEAU SYNOPTIQUE.

SOMMAIRE.

A. ORGANISATION.

I. Nombre des juges.
II. Les juges suppléants.
III. Durée du mandat.
IV. Droit de présenter des candidats.
V. Nombre des candidats.
VI. Eligibilité.
VII. Electeurs.
VIII. Suffrage et mode d'élection des juges et des juges suppléants.
IX. Nationalité des candidats.
X. Nationalité des juges.
XI. Incompatibilité avec d'autres fonctions.
XII. Immunité diplomatique des juges.
XIII. Rémunération des juges.
XIV. Election du Président.
XV. Limite d'âge des juges.
XVI. Constitution d'un tribunal chargé de régler un cas particulier.
XVII. Droit de récusation.
XVIII. Le mode de combler les vacances.
XIX. Révocation, suspension, décès ou démission d'un juge.
XX. Règlement d'organisation.
XXI. Siège de la Cour.
XXII. Bureau de la Cour.

B. COMPÉTENCÉ

I. Accessibilité de la Cour.
II. La Cour peut-elle connaître de conflits dans lesquels une ou deux des parties sont des personnes privées?
III. La Cour est-elle compétente quand une seule des parties a recours à elle?
IV. Caractère des conflits.

C. PROCÉDURE.

I. Règles de procédure.
II. Procédure sommaire.
III. Bases de la sentence.
IV. Droit d'appel.
V. Révision.
VI. Droit d'intervention.
VII. Effet des sentences.
VIII. Comment l'exécution des sentences sera garantie.
IX Frais généraux de la Cour.
X. Frais de procédure.
XI. Langue.
XII. Publication des opinions divergentes dans la sentence.

SYNOPSIS.

TABLE OF CONTENTS.

A. ORGANISATION.

I. Nombre des juges.

1. **Projet 1907.**	. . . .	
2. **Cinq Puissances neutres.**	15.	(art. 4)
3. **Union Interparlementaire.**	15.	(art. 11)
4. **Union Juridique Internationale.**	15.	(art. 2)
5. **Danemark.**	21.	(art. 1)
6. **Norvège.**	21.	(art. 1)
7. **Pays-Bas.**	7.	(art. 2)
8. **Suède.**	15.	(art. 1)
9. **Suisse.**	15.	(art. 13)
10. **Italiè.**	Chaque Etat un juge.	(art. 18)
11. **Allemagne.**	15.	(art. 14)
12. **Autriche.**	15.	(art. 13)

II. Nombre des juges suppléants.

1. **Projet 1907.**	. . . .	
2. **Cinq Puissances neutres.**	6	(art. 4)
3. **Union Interparlementaire.**	15.	(art. 11)
4. **Union Juridique Internationale.**	6.	(art. 2)

A. ORGANISATION.

I. Number of Judges.

1. **1907 draft scheme.**	. . . .	
2. **Scheme of Five Neutral Powers.**	15.	(art. 4)
3. **Draft scheme of the Interparliamentary Union.**	15.	(art. 11)
4. **Scheme of International Law Union.**	15.	(art. 2)
5. **Official Danish scheme.**	21.	(art. 1)
6. **Official Norwegian scheme.**	21.	(art. 1)
7. **Official Dutch scheme.**	7.	(art. 2)
8. **Official Swedish scheme.**	15.	(art. 1)
9. **Official Swiss scheme.**	15.	(art. 13)
10. **Official Italian scheme.**	One state one judge.	(art. 18)
11. **German proposals to the Paris Peace Conference**	15.	(art. 14)
12. **Austrian proposals.**	15.	(art. 13)

II. Number of Deputy Judges.

1. **1907 draft scheme.**	. . . .	
2. **Five Neutral Powers.**	6.	(art 4)
3. **Interparliamentary Union.**	15.	(art. 11)
4. **International Law Union.**	6.	(art. 2)

5. **Danemark.**	15.	(art. 6)
6. **Norvège.**	15.	(art. 6)
7. **Pays-Bas.**	5.	(arts. 2 et 4)
8. **Suède.**	15.	(art. 6)
9. **Suisse.**	. . . .	
10. **Italie.**	. . . .	
11. **Allemagne.**	. . . .	
12. **Autriche.**	8.	(art. 13)

III. La durée du mandat des juges.

1. **Projet 1907.**	12 ans.	(art. 3)
2. **Cinq Puissances neutres.**	9 ans.	(art. 9)
3. **Union Interparlementaire.**	à vie.	(art. 4)
4. **Union Juridique Internationale.**	9 ans.	(art. 3)
5. **Danemark.**	9 ans.	(art. 7)
6. **Norvège.**	= Danemark	(art. 7)
7. **Pays-Bas.**	. . . .	
8. **Suède.**	6 ans.	(art. 7)
9. **Suisse.**	. . . .	
10. **Italie.**	6 ans.	(art. 18)
11. **Allemagne**	9 ans.	(art. 14)
12. **Autriche.**	. . . .	

IV. Droit de présenter des candidats.

1. **Projet 1907.**	. . . .	
2. **Cinq Puissances neutres.**	Les Membres de la Société des Nations.	(art. 6)
3. **Union Interparlementaire.**	Les Puissances.	(art. 12)
4. **Union Juridique Internationale.**	Les Membres de la Société des Nations.	(art. 4)
5. **Danemark.**	Les Gouvernements.	(art 3)
6. **Norvège.**	= Danemark.	(art. 3)
7. **Pays-Bas.**	Certains collèges judiciaires, les facultés de droit des universités nationales et les Gouvernements.	(art. 3)
8. **Suède.**	Les Gouvernements des Etats qui sont Membres de la Société des Nations.	(art. 3)
9. **Suisse.**	Les Etats qui sont Membres de la Société des Nations.	(art. 13)

5. **Denmark.**	15.	(art. 6)
6. **Norway.**	15.	(art. 6)
7. **Netherlands.**	5.	(arts. 2 and 4)
8. **Sweden.**	15.	(art. 6)
9. **Switzerland.**	. . . .	
10. **Italy.**	. . . .	
11. **Germany.**	. . . .	
12. **Austria.**	8.	(art. 13)

III. Term of Office of Judges.

1. **1907 draft scheme.**	12 years.	(art. 3)
2. **Five Neutral Powers.**	9 years.	(art. 9)
3. **Interparliamentary Union.**	Lifetime.	(art. 4)
4. **International Law Union.**	9 years.	(art. 3)
5. **Denmark.**	9 years.	(art. 7)
6. **Norway.**	Same as Denmark.	(art. 7)
7. **Netherlands.**	. . . .	
8. **Sweden.**	6 years.	(art. 7)
9. **Switzerland.**	. . . .	
10. **Italy.**	6 years.	(art. 18)
11. **Germany.**	9 years.	(art. 14)
12. **Austria.**	. . . .	

IV. Nomination of Candidates.

1. **1907 draft scheme.**	. . . .	
2. **Five Neutral Powers.**	The Members of the League of Nations.	(art. 6)
3. **Interparliamentary Union.**	The contracting Powers.	(art. 12)
4. **International Law Union.**	The Members of the League of Nations.	(art. 4)
5. **Denmark.**	The Governments.	(art. 3)
6. **Norway.**	Same as Denmark.	(art. 3)
7. **Netherlands.**	Certain judicial bodies, the Law Faculties of the National Universities, the Governments.	(art. 3)
8. **Sweden.**	The Governments of states Members of the League of Nations.	(art. 3)
9. **Switzerland.**	States Members of the League..	(art. 13)

10. **Italie.**	. . . .
11. **Allemagne.**	Les Etats représentés au Congrès des Etats. (art. 14)
12. **Autriche.**	. . . .

V. Nombre des candidats.

1. **Projet 1907.**	. . . .
2. **Cinq Puissances neutres.**	Chaque membre présente au maximum autant de candidats qu'il y a de mandats à conférer et au minimum la moitié de ce nombre, en tous cas trois au moins. (art. 6)
3. **Union Interparlementaire.**	Chaque Puissance a le droit de présenter autant de candidats qu'il y a de sièges à conférer. (art. 12)
4. **Union Juridique Internationale.**	A concurrence de trois par chaque Etat (art. 4)
5. **Danemark.**	Chaque Gouvernement présente au maximum autant de candidats qu'il y a de mandats et au minimum la moitié de ce nombre. (art. 3)
6. **Norvège.**	Chaque Gouvernement présente autant de candidats qu'il y a de mandats. (art. 3)
7. **Pays-Bas.**	Chaque collège, faculté et Gouvernement présente une recommandation de deux personnes au plus. (art. 3)
8. **Suède.**	= Danemark. (art. 3)
9. **Suisse.**	Chaque Etat propose au moins un et au plus quatre candidats. (art. 13)
10. **Italie.**	. . . .
11. **Allemagne.**	= Suisse. (art. 14)
12. **Autriche.**	. . . .

VI. Eligibilité.

1. **Projet 1907.**	*a*) Des personnes jouissant de la plus haute considération morale et qui tous devront remplir les conditions requises, dans leurs pays respectifs pour l'admission dans la haute magistrature, ou être des jurisconsultes d'une compétence notoire en matière de droit international. *b*) Choisis autant que possible parmi les membres de la C. P. A. (art. 2)
2. **Cinq Puissances neutres.**	Des personnes jouissant de la plus haute considération morale et qui tous doivent remplir les conditions requises, dans leurs pays respectifs, pour l'admission dans la haute magistrature, soit judiciaire, soit administrative, ou être des jurisconsultes d'une compétence notoire en matière de droit international. (art. 4).
3. **Union Interparlementaire.**	*a*) Des personnes jouissant de la plus haute considération morale, et qui tous devront remplir les conditions requises, dans leurs pays respectifs pour l'admission dans la haute magistrature, ou être des jurisconsultes d'une compétence notoire en matière de droit international. (art. 3) *b*) Choisis autant que possible parmi les membres de la C. P. A. (art. 3) *c*) Ne seront éligibles que les candidats présentés par 5 Puissances au moins. (art. 12)

10. **Italy.**	. . . .
11. **Germany.**	States represented at the Congress of States. (art 14)
12. **Austria.**	. . . .

V. Number of Candidates.

1. **1907 draft scheme.**	. . . .
2. **Five Neutral Powers.**	Each member may nominate a number of candidates equal to the number of vacancies and not less than half the number; in no case less than three. (art. 6)
3. **Interparliamentary Union.**	Each Power has the right to present as many candidates as there are seats to be filled. (art. 12)
4. **International Law Union.**	Not more than three for each state. (art. 4)
5. **Denmark.**	Each Government may nominate a number of candidates equal to the number of vacancies and not less than half that number. (art. 3)
6. **Norway.**	Each Government may nominate a number of candidates equal to the number of vacancies. (art. 3)
7. **Netherlands.**	Each judicial body, Faculty of Law and Government recommends not more than two persons. (art. 3)
8. **Sweden.**	Same as Denmark.
9. **Switzerland.**	Each state proposes at least one and at most four candidates. (art. 13)
10. **Italy.**	. . . .
11. **Germany.**	Same as Switzerland. (art. 14)
12. **Austria.**	. . . .

VI. Eligibility.

1. **1907 draft scheme.**	*a)* Persons of the highest moral reputation and all fulfilling conditions qualifying them in their respective countries to occupy high legal posts, or being jurists of recognised competence in matters of international law. *b)* Appointed as far as possible from the members of the P. C. A. (art. 2)
2. **Five Neutral Powers.**	Persons of the highest character who shall possess the qualifications required in their own countries for elevation to high legal office, whether administrative or judicial, or shall be jurists of recognised authority in international law. (art. 4)
3. **Interparliamentary Union.**	*a)* Persons enjoying the highest moral consideration and who all fulfil the conditions requisite in their own countries for admission to the high magistracy, or being jurisconsults of well-known competency on matters of international law. (art. 3) *b)* Chosen as far as possible from among the members of the P. C. A. (art. 3) *c)* Are eligible only candidates who shall have been presented by five Powers at least. (art. 12)

4. **Union Juridique Internationale.**	La liste composée d'une part de candidats présentés par les Gouvernements et d'autre part de membres d'institutions scientifiques internationales n'est pas limitative. (art. 4)
5. **Danemark.**	= Projet 1907 sub *a*). (art. 1)
6. **Norvège.**	= Danemark. (art. 1)
7. **Pays-Bas.**	= Cinq Puissances neutres. L'élection se fait parmi les candidats pourvus de trois recommandations au moins. (arts. 2 et 4)
8. **Suède.**	= Danemark. (art. 1)
9. **Suisse.**	= Des personnes dûment qualifiées, disposées à accepter les fonctions de juges. (art. 13)
10. **Italie.**	. . . .
11. **Allemagne.**	Des personnes aptes et disposées à accepter les fonctions de juge. (art. 14)
12. **Autriche.**	. . . .

VII. Electeurs.

1. **Projet 1907.**	. . . .
2. **Cinq Puissances neutres.**	L'Assemblée de la Société des Nations. (art. 5)
3. **Union Interparlementaire**	Les Puissances contractantes lors d'une session de la Conférence de la Paix. (art. 12)
4. **Union Juridique Internationale.**	L'Assemblée de la Société des Nations. (art. 3)
5. **Danemark.**	L'Assemblée de la Société des Nations. (art. 2)
6. **Norvège.**	= Danemark. (art. 1)
7. **Pays-Bas.**	Un Conseil administratif permanent, composé des représentants des Membres de la Société des Nations à ... et du Ministre des Affaires Etrangères de ... (arts. 2 et 17)
8. **Suède.**	Une Assemblée Electorale où chaque Membre de la Societé des Nations est représenté par le premier dans l'ordre numérique de ses juges à la C. P. A. ou, à son défaut, par le membre suivant qui n'est pas empêché. (art. 2)
9. **Suisse.**	La Conférence des Etats (organe analogue à l'Assemblée de la Société des Nations). (art. 13)
10. **Italie.**	Chaque Etat nomme un juge. (art. 18)
11. **Allemagne.**	Le Congrès des Etats. (art. 14)
12. **Autriche.**	Séance plénière des Membres de la Ligue. (art. 13)

VIII. Le suffrage.

1. **Projet 1907.**	. . . .
2. **Cinq Puissances neutres.**	Egalité de voix. (art. 6)

4. **International Law Union.**	The list, which is composed of candidates presented by the Governments and of persons of scientific national institutions is not limitative. (art. 4)
5. **Denmark.**	Same as 1907 draft, point (*a*). (art. 1)
6. **Norway.**	Same as Denmark. (art. 1)
7. **Netherlands.**	Same as Five-Power plan. The appointments are made among candidates having obtained three nominations at least. (arts. 2 and 4)
8. **Sweden.**	Same as Denmark. (art. 1)
9. **Switzerland.**	Candidates duly qualified for and disposed to accept the office of judge. (art. 13)
10. **Italy.**	. . . .
11. **Germany.**	Persons who are suitable for and ready to accept the office of jûdge. (art. 14)
12. **Austria.**	. . . . . . ; .

VII. The electors.

1. **1907 draft scheme.**	. . . .
2. **Five Neutral Powers.**	The Assembly of the League of Nations. (art. 5)
3. **Interparliamentary Union.**	The contracting Powers during a session of the Peace Conference. (art. 12)
4. **International Law Union.**	The Assembly of the League of Nations. (art. 3)
5. **Denmark.**	The Assembly of the League of Nations. (art. 2)
6. **Norway.**	Same as Denmark. (art. 1)
7. **Netherlands.**	Permanent administrative Council composed of representatives of the Members of the League of Nations at . . . and of the Minister of Foreign Affairs at . . . (arts. 2 and 17)
8. **Sweden.**	An Electoral Assembly wherever every state which is a Member of the League of Nations is represented by its foremost representative in the P. C. A, or, in the event of his being prevented from serving, the representative nearest to him in order who is available. (art. 2)
9. **Switzerland.**	The Conference of States (a body analogous to the Assembly of the League of Nations). (art. 13)
10. **Italy.**	Each State appoints one Judge.
11. **Germany.**	The Congress of States. (art. 14)
12. **Austria.**	A plenary Assembly of the Members of the League. (art. 13)

VIII. Votes.

1. **1907 draft scheme.**	. . . .
2. **Five Neutral Powers.**	The same number of votes for all voters. (art. 6)

3. **Union Interparlementaire.** Egalité de voix. (art. 12)

4. **Union Juridique Internationale.** Egalité de voix. (art. 3 j°. art. 3 du Pacte)

5 **Danemark.** Egalité de voix. (art. 2 j°. art. 3 du Pacte)

6. **Norvège.** = Danemark. (art. 2 j°. art. 3 du Pacte)

7. **Pays-Bas.** Possibilité de différents nombres de votes pour les divers Etats. (art. 4)

8. **Suède.** . . . .

9. **Suisse.** = Danemark. (art. 13 j°. art. 3 du Pacte)

10. **Italie.** . . . .

11. **Allemagne.** Egalité de voix. (art. 14)

12. **Autriche.** Egalité de voix. (art. 13 j°. art. 3 du Pacte)

IX. Mode d'Election.

1. **Projet 1907.** . . . .

2. **Cinq Puissances neutres.** Voir art. 6 par. 6, 7, 8 et art. 7.

3. **Union Interparlementaire.** Les juges et les juges suppléants sont élus au scrutin secret. L'élection des juges suppléants n'aura lieu qu'après que l'élection des juges titulaires sera terminée. Pour être élus, les candidats devront avoir obtenu au moins la moitié des suffrages. Si un nombre plus grand de candidats que celui des sièges à remplir obtiennent un nombre égal de voix, il sera fait application du bénéfice de l'âge. (art. 12)

4. **Union Juridique Internationale.** Les juges sont élus au scrutin secret. L'élection se fait pour les juges d'abord, ensuite pour les suppléants. Au premier tour nul n'est élu sans la majorité absolue, au deuxième tour la majorité relative suffit. (arts. 3 et 6)

Si 2 membres de la même nationalité obtiennent un nombre de voix suffisant pour être élus, celui d'entre eux qui obtient la majorité la plus forte, ou, en cas d'égalité de voix, le plus ancien d'âge est élu. (art. 7)

5. **Danemark.** Voir art. 5.

6. **Norvège.** = Danemark. (art. 5)

7. **Pays-Bas.** = Voir art. 4, sub 3.

8. **Suède.** L'élection a lieu pour un membre à la fois. Pour être déclaré élu le candidat doit avoir obtenu la majorité absolue des suffrages exprimés. Si après deux tours de scrutin aucun candidat n'a obtenu la majorité absolue, l'élection aura lieu au troisième tour à la majorité relative des voix. (art. 6)

9. **Suisse.** Les 15 candidats qui ont recueilli le plus grand nombre de voix sont élus. (art. 13)

10. **Italie.** . . . .

3. **Interparliamentary Union.**	Each power enjoys an equal elective power. (art. 12)
4. **International Law Union.**	An equal number of votes. (art. 3 cf. art. 3 of the Covenant.)
5. **Denmark.**	Equal number of votes for all states. (art. 2 cf. art. 3 of the Covenant.)
6. **Norway.**	Same as Denmark. (art. 2 cf. art. 3 of the Covenant.)
7. **Netherlands.**	Different states may have different number of votes. (art. 4)
8. **Sweden.**	. . . .
9. **Switzerland.**	Same as Denmark. (art. 13 cf. art. 3 of the Covenant.)
10. **Italy.**	. . . .
11. **Germany.**	Equal number of votes. (art. 14)
12. **Austria.**	Equal number of votes. (art. 13 cf. art. 3 of the Covenant.)

IX. Mode of election.

1. **1907 draft scheme.**	. . . .
2. **Five Neutral Powers.**	See Art. 6, pars 6, 7 and 8 and Art. 7.
3. **Interparliamentary Union.**	The judges and deputy judges are elected by secret ballot. The election of deputy judges will take place only after the election of the titular judges is finished. In order to be elected, candidates must obtain at least one half of the votes. If a greater number of candidates than there are seats to be filled receive an equal number of votes, preference will be given to those of greater age. (art. 12)
4. **International Law Union.**	Judges shall be elected by secret vote. First the judges shall be elected, then the deputy judges. At the first ballot an absolute majority to be elected. At the second ballot a bare majority shall suffice (arts. 3 and 6). If two candidates of the same nationality obtain a sufficient number of votes to be elected, the candidate who has the largest majority, or in the case of an equal number of votes, the oldest candidate shall be elected. (art. 7)
5. **Denmark.**	See art. 5.
6. **Norway.**	Same as Denmark. (art. 5)
7. **Netherlands.**	See art 4, sub 3.
8. **Sweden.**	The election shall proceed for one judge at a time. To secure election as a judge a candidate must have an absolute majority of the total number of votes cast. If, however, an absolute majority of the voters has not been reached at two divisions, a bare majority secured by one candidate over any and all of the others at the third division shall suffice for his election. (art 6)
9. **Switzerland.**	The fifteen candidates who have received the greatest number of votes are elected. (art. 13)
10. **Italy.**	. . . .

11. **Allemagne.** Chaque Etat désigne sur la liste générale de proposition 15 personnes; les 15 personnes dont les noms réunissent le plus grand nombre de suffrages sont choisies comme juges. (art 1)

12. **Autriche.** Sont élus ceux qui ont obtenu le plus grand nombre de voix. (art. 15)

X. Nationalité des candidats.

1. **Projet 1907.** . . . .

2. **Cinq Puissances neutres.** Un tiers au plus des candidats proposés peuvent être des ressortissants du membre qui fait la proposition. (art. 6)

3. **Union Interparlementaire.** . . . .

4. **Union Juridique Internationale.** . . . .

5. **Danemark.** Un tiers au plus des candidats proposés par un Gouvernement pourront appartenir à la Puissance en question. (art. 3)

6. **Norvège.** Une Puissance ne peut désigner, à la première élection, qu'un tiers, au maximum, des candidats, qu'elle propose, parmi ses propres ressortissants ; et, aux élections ultérieures, trois au maximum. (art. 3)

7. **Pays-Bas.** . . . .

8. **Suède.** . . . .

9. **Suisse.** Un des candidats proposés par un Etat ne devra pas être ressortissant dudit Etat. (art. 13)

10. **Italie.** . . . .

11. **Allemagne.** = Suisse. (art. 14)

12. **Autriche.** . . . .

XI. Nationalité des Juges.

1. **Projet 1907.** . . . .

2. **Cinq Puissances neutres.** Ne peuvent appartenir à la Cour plus de deux juges ressortissants de la même Puissance. (art. 4)

3. **Union Interparlementaire.** Il ne pourra être élu parmi les juges et les juges suppléants plus de deux candidats d'une même nationalité. (art. 13)

4. **Union Juridique Internationale.** La Cour se compose de 8 juges titulaires et 3 suppléants d'une nationalité européenne, 5 titulaires et 2 suppléants d'une nationalité américaine, 2 titulaires et 1 suppléant d'une nationalité asiatique. (art. 2)

Nul Etat ne peut avoir, ni parmi les juges titulaires ni parmi les suppléants plus d'un juge de sa nationalité. (art. 7)

5. **Danemark.** Il ne pourra siéger à la fois plus de deux juges qui soient nationaux d'une même Puissance. (art. 1)

6. **Norvège.** = Danemark. (art. 1)

7. **Pays-Bas.** La Cour se compose de 7 juges de nationalité différente. (art. 2)

8. **Suède.** Ne pourront appartenir à la Cour plus de deux juges qui soient nationaux d'un même Etat.

11. **Germany.**	From the total list of the proposed each state shall nominate fifteen persons. The fifteen persons who receive the most votes shall be elected as judges. (art. 1)
12. **Austria.**	Those will be considered elected who obtain the largest number of votes. (art. 15)

X. Nationality of Candidates.

1. **1907 draft scheme.**	. . . .
2. **Five Neutral Powers.**	Not more than one third of the candidates nominated may be subjects of the nominating states. (art. 6)
3. **Interparliamentary Union.**	. . . .
4. **International Law Union.**	. . . .
5. **Denmark.**	Not more than one third of the candidates nominated by Governments may belong to the state in question. (art. 3)
6. **Norway.**	Only one third at most of the candidates at the first election may be subjects of the country by which they are nominated, not more than three at succeeding elections. (art. 3)
7. **Netherlands.**	. . . .
8. **Sweden.**	. . . .
9. **Switzerland.**	One at least of the candidates proposed must not be a national of the proposing state. (art. 13)
10. **Italy.**	. . . .
11. **Germany.**	Same as Switzerland. (art. 14)
12. **Austria.**	. . . .

XI. Nationality of Judges.

1. **1907 draft scheme.**	. . . .
2. **Five Neutral Powers.**	Not more than two judges of the same nationality may belong to the Court. (art. 4)
3. **Interparliamentary Union.**	There shall not be elected among the titular judges and deputy judges more than two candidates of the same nationality. (art. 13)
4. **International Law Union.**	The Court shall consist of eight judges and three deputy judges belonging to European states, five judges and two deputy judges belonging to American states, two judges and one deputy judge belonging to Asiatic states. art. 2)
	No state may have more than one judge of each nationality either among the judges or the deputy judges. (art. 7)
5. **Denmark.**	Not more than two judges of the same nationality may sit on the Court at the same time. (art. 1).
6. **Norway.**	Same as Denmark. (art. 1)
7. **Netherlands.**	The Court is composed of seven judges of different nationalities. (art. 2)
8. **Sweden.**	There shall not be more than two judges who are nationals of any one state.

Dans la section de procédure sommaire ne pourront siéger en même temps deux membres appartenant au même Etat. (arts. 1 et 12)

9. **Suisse.**	. . . .
10. **Italie.**	. . . .
11. **Allemagne.**	. . . .
12. **Autriche.**	Aucun Etat ne peut avoir plus d'un membre. (art. 13)

XII. Incompatibilité avec d'autres fonctions.

1. **Projet 1907.**	. . . .
2. **Cinq Puissances neutres.**	Les fonctions de juge sont incompatibles avec toute autre fonction publique ainsi qu'avec toute fonction privée qui comporte un intérêt personnel ou qui poursuit un but politique. En cas de doute, la Cour décide. (art. 13)
3. **Union Interparlementaire.**	. . . .
4. **Union Juridique Internationale.**	Les juges ne peuvent exercer d'autres fonctions d'ordre politique ou judiciaire. (art. 14)
5. **Danemark.**	Aucun membre ne peut exercer d'autres fonctions publiques. (art. 8)
6. **Norvège.**	= Danemark. (art. 8)
7. **Pays-Bas.**	. . . .
8. **Suède.**	= Danemark (art. 10)
9. **Suisse.**	. . . .
10. **Italie.**	. . . .
11. **Allemagne.**	. . . .
12. **Autriche.**	. . . .

XIII. Immunité diplomatique pour les Juges.

1. **Projet 1907.**	Les juges jouissent des privilèges et immunités diplomatiques dans l'exercice de leurs fonctions et en dehors de leurs pays. (art. 5)
2. **Cinq Puissances neutres.**	Les juges jouissent des privilèges et immunités diplomatiques dans l'exercice de leurs fonctions. (art. 13)
3. **Union Interparlementaire.**	. . . .
4. **Union Juridique Internationale.**	. . . .
5 **Danemark.**	. . . .
6. **Norvège.**	. . . .
7. **Pays-Bas.**	= Projet 1907. (art. 7)
8. **Suède.**	. . . .
9. **Suisse.**	. . . .
10. **Italie.**	. . . .

	It shall not be permissible for two judges who are nationals of the same state to serve in the division for summary procedure at one and the same time. (arts. 1 and 12)
9. **Switzerland.**	. . . .
10. **Italy.**	. . . .
11. **Germany.**	. . . .
12. **Austria.**	No state can have more than one member. (art. 13)

XII. Incompatibility with other functions.

1. **1907 draft scheme**	. . . .
2. **Five Neutral Powers.**	The performance of judicial duties shall be incompatible with any other public duties and also with any private duties of a nature entailing personal interest or a political object. In doubtful cases the Court shall decide. (art. 13)
3. **Interparliamentary Union.**	. . . .
4. **International Law Union.**	The members of the Court may not perform any other duties of a political or a judiciary order. (art. 14)
5. **Denmark.**	No member can exercise other public duties. (art. 8)
6. **Norway.**	Same as Denmark. (art. 8)
7. **Netherlands.**	. . . .
8. **Sweden.**	Same as Denmark. (art. 10)
9. **Switzerland.**	. . . .
10. **Italy.**	. . . .
11. **Germany.**	. . . .
12. **Austria.**	. . . .

XIII. Diplomatic Immunity of Judges.

1. **1907 draft scheme.**	The judges enjoy diplomatic privileges and immunities in the exercise of their functions outside their own country. (art. 5)
2. **Five Neutral Powers.**	The judges shall be granted diplomatic privileges and immunities in the performance of their duties. (art. 13)
3. **Interparliamentary Union.**	. . . .
4. **International Law Union.**	. . . .
5. **Denmark.**	. . . .
6. **Norway.**	. . . .
7. **Netherlands.**	Same as 1907 draft. (art 7)
8. **Sweden.**	. . . .
9. **Switzerland.**	. . . .
10. **Italy.**	. . . .

11. **Allemagne.**	. . . .
12. **Autriche.**	. . . .

XIV. Rémunération des Juges.

1. **Projet 1907.**	Une indemnité annuelle de 6.000 florins néerlandais. Pendant l'exercice de leurs fonctions une somme de cent florins par jour. (art. 9)
2. **Cinq Puissances neutres.**	Une indemnité annuelle fixée par l'Assemblée de la Société des Nations. (art. 13)
3. **Union Interparlementaire.**	Une indemnité annuelle de 25 000 florins. (art. 9)
4. **Union Juridique Internationale.**	. . . .
5. **Danemark.**	Les règles seront fixées par l'Assemblée de la Société des Nations. (art. 8)
6. **Norvège.**	= Danemark. (art. 8)
7. **Pays-Bas.**	Une indemnité annuelle et pendant l'exercice de leurs fonctions une certaine somme par jour. (art. 12)
8. **Suède.**	L'indemnité annuelle est fixée par une Convention spéciale. Dans certains cas une pension sera accordée. (art. 9)
9. **Suisse.**	. . . .
10. **Italie.**	. . . .
11. **Allemagne.**	. . . .
12. **Autriche.**	. . . .

XV. Election du Président.

1. **Projet 1907.**	La Cour élit son Président. (art. 8)
2. **Cinq Puissances neutres.**	= Projet 1907. (art. 15)
3. **Union Interparlementaire.**	= Projet 1907. (art. 8)
4. **Union Juridique Internationale.**	. . . .
5. **Danemark.**	La Cour élit son Président. (art. 13)
6. **Norvège.**	= Danemark. (art. 13)
7. **Pays-Bas.**	= Danemark. (art. 11)
8. **Suède.**	= Danemark. (art. 14)
9. **Suisse.**	. . . .
10. **Italie.**	La Cour élit son Président tous les deux ans. (art. 19)
11. **Allemagne.**	. . . .
12. **Autriche.**	. . . .

11. **Germany.**	. . . .
12. **Austria.**	. . . .

XIV. Salary of Judges.

1. **1907 draft scheme.**	An annual salary of 6,000 Netherlands florins. In the exercise of their duties the judges receive the sum of 100 florins a day. (art. 9)
2. **Five Neutral Powers.**	An annual salary to be fixed by the Assembly of the League of Nations. (art. 13)
3. **Interparliamentary Union.**	An annual salary of 25 000 florins. (art. 9)
4. **International Law Union.**	. . . .
5. **Denmark.**	The rules to be fixed by the Assembly of the League of Nations. (art. 8)
6. **Norway.**	Same as Denmark. (art. 8)
7. **Netherlands.**	An annual salary and during the exercise of functions a certain sum a day. (art. 12)
8. **Sweden.**	The amount of the annual salary is to be fixed by special convention. In certain cases a pension shall be paid. (art. 9)
9. **Switzerland.**	. . . .
10. **Italy.**	. . . .
11. **Germany.**	. . . .
12. **Austria.**	. . . .

XV. Election of President.

1. **1907 draft scheme.**	The Court elects its President. (art. 8)
2. **Five Neutral Powers.**	The Court shall elect its own President. (art. 15)
3. **Interparliamentary Union.**	The Court elects its President. (art. 8)
4. **International Law Union.**	. . . .
5. **Denmark.**	The Court elects its President. (art. 13)
6. **Norway.**	Same as Denmark. (art. 13)
7. **Netherlands.**	Same as Denmark. (art. 11)
8. **Sweden.**	Same as Denmark. (art. 14)
9. **Switzerland.**	. . . .
10. **Italy.**	The Court shall elect its President every two years. (art. 19)
11. **Germany.**	. . . .
12. **Austria.**	. . . .

XVI. Limite d'âge des Juges.

1. **Projet 1907.**	. . . .
2. **Cinq Puissances neutres.**	Les juges ayant atteint l'âge de 70 ans prennent leur retraite. (art. 11)
3. **Union Interparlementaire.**	La limite d'âge est fixée à 75 ans. (art. 4)
4. **Union Juridique Internationale.**	. . . .
5. **Danemark.**	Dispositions à fixer par l'Assemblée de la Société des Nations. (art. 8)
6. **Norvège.**	= Danemark. (art. 8)
7. **Pays-Bas.**	. . . .
8. **Suède.**	Les juges ayant atteint l'âge de 70 ans seront tenus de prendre leur retraite. (art. 9)
9. **Suisse.**	. . . .
10. **Italie.**	. . . .
11. **Allemagne.**	. . . .
12. **Autriche.**	. . . .

XVII. Composition du tribunal chargé de juger le litige.

1. **Projet 1907.**	. . . .
2. **Cinq Puissances neutres.**	Le tribunal se compose de 7 juges. (art. 26)
3. **Union Interparlementaire.**	Le règlement déterminera le nombre de chambres qui seront instituées au sein de la Cour. (art. 14)
4. **Union Juridique Internationale.**	La Cour ne juge qu'avec onze membres. (art. 8)
5. **Danemark.**	La Cour ne peut délibérer valablement que si 15 membres au moins sont présents; toutefois elle pourra se prononcer, 11 membres au moins étant présents, si des empêchements ont eu lieu au cours de l'affaire. (art. 11)
6. **Norvège.**	L'audience d'une affaire est ouverte dans la présence de 15 juges; toutefois elle peut délibérer valablement dans la présence de 11 juges au minimum, en cas d'empêchement au cours de l'audience. (art. 11)
7. **Pays-Bas.**	La Cour n'exerce ses fonctions qu'en pleno, (7 juges). (art. 8)
8. **Suède.**	Le tribunal se compose de 7 juges au moins et de 15 juges au maximum. (arts. 11 et 18)
9. **Suisse.**	Le tribunal se compose de 5 juges. (art. 15)
10. **Italie.**	Le tribunal se compose de 7 juges. (art. 21)

XVI. Age limit for Judges.

1. **1907 draft scheme.**	. . . .
2. **Five Neutral Powers.**	The judges shall retire upon reaching the age of 70. (art. 11)
3. **Interparliamentary Union.**	The age limit is fixed at 75 years. (art. 4)
4. **International Law Union.**	. . . .
5. **Denmark.**	Rules to be fixed by the Assembly of the League of Nations. (art. 8)
6. **Norway.**	Same as Denmark. (art. 8)
7. **Netherlands.**	. . . .
8. **Sweden.**	It shall be obligatory on a judge to retire at the age of 70. (art. 9)
9. **Switzerland.**	. . . .
10. **Italy.**	. . . .
11. **Germany.**	. . . .
12. **Austria.**	. . . .

XVII. Composition of the Tribunal for deciding the Case.

1. **1907 draft scheme.**	. . . .
2. **Five Neutral Powers.**	The Court is composed of seven judges. (art. 26)
3. **Interparliamentary Union.**	The standing orders will fix the number of chambers which will be constituted within the Court, which is composed of 15 judges. (art. 14)
4. **International Law Union.**	The quorum of the Court is eleven members. (art. 8)
5. **Denmark.**	The quorum of the Court is fifteen members The Court can, however, decide if not less than eleven members are present if some members have been prevented during the proceedings from taking part in the examination of the case. (art. 11)
6. **Norway.**	The Court is set with fifteen members. Eleven members, however, form a quorum in case of unavoidable absence during the trial of the case. (art. 11)
7. **Netherlands.**	A full session of the Court is required — seven judges. (art. 8)
8. **Sweden.**	A minimum of seven judges of the Court shall constitute a quorum. The Court cannot sit with more than fifteen judges. (arts 11 and 18)
9. **Switzerland.**	The Court consists of five judges when exercising its ordinary jurisdiction. (art. 15)
10. **Italy.**	. . . .

11. **Allemagne.**	Le tribunal se compose de 3 juges.	(art. 15)
12. **Autriche.**	Le tribunal se compose de 9 juges.	(art. 13)

XVIII. Droit de Récusation.

1. **Projet 1907.**	. . . .	
2. **Cinq Puissances neutres.**	Ne sont récusés des juges que pour des motifs bien déterminés (intérêt personnel, etc.)	(art. 28)
3. **Union Interparlementaire.**	. . . .	
4. **Union Juridique Internationale.**	Chaque partie indique 2 juges qui s'abstiendront de siéger. (art. 8) Quand un juge a la nationalité de l'un des Etats, parties au litige, sans qu'aucun autre ait celle de l'adversaire, il cède son siège au premier suppléant qui n'a la nationalité d'aucun des Etats en cause.	(art. 10)
5. **Danemark.**	Chacune des parties a le droit d'exclure jusqu'à trois juges.	(art. 10)
6. **Norvège.**	Chacune des parties doit récuser 3 juges.	(art. 10)
7. **Pays-Bas.**	Aucune influence des parties sur la composition du tribunal.	
8. **Suède.**	Ne sont récusés des juges que pour des motifs bien déterminés (intérêt personnel etc.) Lorsqu'un membre de la Cour appartient à l'une des Parties en litige tandis qu'aucun membre n'appartient à la Partie adverse, il abandonnera pendant la durée de l'instance son siège de juge à la Cour.	(art. 18)
9. **Suisse.**	Chacune des parties doit récuser 5 juges.	(art. 15)
10. **Italie.**	Chacune des parties choisit un juge parmi les 7 juges composant le tribunal.	(art. 21)
11. **Allemagne.**	Parmi les 3 juges sont 2 juges choisis par chacune des parties.	(art. 15)
12. **Autriche.**	Chacune des parties doit récuser 3 juges.	(art. 13)

XIX. Le mode de combler les vacances.

1. **Projet 1907.**	En cas de décès ou de démission d'un juge ou d'un juge suppléant, il est pourvu à son remplacement selon le mode fixé pour sa nomination Dans ce cas, la nomination est faite pour une nouvelle période de 12 ans.	(art. 3)
2. **Cinq Puissances neutres.**	Les juges suppléants entrent en fonctions comme juges d'après le nombre des voix obtenues lors de leur élection En cas d'égalité de voix, c'est le plus âgé qui entre en fonctions.	(art. 12)

11. **Germany.**	The tribunal shall give its decisions through the representation of three members. (art. 15)
12. **Austria.**	The tribunal shall pronounce its decisions by a commissioh of nine members. (art. 13)

XVIII. Right to challenge.

1. **1907 draft scheme.**	. . . .
2. **Five Neutral Powers.**	Judges may be excused by the Court for certain well-defined reasons (personal interest in the subject matter, etc.) (art. 28)
3. **Interparliamentary Union.**	. . . .
4. **International Law Union.**	Each party designates two judges, who will abstain from sitting. (art. 8) When a judge is of the nationality of one of the states parties to the dispute, without any of the other judges being of the nationality of the adverse party he shall give up his seat to the first deputy-judge who is not of the nationality of any state party to the case. (art. 10)
5. **Denmark.**	Each party has the right to challenge not more than three judges. (art. 10)
6. **Norway.**	Each party shall challenge three judges. (art. 10)
7. **Netherlands.**	The parties may have no influence on the composition of the tribunal.
8. **Sweden.**	A challenge cannot be lodged against a judge of the Court save for certain well-defined reasons (personal interest in the subject matter, etc.). In the event of a judge of the Court being a national of one of the states at variance with each other and there being no national of the other state on the bench, the said judge shall withdraw from the Court while the dispute is being dealt with. (art. 18).
9. **Switzerland.**	Each party must challenge five judges. (art. 15)
10. **Italy.**	Each party chooses one judge among the seven judges on the tribunal. (art. 21)
11. **Germany.**	Each party shall choose one of the three members sitting. (art. 15)
12. **Austria.**	Each of the parties shall eliminate three of the fifteen members of the Court. (art. 13)

XIX. Mode of filling vacancies.

1. **1907 draft scheme.**	Should a judge or deputy-judge die or retire, the vacancy is filled in the manner in which the appointment was made. In this case the appointment is made for a fresh period of twelve years. (art 3)
2. **Five Neutral Powers.**	Deputy-judges shall take precedence for duty as judges according to the number of votes received before election. In cases of equality, the eldest shall take precedence. (art. 12)

3. **Union Interparlementaire.** En cas de décès ou de démission d'un juge, il est remplacé par cooptation, à la majorité des juges titulaires en fonctions, parmi les juges suppléants. Le nombre de ces derniers est complété lors de la plus prochaine Conférence de la Paix. (art. 4)

4. **Union Juridique Internationale.** En cas d'empêchement les juges suppléants remplacent de plein droit les titulaires. Le remplacement se fait dans chacune des catégories géographiques. La primauté se détermine par le nombre de voix obtenu ou à égalité de voix par l'ancienneté d'âge. (art. 9)

5. **Danemark.** Lorsqu'un juge est décédé ou autrement a cessé d'être membre de la Cour, il est remplacé par le suppléant qui prend sa place pour le restant de la durée du mandat du membre sortant. (art. 7)

6. **Norvège.** = Danemark. (art. 7)

7. **Pays-Bas.** = Projet 1907. (art. 5)

8. **Suède.** Lorsqu'un juge cesse d'appartenir à la Cour, le premier dans l'ordre numérique des juges suppléants le remplace à vie dans ses fonctions. (art. 7)

9. **Suisse.** En cas de retraite ou de décès des élus les juges suppléants entrent en fonctions en suivant l'ordre des voix qu'ils ont recueillies. (art. 13)

10. **Italie.** . . . .

11. **Allemagne.** Les juges en cas de vacance sont remplacés par les personnes dont les noms, après ceux des 15 élus, ont réuni le plus grand nombre de suffrages et dans l'ordre du nombre des voix obtenues. (art. 14)

12. **Autriche.** . . . .

XX. Règlement d'organisation.

1. **Projet 1907.** La Cour fait elle-même son règlement d'ordre intérieur. (art. 32)

2. **Cinq Puissances neutres.** = Projet 1907. (art. 17)

3. **Union Interparlementaire.** = Projet 1907. (art. 14)

4. **Union Juridique Internationale.** . . . .

5. **Danemark.** = Projet 1907. (art. 14).

6. **Norvège.** = Projet 1907. (art. 14)

7. **Pays-Bas.** = Projet 1907. (art. 24)

8. **Suède.** . . . .

9. **Suisse.** = Projet 1907. (art. 16)

10. **Italie.** . . . .

11. **Allemagne.** . . . .

12. **Autriche.** . . . .

3. **Interparliamentary Union.**	In case of the death or retirement of a judge, he is replaced by co-optation by the majority of the titular judges in office from among the deputy-judges. The number of the latter is completed at the next following Peace Conference. (art. 4)
4. **International Law Union.**	In case a judge is absent his place shall be automatically filled by a deputy-judge This co-optation shall be carried out in each of the geographical categories. Priority shall be determined by the number of votes obtained, or in the case of equality of votes, by age. (art. 9)
5. **Denmark.**	The place of a judge who has died or otherwise ceased to be a member of the Court is taken by the deputy-judge for the remainder of the term of office. (art. 7)
6. **Norway.**	Same as Denmark. (art. 7)
7. **Netherlands.**	Same as 1907 draft. (art. 5)
8. **Sweden.**	On the retirement of any ordinary judge, the supplementary judge who stands first in order of succession shall take his place as ordinary judge for life. (art. 7)
9. **Switzerland.**	In case of resignation or death of a selected candidate the other candidates fill the vacancy in the order of the number of votes received by them. (art. 13)
10. **Italy.**	....
11. **Germany.**	Upon the retirement of judges their places shall be taken by those persons who have received the most votes after the fifteen who had been elected and this in the order of the number of votes obtained. (art. 14)
12. **Austria.**	....

XX. Rules of Court.

1. **1907 draft scheme.**	The Court itself draws up its own rules of procedure. (art. 32)
2. **Five Neutral Powers.**	Same as 1907 draft. (art. 17)
3. **Interparliamentary Union.**	Same as 1907 draft. (art. 14)
4. **International Law Union.**	....
5. **Denmark.**	Same as 1907 draft. (art. 14)
6. **Norway.**	Same as 1907 draft. (art. 14)
7. **Netherlands.**	Same as 1907 draft. (art. 24)
8. **Sweden.**	....
9. **Switzerland.**	Same as 1907 draft. (art. 16)
10. **Italy.**	....
11. **Germany.**	....
12. **Austria.**	....

XXI. Siège de la Cour.

1. **Projet 1907.**	La Cour a son siège à La Haye et ne peut, sauf le cas de force majeure, le transporter ailleurs. (art. 11)
2. **Cinq Puissances neutres.**	La Cour a son siège à . . . . . et ne peut, sauf le cas de force majeure, le transporter ailleurs. (art. 18)
3. **Union Interparlementaire.**	. . . .
4. **Union Juridique Internationale.**	. . . .
5. **Danemark.**	. . . .
6. **Norvège.**	. . . .
7. **Pays-Bas.**	Cinq Puissances neutres. (art. 14)
8. **Suède.**	. . . .
9. **Suisse.**	. . . .
10. **Italie.**	La Haye. (art. 18)
11. **Allemagne.**	. . . .
12. **Autriche.**	. . . .

XXII. Greffe de la Cour.

1. **Projet 1907.**	Le Bureau International de la C. P. A. sert de greffe à la Cour (art 13)
2. **Cinq Puissances neutres.**	La Cour nomme son grffier et les autres fonctionnaires du greffe. (art. 15)
3. **Union Interparlementaire.**	= Projet 1907. (art. 16)
4. **Union Juridique Internationale**	. . . .
5. **Danemark.**	La Cour nomme son Secrétaire et son Bureau. (art. 13)
6. **Norvège.**	= Danemark. (art. 13)
7. **Pays-Bas.**	Un bureau international sert de greffe à la Cour; le Secrétaire Général du bureau remplit les fonctions du greffier. Les secrétaires adjoints au greffier sont désignés par la Cour. (art. 15)
8. **Suède.**	La Cour nomme le Secrétaire Général et le personnel du Secrétariat. (art. 14)
9. **Suisse.**	. . . .
10. **Italie.**	= Projet 1907. (art 20)
11. **Allemagne.**	. . . .
12. **Autriche.**	. . . .

XXI. Seat of the Court.

1. **1907 draft scheme**	The seat of the Court is at the Hague and cannot be transferred, unless absolutely obliged by circumstances, elsewhere. (art. 11)
2. **Five Neutral Powers.**	The Court shall sit at . . . . . . and may not remove elsewhere unless caused by circumstances to do so. (art. 18)
3. **Interparliamentary Union.**	. . . .
4. **International Law Union.**	. . . .
5. **Denmark.**	. . . .
6. **Norway.**	. . . .
7. **Netherlands.**	Same as Five Power plan. (art. 14)
8. **Sweden.**	. . . .
9. **Switzerland.**	. . . .
10. **Italy.**	The Hague. (art. 18)
11. **Germany.**	. . . .
12. **Austria.**	. . . .

XXII. Registry of the Court.

1. **1907 draft scheme.**	The International Bureau of the P. C. A. acts as Registry to the Court of Arbitral Justice. (art. 13)
2. **Five Neutral Powers.**	The Court shall appoint its Registrar and the other officials of the Registry. (art. 15)
3. **Interparliamentary Union.**	Same as 1907 draft. (art. 16)
4. **International Law Union.**	. . . .
5. **Denmark.**	The Court shall appoint its Secretary and other officials. (art. 13)
6. **Norway.**	Same as Denmark. (art. 13)
7. **Netherlands.**	An International Bureau acts as Registry to the Court. The Secretary-General of the Bureau acts as Registrar. The staff at the disposal of the Registrar is appointed by the Court. (art. 15)
8. **Sweden.**	The Court shall appoint the Secretary-General of the Court and shall organise a clerical staff. (art. 14)
9. **Switzerland.**	. . . .
10. **Italy.**	Same as 1907 draft. (art. 20)
11. **Germany.**	. . . .
12. **Austria.**	. . . .

B. COMPÉTENCE.

I. Accessibilité de la Cour.

1. **Projet 1907.**	L'accès de la Cour n'est ouvert qu'aux Puissances contractantes. (art. 21)
2. **Cinq Puissances neutres.**	L'accès de la Cour est ouvert tant aux Membres de la Société qu'aux autres Etats. (art. 20)
3. **Union Interparlementaire.**	. . . .
4. **Union Juridique Internationale.**	. . . .
5. **Danemark.**	. . . .
6. **Norvège.**	. . . .
7. **Pays-Bas.**	L'accès n'est ouvert qu'aux Membres de la Société des Nations et à leurs ressortissants. (arts. 20 et 21)
8. **Suède.**	La Cour ne connaît que des conflits entre les Etats. Un Etat pourra saisir la Cour des demandes fondées sur les droits qu'il fait valoir au nom d'un de ses ressortissants contre un autre Etat. (art. 20)
9. **Suisse.**	Accessible aux Parties Contractantes. (art. 12)
10. **Italie.**	. . . .
11. **Allemagne.**	. . . . Peut-être art. 30 implique que l'accès est limité aux Membres de la Société des Nations.
12. **Autriche.**	. . . .

II. La Cour peut-elle connaître de conflits dans lesquels une ou deux des parties sont des personnes privées.

1. **Projet 1907.**	. . . .
2. **Cinq Puissances neutres.**	La Cour ne connaît que de conflits entre Etats. Cependant un Etat peut saisir la Cour de demandes fondées sur des droits qu'il fait valoir en faveur de ses ressortissants contre un autre Etat. (art. 20)
3. **Union Interparlementaire.**	La Cour est compétente de connaître de conflits entre Etats, entre personnes privées et Etats étrangers, et entre personnes privées. (art. 2)
4. **Union Juridique Internationale.**	Art. 1 implique que la Cour ne connaît que de différends entre Etats.

B. COMPETENCE.

I. Access to the Court.

1. **1907 draft scheme**	The contracting powers only may have access to the Court. (art. 21)
2. **Five Neutral Powers.**	The Court is open both to members of the League and to other states: (art. 20)
3. **Interparliamentary Union.**	. . . .
4. **International Law Union.**	. . . .
5. **Denmark.**	. . . .
6. **Norway.**	. . . .
7. **Netherlands.**	The Court is open only to states Members of the League of Nations, and to nationals of such states. (arts. 20 and 21)
8. **Sweden.**	The Court is only to deal with disputes between states. A state can institute proceedings before the Court to establish a claim on behalf of one of its nationals against another. (art. 20)
9. **Switzerland.**	Accessible to the contracting parties. (art. 20)
10. **Italy.**	. . . .
11. **Germany.**	. . . . It is possible that Art. 30 should be read so as to mean that the access is limited to Members of the League of Nations.
12. **Austria.**	. . . .

II. Can the Court take cognisance of conflicts in which one or two of the parties are private persons.

1. **1907 draft scheme.**	. . . .
2. **Five Neutral Powers.**	The Court shall take cognisance only of inter-state litigation; nevertheless, a state may lay before the Court a suit based upon rights which it claims to put forward on behalf of one of its citizens against another state. (art. 20).
3. **Interparliamentary Union.**	The Court is open to deal with conflicts between private persons and foreign states and between private persons. (art. 2).
4. **International Law Union.**	It follows from art. 1 that the Court has jurisdiction only over conflicts between states.

5. **Danemark.**	Arts. 9 et 15 semblent impliquer que la Cour ne connaît que de différends entre Etats.
6. **Norvège.**	= Danemark.
7. **Pays-Bas.**	La Cour est compétente pour des conflits soit entre Etats, soit entre un Etat et le ressortissant d'un autre Etat, soit entre des ressortissants d'Etats différents qui sont portés devant elle en vertu d'un traité ou d'un accord spécial, soit entre Etats, soit entre un Etat et le ressortissant d'un autre Etat. (art. 21)
8. **Suède.**	La Cour ne connaît que des conflits entre les Etats. Nonobstant cette disposition, un Etat pourra saisir la Cour des demandes fondées sur les droits qu'il fait valoir au nom d'un de ses ressortissants contre un autre Etat. (art. 20)
9. **Suisse.**	Les arts. 12 et 15 impliquent peut-être que la Cour ne connaît que de différends entre Etats.
10. **Italie.**	. . . .
11. **Allemagne.**	La Cour, en dehors des différends entre les Etats, connaît: *a)* des plaintes adressées par des particuliers contre les Etats et les gouvernants de ces Etats lorsque les Tribunaux de ces Etats se sont déclarés incompétents; *b)* des différends entre les ressortissants des divers Etats, dans la mesure ou l'application de traités constitue l'objet de ces différends. (art. 31)
12. **Autriche.**	L'exposé des motifs de M. LAMMASCH semble indiquer que la Cour ne connaît que de différends entre Etats.

III. La Cour est-elle compétente quand une seule des Parties a recours à elle?

1. **Projet 1907.**	La Cour connaît de tous les différends qui sont portés devant elle, en vertu d'une stipulation générale d'arbitrage ou d'un accord spécial. (art. 17. Voir aussi art. 19)
2. **Cinq Puissances neutres.**	La Cour connaît, sans l'assentiment préalable des parties, de différends relatifs à l'interprétation d'un traité ou relatifs à certains autres points. (art. 21)
3. **Union Interparlementaire.**	Art. 2 semble impliquer que la Cour est compétente quand une des parties a recours à elle. (Voir aussi art. 19)
4. **Union Juridique Internationale.**	. . . .
5. **Danemark.**	. . . .
6. **Norvège.**	. . . .
7. **Pays-Bas.**	La Cour connaît des conflits qui sont portés devant elle en vertu d'un traité ou d'un accord spécial, soit entre Etats, soit entre un Etat et le ressortissant d'un autre Etat. (art. 21)
8. **Suède.**	La Cour connaît de tous les litiges pour lesquels les Parties s'accordent à reconnaître sa compétence, tel accord pouvant être établi par convention générale (dans ce cas seulement si aucune des Parties ne proteste devant la Cour contre l'applicabilité de la Convention) ou bien par accord spécial. (art. 15)

5. **Denmark.** It seems to follow from arts. 9 and 15 that the Court has jurisdiction only over conflicts between states.

6. **Norway.** Same as Denmark.

7. **Netherlands.** The Court has jurisdiction over conflicts between states, between one state and a national of another state and over conflicts between nationals of different states, provided the conflict is brought before the Court by virtue of a Treaty or a special agreement concluded either between states or between one state and the national of another state. (art. 21)

8. **Sweden.** The Court has only to deal with disputes between states. This stipulation cannot, however, constitute an obstacle to a state instituting proceedings before the Court, to establish a claim on behalf of its nationals against another state. (art. 20)

9. **Switzerland.** Arts. 12 and 15 may be so construed as to mean that the Court has jurisdiction only over conflicts between states.

10. **Italy.** . . . .

11. **Germany.** Besides jurisdiction over disputes between states, the Court shall be entitled to decide on; (*a*) complaints of private persons against foreign states and heads of states when the state tribunals have declared their incompetence; (*b*) disputes between subjects of different states which are Members of the League of Nations so far as the interpretation of state treaties form the object of the dispute. (art. 31)

12. **Austria.** The explanatory remarks of Mr. LAMMASCH seem to show that the Court has jurisdiction only over conflicts between states.

III. Has the Court jurisdiction when only one of the parties appeals to it?

1. **1907 draft scheme.** The Court is competent to deal with all cases submitted to it in virtue either of a general undertaking to have recourse to arbitration or of a special agreement. (art. 17. See also art. 19)

2. **Five Neutral Powers.** The Court shall have the power to try Members of the League of Nations without their previous consent on all matters relating to the interpretation of a Treaty or to certain other points. (art. 21)

3. **Interparliamentary Union.** It seems to follow from art. 2. that the Court has jurisdiction when one of the parties brings a suit before it. (See also art. 19)

4. **International Law Union.** . . . .

5. **Denmark.** . . . .

6. **Norway.** . . . .

7. **Netherlands.** The Court is competent to deal with conflicts which are submitted to it in virtue either of a Treaty or of a special agreement concluded either between states or between one state and a national of another state. (art. 21)

9. **Suisse.** La Cour connaît de tous les litiges pour lesquels les Parties désignent la Cour comme juge. En outre, si dans le délai de deux mois après l'échec de la tentative de conciliation, les Parties n'ont pu se mettre d'accord sur le compromis prévu à l'art. 52 de la 1ère Convention de la Haye du 18 octobre 1907, la Partie demanderesse peut réclamer le jugement de la Cour. (art. 37)

10. **Italie.** La Cour connaît de différends qui lui sont soumis à la demande d'une seule des parties, en cas de renvoi par le Conseil de la Société des Nations. (art. 22)

11. **Allemagne.** Chaque Membre de la Société des Nations a le droit d'introduire une action à laquelle l'adversaire ne pourra se soustraire. (art. 30)

12. **Autriche.** La Cour connaît de différends qui lui ont été soumis, à moins que la partie adversaire n'objecte, pendant les deux semaines après que le tribunal en a été saisi, que l'affaire touche à ses intérêts vitaux. (art. 12)

IV. Caractère des Conflits.

1. **Projet 1907.** Art. 17 implique que la Cour connaît de différends de toute nature.

2. **Cinq Puissances neutres.** Les différends relatifs à certains points énumérés dans l'art. 21 et en outre les différends d'un caractère international pour lesquels les parties s'accordent à reconnaître sa compétence. (art. 22)

3. **Union Interparlementaire.** Les conflits relatifs à l'interprétation et à l'application des stipulations conventionnelles énumérés dans l'art. 2.

4. **Union Juridique Internationale.** Tous les différends d'un caractère international que les Etats soumettent à la Cour conformément à l'art. XIV du Pacte. (art. 1)

5. **Danemark.** . . . .

6. **Norvège.** . . . .

7. **Pays-Bas.** Conflits juridiques et d'autres conflits que les parties soumettront à la Cour conformément à l'art XIV du Pacte. (art. 21)

8. **Suède.** . . . .

9. **Suisse.** La Cour se déclare non-compétente:

1) si la demande formulée n'est basée ni sur une disposition contractuelle ni sur une norme quelconque tirée du droit des gens et n'est pas de nature à faire l'objet d'une sentence s'inspirant de considérations juridiques;

2) si la demande formulée touche à l'indépendance et aux intérêts vitaux de l'autre partie et si celle-ci réclame, en conséquence que l'affaire soit liquidée par la procédure de médiation. (art 39)

10. **Italie.** Différends de toute nature. (art. 22)

8. **Sweden.**	The Court shall exercise jurisdiction in all cases where the parties are agreed respecting the competence of the Court. Such agreement shall be held to exist if there is a general agreement between the parties, if neither party raises any objection to the agreement being regarded as applicable, or when there is a special agreement. (art. 15)
9. **Switzerland.**	Disputes referred to judicial settlement are decided by the judge whom the parties indicate If within eight weeks after the failure of the attempted conciliation the parties are unable to agree on the *compromis* mentioned in art. 52 of Convention I of the Hague of October 18th, 1907, the plaintiff party may apply for a decision of the International Court of Justice. (art. 37).
10. **Italy.**	Cases referred to the Court by the Council and brought forward by one of the parties only.
11. **Germany.**	Every Member of the League of Nations shall have the right to bring a complaint, which must be answered by the opposite party. (art. 30)
12. **Austria.**	Disputes of a legal character shall be heard and determined by the Court unless one of the parties to the dispute, within two weeks after the Court has been apprised of the matter, raises objections on the ground that its vital interests are involved. (art. 12)

IV. Nature of the Conflicts.

1. **1907 draft scheme.**	It follows from art. 17 that the Court has jurisdiction over all kinds of disputes.
2. **Five Neutral Powers.**	All matters relating to the points in art. 21, and, moreover, any dispute of an international nature, which the parties thereto shall agree to submit to the Court. (art. 22)
3. **Interparliamentary Union.**	Conflicts with regard to the interpretation and application of conventional stipulations enumerated in art. 2.
4. **International Law Union.**	All conflicts of an international character which the states shall submit to the Court according to art. 14 of the Covenant. (art. 1)
5. **Denmark.**	. . . .
6. **Norway.**	. . . .
7. **Netherlands.**	Conflicts of a juridical nature and other conflicts which the parties submit to the Court in conformity with art. 14 of the Covenant (art. 21)
8. **Sweden.**	. . . .
9. **Switzerland.**	The Court has no jurisdiction: (1) if the claim made is based neither on a provision of a contract nor on a rule of international law and the claim is not susceptible of decision on juridical principles; (2) if the claim made touches the honour and vital interests of the defendant party, and if this party demands in consequence that the matter be settled by process of mediation. (art. 39)
10. **Italy.**	All cases. (art. 22)

11. **Allemagne.** L'organe régulier pour la décision de différends d'ordre juridique entre Etats est la Cour. (art. 30).

Si le défendeur objecte que le différend est un simple conflit d'intérêts ou constitue un point de droit ou la question politique domine, la Cour a préalablement à se prononcer sur la légitimité de cette objection. Si elle reconnaît le bien-fondé de cette objection, elle renvoie l'affaire devant l'Office de Conciliation. (art. 33)

12. **Autriche.** Différends de nature juridique, à savoir ceux qui sont susceptibles d'être décidés sur la base des principes du droit international (général ou spécial existant entre eux), à moins que l'une des parties n'objecte que l'affaire touche à ses intérêts vitaux. (art. 12)

11. **Germany.**

The Court shall be the regular official body for the decision of legal disputes between states (art. 30). If the defendant party raises the objection that the question concerns merely a conflict of interest or a legal matter of dominating political significance, the Court must first of all decide on the merits of this objection. Should this objection be well-founded, it shall refer the conflict for settlement to the mediation office. (art. 33)

12. **Austria.**

Disputes of a legal character, namely, those which are suitable for decision on the basis of the principle of international law (general or special existing between them) unless one of the parties raises objections on the ground that its vital interests are involved. (art. 12)

c. PROCÉDURE.

I. Règles de Procédure.

1. **Projet 1907.** La Cour suit les règles de procédure édictée par la Convention pour le règlement pacifique des conflits internationaux sauf ce qui est prescrit par la présente convention (art. 22). La Cour peut proposer des modifications à apporter aux dispositions de la présente Convention qui concernent la procédure. (art. 33)

2. **Cinq Puissances neutres.** Fixées dans la présente convention.

3. **Union Interparlementaire.** La Cour suit les règles de procédure édictées par la Convention pour le règlement pacifique des conflits internationaux. (art. 15)

4. **Union Juridique Internationale.** La Cour arrête elle-même son règlement de procédure que les parties ne peuvent modifier. (art. 13)

5. **Danemark.** Fixées par la Cour. (art. 14)

6. **Norvège.** = Danemark. (art. 14)

7. **Pays-Bas.** Fixées dans la présente Convention, la Cour a le droit de proposer des modifications. (arts. 23 et 26—77)

8. **Suède.** Sauf dispositions contraires il sera fait application par analogie des dispositions de la 1ère Convention de la Haye du 18 octobre 1907, et du Projet de la Cour de justice arbitrale élaboré en 1907. (art. 22)

9. **Suisse.** . . . .

10. **Italie.** Si le compromis est muet sur ce point, ou en l'absence de compromis, le tribunal établira des règles de procédure en tenant compte des circonstances spéciales au cas envisagé. Lorsqu'il n'en est pas décidé autrement, on observera les règles établies par la Convention de la Haye du 18 octobre 1907 pour le règlement pacifique des conflits internationaux, dans la mesure où elles seront applicables. (art. 25)

11. **Allemagne.** La Cour rédige ses règles de procédure d'après les principes de la Convention de la Haye du 18 octobre 1907 sur la solution pacifique des conflits internationaux; ces règles de procédure, pour entrer en vigueur, doivent obtenir l'approbation du Congrès des Etats. (art. 34)

12. **Autriche.** . . . .

C. PROCEDURE.

I. Rules of Procedure.

1. **1907 draft scheme.** The Court follows, the rules of procedure laid down in the Convention for the Pacific Settlement of International Disputes except in so far as the procedure is laid down in the present Convention (art. 22). The Court may propose modifications in the provisions of the present Convention concerning the procedure. (art. 33)

2. **Five Neutral Powers.** Rules laid down by the present Convention.

3. **Interparliamentary Union.** The Court follows the rules of procedure enacted by the Convention for the Peaceful Settlement of International Conflicts. (art. 15).

4. **International Law Union.** The Court shall make its own rules of procedure, which the parties cannot modify. (art. 13)

5. **Denmark.** Laid down by the Court. (art. 14)

6. **Norway.** Same as Denmark. (art. 14)

7. **Netherlands.** Laid down in the present Convention; the Court has the right to propose modifications. (arts. 23 and 26—77)

8. **Sweden.** The provisions contained in the First Hague Convention of 1907 and the draft for a Court of Arbitral Justice except as otherwise stipulated. (art. 22)

9. **Switzerland.** ....

10. **Italy.** When the *compromis* contains no reference to procedure, the pavel shall make whatever regulations it thinks fit, considering the special circumstances of the case, or shall observe those laid down by the Hague Convention of October 18th, 1907 for the pacific settlement of International Disputes, in so far as they are applicable. (art 25)

11. **Germany.** The Court shall draft an order of procedure based upon the Hague Convention of October 18th. 1907, concerning the Pacific Settlement of International Disputes. This procedure shall require for its efficiency the consent of the Congress of States. (art. 34)

12. **Austria.** ....

II. Procédure Sommaire.

1. **Projet 1907.**	La Cour désigne annuellement 3 juges qui forment une délégation spéciale. La délégation est compétente pour juger si les parties sont d'accord pour réclamer l'application de la procédure sommaire. (arts. 6 et 18)
2. **Cinq Puissances neutres.**	La Cour désigne annuellement 3 juges qui forment une section spéciale pour la procédure sommaire. (arts. 16 et 51)
3. **Union Interparlementaire.**	= Projet 1907. (arts 17 et 18)
4. **Union Juridique Internationale.**	. . . .
5. **Danemark.**	La Cour constitue une commission de 3 juges qui est compétente pour la procédure sommaire des affaires que les Parties sont d'accord à soumettre à cette commission. (art. 12)
6. **Norvège.**	= Danemark. (art. 12)
7. **Pays-Bas.**	La Cour désigne annuellement 3 juges qui forment une délégation spéciale qui est compétente pour la procédure sommaire; celle-ci est appliquée, si les Parties sont d'accord pour la réclamer. Chacune des parties a le droit de désigner un juge de la Cour pour prendre part, avec voix délibérative, à l'examen d'une affaire soumise à la délégation. (arts. 9, 22, 23 et 53)
8. **Suède.**	= Danemark. (art. 12)
9. **Suisse.**	. . . .
10. **Italie.**	. . . .
11. **Allemagne.**	. . . .
12. **Autriche.**	. . . .

III. Bases de la Sentence.

1. **Projet 1907.**	Les sentences doivent être motivées. (art. 28)
2. **Cinq Puissances neutres.**	Lorsque la question de droit sur laquelle la Cour doit statuer est prévue directement ou indirectement dans un traité en vigueur entre les parties, ce traité forme la base de la sentence. A défaut de dispositions à cet égard, la Cour applique les règles du droit international en vigueur ou, si des règles de cette nature n'existent pas pour la question dont il s'agit, la Cour juge d'après ce qui, à son avis, devrait être la règle du droit international. (art. 2)
3. **Union Interparlementaire.**	Les sentences sont motivées. (art. 46)
4. **Union Juridique Internationale.**	La Cour juge d'après le droit la justice et l'équité. (art. 12)
5. **Danemark.**	= Cinq Puissances neutres. (arts. 15 et 18)
6. **Norvège.**	= Danemark. (arts. 15 et 18)
7. **Pays-Bas.**	Les sentences doivent être motivées. (art. 45)

II. Summary Procedure.

1. **1907 scheme.**	The Court annually nominates three judges to form a delegation. The delegation is competent to decide if the parties concerned are agreed that the summary procedure is to be applied. (arts. 6 and 18)
2. **Five Neutral Powers.**	The Court shall nominate yearly three judges who shall form a special section of summary procedure. (arts. 16 and 51)
3. **Interparliamentary Union.**	Same as 1907 draft. (arts. 17 and 18)
4. **International Law Union.**	. . . .
5. **Denmark.**	The Court shall nominate a commission of three judges to decide, according to summary procedure, the cases which the parties concerned are agreed to submit to that commission. (art. 12)
6. **Norway.**	Same as Denmark. (art. 12)
7. **Netherlands.**	The Court annually nominates three judges to form a special delegation to be competent to hear and determine cases in summary procedure. This procedure to be applied if the parties are agreed to request its application. Each party has the right to nominate one judge, member of the Court, to take part in the hearing and determination of a case submitted to the delegation. (arts. 9, 22, 23 and 53)
8. **Sweden.**	Same as Denmark. (art. 12)
9. **Switzerland.**	. . . .
10. **Italy.**	. . . .
11. **Germany.**	. . . .
12. **Austria.**	. . . .

III. Basis of the award.

1. **1907 draft scheme.**	The judgment of the Court must give the reasons on which it is based. (art. 28)
2. **Five Neutral Powers.**	Whenever the point of law to be decided by the Court is provided for directly or indirectly by any Treaty in operation between the contesting parties, such Treaty shall form the basis of the judgment. In the absence of such Treaty provisions the Court shall apply the recognised rules of international law, or, should no rules applicable to the case exist, shall enter judgment according to its own opinion of what the rule of international law on the subject should be. (art. 2)
3. **Interparliamentary Union.**	The judgment shall give the reasons on which it is based. (art. 46)
4. **International Law Union.**	The Court shall dispense justice according to the law and to the principles of justice. (art. 12)
5. **Denmark.**	Same as Five-Power Plan. (arts. 15 and 18)
6. **Norway.**	Same as Denmark. (arts. 15 and 18)
7. **Netherlands.**	The judgment of the Court must give the reasons on which it is based. (art. 45)

8 **Suède.** = Danemark. (arts. 17 et 25)

9. **Suisse.** La Cour appliquera en première ligne les conventions existant entre les parties. A défaut de telles stipulations la Cour prendre pour base les principes du droit des gens. S'il n'existe pas de règle généralement connue ou reconnue par les Parties, la Cour prendra pour base les principes généraux de la justice et de l'équité. (art. 42)

10. **Italie.** . . . .

11. **Allemagne.** La Cour s'inspire pour rendre ses arrêts des conventions internationales, des usages du droit international et des principes généraux du droit et de l'équité. (art. 35)

12. **Autriche.** . . . .

IV. Droit d'appel.

1. **Projet 1907.** La sentence dûment prononcée et notifiée aux agents des parties, décide définitivement et sans appel la contestation. (art. 22 jo. art. 81 de la Convention sur le règlement pacifique des conflits internationaux).

2. **Cinq Puissances neutres.** = Projet 1907 (art. 47)

3. **Union Interparlementaire.** = Projet 1907 (art. 15)

4. **Union Juridique Internationale.** . . . .

5. **Danemark.** La sentence décide la contestation définitivement et sans appel. (art. 19)

6. **Norvège.** = Danemark. (art. 19)

7. **Pays-Bas.** = Danemark. (art. 47)

8. **Suède.** = Danemark. (art. 19)

9. **Suisse.** . . . .

10. **Italie.** . . . .

11. **Allemagne.** . . . .

12. **Autriche.** Les décisions sont définitives. (art. 13)

V. Révision.

1. **Projet 1907.** Les parties peuvent se réserver dans le compromis de demander la révision de la sentence arbitrale. Cette révision ne peut être motivée que par la découverte d'un fait nouveau qui eut été de nature à exercer une influence décisive sur la sentence et qui, lors de la clôture des débats, était inconnu du Tribunal lui-même et de la partie qui a demandé la révision. (art. 22 jo. art. 83 de la Convention sur le règlement pacifique des conflits internationaux).

8. **Sweden.**	Same as Denmark	(arts. 17 and 25)
9. **Switzerland.**	The Court applies in the first instance the agreements existing between the parties. In default of such agreements it founds on the principles of the law of nations. If there is on the matter no generally recognised rule of this law, or none recognised by the parties, it decides in accordance with justice and equity.	(art. 42)
10. **Italy.**	. . . .	
11. **Germany.**	The decision of the tribunal is based according to international agreements, international customary law, and according to general principles of law and equity.	(art. 35)
12. **Austria.**	. . . .	

IV. Right of Appeal.

1. **1907 draft scheme.**	The award duly pronounced and notified to the agents of the parties settles the dispute definitively and without appeal (art. 22 cf art 81 of the Convention concerning the Pacific Settlement of International Disputes).	
2. **Five Neutral Powers.**	Same as 1907 draft.	(art. 47)
3. **Interparliamentary Union.**	Same as 1907 draft.	(art. 15)
4. **International Law Union.**	. . . .	
5. **Denmark.**	The award settles the dispute definitely and without appeal.	(art. 19)
6. **Norway.**	Same as Denmark.	(art. 19)
7. **Netherlands.**	Same as Denmark.	(art. 47)
8. **Sweden.**	Same as Denmark.	(art. 19)
9. **Switzerland.**	. . . .	
10. **Italy.**	. . . .	
11. **Germany.**	. . . .	
12. **Austria.**	The awards are final.	(art. 13)

V. Revision.

1. **1907 draft scheme.**	The parties can reserve in the *compromis* the right to demand the revision of the award. The demand can only be made on the ground of the discovery of some new fact which is of a nature to exercise a decisive influence upon the award, and which, at the time the discussion was closed, was unknown to the tribunal and to the party demanding the revision (art. 22 cf. Article 83 of the Convention concerning the Pacific Settlement of International Conflicts).

2. **Cinq Puissances neutres.** Une révision peut être admise à la requête de l'une des parties, si elle est motivée par la découverte d'un fait nouveau antérieur à la sentence, et dont la connaissance, de l'avis de la Cour, aurait été de nature à exercer une influence sur la sentence. (art. 47)

3. **Union Interparlementaire.** = Projet 1907. (art. 15)

4. **Union Juridique Internationale.** . . . .

5. **Danemark.** A la requête de l'une des Parties si elle est motivée par la découverte d'un fait nouveau qui, de l'avis de la Cour aurait pu exercer une influence sur la sentence. (art. 19)

6. **Norvège.** = Danemark. (art. 19)

7. **Pays-Bas.** . . . .

8. **Suède.** = Danemark. (art. 26)

9. **Suisse.** A la requête de l'une des Parties si elle est motivée par la découverte d'un fait nouveau qui eut été de nature à exercer une influence décisive sur la sentence, dans les conditions prévues à l'art. 83 de la 1ère Convention de la Haye du 18 octobre 1907. (art. 45)

10. **Italie.** . . . .

11. **Allemagne.** . . . .

12. **Autriche.** . . . .

VI. Droit d'Intervention.

1. **Projet 1907.** Lorsqu'il s'agit de l'interprétation d'une Convention à laquelle ont participé d'autres Puissances que les parties en litige, chacune des Puissances signataires a le droit d'intervenir. (art. 22 jo. art. 84 de la Convention sur le règlement pacifique des conflits internationaux).

2. **Cinq Puissances neutres.** Lorsqu'un différend soumis à la Cour touche les intérêts d'un Etat tiers, celui-ci a le droit d'intervenir au procès. (art. 48)

3. **Union Interparlementaire.** = Projet 1907. (art. 15)

4. **Union Juridique Internationale.** . . . .

5. **Danemark.** . . . .

6. **Norvège.** . . . .

7. **Pays-Bas.** Lorsqu'il s'agit de l'interprétation d'une convention à laquelle ont participé des Puissances qui ne sont pas parties en litige, chacune de celles-ci a le droit d'intervenir au procès. (art. 49)

8. **Suède** Droit d'intervention dans le cas où le différend est relatif à une convention internationale générale ou concerne à d'autres égards les intérêts d'un Etat tiers. (art. 21).

9. **Suisse.** . . . .

10. **Italie.** . . . .

2. **Five Neutral Powers.** The case may be revised at the request of one of the parties, if such request be based upon the discovery of some new fact which existed before the sentence and which, in the opinion of the Court, would have affected the sentence. (art. 47)

3. **Interparliamentary Union.** Same as 1907 scheme. (art. 15)

4. **International Law Union.** . . . .

5. **Denmark.** At the request of one of the parties, if such request be based upon the discovery of some new fact which, in the opinion of the Court, might have affected the sentence. (art. 19)

6. **Norway.** Same as Denmark. (art. 19)

7. **Netherlands.** . . . .

8. **Sweden.** Same as Denmark. (art. 26)

9. **Switzerland.** Upon the demand of one of the parties, based on the grounds of the discovery of some new fact which is of a nature to exercise a decisive influence upon the award in the circumstances laid down in Art. **83** of the First Hague Convention of October 18th, 1907. (art. 45)

10. **Italy.** . . . .

11. **Germany.** . . . .

12. **Austria.** . . . .

VI. Right of Intervention.

1. **1907 draft scheme.** When there is a question as to the interpretation of a Convention to which Powers other than those in dispute are parties, each of the Powers is entitled to intervene in the case. (art. 22 cf. art. 84 of the Convention for the Pacific Settlement of International Conflicts).

2. **Five Neutral Powers.** Whenever a dispute submitted to the Court affects the interests of a third state, the latter may intervene in the case. (art. 48)

3. **Interparliamentary Union.** Same as 1907 draft. (art. 15)

4. **International Law Union.** . . . .

5. **Denmark.** . . . .

6. **Norway.** . . . .

7. **Netherlands.** When there is a question as to the interpretation of a Convention to which Powers other than those in dispute are parties, each of these Powers is entitled to intervene in the case. (art. 49)

8. **Sweden.** When the dispute bears reference to an international convention or otherwise touches the interests of a third state, such state has the right to intervene in the dispute. (art. 21)

9. **Switzerland.** . . . .

10. **Italy.** . . . .

11. **Allemagne.**	. . . .
12. **Autriche.**	. . . .

VII. Effet des Sentences.

1. **Projet.**	La sentence est obligatoire pour les parties en litige et pour les Puissances qui ont profité de la faculté d'intervention (art. 22 jo. art. 84 de la Convention sur le règlement pacifique des conflits internationaux).
2. **Cinq Puissances neutres.**	La sentence est exécutoire pour les parties en litige, y compris les intervenants, et seulement en l'espèce jugée. (art. 53)
3. **Union Interparlementaire.**	= Projet 1907.
4. **Union Juridique Internationale.**	. . . .
5. **Danemark.**	. . . .
6. **Norvège.**	. . . .
7. **Pays-Bas.**	La sentence est obligatoire pour les parties en litige et les Puissances ayant profité du droit de l'intervention. Réglé soit par décret de l'Assemblée de la Société des Nations soit par les conventions ou accords réglant la compétence de la Cour. (art. 49)
8. **Suède.**	. . . .
9. **Suisse.**	La sentence est seulement exécutoire pour les parties en litige. (art. 46)
10. **Italie.**	. . . .
11. **Allemagne.**	La décision oblige l'Etat, contre lequel elle a été rendue, à en appliquer de bonne foi les termes. (art. 36)
12. **Autriche.**	Les décisions lient les parties à les exécuter en toute bonne foi. (art 13)

VIII. Comment l'exécution des sentences sera garantie.

1. **Projet 1907.**	. . . .
2. **Cinq Puissances neutres.**	Dans les limites fixées par le Pacte l'exécution des sentences est sauvegardée par la Société des Nations. (art. 53)
3. **Union Interparlementaire.**	. . . .
4. **Union Juridique Internationale.**	. . . .
5. **Danemark.**	. . . .
6. **Norvège.**	. . . .
7. **Pays-Bas.**	. . . .
8. **Suède.**	. . . .
9. **Suisse.**	L'exécution des sentences est garantie par la Société des Nations. (art. 43)

11. **Germany.**	. . . .
12. **Austria.**	. . . .

VII. Effect of Judgments.

1. **1907 draft scheme.**	The award is binding on the parties in dispute and on Powers having availed themselves of the right of intervention (art. 22 cf. Art. 84 of the Convention concerning the Pacific Settlement of International Disputes).
2. **Five Neutral Powers.**	The sentence shall only apply to the contesting parties, including any intervening parties, and to the particular case upon which judgment has been delivered. (art. 53)
3. **Interparliamentary Union.**	Same as 1907 draft.
4. **International Law Union.**	. . . .
5. **Denmark.**	. . . .
6. **Norway.**	. . . .
7. **Netherlands.**	The award is binding on the parties in dispute and on the Powers having availed themselves of the right to intervene in the case. Determined either by decree of the Assembly of the League of Nations or by the Conventions or agreements setting forth the competence of the Court. (art. 49)
8. **Sweden.**	. . . .
9. **Switzerland.**	The sentences are executory only for the contesting parties. (art. 46)
10. **Italy.**	. . . .
11. **Germany.**	The decision shall demand of the state in question to carry out its contents in good faith. (art. 36)
12. **Austria.**	The awards bind the parties to carry them out in full good faith. (art. 13)

VIII. Guarantees for the Execution of Judgments.

1. **1907 draft scheme.**	. . . .
2. **Five Neutral Powers.**	The performance of the terms of all sentences is placed under the guarantee of the League of Nations within the limits laid down by the Covenant. (art. 53)
3. **Interparliamentary Union.**	. . . .
4. **International Law Union.**	. . . .
5. **Denmark.**	. . . .
6. **Norway.**	. . . .
7. **Netherlands.**	. . . .
8. **Sweden.**	. . . .
9. **Switzerland.**	Sentences pronounced are guaranteed by the League of Nations. (art. 43)

10. **Italie.**	. . . .
11. **Allemagne.**	. . . .
12. **Autriche.**	Les décisions obligent les Membres de la Ligue à concourir à leur exécution en vertu des dispositions du Statut. (art. 13)

IX. Frais généraux de la Cour.

1. **Projet 1907.**	Les frais généraux de la Cour sont supportés par les Puissances contractantes. (art. 31)
2. **Cinq Puissances neutres.**	Les frais de la Cour sont supportés par la Société des Nations. Les Membres de la Société y contribuent par parts égales. (art. 19)
3. **Union Interparlementaire.**	. . . .
4. **Union Juridique Internationale.**	. . . .
5. **Danemark.**	Les Membres de la Société des Nations supportent une part égale des frais de la Cour. (art. 20)
6. **Norvège.**	= Danemark (art 20)
7. **Pays-Bas.**	Les frais généraux sont supportés par la Société des Nations et figurent sur le budget général de la Société. (arts. 19, 52 et 72)
8. **Suède.**	= Danemark. (arts. 28 et 29)
9. **Suisse.**	. . . .
10. **Italie.**	. . . .
11. **Allemagne.**	. . . .
12. **Autriche.**	. . . .

X. Frais de Procédure.

1. **Projet 1907.**	Chaque partie supporte ses propres frais et une part égale des frais spéciaux de l'instance. (art. 29)
2. **Cinq Puissances neutres.**	Chaque partie supporte ses propres frais de procédure pour chaque affaire. (art. 50)
3. **Union Interparlementaire.**	= Projet 1907. (art. 15)
4. **Union Juridique Internationale.**	. . . .
5. **Danemark.**	Chaque partie supporte des propres frais de procédure pour chaque affaire. (art. 20)
6. **Norvège.**	= Danemark. (art. 20)
7. **Pays-Bas.**	= Projet 1907. (art. 52)
8. **Suède.**	= Danemark. (art. 29)
9. **Suisse.**	. . . .
10. **Italie.**	. . . .
11. **Allemagne.**	. . . .
12 **Autriche.**	. . . .

10. **Italy.**	. . . .
11. **Germany.**	. . . .
12. **Austria.**	The awards oblige the Members of the League to assist in the execution of them in conformity with the regulations of the statute. (art. 13)

IX. General expenses of the Court.

1. **1907 draft scheme.**	The general expenses of the Court are borne by the contracting parties. (art. 31)
2. **Five Neutral Powers.**	The expenses of the Court shall be paid by the League of Nations. Members of the League shall contribute equally. (art. 19)
3. **Interparliamentary Union.**	. . . .
4. **International Law Union.**	. . . .
5. **Denmark.**	The Members of the League of Nations shall contribute equally towards the expenses of the Court. (art. 20)
6. **Norway.**	Same as Denmark. (art. 20)
7. **Netherlands.**	The general expenses are borne by the League of Nations and carried on the general budget of the League. (arts. 19, 52 and 72)
8. **Sweden.**	Same as Denmark. (arts. 28 and 29)
9. **Switzerland.**	. . . .
10. **Italy.**	. . . .
11. **Germany.**	. . . .
12. **Austria.**	. . . .

X. Costs.

1. **1907 draft scheme.**	Each party pays its own costs and an equal share of the costs of the trial. (art. 29)
2. **Five Neutral Powers.**	Every contesting party shall pay its own costs in each case. (art. 50)
3. **Interparliamentary Union.**	Same as 1907 draft. (art. 15)
4. **International Law Union.**	. . . .
5. **Denmark.**	Every contesting party shall pay its own costs in each case. (art. 20)
6. **Norway.**	Same as Denmark. (art. 20)
7. **Netherlands.**	Same as 1907 draft. (art. 52)
8. **Sweden.**	Same as Denmark. (art. 29)
9. **Switzerland.**	. . . .
10. **Italy.**	. . . .
11. **Germany.**	. . . .
12. **Austria.**	. . . .

XI. Langue.

1. **Projet 1907.**	La Cour décide du choix de la langue dont elle fera usage, et des langues dont l'emploi sera autorisé devant elle. (art. 23)
2. **Cinq Puissances neutres.**	La langue est le français, à moins qu'il n'en soit décidé autrement à la demande des parties. (art. 29)
3. **Union Interparlementaire.**	Si le compromis n'a pas déterminé les langues à employer, il en est décidé par le tribunal. (art. 15 jo. art. 61 de la Convention sur le règlement pacifique des conflits internationaux.)
4. **Union Juridique Internationale.**	. . . .
5. **Danemark.**	Le français. Une autre langue pourra être employée du consentement de la Cour et lorsque les deux Parties en sont d'accord. (art. 16)
6. **Norvège.**	= Danemark. (art. 16)
7. **Pays-Bas.**	La Cour décide du choix de la langue dont elle fera usage et des langues dont l'emploi sera autorisé devant elle. (arts. 28 et 54)
8. **Suède.**	= Danemark. (art. 19)
9. **Suisse.**	. . . .
10. **Italie.**	. . . .
11. **Allemagne.**	. . . .
12. **Autriche.**	. . . .

XII. Publication des opinions divergentes dans la sentence.

1. **Projet 1907.**	. . . .
2. **Cinq Puissances neutres.**	Si la sentence n'a pas été rendue à l'unanimité, le sens des opinions dissidentes y est inséré. (art. 46)
3. **Union Interparlementaire.**	. . . .
4. **Union Juridique Internationale.**	. . . .
5. **Danemark.**	Les opinions divergentes ne sont pas publiées. (art. 18)
6. **Norvège.**	Les opinions divergentes sont publiées. (art. 18)
7. **Pays-Bas.**	. . . .
8. **Suède.**	= Norvège. (art. 25)
9. **Suisse.**	. . . .
10. **Italie.**	. . . .
11. **Allemagne.**	. . . .
12. **Autriche.**	. . . .

XI. Language.

1. **1907 draft scheme.**	The Court determines what language it will itself use and what languages may be used before it. (art. 23)
2. **Five Neutral Powers.**	The official language shall be French unless it shall be otherwise decided at the request of the contesting parties. (art. 29)
3. **Interparliamentary Union.**	If the question as to what languages are to be used has not been settled by the *compromis* it shall be decided by a tribunal (art. 15 cf. art. 61 of the Convention for the Pacific Settlement of International Disputes).
4. **International Law Union.**	. . . .
5. **Denmark.**	The French. Another language may be used with the consent of the Court and by agreement between the parties. (art. 16)
6. **Norway.**	Same as Denmark. (art. 16)
7. **Netherlands.**	The Court determines what language it will itself use and what languages may be used before it. (arts. 28 and 54)
8. **Sweden.**	Same as Denmark. (art. 19)
9. **Switzerland.**	. . . .
10. **Italy.**	. . . .
11. **Germany.**	. . . .
12. **Austria.**	. . . .

XII. Publication in the Award of dissenting opinions.

1. **1907 draft scheme.**	. . . .
2. **Five Neutral Powers.**	In case of a judgment by a majority the purport of the dissenting findings shall be included. (art. 46)
3. **Interparliamentary Union.**	. . . .
4. **International Law Union.**	. . . .
5. **Denmark.**	Dissenting findings shall not be made public. (art. 18)
6. **Norway.**	Dissenting findings shall be made public. (art. 18)
7. **Netherlands.**	. . . .
8. **Sweden.**	Same as Norway. (art. 25)
9. **Switzerland.**	. . . .
10. **Italy.**	. . . .
11. **Germany.**	. . . .
12. **Austria.**	. . . .

3ième SÉANCE (non-publique), tenue au Palais de la Paix, à La Haye, le 18 juin 1920.

Présidence de M. le BARON DESCAMPS.

Sont présents: tous les membres du Comité (à l'exception de M. Bevilaqua); Mr. James Brown Scott; les secrétaires particuliers de M. le Baron Descamps et de M. Adatci; les membres du Secrétariat.

La séance est ouverte à $9^1/_2$ heures du matin.

Le PRESIDENT donne lecture du texte revisé de l'article 7 des règles de procédure; (la rédaction définitive de ces règles est reproduite à l'annexe 1). Le nouveau texte est approuvé à l'unanimité.

Le Président communique un questionnaire relatif au problème de l'organisation de la Cour, qu'il a préparé à la demande du Comité. (Annexe 2).

Ce questionnaire est adopté, avec une modification d'ordre et une addition, proposées respectivement par Lord Phillimore et M. Loder. (Voir annexe 3).

Au cours de la discussion, LORD PHILLIMORE dit que dans l'exposé de ses points de vue, qu'il va faire au Comité, il compte traiter exclusivement de la question de la nomination des juges.

M. ADATCI demande la parole pour une courte explication. Il désire souligner le fait que la question de la composition de la Cour est le problème le plus difficile parmi ceux qui se posent devant le Comité. Sous ce rapport, il se permet de rappeler les discussions qui ont eu lieu dans la Commission instituée par la Société des Nations pour élaborer les projets de conventions concernant les communications et le transit. Cette Commission s'était divisée en deux camps: dans l'un, on soutenait la thèse de l'égalité des Etats et dans l'autre, on voulait tenir compte des exigences de la réalité. Après de longs échanges de vues, on tomba d'accord, en ce qui concerne la composition du Comité permanent du Transit etc., sur un texte consigné dans le rapport de la Commission. Ce texte consacre une certaine inégalité entre les Etats.

3rd MEETING (Private), held at the Peace Palace, the Hague, on June 18th, 1920.

BARON DESCAMPS in the chair.

Present: all members of the Committee (with the exception of M. Bevilaqua); Mr. James Brown Scott; the private secretaries of Baron Descamps and of M. Adatci; the members of the Secretariat.

The meeting was opened at 9.30 a.m.

The PRESIDENT read the revised text of article 7 of the rules of procedure (the final form of the rules of procedure is included in Annex 1). The new text was unanimously adopted.

The President communicated to the meeting a questionnaire, prepared by him on the request of the Committee, concerning the question of organisation of the Court. (Annex 2).

His questionnaire was adopted with a re-arrangement of order and an addition, proposed respectively by Lord Phillimore and M. Loder. (See Annex 3).

During the discussion LORD PHILLIMORE said that in the explanation of his views, which he would give to the Committee, he intended to deal solely with the question of the nomination of judges.

M. ADATCI asked to make a short explanation. He wished to emphasize that the question of the composition of the Court is the most difficult problem among those which present themselves to the Committee. In this connection he recalled the discussions which took place at the Commission instituted by the League of Nations to formulate draft conventions dealing with communications and transit. This Commission was divided in its opinion: one element supported the principle of equality of states, the other wished to take into consideration the demand of the real state of things. After prolonged discussion, agreement was reached concerning the composition of the permanent Committee of Transit, etc., on a text included in the report of the Commission. This scheme recognised inequality to a certain extent between the various states.

A la demande du président, M. Adatci se déclare prêt à communiquer aux membres du Comité, à titre confidentiel, le document où sont consignés les résultats des travaux de la Commission des communications et du transit.

M. ANZILOTTI explique que ce document a déjà été envoyé au Comité par la Commission du transit, et qu'il ne tardera pas à arriver.

Le PRESIDENT fait observer qu'il ne s'agit là que d'un comité administratif, tandis que les travaux du Comité actuel ont en vue l'établissement d'une institution d'ordre juridique.

On procède à l'examen de la question de la nomination des juges.

Sur la proposition de LORD PHILLIMORE, il est décidé que tous les membres, dans l'ordre alphabétique, exposeront leurs points de vue sur cette question.

M. ADATCI ne désire rien ajouter, quant à présent, aux communications qu'il a déjà faites.

M. ALTAMIRA est d'accord avec Lord Phillimore en ce qu'il considère la question de la nomination des juges comme la plus importante, spécialement parce qu'elle en entraîne trois autres, à savoir: 1) le criterium d'éligibilité des juges, 2) la détermination du but final à atteindre par la Cour et 3) le caractère volontaire ou obligatoire de la juridiction.

M. Altamira estime qu'en recherchant la solution qu'il convient de donner à ces questions primordiales, il est du devoir du Comité de tenir compte, non seulement de la lettre du Pacte, mais aussi, et en premier lieu, de son esprit et des espérances que la création de la Société des Nations a fait naître parmi les peuples. Il s'agit, à l'heure actuelle, d'écarter toute équivoque; il faudra reconnaître qu'il n'existe pas de questions politiques qui soient hors du droit; toute question politique ou économique est en dernière analyse une question de droit. Au point de vue juridique, la question de la nomination des juges est liée directement à la question de l'égalité des Etats. A ce sujet, M. Altamira se réfère à la formule établie par la Conférence des Associations pour la Société des Nations, tenue à Bruxelles, en décembre 1919. La formule se trouve reproduite au Mémorandum élaboré par le Secrétariat de la Société des Nations, V: F. 16. (Annexe 4).

M. Altamira considère cette formule comme le principe essentiel par lequel il faut se laisser guider pour pouvoir résoudre le problème de la

At the request of the President, M. Adatci announced that he was ready to supply the members of the Committee with the confidential document containing the report of the Commission for communications and transit.

M. ANZILOTTI explained that this document had already been sent to the Committee by the transit Commission, and would shortly arrive.

The PRESIDENT remarked that the Committee referred to was of an administrative nature only, while the present Committee was preparing the establishment of an institution of a juridical nature.

The question of nomination of judges was next brought up for discussion.

Following a proposal of LORD PHILLIMORE it was decided that all members in alphabetical order should express their points of view on this question.

M. ADATCI had nothing at the time to add to his previous remarks.

M. ALTAMIRA agreed with Lord Phillimore in considering the question of the nomination of judges as the most important problem, more particularly because it is closely connected with three other questions, viz: 1) the criterion of eligibility for appointment as judge, 2) definition of the Court's object, 3) the voluntary or compulsory character of the Court's jurisdiction.

M. Altamira considered that it was the duty of the Conference, in searching for a solution of these essential questions, to bear in mind, not only the letter of the Covenant, but also its spirit and the hopes raised in the minds of all nations, by the creation of the League of Nations. It is essential, at the present time, to avoid all uncertainty, it must be recognised that no political questions are outside the scope of justice; all questions, whether political or economic, are in their final analysis questions of law. From the juridical point of view, the method of nomination of judges is directly connected with the principle of equality of States. In this connection M. Altamira referred to the method laid down by the Conference of the League of Nations Societies which took place at Brussels in December 1919. This scheme is reproduced in the Memorandum prepared by the Secretariat of the League of Nations para. V: F. 16. (Annex 4).

M. Altamira considered that this scheme

nomination des juges. Sur les autres points, qui lui semblent secondaires, il préfère réserver son opinion.

Le PRESIDENT constate que M. Bevilaqua n'est pas présent et que M. Fernandes, qui a le droit d'assister aux réunions en qualité de conseiller de M. Bevilaqua, est également absent.

M. HAGERUP dit que son point de départ est le même que celui de M. Altamira. Lui aussi est d'avis que toute question soumise à une cour, peut se résumer en une question juridique. Si cela est, il est impossible de comparer des comités administratifs, tels que le Comité dont a parlé M. Adatci, d'une part, et une Cour de Justice, d'autre part.

M. Hagerup ne va pas jusqu'à dire que les litiges ne possèdent pas d'autres aspects, qui pourraient obliger les membres du Comité à les envisager sous un autre angle. Ces aspects pourraient impliquer la nécessité de conserver la Cour Permanente d'Arbitrage à côté de la Cour de Justice, qu'on est en train de créer.

M. Hagerup laisse cependant de côté ce problème particulier pour faire valoir son opinion que la nouvelle Cour doit être une institution *juridique*. Or, sur le terrain du droit, il y a un principe indiscutable, celui de l'égalité de tous les Etats souverains. Les tentatives de la deuxième Conférence de la Paix, en vue de créer une Cour Permanente, ont échoué, grâce à l'impossibilité où l'on s'est trouvé de donner satisfaction, en même temps, à ce principe, et aux exigences de certaines grandes Puissances qui prétendaient exercer une influence prédominante sur la composition de la Cour. C'est là la difficulté qu'il faut, en premier lieu, envisager.

Le principe de l'égalité des Etats c'est la Magna Charta des Etats secondaires. Et c'est une considération éminemment juridique. Il ne faut pas mêler de la politique aux problèmes d'ordre juridique, et M. Hagerup est fermement convaincu que si l'on tâchait d'introduire un élément d'inégalité dans le projet de l'établissement de la Cour de Justice, ce projet tomberait, comme est tombé le projet de 1907. Les pays scandinaves, la Suisse et probablement les autres Etats de second ordre s'opposeraient à son adoption. Il n'est pas possible d'arriver à un compromis en se plaçant sur le terrain qu'a choisi M. Adatci.

Quant aux modalités de la nomination des juges, M. Hagerup est tout prêt à se rallier à

embodies the main principles for guidance in the solution of the problem of the nomination of the judges. With regard to the other points, which in his opinion are of secondary importance, he reserved his opinion.

The PRESIDENT stated that M. Bevilaqua and M. Fernandes, who was entitled to attend the meetings as the counsellor to M. Bevilaqua, were both absent.

M. HAGERUP said that his starting point was that of M. Altamira. He also thought that every question submitted to a Court could be reduced to a legal question. If this was true, a comparison between the administrative Committees mentioned by M. Adatci and the Court of Justice was impossible.

M. Hagerup did not go so far as to say that disputes do not present other aspects which may make it necessary to consider them from other viewpoints. These other aspects may indeed make it necessary to maintain the Permanent Court of Arbitration along with the Court of Justice which the Committee is in the process of creating.

M. Hagerup, however, did not enter into that particular point. He went on to state that in his opinion the new Court should be a *juridical* organisation; but in the domain of law there is one indisputable principle, that of the equality of sovereign states. The endeavours of the Second Peace Conference to create a Permanent Court did not succeed, because it was found impossible to act at the same time on this principle and to meet the exigencies of certain great Powers, to exercise a predominant influence in the composition of the Court. This is the difficulty which foremost it is necessary to solve.

The principle of the equality of States is the Magna Charta of the smaller States and it is an outstanding juridical argument. Political considerations should not come into account for the solution of juridical problems, and M. Hagerup is convinced that if one tried to introduce an element of inequality into the scheme for the Court of Justice, this scheme would fall to the ground as did the scheme of 1907. The Scandinavian countries, Switzerland, and probably other states of secondary rank would oppose its adoption. It is impossible to strike a compromise in adopting the point of view presented by M. Adatci.

With regard to the details of the nomination of the judges M. Hagerup was prepared to accept any opinion reconcilable with the prin-

toute opinion compatible avec le principe de l'égalité des Etats, qui est pour lui le point essentiel du problème. Son point de vue se trouve exposé en détail dans le projet commun des pays scandinaves, auquel il a collaboré lui-même; mais le projet des Puissances neutres de février dernier et celui de l'Union Juridique Internationale lui semblent pleinement acceptables. L'essentiel, pour M. Hagerup, c'est de trouver — sur la base juridique indiquée — des juges indépendants, possédant la plus haute compétence, la plus vaste expérience, les plus hautes qualités morales.

M. DE LAPRADELLE veut se borner à dire son opinion, sans y ajouter les arguments qui militent en sa faveur. La distinction entre le point de vue politique et le point de vue juridique est selon lui fondamentale. Sur le terrain juridique, les Etats sont égaux; l'égalité des Etats pour la nomination des juges n'est que la conséquence nécessaire de ce principe. A Bruxelles, où dominait surtout l'esprit pacifiste, ainsi qu'à la conférence de l'Union Juridique Internationale à Paris, on s'est rendu compte de cette vérité, et on s'est unanimement prononcé en faveur du principe de l'égalité des Etats. M. de Lapradelle espère vivement que l'échange de vues entre les membres du Comité, aboutira à les rallier tous autour de ce même principe.

M. LODER est heureux de constater que, jusqu'ici, presque tous les membres se sont prononcés en faveur du principe de l'égalité des Etats, principe dont s'inspire également le projet de la Haye de février dernier. Il faut se rendre compte, en premier lieu, du fait qu'il s'agit ici d'une question d'ordre juridique et qu'il faut essayer de trouver les moyens les plus efficaces pour protéger le caractère juridique de la nouvelle institution.

M. Loder se rallie à ce qui a été dit par M.M. Altamira, Hagerup et de Lapradelle.

LORD PHILLIMORE dit que, à son avis, le Comité a la tâche de préparer le plan pour l'établissement d'une Cour Permanente de Justice qui devrait être une Cour de Justice dans le sens véritable du mot, une cour devant laquelle pourraient être cités des Etats ayant contrevenu à la loi des nations, sans leur consentement préalable.

Du principe ainsi posé découlent deux conséquences essentielles.

D'abord il faut de bons juges, ce qui ne veut

ciple of equality of States, which is to him the essential feature of the problem. His particular point of view is set forth in detail in the joint scheme of the Scandinavian countries, in the preparation of which he has taken part himself; but the proposal of the neutral Powers dated February last, and also the proposal of the Union Juridique Internationale seem to him quite acceptable. In the opinion of M. Hagerup the really important thing is to find, on the juridical basis that he had indicated independent judges in possession of the highest competency, the largest experience, and the highest moral character.

M. DE LAPRADELLE wished to state his opinion without adding the arguments which go to support it. In his opinion the distinction between the political and juridical point of view is fundamental. In the domain of law the States are equal, and the equality of States with regard to the nomination of judges is nothing but the necessary consequence of this principle. At Brussels, where the pacifist spirit was predominant, and also at the Paris conference of the Union Juridique Internationale, this truth was taken into consideration, and a unanimous decision pronounced in favour of equality of States. M. de Lapradelle sincerely hoped that the exchange of opinions between the members of the Committee would result in gaining their support for this same principle.

M. LODER was glad to state that up to this point almost all the members had favored the principle of equality of States, the principle which also inspired the Hague scheme of February last. It was necessary to realise first of all that the question to be solved is a juridical question, and that an attempt must be made to find the most effective means to protect the juridical character of the new organisation.

M. Loder wished to support the arguments of M. Altamira, M. Hagerup, and M. de Lapradelle.

LORD PHILLIMORE said that in his opinion the Committee's task is to prepare plans for the establishment of a Permanent Court of Justice which should be a Court of Justice in the true sense of the word, a Court before which it should be possible to call States having broken the law of Nations, without having to obtain their consent in advance.

From the principle so stated, there arose two essential consequences:

1. It is necessary to have good judges; that

pas nécessairement dire des jurisconsultes experts. Un juge doit avoir bien d'autres qualités encore. Il lui faut de la loyauté, de la probité, une certaine largesse de vues, de la patience et du courage. Si les juges sont choisis parmi des jurisconsultes éminents, figurant sur une liste unique, il n'est pas certain que le résultat obtenu soit celui auquel on aspire. Il faut qu'il y ait la possibilité de choisir comme juge, non pas seulement des jurisconsultes, mais aussi, par exemple, des administrateurs.

Deuxièmement, il faut que la Cour ait derrière elle une force matérielle pour assurer l'exécution de ses décisions. Il ne faut pas que les Etats puissent éviter de se conformer aux jugements de la Cour. Dans cet ordre d'idées, il est nécessaire de composer la Cour de telle sorte qu'elle renferme des représentants des grands Etats — expression à laquelle Lord Phillimore donne, pour le moment, le sens commun et étroit d'Etats étendus et populeux. Si la Cour ne comptait pas ces représentants parmi ses membres, il lui manquerait, comme l'on dit en Angleterre, le „backbone", l'épine dorsale.

Lord Phillimore pense aussi à la situation de la Cour vis-à-vis l'opinion publique. Peut-on vraiment concevoir que les peuples des grands Etats admettent que leur patrie se soumette au jugement d'une Cour où elle n'est pas représentée? Le doute qui existe à cet égard est une des raisons pour lesquelles il faut qu'il y ait, derrière la Cour, une grande force matérielle. Lord Phillimore craint que l'Anglais ordinaire ne soit point satisfait d'une Cour au sein de laquelle sa patrie ne serait pas représentée. Pour cette raison Lord Phillimore se rallie à la proposition de M. Adatci. Il déclare que l'observation de celui-ci concernant la nécessité d'assurer la viabilité de la Cour a fait sur lui une impression profonde.

Lord Phillimore n'ignore pas que cette proposition va à l'encontre des vues qui ont trouvé leur expression dans plusieurs projets existants, entre autres dans celui des cinq Etats neutres. Mais d'autre part, le principe sur lequel est basée l'opinion de M. Adatci a été adopté dans la Convention relative à l'établissement d'une Cour Internationale des Prises. D'ailleurs, les intérêts des petites Puissances seraient sauvegardés par le fait que leurs représentants seraient toujours en majorité à la Cour.

Lord Phillimore examine ensuite quelles sont actuellement les grandes Puissances. Il fait observer que le caractère de grands et de petits Etats n'est point permanent. La Russie, par exemple, s'est scindée en plusieurs petits

does not necessarily mean expert jurisconsults. A judge ought to have many other qualities, he must have loyalty, probity, a certain breadth of vision, patience, and courage. If judges are chosen from among eminent jurisconsults named in one single list, it is not certain that the results obtained would be those hoped for. It must be possible to choose judges not only from among jurisconsults but also, for example, from among administrators.

2. The Court must have behind it a material force to ensure the execution of its decisions. Governments must not be able to evade complying with the judgments of the Court. With this in view the Court must be so constructed that it includes representatives of the „Great Powers", an expression to which Lord Phillimore gave at the moment only the common and narrow meaning of the word, — States of large territory and great population. If the Court did not include representatives of these among its members, it would lack what in England is called „back-bone."

Lord Phillimore considered also the relation of the Court to public opinion. Is it possible to conceive the peoples of the Great Powers consenting to have their country submit to the judgment of a Court on which they are not represented? The doubt which exists in this connection is one of the reasons for which it is necessary to have behind the Court a strong material force. Lord Phillimore feared that the ordinary Englishman would not be at all satisfied with a Court on which his country was not represented. For this reason Lord Phillimore agreed with the proposition of M. Adatci. He declared that the observations of M. Adatci concerning the necessity of assuring the Court's practicability had made a profound impression on him.

Lord Phillimore did not disregard the fact that this proposition goes counter to the views which had found expression in several of the existing plans, among others those of the Five Neutral Powers; but on the other hand the principle on which M. Adatci's opinion is based had been included in the Convention relative to the establishment of an International Prize Court. Furthermore the interests of the small Powers would be protected by the fact that their representatives are always in the majority on the Court.

Lord Phillimore proceeded to consider the question of which actually are the Great Powers. He observed that the character of great and small Powers is by no means fixed.

Etats; d'autre part, le jour n'est probablement pas très éloigné où l'Argentine et le Brésil seront de grandes Puissances, ce mot étant toujours employé dans le sens restreint qu'il a défini précédemment, — des Puissances qui seraient certainement aussi grandes que les Dominions Britanniques si celles-ci étaient séparées de la métropole.

Il fait également observer que, si les États-Unis ne formaient pas un seul Etat, ils auraient plus de 40 votes, tandis que, maintenant, ils n'en ont qu'un seul, et que d'autre part, la Monarchie Austro-Hongroise qui autrefois n'avait qu'une voix, dispose de trois voix depuis qu'elle s'est scindée en trois Etats différents.

Lord Phillimore attire aussi l'attention du Comité sur les cas où l'inégalité entre les Etats est déjà acceptée en droit international. Il mentionne les dispositions du Pacte de la Société des Nations, selon lesquelles les Etats n'ont en général qu'une voix, tandis que la Grande Bretagne en a sept. Il mentionne également le nombre inégal de votes donnés par la Convention Postale aux différents membres de l'Union.

Lord Phillimore résume ainsi sa thèse: il faut que la nouvelle Cour ait derrière elle la force matérielle. Elle n'aura cette force que si elle renferme des représentants des grandes Puissances; sinon la nouvelle Cour n'aura pas plus d'autorité que la Cour Permanente d'Arbitrage. Il est vrai que celle-ci, en plusieurs occasions, a évité de petites guerres, mais elle a été insuffisante pour prévenir la grande guerre.

On peut donner aux petites Puissances toutes sortes de satisfactions formelles et leur faire toutes sortes de concessions qui ne touchent pas au fond même du problème, mais Lord Phillimore ne peut admettre le principe sur lequel sont basées les revendications des petits Etats.

Il se rallie à la proposition de M. Adatci.

M. RICCI-BUSATTI déclare que son point de départ n'est pas le même que celui des autres membres. Néanmoins ses conclusions ressembleront peut être à celles de ses collègues. La différence entre la politique et le droit, entre l'équité et la justice, entre un arbitrage et une décision judiciaire, a été fortement mise en relief. Tout de même, il est impossible de la définir exactement. En effet, dans l'opinion de M. Ricci-Busatti il n'y a pas de question qui ne puisse être résolue sur la base du droit; mais il n'y a pas non plus de différend entre Etats entièrement au dehors de toute considération politique. Il est également impossible de

Russia, for example, was cut up into several small States; on the other hand the day was probably not far off, when the Argentine and Brazil would be Great Powers, — the word being employed in the restricted sense which he had earlier defined, — Powers which should be in reality as large as the British Dominions if these were separated from the Mother Country.

He observed also that if the United States did not form one single Government, they would have more than 40 votes, whereas now they have only a single one; and on the other hand, the Austro-Hungarian Monarchy, which formerly had only one vote, now has three after her division into three separate States.

Lord Phillimore also drew the attention of the Committee to the cases of inequality between States already recognised by international law. He mentioned the provisions of the Covenant of the League of Nations, according to which States have generally only one vote, while Great Britain has seven; he mentioned also the inequal number of votes given by the Postal Convention to the different members of the Union.

Lord Phillimore summed up his remarks as follows: The Court must have behind it material force. It will have this force only if it includes representatives of the Great Powers; otherwise the new Court will have no more authority than the Permanent Court of Arbitration. It is true that the latter on several occasions has avoided small wars, but it was unable to prevent the Great War.

It was possible to give to the small Powers all kinds of formal satisfaction and to make all kinds of concessions to them which do not touch the heart of the problem, but the principle on which the claims of the small Powers are based could not be admitted.

He gave his support to the plan of M. Adatci.

M. RICCI-BUSATTI remarked that his starting point was not the same as that of the other members, but that his conclusions were perhaps similar to those of his colleagues. The difference between politics and law, between equity and justice, between arbitration and judicial decision had been sharply pointed out. It was impossible, however, to define the difference exactly. In the opinion of M. Ricci-Busatti all questions might be decided on a legal basis; yet this fact did not exclude political considerations from influencing disputes between States. Similarly it was impossible to trace clearly the line of demarcation between the functions of an arbitrator and those

biën nettement fixer des limites entre le rôle des arbitres et celui des juges; ils exercent, dans bien des cas, les mêmes fonctions; leur origine est commune. L'équité, c'est enfin l'essence même du droit, qui n'en est que la forme.

On ne peut donc pas baser la création de la nouvelle Cour sur des distinctions de cette sorte.

Il faut prendre plutôt en considération le but et la nature des *fonctions* dont il s'agit; savoir: la solution des litiges par une autorité autre que celle des Parties elles-mêmes; il n'y a sur cette base qu'un problème de développements successifs. La Cour de Justice surgira graduellement de la Cour d'Arbitrage, telle qu'elle existe.

Cette nouvelle Cour doit avoir une vie aussi indépendante que possible. En dernière analyse, son autorité découle de la communauté des Etats; mais il est nécessaire de bien distinguer les *fonctions judiciaires* des Etats de leurs *fonctions gouvernementales*. Si cette distinction peut vraiment être réalisée, ce serait un grand avantage pour le développement du droit international, de la Société des Nations et de ses organes. C'est pourquoi M. Ricci-Busatti voudrait écarter toute solution du problème concernant la nomination des juges, qui impliquerait un groupement quelconque des Etats; il préférerait s'en remettre à la Cour d'Arbitrage, selon le projet de M. le Baron Descamps. En ce qui concerne la „viabilité" de l'institution à créer, M. Ricci-Busatti admet que l'opinion de Lord Phillimore et de M. Adatci est, dans une certaine mesure, justifiée: l'égalité entre les Etats n'existe pas *en fait*; mais d'autre part, il est actuellement impossible de nier qu'ils soient tous égaux *en droit*, et il faut maintenir ce principe. L'inégalité réelle aura, automatiquement, l'influence qui lui est dûe; l'influence des différents pays sur la création et sur l'activité de la Cour, sera proportionnée, tout naturellement, à l'importance relative de chacun d'eux, tout comme dans chaque pays, l'inégalité sociale joue son rôle, indépendamment de l'égalité de tous devant la loi. Quant à la force matérielle qui assurera l'exécution des sentences, celle-ci repose sur l'engagement solennel qui a été pris par tous les Gouvernements. En revenant à l'exemple mentionné par M. Adatci, M. Ricci-Busatti fait ressortir la différence qu'il y a entre l'organisation judiciaire et les organisations politiques ou administratives; toute organisation de ce genre doit nécessairement tenir compte des différences entre les intérêts qui sont en jeu et s'y adapter autant que possible. On devra discuter longuement afin d'y réussir: M. Ricci-Busatti rappelle, à cet égard, que les délégués des Pays-Bas réclamaient à juste titre que

of a judge. In many cases they exercise the same functions; their origin is the same. Equity is the very essence of law, which is merely its form.

It is thus impossible to found the new Court on distinctions of this character.

It is the aim and nature of the *function* of the Court that must be considered. The Court was intended to settle disputes between States by an authority other than that of the States themselves. On this basis the problem is only one of successive development: The Court of justice would gradually emerge from the Court of Arbitration as it exists.

The Court must have as independent a life as possible. In final analysis, its authority was derived from the community of States, but it is necessary to distinguish clearly the *judicial* functions of a State from its *governmental* functions. If this could be achieved, it would be a great advantage for the development of international law, of the League of Nations, and of its organs. For this reason M. Ricci-Busatti wished to set aside every solution of the problem of the nomination of judges, which would involve any grouping of States. He should prefer to leave the task to the Court of Arbitration according to the plan of Baron Descamps. In that which concerned the practicability of the institution to be created, M. Ricci-Busatti admitted that to a certain degree the opinion of Lord Phillimore and of M. Adatci was justified: equality between states did not exist *in fact*, but on the other hand it was impossible to deny that they were all equal *in law*, and it was necessary to maintain this principle. Existing inequality would have automatically the influence to which it was entitled; the influence of the different countries on the creation and activities of the Court would be proportional, quite naturally, to the relative importance of each one, exactly the same as in each country social inequality played its rôle quite independently of the equality of all before the law. Regarding the material force to assure the execution of sentences, this execution rested on the formal obligation accepted by the governments. In reverting to the example mentioned by M. Adatci, M. Ricci-Busatti pointed out the differences which exist between the judicial organisations and the political or administrative organisations; all organisations of this nature should take into consideration the weight of the different interests at stake, and adapt themselves to the situation as much as possible. A thorough discussion was required in order to arrive at a successful solution. M. Ricci-Busatti recalled in this connection that the delegates from Hol-

leur pays fût traité en grande puissance, pour les questions qui rentraient dans la compétence de la Commission dont a parlé M. Adatci; également la Belgique avait bien le droit être classée parmi les grandes Puissances, relativement aux questions d'industrie et de travail. Mais lorsqu'il s'agit de réaliser la justice dans la solution des litiges éventuels, il n'y a plus de grands ou de petits Etats: l'intérêt de tous est le même.

Mr. ROOT a l'impression de se trouver maintenant en face de la difficulté qui a empêché la création de la Cour Permanente en 1907.

La difficulté réside, en somme, dans le conflit entre le principe de l'égalité des Etats et la crainte des grandes Puissances d'avoir à se soumettre aux jugements d'une Cour dont la majorité des membres seraient toujours des ressortissants de petits Etats.

Quelques-uns des membres du Comité se sont ralliés à la première manière de voir, quelques autres à la seconde. La simple constatation de ces difficultés ne fournit cependant pas de solution.

Les deux opinions sont, en quelque mesure, justifiées. L'égalité des Etats est le fondement du droit entre nations.

D'autre part, de la décision de la Cour dépendent des intérêts autrement vitaux pour les grands groupements de population que pour les petits Etats.

L'égalité juridique des Etats ne coïncide pas avec l'inégalité des intérêts pratiques qui dépendent de toute leur vie nationale.

Le problème à résoudre est maintenant, selon Mr. Root, de concilier entre eux les deux points de vue.

Mr. Root fait remarquer que des situations semblables se produisent fréquemment dans la vie intérieure des Etats. Il cite comme exemple, les Etats-Unis qui s'étaient trouvés en 1787 devant un problème exactement semblable à celui que le Comité a maintenant à résoudre. Les Etats les plus grands et les plus populeux n'étaient guère disposés à admettre le principe de l'égalité, tandis que les petits Etats ne voulaient pas reconnaître aux autres la suprématie qui leur était dûe, en raison de leur importance et de leur richesse.

On sortit de cette impasse en créant deux chambres. La composition de l'une était fondée sur le principe de l'égalité des Etats, et celle de l'autre, sur le nombre d'habitants, abstraction faite des Etats souverains où ils étaient domiciliés. La méthode, employée ainsi en Amérique, est la

land claimed with all reason that their country be considered as a great Power in regard to the questions which came under the jurisdiction of the Commission mentioned by M. Adatci. Similarly, in the case of the questions of labour, Belgium had the right to be classed as a great Power. But in the administration of justice in eventual cases, great or small Powers did not exist: the interest of all is the same.

Mr. ROOT said that he found himself confronted by the difficulty which prevented the creation of the Permanent Court in 1907.

The difficulty was the conflict between the principle of the equality of States and the Great Powers' fear of finding themselves having to submit to the judgment of a Court in which the majority of the members were representatives of small states.

Some of the members of the Committee supported the first point of view, others the second. However, a simple statement of the problem did not solve the difficulty.

The two opinions were, to a certain extent, justified. The equality of States was the foundation of justice between nations.

On the other hand, the great groupings of population had far more active interests dependent on the decisions of the Court than the smaller ones.

Juridical equality of States did not coincide with the inequality of practical interests which depend upon the whole national life of the peoples.

The problem to be solved by the Committee was, in the words of Mr. Root, to conciliate the two points of view.

Mr. Root made the remark that similar situations were produced frequently in the interior life of states. He mentioned as an example the United States, which found itself in 1787 confronted by a problem exactly analogous to that which the Committee now had to solve. The larger and more populous States were not disposed to accept the principle of equality, while the small States did not wish to recognise the supremacy which was due to the great States by reason of their importance and of their wealth.

The way out of the difficulty was by creating two chambers, the composition of one based on the principle of equality of States and the other on the population, without regard to the sovereign States in which the citizens resided. The method employed in America was the method

méthode de la civilisation: de trouver des moyens de concilier, pour assurer des fins utiles, des théories politiques en conflit.

Mr. Root n'a pas trouvé la solution qu'il cherche, mais il a la conviction que cette solution peut être trouvée. Mr. Root exprime, à ce propos, le désir de pouvoir examiner en détail les propositions du Baron Descamps et de M. Adatci.

Il désire attirer aussi l'attention de ses collègues sur la question de savoir quelles relations il doit y avoir entre la nouvelle Cour, dont l'organisation a été confiée au Comité par la Société des Nations, et les organes politiques de la Société. Il est possible que la solution du problème se trouve dans l'assimilation de l'organisation de la Cour avec les organes politiques de la Société des Nations. Les pouvoirs d'une Cour découlent toujours du pouvoir politique; Mr. Root mentionne quelques exemples de cette vérité. Serait-il possible de confier l'élection des juges à l'Assemblée et en même temps au Conseil de la Société des Nations?

Mr. Root désire soumettre cette idée à la considération de ses collègues. L'effet pratique de l'idée serait d'assurer aux petites Puissances la protection de leurs intérêts par l'Assemblée, où elles sont en majorité, et aux grandes Puissances la protection des leurs par l'activité du Conseil où elles ont la prépondérance.

Un autre avantage pratique de l'idée, c'est qu'elle donnerait les moyens de choisir les meilleurs juges. En effet, elle rend possible la discussion confidentielle des mérites des candidats et elle permet aussi d'apprendre d'avance si un candidat est disposé à accepter le poste qui pourrait lui être offert.

Mr. Root ne prétend pas donner à son idée la valeur d'une conclusion définitive; il l'offre seulement comme une méthode qui s'approche peut-être davantage de la solution qu'on recherche qu'aucune de celles qui ont été proposées jusqu'ici.

Le but des travaux du Comité est de trouver une solution qui permette aux intérêts divergents de prévenir l'injustice et de proposer l'action. Pour arriver à ce but, il faut trouver un moyen pratique, un de ces moyens, qui dans le gouvernement des différents Etats servent à assurer la liberté.

Mr. Root ajoute que son esprit reste ouvert à l'examen des propositions de ses collègues, ainsi qu'à celui des autres systèmes qui ont été proposés.

Le PRESIDENT remercie Mr. Root de son lumineux exposé qui, tous les délégués voudront

of civilisation: to find the means of conciliating, for a useful end, conflicting political views.

Mr. Root had not found the desired solution, but he had the conviction that this solution might be found. Mr. Root expressed, in this connection, the wish to study in detail the proposals of Baron Descamps and M. Adatci.

Mr. Root wanted also to draw the attention of his colleagues to the question of what relationship there should be between the new Court and the political organs of the League of Nations. It was possible that the solution of the problem would be found by articulating the new organisation with the political organisation of the League. Courts derived their powers from the political power; Mr. Root mentioned some examples of this. Would it be possible to vest the power of election of judges both in the Assembly and in the Council?

Mr. Root desired to submit this idea for the consideration of his colleagues. The practical effect of the idea would be to assure to the small Powers the protection of their interests by the Assembly where they are in the majority, and to the great Powers the protection of theirs by the activity of the Council where they are predominant.

Another practical advantage of the idea was that it makes possible the selection of the best men, it allowed for the confidential discussion of the merits of the candidates, and permitted also the finding out in advance whether a candidate would be willing to accept a position that might be offered to him.

Mr. Root did not consider his conclusion as final, but only as a plan which approached more nearly perhaps the desired end than any proposed up to the present time.

The Committee's aim is to find a solution which would allow divergent interests to prevent injustice and to suggest action. To do this, a practical means must be found, one of the means employed by the various governments to guarantee liberty.

Mr. Root added that his mind remained open to examine his colleagues' projects, and also those of the other systems proposed.

The PRESIDENT thanked Mr. Root for his clear explanation, which all the delegates would

bien en convenir, forme une base sérieuse de discussion. Lui-même se propose de l'examiner d'une façon approfondie. Il est heureux que Mr. Root, qui mieux que personne est à même de renseigner les délégués au sujet des institutions américaines, ait bien voulu en exposer les points les plus importants dans leur rapport avec la discussion actuelle.

Le Président, s'adressant ensuite à M. Hammarskjöld, rend hommage à ses qualités de traducteur rapide et clair qui ont permis, même à ceux des membres du Comité qui n'étaient pas aussi complètement au courant de la langue anglaise que les autres, de saisir toute la pensée de Mr. Root.

Comme il avait été entendu que chacun des délégués exposerait à tour de rôle ses idées sur le problème à l'ordre du jour, le Président prend la parole pour expliquer son point de vue. Il dit tout l'intérêt qu'ont eu, pour lui, les idées que les différents délégués ont exposées. Il remarque que quelques-uns de ses collègues s'attachent à bien distinguer les conceptions du droit de celles de la politique, tandis que d'autres disent qu'il n'existe pas de grande différence entre ces deux conceptions. Il voudrait, cependant faire toute réserve à ce dernier égard. Dans le Mémorandum, préparé par la section juridique du Secrétariat Général de la Société des Nations, on a reproduit certain passage d'un discours de Mr. Root, où celui-ci a entrepris de définir les différends d'ordre juridique. (Voir VIII, note, dernier alinéa). Le Président trouve que la définition, ainsi donnée par Mr. Root, est la plus intéressante parmi celles qui ont été formulées dans la discussion pour établir les traits essentiels des questions juridiques. Il rappelle que c'est cette définition qui a été reprise par le Pacte de la Société des Nations, en son article 13. Malheureusement on a, dans le Pacte, ajouté le mot: „généralement", ce qui réduit sensiblement la portée de la définition et en change l'idée. En effet, aux termes du Pacte il est laissé aux Etats de décider si une question est susceptible d'arbitrage ou non. Le Comité devra selon le Baron Descamps voir s'il est possible de se rapprocher du texte de Mr. Root.

La nécessité de sauvegarder l'égalité juridique des Etats étant à peu près universellement admise, comment concilier cette égalité avec ce que le Baron Descamps appelle la nomination „éclectique" des membres de la Cour: tout Etat partie au litige doit avoir un représentant à la Cour. Il faut bien se rendre compte du fait que les juges à la Cour s'occuperont de statuer, non pas de leurs affaires, mais de celles des autres

agree, should provide a serious basis of discussion. He himself intended to study it with great care. He expressed his satisfaction that Mr. Root, preeminently qualified to inform the Committee on American institutions, had explained some of the chief points relating to the present discussion.

The President, speaking then to M. Hammarskjöld, praised his ability as a rapid and accurate interpreter, enabling the members of the Committee who were not as thoroughly familiar with English as other members to grasp thoroughly Mr. Root's thought.

As it had been settled that each of the delegates would in turn present his views on the question on the agenda, the President stated his own views. He expressed his interest in the ideas advanced by the various delegates. He noted the fact that some of his colleagues made a clear distinction between legal and political conceptions, while some others declared that there did not exist any great difference between those two conceptions. He, however, should prefer to reserve entirely his opinion on the latter view. In the Memorandum prepared by the Legal Section of the Secretariat General of the League of Nations, a certain part of a speech by Mr. Root where he undertook to give a definition of „disputes of a legal character" had been reproduced. (See VIII, note, last paragraph). The President thought that this definition of Mr. Root's was the most interesting among those formulated in the discussion of what constitutes the principal features of a juridical question. He recalled that this definition had been taken over by the Covenant of the League of Nations in article 13. Unfortunately in the Covenant the word „generally" had been added — an addition which had reduced considerably the scope of the definition and altered its meaning. According to the Covenant, in fact, it was left to the States themselves to decide whether a question was subject to arbitration or not. Baron Descamps was of the opinion that the Committee should see if it were possible to approach the text of Mr. Root.

The necessity of safeguarding the legal equality of States being almost universally recognised, the question arose as to how this equality was to be reconciled with what Baron Descamps called the "eclectic" nomination of the members of the Court: the mode of nomination according to which each State, party to a dispute, should have a representative on the Court. One must keep in mind the fact that the judges would have to deal not with their own affairs,

Etats; ce qui rendrait un privilège d'autant moins justifiable.

Le Président, reprenant ensuite, afin de les élucider, plusieurs points de l'exposé fait par lui la veille, estime que pour arriver à une solution satisfaisante du problème actuel, il faudra assurer la représentation des grands systèmes juridiques, au sein de la Cour. Ceci n'a rien de contraire à l'égalité juridique des Etats, et atteint, d'autre part, le but visé par les grandes nations.

Le Président ajoute qu'à son avis, en procédant à l'édification de la Cour de Justice, il ne faut pas faire table-rase de tout ce qui a été construit antérieurement dans le même sens.

Il existe une Cour d'Arbitrage, comprenant généralement quatre membres nommés par chaque Etat, et „jouissant de la plus haute considération morale" et „d'une compétence reconnue dans les questions de droit international". Ce sont les termes mêmes des Conventions de 1899 et de 1907. Pourquoi ne pas confier à un tel aréopage la mission de concourir à la formation de juridictions nouvelles, dans des conditions qui sauvegarderaient à la fois l'égalité juridique des Etats et les revendications des grandes nations?

En vue d'atteindre une solution, à coup sûr remarquable, du grand problème des juridictions internationales, le groupe des quatre délégués, nommés par chaque Etat comme arbitres internationaux, désignerait un de ses membres, et l'ensemble des membres ainsi désignés constituerait d'abord une Haute Cour, placée au sommet de la Justice Internationale, et appelée à connaître des crimes contre l'ordre public international et le droit des gens universel.

Les membres de cette Haute Cour choisiraient à leur tour les juges de la Cour Permanente de Justice Internationale, en se conformant à l'obligation, déjà visée par le projet de la Conférence de 1907, de comprendre dans leur choix, des juges représentant les principaux systèmes juridiques du monde, tels que nous les voyons réalisés, notamment dans les principaux Etats.

La Cour Permanente de Justice Internationale ainsi composée pourrait enfin, en considération des exigences pratiques, se répartir en plusieurs chambres, conformément à un règlement d'ordre à approuver par le Conseil et par l'Assemblée de la Société des Nations.

Cette conception n'est sans doute qu'une esquisse susceptible d'améliorations à divers points de vue, mais elle semble de nature à retenir l'attention du Comité en ce qu'elle s'appuie, pour réaliser le progrès, sur une institution qui a fait ses preuves, en ce qu'elle a, pour point de départ, une égale délégation faite par les Etats à des

but with those of other States: a fact which rendered a privilege all the less justifiable.

The President, in order to explain several points of the *exposé* which he had made the day before, continued the discussion. He thought that in order to arrive at a satisfactory solution of the present problem it would be necessary to assure the representation of the great legal systems on the Court. That involved nothing contrary to the legal equality of States, but secured the ends which the great nations wished to attain.

The President added that in his opinion it was not necessary, in proceeding to the construction of the Court of Justice to discard everything which had been done before for the same purpose.

A Court of Arbitration was in existence, made up in general by four members named by each State and "enjoying the highest moral consideration" and "of recognised ability in questions of international law". These are the very terms of the 1899 and 1907 Conventions. Why not entrust to such an aeropagus the mission of co-operating in the formation of new jurisdictions under conditions which protect both the legal equality of States and the claims of the great nations?

In order to arrive at a positive solution of the great problem of international jurisdiction, the group of four delegates named as international arbitrators by each State should designate one of its members, and the group of members so designated should constitute at the outset a High Court, placed at the summit of International Justice and called upon to take cognisance of crimes committed against international good order and the universal law of nations.

The members of this High Court should choose the judges of the Permanent Court of International Justice, in conformity with the obligation already laid down in the plan of the 1907 Conference, to include in its choice judges representing the principal juridical systems of the world such as these systems are in practice notably in the principal States.

The Permanent Court of International Justice thus constituted would be able, in answer to the demand of practical circumstances, to divide itself into several chambers, conforming to rules of procedure to be approved by the Council and by the Assembly of the League of Nations.

This conception was, without doubt, nothing more than an outline, subject to improvements from various points of view; but it seemed to merit the attention of the Committee, because, to make a step in advance, it took for its starting

jurisconsultes considérés comme hors de pair au point de vue de la compétence et de la moralité, en ce qu'elle se développe sur la base d'une cooptation faite par eux et enfin en ce qu'elle assure aux grands Etats une juste représentation dans la composition de la Justice Internationale.

Le Président passe ensuite à la question de l'ordre du jour des deux séances prochaines. On décide que le lendemain, samedi, on continuera l'échange de vues général sur la question de la nomination des juges, en discutant les systèmes déjà suggérés par les membres. Le lundi suivant, les membres communiqueraient autant que possible au Président des propositions formulées.

La séance est levée à 12 h. 35 m.

Le Président:
(signé) Brn. DESCAMPS.

Le Secrétaire-Général:
(signé) D. ANZILOTTI.

point an institution which had proved its worth, because it was founded on an equal delegation sent by the States, of jurisconsults unrivalled from the point of view of competence and morality, because it was developed on a basis of co-optation made by them, and finally, because it assured to the great Powers a just representation in the composition of the Tribunal of International Justice.

The President proceeded to settle the Agenda of the two following meetings. Saturday was decided upon for the continuation of the general exchange of opinion on the question of the nomination of judges; a discussion of the systems already suggested by the different members should take place. On Monday next the members might, if they desired, communicate their plans in writing to the President.

The meeting closed at 12.35 p.m.

The President:
(signed) Brn. DESCAMPS.

The Secretary-General:
(signed) D. ANZILOTTI.

ANNEXE No. 1.

Règles de procédure pour le Comité Consultatif de Juristes.

1. Les séances du Comité ne sont pas publiques; toutefois dérogation pourra être faite à cette règle dans des cas déterminés et par décisions spéciales. Les délibérations sont confidentielles; cependant, le Secrétariat est autorisé à fournir au public des résumés succincts des questions traitées dans chaque séance et du progrès qui a été fait.

2. Les membres du Comité ont seuls le droit de prendre part aux discussions. Le secrétaire du Comité a le droit de fournir lui-même des explications et de charger des membres du Secrétariat d'en fournir.

3. Les conseillers et les secrétaires privés des membres ont le droit d'accompagner les membres aux séances. Avec le consentement du Comité un membre pourra dans des cas déterminés charger ses conseillers de fournir des explications.

4. Les procès-verbaux des séances contiendront un résumé succinct des délibérations et, in extenso, les décisions du Comité, ainsi que les déclarations, projets et amendements déposés par un membre. Un projet de procès-verbal de chaque séance sera présenté aux membres (ronéographié) au commencement de la séance suivante. Ces procès-verbaux ne seront pas lus à la séance.

5. Tous les projets et tous les amendements soumis à la décision du Comité seront, dans la mesure du possible, présentés par écrit au Président.

Si un projet ou un amendement n'a pas été distribué avant le commencement de la séance, l'ajournement de la séance sera prononcé si un membre en exprime le désir.

6. A la fin de chaque séance, le Président soumettra au Comité l'ordre du jour de la séance prochaine. L'ordre du jour une fois adopté ne pourra être modifié que par une décision du Comité.

7. Les décisions du Comité sont prises à la majorité des voix. Les propositions adoptées en première lecture doivent être soumises à un second vote. Les opinions divergentes seront consignées dans les procès-verbaux des séances, et, à la requête des membres directement intéressés, il en sera fait mention, éventuellement motivée, dans le protocole final constatant les résultats des travaux du Comité.

ANNEX No. 1.

Rules of procedure for the Advisory Committee of Jurists.

1. The sittings of the Committee are not public; in certain cases and by special decisions exception may be made to this rule. The deliberations are confidential. However, the Secretariat is authorised to furnish short public statements of the questions treated and of the progress made at each sitting.

2. Only the members of the Committee have the right to take part in the discussions. The Secretary of the Committee has the right to give explanations himself, and to ask the members of the Secretariat to do so.

3. The counsellors and private secretaries of the members are entitled to accompany the members to the sittings. With the consent of the Committee, a member may, in special cases, ask his counsellors to furnish explanations.

4. The procès-verbaux of the sittings shall contain a brief analysis of the deliberations, and, *in extenso*, points adopted by the Committee and declarations, proposals or amendments that may have been made by a member. A draft procès-verbal of each sitting shall be presented to the members (in roneographed copies) at the beginning of the next. These procès-verbaux shall not be read at the meeting.

5. All proposals and all amendments to be discussed by the Committee shall, as far as possible, be presented in writing to the President.

Should a proposal or amendment not have been distributed before the sitting, the adjournment shall be pronounced at the request of any members.

6. At the end of each sitting, the President shall submit to the Committee the agenda of the next sitting. The agenda once having been adopted can be modified only by a decision of the Committee.

7. The decisions of the Committee are taken by a majority of votes. The decisions carried at the first reading will be submitted to a second vote. The divergent opinions will be noted in the procès-verbaux of the sittings and, at the request of the members directly interested, the objections and the reasons therefor shall be included in the final protocol stating the results of the deliberations of the Committee.

ANNEXE No. 2.

Organisation.

(Questionnaire proposé par le Baron Descamps).

Organisation.

1. Nombre de juges permanents.

2. Durée du mandat.

3. Conditions requises pour être juge. Incompatibilités.

4. Mode de nomination des juges:

   a) par l'Assemblée de la Société de Nations ou par le Conseil de cette Société;

   b) par les Etats divisés en groupes et nommant chacun un certain nombre de juges;

   c) modes mixtes comportant d'abord des présentations puis des nominations;

   d) utilisation de la Cour Permanente d'Arbitrage et cooptation par les jurisconsultes de cette Cour pour la formation des diverses juridictions.

5. Participation éventuelle de juges nationaux aux litiges où sont engagés leurs Etats.

6. Composition des chambres. Dispositions à insérer dans le Statut et points à réserver au règlement d'ordre, pour être soumis à l'approbation du Conseil et de l'Assemblée de la Société des Nations.

ANNEX No. 2.

Organisation.

(Questionnaire submitted by Baron Descamps).

Organisation.

1. Number of permanent judges.

2. Term of office.

3. Qualifications for judges. Debarring circumstances.

4. Method of nomination of judges:

   a) by the Assembly of the League of Nations or by the Council of the League;

   b) by the various States in groups, each one naming a certain number of judges;

   c) various methods comprising first presentations, then nominations;

   d) use of the Permanent Court of Arbitration and cooptation by the jurisconsults of this Court for the formation of the various jurisdictions.

5. Participation, under certain conditions, of judges in litigations in which their States are involved.

6. Composition of the chambers. Provisions to insert in the Statute and points to be reserved for the rules of order, to be submitted for approval by the Council and by the Assembly of the League of Nations.

ANNEXE No. 3.

Organisation.

(Questionnaire adopté par le Comité).

Organisation.

1. Mode de nomination des juges:
   a) par l'Assemblée de la Société des Nations ou par le Conseil de cette Société;
   b) par les Etats divisés en groupes et nommant chacun un certain nombre de juges;
   c) modes mixtes comportant d'abord des présentations, puis des nominations;
   d) utilisation de la Cour Permanente d'Arbitrage et cooptation par les jurisconsultes de cette Cour pour la formation des diverses juridictions.

2. Participation éventuelle de juges nationaux aux litiges où sont engagés leurs Etats. Droit de récusation.

3. Caractère permanent de la Cour et domicile des juges.

4. Nombre de juges permanents.

5. Durée du mandat.

6. Conditions requises pour être juge. Incompatibilités.

7. Composition des chambres. Dispositions à insérer dans le Statut, et points à réserver au règlement d'ordre, pour être soumis à l'approbation du Conseil et de l'Assemblée de la Société des Nations.

ANNEX No. 3.

Organisation.

(Questionnaire adopted by the Committee).

Organisation.

1. Method of nomination of judges.
   a) by the Assembly of the League of Nations or by the Council of the League;
   b) by the various States in groups, each one naming a certain number of judges;
   c) various methods comprising first presentations, then nominations;
   d) use of the Permanent Court of Arbitration and cooptation by the jurisconsults of this Court for the formation of the various jurisdictions.

2. Participation, under certain conditions, of judges in litigations in which their States are involved. Right to challenge.

3. Permanent character of the Court, and domicile of the judges.

4. Number of permanent judges.

5. Term of office.

6. Qualifications required for a judge. Debarring circumstances.

7. Composition of the chambers. Provisions to insert in the Statute, and points to be reserved for the rules of order, to be submitted for approval by the Council and by the Assembly of the League of Nations.

ANNEXE No. 4.

Résolution de Bruxelles 1919.

La Conférence des Associations pour la Société des Nations réunie à Bruxelles au début de décembre 1919, a adopté la résolution suivante:

„Dans l'organisation d'une Cour de Justice internationale, il sera stipulé que cette Cour ne comprendra pas plus d'un juge de chaque nationalité; pour l'élection des juges, le principe de l'égalité des Etats sera respecté. Les juges seront choisis sur une liste de candidats proposés par les Etats. Chaque Etat aura le droit de proposer un nombre maximum (à fixer) de candidats de sa nationalité et, afin d'indiquer clairement que le juge est exclusivement au service de la justice, proposera un nombre plus élevé de candidats d'autres nationalités."

ANNEX No. 4.

Brussels Resolution 1919.

At the Conference of the League of Nations Associations held at Brussels early in December 1919 it was resolved:

„In the organisation of the International Court of Justice, it should be stipulated that the Court should not include more than one judge of any one nationality. In the election of judges, the principle of equality of States shall be respected. The election should be made free from a list of candidates nominated by the States. Each State shall have the right to propose a maximum (to be fixed) of candidates of each nationality, and, in order clearly to indicate that the judge is at the exclusive service of justice, it shall propose a higher number of candidates of other nationalities".

4IÈME SÉANCE (non-publique), tenue au Palais de la Paix, à La Haye, le 19 juin 1920.

Présidence de M. le BARON DESCAMPS.

Sont présents: tous les membres du Comité (à l'exception de M. Bevilaqua); Mr. James Brown Scott; les secrétaires particuliers de M. le Baron Descamps et de M. Adatci; les membres du Secrétariat.

Avec l'autorisation spéciale du Président, M. van Hamel, directeur de la Section juridique du Secrétariat Permanent de la Société des Nations, est également présent.

La séance est ouverte à 9.35 h. du matin.

Le PRESIDENT prie M. Hammarskjöld de donner quelques explications au sujet du procès-verbal.

Celui-ci explique que, par suite du surcroît de travail et aussi du non-fonctionnement momentané du service ronéographique une partie du procès-verbal n'a pu être distribuée qu'immédiatement avant la séance.

M. RICCI-BUSATTI demande si les membres peuvent faire des corrections dans les compterendus de leurs propres discours.

Le PRESIDENT ne voit pas d'objection à ce que des retouches soient faites. Après l'approbation du Président et du Secrétaire Général, le bon à tirer sera donné.

M. HAGERUP a remarqué dans les journaux du matin, un communiqué concernant les travaux de la séance de la veille, et dans lequel les opinions des différents membres et les arguments apportés de part et d'autre sont mis en lumière de façon trop visible. Il avait pensé que des communiqués ne seraient donnés à la presse qu'avec l'assentiment du Comité. Sans vouloir insister sur ce point, il suggère que les communiqués ne seront publiés qu'avec l'assentiment du Président et que ces communiqués ne devront pas renseigner sur les opinions émises individuellement par les différents membres.

Le PRESIDENT se propose de faire une enquête au sujet du communiqué en question et d'examiner, d'accord avec le Chef du Secrétariat, tout communiqué qui sera envoyé à la presse.

4TH MEETING (Private), held at the Peace Palace, the Hague, on June 19th, 1920.

BARON DESCAMPS in the chair.

Present: all members of the Committee (with the exception of M. Bevilaqua); Mr. James Brown Scott; the private secretaries of Baron Descamps and of M. Adatci; and the members of the Secretariat.

With the special permission of the President, M. van Hamel, director of the legal section of the Permanent-Secretariat of the League of Nations, was also present.

The meeting opened at 9.35 a.m.

The PRESIDENT asked M. Hammarskjöld to give an explanation concerning the procès-verbal.

The latter explained that, owing to excess of work, and roneographic difficulties, the distribution of a portion of the procès-verbal had not been possible until immediately before the meeting.

M. RICCI-BUSATTI asked whether members could make corrections in the record of their own speeches.

The PRESIDENT saw no objection to slight alterations. The order to print would be given after final approval by the President and the Secretary General.

M. HAGERUP remarked that a communiqué dealing with the work of the previous meeting had appeared in the morning papers; it contained the opinions of different members and arguments pro and con in too great detail. He had thought that press communiqués were not to be issued without the consent of the Committee. Though he did not wish to press the matter, he suggested that communiqués should only be issued with the approval of the President, and that they should not contain the members' individual opinions.

The PRESIDENT said that he would inquire into the matter and would examine, in co-operation with the Secretary-General, any communiqué for the press.

LORD PHILLIMORE demande si le procès-verbal sera rédigé également en anglais.

M. HAMMARSKJÖLD dit que ce texte sera prêt avant la fin de la séance, ou au plus tard, avant la fin de la journée.

Le PRESIDENT ouvre la discussion sur les idées émises la veille par les différents membres, à propos de la question encore à l'ordre du jour.

M. ADATCI désire ajouter quelques remarques que lui permet de faire l'expérience qu'il a acquise récemment dans la Commission des Communications et du Transit.

En ce qui concerne le caractère administratif du Comité Permanent du Transit, il se range, quant au fond, à l'opinion émise la veille par M. de Lapradelle, mais il désire expliquer quelques nuances.

Dans l'article 16 des projets de convention adoptés, il est stipulé que tous les différends seront soumis au Comité Permanent, pour y être jugés, quitte à faire appel, le cas échéant, à la Cour Permanente de Justice Internationale. C'est précisément M. Ricci-Busatti qui a montré, lors des délibérations à Paris, le lien qui, nonobstant cette fonction judiciaire du Comité, devait exister entre le Conseil de la Société des Nations et le Comité.

D'autre part le rôle de la Cour de Justice dont on s'occupe ici, ne sera pas non plus purement judiciaire (dernier paragraphe de l'article 14 du Pacte).

Après de longues discussions, on a décidé d'organiser le Comité Permanent sur une base d'inégalité, réalisant ainsi dans les actes écrits ce qui existe en fait dans le monde.

Au point de vue formel, les Etats sont égaux, mais les membres du Comité actuel doivent traiter l'importante question de l'organisation de la Cour en sociologues plutôt qu'en juristes purs.

Comme il s'agit de créer une institution entièrement nouvelle, il faut avoir le courage et la sagesse d'admettre franchement certaines réalités. Si on exclut l'une des cinq grandes Puissances siégeant au Conseil et représentant divers groupements naturels (races, religions, systèmes juridiques), la nouvelle institution sera mort-née. La postérité sera reconnaissante d'une décision courageuse. Les peuples ont le ferme désir de ne pas se dominer les uns les autres, militairement et économiquement; ils veulent se soumettre à la décision d'une Cour pour réaliser tout ce que l'esprit humain a de généreux.

LORD PHILLIMORE asked if the procès-verbal would be produced also in English.

M. HAMMARSKJÖLD said that this text would be ready before the end of the meeting, or at any rate before the end of the day.

The PRESIDENT opened the debate on the ideas put forward on the previous day by the members, on the subject of the agenda.

M. ADATCI wished to add remarks based on recent experience at the Communications and Transit Committee.

Concerning the administrative character of the Permanent Committee for Transit, he agreed in principle with what M. de Lapradelle had said on the previous day; but he wished to explain some shades of difference.

In article 16 of the draft Conventions adopted, it was laid down that all disputes should be submitted to the Permanent Committee for adjudication, subject to appeal to the Permanent Court of International Justice. It was M. Ricci-Busatti himself who pointed out, during the deliberations at Paris, that notwithstanding this judicial power of the Committee, it must be connected directly with the Council of the League of Nations.

On the other hand the function of the Court of Justice now under consideration would not be of purely judicial character (see last paragraph of Art. 14 of the Covenant).

After long discussions, it was decided to organise the Permanent Committee on an unequal basis, in this way giving documentary recognition of the existing conditions.

Theoretically, States were equal, but the members of the Committee should deal with the important question of the organisation of the Court as sociologists rather than purely as jurists.

As it was a question of creating an entirely new institution, it was necessary to have the courage and wisdom to admit frankly the existence of certain actual conditions. If one of the five great Powers seated on the Council, and representing various natural groups (races, religions, juridical systems), were excluded, the new institution would be still-born. Posterity would be grateful for a courageous decision. The nations desired strongly not to dominate other nations in a military or economic way; they wanted to submit themselves to the decision of a Court in order to give full play to the generosity of the human mind.

M. ALTAMIRA dit que les exposés de Lord Phillimore, de Mr. Root et de M. Adatci, qui représentent un point de vue différent de celui de M. de Lapradelle, de M. Ricci-Busatti et du sien, sont remplis de vues nouvelles: ils traduisent l'expérience et le sens psychologique de quelques-unes des grandes Puissances, et c'est là une considération essentielle, car tout dépend de la bonne volonté, c'est-à-dire de la disposition d'esprit, de ces Puissances.

Ces exposés n'ont pourtant pas convaincu M. Altamira parce que pour lui:

1°. la force du tribunal ne résidera pas dans le nombre plus grand des juges appartenant aux grandes Puissances, mais dans l'opinion publique des peuples qui forment la Société des Nations. Il ne faut pas perdre de vue que l'institution qu'il s'agit de créer, a été réclamée par le Conseil de cette Société lui-même, ce qui prouve déjà que les grandes Puissances sont disposées à respecter ses décisions. Si elles n'ont pas foi dans le nouveau tribunal l'idée de la Société des Nations sera faussée. Le tribunal tirera sa force de l'autorité personnelle des juges: aussi cette autorité en devra-t-elle être la base, sans tenir compte de la nationalité des juges. A ce sujet, il s'appuie sur la résolution adoptée à la Conférence des Associations pour la Société des Nations à Bruxelles. Quant à la comparaison entre les intérêts des grands et des petits Etats, M. Altamira n'est pas d'avis que les intérêts des premiers soient les plus importants. L'importance est la même, mais les nations faibles ont un intérêt supérieur à ce que justice soit rendue, puisque le droit est leur seule arme. M. Altamira attache plus d'importance aux qualités morales qu'aux qualités professionnelles des juges.

2°. pratiquement, les „grandes Puissances" ne sont pas grandes, seulement par leur force militaire et leur développement économique, mais parce qu'elles ont contribué pour une grande part au développement de la civilisation. La minorité d'intellectuels, que l'on trouve dans chaque pays, sera „ipso facto" plus nombreuse dans les pays dont la civilisation est la plus développée. Par conséquent, les grandes Puissances seront toujours suffisamment représentées à la Cour, si l'on s'en tient au principe du choix des meilleurs.

M. Altamira dit enfin que certains des arguments qui avaient été apportés pour combattre sa thèse n'étaient à la vérité, en dernière analyse, pas incompatibles avec celle-ci; et M. Altamira est disposé à accepter toute formule

M. ALTAMIRA said that the statements of Lord Phillimore, Mr. Root and M. Adatci, which represented a point of view different from that of MM. de Lapradelle, Ricci-Busatti and himself, contained new elements: they contained the experience and the psychological sense of some of the great Powers. This was of primary importance, because everything depended on the good-will, in other words on the frame of mind, of these Powers.

However, these statements had not convinced M. Altamira, because in his opinion:

1. the strength of the tribunal would not be derived from a greater number of the judges belonging to the great Powers but from public opinion in the countries which composed the League of Nations. It must not be forgotten that the institution to be created had been demanded by the Council of the League itself; which fact showed that the great Powers were ready to respect its decisions. If those Powers had no faith in the new tribunal, the idea of a Society of Nations would be distorted. The tribunal would derive its strength from the personal authority of the judges. This authority should be the basis of the tribunal without reference to the nationality of the judges. In support of this point he cited the resolution adopted at the Conference of Associations for the League of Nations held at Brussels. Concerning the comparation between the interests of the large and small States, M. Altamira did not share the opinion that the interests of the former were the more important. The importance was equal; but the weaker nations had a greater need that justice be done since the law was their only defence. M. Altamira thought that moral qualities had more importance than professional ability in a judge.

2. in practice, the great Powers were not great because of their military power or economic development only, but because they had contributed more to the development of civilisation. The great Powers, as they had a more developed civilisation, would have *ipso facto* a larger minority of intellectual men. Consequently, they would always be sufficiently represented on the Court, if the simple principle of choosing the best men be adhered to.

M. Altamira finally said that certain arguments put forward against his theory, were not really fundamentally incompatible with it, and M. Altamira was prepared to accept any scheme which, concerning the election of judges,

qui, en ce qui concerne la nomination de juges, a pour criterium le principe exposé par lui, savoir, la nécessité de choisir les meilleurs juges, sans tenir compte de leur nationalité.

Le PRESIDENT demande si M. Fernandes est présent et, comme celui-ci est absent, le Président ajoute que le Comité aurait sans doute consenti à l'entendre.

M. HAGERUP fait observer que lors de la création de la Cour des Prises, on a établi une différence entre les grandes et les petites Puissances. Les grandes auraient eu un juge siégeant à titre permanent, les petites auraient été représentées d'après un système de roulement: c'était là une infraction au principe de l'égalité, mais il ne faut pas perdre de vue, qu'il s'agissait alors de substituer une juridiction internationale aux juridictions nationales, et que, par conséquent, la nouvelle institution représentait en tout cas un progrès immense pour les petits Etats: aussi cette Cour des Prises ne saurait-elle être considérée comme constituant un précédent.

M. Hagerup se range à l'opinion de M. Altamira: nous devons chercher, en dehors de toute considération politique, les juges les mieux préparés à leur tâche. Lord Phillimore a dit également qu'il faut des hommes expérimentés et de haute moralité. Peut-on croire qu'on aurait jamais une Cour ne comprenant pas de juge anglais, ou, de façon générale, de juges des grandes Puissances? Dès lors, pourquoi inscrire dans le projet une règle d'inégalité qui serait contraire au fondement du droit international, irait à l'encontre de l'opinion publique, exprimée unanimement par un grand nombre de corporations internationales, et qui rendrait le projet inacceptable pour la majorité des Etats qui sont membres de la Société des Nations?

M. Hagerup passe ensuite à l'examen des idées exprimées par M. Adatci qui considère la question surtout au point de vue sociologique. M. Hagerup a cru comprendre que M. Adatci, d'accord avec l'évolutionisme moderne, a dit que c'est le plus fort qui survivra. S'il s'agit du développement moral, ceci est vrai plutôt de celui qui est le plus adapté à la civilisation. Dans la conception moderne, les petits Etats sont des éléments indispensables au développement de la civilisation et du droit.

M. ADATCI dit, avec Lord Phillimore, qu'une institution basée sur l'égalité juridique des Etats, n'est pas „viable".

M. HAGERUP ne sait pas exactement ce qui veut dire cette expression. Peut-être veut-on

took as its criterion, the principle laid down by him, namely the necessity of choosing the best, regardless of their nationality.

The PRESIDENT asked if M. Fernandes was present and, as he was not, added that if he had been, the Committee would probably have agreed to hear him.

M. HAGERUP observed that at the time of the establishment of the Prize Court, a difference was recognized between the great Powers and the small ones. The great States would have had one permanent judge, the small ones would have been represented according to a system of rotation: this was a breach of the principle of equality of States, but one must not lose sight of the fact that then it was a question of substituting an international for a national jurisdiction, and that consequently at any rate the new institution represented a great gain for the small States. The Prize Court therefore could not serve as a precedent.

M. Hagerup agreed with the opinions of M. Altamira: we must obtain judges from amongst those best prepared for the task, regardless of political considerations. Lord Phillimore also had said that distinguished men of high moral character were needed. Was it conceivable that a court might exist without an English judge, or, in general, judges of the great Powers? Why then insert in the proposal a rule of inequality which would be contrary to international law and public opinion as expressed unanimously by a large number of international bodies and would render it unacceptable to the majority of the members of the League of Nations?

M. Hagerup then examined the views of M. Adatci who considered the question essentially from the sociological standpoint. M. Hagerup understood that M. Adatci, in accordance with the modern evolutionary theory, had said that it was the strongest who would survive. From the standpoint of moral development, this was more true of the one best adapted to civilisation. According to the modern conception, the small States were indispensable elements in the development of right and civilisation.

M. ADATCI agreed with Lord Phillimore that an institution based on the juridical equality of States was not practicable.

M. HAGERUP was not clear on the meaning of this. Did it mean that the large States would

dire par là, que les grands Etats n'accepteraient pas une telle institution. C'est un point de vue sur lequel M. Hagerup n'a pas compétence pour se prononcer, et il le laisse de côté dans cette discussion. Lord Phillimore a pourtant exposé un argument de fond, à savoir, qu'une Cour où les grandes Puissances ne seraient pas représentées n'aurait pas „d'épine dorsale". A ce sujet M. Hagerup cite le mot de M. Bourgeois, qui a fait observer que „l'épine dorsale" de la Cour, c'est à présent la Société des Nations. C'est là un fait nouveau, qui place le Comité dans une situation toute autre vis-à-vis de cette question que celle dans laquelle on se trouvait lors de la Deuxième Conférence de la Paix.

M. Hagerup ne comprend pas comment „l'épine dorsale" que constitue la Société des Nations, puisse être fortifiée par la représentation à la Cour de telle ou telle Puissance. Il faut distinguer deux cas différents: ou bien la Puissance en question est elle-même l'une des deux parties en cause, ou bien il s'agit d'un différend entre deux autres Puissances. Dans le premier cas, il reste à savoir — le Comité aura à discuter plus tard cette question — si le juge appartenant à la dite Puissance doit assister à la discussion de l'affaire, au cas où l'autre partie n'a pas de représentant parmi les juges; et dans le second cas on ne voit pas comment le fait d'avoir parmi les juges un ressortissant de telle Puissance plutôt que de telle autre, pourrait influer sur la valeur de la sentence prononcée. C'est la qualité du juge, non sa nationalité, qui importe.

La question du corps électoral ne doit être discutée en détail que plus tard. M. Hagerup fait observer cependant qu'en ce qui concerne la composition du collège électoral, il est prêt à se rallier à la proposition du Président, proposition qui se retrouve d'ailleurs dans le projet commun des pays scandinaves. Il estime qu'il s'agit en premier lieu de trouver une solution qui rendrait, autant que possible, les juges indépendants de leurs Etats. C'est pour cette raison qu'il se range de préférence à la proposition du Président, mais il ne serait pas hostile à l'idée de donner à l'Assemblée de la Société des Nations le droit de choisir les juges. Quant à la suggestion de Mr. Root, tendant à faire collaborer en cette matière l'Assemblée et le Conseil, M. Hagerup y voit quelques objections. Toutefois, comme certains détails de cette suggestion lui ont échappé, il doit réserver son opinion.

Mr. ROOT donne quelques explications complémentaires sur sa proposition; il s'agit de „concurrent votes" par l'Assemblée et le Conseil.

not accept such an institution? On this point M. Hagerup could have no opinion, so he refrained from discussing it. Lord Phillimore had advanced, however, an argument to the effect that a Court on which the great Powers were not represented should lack backbone. In that connection, M. Hagerup referred to M. Bourgeois' words that the League of Nations was at present the backbone of the Court. Therein lay a new fact, which in this connection created an entirely different situation from the situation existing at the time of the second Hague Conference.

M. Hagerup could not understand how the "backbone", which was the League of Nations, could be strengthened by the representation on the Court of a given Power. A distinction between two cases must be made: either the Power concerned is or is not a party in the case. In the first case (to be discussed later) the question arises whether the judge representing the said Power should take part in the discussion of an affair in which the other party was not represented among the judges. In the second case it was difficult to understand how the fact that there was among the judges one identified with one Power rather than with another could influence the value of the decision pronounced. It was the qualifications of the judge, and not his nationality, which was important.

Details as to the electoral body should be left to later discussion. M. Hagerup observed, however, that regarding the composition of the electoral college, he was prepared to accept the President's proposition, the same as that included in the joint project of the Scandinavian countries. He believed that it was of primary importance to find a solution which made the judges as far as possible independent of their governments. For that reason he preferred the President's proposition, but he would not object to the idea of giving to the Assembly of the League of Nations the right to choose the judges. Concerning the suggestion of Mr. Root to have the Council and the Assembly co-operate in this matter, he saw several objections. In any case, as certain details of the suggestion had escaped his attention, he would refrain from expressing an opinion now.

Mr. ROOT gave a further explanation of his proposal, saying that "concurrent votes" of the Assembly and the Council should take place.

M. HAGERUP termine en disant qu'il a conscience de la grande responsabilité qui lui incombe comme membre de ce Comité, et qu'il ne manquera pas de prendre en considération toute proposition tendant à concilier les opinions opposées.

M. DE LAPRADELLE, avant d'entamer la discussion des différentes propositions, désire déclarer qu'il entend discuter la question avec la volonté d'arriver à un résultat. Il désire également souligner le fait, que les membres du Comité n'ont pas d'instructions, pas même d'indications de leurs gouvernements. Ils n'ont pas de plans arrêtés à faire triompher. Ce sont des juges siégeant pour délibérer.

Les raisons apportées en faveur de la thèse opposée à la sienne sont groupées autour de deux argumentations; celle de M. Adatci — c'est l'argumentation sociologique, — et celle de Lord Phillimore. Au sujet de la proposition de Mr. Root, M. de Lapradelle dit qu'il trouve prématuré de vouloir concilier avant de savoir s'il y a désaccord.

Dans l'opinion de M. de Lapradelle, l'argumentation sociologique de M. Adatci va à l'encontre des lois de la sociologie. M. Adatci dit que, pour pouvoir vivre, la Cour qu'on est en train de créer doit s'appuyer sur les forts. Les forts sont les grandes Puissances; mais quelles sont les grandes Puissances et quel est leur nombre? On n'en sait rien. Il n'y a pas de critérium scientifique.

M. de Lapradelle se borne à prendre pour critérium la conscience, la force morale. Si ce critérium est adopté, le principe de l'égalité est sauvegardé. Deux Etats qui viennent devant la Cour se sentiront toujours sur un pied de parfaite égalité devant la Justice.

Si les grandes Puissances seules étaient représentées à la Cour, celle-ci n'inspirerait pas de confiance aux autres Puissances et les grands Etats préféreraient voir résoudre leurs conflits par le Conseil plutôt que par la Cour. Si les petits Etats se résignent à se soumettre à la dictature politique des grands Etats, jamais ils ne se soumettront à la dictature judiciaire de ceux-ci. Il faut plus de justice et moins de force.

Les grandes Puissances n'auront pas besoin de réclamer des sièges à la Cour. Ces sièges leur reviendront d'une façon automatique. Ne vaut-il pas mieux, dès lors, obtenir ces mandats par l'effet d'un acte spontané?

M. de Lapradelle cite le *dictum* du juge Sir William Scott dans le cas *Fox* comme exemple de l'esprit de justice internationale qui

M. HAGERUP ended with the remark that he felt the great responsibility resting on him as a member of the Committee and that he would certainly give due consideration to every proposal made with the intention of reconciling opposing opinions.

M. DE LAPRADELLE wished, before discussing the various proposals, to state that he intended to discuss the question in such a way as to arrive at a result. He also wished to emphasize the fact that the members of the Committee had no instructions or even suggestions from their governments. They had no definite policy which they must carry through. They were judges met together for deliberation.

The reasons given for the thesis opposed to his own were divided into two groups; those of M. Adatci, which were sociological, and those of Lord Phillimore. Concerning the proposal made by Mr. Root, he thought it was premature to try to compromise before making sure that real division existed.

In M. de Lapradelle's opinion the sociological line of argument of M. Adatci was contrary to the laws of sociology. M. Adatci said that, if the Court they were about to create were to be a living force, it must rely on strength. Strength was represented by the great Powers; but which were the great Powers, and how many were they? No one knew. Here was no scientific criterion.

M. de Lapradelle was content to take conscience and moral force as his criterion. If this was adopted, the principle of equality would be saved. Two States coming before the Court would always feel that they were on exactly the same footing before Justice.

If only the great Powers were represented on the Court, it would not inspire the other Powers with confidence and the great States would generally prefer to have their disputes settled by the Council than by the Court. Even if the little States agreed to submit to the political leadership of the big States, they would never agree to be dictated to in judicial matters. More justice and less force was required.

The great Powers had no need to claim representation on the Court. They would obtain it automatically. Would it not be better therefore for them to obtain those mandates spontaneously?

M. de Lapradelle quoted the dictum of Sir William Scott in the „Fox" as an example of the spirit of international justice which ought to animate international judges. He thought that

doit animer les juges internationaux. Il ne veut pas qu'on éveille chez les juges l'esprit national, en faisant d'eux des représentants de Puissances déterminées.

M. de Lapradelle s'attache à considérer plus en détail les arguments de M. Adatci et de Lord Phillimore.

Il fait d'abord valoir que le Comité du Transit ne peut être considéré comme analogue à la Cour de Justice.

Examinant ensuite la conception du juge international, tel que le comprend Lord Phillimore, il déclare se ranger à l'avis du dernier et ajoute que ce qui manque aux juges qui ne sont que des jurisconsultes, c'est l'éducation intégrale. Mais il n'est pas d'accord avec Lord Phillimore lorsque celui-ci déclare que la Cour manquerait de force, si elle ne renfermait pas de représentants des grandes Puissances. Lord Phillimore ne tient pas suffisamment compte de la Société des Nations. Si cette Société ne donne pas assez de force à la Cour elle va à un échec certain.

Il n'est pas d'accord non plus avec Lord Phillimore, là où celui-ci dit que s'il n'y a pas de juge anglais à la Cour, aucun anglais ne voudra voir sa patrie se soumettre à une sentence. M. de Lapradelle considère cet argument plutôt comme un argument politique. Le gouvernement anglais aurait des difficultés avec l'opinion publique, mais ce serait une affaire d'ordre intérieur. On voit apparaître derrière l'opinion de Lord Phillimore, la conception d'après laquelle il faut laisser à l'opinion publique la possibilité de reviser les sentences de la Cour.

M. de Lapradelle prie Lord Phillimore et M. Adatci de bien vouloir reconsidérer cette question. Il exprime sa conviction que tous les membres se rallieront à son avis sur la question essentielle de savoir si le privilège d'avoir un juge à la Cour doit être concédé à certains Etats.

Enfin, M. de Lapradelle s'adresse à Mr. Root pour lui demander son avis personnel sur les questions qui ont été discutées. Mr. Root n'a jusqu'ici présenté qu'un projet de conciliation, projet que M. de Lapradelle juge prématuré, puisqu'on ne sait pas si les opinions ont vraiment besoin d'être réconciliées. M. de Lapradelle est persuadé que Mr. Root se ralliera personnellement au principe de l'égalité qui est un des fondements de la constitution de la grande démocratie américaine.

M. LODER dit qu'après le discours de M. de Lapradelle, il ne lui reste pas grand'chose

it would be inopportune to awake the national spirit in the judges by making of them the representatives of certain Powers.

M. de Lapradelle proceeded to consider more in detail the arguments of M. Adatci and of Lord Phillimore.

In his opinion the Transit Committee could not be considered as comparable to the Court of Justice.

M. de Lapradelle, next examining Lord Phillimore's conception of the international judge, concurred and added that judges who were only jurists might not be entirely qualified. He disagreed with Lord Phillimore's statement that the Court would not have strength if it did not include representatives of the great Powers. Lord Phillimore did not take sufficiently into account the League of Nations. If the League did not supply sufficient force to the Court, it certainly would fail.

He did not agree either with Lord Phillimore's opinion that if there were not an English judge on the Court, no Englishman would like to see his country submit to a given sentence. M. de Lapradelle considered this a political argument. The English Government might have some difficulties in dealing with public opinion at home, but this would be an entirely domestic question. Behind Lord Phillimore's opinion, rose the conception of the right to let public opinion correct the judgments of the Court.

M. de Lapradelle requested Lord Phillimore and M. Adatci to reconsider the question. He felt that the members would agree with him on the important question whether the privilege of always having a judge on the Court should be granted to certain Powers.

Finally, M. de Lapradelle asked Mr. Root for his personal opinion on the questions that had been discussed. Up till now Mr. Root had only put forward a proposal for a compromise, a proposal which M. de Lapradelle thought premature, because it was uncertain that there was need for a compromise. M. de Lapradelle was convinced that Mr. Root personally would support the principle of equality which is one of the fundamental principles of the constitution of the great American democracy.

M. LODER said that after M. de Lapradelle's speech he had little to add. He was

à ajouter. Il est frappé du fait que Lord Phillimore et M. Adatci visent le même but que les autres membres du Comité; il croit dès lors; qu'on pourra arriver à une décision unanime. Lord Phillimore et M. Adatci acceptent tous les deux le principe de l'égalité des Etats, mais en même temps ils font valoir la nécessité de tenir compte de la réalité des choses. M. Loder croit qu'on pourrait arriver à concilier les opinions divergentes en établissant des garanties pour que, au cas où, dans la Cour, les représentants des petits Etats seraient en majorité, ces représentants ne contrecarrent point l'action des grandes Puissances.

M. Loder discute ensuite ce qu'a dit Lord Phillimore la veille, au sujet de l'inégalité des Etats; Lord Phillimore est d'opinion que l'égalité des Etats n'existe pas dans le Pacte de la Société des Nations. M. Loder ne peut partager cet avis. Chaque Etat n'a qu'un vote, et la Grande Bretagne ne forme pas une exception, les Dominions étant politiquement indépendants et devant, par conséquent, être considérés comme des Etats séparés. Donc, le premier article du Pacte consacre l'égalité entre les Etats.

M. Loder pense que la proposition faite par Mr. Root au cours de la séance de la veille était un peu prématurée; du reste il ne saisit pas bien la pensée de Mr. Root. Le problème actuel consiste à trouver un système qui garantisse le choix de bons juges et qui maintienne le principe de l'égalité des Etats.

M. Loder discute différents systèmes de nomination des juges; il parle d'abord de celui qui consiste à confier le choix des juges à l'Assemblée de la Société des Nations; c'est la méthode préconisée par le projet de La Haye de février dernier. M. Loder fait ressortir que dans la liste de candidats présentée par chaque Etat un tiers seulement de ces candidats appartiendrait à l'Etat chargé de faire les propositions; les deux autres tiers seraient, par la force des choses, les hommes les plus éminents du monde entier, et parmi ceux-là, il y aurait certainement des représentants des grands Etats.

M. Loder admet cependant qu'il peut y avoir un danger de coalition des représentants des Etats secondaires au sein de l'Assemblée; mais on pourrait certainement trouver le moyen d'écarter ce danger.

Une autre méthode de nomination est celle proposée par le Président, méthode qui rappelle celle recommandée par les Etats scandinaves et qui consiste à faire choisir les juges par les membres de la Cour Permanente d'Arbitrage. Cette méthode avait été longuement discutée lors

struck by the fact that Lord Phillimore and M. Adatci both sought the same end as the other members of the Committee. He thought therefore it would be possible to reach a unanimous decision. Lord Phillimore and M. Adatci accepted the principle of equality of States, but they pointed out that actual facts must receive proper consideration. M. Loder thought that it would be possible to reconcile the different opinions by establishing guarantees to ensure that in a Court where the representatives of small States would form the majority, these representatives should not oppose the activity of the great States.

M. Loder discussed next what Lord Phillimore had said the day before concerning the inequality of States; Lord Phillimore was of opinion that the equality of States did not exist in the Covenant. M. Loder disagreed. Each State had but one vote and Great Britain was no exception, the Dominions being politically independent and, therefore, having to be considered as separate States. So, Article 1 of the Covenant upheld equality between States.

M. Loder considered that Mr. Root's proposal put forward at the preceding meeting was slightly premature. It was also not quite clear to him what Mr. Root's intention was. The question at issue was, to find a system which would ensure good judges, possessing all the necessary qualifications of character and knowledge, and would maintain the principle of equality between States.

M. Loder proceeded to consider possible systems of nomination of judges. One system would be to confer the power of choosing judges on the Assembly of the League of Nations. This was the system recommended by the Hague Plan of last February. M. Loder called attention to the fact that in the list of candidates presented by each State, a third only of the candidates would be nationals of the State making the proposals; the other two thirds would be by the nature of things the most eminent men of all the world, and among these there certainly would be representatives of the great Powers.

M. Loder admitted, however, that this plan might involve the danger of a coalition of the representatives of the secondary States in the Assembly. Means to avert this difficulty, however, might be found.

Another method of nomination was that proposed by the President, similar in form to the recommendations of the Scandinavian countries, to have the members of the Permanent Court

de la Conférence de février, et elle avait été rejetée pour la seule raison qu'on craignait qu'elle ne fût pas adoptée par l'Assemblée. Si, comme semble l'indiquer l'attitude du Président, cette crainte n'est pas fondée, on pourrait reprendre la discussion.

M. Loder est convaincu qu'on pourrait arriver à une décision par cette méthode, ou par une autre du même genre.

LORD PHILLIMORE se sent désarmé par l'hommage adressé à la magistrature anglaise.

Il explique que la veille, en disant qu'il était le délégué britannique, il s'est servi d'une expression qui peut être mal interprétée; il désire faire entendre qu'il n'avait pas reçu d'instructions de son Gouvernement.

Il commencera ses remarques sur le sujet actuellement en discussion par un paradoxe: c'est la Grande Bretagne qui a comparativement le plus souffert de la guerre; jamais jusqu'ici elle n'avait ressenti une commotion telle que celle qui vient d'ébranler jusqu'au cœur le pays tout entier.

Lord Phillimore dit ensuite que s'il se trouve ici, c'est seulement pour travailler à éviter à l'avenir une catastrophe pareille. Il a été président de la commission anglaise qui a préparé le premier plan de la Société des Nations. Ce plan était à certains égards plus complet que celui qu'on a adopté, et il regrette de ne pas être autorisé à le communiquer. — Il est donc venu pour aider à construire une partie de l'édifice de la Paix. A son avis, la paix est plus importante que la justice.

Le PRESIDENT rappelle l'adage: *„justitia et pax osculatae sunt"*.

LORD PHILLIMORE ajoute qu'il a suivi avec le plus grand intérêt l'exposé de M. Altamira. Il respecte son point de vue, mais ne peut s'empêcher de se souvenir que l'Espagne est le pays de Don Quichote.

Lord Phillimore parle ensuite de la difficulté de trouver de bons juges. Une Cour composée de jurisconsultes venus de toutes les parties du monde peut être excellente, mais elle aura toujours ce défaut que les mérites des membres ne seront pas connus, par exemple en Angleterre. On peut très bien être convaincu qu'elle comprend de bons jurisconsultes sans être persuadé qu'elle comprend de bons juges.

Lord Phillimore veut que derrière la Cour il y ait la force: „I want the Sheriff behind me".

S'il arrive qu'une des parties refuse de se soumettre à une sentence qui lui déplait, on

of Arbitration choose the judges. This method had been discussed at length at the February Conference, and had been rejected for the sole reason that it was feared the Assembly would not adopt it. If, as the President's attitude seemed to indicate, this fear was unfounded, the method might be reconsidered.

M. Loder was convinced that a decision could be reached by this or a similar method.

LORD PHILLIMORE said that he felt quite disarmed by the compliments paid to the English Bench.

He felt that he had used an expression liable to misinterpretation at the preceding meeting. He had said that he was a delegate of Great Britain. He wished to explain that he had received no instructions from his Government.

He opened his remarks on the subject under discussion with a paradox: Comparatively speaking, Great Britain had suffered most from the war: never before had she been convulsed by such a disturbance as now had shaken the very foundations of the entire country.

His purpose at this conference was to try to avoid another such catastrophe. He had been President of a Committee in England which drafted the first plan for the League of Nations. This plan was more complete in some respects than that actually adopted and he regretted that he was not authorised to communicate it to the Committee. — He had come here to aid in establishing peace. In his own view, Peace was even more important than Justice.

The PRESIDENT recalled the adage *"justitia et pax osculatae sunt"*.

LORD PHILLIMORE said that he had followed with great interest M. Altamira's proposals, that he respected M. Altamira's view, but that he could not forget that Spain was the land of Don Quixote.

Lord Phillimore then spoke of the difficulty of finding good judges. A Court composed of jurisconsults from all parts of the world might be excellent, but he feared that their merits would not be known, for instance in England. One might be convinced that it included good jurisconsults without being convinced that it included good judges.

Lord Phillimore wanted force to back the Court: "I want the Sheriff behind me".

If a decision was resisted by any State, the League of Nations should intervene. Failure to comply with a sentence constituted an act of

aura recours à la Société des Nations. La non-exécution de la sentence constitue un acte de guerre contre les Membres de la Société. Mais ce n'est pas encore la guerre, et c'est là le point faible. Il y aura toujours des hésitations. La formule du projet auquel Lord Phillimore a fait allusion, était bien plus nette: elle créait dans un cas de ce genre l'état de guerre; mais cette formule a été affaiblie. C'est pour cette raison que Lord Phillimore veut intéresser les grandes Puissances à l'œuvre de la Cour; ce sont elles qui font la police du monde, et, en les obligeant à avoir un intérêt direct, on les amènerait à agir, le cas échéant. Il y a en effet des questions pour le règlement desquelles les grandes Puissances ne seront pas disposées à engager volontairement leur force. Il cite un mot de Bismarck, et donne en exemple certains cas, susceptibles de se présenter dans les circonstances actuelles, et dans lesquels les grandes Puissances pourraient sous l'influence de l'opinion publique être dans l'impossibilité d'agir pour appuyer une sentence de la Cour si elles n'y étaient pas représentées.

M. DE LAPRADELLE demande si la même situation ne se produirait pas au cas où les juges des grandes Puissances se trouveraient faire partie de la minorité, quand la Cour aurait pris une décision.

LORD PHILLIMORE admet le bien-fondé de la question, mais dit qu'il faut se contenter de limiter le danger dans la mesure du possible. Il fait observer combien il est nécessaire aux magistrats de puiser à toutes les sources la force requise pour l'exécution de leurs fonctions. En vue de donner au nouveau tribunal toute la force et toute l'autorité possibles, il désire donner, au sein du tribunal, une position spéciale aux grandes Puissances.

Lord Phillimore rappelle la proposition du Président de faire représenter à la Cour les différents systèmes juridiques. Il admet qu'on arriverait par cette voie au même résultat que celui qu'il avait proposé, mais ce serait une voie difficile et détournée.

Lord Phillimore dit qu'il a cru comprendre du discours de M. de Lapradelle que celui-ci voulait dire qu'il y a déjà une majorité qui veut arriver à un résultat, mais que d'autre part il y a une minorité obstinée; il exprime pour sa part le désir qu'il n'y ait pas une majorité qui s'obstine.

Lord Phillimore considère ensuite la question de la méthode d'élection; il dit que le

war against the Members of the League of Nations, but war did not necessarily follow — that was the weak point. There would always be hesitation. The English draft was clearer: according to it, such a situation would constitute a state of war. This clause, however, was weakened. For this reason Lord Phillimore wished to interest the great Powers in the work of the Court. They are the police of the world, and in obliging them to have a direct interest, they would be compelled to act when the situation demanded. Practically there were questions for the settlement of which the great Powers would not be disposed to act of their own volition. He quoted Bismarck, and gave hypothetical cases in which the great Powers would be prevented by public opinion from taking action in support of a judgment of the Court, unless they were represented on it.

M. DE LAPRADELLE raised the question whether, if the great Powers were among the majority on the Court when it decided a question, the same situation would not arise?

LORD PHILLIMORE admitted the logic of the question, but said that one must be content to confine the dangers within the narrowest possible limits. He pointed out how necessary it was that the magistrates should borrow from all sources the force required for the exercise of their functions. In order to give all possible strength to the tribunal, also to make the tribunal as authoritative as possible in every way, he wished to give a special position to the great Powers.

Lord Phillimore referred to the President's scheme which suggested including on the Court representatives of the different systems of law. He admitted that the same end might be achieved by this means, but he foresaw that it would be a roundabout way.

Lord Phillimore said that from M. de Lapradelle's speech, he had drawn the impression that M. de Lapradelle wished to say that a majority already existed who wished to obtain a certain result but that there was a tenacious minority; — he hoped there would not be a tenacious majority.

Lord Phillimore next considered the

système des élections indirectes n'est pas acceptable.

A l'appui de son opinion à cet égard, il montre l'évolution qu'ont suivie les règles adoptées pour les élections présidentielles en Amérique. On a pensé, au commencement, afin d'éviter une élection directe du Président par le peuple, former un corps électoral composé des citoyens les plus pondérés qui, agissant de leur propre volonté, et sans avoir les mains liées, choisiraient pour Président le meilleur citoyen. Mais en fait on s'est écarté presque tout de suite de cette voie, et maintenant les électeurs ne sont que des chiffres.

Au sujet du système de l'élection par les membres de la Cour Permanente d'Arbitrage Lord Phillimore dit que ces membres ne jouissent pas comme tels d'une grande autorité, que personne ne sait au juste qui sont les membres, et que les membres ignorent parfois eux-mêmes leur situation. Il croit qu'il vaudrait mieux confier le choix des juges aux gouvernements. Sans doute, il est l'avocat du principe de l'égalité des Etats, mais il croit qu'il est avant tout nécessaire de donner de la force à la Cour.

Lord Phillimore ne sait pas s'il a bien compris le système proposé par Mr. Root. Il croit que ce système est le suivant: le Conseil de la Société des Nations dresse une liste de candidats et la communique aux gouvernements; puis les gouvernements dressent leurs listes de candidats. Ces dernières sont combinées par le Secrétaire-Général de la Société des Nations en une liste unique sur laquelle il indique le nombre des voix obtenues par chaque candidat. Si la liste des candidats ayant eu le plus de voix coïncide avec la liste dressée par le Conseil, l'élection sera terminée; sinon, les deux listes seront déférées à un Comité de Conciliation, composé d'un nombre égal de membres du Conseil et de membres de l'Assemblée. La liste définitive, dressée par ce Comité, sera soumise à un vote formel du Conseil et de l'Assemblée.

M. RICCI-BUSATTI pense que M. Adatci, en s'appuyant sur l'exemple du Comité des Communications et du Transit, a apporté à la discussion un élément très utile, parce qu'il amène le Comité à considérer sous tous ses aspects l'organisation de la Société des Nations et les relations entre ses divers organes. Le Comité du Transit et la Cour Permanente de Justice seront deux organes de la Société des Nations, mais, tandis que le Comité dépendra du Conseil auquel il se rattache et dont il ne sera qu'un des instruments techniques, lui permettant d'at-

method of election. He declared that the indirect method of election was not acceptable.

In support of this opinion, he traced the stages through which this method had gone in American presidential elections. Originally it was thought that, to avoid the direct election of the President by the people, an electoral body composed of the most levelheaded citizens should proceed freely and according to its own judgment to choose the best citizen for President. But in practice this method was almost immediately departed from, and now the electors are nothing more than so many figures.

Concerning the system of election by members of the Permanent Court of Arbitration, he said that these members as such did not exercise any great authority, that no one knew exactly who were the members, and that the members themselves sometimes were not conscious of their membership. He thought it better to confer the choice on the governments. Unquestionably he was the advocate of the equality of States, but he thought that it was of primary importance to give strength to the Court.

Lord Phillimore was not entirely certain that he had understood Mr. Root's proposal. In his opinion, this system was as follows: the Council of the League of Nations prepares a list of candidates and communicates it to the governments, then the governments prepare their lists of candidates. These latter lists are combined into one list by the Secretary General of the League, on which list is indicated the number of nominations obtained by each candidate. If the list of candidates receiving most votes coincides with the list prepared by the Council, they are duly elected; otherwise the two lists will be referred to a Conciliation Committee composed of an equal number of members of the Council and of the Assembly. The final list prepared by this Committee will be submitted to a formal vote of the Council and the Assembly.

M. RICCI-BUSATTI thought that M. Adatci, by introducing the example of the Committee for Communication and Transit, had contributed to the discussion a very valuable point, for the reason that the members of the Committee are led by it to consider in all its aspects the organisation of the League of Nations and the relations between its various organs. Both the Committee of Transit and the Permanent Court would be organs of the League of Nations, but while the Committee would depend upon the Council, as one of its many technical branches for

teindre les buts qui sont de son ressort particulier, la Cour doit être indépendante et se rattacher à la Société dans son ensemble; cette dernière représente le „pouvoir judiciaire" qu'il faut bien distinguer du „pouvoir administratif", conformément aux principes qui sont à la base de toute constitution moderne.

M. Ricci-Busatti reprend l'objection opposée par M. Hagerup à Lord Phillimore, lorsque celui-ci voulait, pour étayer la Cour, une force matérielle; il dit qu'au contraire la force dont on aura besoin sera surtout une force morale; il est disposé à admettre, avec Lord Phillimore, que la paix est plus importante que la justice; sauf à bien déterminer leurs rapports. Le but de la Société des Nations est d'assurer la paix et la coopération internationale; le but de la Cour permanente sera d'assurer la justice entre les Etats, et de contribuer par là à maintenir la paix. Il ne faut pas exagérer le rôle de la Cour à cet égard; on ne doit pas s'attendre à ce qu'elle prévienne ou évite toutes les guerres: telle n'a pas été jusqu'ici la tâche de la Cour d'Arbitrage. Les grands conflits politiques d'où pourrait sortir une guerre, seront portés devant le Conseil ou l'Assemblée de la Société; la Cour doit assurer l'empire du droit dans les relations internationales ordinaires; on la compromettrait en lui demandant davantage.

M. Ricci-Busatti, après avoir passé en revue les diverses méthodes proposées pour l'élection des juges, se rallie à la méthode préconisée par le Président, estimant que le collège électoral doit de préférence être la Cour d'Arbitrage, qui est un corps judiciaire, et non pas l'Assemblée de la Société des Nations, qui a un caractère politique trop marqué. Cette méthode n'est point en contradiction avec celle préconisée par la Commission italienne, qui confie aux Etats la nomination des membres de la Cour. Rien ne s'oppose en effet à ce qu'ils exercent cette faculté par l'entremise de leurs représentants respectifs figurant actuellement sur la liste des arbitres. M. Ricci-Busatti se réserve le droit de discuter ultérieurement les détails de l'organisation dont il s'agit.

Mr. ROOT, en raison de l'heure avancée, cède la parole au Président qui n'a que quelques mots à dire.

Le PRESIDENT estime qu'il faut tenir compte, non seulement de l'égalité des Etats, mais aussi de l'importance qu'il y a à assurer aux grands

the attainment of its ends, the Court would be independent and would only be related to the League of Nations as a whole. It represents the "judicial power" which must be distinguished from the "administrative power", in accordance with the principles underlying all modern constitutions.

M. Ricci-Busatti repeated M. Hagerup's objection against Lord Phillimore's view when the latter wished to support the Court by a material force; he said that, on the contrary, the power needed was above all a moral power. M. Ricci-Busatti agreed with Lord Phillimore's belief that peace is more important than justice — only their relative values should be accurately determined. He said that the aim of the League of Nations is to ensure peace and international co-operation; the aim of the Permanent Court will be to ensure justice between States and thereby to contribute to the maintenance of Peace. The rôle of the Court must not be exaggerated in this respect: one must not expect to prevent all future wars. Such has not been up to this time the task of the Court of Arbitration. The great political conflicts from which a war might arise would be taken before the Council or the Assembly of the League of Nations. The Court must establish the reign of law in ordinary international relations. One would only weaken it by demanding more from it.

M. Ricci-Busatti proceeded to consider the methods proposed for the election of the judges. He shared the President's opinion: the electoral body must be preferably the Court of Arbitration (which was a judicial body) and not the Assembly of the League of Nations which had too marked a political character. This method was not in contradiction with that proposed by the Italian governmental Commission, which vested in the States the power of nominating judges. Nothing prevented, indeed, their exercising this authority through their respective representatives who appeared on the present list of arbitrators. M. Ricci-Busatti deferred until later the discussion of the details of the proposed plan.

Mr. ROOT, because of the advanced hour, yielded to the President, who had some short observations to make.

The PRESIDENT thought that not only the equality of States must be considered but also the need to ensure effective representation of

Etats une représentation effective à la Cour. A cet égard il se range à l'avis de Lord Phillimore. Il est vrai que Lord Phillimore apprécie peu l'élection à deux degrés. Mais il ne s'agit pas ici de simples électeurs; l'élection serait faite par des organes constitués en vue d'autres fins que l'élection, qui ne serait pour eux qu'une tâche secondaire.

Le Président attire l'attention du Comité sur le problème de la création d'une Haute Cour de Justice Internationale. Les conditions dans lesquelles on a proposé à la Conférence de Paris d'instituer et de faire fonctionner une telle Cour *ex post facto* ont amené deux Etats à faire leurs réserves à ce sujet. Ces réserves n'ont pas de raison d'être, en présence d'une institution destinée à fonctionner dans l'avenir et poursuivant une fin nettement définie: la répression des délits contre l'ordre public international et le droit des gens universel. Il n'est pas douteux que déjà l'existence seule d'une telle Cour exercerait une heureuse influence préventive sur la perpétration de ces délits. Il est de tout intérêt que le Comité prenne l'initiative d'organiser et de préciser les bases de cette Haute Cour.

S'adressant à Mr. Root, le Président se prononce contre l'assimilation de la Cour, quant à son organisation, aux organes politiques de la Société des Nations. Pareille assimilation serait sans nul doute impopulaire, et l'impopularité atteindrait le Conseil de la Société, ce qu'il faut avant tout éviter.

Le Président expose les avantages du système qu'il a proposé concernant la nomination des juges. Les idées que contient sa proposition ne sont pas précisément nouvelles, comme on peut s'en convaincre en se rapportant aux discussions de la Deuxième Conférence de la Paix et aux projets des pays scandinaves, entre autres. En tout cas, elles ont l'avantage d'offrir un moyen de sauvegarder l'égalité juridique des Etats tout en donnant aux grands Etats la certitude qu'ils seront représentés à la Cour.

the great States on the Court. In this respect he agreed with Lord Phillimore. The President thought that this might be achieved by means of indirect election. He knew that Lord Phillimore did not like this method for the nomination of judges, but in this case it was not a question of having only ordinary electors; the election would be undertaken by bodies created for purposes other than this duty, which would be secondary.

The President called the attention of the members to the problem of creating a High Court of International Justice. The conditions under which it was proposed at the Paris Conference to establish and to set in operation such a Court *ex post facto,* gave rise to certain reservations on the part of two States. These reservations had no *raison d'être* in the presence of an institution proposed for the future with a clearly defined object: the punishment of offenses against international public order and the universal law of nations. There is no doubt that the existence alone of such a Court would exert a beneficial preventative influence on the perpetration of such offences. In any case it was important that the Committee should take the initiative in the organisation of this High Court and in laying down the principles on which it should be based.

Speaking to Mr. Root, the President declared that he opposed the Court in respect to its organisation being likened to the political organs of the League of Nations. This would be without doubt unpopular, and unpopularity would react on the Council and League; this must be avoided.

The President showed the advantages of the system proposed by him for naming the judges. The ideas contained in his proposal were not exactly new, as might be inferred from the discussions of the second Peace Conference and from the Scandinavian projects etc. In any case, they offered a means of safeguarding the legal equality of States, and yet gave the great States an assurance of representation on the Court.

Mr. ROOT demande au Président de vouloir bien formuler par écrit les idées exposées par lui l'autre jour et d'après lesquelles la liberté du choix serait limitée par l'obligation de faire représenter au sein de la Cour les différents grands systèmes juridiques existant dans le monde. Mr. Root ne voit pas comment on pourrait obliger, dans la pratique, les électeurs à restreindre ainsi leur choix. Il serait heureux qu'on lui soumette un texte formel à ce sujet.

Mr. ROOT asked the President kindly to put in writing the ideas expressed by him on a preceding day, according to which liberty of choice would be limited by the necessity of representing on the Court the various legal systems. Mr. Root did not see how, in practice, the electors could be made to limit their choice in this way. He would be glad to have a formal statement of the project.

Le PRESIDENT préparera pour lundi prochain le texte demandé et le soumettra à la discussion du Comité.

M. DE LAPRADELLE fait toutes ses réserves sur l'interprétation de l'expression „systèmes juridiques du monde".

La séance est levée à 12.40 de l'après-midi.

Le Président:
(signé) Brn. DESCAMPS.

Le Secrétaire-Général:
(signé) D. ANZILOTTI.

The PRESIDENT said he would prepare the document asked for, and would submit it on Monday for the consideration of the Committee.

M. DE LAPRADELLE reserved his opinion concerning the construction of the expression "legal systems of the world".

The meeting closed at 12.40 p.m.

The President:
(signed) Brn. DESCAMPS.

The Secretary-General:
(signed) D. ANZILOTTI.

5IÈME SÉANCE, (non-publique), tenue au Palais de la Paix, à La Haye, le 21 juin 1920.

Présidence de M. le BARON DESCAMPS.

Sont présents: tous les membres du Comité (à l'exception de M. Bevilaqua); Mr. James Brown Scott; les secrétaires particuliers de M. le Baron Descamps et de M. Adatci; les membres du Secrétariat.

La séance est ouverte à 9.35 heures du matin.

Le PRESIDENT fait savoir au Comité que Sa Majesté la Reine des Pays-Bas s'est montrée très sensible à l'hommage que le Président Lui a rendu au nom du Comité, dans son discours lors de la séance d'ouverture. Sa Majesté la Reine sera heureuse de recevoir les membres du Comité. Le Président propose au Comité de demander une audience. Cette proposition est acceptée.

Le Président donne quelques explications sur le „Projet d'organisation de la justice internationale" en sept articles, qu'il a composé pour satisfaire à la demande faite par Mr. Root au cours de la dernière séance. (Voir Annexe No. 1).

Il rappelle que tous les membres sont également convaincus de la nécessité d'aboutir. Pour cela, il faut d'abord la bonne volonté et ensuite une méthode, c'est à dire un ensemble de règles directrices. On trouvera une base solide et positive d'organisation dans la Cour Permanente d'Arbitrage actuelle. Il faut procéder plutôt par évolution que par révolution, et non pas renverser un système existant. Il s'agit de concilier, tout en adoptant cette base, le principe de l'égalité des Etats avec la nécessité de donner aux grands Etats une représentation dans la Cour.

Le Président donne lecture des premiers articles de son projet, en faisant observer que la rédaction se rapproche autant que possible du Projet de Convention de 1907. Un simple coup d'œil sur la liste des arbitres internationaux fait voir la haute valeur des personnalités que les Etats ont designées, et, en même temps, combien elles sont qualifiées pour choisir les juges à la Cour de Justice. Quant à l'Assemblée de la Société des Nations, nous ne savons pas d'avance comment elle sera composée, étant donné l'époque encore troublée où nous vivons. En chargeant

5TH MEETING (Private), held at the Peace Palace, the Hague, on June 21st, 1920.

BARON DESCAMPS in the chair.

Present: all members of the Committee (with the exception of M. Bevilaqua); Mr. James Brown Scott; the private secretaries of Baron Descamps and of M. Adatci; the members of the Secretariat.

The meeting opened at 9.35 a.m.

The PRESIDENT informed the Committee that Her Majesty the Queen of the Netherlands had expressed her thanks for the homage paid to her by the President in the name of the Committee, in his speech at the opening meeting. Her Majesty would be pleased to receive the Members of the Committee. The President proposed that the Committee should ask for an audience. This proposal was adopted.

The President gave some explanation concerning the "Project for the organisation of international justice", in 7 articles, which he had drawn up in response to the request made by Mr. Root during the last meeting. (See Annex 1).

He pointed out that all the members of the Committee are equally convinced of the necessity of achieving success. For this, two things were necessary: first of all goodwill, and secondly: a method of work, that is to say, a number of governing rules. The present Permanent Court of Arbitration would be a suitable and positive basis of organisation. Progress must be made rather by evolution than by revolution, not by throwing aside a system already in existence. The principle of equality of States, adopted as a basis, must be reconciled with the necessity of giving the great Powers representation on the Court.

The President read some of the first articles of his project and observed that the wording corresponded as nearly as possible to the Draft Convention of 1907. A single glance at the list of international arbitrators would show the outstanding merits of the persons appointed by the various States, and at the same time would show how well they were qualified to choose the judges for the Court of Justice. As regards the Assembly of the League of

les arbitres internationaux de nommer les juges, on ne privera pas les Etats de justes garanties, car ce sont eux qui désignent ces arbitres.

On s'est demandé s'il est nécessaire de choisir les juges parmi les arbitres. Le Président signale que cette question a été examinée en 1907. Le Projet de Convention de 1907 stipule que les juges seront choisis, autant que possible, parmi les membres de la Cour Permanente d'Arbitrage.

Il faut encore envisager la grave question de la représentation des grands Etats dans la juridiction internationale, et à ce sujet le Président estime qu'il importe de stipuler que les grands systèmes juridiques du monde soient représentés dans la Cour. C'est là une idée d'origine américaine: le Président rappelle les paroles de M. Choate, qui, lors de la Conférence de 1907, s'est prononcé dans ce sens (voir Actes et Documents, Tome II, p. 311, dernier alinéa). Il cite ensuite l'admirable rapport de Mr. James Brown Scott. Le Président donne lecture de quelques extraits de ce rapport. On n'a pas abouti en 1907, parce qu'on a trop oublié l'organisation possible, en pratique, d'une telle garantie. Elle se concilie remarquablement avec la représentation, au sein de la Cour, de l'Angleterre, de la France, de l'Italie, des Etats-Unis d'Amérique et du Japon. Et elle est de nature à donner à la Cour l'aspect mondial qui lui convient, en même temps qu'elle facilite un meilleur jugement des affaires internationales.

En résumant, le Président répète que son projet est en realité fondé sur des idées qui ont déjà été présentées et acceptées antérieurement. Il se rend très bien compte, qu'en général les premières propositions concentrent sur elles toutes les objections. Il n'a cependant pas hesité à formuler un projet, étant donné l'esprit dans lequel travaille le Comité.

Le Projet de 1907 renferme deux lacunes: la composition de la Cour et sa compétence n'ont pas été réglées. Ce sont ces lacunes qu'il faut maintenant s'efforcer de combler.

En ce qui concerne le premier point, l'organisation, tous les Etats demeurent distributivement et à titre égal les électeurs initiaux des juges, puisqu'ils nomment directement les membres de la Cour d'Arbitrage existante. Et le mandat confié à ceux-ci de pourvoir à la représentation dans la Cour nouvelle des principaux systèmes juridiques du monde est de nature à donner, aux grandes Puissances spécialement, tous les apaisements légitimes, en assurant une base vraiment mondiale à l'institution nouvelle.

Nations, one did not at present know how this body would be composed, having regard to the troublous times of the present. By entrusting the international arbitrators with the appointment of the judges, the States would not be deprived of what is due to them, because the arbitrators were chosen by them.

The question had been put whether it was necessary to choose the judges from amongst the arbitrators. The President stated that this question already had been considered in 1907; the Draft of 1907 stipulated that the judges should be chosen as far as possible from among the members of the Permanent Court of Arbitration.

The important question of the representation of the great States in the International Court remained to be considered; and in this respect the President considered a stipulation necessary to the effect that the great legal systems of the world should be represented in the Court. This idea was of American origin. The President recalled the words of Mr. Choate, who at the Conference of 1907 put forward the same view. (See "Actes et Documents", Vol. II, page 311, last paragraph) and also the admirable report of Mr. James Brown Scott. The President read some extracts from this report. Success was not achieved in 1907 for the reason that the possible organisation, in practice, of such a guarantee was too much forgotten. It reconciled itself remarkably with the representation within the Court of England, France, Italy, the United States of America, and of Japan. By its nature, it gave to the Court the world-aspect which it needed, at the same time expediting a better settlement of international affairs.

In conclusion, the President repeated that his plan was founded, in reality, on ideas which already had been presented and formerly accepted. He was quite aware of the fact that in general initial proposals attract all the objections. Nevertheless, he did not hesitate to draw up a plan, knowing as he did the spirit in which the Committee worked.

The 1907 Draft involved two omissions: the Court's composition and its competence were not settled. It was this hiatus which now demanded to be bridged.

Concerning the first point, the organisation, all the States remained, distributively and on an equal footing, the initial electors of judges since they name directly the members of the existing Court of Arbitration. The mandate, imposing upon this body the task of giving representation on the Court to the main legal

systems of the world, had the character of according to the great Powers all just satisfaction by providing a truly world-wide foundation for the new institution.

LORD PHILLIMORE remercie le Président de l'exposé qu'il vient de faire.

Mr. ROOT déclare qu'il apprécie hautement la façon très claire dont le Président a répondu au désir qu'il avait exprimé lui-même, de voir formuler le plan exposé. Mr. Root étudiera ce plan avec le plus grand soin.

Lors de la dernière séance, Mr. Root avait eu l'intention de faire quelques observations théoriques sur le problème qui se pose devant le Comité et de donner ensuite quelques exemples des nécessités imposées au Comité par la tâche qui lui est assignée.

Les membres du Comité ont posé deux principes auxquels ils peuvent tous se rallier: 1) le but de la Cour qu'il s'agit de créer est la réalisation de la justice; 2) l'égalité des Etats doit être sauvegardée. — L'application du premier principe équivaut à l'adaptation de moyens à une fin — de moyens humains à une fin divine. En appliquant l'autre principe, il est nécessaire d'examiner si ce principe couvre la transaction qu'on est en train d'entreprendre. Ce principe veut dire seulement que les Etats sont égaux en tant qu'ils ont tous le droit souverain de contrôler leurs propres actions sans en rendre compte aux autres. Ce droit s'exerce notamment par la faculté d'accepter ou de refuser les arrangements que va proposer le Comité. En procédant à la création d'une Cour, on dépasse les limites des droits souverains. En nommant des juges qui auront le droit de limiter, par leurs jugements, les droits souverains des Etats, on n'exerce pas des droits de souveraineté. Donc, le droit de faire cette nomination doit avoir une autre source; cette source est le consentement mutuel des Etats.

Il faut par conséquent se demander si ce consentement peut être donné, et dans quelles conditions. Dans cet ordre d'idées, on ne peut pas prendre seulement en considération l'égalité des Etats. On sort du domaine de cette égalité pour entrer dans un autre domaine, où tout fait relevant doit entrer en ligne de compte.

Mr. Root prend un exemple: l'Union Postale Universelle. Les Etats qui ont conclu cette Convention étaient incontestablement égaux, mais néanmoins, la Convention consacre une classification des Etats sur la base de leurs ressources et de leurs activités commerciales et autres. La même inégalité a été transportée au sein de la

LORD PHILLIMORE thanked the President for the explanation which he had just made.

Mr. ROOT expressed his appreciation of the clear way in which the President had complied with his request to see the former's proposal formulated. Mr. Root said that he would study this plan with sympathetic appreciation.

At the last meeting, Mr. Root had intended to make some observations upon the theory of the subject now before the Committee, and to make some references to the necessities imposed upon the Committee by the task entrusted to it.

There were two fundamental principles laid down by the members of the Committee, with which all agreed: firstly that the object of the projected Court is to ensure justice, and secondly that the equality of States should be safeguarded. The application of the first principle amounted to an adaptation of means to an end: human means to secure a divine end. In applying the second principle, it was necessary to consider whether the principle covers the transaction we are going to undertake. The principle only meant that States are equal in so far as they have the sovereign right to control their actions without having to account for them to others. This right applied, especially, to the faculty of accepting or refusing the proposals to be made by the Committee. When one came to the creation of a Court, one would infringe on sovereign rights. To appoint judges who are to have the right to make decisions limiting sovereign rights of States, was not an exercise of the powers of sovereignty. Accordingly, the right to make these appointments must have another source: this source was the mutual consent of States.

Consequently we must determine whether such consent can be given, and under what conditions. In this connection, one must not consider only the equality of States. The field to which this principle applies had been passed, and one had come to a state of affairs in which all reasonable considerations must be taken into account as relevant.

Mr. Root took as an example the International Postal Union. The States who made that Convention were undeniably equal, but nevertheless the Convention classed the States according to their resources and commercial and other

Société des Nations, qui, à certains égards, a adopté une classification analogue.

En renonçant au principe de l'unanimité, caractéristique des Conférences diplomatiques, et en soumettant tout litige à la décision d'une majorité des Etats, on se soumet à une règle autre que celle de l'égalité des Etats.

Tous les Etats peuvent, sans rien abandonner de leur souveraineté, se mettre d'accord pour assurer la justice; mais pareil accord ne veut rien dire, à moins que les moyens pratiques donnant le plus de chance de réaliser la justice ne soient trouvés. Le but est d'assurer une institution qui primera la force. Il a toujours existé une division en grands et petits Etats: c'est la force des grandes Puissances qu'il s'agit d'abattre. Les petites nations sentent que leur vie est en danger si le règne de la justice n'est pas assuré. La Cour dominera les grands et protégera les petits. Donc, toutes les nations ne sont pas dans la même situation en présence du problème actuel; les grandes Puissances font de grands sacrifices, les petites Puissances ne sacrifient presque rien, mais obtiennent une protection dont les grands Etats n'ont pas besoin.

Or, un problème qui implique une différence entre les divers Etats ne peut être résolu en appliquant le principe de l'égalité; une Cour composée d'après ce principe mettrait les grandes Puissances à la merci des Etats qui donnent peu et reçoivent beaucoup. Il ne faut pas oublier que les Etats sont composés d'êtres humains; ils sont divisés intérieurement entre un parti militaire et un parti pacifique; ce qu'il faut faire, c'est proposer un plan qui puisse, dans chaque pays, donner le dessus aux principes de Paix et de Justice.

Le principe de l'égalité en a rencontré un autre: le développement de la démocratie, développement qui a fait naître l'idée de l'indépendance des individus. Le projet du Comité concernant l'institution d'une Cour permanente sera soumis non pas aux Ministères des Affaires Etrangères, mais aux démocraties qui les contrôlent; et les individus qui constituent ces démocraties seront toujours persuadés que leur voix doit avoir autant de poids que celle de n'importe quel citoyen d'un autre pays. Dans ces conditions, il serait impossible de proposer un plan selon lequel, par exemple, les cent millions d'habitants des Etats-Unis consentiraient à voir limiter les droits souverains de leur patrie par une Cour où le vote du demi-million de citoyens du Honduras entraînerait pour leur pays la perte du litige.

Il ne faut pas perdre de vue que la question qui va être posée devant l'opinion publique,

activities. The same inequality had been transferred to the League of Nations, which for some matters has adopted a similar classification.

Directly one departed from the basis of unanimous agreement, which is a characteristic of diplomatic conferences, and submits any case to the decision of a majority of States, other rules than that of the equality of States became applicable.

All States could, without giving up any of their sovereign rights, enter into an agreement to ensure justice; but that meant nothing, unless practical means, giving all assurance possible that justice be done, are found. The object was to create an institution which will prevent the use of force. A division into great and small States has always existed. It is the power of the great States which is to be curbed. The little nations feel that their life is in danger, if justice is not established. The Court was to dominate the great Powers and protect the small ones. All nations, therefore, were not on the same footing with regard to this problem; the large Powers made great sacrifice; the little Powers sacrificed practically nothing, and on the other hand obtained a protection of which the great Powers were not in need.

A problem which entails a distinction of this kind between the various States could not be solved by the application of the principle of equality; the formation of the Court on these lines would put the great Powers at the mercy of those States which give little and receive much. It must not be forgotten that the States are composed of human beings, divided among themselves into two groups: one military, one pacifist; the problem to be solved was how to give the upper hand in each country to the principles of Peace and Justice.

The principle of equality had met with another principle: the development of democracy, a development which had given rise to the idea of the independence of the individual. The Committee's plan for a Permanent Court would be submitted, not to Ministries of Foreign Affairs, but to the democracies which control them; and the individuals of which these democracies are composed would always hold the view that each of their votes carries as much weight as the vote of any citizen of another country. Under these circumstances, it would be impossible to put forward a plan in which, for instance, the hundred million inhabitants of the United States would have to consent to have the sovereign rights of their country limited by a Court on which the vote of the half million inhabitants of Honduras

dans les grands pays, c'est la question de la création d'un pouvoir nouveau, accordant aux représentants d'autres Etats un certain droit de contrôle sur l'activité des divers Etats.

Mr. Root ne veut pas paraître pessimiste, ni critiquer aucun pays, mais il croit devoir faire remarquer que les Etats dont la civilisation est la moins avancée, auront aussi leur vote pour la constitution de la Cour, alors même que leur système juridique retarde tellement sur les systèmes généralement acceptés, qu'ils ont dû se soumettre au régime des tribunaux extra-territoriaux.

Mr. Root désire ajouter qu'à son avis l'esprit de ces pays arriérés ne sera pas entièrement dégagé de toute idée préconçue, lorsqu'ils viendront contribuer à la constitution de la Cour. Il fait observer en outre qu'on aura sans doute beaucoup de peine à trouver les hommes vraiment dignes de siéger à la Cour et qu'il faudra insister auprès d'eux pour qu'ils consentent à abandonner leur foyer et leurs occupations, tandis que les hommes moins désirables chercheront par tous les moyens à obtenir la fonction de juge. Le monde n'est pas foncièrement changé.

Mais les gouvernements ne peuvent pas demander à leurs peuples d'accepter une Cour qui sera composée en partie de membres appartenant à cette dernière catégorie. Si les gouvernements abandonnent une partie de leurs pouvoirs souverains il leur faut veiller à ce que ces pouvoirs ne soient cédés que contre de sûres garanties.

Pour les raisons qu'il vient d'exposer, Mr. Root croit qu'il faut concilier d'une façon ou d'une autre les opinions opposées; sinon, une Cour Permanente n'est pas possible.

Le PRESIDENT dit qu'il croit désirable que les membres du Comité soumettent respectivement leurs propositions, puis donnent leur avis sur les divers projets ainsi présentés.

M. HAGERUP et M. ALTAMIRA pensent qu'il convient de trancher d'abord la question actuellement en discussion.

LORD PHILLIMORE se range à leur avis, bien qu'ayant lui-même un avant-projet à soumettre, mais il le fera plus tard.

Le Comité décide de continuer la discussion sur la nomination des juges.

M. ADATCI prend la parole pour fournir une précision. Il commence par dire qu'il est désireux de voir aboutir les travaux du Comité et

might decide a case against the United States.

The questions which would be raised by public opinion in the larger countries must be remembered: namely the creation of a new power giving to representatives of other countries a certain right to control the action of the several states.

Mr. Root did not wish to appear pessimistic, nor to criticise any country, but felt that he must bring out the fact that the States which are most backward in civilisation will also be entitled to vote in the constitution of the Court, even though their legal system is so far different from the generally accepted ones that they have had to submit to a system of extra-territorial tribunals.

Mr. Root added that in his opinion the minds of these backward countries would not be entirely *tabulae rasae* when they would come to contribute their share to the Court. Mr. Root pointed out also that there doubtless would be great difficulty to persuade men really worthy to sit on the Court, and that they would have to be earnestly entreated, before they would consent to leave their homes and their occupations, while less desirable men would try by every available means to obtain these posts. The world had not radically changed.

Governments could not ask the people they represent to accept a Court which would be partly composed of members drawn from this last class. If Governments were to give up part of their sovereign power, they must take due care that these powers are not given up without secure guarantees.

For the reasons he had given, Mr. Root thought that the opposing opinions must be conciliated by some means; otherwise a Permanent Court was impossible.

The PRESIDENT thought it desirable to have the members submit their respective proposals, and express their opinions on the proposals submitted for discussion.

M. HAGERUP and M. ALTAMIRA thought it suitable to begin by the question actually under discussion.

LORD PHILLIMORE agreed; he had a proposal of his own to submit, but would do so later.

The Committee decided to continue the discussion of the nomination of judges.

M. ADATCI wished to clear up certain points. He began by saying that he wished to see the work of the Committee succeed, and for that

que, pour cette raison, il est disposé à faire toutes les concessions possibles. M. Adatci envisage toujours le problème de la nomination des juges au point de vue sociologique.

S'adressant à M. Hagerup, il dit qu'il reconnaît le principe de l'égalité des Etats, ainsi que le fait que le développement de l'humanité tend à la réalisation de ce principe, mais, d'autre part, il faut tenir compte de la réalité. Il faut penser aux peuples lointains, au peuple japonais par exemple, très éloigné du centre de l'activité européenne. Le peuple japonais, dont la civilisation est plusieurs fois millénaire, mais qui est entré, il y a 70 ans seulement, en relations constantes avec l'étranger, et qui récemment encore était sous le régime de l'extraterritorialité, est un peuple très susceptible. Si le Japon n'a pas de représentant à la Cour, il est à craindre que le peuple japonais ne consente jamais à se soumettre à sa juridiction. Il faut bien tenir compte des civilisations différentes, entre autres de la civilisation de l'extrême Orient, dont le Japon est peut-être le principal représentant. On a dit que si les grandes Puissances étaient représentées *ipso jure* à la Cour, certaines Puissances secondaires de l'Europe n'accepteraient pas sa juridiction; ce serait là, sans doute, un fait très regrettable. Mais que dira-t-on si les grandes Puissances ou l'Asie toute entière ne l'acceptent pas? Dans ce cas la Cour aura fait faillite.

M. Adatci termine en disant qu'il est prêt à prendre en considération toute opinion qui pourra se concilier avec son point de vue.

M. LODER présente une motion d'ordre. Il pense qu'on a assez longuement discuté la question de la composition de la Cour et qu'il ne serait pas utile de continuer cette discussion pour le moment. Il propose de la poursuivre dans des conversations privées et que pendant ce temps le Comité, comme tel, s'occupera d'autres questions; autrement on n'aboutira pas.

M. HAGERUP ne veut pas pour l'instant entamer une nouvelle discussion sur le fond de la question. Il veut seulement dire à ce propos qu'il y a sans doute beaucoup de vrai dans la manière de voir de Mr. Root, mais que celui-ci laisse de côté certains points qui ont, surtout pour les Etats de second ordre, de l'importance — plutôt idéale, il est vrai. L'essentiel en ce moment, n'est pourtant pas l'appréciation de ces différents points de vue. Il faut maintenant se placer sur le terrain pratique. Nous sommes en présence de points de vue différents et qui semblent inconciliables si on les maintient avec une rigueur in-

reason he was prepared to make all concessions possible. He always considered the nomination of judges from the sociological point of view.

Speaking to M. Hagerup, he said that, though he recognised the principle of equality of States, as well as the fact that the development of humanity tended to the realisation of this principle, yet realities must be faced. States such as Japan, far from the centre of European activity, must be considered. The Japanese, whose civilisation is several thousand years old, but who entered into definite relation with foreign Powers only 70 years ago and who until recently were under the regime of extra-territoriality, nevertheless were very impressionable. If Japan had no representative at the Court, he feared that the Japanese people would never consent to submit to its jurisdiction. All different kinds of civilisation must be taken into account, among them the civilisation of the Far East, of which Japan was perhaps the principal representative. It had been said that if the great Powers were represented on the Court *ipso jure,* some secondary Powers of Europe would not accept its jurisdiction; this fact would be without doubt very regrettable. But what could be said if the great Powers or the whole of Asia refused to accept? In such a case the Court would fail.

M. Adatci said in conclusion that he was ready to consider all suggestions which could be reconciled with his point of view.

M. LODER raised a motion of order. He thought that the composition of the Court had been sufficiently discussed, and did not think that for the time being it would serve any useful purpose to continue this discussion. He suggested that the discussion be continued in private conversations, and that in the meantime the Committee should take up other questions; otherwise they would never reach a decision.

M. HAGERUP did not wish at the moment, to open a new discussion relating to the question. He only wished to say, in this connection, that no doubt there was a great deal of truth in Mr. Root's views, but that they did not embrace certain points which were of importance — ideally, to be sure, — especially to the secondary Powers. The essential consideration at this stage is not the evaluation of these different points of view; the question must now be considered from a practical standpoint. One was in the presence of different points of view, which seem to be irreconcilable if supported inflexibly. To arrive

flexible. Pour aboutir à un résultat, il faut de toute nécessité trouver une base de conciliation. Nous nous trouvons placés devant cette alternative: accorder quelque chose aux autres points de vue ou bien échouer. M. de Lapradelle a adressé à M. Adatci et à Lord Phillimore un appel éloquent et ému pour les amener à abandonner leur manière de voir. Vous avez entendu les réponses de ces Messieurs et le discours de Mr. Root, ce champion de l'égalité juridique des Etats qui est venu nous dire qu'il serait impossible de soumettre les intérêts des grands Etats aux résolutions d'une majorité des petits Etats. Et il nous en a aussi indiqué les raisons. Il est bien vrai que nous ne sommes pas des représentants de tel ou tel pays, mais nous en sommes les nationaux, et nous ne pouvons pas ne pas tenir compte de l'opinion publique dans notre pays. Si nous ne le faisions pas, notre œuvre serait balayée par le courant démocratique de l'ère actuelle. Donc, si nous, nationaux des Etats de second ordre, ne nous opposons pas à ce que les délibérations du Comité donnent naissance à un projet d'après lequel certains grands Etats auraient droit à un représentant à la Cour, le projet sera d'avance condamné par l'opinion publique dans notre pays.

D'autre part il ne semble pas moins certain que tout projet qui ne tiendra compte de l'opinion publique de certains grands Etats, de la Grande Bretagne par exemple, comme l'a expliqué Lord Phillimore, entraînera l'échec de notre œuvre.

M. Hagerup cite à l'appui de sa thèse l'exemple de la Convention concernant la Cour internationale des Prises, adoptée à la presqu' unanimité par la seconde Conférence de la Paix. Cette Convention, émanant d'une proposition du Gouvernement britannique, appuyée par ses délégués, personnages d'une rare autorité, et finalement signée par ce Gouvernement, n'est cependant jamais entrée en vigueur parce qu'elle s'est heurtée à l'opinion publique en Grande Bretagne.

S'il faut donc chercher une base de conciliation entre les différents points de vue, l'idée suggérée d'abord par Mr. Root et formulée plus en détail par Lord Phillimore, semble à M. Hagerup fournir une base qui mérite d'être prise en considération de façon très sérieuse, bien qu'il ne veuille pas, pour le moment, se prononcer définitivement à ce sujet. M. Hagerup veut seulement indiquer brièvement les raisons pour lesquelles il considère que ce projet peut s'accorder avec son propre point de vue. D'abord il ne donne pas aux grandes Puissances une prépondérance formelle et nette. Ce projet fait appel,

at a successful conclusion, a basis of conciliation must necessarily be found. One was faced by this alternative: to concede some things to other points of view, or else fail. M. de Lapradelle had made a brilliant and earnest appeal to M. Adatci and Lord Phillimore to abandon their points of view. The members had heard the answer of these gentlemen, and the speech of Mr. Root, the champion of legal equality of States, who said that it was impossible to submit the interests of the great Powers to a decision of a majority of the small States; and, furthermore, he gave the reasons therefor. It is true that the members are not the representatives of any given country, but they were their nationals, and they could not fail to take into consideration public opinion in their countries. If one did not consider this, the work would be swept away by the current of democratic opinion of the present time. If the members, nationals of the secondary States, did not oppose the proposals, now before the Committee, to the effect of certain large States having the right to a representative on the Court, the project would be condemned in advance by public opinion in their countries.

On the other hand, it seemed no less certain, that any project, which does not take into consideration public opinion in certain of the great Powers, Great-Britain, for example, as Lord Phillimore had explained, would mark the failure of our work.

M. Hagerup mentioned in support of his idea an example of the Convention concerning the International Prize Court adopted almost unanimously by the Second Peace Conference. This Convention, originaing from a proposition of the British Government, was supported by its delegates, persons of unusual authority, and finally signed by the Government. Nevertheless, it did not come into force, because it ran counter to public opinion in Great-Britain.

If, then, one had to search for a basis of conciliation with different points of view, the idea first suggested by Mr. Root, and formulated later in detail by Lord Phillimore, seemed to M. Hagerup to furnish a basis which deserved to be considered seriously; however, he did not wish at this time to commit himself definitely to any proposal on the subject. M. Hagerup wished only to indicate briefly the reason for which he considered that this proposal could be made to coincide with his own point of view. In the first place, it did not give to the great Powers a clear and formal preponderance. This project appealed, in order to give

pour leur attribuer la fonction de corps électoraux, à des institutions créées par un accord commun de tous les Etats qui ont adhéré à la Société des Nations, et composées également des représentants des petits et des grands Etats. D'autre part, si on institue un seul corps électoral, à savoir l'Assemblée générale de la Société des Nations, les grands Etats pourraient avec quelque raison objecter que tout en voulant établir une égalité de droit de tous les Etats, on finit par établir une inégalité de fait, défavorable aux grands Etats qui sont en minorité dans ladite Assemblée. Cela exige une compensation qui consisterait à associer à l'élection des membres de la Cour, l'autre organe de la Société des Nations, le Conseil, dans lequel les grands Etats ont la majorité. Par ce moyen on peut espérer empêcher qu'un élément ne l'emporte sur l'autre.

LORD PHILLIMORE appuie la proposition de M. Loder.

La chose essentielle pour les membres en ce moment, est de former des convictions. La thèse de Mr. Root l'a fortement impressionné. Elle lui a suggéré une proposition rédigée en anglais qu'il demande la permission de lire en français. (Voir annexe 2).

Il ajoute à cette proposition les remarques suivantes:

La question du choix des juges a jusqu'ici été traitée comme s'il s'agissait toujours de choisir le nombre total des juges dont doit être composée la Cour; mais, en fait, cette circonstance ne se produira qu'une seule fois: la première. Dans la suite, il s'agira seulement de remplir les vacances produites par la démission, ou la mort, d'un juge.

Lord Phillimore n'ignore pas que le nombre total de juges proposé par M. Adatci est de 13, et celui proposé par le Baron Descamps de 9; toutefois il préfère, pour sa part, le nombre de 15.

Considérant la première élection, où sera choisie la totalité des juges qui formeront la Cour, Lord Phillimore précise les moyens d'assurer la collaboration du Conseil et de l'Assemblée, telle que les prévoit le projet qu'il vient de soumettre.

Le Conseil dressera une liste de candidats. Il possède une compétence particulière pour mener à bien cette tâche. Par leurs relations diplomatiques et politiques, les membres du Conseil sont à même de connaître les noms des hommes les plus distingués dans les différents pays.

L'Assemblée, de son côté, dressera une autre liste. Les personnes dont les noms figureront sur

them electoral functions, to institutions created by the consent of all the Members of the League of Nations and equally composed of the representatives of great and small Powers. On the other hand, if a single electoral body is established, viz. the general Assembly of the League of Nations, the great Powers, could, with some truth, object, that in wishing to establish equality of Law between the States an inequality of facts, prejudicial to the great Powers who are in the minority in the Assembly, is established. This demanded a compensating influence, which might consist in making the other body of the League of Nations, that is, the Council in which the great Powers are in the majority, a party in the election. By this means, it might be hoped to prevent one element overriding the other.

LORD PHILLIMORE supported the proposal of M. Loder.

The essential thing at the moment was that the Members should make up their minds. The speech of Mr. Root had greatly impressed him. It had suggested to him a proposal which he had drawn up in English and which he asked permission to read in French (See Annex 2).

To this proposal he added the following remarks:

The question of the choice of judges, up to the present, had been treated as if it were necessary to choose the whole number of judges who should compose the Court, but as a matter of fact, this eventually would only occur once: the first time; afterwards it would only be a question of filling vacancies caused by resignation or death of a judge.

Lord Phillimore was well aware that the total number proposed by M. Adatci was 13, and that proposed by Baron Descamps was 9; however he preferred the number of 15.

In considering the first election at which the whole number of judges which would compose the Court must be chosen, Lord Phillimore explained the means which were set out in the proposal he had just submitted, for ensuring the co-operation of the Council and the Assembly.

The Council would prepare a list of candidates; this body was extremely competent to perform this task. Through their diplomatic and political relations, the members of the Council are in a position to know the names of the most distinguished men in the various countries.

The Assembly on the other hand prepared another list. Those persons whose names ap-

les deux listes seront considérées comme élues. Ainsi sera élue une certaine partie du nombre total de 15.

Pour le reste, le Conseil examinera la liste de l'Assemblée; il retiendra probablement plusieurs des noms ne figurant que sur cette liste: ceux qui ont obtenu le plus de voix. De son côté, l'Assemblée pourra adopter un certain nombre des candidats figurant exclusivement sur la liste du Conseil. On parviendra ainsi à s'entendre pour nommer la plus grande partie des juges.

Si quelque difficulté s'élevait au sujet des derniers sièges à pourvoir, le Conseil et l'Assemblée parviendraient sans doute à se mettre d'accord, au moyen de conversations officielles ou officieuses. A défaut d'accord, il faudrait imaginer un moyen pour désigner, en dernière instance, le ou les titulaires des derniers sièges vacants. On pourra certainement trouver ce moyen.

LE PRÉSIDENT dit que, bien qu'il ait été convenu que les membres formuleraient et soumettraient leurs propositions à la séance de lundi, il ne croit pas qu'il y en ait plus de deux de déposées, celle de Lord Phillimore, et la sienne. Il prie les membres de bien vouloir formuler des projets s'ils en ont. On ne peut arriver à s'entendre que sur la base de propositions bien définies.

M. ALTAMIRA se rallie à l'opinion de M. Loder, disant que des conversations particulières seront fort utiles pour arriver à une solution. Personnellement, il est tout disposé à discuter la question à l'ordre du jour avec les membres, qu'ils soient ou non de son avis. Il est convaincu qu'on aboutira malgré les difficultés actuelles. Les membres du Comité sont des hommes pratiques. Ils sauront bien s'entendre, sans avoir besoin de sacrifier les principes primordiaux qu'ils ont adoptés.

M. Altamira demande ensuite de faire une déclaration relative aux paroles de Lord Phillimore, qui rappela au cours de la dernière séance, que l'Espagne est le pays de Don Quichote. (Voir annexe 3).

M. HAGERUP déclare qu'à son avis il convient de suivre l'ordre du jour proposé par le Président. Il pense qu'il serait prématuré de déposer des projets formulés. Il faut d'abord terminer la discussion de la question fondamentale. Personnellement, M. Hagerup peut se rallier — provisoirement bien entendu — à la proposition de Mr. Root et de Lord Phillimore, mais

peared on both lists were considered as elected; in this way a certain proportion of the total number of 15 would be elected. As concerns the remainder, the Council would consider the list made out by the Assembly; it would probably adopt several of the names which had received the most votes, appearing on this list. On the other hand, the Assembly could adopt a certain number of the candidates appearing only on the list of the Council. In this way the appointment of the greater number of judges to be elected could be arranged.

If any difficulty arose, concerning the election of judges for the last seats on the Court, the Council and Assembly would doubtless be able to come to an agreement by means of official or private discussions. If no agreement could be reached, some means must be found to select ultimately the candidates for the last seats. It was certain that a means could be found.

The PRESIDENT said that although it had been agreed that the members should formulate and submit their proposals at the Monday meeting, he thought that only two had been presented, that of Lord Phillimore and his own. He asked the members who wished to do so to be so good as to formulate their proposals. It was only on the basis of definite proposals that they could come to an understanding.

M. ALTAMIRA was of the same opinion as M. Loder and said that private conversations would be very useful in reaching a solution. He, personally, was quite ready to discuss the question on the agenda with the other Members, whether they were of his opinion or not, but he was convinced that they would eventually succeed in spite of the present difficulties. The members of the Committee were practical men. They would be able to come to an understanding without having to sacrifice the fundamental principles that they had adopted.

M. Altamira then asked to be allowed to make a statement concerning the words of Lord Phillimore the other day, when he said that Spain was the country of Don Quixote (See Annex 3).

M. HAGERUP said that in his opinion the agenda proposed by the President should be followed. He thought that the submission of formulated projects would be premature. First of all, the discussion of the fundamental question must be finished. As far as he was concerned, M. Hagerup felt that he could, provisionally, agree to the proposal of Mr. Root and Lord

c'est là une concession de sa part. Il croit que le moment où l'on est en train de faire des concessions n'est pas celui où il convient de formuler des projets.

M. DE LAPRADELLE est du même avis. Il se rallie à l'idée exprimée par M. Loder de procéder à des conversations particulières. Mais il faut poursuivre l'échange général de vues parallèlement aux conversations privées. On ne peut, par exemple, laisser sans le discuter un discours comme celui de Mr. Root, sous prétexte que le temps fait défaut.

Le PRESIDENT fait observer que Mr. Root a exprimé le désir que l'on discutât sa proposition. Le Président insiste pour qu'on l'examine, de même qu'on examinera, à la prochaine séance, le texte de Lord Phillimore.

LORD PHILLIMORE dit que son texte n'est qu'un squelette. Il invite ses collègues à compléter sa proposition.

M. HAGERUP indique qu'il y a sur le questionnaire du Président des points qui pourraient utilement faire l'objet d'une discussion indépendante; entre temps, on pourrait laisser mûrir la question de la nomination des juges.

M. RICCI-BUSATTI reconnaît la nécessité de serrer la discussion; les conversations particulières seront utiles, mais elles présentent cet inconvénient, que tous les membres ne seraient pas au courant de ce qui se passerait. Il faut trouver autre chose.

Comme exemple d'une solution possible il cite la procédure adoptée par la Commission des communications et du transit. Cette Commission tenait deux sortes de séances: officielles et officieuses.

Il n'y avait pas de procès-verbal des séances officieuses. Tout le monde était plus à l'aise pour parler, et l'on pouvait entendre des experts qui n'étaient pas des délégués en titre. En outre, et pour bien marquer la différence entre les deux sortes de réunions, c'était le Vice-Président qui présidait les séances officieuses. Les décisions, naturellement, étaient prises dans les séances officielles. Les réunions officieuses avaient aussi l'avantage de permettre de continuer en toute liberté la discussion d'une certaine question, tandis que dans les séances officielles on pouvait entamer un autre problème.

Cette procédure fut trouvée très souple et très utile; parfois on changea au cours de la

Phillimore; this however would be a concession on his part. He thought that the time when concessions were being considered was not the time to put forward a project.

M. DE LAPRADELLE was of the same opinion. He agreed with M. Loder's idea that they should have private discussions, but that they should continue the general exchange of views, side by side with the private conversations. For instance, one could not leave a speech like Mr. Root's, without any discussion, on the ground that time was short.

The PRESIDENT remarked that Mr. Root had expressed the wish that the former's proposal should be discussed. The President insisted that it should be criticised, just as Lord Phillimore's text should be criticised at the next meeting.

LORD PHILLIMORE said that his proposal was only an outline, and he asked his colleagues to fill it in.

M. HAGERUP pointed out that there were points on the questionnaire of the President which might usefully be the object of an independent discussion; in the meanwhile, the question of the appointment of judges could be allowed to mature.

M. RICCI-BUSATTI recognised that it was necessary to limit the discussion. Private conversations would be valuable, but they would involve the inconvenience that all the members would not be informed as to what had taken place. Some other means must be found.

As an example of a possible solution he mentioned the plan of procedure adopted by the Commission on Communications and Transit. This Commission held two kinds of meetings: official and unofficial.

There was no procès-verbal of the unofficial meetings. Everyone was more at ease in speaking, and experts who were not official delegates could be heard. Further, in order to mark the difference between the two meetings, it was the vice-president who presided at the unofficial meetings. All decisions of course were taken in the official meeting, but unofficial meetings had also the advantage of allowing free discussion of one question, while in the official meetings another question might be taken up.

This procedure had been found very flexible and useful; at times the character of a meeting was changed according to the exigencies of the moment.

même séance le caractère de la réunion selon les besoins du moment.

Le PRESIDENT insiste sur l'importance qu'il y a de discuter des projets formulés.

M. HAGERUP propose de consacrer la matinée de mardi à discuter les autres points figurant dans le questionnaire du Président.

Le PRESIDENT croit qu'il vaut mieux continuer la discussion commencée.

Il est décidé que dans la séance de mardi on discutera la proposition de Lord Phillimore.

La séance est levée à 12.30 de l'après-midi.

Le Président:
(signé) Brn. DESCAMPS.

Le Secrétaire-Général:
(signé) D. ANZILOTTI.

The PRESIDENT insisted on the importance of discussing definite proposals.

M. HAGERUP proposed to devote Tuesday morning to a discussion of the other points enumerated on the questionnaire of the President.

The PRESIDENT thought it would be better to continue the discussion already begun.

It was decided that at Tuesday's meeting the proposal of Lord Phillimore should be discussed.

The meeting closed at 12.30 p.m.

The President:
(signed) Brn. DESCAMPS.

The Secretary-General:
(signed) D. ANZILOTTI.

ANNEXE No. 1.

Projet du Baron Descamps.

L'organisation de la Justice Internationale.

I. De la Cour d'Arbitrage existante ou Cour des arbitres internationaux.

Art. 1. La Cour d'Arbitrage actuelle, telle qu'elle a été établie par la Convention de 1899 et confirmée par la Convention de 1907 pour le règlement pacifique des conflits internationaux, est maintenue.

En conséquence, et conformément à l'article 44 de la Convention de 1907, „chaque Puissance contractante désigne quatre personnes au plus, d'une compétence reconnue dans les questions de droit international, jouissant de la plus haute considération morale et disposées à accepter les fonctions d'arbitre.

Les personnes ainsi désignées sont inscrites, au titre de Membres de la Cour, sur une liste qui sera notifiée à toutes les Puissances contractantes".

Art. 2. Conformément à l'article 42 de la Convention de 1907: „La Cour permanente est compétente pour tous les cas d'arbitrage, à moins qu'il n'y ait entente entre les Parties pour l'établissement d'une juridiction spéciale".

II. De La Haute Cour de Justice Internationale.

Art. 3. La Haute Cour de Justice Internationale se compose d'un membre par Etat respectivement choisi par le Collège des Délégués de chaque Etat à la Cour d'Arbitrage.

Art. 4. La Haute Cour de Justice Internationale est compétente pour juger les affaires qui, du chef de l'ordre public international, comme lorsqu'il s'agit de crimes contre le Droit des Gens universel, lui sont déférées par l'Assemblée plénière de la Société des Nations ou par le Conseil de cette Société.

III. Du Tribunal permanent de Justice Internationale.

Art. 5. Le Tribunal permanent de Justice Internationale se compose de neuf juges avec six

ANNEX No. 1.

Proposal by Baron Descamps.

The organisation of International Justice.

I. The existing Court of Arbitration, or Court of International Arbitrators.

Article 1. The existing Court of Arbitration, as established by the Convention of 1899, and confirmed by the Convention of 1907 for the pacific settlement of international disputes, is maintained.

Consequently, and in accordance with Article 44 of the Convention of 1907, "each contracting Power selects four persons at the most, of known competency in questions of international law, of the highest moral reputation, and disposed to accept the duties of arbitrator.

The persons thus selected are inscribed, as members of the Court, in a list which shall be notified to all the contracting Powers".

Article 2. In accordance with Article 42 of the Convention of 1907, the Court is competent "for all arbitration cases, unless the parties agree to institute a special tribunal".

II. The High Court of International Justice.

Article 3. The High Court of International Justice is composed of one member for each State, chosen respectively by the group ot delegates from each State to the Court of Arbitration.

Article 4. The High Court of International Justice shall be competent to hear and determine cases which shall be submitted to it by the Assembly of the League of Nations or by the Council of the League, and which concern international public order, for instance: crimes against the universal Law of Nations.

III. The Permanent Tribunal of International Justice.

Article 5. The Permanent Tribunal of International Justice is composed of 9 judges and 6

suppléants choisis par les membres de la Haute Cour de Justice Internationale de manière à former, conformément à l'article 1er du Projet de Convention de 1907, „une juridiction d'un accès libre et facile, basée sur l'égalité juridique des Etats", et réunissant obligatoirement des juges représentant les principaux systèmes juridiques du monde et capable d'assurer la continuité de la jurisprudence internationale.

Art. 6. La compétence du Tribunal permanent de Justice Internationale s'étend à tous les litiges que les parties peuvent se trouver engagées à lui soumettre, sans préjudice des litiges que les parties entendent déférer à une autre juridiction.

Le Tribunal permanent de Justice Internationale peut, dans les conditions déterminées par son règlement d'ordre intérieur, fonctionner comme Commission internationale d'enquête, soit à la demande des Parties, soit en vertu d'une décision de l'Assemblée plénière de la Société des Nations ou du Conseil de cette Société.

Il peut en outre, dans les mêmes conditions, être chargé par l'Assemblée ou le Conseil de donner des avis consultatifs sur tout différend ou tout point dont ils estimeront devoir le saisir.

Art. 7. Pour l'expédition des affaires, le Tribunal permanent de Justice Internationale se répartit, conformément à son règlement d'ordre intérieur, dans les offices suivants:

1. *L'Assemblée plénière.*

2. *Une première chambre* dite des vacations générales, composée de 5 juges avec 3 suppléants.

3. *Une seconde chambre* dite des procédures sommaires, composée de 3 juges avec 2 suppléants, à laquelle pourront être déférés en outre les litiges pour lesquels les parties estimeront qu'une juridiction de 3 juges est suffisante.

4. *Un juge unique* avec un suppléant, pour les cas où les parties, en raison de la nature de l'affaire ou de leur convenance commune, estimeront une telle judicature suffisante.

Le règlement d'ordre intérieur par lequel le Tribunal de Justice Internationale détermine le mode suivant lequel il exerce ses attributions doit être soumis à l'approbation du Conseil de la Société des Nations et de l'Assemblée de cette Société.

supplementary judges, elected by the members of the High Court of International Justice, so as to constitute, in accordance with the first Article of the Convention of 1907, a jurisdiction freely and easily accessible and based on the principle of juridical equality of States. This jurisdiction shall include judges representing the principal legal systems of the world and will be capable of securing the continuity of international jurisprudence.

Article 6. The Permanent Tribunal of International Justice shall be competent to hear and determine all disputes which the parties have engaged themselves to submit to the Court. Nevertheless, the parties shall have the right to agree on submitting their disputes to another jurisdiction.

The Permanent Tribunal of International Justice, under conditions provided for in its rules of procedure, may act as International Commission of Inquiry, either at the request of the Parties, or by virtue of a decision of the Assembly or Council of the League of Nations.

Moreover, it may under the same conditions, be called upon by the Assembly or the Council to give advisory opinions on any dispute or question which the Assembly or Council may deem wise to submit to the Tribunal.

Article 7. For the performance of its duties, the Permanent Tribunal of International Justice shall divide itself, in accordance with its rules of procedure, into the following branches:

1. *The full sitting.*

2. *One first Chamber* (of general vacations) composed of five judges and three deputy judges.

3. *One second Chamber* (of summary procedure) composed of three judges and two deputy judges. This Chamber shall also be competent to hear and determine disputes, which the parties concerned are willing to submit to a Court of only three judges.

4. One single judge, with a deputy, to deal with cases in which, by the nature of the dispute or by common interests, the parties concerned consider such jurisdiction sufficient.

The rules of procedure setting forth the mode in which the Tribunal of International Justice will exercise its competence shall be submitted to the Council of the League of Nations and to the Assembly of the League for approval.

ANNEXE No. 2.

Proposition de Lord Phillimore.

1) Les juges de la Haute Cour sont nommés conjointement par le Conseil et l'Assemblée de la Société des Nations.

2) Le Conseil votera une liste qui sera transmise à l'Assemblée.

3) L'Assemblée prend en considération la liste votée par le Conseil ainsi que tous noms proposés à l'Assemblée par un Etat représenté; puis l'Assemblée vote sa propre liste.

4) Les personnes dont les noms se retrouvent sur les deux listes sont considérées comme élues.

5) Pour le reste, le Conseil procède à un nouveau vote; l'Assemblée procède également à un nouveau vote, et ainsi de suite, jusqu'à ce qu'un accord final soit obtenu.

ANNEX No. 2.

Proposition made by Lord Phillimore.

1) The judges of the High Court are named jointly by the Council and by the Assembly of the League of Nations.

2) The Council shall adopt a list which shall be transmitted to the Assembly.

3) The Assembly shall consider the list adopted by the Council and also any names presented to the Assembly by a State which is a Member of the Assembly. The Assembly shall then adopt a list of its own.

4) Persons the names of whom are found on both lists are thereupon considered as elected.

5) For the other seats to be filled, the Council shall proceed to a new vote; the Assembly shall also proceed to a new vote; and so on, until a final agreement is reached.

ANNEXE No. 3.

Déclaration de M. Altamira.

J'ai quelques mots à dire à notre illustre collègue Lord Phillimore. Il ne s'agit pas d'une réplique parce qu'on ne peut répliquer qu'aux idées qu'on a comprises; et malgré tous mes efforts il m'a été impossible de comprendre le sens et le but de la spirituelle allusion faite à ma patrie et à Don Quichotte. Quoiqu'il en soit, je regretterais d'avoir donné à notre illustre collègue l'impression de défendre une utopie purement nationale, caractéristique de mon pays. Je croyais au contraire, dans tout ce que j'ai dit devant vous, exprimer des idées partagées dans le monde par de nombreux esprits, des idées qu'on retrouve dans la plupart des projets qui nous ont été soumis, dans les conclusions qui ont été adoptées par des congrès tenus par plusieurs associations de tous les pays du monde, et même de l'Angleterre. Souvenez vous, Messieurs, que je n'ai parlé que des qualités juridiques et morales des juges d'élite, et parfois, en me ralliant à des idées de Lord Phillimore, de la possibilité, à mon avis incontestable, de réduire tout conflit à des termes juridiques; de la force qui émane de l'autorité personnelle des juges; des garanties que pourra donner la Cour, et qui dépendront surtout de la bonne volonté et du désir qu'apporteront les grandes Puissances à accomplir et à maintenir ce qu'elles nous ont promis dans le Pacte de la Société des Nations, ce qui a même constitué leur drapeau dans la guerre passée, l'explication morale qu'elles ont donnée au monde de leur engagement dans la lutte.

Je ne pousserai pas le chauvinisme jusqu'à me flatter de supposer que c'est l'esprit de l'Espagne qui s'est imposé, qui ici-même, par exemple, a parlé par la bouche de M. de Lapradelle. Ne sont-ce là que des utopies, des songes ou des mots qu'on prononce au moment du danger et qu'on oublie sitôt qu'il est passé? S'il en était ainsi, je ne donnerais pas un sou pour l'avenir de la Société des Nations.

Mais je ne puis croire qu'il faille interpréter ainsi les mots de Lord Phillimore. Tout au contraire, je crois qu'il n'avait que l'intention de rappeler aimablement et d'une façon qui caractérise si bien l'humour anglais, la signification

ANNEX No. 3.

Statement by M. Altamira.

I have a few words to say to our distinguished colleague Lord Phillimore. It is not a reply, because one can only reply to ideas that are understood; and despite my best endeavours I fail to understand the point of this witty allusion to my country and Don Quixote. Whatever the meaning be, I should be very sorry to have given our distinguished colleague the impression of defending a purely national utopian scheme, characteristic of my country. On the contrary, I thought that, in everything which I have said here, I had expressed ideas shared by many minds throughout the world, ideas contained in most of the proposals which have been put before us, and in the conclusions adopted by Conferences held by several associations in all countries and even in England. I beg you to remember, Gentlemen, that I only spoke of the judicial and moral qualities of the judges to be elected; I spoke also of the possibility — in my opinion a point not open to debate — of reducing all conflicts to terms of law. In this I agreed with Lord Phillimore's own ideas. I likewise spoke of the force which comes from the personal authority of the judges; of the guarantees which the Court can give, and which depend above all on the good-will and earnest desire of the great Powers to accomplish and maintain that which they have promised us in the Covenant of the League of Nations, that which even was inscribed on their standards during the War just ended, the high moral explanation proclaimed before the world, as their reason for taking part in the struggle.

I shall not exaggerate national pride to the extent of flattering myself by supposing that it is the spirit of Spain which has made itself felt, which here, for instance, has spoken through M. de Lapradelle. Are those only Utopian ideas, illusions, words spoken in a moment of danger and forgotten when the danger is passed? If this were the case, I should not give a farthing for the future of the League of Nations.

But I cannot believe that this interpretation must be placed on the words of Lord Phillimore. On the contrary, I believe that he only meant to

idéaliste de notre grand roman espagnol. Il y a toujours eu trop de noblesse dans l'esprit de la Grande-Bretagne pour que je puisse croire que Lord Phillimore puisse faire sien un scepticisme qui supposerait un mépris du sens de la justice que représente Don Quichotte. Lord Phillimore sait très bien que, s'il est toujours facile de lancer un trait contre les grands idéals vers lesquels, aujourd'hui plus que jamais, tend l'humanité, par contre, dans les heures de détresse où l'on foule aux pieds le droit, où l'on ne connaît plus de pitié, où l'on s'attaque à tous les sentiments qui font la noblesse de l'homme, c'est vers ces idéals qu'on tourne les yeux, c'est d'eux qu'on espère le salut, ce sont eux qu'on invoque pour justifier la résistance et l'attaque.

En ce moment et dans cette assemblée, je ne me considère pas comme un compatriote de Don Quichotte, mais comme un citoyen du monde qui sait ce que désirent et ce que pensent, non pas les minorités qui gouvernent les peuples, mais les masses, la jeunesse universitaire de tous les pays, les hommes dont on aura besoin demain pour tout faire et qui voudront connaître de plus en plus, d'une façon précise, les engagements pris en leur nom.

L'utopie de Don Quichotte, voire même son ridicule, ne vient pas de ses idées, mais de la disproportion qui existe entre ses idées et les moyens qu'il emploie pour les réaliser. Certes, ce sont des moyens efficaces que nous cherchons ici, mais les exigences de la réalité ne peuvent pas nous faire oublier ou méconnaître les idéals qui sont nos principes dirigeants.

recall in a friendly and typically British humouristic way the ideal contained in our great Spanish novel. There always has been too much nobility in the character of Great-Britain to allow me to believe that Lord Phillimore would be so sceptical as to despise the real sense of justice represented by Don Quixote. Lord Phillimore knows very well that, though it is always easy to criticize the great ideals to which mankind to-day more than ever appeals, in times of trouble, when justice is trampled under foot, when pity is unknown, when all the nobler sentiments of mankind are attacked, it is then towards these high ideals that eyes are turned, it is on them that all hopes are fixed, they are invoked to justify the attack and the defence.

At this moment and in this meeting, I feel not as a compatriot of Don Quixote, but as a citizen of the world, who knows, not what the minority who govern the peoples, but what the masses and the youth of the universities in all countries know and think. These men whom we shall need in the near future to carry out all these works will insist on knowing more and more exactly what engagements have been taken in their name.

The utopian element of Don Quixote and even that which makes him derisive does not result from his ideas, but from the disproportion between his ideas and the means he employs to realise them. To be sure, we are looking here for practical means, but the requirements of realities must not make us lose sight of, or fail to understand, the ideals which are our guiding principles.

6IÈME SÉANCE (non-publique), tenue au Palais de la Paix, à La Haye, le 22 juin 1920.

Présidence de M. le BARON DESCAMPS.

Sont présents: tous les membres du Comité (à l'exception de M. Bevilaqua); Mr. James Brown Scott; les secrétaires particuliers de M. le Baron Descamps et de M. Adatci; les membres du Secrétariat.

La séance est ouverte à $9^1/_2$ heures du matin.

LORD PHILLIMORE fait remarquer qu'il n'est pour rien dans le communiqué à la presse qui se trouve reproduit dans les journaux d'aujourd'hui.

Le PRESIDENT donne quelques explications sur les relations du Comité avec la presse; les communiqués sont rédigés d'accord avec le Secrétariat; ils sont strictement objectifs et ne contiennent aucun nom.

Le Président a reçu des propositions de Lord Phillimore et de M. Adatci; M. Altamira va en déposer une et M. Loder a demandé la parole pour faire une communication.

M. ALTAMIRA donne lecture de sa proposition. (Voir annexe 1).

M. LODER pour préciser ses idées sur les propositions faites, donne lecture d'une déclaration. (Voir annexe 2).

M. ADATCI se contente de dire qu'il a formulé son point de vue dans un projet en deux articles qu'il vient de déposer et auquel il renvoie. (Voir annexe 3).

M. DE LAPRADELLE dit que les propositions faites par divers membres appellent de sa part quelques réflexions. Il s'adresse d'abord à Mr. Root qui semble avoir nié l'applicabilité du principe de l'égalité au problème de la constitution de la Cour, ceci pour deux raisons: l'égalité des Etats est une conséquence de leur souveraineté, et l'inégalité des Etats a été consacrée par la Société des Nations.

M. de Lapradelle croit qu'il ne faut pas, comme l'a fait Mr. Root, se servir de la notion abstraite de la souveraineté; il faut tenir compte

6TH MEETING (Private), held at the Peace Palace, the Hague, on June 22nd, 1920.

BARON DESCAMPS in the chair.

Present: all members of the Committee (with the exception of M. Bevilaqua); Mr. James Brown Scott; the private secretaries of Baron Descamps and of M. Adatci; the members of the Secretariat.

The meeting opened at 9.30 a.m.

LORD PHILLIMORE observed that he was in no way responsible for the communiqué which appeared in the press to-day.

The PRESIDENT explained the relations existing between the Committee and the Press; the communiqués were prepared in agreement with the Secretariat and were strictly objective, and mentioned no names.

The President had received proposals from Lord Phillimore and M. Adatci. M. Altamira was going to submit one, and M. Loder had asked to be allowed to make a communication to the meeting.

M. ALTAMIRA read his proposal. (See Annex 1).

M. LODER, in order to define his views upon the proposals already made, read a statement. (See Annex 2).

M. ADATCI said that he had given his point of view concrete form in a project consisting of two articles which he had submitted and to which he called the Committee's attention (See Annex 3).

M. DE LAPRADELLE said that the proposals made by various members called for certain remarks from him. In the first place he addressed Mr. Root. The latter seemed to have denied that the principle of equality was applicable to the problem of the constitution of the Court, for two reasons: The equality of States is a result of their sovereignty, and the inequality of States has been sanctioned by the League of Nations.

M. de Lapradelle thought that one ought not, as Mr. Root had done, to use the abstract idea of sovereignty; one must consider public

de l'opinion publique à ce sujet. Pour celle-ci l'égalité des Etats est bien en cause lorsqu'il s'agit de constituer la nouvelle Cour; on l'a vu en 1907.

D'après M. de Lapradelle, il est vrai que l'inégalité a été, jusqu'à un certain degré, consacrée par la Société des Nations, et notamment en ce qui concerne la composition du Conseil. A cet égard, l'inégalité se trouve cependant justifiée par le fait que le Conseil est l'organe exécutif, et que l'exécution des décisions prises incomberait aux grands Etats; ils doivent par conséquent avoir le droit de prendre part d'une façon permanente aux décisions qui pourraient être suivies de mesures coërcitives.

La Cour Permanente au contraire est un organe délibératif.

M. de Lapradelle ne trouve par conséquent pas de raison pour sortir du domaine ordinaire de la notion de l'égalité.

Le Comité se trouve en présence de plusieurs projets provisoires présentés par ses membres. Les projets vont vers deux directions déterminées. La première, c'est la nomination des juges de la Cour Permanente par les membres de la Cour d'Arbitrage. M. de Lapradelle trouve cette idée séduisante pour les raisons suivantes:

Elle tend à renouer le fil de l'histoire que le Pacte de la Société des Nations a rompu en construisant un nouvel édifice international, sans tenir compte des institutions qui existaient déjà. Elle renoue l'avenir au passé, en se basant sur l'œuvre de 1907. Elle a également cet avantage qu'elle prévoit d'une façon bien marquée la coexistence de la nouvelle Cour et de l'ancienne Cour d'Arbitrage. En outre, l'idée en question, qui est celle du projet du Président, sauvegarde d'une façon absolue l'égalité entre les Etats.

Nonobstant ces avantages indiscutables, M. de Lapradelle ne peut pas se rallier au système du projet du Président. Il y trouve en effet les défauts suivants:

Les membres de la Cour d'Arbitrage sont, pour la moitié, non pas des jurisconsultes purs, mais des hommes politiques. Ce fait se fera bien sentir si l'on fait de ces membres un corps électoral. Les membres de la Cour d'Arbitrage proviennent, en partie, de plusieurs pays qui ne font pas partie de la Société des Nations, et d'autre part plusieurs des Membres de la Société n'y sont pas représentés. Il serait bien peu logique de faire élire la Cour de la Société des Nations, établie par la Société des Nations, par un collège électoral qui sort du cadre de la Société.

C'est un fait bien connu que la Cour d'Ar-

opinion on this subject. According to public opinion the principle of the equality of States was at stake in the constitution of the new Court; this was seen in 1907.

M. de Lapradelle said that it was true that the principle of inequality had been, to a certain extent, recognised by the League of Nations, especially in the composition of the Council. In this connection, however, the inequality was justified by the fact that the Council was the executive body, and that the execution of decisions fell to the great States; they must therefore have the right to take part permanently in decisions which might require a certain coercion.

On the other hand, the Permanent Court was a deliberative body.

M. de Lapradelle did not, therefore, think that there was any reason to deviate from the ordinary conception of equality.

The Committee had to consider several provisional proposals put forward by its members. These proposals pointed in two distinct directions. The first was the nomination of the judges of the Permanent Court by the members of the Court of Arbitration. M. de Lapradelle was attracted to this idea for the following reasons:

It tended to renew the historical connection which was broken by the Covenant of the League of Nations when it set up a new international organism, without considering the institutions already in existence. The idea connected the future with the past on the basis of the work of 1907. It had also the advantage of expressly providing for the co-existence of the new Court and the old Court of Arbitration. Further, the idea under consideration, which was that of the project of the President, safeguarded absolutely the equality of States.

In spite of these indisputable advantages M. de Lapradelle could not agree with the system proposed by the President. He found fault with it as follows:

The members of the Court of Arbitration are only half jurisconsults, the other half are politicians. This would have a great effect if the Members of the Court were made an electoral body. The Members of the Court of Arbitration were drawn, in part, from some nations which were not members of the League of Nations; and, on the other hand, several Members of the League were not represented on the Court. It would not be logical to have the Court of the League of Nations, established by the League

bitrage n'est qu'une liste de membres; de là découlent des difficultés d'ordre pratique pour l'organisation de l'élection. En fin de compte, il ne faut pas rendre la Cour Permanente dépendante de la Cour d'Arbitrage, et d'autre part cette dernière Cour ne doit pas être investie d'un pouvoir qui ne pourrait manquer d'être un pouvoir politique. Encore, l'opinion publique trouverait-elle à redire à ce que les juges se nomment les uns les autres.

La Cour d'Arbitrage et la Cour Permanente doivent être deux institutions parallèles et indépendantes avec des missions différentes. Elles ne peuvent pas se confondre, ni s'alimenter à la même source.

Pour toutes ces raisons M. de Lapradelle se voit obligé de retirer son adhésion à la proposition du Président. Il croit qu'il faut chercher la solution dans la direction indiquée par Lord Phillimore, dont la proposition a ce grand avantage qu'elle apaise les susceptibilités, aussi bien de ceux qui désirent voir réaliser le principe de l'égalité des Etats, que de ceux qui veulent qu'on donne une influence spéciale aux Etats qui ont le plus souffert pour la cause du droit.

D'autre part, M. de Lapradelle ne partage pas l'idée de Mr. Root selon laquelle il faut distinguer entre les nations qui renoncent à une partie de leurs droits et celles qui reçoivent une garantie de sécurité.

Mais si M. de Lapradelle trouve que la proposition de Mr. Root, adoptée par Lord Phillimore, représente la solution, il envisage la possibilité d'un conflit entre les deux corps auxquels serait confiée l'élection des juges: l'Assemblée représentant l'égalité des Etats, et le Conseil, où il est tenu compte du prestige spécial de certains Etats. Pour résoudre ce conflit, M. de Lapradelle propose un amendement à la proposition de Mr. Root. Il pense qu'aucun candidat ne devrait être considéré comme élu à moins d'avoir réuni la majorité des deux tiers dans le Conseil et dans l'Assemblée: ceci pour tirer tous les avantages possibles du principe de Mr. Root. Un *deadlock* dans ce cas devient possible, si l'Assemblée et le Conseil tiennent à leurs candidats respectifs. A la première élection, l'élection de la totalité des juges, on peut résoudre la difficulté de la façon suivante: D'abord essayer de concilier les opinions divergentes au moyen d'une de ces commissions mixtes, proposées par Mr. Root et composées de 3 membres du Conseil et 3 membres de l'Assemblée; si cette commission n'aboutit pas, avoir recours à une commission spéciale nommée d'avance parmi les

itself, elected by an electoral body which stood outside the League.

It was well known that the Court of Arbitration is merely a list of members. From this fact practical difficulties arose in connection with the election. Finally, the Permanent Court must not be made dependent on the Court of Arbitration, and on the other hand the latter Court must not be vested with a power which could not avoid being of a political character. Also public opinion would find fault with the appointment of judges by others holding the same position.

The Court of Arbitration and the Permanent Court must be two parallel and independent institutions with different tasks. They must be two separate bodies and must not draw their authority from the same source.

For these reasons, M. de Lapradelle felt himself obliged to withdraw his adherence from the President's proposal. He thought that the solution must be sought on the lines indicated by Lord Phillimore. The latter scheme had the great advantage of satisfying the susceptibilities, both of those who wished to see realised the principle of the equality of States, and those who wished to give a special influence to such States as have suffered the most in the cause of justice.

On the other hand M. de Lapradelle did not share the opinion of Mr. Root that a distinction must be drawn between nations who give up a part of their right, and those who receive a guarantee of security.

But, though M. de Lapradelle thought that the proposal of Mr. Root, adopted by Lord Phillimore, represented the solution, he foresaw the possibility of a disagreement between the two bodies entrusted with the election of judges; the Assembly representing the equality of States, and the Council in whose constitution the special influence of certain States is taken into consideration. In order to solve this difficulty, M. de Lapradelle suggested an amendment to Mr. Root's proposal. M. de Lapradelle thought that no candidate ought to be considered elected, unless he had received a majority of two-thirds in the Council and in the Assembly. The object of this was to obtain as much advantage as possible from the principle laid down by Mr. Root. Under this system a dead-lock would be possible if the Assembly and the Council respectively refused to give up their candidates. At the first election, when all the judges would have to be elected, the difficulty might be solved in the following manner. First

membres de la Cour d'Arbitrage. Pour les élections suivantes, où il ne s'agirait que de remplir un ou plusieurs sièges devenus vacants, on procéderait par co-optation exercée par la Cour elle-même. M. de Lapradelle croit que, plutôt que de se dessaisir ainsi de l'élection, le Conseil et l'Assemblée préféreront se mettre d'accord.

M. de Lapradelle se rallie, sous réserve de l'amendement qu'il vient de proposer, au projet déposé par Lord Phillimore.

En réponse à une question posée par M. Loder au sujet de la composition des listes de nomination, M. de Lapradelle émet l'idée que cette liste pourrait être composée de 3 noms, présentés par chaque gouvernement, dont un serait le nom d'une personne de nationalité autre que celle du gouvernement qui présente les candidats. L'étranger proposé serait régulièrement un homme très éminent. Il serait problablement élu, et les Etats auraient donc la satisfaction de voir élire un candidat présenté par eux-mêmes, si le choix ne tombe pas sur un de leurs nationaux.

Pour terminer, M. de Lapradelle dit que puisqu'il s'agit de créer, dans le cadre de la Société des Nations, un organe nouveau, il est juste que la nomination revienne aux deux organes principaux de cette société. On évitera ainsi de créer de nouveaux privilèges; on ne fera que consacrer une supériorité fondée sur le Pacte même. M. de Lapradelle croit que la meilleure façon pour le Comité de remplir la mission qui lui a été confiée par la Société des Nations est d'adopter ce système.

of all an attempt might be made to reconcile opposing opinions by means of a Joint Conference such as was proposed by Mr. Root, composed of three Members of the Council and three Members of the Assembly. If this Commission did not succeed in its task, recourse might be had to a special Commission appointed beforehand from amongst the members of the Court of Arbitration. For the subsequent elections, when it would only be a matter of filling one or two vacant seats, election would be by a system of co-optation by the Court itself. M. de Lapradelle thought that rather than divest themselves of the election, the Council and the Assembly would prefer to agree.

M. de Lapradelle, subject to the amendment which he had just suggested, was in agreement with the proposal put forward by Lord Phillimore.

In answer to a question of M. Loder relating to the composition of the lists of candidates, M. de Lapradelle put forward the suggestion that this list could consist of three names proposed by each Government; of these names one should be the name of a person not a national of the proposing Government. This foreign candidate would as a rule be a very distinguished man. He would probably be elected and the States would thus have the satisfaction of seeing one of their candidates elected even if none of their own nationals were chosen.

In conclusion M. de Lapradelle said that as the question before the Committee was the creation of a new organism forming a part of the League of Nations, it is only right that the election should be entrusted to the two chief organs of this League. In this way the creation of new privileges would be avoided; it would only acknowledge a superiority already established in the Covenant itself. M. de Lapradelle thought that the Committee would best fulfil the duties which had been entrusted to it by the League of Nations, if it adopted this method.

Mr. ROOT, après réflexion sur les idées de M. de Lapradelle, trouve que quelques unes d'entr'elles répondent assez bien aux exigences de la situation actuelle. C'est pourquoi il a préparé un mémorandum où ces idées, ainsi que l'idée de la proposition du Président qu'il juge la plus utile, ont été incorporées. Mr. Root lit son mémorandum (voir annexe 4). Il ajoute qu'il part de deux idées fondamentales: la nouvelle Cour doit former une partie d'un système judiciaire dont l'ancienne Cour d'Arbitrage, qui con-

Mr. ROOT after reflecting upon the ideas of M. de Lapradelle came to the conclusion that some of them would meet the requirements of the present situation. For this reason he had prepared a memorandum, in which his own ideas and that of the President which to him seemed the most valuable, were incorporated. Mr. Root read his memorandum. (See Annex 4). He added that he had taken two fundamental ideas as his starting point: first the new Court should form part of a judicial system in which the old

tinuerait à exister, fait également partie; et, en même temps, la nouvelle Cour formera une partie du système de la Société des Nations.

Le système judiciaire international doit avoir quatre attributions différentes:

1. Décider des questions de droit pur et des questions résultant de l'interprétation de contrats.

2. Décider des questions à résoudre sur la base des principes de droit applicables en l'absence de règles de droit pur ou de dispositions contractuelles.

3. Décider des questions de fait.

4. Conciliation.

Mr. Root pense que la participation des membres de la Cour Permanente d'Arbitrage à l'œuvre de la constitution de la nouvelle Cour est désirable. Ces membres sont mieux placés que toute autre personne dans les divers pays pour pouvoir juger des questions dont aura à connaître la Cour, ainsi que des mérites des personnes à élire dans les différents pays. Les membres de la Cour d'Arbitrage ont aussi cet avantage, comme électeurs, qu'on ne peut les soupçonner de faire des élections politiques, et que d'autre part, il y a tout lieu de présumer qu'ils sont animés de l'esprit international.

Mais Mr. Root pense que la participation des membres de la Cour d'Arbitrage doit avoir lieu au commencement et non pas à la fin de la procédure, comme l'a proposé M. de Lapradelle. Autrement le rôle du Conseil et de l'Assemblée serait par trop diminué; ce n'est que la décision finale qui est importante.

Mr. Root pense que la nécessité d'arriver à un résultat amènerait le Conseil et l'Assemblée à tomber d'accord sur le choix des juges. D'autre part, il est convaincu qu'on aura toutes les garanties nécessaires pour obtenir des juges compétents, si l'on donne à la Cour d'Arbitrage le droit de proposer des candidats. Si le Conseil et l'Assemblée ne peuvent pas se mettre d'accord sur le choix des derniers noms, le droit qu'ils ont de choisir même des noms ne figurant pas sur les listes proposées, est une garantie suffisante pour qu'un résultat soit obtenu.

Mr. Root pense que sa dernière proposition, à savoir que les électeurs seront dans l'obligation morale d'assurer la représentation des divers systèmes juridiques, donne le moyen de réaliser, autant qu'il est possible, l'idée émise par un des membres du Comité.

Mr. Root termine en disant que la proposition

Court of Arbitration still in existence would also be included; and second, the new Court should also form part of the system of the League of Nations.

The international judicial system should have four different functions:

1. To determine questions of strict law and questions arising from contracts:

2. To determine questions depending upon the principles of justice applicable in the absence of rules of strict law or contract provisions.

3. To determine facts which are unknown or are disputed.

4. Conciliation.

Mr. Root thought that the participation of members of the Permanent Court of Arbitration in the work of constituting the new Court was desirable. They were in a better position than any other persons in the various countries to take into consideration the questions with which the Court will deal, likewise the relative merits of persons to be elected in the several countries. The members of the Court of Arbitration had also this advantage as electors: they could not be suspected of making political choices; on the other hand, there was every reason to believe that they had the international mind.

But Mr. Root thought that the participation of the members of the Court of Arbitration should be at the beginning and not at the end of the procedure, as M. de Lapradelle had proposed. Otherwise the part played by the Council and the Assembly would be too much reduced: it is only the final decision that really counts.

Mr. Root thought that the necessity of reaching a conclusion would lead the Council and Assembly to agree on the choice of judges. On the other hand he was convinced that, if the right of putting forward candidates were given to the Court of Arbitration, there would be a sufficient guarantee that one would obtain competent judges. If the Council and Assembly could not agree on the choice of the last candidates, the right which they had to select candidates not mentioned on the proposed list of nominations would be a sufficient guarantee that a result would be attained.

Mr. Root thought that his last proposal, that the electors should be under the moral obligation to ensure the representation of the various legal systems, provided for the realisation, in as great a degree as possible, of the idea put forward by one of the members of the Committee.

qu'il vient de faire n'est pas sienne. Ce sont des „biens volés".

M. HAGERUP ne peut admettre que l'idée fondamentale de la proposition n'appartient pas à Mr. Root lui-même.

LORD PHILLIMORE dit que la première proposition de Mr. Root a été adoptée par M. Loder, M. de Lapradelle et lui-même. Il n'est pas certain si la proposition de M. Altamira rentre dans la même catégorie; il a l'intention de l'étudier après la séance.

Lord Phillimore fait remarquer que l'idée fondamentale de son projet est empruntée au discours de Mr. Root, mais qu'il a développé le plan exposé par ce dernier.

Il croit que tous les membres du Comité sont d'accord sur le second point du projet déposé au cours de la séance par Mr. Root. Les 4e et 5e points de ce projet reproduisent ses idées propres combinées avec celles de M. de Lapradelle.

Quant au 6e point, il est disposé à l'accepter, mais il désire voir préciser le sens véritable du mot „obligés". S'il ne s'agit que d'une obligation morale, il peut accepter la disposition telle quelle. Si, au contraire, il s'agit d'une obligation réelle, il aura quelques remarques à ajouter.

Le plan de Mr. Root veut assurer, dans la mesure du possible, une représentation à la Cour de tous les systèmes de droit. Lord Phillimore ne sait pas ce qu'il faut entendre par „les différents systèmes de droit". Il fait un exposé des différents systèmes juridiques actuellement en vigueur; il cite les systèmes japonais, italien, scandinave et allemand, et se demande comment il conviendra de choisir des représentants de tous ces systèmes.

Il attire également l'attention sur les systèmes slave, turc et oriental qui doivent être représentés. Il montre la difficulté créée par la question compliquée du droit en vigueur dans les Dominions britanniques d'outre-mer: droit romain-hollandais, ancien droit français, droit hindou, droit mahomédan.

Lord Phillimore croit qu'on ne peut pas imposer aux électeurs une obligation réelle d'assurer la représentation de tous ces systèmes; mais s'il ne s'agit que d'une obligation morale, il se déclare satisfait.

Lord Phillimore ajoute que, bien qu'il se rallie en principe aux projets de Mr. Root et de M. de Lapradelle, il doit à certains égards faire des réserves sur ces projets; — d'une façon

Mr. Root concluded with the remark that the proposals made by him were not his own. They were all "stolen goods."

M. HAGERUP could not agree with this statement and said that the fundamental idea embodied in the proposal had come from Mr. Root himself.

LORD PHILLIMORE said that the first proposal of Mr. Root had been accepted by M. Loder, M. de Lapradelle and himself. He was not quite sure whether M. Altamira's project coincided with that of Mr. Root; he intended to study it after the meeting.

Lord Phillimore said that the original idea of his own project was borrowed from Mr. Root's speech, but he had worked out the details of the plan of Mr. Root.

He thought that all the members of the Committee agreed to the second point of the project submitted at the meeting by Mr. Root. The fourth and fifth points represented his own ideas combined with those of M. de Lapradelle.

As regards the sixth point, he was prepared to accept it, but he wished to have the exact meaning of the word "obligation" defined. If this meant merely a moral obligation, he could accept the provision as it stood, but if a real obligation were meant, he had some remarks to add.

Mr. Root's plan was to ensure, as far as possible, a representation on the Court of all the systems of law. Lord Phillimore did not quite understand what was meant by "the different systems of law". He enumerated the different legal systems, actually in force; he mentioned the Japanese, Italian, Scandinavian and German systems of law, and raised a question as to how representatives of each of these systems were to be chosen.

He also drew attention to the Slav, Turkish and Eastern systems which should be represented. He pointed out the difficulties created by the complicated question of the laws in force in the British Overseas Dominions, Roman-Dutch law, old French law, Hindoo law, Mahommedan law.

Lord Phillimore thought that a definite obligation to ensure the representation of all these systems could not be imposed on the electors. If only a moral obligation were intended, he was quite satisfied.

Although he agreed in principle with the plans of Mr. Root and M. de Lapradelle, he

générale, sa préférence va à celui de M. de Lapradelle.

Parlant de la fonction attribuée par ces projets aux membres de la Cour Permanente d'Arbitrage, il considère l'utilité de cette Cour comme collège électoral. Plusieurs Etats ne sont pas représentés; d'autre part, certains membres à coup sûr ne représentent pas véritablement leurs pays dans la situation où sont aujourd'hui ces pays.

Il est très difficile de trouver en Grande Bretagne des personnes disposées à accepter d'être nommées membres de la Cour Permanente d'Arbitrage. Les hommes compétents ne veulent pas abandonner leur situation actuelle; le cas de Sir Edward Fry était tout à fait spécial. Si l'on fait de la Cour Permanente d'Arbitrage un collège électoral, la Grande Bretagne nommera certainement les quatre membres auxquels elle a droit, mais pour servir d'électeurs, et pour cela seulement.

M. RICCI-BUSATTI déclare que ses préférences vont au premier projet du Président; c'est dans cette voie, croit-il, que l'on doit chercher une solution, parce que le caractère principal du projet du Baron Descamps est le rattachement de la nouvelle Cour à la Cour d'Arbitrage: on peut attribuer au Conseil et à l'Assemblée un certain rôle dans la composition de la nouvelle Cour, mais il faut que la base en soit la Cour d'Arbitrage. L'essentiel, c'est de maintenir l'unité du fond de la juridiction internationale.

La différence entre la Cour de Justice et la Cour d'Arbitrage n'est pas fondamentale. Cette dernière aura la faculté d'appliquer des principes et de suivre des procédures plus larges que l'autre; c'est tout. D'autre part, il est permis de dire que la Cour d'Arbitrage remplace à certains points de vue l'Assemblée de la Société des Nations; la Cour est composée de délégations de quatre juristes désignés par leurs Gouvernements; l'Assemblée, de trois personnages politiques représentant les mêmes Gouvernements; les premiers paraissent évidemment les mieux qualifiés pour le choix des juges.

M. Ricci-Busatti rappelle les raisons qui expliquent pourquoi on a eu si rarement recours à la Cour d'Arbitrage: il espère qu'on fera plus souvent appel à la Cour de Justice à cause du grand nombre de petites questions qui pourront être réglées par son entremise. Cependant, il croit que la nouvelle Cour doit, tout comme la Cour d'Arbitrage, consister en une liste de juges toujours prêts à siéger, mais cette liste

would have to make reservations concerning certain features. In general, his preference was for M. de Lapradelle's plan.

Speaking of the power vested in the members of the Permanent Court of Arbitration by these projects he considered the advantages of this body as an electoral college. Several States were not represented, while certain members, without doubt, did not represent their countries as these countries existed to day.

It was very difficult to find in Great-Britain persons willing to be appointed members of the Court of Arbitration. Competent men were not prepared to give up their present positions. The case of Sir Edward Fry was a very special one. If the Court of Arbitration were made into an electoral college, Great-Britain certainly would name the four members to which she has the right, but with the exclusive view of having them to serve as electors.

M. RICCI-BUSATTI stated that he preferred the first proposal of the President, and he thought that it was along the lines of this proposal that a solution should be sought, for the reason that the principal characteristic of Baron Descamps' project was to attach the new Court to the Court of Arbitration; a certain influence over the composition of the new Court might be given to the Council and to the Assembly, but the Court of Arbitration must be the starting point. The essential point was to maintain a basic unity in international jurisdiction.

The difference between the Permanent Court of Justice and the Court of Arbitration was not fundamental; the latter would be able to apply principles and follow a procedure broader than the former, that was all. On the other hand, it might be said, that the Court of Arbitration replaced from certain points of view the Assembly of the League of Nations. The Court was composed of groups of four jurists chosen by their Governments, the Assembly consisted of three political persons representing the same Governments; the former plainly appeared the better qualified to choose the judges.

M. Ricci-Busatti recalled the reasons which explain why such infrequent use was made of the Court of Arbitration; he hoped that the Court of Justice would be used oftener, considering the great number of small questions which might be settled by its intervention. However, he thought that the new Court, like the Court of Arbitration, should consist of a list of judges

sera bien plus restreinte que la liste des arbitres, et extraite de celle-ci.

Ce sera dans cette nouvelle liste limitée qu'on choisira les juges appelés à connaître d'un cas particulier. Cette manière de composer le tribunal aurait cet avantage qu'elle permettrait de choisir des juges ayant une compétence spéciale pour chaque litige déterminé; il ne faut pas oublier que la nouvelle Cour sera appelée à juger de cas qui lui seront soumis de toutes les parties du monde, et concernant toutes sortes de matières; tout membre peut, dans ces conditions, n'être pas qualifié pour connaître de toutes les questions.

Le PRESIDENT voudrait d'abord élucider une question de procédure. Une des objections contre l'utilisation de la Cour d'Arbitrage comme collège électoral est sa composition actuelle, restreinte à certains égards; mais cette composition peut être étendue. Une procédure spéciale dans ce but a été incorporée dans l'article 94 de la Convention de 1907 pour le règlement pacifique des conflits internationaux. Il donne lecture de cet article.

Le Président examine ensuite la proposition de Lord Phillimore. Le Conseil aurait, d'après cette proposition, le premier et le dernier mot dans la nomination des juges.

Le Président expose comment selon lui, le mécanisme proposé par Lord Phillimore fonctionnera en fait, et il montre comment, si son appréciation est exacte, l'Assemblée n'aura que le rôle d'approuver le choix du Conseil, car celui-ci décide tout dès la première instance, ou peu s'en faut.

Le Président, poursuivant sa critique, attire l'attention de ses collègues sur une certaine incompatibilité qui, dans son opinion, existe entre les fonctions que possède le Conseil aux termes du Pacte, et celles dont on veut l'investir. Il paraît difficile de confier au Conseil, qui en cas de conflit concentre tout le système de la procédure en „recommandation", le pouvoir de nommer en outre les organes de judicature.

Le Président veut bien donner au Conseil toute l'influence qui lui est dûe, mais il n'est pas persuadé que la nouvelle attribution conférée au Conseil dans ces conditions, soit un élément de force pour lui, et il estime en tout cas que la Cour d'Arbitrage est le meilleur collège électoral pour la nomination des juges.

Il importe de s'élever à une conception d'ensemble dans l'organisation de la justice internationale. A ce point de vue on ne saurait faire ab-

always ready to sit. This list, however, should be much more limited than the list of arbitrators and be taken from the latter.

It would be from this new limited list that judges would be chosen to sit in a particular case. This method of constituting the Court would have the advantage of allowing judges to be chosen who possess special qualifications for the particular case; it must not be forgotten that the new Court would be called upon to try cases submitted from all parts of the world and dealing with all kinds of questions; all of the members, under these conditions, could not be supposed to know of all these questions.

The PRESIDENT would first like to elucidate a question of procedure. One of the objections raised against the use of the Court of Arbitration as an electoral college was its present composition, limited in some respects; but this composition could be extended. A special procedure for this purpose was incorporated in article 94 of the Convention of 1907 for the pacific settlement of international disputes. The President read this article.

The President then examined Lord Phillimore's project. The Council would have, according to this proposal, the first and last word in the appointment of judges.

The President explained how, in his opinion, the working of the machinery proposed by Lord Phillimore would be carried out, and he pointed out how, if he understood the plan correctly, the Assembly would limit itself to approving the choice of the Council; for the latter, almost from the outset, would decide everything.

Continuing his criticism, the President drew the attention of his colleagues to a certain incompatibility which, in his opinion, existed between the powers given to the Council under the Covenant and those which it was proposed to give it. It would be difficult to entrust to the Council, in which in the case of a dispute all the procedure in "recommendation" is concentrated, the power also of appointing the judicial organs.

But the President was not convinced that the new function conferred on the Council, in the present conditions, would constitute an element of force for the Council. Anyhow he was of opinion, that the Court of Arbitration would be the best electoral body for the appointment of the judges.

A broad view of the whole situation must be taken in the organisation of the Court of Inter-

straction de la Cour d'Arbitrage, lorsqu'on s'occupe de fonder une Cour nouvelle.

L'omission, qu'on peut appeler systématique, dans les actes de la Conférence de Paris, de toute allusion aux travaux des deux premières Conférences de la Paix est dans les annales diplomatiques un phénomène qu'il est difficile d'expliquer. Il n'est pas sans danger de prétendre créer une œuvre originale à tous égards, sans points d'attache dans le passé et ouvrant vers l'avenir des horizons qu'on représente comme insoupçonnés. Une entreprise présentée dans sa réalité vraie, avec ses tenants historiques, comme une étape dans la voie du progrès, éveille moins d'appréhension et suscite moins d'antagonisme.

Le Président rend hommage au Comité qui a reconnu les liens qui existent entre la nouvelle Cour et la Cour d'Arbitrage. Si cette dernière n'a pas réalisé toutes les attentes, cela tient à de multiples causes dont les Gouvernements sont en partie responsables, et dont, pour une autre partie, nous pouvons précisément, dans l'organisation de la nouvelle Cour, conjurer l'action.

Le Président reconnaît qu'il faut maintenant tâcher de trouver une solution à la question, si importante, de la nomination des juges, et que, pour cela, il faut entrer dans la voie des concessions; mais il croit qu'il serait dangereux de donner au Conseil, sur la nomination des juges, la principale influence effective. Le Président craint que ce plan ne soit pas accepté par l'Assemblée de la Société des Nations, et il ne voit pas bien l'avantage définitif que pourrait en retirer le Conseil.

national Justice. This view must not leave out the Court of Arbitration when the question of establishing a new Court is being considered.

The omission, which may be called systematic, in the acts of the Paris Conference, of any reference to the work of the first two Peace Conferences was a phenomenon of diplomatic history which was difficult to explain. It was not without danger to pretend to create a piece of work original in all respects, a work without connection in the past and opening up in the future horizons which, it was believed, never were suspected of existing. An undertaking, presented in its true light, with its historical connections, and as a step in the march of progress, would waken fewer apprehensions and excite less antagonism.

The President complimented the Committee for having recognised the ties which unite the new Court and the Court of Arbitration. If the latter had not realised all expectations, that was due to numerous causes for which the Governments are in part responsible, and of which the Committee, precisely in the organisation of the new Court, could prevent in part the effect.

The President recognised the necessity of attempting now to find a solution of the important question of the nomination of judges, a question which would require concessions; but he thought that it would be dangerous to give to the Council the main effective influence on the nomination of judges. The President feared that this plan might not be accepted by the Assembly of the League of Nations and he did not see clearly the final advantage which the Council might derive from it.

LORD PHILLIMORE soulève la question de savoir à quel organe de la Société sera soumis le rapport futur du Comité. C'est le Conseil qui a nommé les membres du Comité, et si ce rapport n'est pas accepté par le Conseil, celui-ci ne le renverra pas à l'Assemblée.

LORD PHILLIMORE raised the question as to which organ of the League the future report of the Committee would be submitted. The Council was the organ by which the members of the Committee had been named and if the report was not accepted by the Council, the latter would not refer it to the Assembly.

Le PRESIDENT répond en soulignant la pleine indépendance du Comité. Le Conseil sera le premier à la reconnaître. En tout cas, il serait fort difficile de faire accepter par l'Assemblée un projet qui donne au Conseil une influence trop prépondérante.

The PRESIDENT answered by emphasising the complete independence of the Committee. The Council would be the first to recognise this. In any event it would be very difficult to obtain the consent of the Assembly to a plan which gives to the Council an unduly preponderant influence.

M. HAGERUP dit qu'il ne veut pas être considéré comme ayant des idées préconçues contraires à l'adoption du plan du Président. Ce plan est d'ailleurs assez conforme au projet com-

M. HAGERUP said that he did not wish to be considered as having preconceived ideas against the adoption of the President's plan. This plan, on the contrary, conformed well

mun des 3 commissions des pays scandinaves auquel M. Hagerup a collaboré. Mais il est convaincu qu'on n'aboutira pas si chacun croit devoir défendre les solutions qu'il trouve meilleures. Il faut tâcher de concilier les deux principes exposés, ainsi que tous les intérêts. Pour cela il faut d'abord trouver une base d'entente, mais elle ne saurait être constituée ni par le projet auquel il a collaboré lui-même, ni par celui du Président, ni enfin par celui de M. Ricci-Busatti. La seule proposition qui puisse être utilisée, c'est, à son avis, celle de Mr. Root et de Lord Phillimore. Il faut s'entendre sur la base de cette proposition, en éclaircissant les points qui restent encore douteux.

Bien qu'il soit depuis longtemps jurisconsulte, sa conscience ne lui défend pas, au point de vue purement juridique, de conférer au Conseil de la Société des Nations une part dans la nomination des juges.

Il admet pourtant qu'il y a des objections d'ordre politique. Le Conseil n'est pas populaire, et il se rallie à ce que vient de dire à ce sujet le Président. Cependant, les Etats ont adhéré à la Société des Nations; et il s'agit maintenant de faire le meilleur usage possible de ses institutions.

Si on ne peut pas créer une Cour permanente de Justice sans une collaboration du Conseil — et il semble à M. Hagerup qu'on se trouve actuellement dans cette situation — il est disposé à admettre cette collaboration. Celle-ci ne heurte pas en elle-même le principe de l'égalité juridique des Etats, ce que fait au contraire la proposition de M. Adatci, à laquelle M. Hagerup ne peut pas se rallier. Mais si nous admettons cette égalité de droit, il est pourtant impossible de réaliser une parfaite égalité de fait. Il y a là une question d'équilibre: il est impossible de ne pas faire pencher la balance d'un côté ou de l'autre. Si l'on ne donne pas la prépondérance de fait aux grandes Puissances, ce seront les petits Etats qui en seront investis, et nous devons nous rendre compte, d'après ce qui nous a été dit par plusieurs des membres du Comité, que les grandes Puissances n'accepteront pas toutes cet état de choses. En ce qui concerne la proposition de faire représenter dans la Cour les différents systèmes juridiques, M. Hagerup adopte la manière de voir de M. Loder. La Cour n'a pas à rendre justice d'après des lois nationales, mais d'après le droit international qui, en principe, est commun à tous les Etats.

En résumé, M. Hagerup dit qu'il est impossible d'atteindre l'idéal; si l'on ne veut pas ac-

enough to the Joint Scheme of the three Commissions of the Scandinavian countries, in which M. Hagerup had collaborated. But he was convinced that success would not be attained, if each one felt bound to defend the solutions which he thought best. An attempt must be made to harmonise the two principles presented and all the interests as weil. To accomplish this, a basis for understanding must first be found, but this could be furnished neither by the plan which he had assisted in preparing, nor by the President's, nor finally by that of M. Ricci-Busatti. The only plan which might be of use was, in his opinion, that of Mr. Root and Lord Phillimore. An understanding must be reached on the basis of this proposition, in throwing light on the points which still remained doubtful.

Although a jurisconsult himself for many years, his conscience did not forbid him from a purely legal standpoint to confer on the Council of the League of Nations a part in the nomination of judges.

He admitted nevertheless that there are objections of a political nature. The Council was not popular, and he agreed with what the President had just said on the subject. However, States had adhered to the League of Nations, and it now became a question of using its institutions to the greatest possible advantage.

If it were impossible to create a Permanent Court of Justice without a collaboration of the Council — and that seemed to M. Hagerup to be the situation in which they found themselves — he was prepared to admit this collaboration. This collaboration in itself did not clash with the principle of the legal equality of States, which was involved in the proposition of M. Adatci to which M. Hagerup could not agree. But if this equality in law was admitted, it was impossible to realise a perfect equality in fact. That involved a question of equilibrium: it is difficult not to have the balance tipped to one side or the other. If preponderance in fact were not given to the great Powers, it would be the small Powers who would be invested with it; and the Committee should keep in mind what had been said by several members of the Committee, namely, that all the great Powers would not accept this state of things. Concerning the representation on the Court of the different legal systems, M. Hagerup adopted M. Loder's views. The Court was not to administer justice in accordance with national laws, but in accordance with international law which, in principle, was common to all States.

In conclusion, M. Hagerup said that it was

cepter un compromis, on échouera. Il demande aux membres d'abandonner les idées qui leur sont les plus chères, parce qu'elles leur semblent les plus parfaites, pour se rallier à la proposition de Lord Phillimore qui lui paraît constituer la seule solution possible.

Le PRESIDENT demande si M. Hagerup ne trouve pas qu'il y ait quelqu' incompatibilité entre la tâche normale du Conseil, qui consiste à résoudre des difficultés internationales sur la base d'une action politique, et la nomination des membres de la Cour Permanente qu'on veut maintenant confier au Conseil à titre principal.

M. HAGERUP dit qu'il ne trouve pas qu'il y ait là une incompatibilité plus grande qu'entre les diverses fonctions normales de tout gouvernement national. Le juge idéal serait celui qui tomberait du ciel; mais il faut trouver une solution pratique.

La séance est levée à 12.30 de l'après-midi.

Le Président:
(signé) Brn. DESCAMPS.

Le Secrétaire-Général:
(signé) D. ANZILOTTI.

impossible to achieve the ideal; if a compromise were not accepted, the Committee would fail. He called upon the members to abandon some of their most cherished ideas, those which seemed to them the most perfect, and to adopt Lord Phillimore's proposal, which seemed to him the only possible solution.

The PRESIDENT asked M. Hagerup if he did not think that there was an incompatibility between the normal task of the Council, — that of solving international difficulties on the basis of political considerations, — and the task of appointing members of the Permanent Court which it was now wished to vest in the Council as one of its principal duties.

M. HAGERUP said that he did not see any greater incompatibility between these two tasks than between the normal functions of any national government. The ideal judge would be one that dropped from the skies; what they had to do was to find a practical solution.

The meeting closed at 12.30 p.m.

The President:
(signed) Brn. DESCAMPS.

The Secretary-General:
(signed) D. ANZILOTTI.

ANNEXE No. 1.

Proposition de M. Altamira.

1. Le premier stage consistera dans la présentation ou proposition de personnes, que chacun des Etats fera d'après des listes préparées par:

a) la Cour suprême du pays;

b) les Facultés de droit;

c) les Académies officielles ou Royales (s'il y en a) de Droit et des Sciences morales et politiques.

Une liste sera ainsi dressée par le Gouvernement et présentée au Conseil de la Société des Nations.

2. Ces listes devront comprendre des jurisconsultes nationaux et étrangers, réunissant les conditions essentielles: autorité morale, qualité professionnelle.

Le choix devra donc se fixer sur des personnes remplissant les conditions requises dans chaque pays pour l'admission dans la haute magistrature tant judiciaire qu'administrative. (En Espagne les professeurs dans certaines branches peuvent être admis à ces fonctions après quelques années de service. Dans les pays, où cela n'a pas lieu, on devra choisir dans une certaine proportion des jurisconsultes d'une compétence notoire en matière de droit international, et de préférence ceux qui possèdent déjà une expérience de l'arbitrage international).

3. Tous les Etats auront le droit de présenter une liste du même nombre de candidats; mais il leur sera loisible d'en présenter moins, s'ils le jugent utile.

4. Le choix, en vue de la nomination par le Conseil et l'Assemblée de la Société des Nations, portera sur ces listes d'après une procédure qui pourrait être celle qu'a proposée Lord Phillimore, ou toute autre analogue.

Ainsi, tout en laissant aux grandes et aux petites Puissances une certaine part d'influence, on aurait toujours en vue les noms les plus dignes du monde entier, toute consideration de nationalité mise à part. Dans l'intérêt même de la justice il faut espérer qu'on choisirait les meilleurs, ce qui sera toujours la plus sûre garantie que justice sera faite.

5. Le nombre des juges composant la Cour pourrait être de 15; c'est celui qui revient le plus souvent dans les divers projets connus.

ANNEX No. 1.

Proposal of M. Altamira.

1. The first step shall be the presentation or proposal of candidates which each State shall make from lists prepared by:

a) the Supreme Court of the country;

b) the Law Faculties;

c) the Official or Royal (if any) Academies of Law and moral and political Science.

A list shall be in this way prepared by the Government and presented to the Council of the League of Nations.

2. These lists shall contain national and foreign jurisconsults possessing the essential qualities of moral authority and professional ability.

The persons should be chosen who fulfil the conditions required in each country for appointment to the high legal or administrative magistracy. (In Spain professors on certain subjects are eligible for such duties after some years of service. In countries where this is not so, a certain number of the candidates should be selected from jurisconsults of recognised ability in international law, and preferably from those who have already had experience of international arbitration).

3. Each State shall have the right to submit an equal number of candidates; but they may, if they so desire, submit a smaller number.

4. The Council and Assembly of the League of Nations will elect from these lists. The procedure might be that proposed by Lord Phillimore, or any other similar one.

Thus, although leaving to the great and small Powers a certain amount of influence, there would always be under consideration the most respected and worthy names in the whole world, regardless of their nationality. In the interest of justice it is hoped that the best would be chosen; such choice would be the best guarantee that justice would be done.

5. The number of judges composing the Court might be 15. This number is the most favored in the various known projects.

In order to retain the proportional system which seems to be considered as an essential condition for success in the establishment of the Court, a limit might be fixed for the number of

Pour conserver le système de la proportionnalité qui semble être une condition de réussite pour l'établissement de la Cour, on pourrait fixer un chiffre limité des juges appartenant à une même nationalité. Cette limite pourra porter sur le nombre total des juges de la Cour, ou bien sur le nombre des juges qui devront siéger chaque fois dans chaque affaire particulière.

Par ce moyen, ainsi que par des récusations, on arrivera à donner satisfaction à certaines exigences, qu'il semble impossible de dédaigner, si l'on veut obtenir l'assentiment de certaines Puissances.

Cependant, il serait préférable que soient représentés à la Cour, plutôt que des Etats particuliers, des systèmes de droit qui eux-mêmes représentent des groupements de nations: par exemple le système espagnol qui, au fond, représente le droit de tous les pays américains parlant la langue castillane.

6. Il est entendu que l'établissement de la Cour de Justice internationale ne suppose pas la disparition de la Cour Permanente d'Arbitrage, ces deux corps ayant des fonctions entièrement différentes.

judges belonging to any one nationality. This limit might be fixed with regard to the total number of judges of the Court, or with regard to the number of judges who should sit on any given case.

By this means and also by a system of exclusion, certain demands might be satisfied which seem impossible to disregard if it is desired to obtain the approval of certain Powers.

Nevertheless it would be preferable to represent on the Court systems of law which represent groups of nations, rather than particular States. For instance the Spanish system is the basis of the systems of law of all American countries speaking Spanish.

6. It is understood that the establishment of the Court of International Justice does not presuppose the disappearance of the Permanent Court of Arbitration whose functions are entirely different.

ANNEXE No. 2.

Discours de M. Loder.

Déférant au désir du Président, j'ai l'intention d'expliquer d'abord pourquoi je n'ai pas présenté un projet personnel, et de dire ensuite ce que je pense des deux propositions faites, l'une par le Président, l'autre par Lord Phillimore. Cette dernière proposition pourrait être appelée aussi le projet Root—Phillimore.

Le projet qu'il aurait été naturel de ma part de présenter et de défendre est celui qui a été adopté à La Haye en février dernier. Mais les précieuses informations prises dans le domaine des réalités qu'ont apporté mes honorables collègues ici présents m'ont fait comprendre que le projet des cinq Etats neutres est entaché d'un vice, chaque jour d'ailleurs moins répandu; j'ai nommé l'idéalisme. Nous avions cru que, grâce à la disposition selon laquelle chaque Etat ne peut porter sur sa liste de présentation qu'un tiers de candidats étant ses ressortissants, il arriverait automatiquement que les deux autres tiers ne compteraient que des noms illustres, des *primi inter pares*.

Il n'en est rien, m'a-t-on dit. Il y aura des combinaisons, des conspirations qui réussiront à faire exclure ces lumières, et nous ne voulons pas d'un système qui n'engendrerait que du mal. Je vois que le monde est aussi mauvais qu'il a été toujours, et je retire ma proposition.

J'en viens maintenant à la proposition du Président. Je dirai tout de suite que son idée fondamentale me séduit beaucoup, et cela pour deux raisons.

D'abord parce qu'il rattache la Cour à créer à l'œuvre accomplie à La Haye par les Conférences de la Paix. Il préconise un système d'unification de l'organisation du droit international mondial. Il me paraît que la réalisation de cette idée est hautement désirable. Et, si je ne me trompe, Mr. Root y donnera également son adhésion.

En second lieu, je trouve très heureuse l'idée d'attribuer une part active dans l'élection des juges de la Cour future, à un collège de juristes d'une si haute importance et d'une autorité si universellement reconnue. Il va de soi que je ne parle ici que de ce qu'il a appelé le Tribunal de Justice internationale, et je laisse de côté la Haute Cour qui n'entre pas dans nos discussions ac-

ANNEX No. 2.

Statement made by M. Loder.

In deference to the wish of the President, I intend first to explain why I have not submitted a proposal of my own, afterwards to give my opinion on the two schemes put forward, the one by the President and the other by Lord Phillimore, which I may call the Root—Phillimore project.

The plan which I should most naturally put forward and defend is that which we prepared at the Hague in February. However, the valuable information drawn from the realm of realities and presented by my honorable colleagues here present have made me realise that the project of the five neutral States is tainted by a blemish which after all is daily becoming less and less wide spread — I refer to idealism. We thought that thanks to the arrangement made in that project whereby each State could only put forward on its list of candidates a third of its own subjects, it would work out automatically that the other two thirds would include only the most distinguished, the *primi inter pares*.

I am told that this plan is worthless. There would be combinations and intrigues which would succeed in excluding these luminaries, and we do not desire a system which engenders only evil. I see that the world is still as corrupt as ever, and I withdraw my proposal.

I now come to the proposal of the President. I shall say at the outset that his fundamental idea attracts me very much, and for two reasons:

First, because it links the Court to be created to the work done at the Hague by the Peace Conferences. Also it favors a system of unification of the organisation of international law throughout the world. It seems to me that the realisation of this idea is highly desirable. If I am not mistaken, Mr. Root also will agree.

In the second place, I very much like the idea of giving an active part in the election of judges for the future Court to a body of jurists of such great importance and of such widely recognised authority. It goes without saying that I refer only to the Tribunal of International Justice. I leave aside the High Court, which does not enter into the present discussion and which we can discuss later.

tuelles, mais dont nous pourrons traiter ultérieurement.

Il me semble qu'en effet les meilleurs juristes feront les meilleurs juges.

J'ouvre ici une parenthèse. Je me souviens que, dans une conversation que j'ai eu l'honneur d'avoir avec M. Léon Bourgeois, celui-ci m'a dit: „N'oubliez pas que si vous voulez rester dans le domaine pratique vouz devrez, quel que soit le système que vous adopterez, accorder toujours un rôle plus ou moins actif à l'Assemblée. Car l'Assemblée, c'est l'organe des nations elles-mêmes. D'après le Pacte, c'est elle qui en dernier ressort décide de l'organisation de la Cour, et elle ne consentira jamais à être écartée au moment où il s'agira de choisir les personnes qui devront composer cette Cour."

J'ai senti toute la justesse de ces paroles; l'idée qu'elles expriment est la base du projet des cinq Etats neutres.

Donc, ce que j'approuve dans le projet Descamps, c'est qu'il donne le meilleur moyen de trouver de bons candidats, mais ce que je lui reproche, c'est d'écarter l'Assemblée et d'être une application du principe: „sur vous et sans vous".

J'en viens maintenant au projet Root—Phillimore. Il est basé sur la réalité des choses, et je m'incline respectueusement devant le discours qu'a prononcé hier Mr. Root. L'égalité des Etats, nous dit-il, c'est leur souveraineté. Or, la souveraineté, c'est le droit pour quelqu'un d'être le maître absolu chez lui, de diriger ses propres affaires comme bon lui semble, mais cela ne signifie nullement qu'il aurait le droit de se mêler des affaires des autres et d'exercer un certain pouvoir sur eux.

L'élection faite par un collège qui aura le pouvoir de décider entre des Etats souverains ne peut être basée que sur un accord.

Cet accord se fait entre Etats égaux et souverains, et par le fait même que c'est un accord, l'égalité est sauvée.

Par conséquent, la seule difficulté consiste à trouver pour cette élection une méthode qui protège les grands contre les petits, aussi bien que les petits contre les grands.

Le raisonnement me paraît fondé. Examinons si le projet de Lord Phillimore, qui esquisse les moyens d'arriver à un tel accord, atteint le but qu'il se propose.

Il n'y a pas d'objection à élever, ce me semble, contre l'idée fondamentale qu'il faudrait la collaboration de l'Assemblée et du Conseil. Mais la façon dont cette idée est développée me paraît prêter le flanc à la critique.

L'Assemblée et le Conseil dresseront séparé-

It seems to me that the best jurists will make the best judges.

Here I wish to make a parenthetical remark. I remember, that in a conversation which I had the honor to have with M. Bourgeois, the latter said to me: "Do not forget that if you want to keep in a practical realm, whatever your system may be, you must give a more or less active rôle to the Assembly. For the Assembly is the body representing the nations themselves. According to the Covenant, it is the body which will have the final decision in the matter of the organisation of the Court, and it would never consent to be pushed aside when the time comes to choose the persons of whom the Court is to be composed."

I am aware of the truth of these words, and the ideas which they express are the basis of the Five Neutral Powers' plan.

That which I approve of in the plan of Baron Descamps is that he gives the best means of finding the good candidates, but that which I do not like is the fact that it puts aside the Assembly and amounts to an application of the saying "sur vous, sans vous".

I now come to the Root—Phillimore system. This is based on realities. I compliment Mr. Root sincerely on the speech which he made yesterday. The equality of States, he tells us, is their sovereignty. But sovereignty is the right for someone to be absolutely master at home, to conduct all one's own affairs exactly as may seem best, but this in no way implies the right to mix in other peoples affairs, and to exercise a certain control over them.

An election made by an electoral college which has the power to make decisions between sovereign States can have no other basis than mutual agreement.

This agreement is reached between equal sovereign States, and by the very fact that it is an agreement, equality is preserved.

Consequently, the only difficulty consists in finding for this election a method which will defend the large States against the small, as well as the small against the large.

The argument appears to me well founded. Let us see if the project of Lord Phillimore, which outlines the means of reaching such an agreement, will attain its proposed end.

It seems to me there is no objection which presents itself to the fundamental idea that there must be collaboration between the Assembly and the Council. The method, however, employed in the working out of this idea seems to me open to criticism.

ment des listes. Ceux qui figureront sur les deux listes seront considérés comme élus. En réalité il ne semble pas probable que le cas se présente jamais. La liste du Conseil, où les grands Etats ont la majorité, ne contiendra probablement que des noms de ressortissants des grands Etats. Les grands Etats représentés au Conseil, sachant que les Etats secondaires ont la grande majorité à l'Assemblée, et craignant naturellement les combinaisons et les intrigues, essaieront d'assurer l'élection du plus grand nombre possible de leurs ressortissants. L'Assemblée reçoit la liste du Conseil, et en vertu de l'article 3 du projet elle y ajoute tous les noms proposés par les différents Etats. Après cela la liste définitive est prête. Il est évident que les Etats secondaires ne commenceront point leurs intrigues et leurs combinaisons lorsqu'ils se trouveront réunis en Assemblée. Ils seront plus prudents, ils prépareront leurs combinaisons à l'avance et leur admirable accord se manifestera dans les listes qu'ils dresseront et où ne figureront pas de ressortissants des grands Etats. Et c'est alors seulement que la lutte commence: les grands contre les petits, et les petits contre les grands. Naturellement cela n'avancera pas les choses, et l'on devra inévitablement aboutir à un compromis difficile à établir. De bons juges seront sacrifiés pour donner au moins quelques sièges aux autres. Et puisque d'après l'art. 5, le scrutin doit recommencer tant qu'un résultat n'aura pas été obtenu, le résultat final ne pourra être que déplorable. Mais, en tout cas, et c'est sur ce point que je me permets d'attirer votre attention: ce système qui favorise l'imprévu ne donne pas la certitude que les meilleurs candidats seront élus. La politique, qui devrait être exclue de l'élection du corps de magistrats dont il s'agit, la politique, dis-je, y fera son entrée triomphale.

En résumé donc: ce qui me séduit dans la proposition de Lord Phillimore, c'est qu'il fait collaborer à la décision les deux organes principaux de la Société des Nations, et qu'il les fait travailler ensemble dans l'intérêt public et pour le plus grand bien de la plus haute institution qui soit.

Ce que je n'aime pas, c'est qu'il ouvre la porte toute grande à la politique, et que son projet ne donne aucune garantie et laisse même peu de chance pour que les hommes qui devraient être élus obtiennent la place qui leur est dûe.

Et nous nous trouvons à nouveau en présence de la grande question: comment trouver une solution. Je dis solution — et non pas compromis, parce qu'il serait indigne de baser une institution de si haute importance sur un compromis, c'est-

The Assembly and the Council prepare separately their lists. Those who appear on both lists are considered elected. In reality it does not appear likely that this will ever happen. The list of the Council in which the great States have a majority, probably would contain only the names of subjects of the great States. The large States represented on the Council, knowing that the lesser States have a great majority in the Assembly, and naturally fearing combinations and intrigues would try to ensure the election of as great a number as possible of their representatives. The Assembly receives the list of the Council and, according to Article 3 of the project, adds to it all the names proposed by the different States; and in this way the final list is prepared. It is obvious that the lesser States would not wait to begin their intrigues until they met in the Assembly. They would be most prudent; they would prepare their combinations in advance, and their admirable agreement would manifest itself in the lists which they would prepare and in which subjects of the large States would not appear. And there the struggle begins, of the great States against the small, and the small against the great. Naturally this would not make for progress, and the only ending would be a compromise reached under difficult conditions; suitable judges would be sacrificed so that other States might have at least a few seats. And, as according to Article 5 the ballot should be taken again as long as a definite result is not reached, the final result may be deplorable. But in any case, — and it is to this point I wish to call your attention, — this system which favors the unexpected gives no assurance that the best candidates will be elected. Politics, which ought to be excluded from any influence in the election of this judicial body, politics, I say, would completely gain the upper hand.

In conclusion, then, that which attracts me in the proposal made by Lord Phillimore is that he makes the two principal bodies of the League of Nations work together, and this for common good and for the good if the highest institution which exists.

That which I find to disagree with is that he has opened the door wide to political intrigues, and that his project gives no guarantee and even leaves little chance for men who ought to be elected to obtain the place to which they are entitled.

And we find ourselves confronted by the great question how to find a solution. I say solution, and not compromise, because it would be mean to found an institution of such importance upon

à-dire sur quelque chose qui ne satisfait aucune des parties. Il nous faut une solution, il faut que le Comité puisse crier „Eureka", j'ai trouvé!

Eh bien, Messieurs, ne serait-il pas possible de trouver la solution en combinant les deux systèmes dont je vous parlais? On ne peut pas laisser de côté l'Assemblée et dire à ses Membres: „Vous qui êtes les représentants de tous les pays, vous êtes incapables de choisir des juges; on va nommer vos maîtres sans vous." On ne peut pas dire au Conseil: „Vous qui êtes l'organe de la Société dont l'action se manifeste de façon continue, vous qui réglez les affaires, vous qui conduisez le monde, vous qui représentez les grandes Puissances du monde, vous comprenez bien que vous n'êtes pas assez impartiaux pour qu'on vous confie le choix de juges; cela dépasse vos attributions".

Mais d'autre part nous savons qu'il y a du vrai dans ces propos, nous connaissons la faiblesse morale de tout corps politique, et nous sommes convaincus qu'il serait désastreux de confier à un corps de cette nature la prépondérance dans le choix des juges dont le premier devoir est l'impartialité. Alors, n'est il pas naturel que nous nous tournions vers le projet du Président?

Qui serait mieux à même de choisir les meilleurs juristes, qui doivent être des hommes de valeur, rompus aux affaires, à qui on peut confier la tâche de faire le droit, qui pourrait mieux les choisir, dis-je, que les arbitres internationaux?

C'est donc à eux de composer une liste de candidats; on peut donner à tous les Etats le droit de leur recommander certains noms; on peut prescrire aux arbitres de joindre à la liste des juges qu'ils auront proposés la liste de ceux qu'ils auront rejetés et de faire connaître les motifs qui auront dicté leur choix. Mais la liste qu'ils auront établie sera la liste définitive, en dehors de laquelle il ne sera pas permis de choisir.

Présentez la liste à l'Assemblée et au Conseil. Mettez ensuite en branle la machine électorale construite d'après le projet de Lord Phillimore, et les deux organes tâcheront de s'entendre sur le choix des candidats qui auront au moins le mérite d'être proposés par un corps compétent, exempt de tout parti-pris.

Il me semble que par ce moyen on donnera aux organes de la Société ce qui leur est dû et l'on évitera au monde les dangers qui pourraient résulter de leur impéritie, de leur mauvais vouloir, de leurs combinaisons et de leurs intrigues.

Pour terminer, un mot encore des soi-disant systèmes juridiques différents: le système anglais, ou continental, ou américain, ou japonais. Je ne vois pas très bien à quoi cela peut aboutir.

a compromise, that is to say, on something which is satisfactory to none of the parties. We must find a solution. We must be able to cry to the world: "Eureka", I have found it!

Well, Gentlemen, would it not be possible to find this solution by combining the two systems of which I have spoken? We cannot leave aside the Assembly and say to its members, "You who are the representatives of all the countries, you are incapable of choosing judges; we are going to appoint your masters without consulting you". We cannot say to the Council: "You who are the organism of the League which acts continuously, you who control the affairs, you who lead the world, you who represent the great Powers of the earth, you thoroughly understand that you are not sufficiently impartial to be entrusted with the choosing of judges; that exceeds your power".

On the other hand we know there is some truth in this talk, we know the moral weakness of all political bodies, and we are convinced that it would be disastrous to entrust to a body of this character the preponderant influence in the choice of judges, whose chief duty it is to be impartial. Is it not natural then, for us to turn towards the President's plan?

Who should be more able to choose the best jurists, who must be men of high merit, men with large experience, to whom might be entrusted the task of administering justice; — who could better choose them, I ask, than the international Arbitrators?

It is therefore for them to make up a list of candidates; all States may be given the right of making recommendations to them of certain names: it may be laid down that the list of names recommended by them should be accompanied by the list of names rejected by them and that they should state the reasons which have dictated their choice. But the list prepared by them must be the final list outside of which no selection may be made.

Present the list to the Assembly and the Council, set in motion the electoral machine constructed after the plan of Lord Phillimore, and the two bodies will try to come to an understanding on the selection of candidates, who shall have at least the merit of having been proposed by a competent body, free from prejudice.

It this way, it seems to me we shall have accorded to the principal institutions of the League that which is due to them, and avoided the dangers confronting the world which might result

Le droit mondial ne se divise pas en ces quelques catégories. La division est incomplète. D'ailleurs, nous n'en avons pas besoin. Notre Cour appliquera le droit international. En l'espèce, ce seront les traités, les conventions spéciales, le droit international non écrit. Il pourra se faire qu'on ait à appliquer un droit national quelconque, français ou anglais, grec ou marocain, par exemple. Si le cas se présente, le juge international fera ce que font chaque jour les juges de tous les pays: il se mettra au courant de l'affaire qui lui est soumise.

Je crois que la recherche de quelques spécialistes de telle ou telle conception de droit, ne fera qu'augmenter inutilement les difficultés que nous avons à résoudre.

Voici, Messieurs, de façon générale, ce que je pense des projets qui vous sont présentés. Je m'excuse d'avoir retenu trop longtemps votre attention et vous remercie de la patience avec laquelle vous avez daigné m'écouter.

from their incapacity, ill will, intrigues or conspiracies.

One word in conclusion on the so-called different legal systems, the English system, the Continental, the American, or the Japanese system. I do not quite understand what this should lead to. The law of the world does not divide itself into these classes. The division is incomplete, and there is no need for it. Our Court is to apply International Law; in this particular case it consists of treaties, special conventions, and unwritten International Law. It may happen that a national law, French, English, Greek or Moroccan, for instance, has to be applied. In this case, the international judge will do the same as judges do every day in all countries: he will make himself conversant with the subject before him.

I think that a search for a few specialists in this or that system of law would only quite needlessly increase the difficulties with which we have to deal.

This, Gentlemen, is a general expression of my opinion on the projects presented to you. I ask you to excuse me for having required your attention so long, and I thank you for the patience with which you have listened to me.

ANNEXE No. 3.

Projet présenté par M. Adatci.

Art. . . . La Cour se compose de juges désignés par les Membres de la Société des Nations représentés d'une façon permanente au Conseil, à raison d'un juge pour chacun de ces Membres, ainsi que de huit juges désignés par l'Assemblée d'après les dispositions suivantes: . . . .

Art. . . . Dans le cas où, dans une affaire dont la Cour est saisie, un Membre de la Société ne possède pas de représentant parmi les juges siégeant à la Cour, le dit Membre aura le droit de désigner un de ses ressortissants pour siéger comme juge dans cette affaire.

N.B. Ce droit doit naturellement s'étendre aux cinq Dominions britanniques.

ANNEX No. 3.

Project presented by M. Adatci.

Art. . . . The Court shall be composed of judges, one named by each of the Members of the League of Nations represented permanently on the Council, and eight other judges designated by the Assembly, according to the following provisions: . . . . .

Art. . . . . If, in any case brought before the Court, one Member of the League has not a representative amongst the judges sitting in the Court, the said Member shall have the right to appoint one of its own nationals to sit as judge in the case.

N.B. This right should of course be extended to the five British Dominions.

ANNEXE No. 4.

Proposition de Mr. Root.

1) L'élection doit être faite par l'Assemblée et par le Conseil.

2) Les qualifications des juges seront la haute compétence juridique et le haut caractère moral.

3) Des listes de personnes jugées en possession des qualifications requises seront avant chaque réunion de l'Assemblée présentées par les membres de la Cour Permanente d'Arbitrage de La Haye. Les membres nommés par chaque Etat devront présenter au moins deux, au plus quatre noms, la moitié des noms devant appartenir à des personnes d'une nationalité autre que celle des membres qui font la présentation.

4) Les listes ainsi constituées seront soumises au vote de la manière qui a été proposée par Lord Phillimore.

5) Pour autant que les sièges vacants ne peuvent être remplis par l'élection de personnes figurant sur cette liste, d'autres noms pourront être présentés par l'Assemblée et le Conseil et soumis au vote dans les mêmes conditions que les noms originairement présentés.

6) Dans toutes les élections les électeurs seront moralement obligés de tenir compte de l'existence des qualifications requises et de chercher à assurer dans la Cour une représentation adéquate des différents systèmes juridiques.

ANNEX No. 4.

Proposal of Mr. Root.

1) Election by Assembly and Council.

2) Qualification: juridical eminence, and character.

3) Lists of persons deemed to have qualification to be furnished before a meeting of the Assembly by the members of the Permanent Court of Arbitration at the Hague — the members appointed by each nation to propose not less than two nor more than four names, one half to be from nations other than that by which the proposers are appointed.

4) Votes on the list thus formed as provided by Lord Phillimore.

5) So far as vacancies may not be filled by election from this list, other names may be proposed by the Assembly and the Council and voted upon in like manner.

6) In all elections the electors to be under honorable obligation in regard to the qualifications stated, and to seek adequate representation in the Court for the different systems of jurisprudence.

7IÈME SÉANCE (non-publique), tenue au Palais de la Paix, à La Haye, le 23 juin 1920.

Présidence de M. le BARON DESCAMPS.

Sont présents: tous les membres du Comité (à l'exception de M. Bevilaqua); Mr. James Brown Scott; les secrétaires particuliers de M. le Baron Descamps et de M. Adatci; les membres du Secrétariat.

La séance est ouverte à $9^1/_2$ heures du matin.

LE PRESIDENT prend la parole pour faire une communication au sujet du procès-verbal. Le Secrétariat a fait remarquer que les membres du Comité continuent à lui transmettre des modifications à apporter aux procès-verbaux antérieurs, même des toutes premières séances. Il faut cependant que les procès-verbaux soient clos afin de pouvoir être imprimés. Dans ce but, le Président propose que les modifications à apporter aux procès-verbaux soient notifiées dans les deux jours qui suivront la séance à laquelle a trait chaque procès-verbal.

La proposition du Président est adoptée.

Pour faciliter le travail du Secrétariat, le Président propose également que toute modification soit transmise par écrit, et que toute communication comprenant une modification, de même que tout envoi de pages détachées d'un proçès-verbal, portent la date du procès-verbal auquel la modification est apportée.

Cette proposition est également adoptée.

M. DE LAPRADELLE signale que dans l'édition de Paris du „Chicago Tribune" a paru un article sur les travaux du Comité. Dans cet article les noms de Mr. Root, de Lord Phillimore et de M. de Lapradelle ont été mentionnés. On y a publié les opinions exprimées par M. de Lapradelle en leur donnant une fausse interprétation.

M. de Lapradelle prie le Président de prendre les mesures nécessaires pour empêcher que le fait ne se reproduise.

Le PRESIDENT signale le fait à l'attention du Secrétaire-Général. Il rappelle que les communiqués à la presse ne doivent mentionner aucun nom et que leur rédaction doit être à tel

7TH MEETING (Private), held at the Peace Palace, the Hague, on June 23rd 1920.

BARON DESCAMPS in the chair.

Present: all members of the Committee (with the exception of M. Bevilaqua); Mr. James Brown Scott; the private secretaries of Baron Descamps and of M. Adatci; the members of the Secretariat.

The meeting opened at 9.30 a.m.

The PRESIDENT made a remark concerning the procès-verbal. The Secretariat had pointed out that members of the Committee were still submitting alterations to be made in the earlier procès-verbaux, even in those of the first meetings. But the procès-verbaux must be finished in order to be printed. For this purpose, the President proposed that any alteration to be made in the procès-verbaux should be submitted in writing within two days after the meeting to which the procès-verbal in question relates.

The President's proposal was adopted.

To facilitate the work of the Secretariat, the President also proposed that all amendments should be submitted in writing and that all communications containing an amendment of a procès-verbal, as well as all separate sheets sent in, should be marked with the date of the procès-verbal to which they relate.

This proposal was also adopted.

M. DE LAPRADELLE pointed out that in the Paris Edition of the "Chicago Tribune" an article had appeared dealing with the work of the Committee. In this article the names of Mr. Root, Lord Phillimore and M. de Lapradelle were mentioned. In the article opinions expressed by M. de Lapradelle had been mentioned and a wrong interpretation had been put upon them.

M. de Lapradelle begged the President to take the necessary steps to avoid a repetition of this.

The PRESIDENT directed the attention of the Secretary General to this matter; He repeated that Press Communiqués should not mention names and should be so objective in

point objective que personne ne puisse préjuger des décisions futures.

Le Président, afin de laisser aux membres du Comité le loisir d'étudier les différentes propositions présentées sur le sujet discuté dans les séances précédentes, propose que la discussion porte aujourd'hui sur le second point de l'ordre du jour adopté précédemment, c'est à dire sur la question de la participation éventuelle de juges nationaux aux litiges où sont engagés les Etats. Le Président constate qu'une seule proposition concernant ce sujet, celle de M. Adatci, a été soumise au Comité.

M. RICCI-BUSATTI annonce qu'il a rédigé un projet précisant les idées qu'il avait déjà exprimées. Ce projet sera distribué au cours de la séance. (Voir Annexe 1).

M. HAGERUP dit que, sur le point en question, il existe en effet d'autres projets que celui de M. Adatci. Il mentionne les projets officiels des trois pays du Nord, le projet de l'Union juridique internationale, et d'autres encore. Il demande que la question du droit de récusation soit discutée en même temps que la question mise à l'ordre du jour par le Président, à cause des relations étroites existant entre elles.

LORD PHILLIMORE dit que, par rapport à la question du droit de récusation celle du nombre des juges a de l'importance. Il propose par conséquent que les trois questions de la participation de juges nationaux, du droit de récusation, et du nombre des juges, soient discutées en même temps.

Le Comité décide de se conformer à la proposition du Président complétée par celles de M. Hagerup et de Lord Phillimore.

Le Président donne la parole à M. Adatci.

M. ADATCI fait remarquer que l'article 2 de son projet traite de la question à l'ordre du jour. Il dit que les causes que la nouvelle Cour Internationale aura à juger lui parviendront des diverses parties du monde. Or, il y a des races, des systèmes juridiques, des civilisations très divers: si des juges nationaux ne sont pas admis, l'examen de l'affaire sera incomplet. Des échanges de vue avec des amis et collègues européens et asiatiques lui ont donné la conviction qu'il est nécessaire de faire siéger à la Cour Permanente des ressortissants des parties en litige.

Pour le nombre des juges, il a proposé le chiffre de 13, dont 5 pour les grandes Puissan-

character, that future decisions could not be anticipated.

The PRESIDENT, in order to give members of the Committee the opportunity of studying the different proposals put forward on the subject under discussion in the previous meetings, proposed that the day's discussions should deal with the second point on the Agenda formerly adopted, namely the question of the possible participation of national judges in cases in which their own States were involved; — the President stated that only one proposal on the subject had been submitted to the Committee, namely that of M. Adatci.

M. RICCI-BUSATTI announced that he had prepared a project summing up the ideas which he had already expressed. This project would be distributed during the meeting. (See Annex 1).

M. HAGERUP said that on the point in question other projects besides that of M. Adatci were, as a matter of fact, in existence. He mentioned the official projects of the three Northern countries, the project of the "Union juridique internationale", and others. M. Hagerup asked that the right of challenge should be discussed at the same time as the question put on the Agenda by the President, because of the close relationship between these two questions.

LORD PHILLIMORE said that in connection with the right of challenge the number of judges was very important. He proposed therefore that the three questions: participation of national judges, the right of challenge, and the number of judges, should be discussed at the same time.

The Committee decided to adopt the proposal of the President as completed by those of M. Hagerup and Lord Phillimore.

The PRESIDENT called on M. Adatci.

M. ADATCI said that Art. 2 of this project dealt with the question on the agenda. He said that the cases to be decided upon by the new international Court would come from various parts of the world. Very different races, legal systems and civilisations exist; if national judges were not admitted, the examination of the case would be incomplete. Discussions with European and Asiatic friends and colleagues had convinced him of the necessity of allowing judges of the same nationality as the contesting parties to sit on the Court.

He had proposed 13 as the number of judges, 5 for the great Powers and 8 for the small

ces et 8 pour les petites. Cependant, le nombre idéal serait à son avis 9 ou 7. Le nombre de 15 est trop élevé.

LORD PHILLIMORE est d'avis que le nombre de juges doit être fixé à 15; plus un petit nombre de juges suppléants.

La Cour doit toujours siéger *in pleno*. On devra donner aux parties le droit de récuser chacune deux juges. La Cour sera ainsi composée de 11 membres lorsqu'elle commencera ses délibérations sur une certaine question; si la procédure se prolonge, il se peut que ce nombre se réduise à 9 ou même à 7 par suite d'absences, de cas de maladie, etc. S'il y a plus de deux parties au litige, par exemple 3, chacune peut récuser un juge; le quatrième juge à éliminer serait dans ce cas désigné par le sort ou par le Président. L'essentiel, c'est que la Cour ne se divise pas en plusieurs chambres; elle doit mettre en œuvre toutes ses forces.

Si une seule des parties en cause est représentée à la Cour, il faut permettre à l'autre de désigner un de ses nationaux pour y siéger temporairement. Si aucune des parties n'est représentée à la Cour, il faut permettre à l'une et à l'autre de désigner un juge national. Ces juges siégeront comme assesseurs avec voix délibérative. Pour compenser l'augmentation du nombre des juges résultant de l'adjonction de juges nationaux, on pourrait augmenter de 4 à 6 par exemple, le nombre des juges à éliminer.

En tout cas, le droit d'élimination doit être conservé parce qu'il donne aux Etats un moyen pour éviter que certaines questions délicates ne soient soulevées.

M. LODER croit que si l'on veut fixer le nombre des juges, il faut prendre comme point de départ le caractère de la Cour.

A son avis, cette Cour, qui doit être la plus haute autorité judiciaire du monde, devra être composée d'un nombre très restreint de juges.

Il faut que ses membres puissent travailler en collaboration et qu'ils soient tous des hommes éminents. Il croit qu'il serait difficile de trouver un grand nombre de personnes suffisamment qualifiées et en même temps disposées à accepter la fonction de membre de la Cour. Par conséquent, il est d'avis que le nombre de 9 juges serait le meilleur.

M. Loder pense que la participation des juges nationaux aux délibérations de la Cour pour des litiges déterminés n'est pas nécessaire. On a, ou on n'a pas confiance en la Cour. Le fait que les Etats en cause y sont représentés ne

Powers. However, in his opinion the ideal number would be 9 or 7; the number 15 was too high.

LORD PHILLIMORE was of the opinion that the number of judges should be fixed at 15, plus a small number of deputy judges.

The Court must always sit *in pleno*. Each contesting party should have the right to challenge two judges. The Court would thus be composed of 11 judges at the opening of any case; if the case were prolonged, it might happen that this number would be reduced to 9 or even 7, by absence, illness, etc. If there are more than two parties involved in the case, for instance 3, each may challenge one judge; the fourth judge to be eliminated will in such a case be chosen by lot or by the President. The essential point is that the Court is not divided into several chambers; it should make use of all its resources.

If only one of the parties in any case is represented on the Court the other must be allowed to designate one of its nationals to sit temporarily: if neither of the parties is represented on the Court, they must both be allowed to designate a national judge. These judges will sit as assessors with voting powers. To counterbalance the increased number of judges resulting from the addition of national judges, the number of the judges to be eliminated might be increased from 4 to 6 for instance.

In any case the right of elimination must be maintained, because it gives to States a means to avoid certain delicate questions being raised.

M. LODER thought that if it were desired to fix the number of judges, the character of the new Court should first be considered.

In his opinion, this Court, which should be the highest judicial authority in the world, should be composed of a very limited number of judges.

Its members must be able to work well together and they must all be eminent men. He thought it would be difficult to find a large number of persons sufficiently qualified and at the same time willing to accept the duties of judges. Consequently, he thought that the number 9 would be the best.

M. Loder thought that the participation of national judges in the deliberations of the Court for a given case was not at all necessary. Confidence in the Court either does or does not exist. The fact that States concerned in any dispute were represented would not add to this confi-

saurait rien ajouter à cette confiance. Mais il ne voit pas d'objection à l'adjonction d'assesseurs avec voix consultative.

M. Loder croit qu'on doit exclure de l'organisation de la nouvelle Cour le droit de récusation qui la ferait inévitablement ressembler plus ou moins à une Cour d'arbitrage. Il faut éviter cela, vu que la distinction entre la nouvelle Cour Permanente et l'ancienne Cour d'Arbitrage doit être bien nette. Il va de soi qu'il ne s'agit pas ici des causes d'abstention qu'on trouve dans toutes les législations.

M. HAGERUP fait lecture au Comité des dispositions du projet commun des trois comités des pays scandinaves relatives à la question de la récusation. Il explique que le point de vue auquel on s'était placé primitivement n'a pas été adopté par le Danemark; que plus tard la Norvège a fait défection, et que seul parmi les projets particuliers des trois pays scandinaves celui de la Suède le maintient aujourd'hui. Le projet suédois s'appuie sur les mêmes considérations que celles que M. Loder vient d'exposer.

Le PRESIDENT dit qu'il faut bien distinguer entre la récusation et les incompatibilités.

M. HAGERUP se rallie à cette idée. Il ajoute que, du moment qu'il ne s'agit pas d'une Cour d'Arbitrage, il faut éviter la récusation; autrement, l'autorité d'une Cour Permanente serait par trop amoindrie. Il donne lecture de l'article 28 du projet originaire des trois comités scandinaves. Il croit que le projet de l'Union juridique internationale et celui des cinq Puissances neutres de février dernier ont adopté le même point de vue que celui qui a trouvé son expression dans l'article qu'il vient de lire.

Pour ce qui est du nombre des juges, M. Hagerup fait observer que la plupart des projets ont adopté le nombre de 15. Il remarque que la question du quorum est entièrement séparée de la question du nombre des juges.

Il ajoute qu'à son avis, si l'on adopte un nombre de juges inférieur à 15, on rencontrera de graves difficultés d'ordre pratique, provenant de la nécessité de donner satisfaction aux diverses nations qui demanderont d'être représentées à la Cour.

M. LODER nie qu'il aurait renoncé, comme M. Hagerup le croit, au chiffre de 9 proposé par la Commission néerlandaise dans son projet. Il est vrai que les cinq Puissances neutres

dence, but he saw no objection to the addition of assessors with advisory powers.

M. Loder thought that the right of challenge should be excluded from the organisation of the new Court. It inevitably would cause this Court to resemble more or less a Court of Arbitration. This must be avoided, as there should be a clear distinction between the new Permanent Court and the old Court of Arbitration. It goes without saying that now there is no question of causes of abstention, which are to be found in all legislations.

M. HAGERUP read to the Committee the proposals, contained in the Joint Scheme of the three Scandinavian countries, concerning the question of challenge. He explained that the original view had not been adopted by Denmark; that Norway withdrew her support; and that the Swedish scheme was the only one among the separate schemes of the three Scandinavian countries which still adhered to it. This Swedish project was based on the same grounds as those just explained by M. Loder.

The PRESIDENT said that a distinction must be drawn between the question of challenge and that of incompatibility.

M. HAGERUP agreed with this idea. He added that as soon as there was no longer question of a Court of Arbitration, the right of challenge should be avoided, otherwise the authority of a Permanent Court would be too much diminished. He read Article 28 of the original scheme of the three Scandinavian Commissions. He thought that the project of the "Union juridique internationale" and that of the Five Neutral Powers of February last had adopted the same view as that expressed in the Article he had just read.

With regard to the number of judges, M. Hagerup called attention to the fact that most projects had adopted the number 15. He pointed out that the question of a quorum was quite distinct from that of the number of judges.

He added that in his opinion, if a number of judges smaller than 15 were decided upon, grave difficulties of a practical nature would be encountered arising out of the necessity of giving satisfaction to the various nations who will demand representation on the Court.

M. LODER denied, contrary to M. Hagerup's belief, that he had abandoned the number 9 proposed by the Dutch Commission in its plan. It was true that the Five Neutral Powers had

ont adopté le chiffre de 15, mais, lorsque cette décision fut prise, M. Loder s'est trouvé parmi la minorité; il croit toujours que le nombre de 9 est préférable, car à son avis on trouvera difficilement plus de 9 juges qualifiés.

Le PRESIDENT fait observer que, d'après le projet qu'il a présenté, les juges seront au nombre de 9. Il expose comment, aux termes de ce projet, la Cour pourra se diviser en chambres et comment le tribunal pourra fonctionner même avec un seul juge, si telle est la convenance des parties. Il rappelle que le projet adopté en 1907 par l'assemblée des Etats prévoit déjà, dans son article 6, le fonctionnement d'une Délégation spéciale de la Cour.

LORD PHILLIMORE, de son côté, est d'avis que la Cour doit toujours siéger *in pleno*.

M. DE LAPRADELLE dit que, puisque le projet de l'Union juridique internationale a été mentionné, il désire faire devant le Comité un commentaire succinct des dispositions qui dans ce projet ont trait aux points à l'ordre du jour.

Le projet en question prévoit une Cour composée de 15 juges. La Cour siège toujours en séance plénière; le nombre des juges présents ne doit jamais être inférieur à 9. L'Union avait d'abord pensé au nombre de 11, mais on s'est arrêté au chiffre de 15, afin de pouvoir introduire dans le projet le droit de récusation. Ce droit est nécessaire. Il peut y avoir des motifs tout à fait justifiés pour lesquels l'une des parties en cause désire qu'un certain juge ne prenne pas part aux délibérations au sujet d'un litige déterminé. Ces motifs peuvent être de nature à ne pas devoir être divulgués, sans pour cela rien contenir de blessant pour le juge éliminé.

M. de Lapradelle cite le cas où un juge est intéressé à l'objet du litige, et celui où il a pris part, dans l'intérêt de l'une des parties, aux travaux préparatoires à la solution du litige.

Si les parties n'usent pas du droit de récusation, l'élimination peut se faire par tirage au sort. En tout cas, le nombre de 11 représente un minimum: il faut envisager l'éventualité où, la procédure traînant en longueur, un ou plusieurs des juges seraient empêchés de prendre part aux délibérations. Le quorum des juges doit être 9, ou peut être 7. Il ne faut pas que le nombre des juges descende au-dessous de ce chiffre.

M. de Lapradelle n'ignore pas que les tribunaux internationaux sont ordinairement com-

adopted the number 15, but when this decision was arrived at, M. Loder voted with the minority; he still was of opinion that the number 9 was preferable because he thought that it would be difficult to find more than 9 properly qualified judges.

The PRESIDENT observed that in the project submitted by him, the judges should be 9 in number. He explained that, according to this project the Court was empowered to divide itself into chambers, and that the Tribunal might operate even with only one judge, if such was the desire of the parties. He recalled that the draft plan adopted in 1907 by the assembly of States provided at that time, in its sixth article, for the creation of a special delegation of the Court.

LORD PHILLIMORE stated that in his opinion the Court should always sit *in pleno*.

M. DE LAPRADELLE said that as the project of the "Union juridique internationale" had been mentioned, he wished to make a short *résumé* before the Committee of the dispositions of this project relating to the points on the Agenda.

The project in question provided for a Court of 15 judges. The Court should always meet in full sitting; the number of judges present must never be less than 9. The Union first considered the number 11, but the number 15 had been fixed in order to make it possible to insert in the plan the right of challenge. This right was necessary. One of the parties concerned in a case might have perfectly justified motives for wishing to exclude a certain judge from participation in the particular case. These motives might very well be of such a kind that they should not be divulged though they might contain nothing offensive to the judge excluded.

M. de Lapradelle mentioned as an example a case in which the judge was interested in the matter before the Court, or had taken part, in the interests of one of the parties, in the preliminary work on the case.

If the parties did not use the right of challenge the elimination might be made by drawing lots. In any case the number 11 should be a minimum. The possibility of the case continuing for a long time must be considered, when one or more judges might become unable to take part in the deliberations. The quorum of the judges should be 9 or possibly 7. The number of judges must not drop below this figure.

posés de 5 juges au maximum. Il dit que si l'on propose maintenant de tripler le nombre, c'est en vue de n'être point forcé de voir, à la fin de la procédure, le nombre descendre au-dessous de ce chiffre.

En ce qui concerne la question de la participation de juges nationaux, M. de Lapradelle se réfère à l'article 10 du projet de l'Union juridique. Cet article stipule que, quand un juge est de la nationalité de l'une des parties en litige, sans que l'autre partie soit représentée par l'un de ses nationaux, il doit céder sa place.

Les Etats qui auront le plus souvent à plaider devant la Cour y auront probablement des juges de leur nationalité. Ces juges resteront donc membres de la Cour, lorsque les intérêts de leurs deux pays respectifs seront en cause. C'est là une garantie de justice. M. de Lapradelle ne prétend pas que les juges en question rendent une justice plus juste que les autres; mais il faut ménager les susceptibilités nationales; et, comme l'a remarqué M. Louis Renault, la présence à la Cour de juges appartenant à la nationalité des parties en cause permet de rédiger les sentences de façon à éviter d'irriter les susceptibilités nationales; ainsi les sentences auront un maximum de force conciliatrice.

Si l'une des parties seulement est représentée à la Cour, le problème ne se présente pas sous le même aspect. Pour que les deux parties fussent représentées dans ces conditions il faudrait la présence d'un juge national *ad hoc*; mais il faut éviter les juges siégeant pour l'occasion.

M. de Lapradelle fait remarquer que l'Union juridique a voté son texte à l'unanimité.

Il résume ce texte. Si les deux parties sont représentées à la Cour, les juges nationaux peuvent garder leurs sièges. Si l'une seulement des parties est représentée, le juge de sa nationalité doit céder sa place. Si aucune des parties n'est représentée, on évitera d'y envoyer des assesseurs qui auraient nécessairement une position inférieure à celle des juges réguliers.

M. de Lapradelle was quite aware that international tribunals were usually composed of a maximum of 5 judges. He said that the reason for the present proposal to treble the number was to avoid the possibility of being obliged to go below this figure at the end of the procedure.

Concerning the question of the participation of national judges, M. de Lapradelle referred to Art. 10 of the project of the Union juridique. This Article stipulates that, when a judge is of the same nationality as one of the contesting parties, without the other party being represented by one of its nationals, he should give up his seat.

Those States which will most often be concerned in cases before the Court will probably have judges of their nationality on it. These judges will remain members of the Court when the interests of their respective countries are at issue. Therein will be a guarantee of justice. M. de Lapradelle did not mean that these judges would administer justice more fairly than the others, but national susceptibility must be treated with regard, and as M. Louis Renault has said, the presence on the Court of judges of the same nationality as the contesting parties will allow sentence to be delivered without incensing national susceptibilities; in this way sentences will have as great a conciliatory effect as possible.

If only one of the parties is represented on the Court the problem is not the same.

In order that both parties should be represented, the presence of a national judge *ad hoc* would be necessary; however, care must be taken to avoid judges sitting only for a single case.

M. de Lapradelle pointed out that the Union juridique had adopted its project unanimously.

He summed up: if both parties are represented on the Court the national judges may keep their seats. If one only of the parties is represented the judge of the same nationality must give up his seat. If neither party is represented, the appointment of assessors who necessarily would occupy an inferior position to ordinary judges would be avoided.

Le PRESIDENT regrette qu'on n'ait pas adopté la proposition faite par Mr. Root de prendre le projet de 1907 comme base des discussions. Il lui semble qu'il faudrait s'écarter le moins possible d'un projet accepté par les Puissances. Ce projet institue en vue de faciliter la procédure, une Délégation spéciale de trois ju-

The PRESIDENT regretted that the proposal of Mr. Root to take the project of 1907 as a basis of discussion had not been adopted. It seemed to him that the Committee ought as far as possible to proceed along the lines of a project which had already been adopted by the Powers. This plan provided for a special Dele-

ges. Si l'on compose la Cour de treize juges, on aboutira à une organisation singulièrement compliquée et souvent contraire au désir des parties. La récusation amènerait peut-être l'élimination des meilleurs parmi les juges, peut-être à cause de leur supériorité même.

Il faut distinguer entre la notion de l'incompatibilité, qui a pour conséquence une option nécessaire entre les deux qualités déclarées incompatibles, et celle de la récusation, qui vise l'exclusion d'un juge sans motif défini. S'il est nécessaire de tenir compte des incompatibilités, la récusation, par contre, présente des dangers à cause des calculs et des combinaisons occultes qu'elle peut favoriser; son expérience permet au Président de dire que ce danger n'est pas imaginaire. L'expérience lui enseigne également que s'il y a un grand nombre de juges il en résulte, étant donné les absences, les récusations, les questions de quorum qui en découlent, un grave danger d'arbitraire quant à la composition de la Cour. Pourquoi aller contre ce qui a été décidé par une assemblée unanime des Etats en 1907? Cinq juges ont bien suffi jusqu'à présent; au lieu du droit de récusation, il vaut mieux avoir des cas d'incompatibilité bien définis et dont la réalité serait constatée, le cas échéant, par la Cour elle-même.

M. LODER désire faire part de quelques expériences personnelles. Une Cour composée d'un nombre restreint de juges travaille mieux qu'un tribunal nombreux: les discussions sont plus serrées et les membres ont un sentiment plus net de leur responsabilité. M. Loder termine en rappelant la grande autorité du juge unique en Angleterre.

Après qu'un échange de vues avec le Président eut permis de constater que la question portée au No. 7 du questionnaire, à savoir la division de la Cour en chambres, pouvait, elle aussi, être examinée, comme étant intimement liée aux sujets en discussion, M. HAGERUP poursuit l'exposé de ses vues.

Il a pu constater que les archives de Ministères des Affaires Etrangères renferment de nombreuses questions laissées sans solution parce qu'on a hésité à mettre en branle pour les trancher, le lourd appareil de l'arbitrage. Il désire voir constituer une chambre composée d'un nombre limité de juges pour trancher ces conflits.

En général, il est d'avis qu'un grand nombre de juges n'est pas fait pour augmenter l'autorité de la Cour; pourtant, puisqu'il s'agit d'une juridiction internationale, il faut peut-être prendre en

gation of three judges to expedite procedure. If the Court were composed of 13 judges the result would be a very complicated organisation and often contrary to the wishes of the parties. Challenge might lead to the exclusion of the best of the judges, perhaps because of their superiority.

A distinction must be made between the conception of incompatibility, which entails a necessary choice between the two functions declared incompatible, and the conception of challenge by which a judge is debarred for no stated reason. If it is necessary to take incompatibilities into account, challenging, on the other hand, involved dangers, because of intrigues and hidden combinations which it favours; the President added that in his experience this danger was not at all imaginary. Experience also had taught him that if there were a large number of judges, absences, challenges, and resulting questions of quorum would give rise to the grave danger of having the Court composed in an arbitrary manner. Why proceed in opposition to that which was decided by a unanimous assembly of States in 1907? Five judges have been quite enough up till now; instead of the right of challenge it would be much better to have cases of incompatibility clearly defined, whose existence in fact should be established in particular cases by the Court itself.

M. LODER wished to relate some personal experiences. A Court composed of a limited number of judges works better than a large tribunal: discussions are more to the point and the members have a greater sense of their responsibility. M. Loder ended by alluding to the great authority of single judges in England.

M. HAGERUP said that, after a conversation with the President, he was able to state that the subject considered in number 7 of the questionnaire — namely the division of the Court into chambers — also could be examined as it was closely related to the subject under discussion. He then continued to explain his views.

He stated that the archives of the various Foreign Offices contained many questions left unsolved, because there had been hesitation to set going the cumbersome machinery of arbitration to solve them. He wished to see a chamber composed of a limited number of judges formed to consider these cases.

In general, he was of opinion that a great number of judges does not augment the authority of the Court; however, as the Committee is dealing with an international jurisdiction, he

considération la nécessité d'assurer une représentation plus variée au sein de la Cour.

Sur la question de l'admission de juges nationaux M. Hagerup se rallie à l'opinion de M. de Lapradelle; il se demande, toutefois, comment sera résolue la difficulté qui ne manquera pas de se présenter lorsqu'il y aura plusieurs parties en cause.

Au sujet de la question du droit de récusation M. Hagerup dit qu'il faut tenir compte de la susceptibilité des juges: ceux-ci n'accepteront pas le poste qui pourrait leur être offert, s'ils courent le risque d'être récusés.

M. Hagerup croit que l'on a eu cette raison spéciale d'adopter le droit de récusation: on a voulu rendre la nouvelle Cour compétente pour les litiges de toutes sortes, même pour les questions politiques. Mais M. Hagerup ne pense pas que ce point de vue mérite d'être généralement accepté. Il faut bien distinguer entre les questions de droit et celles qui doivent être résolues par la méthode de conciliation, ou par un tribunal composé pour des buts politiques.

LORD PHILLIMORE dit qu'il n'a pas encore d'idées bien arrêtées sur les questions de la récusation, de la présence de juges nationaux, et du nombre des juges; mais il désire soulever une légère protestation à propos d'une question d'ordre.

On a fait allusion à divers projets arrêtés; le projet des cinq Puissances, le projet scandinave, etc. N'est-ce-pas là préjuger un peu de la solution future? Bien qu'il soit reconnaissant du travail que représentent les projets en question, il désire souligner que, à son avis, il ne faut pas que les membres du Comité se fassent les interprêtes de tel ou tel projet. Le Comité se réunit pour un autre but; si l'on s'en tient à l'œuvre des Conférences antérieures, on n'aboutira pas. Il faut du reste tenir compte du fait que les pays latins auraient pu se concerter sur un projet; qu'on aurait pu faire de même aux Etats-Unis, etc.

Lord Phillimore s'adresse au Président qui veut qu'on s'attache à l'œuvre de La Haye. Certes, cette œuvre mérite des éloges, mais il ne faut pas oublier que lorsqu'elle a été accomplie, la juridiction internationale n'en était encore qu'à ses débuts.

A La Haye, on a fait une tentative plutôt timide; on n'a pas créé un véritable tribunal, on n'a fait qu'établir une liste de juges. Le projet de La Haye ne sort pas du cadre de l'arbitrage. L'idée de 1907 de diviser la Cour en chambres

thought perhaps they should take into consideration the necessity of assuring a more varied representation on the Bench.

Concerning the question of the admission of national judges, M. Hagerup was of the same opinion as M. de Lapradelle; nevertheless, he did not quite see how the difficulty, which would not fail to arise when there were several parties to a dispute, should be solved.

On the subject of the question of the right of challenge, M. Hagerup said that they must take into account the feelings of the judges: they would not accept the positions offered to them if they ran the risk of being challenged.

M. Hagerup thought there had been a special reason for the adoption of the right of challenge: the wish to make the new Court competent to deal with all kinds of disputes, even political disputes. But M. Hagerup did not think that this point of view ought to be generally accepted. A distinction must be drawn between questions of law and questions which must be solved by conciliatory methods, or by a tribunal established for political purposes.

LORD PHILLIMORE said that he had not yet made up his mind definitely on the questions of challenge, the presence of national judges, and the number of judges, but he wished to make a slight protest on a point of order.

Several projects had been mentioned: the Five-Power-Plan, the Scandinavian project, etc. Would not this have the effect of slightly prejudicing the further solution of the problem? Though he thoroughly recognised the value of the work represented by these projects, he wished to emphasise that in his opinion the members of the Committee should not act as propounders of any existing project. The Committee was assembled for another purpose. If they were bound by the work of previous Conferences, they would not succeed. Further, they must take into account the fact that the Latin countries might equally well have united to compose a project; so might the United States, etc.

Lord Phillimore addressed the President, whose wish was to start from the work of the Hague. That work certainly deserved the highest praise, but it must not be forgotten that at the time when it was done international jurisdiction was still in its infancy.

At The Hague a rather timid attempt was made; in fact, a real tribunal had not been created, only a list of judges had been formed. The project of the Hague could only be classed

est également trop liée à celle de l'arbitrage, puisque les chambres seraient composées *in casu*. Pour être une Cour de Justice il faut que la Cour siège *in pleno*.

Pour la même raison, il faut que la Cour soit composée de hauts magistrats, qui consacreront toute leur activité à l'œuvre du tribunal; et il est nécessaire que le nombre en soit très limité, afin qu'ils puissent tous, ou presque tous, prendre part à chaque procès. Pour obtenir de bons juges il faut pouvoir leur donner la certitude qu'ils auront assez de travail.

Au point de vue absolu, le nombre de cinq, ou peut être de sept, serait le meilleur. Il faut cependant tenir compte de la nécessité de faire représenter, dans la mesure du possible, les différents systèmes juridiques; pour cette raison il faut avoir un nombre plus élevé. On peut s'arrêter sur les chiffres de 15, 13, 11.

Lord Phillimore fait valoir qu'en Angleterre, les cours peuvent être composées de trois juges; mais qu'il y a vu des cours composées de 7, de 8 et de 12 juges. Il rappelle que le nombre des juges de la Cour Suprême des Etats-Unis est de 9.

Pour résumer, il dit que le nombre de juges n'a qu'une importance secondaire; l'essentiel c'est que, dans la mesure du possible, tous les juges siègent en même temps.

Le PRESIDENT fait remarquer que son projet prévoit 9 juges et 6 juges suppléants; le nombre total proposé par lui est donc de 15.

LORD PHILLIMORE ne s'oppose pas à ce qu'il y ait des juges suppléants, mais il faut que leur nombre soit très restreint.

M. HAGERUP ne comprend pas l'objet de la protestation de Lord Phillimore. En se référant aux dispositions du projet scandinave, il a cru se conformer aux règles de procédure qui prescrivent que les membres soumettront au Président des propositions par écrit. Au lieu de faire recopier les dispositions par le Secrétariat, il s'est seulement permis de renvoyer à un texte se trouvant entre les mains de tous les membres. Lord Phillimore fait valoir la nécessité de ne point se lier les mains en adoptant tel ou tel projet. M. Hagerup croit que les procès-verbaux témoigneront qu'il ne s'est point inféodé à tel projet particulier. Il rappelle qu'aux termes de l'invitation adressée aux membres, ils sont obligés de tenir compte des projets antérieurs. C'est ce qu'il a fait. Il a soumis un texte inspiré de l'un de ces projets, en expliquant les

as a form of arbitration. The idea of 1907 to divide the Court into chambers, also is too closely bound to the idea of arbitration, since these chambers would be formed *in casu*. The Court must sit *in pleno* to be a real Court of Justice.

For the same reason, the Court must be composed of eminent magistrates, who would devote all their energies to the work of the tribunal, and it was necessary that the number should be very limited to permit all or most of them to take part in each case. In order to get good judges, it must be possible to assure them that they will have enough work.

From an abstract point of view, the number 5, or possibly 7, would be best. However, one must take into account the necessity of representing as far as possible the different legal systems; for this reason there must be a higher number; 15, 13, or 11 might be agreed upon.

Lord Phillimore pointed out that in England courts could be composed of 3 judges, but that he had seen courts composed of 7, 8 and 12 judges. He mentioned that the number of judges on the Supreme Court of the United States was 9.

In conclusion, he said that the number of judges was of secondary importance; the essential thing was that as far as possible all judges should sit at the same time.

The PRESIDENT called attention to the fact that his project allowed for 9 judges and 6 deputy judges; the total number proposed was therefore 15.

LORD PHILLIMORE did not object to there being deputy judges, but thought their number should be very limited.

M. HAGERUP did not understand the object of Lord Phillimore's protest. In referring to the dispositions of the Scandinavian project, he thought that he had conformed to the rules of procedure laid down, namely, that the members should submit their proposals to the President in writing. Instead of having the provisions copied by the Secretariat, he had simply made use of a draft already in the possession of all the members. Lord Phillimore had pointed out the necessity of not tying the hands of the Committee by adopting any particular project. M. Hagerup thought that the procès-verbaux bore witness that he had not bound himself to any particular project. He recalled the fact that in the invitation addressed to the members, they were called upon to take into account previous proposals. That was what he

considérations sur lesquelles ce texte s'appuie. Si cette manière de procéder appelle une protestation, il se demande s'il peut continuer à prendre part aux discussions.

LORD PHILLIMORE explique qu'il y a un malentendu. Il regrette de s'être servi du mot protestation.

M. HAGERUP admet que ce mot lui a fait faire fausse route.

Le PRESIDENT déclare que l'incident est clos. Il résume les méthodes dont on peut se servir pour soumettre une proposition au Comité; ou on la notifie par écrit au Président qui la remet au Secrétariat pour être communiquée à tous les membres, ou bien on fait sien tel ou tel projet déjà existant.

M. HAGERUP poursuit l'exposé de son point de vue. Il souligne d'abord qu'il considère les questions sans aucune idée préconçue.

S'adressant à Lord Phillimore, il dit que les chambres en lesquelles la Cour devrait pouvoir se scinder, ne seraient point choisies par les parties pour tel litige déterminé; il y aurait par exemple, une chambre de procédure sommaire. Pareille chambre est désirable afin de donner une solution rapide et peu coûteuse à maintes questions qui sont jusqu'ici restées dans les archives. Il croit que ce procédé donnera en même temps satisfaction à l'idée exprimée par Lord Phillimore, qu'il ne faut pas laisser les juges inoccupés; il se range entièrement à cette opinion. La création d'une chambre de procédure sommaire a déjà été prévue par la Convention de La Haye. Elle a été préconisée par M. Asser et M. Renault, pour les raisons que vient d'exposer M. Hagerup.

M. DE LAPRADELLE est d'avis qu'on peut parer au besoin d'une procédure sommaire en conférant au Président ou à un membre de la Cour le droit de prendre, seul, des décisions en cas d'urgence; ce système existe en France. M. de Lapradelle fait allusion à la procédure des référés: les parties peuvent, en s'adressant à la Cour, spécifier que le Président, ou un juge désigné par lui, décidera seul.

La méthode qui consiste à scinder la Cour en chambres est plus compliquée. On pourrait arriver au même but d'une façon plus simple, en stipulant que la Cour ne doit siéger qu'*in pleno,* mais que des décisions peuvent être prises, en cas d'urgence et si les parties le désirent,

had done. He had submitted a draft based on one of these projects and explained the principles on which the draft was based. If this procedure gave rise to a protest he did not see how he could continue to take part in the discussions.

LORD PHILLIMORE explained that there was a misunderstanding. He regretted that he had used the word "protest."

M. HAGERUP admitted that this word had misled him.

The PRESIDENT declared the incident closed. He repeated the methods of submitting a proposal to the Committee: either a member shall submit it in writing to the President, who sends it to the Secretariat for distribution to all the members, or else he shall adopt one of the already existing plans as his own.

M. HAGERUP continued the explanation of his point of view. He began by emphasizing that he considered all questions with an open mind.

Addressing Lord Phillimore, he said that the chambers into which the Court should be able to divide itself would not be chosen by the contesting parties in a certain case. There would be, for example, a section of summary procedure. Such a section is desirable in order to make possible a rapid and inexpensive procedure for dealing with many questions which up to this time have remained in the archives. He thought this method would also meet the argument expounded by Lord Phillimore, to keep the judges busy. He was in complete agreement with this idea. The formation of a section of summary procedure had already been foreseen in the Hague Convention. It had been recommended by M. Asser and M. Renault, for the reasons just given by M. Hagerup.

M. DE LAPRADELLE was of opinion that one could meet the need for a summary procedure by conferring on the President or a member of the Court the right to make decisions alone in urgent cases. This system existed in France. M. de Lapradelle mentioned the "procédure des référés". The parties may, when putting the case before the Court, specify that the President or a judge appointed by him shall decide the case by himself.

The method of dividing the Court into sections was more complicated. The same end might be achieved in a simpler way by stipulating that the Court should only sit *in pleno,* but that decisions might be taken, in urgent cases, and

par le Président seul ou par un juge désigné par lui.

LORD PHILLIMORE suggère l'idée de décisions urgentes à prendre par trois juges.

M. DE LAPRADELLE réserve son opinion à ce sujet.

Le PRESIDENT rappelle que la Convention de 1907 a prévu la création d'une procédure sommaire.

M. DE LAPRADELLE répond que ce n'est là qu'une procédure d'arbitrage, non pas une véritable procédure judiciaire.

M. RICCI-BUSATTI fait remarquer que les trois questions qu'on est en train de discuter sont liées entre elles, ainsi qu'à la question fondamentale qui a été discutée tout d'abord.

Pour pouvoir les résoudre, il faut commencer par se rendre compte du caractère de la nouvelle Cour.

On a dit qu'il faut créer une institution complètement différente de la Cour d'Arbitrage, une institution purement juridique, pareille aux Cours nationales de chaque pays. Cette conception présente des difficultés d'ordre théorique et pratique. En théorie, elle présuppose une autorité supérieure, dont elle tiendrait son pouvoir; en l'état actuel des relations internationales, cette autorité n'existe pas. En pratique, elle exige des juges toujours présents au siège de la Cour, afin d'en assurer la permanence effective; mais comme la Cour ne sera probablement occupée que pendant quelques semaines chaque année, il sera bien difficile de trouver des personnes qualifiées pour l'accomplissement de leur tâche, qui soient disposées à accepter un poste de juge.

M. Ricci-Busatti part personnellement d'une conception différente: il maintient son point de vue, à savoir qu'il ne faut pas trop distinguer entre la nouvelle Cour et l'ancienne Cour d'Arbitrage, et qu'il n'y a pas de différence essentielle, surtout dans le domaine des rapports internationaux, entre la fonction arbitrale et la fonction judiciaire. Dans ces conditions, il propose le système suivant: la Cour d'Arbitrage se composerait toujours d'une liste comprenant un nombre de membres assez élevé. La nouvelle Cour se composerait également d'une liste, qui ne comprendrait toutefois que 15 ou 20 noms; le tribunal qui connaîtrait d'un litige déterminé serait composé de juges choisis dans cette dernière liste. Les détails de l'organisation de la Cour devraient permettre aux parties de faire ce choix, voire même s'entendre pour soumettre leurs différends

if the parties wish it, by the President alone, or by a single judge selected by him.

LORD PHILLIMORE suggested that judgments in cases of urgency should be delivered by three judges.

M. DE LAPRADELLE reserved his opinion on this subject.

The PRESIDENT recalled that the Convention of 1907 provided for the creation of a section of summary procedure.

M. DE LAPRADELLE answered that that was only a procedure by arbitration and not really a judicial procedure.

M. RICCI-BUSATTI remarked that the three questions which are under discussion were closely united to one another, and also to the fundamental questions just discussed.

In order to solve them, one must begin by considering the character of the new Court.

It has been said that a new institution, completely different from the Court of Arbitration must be created; a new juridical body similar to the national courts of all countries. This idea presents theoretical and practical difficulties. In theory, it presupposes a superior authority from which it derives its authority; and in the present conditions of international relations this authority does not exist. In practice, it entails a continual presence of judges at the seat of the Court, in order to assure its permanent character, but, as the Court probably would only be occupied during a few weeks in each year, it would be very difficult to find persons qualified for the discharge of their duty who would be willing to accept a post as judge.

M. Ricci-Busatti personally started from an entirely different conception: he maintained his point of view that too much distinction should not be drawn between the new Court and the old Court of Arbitration; that there was no essential difference, especially in international relations, between Arbitration and strict Justice. Under these conditions he proposed the following system: The Court of Arbitration should consist of a list containing a sufficiently large number of members. The new Court should also consist of a list which, however, should contain only 15 or 20 names; the tribunal which was to deal with a particular case should be composed of judges chosen from this last list. The rules laid down for the organisation of the Court must allow contesting parties to choose from this list; they might mutually agree to submit their disputes to a single judge, or even to allow the tribunal

à un seul juge, ou encore de permettre au tribunal de fonctionner automatiquement, quand cet accord n'existe pas, ou dans les cas d'urgence.

M. Ricci-Busatti est heureux de constater que le dernier alinéa du projet qu'il a soumis, concernant la désignation d'un juge unique et le rôle du président de la Cour, se rapproche des propositions que vient de faire M. de Lapradelle.

M. LODER exprime sa reconnaissance à Lord Phillimore pour l'exposé qu'il a fait de ses vues, mais ne peut se déclarer d'accord avec lui au sujet de la question du nombre des juges. Il admet qu'il peut être nécessaire de fixer un nombre supérieur à 9, mais il ne croit pas que la Cour doive toujours nécessairement siéger *in pleno*. Elle peut se diviser en chambres; l'essentiel, c'est de déterminer le quorum des chambres. Il faut qu'il n'y ait aucune incertitude à cet égard. Quant au système de récusation d'office, sans motifs, c'est à son avis un système odieux, auquel il s'opposera de toutes ses forces.

M. Loder pense qu'il est inutile d'assurer la représentation des divers systèmes juridiques dans la Cour. La nouvelle Cour appliquera le droit international; et ce droit est vraiment international. Si le besoin se fait sentir d'élucider un point de droit national, les juges éminents dont la Cour sera composée pourront bien s'en charger.

Les observations de M. Ricci-Busatti ont beaucoup surpris M. Loder. Il faut se placer au point de vue de l'article 14 du Pacte, qui fait une distinction formelle entre la justice stricte et l'arbitrage.

Le PRESIDENT fait remarquer que dans le Pacte tous les différends sont classés en différends arbitrables et non-arbitrables, et que ces derniers relèvent de la procédure en recommandation.

M. LODER donne lecture du texte de l'article 14 du Pacte. Il ne s'agit plus d'établir une liste de membres d'une Cour, il s'agit d'établir une Cour qui aura une permanence réelle et effective.

M. Ricci-Busatti peut personnellement être d'un avis contraire mais il ne faut pas oublier que le Comité a été convoqué en vertu de l'article 14 du Pacte. M. Loder craint que si M. Ricci-Busatti n'adopte pas ce point de vue, il deviendra difficile de poursuivre avec lui la discussion.

M. DE LAPRADELLE se range à l'opinion exprimée par M. Loder. M. Ricci-Busatti

to work automatically when this agreement does not exist, or in urgent cases.

M. Ricci-Busatti was pleased to state that the last paragraph of the project he had submitted concerning the appointment of a single judge and the duties of the president of the Court harmonised with the proposal that M. de Lapradelle had just made.

M. LODER expressed his thanks to Lord Phillimore for the explanation he had given of his views. He could not, however, agree with Lord Phillimore on the subject of the number of judges; he admitted that it might be necessary to appoint a larger number than 9, but he did not think it necessary that the Court should always sit *in pleno*. It might be divided into chambers; the essential thing was to decide on the quorum of the chambers. There must be no doubt on this point. As to the system of exclusion *ex-jure* without reasons given, he thought it was an odious system and he would oppose it in every way.

M. Loder thought that it was useless to have the different legal systems represented on the Court. The new Court will apply international law, and this law is international in the true sense of the word. If the need arises of clearing up a point of national law, the eminent judges composing the Court would be quite able to deal with it.

The remarks of M. Ricci-Busatti very much surprised M. Loder. It is necessary to adopt the point of view of Article 14 of the Covenant which makes a formal distinction between strict Justice and Arbitration.

The PRESIDENT remarked that in the Covenant all the disputes are classified as permitting or not permitting of arbitration; the latter give occasion merely for a recommendation.

M. LODER read the text of Art. 14 of the Covenant. He observed that this Article had not in view the making up of a list of members for a Court, but the creation of a Court of a really permanent character.

M. Ricci-Busatti personally might be of a different opinion, but one should not forget that the Committee had been summoned by virtue of Article 14 of the Covenant. However, M. Loder feared that if M. Ricci-Busatti did not accept this view, it would become difficult to continue the discussion with him.

M. DE LAPRADELLE agreed with the views set forth by M. Loder. M. Ricci-Busatti

est favorable à l'idée d'établir une relation entre la Cour d'Arbitrage et la nouvelle Cour Permanente, qui en serait extraite: cette idée va à l'encontre du Pacte, et aussi du développement du droit international.

En 1907, déjà, on a reconnu que la Cour d'Arbitrage était insuffisante, et on a poursuivi l'idéal de la création d'une Cour Permanente de Justice. C'est cette Cour que veut réaliser le Pacte, et l'opinion publique dans les différents Etats s'attend à voir surgir des discussions du Comité une institution comparable aux institutions nationales de justice. Il faut que le Comité s'éloigne de l'œuvre de La Haye pour bien accentuer le fait qu'il s'agit de créer une institution de justice.

M. Ricci-Busatti a comparé son système à une pyramide. Cette expression a rappelé à M. de Lapradelle la constitution française de l'an VIII, constitution qui n'a certainement pas eu un succès pyramidal. Donc, la comparaison même effraye. Il faut résolument se placer à un autre point de vue. Mais en adoptant cette attitude il faut tenir compte des arguments tirés des susceptibilités nationales. Chaque peuple veut avoir son siège à la Cour. Par conséquent, plus la Cour contient de juges et de juges suppléants, plus les peuples auront confiance en elle, et plus grandes seront sa force et son influence.

M. de Lapradelle est prêt à se rallier à l'opinion de la majorité en ce qui concerne la question du nombre de juges, mais il souligne la nécessité de ne pas tenir compte seulement des exigences de la raison; il faut considérer également les possibilités pratiques et les susceptibilités nationales.

Le PRESIDENT reprend la question des rapports entre la Cour d'Arbitrage et la Cour nouvelle. M. Loder estime que les points de départ des membres sont trop différents pour qu'on puisse s'entendre. Le Président, pour sa part, croit que cette opinion repose à l'origine sur une confusion.

Il n'y a pas de différence essentielle et fondamentale entre la Cour d'Arbitrage et la Cour de Justice au point de vue de leur compétence virtuelle. Les deux juridictions connaissent des questions de droit qui leur sont déférées, et aussi des questions d'une nature non juridique, qui peuvent leur être accidentellement soumises. Normalement les deux juridictions statuent en droit: c'est commettre une erreur que de dire que la Cour d'Arbitrage statue en équité. M. Renault a dit qu'on peut seulement donner à l'arbitre d'une manière accessoire la fonction de conci-

favoured the idea of establishing a connection between the Court of Arbitration and the new Permanent Court, which should be derived from the former: this idea is contrary to the Covenant and also to the development of international law.

It already had been recognised in 1907 that the Court of Arbitration was insufficient. The idea was taken up of creating a Permanent Court of Justice. It was this Court which the Covenant intended to bring into being, and public opinion in all countries expects to see an institution comparable to the national institutions of justice result from the discussions of this Committee. The Committee must keep its work distinct from the work done at the Hague in order to make it quite clear that the present problem is to create a judicial body.

M. Ricci-Busatti had compared his system to a pyramid. This expression reminded M. de Lapradelle of the French constitution of the year VIII of the Revolution, a constitution whose success certainly was not pyramidal. He felt shy, therefore, of this comparison. It was essential to adopt another standpoint, but in doing so it was necessary to consider the arguments based on national susceptibility. Every nation wished to have a representative on the Court. Consequently the larger the number of judges and deputy-judges included in the Court, the greater would be the confidence of the nations in the Court and the greater would be its power and influence.

M. de Lapradelle was ready to agree with the opinion of the majority concerning the question of the number of judges, but he emphasised the necessity of taking into account, not only scientific requirements but also the practical possibilities and national susceptibilities.

The PRESIDENT again dealt with the question of the relations between the Court of Arbitration and the new Court. M. Loder had said that the members' fundamental ideas were too different to permit an agreement. The President, however, thought that this opinion was based on a primary confusion of terms.

There was no essential and fundamental difference between the Court of Arbitration and the Court of Justice with regard to their potential competence. Both jurisdictions dealt with questions of law presented to them, and also with questions not so strictly legal, which might be submitted to them. Normally both jurisdictions decide according to law: it would be a mistake to say that the Court of Arbitration made use only of equity. M. Renault has said that conciliatory functions might be given to the Court of Arbitration only as an accessory to its other

liateur. Il peut bien en être de même en ce qui concerne la Cour Permanente de Justice Internationale.

Les différences entre les deux Cours apparaissent surtout lorsque l'on considère les questions d'organisation et de fonctionnement. En effet, les règles concernant la nomination des juges, la permanence de la juridiction, la procédure et d'autres points encore, ne peuvent pas être les mêmes pour les deux Cours.

Le Président appelle de nouveau l'attention du Comité sur le fait que le Pacte ne connaît que la distinction entre les différends arbitrables et les litiges non arbitrables, ces derniers devant être soumis au Conseil de la Société des Nations.

Il donne lecture des articles 12 et 14 du Pacte et exprime l'avis que, si l'on veut concilier ces deux articles selon les règles ordinaires de l'interprétation juridique, on arrive clairement à ce résultat, que la Cour d'Arbitrage et la Cour Permanente de Justice Internationale peuvent avoir la même compétence et qu'elles ne différeront que dans leur organisation et leur fonctionnement.

L'objet qu'on a en vue en créant une Cour vraiment permanente est surtout, au dire du regretté M. Asser, d'éviter la procédure souvent compliquée, lourde et coûteuse de l'arbitrage, et d'avoir des juges professionnels domiciliés au siège de la Cour.

En terminant, le Président revient à l'œuvre de La Haye. Il rappelle que l'objet de la juridiction internationale projetée en 1907 a été de rendre des jugements sur la base du droit. Il ajoute qu'il est juridiquement impossible de donner à la Cour prévue par l'article 14 du Pacte un caractère radicalement différent à ce point de vue, de celui de la Cour d'Arbitrage.

M. LODER, reprenant l'argument tiré par le Président de l'article 12 du Pacte, fait observer que cet article ne parle que de conflits susceptibles d'entraîner une rupture.

Il poursuit en faisant valoir que l'objet des deux juridictions, arbitrale et judiciaire, est le même; savoir la réalisation de la justice. Mais les fonctions des deux juridictions sont foncièrement différentes; et les différences ne sont pas seulement dans l'organisation. Le but de l'article 14 est en effet de fonder un tribunal devant lequel une partie pourrait citer la partie adverse; la juridiction de la Cour d'Arbitrage est purement facultative.

Le PRESIDENT estime qu'il n'y a pas lieu d'insister davantage sur le texte du Pacte qui paraît clair.

work. The same applied, according to the President, to the Permanent Court of International Justice.

The difference between the two Courts above all appeared when the questions were considered as to how they were organized and how they worked. The rules governing the nomination of judges, the permanence of the jurisdiction and the procedure etc. could not be the same in the two Courts.

The President again called the attention of the Committee to the fact that the Covenant only made a distinction between disputes capable of settlement by arbitration and cases not suitable for arbitration; the latter are to be submitted to the Council of the League of Nations.

He read articles 12 and 14 of the Covenant and said that in his opinion, if these two articles were reconciled according to the ordinary rules of legal interpretation, the result would be that the Court of Arbitration and the Permanent Court of International Justice might have the same competence and would only differ in their organisation and their working.

The object in view when creating a really Permanent Court is above all, according to M. Asser, to avoid the often complicated, slow, and expensive procedure of arbitration, and to have professional judges resident at the seat of the Court.

In conclusion, the President reverted to the subject of the work of the Hague. He recalled that the object of the project of international jurisdiction of 1907 had been to deliver judgments based on law. He added that it was legally impossible to give the Court mentioned in Art. 14 of the Covenant a character radically different in this respect from that of the Court of Arbitration.

M. LODER taking up the argument based by the President on Article 12 of the Covenant, pointed out that this Article mentioned only disputes likely to lead to a rupture.

He continued by pointing out that the object of the two jurisdictions of arbitration and justice was the same; namely — to assure that justice be done. But the functions of the two jurisdictions were fundamentally different, the differences were not only in the organisation. The aim of Article 14 is in reality to found a tribunal before which one party might call the opposing party; submission to the jurisdiction of the Court of Arbitration is purely optional.

The PRESIDENT thought that it was useless to discuss any longer the text of the Covenant, which appeared clear.

M. DE LAPRADELLE donne lecture de l'article 14; d'après lui il ne faut pas exagérer l'idée de M. Loder, puisque, aux termes de l'article précité, la Cour connaîtra de tout litige que les parties lui soumettront. M. de Lapradelle estime que la différence entre les deux tribunaux réside plutôt dans le fait que, tandis que la fonction de la Cour d'Arbitrage est plus large et plus souple, celle de la Cour nouvelle sera strictement juridique.

M. DE LAPRADELLE read Article 14; he thought that the idea put forward by M. Loder should not receive too much stress because, according to the Article he had quoted, the Court will hear any dispute presented to it by the contesting parties. M. de Lapradelle thought that the difference between the two tribunals rested rather on the fact that, whereas the function of the Court of Arbitration was wider and very flexible, that of the new Court would be strictly legal.

Mr. ROOT émet une suggestion au sujet de la question du nombre des juges.

Les conditions dont il faut tenir compte pour régler cette question sont sujettes à des changements. A l'heure actuelle la Société des Nations comprend moins de la moitié de la population de l'Europe; le temps viendra où les autres Etats, représentant la vaste population de l'Europe Orientale, entreront dans la Société. Il faut qu'il en soit ainsi pour que le but de la Société — assurer une meilleure entente entre les nations en vue du maintien de la paix — puisse être réalisé. Mr. Root exprime aussi l'espoir que les objections soulevées dans son pays contre certaines dispositions du Pacte de la Société des Nations pourront être écartées par des amendements, de façon à permettre aux Etats-Unis d'entrer dans la Société. Il ajoute à cet égard qu'il préfère l'expression „Société des Nations" à celle de „Ligue des Nations", parce que l'association entre les nations doit être fondée non pas sur un contrat, mais sur une entente.

L'idée qu'il désire suggérer, c'est que, lorsque le Comité proposera le nombre des juges dont sera composée la Cour, il envisage, non seulement les conditions telles qu'elles seront à ce moment, mais aussi telles qu'elles seront dans un avenir plus lointain. Il propose que le nombre fixé au début soit moins élevé que le chiffre définitif: si l'on veut atteindre finalement le nombre de 15, le chiffre de 9 doit être suffisant pour le moment. En fixant un nombre moins élevé, il faudrait cependant stipuler expressément que ce nombre devra augmenter au fur et à mesure que de nouveaux Etats entreront dans la Société des Nations. Mr. Root n'attache pas trop d'importance au chiffre à fixer; s'il a mentionné les nombres de 15 et 9, c'est seulement afin de donner un exemple de la relation qui, à son avis, doit exister entre le chiffre original et le chiffre définitif.

Mr. Root ajoute que l'augmentation progressive du nombre des juges répondrait de façon heureuse aux exigences du développement natu-

Mr. ROOT presented a suggestion on the subject of the number of judges.

The conditions necessary to consider in settling this question are subject to change. At the present moment, the League of Nations includes less than half of the population of Europe; the time will come when the remainder of the States representing the vast population of Eastern Europe would come into the League. This expectation must be fulfilled if the object of the League — a better understanding between nations and a more effective preservation of peace — are to be realised. Mr. Root also hoped that the objections raised in his own country to certain provisions of the Covenant of the League would be obviated by certain amendments, so that the United States might enter the League. He added in this connection that he preferred the expression "Society of Nations" to "League of Nations", because the association between nations should not be based upon a contract, but on an understanding.

The idea which he wished to suggest was that in recommending the number of judges for this Court, not only actual conditions prevailing at that time, but also those conditions which will prevail in the future, should be taken into consideration by the Committee. He suggested that the number now fixed be smaller than the final number; that if the number 15 was finally to be reached, 9 would be sufficient now. In fixing a lower number, it should, however, be definitely stipulated that it should be increased in proportion to the entrance of new States into the League of Nations. Mr. Root did not attach too much importance to the actual number to be fixed; he merely intended, by mentioning the numbers 15 and 9, to show the relation which he thought ought to exist between the present and the final number.

Mr. Root added that the successive increases in the number of judges would respond easily to the demands of a natural development. The number of members of the League of Nations in-

rel. Le nombre des Membres de la Société s'élevant avec le temps, il sera nécessaire d'avoir un nombre plus élevé de juges.

A l'appui de cette opinion, Mr. Root cite l'exemple du développement de la Cour Suprême des Etats-Unis; il fait aussi allusion à l'histoire du Conseil Privé de la Grande-Bretagne.

Mr. Root fait valoir que si l'on prend pour point de départ la nomination des juges par le vote conjoint du Conseil et de l'Assemblée de la Société des Nations, l'idée qu'il a suggérée aura dans la pratique le même effet que le projet de M. Adatci. Celui-ci a proposé un nombre de 13 juges, dont cinq ressortissants des grandes Puissances et huit provenant des Puissances secondaires. Si l'on adopte le nombre final de 15, il y aura place pour deux nouvelles grandes Puissances, sans ôter la majorité aux petites.

Mr. Root ajoute qu'il faut envisager la possibilité de l'entrée de l'Allemagne, de la Russie et des Etats-Unis dans la Société des Nations, à titre de grandes Puissances.

Répondant à une question du Président, Mr. Root dit qu'il a l'intention de faire quelques observations sur les relations qui existent entre la justice pure et l'arbitrage. Vu l'heure avancée, il préfère cependant remettre ces remarques à la séance prochaine.

Le PRESIDENT déclare qu'à la séance du jeudi, Mr. Root aura la parole le premier.

La séance est levée à 12.30 de l'après-midi.

Le Président:
(signé) Brn. DESCAMPS.

Le Secrétaire-Général:
(signé) D. ANZILOTTI.

creasing as time goes on would necessitate a larger number of judges.

In support of this view, Mr. Root pointed to the example of the development of the Supreme Court of the United States; he alluded also to the history of the Privy Council in Great-Britain.

Mr. Root pointed out that, if election by the concurrent action of the Council and Assembly were adopted as a starting point, the idea he had put forward would have the same effect in practice as the suggestion made by M. Adatci. The latter had proposed 13 judges — 5 for the great Powers and 8 for the small Powers. If the final number 15 were adopted, there would be room for two new great Powers without removing the small Powers' majority.

Mr. Root added that it was necessary to bear in mind the possibility of the entry into the League of Nations, on the footing of Great Powers, of Germany, Russia and the United States.

In answer to a question by the President, Mr. Root said that he intended to discuss the relations existing between justice and arbitration. Because of the lateness of the hour he postponed his remarks until the next meeting.

The PRESIDENT announced that Mr. Root would speak first at Thursday's meeting.

The meeting closed at 12.30 p.m.

The President:
(signed) Brn. DESCAMPS.

The Secretary-General:
(signed) D. ANZILOTTI.

ANNEXE No. 1.

Proposition de M. Ricci Busatti.

Le projet suivant n'est qu'une esquisse, inspirée des considérations brièvement résumées ci-dessous:

1. Il convient que la Cour de Justice se rattache autant que possible à la Cour d'Arbitrage, dont elle ne fait que développer les fonctions.

2. Il paraît nécessaire que le principe fondamental de l'égalité juridique des Etats soit mis en accord avec certains égards dûs aux Puissances qui jouent un rôle prépondérant au sein de la Société des Nations.

3. Il paraît utile que l'Assemblée de la Ligue participe de quelque façon à la constitution de la Cour.

4. Il convient, semble-t-il, pour des raisons d'ordre pratique, de pourvoir, à l'aide de dispositions spéciales, à la constitution du tribunal pour chaque litige particulier; il faudra, à cet égard, tenir compte dans une large mesure des désirs exprimés par les parties en cause.

Article 1.

La Cour Permanente de Justice Internationale sera composée de 15 membres, réunissant les qualités nécessaires pour faire partie de la Cour Permanente d'Arbitrage, aux termes de la Convention de La Haye pour le règlement pacifique des conflits internationaux.

Article 2.

Chaque Etat, Membre de la Société des Nations, aura la faculté de désigner, à cette fin, une personne qui sera choisie par le collège de ses délégués à la Cour d'Arbitrage, soit parmi les nationaux dudit Etat, soit parmi les nationaux d'un autre pays.

Article 3.

Les personnes ainsi designées par les Etats représentés d'une façon permanente au Conseil de la Société, et celles qui auront été désignées au moins par trois Etats seront de plein droit membres de la Cour. Les autres membres seront choisis par l'Assemblée de la Société sur la liste des personnes visées au paragraphe précédent.

Chaque membre de l'Assemblée disposera d'un

ANNEX No. 1.

Proposal of M. Ricci Busatti.

The following scheme is merely a sketch inspired by considerations briefly set out as follows:

1. The Court of Justice should be connected as intimately as possible with the Court of Arbitration, the functions of which it merely develops.

2. It seems necessary that the fundamental principle of the legal equality of States should be made to agree with certain considerations due to the Powers who play a preponderant part within the League of Nations.

3. It seems useful that the Assembly of the League should take part in some way in the composition of the Court.

4. It is desirable, it seems, for practical considerations, to provide, by means of special clauses, for the establishment of a tribunal for each particular case. In this connection, the desires expressed by the parties concerned must be given much consideration.

Article 1.

The Permanent Court of International Justice shall be composed of 15 members possessing the necessary qualifications for membership in the Permanent Court of Arbitration, in accordance with the terms of the Hague Convention for the pacific settlement of international disputes.

Article 2.

All States, Members of the League of Nations, shall have the right to nominate for this purpose, one person, who shall be elected by a college of its delegates to the Court of Arbitration, from among the nationals of the said State or of another State.

Article 3.

The persons thus named by the States represented permanently on the Council of the League, and the persons who shall be named by at least three States shall be members of the Court *de plano*. The other members of the Court shall be chosen by the Assembly of the League from a list of persons named in the preceding paragraph.

nombre de voix égal à celui des juges à choisir; les personnes qui auront obtenu le plus grand nombre de voix seront élues.

Article 4.

La Cour réunie en séance plénière nommera un Président et deux Vice-Présidents; elle se divisera en trois sections composées chacune de cinq membres.

Article 5.

Les parties en cause pourront désigner, d'un commun accord, la section de la Cour qu'elles désirent saisir de l'affaire: elles pourront également demander que le tribunal soit composé de trois juges librement désignés par elles parmi les membres de la Cour, ou que le litige soit soumis à la décision d'un juge unique, également désigné par elles.

Lorsque les parties n'auront exprimé aucun vœu particulier conformément à l'alinéa précédent, le Président désignera la section devant laquelle doit être portée l'affaire.

Each member of the Assembly shall have as many votes as there are judges to be chosen; the persons who shall have received the greatest number of votes shall be elected.

Article 4.

The Court shall elect in full sitting one President, and two Vice-Presidents. It shall divide itself into three sections, each composed of five members.

Article 5.

The parties in dispute shall have the right to designate by mutual agreement which section of the Court they desire to hear the case: they may also demand that the tribunal be composed of three judges nominated by them from among the members of the Court; or that the case be submitted to the decision of a single judge also named by them.

If the parties shall have expressed no special preference, according to the preceding paragraph, the President shall name the section before which the matter should be taken.

8IÈME SÉANCE (non-publique), tenue au Palais de la Paix, à La Haye, le 24 juin 1920.

Présidence de M. le BARON DESCAMPS.

Sont présents: tous les membres du Comité (à l'exception de M. Bevilaqua); Mr. James Brown Scott; les secrétaires particuliers de M. le Baron Descamps et de M. Adatci; les membres du Secrétariat.

La séance est ouverte à $9^1/_2$ heures du matin.

Conformément à ce qui avait été décidé à la fin de la séance précédente, le PRESIDENT donne la parole à Mr. Root.

Mr. ROOT, ayant exposé ce qu'il avait à dire sur la question de la nomination des juges, et préférant remettre ses remarques sur le caractère juridique de l'ancienne et de la nouvelle Cour au moment de la discussion générale de ce point, renonce à la parole.

Le PRESIDENT est d'avis que, les membres ayant exprimé leur opinion sur les questions à l'ordre du jour de la séance précédente, on peut passer à l'examen d'un autre point. Toutes les questions relatives à l'établissement de la Cour s'enchevètrent; il faut avoir recours à un échange général de vues avant de procéder à des votes particuliers. Il propose donc, d'accord avec M. Loder, qu'on commence la discussion concernant la permanence de la Cour et le domicile des juges.

LORD PHILLIMORE désire cependant ajouter qu'après avoir réfléchi sur l'idée de Mr. Root, relative à l'élection des juges, et sur l'opinion des autres membres sur la même question, il pense qu'il faut d'abord constituer la Cour avec un nombre de juges plutôt restreint; ce nombre augmentera à mesure que se développera la Société des Nations. On peut p.e. commencer par 11, pour s'arrêter à 15. La Cour doit siéger avec 9 juges. Il y aura toujours, parmi les membres de la Cour, des juges qui voudront céder leur place dans certains cas parce qu'ils auront des interêts personnels dans l'objet du litige, ou parce qu'ils croiront que leur nationalité ou d'autres raisons les empêchent de siéger. Si, après

8TH MEETING (Private), held at the Peace Palace, the Hague, on June 24th, 1920.

BARON DESCAMPS in the chair.

Present: all members of the Committee (with the exception of M. Bevilaqua); Mr. James Brown Scott; the private secretaries of Baron Descamps and of M. Adatci; the members of the Secretariat.

The meeting opened at 9.30 a.m.

In accordance with the decision taken at the end of the preceding meeting, the PRESIDENT called upon Mr. Root.

Mr. ROOT said that, having explained what he had to say on the question of the nomination of judges and preferring to postpone his remarks on the judicial character of the old and the new Courts until the general discussion of this point, he declined the opportunity to speak.

The PRESIDENT was of opinion that as the members had expressed their views on the subjects on the Agenda for the preceding meeting, the examination of another point could now be taken up. All questions concerning the establishment of the Court were intermingled; a general exchange of opinions must take place before proceeding to any individual vote. Therefore he proposed, in agreement with M. Loder, that they should begin the discussion relating to the permanence of the Court and the domicile of the judges.

LORD PHILLIMORE wished, however, to add that, after having thought over Mr. Root's idea concerning the election of judges, and having considered the opinions of the other members on the same question, he thought that the Court first should be composed of a rather limited number of judges; this number will increase as the League of Nations develops. For instance, the number might at first be 11, in the end 15. The Court should sit with 9 judges. Amongst the members of the Court there would always be some judges who would wish to give up their seat in certain cases, because they had personal interests in the litigation or because they thought that their nationality or other rea-

la réduction ainsi opérée, il en reste plus de 9, il sera facile de s'arranger. Le règlement d'ordre intérieur de la Cour peut prévoir des dispositions à ce sujet en instituant, par exemple, un système de roulement; ou bien encore le droit d'exclusion peut être confié au Président.

Lord Phillimore ajoute qu'il a seulement voulu exprimer un avis et non pas faire une proposition formelle.

M. LODER se rallie en principe à l'idée de Mr. Root. Mais il préfère qu'on décide, dès à présent, qu'il y aura, p.e. de neuf à quinze juges.

M. ALTAMIRA croit qu'il serait avantageux de fixer un chiffre maximum et un chiffre minimum. Il est opposé au droit de récusation; il croit que l'élimination d'un juge devrait avoir lieu seulement pour cause d'incompatibilité.

Le PRESIDENT propose qu'on passe à la discussion de la question de la permanence de la Cour et du domicile des juges; la proposition est acceptée.

M. LODER pense que la permanence de la nouvelle Cour étant prévue par l'article 14 du Pacte, il n'y a pas lieu de la discuter: le Comité est lié par cet article. Cependant, il y a une difficulté, celle de trouver des juges disposés à établir leur domicile au siège de la Cour. Pour parer à cette difficulté, M. Loder propose que la Cour, bien que toujours ouverte, ne siégera que pendant quatre périodes chaque année; ainsi les juges ne seraient obligés d'être au siège de la Cour que pendant ces périodes.

Le PRESIDENT résume la proposition de M. Loder: il admet qu'elle est compatible avec le texte du Pacte.

M. ALTAMIRA prenant comme point de départ le système adopté dans certaines Cours nationales, croit qu'on peut trouver une solution en établissant deux chambres, ou „salles", l'une permanente, dans laquelle les juges siègeraient d'après un système de roulement, l'autre ne se réunissant qu'à une certaine période de l'année.

LORD PHILLIMORE préfère une solution d'après laquelle le greffe et le Président de la Cour seraient en permanence installés au siège de la Cour. Les autres membres de la Cour ne seraient tenus d'y être présents que pendant les sessions ordinaires. Si les membres étaient forcés d'être en contact quotidien sans être occupés par leur travail, des conséquences fâcheuses se-

sons prevented them from sitting. If after the reduction thus effected there should remain more than 9 judges, it would be easy to arrange matters. The Court's rules could include provisions on this subject, in establishing, for instance, a system of rotation; or the right of exclusion might be entrusted to the President.

Lord Phillimore added that he only wished to make a suggestion and not a formal proposal.

M. LODER agreed in principle with Mr. Root's idea. However, he preferred that they should decide now that there should be, for instance, from nine to fifteen judges.

M. ALTAMIRA thought that it would be an advantage to fix a maximum and minimum number. He objected to the right of challenge; he thought that the elimination of any judge should only take place for reasons of incompatibility.

The PRESIDENT proposed that they should pass to the discussion of the question of the permanence of the Court and the domicile of the judges. His proposal was adopted.

M. LODER thought that, the permanence of the new Court being provided for by Art. 14 of the Covenant, there was no need to discuss it: the Committee is bound by this Article. However, a difficulty exists: namely, that of finding judges prepared to establish their homes at the seat of the Court. To overcome this difficulty M. Loder proposed that the Court, although always accessible, should only sit during four separate periods in each year. Thus the judges would be obliged to be present at the seat of the Court only during these periods.

The PRESIDENT summed up the proposal of M. Loder, and admitted that it was compatible with the wording of the Covenant.

M. ALTAMIRA taking as his starting point the system adopted in certain national Courts, thought a solution could be found by establishing two chambers (or "salles"): one permanent, in which the judges would sit according to a system of rotation; the other would not meet except at a given time of the year.

LORD PHILLIMORE preferred a solution according to which the Registrar and the President of the Court should be permanently installed at the seat of the Court. The other members of the Court would be bound to be present only during the ordinary sessions. If the members were compelled to be in daily contact without occupation, he feared that there would be unfor-

raient à craindre. Mieux vaut leur permettre de retourner dans leurs pays dans les intervalles entre les sessions. Ils auraient cependant l'obligation de se rendre au siège aussitôt convoqués par le Président ou lorsque, entre les sessions, un cas urgent serait porté devant la Cour. Une session extraordinaire pourrait être convoquée par le noyau permanent de la Cour résidant à son siège. D'autre part le Président pourrait prévenir les membres, avant le commencement d'une session ordinaire, qu'aucun procès n'ayant été soumis à la Cour, la session est prorogée.

M. DE LAPRADELLE reconnaît que certains fonctionnaires, comme le Président et un ou plusieurs Vice-Présidents, doivent toujours être présents au siège de la Cour. Il n'en est pas de même de tous les juges. Si l'on veut avoir des juges hautement qualifiés on ne doit pas priver totalement leurs pays de leurs services. Sauf dans l'Amérique du Sud la vie nationale des différents Etats est moins active entre le 15 juin et le 15 octobre que pendant l'hiver: on pourrait donc songer à tenir la session de la Cour pendant cette période, et laisser aux juges la liberté de travailler dans leurs propres pays pendant le reste de l'année.

Les cas d'urgence pourraient être traités, d'après une procédure sommaire, par le Président, assisté de deux ou trois membres. Cependant, le besoin d'une telle procédure ne se fera pas souvent sentir.

M. ADATCI se déclare surpris par cette discussion. Il croyait que la Cour serait permanente dans le sens littéral du mot et que les juges quitteraient leurs occupations nationales pour s'internationaliser, se „diviniser", comme il se plait à le dire. Au Japon, où l'on a déjà en vue les hommes sur lesquels pourrait se porter le choix pour remplir le poste de juge, on n'hésiterait pas à demander à ces hommes de quitter leurs occupations nationales, pour consacrer leur vie à la justice internationale. M. Adatci fait valoir les difficultés qui surgiraient pour les pays de l'Extrême Orient, en raison de leur éloignement du siège probable de la Cour, si l'on faisait siéger celle-ci pendant certaines périodes seulement de l'année. Il ajoute que, dans ces pays, on ne considérerait pas comme sérieuse une Cour composée de juges siégeant un jour dans leurs propres pays et l'autre au tribunal mondial.

M. LODER préfère également voir les juges domiciliés au siège de la Cour, bien qu'il sache qu'il soit possible, que, pendant les premiers

tunate consequences. It would be better to allow them to return to their countries in the intervals between the sessions. But they would be bound to proceed to the seat of the Court whenever summoned by the President, or when an urgent case was submitted to the Court. An extraordinary session could be summoned by the permanent nucleus of the Court residing at its seat. On the other hand the President could inform the members, before the beginning of an ordinary session that, no cases having been submitted to the Court, the session was postponed.

M. DE LAPRADELLE admitted that certain officials such as the President and one or more Vice-Presidents always ought to be present at the seat of the Court. It was not the same in the case of all the judges. If one wished to have highly qualified judges one must not deprive their respective countries entirely of their services. Except in South America the national life of the various countries was less active between the 15th June and the 15th October than in the winter. Holding the session of the Court during this period might be considered, allowing the judges to work in their own countries during the rest of the year.

Urgent cases could be dealt with summarily by the President, assisted by two or three members. However, the need for such a procedure would not be felt frequently.

M. ADATCI expressed his surprise at the discussion. He thought that the Court was to be permanent in the literal sense of the word and that the judges were to resign their national occupations in order to internationalise themselves, — as M. Adatci liked to express it, to "deify" themselves. In Japan men already have been considered who would be suitable for judges, and there would be no hesitation in asking these men to leave their national occupations so that they might devote their lives to the administration of international justice. M. Adatci pointed out the difficulties which would arise for the countries of the far East on account of their geographical remoteness from the probable seat of the Court, if the Court were to sit only during certain periods of the year. He added that in these countries a Court composed of judges who one day sat in their own country, the next day on the world Court, would not be taken seriously.

M. LODER also preferred that the judges should be domiciled at the seat of the Court, even though it would be possible, he knew, that

temps, les juges ne seront pas suffisamment occupés. Ce point dépend cependant de la solution qu'on donnera à la question de savoir si non seulement les Etats, mais aussi les particuliers, pourront s'adresser à la Cour.

Pratiquement le problème est le suivant: peut-on trouver des personnes disposées à se donner entièrement aux fonctions de juge international? M. Loder incline, à cet égard, vers l'opinion de M. de Lapradelle.

M. RICCI-BUSATTI pense également que la proposition de M. de Lapradelle est la plus pratique à plusieurs égards, si l'on exige une permanence réelle de la Cour; il se préoccupe cependant des difficultés qui proviennent de l'éloignement des pays orientaux et des pays de l'Amérique du Sud.

Il croit qu'il n'est guère facile de trouver des personnes disposées à se dénationaliser, ou à se „diviniser", selon l'expression de M. Adatci, c'est-à-dire, à se détacher entièrement de leur pays, pour remplir une tâche qui ne les occuperait qu'un court laps de temps. Pour parer à ces difficultés, il conçoit la „permanence" d'une manière plus large; il y aurait une „liste de juges" toujours prêts à siéger, et il y aurait un bureau permanent au sens strict du mot, composé du Président, des Vice-Présidents et du greffe, pour recevoir les recours, organiser le tribunal, prendre toute mesure urgente, pourvoir à l'instruction des affaires et, dans certains cas, les résoudre.

Il est difficile de dire si les cas portés devant la Cour seront nombreux. M. Ricci-Busatti ne croit pas qu'ils seront très nombreux; cette question est liée, cependant, à celle de la compétence de la Cour. Mais il y aura toujours, son expérience personnelle le lui enseigne, des cas urgents (questions d'interprétation d'un tarif douanier, d'émigration, de séquestre d'un navire etc.). Ces cas rendent nécessaire qu'une partie de la Cour soit véritablement permanente, et qu'il soit possible à tout moment de convoquer le tribunal.

M. ADATCI informe le Comité que la Commission des Communications et du Transit a prévu l'intervention d'urgence de la Cour Permanente dans un nombre de cas assez élevé.

Le PRESIDENT cite de nouveaux cas à ajouter à ceux qu'a visés M. Adatci.

M. ALTAMIRA pense que la proposition de M. de Lapradelle soulève des difficultés insurmontables: si elle est adoptée on enlèvera en

the judges would not have sufficient work at first. This point, however, depended upon the solution arrived at concerning the question whether not only States but also individuals might appeal to the Court.

Practically the problem was as follows: were persons to be found, prepared to give their whole time to their work as international judges? On this subject M. Loder was inclined to agree with M. de Lapradelle.

M. RICCI-BUSATTI thought also that the proposal of M. de Lapradelle was the most practical in several respects, if a really permanent Court were required; however, he was concerned with the difficulties which would arise from the distant situation of Eastern countries, and States of South America.

He thought that it would not be easy to find persons prepared to denationalise themselves or to "deify" themselves, as M. Adatci had put it; in other words, to separate themselves completely from their country to discharge a duty which will occupy them for only a short period of time. To avert these difficulties, he took a wider view of the expression "permanence"; there should be a "list of judges" always ready to sit, there should always be a permanent office in the strict sense of the word, composed of the President, Vice-Presidents and Registrar, to receive appeals, organize the tribunal, attend to urgent matters, provide for preliminary hearings and, in certain cases, settle disputes.

It was difficult to say whether the cases brought before the Court would be numerous or not. M. Ricci-Busatti thought that they would not be very numerous. This question, however, is dependent upon that of the competence of the Court. But there would always be, his personal experience taught him, urgent cases (questions concerning the interpretation of a customs tariff, emigration, detention of a ship, etc). These cases make it necessary that one part of the Court should be really permanent, and that it should be possible at any time to call together the tribunal.

M. ADATCI informed the Committee that the Communications and Transit Commission had anticipated the speedy intervention of the Permanent Court in a considerable number of cases.

The PRESIDENT mentioned new cases to add to those referred to by M. Adatci.

M. ALTAMIRA thought that M. de Lapradelle's proposal would cause insurmountable difficulties. If it were adopted the possi-

fait aux pays de l'Amérique du Sud la possibilité d'être représentés à la Cour. Il préfère le système de la Chambre permanente, qui pourrait être constituée en adoptant le roulement des juges.

Un échange de vues a lieu entre M. HAGERUP et M. ALTAMIRA sur la question de savoir comment ce système fonctionnera pour les cas d'urgence.

LORD PHILLIMORE exprime l'avis qu'il ne faut pas exiger des membres qu'ils aient leur domicile au siège de la Cour. Si un Etat a l'honneur d'avoir un de ses grands hommes comme membre de la Cour, cet homme doit sans doute être avant tout un juge international, mais son pays natal ne doit pas être entièrement privé de ses services, dans la mesure où ses occupations internationales lui donnent le loisir de se rendre utile à son pays. Lord Phillimore admet que l'avantage ne profiterait qu'aux pays les moins éloignés du siège de la Cour; mais c'est là une circonstance fortuite, et si le siège est aujourd'hui établi en Europe, qui sait si, un jour, il ne sera pas transféré p.e. dans l'Amérique du Sud. Le fait que tout le monde ne peut tirer avantage de cette disposition, n'est pas une raison suffisante pour empêcher d'en profiter ceux qui le peuvent.

Lord Phillimore insiste donc pour que les sessions de la Cour soient arrangées de façon à permettre au plus grand nombre possible de pays, d'utiliser les services des juges de leur nationalité. Lord Phillimore ne croit pas qu'il y aura besoin d'une procédure spéciale pour les cas d'urgence; mais si le besoin s'en fait sentir, on peut toujours parer à cette difficulté.

M. HAGERUP se demande si, en présence de la difficulté de concilier les opinions divergentes, il est nécessaire que le Comité se prononce définitivement sur la question. Ne peut-on pas se contenter de stipuler que le Président et le greffe résideront en permanence au siège de la Cour? Celle-ci pourrait alors prendre elle-même les décisions ultérieures en tenant compte, entre autres choses, de la provenance de ses divers membres. M. Hagerup qui, jusqu'ici, était partisan d'une réponse affirmative à la question de savoir si tous les juges doivent être domiciliés ou non au siège de la Cour, croit, après les considérations exposées par les membres du Comité, devoir abandonner cette opinion.

bility of being represented on the Court would actually be taken away from the South American countries. He preferred the system of a permanent chamber which could be constituted by adopting a system of rotation of judges.

An exchange of opinion took place between M. HAGERUP and M. ALTAMIRA as to how this system would operate in urgent cases.

LORD PHILLIMORE expressed the opinion that it must not be required of the members to be domiciled at the seat of the Court. If a State should be so honoured as to have one of its great men as a member of the Court, this judge should be no doubt above all an international judge, but his native country should not be entirely deprived of his services in so far as his international work allowed him leisure to be of service to his country. Lord Phillimore admitted that only those countries nearest to the seat of the Court would profit by this chance, but that was only circumstance, and though the seat was now established in Europe, who knows but that one day it might be transferred, for instance, to South America. The fact that everybody is not able to benefit by this arrangement is not a sufficient reason for preventing those who are from doing so.

Lord Phillimore therefore insisted that the sessions of the Court be so arranged as to permit the greatest possible number of countries to make use of the services of judges of their nationality. Lord Phillimore thought there would be no necessity for a special procedure for urgent cases, but if the need made itself felt, this difficulty could always be dealt with.

M. HAGERUP asked, considering the difficulty of conciliating various opinions, whether it was necessary for the Committee to give a final answer to the question. Would it not be enough to stipulate that the President and the Registrar should reside permanently at the seat of the Court? The Court itself then could reach its own ulterior decisions, taking into consideration amongst other things the countries from which its various members came. M. Hagerup who up till now had been in favour of an affirmative answer to the question whether all the judges must be domiciled or not at the seat of the Court, after hearing the arguments of the members of the Committee thought that he would have to give up this opinion.

M. RICCI-BUSATTI fait remarquer que la question de la permanence de la Cour est liée à celles de l'incompatibilité de la fonction de juge avec d'autres fonctions, et de la rémunération des juges.

Le PRESIDENT demande qu'après l'échange de vues qui vient d'avoir lieu sur la question à l'ordre du jour, les membres veuillent bien formuler leurs idées, telles qu'elles résultent de la discussion: celle-ci sera ainsi cristallisée dans des textes, et ceux-ci, le moment venu, formeront les éléments appropriés pour une décision première.

M. LODER propose que les textes, qui seront soumis au Comité, soient déférés à un Comité de rédaction.

Le PRESIDENT ne partage pas cet avis en ordre de procédure préliminaire. Les propositions qui seront formulées serviront à éclaircir la situation, en fixant les points de vue différents. Les textes doivent être présentés au Président qui les fera distribuer par les soins du Secrétariat.

Mr. ROOT partage l'opinion de M. Loder pour ce qui concerne la procédure à suivre; il se range à l'avis de M. Hagerup, qu'en évitant trop de détails, on évitera des discussions inutiles.

M. DE LAPRADELLE pourrait répondre à quelques arguments qui ont été apportés contre sa proposition; il doit cependant admettre la difficulté provenant du temps considérable qu'il faut pour venir en Europe du Japon et des Etats Sud-Américains.

Plusieurs membres donnent des indications à ce sujet.

Le PRESIDENT, avec l'assentiment du Comité, met en discussion la question de la durée des mandats (No. 5 de l'ordre du jour adopté).

LORD PHILLIMORE fait valoir la connexité de cette question avec celle de l'incompatibilité entre la fonction de juge et d'autres fonctions; on convient, par suite, d'ouvrir la discussion sur cette deuxième question.

LORD PHILLIMORE dit que, sans avoir des idées bien arrêtées sur la question de la durée du mandat, il lui semble que, en adoptant un mandat à vie, il faudrait en même temps prendre des précautions pour éviter que des juges, devenus incapables, continuent à exercer leurs fonc-

M. RICCI-BUSATTI pointed out that the question of the permanency of the Court was closely connected with those of the incompatibility of the duties as judge with other functions, and also with that of the remuneration to be given to the judges.

The PRESIDENT asked that after the exchange of views which had just taken place on the questions on the Agenda, members should kindly formulate the ideas they had drawn from this discussion; the discussion would thus be crystallized in the texts, and these, when the time came, would form an appropriate basis for a provisional decision.

M. LODER proposed that the texts submitted to the Committee should be referred to a drafting Committee.

The PRESIDENT did not agree to this in preliminary procedure. The proposals drawn up would serve to throw light on the situation by fixing the different points of view. The drafts should be presented to the President, who would have them distributed by the Secretariat.

Mr. ROOT shared the opinion of M. Loder as concerns the procedure to be followed; he agreed with M. Hagerup that by avoiding too much detail useless discussions would be avoided.

M. DE LAPRADELLE answered several arguments put forward against his proposal. He thought, however, that he must admit the difficulty arising from the long time it would take to come to Europe from Japan and the South American States.

Several members gave information on this subject.

The PRESIDENT, with the consent of the Committee, presented for discussion the question of the term of office (number 5 on the Agenda adopted).

LORD PHILLIMORE pointed out the connection existing between this question and that of the incompatibility of the duties of a judge with other functions; it was agreed, consequently, that the discussion of this second question also was open.

LORD PHILLIMORE said that, although he had not quite made up his mind on the question of the length of the mandate, it seemed to him, that if they adopted a life mandate, they must also take precaution to prevent incapacitated judges from continuing to exercise their function.

tions; si au contraire on préfère un mandat de durée limitée, il recommande une période de dix ans; il ne faut pas que la période soit trop longue.

Au sujet de la question de l'incompatibilité des fonctions, Lord Phillimore croit tout d'abord que la fonction de juge doit être considérée comme incompatible avec toute fonction politique. D'autre part, il y a, à son avis, plutôt avantage pour un juge international à appartenir en même temps à la magistrature de son propre pays. En ce qui concerne notamment l'Angleterre, il faudrait probablement chercher les juges internationaux dans la haute magistrature nationale; mais, comme les hauts magistrats anglais sont très souvent membres de la Chambre des Lords, et que, dans d'autres pays, des magistrats sont dans une situation analogue, il faudrait peut-être renoncer à considérer la qualité de membre de ces Chambres comme une fonction politique.

M. LODER et M. ALTAMIRA fournissent quelques informations sur les institutions judiciaires des Pays-Bas et de l'Espagne.

M. RICCI-BUSATTI croit que la question de l'incompatibilité des fonctions doit être réglée par la législation intérieure des divers Etats, puisqu'il s'agit de fonctions qui se rattachent à la vie nationale de chacun d'eux. Il ne voit d'ailleurs aucun motif pour admettre, en principe, que l'exercice d'une charge, même politique ou gouvernementale, dans un pays quelconque, puisse empêcher son titulaire d'exercer en toute conscience un rôle de juge entre des Etats. Le Comité doit s'occuper seulement de l'incompatibilité entre la fonction de juge international et d'autres fonctions du même ordre, par exemple: celle de membre de l'Assemblée de la Société des Nations ou du Conseil, ou le mandat d'agent d'un certain pays devant la Cour Internationale.

En ce qui concerne la durée des mandats, M. Ricci-Busatti croit qu'une période modérément limitée, entre six et dix ans, serait celle qui conviendrait le mieux.

Le PRESIDENT exprime sa surprise de l'opinion de M. Ricci-Busatti; peut-on vraiment laisser à la législation intérieure des Etats le soin de décider si des fonctionnaires éminemment politiques pourront ou non siéger à la Cour?

M. DE LAPRADELLE se demande si les jurisconsultes attachés aux Ministères des Affaires Etrangères pourront exercer la fonction de juges à la Cour; il ne le croit pas.

If, on the other hand, a limited mandate were preferred, he recommended a period of ten years. The period must not be too long.

Concerning the question of incompatibility of duties, Lord Phillimore thought that, to begin with, a post as judge must be considered as incompatible with any political office. On the other hand, in his opinion, it was rather an advantage for an international judge to belong at the same time to the Bench of his own country. Dealing particularly with England, it would probably be necessary to seek the international judges in the high national magistracy; but as English judges were often members of the House of Lords, and as in other countries judges were in a similar position, it would perhaps be desirable not to consider membership of such a chamber as a political function.

M. LODER and M. ALTAMIRA gave some information concerning the judicial institutions of Holland and Spain.

M. RICCI-BUSATTI thought that the question of incompatibility of duties might be dealt with by legislation in the various States, since it has to do with duties connected with the national life of each one of them. Furthermore, he saw no reason to admit in principle that holding office, even political or governmental, could prevent its holder from discharging conscientiously the duties of a judge between States. The Committee need only deal with the incompatibility between the duties of international judges and other duties of the same kind, for instance: membership of the Assembly of the League of Nations, or of the Council, a mandate as Agent for a certain country before the International Court.

Concerning the term of office, M. Ricci-Busatti thought that a moderately short period, from six to ten years, would be most acceptable.

The PRESIDENT was surprised at the opinion of M. Ricci-Busatti. How could it be left to the internal legislation of States to decide whether an eminently political official could sit on the Court?

M. DE LAPRADELLE wondered whether the jurisconsults attached to Foreign Offices could be judges of the Court. He thought not.

LORD PHILLIMORE pose la question de savoir si les Membres d'un Cabinet peuvent accepter pareilles fonctions. Il estime que la réponse doit être négative.

Le PRESIDENT croit, pour sa part, que toutes fonctions relevant de la direction politique des Etats doivent être incompatibles avec la fonction de juge.

M. LODER donne lecture du dernier alinéa de l'article 13 du projet des Cinq Puissances, de février dernier: „les fonctions de juge sont incompatibles avec toute autre fonction publique, ainsi qu'avec toute fonction privée qui comporte un intérêt personnel ou qui poursuit un but politique; en cas de doute, la Cour décide". Il croit que c'est là la meilleure solution. Pour les raisons exposées par Lord Phillimore, il peut cependant se rallier à l'idée de faire une exception pour les fonctions judiciaires.

M. RICCI-BUSATTI craint qu'une disposition de ce genre n'ait pour résultat de réserver les fonctions de juge à ceux dont leur propre pays ne saura que faire.

Mr. ROOT désire attirer l'attention sur l'article 7 du projet de 1907; il en donne lecture.

On fait cependant remarquer que, dans l'alinéa lu par Mr. Root, il ne s'agit pas de l'incompatibilité entendue dans le même sens que celui qu'on est en train de discuter; ce qu'on discute actuellement, c'est l'incompatibilité entre des fonctions simultanées, tandis que l'alinéa traite de l'interdiction radicale d'exercer certains offices.

LORD PHILLIMORE reprend l'idée de Mr. Root: le fait d'avoir admis l'incompatibilité, telle qu'elle est entendue dans l'article cité, exclut l'existence de tout autre genre d'incompatibilité.

M. ADATCI croit que les fonctions de l'enseignement ne doivent pas être incompatibles avec les fonctions de juge. On doit assurer la collaboration à la Cour des savants qui s'occupent du droit international.

Le PRESIDENT résume les débats et constate qu'on est d'accord pour admettre que la fonction de juge à la Cour n'est pas incompatible avec celles de professeur ou de magistrat. En ce qui concerne les fonctions qui tiennent à la politique, la situation ne paraît pas éclaircie. Il s'agit d'abord de savoir si un siège au Parlement doit être considéré comme un office proprement politique. Le Président appelle l'attention du Comité sur la différence entre la Chambre des Lords, dont on demande que les membres puis-

LORD PHILLIMORE asked whether Cabinet members could accept such a position. He thought that the answer should be "No.".

The PRESIDENT thought that all duties relating to the political direction of states should be incompatible with the duties of a judge.

M. LODER read the last paragraph of Article 13 of the Five-Power-Plan of February last. The performance of judicial duties shall be incompatible with any other public duties, and also with any private duties of a nature entailing personal interests or a political object; in doubtful cases the Court shall decide. He thought that this was the best solution. He was prepared, however, for the reasons given by Lord Phillimore, to accept the idea of making an exception in the case of judicial duties.

M. RICCI-BUSATTI feared that a provision of this sort would result in limiting the choice for the duties of judge to those men for whom their countries had no use.

Mr. ROOT wished to call attention to article 7 of the project of 1907, which he read.

It was pointed out, however, that in the paragraph read by Mr. Root incompatibility was not used in the same sense as in the discussion now in progress: the present meaning concerned an incompatibility between simultaneous duties, while the paragraph dealt with the complete prohibition to occupy certain positions.

LORD PHILLIMORE returned to Mr. Root's idea; the fact of having admitted the incompatibility as it is understood in the article mentioned excludes the existence of all other kinds of incompatibility.

M. ADATCI thought that educational duties should not be incompatible with duties as judge. The co-operation on the Court of authorities on international law should be assured.

The PRESIDENT summed up the discussion and stated that the Committee was agreed that the duty of judge on the Court was not incompatible with the duties of a professor or magistrate. Concerning political duties the situation did not appear to be clear. It must first be decided whether a seat in Parliament must be considered exactly as a political position. The President called the Committee's attention to the difference between the House of Lords, whose Members it is asked should be allowed to sit on the Court,

sent siéger à la Cour, et certaines autres Chambres Hautes. Mais il est d'avis que la différence n'est pas assez profonde pour que l'on fasse une distinction radicale à cet égard. Il faudrait donc en venir à admettre les membres de tous les Sénats. Mais alors se pose dans toute son étendue la question relative aux membres des Parlements. Ce qu'il faut exclure en tout cas, ce sont les personnes revêtues de fonctions gouvernementales proprement dites, et celles qui se trouvent sous la dépendance de leurs chefs.

LORD PHILLIMORE croit qu'il serait désirable de ne point stipuler d'incompatibilité légale. On pourrait se borner à donner aux gouvernements un conseil et leur laisser toute liberté pour l'interprêter.

M. ALTAMIRA croit que quiconque exerce une fonction exécutive doit être exclu.

LORD PHILLIMORE répète qu'il ne croit pas qu'il doive y avoir de règles rigides d'incompatibilité. Il ne faut pas que l'opinion publique d'un pays qui a été partie dans un procès soumis à la Cour, puisse dire que telle sentence a été rendue parce que telle ou telle personne faisait partie de la Cour, et que le Gouvernement puisse soulever des objections contre le jugement en s'appuyant sur les règles d'incompatibilité. Il croit par conséquent qu'il est préférable de se borner à un simple conseil.

M. DE LAPRADELLE est convaincu de la nécessité d'avoir des règles fixes, bien que largement conçues.

M. RICCI-BUSATTI remarque que si l'on admet le droit de récusation on peut se montrer bien plus large sur la question des incompatibilités; il craint que toute disposition à cet égard ne prête à des difficultés et à des recours éventuels contre la validité des jugements.

M. LODER se rallie à l'opinion de M. de Lapradelle.

M. DE LAPRADELLE ajoute qu'on devrait stipuler qu'un juge ayant accepté une fonction incompatible avec la fonction de juge sera considéré comme démissionnaire.

M. ADATCI se rallie à M. Loder et, d'une façon générale, aux dispositions qui se retrouvent dans le projet des Cinq Puissances. Il est convaincu de la nécessité d'avoir des règles d'incompatibilité fixes et précises.

Suit un échange de vues entre M. HAGERUP et M. LODER d'une part et LORD PHILLI-

and certain other upper Houses. But he thought that the difference was not sufficiently great to draw a complete distinction in this respect. Consequently, they should come to admit the members of all Senates. But then there arose the parliamentary question in its full extent. Those who in any case must be excluded are the persons vested with governmental duties in its strict meaning, and those directly responsible to their superiors.

LORD PHILLIMORE thought that it would be desirable not to stipulate a legal incompatibility. They might limit themselves to submitting a recommendation to the Governments, and leave to them full liberty in the interpretation.

M. ALTAMIRA thought that anyone holding an executive position should be excluded.

LORD PHILLIMORE repeated that he did not think that there should be any rigid rules on incompatibility. No chance must be given to public opinion in any country, which had been concerned in a case submitted to the Court, to say that such a sentence was pronounced because such or such a person was included on the Court, nor must the Government be able to raise objections to the judgment on grounds of incompatibility. He thought, therefore, that it was preferable to limit oneself to a simple recommendation.

M. DE LAPRADELLE was convinced of the necessity of having fixed but broad rules.

M. RICCI-BUSATTI remarked that if the right of challenge were admitted they could afford to be less particular on the question of incompatibility; he feared that all provisions in this connection might lead to difficulties and possible recourse against the validity of the judgment.

M. LODER agreed with M. de Lapradelle.

M. DE LAPRADELLE added that it should be stipulated that if a judge accepted a duty incompatible with his duties as a judge he shall be considered as having resigned.

M. ADATCI agreed with M. Loder, and, generally speaking, with the dispositions found in the project of the Five-Powers. He was convinced of the necessity of having definite fixed rules concerning incompatibility.

An exchange of views followed between M. HAGERUP and M. LODER on one hand, and

MORE de l'autre, sur la position des *Law Lords* en Angleterre.

Le PRESIDENT fait observer que la question de la durée des mandats n'a pas encore été traitée à fond. Il suggère l'idée que, au cas où l'on conférerait à l'Assemblée de la Société des Nations le droit d'élire les juges, on pourrait faire coincider la durée des mandats avec la périodicité des réunions de cette Assemblée: si, par exemple, l'Assemblée est convoquée tous les 5 ans, la durée du mandat peut être de 5 ou 10 ans.

M. DE LAPRADELLE est surpris que le Président, qui est partisan de l'idée de donner toute autorité possible à l'Assemblée, semble considérer qu'elle ne se réunira que tous les 5 ans.

Plusieurs autres membres ne partagent pas l'opinion du Président au sujet de l'intervalle entre les réunions de l'Assemblée.

Le PRESIDENT fait remarquer qu'il n'a signalé qu'une hypothèse.

On exprime l'avis que l'Assemblée aura des réunions annuelles.

LORD PHILLIMORE fait valoir que si l'on fait de l'Assemblée le collège électoral, elle doit se réunir dès qu'un siège devient vacant: il n'est par conséquent pas nécessaire d'établir une coïncidence entre la durée des mandats et la périodicité des réunions de l'Assemblée.

Le PRESIDENT prie les membres de présenter des propositions formelles.

M. LODER propose une durée de 10 ans.

M. DE LAPRADELLE soulève la question de savoir si un juge qui a été nommé pour remplir un siège devenu vacant, doit rester en fonction pour une durée égale à la durée ordinaire des mandats ou seulement pendant la période qui reste du mandat de son prédécesseur. M. de Lapradelle est disposé à adopter la première solution.

Le PRESIDENT dit qu'il préfère l'autre solution, qui est la solution traditionelle. Le système préconisé par M. de Lapradelle aurait pour effet l'enchevêtrement des mandats.

M. DE LAPRADELLE et LORD PHILLIMORE voient dans cet enchevêtrement l'avantage principal du système, à cause de la continuité qui en résultera.

Le PRESIDENT préfère une période de 6 ans avec le droit pour les membres sortants d'achever une affaire en cours. Il ne faut pas oublier qu'on

LORD PHILLIMORE on the other, concerning the position of the Law Lords in England.

The PRESIDENT pointed out that the question of the term of office had not been thoroughly gone into. He suggested that if they gave the right of electing the judges to the Assembly of the League of Nations, they might make the term of office coincide with the periodical meetings of this Assembly; if, for example, the Assembly met every 5 years, the term of mandate could be 5 or 10 years.

M. DE LAPRADELLE was surprised that the President, who favoured the idea of giving all possible authority to the Assembly, seemed to think that it will meet only every five years.

Several other members did not share the opinion of the President on the subject of the interval between the meetings of the Assembly.

The PRESIDENT stated that he had mentioned only a hypothetical case.

The opinion was put forward that the Assembly will meet annually.

LORD PHILLIMORE pointed out that, if the Assembly were made the electoral body, it should meet whenever a seat became vacant; it is not necessary therefore to arrange to have the term of mandate and the periodical meetings of the Assembly coincide.

The PRESIDENT asked the members of the Committee to put forward formal proposals.

M. LODER proposed 10 years.

M. DE LAPRADELLE raised the question whether a judge who had been named to fill a vacancy should remain in office for a term equal to the ordinary term of office or only for the remaining term of his predecessor. M. de Lapradelle was disposed to accept the former solution.

The PRESIDENT said that he preferred the latter, which is the traditional method. The system favored by M. de Lapradelle would have the effect of entangling the mandates.

M. DE LAPRADELLE and LORD PHILLIMORE saw in this entanglement the principal advantage of the system because of the continuity which will result from it.

The PRESIDENT preferred a six year period with the right for a retiring member to complete a pending case. It must not be forgotten that

se trouve encore dans une période d'essai. Il convient de ne pas donner de mandats trop longs, du moins au commencement. Il y aurait des juges suppléants pour remplir les sièges devenus vacants.

Sur une question de M. LODER, le PRESIDENT dit qu'il est opposé à l'idée de mandats à vie. M. RICCI-BUSATTI et M. DE LAPRADELLE se rangent à l'avis du Président.

M. HAGERUP constate que le mandat à vie n'a été préconisé par aucun des membres. M. Hagerup, lui-même, qui l'a adopté dans le projet auquel il a collaboré, consent à l'abandonner; mais il désire expliquer les raisons qui militent en faveur d'une durée considérable des mandats. On veut rendre les juges inamovibles pour assurer leur indépendance. C'est un principe universellement admis dans le droit national, et il n'y a pas d'objections contre son application dans la vie internationale. Si l'on fixe la durée du mandat à 10 ans, cela revient pratiquement à un mandat à vie, à cause de l'âge probable des juges à l'époque de leur nomination. Il faut alors penser à une limite d'âge, p. e. 70 ans.

M. Hagerup est d'avis que le Président ne tient pas assez compte de l'importance de l'inamovibilité des juges, ni de la continuité des travaux de la Cour que favorisera une durée plus considérable des mandats; il est disposé à accepter une durée de 9 à 10 ans.

Il y a une autre question qu'il faut considérer: c'est la question des pensions, qui est intimement liée à celle de la durée des mandats. On a proposé de donner aux juges la totalité du traitement à titre de pension. Ce système n'est cependant possible que si l'on adopte les mandats à vie.

Il faut encore considérer la question du traitement à donner aux juges. Cette question se rattache à celle des incompatibilités. Si un juge peut conserver ses fonctions nationales, le traitement peut être moins élevé que dans le cas contraire. On doit tenir compte de ce qu'un juge, qui doit quitter ses occupations dans son propre pays, doit avoir un traitement assez considérable, et qu'une indemnité, en cas de destitution, doit lui être garantie. Il ne faut pas oublier que la question peut être décisive pour des personnes dont les services sont désirables.

M. DE LAPRADELLE fait valoir que l'on doit fixer le traitement des juges non pas en raison de l'importance des services qu'ils rendent, mais en raison de l'importance des occupations qu'ils ont dû abandonner. Il donne comme

this is still a trial period. It is advantageous not to have too long terms, at least not at the outset. There would be deputy judges to fill vacant seats.

In answer to a question of M. LODER, the PRESIDENT said that he was opposed to the idea of holding office for life. M. RICCI-BUSATTI and M. DE LAPRADELLE agreed with the President.

M. HAGERUP said that a life term had not been advocated by any member. M. Hagerup himself, who had adopted it in the project which he had helped to draw up, was prepared to abandon it. But he wished to explain the considerations which weigh in favor of a fairly long term. It is wished to make the judges irremovable in order to ensure their independence. This is a principle universally recognised in national law; there is no objection to its application in international life. If the term of office is fixed at 10 years, in practice that amounts to office for life because of the probable age of the judges at the time of appointment. It is necessary then to consider an age limit — for example 70 years.

M. Hagerup was of opinion that the President had not given due weight to the importance of the irremovability of judges, nor of the continuity of the work of the Court, which would be strengthened by a longer term. M. Hagerup was prepared to accept a 9 or 10 year term.

There is another question to be considered: the question of pensions, which is intimately connected with that of the term of office. It had been proposed to give the judges the whole of their salary as a pension. This system is not possible unless office for life is adopted.

The question of judge's salary must also be considered. This question is connected with that of incompatibility. If a judge were allowed to continue national duties, the salary could be smaller than in the contrary case. It should be kept in mind that a judge who has to leave his occupation in his own country must receive a fairly large salary and that he must have the assurance of receiving an indemnity in case of retirement. It must not be forgotten that this question may be a deciding factor in the case of persons whose services are desirable.

M. DE LAPRADELLE pointed out that the salary of judges ought to be fixed not in relation to the importance of the services rendered, but in relation to the importance of the occupation which the judges have given up. He gave as an

exemple les juges anglais. Ceux-ci sont recrutés parmi les meilleurs membres du barreau. Ils reçoivent des traitements très élevés parce qu'ils doivent abandonner une occupation très lucrative.

M. ADATCI exprime l'avis qu'en vue d'assurer l'indépendance des juges et la continuité du travail, il faut fixer une durée assez longue pour les mandats, tout en ayant soin de spécifier au moment de leur nomination que les juges ne continueront pas à siéger si leurs facultés viennent à baisser. Au sujet du traitement, il pense qu'il faut fournir aux juges les moyens de mener une vie très honorable pendant la durée de leurs fonctions et, leurs fonctions une fois terminées, une vie calme et digne du prestige que doivent conserver les juges.

M. RICCI-BUSATTI suggère l'idée suivante, qui se base sur sa conception de l'organisation et de la permanence de la Cour: le Président et les Vice-Présidents, résidant au siège de la Cour, devraient être largement rémunérés. Les autres membres ne devraient recevoir qu'une somme annuelle très modérée, pour faire face à certaines obligations générales inhérentes à leur charge, mais une allocation journalière assez élevée pendant les périodes ou ils sont en fonction.

M. DE LAPRADELLE émet l'idée de fixer le traitement à une somme égale à deux fois les appointements du juge le mieux rémunéré dans n'importe quel pays.

Le PRESIDENT invite les membres à présenter des propositions formelles au sujet des questions qu'on vient de discuter.

Mr. ROOT soumet aux réflexions du Comité l'idée de laisser à l'Assemblée la tâche de fixer les traitements des juges. Les conditions changent si vite. La valeur en dollars d'une somme en francs n'est maintenant que le sixième de ce qu'elle était il y a sept ans, et en même temps la valeur de l'argent a baissé de moitié.

Si le Comité fixe dès maintenant les traitements, il peut arriver que l'Assemblée se voie dans l'impossibilité de trouver des personnes disposées à accepter le poste de juge.

M. LODER attire l'attention sur les difficultés qui pourraient surgir du fait que l'Assemblée serait appelée à régler, de temps en temps, les traitements des juges: deux juges siégeant en même temps pourraient recevoir des traitements différents, ce qui est inadmissible.

Le PRESIDENT croit que l'idée de Mr. Root est la suivante: le Comité doit poser une règle

example the English judges. They are drawn from among the best members of the bar. They receive very large salaries, because they have to give up a very lucrative profession.

M. ADATCI expressed the opinion that in order to ensure the independence of judges and continuity of work, a fairly long term of office must be fixed, at the same time taking care to specify at the time of their appointment that judges shall not continue to sit if their faculties should deteriorate. With regard to the salaries, he thought that the judges should be afforded the means of living very comfortably during their term of office, and once their duties ended they should be able to live quietly and in keeping with the prestige which the judges should enjoy.

M. RICCI-BUSATTI suggested the following idea based on his conception of the organisation and permanence of the Court: The President and the Vice-President residing at the seat of the Court should receive large salaries. The other members need only receive a very moderate annual salary to meet certain obligations inherent in their duties, but a fairly large daily allowance during the times when they are at work.

M. DE LAPRADELLE put forward the idea of fixing the salary at an amount equal to twice that received by the best paid judge in any country.

The PRESIDENT asked the members to put forward formal proposals relating to the question which had just been discussed.

Mr. ROOT suggested to the Committee that the task of fixing the salaries of the judges should be left to the Assembly. Conditions changed so quickly. The value in dollars of a sum in francs is now only one sixth part of what it had been seven years ago, and at the same time the value of money had decreased by one half. If the Committee were to fix salaries now, the Assembly might find it impossible to find persons willing to accept positions as judges.

M. LODER drew attention to the difficulties which might arise from the fact that the Assembly would be called upon from time to time to adjust the salaries of judges. Two judges sitting at the same time might receive different salaries. This would not be admissible.

The PRESIDENT thought that Mr. Root's idea was the following: The Committee should

générale, mais l'Assemblée et le Conseil de la Société des Nations doivent fixer les sommes selon l'esprit et dans le cadre de cette règle.

lay down a general rule, but the Assembly and the Council of the League of Nations should fix the amounts according to the spirit and within the compass of the rule.

LORD PHILLIMORE partage l'avis de Mr. Root. Il croit qu'il faut donner à l'Assemblée la faculté de régler à nouveau le montant des traitements. Seulement, l'Assemblée doit toujours augmenter et non pas diminuer les sommes.

Quant à la durée du mandat, Lord Phillimore croit, comme M. Loder, que la période de dix ans sera acceptable. Il pense qu'il ne faut pas fixer de limite d'âge: il y a tant d'exemples de juges ayant conservé la plénitude de leurs facultés intellectuelles jusqu'à 80 ans.

Lord Phillimore est donc d'avis que la limite d'âge peut dépasser 70 ans; on pourra l'étendre jusqu'à 75 ans ou davantage: il faut laisser la décision dans les cas particuliers à ceux qui ont à faire l'élection des juges.

LORD PHILLIMORE agreed with Mr. Root; he thought that the power of readjusting the amount of the salaries should be left to the Assembly. But the Assembly ought always to increase and not to diminish the amount.

As to the term of office, Lord Phillimore thought, like M. Loder, that the period of ten years was suitable. He did not think it was necessary to fix an age limit. There were so many examples of judges having kept the full use of their intellectual powers until the age of 80.

Lord Phillimore was therefore of opinion that an age limit over 70 years could be fixed. It might be extended to 75 years or more. The decision in particular cases should be left to those who have to elect the judge.

M. ALTAMIRA se range à l'avis de Lord Phillimore. Il croit qu'une durée de dix ans permettra aux juges de siéger aussi longtemps qu'ils conservent la plénitude de leurs facultés.

M. Altamira suggère l'idée de soumettre à l'Assemblée et au Conseil, à titre de proposition, des chiffres relatifs aux traitements des juges.

M. ALTAMIRA agreed with Lord Phillimore. He thought that a term of ten years would allow the judges to sit as long as they preserved the full use of their Powers.

M. Altamira suggested that an amount for the salaries of judges should be submitted to the Assembly and Council as a proposal.

Après un échange de vues avec les membres, le PRESIDENT propose d'employer le reste de la séance à la discussion de la division de la Cour en chambres: à la séance prochaine on pourrait ouvrir la discussion sur la question de la compétence de la Cour, et plus particulièrement sur la question de savoir qui pourra s'adresser à la Cour.

After exchange of opinion with the members, the President proposed that the rest of the meeting should be devoted to the discussion of the question of dividing the Court into sections. At the next meeting the discussion on the competence of the Court, in particular who could address the Court, would be opened.

M. RICCI-BUSATTI se demande si ce point rentre dans la compétence du Comité.

M. RICCI-BUSATTI asked if this point came within the powers of the Committee.

Le PRESIDENT constate qu'on est d'accord pour reconnaître qu'à raison des rapports qui existent entre la question de la compétence de la Cour et celle de son organisation, le Comité a compétence pour examiner ces deux points.

The PRESIDENT stated that they were agreed that because of the connection which exists between the competence and organisation of the Court, the Committee was competent to examine these two points.

M. DE LAPRADELLE soulève la question de savoir si la discussion sur la présence à la Cour des membres nationaux doit être considérée comme close.

M. DE LAPRADELLE raised the question as to whether the discussion concerning the presence of national members at the Court was to be considered as closed.

Le PRESIDENT prie M. de Lapradelle de bien vouloir exposer ses vues sur cette question.

The PRESIDENT asked M. de Lapradelle to put forward his views on this question.

M. DE LAPRADELLE pose la question de la façon suivante: s'il y a parmi les juges un juge de la nationalité d'une des parties en litige,

M. DE LAPRADELLE did so as follows: If a judge of the nationality of one of the parties in any case were present, should he give up his

doit il céder sa place, ou l'autre partie doit-elle avoir le droit d'envoyer un assesseur pour assister aux délibérations de la Cour? M. de Lapradelle constate la nécessité de rétablir l'égalité entre les deux parties. Il ne croit pas que cette égalité puisse être rétablie par l'envoi des assesseurs, parce qu'un assesseur ne pourra jamais avoir l'autorité d'un juge. L'inégalité n'en sera qu'atténuée. M. de Lapradelle croit que la solution doit être cherchée dans la direction suivante: il faut que le juge de la nationalité d'une des parties cède sa place et que les deux parties envoient des assesseurs avec voix délibérative. Ainsi l'égalité entre elles sera parfaite.

M. ADATCI préfère la disposition contenue dans le second article du projet qu'il a soumis au Comité. Cet article dit que, au cas où dans une affaire dont la Cour est saisie, l'une des parties n'a pas un de ses ressortissants siégeant parmi les juges, cette partie aura le droit de désigner un de ses ressortissants pour siéger dans cette affaire determinée.

M. Adatci croit qu'il ne faut pas attacher trop d'importance à l'objection qui se base sur l'inégalité qu'il y aurait entre un juge ordinaire et un assesseur.

Ce qui est grave, c'est d'exclure de la Cour un juge expérimenté pour le remplacer par un assesseur. Il croit qu'il est bien suffisant, pour rétablir l'égalité, de permettre à la partie non représentée d'envoyer un assesseur.

M. HAGERUP donne lecture de la disposition du projet scandinave relative au point qu'on est en train de discuter. Il résume la proposition de M. de Lapradelle et demande si, dans le cas où ni l'une ni l'autre des parties ne seraient représentées à la Cour, elles auraient toutes les deux le droit d'y envoyer des assesseurs.

M. DE LAPRADELLE n'y voit pas d'objection, et M. ADATCI dit que cette idée est pleinement compatible avec son projet.

M. HAGERUP termine en attirant l'attention sur les délibérations qui ont eu lieu en 1907 sur la constitution de la Cour internationale des prises; il donne lecture de l'article 16 de la Convention pour l'établissement de cette Cour, et dit qu'il voit une certaine analogie entre les dispositions de cet article et la proposition de M. de Lapradelle.

M. Hagerup, sans prétendre que la solution proposée par MM. de Lapradelle et

place or should the other party have the right to send an assessor to take part in the deliberations of the Court? M. de Lapradelle insisted that it was necessary to establish equality between the two parties. He did not think that such equality would be established by the sending of assessors, because an assessor could never have the authority of a judge. This method could only diminish the inequality. M. de Lapradelle thought that a solution should be sought in the following way: the judge of the same nationality as one of the parties should give up his place, and both parties send assessors with deliberative powers. In this way the equality between them would be complete.

M. ADATCI preferred the arrangements contained in the second Article of the project which he had submitted to the Committee. This Article said that if, in any case brought before the Court, a Member State concerned had no representative amongst the judges, the said State shall have the right to appoint a judge of its own nationality for the case in question.

M. Adatci thought that too much importance should not be attached to the objection based on the inequality which would exist between an ordinary judge and an assessor.

What is serious, is to exclude from the Court an experienced judge in order to replace him by an assessor. He thought that in order to establish equality it would be quite sufficient if the party not represented might send an assessor.

M. HAGERUP read the provision of the Scandinavian project relating to the point under discussion. He summed up the proposals of M. de Lapradelle and asked whether, if neither of the two parties was represented on the Court, they both would be allowed to send assessors.

M. DE LAPRADELLE saw no objection to this, and M. ADATCI said that the idea was quite compatible with his project.

M. HAGERUP ended by drawing attention to the discussion which took place in 1907 on the subject of the constitution of the International Prize Court; he read Article 16 of the Convention establishing this Court, and said that he saw a certain parallel between the provisions of this Article and M. de Lapradelle's proposition.

M. Hagerup would not contend that the solution proposed by M. de Lapradelle and M.

Adatci soit parfaite, puisqu'elle ne s'accorde pas très bien avec la notion de la permanence de la Cour, croit cependant que l'adoption de cette proposition serait le seul moyen d'arriver à un accord.

M. DE LAPRADELLE est disposé à amender sa propre proposition dans le sens suivant: on se bornerait à donner le droit d'envoyer des assesseurs, aux parties qui en exprimeraient le désir.

M. LODER remarque que la question qu'on est en train de considérer a été longuement discutée lors de la Conférence en février dernier. On ne réussit pas alors à s'accorder. Ceux qui ont considéré comme superflu le droit d'envoyer des assesseurs sont parties de cette idée que les juges à la Cour Permanente seront des hommes éminents qui sauront faire abstraction de leur nationalité.

M. DE LAPRADELLE partage cet avis; s'il a proposé une solution basée sur d'autres considérations, c'est qu'il n'est pas certain que les différents Etats seront disposés à accepter le point de vue de M. Loder.

M. LODER croit que si, pour la raison avancée par M. de Lapradelle, on accepte l'institution des assesseurs, il ne faut pas leur donner voix délibérative, mais seulement voix consultative.

LORD PHILLIMORE analyse la question et la solution proposée par M. de Lapradelle. Il croit qu'il ne faut pas accepter une solution rigide; il faut tenir compte de nombreuses circonstances. Si un Etat européen et un Etat de l'Extrême Orient sont en conflit, et si ce dernier seulement est représenté à la Cour, l'égalité entre les Etats ne serait pas rétablie du fait que le représentant de l'Etat Oriental céderait sa place. Dans ce cas, les parties en cause ne seraient pas représentées à la Cour, qui serait composée exclusivement de juges provenant de l'Europe ou de l'Amérique. Les Orientaux considéreraient ceci comme une inégalité.

Lord Phillimore se demande si, dans ces conditions, il suffirait de permettre aux deux parties d'envoyer des assesseurs avec voix consultative. Ne faudrait-il pas leur donner voix délibérative?

M. DE LAPRADELLE réplique qu'à la question posée par Lord Phillimore on peut faire deux réponses:

1. Les deux parties pourront toutes deux en-

Adatci was perfect, since it did not quite agree with the conception of the Court's permanence. He thought, however, that the adoption of this proposal would be the only way of coming to an understanding.

M. DE LAPRADELLE was inclined to amend his own proposal to the following effect: that the right of sending assessors should be extended only to parties desirous of so doing.

M. LODER pointed out that the question under consideration had been discussed at length in the Conference of last February. They did not succeed at that time in coming to an agreement. Those who considered superfluous the right of sending assessors held that the judges of the Permanent Court would be distinguished men who would be able to disregard their nationality.

M. DE LAPRADELLE shared this opinion, If he had proposed a solution based on other considerations, it was because he was not certain that the various States would be disposed to accept M. Loder's point of view.

M. LODER thought that if, for the reasons presented by M. de Lapradelle, the institution of assessors were accepted, they should not be given deliberative but only advisory powers.

LORD PHILLIMORE analysed the question and the solution proposed by M. de Lapradelle. He thought that a hard and fast solution was not necessary; many considerations must be taken into account. If a European and a Far-Eastern State were concerned in a dispute, and if the latter only were represented on the Court, the equality between the States would not be readjusted by the fact that the representative of the Eastern State gave up his seat. In this case the parties concerned would not be represented on the Court, which would be composed exclusively of judges coming from Europe or America. The Orientals would consider this as an inequality.

Lord Phillimore wondered whether under these conditions it would be enough to allow the two parties to send assessors with advisory powers. Would they not have to be given the power of voting?

M. DE LAPRADELLE answered that two replies could be given to Lord Phillimore's question:

1. Both parties might send assessors; in this

voyer des assesseurs; ainsi le point de vue oriental serait sans doute suffisamment représenté.

2. On peut songer à introduire dans la Cour une représentation des idées juridiques différentes, peut-être même des idées politiques, des tendances de la civilisation, etc. Ceci n'est pas la même chose que de faire représenter les divers systèmes juridiques. Le droit international a été fortement nationalisé. M. de Lapradelle mentionne le droit des prises en Angleterre et la tendance, relevée par un savant chilien, M. Alvarez, à distinguer entre un droit international américain et un droit international européen. Cependant le droit international doit être un et le rester. Il serait imprudent et même contradictoire d'introduire dans la Cour des systèmes juridiques nationaux. Mais il y a des idées juridiques; c'est cette pensée qu'il faut retenir au lieu de celle des différents systèmes juridiques. Tous les grands types de civilisation doivent trouver leur représentation à la Cour. Il faut adopter l'idée d'une représentation en quelque sorte géographique. Mais seules les contrées qui ont formé des noyaux civilisateurs peuvent être représentées.

Pour assurer cette représentation, il faut avoir un nombre assez élevé de juges. M. de Lapradelle mentionne le chiffre de 15. On doit stipuler que la Cour contiendra tant de juges asiatiques, tant de juges américains, tant de juges européens. Si cette idée est adoptée aucun des grands centres de civilisation ne manquera de représentation.

Il y a donc deux réponses à faire à la question posée par Lord Phillimore; la première est la plus simple: elle représente un moyen de s'entendre; la seconde réponse mène plus loin.

Le PRÉSIDENT fait remarquer que M. de Lapradelle n'a pas suffisamment tenu compte des difficultés qui concernent la répartition des sièges en divisant ceux-ci en groupes européen, américain et asiatique.

M. LODER dit qu'il est impossible de laisser à une partie la faculté de désigner un juge.

Le PRESIDENT demande à M. de Lapradelle comment, dans son plan, les juges suppléants seront utilisés.

M. DE LAPRADELLE répond qu'ils entreront pour occuper un siège vacant jusqu'à l'élection prochaine, ou remplacer un juge empêché jusqu'à la cessation de l'empêchement; puis, si les deux parties ont, l'une un juge titulaire, l'autre un juge

way the Eastern point of view would doubtless be sufficiently represented.

2. The introduction into the Court of a representation of the various juridical ideas might be considered, perhaps even of political ideas, tendencies of civilisation, etc. This would not be the same as the representation of the various legal systems. International law has been decidedly nationalised. M. de Lapradelle mentioned the British Naval Prize Law, and the tendency pointed out by a Chilean authority, M. Alvarez, to distinguish between an American international law and a European international law. But international law ought to be one and remain so. It would be unwise and even contradictory to introduce national systems of law into the Court. But legal ideas exist, and it is this conception which must be retained rather than that of the different legal systems. All the main types of civilisation ought to be represented on the Court; the idea of some sort of a geographical representation must be adopted. However, only the countries which have been the centres of civilisation can be represented.

To assure this representation it is necessary to have a fairly large number of judges. M. de Lapradelle mentioned the number 15. It should be laid down that the Court should contain so many Asiatic judges, so many American judges, so many European judges. If this idea is adopted, none of the great centres of civilisation would be unrepresented.

There are therefore two answers to the questions put forward by Lord Phillimore. The first is the most simple: it offered a basis of agreement; the second goes farther.

The PRESIDENT observed that M. de Lapradelle had not met satisfactorily the difficulties involved in the allotment of seats by dividing them among the European, American, and Asiatic groups.

M. LODER said that it was not possible to allow a contesting party to have the power of appointing a judge.

The PRESIDENT asked M. de Lapradelle what use would be made of the deputy judges in his scheme.

M. DE LAPRADELLE answered that they will first be used to fill a vacant seat until the next election, or to replace a disabled judge until the end of the disability; secondly, if one of the parties has a judge and the other a deputy

suppléant, ou les deux des juges suppléants, celui-ci ou ceux-ci sont appelés de droit au siège, en qualité de juges et non pas d'assesseurs.

Le PRESIDENT propose de mettre à l'ordre du jour de la séance suivante la question de la compétence de la Cour. On pourrait discuter tout d'abord la question de savoir qui pourra saisir la Cour.

M. DE LAPRADELLE préférerait voir ouvrir la discussion sur la question de savoir si une partie pourra citer une autre partie devant la Cour.

LORD PHILLIMORE se range à l'opinion de M. de Lapradelle.

Le PRESIDENT fait observer que l'ordre naturel serait d'examiner d'abord si les Etats auront seuls le droit de s'adresser à la Cour ou s'il faut aller plus loin. On sait que les Etats peuvent prendre fait et cause pour leurs nationaux; mais des particuliers pourront-ils être partie dans un procès devant la Cour?

Ensuite on sera amené à discuter la question de savoir si un Etat peut contraindre un autre Etat à venir devant la Cour.

M. ALTAMIRA déclare qu'il aurait encore quelques mots à dire sur la question des systèmes juridiques.

La séance est levée à 12.30 de l'après-midi.

Le Président:
(signé) Brn. DESCAMPS.

Le Secrétaire-Général:
(signé) D. ANZILOTTI.

judge, or both have deputy judges, the deputy judges shall be called to sit as judges in full right and not as assessors.

The PRESIDENT proposed that the question of competence of the Court should be put on the Agenda for the following meeting. First of all they could discuss the question: who would be entitled to appeal to the Court.

M. DE LAPRADELLE preferred that the discussion should commence by considering whether one party could summon another party before the Court.

LORD PHILLIMORE agreed with M. de Lapradelle.

The PRESIDENT observed that the normal order would be to discuss first of all whether States only should have the right to appeal to the Court, or whether it would be necessary to go farther. It is established that States can appear on behalf of their nationals, but can a private individual be party to a case brought before the Court?

This would lead to consider the question whether a State could compel another State to come before the Court.

M. ALTAMIRA announced that he had still something to say concerning the question of legal systems.

The meeting closed at 12.30 p.m.

The President:
(signed) Brn. DESCAMPS.

The Secretary-General:
(signed) D. ANZILOTTI.

9ième SÉANCE (non-publique), tenue au Palais de la Paix, à La Haye, le 25 juin 1920.

Présidence de M. le BARON DESCAMPS.

Sont présents: tous les membres du Comité (à l'exception de M. Bevilaqua); M. Fernandes; Mr. James Brown Scott; les secrétaires particuliers de M. le Baron Descamps et de M. Adatci; les membres du Secrétariat.

La séance est ouverte à $9^1/_2$ heures du matin.

Le PRESIDENT rappelle que la discussion de la séance précédente a porté sur l'organisation de la Cour. Il tient maintenant à signaler une question qui pourrait être tranchée sans discussion bien longue: celle du siège de la Cour. Il propose au Comité de recommander que La Haye soit choisie comme siège de la Cour Permanente de Justice Internationale. Le Président estime que ce n'est pas là seulement un acte de courtoisie envers le Gouvernement Néerlandais. Il s'appuie sur deux autres arguments: d'une part, La Haye est déjà le siège de la Cour Permanente d'Arbitrage, et d'autre part il y a, dans l'opinion du Président, intérêt à séparer les fonctions politiques de la Société des Nations de ses fonctions judiciaires, en assignant des sièges différents aux deux groupes d'institutions.

Si la proposition est adoptée, on doit naturellement réserver les cas où il pourra devenir nécessaire de convoquer la Cour hors de son siège normal.

M. ADATCI a beaucoup réfléchi sur la question du siège de la Cour. Il a pensé tout d'abord que la Cour devrait être établie au siège de la Société des Nations. Après avoir consulté nombre de ses amis et collègues au Japon, il adopte aujourd'hui l'opinion du Président, et ce faisant, il est certain d'être l'interprête de l'opinion publique chez les peuples asiatiques. Au Japon, quand on parle de La Haye, cela signifie: Paix et Justice. C'est une idée devenue légendaire chez le peuple. Il faut d'ailleurs séparer les délibérations judiciaires des délibérations politiques, afin que la Cour puisse examiner et juger dans le calme les affaires qui lui seront soumises.

9th MEETING (Private), held at the Peace Palace, the Hague, on June 25th, 1920.

BARON DESCAMPS in the chair.

Present: all members of the Committee (with the exception of M. Bevilaqua); M. Fernandes; Mr. James Brown Scott; the private secretaries of Baron Descamps and of M. Adatci; the members of the Secretariat.

The meeting opened at 9.30 a.m.

The PRESIDENT mentioned that the discussion at the previous meeting related to the organisation of the Court. He now wished to put forward a question which could be settled without long discussion: that of the seat of the Court. He proposed that the Committee should recommend that the Hague be chosen as the seat of the Permanent Court of International Justice. The President considered that this was not only an act of courtesy to the Government of the Netherlands. He based his proposal on two other arguments: first, the Hague is already the seat of the Permanent Court of Arbitration; and second, the President thought there was reason to separate the political functions of the League of Nations from its judicial functions by assigning different seats to the two groups of institutions.

If the proposal were adopted, exception of course should be made for cases in which it might be necessary to convene the Court away from its normal seat.

M. ADATCI had thought over thoroughly the question of the seat of the Court. He had thought first that the Court should be established at the seat of the League of Nations. After having consulted a number of his friends and colleagues in Japan, he now shared the President's opinion. If this idea is carried out, it is certain to be the interpretation of public opinion in the Asiatic nations. In Japan, when the Hague is mentioned, it means Peace and Justice. This has become a tradition among the people. Furthermore, it is necessary to separate the judicial from the political deliberations in order to permit the Court to examine and judge in tranquillity the cases submitted to it.

Mr. ROOT, LORD PHILLIMORE et les autre membres se rallient à la proposition du Président.

Le PRESIDENT constate que le Comité est unanime pour recommander le choix de La Haye comme siège de la Cour Permanente.

M. DE LAPRADELLE exprime le désir qu'on décide seulement sur la question de fond et que les motifs ne soient pas inclus dans la décision. Il pourrait, en effet, avoir des réserves à exprimer à leur sujet.

M. LODER fait la déclaration suivante: „Je n'ai pas besoin de vous dire que la proposition faite par notre Président et son adoption par vous tous, Messieurs, me remplissent de joie, et particulièrement à cause des raisons sur lesquelles le Président a bien voulu fonder la résolution. Je crois pouvoir dire, au nom de mon Gouvernement aussi bien qu'au nom de mon pays, que la résolution de ce Comité sera accueillie avec beaucoup de joie, et je crois pouvoir vous assurer que la Hollande, fidèle à ses traditions, fera tout ce qui est en son pouvoir pour accomplir la tâche qu'on lui impose. J'espère que le Conseil et l'Assemblée voudront s'associer également à la résolution prise ici, et j'exprime le vœu que la Cour dont nous préparons l'avènement, soit à l'avenir un bonheur pour le monde entier".

Le PRESIDENT constate l'unanimité de la décision, ainsi que le fait que le Gouvernement Néerlandais est disposé à adhérer au choix qu'on vient de faire.

Le Président passe à la question à l'ordre du jour: la compétence de la Cour. Il a formulé le programme de quelques questions sur la matière afin d'aider le Comité à arriver à un résultat. Il donne lecture du questionnaire (voir Annexe 1). Il propose qu'on procède à la discussion du premier point: „La Cour constituera-t-elle essentiellement une juridiction entre Etats, ou sa compétence s'étendra-t-elle à des litiges concernant des particuliers? Dans quelles conditions ce dernier cas pourrait-il éventuellement se produire?" Le Comité étant d'accord pour discuter cette question, le Président donne la parole à M. Adatci.

M. ADATCI dit que la Commission dite „des nouveaux Etats", qui siégeait à Paris, a étudié la question de la protection des minorités, et particulièrement la question de savoir si les minorités nationales peuvent recourir directement à

Mr. ROOT, LORD PHILLIMORE, and the other members agreed with the President's proposal.

The PRESIDENT stated that the Committee were unanimous in recommending the Hague as the seat of the Permanent Court.

M. DE LAPRADELLE expressed the wish that the decision should be taken only on the actual question at issue, and that the reasons should not be included with the deliberation. He might in fact have some reservations to make concerning the motives of the decision.

M. LODER made the following statement: "There is no need for me to tell you that the proposal made by our President and its adoption by all of you make me very happy, Gentlemen, especially in view of the reasons upon which the President was so good as to base the resolution. I think that I may say, in the name of my Government, as well as in the name of my country, that the resolution adopted by this Committee will be received with joy, and I think I can assure you that Holland, always faithful to its traditions, will do all in its power to accomplish the task given to it. I hope that the Council and Assembly will also adopt the decision taken here, and I give voice to the hope that the Court for whose coming we are preparing the way will be a source of happiness for the whole world."

The PRESIDENT put on record that the decision was unanimous and that the Netherlands Government was prepared to agree with the choice just made.

The President now proceeded to deal with the question on the agenda, namely: the competence of the Court. He had formulated a programme for some questions on the subject in order to aid the Committee to come to a conclusion. He read this questionnaire (see Annex 1). He now proposed that they should proceed to discuss the first point: "Shall the Court constitute essentially a jurisdiction between States, or shall its competence extend to litigation concerning individuals. Under what conditions can the latter eventuality occur?" The Committee having agreed to discuss this question, the President called upon M. Adatci.

M. ADATCI said that the so called commission of new States, which was sitting at Paris, had studied the question of the protection of minorities and in particular the question as to whether national minorities might directly appeal to the

la Cour de Justice. On a fini par donner aux seuls Etats le droit de recours. La décision est importante. Si, en effet, on a laissé aux Etats le devoir de défendre le droit des minorités qu'ils renferment, c'est que l'unique moyen de limiter le recours à la Cour est de donner aux Etats seuls le droit d'y faire appel. D'ailleurs, si les Etats s'intéressent à la cause de leurs ressortissants, ils la prendront en mains.

M. ALTAMIRA ne voudrait faire ses observations qu'après avoir entendu celles de ses collègues. Il croit cependant pouvoir, dès maintenant, se rallier au point de vue adopté dans l'art. 20 du projet suédois, d'après lequel la Cour ne connaît que des litiges entre Etats, mais un Etat peut faire valoir les droits d'un de ses ressortissants contre un autre Etat.

Le PRESIDENT constate l'accord qui existe entre les opinions de M. Adatci et M. Altamira, et ses propres idées.

M. LODER rappelle que le projet des Cinq Puissances contient une disposition analogue.

M. HAGERUP se rallie à M. Adatci. Il rappelle que la formule suédoise, qui est aussi celle du projet commun des premières commissions des pays du Nord, se retrouve dans l'article 30 du projet commun des trois pays scandinaves.

Il tient toutefois à remarquer qu'il y a un précédent international qui va dans une autre direction. Il veut dire la convention pour l'établissement d'une Cour Internationale des Prises, dont l'article 4, 2e alinéa, est plus large que la formule suédoise.

M. DE LAPRADELLE, invité à prendre la parole, se déclare moins éclairé sur les points en question que ses collègues.

La Cour dont on envisage la création est conçue essentiellement comme un tribunal pour trancher des conflits entre Etats. On peut cependant se demander si le droit d'avoir recours à la Cour ne doit pas, dans une certaine mesure, être étendu aux particuliers; à savoir dans les cas de déni de justice. Il arrive quelquefois qu'un particulier, qui a contracté avec un Etat, se trouve dans l'impossibilité de l'assigner en justice en raison d'une sorte de privilège de souveraineté admis par la législation et la jurisprudence de certains pays, comme la France. M. de Lapradelle pose la question de savoir si, dans des circonstances semblables, il ne serait pas utile de donner

Court of Justice. It was decided that States only would have this right of appeal. The decision was important. The reason for leaving to States the duties of protecting the rights of minorities included in them was that the only means of limiting the right of recourse to the Court was to give to States only the right of appearing before the Court. Besides, if the States took an interest in the lawsuits of their subjects, they would take up their cases.

M. ALTAMIRA preferred not to express his views until he had heard those of his colleagues. However, he thought that he could say from now on that he took the same standpoint as Article 20 of the Swedish project in which it was laid down that the Court could only take cognisance of cases between States, but that a State might present the claims of one of its subjects against another State.

The PRESIDENT stated that the opinion of M. Adatci and M. Altamira coincided with his own.

M. LODER recalled that the project of the Five Powers contained a similar disposition.

M. HAGERUP agreed with M. Adatci. He mentioned that the Swedish wording, which is the same as that of the joint plan of the first commissions of the Northern Countries, also appeared in Article 30 of the joint project of the three Scandinavian Countries.

However, he wished to point out that there was an international precedent which pointed in a different direction. He referred to the Convention for the establishment of the International Prize Court, in which Paragraph 2 of Article 4 had a wider bearing than the Swedish project.

M. DE LAPRADELLE, having been asked to speak, said that he was less clear on the points under consideration than his colleagues.

The Court of which the creation was under consideration was essentially a tribunal to deal with disputes between States. However, it might be considered whether the right to have recourse to the Court should not be given to some extent to private individuals, that is to say, in cases of denial of justice. It sometimes happens that a private individual who has made a contract with a State, finds it impossible to obtain justice against it on account of a species of privileged right of sovereignty recognised by the legislation and jurisprudence of some countries, such as France. M. de Lapradelle raised the question whether, under these circumstances,

à la Cour de Justice Internationale une compétence accessoire: la Cour agirait alors sur l'initiative d'un particulier, pourvu que le cas n'ait pas de caractère politique.

M. LODER dit que la législation hollandaise a adopté la même attitude que la législation française sur le point auquel vient de faire allusion M. de Lapradelle.

Ce point a été très discuté en février dernier, lors de la Conférence des Neutres. La solution restreinte qu'on avait alors adoptée n'était pas d'accord avec les vues de M. Loder, qui ne voit pas de raison pour limiter la compétence de la Cour, en exigeant que les particuliers soient couverts par leur gouvernement pour pouvoir avoir accès à la Cour. Il relève la disposition de l'article 14 du Pacte de la Société des Nations, aux termes duquel la Cour est appelée à connaître de tous différends que les parties lui soumettront. Dans le texte anglais, qui est le texte original, le mot „parties" est écrit avec une minuscule; cela montre que les rédacteurs du Pacte n'avaient pas l'intention de limiter aux seuls Etats le droit d'être partie dans un litige soumis à la Cour. Il fait valoir qu'après la création de la Société des Nations les circonstances ne sont plus les mêmes qu'auparavant. La souveraineté des Etats a été invoquée pour empêcher les particuliers de les citer en justice. Après l'établissement d'une institution comme la Cour Permanente de Justice Internationale, ces empêchements ne peuvent plus exister. On a dit que si l'on étend la compétence de la Cour aux procès des particuliers, il s'ensuivra un trop grand nombre de procès. M. Loder passe outre, et s'oppose à l'idée de ne rendre la Cour accessible qu'aux Etats.

LORD PHILLIMORE pense que les litiges internationaux sont toujours des litiges entre des Etats; il se rallie à la formule suédoise qui exprime cette idée. Il lui paraît pourtant inutile de dire explicitement que les Etats peuvent prendre fait et cause pour leurs ressortissants. Il appartient au droit intérieur de déterminer les conditions dans lesquelles cela peut se faire, mais il est du devoir d'un Etat de protéger ses ressortissants. Lord Phillimore montre par des exemples que l'exercice du droit de protection a pu mener jusqu'à la guerre.

Le droit municipal, selon les pays, donne ou ne donne pas aux particuliers le droit de citer l'Etat en justice. Si ce droit n'existe pas, il est inadmissible qu'il soit introduit par le chemin détourné d'une juridiction internationale. Pareil expédient augmentera le nombre des conflits inter-

it might not be beneficial to give the Court of International Justice a supplementary jurisdiction; the Court would then take action at the instance of a private individual, provided that the case was not of a political nature.

M. LODER said that Dutch legislation had adopted the same attitude as the French on the point mentioned by M. de Lapradelle.

This point had been much discussed last February at the time of the Conference of the Neutral Powers. The narrow resolution then adopted was not in accordance with his own views. He saw no reason for limiting the competence of the Court by stipulating that private individuals must be represented by their Governments in order to have access to the Court. He quoted the terms of Article 14 of the Covenant of the League of Nations, in the terms of which the Court was to take cognisance of all disputes that the parties may submit to it. In the English version, which was the original one, the word "parties" was written with a small "p". That showed that the persons who drew up the Covenant had no intention of limiting only to States the right to be a party to a case before the Court. He pointed out that after the creation of the League of Nations circumstances were not the same as before. The sovereignty of the States had been used to prevent private individuals from taking action against them. Once an institution like the Permanent Court of International Justice was established, no such obstacles could exist. It had been said that if the competence of the Court were extended to cases of individuals, too large a number of cases would result. M. Loder disregarded this objection. He was opposed to the idea of allowing only States to appear before the Court.

LORD PHILLIMORE was of opinion that international cases should always be interstate cases; he agreed with the wording of the Swedish project which expresses this idea. It appeared to him, however, useless to state explicitly that States could adopt as their own the case of their subjects. The determination of the conditions under which this could be done was a question of national law, but it was the duty of a State to protect its subjects. Lord Phillimore showed by examples that the exercise of the right of protection could lead even to war.

Municipal law, according to the country, either gives or does not give to individuals the right to sue the State at law. If this right did not exist it was not admissible that it should be introduced by a roundabout method of international jurisdiction. Such an expedient would in-

nationaux; un Etat ne tolérera jamais d'être attaqué devant une Cour par un particulier. Si un particulier se sent lésé dans ses droits, qu'il s'adresse à son Gouvernement; et si celui-ci trouve la plainte justifiée, il ne manquera pas de se mettre en pourparlers avec l'Etat offenseur, et éventuellement de le citer en justice.

crease the number of international disputes. A State would never permit itself to be sued before a Court by a private individual. If a private individual felt that his rights were affected he should appeal to his Government, and if the latter found his complaint justified it would not fail to open communications with the offending State, and possibly, to take legal action against it.

Mr. ROOT est d'accord avec M. Loder et reconnaît l'importance des remarques de M. de Lapradelle; mais il pense que le but qu'on poursuit pourrait être atteint simplement grâce à un système qui donnerait aux Etats seuls le droit de recourir à la Cour, plutôt qu'en étendant la compétence de cette dernière.

Il s'appuie sur deux considérations:

Premièrement, il invoque la règle, découlant du principe de la souveraineté des Etats, qu'aucun Etat ne peut être cité sans son consentement préalable. Il est vrai que le consentement est généralement donné; mais il est sujet à des limitations qui varient selon les Etats. Si le Comité essaie d'établir des règles fixes, il peut s'exposer à enfreindre les idées propres à certains pays; Mr. Root pense que moins on impose de restrictions aux Etats, plus on a de chances de réussir.

En second lieu, le système actuel donne aux particuliers, pour sauvegarder leurs droits, un moyen supérieur à celui qui leur serait fourni si on leur donnait le droit de citer un Etat devant un tribunal international. En effet, si leurs propres gouvernements trouvent leur cause justifiée, ils prêtent aux particuliers tout leur appui et tâchent de régler l'affaire par la voix diplomatique, ce qui réussit dans 99 cas sur 100. D'autre part, il est impossible d'imaginer que des conversations diplomatiques puissent s'engager entre un particulier et un Gouvernement. Mr. Root ne croit pas qu'un particulier puisse avoir aucun avantage à porter devant la Cour Internationale une plainte que son propre Gouvernement ne trouve pas justifiée.

Le mot „international" employé dans l'art. 14 du Pacte caractérise bien la situation; la Cour peut traiter de questions qui affectent les intérêts des individus, mais seulement si le Gouvernement, dont le particulier est le ressortissant, a internationalisé ces intérêts en les prenant en main. Mr. Root rappelle que la majorité des cas portés devant la Cour d'Arbitrage concernaient les intérêts de particuliers, appuyés par leurs Etats respectifs. Mr. Root se demande si la plainte d'un particulier qui ne serait pas soutenu par son Gouvernement, aurait assez de poids

Mr. ROOT stated that he agreed with M. Loder and realised the importance of what M. de Lapradelle had said, but he thought that the end they sought could be reached by a system which gave only to States access to the Court, instead of enlarging the Court's competence.

Two considerations supported this view:

Firstly, he quoted the rule, arising from the principle of sovereignty of States, that no State could be summoned before the Court without its previous consent. It was true that consent generally was given, but it was subject to limitations which varied according to the States. If the Committee tried to fix the definite rules they might expose themselves to infringing on the individual conceptions of certain countries. Mr. Root thought that the less restrictions were imposed on States, the greater would be the chance of success.

Secondly, the present system gave to individuals a means of protecting their rights superior to that which would be given them if they had the right to summon a State before an international tribunal. In practice, if their own Government thought their case justified, they would give the individuals all possible help and would try to settle the affair through diplomatic channels. This would mean success in 99 cases out of 100. On the other hand, it was inconceivable that diplomatic relations should proceed between a private individual and a Government. Mr. Root did not think that a private individual would gain any advantage by taking before the International Court a case which his Government did not consider justified.

The word "international", used in Article 14 of the Covenant, summed up the position very well. The Court could deal with questions affecting private interests, but only if the Government of the country of which the individual was the subject made them international by adopting them as its own. Mr. Root recalled the fact that the majority of cases before the Court of Arbitration related to private interests supported by the respective States.

devant une Cour internationale. Il pense que la force logique de l'argument de M. Loder et du point de vue de M. de Lapradelle feront triompher ces opinions dans l'application du système préconisé par lui-même. Il est impossible qu'un Gouvernement, qui trouve juste la plainte d'un de ses nationaux, ne la fasse pas sienne, et que la Cour internationale ne prenne pas en considération la cause d'un particulier si elle a été embrassée par un Gouvernement.

Mr. Root doubted whether the claim of a private individual which was not supported by his Government would carry enough weight before an international Court. He thought that the logical force of M. Loder's argument and of the point of view put forward by M. de Lapradelle would insure the success of their ideas if the system recommended by him were put in force. It was impossible that a Government, which considered the case of one of its subjects just, would not make it its own, and that the International Court would not give consideration to the case of a private individual if it had been adopted by a Government.

LORD PHILLIMORE remarque que, lorsqu'il a eu la parole, il n'a pas considéré la question, soulevée par M. Loder, relative à l'interprétation de l'article 14 du Pacte.

Lord Phillimore est d'avis, du moins en ce qui concerne le texte anglais du Pacte, que le mot „international" doit être interprété comme signifiant exclusivement des relations entre Etats. Il appuie son interprétation sur les articles 18 et 19 du Pacte, où, d'après lui, il est question d'engagements entre Etats, de rapports entre les Etats.

LORD PHILLIMORE remarked, that when he last spoke, he had in consideration the question raised by M. Loder concerning the interpretation of Article 14 of the Covenant.

Lord Phillimore was of opinion that, at any rate in so far as the English version of the Covenant was concerned, the word "international" must be interpreted as having regard exclusively to relations between States. He based this interpretation on Articles 18 and 19 of the Covenant, which in his opinion dealt with engagements between States and relations among States.

M. RICCI-BUSATTI se rallie à l'opinion de Mr. Root et de Lord Phillimore, à savoir que la Cour ne doit être compétente que pour conflits entre Etats; il approuve entièrement les motifs sur lesquels cette opinion a été fondée.

Il est impossible de mettre les Etats et les particuliers sur le même plan; les particuliers ne sont pas sujets de droit international, et c'est exclusivement dans le domaine de ce droit que la Cour est appelée à fonctionner. Il est vrai qu'on peut donner à la notion de conflit international, diverses interprétations: on a l'habitude de considérer comme telle, à certains égards, toute question où des éléments relevant de pays différents sont en jeu; dans ce sens, même un conflit entre deux ressortissants d'un même Etat peut être international, par exemple, s'il a trait à une propriété située en pays étranger; mais ce n'est pas le sens visé par le Pacte, où il ne s'agit que de relations entre Etats. Pour qu'un conflit entre un Etat et un particulier, ressortissant d'un autre pays, puisse être du domaine de la Cour internationale, il faut que l'Etat auquel appartient le particulier se considère comme lésé lui-même, dans les droits et intérêts de son ressortissant, et que, de ce chef, il „internationalise" le conflit. Même dans ce cas, de l'avis de M. Ricci-Busatti, quelques précautions seraient nécessaires.

M. RICCI-BUSATTI agreed with Mr. Root and Lord Phillimore that the Court must be competent only to deal with disputes between States. He approved entirely of the grounds on which this opinion was based.

It is impossible to put States and private individuals on the same footing; private individuals are not subjects of international law and it is entirely within the realm of that law that the Court is called upon to act. It was true that various interpretations may be given to the words "international disputes"; it is customary to consider in, certain connections, any question as international in which elements relating to different countries are concerned. Under this interpretation, even a conflict between two subjects of the same State may be international, if for example it deals with a piece of property located in a foreign country; but this is not the interpretation meant by the Covenant, which has to do with inter-state relations. To bring a dispute between a State and a private citizen of another State within the domain of the International Court, the State of the private individual must consider itself injured through the rights and interests of its subject; thus it "internationalises" the conflict. Even in this case, M. Ricci-Busatti thought that some precaution would be necessary.

Le PRESIDENT, dans l'examen de la question soumise au Comité, adopte le point de départ suivant: le droit international règle les rapports entre Etats comme tels, et les Etats ont le devoir de protéger leurs nationaux.

L'objet propre du droit des gens, du *jus inter gentes,* ce sont les rapports d'Etat à Etat considérés comme collectivités souveraines et comme membres, à ce titre, de la Société des Nations. La condition des ressortissants de chaque Etat dans d'autres pays, la coordination du droit public et privé de chaque nation avec celui des autres nations, sont l'objet de la sollicitude des nations dans leurs rapports mutuels; mais ces questions ne rentrent que médiatement dans le droit des gens et ne changent pas, en soi, de nature en étant assumées par ce droit.

En cas de lésion de droit dans le chef des ressortissants d'un Etat, l'accomplissement du devoir de protection peut s'exercer d'abord par l'action diplomatique et tout ce qui s'y rattache. Elle peut s'exercer au besoin par l'action en justice d'un Etat qui prend fait et cause pour ses nationaux. On ne conçoit guère en droit international qu'un particulier exerce, de sa propre autorité, une action en justice contre un Etat étranger qui n'a pas accepté une telle judicature, et cela sans aucune entremise de son propre Etat. La voie naturelle à suivre par les particuliers est de s'adresser à la juridiction étrangère en tant qu'elle leur est ouverte, d'épuiser dans cet ordre tous les moyens d'obtenir justice, — ce qui pourrait être visé comme indispensable, — puis de s'adresser au besoin à leur Gouvernement pour entamer une procédure diplomatique et éventuellement judiciaire. Encore faudra-t-il que cette dernière procédure ait été conventionnellement admise ou soit volontairement acceptée. Ces cas sont fréquents: la première cause plaidée devant la Cour d'Arbitrage, où le Président du Comité a représenté les Etats-Unis d'Amérique, en offre un exemple. Mais, même dans ces cas, le procès demeure essentiellement une affaire d'Etat à Etat, quelque soit l'intérêt particulier qui s'y trouve engagé.

Le Président rappelle, à ce propos, que la Convention de 1907 ne donne accès à la Cour qu'aux Etats contractants, et il espère que M. Loder et M. de Lapradelle se rallieront à cette solution.

M. DE LAPRADELLE croit devoir préciser son point de vue. Il envisage deux éventualités principales, où il faudrait, par exemple, donner aux particuliers le droit de citer des Etats en

The PRESIDENT, examining the question submitted to the Committee, took the following starting point: international law governs relations between States as such, and it is the duty of States to protect their nationals.

The real object of the law of nations, of *jus inter gentes,* is the relation of State to State considered as sovereign groups, and, as such, Members of the League of Nations. The conditions of subjects of each State in another country, the co-ordination of public and private law of each State with that of the other nations, these are the concerns of nations in their mutual relations, but these questions enter only indirectly into the realm of the law of nations, and do not change in their essential character by being included in this law.

In case of violation of law through the subject of a given State, the duty to protect the subject first may be fulfilled by diplomatic means and all which this involves. In case of need, it may be fulfilled by a State taking up the cause of its national in a Court of Justice. It is scarcely conceivable in international law that a private citizen brings judicial action by his own authority against a foreign State which has not agreed to such jurisdiction and without the mediation of his own Government. The natural course for an individual to follow is to make his appeal under the foreign jurisdiction to the extent permitted, to exhaust all means of this kind to obtain justice, — which may be considered as indispensable, — and then, if need be, to call on his Government to institute diplomatic proceedings and eventually judicial proceedings. Again, will it be necessary that this last procedure shall have been admitted by convention or be voluntarily accepted. These are frequent cases: the first cause pleaded before the Court of Arbitration, in which the President of the Committee represented the United States of America, furnished an example of this. But even in this case, the action remains essentially an affair between State and State with a certain individual interest incidentally involved.

The President recalled in this connection that the Convention of 1907 affords access only to the contracting States, and he hoped that MM. Loder and de Lapradelle would agree to this solution.

M. DE LAPRADELLE thought that he should define his point of view. He foresaw two general conditions under which the right of suing States at law would have to be given to private

justice. Il a d'abord en vue les cas de double nationalité: si deux Etats réclament la même personne comme leur sujet, il n'y a pas moyen de résoudre le conflit autrement que par une juridiction supérieure. Puisqu'il y a un conflit de droits constitutionnels, il est extrêmement improbable que les Etats aient recours à l'arbitrage; pour régulariser sa situation le particulier devrait donc pouvoir attaquer les deux Etats. En créant la nouvelle Cour, on doit marquer un progrès. Il ne faut pas renoncer à la possibilité d'un développement ultérieur; il est presque certain que les deux Etats qui réclament la même personne comme leur ressortissant ne voudraient pas se soumettre à un arbitrage; mais il faut justement sortir des limites de l'arbitrage.

L'autre éventualité envisagée par M. de Lapradelle est celle où un ressortissant d'un certain Etat se trouve en relations de commerce avec un autre Etat, sans qu'aucun intérêt de la souveraineté soit en jeu. Dans ce cas, il existe une certaine parité entre l'Etat et le particulier; pourtant on a, jusqu'ici, mis l'Etat au-dessus de la justice pour deux raisons: possibilité de difficultés diplomatiques, et défaut de moyens d'exécution. La deuxième objection doit être considérée comme devant être abandonnée après l'établissement de la Société des Nations. Pour ce qui est de l'autre, il ne faut pas perdre de vue qu'il ne s'agit pas d'actes de souveraineté. Cette même considération oblige plus directement le particulier à s'adresser à la Cour, puisque par le fait même que la souveraineté n'est pas en jeu, il serait plus difficile pour lui d'obtenir l'intervention diplomatique de son gouvernement.

La question sort des limites de l'arbitrage ordinaire; aussi a-t-on proposé de créer, pour connaître des questions de cet ordre, une Chambre spéciale. La question de savoir si l'on peut permettre à la Cour de dépasser ces limites, est fort importante. On peut envisager deux possibilités: organiser la nouvelle Cour de façon à ce qu'elle dépasse les limites de l'arbitrage, ou ne pas le faire. Dans la deuxième éventualité, on sait à quoi s'en tenir, puisqu'on a l'expérience; dans l'autre, on ne peut que se borner à faire prendre aux Etats fait et cause pour leurs ressortissants. Ces transformations d'un conflit entre un Etat et un individu en un conflit entre deux Etats, ne peut cependant se faire que pour cause de déni de justice. A ce sujet M. de Lapradelle peut se rallier à la première phrase de l'article 30 du projet scandinave. Par contre il trouve la deuxième phrase superflue, puisque la réclamation de l'individu a été transformée en une réclamation d'Etat à Etat.

individuals. He first dealt with the case of double nationality: if each of two States claimed the same person as a subject, there would be no means of settling the dispute, except by a higher jurisdiction. Since there is a conflict of constitutional Laws, it is extremely improbable that the States would resort to arbitration; the individual in order to define his position must therefore have the power of bringing suit against the two States. A step in advance should be taken with the creation of the new Court. The possibility of subsequent development must not be blocked; it is almost certain that the two States who claim the same person as their subject would not care to submit to arbitration; it becomes necessary to go outside the limits of arbitration.

The other case foreseen by M. de Lapradelle was that of a subject of a certain State having commercial relations with another State, attributes of sovereignty not being affected. In this case a certain equality exists between the State and the individual. However, up to the present time, the State has been considered as above the law, for two reasons: first, the possibility of diplomatic difficulties, second, the absence of means for the execution of the sentence. The second objection should be considered as having to be abandoned after the establishment of the League of Nations. As concerns the other, the fact must not be lost sight of that there is no question of acts of sovereignty. This same consideration demands implicitly that the private individual appeal to the Court, because the very fact that sovereignty is not affected makes it more difficult for him to obtain the diplomatic intervention of his Government.

The question goes outside the bounds of ordinary arbitration; for that reason it has been proposed to create a special Chamber to deal with questions of this kind. It is very important to decide whether power shall be given to the Court to go beyond those limits. Two possibilities are to be considered: either the new Court will be organised in such a way that it may go beyond the limits of arbitration, or it will not be so organised. In the latter case, what may be expected is known from past experience. In the other case, the only thing to do is to have the States take up the cause of their subjects. Such transformation of disputes between States and individuals into disputes between two States can take place only as a consequence of a refusal of justice. On this point M. de Lapradelle was in agreement with the first paragraph of article 30 of the Scandinavian project. However,

M. de Lapradelle se demande jusqu'où s'étend la protection de l'Etat sur son ressortissant, dans le cas ou il a pris fait et cause pour celui-ci. L'Etat doit-il laisser à l'individu le soin de plaider lui-même sa cause devant la Cour où il a pénétré grâce à l'appui de son Gouvernement, ou est-ce que l'Etat, ayant pris fait et cause pour son ressortissant, doit agir seul devant la Cour? M. de Lapradelle prouve par des exemples que les particuliers désirent prendre part eux-mêmes aux procès. En tout cas, c'est là une question de procédure fort importante, qui doit être tranchée.

M. de Lapradelle se résume: même si pour le moment on ne peut pas donner à la Cour une compétence trop étendue, il faut réserver la possibilité d'étendre sa compétence aux conflits provenant des relations d'activité économique entre un Etat et un particulier, et aux cas où un individu est la victime d'un conflit de nationalités. Il ne faut pas trop rester dans le domaine théorique; on doit tenir compte des souffrances individuelles résultant de l'état anarchique des relations internationales.

M. de Lapradelle rappelle l'idée de créer une Haute Cour, compétente pour juger les crimes contre le droit des gens: il espère que les procès devant cette Cour seront intentés à des individus; mais si la juridiction internationale est ainsi rendue compétente pour juger des particuliers, on doit réciproquement ouvrir aux particuliers l'accès à la juridiction internationale pour la protection de leurs intérêts.

he thought the second paragraph superfluous, since the claim of the individual had been turned into a claim of State against State.

M. de Lapradelle wondered how far a State's protection of its citizen extended in case the State took up the cause in his behalf. Should the State leave to the individual the task of pleading his own case before the Court to which he has gained access by the aid of his Government, or should the State, having taken up the case for its subject, conduct the case alone before the Court? M. de Lapradelle proved, by quoting examples, that individuals wished to take part themselves in the proceedings. In any case, this very important question of procedure must be decided.

M. de Lapradelle summarised what he had said: Even if at the present time it is not possible to give the Court a very wide competence, it is necessary to guard the possibility of extending its competence to disputes based on economic relations between a State and an individual, and to cases in which the individual is the victim of a conflict of nationality. One must not remain too much in the realm of theories; wrongs done to individuals resulting from the chaotic conditions of international relations must be taken into account.

M. de Lapradelle recalled the idea of creating a High Court competent to deal with offences against the law of nations. He hoped that the proceedings before this Court would be undertaken against individuals, but if the international jurisdiction is thus made competent to try individuals, access to the International Court should be given reciprocally to individuals for the protection of their interests.

Le PRESIDENT observe que M. de Lapradelle a posé devant le Comité deux cas différents; le premier, c'est le cas d'une personne ayant une double nationalité. Il demande quels moyens il faut employer pour résoudre cette difficulté. On ne peut forcer les Etats à accepter contre leur gré une juridiction à cet égard. Par contre, on peut essayer de rapprocher les législations et de supprimer ainsi la raison même du conflit. On pourrait également avoir recours à des moyens de conciliation volontaire.

Le deuxième cas envisagé par M. de Lapradelle, c'est le cas d'un litige entre un particulier et un Etat considéré comme personne civile. Le Président se demande si on peut avoir recours à la juridiction internationale, lorsque le recours aux tribunaux de l'Etat n'est pas ouvert. Le Président croit que, même dans ce cas, il faut

The PRESIDENT pointed out that M. de Lapradelle had put two different cases to the Committee: the first was the case of a person having a double nationality. He wondered what means should be employed to solve this difficulty; States could not be forced to submit to a jurisdiction on this subject against their will. On the other hand an attempt might be made to bring the laws to agree and thus remove the very cause of the conflict. It might also be possible to resort to voluntary conciliation.

The second case presented by M. de Lapradelle was that of litigation between an individual and a State considered as a civil person. He wondered whether in this case recourse was open to international jurisdiction when there was no recourse to the tribunals of the State. The President thought that, even in this case, it

plutôt songer, soit à des réformes législatives, soit à un arrangement amiable. On ne peut dans un tel cas traduire l'Etat contre son assentiment, exprès ou tacite, mais réel, devant la Cour internationale.

A ce propos, le Président fait observer qu'il ne faut pas se laisser égarer par les mots. On parle de droit international privé; mais en réalité il n'y a pas de droit international proprement dit qui soit en même temps un droit privé; il y a seulement un droit privé, qu'on pourrait appeler de projection extra-nationale, de même qu'il y a un droit public, pénal, administratif etc., de semblable projection.

Le droit privé et le droit public de chaque Etat, originairement limités aux personnes et au territoire d'une nation, débordent, par suite du fractionnement du genre humain en nations, la sphère purement nationale. Ils donnent lieu à des développements et à des complications sur le terrain de la vie extra-nationale, où ils rencontrent le droit privé et le droit public d'autres Etats, au point de vue de la réglementation d'un même rapport juridique. De là la nécessité de les coordonner, non seulement à titre de courtoisie, mais sur la base du droit. La coordination, d'abord jurisprudentielle, tend à devenir conventionnelle. En tant qu'elle concerne le droit civil, on peut l'appeler, dans un certain sens, droit civil international.

On peut parler de même d'un droit maritime, pénal, administratif, etc. international. Ce qu'il importe d'éviter, c'est la distinction entre le droit international privé et le droit international public, comme s'il existait un droit international général dont ces deux parties seraient des subdivisions.

M. DE LAPRADELLE n'a pas parlé de droit international privé: les questions visées par lui touchent à des points du droit constitutionnel, c'est à dire du droit public au premier chef.

M. HAGERUP déclare qu'il est d'accord avec la première partie du discours du Président. Il croit, p. ex., que le cas de double nationalité ne peut pas être porté devant un tribunal sans qu'il y ait entre les deux Etats intéressés une convention préalable.

M. Hagerup, par contre, ne peut pas se rallier à l'opinion du Président lorsqu'il dit qu'on ne peut obliger un Etat, par une sentence internationale, à modifier sa législation. M. Hagerup prend comme exemple la Convention sur la propriété littéraire et artistique: si une des parties contractantes n'a pas passé une législation conforme à la convention, et si, en appliquant sa législation nationale, elle lèse les intérêts des

would be preferable that the matter should be dealt with, either by legislative reforms, or by amicable arrangement. In such a case a State cannot, without its consent — express or tacit, but nevertheless real —, be sued before an International Court.

In this connection, the President observed that one must not be misled by words. Private international law is spoken of; but in reality there is no international law in the strict sense of the word which is at the same time private law; there is only private law which may be said to be projected extra-nationally, just as there are public, penal, administrative, and other kinds of law similarly projected.

Public and private law of each State, originally limited to the people and territory of the nation, have gone outside their purely national sphere as a result of the division of the human species into nations. They give rise to development and complications in the domain of extra-national affairs where they confront public and private law of other States in the settlement of a given legal question. From this arises the necessity of co-ordinating them, not only out of courtesy but also on the basis of law. The co-ordination, at first jurisprudential, tends to become conventional. In so far as it concerns civil law, it may in a certain sense be called international civil law.

International maritime law, penal, administrative, etc. may be spoken of in the same way. What is important is to avoid the distinction between international private law and international public law, just as if there existed a general international law of which these two parts were subdivisions.

M. DE LAPRADELLE had not mentioned private international law. The question dealt with by him concerned points of constitutional law, that is to say, law of an essentially public nature.

M. HAGERUP said that he agreed with the first part of the President's speech. He thought, for instance, that cases of double nationality could not be taken before a Court, without a previous convention between the two States concerned.

M. Hagerup, on the other hand, could not agree with the President when he said that a State could not be compelled to modify its laws by an international sentence. M. Hagerup took as an example a case coming under the artistic and literary Copyright Convention: if one of the contracting parties had not instituted laws in accordance with the terms of the Convention, and if the said party by the application of its

ressortissants d'une autre puissance contractante, une Cour internationale, devant laquelle le cas serait porté, peut bien rendre un jugement qui décide l'obligation pour l'Etat en question de modifier sa législation intérieure.

M. DE LAPRADELLE a la parole pour répondre aux objections soulevées contre ses idées. Il n'a pas voulu formuler un programme. Il a seulement voulu poser des problèmes. Il faut considérer la possibilité de l'élargissement de la compétence ordinaire des Cours d'arbitrage. Cette nécessité s'est longtemps fait sentir: on peut en effet en retrouver les traces dans l'histoire de l'arbitrage, par exemple dans l'affaire de „l'Alabama". Les cas qu'il a exposés sont des cas de droit constitutionnel. Il est d'accord avec M. Hagerup pour reconnaître que dans certains cas de ce genre il faut écarter la compétence de la Cour; mais à côté du droit constitutionnel il y a le droit de la vie qu'il ne faut pas méconnaître.

M. HAGERUP déclare que la 2ième phrase de l'article 20 du projet suédois prévoit que la question ne peut être tranchée par les tribunaux nationaux, ou qu'il y a un cas de déni de justice. Cette réserve se trouve dans plusieurs traités d'arbitrage.

En ce qui concerne la question posée par M. de Lapradelle, de savoir si, dans un cas où un Etat a pris en main devant la Cour de Justice les intérêts d'un de ses ressortissants, le particulier peut plaider devant la Cour, M. Hagerup pense que la pratique actuelle de l'arbitrage admet en général une telle faculté. Mais c'est là une question qui doit être examinée lors de la discussion sur les règles de procédure.

LORD PHILLIMORE observe que si M. de Lapradelle est disposé à se contenter de voir les intérêts des particuliers protégés dans la pratique, tout en donnant aux Etats seulement, le droit d'ester en justice devant la Cour, la discussion a fait du progrès, M. Loder étant seul à ne pas se rallier à ce point de vue. Si, au contraire, M. de Lapradelle veut transporter jusque dans la pratique l'application de ses idées, Lord Phillimore croit devoir faire quelques remarques.

Il examine d'abord le cas de conflit de nationalités. L'individu qui se trouve être la victime de ce conflit, n'est pas à considérer comme un *civis mundi,* il est le ressortissant d'un ou deux Etats déterminés. Mais alors la Cour n'a pas de question pratique à résoudre. La question qui se pose réellement est celle de savoir si la législation de

national law damaged the interests of subjects of another contracting Power, an International Court, before which the case was taken, could impose a sentence, necessitating an alteration in national laws.

M. DE LAPRADELLE spoke in answer to the objections raised to his ideas. He had no intention of formulating a programme. He only wished to suggest some problems. The possibility of widening the ordinary competence of Courts of Arbitration must be considered. This necessity had been felt for a long time; in fact, traces of it could be found in the history of Arbitration, for instance, in the Alabama claims. The cases he had put forward were cases of constitutional law. He agreed with M. Hagerup that in certain cases of this kind the Court could not have competence, but side by side with constitutional law, there were the ordinary laws of life, which must not be overlooked.

M. HAGERUP declared that Paragraph 2 of Article 20 of the Swedish plan provides for the case that the question cannot be settled by the national tribunals or that there is a refusal of justice. This reservation is included in several arbitration treaties.

Concerning the question raised by M. de Lapradelle, whether in a case in which a State has taken up the cause of one of its subjects before the Court of Justice, the private individual can plead before the Court, M. Hagerup thought that present arbitration practice admits in general such right. However, that is a question which should be examined when the rules of procedure are discussed.

LORD PHILLIMORE observed that if M. de Lapradelle would be satisfied to have the interests of private individuals protected in a practical manner, giving only to States the right to bring suit before the Court, progress had been made in the discussion; M. Loder being the only one who did not agree with the point of view. If, on the other hand, M. de Lapradelle wished his ideas to be put into practice, Lord Phillimore felt that he must make some further observations.

First of all he dealt with the case of double nationality. The individual who is the subject of this dispute cannot be considered as a *civis mundi.* He is the subject of one or two particular States. In this case there is no practical question the Court could decide. The point raised really is whether the legislation of any partic-

tel ou tel Etat doit être modifiée ou non. Le problème de la nationalité actuelle de l'individu ne peut être résolu que d'après les lois du pays sous la juridiction duquel il se trouve.

Quant à l'autre cas, celui où il y a conflit entre un individu et un Etat considéré comme personne civile, Lord Phillimore fait remarquer que c'est là un cas très fréquent. Si la législation de l'Etat en question permet à l'individu de le citer en justice devant ses tribunaux nationaux, il n'y a à considérer que l'éventualité où ces tribunaux n'appliquent pas la loi d'une façon juste. Mais une Cour internationale ne pourrait rien faire dans pareil cas; elle n'est pas une Cour d'appel superposée aux Cours nationales. Si, au contraire, l'individu ne peut pas citer l'Etat en justice, il faut tenir compte du fait que le contrat qu'il a conclu avec l'Etat doit être considéré comme ayant été conclu en pleine connaissance de cause. L'étranger doit accepter les mêmes risques que les ressortissants mêmes de l'Etat.

Pour les raisons qu'il vient d'exposer, Lord Phillimore est d'avis qu'il n'est pas nécessaire de tenir compte des deux cas envisagés par M. de Lapradelle.

M. RICCI-BUSATTI dit pour commencer qu'il peut se rallier en principe, à la formule de l'article 30 du projet scandinave.

Il continue en relevant l'opinion de M. Hagerup, selon laquelle on doit laisser aux particuliers le soin de prendre en main la défense de leurs droits devant la Cour. M. Ricci-Busatti n'est pas de cet avis. Il est nécessaire que l'Etat reste toujours le *dominus litis*, la partie en cause. S'il en est autrement, on se heurte à des inconvénients qu'il a lui-même constatés dans la pratique.

Il croit utile de faire remarquer, d'ailleurs, que devant les tribunaux nationaux une partie seulement des pouvoirs de l'Etat est en cause, tandis que dans les rapports internationaux l'Etat figure toujours dans sa totalité et avec la plénitude de ses attributions souveraines.

Sur la question de la double nationalité, M. Ricci-Busatti se rallie à l'avis de Lord Phillimore. Il fait cependant une réserve: il faut tenir compte du cas où le différend porterait sur l'interprétation à donner à un principe de droit international ou à un traité; dans ce cas la compétence de la Cour pourra être reconnue. Mais, en général, il admet que la solution des conflits de cette nature doit être cherchée dans le rapprochement des différentes législations. Il rappelle le travail qui a été poursuivi dans cet ordre d'idées par les Conférences de droit in-

ular State should be amended or not. The question of the nationality of an individual can only be decided according to the laws of the country under whose jurisdiction he is.

With reference to the other case, that in which there was a dispute between an individual and a State, considered as a civil person, Lord Phillimore pointed out that such cases were very frequent. If the laws of the State in question allowed the individual to sue the State before the national Court, it only remained to consider the eventuality in which its Courts might not apply the law with justice. But an international Court could do nothing in such a case; it was not a Court of Appeal placed over national Courts. If, on the other hand, the individual could not sue the State, it must be remembered that the individual entered into the contract with the State, in full knowledge of this fact. Foreigners must accept the same risks as subjects of the State.

For the reasons just given, Lord Phillimore thought that it was not necessary to take into account the two cases considered by M. de Lapradelle.

M. RICCI-BUSATTI began by saying that he agreed in principle with the wording of Article 30 of the Scandinavian project.

He then considered the opinion given by M. Hagerup, according to which the right of defending their own cases before the Court should be given to private individuals. He did not agree. The State should always be the *dominus litis*, the party concerned. If it were otherwise, the same practical difficulties which he himself has experienced would be encountered.

It is unnecessary, moreover, to mention that before national Courts only one part of the State's powers is concerned, while in international affairs the State is always considered as a whole, and in the fullness of its attributes of sovereignty.

Concerning the question of double nationality, M. Ricci-Busatti agreed with Lord Phillimore. He made one reservation, however; the case in which the dispute turns on the interpretation to give to a treaty or principle of international law, must be taken into account; in such cases, the competence of the Court might be recognised. Generally speaking, however, he admitted that the settlement of disputes of this nature should be sought by harmonising the different laws. He recalled the work done in this connection by the Hague Confer-

ternational privé de La Haye. Les conventions qui ont été le résultat de ces conférences, et dont il souhaite que la série soit reprise, posent des principes communs pour la solution des conflits de lois. On a aussi cherché à réaliser dans une certaine mesure l'uniformité du droit matériel, entre quelques Etats. La question de l'établissement de Cours internationales spéciales, pour assurer l'uniformité de la jurisprudence dans ces matières, a été soulevée. Ce sujet sort cependant du cadre de la discussion actuelle.

M. FERNANDES se rallie au point de vue soutenu par Lord Phillimore et par Mr. Elihu Root. A son avis, la formule qui reconnaît aux seuls Etats l'accès à la Cour de Justice Internationale, — tout en s'accordant avec la logique juridique, puisque les Etats seuls constituent des personnes juridiques dans l'ordre international — épuise néanmoins tous les cas qu'on peut envisager comme devant rentrer dans la compétence de la Cour, y compris ceux auxquels ont fait allusion M. de Lapradelle et M. Loder. En effet, les atteintes portées par un Etat au droit individuel, vis-à-vis d'un étranger, constituent maintenant l'objet de réclamations diplomatiques, l'Etat auquel appartient l'individu lésé prenant fait et cause pour lui, ce qui transforme la question privée en question internationale sous cette forme; et, l'Etat se faisant lui-même demandeur, la question pourra être portée devant la Cour, et de ce fait les intérêts très respectables, envisagés par M. de Lapradelle et M. Loder, trouveront protection judiciaire sans que soit dénaturé le caractère propre du tribunal international. Ceci lui paraît tellement évident qu'il s'abstiendrait d'intervenir dans le débat si M. le Président n'avait suggéré la possibilité d'une mention spéciale exigeant que, avant que l'Etat ne prenne en main la défense de son ressortissant, les juridictions nationales aient été épuisées. Or, il y a des Etats en Amérique, dont le Brésil, qui accordent à tout individu sans distinction de nationalité, le droit d'actionner les personnes publiques en dommages intérêts, et même en annulation de ceux de leurs actes qui seraient entâchés d'excès de pouvoir ou d'illégalité, au cas où quelque droit s'en trouve lésé. Cependant, d'autres Etats, et ceux-ci sont les plus nombreux, ne permettent pas une telle action: tout ce que la personne lésée peut faire, c'est d'avoir recours à des juridictions administratives n'ayant pas un caractère nettement contentieux et très loin d'avoir les traits caractéristiques d'une instance judiciaire. Il est évident que dans l'un cas comme dans l'autre, il y a possibilité d'un déni de justice.

ences on private international law. The conventions following on these Conferences, which he hoped to see continued, stated general principles applicable in case of conflicting legal systems. It was also attempted to realise to a certain degree uniformity of law between certain States. The question of the establishment of a special international Court to insure uniformity of jurisprudence in these matters had been raised. However, this subject goes outside the scope of the present discussion.

M. FERNANDES agreed with the point of view upheld by Lord Phillimore and Mr. Root. In his opinion, the clause which conferred only on States access to the International Court of Justice, — agreeing completely with legal logic, since States alone constituted legal persons in international matters, — covers nevertheless all cases which may be considered as coming within the competence of the Court, including those to which Messrs. de Lapradelle and Loder alluded. As a matter of fact, infractions by a State on individual rights in respect to a foreigner now constitute the object of diplomatic claims. The State of which the injured person is a subject takes up the cause for him. This changes the private question into an international one. In this way the State makes itself the plaintiff and the question may be taken before the Court. By this fact the important interests considered by Messrs. de Lapradelle and Loder shall obtain legal protection, without changing the real character of the international tribunal. This seemed so evident to him that he would have refrained from taking part in the debate, had not the President suggested the possibility of including a special clause demanding that, before a State take up the defence of its subject, national jurisdiction should have been exhausted. But there are States in America, Brazil among them, which grant to any person without distinction as to nationality, the right to bring action against public servants for injury of interests, and even the nullification of their acts which exceed their authority or are illegal, in case a right has been violated. However, there are other States, and these are the more numerous, which do not permit such action; all that the injured parties may do is to appeal to administrative jurisdiction, which does not have a clearly judicial character and is far from having the typical features of a suit at law. It is clear that in one case as in the other, there is the possibility of a refusal of justice. However, M. Fernandes should prefer

Mais M. Fernandes préférerait ne pas voir ajouter la condition suggérée par M. le Président: elle pourrait être interprétée dans un sens trop étroit, c'est à dire que, l'épuisement préalable des juridictions nationales étant exigé pour que l'Etat prenne, devant la Cour, fait et cause pour son sujet, on pourrait en conclure que l'instance serait irrecevable quand, faute d'action nationale contre l'Etat, il n'y aura pas de degrés de juridiction interne à épuiser. Cela rendrait précaire la position des Etats qui sont precisément les plus libéraux et dont la législation intérieure en cette matière est la plus avancée.

Le PRESIDENT donne lecture d'une partie de son discours liminaire, où la compétence de la Cour est limitée aux litiges entre Etats. Ces litiges peuvent se diviser en deux classes; litiges entre Etats agissant pour leur propre compte, et litiges entre Etats ayant pris fait et cause pour leurs ressortissants. Il faut, à son avis, que l'Etat demeure le *dominus litis* et que la décision soit rendue entre Etats. Ceci n'exclut pas l'emploi par les particuliers des moyens de sauvegarder leurs propres intérêts sous la direction de l'Etat.

M. RICCI-BUSATTI croit qu'il ne faut pas trop insister sur la différence entre les intérêts de l'Etat et les intérêts des individus pour lesquels il aura pris fait et cause. En réalité, c'est toujours son propre droit que l'Etat fait valoir: le droit à ce que ses ressortissants ne soient pas injustement lésés par un autre Etat.

M. DE LAPRADELLE se rallie à la formule du Président. Il tient à signaler le problème important de la protection des minorités. Elles sont des personnalités de droit international, sans être des Etats. La formule du Président est excellente parce qu'elle est générale. Elle permettra le libre développement du droit: en particulier, elle permettra de tenir compte du droit des minorités, tel qu'il est sanctionné p. ex. dans l'article 69 du traité de St. Germain du 10 septembre 1919.

Le PRESIDENT remarque que ce sont des cas spécifiés par une convention particulière.

LORD PHILLIMORE dit que dans les cas en question c'est toujours un Etat qui vient devant la Cour pour défendre la cause de certaines populations. En général, cependant, Lord Phillimore convient que la formule du Président est supérieure à celle du projet suédois.

not to see the clause added which the President suggested: it might be interpreted in too narrow a sense, that is to say that, the previous exhaustion of national jurisdiction being demanded before a State takes the cause of its subject before the Court, it might be concluded from this that no suit could be brought when it was not allowed to sue the State at law before the national Courts and, consequently, there would be no degrees of internal jurisdiction to be exhausted. This renders precarious the position of States which are precisely the most liberal, and whose domestic legislation on this subject is the most advanced.

The PRESIDENT read part of his introductory speech, in which the competence of the Court was limited to cases between States. These cases could be divided into two classes: cases between the States acting on their own behalf, and cases between States having taken up the cause of their subjects. In his opinion, the State must remain the *dominus litis* and the decision must be given as between States. This did not exclude individuals employing means to protect their own interests under the direction of the State.

M. RICCI-BUSATTI thought it not necessary to insist too much on the difference between a State's interests and an individual's interests which the State had adopted as its own. In reality, a State would always be upholding its own right, the right that its subjects shall not be unjustly injured by another State.

M. DE LAPRADELLE agreed with the President's proposal. He wished to draw attention to the important question of the protection of minorities. They are persons in international law, although they are not States. The clause proposed by the President was excellent, because it was of a general nature. It would allow a free development for law; in particular it would allow the rights of minorities to be taken into account, as laid down, for instance, in Article 69 of the Treaty of St. Germain of September 10, 1919.

The PRESIDENT remarked that these are cases specified by particular conventions.

LORD PHILLIMORE said that in the cases in question, it is always a State which comes before the Court to defend the cause of certain groups of individuals. Generally speaking, however, Lord Phillimore agreed that the clause proposed by the President was preferable to that of the Swedish project.

Mr. ROOT donne lecture de l'article 69 du traité de St. Germain, qui donne lieu à quelques remarques de Mr. Root lui-même et du Président.

A ce propos, M. RICCI-BUSATTI ajoute que, lors de la rédaction du traité de paix avec l'Autriche ainsi que des traités particuliers qui contiennent à cet égard des dispositions analogues, on s'est posé la question de savoir de quelle façon on aurait pu donner aux minorités le moyen de faire valoir leurs droits et intérêts devant la Cour; on s'est arrêté à la formule, selon laquelle tout Membre de la Société des Nations peut s'ériger en protecteur des minorités.

Le PRESIDENT remarque qu'en règle générale un Etat ne peut étendre sa protection que sur ses propres ressortissants. L'article cité comporte une extension au nom de l'humanité. Il y a là une conception remarquable, mais non pas nouvelle: elle se trouvait déjà dans divers traités.

LORD PHILLIMORE demande au Président quel est le sens exact de la seconde question, dans le questionnaire soumis par lui.

Le PRESIDENT explique qu'il a voulu poser la question de savoir si tous les Etats ou seulement les Etats mentionnés à l'annexe du Pacte de la Société des Nations auront le droit d'avoir recours au Tribunal International. Cette question sera discutée la première à la séance prochaine.

La séance est levée à 12.30 de l'après-midi.

Le Président:
(signé) Brn. DESCAMPS.

Le Secrétaire-Général:
(signé) D. ANZILOTTI.

Mr. ROOT read article 69 of the Treaty of St. Germain, which was the occasion of some remarks by Mr. Root and the President.

In this connection, M. RICCI-BUSATTI added that at the time of drafting the Treaty of Peace with Austria, as well as the separate treaties which contain in this connection analogous provisions, the question was considered in what way means might be given to minorities to present their claims before the Court. The clause was adopted according to which any Member of the League of Nations may appear in Court as the protector of minorities.

The PRESIDENT remarked, that as a general rule, a State could not extend its protection beyond its own subjects. The article quoted extended this protection in the name of humanity. It was a notable conception, but was not new. It was to be already found in various treaties

LORD PHILLIMORE asked the President what was the exact meaning of the second question in the questionnaire submitted by him.

The PRESIDENT explained that he wished to present the question, whether all States or only those States named in the Annex of the Covenant of the League of Nations would have the right to appeal to the International Court. This question would be discussed first at the next meeting.

The meeting closed at 12.30 p.m.

The President:
(signed) Brn. DESCAMPS.

The Secretary-General:
(signed) D. ANZILOTTI.

ANNEXE No. 1.

Compétence.

(Questionnaire proposé par le Baron Descamps)

I. La Cour constituera-t-elle essentiellement une jurisdiction entre Etats, ou sa compétence s'étendra-t-elle à des litiges concernant des particuliers? Dans quelles conditions ce dernier cas pourrait-il éventuellement se produire?

II. Quels seront les Etats qui pourront procéder devant la Cour?

III. Faudra-t-il l'accord des deux parties pour procéder juridictionnellement, ou l'action en justice pourra-t-elle être exercée unilatéralement par un Etat contre un autre?

IV. Dans quelle mesure la judicature obligatoire peut-elle être admise?

V. Quelles règles le juge devra-t-il appliquer en rendant sa sentence?

ANNEX No. 1.

Competence.

(Questionnaire submitted by Baron Descamps)

I. Shall the Court constitute essentially a jurisdiction between States, or shall its competence extend to litigation concerning individuals? Under what conditions can the latter eventuality occur?

II. What States may appear before the Court?

III. Shall the consent of the two parties be necessary to undertake judicial proceedings, or may an action in law be brought uni-laterally by one State against another?

IV. To what extent may obligatory jurisdiction be admitted?

V. What law shall the judge apply in delivering his sentence?

10ième SÉANCE (non-publique), tenue au Palais de la Paix, à La Haye, le 26 juin 1920.

Présidence de M. le BARON DESCAMPS.

Sont présents: tous les membres du Comité (à l'exception de M. Bevilaqua); Mr. James Brown Scott; les secrétaires particuliers de M. le Baron Descamps et de M. Adatci; les membres du Secrétariat. M. Fernandes a assisté à la dernière partie de la séance.

La séance est ouverte à $9^1/_2$ heures du matin.

Le PRESIDENT propose au Comité d'ouvrir la discussion sur la question que l'on a décidé de mettre à l'ordre du jour lors de la séance précédente: „quels seront les Etats qui pourront procéder devant la Cour?"

Le Président commence par exposer le problème. Il dit que la Société des Nations est ouverte à tous les Etats; 45 membres en font partie ou peuvent en devenir Membres sans conditions, et tous les autres Etats peuvent entrer dans la Société à condition de fournir certaines garanties. Il y a aussi une procédure prévue pour les cas de différends entre deux Etats dont un seul est Membre de la Société ou dont aucun n'en fait partie. Aux termes de l'article 17 du Pacte l'Etat ou les Etats étrangers à la Société sont invités à se soumettre aux obligations imposées à ses Membres aux fins de règlement, et cela aux conditions estimées justes par le Conseil.

Il faut ajouter que certains grands traités prévoient quelques éventualités, dans lesquelles les juridictions rattachées à la Société des Nations sont accessibles, sans distinction, pour les diverses parties en litige.

Le Président, ayant ainsi montré l'aspect général de la question, se demande quelle solution le Comité doit admettre?

Il appelle l'attention sur trois points: 1. l'article 21 du projet de 1907, aux termes duquel la juridiction est ouverte aux seuls Etats contractants; 2. les considérations financières: les Etats qui ne contribuent pas aux frais de l'institution de la juridiction nouvelle, pourront-ils s'en servir? 3. le projet allemand lui-même réserve aux seuls Membres de la Société des Nations le droit d'intenter un procès auquel l'adversaire ne peut se soustraire.

10TH MEETING (Private), held at the Peace Palace, the Hague, on June 26th, 1920.

BARON DESCAMPS in the chair.

Present: all members of the Committee (with the exception of M. Bevilaqua); Mr. James Brown Scott; the private secretaries of Baron Descamps and of M. Adatci; the members of the Secretariat. M. Fernandes was present during the last part of the meeting.

The meeting opened at 9.30 a.m.

The PRESIDENT proposed to the Committee to open the discussion on the question put on the Agenda at the preceding meeting: "what States may appear before the Court?"

The President began by stating the problem. He said that the League of Nations was open to all States. Forty-five States either have or may become Members without conditions, and all other States may enter the League on condition that they furnish certain guarantees. There is also a procedure for the cases of disputes between two States, neither or only one of which is a Member of the League. According to Article 14 of the Covenant the State or States non-members of the League are invited to assume the obligations imposed on Members, and that upon such conditions as the Council may deem just

It must be added that certain important treaties provide for certain eventualities in which the tribunals attached to the League are available without distinction, for the parties in dispute.

After the President had thus explained the general bearing of the question, he asked what solution the Committee should adopt.

He called attention to three points: 1st. Article 21 of the project of 1907, according to which the jurisdiction of the Court should extend only to contracting States. 2nd. Financial considerations. Should States who do not contribute to the expenses of the institution of the new Court be permitted to make use of it? 3rd. The German project itself, according to which only Members of the League of Nations should have the right to start proceedings to which the defendent would be bound to submit.

En résumant, le Président dit que la procédure est ouverte d'emblée à tous les Membres de la Société des Nations, et aux autres Etats en tant qu'ils sont *invités* — le Président appuie sur ce mot — sauf certains cas sporadiques déterminés dans divers traités de paix.

M. LODER dit que la difficulté surgit quand un Etat non-contractant est en cause. Il croit que l'article 17 du Pacte est conçu dans l'esprit de donner à la juridiction de la Cour toute l'extension possible. Des Etats autres que les Membres de la Société des Nations, doivent être admis bien que, naturellement, à des conditions spéciales relatives aux frais de procédure.

Au cours d'un échange de vues entre M. ADATCI et le PRESIDENT, qui insiste sur l'importance du mot „invitation" employé dans l'article 17, M. LODER exprime l'opinion qu'il faut reconnaître aux Etats qui ne sont pas Membres de la Société des Nations, le droit de procéder devant la Cour Permanente de la Société.

Le PRESIDENT répète que, selon lui, la juridiction de la Cour doit être ouverte à tous les Membres de la Société, que la Cour doit être rendue accessible, à l'aide d'une procédure spéciale, aux Etats qui ne sont pas Membres, et que, en dernier lieu, la Cour aura compétence pour des cas déterminés définis dans les traités de paix.

M. LODER croit que, dans ces conditions, il faudrait mentionner dans l'acte constitutif de la Cour, le droit pour les Etats non-membres d'avoir recours à la nouvelle juridiction, moyennant une procédure spéciale.

M. ADATCI déclare que le principe qui a présidé à l'établissement de la Société des Nations a été qu'elle serait d'abord une Société restreinte créant pour ses Membres des obligations contractuelles. Ce principe a également, malgré quelques hésitations, formé le point de départ de tous les travaux se rattachant à l'œuvre de la Conférence de Paris.

La question visée par le Président peut, selon M. Adatci, être traitée avec avantage dans deux articles différents. Le premier contiendrait des règles générales applicables, sauf stipulations contraires, aux Membres de la Société des Nations. Le second article aurait trait à la question de savoir si la Cour doit être ouverte également aux Etats qui ne sont pas Membres de la Société des Nations. M. Adatci pense que ces deux questions sont entièrement séparées.

In conclusion, the President said that the Court is open at once to all the Members of the League of Nations, and to other States only in so far as they were *invited* — the President laid emphasis on this word — except certain scattered cases defined in the Treaties of Peace.

M. LODER said that difficulty arose when a non-contracting State was concerned. He thought that Article 17 of the Covenant was drawn up with the intention of extending the jurisdiction of the Court as widely as possible. States other than Members of the League of Nations should be admitted, though of course with special conditions regarding the costs of the procedure.

In a discussion with M. ADATCI and the PRESIDENT who laid emphasis on the importance of the word "invitation" used in Article 17, M. LODER stated that he thought that the right of States who were not Members of the League of Nations to take proceedings before the Permanent Court of the League should be recognised.

The PRESIDENT repeated that in his opinion the jurisdiction of the Court should be open to all Members of the League, that the Court should be accessible to States non-members of the League, by means of a special procedure, and that lastly the Court should be competent to deal with the particular cases mentioned in the Treaties of Peace.

M. LODER thought that under these conditions special mention should be made in the constitution of the Court of the right of non-member States to have access to the new jurisdiction by means of a special procedure.

M. ADATCI stated that the principle which had governed the establishment of the League of Nations was that, in the first place, it should be a limited organisation creating conventional obligations for its Members. This principle also, in spite of some hesitation, had been the starting point of all the work connected with the work of the Conference of Paris.

The question put forward by the President, according to M. Adatci, could with advantage be dealt with in two separate articles. The first could contain general rules applicable except for contrary provisions to the Members of the League of Nations. The second article would deal with the question whether the Court should be open on equal terms to States who were not Members of the League of Nations. M. Adatci thought that these two questions were quite

Il est d'accord pour résoudre la dernière dans le sens indiqué par le Président: il croit qu'on peut ouvrir la Cour à tous les Etats, sous réserve naturellement de conditions sagement déterminées.

M. ALTAMIRA se range à l'opinion de M. Adatci.

M. HAGERUP distingue entre les trois hypothèses suivantes:

1. Il y a un différend entre deux Etats Membres de la Société des Nations.

2. Il y a un différend entre un Etat Membre et un Etat non-membre de la Société des Nations.

3. Il y a un différend entre deux Etats dont ni l'un ni l'autre n'est Membre de la Société, mais qui ont été invités par le Conseil de la Société des Nations à procéder devant la Cour.

Dans ces trois hypothèses, la Cour est ouverte aux Etats en litige; mais il y a une quatrième éventualité: celle où deux Etats qui ne sont pas Membres de la Société se mettent d'accord pour soumettre un litige à la Cour, sans être invités par le Conseil de la Société. M. Hagerup est d'avis que ce point est le seul qui reste réellement à discuter; il déclare réserver son opinion sur la solution à lui donner.

M. LODER pose la question suivante. Si deux Etats sont en conflit, ils peuvent être forcés, s'ils sont Membres, — ou invités, s'ils ne le sont pas, à procéder devant la Cour: les portes de la Cour leur sont ouvertes. Alors pourquoi fermer les portes à ces mêmes Etats, s'ils se mettent d'accord pour soumettre leur litige à la Cour?

M. DE LAPRADELLE est d'avis qu'il faut donner à l'article 17 du Pacte une interprétation très serrée. Il donne lecture de cet article. M. de Lapradelle estime que, lorsque les deux parties dans un litige sont d'accord pour soumettre leur différend à la Cour, le conflit a cessé d'exister. En tout cas, toute cause de trouble entre les Membres de la Société des Nations a disparu.

M. de Lapradelle trouve que cette interprétation est corroborée par l'article 14, lorsqu'il dit que tous les litiges que les parties sont d'accord à porter devant la Cour, doivent être tranchés par celle-ci. Il pense qu'il faut étendre le domaine de la juridiction internationale; il faut attirer les plaideurs au lieu de les repousser.

M. de Lapradelle estime cependant qu'il y a une complication: quelle influence y a-t-il lieu de donner aux Etats non-membres de la Société des Nations, sur la composition de la Cour? Il rappelle la discussion sur la présence

separate. He agreed to the solution of the latter on the lines indicated by the President. He thought that the Court might be open to all States, but naturally, under certain well established conditions.

M. ALTAMIRA agreed with M. Adatci.

M. HAGERUP drew a distinction between the three following hypotheses:

1. A dispute between two States Members of the League of Nations.

2. A dispute between a Member State and a non-member of the League of Nations.

3. A dispute between two States, neither of which is a Member of the League of Nations, but which have been invited by the Council of the League to come before the Court.

The Court is open to contesting States in all these three cases; but there is a fourth possibility: that of two States not Members of the League agreeing to submit a case to the Court without an invitation to do so from the Council of the League. M. Hagerup thought that this point was the only one really left to discuss. He said he reserved his opinion as to the solution of it.

M. LODER put the following question: If two States were concerned in a dispute, if Members, they may be compelled, if non-members, they may be invited to come before the Court: the doors of the Court are open to them; why then shut these doors to the same States if they agree to submit their disputes to the Court?

M. DE LAPRADELLE was of the opinion that Article 17 of the Covenant must be given a very strict interpretation. He read this Article. He thought that when two parties in any dispute were agreed to submit the case to the Court, the dispute had ceased to exist. In any case, all cause for concern among Members of the League of Nations had disappeared.

M. de Lapradelle thought that his interpretation was confirmed by Article 14; this article says that all cases which the parties agreed to bring before the Court should be decided by the Court. He thought that the competence of international jurisdiction should be extended; litigants must be drawn to it and not warded off.

M. de Lapradelle thought, however, that there was a complication: what influence in the composition of the Court should be given to States not Members of the League of Nations? He recalled the discussion on the subject of the presence of national judges (or assessors) in

de juges (ou assesseurs) nationaux à la Cour. Pour lui il est clair que si un Etat vient devant la Cour sans y être obligé ou invité, il a accepté par là même la composition de la Cour telle qu'elle est. Donner à un Etat qui n'est pas Membre de la Société le droit d'avoir quelque influence sur cette composition, serait lui donner un droit de Membre, ce qui n'est pas à recommander.

the Court. It was clear to him that a State that came before the Court without being forced or invited to do so, had accepted by this action the existing composition of the Court. To give a State not a Member of the League the right of exerting an influence on the Court's composition would be to give it the right of a Member; this would not be advisable.

LORD PHILLIMORE fait siens les motifs aussi bien que les conclusions de M. Adatci. La Cour dont on est en train de préparer l'organisation, sera établie par un contrat. En premier lieu elle doit donc être ouverte aux parties contractantes, mais celles-ci peuvent, s'ils y trouvent avantage, ouvrir la Cour à d'autres Etats. Le but pratique de l'établissement de la Cour est de prévenir la guerre: pour l'atteindre, il est désirable de donner accès à la Cour au plus grand nombre d'Etats possible. Il n'y a qu'une objection à faire: la question des frais qu'entraînera l'établissement de la Cour; mais cette question est trop peu importante pour être prise en considération.

Lord Phillimore se range à l'avis de M. de Lapradelle, selon lequel une partie qui n'est pas Membre de la Société des Nations, mais qui désire avoir recours à la Cour, doit accepter la Cour telle qu'elle se trouve composée. Mais la question se pose encore dans le cas d'un Etat non-membre de la Société cité devant la Cour par un Etat-Membre.

Il pourra d'ailleurs arriver qu'un Etat non-membre se trouve avoir parmi les membres de la Cour, un de ses ressortissants qui y sera entré à cause de son mérite personnel, ou pour d'autres raisons. Lord Phillimore pense, par exemple, aux Etats-Unis d'Amérique.

M. DE LAPRADELLE n'est pas de cet avis. Il croit que, pour le moment, un juge des Etats-Unis devrait être exclu.

LORD PHILLIMORE, après beaucoup d'hésitations, est arrivé à cette conclusion qu'il faut ouvrir à deux battants les portes de la Cour aux non-membres, aussi bien qu'aux Membres de la Société des Nations, sous la seule réserve qu'il vient d'indiquer.

Au cours d'un échange de vues avec le PRESIDENT, LORD PHILLIMORE déclare qu'il ne fait aucune différence pour le cas où un Etat-Membre de la Société serait assigné par un Etat non-membre.

Mr. ROOT se rallie à l'opinion de M. Adatci et des orateurs qui l'ont suivi. Il pense que le but

LORD PHILLIMORE agreed with M. Adatci both in regard to his motives and his conclusions. The Court in process of organisation will be established by a contract. It must therefore in the first place be open to the contracting parties, but these, if they find it to their advantage, may open the Court to other States. The practical end of the establishment of the Court is the prevention of War; to achieve this end it is desirable to give access to the Court to the largest possible number of States. There was only one objection to this: the question of expenses which the establishment of the Court involves, but this question is of too little importance to be considered.

Lord Phillimore agreed with M. de Lapradelle that a party not a Member of the League of Nations, but desiring recourse to the Court, should accept the Court as it is. The question, however, presents itself again in the case of a State not a Member of the League, being summoned before the Court by a Member.

It might happen that a State not a Member of the League might have among the members of the Court one of its subjects who was there by reason of personal merit, or for other reasons. Lord Phillimore thought of the United States of America as an example.

M. DE LAPRADELLE did not agree. He thought that for the time being a judge from the United States should be excluded.

LORD PHILLIMORE after much hesitation reached the conclusion that the doors of the Court must be wide open to non-members as well as to Members of the League of Nations, under the sole condition which he had just indicated.

In an exchange of views with the PRESIDENT, LORD PHILLIMORE stated that he made no distinction for the case in which a Member State of the League was summoned by a non-member State.

Mr. ROOT agreed with M. Adatci and the speakers who had followed him. He thought that

de la Société des Nations n'est pas simplement de prévenir les guerres entre les Membres, mais plus généralement d'empêcher la guerre. Une nation qui fermerait ses Cours aux étrangers serait avec raison considérée comme une nation fermée aux principes du droit international. Il incline donc à déférer à la Cour tous les différends internationaux, quels que soient les Etats intéressés.

M. RICCI-BUSATTI pense que l'accès de tous les Etats à la Cour est conforme à l'esprit de l'article 17 du Pacte. Il attire l'attention sur le dernier alinéa de cet article, aux termes duquel le rôle du Conseil pour le règlement d'un conflit n'est pas fini lorsqu'un Etat non-membre de la Société des Nations refuse d'accepter l'invitation qui lui a été adressée. Le devoir du Conseil est, en effet, d'assurer la Paix en toutes circonstances et à tout prix.

M. Ricci-Busatti se range à cet égard à l'avis de Mr. Root: or, le meilleur moyen d'atteindre ce but est d'étendre, autant que possible, la juridiction de la Société, même aux Etats qui n'en font pas encore partie.

Il est cependant nécessaire de poser des conditions à deux points de vue:

1. Il faut, pour donner du prestige aux jugements, s'assurer la garantie qu'ils seront observés par les Etats.

2. Il faut régler la question des frais; il ne serait pas juste que les Etats étrangers à la Société puissent profiter gratuitement de la Cour. L'article 17 du Pacte prévoit des conditions de ce genre lorsqu'il parle d'une invitation à adresser aux dits Etats.

M. Ricci-Busatti croit que le statut de la Cour doit contenir des règles au sujet du recours volontaire d'Etats qui ne sont pas Membres de la Société des Nations, ce point étant laissé ouvert par l'article 17.

M. Ricci-Busatti se range pour l'ensemble à l'avis de M. de Lapradelle. Il doit cependant faire une réserve: la composition de la Cour concerne l'intérêt de la justice, plutôt que celui des parties: si l'on pense qu'une représentation des parties au sein de la Cour, sous une forme quelconque, est nécessaire ou recommandable lorsqu'il s'agit d'Etats Membres de la Société, on doit accorder les mêmes droits aux Etats qui ne sont pas Membres.

Le PRESIDENT croit que la discussion sur la première question à l'ordre du jour peut être considérée comme close.

Répondant à Lord Phillimore, il déclare réserver son opinion sur la solution à donner à

the object of the League of Nations was not merely to prevent wars between Members, but more generally to stop War. The nation which closes its courts to foreigners should be considered rightly as a nation opposed to the principles of international law. Therefore, he was disposed to leave to the Court all international disputes, no matter which States were concerned in them.

M. RICCI-BUSATTI thought that the granting of access to all States would coincide with the spirit of Article 17 of the Covenant. He drew attention to the last paragraph of this Article according to which the rôle of the Council in the settlement of a dispute did not end when a State, not a Member of the League of Nations, refused to comply with the invitation addressed to it. The duty of the Council in fact was to assure Peace in all circumstances and at any cost.

On this point M. Ricci-Busatti agreed with the opinion of Mr. Root. The best means of attaining this end is to extend the jurisdiction of the League of Nations as much as possible, even to States which do not yet belong to it.

It is necessary, however, to impose conditions for two purposes:

1. To give prestige to the judgments, guaranties must be provided that they be respected by the States.

2. The question of expenses must be dealt with; it would not be fair that States not belonging to the League should be able to make use of the Court free of cost; Article 17 of the Covenant provides for conditions of this nature when it deals with an invitation to be addressed to the said States.

M. Ricci-Busatti thought that the statute of the Court should contain rules governing voluntary use of the Court by States not Members of the League of Nations, this point being left open by Article 17.

M. Ricci-Busatti agreed in general with M. de Lapradelle. However, he had to make one reservation: the composition of the Court affects rather the interests of justice than those of the contesting parties; if it were considered necessary or advisable that the contesting parties should be represented in some way on the Court in cases concerning Member States of the League, the same rights should be granted to States which are not Members.

The PRESIDENT thought that the discussion on the first question of the Agenda could be considered as closed.

Answering Lord Phillimore, he said that he reserved his opinion on the solution of

cette question. Avant de se décider, il veut examiner dans quelles conditions le texte de l'article 21 du Projet de 1907 a été voté. Il veut également se rendre compte de la compatibilité de la solution favorisée par la majorité du Comité avec l'art. 17 du Pacte.

LORD PHILLIMORE se demande s'il est vraiment nécessaire, d'attacher tant d'importance au texte de 1907; les conditions ont beaucoup changé depuis lors.

Le PRESIDENT fait observer que, si les conditions ont changé, le changement est de nature à inviter à plus de prudence encore qu'en 1907.

Le Président ouvre ensuite la discussion sur le troisième point du questionnaire: „faudrait-il l'accord des deux parties pour procéder juridictionnellement, ou l'action en justice pourrait-elle être exercée unilatéralement par un Etat contre un autre?"

Selon M. LODER, un accord entre les parties n'est pas nécessaire. On doit admettre qu'une partie a le droit de citer la partie adverse en justice sans avoir obtenu son consentement préalable; c'est justement le pas en avant qu'il faut faire, pour sortir des limites de la juridiction arbitrale.

Sur une question du Président, M. Loder explique qu'il désire la judicature obligatoire pour tous les différends.

LORD PHILLIMORE se demande comment l'interprétation de M. Loder serait compatible avec l'article 14 du Pacte. Il ne peut interpréter le mot „parties" contenu dans cet article que comme signifiant: „les deux parties".

M. HAGERUP demande la parole pour déposer une motion d'ordre. Il se demande s'il ne serait pas utile de discuter d'abord le point No. 4 du questionnaire, à savoir: „dans quelle mesure la judicature obligatoire peut-elle être admise?"

Il y a entre cette question et celle sur laquelle le Président a ouvert la discussion d'étroits rapports. M. Hagerup croit préférable de procéder d'abord à un échange de vues sur la compétence matérielle de la Cour, pour examiner ensuite si l'une des parties seulement peut soumettre un litige à l'examen de la Cour. Pour sa part, M. Hagerup pense qu'il faut interprêter l'article 14 dans le sens suivant: une partie en peut assigner une autre unilatéralement chaque fois qu'une convention a obligé les parties à reconnaître la juridiction de la Cour de Justice Internationale.

Le PRESIDENT explique l'ordre qu'il a adopté dans son questionnaire entre les diffé-

the question. Before deciding he wished to ascertain under what conditions the text of Article 21 of the Project of 1907 had been voted upon. He also wished to consider whether the solution preferred by the majority of the Committee was compatible with Article 17 of the Covenant.

LORD PHILLIMORE questioned whether it was really necessary to attach so much importance to the Project of 1907; conditions had much changed since then.

The PRESIDENT observed that if conditions had changed, the change was of such kind as to necessitate still more caution than in 1907.

The President then opened discussion of point 3 in the questionnaire: "Shall the consent of the two parties be necessary to undertake judicial proceedings or may an action in law be brought unilaterally by one State against another?"

According to M. LODER, an agreement between the parties is not necessary. The right of one party to take action against another without having obtained its previous consent, must be recognised. It was just this step forward which must be taken to pass the boundaries of arbitral jurisdiction.

In answer to a question by the President, M. Loder explained that he desired compulsory jurisdiction for all disputes.

LORD PHILLIMORE wondered whether M. Loder's interpretation was compatible with Article 14 of the Covenant. He was unable to interpret the word "parties" contained in this article otherwise than to mean "the two parties".

M. HAGERUP wanted to speak on a point of order. He asked whether it would not be advantageous to discuss the fourth point on the questionnaire first: "To what extent may obligatory jurisdiction be admitted?"

An intimate relation exists between this question and that on which the President opened the discussion. M. Hagerup thought it preferable to begin by an exchange of views on the subject of the material competence of the Court, and then to discuss whether one party only could submit a case for examination by the Court. For his part, M. Hagerup thought that Article 14 should be interpreted in the following sense: one party may summon another party unilaterally whenever a convention requires the parties to submit to the jurisdiction of the International Court of Justice.

The PRESIDENT explained the order of the different questions which he had adopted in his

rentes questions, et pourquoi il préfère s'y tenir. Pour la question de fond, le Président pense qu'il ne serait pas possible de permettre à un Etat d'en citer un autre en justice, à moins qu'il n'y ait entre eux une convention générale ou spéciale à cet effet.

M. ADATCI a toujours eu des opinions très arrêtées sur le point qu'on est en train de discuter. Le Comité est le mandataire du Conseil de la Société des Nations; il est donc lié par le texte du Pacte. A son avis, l'article 14 est clair: il borne la compétence de la Cour au cas où il y a accord entre les deux parties. Il croit que si l'on examine impartialement les articles 13 et 17 du Pacte, on se rendra compte qu'ils indiquent clairement que le Pacte ne vise que les parties prises ensemble. Cette conclusion est corroborée par l'historie du Pacte, telle qu'elle ressort des discussions de la Commission qui le prépara, à la Conférence de Paris. L'interprétation du Pacte mise à part, M. Adatci croit qu'on ne favoriserait pas le progrès en admettant la juridiction sur une initiative unilatérale: le progrès véritable ne se réalise que par degrés. Il se range donc à l'opinion du Président.

M. DE LAPRADELLE remercie M. Adatci d'avoir ramené la question sur son terrain véritable, celui de l'interprétation du Pacte. Il estime qu'une interprétation correcte ouvre la possibilité de traduire un Etat, qu'il le veuille ou non, devant la Cour. L'article 14 exige pour que la Cour soit compétente l'accord entre les parties. Si cet accord existe, la Cour est naturellement autorisée à connaître du litige.

Si l'accord n'existe pas, l'article 12 entre en jeu. En effet, si les parties n'ont pas pu se mettre d'accord pour soumettre leur litige à l'arbitrage, elles sont obligées de le porter devant le Conseil de la Société des Nations; mais si le Conseil reconnaît que la question est de la compétence de la Cour, il s'en dessaisira en faveur de la Cour, en lui demandant un avis consultatif. M. de Lapradelle reconnaît bien la différence entre la décision consultative, ainsi obtenue, et la décision délibérative, qui aurait été obtenue par un jugement, mais il croit que, dans la pratique, les deux décisions auront la même force.

LORD PHILLIMORE regrette que sa conscience de magistrat l'oblige à ne pas se ranger à l'opinion de M. Loder. Il n'a pas d'objection de principe; pour le fond il croit qu'on est d'accord. Il pense qu'il faut étendre la juridiction internationale, et que, d'une façon ou de l'autre, il faut amener les parties à porter les

questionnaire, and preferred to adhere to it. As to the point itself the President thought that it would not be possible to allow a State to call another State into Court, unless a general or special convention existed between them to this effect.

M. ADATCI had always had a very fixed opinion on the point under discussion. The Committee holds its authority from the Council of the League of Nations. It is thus bound by the text of the Covenant. In his opinion Article 14 is clear. It limits the competence of the Court to cases in which both parties agree. He thought that, if Articles 13 and 17 of the Covenant were examined impartially, it would be found that they indicated clearly that the Covenant was only intended to apply to both parties together. This conclusion is confirmed by the history of the Covenant as gathered from the discussions of the Commission which prepared it at the Paris Conference. Apart from the interpretation of the Covenant, M. Adatci thought that progress would be hindered by admitting jurisdiction over cases initiated by one party alone; real progress only is realised by degrees. Consequently he agreed with the President.

M. DE LAPRADELLE thanked M. Adatci for having brought the discussion back to its true field: the interpretation of the Covenant. He thought that a correct interpretation would allow the possibility of suing a State before the Court, whether it were willing or not. Article 14 demands agreement between the parties in order to make the Court competent. If such an agreement exists, the Court naturally is competent to deal with the case.

If no agreement exists, Article 12 comes into operation. In fact, if the parties are not able to agree to submit their case to arbitration, they are obliged to take it to the Council of the League of Nations; but if the Council finds that the question comes within the competence of the Court, it will refer it back to the Court, asking of it an advisory opinion. M. de Lapradelle fully realised the difference between the advisory opinion thus obtained and a judgment of the Court, but the thought that in practice both would have the same force.

LORD PHILLIMORE regretted that his conscience as a judge compelled him to differ with M. Loder. He did not disagree on principle; he thought that fundamentally they agreed. He thought that the international jurisdiction must be widened, and that in one way or another, parties must be induced to bring

questions juridiques devant la Cour. Il se peut que la méthode de M. de Lapradelle soit satisfaisante. Toutefois, s'il voit le but, il ne distingue pas clairement le chemin pour y arriver. On ne doit pourtant pas oublier que la compétence obligatoire de la Cour est déterminée dans des cas sporadiques par les grands traités de paix. Pour le reste, Lord Phillimore croit que la Cour possède la compétence qui lui est attribuée par l'accord des parties. Il pense qu'il serait préférable de ne rien stipuler sur les détails, mais de se borner à dire que la Cour sera compétente pour les questions que les traités en vigueur et les conventions futures lui attribuent ou attribueront. Au point de vue pratique Lord Phillimore fait ressortir la difficulté qu'il y a à déterminer l'objet du litige: il cite l'exemple de l'arbitrage pour les pêcheries de l'Atlantique. Pour cette raison, il croit qu'il serait préférable d'éviter la nécessité de conclure une Convention spéciale, ou compromis, établissant l'accord entre les parties sur la compétence de la Cour. En terminant, il suggère à nouveau l'idée de déterminer la compétence de la Cour par un simple renvoi aux traités et conventions.

M. RICCI-BUSATTI se trouve d'une façon générale d'accord avec Lord Phillimore; il désire cependant ajouter quelques considérations:

Il donne lecture d'un passage du Mémorandum préparé par la Section Juridique du Secrétariat de la Société des Nations [I: (*a*)] et dont il trouve la formule satisfaisante. En effet, bien que l'article 14 du Pacte n'admette pas la compétence sur demande unilatérale, les parties peuvent se mettre d'accord pour reconnaître cette compétence dans une Convention générale, qui pourrait peut-être avec avantage, être le statut constitutionnel de la Cour. Quelques dispositions des traités de paix admettent déjà une compétence de ce genre p. ex. les articles 336, 415 et 416 du traité de Versailles. Dans les cas visés par ces articles il ne s'agit pas évidemment d'un simple avis, mais d'un véritable jugement, rendu sur le recours de l'une des parties intéressées. M. Ricci-Busatti ne voudrait pas assimiler, cependant, comme le fait M. de Lapradelle, les avis consultatifs dont il est question dans la dernière phrase de l'art. 14 du Pacte, aux jugements proprement dits. Il ne s'agit pas, d'ailleurs, d'une disposition entièrement nouvelle dans les rapports internationaux. M. Ricci-Busatti attire l'attention sur deux traités d'arbitrage conclus par l'Italie avec la Hollande et le Danemark. Ces traités rendent non seulement l'arbitrage vraiment obligatoire mais ils contiennent des dispositions pour l'assurer, ne fût-ce que sur la demande d'une seule des parties; cela prouve encore, à son avis, qu'il

legal questions to the Court. The method suggested by M. de Lapradelle might be satisfactory. However, though he saw the object, he did not quite see the way of attaining it. At the same time it should not be forgotten that the compulsory jurisdiction of the Court is laid down for scattered cases by the main Treaties of Peace. Outside these cases, Lord Phillimore thought that the Court had the competence which the parties conferred on it by mutual agreement. He thought that it would be preferable not to specify details, but to limit themselves to saying that the Court shall be competent to deal with cases assigned to it by the treaties in force or by future conventions. From the practical point of view, Lord Phillimore pointed out the difficulty there is to define the point at issue; he quoted the case of the Atlantic Fisheries Arbitration. For this reason he thought it would be preferable to avoid the necessity for a special convention or compromise between the two parties on the competence of the Court. Finally, he again put forward the idea of defining the competence of the Court by a simple reference to treaties and conventions.

M. RICCI-BUSATTI agreed with Lord Phillimore generally speaking; however, he had some additions to make.

He read a portion of the Memorandum, prepared by the Legal Section of the Secretariat of the League of Nations. [I: (*a*)], the wording of which he found satisfactory. In fact, though Article 14 of the Covenant did not admit competence on a unilateral demand, the parties could agree to recognise such a competence by a general convention, which perhaps might very well be the constituent statute of the Court. Some provisions in the Peace Treaties admit already a competence of this kind, for example Articles 336, 415 and 416 of the Treaty of Versailles. In the cases covered by these articles, a mere legal opinion obviously was not intended, but real judgment rendered on the appeal of one of the interested parties, to the Court. M. Ricci-Busatti, however, should not wish to associate as M. de Lapradelle had done, the advisory opinion mentioned in the last paragraph of Article 14 of the Covenant with judgments in the true sense of the word. Moreover, it is not the question of a provision entirely new in international relations; M. Ricci-Busatti drew attention to two Arbitration Treaties made by Italy with Holland and Denmark. These treaties not only make arbitration truly compulsory, but they contain provisions to make ensure it on the request of only one of the parties. This again goes to prove, in his opinion, that there is

n'y a aura pas de différence essentielle entre l'arbitrage et la juridiction de la nouvelle Cour. Ces traités indiquent le chemin à suivre dans le domaine de la justice internationale.

M. HAGERUP commence par se prononcer sur la question de savoir si une partie peut unilatéralement en assigner une autre devant la Cour. En ce qui concerne les Etats non-membres de la Société des Nations, il est évident qu'une telle faculté ne peut pas exister. Le seul cas à considérer est donc celui où il s'agit d'un conflit entre deux Membres de la Société. A cet égard il y a deux éventualités à envisager: ou les Membres ont conclu une convention spéciale ou générale, ou une convention n'existe pas. Si une convention existe, une partie peut sans aucun doute en assigner une autre: le problème se réduit alors à une simple question de procédure. Pour donner un exemple de la façon dont cette question peut être résolue, M. Hagerup donne lecture, à titre de renseignement, de l'article 26 du projet des trois pays scandinaves. Si une convention à cet effet n'existe pas, on ne saurait admettre qu'une partie puisse unilatéralement assigner l'autre partie devant la Cour.

Convient-il de proposer une convention générale fixant les cas de juridiction obligatoire? Tout en réservant son opinion jusqu'au moment où il aura entendu celles de ses collègues, M. Hagerup préférerait s'en tenir aux articles du Pacte et aux traités déjà passés ou qui seront passés à l'avenir entre les Etats. Il est préoccupé surtout par l'expérience des difficultés qui se sont présentées à la Conférence de 1907, lorsqu'on a voulu déterminer les cas d'arbitrage obligatoire.

Le PRESIDENT insiste sur la question de la compétence du Comité. Il envisage le mandat donné au Comité par le Conseil de la Société, de la façon suivante: le Comité doit rédiger un projet à soumettre à la Société des Nations sur la meilleure manière d'organiser la justice internationale. Dans ces circonstances, il considère qu'il est absolument impossible d'écarter des discussions du Comité, la question de la compétence de la Cour et de la judicature obligatoire. Il croit que c'est le devoir du Comité de prendre des résolutions à ce sujet.

Pour donner satisfaction à sa conscience juridique, il soumettra lui-même un projet pour résoudre ces questions. Afin de démontrer que la compétence du Comité a été conçue d'une façon très haute et très large, le Président donne lecture d'un passage du Mémorandum du Secrétariat de la Société des Nations (VII).

En tout cas, le Président croit qu'il est impossible que le Comité se déclare incompétent

no essential difference between arbitration and the jurisdiction of the new Court. These treaties point the road to follow in the realm of international justice.

M. HAGERUP began by speaking on the question whether a party may arraign another before the Court unilaterally. In that which concerns States not Members of the League of Nations, it is evident that such a right cannot exist. Therefore the only case to be considered is that of a dispute between two Members of the League. In this connection there were two possibilities to be taken into account: either the Members have concluded a special or general convention, or such a convention does not exist. If a convention exists, one party no doubt can summon the other to appear; the problem is reduced then to a simple question of procedure. As an example of the way in which that question could be decided, M. Hagerup read Article 26 of the Project of the three Scandinavian countries. If such a convention did not exist, it could not be admitted that one party only could arraign unilaterally another party before the Court.

Ought a general convention to be proposed defining the cases of compulsory jurisdiction? He reserved his opinion until he had heard those of his colleagues. M. Hagerup said he preferred to confine himself to the articles of the Covenant, and to treaties already in force, or future treaties. His experience with the difficulties which arose at the Conference of 1907 when it attempted to define cases in which arbitration should be compulsory had a great weight with him.

The PRESIDENT insisted on the question of the powers of the Committee. He considered the mandate given to the Committee by the Council of the League to be as follows: the Committee should draft a project for submission to the League of Nations stating the best methods of organising international justice. In these circumstances he thought it was quite impossible to leave the question of the competence of the Court and compulsory jurisdiction out of the discussion of the Committee. He thought that it was the Committee's duty to pass resolutions on this subject.

To satisfy his own legal conscience, he would himself submit a proposed solution for these questions. In order to show that the powers of the Committee had been understood as being very extensive, the President read part of the Memorandum of the Secretariat of the League of Nations (VII).

In any case, the President thought it was

pour discuter une question qui a déjà été en partie résolue en 1907. On a reconnu alors unanimement le principe de l'arbitrage obligatoire et on a reconnu aussi que certains différends sont de nature à pouvoir être résolus sans réserve par la voie judicaire. Si le Comité n'essayait pas d'arriver à une décision ferme sur ces points il manquerait à une partie de sa tâche. La judicature obligatoire entre deux Etats est une chose réalisée depuis longtemps: il faut aujourdhui aller plus loin et rechercher dans quelle mesure peut être réalisée la judicature obligatoire entre tous les Etats. C'est ce que l'on attend du Comité.

M. HAGERUP donne lecture de l'article 13 du Pacte. Il remarque que le progrès que le Président estime qu'il convient de faire faire à l'œuvre de 1907 se trouve déjà réalisé dans cet article, où il ne s'agit pas d'un simple vœu, mais où sont énumérés les cas où les parties seront tenues d'avoir recours à la judicature. Pour le moment, on ne peut pas aller plus loin. Si c'est une convention générale qu'on désire, on la trouve justement dans l'art. 13 du Pacte. M. Hagerup n'est pas en désaccord avec le Président quant au fond, mais il pense que, même si le Comité réussissait à se mettre d'accord sur une liste de cas de juridiction obligatoire, on ne pourrait jamais rallier à cette liste la totalité des Etats représentés à l'Assemblée.

M. ADATCI croit qu'il faut bien se rendre compte de la portée exacte de la seconde phrase de l'article 14 du Pacte. L'interprétation adoptée par le Comité devrait être insérée dans un article.

Si cela est impossible, M. Adatci peut se rallier à l'avis de Lord Phillimore.

S'appuyant toujours sur la seconde partie de l'article 14, M. Adatci persiste à penser que la Cour n'est compétente qu'en vertu d'un accord préalable entre les parties: un Etat ne peut s'adresser à la Cour sans s'appuyer sur une convention générale ou spéciale à cet effet.

Cependant M. Adatci voudrait bien étudier de plus près les idées du Baron Descamps qu'il trouve justes et intéressantes. La question de la compétence est à son avis aussi importante que celle de la nomination des juges; il croit qu'il serait nécessaire de fixer unanimement une définition exacte de la compétence de la Cour.

impossible for the Committee to declare that it was unable to discuss a question which had already been partly settled in 1907. In that year, the principle of compulsory arbitration had been unanimously accepted, and it was recognised also that certain disputes were of such a nature that they could always be settled, without reserve, by legal methods. If the Committee does not try to reach a definite decision on these points, they would fail in a part of their task. Compulsory jurisdiction between two States had been recognised for a long time. Now a further step must be taken. It must be found out to what extent compulsory jurisdiction may be realised among all States. That is what is expected of the Committee.

M. HAGERUP read article 13 of the Covenant. He pointed out that the new step from the work of 1907 which the President thought the Committee should take was already taken by this article, where a mere expression of opinion is no longer concerned, but where is enumerated a list of cases which the parties are bound to submit to trial. For the time being it is impossible to go further. If it is a general convention which is desired, exactly that is found in Article 13 of the Covenant. M. Hagerup was not fundamentally opposed to the President, but he thought that even if the Committee should succeed in agreeing on a list of cases for obligatory jurisdiction, all the States represented in the Assembly would never be brought to accept this list.

M. ADATCI thought the exact meaning of the second sentence in Article 14 of the Covenant should be considered. The interpretation adopted by the Committee should be inserted in an article.

If this were impossible, M. Adatci could agree with Lord Phillimore.

Using always as his authority the second part of Article 14, M. Adatci persisted in believing that the Court was not competent except by virtue of a previous agreement between the parties: a State cannot appeal to the Court unless such appeal is based on a general or special convention to this effect.

However, M. Adatci wished to give closer consideration to the ideas of Baron Descamps, as he found them accurate and interesting. The question of the competence of the Court was, in his opinion, quite as important as that of the nomination of judges. He thought that it would be necessary to come to a unanimous decision concerning the exact limits to be given to the competence of the Court.

M. ALTAMIRA est également d'avis que la question qu'on est en train de discuter est de la plus haute importance. M. de Lapradelle et M. Ricci-Busatti ont prouvé que, d'après la lettre et l'esprit du Traité de Versailles, le principe de la juridiction obligatoire a été admis. L'article 13 du Pacte contient une liste de cas pour lesquels ce principe est également reconnu. Mais tout cela n'est pas suffisant, et M. Altamira croit qu'il rentre dans la mission du Comité de combler les lacunes.

Il se place au point de vue des faibles: ce sont eux qui ont besoin de la Cour; on ne peut les priver du moyen d'obtenir justice contre les forts qui se refusent à la leur accorder.

M. LODER croit que l'article 14 a voulu ouvrir la porte de la Cour à toute partie, sans qu'il y ait besoin d'un accord préalable entre elle et la partie défenderesse. A la conférence de février on a été unanime sur ces points.

Selon lui, un projet qui fermerait la Cour aux Etats lorsqu'il n'y a pas entre eux un accord préalable ne serait pas accepté par l'Assemblée de la Société des Nations.

Le PRESIDENT constate que M. Loder veut introduire une judicature obligatoire indépendamment de toute convention.

M. HAGERUP demande si M. Loder maintiendrait ce point de vue même lorsque la partie demanderesse n'est pas Membre de la Société des Nations.

M. LODER répond par la négative.

M. HAGERUP fait alors observer que les Membres de la Société sont en effet liés par une convention générale, le Pacte de la Société des Nations.

Mr. ROOT fait valoir que le progrès ne se fait que pas à pas. Il croit que le Comité se trouve placé devant la question suivante: le temps est-il venu de faire un nouveau pas en avant? Le principe de l'arbitrage obligatoire a été accepté en 1907, et dans de nombreux traités conclus depuis lors entre les Etats. Dans les traités en question on a cependant fait des réserves, pour des questions relatives à l'honneur, à l'indépendance et aux intérêts vitaux des Etats; il pense toutefois que ces réserves ont été dictées par la prudence plutôt que par la nécessité. La formule adoptée dans l'article 13 du Pacte est le résultat de discussions poursuivies depuis longtemps par des jurisconsultes d'un

M. ALTAMIRA also thought that the question under discussion was of the highest importance. M. de Lapradelle and M. Ricci-Busatti had proved that the principle of compulsory jurisdiction was recognised in both the letter and the spirit by the Treaty of Versailles. Art. 13 of the Covenant contains a list of cases in which this principle also is recognised. This, however, is not enough, and M. Altamira thought that it was part of the duty of the Committee to fill up the gaps.

He considered the question from the point of view of the weak. They are the ones who need the Court. They must not be deprived of the means of obtaining justice against the strong who refuse to grant it to them.

M. LODER thought that Art. 14 was intended to open the doors of the Court to any party without any previous consent between it and the defendant party. At the Conference of February a unanimous decision was reached on these points.

According to him, a project which closed the Court to States when no previous agreement existed between them would not be accepted by the Assembly of the League of Nations.

The PRESIDENT stated that M. Loder wished to introduce a compulsory jurisdiction independent of any convention.

M. HAGERUP asked if M. Loder would hold to this view even when the plaintiff was not a Member of the League of Nations.

M. LODER answered "No."

M. HAGERUP then observed that the Members of the League in fact were bound by a general convention, the Covenant of the League of Nations.

Mr. ROOT pointed out that progress could only be made a step at a time. He thought that the Committee had the following question before it: has the time come to take a new step in advance? The principle of compulsory arbitration was accepted in 1907, and has been in numerous treaties ratified between States since that time. In the treaties in question, however, reservations have been made for questions concerning honour, independence, and vital interests of States. He thought, however, that these reservations had been dictated rather by prudence than by necessity. The wording adopted in Article 13 of the Covenant was the result of prolonged discussions between jurisconsults from

grand nombre de pays. La généralisation du principe contenu dans les divers traités d'arbitrage ne constituerait donc pas un très grand progrès, d'abord en considération du grand nombre d'Etats qui, dans les traités conclus par eux, se sont déclarés disposés à soumettre à l'arbitrage les questions de droit. Mais il y a encore une autre raison. Les articles 12 et 13 du Pacte créent pour les Membres de la Société l'obligation de soumettre leurs différends à la judicature et au Conseil. Le Conseil n'est pas dans l'obligation morale d'appliquer les principes de droit; il agit d'après des principes d'opportunité politique. Mais ces principes se prêtent mal à la solution de différends d'ordre juridique. Or il ne faut pas laisser à une nation qui en a lésé une autre, l'option entre la solution juridique et la solution politique du conflit. L'espoir du monde repose sur la réalisation de l'empire du droit. La création d'institutions à cet effet contient le germe d'un développement futur. Les décisions légales s'appuient sur les décisions antérieures du même ordre; c'est ainsi que le progrès est possible. Le monde sera accoutumé à agir selon le droit. Il n'en est pas de même des décisions du Conseil. Le Comité doit donc tâcher d'obtenir l'accord des nations sur une disposition aux termes de laquelle toute question dépendant de l'interprétation d'un contrat ou des principes du droit, doit être résolue par la voie judiciaire; la faculté de choisir entre la voie judiciaire et la décision du Conseil ne serait laissée que pour les questions d'ordre politique. Cette disposition devrait être accompagnée d'une recommandation au Conseil et à l'Assemblée de faire continuer, dans le plus bref délai, le travail des Conférences de la Paix. Une nouvelle conférence de droit international doit être convoquée le plus tôt possible; elle aurait pour tâche d'examiner quelles sont actuellement les règles du droit international. La conférence devrait avoir des sessions périodiques.

Si cette idée pouvait se réaliser, la Cour appliquerait, non seulement des principes généraux, mais du droit positif: le Comité aurait créé une institution dont la valeur s'accroîtrait de plus en plus au cours des siècles. Les décisions de la Cour seront un frein à l'exercice incontrôlé du pouvoir politique; et c'est bien cela qui rend si singulièrement important le développement du droit et son avènement comme le principe qui doit régir l'activité des hommes. Mr. Root ajoute que l'article 21 du projet des Cinq Puissances dont il donne lecture, a toute sa sympathie.

a large number of countries. The generalisation of a principle contained in various arbitration-treaties would not constitute, therefore, a very great advance, because of the large number of States who in treaties concluded by themselves had declared that they were disposed to submit questions of law to arbitration. But there is also another reason. Articles 12 and 13 of the Covenant create the obligation for Members of the League to submit their disputes to trial or to the Council. The Council is not under the honourable obligation to apply principles of law; it follows rather the principles of political expediency. These principles are not suitable for the settlement of differences of a legal nature. However, the choice between a judicial settlement and a political settlement of the dispute should not be given to a nation which had injured another. The hopes of the world rested upon the realisation of the rule of law. The creation of institutions with this object contains the germ of future development. Legal decisions based on previous decisions of the same kind, it is this way that progress is possible. The world would become accustomed to act according to law. This does not apply to decisions taken by the Council. The Committee therefore should try to induce the nations to agree to a provision by which every question relating to the interpretation of a contract or a principle of law must be settled by judicial means; the choice between a judicial procedure and the decision of the Council should only be possible in cases of a political nature. This disposition should be accompanied by a recommendation to the Council and to the Assembly to the effect that the work of the Hague Peace Conferences should be continued with the least possible delay. A new Conference on international law should be called together as soon as possible; it would have the task of examining what actually are the rules of international law. The Conference should meet periodically.

If this idea could be realised, the Court would apply not only general principles but positive law: the Committee would have created an institution whose value would increase more and more throughout the centuries. The decision of the Court would act as a brake upon the uncontrolled use of political powers; it is just this point which makes so singularly important the development of justice and its coming as the principle which must govern the activity of men. Mr. Root added that Article 21 of the project of the Five Powers, which he read, met with his entire approval.

M. HAGERUP se demande si Mr. Root s'est rendu compte que cet article est en somme identique à l'article 13 du Pacte.

Le PRESIDENT souligne la nécessité de réaliser un progrès en matière de judicature obligatoire: les peuples l'attendent. En 1907 déjà on a reconnu le principe de l'arbitrage obligatoire. Il est maintenant du devoir du Comité de réaliser ce principe. Il ne faut pas abandonner cette tâche parce que certains articles du Pacte, qui peuvent d'ailleurs être revisés, prêtent à équivoque.

Mr. ROOT est d'avis que l'article 21 du projet des Cinq Puissances ne fait que reprendre la définition de l'article 13 du Pacte.

M. HAGERUP se rallie à l'idée émise par Mr. Root de demander la convocation d'une nouvelle conférence de droit international. Une organisation permanente de ces conférences a été proposée dans le projet commun des commissions des trois pays du Nord.

M. RICCI-BUSATTI ne croit pas s'écarter des idées de Mr. Root et de M. Hagerup en proposant l'insertion dans le projet du Comité, d'une interprétation des articles dont il s'agit, de nature à renforcer les obligations qui en découlent dans le sens du recours obligatoire à la justice internationale, sans empiéter toutefois sur les attributions de la future conférence de droit international.

M. ADATCI rappelle que le Comité a un mandat de la Société des Nations qu'il ne doit pas dépasser. On est libre d'exprimer des vœux, mais en formulant un projet, il faut se tenir à l'interprétation exacte du Pacte. Il maintient cette opinion bien qu'étant, quant au fond, du même avis que Mr. Root et M. Hagerup.

Le PRESIDENT dit que le Comité ne se trouve pas devant une table rase; sa tâche est de travailler en tenant compte des conventions existantes, ainsi que de l'œuvre des Conférences de La Haye qui ont eu lieu précédemment.

LORD PHILLIMORE déclare partager l'avis de Mr. Root.

Suit une discussion sur la question de savoir si Mr. Root a voulu dire que l'article 21 du projet des Cinq Puissances peut être inséré dans le Pacte. Mr. ROOT dit qu'il pense qu'il faut s'en tenir à cette interprétation et ne pas aller plus loin.

Pour lui, il ne s'agit pas de la compétence du Comité, mais de la compétence du Conseil et

M. HAGERUP asked whether Mr. Root had considered the fact that this Article as a whole is identical with Article 13 of the Covenant.

The PRESIDENT emphasised the necessity of making progress in the matter of compulsory jurisdiction: the nations are waiting for it. As early as 1907 the principle of compulsory arbitration was recognised. It was now the duty of the Committee to realise this principle. They must not neglect this duty because certain articles of the Covenant, which furthermore may be revised, have a doubtful meaning.

Mr. ROOT was of the opinion that Art. 21 of the project of the Five Powers only adopted the definition in Article 13 of the Covenant.

M. HAGERUP agreed with Mr. Root's idea that a new Conference of international law should be called. A permanent organisation of this Conference had been proposed in the joint plan of the Commissions from the three Northern Countries.

M. RICCI-BUSATTI did not think that he was going contrary to the ideas of Mr. Root and M. Hagerup in proposing the insertion in the Committee's project of an interpretation of the Articles concerned, such that the obligations arising out of them in regard to compulsory jurisdiction would be strengthened, without, however, encroaching on the functions of the future Conference of international law.

M. ADATCI recalled that the Committee had a mandate from the League of Nations, which must not be exceeded. Recommendations might be passed but in drafting a plan; the exact interpretation of the Covenant must be followed. He held to this opinion although fundamentally he agreed with M. Hagerup and Mr. Root.

The PRESIDENT said that the Committee was not confronted by a *tabula rasa*; its task must be carried out with due consideration to existing conventions and to the work done by the Hague Conferences which have already been held.

LORD PHILLIMORE declared that he agreed with Mr. Root.

A discussion followed as to whether Mr. Root intended to say that Article 21 of the project of the Five Powers might be inserted in the Covenant. Mr. ROOT thought that they must adhere to this interpretation and not go further.

He was not concerned with the question of the Committee's competence but with the competence of the Council and the Assembly. If

de l'Assemblée. Si ces deux organes ont le pouvoir de créer la judicature obligatoire dans le cadre du Pacte, qu'ils le fassent; si non, ils peuvent s'adresser aux Etats, leurs mandants, pour obtenir ce pouvoir. Le Comité peut leur recommander l'établissement du recours obligatoire à la juridiction internationale, et en même temps leur proposer de se procurer, si nécessaire, les pouvoirs requis pour réaliser ce progrès.

M. ADATCI se rallie à l'avis de Mr. Root; le Comité pourra, s'il le veut, exprimer un vœu demandant la modification de l'article 14 du Pacte, mais n'étant chargé que de rédiger un projet pour l'établissement de la nouvelle Cour, il n'est pas autorisé à proposer des modifications au Pacte.

Mr. ROOT ajoute qu'il croit inévitable une révision du Pacte. Dans ce cas l'introduction d'une disposition interprétant l'art. 14 pourrait faire partie de la révision.

M. ALTAMIRA déclare qu'il ne peut pas partager l'opinion de M. Adatci. Les membres du Comité n'ont pas reçu de mandat. Ils sont absolument libres d'interpréter les articles du Pacte et de faire des recommandations à cet égard.

M. ADATCI maintient que le mandat du Comité est limité par les dispositions du Pacte de la Société des Nations.

Le PRESIDENT répond que le Comité n'a pas les mains liées par certains actes: aussi a-t-il l'intention de déposer une proposition sur la question qui a formé l'objet de la discussion au cours de cette séancce.

On décide que la séance prochaine aura lieu le mardi 29 à 3 heures de l'après-midi. Au cours de cette séance, on reprendra, après avoir épuisé la question de la compétence de la Cour, celle de la nomination des juges.

La séance est levée à 12.30 de l'après-midi.

Le Président:
(signé) Brn. DESCAMPS.

Le Secrétaire-Général:
(signé) D. ANZILOTTI.

these two organs had the power to create compulsory jurisdiction under the terms of the Covenant, let them do it; if not, they could apply to the States from whom they had received their mandate, to receive such power. The Committee could recommend the establishment of compulsory recourse to international jurisdiction, and at the same time it could suggest that, if necessary, the powers required for the realisation of this progress be given.

M. ADATCI agreed with Mr. Root that the Committee could, if it wished, make a recommendation that Article 14 of the Covenant should be modified, but as it is instructed only to draft a project for the establishment of the new Court, it is not authorised to propose modifications of the Covenant.

Mr. ROOT added that he thought a revision of the Covenant was inevitable. In such a case the introduction of a provision interpreting the meaning of Article 14 might form part of the revision.

M. ALTAMIRA declared that he could not agree with M. Adatci. The members of the Committee had not received mandates. They were absolutely free to interpret the articles of the Covenant and to make any recommendations in this connection.

M. ADATCI maintained that the mandate of the Committee was limited by the provisions contained in the Covenant of the League of Nations.

The PRESIDENT answered that the Committee had not its hands tied by certain documents. He consequently intended to submit a proposal on the question under discussion.

It was decided that the next meeting should take place on Tuesday 29th at 3 p.m. At this meeting, after completing the discussion on the subject of the competence of the Court, the question of the appointment of judges would be further dealt with.

The meeting closed at 12.30 p.m.

The President:
(signed) Brn. DESCAMPS.

The Secretary-General:
(signed) D. ANZILOTTI.

11IÈME SÉANCE (non-publique), tenue au Palais de la Paix, à La Haye, le 29 juin 1920.

Présidence de M. le BARON DESCAMPS.

Sont présents: tous les membres du Comité (à l'exception de M. Bevilaqua et M. de Lapradelle); M. Fernandes; Mr. James Brown Scott; les secrétaires particuliers de M. le Baron Descamps et de M. Adatci; les membres du Secrétariat.

La séance est ouverte à 3.10 h. de l'après-midi.

Le PRESIDENT dit qu'on va consacrer encore cette séance à l'examen de la question de la judicature obligatoire, et plus particulièrement à la question de savoir dans quelle mesure il convient de la régler dans le projet du Comité. Certaines propositions ou déclarations ont été introduites par écrit, mais le temps a manqué aux membres pour en prendre connaissance. Le Président croit cependant que les membres qui ont déposé des propositions pourront opportunément développer leur thèse; il donnera à cet effet la parole d'abord à M. Loder, puis à Lord Phillimore.

M. LODER donne lecture de la déclaration qu'il a fait communiquer aux membres par les soins du Secrétariat (voir Annexe 1).

Le PRESIDENT fait une remarque d'ordre général: il constate que le Comité se trouve, pour le moment, en présence de deux questions différentes:

1. Le Comité peut-il se prononcer sur l'introduction d'une action en justice demandée par une seule des parties?

2. Est-ce qu'une judicature de cet ordre est prévue dans le Pacte?

Il semble que quelques membres se soient lancés à ce sujet dans un débat d'orthodoxie juridique extrême; il ne faut pas oublier que le seul mandat du Comité est la recherche de la meilleure solution. On a voulu interpréter les articles 13 et 14 du Pacte de façon à lier les mains au Comité; mais le Comité n'a pas été convoqué pour interpréter le Pacte d'une façon restrictive. Cela est si vrai que le Comité est expressément invité, pour l'accomplissement de sa tâche, à tenir

11TH MEETING (Private), held at the Peace Palace, the Hague, on June 29th, 1920.

BARON DESCAMPS in the chair.

Present: all members of the Committee (with the exception of M. Bevilaqua and M. de Lapradelle); M. Fernandes; Mr. James Brown Scott; the private secretaries of Baron Descamps and of M. Adatci; the members of the Secretariat.

The meeting opened at 3.10 p.m.

The PRESIDENT said that this meeting also would be devoted to the consideration of the question of compulsory jurisdiction, and more particularly to the question to what degree it was desirable to provide for it in the Committee's plan. Certain proposals or statements have been submitted in writing, but the members have not had time to study them. The President thought, however, that the members who had submitted these proposals might profitably explain their plans; he therefore was to call upon M. Loder first of all, and then Lord Phillimore.

M. LODER read the statement which he had communicated to the members through the Secretariat (see Annex 1).

The PRESIDENT made a general remark: he said that the Committee was confronted at present by two different questions:

1. Has the Committee the power to decide on the bringing of judicial suit by only one of the parties?

2. Is an action of this nature provided for in the Covenant?

It appears that some members have engaged in a debate of legal orthodoxy on this subject. It must not be forgotten that the only instruction to the Committee is to find the best solution. It has been desired to interpret Articles 13 and 14 of the Covenant in such a way as to tie the hands of the Committee, but the Committee had not been called together for the purpose of interpreting the Treaty narrowly. This is so true that the Committee expressly is

compte des projets antérieurs. Si le Comité perd de vue l'œuvre de 1899 et de 1907, il n'aboutira pas. Le Président se demande si le Comité doit faire œuvre d'interprétation étroite ou créer une Cour Permanente. La réponse est d'autant plus facile que le Pacte qu'on veut interpréter de la façon la plus restrictive est peut-être sur le point d'être revisé. A quoi bon, dès lors, lier étroitement le travail du Comité à de telles interprétations? Le Président a tenu à faire cette observation parce qu'il estime qu'elle domine le débat.

S'adressant à M. Loder il lui dit: Puisque nous ne sommes pas limitativement astreints, il semble superflu de rechercher si le Pacte comporte ou non une interprétation plus ou moins large. Mais en supposant que M. Loder réussisse à démontrer que le droit d'assigner unilatéralement son adversaire devant la Cour est compatible avec les termes du Pacte, il restera toujours à se demander s'il y a lieu d'admettre ce droit. C'est aller fort loin en droit international que de vouloir créer le droit pour une partie d'en assigner n'importe quelle autre dans n'importe quel litige, sans aucun assentiment exprès ou tacite, mais en tout cas réel, de cette partie.

M. HAGERUP croit que M. Loder a voulu dire qu'une partie pourra toujours assigner une autre en vertu d'une convention générale à laquelle elles auront adhéré.

M. LODER ne peut pas accepter l'interprétation de M. Hagerup; sa thèse a été exposée dans les dernières paroles du Président. On a dit que l'article 14 s'opposerait à cette thèse. Cet avis, d'après lui, repose sur une interprétation erronée du Pacte; mais il croit qu'il faut d'abord se former une opinion définitive sur la question de savoir s'il est compatible avec le Pacte de donner aux parties le droit d'assignation unilatérale; on examinera ensuite la question de l'opportunité de l'admission de ce droit.

Le PRESIDENT insiste sur le fait que le Comité a toute liberté d'interpréter le Pacte, puisqu'il n'existe pas de commentaire officiel. Dans ces conditions, le Président demande aux membres de ne point s'attacher à une interprétation étroite de l'article 14 et du Pacte en général. Autrement, le Comité n'aboutira pas au résultat qu'il doit atteindre.

invited, for the performance of its task, to take into account the previous projects. If the Committee loses sight of the work of the Conferences of 1899 and 1907 it will never succeed. The President asked whether the Committee should work on narrow interpretations or create a Permanent Court. The answer is all the more easy because the Covenant which it is wished to interpret in the narrowest way, perhaps has to be revised. What is the good, then, of restricting the work of the Committee by such an interpretation? The President thought it necessary to make these remarks because in his opinion the whole discussion was dominated by the point.

Addressing M. Loder the President said that as they were not bound by limitations, it seemed superfluous to discuss whether the Covenant permits of a more or less broad interpretation. But supposing that M. Loder succeeded in proving that the right of one party to arraign unilaterally its opponent before the Court was compatible with the terms of the Covenant, it still remains to be decided whether there is reason to admit this right. It would be a very great move in international law to create the right for one party to arraign any other party, in any case whatever, if the said party does not expressly or tacitly consent to it.

M. HAGERUP thought that M. Loder had intended to say that one party always might arraign another in virtue of a general convention to which they had both agreed.

M. LODER could not accept M. Hagerup's interpretation; his intention was as explained by the President's closing remarks. It had been said that Article 14 was in opposition to this view. He thought this was due to a misinterpretation of the Treaty, but he thought first of all a definite opinion should be reached upon the question whether it was compatible with the Covenant to give to the parties the right of unilateral arraignment; afterwards they could consider the question whether it would be opportune to admit this right.

The PRESIDENT laid stress on the fact that the Committee was quite free to interpret the Covenant since no official commentary existed. Under these conditions, the President asked the members not to adopt too narrow an interpretation on Article 14 and of the Covenant as a whole. If they did so, the Committee would never achieve the results they should.

M. LODER remarque qu'il se trouve évidemment d'accord avec le Président puisque l'interprétation qu'il a donnée de l'article 14, à savoir qu'il est compatible avec le droit pour une partie d'assigner son adversaire en justice, est bien loin d'être étroite.

Le Pacte a voulu faire un pas en avant qui consiste à rendre inutile l'accord préalable des parties, requis dans les cas d'arbitrage.

S'adressant à Lord Phillimore, M. Loder dit ne pouvoir pas se rallier au projet soumis par lui car dans ce projet (annexe 2), les articles 13 et 14 du Pacte sont mis sur le même plan, et les deux idées absolument différentes exprimées dans les deux articles s'y trouvent confondues.

Le PRESIDENT dit qu'il a simplement voulu mettre en garde, dès le début de la séance, les membres contre le danger d'une interprétation restrictive.

Il répète qu'à son avis M. Loder a voulu créer, sans aucune restriction, le droit pour une partie d'en assigner une autre en justice. Le Président entend réserver expressément son opinion à cet égard.

LORD PHILLIMORE déclare qu'à ses yeux, il est inutile de trop s'attacher à l'interprétation du Pacte, puisque indépendamment de toute interprétation, on peut arriver au même but. Il veut néanmoins observer en passant que, selon lui, l'article 14 ne peut signifier qu'une chose: l'accord des deux parties est nécessaire pour qu'une affaire puisse être portée devant la Cour.

La langue juridique anglaise ne se sert du pluriel, en parlant des parties, que pour désigner les deux parties en litige. Son interprétation se trouve corroborée par plusieurs juristes anglais et par des membres de la Section Juridique du Secrétariat de la Société des Nations.

Il croit qu'il faut bien distinguer entre le devoir que l'on a de soumettre un différend à la Cour, et le moyen par lequel cette soumission peut être opérée: l'article 13 établit l'obligation de soumettre les disputes; l'article 14 constate — il s'appuie ici sur le texte anglais — que le consentement des deux parties est nécessaire pour que la procédure puisse être entamée. Cette interprétation peut être fâcheuse; mais elle n'en est pas moins exacte.

Comme Lord Phillimore a commencé par le dire, toutes ces questions d'interprétation sont au fond sans importance: le Comité doit propo-

M. LODER said that he evidently agreed with the President, since the interpretation he had given to Article 14, namely that it does admit the right for one party to call his opponent before a Court of Justice, is far indeed from being narrow.

The Covenant was intended to mark a step forward. This step was to consist in making it unnecessary to have a previous agreement between the contesting parties as in cases of arbitration.

M. Loder, addressing Lord Phillimore, said that he could not agree with the project which the latter had submitted, since in this project (Annex 2) Articles 13 and 14 of the Covenant are put on the same plane and the two radically different ideas contained in the two Articles are confused.

The PRESIDENT said that he simply wished to warn the members from the very outset against the danger of a narrow interpretation.

He repeated that in his opinion M. Loder had wished to create the unrestricted right of one party to call another to justice. The President wished to make an express reservation in this connection.

LORD PHILLIMORE said that as he saw it, there was no need to be too much concerned with the interpretation of the Covenant, since he thought the same end could be reached quite apart from any interpretation. Nevertheless he wished to point out in passing that Article 14 could only mean one thing in his opinion: the consent of both parties is necessary before a case can be taken before the Court.

English legal phraseology uses the plural, in speaking of parties concerned in a case, only for the purpose of referring to the two contesting parties. His interpretation was confirmed by several English jurists and by members of the Legal Section of the League of Nations Secretariat.

He thought that a clear division should be drawn between the duty one has to submit a case to the Court and the means by which this submission should be carried out: Article 13 establishes the obligation of submitting disputes, Article 14 states — here he based his argument on the English text — that the consent of both parties is necessary before the case can be dealt with. This interpretation may be regrettable but it is none the less true.

As Lord Phillimore had said at the be-

ser une convention qui n'entrera en vigueur qu'avec le libre assentiment des parties, et il peut insérer dans son projet ce que bon lui semble. Le Pacte, c'est une loi pour la Société des Nations, mais la convention, d'où sortira la Cour, en sera une autre. Il sera utile cependant de marquer dans le rapport que le Comité joindra au projet qu'il doit soumettre au Conseil, les points où le projet s'écarte du Pacte; ceci pourra avoir l'avantage d'amener les Etats-Unis à donner leur adhésion à la convention, avant même d'adhérer au Pacte. Se tenant à son opinion que le Pacte et la convention seront deux lois indépendantes, Lord Phillimore déclare que, pour les Anglais, qui ne connaissent pas de différence entre lois constitutionnelles et lois ordinaires, il n'y aura pas de différence essentielle entre les deux documents.

Lord Phillimore a peur que M. Loder ne soit indigné en l'entendant exprimer ainsi son avis; il regrette que sa connaissance imparfaite du français ne lui ait pas permis de s'exprimer de façon plus courtoise, mais il est convaincu que, pour le fond, son opinion est celle des autres membres, et que M. Loder et lui arriveront au même but, mais par des voies différentes.

Ayant ainsi montré dans quel sens est conçu son projet, il en donne lecture: cette esquisse, du reste, a pour seul objet de réaliser le but même vers lequel tend M. Loder. Lecture faite, Lord Phillimore explique que les cas énumérés dans son projet (lettres *a—e*) et qui ont été empruntés au projet des Cinq Puissances, lui semblent prévoir tous les cas où la solution judiciaire peut être admise. Il ajoute que les quelques lignes qui, dans son projet, suivent l'énumération de ces cas, ont été ajoutées afin d'éviter toute équivoque et de rendre inutile tout essai d'interprétation de l'article 14.

Le PRESIDENT s'adresse à Lord Phillimore en le priant de bien vouloir préciser le sens véritable de la deuxième phrase de la note jointe à son esquisse. Le Président se demande si cette phrase n'est pas la négation même de la compétence de la Cour dans les questions d'interprétation des traités. Il se demande comment on pourra aboutir à un résultat sérieux si l'on accepte la thèse d'après laquelle la Cour devra se déclarer incompétente dès qu'une partie qui

ginning of his remarks, all these questions of interpretation fundamentally had no importance. The Committee had to propose a Convention which would come into force only with the free consent of the parties, and it might put into its project whatever seemed advisable. The Covenant is a law for the League of Nations, but the Convention establishing the Court would be another. Nevertheless, it would be useful to point out in the report, which the Committee will attach to the plan to be submitted to the Council, the respects in which the project differs from the Covenant; this might have the advantage of inducing the United States to give its adherence to the Convention even before adhering to the Covenant. Holding to his opinion, that the Covenant and the Convention would be two independent laws, Lord Phillimore said that for English people who do not recognise any difference between constitutional laws and ordinary laws, there would be no essential difference between the two documents.

Lord Phillimore was afraid that M. Loder might be offended by such an expression of his opinion. He regretted that his imperfect knowledge of French did not permit him to express himself more courteously, but he was convinced that fundamentally his opinion was the same as that of the other members, and that both he and M. Loder would arrive at the same result, though by different routes.

Having thus explained the ideas underlying his project he read it. This outline was as a matter of fact intended to achieve the same end as that to which M. Loder aspired. After reading it, Lord Phillimore explained that the cases enumerated in his project (letters a to e inclusive), which were borrowed from the project of the Five Powers, seemed to him to cover all cases in which a judicial decision would be admissible. He went on to say that the few lines in his draft which follow the enumeration of these cases had been added in order to avoid any misunderstanding and make unnecessary any attempt to interpret Article 14.

The PRESIDENT asked Lord Phillimore to be so good as to explain the real meaning of the second sentence in the note accompanying his draft. The President asked whether this sentence did not deny the competence of the Court to deal with questions concerning the interpretation of treaties. He wondered how a result with any real meaning could be reached if it were laid down that the Court must declare itself incompetent to deal with a case

s'est engagée à soumettre un litige à la Cour, se refuse de paraître devant elle.

LORD PHILLIMORE répond que, malheureusement, l'article 14 du Pacte ne donne compétence à la Cour que pour les questions que les parties lui soumettent réellement, et non pas pour les questions qu'elles se sont engagées à lui soumettre. C'est évidemment là un des défauts de l'article, et c'est justement afin d'écarter les inconvénients qui en résultent que Lord Phillimore a soumis sa proposition.

M. HAGERUP constate que, contrairement à ce qu'il avait cru lors de la dernière séance, il est vraiment nécessaire de se prononcer sur la compétence de la Cour. En effet, il faut arriver à concilier les opinions divergentes qu'ont émises les membres du Comité.

M. Hagerup se rallie, sur la question de fond, à l'avis de Mr. Root, tel qu'il se trouve exprimé dans le projet de Lord Phillimore, projet qui adopte du reste les idées du projet dit des Cinq Puissances.

M. Hagerup fait cependant observer que le projet des Cinq Puissances contient, à côté de l'article 21, un article 22, aux termes duquel les parties soumettront à la Cour, outre les cas visés à l'article 21, tous les cas prévus dans les conventions qui peuvent exister entre elles.

M. Hagerup croit que c'est une disposition de ce genre qu'a visée Lord Phillimore lorsque, dans le premier alinéa de son projet, il parle d'une convention spéciale entre les parties. M. Hagerup se demande donc si le mot „spécial" ne devrait pas être être remplacé par une expression moins restrictive.

LORD PHILLIMORE n'y voyant pas d'objection, M. HAGERUP déclare qu'il peut se rallier entièrement à la première partie de la proposition de Lord Phillimore.

Pour la seconde, M. Hagerup fait remarquer que la différence d'opinion entre Lord Phillimore et certains autres membres provient d'une différence en matière de procédure entre le droit continental et le droit anglais qui ne connaît pas les jugements par contumace.

M. Hagerup croit que, afin d'écarter la possibilité regrettable de voir une partie rendre la Cour incompétente par le seul fait qu'elle se refuserait à paraître devant celle-ci, la fin de la proposition de Lord Phillimore devrait être complétée par une disposition analogue à l'article 26 du projet commun des pays scandinaves; il donne lecture de cet article, qui a été reproduit dans le projet suédois revisé. M. Hagerup pro-

whenever a party which had bound itself to submit a case to the Court refused to appear before it.

LORD PHILLIMORE answered that unfortunately Article 14 of the Covenant only gave the Court competence to deal with questions truly submitted to it by the parties, and not with questions that they had agreed to submit to it. That was one of the evident faults of the Article, and it was precisely in order to avoid the difficulties arising out of this that Lord Phillimore had put forward his proposal.

M. HAGERUP stated that, contrary to his opinion at the last meeting, it is really necessary to decide on the competence of the Court. In fact, they must find some means of conciliating the divergent opinions expressed by the members of the Committee.

M. Hagerup agreed, on fundamental questions, with the view of Mr. Root as expressed in Lord Phillimore's proposal, which also adopts the ideas of the socalled project of the Five Powers.

M. Hagerup pointed out, however, that the project of the Five Powers contained as well as Article 21, an Article 22, according to which the parties shall submit in addition to the cases mentioned in Article 21, all cases mentioned in Conventions which may exist between them.

M. Hagerup thought that it was a disposition of this kind which was intended by Lord Phillimore in the first paragraph of his proposal, which mentions a special Convention between the parties. M. Hagerup wondered therefore whether the word "special" ought not to be replaced by a less restrictive expression.

LORD PHILLIMORE having no objection to this, M. HAGERUP said that he was able to agree entirely with the first part of Lord Phillimore's proposal.

Concerning the second part, M. Hagerup pointed out that the differences of opinion existing between Lord Phillimore and certain other members arise from the difference in matter of procedure between Continental and English law, English law knowing no judgments by default.

M. Hagerup thought that in order to avoid the possibility of having one party render the Court incompetent by merely refusing to appear before it, the end of Lord Phillimore's draft proposal should be completed by a disposition similar to Article 26 of the Joint project of the Scandinavian States. He read this Article, which was reproduced in the revised Swedish project. M. Hagerup proposed that an addition to this

pose qu'une addition dans ce sens soit introduite dans le projet d'article présenté par Lord Phillimore. (Voir annexe 3). Sauf rédaction, et sous réserve de cet amendement, M. Hagerup peut également se rallier à la seconde partie dudit article.

Avant de terminer, M. Hagerup désire attirer l'attention sur une question d'un autre ordre. Il dit que les traités actuellement en vigueur visent seulement la Cour Permanente d'Arbitrage. Il se demande s'il ne serait pas utile d'insérer dans la convention d'où sortira la Cour une disposition générale établissant la compétence de la Cour de Justice pour un certain nombre de différends internationaux qui, si l'on s'en tenait aux termes des traités en vigueur, devraient être portés devant la Cour d'Arbitrage. Pour les Etats signataires de cette convention, cela comporterait une modification des traités d'arbitrage actuellement existants qui pourrait donner à la Cour de Justice une sphère d'activité plus étendue.

Mr. ROOT demande si M. Hagerup a l'intention de substituer la nouvelle Cour à la Cour d'Arbitrage.

M. HAGERUP répond que telle n'est pas son intention; il est parfaitement convaincu qu'il y a des cas où la juridiction de la Cour d'Arbitrage est préférable à celle de la Cour de Justice. Il voudrait cependant introduire une règle générale d'après laquelle la compétence de la Cour de Justice serait étendue, et la compétence de la Cour d'Arbitrage limitée dans une mesure correspondante.

Le PRESIDENT constate qu'il a d'autant moins l'intention de s'opposer à l'idée suggérée par M. Hagerup, qu'une disposition dans ce sens se trouve déjà insérée dans l'article 13, alinéa 3 du Pacte. Le Président croit, sauf vérification, que cette disposition a été introduite lors de la révision du projet de Pacte publié le 14 février 1919. Cette addition au projet n'a certainement pas été faite sans raison. Il remarque cependant qu'il y a une difficulté: est-ce que les gouvernements seront disposés à annuler les conventions antérieures?

M. ADATCI se demande quels sont les traités qui seront atteints par une disposition générale, établissant au lieu de la compétence de la Cour d'Arbitrage, celle de la Cour de Justice. Est-ce qu'il s'agira seulement des traités d'arbitrage? N'y en a-t-il pas d'autres qui contiennent des stipulations du même ordre?

effect should be introduced in the draft Article presented by Lord Phillimore. (See Annex 3). Except in the matter of wording and with this amendment, M. Hagerup entirely agreed also with the second part of this Article.

Before ending his remarks, M. Hagerup wished to call attention to a question of another nature. He said that treaties actually in force only referred to the Permanent Court of Arbitration. He wondered whether it would not be useful to insert in the Convention for the establishment of the new Court a general provision establishing the competence of this Court to deal with a certain number of international disputes which, if the terms of the treaties in force were adhered to, should be submitted to the Court of Arbitration. For States signatory to this Convention, this would involve a modification of arbitration treaties actually existing, which might give a wider sphere of activity to the Court of Justice.

Mr. ROOT wondered whether M. Hagerup intended to substitute the new Court for the Court of Arbitration.

M. HAGERUP answered that this was not his intention; he was quite convinced that there were cases in which the jurisdiction of the Court of Arbitration was preferable to that of the Court of Justice. He should wish, however, to introduce a general rule according to which the competence of the Court of Justice would be extended and the competence of the Court of Arbitration limited to a corresponding degree.

The PRESIDENT stated that he had no intention to oppose the idea suggested by M. Hagerup, since a disposition to the same effect already existed in Article 13, Paragraph 3 of the Covenant. The President thought, without verifying it, that this provision was introduced at the time of the revision of the Draft Covenant published on February 14, 1919. This addition to the Draft was certainly not made without reason. He pointed out, however, that there was a difficulty; would the Governments be disposed to nullify previous conventions?

M. ADATCI wondered which were the treaties to be affected by a general disposition establishing in place of the competence of the Court of Arbitration that of the Court of Justice. Were only Arbitration-Treaties concerned? Were there not others which contain stipulations of the same nature?

M. HAGERUP fait valoir que les gouvernements conservent toujours le droit de modifier les conventions conclues par eux; il croit que, dans le cas présent, ils seront tous disposés à le faire. A la question soulevée par M. Adatci, il répond que, depuis 1907, il y a peu de traités sauf les traités d'arbitrage établissant la compétence de la Cour Permanente d'Arbitrage.

Le PRESIDENT répète que, d'une façon générale, il ne voit pas d'inconvénient à ce qu'on introduise une disposition dans le sens proposé par M. Hagerup. Il fait observer que la Convention de 1907 s'est déjà engagée dans cette voie, en stipulant la compétence de la Cour Permanente d'Arbitrage dans tous les cas où les parties ne se sont pas accordées sur l'établissement d'une juridiction spéciale.

M. LODER a la parole pour répondre à la critique adressée par Lord Phillimore à sa déclaration. Il déclare qu'il ne peut que s'incliner devant l'interprétation que Lord Phillimore a donnée du texte anglais au sujet du mot „Parties", dans l'article 14 et, par conséquent, qu'il renonce à la sienne.

Mais il ajoute que si l'interprétation de Lord Phillimore est justifiée, il y a, dès lors, contradiction entre ce qui a été dit dans l'article et ce qu'on a voulu dire; or, il faut arriver à un résultat raisonnable.

M. Loder ne peut pas adopter l'article proposé par Lord Phillimore. Cet article prend comme point de départ l'article 13 du Pacte, dans lequel il n'est point question de la Cour Permanente de Justice.

M. Loder veut bien reconnaître la différence entre la jurisprudence anglaise, qui cherche à atteindre le but sans se soucier des théories, et la jurisprudence continentale. Mais le premier alinéa de la proposition de Lord Phillimore va trop loin dans cette voie. L'article 13 oblige les Membres à soumettre leurs différends à l'arbitrage; mais, en acceptant le premier alinéa de la proposition en question, on enlèverait aux parties la liberté qui leur est dûe de pouvoir s'adresser à la Cour d'Arbitrage.

LORD PHILLIMORE ne peut pas accepter cette interprétation de sa proposition; il a voulu dire seulement que la Cour de Justice serait la Cour compétente lorsqu'il n'y a pas de stipulation contraire dans une convention en vigueur. La Cour de Justice ne ferait que se substituer à la Cour d'Arbitrage comme juridiction subsidiaire.

M. HAGERUP pointed out that Governments always reserved the right of modifying conventions concluded by them. He thought that in the present case they would all be disposed to do so. To M. Adatci's question he replied that after 1907 there were few Treaties except Arbitration-Treaties establishing the competence of the Permanent Court of Arbitration.

The PRESIDENT repeated that, generally speaking, he saw no objection to the introduction of a provision to the effect suggested by M. Hagerup. He pointed out that the Convention of 1907 had already proceeded along these lines by laying down that the Permanent Court of Arbitration should be competent to deal with all cases which the parties concerned had not agreed to submit to a special jurisdiction.

M. LODER spoke in answer to the criticism of his statement made by Lord Phillimore. He said he could only accept the interpretation which Lord Phillimore had given to the English text regarding the word "parties" in Article 14, and consequently could only abandon his own.

But he added that if Lord Phillimore's interpretation was justified, there would be a contradiction between what was said in the Article, and what it had been intended to mean. However, they must try and arrive at a reasonable solution.

M. Loder could not accept the Article, proposed by Lord Phillimore. This article took as its starting point Article 13 of the Covenant in which there was no question whatever of the Permanent Court of International Justice.

M. Loder was quite prepared to recognise the difference between English jurisprudence, which sought to reach a result without being concerned with theories, and continental jurisprudence. But the first paragraph of Lord Phillimore's proposal went too far in this direction. Article 13 requires Members to submit their disputes to arbitration, but by accepting the first paragraph of the proposal in question, the liberty to which parties are entitled to appeal to the Court of Arbitration would be taken away.

LORD PHILLIMORE could not accept this interpretation of his proposal; he had only meant that the Court of Justice should be the competent authority when no stipulation to the contrary existed in a convention in force. The Court of Justice would only substitute itself for the Court of Arbitration as a subsidiary jurisdiction.

M. LODER fait valoir que l'article 13 concerne l'arbitrage et rien que l'arbitrage. Les Membres de la Société des Nations ne sont pas libres de choisir: c'est à l'arbitrage qu'ils doivent soumettre leurs litiges. Le mot „généralement" ne doit pas être pris trop sérieusement: ce n'est qu'une imprécision. M. Loder estime que son opinion se trouve corroborée par le dernier passage de l'article, par lequel les Membres de la Société s'engagent à exécuter de bonne foi les sentences rendues: s'il s'agissait en effet d'une véritable cour de justice, ces dispositions seraient superflues.

Mais si les parties sont ainsi tenues de soumettre leurs litiges à l'arbitrage, il convient de se demander quelle Cour d'arbitrage sera compétente. La réponse, c'est que la compétence appartient à la cour à laquelle les parties auront convenu de s'adresser; il n'est donc pas question de la Cour Permanente de Justice.

M. Loder pense, en effet, qu'il faut distinguer absolument entre les articles 13 et 14 et ne point se laisser égarer par l'ordre peu logique des dispositions du Pacte, où la question de l'arbitrage est reprise dans l'article 15.

Il croit que si l'on confond les deux articles on fera nécessairement une œuvre de peu de valeur, et se demande comment Lord Phillimore croit pouvoir arriver au même résultat que lui en partant d'une conception des relations entre l'arbitrage et la justice si différente de la sienne.

M. Loder reprend les remarques de M. Hagerup sur le passage de la note de Lord Phillimore, où il est dit que la Cour perdrait sa compétence si l'une des parties se refusait à paraître devant elle. Il ne croit pas qu'il soit possible de forcer la Cour à se déclarer incompétente dans ce cas, à condition qu'il existe entre les parties un engagement de soumettre le litige à la Cour.

Mr. ROOT se déclare disposé à se rallier à tout ce qui a été dit par les membres du Comité. Il considère que le Comité ne doit pas regarder de trop près les dispositions du Pacte. Les articles 12, 13 et 14 étaient, selon lui, destinés plutôt à exprimer une intention générale qu'à formuler des règles précises. Le Comité, n'étant pas chargé d'autre chose que de recommander au Conseil un projet pour l'établissement de la Cour Permanente de Justice, peut se borner à suggérer des idées en harmonie avec la tendance générale des articles en question. Si le Comité trouve que pour réaliser ces idées il est nécessaire de sortir

M. LODER pointed out that Article 13 dealt with arbitration, and nothing but arbitration. Members of the League of Nations were not free to choose; they were bound to submit their disputes to Arbitration. Too much importance must not be attached to the word "generally". It is an inaccuracy. M. Loder thought that his opinion was confirmed by the closing passage of the Article, according to which Members of the League of Nations undertake to carry out in good faith sentences pronounced; if it were a question of a real Court of Justice, this would be superfluous.

But if the parties were thus bound to submit their disputes to Arbitration, the question arises what Court of Arbitration is competent. The answer is that the court to which the parties have agreed to appeal shall be competent. There is no question, therefore, of the Permanent Court of Justice.

In fact, M. Loder thought that a clear distinction must be drawn between Article 13 and 14, and care must be taken not to be led astray by the not quite logical order of the provisions of the Covenant, in which the question of Arbitration is again taken up in Article 15.

He thought that if the two articles were confused, the work of the Committee necessarily would be of little value, and he wondered how Lord Phillimore could expect to arrive at the same result as he did, starting from a conception of the view of the relations between Arbitration and Justice so different from his.

M. Loder dealt with M. Hagerup's remarks concerning the passage in Lord Phillimore's note in which it is said that the Court would lose its competence if one of the parties refused to appear before it. He did not think it was possible to compel the Court to declare itself incompetent in this case, provided that an agreement to submit the dispute to the Court existed between the parties.

Mr. ROOT declared that he was disposed to agree with all that had been said by the members of the Committee. He considered that the Committee ought not to examine too closely the provisions of the Covenant. Articles 12, 13 and 14 were, in his opinion, intended rather to express a general intention than to formulate precise rules. As the Committee was instructed only to submit to the Council a plan for the establishment of the Permanent Court of Justice, it could limit itself to suggesting ideas in harmony with the general trend of the Articles in question. If the Committee found that to accomplish this pur-

du cadre du Pacte, il lui appartient de recommander au Conseil les mesures qui rendront possible leur réalisation. Le Comité peut faire une double recommandation: il peut recommander une certaine solution et, si cette solution dépasse le cadre du Pacte, suggérer l'idée d'une nouvelle convention créant la base nécessaire pour permettre d'adopter cette solution.

Mr. Root pense, d'une façon générale, que les rédacteurs du Pacte avaient seulement une idée générale de la situation actuelle de l'arbitrage et qu'ils ne s'étaient pas rendus compte en détail des dispositions adoptées en 1899 et 1907.

En 1907 on a obtenu trois résultats:

1. on a élargi et perfectionné les dispositions de 1899 relatives à la Cour Permanente d'Arbitrage;

2. on a adopté à l'unanimité un vœu exprimant le principe de l'arbitrage obligatoire; Mr. Root donne lecture de ce vœu;

3. on a adopté un projet de convention relatif à l'établissement d'une Cour de Justice Arbitrale; Mr. Root appuie sur le mot „justice" et donne, pour préciser le but du projet, lecture du premier article. Il fait ressortir que la Conférence de 1907 se faisait de la permanence de la Cour la même conception, que celle qui prévaut au sein du Comité, et fait également observer qu'on a d'abord eu l'intention d'appeler la Cour projetée: Haute Cour de Justice Internationale.

Mr. Root pense que les rédacteurs des articles 12, 13 et 14 du Pacte sont partis de la même conception des relations entre l'arbitrage et la juridiction judiciaire que celle qui a prévalu en 1907. Cette conception a trouvé son expression, imparfaite il est vrai, dans les articles mentionnés. Si le Comité estime que les dispositions de ces articles ne lient pas suffisamment ses membres, il devrait indiquer comment ces dispositions devraient être appliquées pour atteindre le but en vue duquel elles ont été établies.

Mr. Root veut également attirer l'attention du Comité, sans toutefois y insister, sur la question suivante: comment une seule des parties pourra-t-elle soumettre un litige à la Cour sans s'être au préalable mise d'accord à ce sujet avec la partie adverse? Il suggère l'idée que la partie demanderesse soumette à la Cour son exposé du cas; que la partie adverse lui soumette le sien, et que la décision soit laissée à la Cour, au lieu d'obliger les parties à s'accorder entre elles sur l'objet du litige, avant de la soumettre à la Cour; mais Mr. Root ne fait qu'indiquer cette question et revient à la question principale. Il déclare ne pas

pose, it was necessary to go outside the bounds of the Covenant, it should recommend to the Council the measures which would make possible its accomplishment. The Committee may make a double recommendation. It can recommend a certain solution, and if such solution goes beyond the limits of the Covenant, it may suggest the idea of a new Convention creating the necessary basis for the adoption of the solution.

Mr. Root thought that in general the framers of the Covenant had only a general idea of the present state of arbitration and that they have not taken fully into account the provisions adopted in 1899 and 1907.

In 1907 three results were accomplished:

1. The provisions of 1899 concerning the Permanent Court of Arbitration were enlarged and perfected.

2. A *vœu* embodying the principle of compulsory arbitration was adopted unanimously; Mr. Root read this.

3. A draft Convention for the establishment of a Court of arbitral Justice was adopted. Mr. Root laid emphasis on the word "justice", and to show the object of the project read its first article. He laid stress on the fact that the Conference of 1907 had the same idea of the permanence of the Court as that of the Committee, and also pointed out that the first intention had been to call the Court the High Court of International Justice.

Mr. Root thought that the framers of Articles 12, 13 and 14 of the Covenant had the same idea of the relation between arbitration and judicial jurisdiction as that which had prevailed in 1907. This idea had found expression, imperfectly it is true, in the articles mentioned. If the Committee thought that the provisions of these Articles do not bind its members sufficiently, it should point out how the provisions should be supplemented to attain the result in view of which they were established.

Mr. Root wished to call the attention of the Committee, without insisting on it, to the following question: how one party alone could submit a case to the Court without a previous agreement on the subject with the opposite party. He suggested that the plaintiff should submit its version of the case to the Court, that the defendant party should submit his, and that the decision should be left to the Court, instead of requiring the parties to agree between themselves upon the subject of the dispute before submitting it to the Court. However, Mr. Root only mentioned this question, and returned to

s'arrêter aux interprétations du Pacte présentées par Lord Phillimore et M. Loder, puisqu'il est d'accord avec eux sur la conclusion. Il désirerait qu'on évitât de s'attacher aux mots pour se borner à faire les recommandations que l'on juge utiles. Il pense que ce faisant, le Comité accomplira exactement la tâche qu'attendent de lui ceux qui l'ont invité à siéger. Ce point de vue, croit-il, est corroboré par le fait que l'Assemblée de la Société des Nations, lors de sa prochaine réunion, s'occupera du rapprochement des textes anglais et français du Pacte.

Mr. Root se rallie d'une manière générale à la formule proposée par M. Hagerup, et qu'il trouve admirable. Il suggère cependant l'idée d'ajouter à cet effet la recommendation suivante: si le Conseil et l'Assemblée trouvent que de nouveaux engagements entre les Etats sont nécessaires pour réaliser les vues du Comité, il faudra essayer d'obtenir que ces engagements soient pris.

M. ADATCI remarque qu'il y a déjà trois jours que la question qu'on est en train de discuter a été soulevée. Pendant ce temps il l'a étudiée pour savoir s'il pourrait se rallier à l'opinion de ses collègues. Toutefois, il a trouvé qu'il doit maintenir son avis sur le mandat limité du Comité et sur l'interprétation de l'article 14, dont les termes sont trop clairs pour ne pas être respectés.

Il n'a pas entendu sans une émotion respectueuse les paroles de Mr. Root, qui veut qu'on s'efforce de satisfaire les besoins actuels au lieu de s'attacher à des interprétations de texte, et qu'on examine les questions indépendamment de l'interprétation du Pacte. M. Adatci désire cependant réserver son opinion à cet égard. Par contre, à la question de savoir si la Cour peut connaître d'un litige qui lui a été soumis unilatéralement, M. Adatci répond par la négative, se ralliant à la proposition de Lord Phillimore. Les dispositions à cet égard du projet des Cinq Puissances ne lui semblent pas satisfaisantes.

Le PRESIDENT constate les divergences qui existent entre les opinions des membres. Il croit, toutefois, qu'il doit y avoir accord sur ce point que les questions qui concernent la compétence de la Cour, comme celles qui concernent son organisation, rentrent dans les attributions normales du Comité. A cet égard, les termes de l'article 14 sont clairs, puisqu'ils visent distinc-

the main question. He was not concerned with the interpretation of the Covenant given by Lord Phillimore and M. Loder, since he agreed with them as to the conclusion made. He wanted to avoid limiting themselves to strict compliance with wording in making any recommendations which they thought useful. He thought that in this way the Committee would accomplish exactly the task which was expected of them by those who had asked them to meet. He thought that this point of view was confirmed by the fact that the League of Nations at its next meeting would deal with the question of making the English and French text of the Covenant agree.

Mr. Root agreed in a general way with the draft proposed by M. Hagerup, which he thought admirable. However, he suggested the idea of adding in this connection the following recommendation: if the Council and Assembly thought that new agreements between the States were necessary to achieve the Committee's aims, they should try to arrange for these agreements to be made.

M. ADATCI remarked that the question under discussion had been raised three days ago. In the interval he had studied it in order to see if he could come to the same opinion as his colleagues. However, he felt that he must maintain his opinion concerning the limited powers of the Committee and the interpretation of Article 14, the meaning of which was too clear to be disregarded.

He had not listened without a feeling of great respect to the speech of Mr. Root, who wanted to have actual needs satisfied instead of the members devoting themselves to interpretations of texts and who wanted them to examine the question independently of any interpretation of the Covenant. However, M. Adatci wished to reserve his opinion on this point. On the other hand, concerning the question whether the Court could hear a case submitted to it unilaterally, M. Adatci was of opinion that it could not, and gave his adherence to Lord Phillimore's proposal. The provisions of the Five Power's project in this connection did not seem to him satisfactory.

The PRESIDENT stated the divergencies which existed between the opinions of the members. However, he thought that there should be an understanding on the point that the question which concerns the competence as well as those which concern the organisation of the Court should come within the normal powers of the Committee. In this connection, the terms of Ar-

tement les deux points. L'accord doit également exister, ce semble, quant à la nécessité de prendre une décision au sujet de la judicature obligatoire.

Mr. Root nous a dit que les articles 12, 13 et 14 sont vagues et incomplets. Raison de plus pour que le Comité prenne en considération l'œuvre des deux Conférences de La Haye, œuvre que l'on a si étrangement oubliée, lors de la rédaction du Pacte, à Paris. Le Comité a le devoir de réparer cet oubli. Or, la Conférence de La Haye de 1907, il importe de le rappeler, a été unanime:

1. à reconnaître le principe de l'arbitrage obligatoire;

2. à déclarer que certains différends, et notamment ceux relatifs à l'interprétation et à l'application des stipulations conventionelles internationales, sont susceptibles d'être soumis à l'arbitrage obligatoire sans aucune réserve.

Il ne semble pas, d'ailleurs, que l'interprétation simplement littérale de l'article 13 du Pacte, la seule qui ait été mise à notre disposition, soit inconciliable avec l'institution de la judicature obligatoire. Car le terme „généralement", appliqué à tout l'ordre juridique spécifiquement défini, indique en bonne foi une règle simplement sujette à certaines exceptions; et le terme „de leur avis" doit se concilier en toute loyauté avec tout engagement conventionnel antérieurement stipulé.

Le statut que nous élaborons peut, en tout cas, consigner dans son texte un engagement dépouillé de toute équivoque, et le problème qui se pose ici ne consiste qu'à en préciser la mesure acceptable et justifiée. A ce point de vue, le Président estime que les litiges suivants devraient être soumis à la judicature obligatoire:

1. Litiges d'ordre juridique.

2. Litiges qui, bien que n'étant pas en soi d'ordre juridique, sont assimilés au point de vue juridictionnel aux litiges de cet ordre, en vertu d'une convention générale ou spéciale entre les parties.

On peut sans doute considérer dans une catégorie à part:

1. Les litiges qui ne sont pas d'ordre juridique et à l'égard desquels les parties n'ont pas manifesté, par un accord, leur volonté de procéder juridictionnellement.

2. Les litiges, même d'ordre juridique, frappés d'une réserve comme impliquant un droit déclaré inaliénable, — terme qui paraît plus exact que celui d'intérêt vital.

ticle 14 are clear, since they have the two points distinctly in view. Agreement also should exist, it seems, on the necessity of deciding on the question of compulsory jurisdiction.

Mr. Root has said that Articles 12, 13, and 14 were vague and incomplete. All the more reason why the Committee should take into consideration the work of the two Hague Conferences, which so strangely was forgotten in the drafting of the Covenant at Paris. The Committee is under obligation to make good this omission, and it should be recalled that the Hague Conference of 1907 was unanimous:

1. In acknowledging the principle of compulsory arbitration.

2. In declaring that certain disputes, especially those relative to the interpretation and application of international contractual provisions, may be submitted to compulsory arbitration without reservation.

Furthermore, it does not seem that the simply literal interpretation of Article 13 of the Covenant, the only one which has been put at our disposal, is incompatible with the institution of compulsory jurisdiction. The term "generally", applied to all legal matters specifically defined, indicates in good faith a rule subject merely to certain exceptions; and the term "à leur avis" in the French text should be quite loyally reconciled with any conventional agreement formerly made.

The act which we draw up may in any case include in its text an engagement devoid of any ambiguity; and the question which arises here consists only in specifying the degree in which it is acceptable and justified. From this point of view, the President thought that the following cases should be submitted to compulsory jurisdiction:

1. Cases of legal character.

2. Cases which, although not being in themselves of legal character, may be assimilated from a legal point of view to cases of this sort, by virtue of a general or special convention between the parties.

No doubt, the following cases must be considered in a separate category:

1. Cases which are not of legal character, and in regard to which the parties have not shown by an agreement their desire to have recourse to judicial procedure.

2. Cases, even if of legal character, to which a reserve applies involving "inalienable rights", a term which appears to be more exact than that of "vital interests".

Mais pour la première catégorie, à quel titre la soustrairait-on à une stipulation conventionnelle de judicature obligatoire? Quant à la détermination de ce qui fait partie de l'ordre juridique, l'article 13 du Pacte nous donne une définition qu'on peut accepter.

Et quant aux contestations concernant le caractère juridique ou non d'un différend, rien de plus naturel et de plus équitable que d'en confier le jugement à une Cour de justice internationale.

Le Président estime qu'en évitant certaines confusions et en traitant la question de la judicature obligatoire dans un esprit sagement progressif, on peut sans trop de difficulté arriver à s'entendre sur ce terrain. Il donne lecture de quelques passages d'une note qu'il a composée dans ce but. A la demande qui lui en est faite, le Président se déclare disposé à remettre au Secrétariat la note contenant les idées qu'il vient d'exposer, afin qu'elle soit annexée au procès-verbal. (Annexe 4).

LORD PHILLIMORE désire poser deux questions au Président au sujet de son exposé. En premier lieu il voudrait savoir si le Président ne donne la compétence obligatoire à la Cour que dans le cas où il y a un engagement contractuel entre les parties, les obligeant à se soumettre à la juridiction de la Cour.

Le PRESIDENT répond que les cas visés par lui sont ceux où il y a des engagements contractuels, mais que de tels engagements peuvent être multiformes.

LORD PHILLIMORE répète sa question en la formulant ainsi: le statut constitutionnel de la Cour lui donne-t-il compétence pour connaître d'un conflit sans qu'il y ait entre les parties un engagement spécial?

Le PRESIDENT répond en donnant lecture d'un passage de sa note.

LORD PHILLIMORE précise sa question: un Etat déterminé peut-il s'adresser à la Cour, en la priant d'assigner devant elle un autre Etat qui, bien que lié par un engagement formel envers le premier Etat, a refusé de comparaître devant la Cour?

Le PRESIDENT, après avoir expliqué comment il comprend la question de Lord Phillimore, expose son idée en prenant un exemple. Il y a un litige entre deux Etats; tous les moyens pour arriver à une solution amiable ont été loyalement épuisés. Une partie saisit la Cour, l'autre refuse de comparaître. La première peut-elle de-

But concerning the first category, how could they be removed from a conventional provision for compulsory jurisdiction? Concerning the determination of what is of legal character, Article 13 of the Covenant gives a definition which may be accepted.

And concerning contests over the legal or non-legal character of a dispute, nothing is more natural or more just than to confide this to the judgment of an International Court of Justice.

The President thought that in avoiding certain confusions, and by dealing with the question of compulsory jurisdiction in a wisely progressive spirit, it is possible without too great a difficulty to arrive at an understanding on this basis. He read several passages from a note which he had drafted for this purpose. In answer to a request which was made, the President said that he would forward to the Secretariat the note containing the ideas which he had just explained, for the purpose of having it annexed to the proces verbal. (Annex 4).

LORD PHILLIMORE wished to ask the President two questions on the subject of his explanation. First, he wished to know whether the President would give compulsory jurisdiction to the Court only in case contractual agreement existed between the parties, obliging them to submit to the Court's jurisdiction.

The PRESIDENT answered that the cases he included were those in which contractual agreement existed, but that such agreements might be in many forms.

LORD PHILLIMORE repeated his question in the following way: does the act constituting the Court make it competent to deal with a dispute without a previous special agreement between the parties?

The PRESIDENT, in answer, re-read a portion of his note.

LORD PHILLIMORE further explained his question: could a certain State request the Court to summon before it another State, which, though bound by a formal agreement made with the former State, had refused to appear before the Court?

The PRESIDENT, after explaining in what way he understood Lord Phillimore's question, gave an example of what he meant. A dispute existed between two States. All means to reach a friendly solution had been conscientiously exhausted. One party appealed to the Court, the other refused to appear. Can the first demand that

mander à la Cour de décider préjudiciellement s'il y a inexécution d'un engagement, contracté quant à l'adoption de la procédure juridictionnelle et quant au choix de la Cour comme juridiction?

En cas de décision affirmative, la Cour peut statuer définitivement sur l'objet du litige.

LORD PHILLIMORE demande au Président s'il admet cette solution également dans le cas où les parties ne sont pas liées par un engagement contractuel.

Le PRESIDENT répond négativement: dans cette hypothèse la solution proposée ne lui paraît pas admissible. La soumission d'un litige à la Cour sur initiative unilatérale ne peut se faire qu'en vertu d'une Convention entre les parties. A cet égard le Président se range à l'opinion de Mr. Root.

Le Président continue en discutant le discours de Mr. Root. Il croit qu'il faut distinguer entre deux sortes de recommandations: recommandations sur des objets qui sortent manifestement du cadre du statut organique élaboré par le Comité et qu'on peut juger opportunes à tel ou tel égard particulier, et recommandations qui seraient fondées seulement sur l'opinion étroite de quelques-uns des membres concernant les éléments à comprendre dans le statut.

Le Président estime, à ce dernier point de vue, qu'il y a lieu pour le Comité de faire œuvre unitaire et complète et d'éviter de rejeter dans les recommandations une partie de la tâche qui revient légitimement au Comité.

Mr. ROOT exprime le désir de pouvoir prendre connaissance du document si intéressant dont vient de parler le Président.

M. ALTAMIRA fait observer que le projet du Comité ne sera qu'une proposition soumise au Conseil et à l'Assemblée de la Société des Nations.

Dans ces conditions le Comité devra adopter des résolutions fermes: en faisant des distinctions entre principes plus ou moins nécessaires, entre solutions positives et simples recommandations, on risquerait de voir nombre de propositions écartées par le Conseil ou l'Assemblée. Il se réserve de soumettre à la séance prochaine un projet très succinct, s'inspirant des idées de Mr. Root et M. Loder. Il exprime l'espoir que ce projet pourra contribuer à éclaircir la situation.

M. RICCI-BUSATTI dit que le Président a souligné la nécessité de faire œuvre unitaire

the Court render an interlocutory decision on the point whether there has been a breach of an agreement to adopt judicial procedure and to recognise the Court's jurisdiction?

In case of an affirmative decision, the Court may decide on the subject-matter of the case.

LORD PHILLIMORE asked the President whether he considered that this solution also applied in a case in which the parties were not bound by formal agreement.

The PRESIDENT replied in the negative: in such circumstances he did not think the proposed solution admissible. Submission of a case to the Court by only one party could take place only by virtue of a Convention between them. On this point, the President agreed with Mr. Root.

The President continued by commenting on Mr. Root's speech. He thought it necessary to distinguish between two varieties of recommendations: those which arise manifestly from the organic statute drawn up by the Committee, and which may be judged opportune in some particular connection; and recommendations which should be founded only on the narrow opinion of some members concerning the elements to include in the statute.

The President felt that, from the latter point of view, there was occasion for the Committee to make a unified and complete piece of work, and to avoid passing along with recommendations a part of the task which rightfully fell upon the Committee.

Mr. ROOT expressed the desire to be able to familiarise himself with the interesting document just spoken of by the President.

M. ALTAMIRA pointed out that the project of the Committee would only be a proposal for the consideration of the Council and Assembly of the League of Nations.

Under these circumstances the Committee should put forward firm resolutions; by making a distinction between principles which were more or less necessary, also between definite solutions and mere recommendations, they would run the risk of seeing a number of proposals disregarded by the Council or the Assembly. He would submit a very short and clear proposal following the ideas of Mr. Root and M. Loder at the next meeting. He hoped that this proposal would help to elucidate the position.

M. RICCI-BUSATTI said that the President had emphasised the necessity of drawing

intégrale; lui croit au contraire qu'il serait utile de bien distinguer les deux questions contenues dans l'article 14: celle de l'organisation et celle de la compétence. En traitant les deux questions ensemble, on risque de prolonger les discussions, au sein du Comité (il semble cependant qu'à l'exception de M. Loder, les membres se rallieront, sur la question de la compétence, à la solution d'après laquelle la compétence serait déterminée par les engagements des parties). On risque surtout de faire tomber le projet. Dans l'Assemblée il y aura sûrement des Membres qui s'opposeront à la solution proposée de la première question; il y en aura d'autres qui s'opposeront à la solution de la seconde. La combinaison de ces difficultés diminuera ainsi les chances de succès.

M. Ricci-Busatti propose donc, si on les veut traiter l'une et l'autre, qu'on les traite dans deux projets de convention différents.

Le discours du Président porte sur la compétence de la Cour. M. Ricci-Busatti croit qu'il vaudrait mieux s'occuper de l'organisation: il reconnaît cependant que dans une certaine mesure les deux points sont liés. Le Président a soulevé des questions si délicates et si nombreuses qu'on ne voit pas quand finiraient les discussions auxquelles elles donneraient lieu. Que l'on considère par exemple, la formule des droits inaliénables; d'après M. Ricci-Busatti elle soulève les mêmes objections et difficultés que des formules telles que les intérêts vitaux, l'honneur, etc., auxquelles on voudrait la substituer.

Pour le fond de la question, M. Ricci-Busatti préfère la formule de Lord Phillimore à celle du Président, parce que la première est plus simple, et parce qu'elle tend à rapprocher la Cour de Justice de la Cour d'Arbitrage. Il y a une question préliminaire, à laquelle on revient sans cesse: celle de la nature de la nouvelle Cour. M. Ricci-Busatti insiste sur son idée de l'assimilation fondamentale entre les deux juridictions, d'arbitrage et judiciaire.

Il trouve que cette assimilation a été mise en lumière par Mr. Root, lorsqu'il a tracé les origines du Pacte à l'œuvre des Conférences de La Haye. La question même du droit d'assigner en justice la partie adverse n'est pas exclusive de la juridiction proprement dite; elle s'était déjà posée à propos de l'arbitrage obligatoire. Le rapprochement des deux juridictions renferme la solution de la question soulevée par M. Hagerup: la nouvelle Cour de Justice doit-elle être substituée aux tribunaux d'arbitrage visés par les conventions antérieures? Si l'idée de l'assimilation est adoptée, M. Ricci-Busatti peut

up a unified and complete plan. However, he thought it would be useful to distinguish clearly between the two questions contained in Article 14: that of organisation and that of competence. By treating the two questions together they would run the risk of uselessly prolonging the Committee's discussions. (It seemed, however, that the members of the Committee, with the exception of M. Loder would agree, on the question of competence, to the solution according to which the competence shall be determined by the parties' agreements). There is above all the danger of causing the whole scheme to fail. There certainly will be Members of the Assembly who will oppose the solution proposed for the first question; there will be others who would oppose the proposed solution for the second. The combination of these difficulties will decrease the chance of success.

M. Ricci-Busatti therefore proposed that, if it were desirable to deal with both questions, they should be dealt with in two separate draf. Conventions.

The speech of the President dealt with the competence of the Court, M. Ricci-Busatti thought that it would be better to deal with the question of organisation; he recognised however, that to a certain extent the two points were closely related. The President had raised such a number of delicate questions, that the end of the discussions arising out of them could not be foreseen: if, for example, the phrase "inalienable rights" were considered, according to M. Ricci-Busatti this would give rise to the same objections and difficulties as such expressions as "vital interests", "honour" etc., in the place of which the former was to be substituted.

Fundamentally, M. Ricci-Busatti preferred the formula of Lord Phillimore to that of the President, because the former was simpler and tended to increase the resemblance between the Court of Justice and the Court of Arbitration. There was a preliminary question which was always recurring: that of the nature of the new Court. M. Ricci-Busatti insisted on his idea of the fundamental association between the two jurisdictions, Arbitration and Justice.

He thought that this resemblance had been clearly shown by M. Root when he traced the origin of the Covenant to the work of the Hague Conference. The question even of the right to arraign an adversary before a Court is not exclusively limited to the jurisdiction in the proper meaning of the word, it had already been raised in the matter of compulsory arbitration. The close union of the two jurisdictions would solve

répondre à cette question par l'affirmative; sinon, il doit réserver son opinion.

En général, M. Ricci-Busatti est d'avis que, plus on s'éloigne du principe de l'arbitrage pour la solution des conflits entre Etats, plus la Cour risque d'être délaissée ou le projet lui-même de ne pas aboutir.

Avant de finir, M. Ricci-Busatti rappelle un point de détail soulevé par M. Hagerup, concernant la formule de l'article 26 du projet commun des pays scandinaves sur la procédure par contumace: il croit cependant prématuré de discuter actuellement cette question.

M. ADATCI se rallie à M. Ricci-Busatti et insiste sur la séparation qu'il convient d'établir entre les questions de l'organisation et de la compétence de la Cour.

Le PRESIDENT est d'avis que presque toutes les questions importantes à l'ordre du jour du Comité ont maintenant été élucidées. Il invite les membres à formuler des propositions, pour qu'on puisse procéder, aussitôt que possible, au vote préliminaire.

LORD PHILLIMORE fait valoir qu'il y a encore une ou deux questions importantes à discuter: d'abord la question du droit matériel à appliquer par la Cour, puis la question des règles de procédure.

Le PRESIDENT reconnaît l'importance de la première question, qui doit certainement être étudiée par le Comité. Pour ce qui est de la procédure, le Président fait observer que cette question n'a pas été moins de quatre fois déjà discutée d'une façon approfondie: d'abord en 1899, puis en 1907 au sujet de la Cour d'Arbitrage, de la Cour Internationale des Prises et du projet d'établissement d'une Cour permanente de justice arbitrale. Il croit, par conséquent, que le Comité aura sans peine sous la main les éléments principaux nécessaires à l'élucidation des questions qui ont été ainsi discutées.

LORD PHILLIMORE pense cependant qu'il sera nécessaire de présenter des textes.

Mr. ROOT fait une remarque sur la question des règles de procédure. Il pense qu'à cet égard les conclusions du projet dit des Cinq Puissances,

M. Hagerup's question: should the new Court of Justice be substituted in place of the Tribunals of Arbitration provided for by former conventions? If they adopted the idea of assimilation, M. Ricci-Busatti could answer this question in the affirmative; otherwise he must reserve his opinion.

Generally speaking, M. Ricci-Busatti thought that the further they parted from the principle of Arbitration in the solution of disputes between States, the more they ran the risk of having the Court abandoned, or having the plan itself fail.

Finally, M. Ricci-Busatti recalled a question of detail, raised by M. Hagerup, concerning the clause in Article 26 of the joint project of the Scandinavian Countries, dealing with procedure by default: he thought, however, that it was premature actually to discuss this question.

M. ADATCI agreed with M. Ricci-Busatti and insisted on the separation which should be made between the questions of organisation and of the competence of the Court.

The PRESIDENT was of the opinion that nearly all the important questions on the Committee's Agenda had now been explained. He asked the members to formulate proposals so that a preliminary vote might be taken as soon as possible.

LORD PHILLIMORE pointed out that there were still two or three important questions to discuss: first the question of the substantive law to be applied by the Court, then the question of the rules of procedure.

The PRESIDENT recognised the importance of the first question, which certainly should be studied by the Committee. Concerning procedure, the President pointed out that this question had already been discussed thoroughly not less than four times: first of all in 1899, afterwards in 1907, in connection with the Court of Arbitration, with the International Prize Court, and with the scheme for the establishment of a Permanent Court of Arbitral Justice. He thought that consequently the Committee had at hand the main facts necessary for the elucidation of the questions which had been thus discussed.

LORD PHILLIMORE, however, thought that it would be necessary to submit texts.

Mr. ROOT, in connection with the question of rules of procedure, thought that in this respect the conclusions of the so-called Project of the

sont claires et satisfaisantes. Dans ces conditions, et en considération de la façon approfondie dont ces règles ont déjà été étudiées, il suggère l'idée de prendre comme base de discussion les dispositions dudit projet. Ces dispositions pourraient être considérées comme le rapport d'une sous-commission chargée par le Comité de s'occuper d'elles.

Le PRESIDENT exprime l'avis que le Comité ne doit point régler trop en détail la procédure de la Cour. Celle-ci doit formuler elle-même nombre de ces règles dans son règlement d'ordre intérieur. Les dispositions sur la procédure qui devront être soumises à l'approbation des Etats ne doivent porter que sur des points fondamentaux.

M. ALTAMIRA soulève une question d'ordre. Le Secrétariat a communiqué aux membres copie d'une lettre adressée par M. Albert Thomas au Secrétaire-Général de la Société des Nations relative au travail du Comité. (Annexe 5). Que doit faire le Comité à propos de cette communication?

Le PRESIDENT croit qu'il s'agit d'un simple accusé de réception de la lettre.

LORD PHILLIMORE fait observer que la lettre n'est pas adressée au Comité, mais à Sir Eric Drummond qui l'a communiquée au Comité. Dans ces conditions, il croit qu'on doit se borner à accuser réception de la lettre à Sir Eric Drummond.

Le PRESIDENT constate que le Comité adopte l'idée suggérée par Lord Phillimore.

M. HAGERUP, en considération des difficultés résultant pour le Secrétariat du fait que la réunion de ce soir sera suivie d'une autre le lendemain matin, propose que le Secrétariat soit dispensé de déposer le procès-verbal de la présente séance une heure avant la réunion du lendemain et, en outre, que cette réunion se tienne, exceptionnellement, de 11 à 1 heures.

La proposition de M. Hagerup est adoptée, comme une mesure exceptionnelle.

La séance est levée à 6 heures de l'après-midi.

Le Président:
(signé) Brn. DESCAMPS.

Le Secrétaire-Général:
(signé) D. ANZILOTTI.

Five Powers were clear and satisfactory. Under these conditions and considering how thoroughly these questions had already been studied, he suggested that they should take the provisions of this project as a basis for discussion. They might consider these provisions as though they were the report of a sub-committee entrusted by the Committee with the study of these rules.

The PRESIDENT thought that the Committee should not draw up the procedure of the Court in too much detail. The Court itself ought to formulate these rules in its internal regulations. The rules of procedure which ought to be submitted for the States' approval must deal only with fundamental points.

M. ALTAMIRA raised a question of order. The Secretariat had communicated to the members copies of a letter addressed by M. Albert Thomas to the Secretary-General of the League of Nations concerning the work of the Committee. (Annex 5). What should the Committee do in this matter?

The PRESIDENT thought that they need only acknowledge the receipt of the letter.

LORD PHILLIMORE pointed out that the letter was not addressed to the Committee, but to Sir Eric Drummond, who had communicated it to the Committee. Under these conditions he thought that they should only send an acknowledgment to Sir Eric Drummond.

The PRESIDENT declared the adoption of Lord Phillimore's suggestion by the Committee.

M. HAGERUP, in view of the difficulties for the Secretariat resulting from the fact that the meeting of this evening would be followed by another to-morrow morning, proposed that the Secretariat should be excused from delivering the procès-verbal of the present meeting one hour before to-morrow's meeting, and further that that meeting be held between 11 and 1 as an exceptional case.

M. Hagerup's proposal was adopted as an exceptional measure.

The meeting closed at 6 p.m.

The President:
(signed) Brn. DESCAMPS.

The Secretary-General:
(signed) D. ANZILOTTI.

ANNEXE No. 1.

Notice de M. Loder.

Citation unilatérale ou accord préalable.

Sur la question de savoir si, pour avoir accès à la Cour Permanente de Justice Internationale, une citation unilatérale pourra suffire ou s'il faudra un accord préalable des parties, je me permets de soumettre les observations suivantes à la considération bienveillante de mes honorables collègues.

Dans les conversations qui se sont engagées à ce sujet, on s'est exprimé dans le sens suivant: le texte de l'article 14 du Pacte exclut la citation unilatérale et par suite, un accord préalable entre les parties est requis pour entamer le procès et en saisir la Cour.

Il me semble — en toute modestie — que cette opinion n'est pas juste; que cette interprétation de l'article ne ressort pas du texte et que le Pacte lui-même, ainsi que différents articles du Traité de Paix, démontrent que, bien au contraire, les auteurs du Covenant n'ont eu en vue, et pour de bonnes raisons, que la citation unilatérale.

Le texte dit que „la Cour connaîtra de tous différends d'un caractère international que les parties lui soumettront".

Il n'a évidemment pour objet que la détermination générale de la sphère d'activité de la Cour. La première phrase de l'article annonce l'existence future de la Cour, la seconde détermine la nature des différends qu'elle aura à juger. Si dans celle-ci, on avait eu l'intention de mettre en évidence que, pour obtenir justice, il serait nécessaire, comme pour obtenir l'arbitrage, d'avoir un accord préalable, on l'aurait certainement dit, en dépit de la nonchalance qui ne caractérise que trop la rédaction du Pacte. On l'aurait signifié expressément parce que, du fait d'ajouter une Cour permanente de *justice* à une Cour non-permanente *d'arbitrage*, et de les régler séparément, il ne découle pas évidemment que pour obtenir justice contre son adversaire, on devra acquérir préalablement son consentement gracieux. Or, le texte ne le dit pas. Pour le lui faire dire, il faut tenir le raisonnement suivant: l'article dit: „les parties lui soumettront", c'est donc qu'il en faut au moins deux, et qu'elles doivent se présenter ensemble, d'où un accord préalable nécessaire.

ANNEX No. 1.

Memorandum by M. Loder.

Unilateral summons or previous agreement.

Dealing with the question whether unilateral summons is sufficient to have access to the Permanent Court of International Justice, or whether a previous agreement between the parties is required, I take the liberty to present the following observations for the kind consideration of my honoured colleagues.

In the conversations which have taken place on this subject, the following opinion has been expressed: Article 14 of the Covenant excludes unilateral summons, and consequently a previous agreement between the parties is necessary to institute proceedings and bring a case before the Court.

In my humble opinion it seems that this opinion is not correct; that this interpretation does not follow from the text, and that the Covenant itself, as well as various articles of the Treaty of Peace, show that quite on the contrary the authors of the Covenant were only considering, and for good reasons, unilateral summons.

The text says that "the Court shall be competent to hear and determine any dispute of an international character which the parties thereto submit to it."

It evidently has for its object only the determination of the general sphere of the Court's activity. The first sentence of the Article announces the future existence of the Court, the second decides the nature of the disputes which it shall have to decide. If in this it had been intended to show that in order to obtain justice it would be necessary, as in the case of arbitration, to arrive at a previous agreement, it would certainly have been said so, in spite of the carelessness which is only too much a characteristic of the drafting of the Treaty. It would have been expressly stated because by the fact of adding a Permanent Court of *Justice* to a Court of *Arbitration* which is not permanent, and in organising them separately, it does not evidently follow that to obtain justice against one's adversaries, one should have to obtain their gracious consent beforehand. But the text does not say this. To make it say this, the following reasoning must be adopted: The article says

Mais on peut, tout aussi bien, donner à ces mots leur sens le plus simple, le plus naturel et le plus banal aussi, à savoir: que la Cour connaîtra de tous les litiges que les parties, c'est à dire parties A ou B ou C, lui soumettront à l'avenir.

A quoi bon, autrement, créer cette Cour? Pour constituer une doublure de la Cour d'Arbitrage? Pour conserver un état de choses déplorable, et continuer à ne faire justice entre deux adversaires qu'après avoir obtenu leur consentement mutuel, leur accord sur la formule du grief et le choix des juges? Cela n'en valait pas la peine. On ne sait que trop comment ceux qui se sentent coupables aux yeux du droit et de la justice savent profiter de leur situation, n'approuvant jamais rien, et font servir à leurs fins les exceptions et les subterfuges.

La différence entre arbitrage et justice ne se trouve pas dans la nature de la décision rendue. Dans les deux cas le droit et l'équité peuvent être sauvegardés, M. le Président l'a très bien démontré dans son discours au début de nos discussions. Mais dans l'arbitrage, il faut le consentement de la partie adverse pour que justice soit faite et son concours pour la définition du point en litige, ainsi que pour le choix des juges qu'elle peut récuser s'ils n'ont pas l'heur de lui plaire. L'arbitrage, c'est un combat avant le combat.

Le Pacte n'a pas voulu abolir l'arbitrage, mais il a désiré placer à côté de lui une Cour de Justice.

Elle doit être permanente, et laisser la porte ouverte à ceux qui se présenteront pour lui demander de régler tous les différends qui rentrent dans les limites de sa compétence, — mais le concours gracieux de l'adversaire n'est plus requis; on s'arrangera sans lui.

Le Traité de Paix démontre que tel est bien réellement le sens, la signification de la nouvelle institution. Au cours des débats actuels, l'attention des membres du Comité s'est fixée sur différents articles qui renvoient à la décision de la Cour — sans compromis ou rien qui y ressemble.

En 1907 on a vainement essayé de créer une Cour de Justice.

C'était toujours une Cour de Justice Arbitrale. Comment aurait-il pu en être autrement? Le lien entre les Etats manquait.

Ce n'est que par l'avènement de la Société des Nations que la possibilité de l'existence d'une vraie Cour de Justice fut créée, une Cour où le demandeur n'aura plus à attendre le bon vouloir de son adversaire. C'est une telle Cour que le Pacte a voulu, et non point une doublure inutile.

"which the parties shall submit to it", therefore there must be at least two parties, and they must appeal to the Court together, for which a previous agreement is necessary.

But it is just as easy to give these words their simpler meaning, their natural meaning, and also their more common meaning: that is, that the Court will take cognisance of all cases that the parties, that is to say, parties A. or B. or C. will submit to it in the future.

Otherwise, why create this Court? In order to duplicate the Court of Arbitration? To continue a deplorable state of affairs and administer justice between two contesting parties only after having obtained their mutual consent, and their agreement on the wording of the complaint, and on the choice of judges? That is not worth the trouble. It is only too well known that those who feel themselves offenders in the eyes of the law and of justice know how to profit by their position; they never agree to anything, and make exceptions and subterfuges serve their ends.

The difference between arbitration and justice is not to be found in the nature of the decision rendered. In both, law and equity may be protected. The President has shown this very clearly in his speech at the beginning of our discussion. But in arbitration the consent of the opposing party is necessary before justice can be done; his concurrence on the definition of the disputed point is necessary, as well as his agreement to the choice of judges which he may rule out if by chance they do not please him. Arbitration means a combat before the combat.

The Covenant did not intend to abolish arbitration, but it wished to place beside it a Court of Justice.

The latter must be permanent, it must be open to all who present themselves before it for a decision in all cases which come within the bounds of its competence. The gracious consent of the adversary is no longer required: one can do without him.

The Treaty of Peace shows that such is really the meaning of the new institution. During the present discussions the attention of the members of our Committee has been directed to various articles which refer to decision by the Court, without compromise or anything resembling it.

In 1907 a vain attempt was made to create a Court of Justice.

It was still a Court of Arbitral Justice. How could it have been otherwise? The bond between the States was lacking.

It was only the institution of the League of

Ce serait à mon avis lui faire manquer son but, que de suivre toujours l'ancien sillon, que de s'attacher indéfiniment à l'interprétation d'un article, qui, pris dans son sens naturel, ne prête à aucune équivoque.

Le Pacte a voulu faire ce pas en avant, qui constitue un réel progrès. Notre collègue Mr. Root l'a clairement démontré. Et à mon avis il faut déclarer ouvertement que le pas est fait. Je m'associe à la proposition de Mr. Root d'insérer au projet de ce Comité l'article 21 des Cinq Etats.

Quelques-uns de nos collègues prétendent que c'est inutile parce qu'il ferait double emploi avec l'article 14 du Pacte. Je crois que ce n'est pas exact, mais quand il le serait, ce ne serait pas une raison pour nous de nous abstenir de statuer sur ce qui rentre dans notre projet, par la nature même du sujet qu'on y traite.

Nations that made possible a real Court of Justice, a Court where the plaintiff would no longer have to wait upon the good will of his opponent. It is such a Court that is intended in the Covenant, and not a useless duplication.

In my opinion it would cause the Covenant to miss its goal, to follow always in the old track, to adopt a vague interpretation of an article which taken in its natural meaning was unmistakable.

The intention of the Covenant was to take this step which would constitute a real progress. Our colleague, Mr. Root, has shown it clearly. In my opinion, we must openly declare that this step forward has been taken. I agree with the proposal of Mr. Root to insert in the Committee's plan article 21 of the Five Powers.

Some of our colleagues think that it is useless, because it would duplicate article 14 of the Covenant. I do not think this is correct, but even if it were so, it would not be a reason for us to abstain from putting into our project a point which ought to be there from the very nature of the subject dealt with.

ANNEXE No. 2.

Article sur la question de compétence proposé par Lord Phillimore.

S'il n'y a pas de convention spéciale entre les parties, la Cour Permanente de Justice Internationale sera censée être la Cour d'Arbitrage prévue à l'article 13 du Pacte, et sera ainsi compétente pour juger tous les différends entre les parties relatives à:

a. l'interprétation d'un traité;
b. tout point de droit international;
c. la réalité de tout fait, qui, s'il était établi, constituerait la rupture d'un engagement international;
d. l'étendue ou la nature de la réparation dûe pour la rupture d'un engagement international;
e. l'interprétation d'une sentence rendue par la Cour.

La Cour sera également compétente dans les cas que lui sont déférés par le Traité de Versailles.

Dans tous les cas nommés ci-dessus les parties seront censées être convenues de soumettre le différend à la Cour; de sorte que la Cour sera compétente d'en prendre connaissance selon les provisions de l'Article 14 du Pacte, et l'une des parties peut demander à la Cour de prendre connaissance du différend sans autre assentiment préalable de l'autre partie.

Note de Lord Phillimore.

Selon mon idée, et je crois celle de la plupart de mes Collègues, la Cour n'est pas compétente, d'après les termes de l'article 14, à moins que chacune des parties lui soumette le différend. Même si (ce dont je doute excepté dans les cas prévus dans le Traité de Versailles) l'on s'est engagé à soumettre un différend à la Cour, et que si, en fait, on ne le soumette pas, il n'y aura pas de compétence.

Mais il faudra une convention à laquelle les Etats composant la Société des Nations doivent être parties, pour établir la Cour. Par cette convention, on pourra donner à la Cour une compétence quelconque, malgré que cette compétence n'ait pas été donnée par le Pacte original.

Il sera peut-être bien d'ajouter un mot à notre rapport, justifiant nos recommandations par cette raison.

ANNEX No. 2.

Article on the subject of jurisdiction proposed by Lord Phillimore.

In the absence of any special convention between the parties, the Permanent Court of International Justice shall be deemed to be the Court of Arbitration mentioned in Article 13 of the Covenant, and shall have jurisdiction in all cases of disputes between States, which involve:

a. the interpretation of a Treaty;
b. any question of International Law;
c. the existence of any fact, which, if established, would constitute a breach of any International obligation;
d. the extent or nature of the reparation to be made for any such breach;
e. the interpretation of its own judgments.

The Court shall also have jurisdiction in the several cases which are referred to it by the Treaties of Versailles.

In all the cases above mentioned the parties shall be deemed to have agreed to submit the dispute to the Court so that the Court will be competent to hear and determine it according to the provisions of Article 14 of the Covenant, and either of the parties may require the Court to exercise jurisdiction without any further assent on the part of the other party.

Note by Lord Phillimore.

In my view, and that, I think, of most of my Colleagues, no power is given to the Court by Article 14, unless the parties submit the dispute to it. Even if they were bound (which I doubt) to submit any dispute to the Court (except those provided in the Treaties of Versailles) unless, in fact, they submit, there would be no jurisdiction.

But the Court can only be established by a Convention, to which the Members of the League must be parties, and by that Convention they can give the Court any jurisdiction which they please, though it was not given by the Original Covenant.

Perhaps we should append a note to our report, justifying our recommendation by this consideration.

ANNEXE No. 3.

Proposition de Lord Phillimore avec Amendement de M. Hagerup.

S'il n'y a pas de convention contraire entre les parties, la Cour Permanente de Justice Internationale sera censée être la Cour d'Arbitrage prévue à l'article 13 du Pacte, et sera ainsi compétente pour juger tous les différends entre les parties relatives à:

a. l'interprétation d'un traité;

b. tout point de droit international;

c. la réalité de tout fait, qui, s'il était établi, constituerait la rupture d'un engagement international;

d. l'étendue ou la nature de la réparation dûe pour la rupture d'un engagement international;

e. l'interprétation d'une sentence rendue par la Cour.

La Cour sera également compétente dans les cas qui lui sont déférés par le Traité de Versailles, ainsi que lorsque les Parties se sont engagées par une convention à soumettre à la Cour Internationale ou bien tous les conflits survenus entre elles, ou bien certaines catégories d'affaires, ou bien un différend spécial.

Dans tous les cas nommés ci-dessus les parties seront considérées, dans le sens de l'article 14 du Pacte, comme étant convenues de soumettre le différend à la Cour; l'une des parties peut demander à la Cour de prendre connaissance du différend sans autre assentiment préalable de l'autre partie. Par conséquent, lorsqu'une des Parties ne se présente pas à la Cour ou autrement s'abstient de se prononcer dans l'affaire, l'autre partie peut exiger que l'affaire soit jugée par la Cour de Justice Internationale, sur la base de l'exposé des faits fourni par la Partie, pourvu que cet exposé ne soit pas contraire aux preuves présentées à la Cour ou à des faits notoires.

ANNEX No. 3.

Proposal by Lord Phillimore with amendment by M. Hagerup.

In the absence of any Convention to the contrary between the Parties the Permanent Court of International Justice shall be deemed to be the Court of Arbitration mentioned in Article 13 of the Covenant, and shall have jurisdiction in all cases of disputes between States, which involve:

a. the interpretation of the Treaty;

b. any question of International Law;

c. the existence of any fact, which, if established, would constitute a breach of any international obligation;

d. the extent or nature of a reparation to be made for any such breach;

e. the interpretation of its own judgments.

The Court shall also have jurisdiction in the several cases which are referred to it by the Treaties of Versailles, and also in cases in which the parties have bound themselves by a Convention to submit to the International Court, either all disputes arising between them or certain classes of affairs, or a special dispute.

In all the cases above mentioned the parties shall be deemed to have agreed to submit the dispute to the Court, so that the Court will be competent to hear and determine it according to the terms of Article 14 of the Covenant; and either of the Parties may require the Court to exercise jurisdiction without any further assent on the part of the other party. Consequently, if one of the parties does not enter an appearance in the Court, or abstains in any other way from stating its intentions in the case, the other party may demand that the case shall be tried by the Court of International Justice upon the basis of the statement of facts supplied by the latter party, provided that this statement is not contrary to proofs submitted to the Court or to common knowledge.

ANNEXE No. 4.

Note du Baron Descamps sur la question de la Judicature Obligatoire.

La question de savoir dans quelle mesure, indépendamment des conventions qui peuvent lier d'autre part les parties, il y a lieu d'adopter, dans la convention concernant l'Office général de la justice internationale, pour l'ensemble des Etats contractants, la règle de la judicature obligatoire, doit être bien posée et résolue, si possible, en un esprit de sage progrès.

A coup sûr, la procédure juridictionnelle, lorsqu'on la compare à la procédure guerrière, apparaît à tous comme la procédure la plus conforme à la raison, à l'humanité et même à l'intérêt des parties en tant qu'elles ne recherchent que la juste et loyale satisfaction, par la voie la moins aléatoire, de leurs revendications légitimes. Dans la procédure guerrière en effet, chaque Etat s'érige en juge de ses propres revendications et prétend imposer par la force sa manière de voir à l'adversaire, en telle sorte que le triomphe entre les prétentions concurrentes est abandonné au sort violent des armes. Dans la procédure juridictionnelle, la solution du litige est confiée à un juge impartial appelé à fixer le droit des parties. Ce n'est donc pas sans raison que la Première Conférence de La Haye a déclaré que la procédure juridictionnelle — considérée par elle sous les espèces de l'arbitrage — constitue le moyen à la fois le plus équitable et le plus efficace de terminer tout au moins les litiges d'ordre juridique.

Nul ne conteste aujourd'hui que de tels litiges ne doivent relever plutôt d'une juridiction que de la guerre.

Mais ici s'offrent précisément deux observations dont il semble qu'il y ait lieu de tenir compte:

Il y a des litiges qui ne peuvent être formulés ni résolus juridiquement, comme les contestations d'intérêts et les différends d'ordre politique.

Il y a des litiges, même d'ordre juridique, dans lesquels, aux yeux de certains Etats, l'adoption d'une procédure juridictionnelle impliquerait l'abandon de droits considérés, à tort ou à raison, comme inaliénables.

La question qui se pose pratiquement est donc de savoir comment dans un ensemble de dispositions visant un accord général concernant

ANNEX No. 4.

Note by Baron Descamps on the question of Compulsory Jurisdiction.

The following question should be clearly stated and if possible settled in an intelligently progressive spirit: to what extent, independently of existing Conventions between the parties, is it advisable to insert the rule of compulsory jurisdiction for all States in the Convention concerning the general Office of International Justice?

Judicial procedure, when compared to belligerent methods, appears unmistakably to all as the method conforming more to reason, to humanity, and even the interest of parties, in so fai as they seek fair and just satisfaction by the least aleatory way for their legitimate claims. By the use of belligerent methods each State in fact erects itself as judge of its own claims and undertakes to impose by force its viewpoint on the opponent, in such a way that the force of arms decides which of the conflicting demands shall predominate. By use of judicial methods the decision of a case is left to an impartial judge, called upon to administer justice between the parties. It was therefore not without cause, that the First Hague Conference stated that judicial procedure, considered by it in the form of arbitration, constituted both the most equitable and at the same time the most efficient means of settling at least all cases of legal character.

To-day no one disputes the fact that such cases should be settled by trial rather than by War.

Here however two points arise which should be considered:

There exist cases which can neither be stated nor decided legally, such as conflicts of interest and political disputes.

There exist cases even of legal character, in which the adoption of legal methods would imply, according to certain States' view, the abandonment of rights considered rightly or wrongly inalienable.

The question therefore which arises in practice is to ascertain to what extent it is possible in a body of provisions providing for a general agreement on Compulsory Jurisdiction to give such jurisdiction all the scope to which it is entitled, considering in an appropriate degree

la judicature obligatoire, il est possible de donner à cette judicature l'extension qu'elle peut revendiquer à tant de titres, en tenant compte, dans une mesure convenable, de réserves qui, si elles ne pouvaient se formuler, menaceraient de réagir sur la conclusion d'un accord international général.

Voici l'indication de quelques points dont l'élucidation pourrait peut-être donner satisfaction à la diversité des opinions en présence.

I. Doivent être soumis à la procédure juridictionnelle excluant toute autre procédure comme moyen définitif de solution:

1. Les différends d'ordre juridique sauf une réserve à envisager comme possible.

   Sont essentiellement reconnus comme différends d'ordre juridique, les litiges relatifs à l'interprétation d'un traité, à toute question de droit international, à la réalité de tout fait qui, s'il était établi, constituerait la violation d'une obligation internationale, ou à l'étendue ou à la nature de la réparation dûe pour une telle violation.

2. Les différends qui, bien que ne pouvant être formulés et résolus juridiquement, sont assimilés au point de vue juridictionnel aux différends d'ordre juridique en vertu d'un accord général ou spécial intervenu entre les parties en litige.

II. Doivent être considérés à part les différends qui ne sont pas d'ordre juridique et à l'égard desquels les parties en litige n'ont pas manifesté par un accord la volonté de procéder par la voie juridictionnelle.

III. Peuvent encore occuper une place à part les différends, même d'ordre juridique, frappés d'une réserve du chef d'implication dans le litige d'un droit déclaré inaliénable.

IV. En cas de contestation concernant le caractère juridique ou non d'un différend, ce point doit faire l'objet, en ordre préjudiciel, d'une décision par la voie juridictionnelle.

Il en est de même en cas de contestation sur le point de savoir si un différend qui n'est pas en soi de nature juridique a été assimilé par les parties aux différends d'ordre juridique, et en cas d'exception fondée sur une réserve du chef d'implication dans le litige d'un droit déclaré inaliénable.

V. Au cas où l'une des parties en litige refuse de procéder par la voie juridictionnelle, alors que l'autre partie soutient qu'il y a engagement con-

reserves which if they may not be made, may threaten to jeopardise a general international understanding.

Below is a list of points concerning which an explanation may satisfy present differences of opinion.

I. The following should be submitted to judicial procedure exclusively:

1. Disputes of a legal character, with a possible reservation.

   Cases considered as essentially of legal character are, disputes relating to the interpretation of a Treaty, any question of International Law, the reality of any fact, which, if established, would constitute a violation of an international obligation, or the extent or nature of reparation due for such violation.

2. Disputes which, although unable to be stated or settled legally, are comparable from the point of view of jurisdiction to disputes of legal character by virtue of a general or special agreement arrived at by the parties concerned.

II. Disputes which are not of legal character and regarding which the parties concerned have not manifested by mutual consent their willingness to proceed by judicial methods should be considered separately.

III. Separate consideration may also be given to disputes even of a legal character, affected by the reservation of a right declared inalienable.

IV. In case of a contest concerning the legal or non-legal character of a dispute, this point should be the subject of an interlocutory decision rendered judicially.

The same procedure should be followed in cases of contest on the point whether a dispute not itself of legal character has been made comparable to one of legal character by the parties concerned, and in case of an exception founded on the reservation of a right declared inalienable.

V. In case one of the parties concerned refuses to proceed by judicial methods when the other party maintains that there is a conventional

ventionnellement pris à cet égard vis-à-vis d'elle, cette dernière, après avoir exercé le recours normal par les voies diplomatiques, peut citer la première devant la juridiction reconnue compétente, à l'effet de faire décider s'il y a inexécution d'un engagement assumé. Et en cas de décision affirmative, elle a titre autorisé pour demander au juge de statuer définitivement sur le fond du litige.

agreement to this effect between the parties, the latter, if it has been impossible to settle the dispute by diplomatic means, may summon the former before the recognised competent jurisdiction, for the purpose of obtaining a decision whether there is a breach of contract. In case of an affirmative decision the latter is entitled to demand that the judge render a final decision on the question at issue.

ANNEXE No. 5.

Lettrè de M. Albert Thomas à Sir Eric Drummond.

Bureau International du Travail
7, Seymour Place
W. 1.

Le 23 Février 1920.

Mon cher Secrétaire Général,

Le Conseil de la Société des Nations a décidé d'étudier la constitution, le plus rapide possible, de la Cour Permanente de Justice Internationale.

Le Conseil a confié, je crois, à une Commission de Juristes le soin de rédiger un avant-projet.

Puis-je vous demander de faire parvenir à la Commission quelques observations ou quelques demandes de la part du Bureau International du Travail?

En vertu de l'article 415 du Traité de Paix, en effet, lorsque les recommandations faites à un ou plusieurs Gouvernements dans un différend concernant les questions du travail ne sont pas acceptées par ces Gouvernements, ceux-ci peuvent, s'ils le désirent, „soumettre le différend à la Cour Permanente de Justice Internationale de la Société des Nations".

De même, en vertu de l'article 416, tout Membre de l'organisation Permanente du Travail a le droit de soumettre à la Cour Permanente de Justice Internationale le cas d'un autre Membre qui ne respecte pas les recommandations ou les conventions.

L'article 417 spécifie que la décision de la Cour Permanente de Justice Internationale, dans de pareils cas, n'est pas susceptible d'appel.

Et, en vertu de l'article 418 et de l'article 419, les sanctions d'ordre économique peuvent être prises contre les Etats qui violent les décisions.

Ces articles soulèvent deux séries de questions sur lesquelles je me permets d'attirer l'attention du Conseil de la Société des Nations et de la Commission des Juristes qui travaille pour lui:

1. Il importerait d'abord de définir le rôle du Bureau International du Travail. C'est à lui, évidemment, qu'il appartiendra, dans ce cas, d'in-

ANNEX No. 5.

Letter from M. Albert Thomas to Sir Eric Drummond.

International Labour Bureau.
7 Seymour Place,
W. 1.

February 23rd, 1920.

My dear Secretary-General,

The Council of the League of Nations has decided to study the question of establishing the Permanent Court of International Justice as speedily as possible.

I believe the Council has entrusted the task of preparing a draft-scheme to a Committee of Jurists.

May I ask you to acquaint the Committee with certain observations or requests, put forward by the International Labour Bureau?

By virtue of Article 415 of the Treaty of Peace, if recommendations made to one or more Governments in a dispute concerning Labour questions are not accepted by these Governments, they may, if they wish to, "submit the dispute to the Permanent Court of International Justice of the League of Nations."

In the same way, by virtue of Article 416, any Member of the permanent Labour organisation has the right to submit to the Permanent Court of International Justice the case arising when another Member does not respect recommendations or conventions.

Article 417 lays down that the decision of the Permanent Court of International Justice in such cases is final.

Further, by virtue of Articles 418 and 419, economic penalties can be enforced against States who violate the Court's decisions.

These articles raise two series of questions, to which I take the liberty of calling the attention of the Council of the League of Nations, and of the Committee of Jurists working for it:

1. First of all, the rôle of the International Labour Bureau must be defined. Evidently, it will be the task of the Labour Bureau, in such cases,

troduire la plainte et, si j'ose le dire, d'établir le réquisitoire.

En vertu des articles 409 et suivants c'est en effet au Bureau que revient le soin de suivre toute la procédure avant qu'il ne soit recouru à la Cour Permanente de Justice Internationale.

2. Pour que la Cour Permanente puisse appuyer des décisions sur une connaissance exacte des faits en matière de Travail, et pour qu'elle offre ainsi toute garantie, il importe ou bien que des patrons et des ouvriers fassent partie de la Cour de Justice, ou bien des Conseillers Techniques ou de Groupements d'Experts soient prévus.

La présente lettre a simplement pour objet de ne pas laisser les travaux de la Commission de Juristes sans qu'elle ait été saisie de nos observations ou de nos demandes. Nous nous réservons ultérieurement de vous faire parvenir sur le sujet les résultats d'études nouvelles.

Veuillez agréer, mon cher Secrétaire Général, l'assurance de ma considération bien distinguée et mes sentiments très cordiaux.

(*signé*) ALBERT THOMAS.

to make the accusation, and, if I may say so, to act as prosecutor.

By virtue of Article 409 and the following articles, the task of carrying out the procedure, before recourse is had to the Permanent Court of International Justice, falls upon the Labour Bureau.

2. In order that the Permanent Court may base its decisions upon an exact knowledge of the facts in Labour questions, and in order that a just decision may be guaranteed, it is necessary, either that employers and workmen should form part of the Court of Justice, or that expert advisers, or groups of experts should be provided.

This letter is simply intended to inform the Committee of Jurists of our observations or requests, so that its labours may not be carried out in ignorance of them. We reserve the right to inform you later of results of any fresh consideration of the question.

I have the honour to be, my dear Secretary-General,

Your most obedient servant,

(*signed*) ALBERT THOMAS.

12IÈME SÉANCE (non-publique), tenue au Palais de la Paix, à La Haye, le 30 juin 1920.

Présidence de M. le BARON DESCAMPS.

Sont présents: tous les membres du Comité (à l'exception de M. Bevilaqua et de M. de Lapradelle); M. Fernandes; Mr. James Brown Scott; les secrétaires particuliers de M. le Baron Descamps et de M. Adatci; les membres du Secrétariat.

La séance est ouverte à 11 heures du matin.

Le PRESIDENT dit qu'en vertu du mandat que le Comité lui a confié au cours de la séance précédente, il a conféré avec ses collègues, et notamment avec Lord Phillimore, sur la possibilité de trouver une formule transactionnelle au sujet de la question de la compétence de la Cour. Le résultat a été un projet qui a été préparé en collaboration avec Lord Phillimore et distribué aux membres du Comité. Ce projet semble constituer un progrès dans l'ordre de la juridiction internationale, et il a paru de nature à donner satisfaction à la plupart des membres du Comité. En vue d'arriver à ce résultat, le Président n'a pas cru devoir insister spécialement sur la réserve des droits inaliénables.

Les membres du Comité n'ayant guère eu le temps de prendre connaissance du projet, le Président en donne lecture. Il fait remarquer que les littéra *a, b, c, d,* du premier article du projet sont empruntés au Pacte, et que le littéra *e* a été pris au projet des Cinq Puissances.

(Le projet est reproduit à l'annexe 1ère).

LORD PHILLIMORE répète que le projet a été préparé en collaboration avec lui. Il est d'accord avec ce qu'a dit le Président, et tout en se réservant sur la rédaction du projet, il prie les membres de le prendre en sérieuse considération.

M. LODER trouve que, par ces transactions, le Comité est entré dans la bonne voie, et il s'en félicite. Pour le moment il désire faire une seule remarque. Lorsque le projet dit que tous les moyens diplomatiques doivent être épuisés avant le recours au tribunal, il adopte le système des

12TH MEETING (Private), held at the Peace Palace, the Hague, on June 30th, 1920.

BARON DESCAMPS in the chair.

Present: all members of the Committee (with the exception of M. Bevilaqua and M. de Lapradelle); M. Fernandes, M. James Brown Scott; the private secretaries of Baron Descamps and of M. Adatci; the members of the Secretariat.

The meeting opened at 11 a.m.

The PRESIDENT said that by virtue of the instructions given to him by the Committee at the preceding meeting, he had conferred with his colleagues, especially with Lord Phillimore, concerning the possibility of finding a transactional formula dealing with the question of the Court's competence. The result of his efforts was a proposal which he had worked out in conjunction with Lord Phillimore and had had distributed to the members of the Committee. This project seemed to him to constitute an advance in the matter of international jurisdiction and to be of such nature as to satisfy most of the members of the Committee. In order to attain this result the President had not thought it necessary to insist especially on the reservation of inalienable rights.

As the members of the Committee had hardly had time to study the project, the President read it. He pointed out that the first four points of the first Article of the project were borrowed from the Covenant and that the fifth point was taken from the project of the Five Powers.

(The project is contained in the Annex 1).

LORD PHILLIMORE said that the project had been prepared with his collaboration. He agreed with what the President had said, and though he reserved his judgment as to the drafting of the project, he asked the members to give it their serious consideration.

M. LODER thought this work had started the Committee along the right road and expressed his satisfaction. For the moment he wished to make only one observation. When the project stated that all diplomatic means must be exhausted before recourse to the Court, it was

preuves négatives, système toujours susceptible d'amener des difficultés.

Mr. ROOT trouve également, d'une façon générale, le projet satisfaisant. Le sens exact de quelques passages devra cependant être précisé.

M. ALTAMIRA rappelle qu'il a promis lors de la séance précédente de soumettre un projet formulé. Comme ses propositions se trouvent entièrement reprises dans le troisième article du projet du Président, il communique sa formule exclusivement en vue de l'utilité qu'elle pourrait avoir pour la rédaction finale (voir annexe 2), et déclare se rallier au projet.

M. ADATCI dit qu'à première vue, ce projet lui semble bon. Avant de se prononcer, il veut cependant avoir le temps de réfléchir.

M. RICCI-BUSATTI est disposé à accepter en principe le projet qui lui semble correspondre à la tâche du Comité et reproduire, quant au fond, les idées de ses membres. Il fait cependant des réserves quant aux différentes formules; et tout d'abord il demande des éclaircissements au sujet de l'article 2.

Le PRESIDENT répond qu'à propos de certains conflits, il pourra s'élever des contestations sur la question de savoir s'ils rentrent dans les cas énumerés à l'article 1er; la Cour devra alors examiner cette question en ordre préjudiciel, et si le différend ne rentre pas dans les catégories de l'article 1er, elle renverra les parties devant le Conseil de la Société des Nations.

Le Président explique ensuite l'économie générale des articles proposés.

M. RICCI-BUSATTI persiste à penser qu'il y a une certaine contradiction entre les articles 1 et 2, tels qu'ils sont rédigés, mais reconnaît d'autre part la possibilité de les concilier par des amendements. Il n'approuve pas entièrement la formule „questions d'ordre juridique": d'une part elle est beaucoup trop vague et de l'autre elle suppose une distinction nette entre les différends d'ordre juridique et ceux d'un autre ordre, distinction qui, selon M. Ricci-Busatti, n'existe pas dans le domaine des rapports internationaux. Le second alinéa de l'article 1er augmente encore, à son avis, les défauts de rédaction du projet.

LORD PHILLIMORE observe que toute question peut être contestée. Il faut qu'il y ait une juridiction pour trancher les difficultés. Si un

adopting a system of negative proof, a system which was always liable to cause difficulties.

Mr. ROOT also thought that the project was generally satisfactory. However, the exact meaning of certain passages must be made clear.

M. ALTAMIRA recalled that he had promised at the preceding meeting to submit a written plan. As his plan was entirely covered by the third Article of the President's project, he submitted it solely for the purpose of being useful in the final drafting. (See Annex 2). He accepted the project.

M. ADATCI said that at first sight the project seemed to him to be a good one. Before definitely committing himself, however, he wished to have time to think it over.

M. RICCI-BUSATTI was disposed to accept the project in principle; it seemed to him to correspond to the duty of the Committee and the fundamental ideas of its members. However, he wished to make reservations in respect to different clauses, and first of all he asked for enlightenment on Article 2.

The PRESIDENT replied that in regard to certain conflicts, disputes might arise over the question whether they were included in the cases named by Article 1: the Court then should examine this question as interlocutory, and if it found that the dispute did not come within one of the categories of Article 1, it would send the contesting parties to the Council of the League of Nations.

The President then explained the general effect of the Articles proposed.

M. RICCI-BUSATTI persisted in thinking that there was a certain contradiction between Article 1 and 2 as they were worded; he admitted however that it was possible to reconcile these two Articles by means of amendments. He did not entirely approve of the expression, "questions of a legal nature": for one reason it was much too vague, for another thing it supposed a clear distinction between disputes of a legal nature and others, a distinction which in his opinion did not exist in the field of international relations. Paragraph 2 of Article 1 increases even more, in his opinion, the faulty drafting of the project.

LORD PHILLIMORE observed that every question could be disputed. There must be a jurisdiction to settle these difficulties. If a State

Etat juge qu'un conflit entre lui et un autre Etat a trait à l'interprétation d'un traité et si l'autre n'en juge pas ainsi, il doit y avoir un tribunal pour écarter la difficulté.

M. LODER est de cet avis, mais remarque que la solution serait identique même si l'article 2 n'existait pas.

M. HAGERUP se rallie, sauf rédaction, à la proposition. Il désire cependant signaler que, d'après lui, on n'a pas suffisamment tenu compte de l'existence d'un certain nombre de traités qui obligent les parties à avoir recours à l'arbitrage dans des cas qui sortent du cadre du premier article du projet. Il serait donc plus logique de stipuler expressément la compétence de la Cour, même pour les questions non-juridiques, dans les cas visés par lesdits traités, que de déterminer la compétence de la Cour comme le fait le dernier alinéa de l'article 1er. D'autre part il se rallie complètement à l'idée de conférer à la Cour le droit de décider si un différend rentre ou non dans les catégories de l'article 1er.

M. Hagerup voudrait pourtant substituer, dans le deuxième article, les mots „sur le point de savoir si le différend entre dans le cadre de l'article 1er" aux mots „concernant le caractère juridique ou non d'un différend".

M. Hagerup rappelle que si l'on adopte le système qui a trouvé son expression à l'article 3 du projet, il faudrait envisager la question de l'établissement d'une procédure dans le sens de l'article 26 du projet des trois pays scandinaves.

Le PRESIDENT croit qu'on pourrait aisément donner satisfaction à M. Hagerup en insérant au début de l'article 1er les mots: „sans préjudice des dispositions générales ou spéciales établissant un ordre différent".

LORD PHILLIMORE se rallie à cette proposition.

M. HAGERUP déclare cependant que la rédaction proposée ne lui semble pas suffisamment claire. Il suggère l'idée suivante: au lieu d'insérer les mots proposés par le Président, substituer, dans le dernier alinéa de l'article 1er, les mots: „même lorsqu'ils ne peuvent" aux mots „bien que ne pouvant".

Le PRESIDENT explique qu'il faut distinguer entre les cas vraiment juridiques et les cas d'ordre non juridique qui, à la suite d'un accord entre

believes that a dispute between it and another State refers to the interpretation of a treaty, and if the other State was not of the same opinion, there must be a tribunal to remove the difficulty.

M. LODER was of the same opinion; but he pointed out that the solution would be the same, even if Article 2 did not exist.

M. HAGERUP agreed to the President's proposal, drafting excepted. He wished, however, to point out that in his opinion the existence of a number of treaties, which bind the contracting parties to use arbitration in cases other than those contained in the first Article of the project, was not sufficiently taken into account. Therefore it would be more logical to stipulate expressly the competence of the Court, even for non-legal questions in cases dealt with by the said treaties, than to determine the competence of the Court as the last paragraph of the Article specifies. Otherwise he quite agreed with the idea of giving the Court the right to determine whether a dispute did or did not come under one of the headings in Article 1.

M. Hagerup however, wished to substitute in Article 2 the words "when it is disputed whether the case is included in Article 1", for the words "when the legal nature of a case is disputed".

M. Hagerup pointed out that if the system expressed by Article 3 of the project were adopted, it would be necessary to consider the question of establishing a procedure of the kind indicated in Article 26 of the project of the three Scandinavian countries.

The PRESIDENT thought that they could easily satisfy M. Hagerup's wish by inserting at the beginning of Article 1 the words: "without prejudice to general or special dispositions laying down a different classification".

LORD PHILLIMORE agreed with this proposal.

M. HAGERUP, however, said that the proposed wording did not appear to him to be sufficiently clear. He suggested the following idea: instead of inserting the words proposed by the President, to substitute in the last paragraph of Article 1 for the words "though they cannot" the words "even should they be unable to".

The PRESIDENT explained that a distinction must be drawn between real legal cases and cases of a non-legal nature, which as a result

les parties, sont assimilés aux questions juridiques.

M. HAGERUP estimant qu'il est nécessaire de s'exprimer bien clairement pour le cas où, en vertu d'une convention entre les parties, des conflits d'ordre non juridique seront assimilés aux questions juridiques, propose de substituer une disposition dans le sens de l'article 22 du projet des Cinq Puissances, au dernier alinéa du projet actuel.

LORD PHILLIMORE fait valoir que le dernier alinéa de l'article 1er n'introduit point de restriction au premier alinéa; la stipulation du second alinéa est purement facultative: les parties pourront, si elles le désirent, assimiler des questions d'ordre non juridique aux questions juridiques. Il trouve que cet alinéa correspond à cet article 22 du projet des Cinq Puissances que M. Hagerup a proposé d'ajouter au projet soumis par Lord Phillimore au cours de la séance précédente.

M. HAGERUP croit qu'on est d'accord quant au fond; on pourra laisser au Comité de rédaction le soin de trouver la formule. Il demande si le dernier alinéa de l'article 3 est destiné à donner satisfaction au point de vue de Lord Phillimore.

Le PRESIDENT explique qu'à son avis cet alinéa n'est pas indispensable, mais qu'il a son utilité.

M. HAGERUP propose, afin d'éviter toute équivoque, d'insérer dans le dernier alinéa de l'article 3 les mots: „dans le sens de l'article 14 du Pacte".

Le PRESIDENT dit qu'il faut examiner si ces mots ne feraient pas double emploi avec l'expression déjà introduite à cet effet à l'alinéa 2.

M. HAGERUP demande si la compétence de la Cour, telle qu'elle résulterait de l'adoption du projet, devra s'étendre à tous les Etats ou seulement aux Membres de la Société des Nations.

M. LODER croit qu'il faut maintenir le dernier alinéa du premier article. En effet, une Cour de Justice ne peut, d'après sa nature, connaître que des différends juridiques; si l'on veut étendre sa compétence au delà de ces limites, il est nécessaire de le spécifier explicitement. Si tel n'est pas l'avis de M. Hagerup, M. Loder ne peut pas se rallier à lui.

M. HAGERUP croit que M. Loder n'a pas compris toute sa pensée. Il a seulement voulu sig-

of agreement between the parties are assimilated to legal questions.

M. HAGERUP thought it necessary expressly to mention cases in which, by virtue of a Convention between the parties, disputes of a non-legal nature were classed with disputes of a legal nature, and proposed to substitute a provision to the effect of Article 22 of the project of the Five Powers for the last paragraph of the present project.

LORD PHILLIMORE pointed out that the last paragraph of Article 1 introduced no restriction on the first paragraph; the stipulation of the second paragraph was purely optional: the parties could, if they wished, class questions of a non-legal nature with questions of a legal nature. He thought that this paragraph corresponded to Article 22 of the Five Power's project, the Article M. Hagerup had proposed to add to the proposition submitted by Lord Phillimore during the previous meeting.

M. HAGERUP thought that as they were agreed upon principles, they might leave the task of finding a suitable wording to the drafting Committee. He asked whether the last paragraph of Article 3 was intended to give satisfaction to Lord Phillimore's point of view.

The PRESIDENT said that in his opinion the paragraph was not indispensable, but that it had its use.

M. HAGERUP, in order to avoid any ambiguity, proposed to insert in the last paragraph of Article 3 the words "according to Article 14 of the Covenant".

The PRESIDENT said that it was necessary to examine whether these words would not duplicate the expression to the same effect already found in paragraph 2.

M. HAGERUP asked whether the competence of the Court, such as it would result from the adoption of the project, should apply to all States or only to Members of the League of Nations.

M. LODER thought it necessary to keep the last paragraph of the Article 1. Practically a Court of Justice, by its nature, could only hear legal disputes; if it was desired to extend its competence beyond these limits the fact must be expressly stated. If M. Hagerup did not think so, M. Loder could not agree with him.

M. HAGERUP thought that M. Loder did not quite understand his idea. He had only

naler une petite inexactitude dans le texte proposé. On n'a pas tenu suffisamment compte de ce que les traités auxquels le texte fait allusion, concernent en premier lieu des questions juridiques, bien que, au moins dans quelques cas — sinon dans tous — ils visent aussi des questions d'ordre politique.

Le PRESIDENT est d'avis que l'expression „un accord intervenu entre les parties" dans le dernier alinéa de l'article 1er, couvre le cas visé par M. Hagerup.

LORD PHILLIMORE déclare que l'importance des cas de ce genre ne lui a pas échappé. Il reconnaît qu'il peut y avoir des traités qui soumettent à la juridiction internationale des questions autres que des questions juridiques; dans ces cas il n'est pas certain que la juridiction compétente soit la Cour Permanente de Justice. C'est justement ce qui rend nécessaire la formule qui a trouvé sa place au 2ème alinéa de l'article 1.

M. HAGERUP fait observer que c'est bien là le point qu'il a eu en vue. Il fait sienne l'idée contenue au 2e alinéa de l'article 1er, mais il en trouve l'exposition un peu défectueuse.

M. FERNANDES demande au Président d'expliquer un point qui touche au fond même de la question: Est-ce qu'une question ne peut être portée devant la Cour que si toutes les voies diplomatiques ont été tentées?

Le PRESIDENT explique que les moyens diplomatiques, dans le sens ordinairement donné à ces mots, doivent être épuisés avant le recours à la Cour.

Mr. ROOT fait observer que la formule selon laquelle toutes les voies diplomatiques doivent avoir été tentées est d'un emploi fréquent dans la vie internationale et qu'elle n'a jamais donné lieu à des difficultés. L'éventualité visée par cette formule se présente lorsqu'une des deux parties a demandé à l'autre de formuler par écrit son point de vue, et que l'autre se refuse à le faire.

Le PRESIDENT déclare que Mr. Root a mis à la fois en lumière la nécessité de la méthode diplomatique et ses limites naturelles.

M. RICCI-BUSATTI se borne à proposer une série d'amendements au texte soumis par le Président; ces amendements s'expliqueront d'eux-mêmes. Il en donne lecture (voir l'annexe 3), en

wished to point out a slight inaccuracy in the proposed text. Sufficient account had not been taken of the fact that the treaties referred to by the text deal in the first place with legal questions, although — in some cases at least, if not in all — they include also questions of political character.

The PRESIDENT was of the opinion that the expression "the subject of an agreement between the parties" in the last paragraph of Article 1 would cover the case mentioned by M. Hagerup.

LORD PHILLIMORE said that he had not lost sight of the importance of this kind of cases. He admitted that there might be treaties which submitted other than legal questions to the international jurisdiction; in such a case he was not sure that the competent jurisdiction was the Permanent Court of Justice. It is exactly that which necessitates the clause found in the second paragraph of Article 1.

M. HAGERUP pointed out that this was exactly the point which he had in mind. He adopted the idea contained in Paragraph 2 of Article 1, but he felt the wording slightly defective.

M. FERNANDES asked the President to explain a point which touches the heart of the question: Could a question be taken before the Court only when all diplomatic means of settlement had been tried?

The PRESIDENT explained that diplomatic means, in the ordinary sense of these words, should be exhausted before the appeal to the tribunal.

Mr. ROOT pointed out that the clause stating that all diplomatic means must be exhausted was very frequently used in international affairs, and that it had never given rise to any difficulties. The eventuality referred to by this clause arises when one party requests the other party to state its views in writing and the other party refuses to do so.

The PRESIDENT said that Mr. Root had explained the necessity for diplomatic methods and at the same time its natural limits.

M. RICCI-BUSATTI confined himself to proposing a series of amendments to the texts submitted by the President. These amendments were self-explanatory. M. Ricci-Busatti

ajoutant quelques mots à propos du 1er article, pour bien fixer son point de vue au sujet de la nature des différends dont il s'agit.

Le PRESIDENT ne voit pas la nécessité d'éliminer de la formule les termes: „les différends d'ordre juridique" qui ont été adoptés en 1899 et en 1907 (Articles 16 et 38 de la première Convention).

LORD PHILLIMORE observe que le Pacte de la Société des Nations contient la même formule.

M. HAGERUP se rallie complètement aux amendements de M. Ricci-Busatti.

Le PRESIDENT proteste contre les amendements à l'article 1er. Il ne comprend pas pourquoi on s'élèvait si fort contre des formules antérieurement admises sans difficulté.

Au sujet des amendements de M. Ricci-Busatti sur le 2ème alinéa de l'article 1er, il se demande si M. Ricci-Busatti à l'intention de nier la distinction entre les questions de droit et les questions non-juridiques. A cet égard, il rappelle deux faits: les Traités généraux d'arbitrage qui ne bornent pas aux questions de droit la compétence du tribunal arbitral, et un article de M. Louis Renault où celui-ci fait valoir la nécessité de donner à la Cour Internationale une compétence subsidiaire pour des questions autres que les questions juridiques.

Ces deux points démontrent qu'il ne faut pas renoncer à la formule introduite à l'alinéa 2 de l'article 1er. En effet, si dans des cas de ce genre les parties préfèrent la justice à l'arbitrage la porte de la Cour ne doit pas leur être fermée. —

Après cette déclaration du Président, une discussion de détail s'engage sur les amendements de M. Ricci-Busatti. Il s'en dégage l'impression que les membres sont d'accord sur le fond des questions contenus dans le texte du projet et sur ce que les amendements de M. Ricci-Busatti visent plutôt leur rédaction.

Cette discussion terminée, le PRESIDENT fait valoir que le texte proposé se fonde sur les précédents fournis par l'œuvre de La Haye et par le Pacte de la Société des Nations. Il trouve qu'il serait peu sage d'abandonner cette base. La formule „tout point de droit international" (paragraphe *b* de l'article 1er) a été sans doute suggérée par le souvenir qu'il y a deux sortes de droit international: le droit conventionnel spécial et le droit international général. Le Président pense qu'on ne saurait se passer de cette formule.

read his amendments (see Annex 3) and added a few words with respect to Article 1 to make clear his viewpoint regarding the disputes concerned.

The PRESIDENT saw no necessity to strike out from the clause the term, "cases of a legal nature", which was adopted in 1899 and 1907 (Articles 16 and 38 of the first Convention).

LORD PHILLIMORE pointed out that the Covenant of the League of Nations contained the same clause.

M. HAGERUP agreed completely with the amendments made by M. Ricci-Busatti.

The PRESIDENT protested against the amendments to Article 1. He did not understand why such strong objection was raised to a clause formerly admitted without difficulty.

Concerning M. Ricci-Busatti's amendment to the second Paragraph of Article 1, he asked whether M. Ricci-Busatti intended to deny the distinction between legal and non-legal questions. In this connection he recalled two points: the general treaties of arbitration which do not limit to questions of law the competence of the Court of Arbitration, and an Article by M. Louis Renault in wich the latter points out the necessity of giving the international Court an additional competence to deal with other than legal questions.

These two points prove that the clause inserted in Paragraph 2 of Article 1 must not be rejected. If in cases of this nature the parties in practice prefer justice to arbitration, the doors of the Court must not be closed to them.

After the President's speech, a discussion took place concerning the details of M. Ricci-Busatti's amendments. It appeared that the members were agreed concerning the fundamental questions dealt with in the text of the draft, and that the amendments suggested by M. Ricci-Busatti affected rather the drafting.

At the end of this discussion, the PRESIDENT pointed out that the text proposed was based on precedents supplied by the work at the Hague and by the Covenant of the League of Nations. He thought it would be unwise to abandon this basis. The phrase: "Any point of international law" (Paragraph *b* of Article 1) no doubt was suggested by the fact that there are two kinds of international law: the law founded on special conventions, and general international law. The President thought that this formula could not be omitted.

LORD PHILLIMORE croit que les amendements de M. Ricci-Busatti aux articles 2 et 3 du texte défendu par le Président concernent purement leur rédaction; il les juge utiles et pense qu'on doit les accepter.

Il est disposé également à retoucher le 2ème alinéa de l'article 1er. Par contre, en ce qui concerne le premier alinéa de cet article, il croit qu'il faut maintenir la formule du Pacte.

M. RICCI-BUSATTI répond qu'il trouve cette formule défectueuese et qu'elle a besoin d'être corrigée.

Le PRESIDENT prie M. Ricci-Busatti de lui présenter ses amendements par écrit. (Voir annexe 3*bis*).

M. HAGERUP signale un autre point défectueux de l'article 1er du texte proposé. Le premier alinéa est en effet si large qu'il ne distingue pas entre les conflits dans lesquels seuls des membres de la Société des Nations sont parties, et ceux dans lesquels d'autres Etats se trouvent être parties.

LORD PHILLIMORE explique que c'est à dessein qu'il n'a pas fait entrer dans le projet une disposition comblant la lacune qui vient d'être signalée: il a eu, en effet, l'impression que le Président n'était pas prêt à adhérer à une solution donnant à tous les Etats le droit d'avoir recours à la Cour. La question sera certainement tranchée plus tard.

M. HAGERUP signale encore que l'article 3 du projet ne peut viser que les cas où il y a accord entre les parties. Si l'on ouvre la Cour aux Etats non-membres de la Société, comme il ressort de la rédaction actuelle de l'article 1er, il faut cependant éviter de leur donner le droit d'assigner un Membre de la Société devant la Cour. A cet effet, M. Hagerup propose de rédiger la première phrase de l'article 3 de la manière suivante: „lorsqu'un différend, tel qu'il est prévu à l'article 1er, s'élève entre deux Etats Membres de la Société des Nations". etc.

Le PRESIDENT ne s'oppose pas à l'idée suggérée par M. Hagerup.

LORD PHILLIMORE demande à réfléchir encore sur le point.

M. LODER croit que M. Hagerup a raison. Il est d'avis que l'amendement ne doit pas être introduit à propos de l'article 1er, qui a trait à la compétence matérielle, mais à propos de l'article 3, où il s'agit de la compétence *ratione personarum.*

LORD PHILLIMORE thought that the amendments of M. Ricci-Busatti to articles 2 and 3 of the text advocated by the President concerned only matters of drafting; he thought that they were useful and should be accepted.

He was disposed also to correct Paragraph 2 of Article 1. On the other hand, concerning the first paragraph of this article, he thought it necessary to follow the wording of the Covenant.

M. RICCI-BUSATTI answered that he thought this wording defective, and that it should be amended.

The PRESIDENT asked M. Ricci-Busatti to submit his amendments in writing. (See Annex 3*bis*).

M. HAGERUP pointed out another defect in Article 1 of the proposed text. The first paragraph is so wide in its bearing that it does not distinguish between disputes in which only Members of the League of Nations were parties and those in which other States were parties.

LORD PHILLIMORE stated that it was with intention that he had not included in the project a provision bridging the gap just mentioned. He had had the impression that the President was not prepared to adhere to a solution giving all States the right to appeal to the Court. The question certainly would have to be decided later.

M. HAGERUP pointed out also that Article 3 of the project could only refer to cases in which there was an agreement between the parties. If the Court were open to States non-members of the League, as it appears from the present draft of Article 1, they must in any case not be given the right of summoning a Member of the League before the Court. With this object, M. Hagerup proposed to frame the first sentence of Article 3 in the following way: "When a dispute, as provided in Article 1, arises between two States Members of the League of Nations, etc. . . . .".

The PRESIDENT was not opposed to M. Hagerup's idea.

LORD PHILLIMORE asked to consider the point further.

M. LODER thought that M. Hagerup was right. He thought that the amendment ought not to be introduced in connection with Article 1, which deals with the material competence of the Court, but in connection with Article 3, which is concerned with competence *ratione personarum.*

M. ALTAMIRA fait observer que dans l'article 3 les mots „voies diplomatiques" ont deux sens différents: un sens étroit et un sens large, selon qu'il signifient des démarches entre les agents diplomatiques, ou tous les moyens pacifiques mis en œuvre pour le règlement d'un conflit. M. Altamira voudrait voir consacrer une formule qui comprît tous les moyens d'apaisement: c'est pourquoi il recommande à l'attention des membres certains passages du projet qu'il a soumis.

Le PRESIDENT fait valoir que la proposition de M. Altamira se heurte à deux difficultés: d'abord l'expression „voies diplomatiques" est, comme l'a fait remarquer Mr. Root, acceptée dans la langue officielle et consacrée par la Convention de 1907; puis, l'expression „moyens pacifiques" pourrait aller jusqu'à comprendre même les voies de fait qui sont généralement regardées comme compatibles avec l'état de paix, ce qui ne serait guère admissible.

Le Président fait encore remarquer que, l'expression „voies diplomatiques" ayant été reproduite dans un grand nombre de traités, on se demanderait quelle a été l'intention du Comité en lui substituant une autre expression.

M. HAGERUP trouve que la formule proposée par M. Altamira est trop large. Elle ouvre à une partie de mauvaise foi la possibilité de créer des difficultés, en s'adressant, pour régler un conflit déterminé, à la conciliation, à la médiation etc.; et cela malgré l'existence d'une clause d'arbitrage obligatoire, qui serait ainsi rendue illusoire.

LORD PHILLIMORE fait observer qu'on a voulu créer un droit facultatif: quand les voies diplomatiques auront été tentées, les parties auront le droit de s'adresser à la Cour, si elles le jugent utile. L'adoption de la formule de M. Altamira créerait des délais qu'il vaut mieux éviter.

M. ALTAMIRA insiste pour que tous les moyens diplomatiques soient épuisés avant le recours obligatoire à la Cour.

LORD PHILLIMORE souligne les difficultés soulevées par les délais qui résulteraient de là.

M. HAGERUP ajoute que la formule de M. Altamira augmente inutilement le nombre des conditions requises pour obtenir le droit de recourir à la Cour.

M. FERNANDES reprend le point sur lequel il a déjà demandé un renseignement au Pré-

M. ALTAMIRA pointed out that in Article 3 the words "diplomatic means" have two different meanings: a narrow and a wide meaning, according to whether they refer to negotiations between diplomatic representatives or all peaceful means put into operation for settling a conflict. M. Altamira desired to have a clause covering all peaceful means of obtaining a solution. For this reason he drew the attention of the members to certain passages of the project which he had submitted.

The PRESIDENT pointed out that M. Altamira's proposal was confronted by two difficulties: first of all the expression "diplomatic means", as Mr. Root had observed, was accepted in official language and sanctioned by the Convention of 1907; while the expression "pacific means" might go as far as to include all violent means generally looked upon as compatible with a state of peace, which would hardly be admissible.

The President also pointed out that as the expression "diplomatic means" had been used in a large number of treaties, it would be asked what was the intention of the Committee in substituting another expression.

M. HAGERUP thought that the formula proposed by M. Altamira was too broad. It opens to a party acting in bad faith the possibility of creating difficulties by appealing, for the settlement of a given conflict, to conciliation, to mediation etc., and that in spite of the existence of a clause for compulsory arbitration, which thus would be rendered illusory.

LORD PHILLIMORE said that they had wished to create an optional right: when diplomatic means had been tried, the parties would have the right to appeal to the Court, if they thought it useful. The adoption of M. Altamira's proposal would create delays, which might better be avoided.

M. ALTAMIRA insisted that all diplomatic means should be exhausted before obligatory recourse to the Court.

LORD PHILLIMORE laid emphasis on the difficulties caused by the delays which would result from this.

M. HAGERUP added that the formula proposed by M. Altamira would uselessly add to the conditions required to obtain the right of appeal to the Court.

M. FERNANDES again considered the point concerning which he had already asked the

sident, à savoir la nécessité de tenter toutes les voies diplomatiques avant de recourir à la Cour. Il est évident, d'après lui, qu'avant d'aller devant la Cour il faut essayer les moyens amicaux, mais d'autre part il pense que l'expression „toutes les voies diplomatiques" serait dangereuse. On devrait se contenter d'une recommandation, parce qu'une stipulation ferme ouvrirait à une partie de mauvaise foi le moyen de contester la compétence de la Cour, en faisant valoir qu'au cours du conflit en question, un moyen diplomatique a été laissé de côté. Le moins habile des défendeurs pourra traîner indéfiniment en longueur les négociations diplomatiques, en en parcourant d'ailleurs obligatoirement toute la série, avant que le différend puisse être porté devant la Cour de Justice. L'intervention de celle-ci serait dès lors, sinon pratiquement écartée, du moins beaucoup trop retardée. Il ne serait d'ailleurs pas facile de passer, dans tous les cas, par la filière de toutes les voies diplomatiques — négociations directes, bons offices, médiation, enquête — qui ne conviennent pas également à tous les différends.

Le PRESIDENT est d'avis que la remarque de M. Fernandes est bien fondée et qu'on doit reprendre la formule de 1907 et celle du Pacte. Il préfère cependant la première qui dit: „les différends internationaux qui n'ont pu être réglés par la voie diplomatique. . . . ."

M. RICCI-BUSATTI prend acte de ce que le Président est disposé à amender une formule du Pacte.

Le PRESIDENT déclare qu'il est tout prêt à s'entendre avec les autres membres, comme il a essayé de s'entendre avec Lord Phillimore.

M. FERNANDES exprime quelques inquiétudes sur l'avis exprimé par M. Hagerup qu'il serait injuste de donner aux Etats non-membres de la Société des Nations le droit de citer un Membre devant la Cour, et qui semble avoir rallié la majorité des membres du Comité. M. Fernandes envisage le cas où un Etat non-membre de la Société des Nations, p. ex. les Etats-Unis d'Amérique, adhérerait à la convention établissant la Cour. Serait-il juste dans ces conditions de le priver du droit de citer un Membre en justice? S'il en était ainsi, les Etats non-membres de la Société des Nations ne seraient pas disposés à donner leur adhésion à la convention établissant la Cour. En effet, en donnant leur adhésion, ils s'engagent à comparaître devant la Cour sur citation d'un autre Etat. Si,

President for information: — the necessity of trying all diplomatic means before resorting to the Court. According to him, it was obvious that before going to the Court, amicable means must be tried; but, on the other hand, he thought that the expression "all diplomatic means" would be dangerous. They should be satisfied with a recommendation, because a definite stipulation would furnish to a party acting in bad faith grounds for contesting the competence of the Court by stating that at a stage in the conflict in question a diplomatic means had been neglected. The least skillful defendant could prolong indefinitely the length of diplomatic negotiations, by running through the whole series, before a dispute could be brought before the Court of Justice, and by being obliged to do so. The intervention of the Court then would be, if not practically set aside, at least too much delayed. Furthermore it would not be possible to pass, in any case, through the whole series of diplomatic means — direct negociations, good offices, mediation, inquiries, — which are not equally suited to all disputes.

The PRESIDENT thought that M. Fernandes' statements were well founded and that the wording of 1907 and of the Covenant should be adopted. He preferred the former, which states: "international differences which it has not been possible to settle by diplomacy . . . ."

M. RICCI-BUSATTI drew attention to the fact that the President was disposed to amend a formula of the Covenant.

The PRESIDENT stated that he was ready to come to an understanding with the other members as he had attempted to do with Lord Phillimore.

M. FERNANDES expressed some anxiety concerning the opinion of M. Hagerup when the latter stated that it would be unfair to give States not Members of the League of Nations the right to summon a Member before the Court, an opinion which seemed to be shared by the majority of the members. M. Fernandes considered a case in which a State, not a Member of the League of Nations, for instance, the United States, might adhere to the Convention establishing the Court. Would it be fair, under these circumstances, to deprive it of the right of summoning a Member to justice? If this were done, States non-members of the League of Nations would not be disposed to adhere to the Convention establishing the Court. Practically, by their adhering, they agreed to appear before

quand ils se présenteront en demandeurs, l'assentiment du défendeur est exigé pour que la Cour puisse être saisie, on leur aura fait une situation tellement inégale, qu'il sera de leur intérêt, et même de leur dignité, de ne pas s'associer à l'organisation projetée. Or, il paraît que cela n'entre pas dans l'intention du Comité.

M. HAGERUP remarque que c'est en vue d'écarter cette difficulté qu'il a proposé d'insérer à l'article 3 les mots: „dans le sens de l'article 14 du Pacte".

LORD PHILLIMORE admet que le texte de l'article 3 est défectueux. Il doit cependant être compris de la façon suivante: tout Etat ayant adhéré à la convention établissant la Cour sera assimilé aux Membres de la Société des Nations.

M. FERNANDES déclare qu'il est parfaitement d'accord avec Lord Phillimore et qu'il a seulement voulu s'élever contre l'avis exprimé par M. Hagerup.

LORD PHILLIMORE croit qu'on peut résumer la question ainsi: la Cour sera-t-elle ouverte aux nations qui ne sont pas Membres de la Société des Nations et qui n'ont pas non plus signé la convention qui la crée? Cette question n'a jusqu'ici pas été tranchée.

M. HAGERUP croit qu'on pourra donner satisfaction à M. Fernandes en formulant les premières lignes de l'article 3 de la manière suivante: „lorsqu'un différend tel qu'il est prévu à l'article 1er, s'élève entre deux Etats, Membres de la Société des Nations ou signataires du présent acte", etc.

M. FERNANDES préfère la formule qui se trouve dans le texte original de l'article.

Le PRESIDENT voudrait dire un mot concernant les Etats qui ne sont pas Membres de la Société des Nations et qui ne sont pas non plus mentionnés à l'annexe du Pacte. Ces Etats ne se trouvent pas dans la même situation que les autres, et ils n'ont le droit de procéder devant la Cour que dans les conditions déterminées par l'article 17 du Pacte. Le droit plein leur doit-il être accordé par le statut concernant la Cour, ou, autrement dit, ce statut peut-il assimiler ces Etats aux autres Etats?

Le Président déclare qu'il a, à cet égard, de graves scrupules.

Le Pacte n'exclut personne; la Société des Nations est une Société ouverte, mais en assimilant d'emblée aux autres Etats les Etats qui ne sont

the Court at the summons of another State. If when they appear as plaintiffs, the consent of the defendant was required for the Court to hear the case, such an unequal situation would be created that it would be to their interest, and that even their dignity would require them, not to take part in the proposed organisation. But it seems that that is not the Committee's intention.

M. HAGERUP pointed out that it was for the purpose of disposing of this difficulty that he had proposed to insert in Article 3 the words "according to Article 14 of the Covenant".

LORD PHILLIMORE admitted that the text of Article 3 was defective. It should, however, be understood in the following manner: any State having adhered to the Convention establishing the Court would be classed with the Members of the League of Nations.

M. FERNANDES declared that he quite agreed with Lord Phillimore, and had only wished to oppose the opinion expressed by M. Hagerup.

LORD PHILLIMORE thought that the question could be summarised thus: Should the Court be open to Nations which are not Members of the League of Nations, and which have not signed the Convention of the Court? This question had not yet been resolved.

M. HAGERUP thought that satisfaction could be accorded to M. Fernandes by framing the first lines of Article 3 in the following way: "When a dispute, as provided in Article 1, arises between two States, Members of the League of Nations, or signatories of the present Act, etc."

M. FERNANDES preferred the wording in the original text of the Article.

The PRESIDENT desired to deal briefly with States which are neither Members of the League of Nations nor mentioned in the Annex to the Covenant. These States are not in the same situation as others, and they have not the right to take action before the Court except under the special conditions determined by Article 17 of the Covenant. Should full right be given them by the Statute dealing with the Court; in other words, could this Statute make these States equal to other States?

The President had grave doubts on this point.

The Covenant excludes nobody; the League of Nations is an open League, but to include at the outset the States not mentioned in the An-

pas mentionnés à l'annexe, on irait à l'encontre du Pacte, dans des conditions d'ailleurs injustifiables.

Il ne s'agit pas ici d'une simple modification, il s'agit du renversement d'un système.

M. ADATCI trouve que les paroles du Président expriment la sagesse et la justice. Pour lui la chose est parfaitement claire; il faut faire une distinction entre les Etats Membres de la Société et les Etats non-membres. Il croit devoir approfondir cette question; il le fera au cours d'une prochaine séance.

M. FERNANDES tient à faire remarquer au Président qu'il n'a visé dans sa remarque que les Etats dont l'accès à la Société des Nations est admis *de plano*.

M. HAGERUP tient à faire une réponse aux remarques de M. Fernandes. Il se place exclusivement au point de vue juridique. La faculté d'assigner unilatéralement un Etat devant la Cour ne peut être donnée qu'aux Etats qui ont accepté les obligations découlant de la Convention. Le dernier alinéa de l'article 3 ne lui donne pas satisfaction. En effet, cet alinéa n'établit que l'obligation d'avoir recours à l'arbitrage; il n'a pas trait à l'assignation unilatérale.

M. Hagerup ajoute qu'il pense qu'au fond, il n'y a pas de divergence de vues entre M. Fernandes et lui. M. Fernandes a signalé que la formule „Membres de la Société des Nations" est trop limitée, et en cela il a raison. Il faut dire „tout Etat signataire du présent acte est consideré comme acceptant de soumettre à la Cour Permanente tout différend caractérisé par l'article 1er entre cet Etat et un autre Etat signataire".

LORD PHILLIMORE propose une nouvelle rédaction du dernier alinéa et en donne lecture (voir annexe 4).

M. HAGERUP propose de faire de cette nouvelle rédaction un nouvel article 4. On doit en effet avoir en vue, non seulement les dispositions de l'article 3, mais aussi celles de l'article 1er.

LORD PHILLIMORE accepte cette idée.

Le PRESIDENT engage les membres à lui faire parvenir par écrit les propositions d'amendement qu'ils désirent faire au sujet du projet de texte qu'il a lu au début de la séance.

Il propose que la question de la situation des Etats non-membres de la Société, soulevée par M. Adatci à propos de l'article 17 du Pacte, soit discutée à la réunion prochaine. A cet

nex would be unjustifiably contrary to the Covenant.

It is not a question here of mere modification, but of the reversal of the system.

M. ADATCI thought that the President's remarks were both wise and just. It was perfectly clear to him that a distinction must be drawn between States Members of the League and States which are not Members. He thought they must go more deeply into the question. He would do so at a future meeting.

M. FERNANDES desired to assure the President that his remarks had reference only to States whose access to the League of Nations was admitted *de plano*.

M. HAGERUP wished to answer M. Fernandes. His point of view was purely legal. The power of summoning uni-laterally a State before the Court could only be given to States which had accepted the obligations arising from the Convention. The last paragraph of article 3 was not satisfactory to him. This paragraph only laid down obligatory recourse to Arbitration; it did not deal with unilateral arraignment.

M. Hagerup added that he thought that there was no fundamental difference of opinion between M. Fernandes and himself. M. Fernandes had only shown that the clause "Members of the League of Nations" was too narrow, and concerning that he was correct. The clause should read: "Any State signing the present Act is considered as having accepted the obligation to submit to the Permanent Court any dispute described by Article 1 between this State and another signatory State".

LORD PHILLIMORE proposed a new wording for the last paragraph and read it. (See Annex 4).

M. HAGERUP proposed that this new draft should constitute a new Article 4. Not only the disposition of Article 3, but also those of Article 1 must be taken into account.

LORD PHILLIMORE accepted this suggestion.

The PRESIDENT requested the members to submit to him in writing any proposed amendments which they desired to put forward with reference to the project which he had read at the beginning of the meeting.

He proposed that the question of the situation of States not Members of the League raised by M. Adatci with reference to Article 17 of the

égard il attire l'attention du Comité sur le fait qu'au point de vue de la solution de leurs différends les Etats non-membres n'entrent pas, aux termes du Pacte, *de plano* en rapport avec les Membres: une invitation spéciale est requise à cet effet. Toujours aux termes de l'article 17, les dispositions des articles 12 à 16 et suivants ne seront applicables aux Etats non-membres, qu'aux conditions prévues par ce même article.

LORD PHILLIMORE pense qu'il s'agit seulement d'une recommandation à faire aux non-membres, et non pas d'une obligation à leur imposer.

Le Conseil de la Société des Nations ne doit que conseiller aux Etats non-membres de se soumettre à la juridiction de la Cour.

Une discussion s'engage entre LORD PHILLIMORE et le PRESIDENT sur les conditions dans lesquelles les Etats non-membres peuvent être admis devant la Cour. On est d'accord pour reconnaître que l'égalité absolue ne saurait être établie.

M. ALTAMIRA fait valoir que l'acte établissant la Cour devant être signé par les Etats, c'est au Conseil qu'il appartiendra de poser les conditions auxquelles les différents Etats peuvent être admis à signer.

Le PRESIDENT propose qu'à la séance de jeudi on discute la question soulevée par M. Adatci, et qu'au cours de la séance suivante la question de la nomination des juges soit reprise, à condition qu'on arrive demain à s'entendre sur une formule au sujet de la première question. Il suggère l'idée de tenir des réunions en Chambre du Conseil en vue de hâter le travail.

M. ALTAMIRA demande à Lord Phillimore de rédiger un texte sur la compétence de la Cour, en tenant compte des divers amendements présentés au début de la séance. (Voir annexe 5).

M. RICCI-BUSATTI communiquera ses amendements au Président.

Le PRESIDENT donne lecture d'une lettre adressée à M. Loder par M. Schuurman. Le Comité décide qu'il n'y a pas lieu d'en tenir compte. (Voir annexe 6).

M. RICCI-BUSATTI fait remarquer que le Comité doit encore discuter la question du droit matériel à appliquer par la Cour.

Le PRESIDENT approuve et exprime l'avis que, lorsque les grandes questions auront été

Covenant should be discussed at the next meeting. In this connection he drew the Committee's attention to the fact that from the standpoint of settling their disputes, non-member States do not enter into relations with Members *de plano* according to the Covenant; special invitation to do so was necessary. According to the terms of Article 17, the provisions of Article 12 to 16 and following were applicable to non-member States only under conditions provided by this same Article.

LORD PHILLIMORE thought that a recommendation only should be made to non-members and that a definite obligation should not be imposed upon them.

The Council of the League of Nations could only advise non-member States to submit to the jurisdiction of the Court.

Discussion took place between LORD PHILLIMORE and the PRESIDENT concerning conditions under which non-member States could be admitted before the Court. The Committee was agreed in recognising that absolute equality could not be established.

M. ALTAMIRA pointed out that as the Act establishing the Court must be signed by the States, the Council would have to fix the conditions under which the various States should be permitted to sign.

The PRESIDENT proposed that at the Thursday meeting the question raised by M. Adatci should be discussed, and that at the following meeting the question of the nomination of judges should be taken up again, provided that on Thursday a solution for the first question was obtained. He suggested that unofficial meetings should be held to hasten the work.

M. ALTAMIRA asked Lord Phillimore to draft a text on the competence of the Court, taking into account the various amendments presented at the beginning of the meeting. (See Annex 5).

M. RICCI-BUSATTI would send his amendments to the President.

The PRESIDENT read a letter addressed to M. Loder by M. Schuurman. The Committee decided that the letter did not call for its attention. (See Annex 6).

M. RICCI-BUSATTI pointed out that the Committee had yet to discuss the question of the substantive law to be applied by the Court.

The PRESIDENT agreed and thought that when the first reading of the important questions

résolues en première lecture, le Comité pourra résoudre la question des règles de procédure en peu de séances. Il dit qu'il est entendu que la base de discussion à cet égard sera le projet des Cinq Puissances.

M. HAGERUP suggère l'idée de discuter plus à fond la question des règles de procédure. Il croit que les questions de la compétence et du droit matériel à appliquer n'occuperont pas, à elles deux, une séance entière. Dans ces conditions, on pourra commencer la discussion des règles de procédure dans la séance qui sera consacrée aux autres questions.

M. Hagerup est moins optimiste que le Président au sujet de la facilité de régler les questions de procédure. Il croit que sur plusieurs points, la discussion pourra se prolonger.

Le PRESIDENT propose de faire procéder à une comparaison des dispositions concernant la procédure contenues dans le projet des Cinq Puissances, avec celles de la Convention de 1907: les stipulations du projet pourront être mises en regard des articles de la Convention. Il faudrait éviter les confusions résultant de multiples numérotages.

LORD PHILLIMORE fait observer que le numérotage des articles formant la future Convention établissant la Cour sera tout à fait indépendant du numérotage de la Convention de 1907.

La prochaine séance sera tenue jeudi à 9.30 du matin.

La séance est levée à 1 heure 10 de l'après-midi.

Le Président:
(signé) Brn. DESCAMPS.

Le Secrétaire-Général:
(signé) D. ANZILOTTI.

had been passed, the Committee could easily settle the question of rules of procedure in a few meetings. He said that it would be understood that the basis of discussion on this subject would be the project of the Five Powers.

M. HAGERUP suggested that the question of the rules of procedure should be more deeply discussed. He thought that the questions of competence and of the law to be applied would not together take up a whole meeting. Therefore they might begin the discussion of rules of procedure at the meeting which was devoted to the other questions.

M. Hagerup was less optimistic than the President as to the ease with which the questions of procedure could be arranged. He thought that on several points the discussion might be a protracted one.

The PRESIDENT proposed to have a comparison made of the dispositions relating to procedure contained in the project of the Five Powers with those of the Convention of 1907; the provisions of the project might be arranged according to the articles of the Convention. Confusion resulting from too many systems of numbering must be avoided.

LORD PHILLIMORE pointed out that the numbering of the articles which were to form the new Convention establishing the Court would be quite independent of the numbering of the Convention of 1907.

The next meeting will be held Thursday at 9.30 a.m.

The meeting closed at 1.10 p.m.

The President:
(signed) Brn. DESCAMPS.

The Secretary-General:
(signed) D. ANZILOTTI.

ANNEXE No. 1.

Proposition transactionnelle communiquée par le Baron Descamps.

Article 1er.

La Cour Permanente de Justice Internationale est compétente pour statuer sur les contestations concernant les différends qui sont d'ordre juridique, c'est-à-dire ceux qui concernent:

a. l'interprétation d'un traité;

b. tout point de droit international;

c. la réalité de tout fait qui, s'il était établi, constituerait la rupture d'un engagement international;

d. l'étendue ou la nature de la réparation dûe pour la rupture d'un engagement international;

e. l'interprétation d'une sentence rendue par la Cour.

Sont assimilés aux différends d'ordre juridique, au point de vue juridictionnel, les différends qui, bien que ne pouvant être formulés et résolus juridiquement, sont l'objet d'un accord intervenu entre les parties quant à leur solution par voie de judicature.

Article 2.

En cas de contestation concernant le caractère juridique ou non d'un différend, la Cour Permanente décide cette question en ordre préjudiciel.

Article 3.

Lorsqu'un différend tel qu'il est prévu dans l'article 1er s'élève entre deux Etats, que toutes les voies diplomatiques pour arranger ce différend ont été épuisées, et que l'on n'est pas convenu de choisir une Cour d'arbitrage dans le sens de l'article XIII du Pacte, la partie qui se prétend lésée peut en saisir la Cour Permanente.

Si l'autre partie refuse de soumettre le différend à la Cour, celle-ci décide en premier lieu s'il y a ou non engagement de soumettre le différend, selon l'article XIV du Pacte, à la procédure juridictionnelle.

Tout Etat signataire du présent Acte est considéré comme acceptant de résoudre juridictionnellement tout différend caractérisé par l'article 1er.

ANNEX No. 1.

Transactional proposal submitted by Baron Descamps.

Article 1.

The Permanent Court of International Justice is competent to decide disputes concerning cases of a legal nature, that is to say those dealing with:

a. the interpretation of a treaty;

b. any question of international law;

c. the existence of any fact which, if established, would constitute a breach of any international obligation;

d. the extent and nature of reparation to be made for the breach of an international obligation;

e. the interpretation of a sentence rendered by the Court.

Cases, though they cannot be stated and decided according to strict law, which are the subject of an agreement between the parties to submit them for decision by judicial means, are classed with cases of a legal nature, for the purpose of submission to jurisdiction.

Article 2.

When the legal nature of a case is disputed, the Permanent Court will decide the point as an interlocutory question.

Article 3.

When a dispute as provided in Article 1 arises between two States and when all diplomatic means to settle the case have been exhausted, and provided that no agreement has been made to choose a Court of Arbitration as indicated in Article XIII of the Covenant, the party alleging injury may appeal to the Permanent Court.

If the other party refuses to submit the case to the Court, the latter will first of all decide whether an engagement to submit the case to jurisdiction does or does not exist in accordance with Article XIV of the Covenant.

Any State subcribing to the present Act is considered as having agreed to settle by legal means all disputes described in Article 1.

ANNEXE No. 2.

Projet de M. Altamira.

Dans tous les cas susceptibles d'une sentence en droit ou en équité, tout Etat ayant un différend avec un autre Etat, pourra demander à la Cour Permanente de Justice Internationale la connaissance de l'affaire, même sans l'assentiment de l'autre Etat, *si celui-ci ne convient pas de le résoudre par tout autre moyen pacifique* et refuse de se rendre à la Cour. La Cour ainsi saisie sera de plein droit compétente.

ANNEX No. 2.

Draft of M. Altamira.

In all cases permitting of a sentence in law or in equity any State in conflict with another State may bring the case before the Permanent Court of International Justice even without the consent of the other State *provided the latter does not agree to have the conflict settled by any other pacific means,* and refuses to appear before the Court. The Court thus appealed to shall be competent *ipso facto.*

ANNEXE No. 3.

Amendements au texte communiqué par le Baron Descamps proposés par M. Ricci-Busatti, le 30 juin.

Article 1er.

Supprimer les mots: „les différends qui sont d'ordre juridique c'est-à-dire ceux qui concernent" (ces mots ne figurent pas dans le projet des Cinq Puissances Neutres, ni dans l'article 13 du Pacte). Il serait peut-être utile d'ajouter, après le mot „contestation", les mots „entre Etats".

Ajouter à la lettre *a*) les mots „l'application ou".

Remplacer à la lettre *b*) les mots „tout point de" par les mots suivants „l'application ou l'interprétation d'une règle générale de . . ."

Remplacer le dernier alinéa par le suivant: „Elle est également compétente pour statuer sur tous différends, quelle que soit leur nature, qui sont l'objet d'un accord entre les parties, quant à leur solution par voie judiciaire".

Article 2.

Remplacer les mots „concernant le caractère juridique ou non, d'un différend" par les suivants: „sur le point de savoir si tel différend rentre, oui ou non, dans les catégories visées au paragraphe précédent".

Article 3.

2e alinéa: substituer aux deux derniers mots: „procédure juridictionelle" les suivants: „Cour de Justice Internationale".

3e alinéa: substituer également aux mots: „résoudre juridictionnellement" les suivants: „soumettre à la Cour de Justice Internationale".

J'ajoute que, à part les autres amendements qui ont été proposés et agréés au texte de l'article 3, la disposition de son deuxième alinéa gagnerait, peut-être, à être rapprochée des dispositions de l'article 2, puisque l'un et l'autre se réfèrent de quelque façon à l'engagement visé au dernier alinéa de l'article 1er. Le dernier alinéa de l'article 3 mériterait, à mon avis, d'être l'objet d'un article séparé.

(*signé*) A. RICCI-BUSATTI.

ANNEX No. 3.

Amendments to the text submitted by Baron Descamps, proposed by M. Ricci-Busatti on June 30th.

Article 1.

Strike out the words "disputes concerning cases of a legal nature, that is to say, those dealing with" (these words are not to be found in the scheme of the Five Neutral Powers nor in Article 13 of the Covenant). It might perhaps be useful to add after the word "disputes" the words "between States".

Add under letter *a*) the words "the application or".

Substitute under letter *b*), for the words "any question", the words "the application or interpretation of a general rule of".

Substitute for the last paragraph the following phrase: "It will also be competent to decide on all disputes, no matter of what description, which the parties have agreed to submit to a judicial decision".

Article 2.

Substitute for the words "when the legal nature of a case is disputed", the words "if a question arises whether a certain dispute is or is not included in the categories enumerated in the preceding article".

Article 3.

Second paragraph. Substitute for the two words "to jurisdiction" the following words "to the Court of International Justice".

Third paragraph. Substitute for the words "to settle by legal means" the following words "to refer to the Court of International Justice".

I add that, apart from the other amendments to Article 3 proposed and agreed to, the provision of its second paragraph might perhaps with advantage be connected with the provisions of the second Article, both of them having regard, to a certain extent, to the engagement laid down in the last paragraph of the first Article. The last paragraph of Article 3, in my opinion, deserves to be made a separate Article.

(*signed*) A. RICCI-BUSATTI.

ANNEXE No. 3*bis.*

Le texte du Baron Descamps amendé par M. Ricci-Busatti.

Article 1er.

La Cour Permanente de Justice Internationale est compétente pour statuer sur les contestations entre Etats concernant les différends d'ordre juridique qui ont pour objet:

a. l'interprétation ou l'application d'un traité;

b. l'interprétation ou l'application d'une règle générale de droit international (*réservé*);

c. la réalité de tout fait qui, s'il était établi, constituerait une infraction à une obligation internationale;

d. l'étendue ou la nature de la réparation dûe pour l'infraction à une obligation internationale;

e. l'interprétation d'une sentence rendue par la Cour.

Elle sera également compétente pour statuer sur tous différends qui, bien que n'ayant pas un caractère exclusivement juridique, sont l'objet d'un accord intervenu entre les Parties quant à leur solution par voie judiciaire.

Article 2.

En cas de contestation sur le point de savoir si un différend rentre, oui ou non, dans les catégories visées à l'article 1er, la Cour Permanente décide cette question en ordre préjudiciel.

Article 3.

Lorsqu'un différend tel qu'il est prévu à l'article 1er s'élève entre deux Etats, que tous les moyens diplomatiques pour arranger ce différend ont été épuisés, et que l'on n'est pas convenu de choisir une Cour d'arbitrage dans le sens de l'article 13 du Pacte, la partie qui se prétend lésée peut en saisir la Cour Permanente.

Si l'autre partie refuse de soumettre le différend à la Cour, celle-ci décide en premier lieu s'il y a ou non engagement de soumettre le différend à la Cour Permanente de Justice Internationale.

Article 4.

Tout Etat signataire du présent Acte est considéré comme acceptant de soumettre à la Cour Permanente de Justice Internationale, conformément aux dispositions qui précèdent, tout différend visé à l'article 1er, qui s'élève entre cet Etat et un autre Etat signataire.

ANNEX No. 3*bis.*

Baron Descamps text as amended by M. Ricci-Busatti.

Article 1.

The Permanent Court of International Justice is competent to decide disputes between States concerning cases of a legal nature which deal with:

a. the interpretation or application of a treaty;

b. the interpretation or application of a general rule of international law (*reserved*);

c. the existence of any fact which, if established, would constitute an infraction of an international obligation;

d. the extent and nature of reparation to be made for the infraction of an international obligation;

e. the interpretation of a sentence rendered by the Court.

It will also be competent to decide on all disputes which, though not of an exclusively legal nature, the parties have agreed to submit to a judicial decision.

Article 2.

If a question arises whether a certain dispute is or not included in the categories enumerated in the first Article, the Permanent Court shall decide it as an interlocutory question.

Article 3.

When a dispute, as provided in Article 3, arises between two States, and when all diplomatic means to settle the case have been exhausted, and provided that no agreement has been made to choose a Court of Arbitration as indicated in Article 13 of the Covenant, the party alleging injury may appeal to the Permanent Court.

If the other party refuses to submit the case to the Court, the latter will first of all decide whether an engagement to submit the case to the Permanent Court of International Justice exists.

Article 4.

Any State subscribing to the present Act is considered as having undertaken to submit to the Permanent Court of International Justice, in accordance with the foregoing dispositions, any dispute mentioned in Article 1, which arises between it and another signatory State.

ANNEXE No. 4.

Amendement de Lord Phillimore au dernier alinéa du texte du Baron Descamps (Annexe 1er).

Tout Etat signataire du présent Acte est considéré comme acceptant de soumettre à la Cour Permanente tout différend, caractérisé par l'article 1er, entre cet Etat et un autre Etat signataire.

ANNEX No. 4.

Lord Phillimore's Amendment to the last paragraph of Baron Descamps' text (Annex 1).

Any State signing the present Act, is considered as having agreed to submit to the Permanent Court any dispute between itself and another signatory State, as described by Article 1.

ANNEXE No. 5.

Texte amendé par Lord Phillimore.

Article 1er.

La Cour Permanente de Justice Internationale est compétente pour statuer sur les contestations entre Etats concernant les différends qui sont d'ordre juridique, c'est-à-dire ceux qui concernent:

a. l'interprétation d'un traité;

b. tout point de droit international;

c. la réalité de tout fait qui, s'il était établi, constituerait la rupture d'un engagement international;

d. l'étendue ou la nature de la réparation dûe pour la rupture d'un engagement international;

e. l'interprétation d'une sentence rendue par la Cour.

Sont assimilés aux différends d'ordre juridique, au point de vue juridictionnel, les différends qui, bien que ne pouvant être formulés et résolus juridiquement, sont l'objet d'un accord intervenu entre les parties quant à leur solution par voie judiciaire.

Article 2.

En cas de contestation sur le point de savoir si tel différend rentre, oui ou non, dans les catégories visées à l'article précédent, la Cour Permanente décide cette question en ordre préjudiciel.

Article 3.

Lorsqu'un différend tel qu'il est prévu à l'article 1er s'élève entre deux Etats, que tous les moyens diplomatiques pour régler ce différend ont été épuisés, et que l'on n'est pas convenu de choisir une Cour d'arbitrage dans le sens de l'article 13 du Pacte, la partie qui se prétend lésée peut en saisir la Cour Permanente.

Si l'autre partie refuse de soumettre le différend à la Cour, celle-ci décide en premier lieu s'il y a, oui ou non, engagement, positif ou négatif, de soumettre le différend, en conformité avec les exigences de l'article 14 du Pacte, à la Cour Permanente.

ANNEX No. 5.

Draft amended by Lord Phillimore.

Article 1.

The Permanent Court of International Justice is competent to decide disputes between States concerning cases of a legal nature, that is to say those dealing with:

a. the interpretation of a treaty;

b. any point of International Law;

c. the existence of any fact, which, if established, would constitute a breach of an international contract;

d. the extent or nature of reparation due for the breach of an international contract;

e. the interpretation of a sentence rendered by the Court.

Cases, though they cannot be stated and decided according to strict law, which are the subject of an agreement between the parties to submit them for decision by judicial means, are classed with cases of a legal nature, for the purpose of submission to jurisdiction.

Article 2.

In cases of a dispute on the question whether a given case does or does not fall within the classification of the preceding article, the Permanent Court will render an interlocutory decision.

Article 3.

When a case under the provisions of Article 1 arises between two States and after all diplomatic means of settling such dispute have been exhausted and it is not agreed to select a Court of Arbitration as defined in Article 13 of the Covenant, the party alleging injury may submit the case to the Permanent Court.

If the other party refuses to submit the case to the Court, the Court decides in first instance if there exists an affirmative or negative engagement to submit to the Permanent Court the case in conformity with the demands of Article 14 of the Covenant.

Article 4.

Tout Etat signataire du présent acte est considéré comme acceptant de soumettre à la Cour Permanente tout différend caractérisé par l'article 1er qui s'élève entre cet Etat et un autre Etat signataire, si on n'est pas déjà convenu de choisir une Cour d'Arbitrage, comme il est indiqué à l'article 3.

Article 4.

Any State subscribing to the present Act is considered as having agreed to submit to the Permanent Court all cases, described in Article 1, arising between this State and another signatory State, unless it is not already agreed to select a Court of Arbitration according to Article 3.

ANNEXE No. 6.

La Haye, le 29 juin 1920.

Aux Membres de la Commission des Juristes Internationaux.

Messieurs,

J'ai l'honneur de vous communiquer la traduction d'une lettre que je viens de recevoir. Elle m'est adressée en ma qualité de Vice-Président de notre Commission, et je crois qu'il est de mon devoir de porter son contenu à votre connaissance.

Le Vice-Président,
(*signé*) LODER.

(ANNEXE A LA LETTRE PRÉCÉDENTE.)

Hoek van Holland, 27—6—'20.

Monsieur,

Je me permets de vous communiquer en votre qualité de Vice-Président de la Commission des Juristes Internationaux, l'observation suivante que vous voudrez bien transmettre à la Conférence.

On regrette infiniment que l'organisation de la future Cour de Justice Internationale sera probablement telle que seuls des Etats pourront être parties au procès.

Lorsqu'un particulier a le sentiment de la présence d'une injustice, la voie de recours, ne fût-ce que par une sentence déclaratoire, ne doit pas être entravée. Et c'est certainement une entrave si le concours de son Gouvernement est requis pour obtenir ce recours. Quelles possibilités de divergences d'opinion, de considérations politiques! Non, pour que les institutions de la Société des Nations puissent fleurir la sève leur doit venir du sein des peuples. Car, puisqu'il s'agit de détrôner les Etats, comment pourrait-on compter sur leur dévouement? Les arguments allégués par le communiqué dans les journaux pour la conception que seuls les Etats pourront procéder, se rangent dans le cadre que nous espérons de quitter, et s'éloignent du principe fondamental

ANNEX No. 6.

The Hague, 29th June 1920.

To the Members of the Commission of International Jurists.

Gentlemen,

I have the honour to lay before you a translation of a letter that I have just received. It was sent to me in my capacity as Vice-President of our Committee, and I think that it is my duty to communicate its contents to you.

The Vice President:
(*signed*) LODER.

(ANNEX TO ABOVE LETTER.)

Hook of Holland, 27—6—'20

Sir,

I am taking the liberty of bringing to your notice, in your capacity as Vice-President of the Committee of International Jurists, the following remarks, and would beg you to convey them to the Committee.

It is deeply regretted that the organisation of the new Court of International Justice will probably be such that States only may appear before it.

When an individual feels that an injustice exists there should be nothing to hinder recourse to justice, even though the sentence were only of declaratory nature. The necessity of obtaining the support of his Government before such recourse is possible is certainly a hindrance. What opportunities there are for differences of opinion, and for the intervention of political considerations! If the institutions of the League of Nations are to meet with success, they must draw their strength from the nations themselves. Since it is a question of dethroning the States, how can their support be relied on? The arguments put forward in the Communiqué to the Press, in support of the principle that States only may

de la Société des Nations, qui doit devenir une société de *nations* et non pas *d'Etats souverains*. Si ce n'est pas trop indiscret je serai prêt à développer verbalement l'opinion préconisée dans ces lignes, soit devant vous-même, soit devant la Commission.

J'ai l'honneur, etc.

(*signé*) W. ELINK SCHUURMAN.

A Monsieur
le Dr. B. C. J. LODER,
La Haye.

take action before the Court, are all part of the system that we were hoping to leave behind; they are opposed to the fundamental principle on which the League of Nations is based: it is to be a League of *Nations,* not a League of *Sovereign States*. I trust I am not taking too much upon myself in saying that I am quite prepared to develop orally the ideas put forward in this letter, either to you personally, or before the Commission.

I have the honour etc.

(*signed*) W. ELINK SCHUURMAN.

A Monsieur
le Dr. B. C. J. LODER,
La Haye.

13ième SÉANCE (non-publique), tenue au Palais de la Paix, à La Haye, le 1er juillet 1920.

Présidence de M. le BARON DESCAMPS.

Sont présents: tous les membres du Comité (à l'exception de M. Bevilaqua); M. Fernandes; Mr. James Brown Scott; les secrétaires particuliers de M. le Baron Descamps et de M. Adatci; les membres du Secrétariat.

La séance est ouverte à $9^1/_2$ heures du matin.

Le PRESIDENT propose qu'en vue de hâter les travaux du Comité, un quart d'heure seulement soit accordé à chaque orateur pour exprimer son point de vue sur une question déterminée. Dans les cas où doit se faire la traduction orale du discours dans une autre langue, le temps de la traduction n'est pas compris dans le quart d'heure.

Cette proposition est adoptée.

Mr. ROOT rappelle les paroles de plusieurs membres, notamment de M. Hagerup, exprimant l'avis que le Comité est maintenant près d'arriver à des conclusions déterminées.

Lord Phillimore et lui-même, suivant la règle parlementaire qui veut que ceux qui ont proposé certaines mesures, se chargent de les mettre au point, ont préparé un projet formulé sur l'organisation de la Cour, afin de compléter la proposition fragmentaire déjà soumise par eux.

Mr. Root a fait distribuer le nouveau projet aux membres (voir annexe 1). Il a l'intention de proposer qu'il soit adopté, et qu'il soit soumis au vote du Comité, article par article. Il demande auparavant à M. Hammarskjöld de donner lecture de la traduction française du projet.

M. Hammarskjöld ayant donné lecture du document, Mr. Root qui veut saisir le Comité du projet pour lui permettre de se prononcer à son sujet quand bon lui semble, propose que le premier article soit soumis au vote.

Le PRESIDENT exprime son regret de ne pouvoir agréer la proposition de Mr. Root. Il rappelle que le Comité a décidé de n'aborder que samedi la question de l'organisation. Les séan-

13th MEETING (Private), held at the Peace Palace, the Hague, on July 1st, 1920.

BARON DESCAMPS in the chair.

Present: all members of the Committee (with the exception of M. Bevilaqua); M. Fernandes, Mr. James Brown Scott; the private secretaries of Baron Descamps and of M. Adatci; the members of the Secretariat.

The meeting opened at 9.30 a.m.

The PRESIDENT proposed that in order to hasten the work of the Committee a quarter of an hour only should be allowed to each speaker to express his views on a given question. When an oral translation of the speech in an other language had to be made, the time taken by the translation would not be included in the quarter of an hour.

This proposal was adopted.

Mr. ROOT recalled that several members, in particular M. Hagerup, had expressed the opinion that the Committee was now ready to come to definite conclusions.

Lord Phillimore and himself, in accordance with the parliamentary rule, that those who have proposed certain measures undertake the task of perfecting them, had prepared a definite project dealing with the organisation of the Court, for the purpose of completing the fragmentary plan already submitted by them.

Mr. Root had caused the new project to be distributed to the members. (Annex No. 1). He intended to propose its adoption, and that it should be voted upon by the Committee article by article. He first asked M. Hammarskjöld to read the French version of the project.

M. Hammarskjöld having read the document, Mr. Root, desiring to bring the matter formally before the Committee and to permit it to express its opinion about it when the Committee thought fit, proposed that Article 1 be put to a vote.

The PRESIDENT regretted that he could not admit Mr. Root's proposal. He recalled that the Committee had decided that the question of organisation should not be dealt with

ces antérieures doivent être consacrées aux questions de la compétence et des règles de procédure. En outre, avant de demander aux membres du Comité de voter sur la proposition, il faut leur donner le temps matériel de la connaître.

Mr. ROOT explique qu'il n'a pas eu l'intention de demander au Comité de voter immédiatement sur son projet. Afin d'arriver à un résultat définitif, il a seulement voulu saisir le Comité de sa proposition, et il sera satisfait si l'on en met le vote à l'ordre du jour d'une séance déterminée, dans un délai de quelques jours.

M. LODER souligne que Mr. Root a seulement voulu mettre sa proposition à l'ordre du jour d'une façon permanente.

Le PRESIDENT se rallie à cette manière de voir et se propose, d'accord avec le Comité, de mettre la proposition de Mr. Root à l'ordre du jour du lundi 5 juillet.

LORD PHILLIMORE demande s'il est bien entendu que la proposition déposée par Mr. Root sera discutée en premier lieu à la séance du lundi.

Le PRESIDENT fait remarquer qu'il est possible que des projets plus complets soient déposés avant lundi, et dans ce cas il appartiendrait au Comité de décider quel projet formera la base des discussions.

M. HAGERUP insiste pour que, le lundi suivant, on ne rouvre pas la discussion générale sur la question de l'organisation, mais qu'on procède tout d'abord à un vote pour savoir quel projet servira de base de discussion.

LORD PHILLIMORE insiste encore pour que le projet déposé par Mr. Root soit pris comme point de départ: ce projet exprime les idées émises par la plupart des membres.

M. RICCI-BUSATTI demande au Président si le projet que celui-ci a déposé il y a quelque temps est maintenu. Il déclare qu'il vient lui-même de déposer un nouveau projet au bureau du Secrétariat, projet qui remplace et complète celui qu'il avait proposé auparavant (annexe 2).

Le PRESIDENT répond affirmativement et ajoute qu'il se réserve le droit de présenter de nouveau son projet sous une forme amendée.

Il engage les membres à déposer tous leurs projets relatifs à l'organisation au plus tard samedi matin, pour qu'ils puissent être distribués le même jour.

until Saturday. The previous meetings would be devoted to the questions of competence and of the rules of procedure. Besides, before asking members of the Committee to vote on the proposal, they must be given time to become familiar with it.

Mr. ROOT explained that he had not intended to ask the Committee to vote upon the project immediately. In order to obtain a definite result, he simply had wished to bring it officially before the Committee and he would be satisfied if the vote were put on the Agenda for a definite meeting some days ahead.

M. LODER emphasised the fact that Mr. Root had only wished to record his proposal formally upon the Agenda.

The PRESIDENT agreed to this view and proposed, with the Committee's approval, that Mr. Root's plan be put on the Agenda for Monday, July 5.

LORD PHILLIMORE asked whether it was quite understood that the plan presented by Mr. Root should be discussed first of all at the Monday meeting.

The PRESIDENT remarked that it was possible that some more complete projects might be submitted before Monday, and in that case it would be left to the Committee to decide which project should form the basis of discussion.

M. HAGERUP insisted that the general discussion of the question of organisation should not be reopened on Monday next, but that they should begin by taking a vote to decide which project should serve as the basis of discussion.

LORD PHILLIMORE insisted again that the project submitted by Mr. Root should be used as the starting point: this project expressed the ideas of most of the members.

M. RICCI-BUSATTI asked the President whether the project put forward by the President some time ago still held good. He announced that he had just handed in a new project to the Secretariat which superseded and completed the one which he had proposed formerly. (Annexe 2).

The PRESIDENT replied in the affirmative and added that he reserved the right to put forward again his plan in an amended form.

He requested the members to hand in all their projects dealing with organisation by Saturday morning at the latest, so that they could be distributed the same day.

Le Président rouvre la discussion sur la question de la judicature obligatoire. Il dit que Lord Phillimore et lui-même ont pris en considération les amendements présentés par M. Ricci-Busatti, au projet qu'ils ont déposé au début de la séance de la veille.

Lord Phillimore et lui sont d'accord pour reconnaître que les amendements ne touchent pas au fond de la question, mais concernent plutôt la rédaction. Toutefois le Président, d'accord avec Lord Phillimore, demande à M. Ricci-Busatti, de ne point insister sur les deux points suivants: 1. la suppression de l'expression „questions d'ordre juridique": il faut tenir compte du grand rôle que cette expression a joué lors des conférences de 1899 et 1907; il faut tenir compte aussi de la conscience juridique et de l'opinion mondiale, qui s'étonneraient de ne point retrouver ce terme dans le projet du Comité. — 2. la substitution, au paragraphe *b* de l'article 1er, d'une autre terminologie aux mots: „tout point de droit international"; il faut s'appuyer autant que possible sur des documents positifs antérieurs, et il ne faut pas oublier que l'expression employée dans le projet se trouve dans l'article 13 du Pacte. — Quant à l'amendement de M. Ricci-Busatti au dernier alinéa de l'article 1er, le Président se demande s'il constituerait vraiment une amélioration.

M. DE LAPRADELLE se prononce contre la proposition de M. Ricci-Busatti de faire insérer à l'article 1er, paragraphe *b*, l'expression „application et interprétation etc.". Cette expression a un double désavantage: elle pourrait en premier lieu créer l'impression que la Cour est chargée de donner des interprétations en dehors de toute application à un cas déterminé; et, en second lieu, elle est illogique, parce que l'interprétation est incluse dans l'application.

Tout en reconnaissant qu'il y a du vrai dans les observations de M. de Lapradelle, le PRESIDENT fait remarquer qu'il s'agit d'une expression traditionnelle et dont l'usage est général. D'ailleurs, même en admettant qu'il n'est pas nécessaire de mentionner l'interprétation à côté de l'application, il est certain qu'il n'y a aucun inconvénient à le faire.

M. RICCI-BUSATTI accepte les raisons exposées par le Président.

Mr. ROOT fait valoir que la terminologie que veut maintenir le Président est celle du Pacte. Il pense qu'il serait peu prudent d'en accepter une autre qui, si elle était adoptée, semblerait impliquer qu'on veut exprimer un avis différent de celui des rédacteurs de ce document; il se

The President re-opened the discussion on the question of compulsory jurisdiction. He said that Lord Phillimore and he had considered the amendments put forward by M. Ricci-Busatti to the plan which they had presented at the opening of the preceding day's meeting.

Lord Phillimore and he had agreed that the amendments did not affect the heart of the question, but concerned rather the drafting. However, the President in agreement with Lord Phillimore requested M. Ricci-Busatti not to insist on the two following points: 1. The omission of the expression "questions of a legal nature." Regard must be had also for the important part this expression played in the Conferences of 1899 and 1907; as well as for legal conscience and world opinion which would be astonished not to find this term in the Committee's plan. — 2. The substitution in Paragraph *b*, Article 1 of another expression for the words "any point of international law." Definite previous documents must be followed as much as possible, and it must not be forgotten that the expression used in the project is contained in Article 13 of the Covenant. Concerning M. Ricci-Busatti's amendment to the last paragraph of Article 1, the President doubted whether the amendment would really be an improvement.

M. DE LAPRADELLE opposed M. Ricci-Busatti's proposal to insert in Article 1, Paragraph *b*, the expression "application and interpretation, etc." This expression had two disadvantages; first it might create the impression that it was the duty of the Court to give interpretations apart from their application to a particular case; and second it was illogical because interpretation is included in application.

Though admitting that there was truth in M. de Lapradelle's remarks, the PRESIDENT pointed out that the Committee were dealing with a traditional expression which was in general use. Further, even if it were admitted that it was not necessary to mention interpretation as well as application, there was certainly no objection to doing so.

M. RICCI-BUSATTI accepted the reasons advanced by the President.

Mr. ROOT pointed out that the phraseology which the President wished to adhere to was that of the Covenant. He thought it would not be wise to accept another which, if adopted, would seem to imply that they wished to express a different meaning from that of the framers of

demande si c'est vraiment là l'intention du Comité.

M. ADATCI se rallie à l'opinion de Mr. Root qui est celle du bon sens. Il serait en effet dangereux de modifier la terminologie.

M. RICCI-BUSATTI fait observer que les membres du Comité ne sont pas liés sur tous les points par le Pacte. Mr. Root lui-même a souligné le besoin qu'on peut avoir, dans certains cas, de s'en écarter. Le Comité manquerait à son devoir si, lorsqu'un de ces cas se présente, il ne le faisait pas.

Le PRESIDENT se range à l'avis de Mr. Root. Si l'on se trouve en face de deux textes, dont l'un a pour lui la tradition, tandis que l'autre est improvisé, c'est le premier qu'il convient d'adopter.

M. RICCI-BUSATTI insiste sur la nécessité de substituer, au paragraphe *b* de l'article 1er du projet du Président, l'expression „tout point de droit international", par les mots: „l'application d'une règle générale de droit international". Toutes les questions soumises à la Cour touchent à des points de droit international. Ce qu'on a voulu dire au paragraphe *b*, c'est évidemment que la Cour est compétente lorsqu'il s'agit de l'application d'une règle générale de droit international coutumier, tandis que le paragraphe *a* vise le droit conventionnel. Quant à la formule de ce dernier paragraphe, ainsi que le Président l'a remarqué, l'expression proposée par M. Ricci-Busatti a pour elle la tradition et l'usage: toutefois il n'insiste pas pour qu'elle soit adoptée; il se contente du mot „application".

M. DE LAPRADELLE appuie énergiquement le point de vue de M. Ricci-Busatti. La terminologie de l'article 13 du Pacte est extrêmement défectueuse. Il est en effet peu logique de dire „tout point de droit international", lorsqu'on établit en même temps une liste de points précis, qui sont compris dans cette expression.

M. HAGERUP s'associe à l'opinion de MM. Ricci-Busatti et de Lapradelle.

Le PRESIDENT préfère conserver l'expression qui se trouve dans l'article 13. Il ne conteste pas qu'on en puisse trouver une meilleure au point de vue juridique, mais il y aurait danger à introduire une modification. En effet, s'il est hors de doute que l'expression „tout point de droit international" peut s'appliquer à toutes les éventualités possibles, une autre expression, par contre, pourrait être interprêtée de façon trop restrictive.

the Covenant. He doubted whether this was really the intention of the Committee.

M. ADATCI agreed with Mr. Root: he thought his was the sensible point of view. Practically it would be dangerous to alter the terminology.

M. RICCI-BUSATTI pointed out that the members of the Committee were not bound on all points by the Covenant. Mr. Root himself had emphasised the possible need of departing from it. The Committee would neglect its duty if, when such a need arose, it failed to meet it.

The PRESIDENT agreed with Mr. Root. If the choice lay between two phrases of which one was a traditional phrase, while the other was improvised, the former should be adopted.

M. RICCI-BUSATTI insisted that it was necessary to substitute in Paragraph *b*, Article 1, of the President's project the words "the application of a general rule of international law" for the expression "any point of international law." All questions submitted to the Court concern points of international law. Paragraph *b* evidently intended to say that the Court was competent to deal with cases concerning the application of a general rule of customary international law, while Paragraph *a* dealt with conventional law. Concerning the phrase in the last paragraph, the expression proposed by M. Ricci-Busatti had as the President said, both tradition and usage in its favour; however, he did not insist on its adoption; he would be satisfied with the word "application".

M. DE LAPRADELLE vigorously supported M. Ricci-Busatti's point of view. The terminology of Article 13 of the Covenant was extremely defective. Indeed it was hardly logical to mention "any point of international law" when a list of definite points has been laid down and these points are included in the said expression.

M. HAGERUP agreed with Messrs. Ricci-Busatti and de Lapradelle.

The PRESIDENT preferred to retain the expression used in Article 13. He did not deny that one better from a legal standpoint could be found, but it would be dangerous to introduce an alteration. Indeed, if there is no doubt that the expression "any point of international law" may apply to all possible eventualities, another expression, on the other hand, might be interpreted in too limited a manner.

LORD PHILLIMORE rappelle que „le mieux est parfois l'ennemi du bien". Il convient que le texte de l'article 13 est probablement défectueux, mais il croit qu'il faut néanmoins le maintenir, pour les raisons exposées par Mr. Root, pour son élasticité indéniable, et enfin pour éviter d'avoir à abandonner une formule adoptée par le Pacte.

M. DE LAPRADELLE constate que le Comité à la mission d'établir clairement et en bon langage juridique la compétence de la Cour. Le texte français du Pacte est très obscur; celui du Covenant anglais est meilleur. En tous cas, il est possible de retrouver la pensée du rédacteur français.

M. de Lapradelle expose ce qu'on a voulu, selon lui, exprimer par l'article 13 du Pacte: On a voulu établir l'obligation pour les Etats de soumettre à l'arbitrage les points suivants:

1. les questions dépendant d'un traité;
2. les questions dépendant du droit international général;
3. les questions de fait, d'où peuvent découler des responsabilités juridiques;
4. les questions concernant le *quantum* dans les cas où l'obligation est reconnue.

Mais il faut exprimer ces idées d'une façon plus satisfaisante.

M. RICCI-BUSATTI répond à Lord Phillimore: Il se rallierait à son avis que „le mieux est parfois l'ennemi du bien", si le Pacte était „le bien", mais selon lui, le Pacte, sur ce point, est fort mal rédigé.

Il continue en disant que même l'expression „engagement international" ne lui semble pas bien choisie; il aurait préféré le mot „obligation". Le mot „engagement" est trop étroit, puisqu'il signifie une obligation volontaire.

Le PRESIDENT fait valoir qu'au contraire, le mot „engagement" est souvent considéré comme plus large que le mot „obligation". Il peut y avoir engagement dans certains rapports juridiques sans qu'il y ait obligation par un accord des volontés.

M. DE LAPRADELLE ne partage pas l'avis du Président. Il pense avec M. Ricci-Busatti que l'engagement présuppose la volonté de s'engager, tandis qu'une obligation peut naître sans qu'il y entre une part de volonté. Par conséquent l'expression „obligation" est plus large que l'expression „engagement".

LORD PHILLIMORE recalled that "something better is often the enemy of something good." He agreed that the wording of Article 13 was probably defective, but he thought they should keep it nevertheless for the reasons given by Mr. Root, for its undeniable elasticity, and finally to avoid having to abandon a phrase adopted by the Covenant.

M. DE LAPRADELLE stated that the Committee's task was to define clearly and in good legal language the competence of the Court. The French version of the Covenant was very obscure. The English version was better. In any case, it was possible to follow the thoughts of the draftsman of the French text.

M. de Lapradelle explained what he thought Article 13 of the Covenant was intended to convey: the intention was to establish an obligation for States to submit the following points to arbitration:

1. questions arising out of a treaty;
2. questions connected with general international law;
3. questions of fact from which legal responsibility followed;
4. questions concerning the *quantum* in cases in which an obligation is admitted.

But these ideas must be expressed in a more satisfactory way.

M. RICCI-BUSATTI answered Lord Phillimore. He would agree with his belief about "better opposed to good" if the Covenant were the "good", but in his opinion the Covenant on this point is very badly drafted.

He went on to say that even the expression (in the French text) "international engagement" did not seem to him to be well chosen. He would have preferred the word "obligation". The word "engagement" had too narrow a meaning since it meant an obligation freely undertaken.

The PRESIDENT said that on the contrary (in French) the word "engagement" often is considered as having a broader meaning than the word "obligation". There might be an engagement in certain legal relations without an obligation by voluntary agreement.

M. DE LAPRADELLE did not share the opinion of the President. Like M. Ricci-Busatti he thought that engagement presupposed will to make engagement, while an obligation might arise without any will entering into it. Consequently, the expression "obligation" was wider than the expression "engagement."

Mr. ROOT fait observer que le texte anglais se sert du mot „obligation".

M. RICCI-BUSATTI n'est pas satisfait non plus de l'expression „rupture" d'un engagement international. Il propose, d'accord avec M. Hagerup, la formule „infraction à un devoir international".

M. DE LAPRADELLE et M. FERNANDES, s'opposent à cette proposition en faisant valoir que le mot „devoir" est plutôt du domaine moral. M. de Lapradelle ajoute que, selon lui, il faudrait prendre le texte anglais comme point de départ et en faire une traduction française meilleure que celle qui existe.

LORD PHILLIMORE se rallie à cette idée. Il est d'avis que le mot anglais „obligation" exprime tout lien juridique.

Mr. ROOT rappelle l'allusion faite par M. Ricci-Busatti à des paroles prononcées par lui au sujet de la réalisation des intentions des rédacteurs du Pacte, et dans lesquelles il se bornait à envisager la création d'une Cour qui serait compétente pour exercer la juridiction obligatoire. Il est certain que les membres du Comité s'accordent pour reconnaître à la Cour une compétence de cette nature.

Il a fallu beaucoup de temps pour arriver à l'accord sur ce point. Il s'agit maintenant de sauvegarder le progrès qui a été ainsi réalisé. Pour cela, il faut définir d'une façon nette les limites de la juridiction obligatoire. Si l'on substitue au mot „règle" le mot „principe", on élargira tellement les limites de la juridiction obligatoire qu'on les fera disparaître.

Les Etats n'accepteraient pas une Cour qui aurait le droit de trancher les différends d'après des règles élaborées par la Cour elle-même, et en interprétant des principes plus ou moins vagues. On se heurterait aux difficultés qui ont empêché l'adoption de la Convention redigée en vue de l'établissement d'une Cour internationale des Prises. Mr. Root donne lecture de l'article 7 de cette convention et ajoute que si elle n'a pas été appliquée, c'est que certains pays n'ont pas voulu soumettre leurs droits à une Cour sans savoir comment celle-ci appliquerait les principes du droit, de la justice et de l'équité. La Conférence Navale de Londres avait été convoquée afin de définir ces principes; mais comme la Déclaration qui fut publiée ne précisait pas assez certains points, les Etats ne la ratifièrent pas. Les membres du Comité doivent tenir compte de la leçon qui se dégage de l'histoire de cette Déclaration.

Les nations en effet, se soumettront au droit

Mr. ROOT pointed out that the English version used the word "obligation."

M. RICCI-BUSATTI also was not satisfied with the word "breach" of an international engagement. He suggested, in agreement with M. Hagerup, the expression "infraction of any international duty."

M. DE LAPRADELLE and M. FERNANDES opposed this suggestion and pointed out that the word "duty" is rather in the realm of morals. M. de Lapradelle added that in his opinion the English version should be taken as a basis, and that from it a French translation better than the existing one should be made.

LORD PHILLIMORE agreed. He thought that the English word "obligation" included all legal responsibility.

Mr. ROOT recalled the reference made by M. Ricci-Busatti to Mr. Root's remark concerning the realisation of the intentions of those who had drawn up the Covenant, in which he confined himself to considering the creation of a Court which should be competent to exercise compulsory jurisdiction. He feels sure that the members of the Committee agree to recognise the Court's competence in this respect.

It had taken a long time to agree on this point. They must now take steps to preserve the progress thus made. To do this the limits of compulsory jurisdiction must be clearly laid down. If the word "principle" were substituted for the word "rule", the limits of obligatory jurisdiction would be widened to such an extent that they would be destroyed.

The States would not accept a Court which had the right to settle disputes in accordance with rules established by the Court itself, and by the interpretation of more or less vague principles. The same difficulties would be encountered which prevented the acceptance of the Convention drafted to establish an International Prize Court. Mr. Root read Article 7 of that Convention, and added that the reason it had not been applied was that certain countries had not been willing to agree to submit their rights to a Court without knowing how this Court would apply the principles of law, justice and equity. The Naval Conference of London was called together to define these principles; but as the declaration which was published did not make certain points sufficiently clear, the States did not ratify it. Members of the Committee must bear in mind the lesson which the history of this Declaration teaches.

positif, mais ne se soumettront pas à des principes tant que ceux-ci ne se seront pas développés de façon à devenir des règles positives, soutenues par l'accord de tous les Etats. L'avantage des formules contenues dans le Pacte de la Société des Nations, c'est justement qu'elles ont fait sur elles l'accord des Etats convoqués à Paris. Il ne faut pas méconnaître la force de ces faits si l'on veut que la convention proposée par le Comité obtienne l'assentiment général.

Mr. Root admet, avec M. de Lapradelle, que l'on pourrait certainement améliorer la formule du Pacte; mais si grandes que soient l'autorité et la réputation de M. de Lapradelle, il leur serait difficile de contrebalancer l'autorité d'un texte sur lequel les Etats se sont mis d'accord.

Le PRESIDENT fait observer que les questions soulevées par Mr. Root seront traitées lors de la discussion sur les normes matérielles que devra appliquer la Cour.

M. DE LAPRADELLE est du même avis et dit qu'en mentionnant l'article 7 de la Convention sur la juridiction des Prises, Mr. Root a transporté la discussion sur un nouveau terrain: la question des règles qui doivent servir de base aux sentences est en effet entièrement distincte de celle de la compétence de la Cour. M. de Lapradelle ajoute qu'il ne saurait partager l'avis de Mr. Root au sujet des raisons qui ont déterminé l'échec de la déclaration de Londres. Pour sa part, il se félicite que la déclaration n'ait pas été ratifiée; si elle ne le fut pas, dit-il, c'est parce qu'il fut impossible de formuler des règles de droit matériel qui satisfissent l'opinion publique en Angleterre. Il remarque que la situation n'est plus la même: on travaille maintenant dans un esprit de confiance et de conciliation.

Le PRESIDENT propose de s'en tenir, en première lecture, au texte de l'article 13 du Pacte, sauf à substituer s'il est nécessaire, en deuxième lecture, une formule plus satisfaisante: il invite les membres à faire des propositions à cet égard.

M. DE LAPRADELLE suggère l'idée de décider dès à présent qu'on n'est pas lié par le texte français du Pacte et qu'on doit prendre le texte anglais comme base des discussions: on pourra alors essayer de trouver une meilleure traduction française.

Le PRESIDENT ne voit pas d'objection à la proposition de M. de Lapradelle.

LORD PHILLIMORE pense qu'on a assez discuté les questions de détail et qu'il faut revenir

Nations will submit to positive law, but will not submit to such principles as have not been developed into positive rules supported by an accord between all States. The advantage of the phrases in the Covenant of the League of Nations was that they had been agreed upon by the States met together in Paris. The force of these arguments must not be underestimated if the Convention proposed by the Committee is to gain general support.

Mr. Root agreed with M. de Lapradelle that the wording of the Covenant could certainly be improved, but great as might be the reputation of M. de Lapradelle, it would be difficult for it to outweigh the authority of a text agreed on by the States.

The PRESIDENT pointed out that the questions raised by Mr. Root would be dealt with at the time of the discussion of the rules which the Court should apply.

M. DE LAPRADELLE was of the same opinion and said that by mentioning Article 7 of the Convention for the Prize Court, Mr. Root had shifted the discussion to another subject: the question of the rules which must form the basis for sentences was quite distinct from that of the competence of the Court. M. de Lapradelle added that he could not share Mr. Root's view of the reasons which led to the failure of the Declaration of London. For his part, he congratulated himself that the Declaration had not been ratified; the reason why it was not was because it had been impossible to draw up rules of prize law which satisfied public opinion in England. He pointed out that the situation was no longer the same; they were now working in a spirit of confidence and conciliation.

The PRESIDENT proposed to adhere in the first reading to the wording of Article 13 of the Covenant; if necessary they were free to substitute in the second reading a more satisfactory wording. He asked the members to draw up proposals in this connection.

M. DE LAPRADELLE suggested that they decide that from now onwards they were not to be bound by the French text of the Covenant, and that they should take the English text as a basis for discussion; efforts could then be made to find a better French translation.

The PRESIDENT saw no objection to M de Lapradelle's proposal.

LORD PHILLIMORE thought that questions of detail had been sufficiently discussed,

au texte du projet sur la compétence de la Cour, déposé la veille par le Président.

A cet égard, il propose l'adoption des amendements de M. Ricci-Busatti aux articles 2 et 3 du texte. Il propose également qu'on donne satisfaction au désir exprimé par M. Ricci-Busatti d'insérer dans la première phrase de l'article 1er les mots „entre Etats".

Lord Phillimore propose l'adoption, comme un nouvel article 4, de la nouvelle rédaction du dernier alinéa de l'article 3 qu'il a soumise la veille, ainsi conçue: „Tout Etat signataire du présent acte est considéré comme acceptant de soumettre à la Cour permanente tout différend, caractérisé par l'article premier, qui s'élève entre cet Etat et un autre Etat signataire".

Ce texte est destiné à ne pas accorder aux Etats non-signataires de la convention pour l'établissement de la Cour internationale de Justice, le droit d'assigner unilatéralement un autre Etat.

Le PRESIDENT remarque que Lord Phillimore a ramené la discussion sur la question du traitement à donner aux Etats qui ne sont pas mentionnés à l'annexe du Pacte. Il a lui-même formulé le résultat, auquel il est arrivé en étudiant cette question, dans une déclaration conçue en ces termes:

„Je voudrais signaler les raisons pour lesquelles il est, à mon sens, impossible au Comité de reconnaître un droit direct d'accès aux juridictions internationales, prévues par le Pacte, au bénéfice des Etats qui ne sont pas Membres de la Société des Nations. Ce serait là, à mon avis, le renversement de toute l'économie du système positivement et nettement établi par le Pacte au sujet de ces Etats.

En effet, l'article 17 prévoit précisément le cas de différends où peuvent se trouver engagés les Etats dont il s'agit, et il définit, sans l'ombre d'un doute possible, la situation de ces Etats au point de vue de la solution de leurs différends. En cas de différend les concernant, dit expressément cet article, ils sont invités à se soumettre aux obligations qui s'imposent aux Membres de la Société, aux conditions estimées justes par le Conseil. Ils ont alors le choix d'accepter ou de refuser cette invitation. S'ils l'acceptent, les articles 12 à 16 du Pacte leur deviennent occasionnellement applicables, sous réserve des modifications jugées nécessaires par le Conseil. Or, les articles 12 à 16 comprennent spécialement tout le régime des institutions arbitrales et judi-

and that they should now return to the text of the draft regarding the competence of the Court, submitted on the previous day by the President.

In this connection, he proposed that the amendments of M. Ricci-Busatti to Articles 2 and 3 of the draft should be adopted. He also proposed that they should satisfy M. Ricci-Busatti's wish for the insertion in the first sentence of the first Article, of the word "between States".

Lord Phillimore proposed the adoption as a new Art. 4 of the new wording of the last paragraph of Article 3, suggested by him the previous day, as follows: "Any State signing the present Act is considered as having agreed to submit to the Permanent Court any dispute between itself and another signatory State, as described by Art. 1."

This text is intended to exclude States which have not subscribed to the Convention for the establishment of the International Court of Justice, from the right of summoning unilaterally another State.

The PRESIDENT remarked that Lord Phillimore had brought the discussion round to the question of treatment to be afforded to States which were not mentioned in the Annex to the Covenant. As a result of his study of this question, the President had drawn up a declaration as follows:

"I wish to state the reasons which in my opinion make it impossible for the Committee to admit that States not members of the League of Nations have right of direct access to the international jurisdictions. To do so, in my opinion, would amount to a complete overthrow of the arrangement of the whole system which has been clearly and definitely put in force by the Covenant regarding these States.

In fact, Article 17 deals precisely with the disputes, in which the States referred to may be involved, and it lays down, without the slightest possibility of doubt, the position of such States with regard to the settlement of their disputes. The article expressly states that, should disputes in which they are concerned arise, they are invited to submit to the obligations imposed on Members of the League, under conditions which are considered reasonable by the Council. They may then choose whether they will accept or refuse this invitation. If they accept, they become subject to the conditions of articles 12 to 16 of the Covenant for the particular case, except in so far as the Council may consider modifications necessary. Articles 12 to 16, however, contain

ciaires instauré par le Pacte. Il est manifeste qu'accorder aux Etats dont nous parlons un accès d'emblée aux juridictions établies par le Pacte, c'est leur accorder cet accès sans qu'ils soient invités dans les conditions spéciales déterminées par l'article 17, et sans que les articles 12 et 16 subissent éventuellement les modifications jugées nécessaires par le Conseil.

En dehors de l'article 17, on ne peut relever que des cas sporadiques où les Etats qui ne sont pas Membres de la Société des Nations peuvent bénificier d'un accès direct aux juridictions prévues par le Pacte. Dans ces conditions je ne vois que deux moyens pour nous d'aboutir à une solution satisfaisante. Le premier est de préciser que l'accès aux juridictions établies par le Pacte est ouvert aux Etats qui ne sont pas Membres de la Société des Nations sous les conditions générales déterminées par l'article 17.

Le second est de ne pas résoudre cette question, comme étant une question transitoire. Il est certain, en effet, que la Société des Nations est une Société ouverte en soi à tous, et que la seule différence admise est une différence transitoire pour laquelle nous pourrons en conséquence nous abstenir de formuler des règles dans un Projet qui, dans notre intention, doit revêtir le caractère d'une œuvre définitive".

LORD PHILLIMORE se rallie à l'avis exprimé par le Président. Les Etats qui ne sont pas Membres de la Société des Nations ne doivent pouvoir se prévaloir de la juridiction de la Cour qu'aux conditions fixées par l'article 17; mais, d'autre part, il faut décider d'une façon définitive qu'à ces conditions, ces Etats ont le droit de procéder devant la Cour. Il ne restera plus ensuite qu'une question de rédaction.

Le PRESIDENT ne s'oppose pas à cette solution, à condition que l'on mentionne l'article 17 du Pacte.

LORD PHILLIMORE continue: Le Conseil pourra imposer aux Etats non signataires l'observance de certaines conditions; mais il ne pourra pas obliger les Etats signataires à ester en justice devant la Cour avec les Etats non signataires, même si ces derniers ont accepté les conditions qui leur ont été imposées.

A ce propos, Lord Phillimore donne de nouveau lecture du nouvel article 4 qu'il a proposé d'ajouter au texte soumis par le Président: „Tout Etat signataire du présent acte est considéré comme acceptant de soumettre à la

in particular the whole system of judicial and arbitral institutions inaugurated by the Covenant. It is obvious that to grant the States referred to free access to the jurisdictions set up by the Covenant would amount to giving them this right, regardless of the special conditions under which they should be invited according to Article 17, and without reference to the eventual modifications of Articles 12 to 16, which might be considered necessary by the Council.

Apart from Article 17, only occasional cases can be remarked in which States which are not Members of the League of Nations could profit by direct access to the jurisdictions provided by the Covenant. Under these circumstances, I can only see two ways in which we can come to a satisfactory conclusion. The first is to state definitely that access to the jurisdiction set up by the Covenant is open to States not Members of the League of Nations under the general conditions laid down in article 17.

The second is not to deal with this question, because it is only transitory. Indeed, it is certain that the League of Nations is a League in principle open for all; the only distinction recognised is of a transitory nature, and we may therefore disregard it in drawing up the rules for our Project, which we must intend to be of a permanent nature."

LORD PHILLIMORE agreed with the opinion expressed by the President. States which are not Members of the League of Nations should not be able to make use of the jurisdiction of the Court except under the conditions laid down by Article 17; but, on the other hand, it must be clearly stated, that under these conditions these States have the right to take action before the Court. The question would then be only one of drafting.

The PRESIDENT had no objection to this solution, provided that reference were made to Article 17 of the Covenant.

LORD PHILLIMORE continued: The Council might impose the observance of certain conditions upon non-signatory States; but it could not oblige signatory States to appear in Court at the suit of non-signatory States, even if the latter had accepted the conditions imposed on them.

In this connection, Lord Phillimore again read the new Article 4 which he proposed to add to the project submitted by the President:

"Any State signing the present Act is considered as having agreed to submit to the Perman-

Cour tout différend, caractérisé par l'article premier, qui s'élève entre cet Etat et un autre Etat signataire".

Il rappelle que le Comité s'est déjà mis d'accord sur la compétence personnelle de la Cour: tous les Etats, et non pas quelques-uns seulement, doivent avoir le droit de procéder devant la Cour. Le texte soumis par le Président vise à établir également l'accord sur la compétence matérielle de la Cour. L'accord sur la compétence personnelle n'a pas été formulé jusqu'ici; afin d'avoir un texte complet, Lord Phillimore se déclare disposé à rédiger aussi une formule à cet égard.

Sur une remarque du PRESIDENT qui relève une ambiguité dans le texte relatif à la compétence matérielle, LORD PHILLIMORE dit qu'il y a bien dans ce texte un ou deux points qui ont besoin d'être remaniés. Lord Phillimore s'en charge, d'accord avec le Président.

M. HAGERUP demande s'il est dans l'intention du nouvel article 4, proposé par Lord Phillimore, d'obliger les Etats à aller toujours devant la Cour Permanente de *Justice*, même lorsque les parties en litige sont liées entre elles par un traité, aux termes duquel le litige serait soumis à un Tribunal *d'Arbitrage*.

LORD PHILLIMORE répond que s'il existe des traités de cette nature, ils doivent sans doute être exécutés, à moins que les parties ne se soient mises d'accord pour reconnaître la compétence de la nouvelle Cour, même dans les cas visés par les traités d'arbitrage. A cet égard Lord Phillimore rappelle le premier alinéa de l'article 3.

M. HAGERUP demande alors si, dans ces circonstances, le renvoi à l'article 1er ne doit pas être remplacé par un renvoi à l'alinéa 1er de l'article 3. Il suggère l'idée d'ajouter une réserve à l'alinéa 3 de l'article 3.

LORD PHILLIMORE répond que l'article 3 a trait simplement aux cas énumérés à l'article 1er. Ces cas sont les seuls dans lesquels la Cour Permanente de Justice est compétente, et elle est seule à l'être, sauf convention contraire.

M. HAGERUP préférerait un renvoi à toutes les dispositions précédentes. Il ajoute une autre question: Si deux Etats, qui ne sont pas mentionnés à l'annexe du Pacte, sont d'accord pour soumettre un litige à la Cour, la Cour sera-t-elle compétente pour connaître de cette affaire?

ent Court all disputes between itself and another signatory State, as described by Article 1."

He recalled that the Committee had already come to an agreement on the subject of the personal competence of the Court: all States, and not only a few should have the right to take action before the Court. The project submitted by the President was intended to establish also an agreement concerning the material competence. The agreement concerning the personal competence had not yet been drafted; in order to make the text complete, Lord Phillimore said that he was prepared to draw up a formula on this subject also.

Following a remark by the PRESIDENT on an ambiguity in the text relative to material competence, LORD PHILLIMORE said that there were still one or two points in this draft which needed to be altered. He undertook to carry this out in collaboration with the President.

M. HAGERUP asked if it were intended in the new Article 4 proposed by Lord Phillimore to oblige States always to resort to the Permanent Court of *Justice*, even when the contesting parties were bound by a treaty to submitting the case to a Court of *Arbitration*.

LORD PHILLIMORE answered that if there were treaties of this nature, they should doubtless be carried out, unless the parties had agreed to recognise the competence of the New Court even in the cases covered by the Treaties of Arbitration. In this connection, Lord Phillimore recalled the first paragraph of Article 3.

M. HAGERUP asked whether, under these circumstances, the reference to Article 1 should not be replaced by a reference to paragraph 1, Article 3. He suggested adding a reservation to paragraph 3 of Article 3.

LORD PHILLIMORE answered that Article 3 simply dealt with cases enumerated in Article 1. These were the only cases which the Permanent Court of Justice was competent to deal with, and it alone would be competent except for a convention to the contrary.

M. HAGERUP preferred that reference should be made to all the preceding dispositions. He asked another question: if two States, which were not mentioned in the Annex of the Covenant, agreed to submit a case to the Court, would the Court be competent to deal with the case?

LORD PHILLIMORE croit qu'on peut laisser ce point à la décision de la Cour.

M. LODER pense au contraire qu'il faut arriver à une solution ferme.

M. HAGERUP est d'avis que la Cour doit être ouverte également aux Etats non signataires, sous réserve de la question des frais.

Il distingue deux cas où les Etats non-signataires pourront venir devant la Cour:

1. Invitation par le Conseil aux termes de l'article 17;
2. Accord entre deux Etats non-membres.

Dans les deux cas la Cour serait, non seulement compétente, mais obligée de trancher le litige.

M. LODER se range à l'opinion de M. Hagerup.

M. DE LAPRADELLE croit qu'il faut stipuler expressément la compétence de la Cour à connaître des litiges que deux Etats non-signataires se sont mis d'accord pour lui soumettre.

Le PRESIDENT remarque qu'à son avis le Conseil devrait auparavant intervenir: l'article 12 du Pacte est applicable seulement dans la mesure où le Conseil est de cet avis.

M. DE LAPRADELLE croit que, dans le cas visé par M. Hagerup, il faut stipuler également que les conditions à fixer par le Conseil ne peuvent viser que la question des frais.

Le PRESIDENT répète que les articles 12 à 16 du Pacte ne sont applicables aux Etats non-membres que dans la mesure ou cela a été admis par le Conseil. Il est difficile d'assimiler d'emblée les Etats non-signataires aux Etats signataires.

M. DE LAPRADELLE pense que le Conseil ne peut pas poser de conditions aux Etats non-membres qui viennent devant la Cour de leur plein gré. Les dispositions de l'article 17 ne sont pas applicables dans ce cas.

Le PRESIDENT croit au contraire que ce cas est inclus dans l'hypothèse de l'article 17; il faut, dit-il, considérer de la même façon le cas où un Etat non-membre a été invité par le Conseil à se présenter devant la Cour et celui où deux Etats non-membres se sont mis d'accord pour venir devant elle.

M. DE LAPRADELLE répond qu'une invitation dans chaque cas particulier n'est certaine-

LORD PHILLIMORE thought that this point might be left for the Court to decide.

M. LODER thought, on the contrary, that a definite solution was necessary.

M. HAGERUP thought that the Court would be open also to a non-signatory State, subject to the question of expenses. He distinguished between two cases in which non-signatory States might come before the Court:

1. At the invitation of the Council, according to Article 17;
2. As the result of an agreement between two non-member States;

In both cases the Court would be not only competent but compelled to hear the case.

M. LODER agreed with M. Hagerup.

M. DE LAPRADELLE thought that it should be expressly stipulated that the Court was competent to deal with cases which non-signatory States agreed to submit to it.

The PRESIDENT said that in his opinion the Council ought first to intervene; Article 12 of the Covenant was only applicable to the extent which the Council thought fit.

M. DE LAPRADELLE thought that in the case suggested by M. Hagerup, it should also be stipulated that the conditions to be fixed by the Council should deal only with the question of expense.

The PRESIDENT repeated that Articles 12 to 16 of the Covenant were applicable to non-members only in so far as admitted by the Council. It is difficult to assimilate at the outset non-signatory States with signatory States.

M. DE LAPRADELLE thought that the Council could not impose conditions upon non-member States which come before the Court of their own free will. The provisions of Article 17 would not apply in this case.

The PRESIDENT thought, on the contrary, that this case was included in the hypothesis of Article 17; it is necessary, he said, to consider in the same way the case of a non-member State being invited by the Council to appear before the Court, and the case of two non-member States agreed to come before the Court.

M. DE LAPRADELLE replied that an invitation for each individual case was certainly not

ment pas nécessaire. L'invitation peut être faite *in globo* et à des conditions qu'on fixera une fois pour toutes: la condition à fixer dans le cas actuel devrait être seulement l'obligation de supporter une partie des frais.

M. LODER se range à l'avis de M. de Lapradelle. Il croit que l'article 17 ne vise pas l'éventualité ou deux Etats non-membres sont d'accord pour s'adresser à la Cour.

Il pense donc, qu'il sera suffisant de stipuler, dans la convention établissant la Cour, que celle-ci devra connaître des cas qui seront ainsi soumis.

M. RICCI-BUSATTI prend acte du fait que ses amendements aux articles 2 et 3 du projet déposé par le Président ont été acceptés. Par contre, l'accord ne s'est pas fait sur les amendements à l'article 1er. M. Ricci-Busatti est disposé à se rallier, sous réserve de quelques améliorations de pure forme, à l'opinion de la majorité en ce qui concerne le mot „juridique". Mais il croit devoir insister jusqu'au vote final, sur la nécessité de modifier la formule du paragraphe *b*.

Pour ce qui est de la situation des Etats non-membres de la Société des Nations, M. Ricci-Busatti se rallie, en général, à M. de Lapradelle. Il croit d'ailleurs, que l'article 17 ne se prononce pas clairement sur ce point; les articles 12 à 16 ont trait surtout à la procédure devant le Conseil et aux sanctions; la Cour prévue par l'article 14 n'étant pas encore constituée, l'article 17 ne vise pas directement la procédure dans les affaires qui lui seront soumises. Les traités de paix contiennent en effet des dispositions qui confèrent à la Cour de Justice la compétence pour résoudre des litiges auxquels des Etats non-membres de la Société des Nations peuvent être parties, sans soumettre à des conditions spéciales le droit qu'ont ces Etats de faire appel à la Cour.

Le PRESIDENT admet la justesse de l'observation de M. Ricci-Busatti; mais il dit que ce sont là des cas sporadiques, et que d'ailleurs les exceptions confirment la règle. En général il faut toujours l'autorisation du Conseil pour que des Etats non-signataires puissent avoir accès à la Cour. Si deux Etats de cette catégorie se sont mis d'accord pour aller devant la Cour, le Conseil les invitera en y mettant certaines conditions.

M. DE LAPRADELLE peut se ranger à cette opinion, mais il croit que l'invitation du Conseil peut être faite une fois pour toutes.

Le PRESIDENT réplique que M. de Lapradelle préjuge la question de savoir si le Con-

necessary. The invitation could be made general and under conditions fixed once and for all: the only condition to be imposed in the present case should be the obligation to share in the expenses.

M. LODER agreed with M. de Lapradelle. He thought that Article 17 did not refer to a case in which two non-member States agreed to appeal to the Court.

He thought therefore, that it would be sufficient to stipulate in the Convention establishing the Court that it should hear cases thus submitted to it.

M. RICCI-BUSATTI stated that his amendments to Articles 2 and 3 of the plan submitted by the President had been accepted. On the other hand his amendment to Article 1 had not been agreed to. M. Ricci-Busatti was disposed to adopt the opinion of the majority on the word "legal" except for some changes purely relating to form. He felt that he must insist even up to a final vote upon the necessity of amending the wording of paragraph *b*.

Concerning the situation of States non-members of the League of Nations, M. Ricci-Busatti agreed generally with M. de Lapradelle. He thought however, that Article 17 was not clear on this point; Articles 12 to 16 dealt primarily with the procedure before the Council and with sanctions; the Court mentioned in Article 14 not yet being constituted, Article 17 does not provide directly the procedure for the affairs submitted to it. The Treaties of Peace as a matter of fact contained provisions conferring on the Permanent Court of Justice competence to deal with cases to which States non-members of the League of Nations may be parties, without submitting to special conditions the right of these States to appeal to the Court.

The PRESIDENT admitted the accuracy of M. Ricci-Busatti's remarks, but he said that these were only isolated cases, and further that exceptions proved the rule. In general the Council must always authorise non-signatory States to have access to the Court. If two States of this class agreed to submit their case to the Court, the Council would invite them under certain conditions.

M. DE LAPRADELLE could agree to this opinion, but he thought that the invitation of the Council might be given, once and for all.

The PRESIDENT answered that M. de Lapradelle anticipated that the Council would

seil sera disposé à établir à cet effet un règlement général qui permettrait aux Etats non-signataires d'aller naturellement et *de plano* devant la Cour.

M. DE LAPRADELLE l'admet volontiers.

LORD PHILLIMORE propose que le Comité examine maintenant la question des normes matérielles à appliquer par la Cour.

Le PRESIDENT appelle à cet égard l'attention du Comité sur le projet qu'il leur a fait distribuer (voir annexe 3). Il ajoute que la question a déjà été examinée lors de la première Conférence de La Haye, mais qu'on n'est pas parvenu à la résoudre. Si l'on arrive aujourd'hui à un résultat positif, on aura réalisé un progrès. Comme l'a fait observer M. de Lapradelle, deux questions se posent:

1. Quelle est l'objet de la compétence de la Cour?
2. Quelles sont les règles que la Cour doit appliquer?

La première question a déjà été étudiée et résolue. Le Comité doit maintenant procéder à l'examen de la seconde.

Le Président a formulé quatre règles pour servir de base à la discussion. Il en donne lecture.

Mr. ROOT rappelle la remarque qu'il vient de faire à propos d'une autre question, à savoir que, pour faire accepter aux Etats la disposition établissant la judicature obligatoire, il faut bien définir les limites de cette judicature.

Les rédacteurs du Pacte n'ont pu se mettre d'accord pour établir une autre juridiction que celle qui serait compétente pour des questions d'interprétation des traités, et en général, pour des questions de droit international. De l'avis de Mr. Root, le Comité ne doit pas essayer d'aller plus loin. Si le Comité entreprenait de fixer les normes matérielles qui doivent guider les juges, il dépasserait son mandat, qui est d'organiser la Cour et non pas de légiférer.

Mais si le Comité entreprend cette tâche, Mr. Root ne trouve, en première lecture, rien à redire aux clauses 1 et 2 du projet du Président; mais si, personnellement, il accepte la clause relative aux coutumes internationales, il n'est pas certain que 50 Etats s'accordent à son sujet. Par contre, Mr. Root ne parvient pas à comprendre le sens exact de la 3ème clause. Fait-elle allusion à quelque chose qui a été reconnu, sans avoir pour cela revêtu le caractère d'une règle de droit positif? De même en ce qui concerne la 4ème clause. Les deux clauses constituent un élar-

be disposed to make a general rule to this effect, which would allow non-signatory States naturally to go before the Court *de plano*.

M. DE LAPRADELLE admitted this willingly.

LORD PHILLIMORE proposed that the Committee now proceed to consider the question of the rules to be applied by the Court.

The PRESIDENT in this connection called the attention of the Committee to the project which had already been distributed to them. (See Annex 3). He added that the question had already been examined at the first Hague Conference, but had not been decided upon. If to-day they reached a definite decision, they would have made a step forward. As M. de Lapradelle had observed, two different questions arise:

1. What is the subject-matter of the competence of the Court?
2. What are the rules that the Court must apply?

The first question already had been examined and settled. The Committee must now proceed to consider the second.

The President had formulated four rules to serve as a basis for the discussion. He read them.

Mr. ROOT recalled the remark he had just made on another subject, that is to say, that in order to induce the States to accept the establishment of compulsory jurisdiction, the limits of this jurisdiction must be clearly defined.

The authors of the Covenant could only agree upon the establishment of a jurisdiction which would be competent to deal with questions concerning the interpretation of treaties and questions of international law generally. In Mr. Root's opinion, the Committee should not try to go further. If the Committee undertook to establish the actual rules to be followed by the judges, they would exceed their mandate, which was to organise the Court and not to make laws for it.

But if the Committee did undertake this task, Mr. Root at a first reading found nothing in clauses 1 and 2 of the President's project which required amendment, but even if, personally, he should accept the clause relative to international customs, he was not certain that 50 States would agree on the subject. On the contrary, Mr. Root could not understand the exact meaning of clause 3. Did it refer to something which had been recognised but nevertheless had not the character of a definite rule

gissement de la juridiction de la Cour, qui menace de la faire éclater tout entière. Si ces clauses sont acceptées, cela revient à dire aux Etats: „Vous abandonnez votre droit de déterminer le contenu du droit international". Est-il possible d'obliger les nations à soumettre leurs différends à une Cour qui n'appliquerait pas seulement le droit, mais ce qu'elle considère comme la notion du droit, telle qu'elle existe dans la conscience des peuples civilisés?

Mr. Root, pour terminer, fait appel à ses collègues et leur demande de s'en tenir au progrès qu'ils viennent de réaliser: il faut avant d'aller plus loin amener le monde à accepter les sentences de la Cour dans le domaine du droit.

M. LODER déclare que le discours de Mr. Root a fait sur lui une grande impression. Il a cependant quelques questions à poser à propos de ce discours. Il ne voit pas exactement en effet, les limites que Mr. Root veut fixer à la compétence de la Cour.

Mr. Root avait dit qu'il faut que le Comité se borne aux règles conventionnelles et au droit international positif, — aux lois; mais il n'y a pas de lois en matière de droit international.

LORD PHILLIMORE fait remarquer qu'il y a des coutumes.

M. LODER ne croit pas que la différence soit grande entre lois et coutumes en matière de droit international.

Mr. ROOT craint que si le Comité fait des innovations les nations n'acceptent pas son projet.

M. LODER comprendrait cette objection, si l'on était encore en 1907, avant l'avènement du Pacte. Le Pacte veut établir la Cour Permanente de Justice Internationale, pour appliquer le droit international; c'est le devoir du Comité d'indiquer à la Cour comment elle devra accomplir sa tâche.

M. Loder examine alors le projet soumis par le Président. Il constate que les points 1 et 2 ne rencontrent pas d'objection. Par contre Mr. Root avait trouvé trop vagues les clauses 3 et 4.

M. Loder ne partage pas cet avis. On a parlé de règles reconnues et respectées du monde entier, qui n'ont pas encore le caractère de droit positif; mais la Cour a justement le devoir de développer le droit, de faire „mûrir" les coutumes et les principes universellement reconnus, et de les cristalliser sous la forme de règles positives; en un mot, de fixer la jurisprudence internationale. M. Loder ne croit donc pas que les craintes de Mr. Root soient fondées.

of law? It was the same with clause 4. These two clauses constituted an enlargement of the jurisdiction of the Court which threatened to destroy it. If these clauses were accepted, it would amount to saying to the States: "You surrender your rights to say what justice should be." Was it possible to compel nations to submit their disputes to a Court which would administer not merely law, but also what it deems to be the conscience of civilised peoples.

Mr. Root ended by appealing to his colleagues to confine themselves to the step forward which had just been made. Before going further, the world must be induced to accept the judgments of the Court upon questions of law.

M. LODER said that Mr. Root's speech had made a deep impression upon him. However, he had some questions to ask concerning it. He did not understand exactly what limits Mr. Root wished to fix for the Court's competence.

Mr. ROOT had said that the Committee must limit itself to rules contained in Conventions and positive international law; but there are no statutes in international law.

LORD PHILLIMORE pointed out that there were customs.

M. LODER did not think there was any great difference between statutes and custom in international law.

Mr. ROOT feared that if the Committee made innovations the nations would not accept its project.

M. LODER would have understood this objection if the position were still the same as it was in 1907, before the Covenant. The Covenant intended to establish the Permanent Court of International Justice to apply international law; it was the duty of the Committee to point out to the Court how it should carry out its task.

M. Loder considered the proposal put forward by the President. He said the points 1 and 2 met with no opposition. On the other hand, Mr. Root thought that clauses 3 and 4 were too vague.

M. Loder did not share this opinion. Rules recognised and respected by the whole world had been mentioned, rules which were, however, not yet of the nature of positive law, but it was precisely the Court's duty to develop law, to "ripen" customs and principles universally recognised, and to crystallise them into positive rules; in a word, to establish an international jurisprudence. M. Loder therefore, did not think that Mr. Root's fears were well-founded.

LORD PHILLIMORE croit que, bien que partant d'un point de vue différent, il est arrivé au même but que Mr. Root. Il préfère prendre pour base le projet dit des Cinq Puissances. Il se rallie à la première partie de l'article 2 de ce projet, mais ne peut accepter entièrement la seconde.

Celle-ci en effet, confère à la Cour un pouvoir législatif; mais la législation, en matière de droit international, ne peut se faire que par l'accord universel de tous les Etats. A défaut de cette législation que reste-t-il?

En premier lieu, le droit conventionnel, et en second lieu, le droit international actuellement en vigueur. Ces deux points correspondent aux deux premières clauses du projet du Président. Mais ce projet a le tort d'introduire une distinction qui n'a pas de raison d'être. La coutume internationale étant une pratique commune acceptée comme loi par les nations, constitue en somme le droit international. Dans ces conditions, les clauses 3 et 4 ou rentrent dans la clause, 2 ou constituent des additions à cette clause. Mais, d'après Lord Phillimore, on ne peut pas sortir du cadre de cette dernière clause.

Aussi croit-il qu'il vaut mieux s'en tenir à la formule du projet des Cinq Puissances.

En effet, les conflits qui ne peuvent pas être tranchés en appliquant des règles de droit, doivent être portés devant le Conseil de la Société des Nations.

En résumé, Lord Phillimore est disposé à adopter la règle du projet des Cinq Puissances et à faire ainsi appliquer par la Cour, à défaut de droit conventionnel, le droit international en vigueur. Pour rappeler que non seulement le droit écrit, mais aussi le droit coutumier doit entrer nécessairement en ligne de compte, — étant donnée la conception que se font les pays anglo-saxons en matière de droit, — il voudrait cependant ajouter à la formule, après les mots „règles de droit international", les mots suivants: „quelle que soit la source d'où ils découlent".

M. DE LAPRADELLE préférerait une formule brève, par exemple celle-ci: „La Cour statue d'après le droit, la justice et l'équité".

Le juge en effet, doit statuer en droit. Il n'y a donc qu'à definir le droit. Mais ce soin doit être laissé aux juges. En tout cas il n'y a pas lieu de se préoccuper des sources de ce droit. Le document déposé par le Président définit le droit et en indique les sources. C'est intéressant, mais inutile. Il est inutile, par exemple, de mentionner que la Cour doit tenir compte des traités; cela

LORD PHILLIMORE thought that, though he started from a different conception he arrived at the same point as Mr. Root. He preferred to take as a basis the so-called project of the Five Powers. He agreed with the first part of Article 2 of that project, but could not accept the whole of the second part.

The second part, in fact, gave the Court a legislative power, but legislation in matters of international law could only be carried out by the universal agreement of all States. Apart from this legislation, what remains?

In the first place Conventional law, and in the second place, international law actually in force. These two points corresponded to the first clauses of the President's project. But the plan made a mistake by introducing an unjustifiable distinction. International custom, that is, a general practice accepted as law by nations, constitutes in the main international law. Under these conditions clauses 3 and 4 either came within the limits of clause 2 or else were additions to this clause. But Lord Phillimore thought that it was not possible to go beyond the bounds of this last clause.

He also thought it better to adhere to the wording of the Five Power's plan.

Disputes which could not be settled by the application of rules of law should be taken before the Council of the League of Nations.

Summing up, Lord Phillimore said that he was disposed to adopt the rule of the Five Power's project, to make the Court apply international law in force in the absence of any conventional law. In order to record the fact that not only written law but also customary law must be taken into account, — a point which was necessary considering the Anglo-Saxon conception of law, — he wished, however, to add to the draft after the words "rules of international law", the following words: "from whatever source they may be derived".

M. DE LAPRADELLE preferred a short wording, for instance this: "the Court shall judge in accordance with law, justice, and equity."

A judge must, of course, judge according to law. It only remained therefore to define law. But this duty must be left to the judges. In any case there was not occasion now to consider the sources of this law. The document submitted by the President defined law and indicated its sources. This was interesting but useless. It was useless, for instance, to mention that the Court

va de soi. Il pourrait être utile au contraire de spécifier que la Cour ne doit pas agir en législateur. Il est nécessaire de donner aux parties l'assurance que la Cour ne se préoccupera que d'appliquer le droit, de rendre justice, et qu'elle ne cédera pas à la tentation d'agir en diplomate. Il faut éviter qu'on puisse adresser à la nouvelle Cour le reproche qu'on a adressé à cet égard à la Cour d'Arbitrage.

Cependant il serait trop strict et même injuste d'obliger la Cour à ne tenir compte que du droit. Il n'y a pas de danger à laisser à la Cour la faculté d'examiner si telle ou telle solution en droit est juste et équitable, et de corriger, le cas échéant, cette solution d'après les exigences de la justice et de l'équité. Il faut faire confiance aux juges et leur laisser la liberté de tenir compte eux-mêmes de ces différents éléments.

M. HAGERUP attire l'attention sur la considération qui est à la base du projet des Cinq Puissances, du projet commun des commissions des pays du Nord, ainsi que du projet suédois, à savoir qu'il peut y avoir des cas où aucune règle de droit conventionnel ou général n'est applicable. Il faut établir une règle pour répondre à cette éventualité, afin d'éviter que la Cour ne se déclare incompétente (*non liquet*) faute de normes matérielles. La convention établissant la Cour internationale des Prises a envisagé cette éventualité dans son article 7, aux termes duquel la Cour est dans ce cas obligée de statuer en justice et en équité.

Le projet scandinave a adopté alternativement cette même solution et celle qui, empruntée au Code civil suisse, a été reprise plus tard par le projet des Cinq Puissances. Pour sa part, M. Hagerup peut se rallier aux deux solutions. En effet, comme l'a indiqué M. de Lapradelle, il faut que la Cour ait la faculté d'appliquer des principes, pour combler les lacunes du droit positif.

M. Hagerup insiste sur les deux points suivants:

1. il ne faut pas que la Cour puisse renoncer à prononcer une décision en alléguant qu'il n'y a pas de règles positives applicables;
2. s'il y a une règle de droit, il faut que la Cour soit obligée de l'appliquer. La Cour ne devrait recourir à l'équité que si elle y a été autorisée par les parties.

M. Hagerup ajoute que l'équité est une conception très vague et qui ne se trouve pas tou-

must take treaties into account. That goes without saying. On the other hand it would be useful to specify that the Court must not act as a legislator. It was necessary to give parties an assurance that the Court would concern itself only with the application of law, to administer justice, and would not succumb to a temptation to deal with diplomacy. The reproach which had been levelled in this respect against the Court of Arbitration must not be allowed to apply to the new Court.

However, it would be too strict and even unjust to force the Court to consider only law. There would be no danger in allowing the Court to consider whether any particular legal solution were just and equitable, and if necessary to modify, if the situation arose, the legal solution according to the exigencies of justice and equity. Confidence must be put in the judges, and they must be allowed to consider these different elements for themselves.

M. HAGERUP called attention to the considerations which formed the basis for the project of the Five Powers, the joint plan of the Northern countries commissions, as well as the Swedish plan: there might be cases in which no rule of conventional or general law was applicable. A rule must be established to meet this eventuality, to avoid the possibility of the Court declaring itself incompetent (*non liquet*) through lack of applicable rules. The Convention establishing the international Prize Court, in its Article 7, took this eventuality into account by the provision that in this case the Court must render judgment according to justice and equity.

The Scandinavian project had adopted alternatively this same solution and the one borrowed from the Swiss civil code, which was adopted later by the project of the Five Powers. For his part, M. Hagerup was prepared to agree with both solutions. In fact as M. de Lapradelle had indicated, the Court must have the power to apply principles to fill the gaps in positive law.

M. Hagerup insisted on the two following points:

1. it must not be possible for the Court to abstain from giving a decision, alleging that no positive applicable rule exists;
2. if there is a rule of international law, the Court must apply it. The Court should only have recourse to equity if authorised to do so by the parties.

M. Hagerup added that equity was a very vague conception and was not always in harmony

jours en harmonie avec la justice; il en fournit un exemple puisé à son expérience d'arbitre international. Il convient avec M. de Lapradelle qu'il faut une formule aussi courte, aussi simple, aussi peu doctrinaire que possible. Avant tout il faut éviter de fixer dès maintenant une formule qui limiterait l'action de la Cour.

Le PRESIDENT dit qu'on poursuivra cette discussion au cours de la séance prochaine.

LORD PHILLIMORE demande si, lorsque cette discussion sera terminée, on entamera la question des règles de procédure.

Le PRESIDENT répond affirmativement.

La séance est levée à 12.40.

Le Président:
(signé) Brn. DESCAMPS.

Le Secrétaire-Général:
(signé) D. ANZILOTTI.

with justice, he gave an example taken from his experience as an international arbitrator. He agreed with M. de Lapradelle that a formula was required as short, as simple, and as little theoretical as possible. Above all, they now must avoid the laying down of a formula which would limit the activity of the Court.

The PRESIDENT said that the discussion would be continued at the next meeting.

LORD PHILLIMORE asked if, when this discussion was finished, they would deal with the question of the rules of procedure.

The PRESIDENT replied in the affirmative.

The meeting closed at 12.40.

The President:
(signed) Brn. DESCAMPS.

The Secretary-General:
(signed) D. ANZILOTTI.

ANNEXE No. 1.

Projet d'organisation de la Cour Permanente de Justice Internationale, soumis par Mr. Root et Lord Phillimore („projet Root-Phillimore"). [1])

Article 1.

La Cour Permanente de Justice Internationale visée par l'article 14 du Pacte de la Société des Nations, sera formée de juges indépendants, choisis sans tenir compte de leur nationalité. Il devront remplir les conditions requises dans leurs propres pays pour l'admission dans la haute magistrature administrative ou judiciaire, ou être des jurisconsultes d'une compétence notoire en matière de droit international.

Article 2.

Il y aura 11 juges et 4 juges suppléants. Ils seront élus pour une période de 9 ans par l'Assemblée et le Conseil de la Société. Chacun de ces deux corps votera séparément. Seront élus ceux qui auront réuni la majorité des voix des membres présents et exerçant leur droit de vote dans les deux corps.

Article 3.

Si, après le premier tour de scrutin dans chacun des corps électoraux, des sièges restent à remplir, on procèdera de la même façon à un second tour de scrutin, en vue de pourvoir les sièges inoccupés. On procèdera de la même manière à autant de scrutins qu'il sera nécessaire pour remplir tous les sièges.

Article 4.

En vue de réconcilier les divergences d'opinion qui pourront surgir entre les deux collèges électoraux au sujet des candidats, ces collèges auront le droit de nommer, quand bon leur semble, une commission composée de trois membres de chacun des deux corps. Cette commission aura la tâche de délibérer et de proposer la conciliation des divergences en question. S'il est impossible de concilier les divergences, il appartiendra aux juges déjà élus de nommer les titulaires des sièges laissés inoccupés.

1) Le projet était originairement rédigé en anglais; le texte français en est une traduction.

(Note du secrétariat).

ANNEX No. 1.

Proposed organisation of the Permanent Court of International Justice, submitted by Mr. Root and Lord Phillimore ("Root-Phillimore plan"). [1])

Article 1.

The Permanent Court of International Justice provided for by Article 14 of the Covenant of the League of Nations shall consist of independent judges who shall be chosen regardless of their nationality and who shall possess the qualifications required, in their own countries, for elevation to high legal office whether administrative or judicial, or shall be jurisconsults of recognised authority in international law.

Article 2.

There shall be eleven judges and four supplementary judges who shall hold office for a term of nine years and who shall be elected by the Assembly and the Council of the Society of Nations. Each of these bodies shall vote separately and the votes of a majority of the members present and voting in each body shall be necessary to an election.

Article 3.

If, after the first vote in each electoral body, it shall appear that any vacancies in the Court remain unfilled, a second vote shall be taken in like manner to fill such vacancies; and separate votes shall be taken in like manner until all the existing vacancies are filled.

Article 4.

For the purpose of reconciling any differences which may arise between the two electoral bodies in regard to the persons to be elected, they may, at any time when they deem it suitable, appoint a Committee composed of three from each body for the purpose of conferring and recommending the conciliation of such differences. If such differences should prove ultimately irreconcilable, the appointment to the vacancies unfilled shall devolve upon the judges who have already been agreed upon.

1) The plan was drafted in English; the French text is a translation.

(Note by secretariat).

Article 5.

Les juges suppléants seront élus de la même manière, mais séparément.

Article 6.

Une liste de personnes remplissant les conditions requises et en état de pouvoir exercer les fonctions de juge, sera présentée, à l'Assemblée et au Conseil respectivement, avant la date de l'élection. La liste sera composée de la manière suivante: trois mois au moins avant la date de l'élection, le Secrétaire-Général de la Société des Nations adressera par écrit aux membres de la Cour Permanente d'Arbitrage de La Haye, la requête de procéder par groupes, chaque groupe comprenant les membres nommés par un pays déterminé, à la présentation de quatre noms, au plus, de personnes qui, à leur avis, remplissent les conditions requises et sont disposées à accepter le poste de juge.

Article 7.

La totalité des personnes ainsi proposées composeront la liste à présenter à l'Assemblée et au Conseil; les juges seront choisis sur cette liste. Si, cependant, l'Assemblée et le Conseil ne se mettent pas d'accord sur l'élection, la Commission de conciliation aura la faculté de proposer à l'Assemblée et au Conseil l'élection d'une personne qui ne figure pas sur la liste.

Article 8.

Les membres représentants de chaque pays à la Cour Permanente d'Arbitrage seront priés de consulter les titulaires des plus hautes fonctions judiciaires, les doyens, directeurs ou présidents des universités et des sociétés scientifiques, afin d'assurer la présentation des personnes les plus compétentes et les plus expérimentées, possédant la plus haute considération juridique et morale.

Article 9.

Les juges ou juges suppléants termineront, même après l'expiration de leur mandat, l'instruction des affaires dont ils ont été appelés à connaître.

Article 10.

Si un juge ou juge suppléant devient incapable de faire fonction de juge, ou s'il devient indésirable qu'il remplisse pareille fonction, les autres membres de la Cour pourront notifier ce fait au Secrétaire-Général de la Société des Na-

Article 5.

The supplementary judges shall be separately elected in like manner.

Article 6.

A list of persons qualified and fit to exercise the judicial office shall be laid before the Assembly and the Council respectively before the time of election. Such list shall be made up in the following manner: At least three months before the time of election, the Secretary-General of the League of Nations shall apply in writing to the members of the Permanent Court of Arbitration at The Hague from each country which shall have appointed such member, requesting the members from each country, acting as a body, to propose not more than four names of persons whom they deem to be qualified and available for judges.

Article 7.

All of the persons so proposed shall form the list to be laid before and considered by the Assembly and Council and the judges shall be elected from that list. In the event, however, of the Assembly and Council not agreeing, the Committee of Conference shall be at liberty to recommend to the Assembly and Council a person outside the list.

Article 8.

The members of the Permanent Court of Arbitration in each country are requested to consult with the highest judicial officers, the heads of universities and learned societies, to the end that the nominations made may be of persons who are the most competent and experienced and of the highest judicial character and reputation.

Article 9.

Judges or supplementary judges shall complete the hearing of cases of which they have cognisance even though the period for which they have been elected shall have expired.

Article 10.

In case any judge or supplementary judge shall become incapable or unfit for the performance of a judicial office, upon the unanimous representation of this fact by the Court to the Secretary-General the place of the judge shall become

tions. Si cette notification est faite à l'unanimité, le siège du juge sera considéré comme vacant, et l'élection d'un nouveau titulaire sera fixée pour la réunion prochaine de l'Assemblée et du Conseil.

vacant and notice shall be given of an election to fill the vacancy at the next meeting of the Assembly and Council.

Article 11.

Dans toute élection de juges ou de juges suppléants, les électeurs seront moralement obligés d'assurer que les juges élus sont en possession des conditions requises, et de chercher à assurer, dans la mesure du possible, la représentation à la Cour des différentes formes de civilisation et des différents systèmes juridiques des Membres de la Société des Nations. Cependant, tous les juges doivent appartenir à des Etats différents.

Article 11.

In all elections of judges and supplementary judges the electors shall be under honorable obligation to take into account the existence of the necessary qualifications and to seek so far as practicable to have represented in the Court the different forms of civilisation and juridical systems which exist among the Members of the Society of Nations; but there shall be but one member of the Court elected from any one State.

Article 12.

La Cour élira son Président et son Vice-Président; elle nommera son greffier: elle aura la faculté de nommer comme greffier le greffier de la Cour Permanente d'Arbitrage.

Article 12.

The Court shall elect its own President and Vice-President. It shall also appoint its Registrar or may designate the Registrar of the Permanent Court of Arbitration to be its Registrar.

Article 13.

Le Président et le Vice-Président seront élus pour une période de trois ans. Ils seront rééligibles.

Article 13.

The President and Vice-President shall be elected for a term of three years and shall be eligible for re-election.

Article 14.

Un juge ne pourra pas fonctionner comme tel dans une affaire au règlement de laquelle il aura pris part auparavant, d'une façon quelconque, dans une Cour nationale, un tribunal d'arbitrage ou une commission d'enquête, ou dans laquelle il a fait fonction d'agent ou de conseiller de l'une des parties. Un juge ne pourra faire fonction d'agent ou d'avocat dans aucune affaire internationale pendant la durée de son mandat.

Article 14.

A judge may not exercise his judicial functions in any case in which he has, in any way whatever, taken part in the decision of a national tribunal, of a tribunal of arbitration, or of a commission of inquiry, or has figured in the suit as counsel or advocate for one of the parties. A judge cannot act as agent or advocate in any international cause during his term of office.

Article 15.

Il sera pourvu à la nomination aux sièges de juge ou de juge suppléant devenus vacants, selon la méthode adoptée pour la 1ère élection. Dans chaque cas spécial, l'élection visera la période de neuf ans.

Article 15.

Vacancies in the office of judge and supplementary judge shall be filled as in the case of original appointments, and in every case the appointment shall be for the full term of nine years.

Article 16.

Les parties ne pourront récuser un juge, membre de la Cour Permanente de Justice Internationale. Si pour des raisons déterminées, le Président de la Cour est d'avis que l'un des juges

Article 16.

The parties cannot challenge a judge of the Permanent Court of International Justice. If, for a specific reason, the President of the Court considers that one of the judges ought not to sit

doit céder sa place dans une certaine affaire, il lui fera part de cette opinion. Un juge ayant été ainsi averti aura le devoir de s'abtenir de siéger à la Cour. Un juge qui pense qu'il doit céder sa place dans une affaire déterminée, aura la faculté de prendre auprès du Président l'initiative que cet avis comporte. Si le Président et le juge ne sont pas d'accord à cet égard, chacun d'eux aura la faculté d'en appeler à la Cour pour qu'elle tranche la question en session plénière.

Article 17.

Le nombre des juges peut être augmenté par l'Assemblée de temps à autre, mais ne doit pas excéder, en tout, quinze juges et six juges suppléants.

in a particular case, he shall so inform him and thereupon it becomes the duty of the judge to abstain from sitting. A judge who believes that he ought not to sit in a particular case can take the initiative with the President with reference thereto. In case of disagreement on this point between the President and the judge it is competent for either to appeal to the Court in plenary session for a decision of the question.

Article 17.

The number of judges may be increased by the Assembly from time to time not to exceed fifteen judges and six supplementary judges in the aggregate.

ANNEXE No. 2.

Le projet suivant remplace et complète, en ce qui concerne l'organisation de la Cour (sauf additions éventuelles ultérieures) celui que j'ai eu l'honneur de déposer le 23 de ce mois.

A. RICCI-BUSATTI.

Le 30 juin 1920.

Article 1.

La „Cour Permanente de Justice Internationale" est composée de juges réunissant les qualités nécessaires pour faire partie de la „Cour Permanente d'Arbitrage", aux termes de la Convention de La Haye pour le règlement pacifique des conflits internationaux, et qui seront nommés conformément aux dispositions qui suivent. Ils tiennent leur mandat de la Société des Nations devant laquelle ils répondent de tout ce qui concerne l'accomplissement de leur tâche.

Article 2.

Chaque Membre de la Société des Nations pourra désigner une personne, choisie par ses délégués à la Cour Permanente d'Arbitrage conformément à l'article précédent, soit parmi ses nationaux, soit parmi les nationaux d'un pays différent.

Si ces délégués ne sont pas d'accord sur la personne à choisir, le Gouvernement désignera la personne qu'il préfère, parmi celles dont ils lui auront proposé les noms.

Article 3.

Les personnes désignées par les Etats représentés d'une façon permanente au Conseil de la Société, et celles qui auront été désignées au moins par trois Membres, seront de plein droit juges de la Cour.

L'Assemblée de la Société choisira, parmi les autres personnes qui ont été désignées, un certain nombre de juges qui ne devra pas excéder le tiers de celui des personnes désignées ci-dessus. Chaque Membre disposera, à cet effet, d'un nombre de voix égal à celui des juges à choisir; ceux qui auront obtenu le plus grand nombre de voix, et en cas d'égalité de voix, les plus âgés, seront considérés comme élus.

ANNEX No. 2.

The following proposals supersede and complete, in so far as they concern the organisation of the Court (with the exception of possible later additions), those which I had the honor to submit on the 23rd day of this month.

A. RICCI-BUSATTI.

June 30th, 1920.

Article 1.

The "Permanent Court of International Justice" is composed of judges having the qualifications required for membership in the "Permanent Court of Arbitration" as defined in the Hague Convention for the pacific settlement of international disputes, and who shall be named in conformity with the following provisions. They derive their authority from the League of Nations, and they are responsible to the League for the discharge of their duties.

Article 2.

Each member of the League of Nations may nominate one person, chosen by its delegates at the Permanent Court of Arbitration in conformity with the preceding article from among either its own nationals or the nationals of another State.

If these delegates are not agreed on the person to be chosen, the Government shall designate the person it prefers from among those whose names the delegates shall have proposed to it.

Article 3.

The persons named by the States represented permanently on the Council of the League, and those who shall have been named by at least three members, shall be judges in full right on the Court.

The Assembly of the League shall choose from among the other persons who have been designated a certain number of judges not exceeding one third of the aforesaid persons. Each Member will for this purpose be entitled to a number of votes equal to the number of judges to be elected; those who shall receive the largest number of votes, and in case of equality of votes the oldest, shall be considered elected.

Article 4.

Les juges sont nommés pour une période de six ans; ils continueront cependant à faire partie de la Cour pour la connaissance des affaires dont ils auront été saisis conformément aux dispositions qui suivent, jusqu'à ce que ces affaires soient terminées. Leur mandat peut être renouvelé.

Article 5.

La qualité de membre de la Cour de Justice Internationale est incompatible avec toute autre charge se rattachant aux différents organes de la Société des Nations ou aux relations internationales des Etats, sauf celle de membre de la Cour Permanente d'Arbitrage ou d'un tribunal arbitral international.

Tout membre de la Cour de justice se trouvant dans un des cas d'incompatibilité visés à l'alinéa précédent sera considéré comme démissionnaire de ses fonctions de juge.

Article 6.

Lorsqu'un juge cessera, pour quelque motif que ce soit, de faire partie de la Cour, il sera pourvu à la nomination de son remplaçant d'après les règles suivantes.

S'il s'agit de juges nommés conformément au 1er alinéa de l'article 3, les Membres de la Société des Nations par lesquels ils avaient été désignés, seront invités à pourvoir à la nouvelle nomination conformément à l'article 2 et à l'alinéa précité. S'il s'agit de juges élus par l'Assemblée, ou si, dans le premier cas, aucune désignation n'a été faite dans un délai d'un mois, les Membres de la Société, autres que ceux par lesquels ont été désignés les juges restant en charge, seront invités à faire une nouvelle désignation conformément à l'article 2, et la nouvelle nomination des juges dont il s'agit sera faite conformément au 2ème alinéa de l'article 3.

Article 7.

Lorsque de nouveaux Membres seront admis à faire partie de la Société des Nations ou auront une représentation permanente au Conseil, conformément aux articles 1er et 4 du Pacte, la nomination de nouveaux juges pourra avoir lieu, conformément aux dispositions qui précèdent.

Article 8.

La Cour se divise en trois sections. Chaque section est composée d'un Président et d'un nombre de juges, titulaires et suppléants, à déter-

Article 4.

The judges shall be elected for a period of six years; however, they shall continue as members of the Court, to deal with matters brought before them, in conformity with the following conditions, until such time as those matters are decided. They are eligible for re-election.

Article 5.

Membership on the Court of International Justice is incompatible with any other duty connected with the various organs of the League of Nations, or States, international relations, except duties as a member of the Permanent Court of Arbitration or as a member of an International Arbitration Court.

Any member of the Court of Justice affected by one of the cases of incompatibility named in the preceding paragraph shall be considered as having resigned in his capacity as judge.

Article 6.

When a judge shall cease, for any cause whatsoever, to be a member of the Court, the election of his successor shall be provided for by the following regulations.

In case of a judge elected under the provisions of paragraph 1 of Article 3, the Members of the League of Nations by whom he was named shall be invited to proceed to a new election in conformity with Article 2 and the aforesaid paragraph. In case of a judge elected by the Assembly, or if in the first case no election has been made within one month, the Members of the League, other than those who have named the judges remaining on the Court, shall be invited to proceed to a new election in conformity with Article 2, and the new election of the said judges shall be carried out in conformity with Article 3, paragraph 2.

Article 7.

When new members shall be admitted as Members of the League of Nations or shall have permanent representation on the Council, in conformity with Articles 1 and 4 of the Covenant, the election of new judges shall take place in conformity with the conditions provided above.

Article 8.

The Court is divided into three sections. Each section is made up of a President and a number of judges and supplementary judges to

miner, selon les circonstances, par la Cour elle-même. Aucun des membres ne peut appartenir à plus de deux sections. Les trois Présidents sont élus par la Cour à la majorité des voix: si cette majorité n'est pas obtenue au premier tour de scrutin, on procédera à l'élection à la majorité relative; en cas d'égalité de voix, les plus âgés seront considerés comme élus. Leur collège forme la „Présidence de la Cour".

Article 9.

La durée du mandat présidentiel est de deux ans; il peut être renouvelé. En cas de vacance, il sera pourvu aussitôt que possible à la nouvelle élection conformément à l'article qui précède. Le juge le plus âgé, dans chaque section, remplacera le Président en cas d'absence, pour la connaissance des affaires dont la section est saisie. Les Présidents désignent tous les six mois, celui d'entre eux qui aura la préséance, et auquel il appartiendra de décider, faute d'accord, toute question de leur ressort concernant la procédure et le fonctionnement de la Cour. Lorsque cette désignation ne pourra pas avoir lieu par entente amicale, on procédera à l'élection, et si on ne peut obtenir une majorité, le sort décidera.

Article 10.

Les Présidents doivent résider, normalement, au siège de la Cour. Les autres juges doivent être toujours prêts à s'y rendre, chaque fois qu'ils y seront appelés pour exercer leurs fonctions, à moins que leur abstention ne soit justifiée par des raisons qu'ils seront tenus de faire connaître.

Les Présidents recevront, chaque mois, une rémunération fixe, qui sera déterminée de temps en temps par le Conseil de la Société. Les autres juges recevront une rémunération proportionnelle à l'exercice effectif de leur charge, le remboursement de tous frais de voyage, et une indemnité fixe par an, déterminée également selon les circonstances.

Tous les membres de la Cour jouissent dans l'exercice de leurs fonctions, des privilèges et immunités diplomatiques.

Article 12.

Dans chaque affaire particulière, les Parties en cause pourront désigner, d'un commun accord, la section de la Cour devant laquelle l'affaire doit être portée; elles pourront demander également que le tribunal soit composé de trois juges — deux designés par les Parties elles-mêmes et le troisième par la Présidence parmi les mem-

be determined according to circumstances by the Court itself. No member shall belong to more than two sections. The three Presidents shall be elected by majority vote; if this majority is not obtained on the first ballot, election shall be by plurality vote; in case of tie, the senior shall be considered elected. Their college shall form the "Presidency of the Court."

Article 9.

The Presidential term of office shall be two years; they are eligible for re-election. In case of a vacancy, the new election shall be provided for as soon as possible in conformity with the preceding article. The senior judge in each section shall act in the absence of the President for such matters as the section has to consider. The Presidents shall determine every six months who among them shall rank first and shall in absence of an agreement decide on all questions within their competence concerning the procedure and working of the Court. In case this designation cannot be arrived at by amicable agreement, a ballot shall be taken, and if it is impossible to obtain majority, the decision shall be by lot.

Article 10.

The Presidents shall reside normally at the seat of the Court. The other judges shall hold themselves in readiness to present themselves there whenever called upon for the discharge of their duties, unless their absence is justified by causes which they shall be called upon to explain.

The Presidents shall receive monthly a fixed remuneration, which shall be determined from time to time by the Council of the League. The other judges shall receive a renumeration proportional to the actual exercise of their duties, reimbursement for all travelling expenses, and a fixed annual salary, determined also according to circumstances.

All members of the Court in the discharge of their duties shall enjoy diplomatic privileges and immunities.

Article 12.

In each individual case the parties concerned may decide by mutual agreement the section of the Court to which their case is to be presented; they may demand also that the tribunal be composed of three judges, two designated by the parties themselves and the third by the Presidency from among the members of the Court,

bres de la Cour — ou bien que l'affaire soit tranchée par un seul juge, désigné par elles ou par la Présidence.

Lorsque les Parties n'auront fait aucune désignation conformément à l'alinéa précédent, et lorsque la Cour aura été saisie sur la demande d'une seule des Parties, la Présidence désignera la section devant laquelle l'affaire doit être portée; elle aura aussi la faculté de retenir le jugement de l'affaire en se constituant elle-même comme tribunal.

Article 13.

Lorsque les Parties en cause n'ont pas un de leurs ressortissants parmi les membres de la section qui a été saisie de l'affaire, elles auront le droit, soit de désigner un de leurs ressortissants comme assesseur pour prendre part, sans voix délibérative, au jugement, soit de demander que les ressortissants des Parties adverses, s'il y en a parmi les juges, en soient exclus.

Chacune des Parties aura le droit de demander l'exclusion d'un juge de la section qui aura été saisie de l'affaire, dans les cas visés au second alinéa de l'article 12.

Si un des Présidents appartient à l'une des Parties en cause, il s'abstiendra de toute participation au jugement de l'affaire.

Article 14.

Le Bureau de la Cour Permanente d'Arbitrage sert de greffe à la Cour de Justice Internationale. Chaque section pourra toutefois nommer un greffier adjoint, pour les affaires dont elle a été saisie, lorsqu'elle le jugera utile.

Article 15.

La Cour de Justice Internationale a son siège à La Haye. Chaque section, tribunal ou juge, désignés conformément à l'article 12, peuvent toutefois, avec l'assentiment des Parties, choisir un autre lieu pour leurs réunions, si les circonstances l'exigent.

Article 16.

Toute autre disposition concernant l'application des règles précédentes sera établie par la Cour, et tant qu'elle n'aura pas été constituée, par le Conseil de la Société des Nations.

La Cour établira son règlement de procédure.

or that the case be decided by a single judge, designated by them or by the Presidency.

When the Parties shall not have made any designation in conformity with the preceding paragraph, and when the case has been brought before the Court on the request of a single party, the Presidency shall decide what section shall hear the case; it also shall have the power to reserve for itself decision of the case, constituting itself as a tribunal.

Article 13.

When the parties concerned have not one of their representatives among the members of the section before which the case has been brought, they shall have the right either to designate one of their nationals as assessor to take part in the procedure without voting powers, or to demand that nationals of the opposing parties, if any, be excluded from among the judges.

Each one of the parties shall have the right to demand the exclusion of a judge from the section before which the case has been brought, in cases provided by Article 12, Paragraph 2.

If one of the Presidents is the national of one of the States concerned, he shall take no part in the decision of the case.

Article 14.

The Bureau of the Permanent Court of Arbitration shall serve as the Registry of the International Court of Justice. Each section may for the matters brought to its attention name an assistant Registrar whenever it deems it advisable.

Article 15.

The seat of the International Court of Justice shall be established at the Hague. Each section, tribunal, or judge designated in conformity with Article 12 may always, with the consent of the parties, select another place of meeting, if circumstances demand it.

Article 16.

All other provisions concerning the applicition of the preceding rules shall be decided on by the Court, and until the Court is established, by the Council of the League of Nations.

The Court shall establish its rules of procedure.

ANNEXE No. 3.

Proposition du Baron Descamps.

Les règles à appliquer par le juge pour la solution des différends internationaux sont les suivantes, dans l'ordre successif où elles s'imposent à son examen:

1. le droit international conventionnel, soit général, soit spécial, comme manifestation de règles expressément adoptées par les Etats;
2. la coutume internationale, comme attestation d'une pratique commune des nations, acceptée par elles comme loi;
3. les règles de droit international telles que les reconnaît la conscience juridique des peuples civilisés;
4. la jurisprudence internationale, comme organe d'application et de développement du droit.

ANNEX No. 3.

Proposal by Baron Descamps.

The following rules are to be applied by the judge in the solution of international disputes; they will be considered by him in the undermentioned order:

1. conventional international law, whether general or special, being rules expressly adopted by the States;
2. international custom, being practice between nations accepted by them as law;
3. the rules of international law as recognised by the legal conscience of civilised nations;
4. international jurisprudence as a means for the application and development of law.

14IÈME SÉANCE (non-publique), tenue au Palais de la Paix, à La Haye, le 2 juillet 1920.

Présidence de M. le BARON DESCAMPS.

Sont présents: tous les membres du Comité (à l'exception de M. Bevilaqua); M. Fernandes; Mr. James Brown Scott; les secrétaires particuliers du Baron Descamps et de M. Adatci; les membres du Secrétariat.

La séance est ouverte à 9.35 heures du matin.

Le PRESIDENT rappelle que les projets présentés par les membres doivent lui être communiqués, comme le prescrivent les règles de procédure adoptées par le Comité.

Il remercie M. Altamira et M. Ricci-Busatti de l'avoir fait.

Son propre point de vue sur la question des normes matérielles à appliquer par la Cour, qu'il a formulé dans le document soumis aux membres lors de la dernière séance, ayant été contesté, le Président désire le préciser dans une déclaration dont il donne lecture. (Voir annexe 1).

M. HAGERUP rend hommage aux paroles que vient de prononcer le Président. Il se rallie en principe aux opinions qu'il a exprimées. Il désire cependant ajouter quelques observations.

Si les membres du Comité se trouvent vraiment d'accord sur le fond du problème, la tâche se réduit à trouver une formule qui exprime cet accord: cette tâche est relativement facile. Mais M. Hagerup croit que, sur le point actuel, cet accord n'existe pas. Voici, pour sa part, comment il a compris le discours prononcé la veille par Mr. Root, et son impression a été confirmée par une conversation qu'il a eue avec Mr. Root lui-même.

Selon lui, Mr. Root a voulu dire que, si dans un cas déterminé, il n'existe pas de règles matérielles, la Cour peut déclarer: *non liquet* — je ne puis pas décider. Ce point de vue peut être gros de conséquences. Il restreint sensiblement la compétence de la Cour et la place dans une situation tout autre que celle d'une Cour ordinaire qui ne peut pas dire: *non liquet*. M. Hagerup ne fait que répéter ce qu'il a dit la veille: la nouvelle Cour aura, entre autres, la tâche de développer la jurisprudence. Or, Mr. Root a précisé que, s'il n'y a pas de règles de droit

14TH MEETING (Private), held at the Peace Palace, the Hague, on July 2nd, 1920.

BARON DESCAMPS in the chair.

Present: all members of the Committee (with the exception of M. Bevilaqua); M. Fernandes, Mr. James Brown Scott; the private secretaries of Baron Descamps and of M. Adatci; the members of the Secretariat.

The meeting opened at 9.35 a.m.

The PRESIDENT reminded the members that their projects should be sent to him in accordance with the rules of procedure adopted by the Committee.

He thanked M. Altamira and M. Ricci-Busatti for having done so.

His own point of view upon the questions of the rules to be applied by the Court, which he had formulated in the document submitted at the preceding meeting, had been opposed. He desired therefore to explain them in a vote which he read. (See Annex 1).

M .HAGERUP expressed his appreciation of the observations the President had just made. He agreed in principle with the opinions which he had expressed. However, he wished to add certain observations.

If the members of the Committee were really agreed upon the heart of the question, their task was reduced to finding an expression of their agreement. This task was comparatively easy. But M. Hagerup thought that they were not agreed upon the point under discussion. That was the impression he had drawn from Mr. Root's speech on the preceding day, and his impression had been confirmed by conversations which he had had with Mr. Root himself.

According to him, Mr. Root had meant to say that if in a given case there were no actual rules, the Court might declare: *non liquet*—we cannot decide. This attitude might involve important consequences. It limits appreciably the Court's competence and places the Court in an entirely different position from that of an ordinary Court, which may not declare *non liquet*. M. Hagerup merely repeated what he had said the preceding day: one of the tasks of the new Court would be to develop jurisprudence. On

positives, la Cour sera incompétente, car s'il en était autrement, certains Etats n'accepteraient pas la convention établissant la Cour. M. Hagerup croit que, dans ces conditions, il sera impossible à la Cour de contribuer au développement du droit. Il termine en demandant s'il a bien saisi l'idée de Mr. Root.

M. ADATCI voulait, dit-il, poser la même question, c'est à dire celle de savoir si, d'après Mr. Root, la Cour pourra ne pas juger quand il n'y aura pas de règles, soit conventionnelles, soit de droit international général.

Mr. ROOT déclare pour commencer qu'en faisant distribuer la veille aux membres du Comité le document préparé par lui et par Lord Phillimore, il n'avait fait que suivre la coutume américaine et anglaise: il ignorait qu'il y eût une autre procédure à suivre; il ne manquera pas de se conformer désormais à la règle que vient de rappeler le Président.

Le PRESIDENT a simplement voulu attirer l'attention des membres sur les dispositions qui intéressent la bonne marche des travaux.

Mr. ROOT passe ensuite à l'examen de la question à l'ordre du jour. Le discours éloquent du Président se trouve entièrement d'accord avec ses propres opinions. Cependant, la question qu'il faut considérer n'est pas, croit-il, la question de la base matérielle de la juridiction, mais bien la question de savoir dans quelle mesure le monde est prêt à entrer dans la voie de la juridiction obligatoire. Il a l'impression qu'il est encore trop tôt pour aller jusqu'où le veut le Président. Mr. Root pense que le monde est préparé à accepter la juridiction obligatoire d'une Cour qui appliquerait les règles universellement reconnues du droit international. Mais il ne croit pas qu'il soit disposé à accepter la juridiction obligatoire d'une Cour qui appliquerait des principes qui sont compris différemment selon les pays.

Mr. Root croit que, dans la plupart des cas, les Etats se soumettront en réalité à la juridiction obligatoire; mais ceci n'est pas la même chose que de l'accepter d'avance pour tous les cas, sans exception, même pour ceux qui impliquent des principes diversement interprétés dans les pays. Ces cas devraient être soumis à l'arbitrage obligatoire.

L'opinion de Mr. Root à cet égard s'appuie sur deux faits d'expérience personnelle. En 1907 d'abord deux traités d'arbitrage signés par les

the other hand Mr. Root had specified that if there were no positive rules of law, the Court would not be competent; otherwise certain States would not accept the convention establishing the Court. M. Hagerup thought that under these conditions the Court would be unable to contribute to the development of law. In conclusion, M. Hagerup asked if he had rightly understood Mr. Root's idea.

M. ADATCI wished, he said, to put the same question, whether according to Mr. Root the Court could not judge when there were no conventional or general rules of International Law.

Mr. ROOT began by saying that in distributing on the preceding day to the members of the Committee the document prepared by Lord Phillimore and himself, he merely had followed the American and English custom; he had no idea that there was any other procedure to follow. In the future he would not fail to comply with the rule just mentioned by the President.

The PRESIDENT desired only to call the members' attention to the provisions for expediting the work.

Mr. ROOT then went on to consider the question on the Agenda. The President's eloquent speech agreed entirely with his own opinions. However, the question which ought to be considered was not, he felt, the question of the material basis of jurisdiction, but rather the question to what extent the world was ready to take up compulsory jurisdiction. He thought that it was still too soon to go as far as the President wished. Mr. Root thought that the world was prepared to accept the compulsory jurisdiction of a Court which applied the universally recognised rules of International Law. But he did not think that it was disposed to accept the compulsory jurisdiction of a Court which would apply principles, differently understood in different countries.

Mr. Root thought that in most cases States would actually submit to the compulsory jurisdiction, but this was not at all the same thing as accepting it in advance for all cases without exception, even those entailing principles which were differently interpreted in the different countries. Such cases ought to be submitted to compulsory arbitration.

Mr. Root based his opinion of this subject upon two personal experiences. In 1907 two Treaties of Arbitration signed by the United States on one hand, and by Great Britain and

Etats-Unis d'une part, par la Grande Bretagne et la France d'autre part, n'ont pu être ratifiés par les Etats-Unis; ils contenaient en effet une clause, d'après laquelle tout conflit „justiciable" serait soumis à l'arbitrage. Cette formule souleva de très vives objections, car on considéra qu'elle donnait à la Cour des pouvoirs illimités et lui permettait d'appliquer des notions de justice incompatibles avec celles qui sont admises aux Etats-Unis. Au cours des débats qui aboutirent à la non-ratification de ces traités, Mr. Root défendit le point de vue que le Président vient d'exposer avec plus d'habileté et de force logique qu'il n'avait fait lui-même. C'est pourquoi Mr. Root a la conviction que l'Amérique n'adhérerait jamais à un traité de juridiction obligatoire qui dépasserait les limites des règles reconnues. Il faut commencer modestement, et avant de donner à la Cour des pouvoirs plus étendus, lui permettre de justifier la confiance en elle qu'impliquerait une telle extension.

Mr. Root cite ensuite, à l'appui de son opinion, les tentatives faites pour établir une Cour internationale des prises. Cette Cour n'a pu être constituée, parce que la Grande-Bretagne a voulu connaître la portée des principes de justice et d'équité que la Cour devrait appliquer, et elle n'a pas pu recevoir satisfaction sur ce point. Mr. Root se résume en disant qu'à son avis, il vaut mieux établir une Cour avec une juridiction relativement restreinte que d'établir une Cour avec une compétence très large, mais qui ne pourra pas fonctionner.

Mr. Root répond ensuite à M. Adatci. La juridiction de la Cour comprendra, en premier lieu, dans tous les cas où il y a accord entre les parties, toutes les catégories visées par le Baron Descamps; en fait, toutes les questions justiciables. Cette expression ne vise pas seulement les cas où il y a accord entre les parties, mais aussi ceux où la règle ou principe de droit impliqués sont universellement reconnus. Mais il y a des cas exceptionnels où la Cour, pour se prononcer, serait obligée de s'appuyer sur des principes généraux qui sont compris diversement selon les pays. Ce sont les cas de ce genre que les Gouvernements doivent envisager avant de conclure des traités de juridiction obligatoire. Il est inconcevable qu'un Gouvernement puisse accepter d'être assigné devant une Cour qui se fonderait, dans sa sentence, sur sa conception subjective des principes de la justice. La Cour ne doit pas avoir le pouvoir de légiférer.

Si un Etat est assigné en justice dans des cas de cette nature, il y a, selon Mr. Root, deux solutions possibles: Ou la Cour se déclare incom-

France on the other, could not be ratified by the United States. They contained, in fact, a clause according to which every justiciable dispute should be submitted to arbitration. This clause gave rise to strong opposition because it was felt to give the Court unlimited powers and allowed it to apply conceptions of justice incompatible with those recognised by the United States. During the debates which led to the non-ratification of these treaties, Mr. Root defended the point of view which the President had just explained with an ability and force of logic superior to his own. This was the reason why Mr. Root was convinced that America would never give its adherence to a treaty for compulsory jurisdiction outside the limits of recognised rules. The beginning must be modest; before conferring broad powers on the Court, it must be permitted to justify the confidence in it which would warrant such an extension.

Mr. Root then mentioned in support of his opinion the attempts made to establish an International Prize Court. It had been impossible to establish this Court because Great Britain wished to know the scope of the principles of justice and equity which the Court was to apply, and she had been unable to receive satisfaction on this point. Mr. Root summed up his remarks by saying that in his opinion it was better to establish a Court with a relatively limited jurisdiction than to establish a Court with a very wide competence but which would not work.

Mr. Root then answered M. Adatci. The jurisdiction of the Court would include in the first place all cases coming under the categories laid down by Baron Descamps which the parties concerned agreed to submit; in fact all justiciable questions. This expression not only included cases in which an agreement existed between the parties, but also cases in which the rule or principle of law concerned was universally recognised. But there were exceptional cases, in which the Court, in order do decide, would be compelled to rely on general principles, which are interpreted differently in different countries. It is these exceptional cases which the Governments must consider before concluding treaties for compulsory jurisdiction. It is inconceivable that a Government would agree to allow itself to be arraigned before a Court which bases its sentences on its subjective conceptions of the principles of justice. The Court must not have the power to legislate.

If a State were called to justice in a case of this nature, Mr. Root saw two possible solutions: either the Court would declare itself in-

pétente; ou bien elle se borne à faire une recommandation au lieu de prononcer une sentence. En allant plus loin, le Comité effacera lui-même les limites de la juridiction sur lesquelles on vient de faire l'accord, puisque la portée de l'expression „principes de justice" change avec les pays.

Mr. Root serait disposé à accepter les principes exprimés dans le document soumis par le Président, s'il s'agissait de toute autre juridiction que la juridiction obligatoire. Les rédacteurs du Pacte ont déjà tracé des limites que le Comité a acceptées et qu'on effacerait en voulant ainsi élargir le domaine où ces principes sont applicables.

Mr. Root fait observer que dans tous les pays l'opinion publique est divisée en deux camps au sujet du règlement des conflits internationaux. Il faut formuler le projet du Comité de façon à aider les amis du règlement pacifique à l'emporter sur leurs adversaires.

Le PRESIDENT remercie Mr. Root des paroles trop élogieuses pour lui, que Mr. Root vient de prononcer. Il est heureux de constater que Mr. Root a défendu autrefois la thèse actuellement débattue. Il est convaincu que Mr. Root restera fidèle aux grandes et justes idées dont il s'est fait le champion, et aussi que sa haute autorité en Amérique les fera triompher. Le Président voudrait maintenant dissiper le malentendu qui est au fond de la discussion. On semble avoir l'impression que les normes formulées par le Président donnent aux juges un pouvoir nouveau, qui n'a jamais été reconnu par l'assemblée des Etats. Le Président rappelle cependant que, même en ce qui concerne les lois de la guerre, les Etats assemblés en 1907 ont fait appel au droit des gens tel qu'il résulte non seulement des usages établis entre les nations civilisées, mais des exigences de la conscience publique. L'application des normes signalées par le Président est d'ailleurs de pratique constante dans les juridictions internationales: on ne voit pas les juges s'abstenir de rendre justice sous prétexte d'insuffisance du droit conventionnel ou coutumier. Le Président rappelle à ce propos le cas de l'arbitrage des fondations californiennes.

Quand Mr. Root dit que les principes de justice varient avec les pays, cela peut être vrai en partie, lorsqu'il s'agit de certaines règles secondaires. Mais ce n'est plus vrai lorsqu'il s'agit le la loi fondamentale du juste et de l'injuste, profondément gravée au cœur de tout être humain et qui reçoit son expression la plus haute et la plus

competent to deal, or else the Court would limit itself to making a recommendation instead of pronouncing sentence. If the Committee went further, it would abolish the limits of the jurisdiction which they had just agreed upon, since the scope of the expression "principles of justice" varied with the countries.

Mr. Root was disposed to accept the principles contained in the document submitted by the President if it referred to all other jurisdiction than compulsory jurisdiction. The authors of the Covenant already have defined the limits which the Committee has accepted and which would be destroyed by enlarging the scope of application of these principles.

Mr. Root pointed out that in all countries public opinion was divided into two fields on the subject of settling international disputes. The project of the Committee must be drafted in such form as to aid the supporters of peaceful settlement to overcome their opponents.

The PRESIDENT thanked Mr. Root for the too kind remarks he had just made. The President was pleased to state that Mr. Root formerly had defended the proposition now being debated. He was convinced that Mr. Root should remain faithful to the just and lofty ideas of which he had made himself the champion and that his great authority in America would cause his ideas to prevail. The President wished to put an end to the misunderstanding which underlies the discussion. The impression appeared to exist that the rules drawn up by the President gave to the judges a new power which had never been admitted by the assembly of States. The President pointed out, however, that even in relation to the rules of War, the States assembled in 1907 had appealed to the law of nations, as formed not only by rules recognised by the civilised nations, but also by the demands of public conscience. The application in practice of the rules mentioned by the President, is moreover constant in international jurisdictions; you never would see a judge failing to administer justice on pretext of a lack of conventional or customary law. The President recalled in this connection the arbitration case of the California Pious Funds.

Concerning Mr. Root's statement that the principles of justice varied from country to country, that might be partly true as to certain rules of secondary importance. But it is no longer true when it concerns the fundamental law of justice and injustice deeply engraved on the heart of every human being and which is given its highest

autorisée dans la conscience juridique des peuples civilisés. C'est là une loi dont le juge ne peut faire abstraction, et dont en fait, qu'on le veuille ou non, il ne fera jamais abstraction.

Le Président ajoute que bien loin de donner aux juges une trop grande liberté pour leurs jugements, sa proposition limite cette liberté. En effet elle impose aux juges un devoir qui les empêche de trop se fier à leur propre opinion subjective: il leur est enjoint de rechercher si les données de leur conscience se trouvent en harmonie avec les dictamens de la conscience juridique des peuples civilisés.

M. LODER constate que, dans la séance précédente Mr. Root a dit qu'il ne pouvait se rallier aux points proposés par le Président, parce que, si l'on donnait à la Cour la compétence qu'il veut lui donner, la Cour aurait des pouvoirs de législateur. On a répondu à Mr. Root que ce n'était pas là l'idée du projet du Président. Aujourd'hui Mr. Root a développé sa thèse, et il faut reconnaître la valeur de son argumentation; mais il y a peut être un malentendu: après avoir formulé des craintes à l'égard de la proposition du Président, Mr. Root a omis de dire jusqu'où il voudrait lui-même que l'on étendît la juridiction de la Cour. Il a parlé d'arbitrage obligatoire; mais, selon M. Loder, cette question n'est pas de la compétence du Comité, qui doit s'en tenir là-dessus à la réponse, plus ou moins nette, du Pacte. Il s'agit maintenant des normes matérielles à appliquer par la Cour; ce qui est une chose essentiellement différente. Le Comité semble être d'accord sur l'application des traités et du droit international: mais cela est-il suffisant? Croit-on qu'il serait possible de créer une Cour qui, à un moment donné, se refuserait à juger parce qu'il n'y aurait pas de règle applicable?

LORD PHILLIMORE fait observer que les points 3 et 4 du projet rentrent dans le point 2 qui a trait à la coutume internationale. Dans ces conditions il pourrait y avoir accord également sur ces points.

M. LODER répète qu'il faut éviter toute confusion entre la question de l'arbitrage obligatoire et celle des normes à appliquer par la Cour. Le domaine de l'arbitrage obligatoire ne saurait être limité par les règles du droit matériel qui serviront de base aux sentences. Il prie Mr. Root de bien vouloir tracer lui-même des limites.

M. Loder pense que l'histoire de la Convention relative à l'établissement de la Cour des

and most authoritative expression in the legal conscience of civilised nations. That was the law which could not be disregarded by a judge, a law which in practice, whether it is wished to or not, a judge never would disregard.

The President added that far from giving too much liberty to the judges' decision, his proposal would limit it. As a matter of fact it would impose on the judges a duty which would prevent them from relying too much on their own subjective opinion; it would be incumbent on them to consider whether the dictates of their conscience were in agreement with the conception of justice of civilised nations.

M. LODER stated that at the preceding meeting, Mr. Root had said that he could not agree with the points proposed by the President, because if the Court were given the competence which he wished to give it, the Court would have legislative powers. Mr. Root had been told that this was not the intention of the President's project. To-day, Mr. Root had developed his idea and the value of his arguments must be admitted. But there had perhaps been a misunderstanding; after having stated his misgivings with regard to the President's proposal, Mr. Root had omitted to say how far he himself wished to have the jurisdiction of the Court extended. He had spoken of compulsory arbitration, but in M. Loder's opinion, this did not come within the competence of the Committee, which should confine itself to the more or less clear statement of the Covenant. They were now concerned with the rules to be applied by the Court; this was an essentially different thing. The Committee seemed to be agreed on the application of treaties and international law, but was that enough? Did the Committee think it would be possible to create a Court which might at a given moment refuse to pronounce judgment because no applicable rule existed?

LORD PHILLIMORE pointed out that points 3 and 4 of the project were included in point 2, which dealt with international custom. Under these conditions it should be possible to come to an agreement also on these points.

M. LODER repeated that all possible confusion between the question of compulsory arbitration and that of the rules to be applied by the Court must be avoided. The field of compulsory arbitration could not be limited by the rules of law which would be used as a basis for sentences. He asked Mr. Root to be so good as to define the limits himself.

M. Loder thought that the history of the

Prises ne peut pas servir ici de précédent. Ce qu'il fallait alors, c'était bien des règles matérielles nettement fixées; la Convention n'a pu entrer en vigueur parce qu'on n'a pas réussi à Londres à se mettre d'accord sur ces règles.

M. Loder reprend la proposition de Mr. Root qui permettrait à la Cour de faire une recommandation dans les cas où, faute de règles positives, elle ne pourrait prononcer une sentence. M. Loder croit qu'il serait peu logique de faire une recommandation là où l'on reconnaît qu'il n'y a pas de base suffisante pour fonder un jugement.

En terminant M. Loder dit que le droit néerlandais ne donne pas aux juges le droit de se déclarer incompétents à trancher un litige sous prétexte que la loi garde le silence à son sujet. Il croit que cette éventualité, qui équivaut à un déni de justice, devrait être inadmissible aussi bien dans le domaine international que dans le domaine national.

M. DE LAPRADELLE demande la parole pour répondre au discours de Mr. Root. Il dit que sa réponse sera dictée par le seul désir de trouver un terrain d'entente.

Il désire d'abord faire deux déclarations:

1. il n'est pas possible d'admettre le *non liquet* de la part d'une Cour Internationale; le déni de justice doit être exclu du domaine international comme du domaine national;
2. le principe de l'arbitrage obligatoire doit être favorisé en donnant à la Cour la plus large compétence possible, dans les deux directions de l'obligation pour les Etats de recourir à la Cour et des normes matérielles à appliquer par elle. On ne peut s'arrêter qu'à des considérations de possibilité pratique; on doit aller aussi loin que possible, dans la mesure où l'on est sûr d'être suivi par les Etats.

Dans cette voie, on pourra bien vaincre des résistances d'ordre secondaire, mais il y a des oppositions telle que celle des Etats-Unis qui sont irréductibles. Mr. Root, en voulant démontrer la nécessité de limiter la juridiction obligatoire de la Cour, a posé le dilemme suivant: ou le juge applique d'autres normes que les règles reconnues du droit international, ce qui serait inacceptable, p. ex. aux Etats-Unis, ou il se tient dans les limites de ces règles, et refuse de se prononcer sur les questions où le principe de droit applicable serait un principe contesté.

M. de Lapradelle a l'impression que Mr. Root n'a pas d'objection à faire, lorsqu'il s'agit

Convention for the establishment of the Prize Court could not be used here as a precedent. What was needed at the time was clearly defined rules; the Convention could not be put in force because it was found impossible at London to agree upon these rules.

M. Loder dealt again with Mr. Root's proposal allowing the Court to make a recommendation in cases in which through lack of definite rules it could not pass sentence. M. Loder thought that it would be illogical to make a recommendation where it was recognised that there was not sufficient basis on which to found a judgment.

In conclusion, M. Loder said that Dutch Law does not allow judges the right to declare themselves incompetent to decide a case by reason of law being silent on the matter. He thought that this eventuality, which amounted to a denial of justice, should be inadmissible as well in international law as in national law.

M. DE LAPRADELLE requested to speak in answer to Mr. Root's speech. He said that his answer was inspired by the single desire to find ground for an understanding.

He desired first of all to make two statements:

1. it is not possible to admit a declaration of *non-liquet* by an international Court; denial of justice must be excluded from the international court just as from National Courts;
2. the principle of compulsory arbitration must be favoured by giving the Court the widest possible competence as concerns both the obligation of States to make use of it and the actual rules to be applied by it. The only limit should be imposed by practical possibilities; they should go as far as they felt sure the States would follow them.

Following this method, it might be possible to cope with minor difficulties, but some opposition such as that of the United States could not be overcome. Mr. Root, wishing to show the necessity of limiting the compulsory jurisdiction of the Court, had put the following dilemma: the judge would apply other rules than those recognised by international law, which would be unacceptable to the United States, for instance; or else he would keep within the limits of these rules and refuse to decide questions to which the principle of law applicable was a disputed point.

M. de Lapradelle thought that Mr. Root

de laisser aux juges toute liberté de jugement dans les questions visées aux paragraphes *a, c, d* et *e* du texte soumis par Lord Philllimore. Ce n'est qu'en ce qui concerne le paragraphe *b*: „tout point de droit international", que Mr. Root croit devoir s'opposer à l'application des principes mentionnés aux nos. 3 et 4 du texte du Président, relatif aux normes matérielles.

M. de Lapradelle demande à Mr. Root, s'il a bien rendu son idée.

Mr. ROOT répond affirmativement.

M. DE LAPRADELLE continue en disant que Mr. Root a voulu faire ressortir la correspondance qui existe entre la compétence obligatoire de la Cour, d'une part, et, d'autre part, la liberté pour le juge de statuer, en l'absence de règles positives, d'après les règles qu'il tire des principes de justice. Mr. Root veut que les juges statuent seulement d'après les règles reconnues, et que, si des règles font défaut, ils prononcent un *non liquet*. Cette solution paraît inadmissible à M. de Lapradelle.

Il croit devoir rechercher les cas où vraiment il n'existe pas de règles universellement reconnues. Mr. Root a choisi l'exemple du droit maritime, mais cet exemple présente des difficultés particulières parce que, non seulement des points théoriques, mais des contestations nationales sont en jeu. M. de Lapradelle fait allusion aux questions de la contrebande de guerre, du voyage continu, et de la saisissabilité de la propriété ennemie. Il est compréhensible qu'on hésite à donner à une Cour internationale la compétence en ces matières, en dehors de règles fixes et universellement reconnues.

Mais la Cour Permanente de Justice ne supprimera pas la Cour des Prises, de même qu'elle ne supprimera pas non plus la Cour d'Arbitrage. La Cour des Prises doit être maintenue, à côté de la nouvelle Cour, tout comme la Cour d'Arbitrage. Le Pacte n'abolit pas la guerre; il prévoit la possibilité de guerres légitimes, bien que dans des cas exceptionnels. Mais si l'on maintient, parallèlement avec la Cour Permanente, la Cour des Prises, rien ne semble s'opposer à ce qu'on donne aux juges de la Cour Permanente plus de liberté en ce qui concerne les règles à appliquer.

M. de Lapradelle passe à l'autre exemple choisi par Mr. Root: la faillite, en 1907, des traités d'arbitrage entre les Etats-Unis d'une part et la France et la Grande-Bretagne de l'autre. Ces traités se sont heurtés à la grande susceptibilité de la nation américaine qui, en vertu de

had no objection to giving the judges complete freedom of judgment in the questions dealt with in Paragraphs *a, c, d* and *e* of the text submitted by Lord Phillimore. It was only in connection with Paragraph *b*: "any point of international law", that Mr. Root felt he must oppose the application of the principles mentioned in numbers 3 and 4 of the President's draft, dealing with the rules to be applied.

M. de Lapradelle asked Mr. Root if he had rightly understood his ideas.

Mr. ROOT replied in the affirmative.

M. DE LAPRADELLE went on to say that Mr. Root had wished to emphasize the relation which existed between the compulsory competence of the Court on the one hand, and, on the other, the freedom of a judge to pass sentences, in the absence of positive rules, according to rules derived from the principles of justice. Mr. Root wished that the judges should only act in accordance with recognised rules, and if such rules did not exist they should pronounce a *non-liquet*. This solution seemed inadmissible to M. de Lapradelle.

He thought it was necessary to find out in which cases no universally recognised rules really existed. Mr. Root had chosen an example of maritime law, but this example presented individual difficulties because not only theoretical points but opposing national views were concerned. M. de Lapradelle alluded to contraband of war, continuous voyage, and the seizure of enemy property. It was quite understandable that there should be hesitation to give an international Court competence in these matters, outside fixed and universally recognised rules.

But the Permanent Court of Justice will not abolish the Prize Court, just as it will not abolish the Court of Arbitration. The Prize Court must be kept side by side with the new Court, as must the Court of Arbitration. The Covenant did not abolish war, it admits the possibility of legitimate wars but under exceptional circumstances. However, if the Prize Court is maintained side by side with the Permanent Court, there seems to be no reason why the judges of the Permanent Court should not be given more freedom in the rules they have to apply.

M. de Lapradelle went on to the other example given by Mr. Root; the failure in 1907 of the Arbitration Treaties between the United States on one hand, and France and Great Britain on the other. These Treaties encountered the susceptibilities of the American nation, which,

la doctrine de Monroe, ne voulait pas voir soumettre à la juridiction internationale des cas d'un certain ordre.

Mais la doctrine de Monroe c'est le nationalisme américain qui a revêtu une forme continentale inconnue aux pays de l'Europe. On ne peut pas céder devant ce nationalisme, on ne peut pas abandonner les vrais principes: il faut plutôt essayer de faire comprendre aux Etats-Unis qu'une grande nation ne peut pas se borner à être continentale, elle doit prendre sa place mondiale. Cependant, pour ne point empêcher les Etats-Unis de se joindre à la Société des Nations, il faut trouver une solution qui ménage leurs susceptibilités. A cet égard, M. de Lapradelle suggère l'idée suivante: la nouvelle Cour doit être limitée d'un côté par la Cour des Prises, et de l'autre par la Cour d'Arbitrage.

La Cour Permanente pourrait renvoyer à la Cour d'Arbitrage les questions sur lesquelles elle ne pourrait elle-même statuer, faute de règles positives en vigueur: le mandat d'un tribunal d'arbitrage contient, entre autres, les bases sur lesquelles le tribunal doit fonder sa sentence.

On peut limiter la compétence des arbitres, mais non pas celle des juges. En plaçant ainsi la Cour de Justice entre la Cour des Prises et la Cour d'Arbitrage, on pourrait, en dressant le statut des trois Cours, parvenir à établir pour la Cour Permanente un statut établissant sa compétence obligatoire en donnant aux autres des statuts plus souples.

M. RICCI-BUSATTI commence par rendre hommage au discours du Président et dit qu'il peut se rallier, à plusieurs égards, au point de vue de Mr. Root; notamment en ce qui concerne l'impossibilité pour la Cour d'agir en législateur. Il ne faut pas mêler les compétences; la législation en matière de droit international est du domaine des Etats. Ceci n'empêche pas que justice soit rendue. En constatant l'absence d'une règle positive de droit international, c'est-à-dire d'une limite internationale à la liberté des Parties, on établit tout de même une situation juridique. Ce qui n'est pas défendu est permis; voilà un principe général de droit que la Cour aura à appliquer. Si un litige est porté devant elle et si elle trouve qu'il n'y a pas de règle qui le concerne, elle déclarera qu'il n'existe pas de droits à faire valoir par l'une des parties contre l'autre, que la conduite de l'Etat mis en cause n'était contraire à aucune règle admise. Il y a d'ailleurs d'autres principes du même ordre (celui

influenced by the Monroe Doctrine, did not wish to have cases of a certain kind submitted to international jurisdiction.

But the Monroe Doctrine was the expression of American nationalism, which had assumed a continental form unknown to European countries. No surrender can be made to this nationalism; the true principles must not be abandoned. Rather must an effort be made to make the United States understand that great nations must not limit themselves to being continental, they must take their proper place in the world. Nevertheless, in order not to prevent the United States from joining the League of Nations, a solution must be found which has regard for their susceptibilities. With this object M. de Lapradelle suggested the following idea: the new Court should be limited by the Prize Court on one side, and the Court of Arbitration on the other.

The Permanent Court could send to the Court of Arbitration questions on which it could not decide itself through lack of positive rules in force: the mandate of the Court of Arbitration would include, amongst other things, the elements upon which the Court should base its sentences.

The competence of arbitrators might be limited, but not that of the judges. By thus interposing the Court of Justice between the Prize Court and the Arbitration Court, it would be possible, in drawing up the Statute of the three Courts, to arrive at establishing for the Permanent Court a compulsory competence and for the others a more flexible one.

M. RICCI-BUSATTI began by complimenting the President on his speech and said that he could agree with Mr. Root's point of view in several respects, especially concerning the impossibility of the Court acting as legislator. The competences must not be confused; legislation dealing with International Law comes within the power of the States. That fact does not prevent the administration of Justice. By declaring the absence of a positive rule of international law, in other words an international limitation on the freedom of the parties, nevertheless a legal situation is established. That which is not forbidden is allowed; that is one of the general principles of law which the Court shall have to apply. If a case is brought before the Court and if the latter finds that no rules exist concerning it, the Court shall declare that one party has no right against the other, that the conduct of the accused State was not contrary to any admitted rule. Furthermore, there are other prin-

qui défend l'abus du droit, ou celui de la chose jugée etc.), et certaines règles générales d'équité et de justice qui entrent en jeu dans chaque cas. Il ne s'agit donc pas de créer des règles inexistantes, mais d'appliquer des règles générales qui permettent de résoudre toute question.

Il donne comme exemple la question de l'étendue des eaux territoriales. Il n'y a pas de règle de droit international qui fixe les limites des eaux territoriales; si une question à ce sujet était portée devant la Cour, celle-ci ne devrait pas accepter l'une ou l'autre des différentes règles en vigueur dans les différents pays: elle devrait tout simplement constater qu'une règle généralement admise n'existe pas, et, après cette constatation, reconnaître que les dispositions adoptées dans les différents pays sont également licites, tant qu'elles n'empiètent pas sur d'autres principes, tel que celui, par exemple, de la liberté de la mer. En priant le Comité de ne point mal interpréter sa pensée, M. Ricci-Busatti ajoute que le principe d'après lequel dans certaines situations particulières le plus fort prime de droit le plus faible, est également une de ces règles générales auxquelles il fait allusion.

M. DE LAPRADELLE se déclare hostile à cette idée.

Dans sa conclusion, M. RICCI-BUSATTI dit qu'il faut trouver une formule qui réunisse les différents éléments qui devront guider la Cour, sans établir entre eux aucune gradation.

A ce propos il admet qu'il serait utile d'insérer dans la formule un renvoi à la jurisprudence internationale.

LORD PHILLIMORE constate qu'il y a des divergences d'opinion assez graves. Ces divergences proviennent, selon lui, de la conception continentale de la justice: on commence par imposer aux juges de strictes limites, puis, craignant qu'ils ne soient trop étroitement liés, on leur donne pleine liberté à l'intérieur de ces limites. Le système anglais est différent: le juge doit prêter serment "de rendre la justice selon la loi" ("to do justice according to law").

Lord Phillimore juge inutile cependant de discuter cette question. Le Comité a pour tâche d'établir la Cour, et non pas de lui prescrire des lois. On a déterminé la compétence de la Cour; on peut lui confier le reste. Cependant, si le Comité ne suit pas son conseil, et considère que sa tâche ne se borne pas là, deux questions se posent à lui:

ciples of the same character, (that which forbids the abuse of right or that of *res judicata,* etc.), and certain general rules of equity and justice which come into play in each case. Therefore it is not a question of creating rules which do not exist, but of applying the general rules which permit the solution of any question.

He gave as an example the question of the extent of territorial waters. There is no rule of International Law which defines the limits of territorial waters; if a question of this kind were taken before the Court, the Court must not accept one or other of the different rules in force in the different countries: it must simply state that a rule generally admitted does not exist, and, after this statement, that rulings of different countries are equally legitimate in so far as they do not encroach on other principles, such for instance, as that of the freedom of the seas. After requesting the Committee not to misinterpret his idea, M. Ricci-Busatti added that the principle, according to which under certain special conditions the stronger takes rightful precedence over the weaker, was also one of those general rules to which he alluded.

M. DE LAPRADELLE disagreed with this.

In conclusion, M. RICCI-BUSATTI said that a formula must be found uniting the various elements which should guide the Court, without making any distinction between them.

In this connection he admitted that it would be advisable to include in the formula a reference to international jurisprudence.

LORD PHILLIMORE thought that serious differences of opinion existed. In his view these divergences arose from the continental idea of justice; at the outset strict limitations are imposed on the judges, then through fear of restricting them too much they are given complete freedom within these limits. The English system is different: the judge takes an oath "to do justice according to law."

Lord Phillimore, however, thought it useless to discuss this question. The Committee has as its task to establish the Court, not to make laws for it. The competence of the Court had been fixed, the rest might be left to it. However, if the Committee did not follow his advice, and considered that its task did not end there, two questions presented themselves:

1. Les normes matérielles à appliquer doivent-elles être élargies?

2. De quelle manière cela peut-il se faire; est-ce le devoir du juge de s'en occuper?

Il faudrait stipuler que le juge international aura, à cet égard, le même droit que le juge national; et il ne s'agit pas de donner au juge le pouvoir de juger d'après les principes de la justice et de l'équité; cela ne réussirait pas: l'échec de la Convention pour l'établissement d'une Cour Internationale des Prises en est la preuve. Cette Cour aurait eu le pouvoir de juger ainsi, mais on peut tenir pour certain que ces principes auraient été appliqués de façon différente, selon que les neutres ou les belligérants y eussent été en majorité.

Lord Phillimore reprend le discours du Président. Celui-ci a cité l'exemple des „fondations pieuses de Californie", où la sentence a été rendue d'après le principe de droit commun de la chose jugée. C'est un principe qui a le même caractère de droit que n'importe quelle règle formulée. En général tous les principes du droit commun sont applicables aux rapports internationaux. Ce sont en fait des règles de droit international.

Un autre principe du même ordre est celui d'après lequel la partie demanderesse doit prouver son argument, sous peine d'être déboutée. Il faut remarquer qu'il ne s'agit pas d'un déni de justice, qui est inadmissible. Il peut être regrettable de se trouver dans la nécessité de débouter la partie demanderesse, faute d'une règle admise sur laquelle elle puisse appuyer sa demande; mais dans ce cas, la Cour pourrait seulement dire qu'aucune injustice n'a été commise; l'éventualité se présente assez souvent devant les tribunaux nationaux, lorsqu'il s'agit de préventions d'ordre moral plutôt que juridique. L'éventualité se présentera peut-être plus souvent dans le domaine international; on ne courra pas le risque de voir commettre des injustices, car la partie lésée pourra en appeler à une autre instance, à savoir le Conseil. Le Conseil est là pour donner satisfaction dans les cas où il est juridiquement impossible de rendre la justice.

Lord Phillimore n'est pas sûr d'avoir bien suivi la pensée de M. Ricci-Busatti, mais il a l'impression de se trouver d'accord avec lui. Il croit, en effet, que M. Ricci-Busatti ne veut pas donner au juge international une compétence plus large que celle du juge national: il ne veut pas, en tout cas, que le juge international ait le droit de légiférer.

En achevant, Lord Phillimore dit qu'il

1. Should the rules to be applied be extended?

2. How should this be done? Is it the duty of the judge to consider it?

It must be stipulated that the international judge shall have in this respect the same rights as the national judge, and it is not a question of giving to the judge the power to decide according to the principles of justice and equity. Such a step would not bring success: the proof of this is the failure of the Convention for the establishment of the International Prize Court. This Court would have had the power to judge thus, but it may be considered as certain that these principles would have been applied differently, according to whether the neutrals or belligerents were in the majority.

Lord Phillimore considered the President's speech. The latter had quoted the case of the California Pious Funds, in which sentence had been rendered in accordance with a principle of common law: *res judicata*. This was a principle which had the same character of law as any written law. Generally speaking, all the principles of common law are applicable to international affairs. They are in fact part of international law.

Another principle of the same kind is that by which the plaintiff must prove his contention under penalty of having his case refused. There is no question of a refusal of justice: this is inadmissible. It may be regrettable to be obliged to refuse to hear a plaintiff's case through lack of any recognised law on which it can be based; but in such case the Court could only say that no injustice had been done. This eventuality arises frequently enough before municipal Courts, when the charge is rather of a moral than a legal nature. The eventuality would possibly arise more often in international affairs; there would, however, be no danger of injustice being done because the injured party could appeal to another body, the Council. The Council is the body which must give satisfaction in cases which cannot be dealt with according to law.

Lord Phillimore was not sure that he had quite grasped M. Ricci-Busatti's train of thought, but believed that he agreed with him. He gathered that M. Ricci-Busatti did not wish to give international judges wider powers than municipal judges: he did not wish, in any case, to give international judges legislative powers.

Finally, Lord Phillimore said that he would accept a formula based on Article 2 of

accepterait une formule s'inspirant de l'article 2 du projet des Cinq Puissances; on pourrait reproduire l'article depuis le commencement jusqu'au mot „vigueur"; en ajoutant cependant une phrase pour indiquer que les règles du droit international en vigueur seraient applicables, indépendamment de la source d'où elles découlent.

M. HAGERUP constate qu'il se trouve entièrement d'accord avec Lord Phillimore. Il serait heureux de voir les juges de la Cour permanente juger d'après les mêmes principes que les juges anglais, et que les juges nationaux en général. Ils doivent décider d'après les règles du droit, mais non pas déclarer qu'il leur est impossible, faute de règles, de se prononcer. Il ne faut pas qu'un déni de justice soit possible.

LORD PHILLIMORE pense que M. Hagerup n'a pas bien saisi la pensée de Mr. Root.

M. HAGERUP continue; il accepte, dit-il, l'idée de débouter une partie lorsqu'il n'y a pas de règle de droit en sa faveur. Mais il croit, d'autre part, qu'il faut adopter le principe anglais du droit fait par le juge: avant de débouter une partie pour la raison qu'il n'existe pas de droit positif, le juge doit rechercher s'il n'existe pas d'analogies, de précédents etc. Il croit, en somme, que si l'on réussit à se mettre d'accord sur la base proposée par Lord Phillimore, on aura trouvé la solution. La question grave à résoudre est celle du *non liquet*. Pour sa part, M. Hagerup ne s'est pas attaché à une formule spéciale, mais il pense qu'il est essentiel de bien distinguer entre la compétence matérielle de la Cour et les normes à appliquer par elle. A cet égard il peut se rallier aux opinions que viennent d'exprimer certains membres.

M. Hagerup, comme M. de Lapradelle, ne croit pas que l'échec de la Convention sur la Cour des Prises puisse ici être considéré comme un précédent. Il s'agissait alors non pas de soumettre à une juridiction toute nouvelle des matières qui jusque-là n'avaient pas été résolues par la voie judiciaire; il s'agissait d'abandonner des juridictions nationales pour une juridiction internationale, chargée d'appliquer des normes entièrement nouvelles pour une partie des Etats intéressés. Tel était le cas surtout pour la Grande-Bretagne. Dans le cas de la nouvelle Cour, la question n'est pas la même puisqu'il ne s'agit pas de juridictions nationales à abolir. M. Hagerup suggère, en terminant, l'idée de différer la discussion jusqu'à ce qu'une formule ait été présentée, et il prie Mr. Root d'en soumettre une.

Mr. ROOT se déclare disposé à formuler un texte, et se sent en devoir d'expliquer ses remar-

the project of the Five Powers. This Article might be reproduced from the commencement to the word "operation"; adding, however, a phrase to indicate that rules of international law in operation would be applicable, regardless of the source from which they were derived.

M. HAGERUP stated that he entirely agreed with Lord Phillimore. He would be pleased to see the judges of the Permanent Court judge according to the same principles as English judges, and national judges generally. They must give judgment according to rules of law, but they must not declare that it is impossible for them to decide because of the absence of rules. There must be no possibility of a denial of justice.

LORD PHILLIMORE thought M. Hagerup had not quite grasped Mr. Root's intention.

M. HAGERUP went on to say that he accepted the position of refusing to admit a claim if no law exists applicable to the case. But he thought that the English principle of judge-made law should be adopted: before refusing to admit a claim because no positive law exists, the judge must seek to find analogies, precedents, etc. In fact he thought that if an agreement could be reached on the basis of Lord Phillimore's proposal, the solution would have been found. The serious question to be considered was that of *non-liquet*. Personally, M. Hagerup was not bound to any particular formula, but he thought that it was essential to draw a clear distinction between the material competence of the Court and the rules to be applied by it. On this subject he agreed with the opinions recently expressed by certain members.

He thought with M. de Lapradelle that the failure of the Prize Court Convention could not be considered as a precedent. The question then was not one of submitting matters, which had not been previously settled by judicial methods, to an entirely new jurisdiction; it was a question of abandoning national jurisdiction in favour of an international one entrusted with the application of rules entirely new, in part, to the States concerned. This was especially the case of Great Britain. The establishment of the new Court was not on the same footing, as there were no national jurisdictions to abolish. Finally, M. Hagerup suggested that further discussion should be postponed until a draft had been submitted. He asked Mr. Root to submit one.

Mr. ROOT said that he would do so, and went on to explain his previous remarks. He had not

ques antérieures. Il n'a pas voulu dire que la Cour pourrait refuser de prendre une décision dans certains cas, mais qu'elle doit agir conformément au second article du texte relatif à la compétence qui a été soumis par le Président, et d'après lequel la Cour décide si la question soulevée par la partie demanderesse est comprise ou non dans les catégories prévues à l'article 1er de ce texte. Dans la négative, la Cour renvoie la question devant le Conseil de la Société des Nations; dans l'affirmative, elle décide conformément au droit et à la coutume.

Le PRESIDENT demande à Mr. Root s'il ne croit pas nécessaire de distinguer entre la compétence *ratione materiae* et les sources auxquelles le juge doit puiser pour fonder son jugement. Il a d'autre part l'impression que le droit international tel que le conçoit Lord Phillimore, se rapproche du droit naturel.

LORD PHILLIMORE en convient.

Le PRESIDENT reconnaît avec Mr. Root qu'il serait dangereux d'abandonner exclusivement à l'appréciation subjective des juges l'application de la loi du juste et de l'injuste. C'est précisément pour cette raison que le Président a voulu tracer aux juges une voie à suivre, et les obliger à se conformer aux dictamens de la conscience juridique des peuples civilisés. Lorsque l'opinion universelle reconnaît la justice de telle ou telle décision, alors le juge est fondé à l'appliquer.

Le Président croit que ce serait compliquer inutilement la question que d'établir, avec M. de Lapradelle, une sorte de compétence subsidiaire, pour la Cour d'Arbitrage. On ne peut pas enlever aux juges le pouvoir de statuer en justice, mais on peut et on doit chercher une formule qui éclaire et dirige ce pouvoir. Si le Comité réussit, il aura bien mérité de l'humanité.

Contrairement à l'opinion de M. Ricci-Busatti, le Président croit que le juge doit pratiquer la méthode successive, en puisant aux diverses sources de droit. La première règle, c'est que, s'il existe un texte, une règle conventionnelle, on doit l'appliquer. A défaut d'une règle de ce genre, il faut appliquer les coutumes internationales. S'il n'y a ni loi ni coutume, le juge peut-il prononcer un *non liquet*? Le Président est convaincu que non: le juge devra alors appliquer les principes généraux du droit. Mais il faut soustraire le juge à la tentation d'appliquer ces principes à sa guise. C'est pourquoi il lui est

meant to say that the Court could refuse to pass sentence in particular cases, but that it must act in accordance with the second Article of the draft dealing with competence, which had been submitted by the President, according to which the Court would decide whether the question raised by the plaintiff was or was not included in the categories enumerated in Article 1 of this draft. If the answer were in the negative, the Court would send the case to the Council of the League of Nations; if in the affirmative, it would decide according to law and custom.

The PRESIDENT asked Mr. Root if he did not think it would be necessary to distinguish between the competence *ratione materiae* and the sources from which the judge should draw to base his judgment. He had formed the impression in another connection that international law as understood by Lord Phillimore resembled natural law.

LORD PHILLIMORE agreed.

The PRESIDENT agreed with Mr. Root that it would be dangerous to allow the judges to apply the law of right and wrong exclusively according to their own personal understanding of it. It was exactly for this reason that the President wished to indicate the lines which the judges must follow; and compel them to conform to the dictates of the legal conscience of civilised nations. When a certain solution is approved by universal public opinion, the judge is justified in applying it.

The President thought that it would only unnecessarily complicate the question if, as M. de Lapradelle suggested, subsidiary powers were given to the Court of Arbitration. The power to administer justice must not be taken away from the judges, but a formula defining and guiding this power can and must be looked for. If they succeeded, they would merit the gratitude of humanity.

The President, in opposition to M. Ricci-Busatti, said that the various sources of law should be examined successively. The first rule was that if there were a text, a conventional rule, it must be applied. Failing a rule of this kind, international custom must be applied. If neither law nor custom existed, could the judge pronounce a *non-liquet*? The President was convinced that he could not; the judge must then apply general principles of law. But he must be saved from the temptation of applying these principles as he pleased. For that reason he

enjoint de statuer en harmonie avec les prescriptions de la conscience juridique des peuples civilisés et de se servir, à cette même fin, comme auxiliaire, de la doctrine des publicistes qui font autorité.

Le Président termine en remarquant que, lors de la première Conférence de La Haye, on s'est déjà occupé des normes qui doivent guider les juges.

M. HAGERUP, désirant se rendre compte s'il a bien compris la pensée de Lord Phillimore, prend un exemple. Un navire anglais se trouve dans la zone comprise entre le 3e et 4e mille marin, au large de la côte norvégienne. La Norvège, prétendant que ses eaux territoriales s'étendent jusqu'à une distance de 4 milles de la côte, expulse le navire anglais. L'Angleterre, se plaignant du traitement subi par son navire, porte le cas devant la nouvelle Cour. Est-ce que celle-ci pourra la débouter de sa demande en expliquant qu'il n'y a pas de règles admises au sujet de l'étendue des eaux territoriales?

LORD PHILLIMORE répond que non. Le cas sera jugé conformément aux principes reconnus; il y a, par exemple, un principe d'après lequel il existe toujours des eaux territoriales, indépendamment de leur étendue. Cependant Lord Phillimore admet qu'il y a des cas qui ne pourront pas être résolus de cette façon, par exemple, lorsque deux lois nationales sont en conflit ou lorsqu'aucune coutume ou règle internationale n'est applicable.

M. HAGERUP croit pouvoir se dire maintenant d'accord, quant au fond, avec Lord Phillimore.

Il tient à faire observer que l'exemple cité par lui démontre que peut-être la formule des Cinq Puissances neutres va trop loin, en donnant à la Cour la faculté de suivre, à défaut d'une règle généralement admise, la règle qui à son avis devait être la loi. M. Hagerup n'admettrait pas, par exemple, que la Cour pût fixer une limite quelconque aux eaux territoriales.

M. DE LAPRADELLE a la parole pour répondre au discours de Lord Phillimore. Il dit que ce dernier s'est montré habile politicien; il essaie de concilier les opinions divergentes en supprimant les difficultés. C'est là une solution de suprême détresse. M. de Lapradelle croit qu'il sera extrêmement utile de creuser la question: c'est seulement par cette voie qu'on peut arriver à concilier les divergences et à s'arrêter à une conclusion définitive.

M. de Lapradelle déclare ensuite, que

urged that the judge render decisions in keeping with the dictates of the legal conscience of civilised peoples and for this same purpose make use of the doctrines of publicists carrying authority.

The President concluded with the remark that ever since the First Hague Conference attention has been given to the rules which should guide the judges.

M. HAGERUP, desiring to make sure that he had quite understood Lord Phillimore, cited an example: an English vessel arrives within the zone between the three and four sea mile limit off the Norwegian coast. Norway, maintaining that her territorial waters extend to a distance of four miles from the coast, expels the English vessel. England protesting against the treatment of its vessel brings the case before the new Court. Should the Court declare that its complaint was not cause for a suit because there existed no admitted rules on the subject of territorial waters' extent.

LORD PHILLIMORE answered "No." The case would be decided in conformity with recognised principles; there is, for example, a principle according to which territorial waters always exist, regardless of their extent. However, Lord Phillimore admitted that there were cases which could not be decided in this way, for example, two conflicting national laws or cases to which no international rule or custom applied.

M. HAGERUP felt that he could agree then with Lord Phillimore on the basic principles.

He observed that the example cited by him indicated perhaps that the clause of the Five Neutral Powers goes too far in giving to the Court the right to act, in the absence of a generally admitted rule, according to the rule which it thinks should be the law. For example, M. Hagerup did not admit that the Court could fix any limit whatever for territorial waters.

M. DE LAPRADELLE spoke in answer to Lord Phillimore's speech. He said that it was a skilful political method that tried to conciliate the various opinions by eliminating the difficulties. That was a solution to be used in dire straits. M. de Lapradelle thought it would be very profitable to discuss the question thoroughly; this was the only means of conciliating different views and coming to a definite conclusion.

M. de Lapradelle said that according to

d'après la thèse de Lord Phillimore, le juge prononcera contre le demandeur dans le cas où il n'y a pas de loi, d'où il résulte que là où il n'y a pas de droit, le fort fera la loi. La tâche de la Cour se bornerait donc à enregistrer les actes des puissants.

LORD PHILLIMORE répond que dans la vie ordinaire on se trouve en présence de beaucoup de cas où il existe un droit, ou un quasi-droit, d'ordre moral; on peut justifier une plainte sans parvenir à la faire rentrer dans des catégories juridiques et, partant, sans parvenir à avoir raison. Le résultat est parfois la création d'une nouvelle loi; parfois aussi, le juge considère qu'il peut juger sans loi. Si des cas de çe genre se produisent dans la vie internationale, deux solutions sont possibles: on peut demander à l'Assemblée de remplir la lacune par voie de législation, ou bien on peut saisir le Conseil de la difficulté.

Lord Phillimore croit que Mr. Root a emprunté l'opinion qu'il a exprimée, à la pratique anglo-américaine des „demurrers": l'une des parties accepte l'exposé des faits par l'autre partie, mais prétend que, en dépit de ces faits, l'argument de l'adversaire n'est pas justifié.

Lord Phillimore examine l'idée qui a été émise de ne rien spécifier, dans la convention établissant la Cour, sur les règles matérielles à appliquer par elle. Il propose qu'au lieu d'avoir recours à cet expédient, on fasse entrer dans la formule du serment des juges, ce qu'on estime nécessaire au sujet du droit matériel à appliquer, sans énumérer autrement les normes dans la convention.

M. DE LAPRADELLE n'est pas hostile à cette idée, mais exprime des doutes sur sa valeur pratique. Il croit qu'il faut distinguer les cas qui peuvent être considérés comme impliquant des intérêts nationaux d'une importance vitale et ceux qui ne le peuvent pas. Il propose que chaque membre dresse une liste des cas qui, d'après lui, rentrent dans l'une ou l'autre de ces deux catégories; en comparant ces listes on pourrait probablement parvenir à trouver une formule qui les réunisse tous.

Le PRESIDENT pense que les difficultés de la question actuelle proviennent de la diversité des cas dont la Cour aurait à connaître; si l'on enfermait la compétence de la Cour dans les limites des règles positives reconnues, elle aurait trop souvent à débouter les parties.

Lord Phillimore's theory the judge delivered judgment against the plaintiff in a case in which no law existed, from which it follows that where there is no law, the strong make the law. The task of the Court would be limited to registering the acts of the powerful.

LORD PHILLIMORE answered that in every day life many cases appear in which there exist a right, or quasi right, of a moral order; a complaint could be justified, though it might not fall within the bounds of actual law, and consequently could not be recognised according to law. The result sometimes was the creation of a new statute; sometimes also the judge considered that he could judge without law. If cases of this nature arise in international affairs, two solutions are possible: either the Assembly may be asked to fill the gap by means of legislation, or the question may be submitted to the Council for decision.

Lord Phillimore thought that Mr. Root had borrowed the opinion he had formerly expressed from the "demurrers" of Anglo-American practice: one of the parties accepts the facts stated by the other party, but claims that, in spite of these facts, the opponent's argument is not justified.

Lord Phillimore considered the idea expressed that no stipulation should be made of rules to be applied by the Court, in the Convention establishing it. He proposed that instead of resorting to this expedient, there should be inserted in the form of the oath taken by the judges all that might be considered necessary concerning the law to be applied, and that no other mention of the rules should be made in the convention.

M. DE LAPRADELLE was not opposed to this idea, but doubted its practical value. He thought that distinction must be made between cases which may be considered as entailing national interests of vital importance, and those which may not. He proposed that every member should make a list of cases which in his opinion fell under one or other of these two categories; by comparing these lists it would probably be possible to draw up a wording covering them all.

The PRESIDENT thought that the difficulties of the present question arose from the diversity of cases which the Court would have to deal with; if the competence of the Court were confined within the limits of positive recognised rules, too often it would have to non-suit the parties.

On continuera, au cours de la séance prochaine la discussion sur la question des normes matérielles applicables par la Cour.

M. LODER a été chargé par M. van Karnebeek de communiquer que Sa Majesté la Reine des Pays-Bas a l'intention d'inviter le Comité à prendre le thé jeudi prochain à 4 heures de l'après-midi à la Huis ten Bosch; les invitations formelles seront envoyées plus tard.

Le PRESIDENT remercie M. Loder de la communication qu'il vient de faire, exprime la reconnaissance des membres pour la gracieuse invitation de Sa Majesté et prie M. Loder de faire parvenir les remerciements du Comité à M. van Karnebeek.

La séance est levée à 12 heures 35 de l'après-midi.

Le Président:
(signé) Brn. DESCAMPS.

Le Secrétaire-Général:
(signé) D. ANZILOTTI.

The discussion of the question of the rules to be applied by the Court would be continued at the next meeting.

M. LODER had been requested by M. van Karnebeek to inform the Committee that Her Majesty the Queen of the Netherlands intended to invite the Committee to take tea on the following Thursday at 4 o'clock in the afternoon at the Huis ten Bosch. Formal invitations would be sent later.

The PRESIDENT, thanking M. Loder for the message, expressed the thanks of the members of the Committee for Her Majesty's gracious invitation; and asked M. Loder to convey the thanks of the Committee to M. van Karnebeek.

The meeting closed at 12.35 p.m.

The President:
(signed) Brn. DESCAMPS.

The Secretary-General:
(signed) D. ANZILOTTI.

ANNEXE No. 1.

Discours de M. le Baron Descamps concernant les normes d'application du droit.

L'importance des normes que doit suivre le juge dans la solution des différends qui lui sont soumis, est capitale. Elle a été signalée dès la première Conférence de la Paix, et c'est une des tâches les plus dignes de notre Comité que d'essayer de l'éclairer d'un de ces jets de lumière qui défient la contradiction.

Chose étrange pourtant, il me semble qu'au moment où nous voulons donner aux juges dans cet ordre d'idées des règles qui précisent leur activité en la limitant, il semble que ce soit à nous qu'on reproche de livrer à l'arbitraire la distribution internationale de la Justice. Pareil reproche est, à notre sens, la méconnaissance de l'état actuel du droit international, et de la mission du juge.

Constatons les points sur lesquels nous sommes d'accord et les points où commencent les divergences. Nul ne conteste que, lorsque le juge se trouve en face d'une règle expressément consacrée par un traité, soit général, soit spécial, entre parties, son devoir primordial soit de l'appliquer.

Il ne paraît pas davantage contestable que, lorsque le juge se trouve en présence d'une coutume nettement caractérisée, d'une règle établie par la pratique constante, générale, des nations, devenue, à ce titre, une loi pour elles, le devoir du juge soit encore de l'appliquer. La coutume a toujours eu beaucoup d'importance, d'extension, particulièrement dans le domaine du droit des gens, précisément parce qu'à défaut d'une législation en cette matière, et en présence du peu de développement du droit conventionnel entre les Etats, c'est sous cette forme que s'est affirmé et développé le droit des gens. Forme d'ailleurs naturelle, et éminemment respectable, puisqu'elle n'est que l'expression des conventions juridiques et des besoins sociaux des nations, s'affirmant dans leur commune et constante manière d'agir. Ce serait méconnaître la physionomie vraie et toute l'histoire du droit des gens, que de ne pas admettre, comme norme qui s'impose au juge, le droit coutumier international, lorsqu'il n'est pas primé par un droit conventionnel expressément formulé.

Ce serait encore, à mon sens, priver le juge d'un de ses auxiliaires les plus précieux que de ne pas le convier à faire appel à la jurisprudence

ANNEX No. 1.

Speech by Baron Descamps on the Rules of Law to be applied.

The principles which must guide the judge, in the solution of the disputes submitted to him, are of vital importance. Their importance was recognised at the First Peace Conference, and one of the most important tasks of the Committee is to try to make them so clear as to be proof against dispute.

It is a strange thing but it seems to me that, directly we try to create rules of this kind to define and at the same time limit the powers of judges, we are reproached with making the administration of International Justice arbitrary. Such a reproach in our opinion implies a misunderstanding of present conditions, of international law, and the duties of a judge.

Let us consider the points on which we are agreed, and those where we begin to differ. All agree that, when rules are expressly laid down by a general or special treaty between the parties, it is the first duty of a judge to apply them.

It is equally evident that, when a clearly defined custom exists or a rule established by the continual and general usage of nations, which has consequently obtained the force of law, it is also the duty of a judge to apply it. Custom has always played an important part in, and been especially applicable to the law of nations, because in the absence of legislation and in view of the limited development of conventional law between States, the development and establishment of the law of nations has taken this form. It is a very natural and extremely reliable method of development since it results entirely from the constant expression of the legal convictions and of the needs of the nations in their mutual intercourse. Not to recognise international custom as a principle which must be followed by the judge in the absence of expressed conventional law, would be misconstrue the true character and whole history of the law of nations.

Not to allow the judge to make use of existing international jurisprudence as a means of defining the law of nations is, in my opinion, to deprive him of one of his most valuable resources.

The only question which it seems to me ought to be elucidated is whether after having recorded as law conventions and custom, objective justice

internationale existante, en tant qu'instrument de précision du droit des gens.

La seule question qui me paraisse devoir être élucidée est celle de savoir, si, après avoir signalé comme normes les conventions et la coutume, il y a lieu de signaler, à titre complémentaire, la norme de la justice objective dans des conditions qui soient précisément de nature à prévenir l'arbitraire.

C'est une grande erreur de se figurer que les nations ne puissent être engagées que dans des rapports qu'elles ont constitués par leur volonté concertée. Il suffit de jeter un regard sur la vie internationale dans sa réalité, pour être frappé de la part très grande occupée dans cette vie par les obligations qui ne résultent pas du fait concordant des deux parties, mais du fait unilatéral de l'une d'elles (qu'on l'appelle quasi-contrat, délit, quasi-délit) du fait des tiers, etc.

Dans tous ces cas, la justice objective est la norme naturelle dont l'application s'impose au juge. La question est seulement de savoir comment on peut, dans cet ordre, attacher le juge à des règles de nature à le guider sûrement. Car il est en vérité impossible, et il serait souverainement odieux, de dire au juge en face d'une solution manifestement conforme à la justice: „votre tâche consiste à commettre un véritable déni de justice", sous prétexte qu'on ne trouve pas de convention ou de coutume déterminées. Quelle est donc ici la différence entre mon éminent contradicteur et moi? C'est qu'il abandonne le juge à une sorte d'aveuglement forcé ou à des opinions subjectives, et que je lui donne deux yeux pour voir clair dans les affaires qu'il doit juger. L'un de ces clairs regards, c'est la doctrine concordante des auteurs qui font l'autorité: et ici je me permets d'invoquer la mémorable et typique parole du grand Chancelier Kent:

„Quand la plupart des jurisconsultes sont d'accord sur une règle, la présomption en faveur de cette règle prend une telle force qu'elle ne peut être contredite que par une nation qui se ferait un jeu de la justice."

Le second des clairs regards que je donne au juge, c'est la conscience juridique de nations civilisées dans ses éclatantes manifestations. Et remarquez bien qu'il n'y a là rien qui ne soit approuvé déjà par l'assemblée des Etats civilisés dans d'unanimes déclarations, soit concernant l'état de paix, soit concernant l'état de guerre. Je ne veux pas rappeler l'article 7 de la convention relative à l'établissement d'une Cour Internationale des Prises qui distingue des stipulations conventionnelles, la justice et même l'équité. Il serait facile de multiplier de telles citations.

should be added as a complement to the others under conditions which are calculated to prevent arbitrary decisions.

It would be a great mistake to imagine that nations can be bound only by engagements which they have entered into by mutual consent. One glance at international life as it really is suffices to show what a great part is played in it by obligations created, not by a mutual agreement between the two parties, but by some act on the part of one of them only (which is called a quasi-contract, tort, or quasi-tort) or from some act of a third party etc.

In all these cases, objective justice is the natural principle to be applied by the judge. The only question is, — how to make unerring rules for the judge's guidance. For it is absolutely impossible and supremely odious to say to the judge that, although in a given case a perfectly just solution is possible: "You must take a course amounting to a refusal of justice" merely because no definite convention or custom appeared. What, therefore, is the difference between my distinguished opponent and myself? He leaves the judge in a state of compulsory blindness forced to rely on subjective opinions only; I allow him to consider the cases that come before him with both eyes open. In the first place, I would allow him to make use of the concurrent teaching of the authors whose opinions have authority: at this point allow me to recall the memorable and characteristic words of the great Chancellor Kent, to the effect that when the greater part of jurisconsults agree upon a certain rule — the presumption in favour of that rule becomes so strong, that only a person who makes a mock of justice would gainsay it.

In the second place I would allow him to take into consideration the legal conscience of civilised nations, which is illustrated so strikingly on certain occasions. And I would point out that there is nothing in the foregoing, which has not already been approved by unanimous declarations of the assembly of civilised States, both with reference to peace and war. I will not remind you of Article 7 of the Convention for the establishment of an International Prize Court, which distinguished between the conventional stipulations and justice, and even equity. It would be easy to repeat such instances. However, listen to this solemn declaration of the Powers, placed at the beginning of the Convention dealing with laws and customs of war on land:

"Until a more complete code of the laws of war has been issued, the high contracting Parties deem it expedient to declare that, in cases not

Mais écoutez cette déclaration solennelle des Puissances, placée en tête de la Convention concernant les lois et coutumes de la guerre sur terre:

„En attendant qu'un Code plus complet des lois de la guerre puisse être édicté, les Hautes Parties contractantes jugent opportun de constater que, dans les cas non compris dans les dispositions réglementaires adoptées par elles, les populations et les belligérants restent sous la sauvegarde et sous l'empire des principes du droit des gens, tels qu'ils résultent des usages établis entre nations civilisées, des lois de l'humanité et des exigences de la conscience publique."

Et quand le droit des gens affirme que les traités sont essentiellement des conventions de bonne foi, il érige en règle pour le juge l'obligation de les interpréter avec toutes les conséquences que leur donne suivant leur nature la justice objective, — je dirais l'équité, si je ne craignais d'ouvrir la voie à des équivoques, sachant que ce terme est diversement interprété.

C'est une des convictions les plus profondes de ma vie vouée à l'étude et à la pratique du droit international, qu'il n'est pas possible de chasser du domaine de l'ordre juridique, en ses applications, une loi fondamentale de justice, dans la mesure où sa voix est assez claire pour promulguer certaines règles comme nécessairement liées à l'économie essentielle des rapports sociaux dans la vie internationale; et comme s'appliquant à la diversité des faits qu'embrasse cette vie. Et certes, ce n'est pas au moment où l'ensemble des Etats civilisés entend précisément substituer au système instable et aléatoire de la pure balance des forces, le régime de la coordination des peuples dans une société réglée selon la justice, — ce n'est pas au moment où nous sommes appelés à organiser cette justice, que je pourrais — laissez-moi dire: que nous pourrions — faire litière de telles convictions.

J'ai la ferme assurance, que ce que l'assemblée universelle des Etats a entendu consacrer si clairement pour l'état de guerre, elle n'entend pas, elle ne pourrait entendre le renier, pour l'état de paix.

N'hésitons donc pas — je voudrais mettre dans cet appel toute l'ardeur et toute la clairvoyance de mon âme de jurisconsulte — à placer, parmi les normes que doit suivre le juge dans la solution des différends qui lui sont soumis, la loi de la justice objective, en tant, tout au moins, que, doublement et remarquablement précise, et par la doctrine concordante des jurisconsultes

included in the Regulations adopted by them, populations and belligerents remain under the protection and the rule of the principles of the law of nations, as they result from the usages established among civilised peoples, from the laws of humanity, and the dictates of the public conscience."

The Law of Nations in stating that treaties are essentially conventions in good faith, makes the obligation binding on the judge to interpret them in the light of and with all the consequences deriving from their nature according to objective justice — I should say equity, if I did not fear that a misunderstanding might occur, owing to the various meanings put upon that word.

One of the most profound convictions of my life, which has been devoted to the study and application of international law, is that it is impossible to disregard a fundamental principle of justice in the application of law, if this principle clearly indicates certain rules, necessary for the system of international relations, and applicable to the various circumstances arising in international affairs. At any rate, — now that we are called upon to organise international justice, now that all civilised States have agreed to adopt a co-ordinated system based on principles of justice in international affairs, in place of the inevitably unreliable system of the balance of power, I cannot — let me say rather — we cannot, discard this convention.

I am convinced that the assembly of all the States does not and cannot intend, in dealing with the state of peace, to abjure principles which are clearly intended to be applied in war.

Let us therefore no longer hesitate — I would put in this appeal all the ardour and all the foresight that my mind as a jurisconsult gives me — to insert, amongst the principles to be followed by the judge in the solution of the dispute submitted to him, the law of objective justice, at any rate in so far as it has twofold confirmation of the concurrent teachings of jurisconsults of authority and of the public conscience of civilised nations.

On the threshold of the Palace of Peace where we meet daily there is a mosaic bearing the inscription *Sol Justitiæ Illustra Nos*. Let us draw inspiration and encouragement from this, and let us recognise that the conception of justice and injustice as indelibly written on the hearts of civilised peoples, and with the two additional guarantees that I would give it, is not only the element *par excellence* making for pro-

qui font autorité, et par la conscience juridique des peuples civilisés.

Il y a au seuil du Palais de la Paix où nous venons chaque jour, une mosaïque avec cette inscription: *Sol justitiæ illustra nos*. Eclaironsnous et réchauffons-nous à ce soleil, et reconnaissons que la loi du juste et de l'injuste, telle qu'elle est gravée et tracée de façon ineffaçable au cœur des peuples civilisés, et sous les deux garanties que je lui donne, est non seulement l'élément générateur par excellence du progrès du droit international, mais le complément indispensable pour le juge de l'application du droit, dans la haute mission qui lui est conférée.

gress in international law, but an indispensable complement to the application of law, and as such essential to the judge in the performance of the great task entrusted to him.

ANNEXE No. 2.

Deuxième partie du Projet Root-Phillimore. [1])

Article 18.

Tout juge ou juge suppléant devra, lors de la première séance à laquelle il sera présent, faire une déclaration solennelle de son intention de se conformer dans l'exercice de ses fonctions, au droit international.

Article 19.

Le Président résidera au siège de la Cour.

Article 20.

Les juges et juges suppléants jouiront, dans l'exercice de leurs fonctions, en dehors de leur propre pays, des privilèges et immunités diplomatiques.

Article 21.

Les juges et juges suppléants toucheront une indemnité annuelle à fixer par le Conseil de la Société des Nations.

Article 22.

Leurs fonctions terminées, les juges auront droit à une pension dont le montant sera déterminé d'après un plan qui sera dressé par le Conseil de la Société des Nations.

Article 23.

Les frais de la Cour seront supportés par la Société des Nations.

Article 24.

Le siège de la Cour sera établi à La Haye.

Article 25.

La Cour aura une session chaque année, sauf dispositions contraires dans le règlement d'ordre de la Cour. Cette session commencera le 15 juin et continuera jusqu'à ce que l'ordre du jour de la Cour soit épuisé. Le Président aura le droit de convoquer la Cour en session extraordinaire quand cela lui paraîtra nécessaire.

Article 26.

A la première audition d'un cas, neuf juges au moins devront être présents. S'il n'y a pas

1) Voir Annexe 1ère au Procès-Verbal de la 13ème séance.

ANNEX No. 2.

Second part of the Root-Phillimore plan. [1])

Article 18.

Every judge or supplementary judge shall, at the first sitting at which he is to be present, solemnly declare that he will exercise his functions in accordance with international law.

Article 19.

The President shall reside at the seat of the Court.

Article 20.

The judges and supplementary judges shall enjoy diplomatic privileges and immunities in the exercise of their functions, outside their own country.

Article 21.

The judges and supplementary judges shall draw an annual salary to be fixed by the Council of the League of Nations.

Article 22.

After the termination of the judicial functions the judges shall be entitled to a pension on a scale to be fixed by the Council of the League of Nations.

Article 23.

The expenses of the Court shall be borne by the League of Nations.

Article 24.

The seat of the Court shall be established at The Hague.

Article 25.

The Court shall have one session each year, unless otherwise provided by rule of Court. This session shall open on the fifteenth day of June and continue until the business before the Court is disposed of. The President shall have the power to convoke an extraordinary session of the Court when he deems it necessary.

Article 26.

There shall be present at the first hearing of a case not less than nine judges and, if there

1) See Annex 1 to Procès-Verbal of 13th meeting.

neuf juges disponibles, les juges suppléants entreront en fonctions jusqu'à concurrence de ce nombre. Les juges suppléants seront appelés à siéger d'après un système de roulement, et par ancienneté.

Si, pour une raison quelconque, un ou plusieurs des juges se trouvent hors d'état de continuer à siéger pendant toute l'audition du cas, l'audition pourra néanmoins être poursuivie, à condition qu'il y ait un quorum de sept juges présents.

be less than this number available, their places shall be filled by supplementary judges called in rotation in the order of age.

If, for any reason, any of the judges are unable to continue during the hearing, the remaining judges, provided there is a quorum of seven, can continue the case.

Article 27.

Si, lors de l'instruction d'un cas déterminé, la Cour ne renferme pas de juge de la nationalité d'un des Etats parties en litige, cet Etat nommera, en vue de l'instruction, un juge qui prendra part à la décision du litige sur un pied de parfaite égalité avec les autres juges, membres de la Cour.

Si la Cour ne renferme aucun juge de la nationalité des parties en litige, chacune d'elles nommera un juge qui prendra part à la procédure concernant le litige et à la décision prise à son sujet.

S'il y a plus de deux parties et que deux ou plusieurs des parties fassent cause commune, elles seront représentées à la Cour par un juge seulement. Ce juge sera nommé d'un commun accord par les parties.

Article 27.

If, on the trial of a case, there is no judge upon the Court belonging to one of the litigating States, that State shall, for the purpose of the trial, appoint a judge who shall take part in the decision of the case on a footing of absolute equality with the other judges on the Bench.

If neither of the parties in litigation before the Court had a judge, each shall appoint a judge to take part in the proceedings and the decision of the case.

If two or more of the parties are in the same interest, they shall have but one judge, to be agreed upon between them.

Article 28.

La Cour est accessible à tous les Etats qui sont Membres de la Société des Nations et aux Etats qui ne sont pas Membres de la Société, mais qui acceptent les conditions posées par le Conseil de la Société, en conformité avec l'article 17 du Pacte. La Cour connaîtra seulement des litiges entre Etats, mais un Etat pourra soumettre à la Cour les droits qu'il fait valoir au nom de ses ressortissants ou au nom de ressortissants d'un autre Etat que le dit Etat a le droit de représenter en vertu d'un traité.

Article 28.

The Court is open to all States who are Members of the League of Nations and to States non-members of the League of Nations who comply with the conditions laid down by the Council, in accordance with Article 17 of the Covenant. The Court shall take cognisance only of suits between States, but the State may put forward rights which it claims on behalf of any of its citizens or for the nationals of another State on whose behalf it is entitled by treaty to appear.

Article 29.

(Les autres questions relatives à la compétence de la Cour sont traitées dans l'article rédigé par le Président et par Lord Phillimore, et amendé par M. Ricci-Busatti.) [1]

1) Voir Annexes au Procès-Verbal de la 12me séance.

Article 29.

(The rest of the subject of competency is covered by the Article drawn up by the President and Lord Phillimore and amended by M. Ricci-Busatti). [1]

1) See Annexes to Proces-Verbal of 12th meeting.

Article 30.

La Cour aura le droit de donner des avis consultatifs au sujet de conflits ou questions soumis à elle par le Conseil ou l'Assemblée de la Société des Nations. Elle pourra également connaître de toutes questions qui lui auront été soumises en vertu d'un traité auquel un Membre de la Société des Nations est partie.

Article 30.

The Court may give an advisory opinion upon any dispute or question referred to it by the Council or the Assembly of the League of Nations and may take jurisdiction in any question submitted to it, pursuant to the provisions of any treaty to which any member of the League of Nations is a party.

ANNEXE No. 3.

Remarques et amendements au projet d'organisation de la Cour Permanente de Justice Internationale (projet Root-Phillimore), par M. Altamira.

A l'Article 1. — Ajouter, après la catégorie des „jurisconsultes d'une compétence, etc." — *ou s'étant exercés, dans les fonctions d'arbitre dans des affaires d'un caractère international.* (Autre rédaction de la même idée: *ou des arbitres exercés dans des affaires d'un caractère international*).

Dans certains pays, sauf quelques professeurs, possédant le titre plutôt que la compétence, il n'y aura d'autre personnes spécialisées en droit international que celles qui ont rempli des fonctions arbitrales.

Il convient en tout cas, d'ajouter la possibilité (même l'obligation) d'indiquer sur les listes de présentation des noms étrangers à côté des noms nationaux.

A l'Article 7. — Il faut réfléchir sur la faculté de libre élection donnée ici à la Commission de conciliation. N'est-ce pas courir le risque de voir la majorité ou même la totalité des juges élus en dehors de la liste dont parle le premier alinéa de ce même article, et en conséquence, l'intervention de la Cour d'arbitrage ainsi éludée et rendue inutile?

A l'Articles 8. — Au lieu de: „les doyens, directeurs et présidents des universités" (il y aurait en tout cas à y joindre les *recteurs* pour les pays où ce nom seul existe) écrire: *les doyens des Facultés ou Ecoles de Droit.* Autrement on ne consultera pas les personnes vraiment qualifiées pour connaître les jurisconsultes désirables, parce que souvent les recteurs n'appartiennent pas à la carrière juridique et, même s'ils sont professeurs, ils ont peu de rapports, étant donnée l'organisation universitaire de certains Etats, avec d'autres Facultés que la leur.

Afin de ne pas exclure les pays où la division en Facultés n'existe pas, mentionner les deux régimes, en faisant une distinction parfaite entre eux pour ne pas avoir une double consulation. Les mots „sociétés scientifiques" sont très vagues, en ce qui concerne certains pays où ils embrasseront des Sociétés multiples sans autorité réelle, mais prétendant en avoir. Pour écarter ce danger, il serait préférable de dire: *Les Académies nationales ou royales vouées à l'étude du Droit.*

ANNEX No. 3.

Remarks and amendments to the plan of organisation for the Permanent Court of International Justice (Root-Phillimore plan), by M. Altamira.

To Article 1. — Following the category of "jurisconsults of recognised authority, etc." add the following *"or experienced as arbitrators in affairs of an international character."* (Another draft of the same idea: *"or arbitrators experienced in affairs of an international character"*).

In some countries there will exist no persons versed in international law (except a few professors possessed of the title rather than ability) other than those who have taken part in matters of arbitration.

It is expedient in any case to add the possibility (even the obligation) to mention on the list of candidates the names of foreigners along with those of nationals.

To Article 7. — It is necessary to consider the power of free election here given to the Commission of conciliation. Is that not to run the risk of having the majority, even the entire number, of judges, elected from outside the list mentioned in Paragraph 1 of this same Article, with the consequence that the intervention of the Court of Arbitration would thus be evaded and rendered useless?

To Article 8. — In place of (the English equivalent for) "les doyens, directeurs, et présidents des universités" (*"recteurs"* will always have to be added for the countries where there is only this term), insert *"the deans of law-faculties or law schools."* Otherwise there will not be included the persons really knowing the desirable jurisconsults because often the recteurs are not of the legal profession (even if professors) and have slight relation under the university organisation of certain states with other than their own faculty.

In order not to exclude the countries where the division into faculties does not exist, one had better mention the two systems, in making a clear distinction between them, to avoid having a double consultation. The words "learned societies" are very vague with reference to certain countries where they include various societies not endowed with real authority but pretending to have it. To avoid this danger, it would be preferable to say: *National or Royal Academies devoted to the study of law.*

En tout cas, si on veut comprendre aussi les pays où il n'existe pas d'Académies, mentionner les deux choses, mais en précisant qu'elles sont exclusives l'une de l'autre, pour ne pas les voir consulter toutes deux dans un même pays.

A l'Article 10. — Il faudrait préciser à qui le juge devient indésirable, pour éviter des démarches de personnes en dehors de la Cour.

In any case, if it is wished to embrace also the countries where Academies do not exist, the two things should be stated in such manner as to exclude one from the other in order not to have both consulted in the same country.

To Article 10. — It should be specified to whom the judge is to be "indésirable" in order to avoid steps being taken by persons outside the Court.

15IÈME SÉANCE (non-publique), tenue au Palais de la Paix, à La Haye, le 3 juillet 1920.

Présidence de M. le BARON DESCAMPS.

Sont présents: tous les membres du Comité (à l'exception de M. Bevilaqua); M. Fernandes; Mr. James Brown Scott; les secrétaires particuliers du Baron Descamps et de M. Adatci; les membres du Secrétariat.

La séance est ouverte à 9.35 heures du matin.

Le PRESIDENT rouvre la discussion sur les normes matérielles à appliquer par la Cour Permanente de Justice Internationale.

Mr. ROOT rappelle que M. Hagerup lui a demandé la veille de formuler ses idées à ce sujet. Il présente au Président un texte qu'il a préparé en collaboration avec Lord Phillimore.

Le PRESIDENT donne lecture de ce texte (voir annexe 1). Il déclare qu'il s'y rallie sous réserve d'une modification au No. 4 dans lequel il voudrait que les mots „doctrines concordantes" fussent substitués aux mots: „les opinions".

LORD PHILLIMORE approuve cette modification.

M. FERNANDES a rédigé un projet qui avait pour objet de fournir un terrain d'entente entre le Président et Mr. Root. Il se déclare heureux que l'accord soit déjà fait.

Le PRESIDENT engage M. Fernandes à donner lecture de son projet.

M. FERNANDES lit l'exposé, qui se trouve reproduit à l'annexe 2.

Le PRESIDENT remercie M. Fernandes de ses observations intéressantes; il remarque qu'elles cadrent avec les idées générales du Comité et avec le projet déposé par Mr. Root.

Le Président commente alors de manière succincte le texte soumis par Mr. Root. Il explique la mission délicate du juge international. Le juge devra d'abord rechercher si un fait donné rentre dans la catégorie des faits prévus par la loi internationale, puis apprécier ce fait conformément à cette loi.

15TH MEETING (Private), held at the Peace Palace, the Hague, on July 3rd, 1920.

BARON DESCAMPS in the chair.

Present: all members of the Committee (with the exception of M. Bevilaqua); M. Fernandes; Mr. James Brown Scott; the private secretaries of Baron Descamps and of M. Adatci; the members of the Secretariat.

The meeting opened at 9.35 a.m.

The PRESIDENT reopened the discussion on the question of the rules to be applied by the Permanent Court of International Justice.

Mr. ROOT recalled that M. Hagerup had asked him on the previous day to put his ideas on the subject in writing. He presented a draft to the President which he had prepared in collaboration with Lord Phillimore.

The PRESIDENT read the draft. (See annex 1). He declared that he agreed with it, except that in Number 4 he wished to substitute for the words "the opinions" the words "coinciding doctrines".

LORD PHILLIMORE approved of this change.

M. FERNANDES had prepared a plan the object of which was to furnish a basis of agreement between the President and Mr. Root. He was very glad that an agreement had already been reached.

The PRESIDENT asked M. Fernandes to read his statement.

M. FERNANDES read the plan, which is printed in the Annex 2.

The PRESIDENT thanked M. Fernandes for his interesting remarks. He said that they coincided with the general ideas of the Committee and with the project put forward by Mr. Root.

He then commented briefly on the draft submitted by Mr. Root. He explained the delicate task of an international judge. First of all the judges had to decide whether an act was included under one of the classifications of international law; then proceed to appreciate the fact in conformity with the said law.

Le juge doit souvent, comme Lord Phillimore l'a dit, se demander s'il y a une question à résoudre; ensuite, quelle est la question à résoudre.

Il doit réunir tous les éléments nécessaires pour caractériser les faits et pour préciser le droit. Et à ce dernier point de vue il doit déterminer, dans l'ordre successif où elles s'imposent à son examen, les règles applicables.

En exposant cet ordre, le Président remarque qu'au No. 3 il peut accepter la formule proposée par Mr. Root, et qu'au No. 4 l'autorité des décisions judiciaires et la doctrine concordante des juristes ne doivent être employées par le juge qu'à titre auxiliaire et supplétif. En finissant, le Président déclare qu'à son avis le texte de Mr. Root est fait pour donner satisfaction à tous les membres, et que ce texte obvie aux différents inconvénients sur lesquels ont porté les objections, et visant notamment l'impasse du *non liquet*.

LORD PHILLIMORE exprime l'avis qu'on peut considérer ce texte comme adopté en première lecture.

M. RICCI-BUSATTI regrette de devoir faire des réserves. Ce n'est d'ailleurs pas contre le fond du texte qu'il s'élève. Ce texte ne prétend en effet qu'à indiquer exactement les sources diverses auxquelles doit puiser le juge. Mais c'est contre quelques-unes des sources mentionnées et contre leur classification successive que sa conscience juridique s'élève.

Pour ce qui est du préambule, il ne peut pas approuver l'expression „ordre successif, etc.". Le juge doit tenir compte simultanément des diverses sources du droit, l'une complétant l'autre.

Il n'a pas de sérieuses objections contre les points 1 et 2.

Quant au No. 3, il comprend l'expression „les principes généraux du droit" de la manière qu'il a indiquée dans la séance précédente. Il regrette qu'on n'ait pas mentionné les principes de l'équité, qui ne sont pas toujours les mêmes que ceux du droit.

Quant au No. 4, M. Ricci-Busatti ne croit guère qu'il puisse y avoir des doctrines concordantes sur des points où il n'y a pas de règles universellement reconnues. Il nie d'ailleurs, de la manière la plus absolue, que les opinions des auteurs puissent être considérées comme une *source de droit,* à appliquer par la Cour, et surtout il s'étonne que Mr. Root se soit rallié à une formule exprimant cette idée.

M. Ricci-Busatti a rédigé un texte

The judge, as Lord Phillimore had said, must often ask himself if there is a question at issue, and then what it is.

He must bring together all the details necessary to ascertain the facts and to make sure of the law. For the latter purpose, he should determine what rules apply, in the order in which they present themselves to his mind.

In dealing with this order, the President pointed out that in No. 3 he could accept the clause proposed by Mr. Root, and that in No. 4 the judge must use the authority of judicial decisions, and the coinciding doctrines of jurists, as auxiliary and supplementary means, only. Finally, the President said that he thought that Mr. Root's scheme was likely to satisfy all the members, and that it avoided the difficulties that had been pointed out, especially the blind alley of *non liquet.*

LORD PHILLIMORE expressed the opinion that the project might be considered as adopted in first reading.

M. RICCI-BUSATTI regretted that he had to make reservations. Nevertheless he was not opposed to the substance of the project. The text was as a matter of fact intended only to indicate exactly the various sources which the judge might use. But it was to some of the sources mentioned, and the order in which they were classified, that this legal conscience objected.

As concerned the preamble, he did not approve of the expression "ordre successif", etc. He thought that the judge should consider the various sources of law simultaneously in relation to one another.

He had no serious objection to points 1 and 2.

As to number 3 he understood the expression "general principles of law" in the way he had indicated at the last meeting. He regretted that the principles of equity, not always the same as law, were not mentioned.

As to number 4, he hardly thought that it would be possible to find coinciding doctrines concerning points in relation to which no generally recognised rules existed. Further, he denied most emphatically that the opinions of authors could be considered as a *source of law,* to be applied by the Court, and he was above all astonished that Mr. Root had agreed to a formula containing this idea.

M. Ricci-Busatti had drafted an amen-

amendé. Il le présente au Président et en donne lecture. (Voir annexe 4) [1]).

LORD PHILLIMORE a lu dans le procès-verbal le discours prononcé la veille par M. Ricci-Busatti. Il est, d'une manière générale, d'accord avec les idées exprimées dans ce discours. Il désire cependant expliquer les considérations qui sont à la base du texte qu'il a formulé d'accord avec Mr. Root, et répondre aux objections de M. Ricci-Busatti concernant ce texte.

Lord Phillimore n'attache pas trop d'importance à l'ordre successif des sources. La formule adoptée a simplement été enpruntée au texte du Président et, d'après lui, l'ordre signalé représente seulement l'ordre logique dans lequel ces sources se présenteront à l'esprit du juge.

M. Ricci-Busatti a exprimé le désir de voir ajouter au No. 3 „les principes de l'équité". Lord Phillimore rappelle d'abord le sens technique qu'a, en Angleterre, le mot „équité". L'adoption de „l'équité" comme source de droit aurait pour résultat de laisser trop de liberté au juge, si l'on donnait à ce mot une acception autre que l'acception technique qui'il vient de définir.

Lord Phillimore et Mr. Root sont allés aussi loin qu'ils le pouvaient quand s'est posée la question de la liberté qu'il y a lieu d'accorder aux juges. Tout nouveau progrès dans cette voie leur est impossible.

Quant à l'importance de la doctrine, Lord Phillimore fait remarquer qu'elle est universellement reconnue comme source de droit international. Il n'est pas besoin de dire qu'il s'agit exclusivement des opinions des auteurs les plus autorisés. A son avis, le changement apporté par le Président est une amélioration très remarquable du texte rédigé par Mr. Root et par lui-même.

M. RICCI-BUSATTI demande à Lord Phillimore si l'Angleterre accepterait une sentence fondée, non pas sur une règle de droit admise comme telle, mais sur une doctrine d'auteurs juristes.

LORD PHILLIMORE le croit possible.

M. RICCI-BUSATTI doute que les Etats acceptent vraiment des règles qui seraient l'œuvre

1) Cette annexe contient le texte amendé par M. Ricci-Busatti dans sa forme *définitive*, présentée vers la fin de la séance. Les différences entre cette forme et la forme originaire résultent de la discussion.

ded text. He presented it to the President and read it. (See Annex 4) [1]).

LORD PHILLIMORE had read in the procès-verbal the speech made by M. Ricci-Busatti on the previous day. He agreed generally with the ideas expressed in this speech. However, he wished to explain the considerations which formed the basis of the draft which he had formulated in collaboration with Mr. Root, and to answer M. Ricci-Busatti's objections to this draft.

Lord Phillimore did not attach much importance to the successive order in which the sources were to be used. The formula adopted, had simply been taken from the draft of the President, and in his opinion the order mentioned simply represented the logical order in which these sources would occur to the mind of the judge.

M. Ricci-Busatti had expressed the desire to have "the principles of equity" included in number 3. Lord Phillimore first recalled the technical meaning which the word "equity" has in England. The adoption of "equity" as a source of law would result in giving too much liberty to the judge, unless the technical meaning just mentioned were adopted.

Lord Phillimore and Mr. Root had gone as far as they felt they could on the subject of the liberty to give the judge. Any further advance in this direction would be impossible.

As to the importance to be attached to doctrine, Lord Phillimore pointed out, that it is universally recognised as a source of international law. There is no need to say, that only the opinions of widely recognised authors were in question. In his opinion, the change suggested by the President was a very remarkable improvement to the draft prepared by Mr. Root and himself.

M. RICCI-BUSATTI asked Lord Phillimore whether England would accept a sentence based not on a rule of law accepted as such, but upon the doctrine of legal writers.

LORD PHILLIMORE thought that this was possible.

M. RICCI-BUSATTI doubted whether States would really accept rules which would be the

1) This Annex contains the text amended by M. Ricci-Busatti in its *final* form, submitted later on during the meeting. The divergencies between this form and the original one result from the discussion.

de la doctrine et non de leur propre volonté ou de leur coutume.

LORD PHILLIMORE explique qu'en acceptant le texte du Président, qui est le squelette du texte soumis par Mr. Root, on en a aussi accepté la division qui est quelque peu fautive. Lord Phillimore croit, par exemple, que les sources mentionnées dans le No. 3 peuvent rentrer dans l'énumération du No. 2 parce que c'est par la coutume qu'on arrive à la reconnaissance des principes généraux, et d'autre part la coutume se forme par la pratique suivie dans les différents documents publics et solennels et par les œuvres des écrivains qui s'accordent sur un point déterminé.

Le PRESIDENT insiste sur le caractère auxiliaire, au point de vue de l'interprétation, des éléments signalés au No. 4.

M. RICCI-BUSATTI fait observer que ce que vient de dire Lord Phillimore concorde avec ses idées personnelles. Il admet bien la nécessité de tenir compte de la jurisprudence et de la doctrine, mais il croit qu'il est inadmissible de les mettre sur le même plan que les règles positives de droit.

M. DE LAPRADELLE croit pouvoir constater qu'on est actuellement arrivé à une solution commune, puisque Mr. Root a accepté, dans un esprit de conciliation, les points 1 et 2 du projet du Président.

LORD PHILLIMORE remarque que Mr. Root a également accepté le No. 4 du projet du Président; comme, cependant, le mot „jurisprudence" a un sens différent en Anglais et en Français, on a inséré dans le texte soumis par Mr. Root une formule qui définit ce mot, tel qu'on l'use en droit français.

M. DE LAPRADELLE est heureux de l'entente qui s'est produite entre les membres. Il croit cependant pouvoir remarquer que les résultats des accords auxquels arrive le Comité, doivent être irréprochables; le texte actuel ne lui donne pas pleine satisfaction, au point de vue pratique et logique. Les amendements de M. Ricci-Busatti sont en grande partie justifiés, mais ils contiennent également des points qui, s'ils étaient introduits dans le projet ne l'amélioreraient pas; au contraire.

M. de Lapradelle cite des exemples. M. Ricci-Busatti propose que la Cour tienne compte „autant que possible" des décisions judiciaires etc. M. de Lapradelle ne trouve pas cette rédaction suffisamment précise.

result of the doctrine rather than of their own will, or of their usages.

LORD PHILLIMORE explained that by accepting the President's draft, which was the framework of the draft submitted by Mr. Root, they had also accepted the method of division, which was somewhat faulty. Lord Phillimore thought, for instance, that the sources mentioned in point 3 might be included in point 4, because it was through custom that general principles came to be recognised, and on the other hand, custom is formed by the usage followed in various public and formal documents, and from the works of writers who agree upon a certain point.

The PRESIDENT emphasised the auxiliary character of the elements in No. 4 as elements of interpretation.

M. RICCI-BUSATTI observed that what Lord Phillimore had just said coincided with his own ideas. He fully admitted the necessity of taking jurisprudence and doctrine into account, but he thought it was inadmissible to put them on the same level as positive rules of law.

M. DE LAPRADELLE felt he could say that they had actually reached a unanimous solution, since Mr. Root had accepted in a conciliatory spirit the first and the second points of the President's plan.

LORD PHILLIMORE said that Mr. Root had accepted also the fourth point of the President's plan, but, as the word "jurisprudence" had a different meaning in English and French, a clause had been inserted in the draft submitted by Mr. Root, which defines the word according to the French legal meaning.

M. DE LAPRADELLE welcomed the agreement which the members had reached. He thought, however, that he might mention that the results of the agreements reached by the Committee should be above criticism; the actual wording did not give him complete satisfaction from a practical and logical point of view. The amendments of M. Ricci-Busatti were to a great extent justified, but they also contained points which, if introduced in the plan, would not improve it, but would do quite the contrary.

M. de Lapradelle quoted examples. M. Ricci-Busatti had proposed to insert that the Court should take into account "as much as possible" judicial decisions, etc. M. de Lapradelle did not think this wording sufficiently precise.

Le PRESIDENT partage l'avis de M. de Lapradelle à cet égard.

M. DE LAPRADELLE désapprouve également la proposition de M. Ricci-Busatti concernant l'insertion, parmi les sources, des „principes généraux de l'équité". M. de Lapradelle ne connaît pas ces principes: l'équité varie d'espèce en espèce; en général il faut se garder d'employer des mots qui aient une signification particulière: qui dit justice, dit équité.

M. de Lapradelle constate ensuite qu'on est d'accord sur le texte jusqu'au No. 2 inclusivement. On est également d'accord sur les premiers mots du No. 3: „les principes généraux du droit"; c'est alors que les difficultés commencent. Il relève les mots „peuples civilisés" au No. 3.

LORD PHILLIMORE constate que M. Ricci-Busatti s'est servi de la même formule.

M. DE LAPRADELLE la croit superflue puisque qui dit droit dit civilisation.

Hormis ce point spécial, M. de Lapradelle remarque que la coutume se trouve mentionnée comme source dans tous les textes proposés. Il croit que cette mention est nécessaire, mais il se demande, d'autre part, comment on dégage les principes généraux, si ce n'est de la coutume. Les Nos. 2 et 3 devraient changer de place. Si l'on a déjà considéré le droit coutumier, d'où peut-on alors dégager les principes généraux si ce n'est de la lecture des jugements et des auteurs?

LORD PHILLIMORE fait observer que les principes généraux visés par le No. 3 sont ceux qui sont acceptés par toutes les nations *in foro domestico*; tels certains principes de procédure, le principe de la bonne foi, le principe de la chose jugée etc.

M. DE LAPRADELLE observe qu'on touche à la question si difficile et encore si obscure des limites de la coutume.

Le PRESIDENT rappelle qu'une grande partie du droit international, sauf les quelques points qui sont réglés par des stipulations conventionnelles, est le produit de la coutume.

LORD PHILLIMORE explique que, par „principes généraux du droit", il a voulu dire „maximes du droit".

M. DE LAPRADELLE admet que les principes qui sont à la base du droit national, constituent aussi des sources de droit international. Mais il n'y a en fait de principes généraux reconnus, que ceux qui ont réuni autour d'eux l'unanimité ou la quasi-unanimité. Comme les auteurs

The PRESIDENT shared the opinion of M. de Lapradelle in this respect.

M. DE LAPRADELLE also disapproved of M. Ricci-Busatti's proposal to insert among the sources "the general principles of equity". M. de Lapradelle did not know these principles; equity varied from case to case; generally speaking, care must be taken not to employ words with a special meaning; justice includes equity.

M. de Lapradelle stated that agreement had been reached upon the draft up to and including the second point. They also agreed concerning the first words of point 3: "the general principles of law". The difficulties then began at that point. He referred to the words "civilised nations" in point 3.

LORD PHILLIMORE stated that M. Ricci-Busatti's scheme used the same phrase.

M. DE LAPRADELLE thought it superfluous, because law implies civilisation.

Apart from this special point, M. de Lapradelle remarked that custom was mentioned as a source in all the drafts proposed. He thought that a mention of this was necessary, but on the other hand wondered, how were general principles obtained, unless it was from custom. Points 2 and 3 ought to change place. If customary law had already been dealt with, from whence could general principles be derived, unless it were from the reading of judicial decisions and writers?

LORD PHILLIMORE pointed out that the general principles referred to in point 3 were these which were accepted by all nations *in foro domestico*, such as certain principles of procedure, the principle of good faith, and the principle of *res judicata*, etc.

M. DE LAPRADELLE pointed out that they were now bordering on the very difficult and obscure question of the limits of custom.

The PRESIDENT recalled that a large part of international law, except a few points which are regulated by conventional stipulations, is the outcome of custom.

LORD PHILLIMORE explained, that by "general principles of law" he had intended to mean "maxims of law".

M. DE LAPRADELLE admitted that the principles which formed the bases of national law, were also sources of international law. The only generally recognised principles which exist, however, are those which have obtained unanimous or quasi-unanimous support. As the

ne sont presque jamais d'accord sur un point de droit, une disposition telle que celle contenue dans le No. 4 du texte présenté par Mr. Root ôterait toute importance à leurs ouvrages.

M. de Lapradelle croit que la jurisprudence est plus importante que la doctrine, puisque les juges, en rendant leur sentence, ont en vue un but pratique. Si l'on veut indiquer la doctrine comme une source, il faudrait du moins se borner à la doctrine concordante des auteurs qualifiés dans les pays en litige. Il serait certainement nécessaire de faire une classification graduée des diverses manifestations de la doctrine, d'après leur importance. Il faudrait, p. e., tenir compte, dans une mesure assez large, des résolutions de l'Institut de Droit International.

Pour éviter d'entrer dans trop de détails, M. de Lapradelle croit cependant préférable de s'en tenir à une formule simple telle que, p. e. „les principes généraux du droit", sans indiquer expressément les sources où il faut puiser afin de déterminer ces principes.

En achevant, M. de Lapradelle observe que la grande question qui se pose est celle de savoir quelle attitude la Cour devra prendre si, dans un cas déterminé, la jurisprudence fait défaut et s'il n'y a pas d'accord général sur un principe à appliquer. M. de Lapradelle croit qu'il faudrait ajouter un No. 5 au texte pour régler cette question.

Le PRESIDENT répond d'abord aux objections soulevées par M. Ricci-Busatti. Celui-ci déclare qu'il faut appliquer cumulativement les différentes sources du droit. Cela peut être vrai dans un cas donné. Néanmoins une classification graduée des sources s'impose.

M. Ricci-Busatti formule aussi des objections contre le No. 3, mais le Président fait observer que ce numéro est nécessaire pour parer à l'éventualité d'un *non liquet*. Quant aux objections formulées au sujet du No. 4, le Président s'étonne de voir que M. Ricci-Busatti n'accepte pas la doctrine comme élément d'interprétation. Cet élément ne doit avoir qu'un caractère subsidiaire; le juge ne doit s'en servir qu'à titre supplétif en vue d'élucider les règles du droit international. La doctrine et la jurisprudence ne créent pas de règles, sans doute, mais elles concourent à la détermination des règles qui existent. Le juge devra recourir au double trésor de l'interprétation jurisprudentielle et doctrinale, mais ces trésors conservent un caractère élucidateur.

publicists are hardly ever agreed upon a point of law, such a provision as that contained in point 4 of the project put forward by Mr. Root took away any importance from their works.

M. de Lapradelle thought that jurisprudence was more important than doctrine, since the judges in pronouncing sentence had a practical end in view. If it were wished to include doctrine as a source it should be at any rate limited to coinciding doctrines of qualified authors in the countries concerned in the case. It certainly would be necessary to make a classification: the various expressions of doctrine would be arranged according to their importance. The resolutions of the Institute of International Law, for example, would have to be taken into account to a considerable extent.

To avoid going too much into detail, M. de Lapradelle thought it preferable to keep to a simple phrase: such, for example, as "the general principles of law", without indicating exactly the sources from which these principles should be derived.

Finally, M. de Lapradelle observed that the great question which presented itself was what attitude the Court would take if in a certain case, jurisprudence failed and there was no generally accepted principle applicable. M. de Lapradelle thought that there ought to be added to the draft a fifth point to deal with this question.

The PRESIDENT first of all answered the objection made by M. Ricci-Busatti. The latter had said that the different sources of law should be made use of simultaneously. That might be done in given cases. Nevertheless a classified graduation of sources is necessary.

M. Ricci-Busatti also had raised objections to point 3, but the President observed that this Article was necessary to meet the possibility of a *non-liquet*. As to the objections raised to point 4, the President was astonished to find that M. Ricci-Busatti did not accept doctrine as an element of interpretation. This element could only be of a subsidiary nature; the judge should only use it in a supplementary way to clarify the rules of international law. Doctrine and jurisprudence no doubt do not create law; but they assist in determining rules which exist. A judge should make use of both jurisprudence and doctrine, but they should serve only as elucidation.

The President added that if Mr. Root's text were accepted they would have done a satisfac-

Le Président ajoute que si l'on accepte le texte de Mr. Root, on fera une œuvre satisfaisante et on fournira au juge une base solide pour ses jugements.

Le Président regrette que M. de Lapradele ne voie pas la valeur du No. 4. La faculté pour le juge de se servir des éléments mentionnés dans ce paragraphe n'est pas dangereuse, parce qu'on n'y a recours qu'à titre élucidateur et supplétif. Pour donner satisfaction à M. de Lapradelle, le Président et Lord Phillimore ne s'opposeront pas à supprimer dans ce paragraphe le mot „concordante" et à le remplacer par des termes meilleurs, mais il prie M. de Lapradelle de ne point insister sur une modification plus radicale.

Une discussion s'engage alors entre M. de Lapradelle, le Président et Lord Phillimore, à la suite de laquelle le No. 4 est libellé comme suit: „L'autorité des décisions judiciaires et la doctrine des publicistes les plus qualifiés des différentes nations."

M. RICCI-BUSATTI croit que le texte devrait encore être retouché. Il préférerait une formule aussi brève que possible.

Il maintient en partie ses amendements et insiste notamment sur la suppression des mots „dans l'ordre successif" etc. du préambule du texte de Mr. Root. Non seulement ces mots sont superflus, mais ils pourraient aussi suggérer l'idée que le juge ne serait pas autorisé à puiser à une source mentionnée, p. e., dans le No. 3, avant d'avoir appliqué les Conventions et les coutumes, mentionnées respectivement dans les Nos. 1 et 2, ce qui serait méconnaître les intentions du Comité.

Le PRESIDENT remarque qu'il existe cependant une gradation naturelle. Si deux Etats ont conclu un traité dans lequel se trouve la solution du différend, la Cour ne peut pas appliquer la coutume, et laisser de côté le traité. S'il existe une coutume notoire, il n'y a pas lieu de recourir aux principes généraux du droit. Nous indiquons un ordre de précellence naturel sans proscrire éventuellement la concordance de plusieurs sources.

M. RICCI-BUSATTI maintient son point de vue. Si par l'expression „ordre successif" on veut dire seulement qu'une convention prime, p. ex. le droit coutumier, elle est inutile: c'est un principe fondamental du droit que la loi spéciale prime la loi générale; mais elle semble méconnaître l'application simultanée qui peut être faite de ces catégories, ainsi que le caractère différent des unes et des autres.

tory piece of work and would have given the judge a substantial basis for his decisions.

The President regretted that M. de Lapradelle did not see the value of the 4th point. The judge's right to make use of the elements mentioned in this paragraph is not a dangerous one as it would only be for elucidating and supplementary purposes. In order to satisfy M. de Lapradelle, the President and Lord Phillimore would not object to omitting under this paragraph the word "coinciding" and to replace it by a better word, but he begged M. de Lapradelle not to insist upon a more radical alteration.

A discussion followed between M. de Lapradelle, the President and Lord Phillimore, as a result of which point 4 was worded as follows: "The authority of judicial decisions and the doctrines of the best qualified writers of the various nations".

M. RICCI-BUSATTI thought that the text should have further revision. He preferred a formula as short as possible.

He sustained some of his amendments and insisted especially on the suppression of the words "dans l'ordre successif" etc. in the preamble of Mr. Root's draft. These words were not only superfluous, but they might also suggest the idea that the judge was not authorised to draw upon a certain source, for instance point 3, before having applied conventions and customs mentioned respectively in points 1 and 2. That would be a misinterpretation of the Committee's intentions.

The PRESIDENT remarked however, that there was a natural classification. If two States concluded a treaty in which the solution of the dispute could be found, the Court must not apply international custom and neglect the treaty. If a well known custom exists, there is no occasion to resort to a general principle of law. We shall indicate an order of natural *précellence,* without requiring in a given case the agreement of several sources.

M. RICCI-BUSATTI held to his opinion. If the expression "ordre successif" only meant that a Convention should be considered before, for instance, Customary law, it is unnecessary. It is a fundamental principle of law that a special rule goes before general law. This expression also seems to fail to recognise that these various sources may be applied simultaneously, and also that the nature of each source differs.

Il signale quelques autres modifications qu'il serait utile, selon lui, d'apporter au texte: bien des phrases sont superflues; tandis que, d'autre part, le projet, tel qu'il est rédigé, n'exclut pas la possibilité d'un *non liquet*; il s'agit de „sources" plutôt que de „règles" du droit; enfin, la jurisprudence et la doctrine ne peuvent être mises au même rang que les autres sources, et ne doivent pas être utilisées de la même façon, bien qu'elles doivent toujours être présentes à l'esprit du juge.

He pointed out some other modifications which it seemed to him advisable to introduce in the text; many phrases were superfluous, while on the other hand the project as drafted did not prevent the possibility of a *non-liquet;* it dealt rather with "sources" than with "rules" of law; at any rate jurisprudence and doctrine may not be placed on the same level as the other sources and must not be used in the same way; although they must always be borne in mind by the judge.

LORD PHILLIMORE estime qu'il est d'accord avec M. Ricci-Busatti. Tous les membres, d'ailleurs, sont d'accord sur le fond, et la critique ne peut porter que sur la forme. Dans ces circonstances, il propose qu'on abandonne, pour le moment, la discussion de la question des règles à appliquer, pour aborder celle des règles de procédure.

LORD PHILLIMORE felt that he agreed with M. Ricci-Busatti; furthermore all the members were agreed upon the principle, and form only could be criticized. Under these conditions he proposed that the discussion of the question of the law to be applied should be left for the moment, in order to consider the rules of procedure.

M. HAGERUP déclare que, se ralliant au désir de M. Ricci-Busatti, il voudrait que l'on supprimât l'expression „ordre successif".

M. HAGERUP declared that he agreed with M. Ricci-Busatti and wished to have the expression "ordre successif" suppressed.

M. DE LAPRADELLE observe qu'on peut regarder cette expression comme superflue, puisque l'ordre dans lequel on doit consulter les sources est indiqué déjà dans l'énumération.

M. DE LAPRADELLE observed that this expression might be considered superfluous since the order in which the sources should be consulted was already indicated in the enumeration.

Le PRESIDENT désirerait maintenir l'expression, mais attache peu d'importance à ce point.

The PRESIDENT wished to keep the expression but attached little importance to it.

M. ALTAMIRA fait observer que le langage juridique procède partout par pléonasmes. En maintenant cette expression on ne ferait donc que suivre une tradition séculaire.

M. ALTAMIRA pointed out that legal language always uses pleonasms. By keeping this expression, therefore, they would only be following an age-old tradition.

Le PRESIDENT constate, après avoir consulté les membres du Comité, que, sous le bénéfice des observations faites, le texte peut être considéré comme voté, sauf rédaction finale en seconde lecture.

The PRESIDENT, after having consulted the members of the Committee, stated that, with the modifications following from the observations made, the draft might be considered as agreed upon, except as concerned final drafting for the second reading.

M. DE LAPRADELLE propose de faire insérer dans le premier alinéa du préambule les mots „de droit"; l'alinéa serait ainsi conçu: „les règles de droit à appliquer" etc.

M. DE LAPRADELLE proposed to insert in the first paragraph of the preamble the words "of law"; the paragraph would then run: "the rules of law to be applied" etc.

M. HAGERUP, LORD PHILLIMORE et Mr. ROOT se rallient à cette proposition, à laquelle le PRESIDENT ne s'oppose pas.

M. HAGERUP, LORD PHILLIMORE and Mr. ROOT agreed with this suggestion. The PRESIDENT did not oppose it.

Le PRESIDENT ouvre la discussion sur les règles de procédure. Il remarque qu'on a proposé de prendre comme base des discussions le projet dit des „Cinq Puissances". Le Président ne s'oppose pas à cette proposition, bien que personnellement il eût préféré le texte officiel de 1907.

The PRESIDENT opened the discussion on the rules of procedure. He said that it had been proposed to take the project of the Five Powers as the basis for the discussion. He did not oppose this suggestion, although personally he would have preferred the official text of 1907.

Il observe, en effet, que le texte du projet des Cinq Puissances ne fait que reproduire, avec quelques modifications, les règles de procédure de la Convention de 1907.

Mr. ROOT rappelle que, lors de la première séance du Comité, il a proposé de prendre pour base des discussions cette Convention. Cependant le Comité est maintenant d'accord pour prendre comme base le projet des Cinq Puissances.

Mr. Root croit que les deux choses reviennent à peu près au même, d'autant plus qu'on a convenu de considérer le projet des Cinq Puissances comme un rapport de commission sur les textes antérieurs.

Avant de quitter les Etats-Unis, Mr. Root et Mr. Brown Scott ont fait préparer un tableau synoptique comprenant les dispositions de tous ces textes, y compris le projet des Cinq Puissances, relatives à la procédure. Si le Comité n'a pas d'objection, il fera distribuer ce tableau. (Voir annexe 3).

Le PRESIDENT remercie Mr. Root au nom du Comité. Il désire cependant qu'il soit bien entendu que c'est seulement pour les règles de procédure que le projet des Cinq Puissances servira de base aux discussions.

Les dispositions de ce projet relatives à la procédure sont alors prises en considération.

Article 29:

Après une courte discussion, au cours de laquelle on s'est entendu pour supprimer les mots „de la section pour la procédure sommaire" et pour reconnaître que la question de la langue à employer par les parties doit être considérée dans chaque cas spécial, on tombe d'accord sur le texte suivant:

„La langue de la Cour est le Français, à moins qu'il n'en soit décidé autrement à la demande des parties."

Article 30:

Après un échange de vues entre les membres, au cours duquel on reconnaît la nécessité de stipuler que la partie demanderesse doit toujours, soit directement soit par l'intermédiaire de la Cour, notifier à la partie adverse l'objet du litige et les fondements des prétentions, et au cours duquel on reconnaît que, même au cas où les deux parties conviennent d'aller devant la Cour, l'une d'elles peut toujours être considérée comme demanderesse, les membres du Comité se mettent d'accord sur la rédaction suivante:

He pointed out that as a matter of fact th text of the project of the Five Powers, only re produced, with some modifications, the rules o procedure of the Convention of 1907.

Mr. ROOT recalled that at the first meetin of the Committee he had proposed to take tha Convention as a basis for discussion. However the Committee was now agreed to take the pro ject of the Five Powers as base.

Mr. Root thought that the two things amoun ted to about the same, especiall since i had been decided to consider the project of th Five Powers as the report of a sub-Committee o previous schemes.

Before leaving the United States, Mr. Roo and Mr. James Brown Scott had prepared table of synopses containing the provisions o all these texts regarding procedure, includin the project of the Five Powers. If the Committe had no objection he would have this table dis tributed. (See Annex 3).

The PRESIDENT thanked Mr. Root i name of the Committee. He wished it to b clearly understood, however, that it was onl in connection with the rules of procedure tha the project of the Five Powers would serve as a basis for discussion.

The dispositions of this project relating to pro cedure were then considered:

Article 29:

After a short discussion during which it wa agreed to omit the words "by the section o summary procedure", and to recognise that th question of the language to be used by the partie must be considered in each separate case, th following was agreed upon:

"The language to be used by the Court shall b French, unless at the request of the contesting parties it shall be otherwise decided".

Article 30:

After the members had discussed the matter it was agreed that the plaintiff must always eithe directly, or through the Court, notify the op posing party of the subject of the case and th grounds upon which the case was based. It wa also recognised that even when both partie agree to appeal to the Court, one of them migh always be considered as the plaintiff. The mem bers of the Committee agreed upon a wording corresponding to the following:

„La Cour est saisie, sous forme d'une requête, adressée par la partie demanderesse au greffe de la Cour. Cette requête indique l'objet du différend; elle désigne les parties en cause.

La Cour notifie d'office et sans délai à la partie adverse copie certifiée conforme de la requête."

Article 31:

Lors de la discussion de cet article on a considéré, entre autres, la question, débattue à une séance antérieure, du droit que les particuliers auraient de se faire représenter devant la Cour dans des cas où leurs Gouvernements auront pris fait et cause pour eux. On est d'accord pour reconnaître:

1. qu'il doit toujours y avoir un agent, chargé de représenter la partie, de conserver et rédiger les documents, de recevoir les notifications, etc.;
2. qu'il ne doit y avoir qu'un agent pour chaque partie et que, le Gouvernement étant toujours *dominus litis,* l'agent doit être le représentant du Gouvernement;
3. que la question du droit qu'un particulier, associé avec son Gouvernement dans un litige, aurait de se faire représenter dans le procès, est une question d'ordre intérieur, entre le particulier et le Gouvernement.

Le Comité a adopté la rédaction suivante:

„Les parties nomment des agents pour les représenter auprès de la Cour; elles peuvent en outre charger des conseils ou avocats de la défense de leurs droits et intérêts devant la Cour."

Article 32:

Au cours de la discussion sur cet article, on convient d'abord de faire de l'alinéa 4 un article séparé à insérer entre les articles 33 et 34 actuels. On convient ensuite que le mot „instruction", dont se sert l'article 32, prête à interprétation.

On reconnaît également qu'en général, il faut s'en tenir autant que possible aux textes adoptés en 1899 et en 1907 et par le projet des Cinq Puissances; on reconnaît spécialement l'utilité de maintenir la règle appliquée, dans la pratique, devant les tribunaux d'arbitrage, de joindre aux mémoires et contre-mémoires toutes les pièces justificatives.

MM. FERNANDES et ALTAMIRA signalent qu'on pourrait avec avantage tenir compte de la règle de procédure du droit ibérien, d'après

"Recourse to the Court shall take the form of an application addressed by the plaintiff party to the registry of the Court. Such application shall indicate the subject of the dispute; it shall also name the contesting Parties.

The Court shall forthwith furnish the opposing party with a certified copy of the application".

Article 31:

During the discussion of this Article, among others, the question raised at an earlier meeting, whether private individuals should have the right to be represented before the Court in cases which their Governments had adopted in their behalf, was discussed. It was agreed that:

1. there must always be an agent appointed to represent a party, to keep and prepare documents, and to receive communications etc.;
2. there must always be but one agent for each party, and as the Government is always the *dominus litis,* the agent must be the representative of the Government;
3. the right of a private individual, associated with his Government in a suit, to have an agent of his own, is a domestic question concerning the individual and the Government.

The Committee adopted the following:

"The parties shall appoint agents to represent them on the Court; further they may entrust the defence of their rights and interests before the Court to counsel or advocates".

Article 32:

During the discussion on this Article it was agreed first to make Paragraph 4 into a separate Article to be inserted between the present Articles 33 and 34. It was then agreed that the word "instruction" (preliminary proceedings), used in Article 32, is liable to misunderstanding.

It was also recognised that, generally speaking, the text adopted in 1899, 1907 and in the Five Powers' plan must be retained as far as possible; and the advantage of retaining the rule applied in practice before Courts of Arbitration, that is to say, attaching all supporting documents to cases and counter-cases, was especially recognised.

MM. FERNANDES and ALTAMIRA pointed out that use might with advantage be made of the rule of procedure of the Iberian Law,

laquelle le procès comprend trois phases distinctes: la position de la question, la présentation des preuves et les débats. La position de la question, d'autre part, comprend trois éléments; l'exposition des faits, le fondement de droit et la conclusion ou demande.

Sur la base de ce précédent, M. Fernandes soumet le projet de texte suivant: „L'instruction comprend trois phases:

1. la position de la question par l'introduction des mémoires et des conclusions des parties;
2. la production des preuves;
3. les débats oraux."

Le PRESIDENT hésite à approuver ici ce texte.

D'autre part, LORD PHILLIMORE et M. HAGERUP s'y rallient en principe. Il est convenu de réserver la rédaction finale de l'article 32, ainsi que celle de l'article à insérer après l'article 33. Cependant, on tombe d'accord sur les formules suivantes, qui serviront de base à la rédaction finale:

Article 32.

„La procédure devant la Cour comprend deux phases, l'une écrite, l'autre orale.

La phase écrite consiste dans la communication faite aux juges et à la partie adverse de conclusions détaillées et précises, des mémoires, des contre-mémoires, et, au besoin, des répliques.

Les parties joignent toutes pièces et tous documents invoqués par elles à l'appui de leur cause. Cette communication a lieu directement ou par l'intermédiaire du greffe, dans l'ordre et dans les délais déterminés par la Cour".

Article 33*bis*.

„La phase orale consiste dans l'audition de toute personne, témoin ou expert, que la Cour décide d'entendre à la demande des Parties, et dans les explications que les parties fournissent à la Cour, soit sur sa demande, soit spontanément".

M. HAGERUP remarque qu'il n'y a pas de divergences d'opinions sur le fond; les objections ne visent que des questions de rédaction. Il propose qu'un Comité de rédaction soit nommé pour examiner les règles de procédure.

Le PRESIDENT suggère l'idée de se réunir de nouveau à 5 heures de l'après-midi pour considérer les règles de procédure. Il demande au Secrétaire du Comité si le Secrétariat serait en mesure d'exécuter le surcroît de travail que cette réunion entraînerait.

which laid down that the process includes three distinct phases: the presentation of the case, the submission of evidence, and the debate. The presentation of the case also includes three points: the statement of facts, the legal grounds, and the conclusion.

Upon this basis, M. Fernandes submitted the following draft: "The preliminary proceedings shall include three phases:

1. the statement of the question by the introduction of the cases and conclusions of the parties;
2. the submission of evidence;
3. the oral discussions".

The PRESIDENT hesitated to approve here of this draft.

On the other hand, LORD PHILLIMORE and M. HAGERUP agreed with it on principle. It was agreed to postpone the final drafting of Article 32, and also of the article to be inserted after Article 33. However, the following clauses were agreed on to serve as basis for the final drafting:

Article 32.

"The procedure before the Court to be divided into 2 phases, one written, one oral.

The proceedings in writing to include the communication to the judges and to the opposing party of all detailed conclusions, cases, counter-cases, and, if necessary, replies.

The parties to attach thereto all evidence and documents used by them in support of the case. These communications to be made direct or through the registrar in the order and within the periods to be fixed by the Court".

Article 33*bis*.

"The oral phase shall consist of the hearing of all witnesses and experts whom the Court may decide to hear at the request of the parties, and of the explanations made by the parties to the Court, whether at its request or spontanously".

M. HAGERUP pointed out there was no difference of opinion on the principles, but simply on points of drafting. He proposed that a drafting Committee should be appointed to examine the rules of procedure.

The PRESIDENT suggested that they should meet again at 5 o'clock in the afternoon to consider the rules of procedure. He asked the Secretary of the Committee whether the Secretariat would be able to carry out the additional work caused by this meeting.

M. ANZILOTTI répond négativement.

Le PRESIDENT, dans ces circonstances, retire sa suggestion.

LORD PHILLIMORE propose également la nomination d'un Comité de rédaction. Tous les membres devraient envoyer par écrit à ce Comité leurs projets d'amendements au texte qui sert de base de discussion.

Le PRESIDENT exprime des doutes sur l'efficacité de cette méthode.

Mr. ROOT constate qu'il n'y a pas de divergences d'opinions véritables. Il croit que les divergences qui existent tirent en grande partie leur origine des différences qui existent entre le droit continental et le droit anglo-américain. Ces différences sont à la base de la plupart des controverses.

Pour cette raison, il suggère l'idée de laisser à un Comité comprenant un représentant de l'école continentale et un de l'école anglo-américaine, le soin de concilier les divergences.

M. DE LAPRADELLE ne partage pas l'avis de Mr. Root. Il croit qu'il s'agit seulement de trouver un meilleur texte pour exprimer des règles sur lesquelles on est en somme d'accord. Il pense partant qu'il est préférable de continuer la discussion des règles de procédure.

M. ADATCI est d'avis que la méthode suggérée par M. de Lapradelle est la plus pratique.

Le PRESIDENT dit que le Comité discutera lundi prochain les différents projets qui ont été soumis par les membres relativement à l'organisation de la Cour. Entre temps, la discussion sur les règles de procédure sera suspendue. Lorsque le Comité sera parvenu à un résultat quant à l'organisation, on discûtera la compétence de la Cour, question qui est du reste presque résolue. Enfin on discutera de nouveau les règles de procédure. Les discussions auront lieu de préférence en séance plénière.

LORD PHILLIMORE désire hâter les travaux du Comité. Dans cet esprit, il propose la nomination d'un petit Comité; il propose également que des séances aient lieu l'après-midi.

M. HAGERUP se rallie à la proposition de la nomination d'un Comité de rédaction qui aurait à s'occuper de la rédaction des textes à formuler par le Comité. Il croit aussi qu'il serait

M. ANZILOTTI replied in the negative.

The PRESIDENT therefore withdrew his proposal.

LORD PHILLIMORE also proposed the appointment of a drafting Committee. All members should send in writing to this sub-Committee their proposed amendments to the text which formed the basis of discussion.

The PRESIDENT doubted whether this method would be efficacious.

Mr. ROOT said there were no real differences of opinion. He thought that the differences which existed mainly derived from the difference which exists between Continental law and Anglo-American law. These differences are for the most part the basis of the controversies.

For this reason, he suggested that it should be left to a Committee consisting of a representative of the Continental school and one of the Anglo-American school to reconcile these differences.

M. DE LAPRADELLE did not agree with Mr. Root. He thought it was only a question of finding a better wording to express the rules that they had already virtually agreed upon. He thought therefore that it would be preferable to continue the discussion on the rules of procedure.

M. ADATCI thought that the method proposed by M. de Lapradelle was more practical.

The PRESIDENT said that the Committee would discuss on the following Monday the different proposals submitted by members concerning the organisation of the Court. Meanwhile, the discussion on the rules of procedure would be suspended. When the Committee had come to an agreement on the question of organisation, the competence of the Court would be considered; this question was almost decided. Lastly they would again take up the question of the rules of procedure. Discussions preferably should take place at full meetings of the Committee.

LORD PHILLIMORE wished to hasten the work of the Committee. Therefore he proposed to appoint a small sub-Committee. He also proposed that meetings should be held in the afternoon.

M. HAGERUP supported the proposal for the appointment of a drafting Committee which should undertake the preparation of all the Articles to be drawn up by the Committee. He

nécessaire de nommer dès maintenant un rapporteur. A cet égard il propose le nom de M. de Lapradelle. Le Comité de rédaction devrait être composé, selon M. Hagerup, du Président, du Vice-Président, du rapporteur et d'un membre anglais ou américain.

M. ALTAMIRA se rallie à l'opinion de Lord Phillimore dans son désir de hâter les travaux du Comité.

M. RICCI-BUSATTI suggère que le Comité pourrait se réunir l'après-midi; mais ces réunions devraient être seulement officieuses, et un procès-verbal ne serait pas nécessaire.

LORD PHILLIMORE se rallie à cette proposition.

M. RICCI-BUSATTI présente un texte relatif aux règles à appliquer par la Cour. Il a rédigé ce texte de façon à se rapprocher autant que possible du texte de Mr. Root et de Lord Phillimore. Il en donne lecture. Si l'on ne peut se mettre d'accord sur ce texte, il exprime le désir qu'un vote soit émis. (Voir annexe 4).

M. LODER, d'accord avec M. Hagerup, dit qu'il ne suffit pas que le Comité prépare un texte complet; il doit faire accompagner ce texte par un exposé des motifs, ou rapport, signé par autant de membres que possible.

LORD PHILLIMORE prie le Comité de ne s'occuper, pour le moment, que des règles de procédure. Ces règles pourraient être étudiées par un Comité, qui tiendrait des réunions officieuses en présence d'un secrétaire seulement et sans procès-verbal, ou avec un procès-verbal très succinct.

Le PRESIDENT se rallie à la proposition de Lord Phillimore et décide qu'il y aura une réunion officieuse lundi à 5 heures de l'après-midi au Palais de la Paix.

Les projets que les membres voudraient voir prendre en considération lors de cette réunion, doivent être présentés par écrit au Président.

La séance est levée à 12 heures 40 de l'après-midi.

Le Président:
(signé) Brn. DESCAMPS.

Le Secrétaire-Général:
(signé) D. ANZILOTTI.

thought also that it would be necessary to appoint at once the member to make the report. He proposed M. de Lapradelle for this appointment. The drafting Committee should be composed, in M. Hagerup's opinion, of the President, the Vice-President, the Reporter and an English or American member.

M. ALTAMIRA supported Lord Phillimore in his desire to hasten the work of the Committee.

M. RICCI-BUSATTI suggested that the Committee might meet in the afternoon, but that these meetings should only be unofficial, and that a procès-verbal would not be necessary.

LORD PHILLIMORE agreed to this proposal.

M. RICCI-BUSATTI presented a text concerning the rules to be applied by the Court. He had prepared this text so as to agree as far as possible with the wording adopted by Mr. Root and Lord Phillimore. He read his proposal. If the text could not be agreed on, he wished that a vote should be taken upon it. (See Annex 4).

M. LODER, supported by M. Hagerup, said that it was not sufficient for the Committee to prepare a complete text; this text must be accompanied by a statement of reasons, or report, signed by as many of the members as possible.

LORD PHILLIMORE requested that the Committee confine themselves for the moment to the question of the rules of procedure. These rules might be considered by a sub-Committee at unofficial meetings with only one Secretary and no procès-verbal, or with a very short procès-verbal.

The PRESIDENT agreed with Lord Phillimore's proposal and decided that there should be an unofficial meeting at 5 o'clock on Monday afternoon at the Peace Palace.

Any proposals that members wished to have considered at this meeting must be sent in writing to the President.

The meeting closed at 12.40 p.m.

The President:
(signed) Brn. DESCAMPS.

The Secretary-General:
(signed) D. ANZILOTTI.

ANNEXE No. I.

Texte amendé présenté par Mr. Root. [1])

(Voir annexe 3 au procès-verbal de la 13ième séance.)

Les règles à appliquer par la Cour, dans les limites de la compétence ci-dessus prévue, pour la solution des différends internationaux sont les suivantes, dans l'ordre successif où elles s'imposent à son examen:

1. le droit international conventionnel, soit général, soit spécial, comme constituant des règles expressément adoptées par les Etats parties au litige;
2. la coutume internationale comme attestation d'une pratique commune des nations, acceptée par elles comme loi;
3. les principes généraux de droit reconnus par les peuples civilisés;
4. l'autorité des décisions judiciaires et les opinions des publicistes, comme organes d'application et de développement du droit.

1) Ce texte a été provisoirement adopté sauf rédaction finale en seconde lecture, et avec les modifications suivantes:
a) Préambule; lire: „Les règles *de droit* à appliquer" etc.
b) No. 4; lire: „l'autorité des décisions judiciaires et *la doctrine des publicistes les plus qualifiés des différentes nations*, comme" etc.

ANNEX No. I.

Amended text submitted by Mr. Root. [1])

(See Annex 3 to Procès-Verbal of the 13th meeting.)

The following rules are to be applied by the Court within the limits of its competence, as described above, for the settlement of international disputes; they will be considered in the undermentioned order:

1. conventional international law, whether general or special, being rules expressly adopted by the States which are parties to a dispute;
2. international custom, being recognised practice between nations accepted by them as law;
3. the general principles of law recognised by civilised nations;
4. the authority of judicial decisions and the opinions of writers as a means for the application and development of law.

1) This text was provisionally adopted, except as concerned final drafting for the second reading, and with the following alterations:
a) Preamble; read: "The following rules *of law* are to be applied".
b) No. 4; read: „the authority of judicial decisions, and the *doctrines of the best qualified writers of the various nations*, as" etc.

ANNEXE No. 2.

Déclaration de M. Fernandes.

Il me semble indispensable de trouver à tout prix un terrain d'entente pour concilier les points de vue exprimés, d'un côté, par M. le Président, et, de l'autre, par Mr. Root.

La question en vaut la peine, car elle engage l'avenir de la Cour.

Mr. Root s'oppose, en s'appuyant sur d'excellentes raisons, à ce que les juges, sortant de leur rôle spécifique, puissent, non seulement appliquer la loi internationale, mais en quelque manière la créer. Il croit qu'un grand État ne pourra jamais adhérer à un système qui l'expose à voir ses différends tranchés par l'application d'une règle de droit qui n'a pas reçu son approbation, ou — ce qui serait plus grave — dont il a contesté la légitimité d'une façon systématique et traditionnelle.

Je crois que l'honorable Mr. Root pourrait en dire autant de n'importe quel État, et peut-être à plus forte raison, de ceux qui sont dépourvus de puissance militaire.

Mais, d'autre part, il faut reconnaître ce qu'il y a de vrai et de sage dans la proposition de M. le Président, surtout si on l'interprête par l'éloquent et généreux discours qu'il a adressé hier au Comité.

Car il est manifeste que si, en mettant à part le droit conventionnel, les juges restent confinés dans le domaine strict de la coutume internationale (et telle est la pensée de Mr. Root), ils se verront enlever la possibilité de rendre justice dans nombre de cas qui impliquent des rapports de droit entre les Etats en litige et, de ce fait, nettement susceptibles d'une décision judiciaire.

Je vise les différends qui, sans être régis par des coutumes — soit parce qu'ils sont sans précédents, soit parce que les précédents ne sont pas assez nombreux et suivis pour qu'il s'en dégage une règle coutumière — relèvent cependant de certains principes de droit, supérieurs à toute controverse.

La variété multiforme de la vie quotidienne, en dépassant toujours les prévisions du législateur, présente fréquemment de telles espèces aux tribunaux nationaux; et je n'exagère pas si je dis que, le plus souvent, le juge ne trouve pas de prescription légale *topique* pour trancher la question, et se trouve dans la nécessité de la juger

ANNEX No. 2.

Statement of M. Fernandes.

It seems to me essential to find at any cost a basis for conciliating the views expressed on the one hand by the President and on the other by Mr. Root.

The question merits the effort because the whole future of the Court depends upon it.

For very good reasons. Mr. Root opposes granting to the judges — in addition to their ordinary task of applying international law, — the power to some extent to create it. He believes that a great Power could never agree to a system, which would lay it open to having its disputes settled by the application of a rule which had not been approved by it; or, what will be more serious, of a rule whose legality it had systematically contested at all times.

I think that Mr. Root might say the same thing of any State whatever, and perhaps with even more reason of those not provided with military power.

But, on the other hand, all that is true and wise in the President's proposal must be recognised, especially if one considers it in the light of the eloquent and noble speech which he addressed to the Committee yesterday.

For it is obvious that if the judges are strictly confined, apart from law derived from Conventions and Treaties, to the use of international custom (and such is Mr. Root's idea) the possibility of administering justice in many cases which involve legal relations between the States concerned, and from that fact clearly capable of legal decision, is taken away from them.

I include disputes which, though not regulated by usage — either because there is no precedent or perhaps the precedents are not numerous or consecutive enough to establish custom — nevertheless are founded on certain incontrovertible principles of law.

The many sides of daily life which constantly present cases unprovided for by legislation, often bring such cases before National Courts; and I should not exaggerate if I said, that more often than not, the judge cannot find a rule intended to deal with the question, and finds it necessary to pass sentence on a rule derived from the general principles which guide and give life to national law. Nor should I exaggerate if I said.

d'après une règle déduite des principes généraux qui inspirent et vivifient le droit national. Je n'exagère pas non plus en disant que les sentences ainsi fondées sont en règle générale les plus justes; car les principes s'inspirent toujours de la justice, tandis que la loi formelle s'en écarte souvent.

Qu'est-ce à dire? Que le juge, dans l'hypothèse envisagée, a fait œuvre de législateur et a *créé* une règle juridique? Nullement: il s'est borné à mettre en lumière une règle *latente*, selon l'expression de Ihering. Et cette règle là est légitime, car elle était contenue logiquement dans un principe auquel le consentement national était acquis.

Ce qui est vrai et légitime dans le domaine national, par des raisons qui tiennent de la logique, et non par concession arbitraire de la souveraineté, ne peut pas être faux et illégitime dans le domaine international, où, d'ailleurs, la législature faisant défaut et la règle coutumière étant de formation très lente, la nécessité pratique d'admettre l'empire d'une telle vérité s'imposera davantage. Il est tout à fait superflu de donner des exemples de règles qui ne sont établies ni par convention ni par coutume, et pourtant s'imposent irrésistiblement à la raison des peuples par la force des principes desquels on les a déduites.

Je demande toutefois à en citer un qui est particulièrement frappant parce qu'il illustre cette doctrine à la fois *ad rem* et *ad hominem*: c'est celui que nous trouvons dans la „déclaration américaine des droits et devoirs des Nations" et surtout dans les commentaires de cette déclaration dont la paternité revient, si je ne me trompe, au très compétent Mr. Brown Scott, ici présent.

Je crois que le projet donnerait satisfaction aux deux thèses en présence en accordant à la Cour de justice le pouvoir de juger — à défaut de droit conventionnel ou coutumier — selon les principes de droit international non rejetés avant le différend par la tradition juridique de l'un des Etats en conflit.

Cette formule, me semble-t-il, écarterait l'objection de l'honorable Mr. Root, et en même temps éviterait à la Cour de devenir, dans de nombreux cas, „le greffe de la violence des forts contre les faibles", selon la phrase aussi vive que juste de M. de Lapradelle.

that the sentences thus passed were generally the more just; because the principles are always based on justice, while strict law often departs from it.

What does this amount to? Has the judge under these circumstances acted as a legislator and created a juridical rule? Not at all, he has merely brought to light a *latent* rule, as Ihering has put it. Such a rule is quite legitimate because it is logically contained in a principle already recognised by the Nation concerned.

What is true and legitimate in national affairs, for reasons founded in logic and not in the arbitrary exercise of sovereignty, cannot be false and illegal in international affairs, where, moreover, legislation is lacking and customary law is being formed very slowly, so that the practical necessity of recognising the application of such principles is much greater. It is quite superfluous to give examples of rules not established either by convention or custom, which nevertheless must inevitably be accepted in the minds of the Nations, because of the principles on which they are based.

I desire, nevertheless, to mention one which is particularly striking because it illustrates this theory both *ad rem* and *ad hominem*: it is that of the "American declaration of rights and duties of Nations" and especially the commentaries on this declaration, a work due, if I am not mistaken, to the very able lawyer Mr. James Brown Scott, who is present.

I think that the project would give satisfaction to both the opposing theses in giving to the Court of justice the power to base its sentences — in the absence of any conventional or customary law — on those principles of international law which, before the dispute, were not rejected by the legal traditions of one of the States concerned in the dispute.

It seems to me that this formula would remove Mr. Root's objection and at the same time would prevent the Court from becoming in many cases a "registry for the high-handed acts of the strong against the weak", as M. de Lapradelle has said so expressively and well.

ANNEXE No. 3.

Projet des Cinq Puissances neutres, pour l'établissement d'une Cour Internationale de Justice.

Annotations.

Titre I.

Du Caractère général de la Cour.

Titre II.

De l'Organisation de la Cour.

Titre III.

De la Compétence de la Cour.

Titre IV

(basé sur et donnant exécution à l'article 22 du Projet de Convention 1907).

De la Procédure de la Cour.

Article 29.

Nouveau; cf. Art. 23, Projet de Convention 1907; Art. 7, Projet de La Haye, Annexe 2, 1910 (Une Cour de Justice Internationale, p. 142); Art. 24, Convention Cour des Prises 1907.

Article 30.

Par. 1, Nouveau; cf. Art. 28, Par. 1, Convention Cour des Prises, 1907.

Par. 2, cf. Art. 32, Convention Cour des Prises, 1907.

Article 31.

Basé sur Art. 37, Convention sur le Règlement Pacifique, 1899; Art. 62, Par. 1 et 2, idem, 1907; Art. 25, Convention Cour des Prises, 1907.

Article 32.

Basé sur Art. 39, Convention sur le Règlement Pacifique, 1899; Art. 63, idem, 1907; cf. Art. 34, Convention Cour des Prises, 1907.

Article 33.

Basé sur Art. 40, Convention sur le Règlement Pacifique, 1899; Art. 64, idem, 1907; cf. Art. 34, Par. 3, Convention Cour des Prises, 1907.

ANNEX No. 3.

Five Power plan for the establishment of an International Court of Justice.

Annotations.

Title I.

General Character of the Court.

Title II.

Organisation of the Court.

Title III.

Jurisdiction of the Court.

Title IV

(is based upon and gives effect to Article 22, Draft Convention, 1907).

Procedure of the Court.

Article 29.

New; cf. Art. 23, Draft Convention. 1907; Art. 7, Hague Project, Annex 2, 1910 (Une Cour de Justice Internationale, p. 142); Art. 24, Prize Court Convention, 1907.

Article 30.

Paragraph 1, new; cf. Art. 28, Paragraph 1, Prize Court Convention, 1907.

Paragraph 2, cf. Art. 32, Prize Court Convention, 1907.

Article 31.

Based upon Art. 37, Pacific Settlement Convention, 1899; Art. 62, Paragraphs 1 and 2, idem, 1907; Art. 25, Prize Court Convention, 1907.

Article 32.

Based upon Art. 39, Pacific Settlement Convention, 1899; Art. 63, idem, 1907; cf. Art. 34, Prize Court Convention, 1907.

Article 33.

Based upon Art. 40, Pacific Settlement Convention, 1899; Art. 64, idem, 1907; cf. Art. 34, Paragraph 3, Prize Court Convention, 1907.

Article 34.

Par. 1, basé sur Art. 26, Par. 1, Projet Convention, 1907; Art. 41, Par. 1, Convention sur le Règlement Pacifique, 1899; Art. 66, Par. 1, idem, 1907; Art. 38, Par. 1, Convention Cour des Prises, 1907.

Par. 2, cf. Art. 41, Par. 2, Convention sur le Règlement Pacifique, 1899; Art. 66, Par. 2, idem, 1907; Arts. 35 et 39, Par. 1, Convention Cour des Prises, 1907.

Article 35.

Basé sur Art. 41, Par. 3, Convention sur le Règlement Pacifique, 1899; Art. 66, Par. 3, idem, 1907; Art. 39, Par. 2, Convention Cour des Prises, 1907.

Article 36.

Par. 1, basé sur Art. 42, Convention sur le Règlement Pacifique, 1899; Art. 67, idem, 1907.

Par. 2, basé sur Art. 43, Convention sur le Règlement Pacifique, 1899; Art. 68, idem, 1907.

Article 37.

Pratiquement identique à Art. 44, Convention sur le Règlement Pacifique, 1899; Art. 69, idem, 1907.

Article 38.

Par. 1, 1ère phrase basée sur Art. 45, Convention sur le Règlement Pacifique, 1899; Art. 70, idem, 1907; 2nde phrase, cf. Art. 23, Par. 2, 1907, Convention sur le Règlement Pacifique.

Par. 2, pratiquement identique à Art. 46, Convention sur le Règlement Pacifique, 1899; Art. 71, idem, 1907.

Article 39.

Cf. Art. 20 et 21, Convention sur le Règlement Pacifique, 1907; Art. 11, Par. 2, Projet de Convention, 1907.

Article 40.

Substantiellement identique Art. 47, Convention sur le Règlement Pacifique, 1899; Art. 72, idem, 1907.

Article 41.

Pratiquement identique à Art. 49, Convention sur le Règlement Pacifique, 1899; Art. 74, idem, 1907.

Article 42.

Basé sur Art. 75, Convention sur le Règlement Pacifique, 1907.

Article 34.

Paragraph 1, based upon Art. 26, Paragraph 1, Draft Convention, 1907; Art. 41, Paragraph 1, Pacific Settlement Convention, 1899; Art. 66, Paragraph 1, idem, 1907; Art. 38, Paragraph 1, Prize Court Convention, 1907.

Paragraph 2, cf. Art. 41, Paragraph 2, Pacific Settlement Convention, 1899; Art. 66, Paragraph 2, idem, 1907; Art. 35 and 39, Paragraph 1, Prize Court Convention, 1907.

Article 35.

Based upon Art. 41, Paragraph 3, Pacific Settlement Convention, 1899; Art. 66, Paragraph 3, idem, 1907; Art. 39, Paragraph 2, Prize Court Convention, 1907.

Article 36.

Paragraph 1, based upon Art. 42, Pacific Settlement Convention, 1899; Art. 67, idem, 1907.

Paragraph 2, based upon Art. 43, Pacific Settlement Convention, 1899; Art. 68, idem, 1907.

Article 37.

Practically identical with Art. 44, Pacific Settlement Convention, 1899; Art. 69, idem, 1907.

Article 38.

Paragraph 1, first sentence based upon Art. 45, Pacific Settlement Convention, 1899; Art. 70, idem, 1907; second sentence, cf. Art. 23, Paragraph 2, 1907, Pacific Settlement Convention.

Paragraph 2, practically identical with Art. 46, Pacific Settlement Convention, 1899; Art. 71, idem, 1907.

Article 39.

Cf. Art. 20 and 21, Pacific Settlement Convention, 1907; Art. 11, Paragraph 2, Draft Convention, 1907.

Article 40.

Identical in substance with Art. 47, Pacific Settlement Convention, 1899; Art. 72, idem, 1907.

Article 41.

Practically identical with Art. 49, Pacific Settlement Convention, 1899; Art. 74, idem, 1907.

Article 42.

Based upon Art. 75, Pacific Settlement Convention, 1907.

Article 43.

Basé sur Art. 40, Convention Cour des Prises, 1907.

Article 44.

Identique à Art. 50, Convention sur le Règlement Pacifique, 1899; Art. 77, idem, 1907.

Article 45.

Par. 1, pratiquement identique à Art. 78, Convention sur le Règlement Pacifique, 1907.

Par. 2, Basé sur Art. 51, Par. 1, 2me phrase, Convention sur le Règlement Pacifique, 1899; Art. 78, Par. 2, idem, 1907.

La dernière phrase semble être nouvelle.

Cf. Par. 1 et 2 à Art. 27, Projet de Convention, 1907, et Art. 43, Convention Cour des Prises, 1907.

Article 46.

Par. 1, pratiquement identique à Art. 28, Projet de Convention, 1907; Basé sur Art. 79, Convention sur le Règlement Pacifique, 1907; pareil en principe à Art. 44, Convention Cour des Prises, 1907.

Par. 2, pratiquement identique à Art. 53, Convention sur le Règlement Pacifique, 1899; Art. 80, idem, 1907; cf. Art. 45, Par. 1, Convention Cour des Prises, 1907.

Par. 3, basé sur Art. 52, Par. 2, Convention sur le Règlement Pacifique, 1899.

Article 47.

Par. 1, pratiquement identique à Art. 54, Convention sur le Règlement Pacifique, 1899; Art. 81, idem, 1907; cf. Art. 9, Convention Cour des Prises, 1907.

Par. 2, basé sur principes exprimés Art. 55, Convention sur le Règlement Pacifique, 1899; Art. 83, idem, 1907.

Article 48.

Par. 1, basé sur principe exprimé Art. 56, Convention sur le Règlement Pacifique, 1899; Art. 84, idem, 1907.

Article 49.

Par. 1, pratiquement identique à Art. 25, Par. 1, Projet de Convention, 1907; Art. 27, Par. 1, Convention Cour des Prises, 1907.

Par. 2, la 1ère phrase est nouvelle.

La 2nde phrase est pratiquement identique à Art. 25, Par. 2, 1ère phrase, du Projet de Convention, 1907; Identique en principe et pres-

Article 43.

Based upon Art. 40, Prize Court Convention, 1907.

Article 44.

Identical with Art. 50, Pacific Settlement Convention, 1899; Art. 77, idem, 1907.

Article 45.

Paragraph 1, practically identical with Art. 78, Pacific Settlement Convention, 1907.

Paragraph 2, based upon Art. 51, Paragraph 1, second sentence, Pacific Settlement Convention, 1899; Art. 78, Paragraph 2, idem, 1907.

Last sentence appears to be new.

Cf. Paragraphs 1 and 2 with Art. 27, Draft Convention, 1907, and Art. 43, Prize Court Convention, 1907.

Article 46.

Paragraph 1, practically identical with Art. 28, Draft Convention, 1907; based upon Art. 79, Pacific Settlement Convention, 1907; same in principle as Art. 44, Prize Court Convention, 1907.

Paragraph 2, practically identical with Art. 53, Pacific Settlement Convention, 1899; Art. 80, idem, 1907; cf. Art. 45, Paragraph 1, Prize Court Convention, 1907.

Paragraph 3, based upon Art. 52, Paragraph 2, Pacific Settlement Convention, 1899.

Article 47.

Paragraph 1, practically identical with Art. 54, Pacific Settlement Convention, 1899; Art. 81, idem, 1907; cf. Art. 9, Prize Court Convention, 1907.

Paragraph 2, based upon principles set forth in Art. 55, Pacific Settlement Convention, 1899; Art. 83, idem, 1907.

Article 48.

Paragraph 1, based upon principle laid down in Art. 56, Pacific Settlement Convention, 1899; Art. 84, idem, 1907.

Article 49.

Paragraph 1, practically identical with Art. 25, Paragraph 1, Draft Convention of 1907; Art. 27, Paragraph 1, Prize Court Convention, 1907.

Paragraph 2, first sentence is new.

Second sentence is practically identical with Art. 25, Paragraph 2, first sentence, of Draft Convention, 1907; identical in principle and

qu'identique en forme à Art. 27, Par. 2, 2me phrase, de la Convention Cour des Prises, 1907.

Par. 3, pratiquement identique à Art. 25, Par. 3, Projet de Convention, 1907; identique en substance à Art. 27, Par. 3, Convention Cour des Prises, 1907.

Par. 4, pratiquement identique à Art. 25, Par. 4, Projet de Convention, 1907, et à Art. 27, Par. 4, Convention Cour des Prises, 1907; cf. Art. 76, Convention sur le Règlement Pacifique, 1907.

Article 50.

Basé sur Art. 29, 1ère phrase Projet de Convention, 1907; Art. 57, Convention sur le Règlement Pacifique, 1899; Art. 85, idem, 1907.

Article 51.

Nouveau; basé sur principe contenu Art. 89 et 90, Convention sur le Règlement Pacifique, 1907.

Titre V.

De l'effet des Sentences de la Cour.

Titre VI.

Dispositions finales.

nearly identical in form with Art. 27, Paragraph 2, second sentence of Prize Court Convention, 1907.

Paragraph 3, practically identical with Art. 25, Paragraph 3, Draft Convention, 1907; Identical in substance with Art. 27, Paragraph 3, Prize Court Convention, 1907.

Paragraph 4, practically identical with Art. 25, Paragraph 4, Draft Convention, 1907, and with Art. 27, Paragraph 4, Prize Court Convention, 1907; cf. Art. 76, Pacific Settlement Convention, 1907.

Article 50.

Based upon Art. 29, first clause, Draft Convention, 1907; Art. 57, Pacific Settlement Convention, 1899; Art. 85, idem, 1907.

Article 51.

New; based upon principle contained in Art. 89 and 90, Pacific Settlement Convention, 1907.

Title V.

Effect of Sentences of the Court.

Title VI.

Final Provisions.

ANNEXE No. 4.

Propositions présentées par le Président et Lord Phillimore, avec amendements de M. Ricci-Busatti.

(Voir annexe 3 au procès-verbal de la 13ième séance.)

Les règles à appliquer par la Cour pour la solution de tout différend international dont elle sera saisie, découlent des sources suivantes:

1. les conventions internationales, soit générales soit spéciales, comme constituant des règles expressément adoptées par les Etats parties au litige;
2. la coutume internationale, comme attestation d'une pratique commune des dits Etats, acceptée par eux comme loi;
3. les principes généraux de droit reconnus par les peuples civilisés.

La Cour tiendra compte des décisions judiciaires émises par elle dans des cas analogues et des opinions des publicistes les plus qualifiés des différents pays, comme organes d'application et de développement du droit.

ANNEX No. 4.

Proposals presented by the President and Lord Phillimore, as amended by M. Ricci-Busatti.

(See Annex 3 to Procès-Verbal of 13th meeting.)

The rules to be applied by the Court for the settlement of any international dispute brought before it, arise from the following sources:

1. international conventions, either general or special, as constituting rules expressly adopted by the States which are parties to a dispute;
2. international custom as evidence of common practice among said States, accepted by them as law;
3. the general principles of law recognised by civilised nations.

The Court shall take into consideration the judicial decisions rendered by it in analogous cases, and the opinions of the best qualified writers of the various countries, as means for the application and development of law.

16IÈME SÉANCE (non-publique), tenue au Palais de la Paix, à La Haye, le 5 juillet 1920.

Présidence de M. le BARON DESCAMPS.

Sont présents: tous les membres du Comité (à l'exception de M. Bevilaqua); M. Fernandes; Mr. James Brown Scott; les secrétaires particuliers du Baron Descamps et de M. Adatci; les membres du Secrétariat.

La séance est ouverte à 9.40 heures du matin.

Le PRESIDENT exprime l'avis que le moment est venu pour le Comité de nommer un rapporteur. Il propose le nom de M. de Lapradelle.

Cette proposition est adoptée à l'unanimité.

M. DE LAPRADELLE remercie les membres du Comité de la confiance qu'ils lui témoignent. Sur l'invitation du Président, M. de Lapradelle prend place à ses côtés.

M. HAGERUP rappelle la proposition qui avait été faite lors de la dernière séance, de nommer un Comité de rédaction qui serait composé du Président, du Vice-Président, du Rapporteur et d'un membre anglais ou américain. Les membres anglais et américain du Comité s'arrangeraient eux-mêmes pour désigner celui qui fera partie du Comité de rédaction.

M. Hagerup soumet de nouveau cette proposition. Elle est adoptée à l'unanimité.

Le PRESIDENT, conformément à l'ordre du jour adopté pour la séance, ouvre la discussion sur la question de l'organisation de la Cour. Il a fait distribuer aux membres un avant-projet qui a le caractère d'une transaction entre les diverses opinions qui se sont manifestées. (Annexe 1er). Il croit qu'il sera facile de combiner la discussion de cet avant-projet avec celle des projets déposés par Mr. Root et Lord Phillimore, et par M. Ricci-Busatti.

Le Président appelle l'attention du Comité sur le fait que l'article 5 de son projet est relatif aux mêmes questions que celles qui sont traitées dans les articles 1 à 9 du projet Root—Phillimore et dans les articles 2 et 3, 6 et 7 du projet Ricci-Busatti. Il explique ensuite le premier article de son avant-projet. Il croit qu'il est

16TH MEETING (Private), held at the Peace Palace, the Hague, on July 5th, 1920.

BARON DESCAMPS in the chair.

Present: all members of the Committee (with the exception of M. Bevilaqua); M. Fernandes; Mr. James Brown Scott; the private secretaries of Baron Descamps and M. Adatci; the members of the Secretariat.

The meeting opened at 9.40 a.m.

The PRESIDENT said that he thought that the time had come when it would be useful for the Committee to appoint a rapporteur. He suggested the name of M. de Lapradelle.

The President's proposal was unanimously adopted.

M. DE LAPRADELLE thanked the members of the Committee for the confidence placed in him. At the invitation of the President, M. de Lapradelle took a seat at his side.

M. HAGERUP recalled the proposal he had made at the last meeting: to appoint a drafting Committee composed of the President, Vice-President, the Rapporteur and an English or American representative; the English and American members of the Committee to arrange among themselves who should take part in the work of the drafting Committee.

M. Hagerup again put forward this proposal; it was unanimously adopted.

The PRESIDENT, in accordance with the Agenda adopted for the meeting, opened the discussion of the question of the organisation of the Court. He had had distributed to the members a draft scheme which was in the nature of a compromise between the various motions which had been put forward. (Annex 1). He thought it would be easy to combine the discussion of this draft scheme with that of the schemes submitted by Mr. Root and Lord Phillimore, and by M. Ricci-Busatti.

The President called the Committee's attention to the fact that Article 5 of his project covers the same question as Articles 1 to 9 of the Root—Phillimore proposal and as Articles 2, 3, 6 and 7 of the Ricci-Busatti proposal. He then explained the first article of his

utile de constater que les anciennes institutions juridictionnelles sont maintenues, et d'indiquer la place de la nouvelle Cour au milieu d'elles. Il est utile également de faire ressortir le progrès réalisé par l'institution de la nouvelle Cour; c'est à cet effet qu'il a expressément marqué que la Cour est directement accessible aux parties et qu'elle est appelée à assurer la continuité et le progrès de la jurisprudence internationale des arrêts. Les mots „des arrêts" ont été ajoutés à cause de la divergence qui existe entre la signification du mot jurisprudence en anglais et en français.

M. ADATCI a parcouru l'avant-projet du Président et constate qu'il renferme beaucoup de choses nouvelles; mais le temps ne lui a pas permis de l'examiner à fond. Par contre, il a pu étudier d'une façon plus approfondie les projets Root—Phillimore et Ricci-Busatti. Il préfère ce dernier à cause de la stipulation contenue à l'article 3, et qui est indispensable si l'on veut assurer la viabilité de la Cour. Il voudrait qu'on prît ce projet comme base de discussion. Cependant, il peut aussi accepter le projet Root—Phillimore à condition qu'on y insère, après l'article 11, l'article 3 du projet Ricci-Busatti. Il demande à M. Ricci-Busatti de bien vouloir informer le Comité si cette solution lui agrée.

Le PRESIDENT propose que, au cours de la discussion qui vient de s'ouvrir sur la question de l'organisation de la Cour, on prenne en considération simultanément les 3 projets qui ont été présentés. Il pense qu'il serait utile d'insérer au commencement du projet qui sera adopté une déclaration générale analogue à celle qui est contenue à l'article 1er de son avant-projet.

M. RICCI-BUSATTI croit que l'idée suggérée par M. Adatci touche au fond de la question, tandis que celle du Président n'a trait qu'à des questions de rédaction. Pour le moment, il croit devoir simplement maintenir l'article 3 de son projet, tout en se réservant d'y insister s'il le juge à propos lorsque la question sera abordée dans la discussion générale. Il se borne pour l'instant à constater que cet article peut se rattacher à tous les systèmes.

M. Ricci-Busatti partage l'avis du Président sur l'utilité d'une déclaration générale rappelant les institutions juridictionnelles existantes: il a fait lui-même une proposition du même genre. Par contre, il ne juge pas opportun d'in-

draft scheme. He thought it was advisable to state that the former institutions of justice were te be maintained, and to indicate generally the position of the new Court in the system. It would also be desirable to show the progress achieved by the institution of the new Court; for this reason he had expressly stated that the Court would be directly accessible to parties, and that it was its duty to ensure continuity and progress in international jurisprudence based on judgments; these last words had been added in view of the difference between the meaning of the word jurisprudence in English and French.

M. ADATCI had looked through the draft scheme of the President and had seen that it contained many new features; but he had not had time to examine it thoroughly. On the other hand he had been able to study more deeply the Root—Phillimore and Ricci-Busatti projects. He preferred the latter, because of the stipulation contained in Article 3, which cannot be dispensed with if it is desired to make the Court practicable. He wished that this project should be taken as a basis for discussion. However, he was also prepared to accept the Root—Phillimore project, provided that Article 3 of the Ricci-Busatti project was inserted after Article 11. He asked M. Ricci-Busatti to be so good as to inform the Committee whether this solution met with his approval.

The PRESIDENT proposed that, during the discussion just opened on the question of the Court's organisation, all three of the projects presented should be considered simultaneously. He thought that it would be advisable to insert at the beginning of the project to be adopted, a general declaration similar to that contained in the first Article of his draft scheme.

M. RICCI-BUSATTI thought that the idea expressed by M. Adatci affected the heart of the question, while the President's dealt only with matters of drafting. For the moment he felt that he should only support Article 3 of his project, though he reserved the right to insist on it if he saw fit when the question was dealt with in the general discussion. For the present he would limit himself to saying that this Article was equally suitable for inclusion in any of the systems.

M. Ricci-Busatti agreed with the President that a general declaration mentioning the existing institutions of justice would be advisable. He had himself made a proposal of the

sérer les autres déclara...... générales contenues dans le premier article de l'avant-projet du Président.

same kind; on the other hand, he did not think that the other general declarations contained in the first Article of the President's draft scheme were advisable.

Mr. ROOT fait valoir que les dispositions des différents projets visent toutes à répondre à une seule question fondamentale: par quel collège électoral les membres de la Cour seront-ils élus? Beaucoup de ces dispositions diffèrent par la forme plutôt que par le fond. Puisqu'il en est ainsi, Mr. Root propose que le Comité prenne une décision sur la question vitale du mode d'élection des juges. Il ne restera plus ensuite qu'une question de rédaction, toutes les autres questions dépendent dans une large mesure de la façon dont sera résolue la question principale. Mr. Root désire donc faire une proposition; il ne la fait pas, dit-il, sans une certaine hésitation, dûe à son manque d'expérience en ce qui concerne les méthodes européennes de procédure. Il propose qu'avant d'aborder les détails, le Comité prenne une décision sur la question suivante: les membres de la Cour seront-ils élus par l'Assemblée et le Conseil, dans les conditions proposées par le Comité, ou le seront-ils par l'Assemblée seule, d'après une liste dressée par un collège de délégués de la Cour Permanente d'Arbitrage? Mr. Root prie le Président de vouloir bien s'assurer si la procédure qu'il propose agrée au Comité.

Mr. ROOT pointed out that all the provisions of the various projects were intended to answer one single fundamental question: What electoral body was to elect the members of Court? Many of the dispositions differed rather in form than in principle. Since this is the case, Mr. Root proposed that the Committee should come to a decision upon the vital question, the method of electing the judges. There would remain then only the question of drafting; all the other questions largely depended upon the way in which the main question was settled. Mr. Root desired therefore to make a proposal. He did not do so, he said, without a certain amount of hesitation due to his lack of experience in European methods of procedure. Mr. Root proposed that before dealing with the details the Committee should decide on the following question: shall the members of the Court be elected by the Assembly and the Council, under the conditions proposed by the Committee, or shall they be elected by the Assembly alone from lists prepared by a college of delegates from the Permanent Court of Arbitation? Mr. Root asked the President to be so good as to make sure that the proposed procedure was agreeable to the Committee.

Le PRESIDENT pense avec Mr. Root qu'il est désirable de résoudre tout d'abord la question de la nomination des juges.

Il rappelle qu'on se trouve en présence de 3 propositions: celle des articles 1 à 9 du projet Root—Phillimore, celle de l'article 3 du projet Ricci-Busatti et celle de l'article 5 de son propre avant-projet. Il croit que toutes ces propositions peuvent être discutées en même temps, sauf à déterminer, au moment du vote, la manière de se prononcer successivement sur chacune d'elles.

La proposition que vient de soumettre Mr. Root relativement à la procédure à suivre, équivaut à une proposition de procéder à un vote de principe. Un vote de cette nature présente des inconvénients, car il obligerait peut-être certains membres à s'abstenir: tel serait, par exemple, le cas du Président. A son avis, les votes doivent porter sur des textes. Si, cependant, Mr. Root insiste, qu'il veuille bien formuler sa proposition par écrit, et le Président la soumettra au Comité.

The PRESIDENT agreed with Mr. Root that it was very desirable to commence by settling the question of the nomination of judges.

He said that they had before them three proposals: first that contained in Articles 1—9 of the Root—Phillimore plan; second, that contained in Article 3 of the Ricci-Busatti plan; and third, that contained in Article 5 of his own plan. He thought that all these proposals could be discussed at the same time, the order in which they should be voted on to be determined at the moment of voting.

The proposal made by Mr. Root concerning the procedure to be adopted amounted to a proposal to take a vote on the question of principle. Such a vote would cause difficulties because it might compel some members to abstain from voting; as for example the President. In his opinion votes must be taken upon the texts. If, however, Mr. Root insisted, the President requested that he kindly put his plan in writing, and the President would submit it to the Committee.

Mr. ROOT rédige une formule et en donne lecture (voir annexe 2).

Le PRESIDENT adoptera la procédure sur laquelle le Comité se mettra d'accord. Mais il fait observer qu'en adoptant la proposition de Mr. Root on votera sur le principe sans prendre en considération les modalités qui, pour certains membres, rendraient seules le principe acceptable. En discutant au contraire des textes complets, on pourrait, par exemple, examiner si la représentation des grandes Puissances est suffisamment garantie dans tel ou tel projet. Aussi préfère-t-il que la discussion porte sur le texte des trois projets. Les auteurs de ces projets seraient invités à les expliquer, fournissant ainsi aux autres membres du Comité l'occasion de les critiquer. Le vote final porterait sur les 3 textes, dans l'ordre fixé par le Comité. Le Président fait remarquer qu'en adoptant la proposition de Mr. Root il faudrait toujours, après le vote de principe, revenir à la discussion des textes.

Pour M. HAGERUP, la procédure de Mr. Root a l'avantage de faire l'accord sur le principe avant la discussion des textes.

Le PRESIDENT insiste pour qu'on discute simultanément les trois textes, méthode qui lui semble la plus simple et la plus claire.

LORD PHILLIMORE demande au Président s'il est certain que son projet garantit la représentation des grandes Puissances.

Le PRESIDENT répond affirmativement, à condition qu'à la fin de l'article 5 de ce projet se trouve la formule suivante: „en assurant la représentation à la Cour des grandes formes de civilisation et des principaux systèmes juridiques du monde".

Cette formule pourrait avec avantage être expliquée encore dans le rapport du Comité.

LORD PHILLIMORE croit qu'il ne faut pas laisser au rapport le soin de résoudre les questions importantes: leur solution doit se trouver dans le texte. Il désire que le Président précise ses idées, notamment sur la question de la représentation dont il a parlé.

Le PRESIDENT se déclare disposé à préciser davantage, au besoin; mais il croit nécessaire d'abord de rencontrer la proposition de Mr. Root, qui est une proposition de procédure, tandis que la question soulevée par Lord Phillimore touche au fond du débat.

Mr. ROOT prepared a proposal and read it (see Annex 2).

The PRESIDENT said he would adopt any procedure agreed upon by the Committee but he pointed out that by adopting the proposal of Mr. Root they would be voting on the principle without taking into consideration such points of detail as might in the case of some members be a condition for accepting the principle. On the other hand, by discussing the complete texts, it would be possible for instance to find out whether the representation of the great Powers was sufficiently guaranteed in a particular project. For this reason he preferred that the discussion should deal with the text of the three projects. The authors of the projects would be asked to explain them, thus giving other members of the Committee an opportunity to criticise them. A final vote would be taken on the three projects in an order fixed by the Committee. The President pointed out that in adopting Mr. Root's proposal, they would have to return to the discussion of the texts after the vote on principle.

M. HAGERUP said that the procedure suggested by Mr. Root had the advantage of facilitating an agreement on principle before the texts were dealt with.

The PRESIDENT insisted that they discuss the three projects simultaneously, the method which seemed to him clearest and simplest.

LORD PHILLIMORE asked the President whether it was certain that his project guaranteed the representation of the great Powers.

The PRESIDENT replied in the affirmative, on condition that at the end of Article 5 of this project the following clause was added: „so as to ensure that the main forms of civilisation and the principal legal systems in the world be represented on the Court".

This wording might usefully be explained again in the Committee's report.

LORD PHILLIMORE thought that a solution of important questions must not be left to the report; their solution must be included in the text. He asked the President to define his ideas especially on the question of the representation mentioned.

The PRESIDENT said that he was prepared to be more precise if necessary. However he thought that first of all it was important to deal with the proposal submitted by Mr. Root, which was one of procedure, while the question raised by Lord Phillimore touched the heart of the question.

M. DE LAPRADELLE prend la parole sur la question de la méthode à suivre. S'il a bien compris Mr. Root, celui-ci désire qu'on résolve d'abord la question de principe, tandis que certains autres membres préféreraient que l'on discutât un texte, article par article. M. de Lapradelle croit possible de concilier les deux méthodes: il suffit d'indiquer dans les divers textes les articles qui se rapportent à la question qu'on veut résoudre. Les auteurs des projets pourraient alors expliquer leurs idées, et l'on pourrait ensuite procéder au vote.

Le PRESIDENT et LORD PHILLIMORE se rallient à la proposition de M. de Lapradelle.

Le PRESIDENT ajoute qu'il croit se souvenir qu'on a décidé précédemment de ne discuter dans cette séance que sur des textes, la discussion des principes ayant été achevée dans les séances précédentes.

LORD PHILLIMORE propose qu'on commence par discuter la question traitée à l'article 5 de l'avant-projet du Président et dans les articles correspondants des autres projets.

Le PRESIDENT indique quels sont ces derniers articles.

M. DE LAPRADELLE remarque que, chaque fois qu'une question sera soulevée, les auteurs de chaque projet pourront indiquer les articles qui dans leur travail, ont trait à cette question.

M. HAGERUP craint qu'on ne se perde dans une discussion de questions d'ordre secondaire.

Le PRESIDENT insiste encore sur la nécessité qu'il y a de discuter et de voter sur des textes précis, et appuie la proposition de M. de Lapradelle.

LORD PHILLIMORE montre qu'il s'agit, en somme, d'une contestation entre l'article 5 de l'avant-projet du Président, des articles 2 et 3 du projet Root—Phillimore et des articles 2 et 3 du projet Ricci-Busatti.

M. DE LAPRADELLE observe qu'il faut d'abord décider sur quel texte aura lieu le vote final. Les autres textes doivent être considérés comme des amendements à celui qui sera soumis au vote. M. de Lapradelle propose qu'on considère comme texte original, le texte du projet qui a été déposé le premier.

Le PRESIDENT voit des objections à la procédure proposée par M. de Lapradelle.

M. DE LAPRADELLE dealt with the question of the method to be followed. If he had rightly understood Mr. Root, the latter desired that questions of principle should first be decided, while certain other members preferred that a text should be discussed, article by article. He thought that the two methods could be brought together: it would be necessary only to indicate which Articles in the various projects dealt with the question to be decided. The authors of the projects could then explain their ideas and afterwards a vote could be taken.

The PRESIDENT and LORD PHILLIMORE supported M. de Lapradelle's proposal.

The PRESIDENT added that he thought he recalled that they had decided formerly to discuss only texts, as the discussion of questions of principle had been completed in preceding meetings.

LORD PHILLIMORE proposed that they begin by discussing the questions dealt with in Article 5 of the President's project and the corresponding Articles in the other projects.

The PRESIDENT enumerated the latter Articles.

M. DE LAPRADELLE said that each time a fresh question was brought up the respective authors of the project could point out those Articles which in their schemes dealt with the question.

M. HAGERUP feared that they would get too much involved in a discussion of questions of minor importance.

The PRESIDENT emphasised again the necessity of voting on exact texts, and supported M. de Lapradelle's proposal.

LORD PHILLIMORE showed that it was really a question of comparing Article 5 of the President's project, Articles 2 and 3 of the Root—Phillimore project, and Articles 2 and 3 of the Ricci-Busatti project.

M. DE LAPRADELLE pointed out that they must first of all decide, upon which project the final vote would be taken. The other projects must be considered as amendments to that which was to be voted upon. He proposed that the project which had been submitted first should be considered as the orginal.

The PRESIDENT saw objections to the procedure suggested by M. de Lapradelle.

Mr. ROOT est indécis, car il connaît mal les règles de la procédure continentale. Dans la procédure américaine et anglaise, le projet qui a été déposé le premier ne peut être écarté que par un vote ou par un amendement. Un projet ne peut être abandonné sans avoir fait l'objet d'une décision. Il se rallie par conséquent à la proposition de M. de Lapradelle.

Le PRESIDENT ne s'oppose pas à ce qu'un texte soit pris comme base de la discussion, mais il insiste pour que les trois textes soient discutés en même temps. Les auteurs des projets doivent pouvoir les défendre et demander un vote sur eux, par voie d'amendement au besoin.

Après un bref échange de vues au sujet de la date à laquelle ont été déposés les différents projets, LORD PHILLIMORE constate qu'on est d'accord pour prendre comme base de discussion le projet Root—Phillimore. Il propose que la discussion soit ouverte sur la 2ème phrase de l'article 2 de ce projet, ainsi que sur les articles suivants.

M. ADATCI demande si sa proposition relative à l'insertion dans le projet Root—Phillimore de l'article 3 du projet Ricci-Busatti a été adoptée.

M. DE LAPRADELLE constate que le texte Root—Phillimore fera en dernier lieu l'objet du vote et que les autres textes seront considérés comme des amendements à ce texte.

D'accord avec leurs auteurs, le PRESIDENT indique quelles sont dans les différents projets les dispositions qui se rapportent à la question de la nomination des juges. Ce sont: dans le projet Root—Phillimore, les articles 2 à 8 et l'article 11; dans le projet Ricci-Busatti, les articles 2 et 3, 6 et 7; dans l'avant-projet du Président l'article 5.

Le Président ouvre la discussion sur la question à laquelle ont trait ces articles. Il invite d'abord les auteurs des différents projets à exposer leurs propres propositions et à rencontrer celles des autres membres.

D'après LORD PHILLIMORE, puisqu'on se trouve en présence d'un projet qui fera l'objet d'un vote, et de deux textes ayant le caractère d'amendements, il est nécessaire d'établir une comparaison entre les trois textes.

Lord Phillimore fait d'abord valoir que le projet Root—Phillimore concilie les diverses idées émises par les différents membres du Comité. L'idée fondamentale qui est à la base du projet tout entier, est celle que Mr. Root a

Mr. ROOT felt uncertain, as he was unfamiliar with the rules of continental procedure. In English and American procedure, the proposal submitted first could not be set aside except by a vote or by an amendment. No proposal could be abandoned without being voted upon. He consequently agreed with M. de Lapradelle.

The PRESIDENT had no objection to one text being taken as basis for discussion, but he insisted that the three texts should be discussed at the same time. The authors of the projects must be able to defend them and to ask that a vote be taken on them, as amendments if necessary.

After a short discussion concerning the date of the submission of the different projects, LORD PHILLIMORE said he thought that the Committee was agreed to take the Root-Phillimore scheme as a basis for discussion. He proposed that the discussion should be opened on the second sentence of Article 2 of this project and on the following Articles as well.

M. ADATCI asked if his proposal that Article 3 of the Ricci-Busatti plan should be inserted in the Root—Phillimore project had been adopted.

M. DE LAPRADELLE stated that the Root—Phillimore project would be voted upon last and that the other projects would be considered as amendments to this text.

With the approval of the authors, the PRESIDENT pointed out the different dispositions in the various schemes which dealt with the question of the nomination of judges. These were: in the Root—Phillimore project Articles 2 to 8 and Article 11; in the Ricci-Busatti project Articles 2, 3, 6 and 7; in the President's project Article 5.

The President opened the discussion upon the question dealt with by them. First of all he asked the authors of the various projects to explain their own propositions and to criticise those of the others.

LORD PHILLIMORE said that as there was one project which was to be voted upon and two others to be considered as amendments, it would be necessary to compare all three.

First of all he pointed out that the Root—Phillimore project conciliates the various ideas put forward by different members of the Committee. The fundamental idea which formed the basis of the whole project was that developed by Mr. Root: this idea was to try to conciliate

développée: elle tâche de concilier les droits et les devoirs de tous les Etats à l'égard de la constitution de la Cour, en adoptant le principe bien connu du droit intérieur, d'après lequel les juges sont nommés par le pouvoir politique; comme dans la Société des Nations ce pouvoir est confié à deux organes différents, le Conseil et l'Assemblée, ils doivent avoir tous les deux une influence sur l'élection des juges.

En second lieu, le projet reprend l'idée si féconde du Président de donner à la Cour Permanente d'Arbitrage une part dans l'élection.

En outre, on y retrouve l'idée suggérée par M. Altamira de consulter, lors de l'élection, les corps scientifiques, etc.

Il contient également des idées empruntées au projet des Cinq Puissances, auquel ont collaboré MM. Loder et Hagerup.

Enfin le projet adopte l'idée de M. Ricci-Busatti sur les liens qui doivent exister entre la nouvelle Cour et l'ancienne Cour d'Arbitrage, ainsi que sa pensée de donner aux deux Cours un greffier commun.

Lord Phillimore ajoute que MM. Adatci et Fernandes sont avec lui-même les seuls dont les idées ne soient pas représentées dans le projet Root—Phillimore.

Le PRESIDENT estime qu'il doit relever cette appréciation trop modeste. Il fait ressortir la grande part qu'a eue Lord Phillimore à la préparation de ce projet; et il ajoute que Lord Phillimore doit assumer également sa part de responsabilité.

LORD PHILLIMORE accepte les responsabilités. MM. Adatci et Fernandes, et lui-même, n'ayant pas contribué au projet, ont le droit de s'ériger en critiques.

Il commence par faire l'examen du projet de M. Ricci-Busatti. L'idée dont part ce projet, à savoir, la représentation des grandes Puissances, n'est pas faite pour lui déplaire personnellement; mais il croit que l'idée ne serait pas acceptée par quelques-uns de ses collègues. Ce projet prévoit en outre un nombre trop élevé de juges.

Quant à l'avant-projet du Président, Lord Phillimore observe d'abord qu'il est assez difficile de se prononcer à son sujet, le Président ayant légèrement modifié le texte original. Si, par l'addition à l'article 5 suggérée par le Président, on arrive à assurer d'une façon effective une représentation permanente des grandes Puissances, le projet rencontrera de la part des Puissances secondaires les mêmes critiques que celui de M. Ricci-Busatti. Ceux au con-

the rights and duties of all States in relation to the constitution of the Court, by adopting the well known principle of municipal law, according to which judges are appointed by the political powers; since in the League of Nations this power is in the hands of two different bodies, the Council and the Assembly, they must both have an influence in the election of judges.

In the second place the project embodied the happy idea of the President to give to the Permanent Court of Arbitration a share in the election.

In addition, there was the idea suggested by M. Altamira of consulting scientific bodies, etc., at election time.

It also contained ideas taken from the plan of the Five Powers, in the preparation of which plan M. Loder and M. Hagerup had assisted.

Finally the project adopts the idea of M. Ricci-Busatti concerning the relations which should exist between the new Court and the old Court of Arbitration, as well as his suggestion that the two Courts should have one common registry.

Lord Phillimore added that MM. Adatci and Fernandes, and himself were the only ones whose ideas were not represented in the Root—Phillimore proposal.

The PRESIDENT felt he should object to this excessive modesty. He pointed out the large part that Lord Phillimore had had in the proparation of this project, and he added that Lord Phillimore ought to take also his share of responsibility.

LORD PHILLIMORE accepted the responsibility. M. Adatci, M. Fernandes and himself, not having contributed to the project, had the right to constitute themselves as critics of it.

He began by examining M. Ricci-Busatti's project. The idea upon which this plan was based, namely the representation of the Great Powers, did not displease him personally, but he thought that it would not be accepted by some of his colleagues. The system furthermore provided for too large a number of judges.

Concerning the President's project, Lord Phillimore first of all said that it was rather difficult for him to give an opinion as the President had slightly modified the original text. If by the addition to Article 5 suggested by the President it were possible to assure effectively the permanent representation of the Great Powers, the project would be subject to the same criticism from the secondary Powers as that of M. Ricci-Busatti. On the other hand, those

traire qui, comme Lord Phillimore lui-même, estiment que la représentation permanente des grandes Puissances est nécessaire, trouveront la formule du Président trop vague. Pour sa part, il ne pourrait accepter un projet qui ne donne pas aux grandes Puissances une entière sécurité à cet égard. Enfin il trouverait à redire à la disposition qui, dans l'avant-projet du Président, met sur le même plan le Conseil de la Société des Nations, qui est un organe de la Société, et la Cour Permanente d'Arbitrage, qui n'en est pas un. Il admet d'ailleurs que c'est là un point de vue plutôt théorique.

M. RICCI-BUSATTI déclare qu'il était parti du principe de l'égalité des Etats, croyant qu'on pourrait se fier au libre jeu des influences naturelles pour arriver au résultat désiré. Après avoir entendu ses collègues, il a compris, pourtant, que c'était là une idée un peu utopiste; qu'il fallait bien faire des concessions à la réalité et établir des règles précises si l'on veut atteindre le but vers lequel on tend.

Ce but est la représentation des grandes Puissances au sein de la Cour. A son avis, la concession la moins grave, c'est la constatation franche et loyale de la vérité, c'est-à-dire du privilège que les grandes Puissances réclament d'être représentées à la Cour d'une façon permanente. L'influence accordée au Conseil dans la nomination des juges lui paraît plus dangereuse. C'est pourquoi il a inséré dans son projet la formule contenue à l'article 3. Cet article peut, sans aucun inconvénient, être considéré, ainsi que l'a proposé M. Adatci, comme un amendement aux autres projets.

M. Ricci-Busatti s'étonne que les défenseurs des petites Puissances soient satisfaits de l'influence qu'on veut donner au Conseil qui est l'organe de l'inégalité dans la Société des Nations. Mais puisqu'il en est ainsi, M. Ricci-Busatti ne veut point s'y opposer.

Il déclare que le projet du Président a toute sa sympathie. Il lui reproche seulement de ne pas garantir la représentation des grandes Puissances à la Cour, et d'être à cet égard, comme l'a déjà fait remarquer Lord Phillimore, trop vague et trop imprécis.

M. Ricci-Busatti ajoute que si l'article 3 de son projet n'est pas accepté comme amendement à l'article 11 du projet Root—Phillimore, il proposera un nouvel amendement au premier.

Le PRESIDENT déclare qu'au moment où s'engage sur des textes l'examen de la question la plus importante que le Comité ait à résoudre,

who like himself thought that the permanent representation of the Great Powers was necessary, would find the President's clause too vague. For himself he could not accept a project which would not give the Great Powers every safeguard in this respect. Finally, he would have to object to the provision in the President's project which put the Council of the League of Nations, which is one of the institutions of the League, and the Permanent Court of Arbitration, which is not, upon the same footing. He admitted, however, that this point of view was rather a theoretical one.

M. RICCI-BUSATTI stated that he was in favour of the principle of equality of States, believing that the desired result would be obtained by allowing free play to natural influences. After having heard the views of his colleagues, he had realised, however, that this idea was slightly utopian; that concessions would have to be made to realities, and that definite rules would have to be established if the desired result were to be reached.

This result is the representation of the Great Powers on the Court. In his opinion the best way of making this concession was by a frank and honest statement of the truth; that is to say, of the privileges that the Great Powers claimed to be represented on the Court permanently. The influence given to the Council in the appointment of Judges seemed to him more dangerous. This was the reason for which he had inserted in his project the clause contained in Article 3. This Article could without difficulty be considered, as M. Adatci had proposed, as an amendment to the other projects.

He was astonished, that the champions of the small Powers were content with the influence which was intended to be given to the Council, the Council being the organ of inequality in the League of Nations. But, as they were satisfied, M. Ricci-Busatti would not oppose it.

He stated that he was in complete sympathy with the President's project. He objected only to the fact that it did not guarantee the representation on the Court of the Great Powers, and, as Lord Phillimore had pointed out already, that it was too vague and indefinite in this respect.

M. Ricci-Busatti added, that if Article 3 of his plan were not accepted as an amendment to Article 11 of the Root—Phillimore project, he would amend his amendment.

The PRESIDENT said that now that the time had come to discuss on the basis of texts one of the most important questions that the Commit-

il voudrait préciser brièvement la portée de la proposition nouvelle, d'un caractère transactionnel, qu'il a communiquée à ses collègues, en ce qui concerne le point capital qui sollicite actuellement l'attention des membres, à savoir la nomination des juges de la Cour Permanente de Justice Internationale. Le Président avait pensé d'abord que les Etats, ayant une confiance à coup sûr bien placée dans les membres de la Cour Permanente d'Arbitrage nommés par eux, pouvaient leur déléguer en toute sécurité la tâche de désigner les jurisconsultes appelés à faire partie de la Cour nouvelle, sauf à préciser les conditions de nature à sauvegarder l'équitable et nécessaire représentation des Puissances que le Pacte de la Société des Nations appelle „Principales".

Le Président s'était demandé s'il pouvait exister un aréopage plus compétent et garantissant plus sûrement, dans le respect de l'égalité juridique des Etats, la séparation que tous désirent voir se réaliser, de la politique et de la justice.

On lui a signalé l'importance qu'il y a à assurer aux Etats une action plus directe sur le choix des juges internationaux. C'est pourquoi il a, dans son avant-projet, introduit une disposition ne laissant au collège des membres de la Cour Permanente d'Arbitrage qu'un droit de présentation des candidats aux places de membres de la Cour. De cette façon les membres de la Société des Nations ont le premier et le dernier mot dans la nomination des nouveaux juges, puisqu'ils nomment eux-mêmes les membres de la Cour Permanente d'Arbitrage et élisent directement tous les membres titulaires et suppléants de la Cour Permanente de Justice Internationale.

La part réservée au Conseil de la Société des Nations ne laisse pas d'être également importante dans le Projet. C'est à lui que le Collège des membres de la Cour Permanente d'Arbitrage fait les présentations, et il est en mesure de les contrôler, de les approuver, de les rectifier au besoin, en ajoutant une nouvelle liste à la première, de façon que le nombre des candidats soit le double du chiffre des premières présentations.

Le Président croit qu'il serait moins heureux et plus aléatoire d'organiser ici un mécanisme compliqué, fondé sur le paritétisme du Conseil et de l'Assemblée, et d'où résulteraient probablement des difficultés, auxquelles ne remédierait qu'imparfaitement une commission médiatrice entre les deux corps électoraux, surtout lorsqu'il s'agit d'un nombre de candidats qui peut s'élever jusqu'à deux cents.

Il estime d'ailleurs que, le Conseil de la Société

tee had to decide, the nomination of the judges of the Permanent Court of International Justice, he wished to define briefly the scope of the new proposal, which was in the nature of a compromise, dealing with this cardinal point, and which he had already communicated to his colleagues. The President first of all had thought that the States, having complete confidence in the members of the Permanent Court of Arbitration appointed by themselves, could safely delegate to them the task of choosing the jurisconsults called upon to form part of the new Court, provided that guarantees were established to safeguard the equitable and necessary representation of those States designated „Principal Powers" by the Covenant of the League of Nations.

The President did not think that a more competent areopagus existed, which guaranteed with more certainty the desired separation between politics and justice in the interests of the legal equality of States.

The importance of according to the States a more direct influence on the choice of international judges had been brought to his attention. For that reason he had introduced in his plan a provision leaving to the college of members from the Permanent Court of Arbitration only the right of nominating the candidates for places on the Court. In this way the members of the League of Nations have the first and last word in the nomination of the new judges, since they themselves name the members of the Permanent Court of Arbitration and elect directly all the judges and supplementary judges of the Permanent Court of International Justice.

The part which the project reserves to the Council of the League of Nations is also important: it is to the Council that the college of members of the Permanent Court of Arbitration submit the nominations, and it is possible for the latter to regulate them, to approve of them, to correct them if need be by adding a new list to the first in such a way that the number of candidates is twice the number first nominated.

The President thought that it would be less desirable and more hazardous to organise now a complicated piece of mechanism based on the equality of the Council and the Assembly, from which probably would arise difficulties for which a Commission of Mediation between the two electoral bodies would furnish only an unsatisfactory remedy, especially since a number of candidates which might reach 200 was involved.

He thought furthermore that the Council of the League of Nations fulfilled in the general

des Nations remplissant dans l'économie générale du règlement des conflits internationaux, une mission capitale, distincte précisément de la judicature, on introduit une certaine confusion des pouvoirs en faisant intervenir ce Conseil d'une manière trop directe, et sur un pied d'égalité avec l'Assemblée, dans la nomination des juges.

Il ne suffit pas d'invoquer des analogies, d'ailleurs contestables, entre l'ordre international et l'ordre national pour justifier un tel système.

Il paraît évident au Président que la représentation des grands Etats au sein de la Cour sera assurée si l'on impose à tous ceux, y compris le collège des membres de la Cour Permanente d'Arbitrage, qui concourent à la nomination des juges, l'obligation de pourvoir à la représentation des grandes formes de civilisation et des principaux systèmes juridiques du monde. Il ne faut pas sous prétexte de prévenir des abus, qui ne se présenteront pas, porter une atteinte grave à l'égalité juridique des Etats. Le Président regretterait que le Comité ne reconnût pas ce qu'il y a de transactionnel et d'harmonique dans le projet qu'il préfère, et s'abandonnât aux hasards d'un système qui, loin d'assurer le résultat poursuivi, pourrait semer des germes de discorde entre le Conseil et l'Assemblée et peut-être compromettre la grande œuvre de justice, à l'organisation de laquelle se consacre le Comité.

En fait le Conseil et la Cour sont loin d'être sur le même pied, puisque le Conseil, intervenant en quelque sorte comme institution d'appel, peut contrôler l'œuvre de la Cour et la réédifier au besoin, grâce à la formation d'une liste nouvelle de candidats. Et quant aux garanties, il faudrait supposer, pour contester leur existence, qu'un aréopage de jurisconsultes, tel que celui de la Cour, violerait les obligations qui lui sont imposées. Et encore doit-on constater, que même dans cette hypothèse impossible, l'intervention du Conseil d'abord, puis celle de l'Assemblée, peuvent servir de suprême garantie. Il semble enfin absurde d'admettre que la Cour d'Arbitrage et le Conseil ayant rempli leur devoir quant à la représentation des grands Etats à la Cour à établir, l'Assemblée refuse de remplir le sien, alors que par le statut de l'institution nouvelle, accepté par elle, elle s'est imposé ce devoir.

En réalité, les puissances principales ont toute sécurité quant à leur représentation à la Cour nouvelle, et les Etats secondaires peuvent, dans le système proposé, sans qu'aucune atteinte soit portée à l'égalité juridique, accepter une telle représentation comme une condition de vitalité de l'institution nouvelle qu'il s'agit de créer.

system for settlement of international disputes an essential function, completely distinct from judicial proceedings. A certain confusion of powers would be introduced if in the nomination of judges the Council could act in too direct way and on a footing of equality with the Assembly.

It is not sufficient to cite analogies not above question, between national and international affairs, to justify such a system.

It seemed obvious to the President that the representation of the Great Powers on the Court would be ensured if the obligation of providing for the representation of the great forms of civilisation and the principal legal systems of the world were imposed on those who take part in the nomination of judges, including the members of the Permanent Court of Arbitration. It is unnecessary under pretext of an abuse which will not arise to inflict a severe injury on the legal equality of States. The President regretted that the Committee had not observed the qualities of compromise and harmony contained in the project which he preferred, and had given itself up to the dangers of a system which far from ensuring the desired results might sow the seeds of discord between the Council and the Assembly and perhaps compromise the great work of justice to the organisation of which the Committee had to devote itself.

In fact the Council and the Court are far from being on the same footing since the Council, intervening in a certain respect as an institution to which appeal can be made, might control the work of the Court, re-erect it if need be by means of the formation of a new list of candidates. And as regards guarantees, it would be necessary to suppose, in order to justify their existence, that an areopagus of jurisconsults such as those who form the Court would violate the obligations which have been imposed upon them. Furthermore it should be stated that even in this impossible hypothesis the intervention first of the Council and then of the Assembly might serve as a supreme guarantee. It seems absurd, therefore, to admit that the Court of Arbitration and the Council, having fulfilled their duties regarding the representation of the great States on the Court to be established, the Assembly would refuse to fulfil its duties when it has imposed upon itself this duty by the statute establishing the new institution which it has accepted.

In reality all the principal Powers have every security in regard to their representation on the new Court, and the secondary States may in the proposed system, without any injury being done to legal equality, accept such a representation as

a condition necessary for the practicability of the new institution with the creation of which they are concerned.

M. LODER se rallie au projet Root—Phillimore avec les amendements qu'il a proposés lui-même. (Voir annexe 3).

Le Comité, au début de ses discussions, était d'accord pour reconnaître que le temps de l'inégalité est passé. Mr. Root a fait alors observer qu'il faut tenir compte de la réalité des choses, et que le projet des Cinq Puissances pêchait par trop d'idéalisme. L'Assemblée n'assurera pas l'élection des meilleurs juges. Il y aura dans son sein des coalitions et des intrigues. On a donc émis l'idée de confier la nomination au Conseil, mais cette idée a été jugée inacceptable étant donné le caractère hautement politique de cette institution. Le premier projet Root—Phillimore a établi la collaboration entre le Conseil et l'Assemblée, en vue d'assurer le choix des meilleurs.

Ce qui importe, en effet, c'est d'avoir de bons juges, abstraction faite de leur nationalité. Mais, d'autre part, il est probable que les candidats élus appartiendront souvent aux grandes Puissances, puisque dans ces Puissances, qui représentent les grandes civilisations, la minorité intellectuelle est plus nombreuse que dans les petits Etats.

En tout cas, il faut éviter que les juges se considèrent comme des représentants de leur pays: pour cette raison M. Loder croit devoir rejeter la proposition contenue dans l'article 3 du projet de M. Ricci-Busatti, que n'accepteraient jamais les petites Puissances.

L'avant-projet du Président ne lui semble pas non plus satisfaisant. Le rôle qu'il donne au Conseil n'est pas suffisant: l'Assemblée pourra ne tenir aucun compte de la liste présentée par le Conseil. M. Loder trouve que ce projet rappelle, à cet égard, le plan communiqué par M. Bevilaqua.

Enfin, M. Loder s'élève contre l'idée de faire représenter les différents systèmes juridiques. On a beaucoup parlé de cette idée sans jamais bien en élucider le sens, et M. Loder déclare qu'il ne sait pas au juste ce qu'elle veut dire.

Il ajoute qu'on pourra discuter plus tard les amendements qu'il a soumis, puisqu'ils ne touchent pas au fond du projet Root—Phillimore.

M. LODER accepted the Root—Phillimore project with the amendments he had himself proposed. (See Annex 3).

At the beginning, the Committee had agreed to recognise the fact that the period of inequality had passed. Mr. Root had stated that realities must be taken into account and that the project of the five Powers was inclined too much toward the idealistic. Election by the Assembly would not ensure the best judges. There would be intrigues and coalitions within it. The idea therefore had been put forward of giving the power of nomination to the Council, but this idea had not been accepted on account of the highly political nature of this institution. The first Root—Phillimore project had established collaboration between the Council and the Assembly, in order to insure that the best judges were chosen.

The important point was to have good judges regardless of their nationality. But on the other hand it was probable that the candidates elected often would belong to the Great Powers since in these countries, which represent the great civilisations, the intellectual minority is more numerous than in the smaller States.

In any case, the judges must not consider themselves representatives of their countries: for this reason M. Loder thought that he must reject the proposal contained in Article 3 of M. Ricci-Busatti's project. The Article would never be accepted by the smaller States.

The President's project did not seem to him satisfactory either. The part which he gave to the Council was not sufficient; the Assembly might take no notice whatever of the list presented by the Council. M. Loder thought that the project resembled in this respect the plans submitted by M. Bevilaqua.

Finally M. Loder was opposed to the idea of representing the various legal systems. This idea had been talked of a great deal without its meaning ever being clearly explained. M. Loder said that he did not exactly know what it meant.

He added that the amendments he had submitted could be discussed later since they did not affect the underlying principle of the Root—Phillimore project.

M. RICCI-BUSATTI fait observer que la critique de M. Loder n'est pas tout à fait exacte, puisque le projet soumis par M. Ricci-Bu-

M. RICCI-BUSATTI pointed out that the criticism of M. Loder was not entirely accurate since his project did not contain exactly what

satti n'a pas exactement le contenu que lui a prêté M. Loder. Il prévoit par exemple un nombre de 15 juges seulement.

M. HAGERUP désire préciser son attitude envers le projet que l'on est en train d'examiner, et envers le problème en général.

Il croit que dans le projet qu'ils ont à soumettre au Conseil et à l'Assemblée de la Société des Nations, les membres du Comité doivent faire abstraction de leurs préférences personnelles. S'ils ne le faisaient pas, on se trouverait exactement dans la même situation qu'à la fin de la Conférence de 1907, on n'aurait pas fait un seul pas en avant. Il répète ce qui a été dit bien souvent au sein du Comité: il faut arriver à un accord. Il est impossible d'élaborer un projet qui satisfasse l'opinion du monde entier. Mais il faut en préparer un qui réunisse les membres du Comité et dont ces membres puissent accepter la pleine responsabilité. C'est le seul moyen d'aboutir. Aussi M. Hagerup est-il heureux de voir l'accord qui semble se faire autour du projet Root—Phillimore grâce au sacrifice de certaines opinions personnelles. Il sait que Lord Phillimore a sacrifié des idées qui lui étaient chères, et M. Hagerup lui-même est disposé à accepter ce projet, bien qu'il ne soit pas l'idéal, parce qu'il constitue le seul terrain d'entente possible. A cet égard M. Hagerup se rallie à Lord Phillimore. Il croit cependant que M. Ricci-Busatti a raison dans une certaine mesure. Il admet que faire une part au Conseil dans l'élection des juges, c'est donner une influence prépondérante aux Puissances qui sont Membres des deux corps et qui par conséquent auront un double vote. Mais, de l'autre côté, il est impossible de donner pleins pouvoirs à la majorité de l'Assemblée, telle qu'elle est actuellement constituée: on ne serait pas sûr que les juges fussent bien choisis. Il faut un contre-poids à ce pouvoir, et ce contre-poids ne peut être trouvé que dans l'influence à donner au Conseil, si l'on doit se tenir aux institutions de la Société des Nations, agréées par tous les Membres de la Société.

D'autre part M. Hagerup approuve la critique de M. Loder sur le projet de M. Ricci-Busatti, lorsqu'il a fait ressortir qu'une disposition telle que celle contenue à l'article 3 de ce projet, le rendrait inacceptable à un certain nombre d'Etats. L'expérience de 1907 en est une preuve suffisante.

M. Hagerup se déclare très sympathique à l'avant-projet du Président. Il voterait pour lui, s'il croyait que ce plan puisse servir de base d'entente.

M. Loder had stated. For instance he contemplated a number of only 15 judges.

M. HAGERUP wished to define his position with regard to the projects under discussion and with regard to the problem as a whole.

He thought that in the plan which they would submit to the Council and the Assembly of the League of Nations, the members of the Committee should disregard their personal preferences. If they did not, they would be in exactly the same position as that reached at the end of the Conference of 1907. They would not have made a single step in advance. He repeated a phrase often heard at the meetings of the Committee: An agreement must be reached. It was impossible to prepare a project which would satisfy opinion all over the world. But they must prepare one which had the support of the members of the Committee and for which the members could accept full responsibility. This was the only way to succeed. For this reason M. Hagerup was happy to see that unanimity appeared to exist on the subject of the Root—Phillimore project, thanks to the sacrifices of certain personal opinions. He knew that Lord Phillimore had sacrificed cherished ideas, and he himself was prepared to accept the scheme even though it were not ideal, because he thought it was the only possible means of coming to an understanding. Here he agreed with Lord Phillimore, but he thought that M. Ricci-Busatti was right to a certain extent. He admitted that to allow the Council to play a part in the election of the judges would amount to giving a preponderant influence to the Powers which are members of the two bodies and which consequently would have a double vote. But, on the other hand, it would be impossible to give all power to the majority of the Assembly as constituted at present; there would be no guarantee that the judges would be well chosen. There must be some compensation, and this compensation could only be found in the influence to be given to the Council, if they were bound to confine themselves to the institutions of the League of Nations accepted by all the Members of the League.

On the other hand M. Hagerup approved of M. Loder's criticism concerning the project of M. Ricci-Busatti in that he thought that a provision such as was contained in Article 3 of that project would make it unacceptable to a certain number of States. The experience of 1907 was sufficient proof of this.

M. Hagerup désire relever un point spécial dans le projet du Président. Celui-ci a inséré à la fin de l'article 5 quelques mots, qui se retrouvent également dans le projet Root—Phillimore, au sujet de la représentation des différents systèmes juridiques. M. Hagerup croit, comme M. Loder, qu'il y a là une idée fausse. La Cour jugera d'après le droit international; par conséquent, les systèmes nationaux n'ont pas besoin d'être représentés dans son sein. Lord Phillimore a du reste démontré la difficulté de définir ce qu'il faut entendre par cette expression.

M. Hagerup est opposé également à la formule de M. de Lapradelle sur la représentation des différentes formes de civilisation. Il y a dans tous les pays civilisés — en Norvège aussi bien qu'au Japon — une civilisation d'origine nationale sur laquelle se greffe une civilisation d'un caractère général plus ou moins commune à tous les pays.

Dans cet ordre d'idées, M. Hagerup propose un amendement à l'effet de supprimer à l'article 11 du projet Root—Phillimore, les mots: „et de chercher à assurer dans la mesure du possible la représentation à la Cour des différentes formes de civilisation et des différents systèmes juridiques des Membres de la Société des Nations. Cependant. . ."

M. Hagerup declared that he much appreciated the President's scheme. He would vote for it if he thought that it could serve as the basis of an understanding.

He wished to deal also with a particular point. in the President's project. The latter had inserted at the end of Article 5 several words which also were found in the Root—Phillimore project, concerning representation of different legal systems. He agreed with M. Loder that the idea was unsound. The Court was to deliver judgment according to international law; consequently there was no need to have national systems of law represented on it. Lord Phillimore moreover had shown the difficulty of defining what was meant by this expression.

M. Hagerup also was opposed to the clause proposed by M. de Lapradelle dealing with the representation of different forms of civilisation. There exists in all civilised countries — in Norway as well as in Japan — a civilisation national in origin, on which there has been grafted a civilisation general in character, and more or less common to all countries.

In this connection M. Hagerup proposed an amendment suppressing in Article 11 of the Root—Phillimore plan the words: "and to seek as far as practicable to have represented in the Court the different forms of civilisation and juridical systems which exist among the Members of the League of Nations; but . . .".

M. FERNANDES croit devoir présenter le point de vue du Brésil, qui, à son avis, est celui de l'Amérique latine en général. Il doit au préalable examiner les systèmes proposés. MM. Adatci et Ricci-Busatti préconisent la représentation directe à la Cour de Justice des Etats qui sont membres permanents du Conseil de la Société des Nations, en réservant aux autres Etats une représentation indirecte, au moyen de l'élection d'un certain nombre de juges par l'Assemblée de la Société. M. Fernandes a été étonné d'entendre M. Adatci recommander ce système, et dire qu'il fallait tenir compte d'une réalité incontestable, à savoir qu'une Cour sans représentation des dites Puissances serait nécessairement non-viable. Certes, il est désirable que le projet soumis pour l'organisation de la Cour donne aux Etats en question une garantie complète en ce qui concerne l'impartialité, l'indépendance et la compétence des juges; et cela, non pas parce qu'ils constituent les „grandes Puissances" selon la fâcheuse dénomination introduite dans la terminologie diplomatique, mais

M. FERNANDES thought that he should present Brazil's point of view which in his opinion was the same as Latin America's in general. First of all he would examine the proposed systems. MM. Adatci and Ricci-Busatti provided for the direct representation on the Court of Justice of the States which are permanent members of the Council of the League of Nations, reserving to the other States an indirect representation by means of the election of a certain number of judges by the Assembly of the League. M. Fernandes was astonished to hear M. Adatci advocate this system and say that consideration must be had for undeniable realities, namely that a Court on which the said Powers were not represented would necessarily be impracticable. Certainly it is desirable that the plan submitted for the organisation of the Court should give to the States in question a complete guarantee concerning the impartiality, the independence, and the ability of the judges; not because they are the great Powers, according to the regrettable terminology introduced in di-

parce que, le cas échéant, leur responsabilité et leurs intérêts seront les plus affectés lorsqu'il faudra, pour assurer l'exécution des jugements, prendre des mesures coercitives d'ordre militaire ou économique.

Mais, pour que la Cour soit viable, elle devra satisfaire à toutes les conditions de viabilité. MM. Adatci et Ricci-Busatti pensent remplir une de ces conditions en sacrifiant sans ménagement le principe de l'égalité juridique des Etats souverains; mais ils aboutissent précisément au résultat contraire, car on doit tenir pour certain que la majorité des membres de la Société des Nations s'opposeront de façon irréductible à tout règlement impliquant la méconnaissance dudit principe. Si les „grandes Puissances" veulent une Cour qui ne juge que leurs différends, elles sont dans la bonne voie. Mais, si, au contraire, elles veulent une Cour dont la compétence embrasse un aussi grand nombre d'Etats que ceux dont est constituée la Société des Nations, il leur faudra bien alors accorder leur légitime intérêt avec l'application franche du principe de l'égalité de tous les Etats souverains.

M. Fernandes lui-même n'a pas de vote à émettre; il le constate sans embarras, puisque il n'a commencé à siéger qu'après que le Secrétaire Général de la Société des Nations eût fait savoir au Comité que son droit de voter ne dépendait que de son éminent compatriote M. Bevilaqua. Mais, que le Comité n'en doute pas un instant: si, ce qu'il ne croit pas, les suggestions qu'il critique étaient acceptées par le Comité, le Brésil, d'accord avec la majorité des Etats intéressés, voterait immanquablement, le moment venu, contre le projet, faisant ainsi crouler l'édifice que tout le monde désire solide et durable.

M. Fernandes passe ensuite au projet du Président. Ce projet se préoccupe de satisfaire à la fois les grands Etats représentés au Conseil de la Société des Nations et l'ensemble des Etats représentés à l'Assemblée en faisant collaborer à l'élection le Conseil qui présente une liste de candidats, et l'Assemblée à qui il appartiendra de choisir. Mais il ne faut pas oublier que, concurremment avec la liste formée par le Conseil, une autre liste, dressée par la Cour d'Arbitrage de La Haye, sera présentée à l'Assemblée.

En fait, l'Assemblée demeurera donc libre de laisser de côté la liste présentée par le Conseil et de ne faire porter son choix que sur celle de la Cour d'Arbitrage; le Conseil se trouverait ainsi évincé de toute participation à l'élection. Il est manifeste que la garantie accordée aux grandes Puissances sera illusoire et, dans ces conditions, M. Fernandes pense que le projet n'aura

plomatic language, but because in a given case their responsibility and their interests are more deeply affected, since it would be necessary in order to enforce the execution of a sentence that they take coercive measures of a military and economic character.

However, in order that the Court be practicable, it should satisfy all the conditions of success. MM. Adatci and Ricci-Busatti thought that they would fulfil one of these conditions by sacrificing without consideration the principle of legal equality of sovereign States; but they would arrive at the diametrically opposite result, because it should be kept firmly in mind that the majority of Members of the League of Nations are immutably opposed to any rule involving disregard for this principle. If the Great Powers desire a Court which shall judge only their disputes they are on the good road. But if, on the contrary, they desire a Court whose competence covers a number of States equal to that which forms the League of Nations, it would then be necessary for them to adjust their legitimate interests with the frank application of the principle of equality of all sovereign States.

M. Fernandes himself had no vote to cast; he felt no hesitation in stating this since he had not taken his seat until the Secretariat-General of the League of Nations had explained to the Committee that this right to vote was dependent on his eminent fellow-countryman, M. Bevilaqua. However, in order that the Committee might no be in doubt for an instant, he wished to say that if, which he did not think possible, the proposals which he objected to were accepted by the Committee, Brazil, in agreement with the majority of States interested, when the time came, would, without fail, vote against the project, thus causing the fall of the institution which the whole world wished to see powerful and lasting.

M. Fernandes then turned to the President's plan. This plan aims to satisfy both the large States represented on the Council of the League of Nations and the bulk of States represented on the Assembly by making the Council and the Assembly cooperate in the election, the Council preparing the list of candidates from which the Assembly shall make its choice. But it must not be forgotten that concurrent with the list prepared by the Council another list drawn up by the Hague Court of Arbitration shall be presented to the Assembly.

Therefore in fact the Assembly shall remain free to disregard the list presented by the Council

aucune chance d'être agréé. Peut-on l'amender en supprimant la liste à former par la Cour de La Haye? Cela écarterait probablement l'opposition des grands Etats, Membres permanents du Conseil, mais susciterait celle des Etats qui composent l'Assemblée. Ceux-ci, en effet, ne se trouveraient plus en face d'un choix ou d'une élection à faire dans des conditions de liberté satisfaisantes, puisque leur rôle se bornerait à une simple déclaration de préférence de 15 candidats sur les 30 proposés par le Conseil.

M. Fernandes est d'avis que le projet Root—Phillimore réussit mieux dans la tâche très délicate de concilier tous les intérêts en présence. En faisant le choix des juges dépendre du vote concordant de la majorité des membres du Conseil et de l'Assemblée de la Société des Nations, ce projet donne aux deux organes de la Société une égale participation à la composition de la Cour. On y envisage la création d'une Cour peu nombreuse, condition *sine qua non* de son autorité et de sa permanence réelle. Cela implique nécessairement que de nombreux Etats ne pourront pas avoir de leurs ressortissants parmi les élus, mais par là même la représentation des Etats se trouve sagement écartée, les juges étant élus sans égard à leur nationalité, qui n'entre en ligne de compte que lorsqu'il s'agit d'empêcher qu'un Etat ait plus d'un de ses ressortissants à la Cour.

Ainsi se trouve assurée également, dans la plus large mesure, la représentation des différents systèmes juridiques et des principales civilisations. Ce plan ménage en même temps les susceptibilités qui, dans le passé, ont fait échouer un Tribunal où certains Etats étaient représentés par des juges qu'ils désignaient pour y siéger, tandis que d'autres restaient, ou peu s'en faut, en dehors.

M. Fernandes pense que le projet Root—Phillimore fait le pas décisif pour l'avènement de la justice internationale en rompant avec le préjugé de la représentation des Etats comme Puissances publiques à la Cour. C'est là son idée essentielle; et M. Fernandes est heureux de constater qu'il est d'accord en cela avec le projet envoyé par son éminent compatriote M. le professeur Bevilaqua.

Il est très probable que les grandes Puissances auront de leurs ressortissants parmi les 15 élus. On peut même dire que cela est certain, car l'autorité des sentences de la Cour — en ce qui concerne leur application pratique — en dépendra; et les autres Etats, qu'on sous-estime injustement, ont assez de sens politique pour s'en rendre compte. Mais il n'en reste pas moins que le mécanisme du projet n'écarte d'avance les ressor-

and limit its choice to that of the Court of Arbitration; the Council would thus find itself isolated from any participation in the election. It is obvious that the guarantee given to the Great Powers would be deceptive and under these circumstances M. Fernandes thought that the project would have no chance whatever of being accepted. Could it be amended in suppressing the list to be prepared by the Court? That probably would remove the opposition of the Great States, permanent members of the Council, but would excite the opposition of the States who made up the Assembly. The latter in practice would no longer find themselves in position to exercise their choice or carry out an election under satisfactory conditions of freedom, since their part would be limited simply to a statement of preference for 15 candidates among the 30 nominated by the Council.

M. Fernandes was of the opinion that the Root—Phillimore project succeeded better in the very delicate task of conciliating all the interests concerned. By making the choice of judges dependent on the concurrent vote of the majority of members both of the Council and of the Assembly of the League of Nations, this plan gives to the two organs of the League an equal participation in the composition of the Court. The creation of a small Court is anticipated, a condition *sine qua non* of its authority and its real permanence. This implies necessarily that many States will not be able to have their subjects among those elected; but by this very fact the representation of States is wisely avoided, the judges being elected regardless of their nationality, which is taken into account only when it is a question of preventing one State having more than one of its subjects on the Court.

Thus in the largest degree possible the representation of the various legal systems and the principal forms of civilisation is assured. This plan at the same time makes allowance for the susceptibilites which in the past have brought about the failure of a tribunal on which certain States were represented by judges which they named to sit upon it, while other States remained practically outside.

M. Fernandes thought that the Root—Phillimore plan took the necessary step for the advent of international justice by breaking with the prejudice of having the States as Powers openly represented on the Court. That was his fundamental idea, and M. Fernandes was pleased to state that he was in that respect

tissants d'aucun Etat, de même qu'il n'assure d'emblée à aucune grande Puissance l'entrée d'un de ses ressortissants à la Cour. Pour la première fois, sous cet aspect, le principe de l'égalité juridique des Etats souverains se trouvera appliqué dans toute son étendue.

Il y a malheureusement une ombre à ce magnifique tableau: le projet revient à donner un double vote aux Etats représentés à la fois au Conseil et à l'Assemblée, dans une élection où ceux qui sont représentés seulement à l'Assemblée n'en auront qu'un. On porte ici atteinte, et de façon flagrante, au principe de l'égalité; il est impossible de le dissimuler. D'ailleurs, même si on le voulait, cela serait inutile, car l'Assemblée ne manquerait pas de le relever.

D'autre part, M. Fernandes se croit lié par les traditions de son pays, respectées scrupuleusement dans le projet de M. Bevilaqua, et il est ici d'autant plus à l'aise que le Brésil étant à la fois membre du Conseil et de l'Assemblée de la Société des Nations, se trouve précisément être un des Etats qui bénéficieraient de la dite inégalité.

En terminant, M. Fernandes suggère que si, comme il le suppose, l'intervention du Conseil n'a d'autre but que d'assurer aux grandes Puissances un contrôle effectif sur l'organisation de la Cour, on pourrait arriver au même résultat en confiant l'élection à l'Assemblée seule, mais en exigeant une majorité assez forte, une majorité des deux-tiers ou des trois-quarts par exemple. Si l'on considère que la prochaine Assemblée comptera 43 membres dont 10 représentants des grandes Puissances, y compris les Cinq Dominions britanniques, on voit qu'on peut arriver très facilement au résultat cherché, en exigeant une majorité déterminée.

Sauf cette importante réserve, qui exige un amendement, M. Fernandes se rallie au projet Root—Phillimore.

in agreement with the plan sent by his distinguished fellow-countryman, Professor Bevilaqua.

It is very probable that the Great Powers will have their subjects among the 15 judges elected. It might even be said that it is certain, because the authority of the Court's sentences in so far as their practical execution was concerned, would depend on these States; and the other States which are unjustly underrated have enough political sense to take this into consideration. But it remains, nevertheless, that the machinery of the plan does not exclude in advance the subjects of any States, just as it does not provide at the outset for the entrance of a subject of any Great Power into the Court. For the first time, by this means, the principle of legal equality of sovereign States is completely applied.

Unfortunately a shadow is cast over this beautiful picture: the project gives a double vote to States represented both in the Council and in the Assembly in an election in which those who are represented only in the Assembly have but one vote. A flagrant wrong here is done to the principle of equality; it is impossible to hide the fact.

Even should there be any desire to conceal it, the Assembly would not fail to point it out.

On the other hand M. Fernandes felt that he was bound by the traditions of his country scrupulously respected in the plan of M. Bevilaqua, and in this respect he felt all the more at his ease because Brazil, being a member both of the Council and of the Assembly of the League of Nations, found itself precisely to be one of those States which would benefit by the said inequality.

In conclusion M. Fernandes suggested that if, as he supposed, the intervention of the Council had no other object than to ensure to the Great Powers an effective control over the organisation of the Court, the same result might be reached by vesting the election in the Assembly alone, by insisting on a sufficiently large majority, a majority of two-thirds or of three-fourths, for example. If it is borne in mind that the next Assembly will have 43 members, 10 of which represent the Great Powers including the 5 British Dominions, it will be observed that the desired result may very easily be reached by demanding a given majority.

Except for this important reservation, which requires an amendment, M. Fernandes supported the Root—Phillimore plan.

M. ALTAMIRA déclare qu'il avait auparavant des idées bien arrêtées sur la présentation

M. ALTAMIRA said that formerly he had had quite definite ideas concerning the method of

des candidats et la nomination des juges, mais qu'après avoir entendu les opinions des autres membres du Comité, il conçoit maintenant des doutes; il croit qu'il faut rechercher le moyen de concilier la nécessité d'obtenir de bons juges avec les exigences de certaines réalités fâcheuses, qu'a signalées Mr. Root; il voit qu'il faut avant tout donner aux grandes Puissances l'assurance qu'elles ne seront pas dominées par les petites.

M. Altamira se rallie donc au principe de la collaboration entre le Conseil et l'Assemblée, adopté dans le projet Root—Phillimore; mais s'il se plie ainsi devant les réalités, c'est exclusivement parce qu'il faut faire accepter le projet du Comité. Il ne croit pas que, comme l'a dit le Président, les petites Puissances auraient intérêt à ce que les grandes Puissances fussent toujours représentées au sein de la Cour.

Ce qu'il faut avant tout éviter, c'est que les juges se considèrent comme des représentants de leur pays. On doit seulement chercher à obtenir les meilleurs; mais on ne peut pas arriver à ce résultat en donnant trop d'influence à l'Assemblée, parce que dans son sein l'esprit de clocher pourrait se faire trop sentir: chaque Etat voudra satisfaire son point d'honneur national, en assurant l'élection d'un de ses ressortissants. Si l'on se met loyalement à rechercher les meilleurs juges, on les trouvera probablement la plupart du temps dans les grands pays, pour cette simple raison que les minorités intellectuelles sont plus nombreuses dans ces Etats que dans les pays moins peuplés. Pour cette raison, M. Altamira ne croit pas pouvoir s'opposer à l'influence donnée aux Membres du Conseil dans le choix des juges, bien que cette influence porte atteinte au principe de l'égalité. Seulement, il doit maintenir les amendements qu'il a proposés et qui montrent l'importance qu'il attache à la méthode d'élection des juges.

M. Altamira reprend la discussion sur l'utilité d'introduire la disposition aux termes de laquelle les différentes formes de civilisation et les divers systèmes juridiques seraient représentés à la Cour. M. Altamira pense qu'il y a des civilisations diverses et des systèmes de droit différents, même au point de vue international; ce sont les nuances des civilisations qui groupent les peuples entre eux: ainsi la civilisation ibérienne a marqué un sillon dans l'histoire de la civilisation du monde et est représentée aujourd'hui par l'ensemble des pays américains qui parlent le portugais et l'espagnol, et des pays qui en Europe ont été jadis leur métropole. Il en est peut-être de même de la forme de civilisation qui caractérise les peuples dont l'anglais est la langue maternelle.

choosing candidates and appointing judges, but after having heard the opinions of the other members of the Committee, he now was filled with doubt, he thought that it was necessary to find a means of reconciling the need of obtaining good judges, with the exigencies of certain realities which Mr. Root had mentioned. He saw that it was necessary above all to give to the Great Powers assurance against domination by the smaller Powers.

M. Altamira accepted therefore the principle of collaboration between the Council and the Assembly, which had been adopted in the Root—Phillimore plan, but his sole reason for bowing before the inevitable was his wish to have the Committee's plan accepted. He did not share the President's view that the interests of the smaller Powers would be served by the constant representation of the Great Powers in the Court.

The most important thing to avoid was the possibility of the judges considering themselves as representatives of their countries. The only object should be to find the best judges, but this result would not be attained by giving too much influence to the Assembly, because in this body the spirit of nationalism might make itself felt too strongly; each country would wish to gratify its national pride by obtaining the election of one of its subjects. If an earnest endeavour were made to find the best judges, they would probably be found for the most part in the large countries, for the simple reason that the intellectual minority is more numerous in these countries than in the less populous ones. For this reason M. Altamira was not disposed to oppose the influence given to the members of the Council in the choice of judges, even though this influence was contrary to the principle of equality. But he felt that he must support the amendments he had proposed, which showed the importance he attached to the method of electing judges.

M. Altamira went on to consider the value of introducing the provision for representing the different types of civilisation and the different legal systems on the Court. M. Altamira thought that even from an international point of view there were different types of civilisations and different systems of law; it is the various shades of civilisation which create national groups: in this way the Iberian Civilisation has made its mark upon the history of the civilisation of the world, and is represented to-day by the group of American Countries which use the Portuguese or Spanish language, and by the States in Europe which were formerly their mother

M. Altamira croit donc que, s'il est discutable qu'une règle stricte dans ce sens puisse être établie, une indication à ce sujet pourrait donner à ceux qui auront à élire les juges une orientation utile.

Le PRESIDENT désire poser deux questions Lord Phillimore:

1. Le projet Root—Phillimore donne-t-il des garanties complètes pour la représentation des grandes Puissances, et quelles sont ces garanties?
2. Aux termes de ce projet, qui, du Conseil et de l'Assemblée, votera le premier?

Le vote simultané est impossible, les deux corps ayant des membres en commun.

Le Président revient sur la question de la représentation des différents systèmes juridiques. Il dit que cette idée, ainsi que celle de la représentation des civilisations diverses, est d'origine américaine, M. Choate l'ayant proposée en 1899 sur l'initiative du gouvernement des Etats-Unis. Le Président voudrait l'exprimer en disant que les *grandes* formes de civilisation et les *principaux* systèmes juridiques doivent être représentés. Il croit que cette modification rend la formule beaucoup plus précise et permet d'éviter nombre de discussions.

La différence entre les systèmes juridiques a, selon le Président, un fondement réel dans les relations qui existent entre le droit et la civilisation qu'il reflète. Les systèmes juridiques sont nécessairement différents, puisque les civilisations diffèrent entre elles; et cette différence n'est ni récente ni arbitraire: elle a, comme l'a rappelé M. Altamira, de profondes racines historiques. En adoptant ce système, et en dirigeant dans ce sens et le choix des présentations et le choix de l'élection définitive on arriverait à un régime donnant toute garantie.

LORD PHILLIMORE prend la parole pour répondre aux questions que le Président lui a posées. D'accord avec Mr. Root, il reconnaît qu'il n'y a pas dans leur projet commun des garanties complètes pour la représentation des grandes Puissances, mais on y retrouve une garantie raisonnable. Comme l'a démontré M. Ricci-Busatti, il peut arriver qu'un grand Etat vienne à perdre le juge qui le représente, et qu'on choisisse un successeur d'une autre nationalité. Mais il ne faut pas oublier que la Cour doit être composée de bons juges, qui ne doivent pas être accessibles à certains sentiments de jalousie qui règnent entre les grands Etats.

country. The same applies perhaps to the form of civilisation which characterises the English speaking nations. M. Altamira thought therefore, that if the establishment of a definite rule might be objected to, an indication of this point might serve as a valuable guide to those who would have to elect the judges.

The PRESIDENT wished to ask Lord Phillimore two questions:

1. Does the Root—Phillimore project offer complete guarantees for the representation of the Great Powers, and if so, what are these guarantees?
2. According to this scheme, would the Council or the Assembly vote first?

A simultaneous vote would be impossible, the two bodies having members in common.

The President then returned to the question of the representation of various legal systems. He said that this idea as well as that of the representation of different civilisations was of American origin. M. Choate had proposed it in 1899 under the instructions of the United States Government. The President wished to express it by saying that the *main* forms of civilisation and the *principal* legal system should be represented. He thought that this modification would make the clause much more precise and make it possible to avoid much discussion.

The difference between the various legal systems, according to the President, was based upon the relation between law and the civilisation of which it was the reflection. The legal systems are necessarily different because civilisations differ. This difference is neither of recent nor arbitrary origin. As M. Altamira had remarked, it was deep rooted in history. By adopting this method, and by giving instructions to this end for both the nomination and final election of judges, a method will be found which gives every guarantee.

LORD PHILLIMORE answered the questions put to him by the President. He and Mr. Root both admitted that complete guarantee for the representation of the Great Powers was not given in the Root—Phillimore project, but there was a reasonable security. As M. Ricci-Busatti had shown, it might happen that a Great Power would lose the judge representing it, and that a successor might be chosen from another nationality. But it must not be forgotten that the Court must be composed of good judges who would not be influenced by certain jealousies which exist between the Great Powers.

Pour la seconde question, Lord Phillimore fait valoir qu'on peut procéder par amendement. Il est inutile de discuter déjà les détails. A ce propos, Lord Phillimore exprime le désir que les amendements soumis par MM. Loder, Hagerup et Altamira, soient considérés seulement lorsque leur tour sera venu.

Au sujet de la question de la représentation des systèmes juridiques, Lord Phillimore fait observer que la formule insérée dans le projet Root—Phillimore est de caractère transactionnel. Elle a été adoptée parce qu'elle se trouvait dans le projet original du Président, et parce qu'elle donnait satisfaction aussi à M. Adatci. Elle doit du reste être considérée seulement comme une recommandation.

Lord Phillimore, sans s'opposer à l'adoption de la formule, n'y tient pas absolument.

Il désire, avant de terminer, poser à son tour au Président une autre question: le Président donne-t-il la prédominance à l'Assemblée ou au Conseil?

Le PRESIDENT croit que la formule qu'il a proposée sur la représentation des civilisations et des systèmes juridiques, donnerait, autant que cela est humainement possible, la certitude d'obtenir le résultat désiré, c'est-à-dire la représentation des grandes Puissances.

Il pense que Lord Phillimore aurait quelque peine à justifier l'égalité complète du Conseil et de l'Assemblée, étant donné la prédominance qu'il accorde au Conseil auquel sa proposition initiale accorde le privilège du premier vote.

M. DE LAPRADELLE constate qu'on est d'accord sur la nécessité d'établir un équilibre entre les intérêts et les susceptibilités des Etats représentés au Conseil, d'une part, les intérêts et les susceptibilités des Etats qui ne le sont pas, d'autre part. Cet équilibre est le criterium qui doit servir pour l'examen des projets en présence desquels on se trouve actuellement.

M. de Lapradelle reprend d'abord l'idée suggérée par M. Fernandes. Celui-ci ne tient pas compte de cet équilibre, et pour cette raison il manque précisément le but qu'il veut atteindre. Il ôte au Conseil toute influence sur l'élection des juges et donne tout le pouvoir à l'Assemblée, bien qu'exigeant une très forte majorité. Mais, à moins qu'on n'exige l'unanimité, cette exigence ne serait pas satisfaite: l'Assemblée l'emporterait toujours sur le Conseil. Or, M. de Lapradelle croit que le jour où l'équilibre entre les deux organes serait rompu, la Société des

Regarding the second question, Lord Phillimore pointed out that a solution might be reached by way of an amendment. It was useless to discuss the details at the present stage. In this connection Lord Phillimore expressed the wish that the amendments put forward by MM. Loder, Hagerup and Altamira should only be brought up for consideration in their proper turn.

Concerning the question of representation of legal systems, Lord Phillimore observed that the formula inserted in the Root—Phillimore plan was of the nature of a compromise. It had been adopted because it was contained in the President's original plan, and also because it gave satisfaction to M. Adatci. In any case it should only be considered as a recommendation.

Lord Phillimore, without opposing the expression, did not attach much importance to it.

He wished before leaving off, to ask the President another question: Did he give predominance to the Assembly or to the Council?

The PRESIDENT thought that the clause which he had proposed with reference to the representation of civilisations and legal systems would ensure in so far as humanly possible the desired result; that is to say the representation of the Great Powers.

He thought that Lord Phillimore would have some difficulty in proving the complete equality between the Council and the Assembly, taking into account the predominance he gives to the Council; his first proposal, in fact, granted to the Council the privilege of a first vote.

M. DE LAPRADELLE said that there was no question as to the necessity of striking a balance between the interests and susceptibilities of the States represented on the Council on the one hand, and the interests and susceptibilities of the States not represented on the other. This balance is the criterion which should be used in the examination of the projects now before the Committee.

He first of all referred to the idea suggested by M. Fernandes, who did not take this balance into account and therefore failed to achieve exactly the object he was aiming at. He would deprive the Council of any influence in the election of judges and give all the power to the Assembly, even though insisting on a very high majority, Nothing short of unanimity would be sufficient. The Assembly would always have the upper hand of the Council; but M. de Lapradelle thought that if the balance between the

Nations traverserait une crise grave. Ce qu'il faut éviter, c'est que la grande majorité des nations représentées à l'Assemblée, qu'elles soient représentées ou non au Conseil, se coalisent contre un Etat déterminé; mais cette possibilité n'est pas écartée même si l'on exige la majorité des trois quarts. Pour ces raisons, M. de Lapradelle est hostile à la proposition de M. Fernandes.

Il se trouve alors en présence de l'avant-projet du Président. La forme de collaboration entre le Conseil et l'Assemblée, adoptée par ce projet, est celle qu'il trouve la moins satisfaisante: en effet, elle peut amener l'exclusion d'un candidat des grandes Puissances; celui-ci se trouverait ainsi éliminé de façon humiliante. M. de Lapradelle préférerait à cette méthode celle qu'a proposée M. Fernandes, parce que, à son avis, il vaut beaucoup mieux écarter complètement le Conseil que faire bafouer ses candidats par l'Assemblée. On doit lui épargner pareil soufflet: les grandes Puissances ont bien le droit, elles aussi, qu'on tienne compte de leurs susceptibilités.

Après une discussion sur la procédure qu'il conviendra de suivre la prochaine fois qu'on examinera la question de l'organisation de la Cour, le Comité décide, d'un commun accord, que l'on procédera à un vote à la séance du mardi suivant, à onze heures, et que le texte Root—Phillimore sera considéré comme base et les autres textes comme des amendements à ce projet; on soumettra d'abord au vote les amendements qui s'écartent le plus de cette base.

Le PRESIDENT rappelle que le Comité se réunira ce jour à 5 heures de l'après-midi en Chambre du Conseil.

La séance est levée à 12.40 de l'après-midi.

Le Président:
(signé) Brn. DESCAMPS.

Le Secrétaire-Général:
(signé) D. ANZILOTTI.

two bodies were destroyed, the League of Nations would pass through a serious crisis. The point to avoid was a coalition composed of the great majority of the States represented in the Assembly, whether represented on the Council or not, against a particular State; but even a three-quarters majority would not exclude this possibility. For these reasons M. de Lapradelle opposed M. Fernandes' proposal.

He then came to the President's scheme. The form of collaboration between the Council and the Assembly adopted in this scheme was in his opinion the least satisfactory; it might lead to the exclusion of some candidate of the Great Powers: he would thus be rejected under humiliating circumstances. M. de Lapradelle would prefer the method suggested by M. Fernandes to this method, because in his opinion it would be much better to put the Council completely on one side, rather than to allow the Council's candidates to be scorned by the Assembly. The Council must be spared from such insults: even the Great Powers are entitled to have their feelings considered.

After a discussion concerning the procedure to be adopted for the subsequent consideration of the question of the organisation of the Court, the Committee agreed that a vote should be taken at 11 o'clock at the Tuesday meeting. The Root—Phillimore project would be considered as the original draft and the other texts as amendments to this draft. The amendments which differed most from the original project would be voted upon first.

The PRESIDENT reminded the Committee that it would meet unofficially at 5 o'clock in the afternoon.

The meeting closed at 12.40 p.m.

The President:
(signed) Brn. DESCAMPS.

The Secretary-General:
(signed) D. ANZILOTTI.

ANNEXE No. 1.

Avant-Projet concernant la Cour Permanente de Justice Internationale, présenté par le Baron Descamps.

Article 1.

Indépendamment de la Cour Permanente d'Arbitrage organisée par les Conventions de 1899 et de 1907, et des tribunaux spéciaux d'arbitres que les Etats demeurent libres d'instaurer pour la solution de leurs différends, il est institué, conformément à l'article 14 du Traité de Versailles du 28 juin 1919, une Cour Permanente de Justice Internationale, toujours accessible directement aux parties, et en mesure d'assurer la continuité et le progrès de la jurisprudence internationale des arrêts.

CHAPITRE 1.

Organisation de la Cour.

Article 2.

La Cour Permanente de Justice Internationale, est un corps de magistrats indépendants, choisis sans égard à leur nationalité, et constitués dans des conditions de réelle permanence.

Ses membres doivent jouir de la plus haute considération morale et posséder une expérience reconnue.

Ils doivent réunir les conditions requises dans leur pays pour l'admission dans la haute magistrature administrative ou judiciaire, ou être des jurisconsultes d'une compétence notoire en droit international.

Article 3.

La Cour se compose de onze juges et de quatre suppléants.

Le nombre des juges et des suppléants peut être éventuellement augmenté par l'Assemblée sur la proposition du Conseil de la Société des Nations, à concurrence de quinze juges et de six suppléants.

Article 4.

La durée du mandat de membre de la Cour est de neuf années. Ce mandat peut être renouvelé.

Les membres de la Cour terminent les affaires

ANNEX No. 1.

Draft Scheme concerning the Permanent Court of International Justice, submitted by Baron Descamps.

Article 1.

Independently of the Permanent Court of Arbitration organised by the Conventions of 1899 and 1907, and of the special Tribunals of Arbitrators which the States are free to establish for the settlement of their disputes, a Permanent Court of International Justice, which will always be available to States, and have for its purpose to assure the continuity and progress of international jurisprudence based on judgments, is hereby established in accordance with Article 14 of the Treaty of Versailles of June 28th 1919.

CHAPTER 1.

Organisation of the Court.

Article 2.

The Permanent Court of International Justice is a body of independent magistrates chosen regardless of their nationality and established under conditions of real permanence.

Its members must possess the highest moral qualities and be of recognised experience.

They must have the qualifications required in their own countries for admission to the highest administrative or judicial magistracy, or must be international jurisconsults of established repute in international law.

Article 3.

The Court is composed of eleven judges and four supplementary judges.

The number of judges and supplementary judges may eventually be increased by the Assembly, on the proposal of the Council of the League of Nations, to a number of fifteen judges and six supplementary judges.

Article 4.

The term of office for the members of the Court is nine years; they are eligible for reelection.

The members of the Court shall complete the

dont ils sont saisis même si la durée de leur mandat expire avant cette terminaison.

Article 5.

Les membres de la Cour sont élus par l'Assemblée de la Société des Nations, sur deux listes doubles de candidats, présentées l'une par le Conseil de la Société, l'autre par un Collège de Délégués de la Cour Permanente d'arbitrage dans les conditions suivantes:

Trois mois avant la date de l'élection, le Secrétariat Général de la Société des Nations invite par écrit les groupes de délégués nommés à la Cour Permanente d'Arbitrage par chaque Etat, à choisir respectivement un de leurs membres.

Ce membre a pour première mission de consulter les Hautes Cours de Justice, les facultés de droit des universités, les académies ou sections d'académies vouées au culte du droit, ainsi que les autres grands organes de la vie juridique, estimés particulièrement compétents, et de recevoir les présentations de personnes réunissant les conditions requises pour être membre de la Cour et en état de pouvoir en exercer les fonctions.

Le collège des membres de la Cour Permanente d'Arbitrage ainsi choisis, réuni à La Haye deux mois avant la date de l'élection sur convocation du Secrétariat Général, procède à la discussion des candidatures présentées par ses membres et à la formation d'une liste de candidats en nombre double du chiffre des mandats à conférer, de manière que les juges et suppléants appartiennent à des Etats différents, et que les grandes formes de civilisation et les principaux systèmes juridiques du monde soient autant que possible représentés sur cette liste.

Les membres du collège empêchés d'assister à la réunion peuvent envoyer chacun deux noms avec recommandation motivée.

Le collège détermine par un règlement d'ordre le mode suivant lequel il exerce ses pouvoirs dans les conditions ci-dessus déterminées.

La liste des candidats arrêtée par lui, est notifiée sans délai par l'intermédiaire du Secrétariat Général, au Conseil de la Société des Nations, et celui-ci, après toute information estimée opportune, telle que la consultation des grands instituts juridiques internationaux, procède, conformément à un règlement d'ordre adopté par lui, à la formation d'une liste de candidats, également en nombre double du chiffre des mandats à conférer.

L'Assemblée de la Société des Nations procède à son tour, sur la double liste qui lui est

cases brought before them, even if their term of office has expired before the completion of the case.

Article 5.

The members of the Court are elected by the Assembly of the League of Nations from a double list of candidates, one presented by the Council of the League, the other by a College of delegates of the Permanent Court of Arbitration under the following conditions:

Three months before the date of the election, the Secretary-General of the League of Nations shall request in writing the group of delegates appointed to the Permanent Court of Arbitration by each State to name one of its members.

The first duty of this person is to consult the highest Courts of Justice, the University Law Faculties, the Academies, or branches of Academies, devoted to the study of Law, as well as other great institutions of specially recognised merit in the juridical world, and to receive the names of persons combining the qualities necessary to act as a member of the Court and available for an appointment.

The College of members thus chosen from the Permanent Court of Arbitration shall be convened at the Hague two months before the date of the elections, by the Secretary-General, and shall proceed to the discussion of the candidates submitted by its members, and to the preparation of a list of twice as many candidates as the number of the vacancies to be filled. This list shall be prepared in such a way that the judges and supplementary judges shall be drawn from various States and that the great forms of civilisation and the principal legal systems in the world be represented as far as possible.

The members of the College prevented from taking part in the meeting may each send two names together with the reasons for their recommendations.

The College shall determine rules governing the method in which it will exercise its powers, following the conditions here laid down.

The list of candidates drawn up by the College shall be communicated without delay through the Secretary-General to the Council of the League of Nations, and this body, after taking steps to gather all necessary information, such as the consultation of great international law institutions, shall proceed in accordance with the procedure adopted by it to prepare a list of twice as many candidates as the number of the appointments to be filled.

The Assembly of the League of Nations shall

soumise, à la nomination définitive des juges, puis à celle des suppléants, conformément aux dispositions règlementaires qu'elle détermine [1]) en assurant la représentation à la Cour des grandes civilisations et des principaux systèmes juridiques du monde.

proceed in its turn to elect the judges from the double list submitted to it, and to elect the supplementary judges, in conformity to such rules as it shall itself adopt [1]), so as to ensure that the main forms of civilisation and the principal legal systems in the world be represented on the Court.

Article 6.

Il est pourvu régulièrement aux vacances qui peuvent se produire dans la Cour, à la plus prochaine Assemblée de la Société des Nations.

Jusqu'à la réunion de cette Assemblée, les membres en fonction dont le mandat serait expiré peuvent, en cas de nécessité, par décision de la Cour, continuer l'exercice de leurs attributions et assurer ainsi le fonctionnement permanent de la Judicature Internationale.

Article 6.

The Assembly of the League of Nations shall fill any vacancies that may occur, at the first meetings following such vacancies.

Until such meeting of the Assembly, members whose term has expired may, if the Court decides that it is necessary, continue to perform their duties, and thus assure the continuous administration of international jurisdiction.

Article 7.

Les suppléants entrent éventuellement en fonction comme juges dans l'ordre du tableau dressé d'après le nombre de voix obtenu par eux lors de leur élection. En cas de parité de voix, le plus âgé prend rang de préférence.

Au cas où, par suite de modifications survenues, le nombre des suppléants deviendrait insuffisant, au jugement de la Cour, celle-ci peut pourvoir provisionnellement à la désignation d'un ou de plusieurs suppléants, en portant son choix autant que possible sur les candidats compris dans les listes antérieurement présentées à l'Assemblée.

Article 7.

Supplementary judges shall when required assume the duties of judges in the order of a list prepared according to the number of votes obtained by them at their election; in case of equality of votes, the senior shall take precedence.

If, as a result of changed conditions, the number of supplementary judges becomes insufficient in the judgment of the Court, the Court may appoint provisionally one or more supplementary judges, choosing, as far as possible, candidates included in lists previously submitted to the Assembly.

Article 8.

Les membres de la Cour sont inamovibles pendant toute la durée de leur mandat. Ils ne peuvent être relevés de leurs fonctions que si, au jugement unanime des autres membres de la Cour exerçant des fonctions effectives, ils sont manifestement devenus incapables de satisfaire à leur office, ou s'ils ne peuvent plus être considérés comme qualifiés pour le remplir.

Le fait est dans ce cas notifié au Secrétariat Général de la Société des Nations. Cette notification emporte vacance du siège. Cette vacance est aussitôt portée par le Secrétariat Général à la connaissance du membre qui a été l'objet de la notification.

Article 8.

Members of the Court cannot be removed during their term of office; they may only be relieved of their duties if in the unanimous judgment of the other members of the Court they have become manifestly incapable of fulfilling such duties, or if they can no longer be considered as qualified to do so.

In such a case, the fact is communicated to the Secretary-General of the League of Nations. This notification makes the seat vacant. The member concerned shall be informed forthwith by the Secretary-General.

Article 9.

Les membres de la Cour ne peuvent exercer aucune fonction d'ordre diplomatique ou gou-

Article 9.

Members of the Court may not hold any diplomatic or Governmental office, nor discharge any

1) Les mots qui suivent ont été ajoutés au cours de la séance (Note du Secrétariat).

1) The words following were added during the deliberations. (Note by the Secretariat).

vernemental ni être chargés d'aucun service relevant de la direction politique des Etats.

Ne sont pas considérées comme incompatibles avec la qualité de membre de la Cour, les fonctions judiciaires, parlementaires ou d'enseignement.

duties belonging to the political direction of States.

Judicial, parliamentary, or professoral duties, are not considered incompatible with membership of the Court.

Article 10.

Les membres de la Cour ne peuvent, pendant la durée de leur mandat, exercer les fonctions d'agent ou de conseil dans aucune affaire d'ordre international.

Ils ne peuvent participer au règlement d'aucune affaire dans laquelle ils sont intervenus, avant d'être membre de la Cour, comme agents ou conseils de l'une des parties, comme membre d'une Cour Judiciaire, d'un Tribunal d'arbitres, d'une Commission d'enquête, ou à tout autre titre.

Ils ne peuvent prendre part au règlement des affaires dans lesquelles eux ou leurs parents ou alliés jusqu'au troisième degré inclusivement ont un intérêt personnel direct.

En cas de doute, la Cour décide.

Article 10.

Members of the Court cannot during their tenure of office act as agent or counsel in any matter of an international character.

They may not take part in the decision of any case, with which they have been connected, before becoming members of the Court, as agent or counsel for one of the parties concerned, as a member of a judicial Court, of an Arbitration Tribunal, of a Commission of Enquiry or in any other capacity.

They may not take part in the decision of any case in which they, members of their family or their connections up to and including the third degree, have a direct personal interest.

In case of doubt the Court shall decide.

Article 11.

Aucun membre de la Cour ne peut prendre part à une procédure ou à un jugement dans lesquels l'Etat dont il est le ressortissant, est partie. Il est pourvu, le cas échéant, aux remplacements devenus nécessaires à cet effet, par le fonctionnement des suppléants dans l'ordre du tableau indiqué à l'article 7.

Néanmoins tout Etat a le droit de désigner un assesseur ayant la mission de prendre part, avec voix consultative, à l'examen et à la solution des affaires dans lesquelles il est partie.

Article 11.

No member of the Court may take part in any procedure or in any judgment in which the State, of which he is a subject, is a party; in such cases judges thus disqualified shall be replaced by the supplementary judges in the order laid down in Article 7.

Nevertheless, any State has the right to appoint a representative having the right to take part in an advisory capacity in the hearing and determination of a case to which it is a party.

Article 12.

Les membres de la Cour Permanente de Justice Internationale jouissent des privilèges et immunités diplomatiques dans l'exercice de leurs fonctions.

Article 12.

Members of the Permanent Court of International Justice shall enjoy diplomatic privileges and immunities in the exercise of their duties.

Article 13.

Le Siège de la Cour est fixé à La Haye. La Cour ne peut transporter son siège ailleurs qu'en cas de nécessité et en vertu d'une décision motivée.

Les membres de la Cour doivent avoir une résidence à La Haye, de manière que toute communication puisse leur être régulièrement et constamment faite.

Article 13.

The seat of the Court shall be established at the Hague; the seat may not be moved elsewhere except in case of necessity and by virtue of a decision, the reasons for which must be stated.

Members of the Court shall have a domicile at the Hague, so that regular and constant communication with them may be maintained.

Article 14.

Les membres de la Cour jouissent d'une indemnité annuelle fixée par l'Assemblée de la Société des Nations.

Ils ont droit à l'éméritat à la cessation de leurs fonctions.

Article 15.

La Cour élit son Président et son Vice-Président. Ils sont nommés pour le terme de trois ans. Ils sont rééligibles.

La Cour nomme également son Greffier et les autres fonctionnaires du greffe. Elle a la faculté de choisir comme Greffier, le Greffier de la Cour Permanente d'Arbitrage.

Article 16.

La Cour détermine par son règlement d'ordre intérieur le mode suivant lequel elle exerce ses attributions.

Pour l'expédition des affaires elle peut, suivant les cas, soit délibérer en séance plénière, soit se répartir en plusieurs chambres, dont une est affectée au jugement des affaires en procédure sommaire, soit même constituer une ou plusieurs juridictions composées respectivement d'un juge unique, à la disposition des parties qui estimeraient, pour certaines affaires, une telle juridiction suffisante.

Article 17.

Les frais de la Cour sont supportés par la Société des Nations.

Les Membres de la Société y contribuent par parts égales.

Article 14.

Members of the Court shall have an annual salary fixed by the Assembly of the League of Nations.

At the end of their term of office they shall have the right to their salary as a pension.

Article 15.

The Court shall elect its President and Vice-President; they shall hold office for a term of three years; they are eligible for re-election.

The Court shall also appoint its Registrar and the other officials of the Registry. The Court may choose as Registrar the Registrar of the Permanent Court of Arbitration.

Article 16.

The Court shall determine in its rules of order the manner in which it shall exercise its functions.

For the settlement of cases, it may, according to the nature of the case, deliberate in full session, or divide itself into several chambers, one of which shall render judgments according to a summary procedure, or it may vest jurisdiction in one or several single judges for certain cases which the parties concerned consider suitable to be dealt with in this way.

Article 17.

The expenses of the Court shall be defrayed by the League of Nations. The Members of the League shall contribute equally to these expenses.

ANNEXE No. 2.

Proposition de Mr. Root.

Le Comité est-il favorable à un système selon lequel l'élection des juges se fera par le vote séparé et conjoint de l'Assemblée et du Conseil de la Société des Nations sur une liste composée de tous les candidats proposés par les membres de la Cour Permanente d'Arbitrage de La Haye,

ou

le Comité est-il favorable à un système d'élection d'après lequel l'Assemblée seule fera l'élection sur une liste comprenant un nombre de noms deux fois plus grand que le nombre des sièges à remplir, cette liste devant comprendre les noms proposés par une conférence de délégués des membres de la Cour Permanente d'Arbitrage, et sur une autre liste comprenant le même nombre de noms proposés par le Conseil,

ou, en dernier lieu,

le Comité est-il favorable à un système d'élection selon lequel l'Assemblée seule fera l'élection sur une liste proposée par les membres de la Cour Permanente d'Arbitrage, avec les restrictions proposées par M. Ricci-Busatti.

ANNEX No. 2.

Proposal by Mr. Root.

Question, whether the Committee favors the election of the judges:

by separate and concurrent votes of the Assembly and the Council, from a list composed of all the candidates proposed by the members of the Permanent Court of Arbitration at the Hague,

or

by the Assembly alone from a list of double the number of vacancies, proposed by a Convention of delegates of the members of the Permanent Court of Arbitration, and a list of double the number of vacancies, proposed by the Council,

or

by the Assembly alone from a list proposed by members of the Permanent Court of Arbitration under the limitations proposed by M. Ricci-Busatti.

ANNEXE No. 3.

Amendements proposés par M. Loder au Projet Root-Phillimore.

(Voir annexes aux procès-verbaux des 13ième et 14ième séances.)

Les amendements que j'ai l'honneur de proposer au projet ci-dessus mentionné ne se rapportent point à sa teneur générale, ni aux idées sur lesquelles il repose.

Il me semble réunir, en effet, les éléments nécessaires pour assurer le choix des meilleurs juges. L'égalité des Etats n'y est pas atteinte, et la possibilité des combinaisons néfastes semble être exclue.

Je crois cependant — pure question de rédaction — qu'il serait bon de changer l'ordre des articles, afin qu'il corresponde à l'ordre des différentes étapes de l'élection.

En ce qui concerne le nombre des juges, je persiste à croire, qu'étant donnée la difficulté de trouver des juges de premier ordre, il est préférable d'en fixer le nombre à neuf, avec la faculté de l'élever au besoin jusqu'à quinze.

Le rapport entre les articles 3 et 4 n'est pas parfaitement clair.

Aux termes de l'article 3 on devra voter à l'infini tant que les mêmes personnes ne parviennent pas à réunir sur elles la majorité des voix dans chaque collège électoral.

D'après l'article 4 ces collèges pourront mettre fin à ces scrutins réitérés quand bon leur semblera. Mais il paraît que pour cela ils devront d'abord se mettre d'accord.

La disposition finale de l'article punit les six membres de la Commission de leur ténacité en leur enlevant finalement la faculté de choisir. Mais elle ne dit pas à quel moment on pourra prouver que l'accord est impossible.

Dans l'article 1er, il serait bon de biffer les mots „et remplissant . . . ou". Il s'agit de composer la Cour de personnes répondant à ce qui est exprimé à la fin de l'article.

Je voudrais exclure toute personne qui ne se trouve pas sur la liste.

Article 11 du Projet: Je ne crois pas nécessaire d'exiger que tous les juges doivent appartenir à des nations différentes.

L'article 16 concerne les récusations dont il est question dans différents projets.

Le Projet les rejette — et à juste titre. Mais puis-

ANNEX No. 3.

Amendments proposed by M. Loder to the Root-Phillimore plan.

(See Annexes to Procès-Verbaux of 13th and 14th meetings.)

The amendments which I have the honour to propose to the above-mentioned scheme have no relation to its general principles nor to the underlying ideas.

The plan appears to me to unite the necessary elements to assure the choice of the best judges. Equality of States is not interfered with, and the possibility of harmful combinations seems to be excluded.

I believe, however, purely from the standpoint of drafting, that it will be advantageous to change the order of the Articles so that it will correspond to the order of the various steps in the election.

Concerning the number of judges I still believe that, because of the difficulties connected with finding judges of the highest quality, it is preferable to fix the number at nine, with a right of increasing this number in case of need up to fifteen.

The relation between Articles 3 and 4 is not perfectly clear.

By the terms of Article 3, voting would continue indefinitely until a majority of votes has been obtained by the same persons in each of the electoral colleges.

According to Article 4 these colleges may cease balloting when it seems desirable to them, but it appears that they should first mutually agree to this.

The last provision of the Article punishes the six members of the Commission for their tenacity, by finally removing from them the power to choose; but it does not state the time when it will be possible to prove that the accord cannot be reached.

In Article 1 it seems desirable to strike out the words "and who shall possess . . . . or". The Court should be composed of persons fulfilling the conditions laid down at the end of the Article.

I should exclude all persons not on the list.

In Article 11 of the project, I do not believe it necessary to insist that all judges should belong to different nationalities.

que ces récusations n'entrent pas dans le système adopté, on ne peut que créer des confusions en mentionnant qu'elles sont repoussées. D'autre part, l'article ne peut pas rester tel qu'il est, puisque les récusations *processuelles,* reconnues dans toutes les législations, doivent être maintenues ici comme ailleurs. Seulement ces stipulations ne pourront trouver place que dans le règlement de la *procédure*.

En ce qui concerne la deuxième partie du premier alinéa de l'article, il me semble qu'il vaut mieux ne rien régler, et laisser ce soin aux juges qui composeront la Cour et dont le caractère est une garantie suffisante contre des abus.

AMENDEMENTS.

Article 1.

La Cour Permanente de Justice Internationale visée par l'article 14 du Pacte de la Société des Nations se compose de juges indépendants choisis sans égard à leur nationalité et jouissant d'une compétence notoire en matière de droit international. Les juges sont nommés par le concours de l'Assemblée et du Conseil de la Société des Nations d'après les prescriptions des articles suivants.

Article 2.

Trois mois au moins avant l'élection, le Secrétaire Général de la Société invite les membres de la Cour Permanente d'Arbitrage à La Haye, à procéder par groupes, — chaque groupe renfermant les membres nommés par un pays déterminé, — à la présentation de six noms de personnes au plus, remplissant à leur avis les conditions requises et disposées à accepter la dignité de juge [1]), aucun groupe ne pourra présenter plus de deux ressortissants du pays que ce groupe représente.

Article 3.

Le Secrétaire Général dresse une liste comprenant les noms de toutes les personnes ainsi recommandées. A côté du nom de ceux qui auront obtenu plusieurs recommandations, le chiffre de

1) Les mots qui suivent ont été ajoutés pendant les délibérations. De même les mots „l'élection *d'un ou plusieurs juges,* le", qui se trouvaient originairement à la 1ère ligne de l'article. (Note du Secrétariat).

Article 16 is concerned with the rights of challenge referred to in the different projects.

The projects rejects these rights, and rightly so; but as they do not enter into the system adopted, nothing but confusion can be caused by mentioning that they are inadmissible. Furthermore, the Article cannot remain as it is, since the right of challenge *arising out of rules of procedure* must be maintained here, es elsewhere. But these stipulations should be included with the rules of *procedure.*

Concerning the second part of Paragraph 1 of the Article, it appears to me better to make no provisions and to leave the task to the persons who compose the Court. Their character gives sufficient security against abuse.

AMENDMENTS.

Article 1.

The Permanent Court of International Justice provided for by Article 14 of the Covenant of the League of Nations shall consist of independent judges who shall be chosen regardless of their nationality, and who shall be of recognised ability in international law. The judges are appointed by the Assembly and the Council of the League of Nations jointly, according to the provisions of the following Articles.

Article 2.

At least three months before the election, the Secretary-General of the League shall invite the members of the Permanent Court of Arbitration at the Hague to undertake by groups, each group embodying the members named by a given country, the presentations of six names at most for each vacancy, who, in their opinion, possess the qualifications required and who are prepared to accept a post upon the Court [1]). No group may present more than two subjects of the Country which the group represents.

Article 3.

The Secretary-General shall prepare a list containing the names of all the persons so recommended. Following the names of those persons who shall have obtained more than one recom-

1) The words following were added during the deliberation. Similarly, the words "the election *of one or more judges,* the", which formed originally part of the first sentence, were struck out. (Note by the Secretariat).

ces recommandations sera mentionné, sans toutefois indiquer les groupes d'où provient la recommandation. Le Secrétaire Général envoie la liste à l'Assemblée et au Conseil. Seules les personnes mentionnées sur la liste sont éligibles.

Article 4.

L'Assemblée et le Conseil procèdent à l'élection indépendamment l'une de l'autre. Sont élus ceux qui ont réuni dans chaque corps électoral la majorité absolue des voix des membres présents.

Article 5.

Si, en appliquant ce système des sièges restent à remplir, après le premier tour de scrutin dans chacun des corps électoraux on procédera de la même façon à un second tour de scrutin.

Article 6.

Si après le 2me tour de scrutin il reste encore des vacances à remplir, une Commission sera formée composée de six membres, trois pour l'Assemblée et trois pour le Conseil, choisis parmi les personnes qui y siègent comme représentants de leurs Etats. Cette Commission remplit les vacances encore existantes. Sont élus ceux qui ont obtenu la majorité absolue des voix. Si après trois jours consécutifs la Commission n'a pas réussi à choisir les juges manquants, ils seront choisis par cooptation par les juges déjà élus.

Article 7.

Le nombre des juges dont la Cour se compose est de neuf, plus six suppléants. A mesure, cependant, que le besoin s'en fait sentir, le nombre des juges peut être augmenté jusqu'à un maximum de quinze. Les juges suppléants sont nommés suivant le même procédé que les juges.

Article 8 conforme à l'article 10 du Projet.

Article 9 conforme à l'article 11 du Projet.

Article 10 conforme à l'article 12 du Projet.

Article 11 conforme à l'article 13 du Projet.

Article 12 conforme à l'article 14 du Projet.

Article 13 conforme à l'article 15 du Projet.

mendation, the number of such recommendations shall be given, without however indicating by which group any recommendation is made. The Secretary-General shall send the list to the Assembly and to the Council. Only the persons mentioned on the list shall be eligible.

Article 4.

The Assembly and the Council shall carry out the election independently of each other. Those candidates who obtain an absolute majority of the votes of the members present in both electoral bodies, are elected.

Article 5.

If, in the application of this system, vacancies still exist after the first ballot in each of the electoral bodies, a second ballot shall be taken in the same manner.

Article 6.

If, after the second ballot, vacancies still remain to be filled, a Commission shall be formed, composed of six members — three named for the Council and three for the Assembly — chosen amongst the members of each body in their capacity as representatives of their States. This Commission shall fill the outstanding vacancies. An absolute majority of votes is required for election. If, after three consecutive days, the Commission has not succeeded in choosing the judges required, they shall be chosen by the cooptation of the judges already elected.

Article 7.

The number of judges of which the Court is composed is nine, plus six supplementary judges. If, however, it should become necessary, the number of judges may be increased to a maximum of fifteen. The supplementary judges are appointed in the same manner as the judges.

Article 8 conforms to Article 10 of the project.

Article 9 conforms to Article 11 of the project.

Article 10 conforms to Article 12 of the project.

Article 11 conforms to Article 13 of the project.

Article 12 conforms to Article 14 of the project.

Article 13 conforms to Article 15 of the project.

17ième SÉANCE (non-publique), tenue au Palais de la Paix, à La Haye, le 6 juillet 1920.

Présidence de M. le BARON DESCAMPS.

Sont présents: tous les membres du Comité (à l'exception de M. Bevilaqua); M. Fernandes; Mr. James Brown Scott; les secrétaires particuliers de M. le Baron Descamps et de M. Adatci; les membres du Secrétariat.

La séance est ouverte à 9.40 heures du matin.

Le PRESIDENT rappelle la décision prise la veille, de ne commencer le vote sur la question de la nomination des juges qu'à 11 heures. Afin de permettre à chacun d'exprimer son opinion avant cette heure, il propose d'admettre qu'aucun membre ne soit autorisé à parler pendant plus de 10 minutes.

Cette proposition est adoptée.

En ce qui concerne la procédure à suivre, le Président déclare que le projet Root—Phillimore servira de base pour le vote. Il propose que le vote se fasse article par article; qu'on puisse faire des amendements à chaque article; que ces amendements soient soumis au vote d'abord; qu'il y ait un vote d'ensemble sur chaque article; qu'il soit permis aux membres de demander avant chaque vote des explications succinctes, et après le vote de motiver brièvement, s'il y a lieu, leur abstention. Le Président rappelle ensuite que ces votes n'ont qu'un caractère provisoire, c'est-à-dire de première lecture.

Cette méthode est adoptée.

M. LODER dit que le Comité se trouve en présence de trois systèmes différents. Dans ces conditions, il se demande s'il ne vaudrait pas mieux voter d'abord sur les systèmes.

Le PRESIDENT observe qu'il en a déjà été décidé autrement dans la dernière séance. Il pense que la procédure qu'il vient d'exposer est la seule qui permette d'arriver à un rapide et loyal résultat. Le Président souligne encore le caractère provisoire du vote. Il sera possible aux membres d'accorder leur voix à des propositions figurant dans des projets différents. S'il s'élevait des difficultés, le Président a l'inten-

17th MEETING (Private), held at the Peace Palace, the Hague, on July 6th, 1920.

BARON DESCAMPS in the chair.

Present: all members of the Committee (with the exception of M. Bevilaqua); M. Fernandes; Mr. James Brown Scott; the private secretaries of Baron Descamps and of M. Adatci; the members of the Secretariat.

The meeting opened at 9.40 a.m.

The PRESIDENT drew attention to the decision taken on the previous day, namely that a vote should be taken upon the question of the nomination of judges at 11 o'clock. In order to allow each member to speak before this time, he proposed a ten minute limit on debate.

This proposal was adopted.

Concerning the procedure to be followed, the President said that the Root—Phillimore project would be used as a basis for the vote. He proposed that the vote be taken on one Article at a time, that the members might submit amendments to each Article, that these amendments first should be voted upon, that then the Articles as a whole should be put to the vote. Each member should be allowed to ask for a short explanation before each vote, and after the vote they should be allowed to state briefly their reasons if they abstained from voting. The President then reminded the Committee that the votes were only of a provisional nature, in other words first reading.

This method of procedure was adopted.

M. LODER said that the Committee had to deal with three different systems. Under these conditions, he wondered if it would not be better to commence by a vote upon the systems.

The PRESIDENT said that it had already been otherwise decided at the last meeting. He thought that the procedure which he had just explained was the only one which permitted reaching a rapid and fair result. Further he emphasised the provisional nature of the vote. It would be possible for members to vote in favour of proposals contained in different projects. If difficulties arose, the President in-

tion d'appliquer les règles adoptées par l'Institut de Droit International, qui ont toujours donné de bons résultats.

Mr. ROOT désire faire une communication avant que la discussion ne soit ouverte. Il dit que, à la suite de la décision prise la veille par le Comité, Lord Phillimore et lui se sont mis d'accord pour prier Mr. James Brown Scott de les représenter au Comité de rédaction.

Le PRESIDENT prend acte de cette communication et constate qu'il n'y a pas d'objection de la part des membres. Par conséquent, Mr. James Brown Scott représentera Mr. Root et Lord Phillimore au Comité de rédaction.

Le Président ouvre ensuite la discussion sur la question à l'ordre du jour, à savoir celle de la nomination des juges. Il donnera la parole aux membres par ordre alphabétique, à moins qu'un membre ne désire se prononcer que plus tard. Il donne la parole à M. Adatci.

M. ADATCI aurait désiré ne parler qu'après M. Ricci-Busatti. Mais, comme il a déjà eu l'occasion d'exposer en toute franchise son point de vue et ses motifs, il sera bref; aussi ne croit-il pas devoir laisser passer son tour.

Il tient à exprimer ses remerciements pour l'accueil sympathique qu'il a rencontré, bien qu'il ait montré trop de franchise, peut-être, dans l'expression de ses idées. Sa seule préoccupation a été de trouver une solution qui garantît la viabilité de la Cour en assurant la représentation, dans son sein, des Etats représentés de façon permanente au Conseil de la Société des Nations. C'est dans cet esprit qu'il a étudié avec beaucoup de soin les différents projets.

M. Adatci professe beaucoup de sympathie et un grand respect pour le projet du Président, qui, tout en sauvegardant l'égalité juridique des Etats, assure la représentation des grandes civilisations et des principaux systèmes juridiques. Il rappelle que le système japonais diffère essentiellement des systèmes occidentaux. On y a bien introduit des éléments importés d'Europe ou d'Amérique pour régler les choses de la vie quotidienne; mais ces éléments ont été ajoutés à l'ancien fond patriarcal et coutumier qui est toujours prédominant. A ce titre, il semble à M. Adatci que le système japonais aurait bien le droit d'être représenté à la Cour, d'autant plus qu'il a une tendance très nette à se répandre en Asie. Ainsi, ce sont les juristes japonais qui ont préparé la nouvelle constitution de la Chine et élaboré les lois de ce pays. Mais, en dépit de la sympathie qu'il éprouve à ce point de vue pour

tended to apply the rules adopted by the Institute of International Law which had always been found to be satisfactory.

Mr. ROOT wished to make a communication before the discussion was opened. He said that in accordance with the decision taken on the previous day by the Committee, Lord Phillimore and he had agreed to ask Mr. James Brown Scott to represent them upon the drafting Committee.

The PRESIDENT noted this and stated that the members had no objection. Consequently Mr. James Brown Scott would represent Mr. Root and Lord Phillimore upon the drafting Committee.

The President then opened the discussion on the question on the Agenda: the nomination of judges. He said that he would call upon the members to speak in alphabetical order unless a member wished to speak later. He first of all called upon M. Adatci.

M. ADATCI would have preferred to speak after M. Ricci-Busatti. As he had already stated his opinion and his motives quite openly he would be brief, and so he thought he ought not to let his turn pass.

He expressed his thanks for the sympathetic reception afforded to his almost too frank statement of his ideas. He was solely concerned in trying to find a solution which would guarantee the practicability of the Court by assuring the representation upon it of those States permanently represented upon the Council of the League of Nations. It was in this frame of mind that he had very carefully studied the different proposals.

M. Adatci said that he had studied the President's project with great respect and interest. This project, whilst protecting the legal equality of States, assured the representation of the great forms of civilisation and the principal legal systems. He said that the Japanese system was essentially different from Western systems. Many elements had been borrowed from Europe or America for the regulation of daily life, but these elements had been added to the ancient patriarchal customs which still predominated. For this reason M. Adatci thought that the Japanese system was fully entitled to be represented upon the Court, more especially as there was a distinct tendency for it to spread throughout Asia. Thus it was Japanese jurists who had prepared the new constitution of China and who had drafted the laws of that country. But in spite of the sympathy from this standpoint which

le projet du Président, il le trouve insuffisant, parce qu'il ne garantit pas de façon satisfaisante que les grandes Puissances seront représentées à la Cour.

M. Adatci s'est donc tourné vers le projet Root—Phillimore. Il trouve ce projet admirable par son organisation et par les nouveautés qu'il renferme. Toutefois il élève contre ce projet les mêmes objections que contre celui du Président: les garanties pour la représentation des grands Etats ne sont pas suffisantes, bien qu'il donne peut-être, comme l'a dit Lord Phillimore, une garantie raisonnable.

Si ces deux projets ne satisfont pas entièrement M. Adatci, il adhère par contre avec la plus vive sympathie au projet présenté par M. Ricci-Busatti, le seul qui présente la garantie absolue que les grandes Puissances soient représentées à la Cour. Si ce projet n'est pas adopté, M. Adatci se réserve, d'accord avec M. Ricci-Busatti, de soumettre une nouvelle proposition. En achevant, M. Adatci affirme qu'il est animé du meilleur esprit de conciliation et ne demande qu'à arriver à un accord avec les autres membres.

M. ALTAMIRA n'a rien à ajouter aux explications qu'il a données antérieurement; mais, pour bien s'éclairer sur le fond de la question, il demande à Mr. Root de bien vouloir fournir quelques explications sur deux points, à savoir:

1. la garantie de la représentation des grands Etats à la Cour, telle qu'il la conçoit, et
2. la représentation des différents systèmes juridiques.

M. FERNANDES déclare qu'il n'a rien à ajouter aux déclarations qu'il a déjà faites.

M. HAGERUP n'a rien à ajouter non plus quant au fond de la question. Il désire cependant expliquer qu'il lui aurait été plus facile de se rallier au projet Root—Phillimore si l'on avait voulu tenir compte des observations de M. Fernandes, sur le double vote donné aux Etats Membres du Conseil de la Société des Nations. C'est uniquement parce qu'il sait qu'il n'y a pas de chance de voir triompher les idées de M. Fernandes, qu'il s'abstient de les reprendre sous forme d'amendements. Il désire en outre signaler — car le Comité rencontrera des critiques à ce propos — que l'idée d'exclure du scrutin dans l'Assemblée les Etats déjà représentés au Conseil, a été émise, et qu'elle n'a été abandonnée que devant l'évidence qu'un vote à son sujet serait défavorable.

M. Hagerup ajoute qu'il se trouve en complet désaccord avec M. Adatci sur la question

he felt for the President's plan, he thought that it did not go far enough, because it did not guarantee satisfactorily the representation of the Great Powers upon the Court.

Therefore, M. Adatci had turned to the Root—Phillimore scheme. He thought this scheme admirable both as regards its organisation and the new ideas it contained. Nevertheless he had the same objections to this scheme as to that of the President: the guarantees for the representation of the Great States were not sufficient, though, as Lord Phillimore had said, it perhaps gave a reasonable guarantee. As these two plans did not entirely satisfy M. Adatci, he approved very heartily of the plan presented by M. Ricci-Busatti. It was the only one containing a complete guarantee that the Great States would be represented on the Court. If this project were not adopted, M. Adatci reserved the right of submitting a new proposal in agreement with M. Ricci-Busatti. Finally M. Adatci emphasised the fact that he was moved by the strongest desire for reconciliation and that he cared only to reach an agreement with the other members.

M. ALTAMIRA had nothing to add to the explanation he had already given, but in order to get a thorough understanding of the question he asked Mr. Root to be so good as to explain his views on two points:

1. the guarantee of the representation of the Great Powers upon the Court, as conceived by him, and
2. the representation of the different legal systems.

M. FERNANDES said that he had nothing to add to the statements he had already made.

M. HAGERUP also had nothing to add concerning the heart of the question. He wished however to say that it would have been easier for him to adopt the Root—Phillimore project if the remark of M. Fernandes on the subject of the double vote given to States which were Members of the Council of the League of Nations had been taken into account. The fact that there was no chance of M. Fernandes' ideas prevailing was the sole reason why he abstained from proposing them as an amendment. On the other hand he wished to call attention to the fact — because the Committee would surely be criticised on this subject — that the idea of excluding from voting in the Assembly the States already represented in the Council had been advanced, and was given up only after it was apparent that a vote on the matter would be adverse.

de la représentation des systèmes juridiques et des formes de civilisation. Il admet cependant que M. Adatci a fait des concessions, et il croit donc devoir en faire autant. C'est pourquoi il n'insiste pas sur le désir qu'il a exprimé la veille, de voir supprimer dans l'article 11 du projet Root—Phillimore la disposition relative à la représentation des civilisations et des systèmes juridiques. Il y met cependant une condition: c'est qu'à l'expression qui figure actuellement à cet article, on substitue une formule dans le genre de celle proposée par le Président comme addition à l'article 5 de son avant-projet.

En terminant, M. Hagerup demande au Président si l'article 2 du projet Root—Phillimore sera mis aux voix avec les amendements qui s'y rapportent, mais sous la réserve que le nombre des juges et la durée du mandat seront fixées plus tard.

Le PRESIDENT répond affirmativement. Il proposera l'article 5 de son projet comme amendement à l'article 2 du projet Root—Phillimore.

M. HAGERUP fait valoir que cette manière de procéder créera des difficultés: on peut préférer d'une façon générale le projet Root—Phillimore, tout en approuvant plus volontiers le système de la présentation des candidats adopté dans l'avant-projet du Président.

Le PRESIDENT déclare que le procédé qu'il a préconisé est le seul moyen de faire voter sur son système tel qu'il le propose. On pourra ultérieurement faire telle ou telle proposition particulière.

M. HAGERUP se réserve, dans ces conditions, de reprendre la discussion sur la présentation des candidats, par exemple, lorsque l'article 6 du projet Root—Phillimore sera mis aux voix.

Le PRESIDENT n'y voit pas d'inconvénient. Le vote auquel on procède actuellement est purement provisoire.

M. HAGERUP remarque que la question du nombre des juges, traitée dans la première phrase de l'article 2 du projet Root—Phillimore, n'a pas encore été discutée.

LORD PHILLIMORE fait observer que les dispositions de cet article relatif au nombre des juges et à la durée du mandat ne seront pas soumises au vote à présent.

He added that he entirely disagreed with M. Adatci on the question of the representation of legal systems and the forms of civilisation. He admitted however, that M. Adatci had made concessions, and therefore he thought he ought to do the same. For this reason he did not insist on the wish he had expressed on the previous day, to suppress in Article 11 of the Root—Phillimore project the clause concerning the representation of civilisations and legal systems. He made one condition, however; that the expression actually contained in the Article should be replaced by a clause similar to that which the President had proposed as an addition to article 5 of his draft scheme.

In conclusion, M. Hagerup asked the President whether article 2 of the Root—Phillimore project would be put to a vote together with the amendments concerning it, but with the reservation that the number of judges and the term of office should be decided on later.

The PRESIDENT replied in the affirmative. He would put forward article 5 of his project as an amendment to article 2 of the Root—Phillimore plan.

M. HAGERUP pointed out that this method of procedure would create difficulties; it was quite possible to prefer the Root—Phillimore project generally, while preferring the system adopted in the President's scheme for the selection of candidates.

The PRESIDENT said that the procedure which he had explained was the only way of voting on his system as he had presented it. Later on, individual proposals might be submitted.

M. HAGERUP under these conditions reserved the right to continue the discussion of the question of the selection of candidates, when for instance article 6 of the Root—Phillimore plan was voted upon.

The PRESIDENT saw no objection. The vote which was about to be taken was of a purely provisional nature.

M. HAGERUP said that the question of the number of judges dealt with in the first sentence of article 2 of the Root—Phillimore plan had not yet been discussed.

LORD PHILLIMORE said that the provisions of this article concerning the number of judges and the length of their mandates would not be voted upon at present.

M. DE LAPRADELLE n'a rien à ajouter pour le moment. Il se réserve de donner des explications lorsqu'on discutera sur la représentation des civilisations et des systèmes juridiques. Pour lui la question de principe impliquée dans le vote sur l'article 2 du projet Root—Phillimore se résume ainsi: les juges doivent-ils être désignées simultanément par le Conseil et l'Assemblée? Lorsqu'on procèdera au vote sur cette question, il votera „oui".

M. LODER déclare qu'il votera comme M. de Lapradelle.

Il désire répondre à une objection qu'on a adressée au projet Root—Phillimore. On a dit que ce projet donne un double vote aux Etats représentés au Conseil de la Société des Nations. M. Loder croit que cette objection est injuste. Le Conseil et l'Assemblée sont deux corps différents et composés de personnes différentes; par conséquent, il s'agit de deux votations diverses. D'ailleurs, ce ne seront pas les Etats qui feront l'élection par l'intermédiaire du Conseil et de l'Assemblée. M. Loder attire aussi l'attention sur la Commission qui aura pour tâche de concilier les opinions divergentes de l'Assemblée et du Conseil. Cette Commission est entièrement indépendante et constituée sur un pied de parfaite égalité.

M. DE LAPRADELLE se rallie au point de vue de M. Loder, et particulièrement à ce qu'il vient de dire sur le rôle de la Commission de conciliation.

MM. HAGERUP et FERNANDES pensent, contrairement à MM. Loder et de Lapradelle, que les Membres du Conseil et de l'Assemblée sont bien les Etats, et non pas leurs représentants.

M. DE LAPRADELLE déclare qu'il a été vivement frappé par l'idée suggérée par M. Hagerup, d'exclure du vote, dans l'Assemblée, les délégués des Etats dont les représentants ont déjà voté au Conseil. Il se demande comment cette idée qui, à son avis, établirait une égalité absolue, pourrait être réalisée. Il croit qu'il serait dangereux de mettre en discussion le titre de tel ou tel membre de l'Assemblée à prendre part avec voix délibérative à la procédure de l'Assemblée, et il serait peu normal d'ôter aux représentants des grands Etats le droit d'émettre un vote. Mais c'est là une des solutions possibles. L'autre consiste à exclure entièrement les membres des grandes Puissances représentées au Conseil, de la discussion dans l'Assemblée. Au-

M. DE LAPRADELLE had nothing to add at the moment. He would wait until the discussion of the question of the representation of civilisations and legal systems. From his point of view the principle involved in the vote upon article 2 of the Root—Phillimore plan might be summed up as follows: should the judges be appointed by the Council and the Assembly simultaneously? If a vote were taken upon this question he would vote in the affirmative.

M. LODER said that he would vote in the same way as M. de Lapradelle.

He wished to answer an objection raised against the Root—Phillimore plan. It had been said that this plan gave a double vote to the States represented on the Council of the League of Nations. M. Loder thought that this objection was unjust. The Council and the Assembly were two different bodies and composed of different persons; therefore it was a question of two separate votes. Besides, the election was not being carried out by the States through the medium of the Council and the Assembly. M. Loder also called attention to the Commission intended to reconcile the divergent opinions of the Assembly and the Council. This Commission would be entirely independent and would be constituted upon a basis of perfect equality.

M. DE LAPRADELLE agreed with M. Loder and especially on what he had just said concerning the task of the joint conciliation Commission.

M. HAGERUP and M. FERNANDES disagreed with M. Loder and M. de Lapradelle; they held that the States and not their representatives were the Members of the Council and the League.

M. DE LAPRADELLE declared that he was much impressed by the idea advanced by M. Hagerup, namely, to exclude the delegates of those States whose representatives had already voted on the Council, from voting in the Assembly. He wondered how this idea, which in his opinion would create an absolute equality, could be realised. He thought that it would be dangerous to question the right of any particular member of the Assembly to take part in the voting of the Assembly; and it would be hardly normal to deprive the representatives of the Great Powers of the right of voting. But this was one of the two possible solutions. The other was to exclude entirely the members of the Great Powers represented on

cune de ces solutions ne paraît acceptable. Ces membres sont des éléments de conciliation entre les deux corps, et cette communauté semble désirable. Du reste, en la supprimant on déformerait un des organes de la Société des Nations, et on altérerait le fonctionnement normal de tous les deux. M. de Lapradelle fait enfin valoir que l'idée de M. Hagerup pourrait constituer un précédent dangereux; et si séduisante qu'elle paraisse, il croit devoir faire bien des réserves à son sujet.

LORD PHILLIMORE dit qu'il n'a presque rien à ajouter. Il désire seulement répéter que le vote auquel on va procéder sera un vote de principe sur la question de savoir si les juges seront élus ou non par l'Assemblée et le Conseil. Les amendements, ceux de MM. Loder et Adatci, et les autres, seront pris en considération plus tard.

Après un échange de vues entre le PRESIDENT, LORD PHILLIMORE et M. DE LAPRADELLE, pour bien spécifier si le vote sera un vote de principe ou s'il portera sur des textes, M. Ricci-Busatti obtient la parole.

M. RICCI-BUSATTI rappelle qu'il s'est réservé la veille le droit de proposer, le cas échéant, des amendements à son projet. Après les discours de ses collègues il retire ce projet, qu'il considère déjà comme rejeté, en ce qui concerne la nomination des juges. Si cependant M. Adatci, qui a bien voulu l'appuyer, veut le reprendre pour le soumettre au vote, M. Ricci-Busatti s'y ralliera; mais il déclare qu'il se contente de le remplacer par des amendements. En effet, la garantie qu'il avait estimé nécessaire à la suite des discussions précédentes, pour assurer la représentation de tous les grands Etats dans la nouvelle Cour, n'avait été proposée par lui qu'à contre-cœur, puisqu'elle se trouve en contradiction avec le point d'où il était parti, à savoir le principe général de l'égalité des Etats. Les amendements qu'il vient de formuler constituent en réalité une nouvelle proposition qui se rapproche, sur ce point, du projet soumis par la délégation italienne à la Conférence de Paris, ainsi que des principes qu'il a développés dans ses premiers discours: son idée fondamentale reste toujours, en effet, de relier la Cour de Justice à la Cour d'Arbitrage, et d'en assurer l'indépendance en excluant toute influence politique.

M. Ricci-Busatti croit que des corps politiques, tels que le Conseil et l'Assemblée, vote-

the Council from the discussion in the Assembly. Neither of these solutions seemed acceptable. These members would be an element tending to conciliation between the two bodies, and this connecting link seemed very desirable. Besides, by doing away with this, one of the organisms of the League of Nations would be distorted and the normal working of both would be upset. M. de Lapradelle pointed out that M. Hagerup's idea might create a dangerous precedent, and however attractive it might appear, he felt that he must make a firm reservation concerning it.

LORD PHILLIMORE said that he had practically nothing to add. He only wished to repeat that the vote about to be taken would be one upon the question of principle, namely whether the judges should or should not be elected by the Assembly and Council. The amendments proposed by M. Loder, M. Adatci, and others would be considered later.

After an exchange of views between the PRESIDENT, LORD PHILLIMORE and M. DE LAPRADELLE to make certain whether the vote was on principle or on the texts, M. Ricci-Busatti spoke.

M. RICCI-BUSATTI recalled that he had reserved for himself the right to propose amendments to his project, should occasion arise. After the speeches of his colleagues, he withdrew his project. As far as the nomination of judges was concerned, he considered that it already had been rejected. However, if M. Adatci, who had given it his kind support, wished to revive it in order to make it the subject of a vote, M. Ricci-Busatti would agree; nevertheless he said that he would be satisfied to replace it by amendments. As a matter of fact the guarantee, which he felt necessary following the earlier discussions, for the representation of the large States on the new Court, had been proposed by him reluctantly, since it was contradictory to his original point of view on the equality of States. The amendments which he had just drafted, in reality constituted a new proposition which resembled in this respect the project submitted by the Italian delegation at the Paris Conference as well as the principles which he had developed in his first speeches. His fundamental idea always remained to link the Court of Justice with the Court of Arbitration and to guarantee its independence by excluding all political influence.

M. Ricci-Busatti thought that such political bodies as the Council and the Assembly

ront toujours sur des pays plutôt que sur des personnes, dont d'ailleurs les électeurs ne connaîtront pas exactement les qualités.

Ces considérations ont amené M. Ricci-Busatti à proposer une Cour où chaque Etat aura un représentant; la Cour sera divisée en plusieurs sections; les Présidents de ces sections, élus en séance plénière, formeront le noyau de la Cour.

Cette élection, faite entre personnes qui se connaissent, garantira de façon bien supérieure que le choix des meilleurs sera assuré. Il lui est d'ailleurs indifférent que l'on considère la totalité des juges ou seulement le collège présidentiel comme la vraie „Cour Permanente". (Voir annexe 1ère).

Le PRESIDENT donne lecture d'une communication relative à la présentation des dames des membres du Comité à S. M. la Reine des Pays-Bas.

Mr. ROOT déclare qu'il a déjà dit tout ce qu'il avait à dire sur la question à l'ordre du jour. Il veut cependant répondre aux questions qui lui ont été adressées par M. Altamira.

Mr. Root rappelle que le point qui forme l'objet de ces questions a été traité par lui dans les instructions qu'il a données en qualité de Ministre des Affaires Etrangères à la Délégation américaine à la 2ème Conférence de la Paix. Pour ne pas retarder le vote sur la question de la nomination des juges, il attendra pour s'expliquer, si M. Altamira le veut bien, qu'un amendement ait été soumis au sujet de ce point particulier.

Néanmoins, sur les instances de Lord Phillimore, Mr. Root prie Mr. James Brown Scott de donner lecture du passage qui, dans ces instructions, a trait à la représentation des divers systèmes juridiques. (Voir annexe 2).

Mr. Root ajoute qu'il maintient toujours l'avis exprimé dans ce passage. Il fait valoir que le projet Root—Phillimore a encore l'avantage d'écarter toute possibilité de déloyauté, en donnant aux petites nations un droit de véto sur tout ce qui se passe dans le Conseil, et aux grandes nations un droit de véto sur les décisions de l'Assemblée, et cela sans toucher à l'organisation existante: la Cour ne doit pas être fondée sur des présuppositions de désaccord ou d'intrigue. Tout ce qui tend à donner de droit tel ou tel avantage aux grandes ou aux petites nations introduit dans le fondement de la Cour le principe qu'on désire en exclure. Dans le système du projet, les juges ne seront pas élus par un pays déterminé; ils seront tous élus par le vote

would always vote on the country rather than on the man, whose ability would not be exactly known by the electors.

These considerations had led M. Ricci-Busatti to propose a Court on which each State would have one representative; the Court would be divided into several sections; the Presidents of these sections, elected in full session, would form the nucleus of the Court.

This election carried out by people who knew each other would be a far superior guarantee that the best men would be elected. Otherwise it was immaterial to him whether all the judges or merely the college of Presidents were considered as the true "Permanent Court". (See Annex 1).

The PRESIDENT read a communication concerning the presentation of the ladies of members of the Committee to Her Majesty The Queen of the Netherlands.

Mr. ROOT stated that he had already said all that he wished to say concerning the questions on the Agenda. However, he wished to answer the questions put to him by M. Altamira.

Mr. Root reminded the Committee that the point which was the object of these questions had been dealt with by him in the instructions he had given as Secretary of State to the American Delegation to the Second Peace Conference. In order not to delay the vote upon the question of the appointment of judges, he would, with M. Altamira's permission, wait until an amendment had been submitted dealing with this point, before he gave his explanation.

Nevertheless, at the request of Lord Phillimore, Mr. Root asked Mr. James Brown Scott to read the passage in these instructions dealing with the representation of the various legal systems. (See Annex 2).

Mr. Root added that he still held the opinion expressed in it. He pointed out that the Root—Phillimore plan also had the advantage of removing any possibility of unfairness by giving the small nations the veto on everything which took place in the Council, and by giving the large nations a veto on all the decisions taken by the Assembly: this advantage was obtained with the aid of an existing organisation: the Court should not be founded on a supposition of discord and intrigue. Anything which tends to give a particular thing to the great or small nations introduces a principle into the constitution of the Court which it is most desirable

concordant des membres de ces deux corps, qui existent déjà. Ainsi la Cour méritera la confiance de l'humanité.

M. ALTAMIRA remercie Mr. Root. Il fait remarquer cependant que le passage des instructions de la délégation américaine, qu'on vient de lire, lui était bien connu.

Tous les membres ayant exprimé leur opinion sur les projets en présence, le PRESIDENT désire à son tour formuler brièvement son appréciation sur ces projets.

Le projet Adatci a le mérite d'assurer d'une manière absolue un résultat important pour la viabilité de la Cour. Il ne le fait, malheureusement, qu'en portant une nouvelle et grave atteinte à l'égalité juridique des Etats.

Le projet Ricci-Busatti ne prétend pas formuler des conclusions définitives, mais il constitue un louable effort pour arriver à la séparation de la politique et de la justice en conférant des attributions remarquables aux jurisconsultes composant la Cour Permanente d'Arbitrage.

Et, à ce point de vue, le Président doit reconnaître que ce projet poursuit le but que lui-même a, dès le début, cherché à atteindre.

Quant au projet Root—Phillimore, le Président tient à l'examiner de façon plus précise en se plaçant au double point de vue du mode de présentation des candidats et du mode d'élection définitive.

En ce qui concerne le premier, il lui adresse un triple reproche. Ce projet rend illusoire et dangereux le droit de présentation reconnu aux membres de la Cour Permanente d'Arbitrage. Le nombre de deux cents candidats, calculé en accordant à tous les Etats, au nombre de cinquante environ, le droit de présenter quatre candidats, est trop considérable pour ne pas prêter à d'inévitables et regrettables combinaisons. Cette observation est d'autant plus fondée que les choix seront fatalement empreints d'un caractère national. Enfin, à moins de supposer que les quatre membres électeurs de la Cour Permanente d'Arbitrage se choisissent eux-mêmes, on peut arriver à une sorte d'exclusion de la Cour à créer, des membres de la Cour existante.

LORD PHILLIMORE ne partage pas l'avis du Président sur ce dernier point.

M. DE LAPRADELLE fait remarquer que le reproche à cet égard s'applique avec la même force au projet du Président lui-même.

to exclude. According to the system of this plan, the judges are not elected by a particular country. They are all elected by the concurrent votes of the members of these two already existing bodies. In this way the Court will merit the confidence of mankind.

M. ALTAMIRA thanked Mr. Root. He stated, however, that he was familiar with the passage from the instructions to the American Delegation which had just been read.

When all the members had stated their opinion upon the plans before the Committee, the PRESIDENT, in turn, wished to make a brief comment on them.

The Adatci project had the merit of definitely assuring a condition most important for the practicability of the Court. Unfortunately, it accomplished this only by dealing a new and severe blow to the legal equality of States.

The Ricci-Busatti plan did not pretend to be a complete work but it represented a praiseworthy attempt to separate politics and justice, by giving remarkable powers to the jurisconsults composing the Permanent Court of Arbitration.

From this point of view, the President admitted that it aimed at the result which he himself had sought to attain since the beginning.

Turning to the Root—Phillimore plan, the President wished to consider it more fully in the following two aspects: the method of selecting candidates, and the method of actual election.

Dealing with the first, he raised three objections. The project makes the right of nomination granted to the members of the Permanent Court of Arbitration both illusory and dangerous. Counting on fifty States, each nominating four candidates, the number of two hundred is so large as to lend itself to inevitable and regrettable intrigues. This remark is all the truer because of the fact that the choices would inevitably bear a strong national tinge. Finally, unless it were assumed that the four elector-members of the Court of Arbitration would choose themselves, there might arise a kind of exclusion, from the Court to be created, of the members of the existing Court.

LORD PHILLIMORE did not share the opinion of the President on this point.

M. DE LAPRADELLE pointed out that this reproach applied with the same force to the President's own plan.

Le PRESIDENT maintient qu'à son avis une certaine délicatesse pourrait empêcher les membres de la Cour d'Arbitrage de présenter leurs collègues. Il poursuit en disant que ceux, des membres du Comité, qui soutiennent que la part faite dans le projet du Président, au Collège des membres de la Cour Permanente d'Arbitrage, se rapproche trop de celle que le même projet accorde au Conseil de la Société des Nations, oublient peut-être un peu vite qu'il s'agit de nominations judiciaires, que le Conseil est un corps essentiellement politique, qu'il a une mission fort distincte de la judicature et qui ne semble pas comporter une trop grande immixtion dans la distribution de la justice. Dans son projet le Conseil joue plutôt, au point de vue des présentations, le rôle d'une Cour d'appel ayant mission de vérifier et de contrôler les présentations précédemment faites, et de corriger précisément ce qu'elles pourraient avoir de défectueux, en présentant une liste nouvelle de candidats en nombre double des places à attribuer. Il semble d'ailleurs facile d'accentuer au besoin ce caractère de manière à répondre à toutes les objections.

Ce qui est plus difficile à justifier, c'est l'égalité juridique du Conseil et de l'Assemblée, à tous égards, dans la nomination définitive des membres de la Cour nouvelle, c'est le double vote accordé à la fois aux Etats, figurant d'une manière fort étroite et très inégale dans la composition du Conseil. Le Président croit qu'en consacrant le système du véto réciproque, on pourrait n'aboutir qu'à un antagonisme organisé et à cette alternative peu séduisante: collision ou collusion. Toutes les interventions de facteurs internes, comme une commission de conciliation, et de facteurs externes, comme le recours à la nomination par les juges, déjà élus, de la Cour, quelque minime que soit le nombre de ceux-ci — et le Président insiste sur ce point — ne font que confirmer des prévisions qui n'ont rien de rassurant. Qui sait si le Conseil, en voulant faire échec à l'Assemblée, ne soulèvera pas contre lui des oppositions plus générales qu'il pourrait être prudent d'éviter?

Ce qui paraît certain, c'est que le résultat final, et même le but poursuivi par les grands Etats est moins assuré par la procédure d'antagonisme préconisée dans le projet Root—Phillimore que par la procédure simple que le Président s'est permis de proposer et qui repose sur l'obligation fondamentale pour le collège des membres de la Cour Permanente, puis finalement pour l'Assemblée des Etats, d'assurer la présence au sein de la Cour de juges représentant les grandes formes de civilisation et les principaux systè-

The PRESIDENT said that in his opinion a certain delicacy of feeling might prevent the members of the Court of Arbitration from nominating their own colleagues. He then went on to say that the members of the Committee, who thought that the functions given in the President's plan to the members of the Permanent Court of Arbitration bore too close a resemblance to those given by the same plan to the Council of the League of Nations, forgot too soon perhaps, that it was a question of judicial appointment, and that the Council was essentially a political body, that its duties were quite distinct from judicial duties, and should not be combined too much with the administration of justice. In the plan, the Council rather plays the part of a court of appeal whose duty is to verify and control the lists of candidates already made and to amend any defects in these lists by the preparation of a new list containing twice as many candidates as there are appointments to be made. Further it would seem easy to accentuate, if necessary, this characteristic in such a way as to meet all possible objections.

The point which was more difficult to justify was the legal equality of the Council and the Assembly in the appointment of the members of the new Court; also the double vote given to some States which figure in a very narrow and unequal way in the composition of the Council. The President thought that by introducing a system of reciprocal veto, the only result would be organised antagonism, and the very unattractive alternative of open conflict or collusion. The intervention of any internal element such as a conciliatory Commission, or of any external element such as nomination by these judges of the Court who are already elected, no matter how few in number — the President laid emphasis on this point — did nothing to reassure him and only confirmed his forebodings. Who knows that the Council, in an attempt to checkmate the Assembly, would not stir up widespread opposition against itself, which would be wise to avoid?

He felt certain that the final result and the end sought by the Great States was less likely to be achieved by the antagonistic method described in the Root—Phillimore plan than by the simple procedure proposed by the President. This method relies upon a fundamental obligation binding the members of the Permanent Court and finally the Assembly of States, to ensure that judges representing the great civilisations and the principal legal systems of the world are included in the Court. It was this idea the President had in mind from the outset, and

mes juridiques du monde. C'est là l'idée que le Président a préconisée, dès le début, et il ne peut que remercier ses collègues de l'avoir agréée, comme il tient à les remercier aussi d'avoir accordé un droit de présentation à la Cour actuelle d'Arbitrage.

Ayant achevé son exposé, le Président propose qu'on procède au vote.

M. HAGERUP déclare qu'il doit s'abstenir de voter sur le nouveau projet Ricci-Busatti, qui lui paraît intéressant, mais dont il n'a pas eu le temps de prendre suffisamment connaissance.

Sur l'invitation du PRESIDENT, M. RICCI-BUSATTI donne quelques explications supplémentaires sur l'économie de son projet, qui se rapproche aussi du système de l'ancienne *Rota romana*: un collège de juges qui siégeaient à tour de rôle, selon certaines règles de procédure déterminées. Les différentes sections pourraient être constituées de manière à présenter une compétence spéciale pour certaines affaires; tout juge ne peut pas être également compétent pour tous les litiges. Les parties auraient la plus grande influence sur le choix du tribunal qui devrait connaître de leur cas; si elles n'étaient pas d'accord à ce sujet la Présidence de la Cour désignerait la section compétente, à moins qu'elle ne préfère retenir elle-même le litige.

M. DE LAPRADELLE pose à M. Ricci-Busatti les trois questions suivantes: croit-il assurer par son système la permanence de la Cour? croit-il assurer l'unité de la jurisprudence? croit-il donner au monde la Cour qu'attend l'opinion publique?

M. RICCI-BUSATTI répond qu'à son avis la permanence est assurée par le noyau formé par le collège présidentiel; il croit que l'unité de la jurisprudence sera sauvegardée par son système (dans la mesure où cette unité est possible et désirable dans des rapports entre Etats), d'une façon aussi efficace que par n'importe quel autre; il croit enfin qu'une Cour constituée d'après ses idées répondrait bien aux sentiments et à l'attente des peuples. Elle répondrait, à son avis, à la réalité des choses, tandis que tous les autres systèmes s'en écartent.

M. LODER trouve que les amendements de M. Ricci-Busatti vont à l'encontre de tout ce qui a été dit au sein du Comité. Il observe que la Cour serait constituée de quarante cinq juges, choisis par leurs gouvernements.

he felt bound to thank his colleagues for having accepted it. He wished to thank them also for having conferred the right of nomination on the present Court of Arbitration.

Having completed his summary, the President proposed that the vote should be taken.

M. HAGERUP stated that he must abstain from voting upon the Ricci-Busatti plan because, although it seemed very interesting, he had not yet had the time to study it sufficiently.

At the request of the PRESIDENT, M. RICCI-BUSATTI gave some additional explanations concerning the arrangement of his plan, which resembles the system of the ancient *Rota romana*, a college of judges who sit in turn according to certain rules of procedure. The different sections could be composed in such a way as to be specially competent to deal with certain classes of cases. No judge can be equally competent to deal with all cases. The contesting parties would have the largest influence in the choice of tribunals which would deal with their case: if they were not agreed on this subject, the Presidency of the Court would designate which section was competent, unless it preferred to hear the case itself.

M. DE LAPRADELLE put the three following questions to M. Ricci-Busatti: did he think that his system would ensure the permanence of the Court? did he think it would ensure the unity of jurisprudence? did he think that his system would give the nations a Court such as was expected by public opinion?

M. RICCI-BUSATTI answered that in his opinion the permanence was assured by the permanent nucleus of the presidential body. He thought that the unity of jurisprudence would be assured (to the degree this unity is possible and desirable in relations between States) by his system just as effectively as by any other system. Finally he thought that a Court constituted in accordance with his ideas would fulfil the wishes and expectations of the nations. It answered the demands of realities, while all the others kept away from them.

M. LODER thought that M. Ricci-Busatti's amendments were directly opposed to all that had been said during the discussions of the Committee. He noticed that the Court was to consist of forty-five judges chosen by their Governments.

M. RICCI-BUSATTI remarque que les juges ainsi nommés éliront dans leur sein un tribunal vraiment permanent.

M. FERNANDES fait valoir que les amendements de M. Ricci-Busatti n'excluent pas la possibilité d'arriver à une conciliation. Il voit néanmoins une grave objection contre le projet, à propos duquel il désire poser une question: il se demande en effet, quand les parties ne tomberont pas d'accord sur le choix de la section à qui elles voudront soumettre l'affaire, comment s'effectuera ce choix. Dans la plupart des cas, il arrivera que la cause renfermera des éléments assez complexes pour ne pas pouvoir rentrer dans la compétence spéciale d'une des sections. Comment, dans ces conditions, désigner une section particulière?

M. RICCI-BUSATTI dit que si les parties ne sont pas d'accord sur le choix de la section, celle-ci sera désignée par le collège des Présidents.

M. FERNANDES l'admet, mais observe que la plupart des juges seront ainsi inutiles.

M. RICCI-BUSATTI fait valoir que les Présidents changeront tous les deux ans.

M. DE LAPRADELLE dit que si l'on acceptait le projet de M. Ricci-Busatti on tromperait le monde en donnant à la nouvelle institution le nom de Cour permanente de Justice, de même qu'on l'a trompé avec le nom de Cour permanente d'Arbitrage.

Le PRESIDENT déclare qu'on va procéder au vote. Le vote portera sur une partie de l'article 2 du projet Root—Phillimore, à savoir le passage suivant: „Ils (les juges) seront élus . . . . . par l'Assemblée et le Conseil de la Société. Chacun de ces deux corps votera séparément. Seront élus ceux qui auront réuni la majorité des voix des membres présents et exerçant leur droit de vote dans les deux corps".

Les amendements suivants se rapportent à ce passage:

1. L'amendement de M. Adatci:

   „La Cour se compose de juges désignés par les Membres de la Société, représentés d'une façon permanente au Conseil, à raison d'un par chacun de ces membres, ainsi que de huit juges désignés par l'Assemblée . . . ."

2. L'amendement de M. Ricci-Busatti:

   (Voir contre-projet déposé le 6 juillet; annexe 1ère ci-après.)

M. RICCI-BUSATTI pointed out that the judges thus appointed would elect from amongst their number a really permanent Court.

M. FERNANDES remarked that M. Ricci Busatti's amendments did not exclude the possibility of reconciliation. He saw nevertheless a serious objection to the project, with respect to which he wished to ask a question: he wondered how a choice would be effected when the parties failed to agree on the section which they wished to hear their case. In most cases it would happen that the case involved elements sufficiently complicated, to prevent its being included within the special competence of one of the sections. How, under these conditions, designate an individual section?

M. RICCI-BUSATTI said that if the parties were not agreed on the choice of the section, it would be determined by the college of Presidents.

M. FERNANDES admitted this, but observed that most of the judges would thus be useless.

M. RICCI-BUSATTI pointed out that the Presidents would change every two years.

M. DE LAPRADELLE said that if the project of M. Ricci-Busatti were accepted, mankind would be deceived by the name Permanent Court of Justice given to the new institution, just as it had been deceived by the name Permanent Court or Arbitration.

The PRESIDENT said they would proceed to the vote. The first vote would be taken upon a portion of Article 2 of the Root—Phillimore plan, namely the following passage: "who (the judges) shall be elected by the Assembly and the Council of the League of Nations. Each of these bodies shall vote separately, and the votes of a majority of the members present and voting in each body shall be necessary to an election".

The following amendments refer to this clause:

1. M. Adatci's amendment:

   "The Court shall be composed of judges one named by each of the members of the League of Nations represented permanently on the Council, and eight other judges designated by the Assembly . . . .".

2. M. Ricci-Busatti's amendment:

   See the counter-plan submitted on July 6th. (Annex 1).

3. L'amendement du Président:

(Voir article 5 de l'avant-projet du Président.)

Le Président répète qu'il est bien entendu que le vote sera provisoire, que tous les membres pourront joindre des réserves à leur vote, qu'ils peuvent s'abstenir de voter et motiver leur abstention.

Le Comité décide d'un commun accord que le vote aura lieu par appel nominal.

Le Président met d'abord au vote le premier amendement (amendement Adatci).

M. ADATCI retire cet amendement.

Le PRESIDENT met ensuite au vote le second amendement (amendement Ricci-Busatti).

Cet amendement est rejeté par 6 voix contre 2 et une abstention.

Ont voté contre: MM. Adatci, Altamira, de Lapradelle, Loder, Lord Phillimore et Root.

Ont voté pour: M. Ricci-Busatti, le Président.

S'est abstenu: M. Hagerup.

Le PRESIDENT met ensuite au vote le troisième amendement (amendement Descamps).

Avant le vote une courte discussion s'engage au sujet de la portée du vote. Le PRESIDENT désire qu'on vote sur l'article 5 de son projet comme amendement, tandis que plusieurs membres font valoir que le vote aura le caractère d'une décision entre le principe qui est à la base du projet Root—Phillimore et celui de l'avant-projet Descamps.

Au cours de cette discussion Mr. ROOT demande si un vote qui est sujet à des réserves futures et à des amendements déjà prévus, n'a pas le caractère d'un vote de principe, question à laquelle le PRESIDENT répond en disant qu'il s'agit bien d'un vote provisoire, mais pas d'un vote illusoire.

L'amendement, mis aux voix, est rejeté par 5 voix contre 3 et une abstention.

Ont voté contre: MM. Adatci, de Lapradelle, Loder, Lord Phillimore et Root.

Ont voté pour: MM. Altamira, Ricci-Busatti (sous réserves d'amendements futurs) et le Président.

S'est abstenu: M. Hagerup.

Le PRESIDENT déclare qu'il va être procédé au vote de la proposition principale (Root—

3. The President's amendment:

See Article 5 of the President's draft.

The President repeated that it must be clearly understood that the voting would be provisional. All members should have the right to make reservations when casting their vote, or they might abstain from voting and give their reasons for their abstention.

The Committee agreed that the vote should be by roll call.

The President first of all put the first amendment to the vote. (Adatci amendment).

M. ADATCI withdrew this amendment.

The PRESIDENT then put the second amendment to the vote (Ricci-Busatti amendment).

This amendment was rejected by 6 votes to 2 with one abstention.

The following voted against: MM. Adatci, Altamira, de Lapradelle, Loder, Lord Phillimore and Mr. Root.

The following voted in favour: M. Ricci-Busatti and the President.

M. Hagerup abstained from voting.

The PRESIDENT then put the third amendment to the vote (Descamps amendment).

Before the vote a short discussion took place concerning the scope of the vote. The PRESIDENT wished that a vote should be taken upon Article 5 of his project as an amendment, whereas several members pointed out that the vote would be of the nature of a decision between the respective principles underlying the Root—Phillimore plan and that of the President.

During this discussion Mr. ROOT asked whether a vote which was subject to reservations and to amendments already contemplated, would not be of the nature of a vote upon principle. The PRESIDENT answered that it was indeed a provisional vote but it must not be made a misleading one.

The amendment was rejected by 5 votes to 3 with one abstention.

The following voted against: MM. Adatci, de Lapradelle, Loder, Lord Phillimore and Root.

The following voted for: MM. Altamira, Ricci-Busatti (reserving the right to make future amendments) and the President.

M. Hagerup abstained from voting.

The PRESIDENT stated that he would proceed to the vote on the main project (Root—

Phillimore). Avant d'y procéder il désire demander une explication. Il désire savoir qui élira le premier, du Conseil ou de l'Assemblée, selon l'intention des auteurs de la proposition. Il estime que la réponse est importante au point de vue du vote qu'il pourra émettre.

LORD PHILLIMORE répond en son nom et au nom de Mr. ROOT, que c'est là une question de détail qui peut être réglée, lorsque la question aura été tranchée en principe.

M. DE LAPRADELLE suggère l'idée de la division de la question. Il propose qu'on mette au vote seulement la phrase suivante: „Ils (les juges) seront élus par l'Assemblée et le Conseil de la Société".

Cette procédure est adoptée.

Le vote sur la proposition ainsi formulée a pour résultat son adoption par 8 voix contre une.

Ont voté pour: MM. Adatci, Altamira, Hagerup, de Lapradelle, Loder, Lord Phillimore, M. Ricci-Busatti (sous réserve d'amendements futurs) et Mr. Root.

A voté contre: le Président.

Avant d'engager la discussion sur la dernière partie de l'article 2 du projet Root—Phillimore: „Chacun de ces deux corps votera séparément. Seront etc.", des membres demandent à quel moment on se prononcera sur le nombre des juges et la durée de leur mandat.

LORD PHILLIMORE ne croit pas que l'on doive voter maintenant sur la première de ces questions, qui est contestée.

Le PRESIDENT désirerait que ce vote eût lieu en même temps que le vote sur l'article 3 du projet Root—Phillimore. Il invite les auteurs du projet à expliquer comment se fera, d'après eux, l'élection séparée, mais cumulative, du Conseil et de l'Assemblée.

A la demande de LORD PHILLIMORE, Mr. ROOT explique qu'on suivra la méthode adoptée dans tous les Parlements du monde. Le jour de l'élection les deux corps se réuniront pour considérer les listes et pour voter sur elles. Ensuite ils compareront les résultats. Mr. Root ne croit pas nécessaire que le Comité règle cette question en détail.

Le PRESIDENT fait observer qu'il y a des Etats qui sont en même temps membres du Conseil et de l'Assemblée, et qu'il faut d'ailleurs une règle préalable, aucun des deux corps ne pouvant trancher lui-même la question de sa propre autorité.

Phillimore). Before the vote he wished to ask one question. He wished to know whether the authors intended to have the Council or the Assembly elect first. He felt the answer was important in its bearing on the vote he would cast.

LORD PHILLIMORE answered on behalf of himself and Mr. ROOT that that was a question of detail which could be arranged after the question of principle had been decided.

M. DE LAPRADELLE suggested that the question should be divided. He proposed that only the following phrase should be voted upon: "who (the judges) shall be elected by the Assembly and the Council of the League".

This procedure was adopted.

The vote upon this proposition resulted in its adoption by 8 votes to 1.

The following voted for: MM. Adatci, Altamira, Hagerup, Loder, Lord Phillimore, M. Ricci-Busatti (reserving the right to submit future amendments), and Mr. Root.

The President voted against.

Before commencing the discussion upon the last part of Article 2 of the Root—Phillimore plan: "Each of these two bodies shall vote separately, etc." certain members asked at what time the decision would be made on the number of judges and the term of office.

LORD PHILLIMORE felt that a vote should not be taken now upon the first of these questions which was the subject of dispute.

The PRESIDENT desired that this vote take place at the same time as the vote on Article 3 of the Root—Phillimore plan. He requested the authors of the plan to explain how, in their opinion, the separate but concurrent election by the Council and the Assembly should take place.

At LORD PHILLIMORE's request, Mr. ROOT explained that the method adopted by all the Parliaments of the world would be followed. On the day of the election the two bodies would meet to consider the lists and to vote upon them. Then they would compare the results. Mr. Root did not think it was necessary for the Committee to arrange this matter in detail.

The PRESIDENT observed that there were States which were members both of the Council and of the Assembly; and furthermore a preliminary ruling was necessary. Neither body could take up the matter by its own authority.

M. LODER pense que, chaque délégation de l'Assemblée comprenant plusieurs personnes qui ne disposent que d'un vote, l'absence de quelques membres qui représentent leur Gouvernement au Conseil ne peut pas empêcher que l'élection se fasse.

M. Loder croit que le moment est venu de proposer l'amendement figuré par l'article 4 des amendements qu'il a soumis. Cet amendement est ainsi conçu:

„L'Assemblée et le Conseil procèdent à l'élection indépendamment l'un de l'autre. Sont élus ceux qui ont réuni dans chaque corps électoral la majorité absolue des voix des membres présents".

Le PRESIDENT donne lecture d'un nouvel amendement présenté par M. Adatci. Cet amendement est ainsi conçu:

„2. . . . . à insérer entre la troisième phrase terminant par le mot „séparément" et la quatrième phrase commençant par le mot „seront":

„Le Conseil votera le premier jour et transmettra à l'Assemblée la liste des élus. Celle-ci votera le deuxième jour sur les noms figurant sur la dite liste, ainsi que sur tous les autres présentés par un Membre quelconque de la Société des Nations".

M. DE LAPRADELLE propose que l'amendement de M. Adatci soit divisé. On doit considérer d'abord la première phrase: „Le Conseil votera le premier jour et transmettra à l'Assemblée la liste des élus". Cette phrase implique le principe du vote successif.

Mr. ROOT déclare qu'il n'a aucune objection contre la proposition de M. Adatci. Quant à l'amendement de M. Loder, Mr. Root observe que l'expression „indépendamment" a la même signification que l'expression „séparément": c'est une question de rédaction.

En ce qui concerne le fond de la question actuelle, Mr. Root n'a une opinion bien arrêtée que sur un seul point: le Comité ne doit pas entreprendre de donner des directives trop détaillées. Chaque Assemblée peut et doit régler elle-même les détails de sa procédure: chaque directive detaillée que le Comité entreprendrait de fixer pourrait donner lieu à des objections, et le Comité désire voir adopter son projet. D'une façon générale, Mr. Root observe que chaque disposition qui n'est pas absolument nécessaire constitue un danger de plus pour le projet.

Donc, maintenant qu'on a décidé que le Conseil et l'Assemblée voteront séparément ou in-

M. LODER remarked that each delegation to the Assembly included several persons possessing between them one single vote. The absence of some members who represented their Governments upon the Council would not prevent the election from being carried out.

M. Loder thought that the time had come to propose the amendment contained in Article 4 of the amendments he had submitted. This amendment was worded as follows:

"The Assembly and the Council shall carry out the election independently of each other. Those candidates who obtain an absolute majority of the votes of the members present in both electoral bodies are elected".

The PRESIDENT read a new amendment submitted by M. Adatci. This amendment was worded as follows:

"2 . . . . . The following to be inserted in the last sentence after the word "separately"; a new sentence shall begin with the words "the votes":

"The Council shall vote upon the first day and send the list resulting from the votes taken to the Assembly. The latter shall vote, on the second day, upon the names contained in the above mentioned list, and upon any names submitted by any member of the League of Nations".

M. DE LAPRADELLE proposed that M. Adatci's amendment should be divided. The first sentence must be considered first. "The Council shall vote upon the first day and send the list resulting from the votes taken to the Assembly". This sentence implied the principle of successive voting.

Mr. ROOT said that he had no objection to M. Adatci's proposal. Concerning M. Loder's amendment he pointed out that the expression "independently" had the same meaning as the expression "separately": it was only a question of drafting.

Concerning the heart of the question itself Mr. Root had decided views upon one point only: the Committee must not try to lay down too detailed regulations. Each Assembly could and should arrange the details of its procedure for itself. Every detailed regulation that the Committee made might give occasion for objections; and the Committee wished to have its scheme accepted. Generally speaking Mr. Root observed that every provision which was not absolutely necessary would be an added danger to the success of the project.

Therefore, having decided that the Council and the Assembly should vote separately or in-

dépendamment l'un de l'autre, il est inutile d'entrer dans plus de détails; ces corps ne voudront pas recevoir du Comité des instructions sur la manière dont ils doivent accomplir leur devoir.

LORD PHILLIMORE remarque que dans l'amendement de M. Adatci il y a plusieurs questions d'ordre secondaire, au sujet desquelles il se rallie à l'opinion que vient d'exprimer Mr. Root, mais il y a aussi deux questions de principe:

1. Doit-on stipuler que le Conseil et l'Assemblée voteront successivement?
2. Dans l'affirmative, quel sera l'ordre des votes?

Lord Phillimore se rallie en principe à l'idée que le premier vote sera émis par le Conseil; il croit que ce corps, qui est composé d'hommes d'Etat qui se voient souvent et qui ont tous les éléments nécessaires pour faire un bon choix, devrait avoir la préférence mais, d'autre part, il conçoit que les petites Puissances pourraient avoir des objections contre une telle solution et, comme elles ont déjà fait des concessions, Lord Phillimore croit qu'on devrait, par égard pour elles, donner le premier vote à l'Assemblée.

Pour ce qui est de la formule, il préfère celle contenue dans l'amendement de M. Loder à celle qui est adoptée dans le texte français du projet Root—Phillimore.

Enfin, Lord Phillimore attire l'attention sur la dernière partie de l'amendement Adatci, qui soulève une question nouvelle: sur quoi portera le vote du corps qui votera en second lieu? Lord Phillimore est d'avis que cette question ne doit pas être discutée en même temps que le mode d'élection.

M. HAGERUP est du même avis; la dernière partie de l'amendement de M. Adatci ne doit pas être considérée maintenant. En ce qui concerne le fond de la question, M. Hagerup peut se rallier à la formule du projet Root—Phillimore ou à celle de l'amendement Loder. Il préfère le mot „séparément" au mot „indépendamment", mais il acceptera ce dernier s'il obtient l'assurance que tous deux, dans ce texte, signifient la même chose. Il voudrait en tous cas voir insérer dans la formule Root—Phillimore le mot „absolue" qui se trouve dans l'amendement Loder: l'élection doit avoir lieu à la majorité absolue des voix.

M. ADATCI retire son amendement; mais il tient à expliquer les motifs pour lesquels il l'avait proposé.

dependently of each other, it was useless to go into further details. These bodies would resent receiving instructions from the Committee as to the method in which they should carry out their duties.

LORD PHILLIMORE said that in M. Adatci's amendment there were several questions of secondary importance concerning which he agreed with Mr. Root, but there were also two questions of principle:

1. Should it be stipulated that the Council and the Assembly should vote successively?
2. If the answer were in the affirmative, in what order should they vote?

Lord Phillimore agreed in principle with the idea that the first vote should be cast by the Council; he thought that this body, which was composed of statesmen who often met and who possessed all the facilities necessary for making a good choice, ought to have precedence; but on the other hand he thought that the smaller Powers might object to this solution, and as they had already made concessions, Lord Phillimore thought that out of consideration to them the first vote should be given to the Assembly.

Concerning the drafting, he preferred that contained in M. Loder's amendment to that adopted in the French version of the Root—Phillimore plan.

Finally he called attention to the last part of the Adatci amendment, which raises a fresh question: the vote of the second body would be on what list? Lord Phillimore thought that this question should not be considered at the same time as the method of election.

M. HAGERUP was of the same opinion. The last part of M. Adatci's amendment should not be considered now. Concerning the principle underlying the question, M. Hagerup supported the clause of the Root—Phillimore plan or of the Loder amendment. He preferred the expression "separately" to "independently", but was prepared to accept the latter if he were assured that both the words in this text meant the same thing. He wished in any case that the word "absolute" contained in the Loder amendment should be inserted in the Root—Phillimore wording: election should be by an absolute majority of votes.

M. ADATCI withdrew his amendment but in doing so wished to give the reasons for which he had proposed it.

Le Conseil est l'organe le plus capable d'assurer un bon résultat et celui qui a le sentiment le plus profond de sa responsabilité. M. Adatci cite, à l'appui de ses idées, quelques mots prononcés par M. Larnaude à la Commission pour l'établissement de la Société des Nations, le 1er avril 1919. C'est pour cela que sa proposition tendait à faire le Conseil voter le premier.

S'il retire cette proposition, c'est à cause de la nécessité de se plier aux réalités inéluctables qui l'ont déjà amené à se rallier au projet Root—Phillimore.

Le PRESIDENT constate que la rédaction de l'amendement Loder paraît avoir la préférence des membres.

LORD PHILLIMORE et Mr. ROOT acceptent la formule „indépendamment l'un de l'autre" au lieu de l'expression „séparément".

M. LODER donne à Lord Phillimore les explications qu'il demande sur la portée qu'a dans son amendement la formule „majorité absolue".

Le PRESIDENT constate que l'amendement Loder (article 4 des amendements soumis par M. Loder le 5 juillet) est adopté. Le Président constate également qu'en conséquence, le Comité se trouve en présence d'un texte dont le fond est l'article 2 du projet Root—Phillimore. Dans cet article, la troisième phrase est remplacée par la première phrase de l'amendement Loder. Dans la dernière phrase de l'article, à l'expression „majorité" est substituée l'expression „majorité absolue".

Le Président met au vote le texte ainsi établi. Il est adopté à mains levées.

On procède ensuite au vote sur les articles 3 et 4 du projet Root—Phillimore. A ces articles se rattachent, comme amendements, les articles 5 et 6 des amendements déposés par M. Loder le 5 juillet.

A la demande de Lord Phillimore, M. LODER fournit des explications sur la différence entre ces amendements et le texte original; M. Loder a adopté un système limité à deux tours de scrutin, tandis que le projet Root—Phillimore prévoit autant de scrutins qu'il sera nécessaire pour remplir tous les sièges. La différence entre l'article 3 du projet Root—Phillimore et l'article 5 des amendements Loder est surtout d'ordre rédactionnel.

LORD PHILLIMORE remarque que, au cas où les deux collèges électoraux n'ont pu se met-

The Council was the organisation best fitted to assure a satisfactory result and also had the deepest feeling of responsibility. In support of his ideas he quoted some words used by M. Larnaude at the Commission for the establishment of the League of Nations on April 1st 1919. It was for this reason that his plan proposed to have the Council vote first.

He withdrew his proposal because of the necessity of bowing before the irresistible realities which had led him to support the Root—Phillimore plan.

The PRESIDENT stated that the drafting of the Loder amendment appeared to be preferred by the members.

LORD PHILLIMORE and Mr. ROOT accepted the expression "independently of each other "instead of the expression" separately".

M. LODER gave in answer to Lord Phillimore's request an explanation of the meaning of the phrase "absolute majority" in the Loder amendment.

The PRESIDENT stated that the Loder amendment (Article 4 of the amendment submitted by M. Loder on July 5th) was adopted. The President also stated that consequently the Committee had now to consider a text based on Article 2 of the Root—Phillimore scheme. The first part of the second sentence of this Article had been replaced by the first sentence of the Loder amendment. In the last part of the Article the expression "absolute majority" had been substituted in place of the word "majority".

The article as thus amended was put to the vote by the President. It was adopted by a show of hands.

Articles 3 and 4 of the Root—Phillimore plan were next voted upon. The fifth and sixth Articles of the amendments submitted by M. Loder on July 5th should be considered as amendments to these.

At Lord Phillimore's request, M. LODER explained the difference between these amendments and the original text. M. Loder had adopted a system limited to two ballots, whereas the Root—Phillimore plan allowed for as many ballots as might be necessary to fill all the vacancies. The difference between Article 3 of the Root—Phillimore plan and Article 5 of the Loder amendment was more than anything else a question of drafting.

LORD PHILLIMORE said that if the two electoral bodies could not come to an agreement,

tre d'accord, la conférence de conciliation, ou commission médiatrice, nommera, selon M. Loder, les titulaires des sièges qui restent à remplir. Lord Phillimore croit cependant que la nomination formelle doit toujours être laissée aux deux corps.

Après la discussion à laquelle ces remarques donnent lieu, on se trouve d'accord sur les points suivants:

1. La commission médiatrice ne doit pas faire de nominations.
2. L'élection des titulaires des sièges qui restent à remplir doit être faite, sur la base d'un rapport à dresser par la commission médiatrice, par le Conseil et par l'Assemblée. Cette procédure sera expressément stipulée dans le texte.
3. Si le Conseil et l'Assemblée ne réussissent pas à se mettre d'accord, les sièges seront remplis par cooptation, par les membres de la Cour, si elle est déjà instituée, ou, autrement, par les juges qui ont été élus par l'Assemblée et par le Conseil.
4. S'il y a des partages de voix dans la Cour ou parmi les juges, il faudrait introduire un moyen pour les départager. Ce moyen sera expressément mentionné dans le texte.
5. Il est entendu que la cooptation de la Cour ou des juges ne peut porter que sur des noms désignés par la commission médiatrice. La Cour sera ainsi arbitre entre l'Assemblée et le Conseil.

Le PRESIDENT, en constatant cet accord, déclare que les articles 3 et 4 du projet Root—Phillimore sont adoptés, sauf rédaction et les amendements relatifs aux Nos. 2 et 4 ci-dessus.

Le Président met au vote l'article 5 du projet Root—Phillimore.

M. RICCI-BUSATTI pense qu'il n'est pas désirable de faire la distinction entre juges titulaires et juges suppléants au moment de l'élection; à ce moment-là ils doivent se trouver tous sur le même pied. Les élections devant être faites par le Conseil et l'Assemblée, seront, à son avis, forcément de nature politique; c'est pour cela que l'institution de juges de second ordre — pour, ainsi dire — peut amener des difficultés et des complications qu'il serait bon de prévenir. Il vaut mieux laisser à la Cour le soin d'introduire plus tard cette distinction en donnant à un certain nombre de ses membres le caractère de juges suppléants, selon des considérations

the Committee of conciliation or mediation would, according to M. Loder, make the appointments to the vacancies still existing. Lord Phillimore, however, thought that the formal appointment should always be left to the two bodies.

After a discussion arising out of these remarks an agreement was reached upon the following points:

1. The Committee of mediation must not make appointments.
2. The appointments to the seats still vacant must be made by the Council and the Assembly upon the basis of a report prepared by the Committee of mediation. This procedure should be expressly laid down in the text.
3. If the Council and Assembly do not succeed in coming to an agreement, the seats shall be filled by co-optation by the Court, it already formed, or otherwise by the judges who have been elected by the Assembly and the Council.
4. If there should be a tie of vote in the Court or amongst the judges, a means must be introduced to settle the tie. This means shall be expressly stated in the text.
5. It is to be understood that the co-optation by the Court or the judges is limited to the names designated by the Committee of mediation. Thus the Court is to decide between the Assembly and the Council.

The PRESIDENT in stating this agreement said that Articles 3 and 4 of the Root—Phillimore plan were adopted, subject to alterations in drafting and to amendments relating to numbers 2 and 4 above.

The President put Article 5 of the Root—Phillimore plan to the vote.

M. RICCI-BUSATTI thought that it was not desirable to make distinctions between judges and deputy judges at the time of election. At that time they must all be on the same footing. As the elections had to be made by the Council and the Assembly he thought that they must necessarily be of a political nature. For this reason the institution of second rank judges, so to speak, might lead to difficulties which it would be wise to avoid. It would be better to allow the Court to make this distinction later, by giving a certain number of its members the character of deputy judge according to personal considerations which no-one will be better able to make.

personnelles qu'aucun ne sera mieux à même de prendre.

LORD PHILLIMORE dit que l'institution des suppléants est une idée continentale, et que pour sa part il n'y tient pas; il croit cependant que la coutume continentale exigera qu'ils soient maintenus.

Dans ces conditions, il préfère les élections séparées des juges suppléants. Une autre méthode est concevable: celle de faire des juges nommés en dernier lieu des juges suppléants; mais cela serait les soumettre à une humiliation, qu'on évite en adoptant la méthode d'élection directe.

M. RICCI-BUSATTI croit que l'humiliation n'est pas exclue par l'élection directe: l'institution des juges suppléants créera des difficultés politiques par suite des susceptibilités nationales, certains Etats ne se contentant pas de n'avoir qu'un juge suppléant de leur nationalité.

M. ALTAMIRA signale un désaccord entre l'article 5 et le commencement de l'article 2 du projet Root—Phillimore. On décide, sur la proposition de M. HAGERUP, de laisser la solution de cette difficulté au Comité de rédaction.

LORD PHILLIMORE exprime l'avis que si M. Ricci-Busatti désire supprimer l'article 5, et, dans la première phrase de l'article 2, ce qui se rapporte aux juges suppléants, il faudrait mettre cette proposition au vote. Le vote pourrait avec avantage porter sur cette première phrase.

M. LODER fait valoir qu'au point de vue honorifique, les juges titulaires et les juges suppléants se trouvent sur un pied d'égalité; il signale en outre qu'il y a sans doute des personnes qu'il serait désirable d'attacher à la Cour et qui pourront accepter un poste de juge suppléant, mais non pas un poste de juge effectif.

M. RICCI-BUSATTI croit qu'on peut laisser à la Cour elle-même le soin de tenir compte des considérations de cet ordre: autrement on en reviendra toujours à des questions épineuses entre les Etats.

M. DE LAPRADELLE veut maintenir l'institution des suppléants qu'il croit nécessaire au progrès de la Cour et au développement de l'institution. En vue de former de futurs juges à l'esprit qui doit caractériser la Cour, il faut des juges jeunes qui puissent servir de temps en temps à la Cour et se trouver en contact permanent avec

LORD PHILLIMORE said that the appointment of deputies was a continental idea and that personally he did not believe in it; he thought, however, that continental custom made it necessary to maintain them.

Under these conditions he preferred that deputy judges should be elected separately. Another method was possible, namely to give the last judges chosen the character of deputy judges, but this would submit them to a humiliation which was avoided by the method of direct election.

M. RICCI-BUSATTI thought that this humiliation was not eliminated by the method of direct election: the appointment of deputy judges would cause difficulties of a political nature, because of national susceptibilities, certain States not being satisfied to have only a deputy judge of their nationality.

M. ALTAMIRA pointed out that Article 5 and the beginning of Article 2 of the Root—Phillimore plan disagreed. It was agreed, on the proposal of M. HAGERUP, to leave this difficulty to the drafting Committee.

LORD PHILLIMORE said that if M. Ricci-Busatti wished to eliminate Article 5 and the reference to deputy judges in the first sentence of Article 2, this proposal should be voted upon. It would be better if the vote were taken with reference to this first sentence.

M. LODER pointed out that, from the point of view of honours, judges and deputy judges would be equal; he also pointed out that there would doubtless be persons whom it would be desirable to attach to the Court who might be able to accept a post as a deputy judge but not as a judge.

M. RICCI-BUSATTI thought that the Court itself might be left to deal with such matters: otherwise thorny questions would always be arising between States.

M. DE LAPRADELLE wished to keep the institution of deputy judges; he thought they were necessary for the progress and development of the Court. In order to imbue future judges with the spirit which must pervade the Court there must be young judges who can from time to time do duty on the Court and keep in constant

elle. Pour cette raison on doit avoir deux listes séparées; une pour les juges titulaires, et une pour les juges suppléants. Le système préconisé par M. Ricci-Busatti ne pourra pas fonctionner à cause des intrigues inévitables.

M. RICCI-BUSATTI signale une difficulté fondamentale du système des deux listes: une personne qui n'aura pas été élue juge effectif ne pourrait être élue juge suppléant.

Après une courte discussion au cours de laquelle on exprime l'avis qu'il ne faut pas établir une distinction trop étroite entre les deux catégories de juges, M. Ricci-Busatti demande qu'on mette au vote la question de savoir s'il y aura seulement une catégorie de juges au moment de l'élection.

Le PRESIDENT met au vote à mains levées cette question, à laquelle le Comité répond par la négative.

Le Président met ensuite au vote l'article 5 du projet Root—Phillimore. Cet article est adopté, également à mains levées, sauf rédaction.

La séance est levée à 12.30 heures de l'après-midi.

Le Président:
(signé) Brn. DESCAMPS.

Le Secrétaire-Général:
(signé) D. ANZILOTTI.

touch with it. For this reason there must be two separate lists: one for the judges and one for the deputy judges. The system suggested by M. Ricci-Busatti was not practicable on account of inevitable intrigues.

M. RICCI-BUSATTI pointed out a fundamental difficulty in the system of the two lists: a person who had not been elected as a judge could not be elected deputy judge.

After another short discussion during which the opinion was expressed that a too sharp distinction must not be drawn between two classes of judges, M. Ricci-Busatti asked that a vote should be taken on the question as to whether there should only be one class of judges for the purposes of election.

The PRESIDENT put this to the vote by a show of hands. The Committee decided against it.

The President then put Article 5 of the Root—Phillimore project to the vote. This article was adopted, subject to drafting amendments, also by a show of hands.

The meeting closed at 12.30 p.m.

The President:
(signed) Brn. DESCAMPS.

The Secretary-General:
(signed) D. ANZILOTTI.

ANNEXE No. 1.

Contre-Projet de M. Ricci-Busatti.

La proposition suivante remplace les articles 2, 3, 6, 7 et 8 du projet soumis par M. Ricci Busatti au Comité le 30 juin.

Chaque Membre de la Société des Nations, partie contractante à la convention de La Haye pour le règlement pacifique des conflits internationaux, pourra désigner un juge, choisi par ses délégués à la Cour Permanente d'arbitrage, soit parmi ses nationaux, soit parmi les nationaux d'un Etat différent. Si ces délégués ne sont pas d'accord sur la personne à choisir, le gouvernement désignera la personne qu'il préfère, parmi celles dont ils lui auront proposé les noms.

Lorsqu'un juge cessera, pour quelque motif que ce soit, de faire partie de la Cour, l'Etat par lequel il avait été désigné procédera à la nouvelle désignation conformément à l'alinéa précédent.

La Cour, réunie tous les deux ans en séance plénière, se divise en cinq sections. Chaque section sera composée d'un Président et d'un nombre de juges, ordinaires et suppléants, à déterminer selon les circonstances par la Cour elle même, eu égard à la compétence particulière et à la nationalité de chaque juge. Aucun d'eux ne peut appartenir à plus de deux sections.

Les Présidents des cinq sections sont élus par la Cour à la majorité des voix. Si cette majorité n'est pas obtenue au premier tour de scrutin, on procédera à l'élection par majorité relative. En cas d'égalité de voix, le plus âgé est considéré comme élu. Leur collège forme la „Présidence de la Cour".

ANNEX No. 1.

Substituted proposal of M. Ricci-Busatti.

The following propositions replace Article 2, 3, 6, 7 and 8 of the project submitted by M. Ricci-Busatti to the Committee on the 30th June.

Each member of the League of Nations, contracting parties to the Convention of the Hague for the pacific settlement of international disputes, shall have the right to name one judge chosen by its delegates at the Permanent Court of Arbitration, either from among its nationals or from among the nationals of a different State. If these delegates are not agreed in their choice of a person, the government shall designate the person which it prefers from among those whose names have been proposed.

As soon as the judge shall cease for any reason whatsoever to be a member of the Court, the State by which he was named shall proceed to a new appointment in accordance with the preceding paragraph.

The Court shall meet in full session every two years, and shall be divided into five sections. Each section shall be composed of a President and a number of judges and deputy judges to be determined, according to circumstances, by the Court itself, the individual ability and nationality of each judge being taken into consideration. No judge may belong to more than two sections.

The Presidents of the five sections are elected by the Court by an absolute majority. If this majority is not obtained on the first ballot, a simple majority shall decide. In case of a tie the senior shall be considered as elected. Their college shall form the "Presidency of the Court".

ANNEXE No. 2.

Extrait des instructions de la Délégation américaine à la Conférence de 1907.

Vous devriez vous efforcer d'effectuer dans la deuxième Conférence le développement du tribunal de La Haye en un tribunal permanent composé de juges qui fussent des fonctionnaires et rien d'autre, rétribués par un traitement adéquat, qui n'eussent aucune autre occupation et consacrassent la totalité de leur temps à l'examen et au jugement des affaires internationales, selon la méthode judiciaire, et dans un esprit de responsabilité juridique. Ces juges devraient être choisis parmi les différentes nations, afin que les principaux langages fussent équitablement représentés. La Cour, ainsi constituée, aurait une dignité, emporterait une considération, occuperait un rang tel, que les meilleurs et les plus capables d'entre les juristes accepteraient d'y être nommés, et que le monde entier aurait dans ses jugements une absolue confiance.

ANNEX No. 2.

Extract of the instructions to the American Delegates to the Hague Conference, 1907.

It should be your effort to bring about in the Second Conference a development of The Hague Tribunal into a permanent tribunal composed of judges who are judicial officers and nothing else, and who are paid adequate salaries, who have no other occupation and who will devote their entire time to the trial and decision of international causes by judicial methods and under a sense of judicial responsibility. These judges should be so selected from the different countries that the different systems of law and procedure and the principal languages shall be fairly represented. The Court should be made of such dignity, consideration and rank that the best and ablest jurists will accept appointment to it, and that the whole world will have absolute confidence in its judgments.

ANNEXE No. 3.

Proposition de M. Adatci.

2. . . . . . à insérer entre la troisième phrase terminant par le mot „séparément" et la quatrième phrase commençant par le mot „seront":

„Le Conseil votera le premier jour et transmettra à l'Assemblée la liste des élus. Celle-ci votera le deuxième jour sur les noms figurant sur la dite liste ainsi que sur tous les autres présentés par un membre quelconque de la Société des Nations."

ANNEX No. 3.

Proposal by Mr. Adatci.

2 . . . . . . The following to be inserted in the last sentence, after the word "separately"; a new sentence shall begin with the words "the votes":

"The Council shall vote upon the first day and send the list resulting from the votes taken to the Assembly. The latter shall vote, on the second day, upon the names contained in the above mentioned list, and upon any names submitted by any member of the League of Nations".

18IÈME SÉANCE (non-publique), tenue au Palais de la Paix, à La Haye, le 7 juillet 1920.

Présidence de M. le BARON DESCAMPS.

Sont présents: tous les membres du Comité (à l'exception de M. Bevilaqua); M. Fernandes; Mr. James Brown Scott; les secrétaires particuliers du Baron Descamps et de M. Adatci; les membres du Secrétariat.

La séance est ouverte à 9.50 heures du matin.

LORD PHILLIMORE observe que le Comité se trouve maintenant en face de l'article 6 du projet Root—Phillimore. Lord Phillimore a beaucoup réfléchi sur l'objection avancée la veille par le Président, à savoir que, si chaque groupe national composé des membres de la Cour Permanente d'Arbitrage présentait quatre noms, il y aurait un nombre excessif de candidats. Lord Phillimore, cependant, croit que le nombre des présentations n'atteindra presque jamais le chiffre de 4. Il fait remarquer d'abord que, avec le projet Root—Phillimore et les amendements de M. Loder, il ne pourrait y avoir plus d'un ou de deux candidats de la nationalité du groupe qui fait la présentation. Il serait d'ailleurs très imprudent de la part d'un groupe qui voudrait voir élire un de ses nationaux, de désigner plus d'un candidat choisi parmi eux; il se produirait autrement un éparpillement des votes, qui entrainerait la défaite. Pour le reste des candidats, chaque Etat s'arrangera avec ses voisins pour avoir son candidat national inséré dans leur liste, et vice versa. De cette manière il est probable que le nombre de candidats ne dépassera guère 75.

Pour toutes ces raisons, Lord Phillimore maintient son chiffre de 4. Il y en a d'ailleurs une autre: si chaque Etat se borne à nommer en premier lieu un de ses nationaux, les autres noms de la liste comprendront les hommes les plus éminents du monde. Dans ces conditions, on peut espérer que certains candidats seront désignés plusieurs fois, et l'élection se fera ainsi naturellement.

18TH MEETING (Private), held at the Peace Palace, the Hague, on July 7th, 1920.

BARON DESCAMPS in the chair.

Present: all members of the Committee (with the exception of M. Bevilaqua); M. Fernandes; Mr. James Brown Scott; the private secretaries of Baron Descamps and of M. Adatci; the members of the Secretariat.

The meeting opened at 9.50 a.m.

LORD PHILLIMORE pointed out that the Committee had now reached Article 6 of the Root—Phillimore plan. Lord Phillimore had given much reflection to the objections put forward by the President on the previous day, that is to say, that if each national group of members of the Permanent Court of Arbitration were to submit four names, the number of candidates would be excessive. However, Lord Phillimore thought that the number of names submitted would hardly ever reach four. He first pointed out that according to the Root—Phillimore plan and M. Loder's amendment, there would not be more than one or two candidates of the same nationality as the group submitting their names; apart from that, it would be very imprudent for a group which wished to have one of its own nationality elected to submit the name of more than one person of that nationality. A greater number of candidates would lead to a division of votes and consequent defeat. Concerning the remaining candidates, each State would arrange with its neighbours to have its national candidate inserted upon their list, and vice versa. Accordingly, it was probable that the number of candidates would hardly ever exceed 75.

For the above reasons Lord Phillimore continued to support the number 4. He added that there was also another reason in favour of this number: if each State limited itself in the first place to nominating one of its subjects, the other names on its list would be chosen from among the most distinguished men in the world. Under these circumstances it might be hoped that certain candidates would be nominated in many lists, which would bring about their election automatically.

M. LODER veut simplement faire remarquer qu'il est étonné d'entendre défendre par Lord Phillimore une idée qui fut adoptée à la Conférence de février, mais qu'on abandonna comme naïve et trop idéaliste, celle de limiter le nombre des candidats nationaux, présentés par chaque Etat, au tiers du nombre total.

M. Loder attire l'attention sur l'article 2 de ses amendements. Cet article renferme un amendement à l'article 6 du projet Root—Phillimore.

A la suite des observations que vient de faire Lord Phillimore, M. Loder présente un sous-amendement à son article 2, ajoutant à la fin de l'article les mots suivants: „de sorte que chaque groupe ne pourra présenter plus d'un juge ressortissant du pays représenté par ce groupe".

M. ALTAMIRA préfère le texte du projet Root—Phillimore, à condition qu'on y fasse une addition exprimant l'idée que vient de formuler M. Loder. On devrait stipuler expressément que les listes des candidats doivent contenir obligatoirement des noms de jurisconsultes étrangers.

M. HAGERUP remarque qu'on se trouve en présence de plusieurs systèmes. Celui de l'avant-projet du Président a été présenté comme amendement au projet Root—Phillimore, mais a été rejeté. Rappelant la réserve qu'il a formulée lors la discussion de cet amendement, M. Hagerup veut maintenant soumettre de nouveau à la considération du Comité la partie du système du Président, relative à la présentation des candidats.

M. Hagerup constate que les membres qui se sont prononcés jusqu'ici, se trouvent d'accord sur le principe que les candidats doivent être présentés par les membres de la Cour Permanente d'Arbitrage.

Mais tandis que le Président a proposé que la présentation à la première élection fût faite par un membre pour chaque pays représenté à la Cour d'Arbitrage in pleno, le projet Root—Phillimore prévoit des présentations distinctes par les différents groupes nationaux.

Les deux systèmes ont des avantages et des inconvénients. Le projet Root—Phillimore a l'avantage de ne pas obliger les membres de la Cour à se rendre à La Haye pour une simple présentation des candidats. A ce propos, M. Hagerup rappelle que le projet des trois pays scandinaves a adopté le système de la réunion des membres de la Cour comme collège électoral, mais pour les élections définitives. On pourrait alors

M. LODER wished merely to say that he was astonished to hear Lord Phillimore advocate an idea which had been adopted by the Conference in February, but afterwards abandoned because it was considered too ingenuous and idealistic; namely the idea of limiting the number of national candidates submitted by each State to one third of the total number.

He called attention to Article 2 of his amendments. This Article contained an amendment to Article 6 of the Root—Phillimore plan.

In consideration of the remarks just made by Lord Phillimore, M. Loder put forward an amendment to his second Article, by the addition of the following at the end of the Article: "so that each group shall not be able to submit more than one judge of the nationality of the State represented by the group".

M. ALTAMIRA preferred the wording of the Root—Phillimore plan provided that an addition was made to it, containing the idea just suggested by M. Loder. It should be expressly stipulated that the lists of candidates must necessarily contain the names of foreign jurisconsults.

M. HAGERUP remarked that they had several systems to consider; that contained in the President's draft had been put forward as an amendment to the Root—Phillimore plan, but had been rejected. Reminding the Committee of the reservations he had made when this amendment had been discussed, M. Hagerup now wished to submit afresh that part of the President's system dealing with the nomination of candidates to the reconsideration by the Committee.

He said that the members of the Committee were agreed upon the principle that the candidates should be nominated by the members of the Permanent Court of Arbitration.

But whereas the President had proposed that the nominations for the first election should be made by a meeting of one member for each State represented on the Court of Arbitration, the Root—Phillimore plan arranged for the submission of separate lists by the different national groups.

Both systems had advantages and disadvantages. The Root—Phillimore plan had the advantage that it did not force the members of the Court to come to the Hague for the sole purpose of nominating candidates. In this connection M. Hagerup recalled that the project of the three Scandinavian countries had adopted a system whereby the members of the Court

avec plus de raison compter sur la présence des membres, parce qu'il s'agirait d'un devoir plus important qu'une simple présentation de candidats. Par contre, le projet du Président a l'avantage de permettre une discussion avant la présentation.

La présentation par les groupes nationaux se heurte à une difficulté: il sera difficile pour les membres de chaque groupe de connaître très bien les candidats, comme il le faudrait pour qu'ils fussent à même de faire leurs propositions en toute connaissance de cause. Cette difficulté augmente si, comme on l'a recommandé, on borne le nombre des candidats nationaux à un seul.

M. Hagerup trouve d'ailleurs qu'il y a des inconvénients à ramener à quatre le nombre total des candidats à proposer par chaque groupe. Une telle restriction mettra ceux-ci dans un certain embarras quand il s'agira de faire un choix entre les pays chez lesquels ils doivent choisir leurs candidats. M. Hagerup n'est pas convaincu non plus qu'avec cette restriction les corps électoraux auraient toujours un nombre total suffisant de candidats.

Pour ces raisons, M. Hagerup suggère l'idée d'insérer, à la fin de l'article 6 du projet Root—Phillimore, une disposition qui corresponde à l'article 6, alinéa 2, du projet des Cinq Puissances et qui serait ainsi conçue: „Chaque groupe présente au maximum autant de candidats qu'il y a de mandats à conférer et au minimum la moitié de ce nombre; en tout cas trois au moins". En même temps on devrait biffer dans l'article du projet Root—Phillimore les mots: „de quatre noms au plus".

Mr. ROOT déclare qu'il est d'accord avec M. Hagerup au sujet des difficultés de ménager une réunion à La Haye, et qu'il se range aux propositions de M. Loder. Il pense qu'il ne faut pas que les candidats présentés appartiennent exclusivement à la nationalité de ceux qui font la présentation. D'autre part, les membres de la Cour ne trouveraient pas la présentation des candidats un motif suffisant pour se rendre à La Haye, et c'est en outre une grande affaire et une affaire coûteuse que de convoquer une réunion de ce genre. Les pays éloignés ne pourraient envoyer leurs représentants; le résultat serait qu'il n'y aurait pas de réunion du tout, ou qu'elle serait peu nombreuse, ou formée seulement d'hommes de second ordre. Or, il faut éviter de dis-

should meet as an electoral college; but this was for the actual election. Under such circumstances more reliance could be placed upon the presence of the members, since the duty to be carried out was more important than the mere nomination of candidates. On the other hand the President's plan had the advantage of allowing a discussion before the submission of the nominations.

Nomination by national groups meets with this difficulty: it would be difficult for the members of each group to have that thorough knowledge of the candidates which is essential if their proposals are to be made with a full knowledge of the circumstances. This difficulty would be increased if, as had been proposed, the number of national candidates were limited to one.

Further M. Hagerup thought that the limitation of the total number of candidates to be nominated by each group to four would lead to difficulties. Such a restriction would cause the groups some embarassment when the question arose of choosing between the States from which they must select their candidates. He was not sure either, that, if this restriction were enforced, the electoral bodies would always have a sufficently large number of candidates.

For the reasons he had just given, M. Hagerup suggested that, at the end of Article 6 of the Root—Phillimore plan, a clause corresponding to Article 6, Paragraph 2 of the plan of the Five Powers, should be inserted. This clause should be as follows: "Each group shall submit as a maximum a number of candidates equal to the number of appointments to be made, and as a minimum, the half of that number; in no case less than three". At the same time, in the Article of the Root—Phillimore plan, the following words should be struck out: "not more than four names".

Mr. ROOT declared that he agreed with M. Hagerup concerning the difficulties of arranging a meeting at the Hague, and that he supported M. Loder's proposals. He thought that the candidates nominated should not belong exclusively to the same country as those who nominated them. On the other hand members of the Court would not consider the nomination of candidates a sufficient reason for coming to the Hague. Besides it was a considerable and costly undertaking to call a meeting of this nature. Distant countries could not send their representative, and the result would be either that there would be no meeting, or that it would be very small, or would consist of second rate men; but the Court must not be discredited, and

créditer la Cour et avant tout ne pas lui assigner une tâche qu'elle serait hors d'état d'accomplir de façon satisfaisante.

On a besoin de l'opinion éclairée d'hommes venant des régions où vivent les candidats éventuels; pas nécessairement du même pays, mais de contrées appartenant au même système juridique. Il sera difficile de trouver des juges parce qu'il faut des hommes qui soient en même temps dignes de cette haute fonction et disposés à la remplir. On obtiendra à cet égard les renseignements les plus satisfaisants en s'adressant au groupe d'Etats auquel appartient le pays du candidat. Les membres de la Cour permanente provenant de ce groupe d'Etats, pourront donner tous les détails nécessaires, mais ils seront mieux placés pour les donner dans leur milieu normal qu'à La Haye. Ils auront à s'assurer, non seulement qu'un individu a la compétence requise, mais aussi qu'il est disposé à accepter le poste qu'on lui offre.

Mr. Root pense qu'à cet égard, les membres de la Cour venant de pays appartenant au même groupe, pourront utilement se consulter; comme groupes de cet ordre, il mentionne: les Etats-Unis et le Canada, l'Amérique du Sud et l'Espagne, les pays de l'Europe orientale et de l'Europe septentrionale etc.

Mr. Root croit que ces conférences officieuses formeraient la source la plus précieuse d'informations à laquelle puissent puiser les électeurs. Chaque pays ne doit donc pas nommer exclusivement ses nationaux; il admet cependant que la formule proposée à cet effet par M. Loder se heurte à des difficultés d'ordre pratique. Aussi Mr. Root propose-t-il qu'une moitié seulement des candidats soit composée d'étrangers. Il voudrait également fixer à quatre le maximum des candidats à présenter.

M. HAGERUP montre le danger qu'il y aurait à avoir un nombre trop restreint de candidats.

Mr. ROOT ne croit pas que ce danger existe. Le Président craint même que le nombre des candidats ne soit trop grand. A cet égard Mr. Root remarque que chaque Etat a le droit de nommer quatre membres à la Cour d'arbitrage, et pourtant le nombre total de ces membres est seulement de 130. Il ne croit pas qu'il y ait des difficultés à faire le choix sur une liste de cette étendue. D'autre part, il croit qu'on pourrait stipuler que si un Etat manquait à son devoir de présenter le nombre requis de candidats, le Secré-

it would be a most dangerous thing to impose a task upon it that it could not carry out in a satisfactory way.

There was need for the enlightened opinion of men coming from those parts of the world where the prospective candidates lived; not necessarily from the same country, but from countries belonging to the same legal system. It would be very difficult to find judges, because men who were at the same time worthy and willing to accept appointment were required. Information on this point would be best obtained from the group of States to which the native country of the candidate belonged. The members of the Permanent Court coming from these groups of States could give all the information necessary, but they would be better able to give this information in their own country than at the Hague. They would have to make sure, not only that an individual possessed the required qualifications, but also that he was willing to accept the appointment offered.

Mr. Root thought that, in this connection, the members of the Court coming from countries belonging to the same group, might profitably consult each other; such groups were: the United States and Canada, South America and Spain, the countries of Eastern Europe and those of Northern Europe etc.

He thought that such private conferences would be the most valuable source of information upon which the electors could draw. Mr. Root thought therefore that each country should not exclusively nominate its own subjects. He acknowledged however that the clause proposed by M. Loder with this object, would encounter difficulties of a practical nature. Mr. Root therefore proposed that one half only of the candidates should be foreigners. He also wished to fix the maximum number of candidates at four.

M. HAGERUP pointed out the danger of restricting the number of candidates to too low a figure.

Mr. ROOT did not think that this danger existed. The President even feared that the number of candidates would be too large. In this connection Mr. Root said that each State had the right to appoint four members of the Court of Arbitration, and yet the whole number of these members only amounted to 130. He did not think there would be any difficulty in making a choice from a list of this size. On the other hand he thought that it might be stipulated that if a State did not fulfil its duty of nominating

taire-Général de la Société des Nations devrait le lui rappeler.

Mr. Root fait valoir que le nombre de 4 aurait un autre avantage; on pourrait espérer rencontrer dans les divers pays une concordance d'opinions telle que l'élection se trouverait assurée *ipso facto*; l'Assemblée et le Conseil n'oseraient pas aller à l'encontre de cette opinion. A ce propos il rappelle l'expérience qu'il a faite aux Etats-Unis, lorsqu'il a dû seconder le Président dans le choix des juges fédéraux pour la partie du pays à laquelle il appartient. Il s'y est rendu et a consulté les hommes les plus autorisés; il s'est assuré si les personnes qu'on lui désignait étaient disposées à accepter la nomination, et après maintes tentatives, il est parvenu à trouver un candidat de valeur, et disponible.

Mr. Root croit qu'il faut procéder de la même façon pour l'élection des juges à la Cour permanente. Il est convaincu que ce ne sera qu'après la première élection que les Etats chercheront à faire entrer, dans la Cour, un de leurs ressortissants. Plus tard, la Cour elle-même, par l'intermédiaire du Secrétaire Général de la Société des Nations, demandera aux peuples des diverses parties du monde de désigner un homme compétent qui soit disposé à siéger à la Cour.

the required number of candidates, the Secretary-General of the League of Nations should remind this State of its duty.

Mr. Root pointed out that the number 4 would have another advantage: it might be hoped that so many concordant expressions of opinion would be obtained from the various countries, that the election would be thereby virtually decided; the Assembly and the Council would not venture to go against this opinion. At this point Mr. Root recalled the experience he had had in the United States, when assisting the President in the choice of federal judges for that part of the country to which he belonged. He visited the district, and consulted the men who had most knowledge on the subject; he assured himself that the persons suggested to him were willing to accept an appointment, and after many attempts he succeeded in finding a candidate who was both desirable and available.

Mr. Root thought that the same method should be used in the election of the judges of the Permanent Court. He was convinced that it would only be on the first occasion that the States would try to obtain the appointment of one of their own subjects to the Court. Later on the Court itself, through the agency of the Secretary-General of the League of Nations, would ask the peoples of the different parts of the world to name a man who was both competent and willing to accept appointment to the Court.

Le PRESIDENT donne lecture d'un sous-amendement à l'amendement de M. Loder déposé par M. de Lapradelle.

Le sous-amendement de M. de Lapradelle est ainsi conçu: „Trois mois avant l'élection d'un ou de plusieurs juges, le Secrétaire Général de la Société des Nations demande par écrit au gouvernement des Etats Membres de la Société des Nations, de lui adresser une liste de quatre personnes, dont seulement deux nationaux, au plus, qualifiées, d'après lui, pour remplir les fonctions de juge".

Le Président dit qu'avant le dépôt de cet amendement, il avait eu l'impression que l'accord était fait sur l'intervention des membres de la Cour Permanente d'Arbitrage en ce qui concerne la présentation des candidats. Il continue à estimer, pour sa part, qu'en accordant cette présentation à l'aréopage des grands arbitres internationaux, non seulement on aurait toutes chances d'assurer un bon choix, mais on rendrait service aux Gouvernements eux-mêmes, qui seraient ainsi déchargés d'une tâche qu'ils ne doivent pas désirer remplir, dont ils ne s'acquitteraient pas aisé-

The PRESIDENT read an amendment to M. Loder's amendment, submitted by M. de Lapradelle.

M. de Lapradelle's amendment was as follows: "Three months before the election of one or more judges, the Secretary-General of the League of Nations shall request the Governments of the States which are Members of the League of Nations, in writing, to send him a list of four persons, of whom two at most shall be of the nationality of the respective States, duly qualified in the opinion of the nominating Government to perform the duties of a judge".

The President said that, before the submission of this amendment he had been under the impression that the Committee was agreed upon the subject of the intervention of the members of the Permanent Court of Arbitration in the nomination of candidates. He held to his opinion that, by entrusting this task to the areopagus formed by the great international arbitrators, not only would there be every probability that a good selection would be made, but a service would be rendered to the Governments

ment, qui prêterait à de graves critiques, engagerait prématurément leur responsabilité et préjugerait à bien des égards leur attitude lors du vote définitif. Et cette tâche se compliquerait peut-être de façon fâcheuse, s'il s'agissait de choisir des candidats dont certains appartiendraient à des Etats étrangers.

Le Président désire remercier M. Hagerup de l'appui qu'il a bien voulu donner à diverses reprises à ses propositions. Sans revenir sur le fond des idées qu'il a développées, le Président tient à signaler que son but a été d'assurer la meilleure sélection possible des candidats et qu'à ce point de vue, après une enquête approfondie dans les divers pays, une discussion préparatoire par un collège composé de membres de la Cour d'Arbitrage à raison d'un par Etat, lui a paru la meilleure solution.

Certains membres considèrent qu'au point de vue pratique une telle réunion serait difficile. Elle paraît cependant au Président beaucoup facilitée par le fait qu'un seul des quatre membres de la Cour nommés par chaque Etat, devrait y assister. Les quatre membres choisiraient ainsi entre eux celui qui pourrait le plus facilement se déplacer pour quelques jours.

On pourrait croire, à première vue, que la tâche à remplir n'est pas assez importante pour justifier un tel déplacement; mais il convient d'observer qu'il s'agit de former une liste de sélection limitée de candidats à la Cour, ce qui donne à cette liste une grande importance. Le Président estime que le sentiment d'un devoir important à remplir, et l'intérêt considérable qui est en jeu suffiraient pour donner l'assurance que la majorité des membres seront présents. Il est d'ailleurs prévu dans son avant-projet que les membres empêchés pourraient envoyer deux noms avec recommandation motivée. Le Président ne doute pas qu'une importante Assemblée ne se réunisse pour la première élection où tous les sièges seront à remplir, et pour les élections partielles qui pourraient survenir en dehors du renouvellement général, le règlement à adopter par le collège pourrait prévoir le vote par correspondance, comme l'a fait dans des conditions remarquables et fort intéressantes l'Institut de Droit International. Nous savons tous par expérience que des difficultés représentées *a priori* comme graves se résolvent d'elles-mêmes par le jeu des institutions. Que le Comité ne renonce donc pas trop vite à un procédé de sélection qu'on a déclaré excellent, qu'il vise plutôt à l'améliorer au point de vue pratique.

Le Président croit qu'une liste de candidats démesurément longue n'embarrassera guère peut-

themselves; they would be relieved of a task which they ought not to desire, which they could not easily perform, which would subject them to serious criticism, prematurely commit them to responsibility, and in many respects prejudice their attitude at the actual elections. In addition, further complications might arise out of this task if it were a question of choosing candidates some of whom belonged to foreign States.

The President wished to thank M. Hagerup for the support he had given, on many occasions, to the President's proposals. Without again going deeply into the ideas which he had formulated, the President wished to point out that his object had been to assure the best possible choice of candidates, and for this purpose, after exhaustive enquiries in the various countries, it seemed to him that a preliminary discussion, by an electoral body composed of one member of the Court of Arbitration for each State, was the best solution.

He said that some members considered that such a meeting would be difficult from a practical point of view. The President thought however that it would be much facilitated by the fact that one only of the four members of the Court appointed by each State would have to take part. The four members would choose from amongst their number that one who could most easily spare the time.

It might be thought at first sight that the task was not sufficiently important to justify a trip to the Hague, but he would point out that it was a question of drawing up a limited list of specially selected candidates for the Court, so that this list would be very important. The President thought that the fact that it was such an important duty, and the great interests at stake, would suffice to ensure the presence of most of the members. It was also laid down in his scheme that members who could not attend, might send two names with detailed recommendations. For the first election, at which all the seats must be filled, the President did not doubt that there would be a very full meeting; in the case of by-elections, which might occur apart from the periodical general elections, the rules to be adopted by the college might provide for voting by correspondence, as had been done by the "Institut de Droit International" under noteworthy and extremely interesting conditions. We all know by experience that difficulties represented beforehand as serious often disappear of their own accord by the normal working of institutions. Let us not give up too soon a method of

être certains grands Etats, comme la Grande-Bretagne qui a une clientèle puissante gravitant plus ou moins dans sa sphère; mais il n'en est pas de même pour les Etats de moindre importance, dont les présentations seront, en quelque sorte, noyées dans un flot de candidats.

Le Président voit bien le but louable poursuivi par M. Loder quand il préconise l'obligation de faire porter en partie le choix sur des candidats étrangers. Mais il prévoit un monde de difficultés, d'où résulteront probablement des combinaisons et des manœuvres regrettables. Le Président préférerait laisser, en cette matière, la liberté du choix.

Le Président fait observer que les questions que le Comité doit résoudre ont des aspects fort multiples: il faut tâcher de ne pas s'engager dans des voies qui seraient impraticables.

Le Président attendra, pour apprécier le nouveau système proposé par M. de Lapradelle, que son auteur l'ait exposé. A première vue, ce système apparaît au Président comme une formidable régression sur les idées autour desquelles semblaient se rallier les membres du Comité et comme une tendance regrettable à consacrer l'absolutisme politique des gouvernements en matière de justice internationale.

selection which has been admitted to be excellent: let us rather try to see if it cannot be adapted to practical use by means of improvements.

The President thought that an unduly long list of candidates would not perhaps embarrass certain great States like Great Britain which was in close relationship with many important countries and had a wide sphere of influence, but it was not the same for States of lesser importance; their nominations would be, so to speak, drowned in the flood of candidates.

As to the obligation to choose a certain number of foreign candidates, which had been suggested by M. Loder, the President clearly saw the praiseworthy end he had in view, but also foresaw a host of difficulties, which would probably result in collusion between neighbouring States and very undesirable intrigues. The President preferred to leave a free choice open.

The President pointed out that the questions for the Committee to solve were many-sided: they must try not to commit themselves to methods which might prove impracticable.

The President would not give an appreciation of the new system proposed by M. de Lapradelle until its author had explained it. At first sight this system appeared to be tremendous backsliding from the ideas upon which it seemed that the members of the Committee were agreed, and to tend most regrettably to give full sway to the absolutist political ideas of governments, in the administration of international justice.

M. DE LAPRADELLE a la parole pour défendre l'amendement qu'il vient de présenter.

Il a été frappé, dit-il, de l'impossibilité d'aboutir sur la base d'un plan qui l'avait d'abord satisfait. Il avait été séduit par l'idée de réunir à La Haye un grand collège électoral composé d'un membre par Etat, investi de la confiance de son gouvernement. Ainsi des hommes d'une haute compétence juridique et d'une grande autorité morale présenteraient une double liste, et aucune présentation faite en dehors de cette réunion, ne serait possible. On se donnerait mutuellement tous les renseignements possibles sur les candidats, on discuterait, et puis on procéderait à un vote qui sélectionnerait parmi les candidats un nombre déterminé de personnes. S'il y avait un moyen pratique de réaliser ces réunions, M. de Lapradelle n'hésiterait pas à se rallier à ce système.

Mais il faut tenir compte de la réalité. Tous les pays représentés à la Cour d'Arbitrage ne se

M. DE LAPRADELLE obtained permission to speak to defend the amendment he had put forward.

He had been struck by the impossibility of success upon the basis of a plan which had at first sight appeared satisfactory to him. He had been much attracted by the idea of assembling a great electoral body at the Hague, consisting of one member, in whom the confidence of his government was placed, for each State. By this method men possessing great legal ability and moral authority would submit a double list, and no nominations could be made except by means of this meeting. All possible information concerning the candidates would be obtained, a discussion would follow, and then a vote would be taken by which a certain number of persons would be chosen from amongst the candidates. If there were any practical means of bringing these meetings about, M. de Lapradelle would not hesitate to support this system.

trouvent pas assez près du lieu de réunion pour pouvoir envoyer des représentants qualifiés. Ils pourraient envoyer des représentants *ad hoc,* par exemple leurs agents diplomatiques, mais cela ne suffirait pas. Il faut que les membres du collège électoral soient des jurisconsultes spécialisés, capables de discuter les noms des candidats en pleine connaissance de cause. Or, cet idéal est irréalisable. La réunion comprendrait probablement des hommes de second ordre; ceux qui se trouvent à proximité et ceux qui sont inoccupés. Il en résulterait des coalitions et des intrigues, surtout si l'on devait présenter un juge par Etat. Plus tard, les Etats non-représentés à la réunion se révolteraient contre des décisions auxquelles ils n'ont pas participé. M. de Lapradelle croit donc que l'idée d'un grand collège électoral est impossible à réaliser.

Il se tourne alors vers le système du projet Root—Phillimore, tel qu'il a été amendé par M. Loder, d'après lequel les présentations se feraient par groupes nationaux et par écrit. Ce système a l'avantage d'être simple, mais il présente en même temps des inconvénients d'ordre pratique. Rien n'est plus facile que de prier les membres de la Cour d'Arbitrage d'un certain pays de désigner un ou deux candidats de leur nationalité. Mais alors se pose la question: peuvent-ils se désigner eux-mêmes? M. de Lapradelle ne le croit pas; et pour les autres jurisconsultes de la même nationalité à désigner, il fait valoir que tous les juristes d'un pays éprouvent, à l'égard les uns des autres, des sentiments d'amitié ou d'antipatie, ce qui rendrait difficile d'arriver à une présentation unanime et loyale.

En ce qui concerne la désignation de juristes étrangers, le cas n'est plus le même. Les membres d'un certain groupe national se sentiront plus indifférents, et il leur sera par conséquence plus facile d'arriver à l'unanimité.

M. de Lapradelle est favorable à la formule du projet Root—Phillimore, avec l'amendement de M. Loder, parce qu'il est favorable à l'idée de faire désigner les candidats par des groupes étrangers. Il fait valoir qu'il y a de jeunes Etats qui n'ont pas encore parmi leurs nationaux des candidats d'une compétence suffisante. Ces Etats ne voudront cependant pas renoncer à leur droit de présentation, et désigneront forcément des candidats étrangers. M. de Lapradelle croit qu'on obtiendra ainsi les meilleures présentations. Ce seront en effet les présentations les plus désintéressées, et les plus conformes à l'esprit international.

Dans cet ordre d'idées, M. de Lapradelle préfère une consultation nationale sans avoir re-

But realities must be taken into account. All the countries represented on the Court of Arbitration are not sufficiently near the meeting place to be able to send qualified representatives. They might send representatives *ad hoc*; for instance their diplomatic agents; but that would not suffice. The members of the electoral body must be specialised jurisconsults, able to discuss the various candidates with a full knowledge of their respective merits. But this ideal could not be realised. The meeting would probably include second rate men: those who happened to be near and those who were unoccupied. Coalitions and intrigues would follow, especially if each State had to nominate one judge only. Later on those States which were not represented at the meeting would object to decisions in which they had not taken part. For this reason M. de Lapradelle thought that the idea of a great electoral college could not be realised.

He then turned to the system of the Root—Phillimore plan, as amended by M. Loder. According to this system, the nomination of candidates would be made by each national group and in writing. It had the advantage of being simple, but also involved difficulties of a practical nature. Nothing was more easy than to ask the members of the Court of Arbitration, belonging to a certain country, to nominate one or two candidates of their own nationality. The question however then arose: could they nominate themselves? M. de Lapradelle did not think so; further, in connection with the nomination of other jurisconsults of the same nationality, he pointed out that all the jurists of a country are either bound by ties of friendship or have a feeling of antipathy towards each other; under such circumstances a thoroughly unanimous and disinterested selection would be difficult. As to the choice of foreign jurists the position was quite different. The members of a particular national group would be more impartial towards them; it would be easier for it, therefore, to come to an unanimous decision.

M. de Lapradelle was well disposed to the formula of the Root—Phillimore plan as amended by M. Loder, because it favoured the idea of the nomination of candidates by groups of foreigners. He pointed out that there were young States who did not yet possess candidates of their own nationality with the required qualifications; nevertheless such States would not wish to renounce their right of nominating candidates and would be obliged to select foreign candidates. M. de Lapradelle thought that the best candidates would be obtained in this

cours aux membres nationaux de la Cour d'Arbitrage. Il ne faut pas perdre de vue que ces membres sont nommés par des gouvernements et que par conséquent ce seront les gouvernements qui agiront par leur intermédiaire. Dans ces conditions, ne vaut-il pas mieux remonter à la source et confier directement aux gouvernements la présentation des candidats?

Aux termes de l'amendement présenté par M. de Lapradelle, les gouvernements désigneraient quatre candidats dont un ou deux de leur propre nationalité. Afin d'assurer la présentation d'étrangers, la présentation devrait être rendue obligatoire, et l'obligation garantie par une sanction: l'Etat qui n'exerce pas son droit de présentation perdrait son droit de vote à l'élection définitive. Les gouvernements devraient consulter les corps scientifiques les plus compétents. Ainsi on assurerait, dans la mesure du possible, des présentations désintéressées et portant sur des personnes autorisées.

La désignation par les gouvernements serait une sorte de plébiscite. Elle aurait, entre autres, les avantages suivants: on serait certain que les candidats proposés sont disposés à accepter une nomination; on serait sûr que les meilleurs candidats seront présentés, et on n'aurait pas à craindre le mécontentement des gouvernements, dont on ménagerait les susceptibilités en leur confiant la présentation.

M. de Lapradelle voit bien les difficultés du système qu'il propose, mais il croit cependant que les avantages l'emportent. C'est pourquoi il recommande à l'attention du Comité son amendement, qu'il propose qu'on considère comme un sous-amendement à celui de M. Loder.

way. Such nominations would be the most disinterested, and the most in accordance with a true international spirit.

For these reasons, M. de Lapradelle preferred a system of selection by consultation within a State without recourse to the national members of the Court of Arbitration. It must be remembered that these members are appointed by the governments and that consequently, they would only be the agents of the governments. Under these circumstances, would it not be better to go to the source and entrust the selection of candidates directly to the governments themselves?

According to the amendment presented by M. de Lapradelle, governments would nominate four candidates, of whom one or two would be of their own nationality. In order to ensure the inclusion of foreigners, the nominations should be made compulsory, and compliance should be enforced by a penalty: any State which did not use its right of nomination should lose its right to vote at the actual election. The governments should consult the most competent scientific bodies. In this way the disinterested nomination of duly qualified persons would be assured as far as possible.

The selections made by the governments would be of the nature of a plebiscite. The following advantages, among others, would accrue: it would be certain that the proposed candidates were prepared to accept an appointment; it would also be certain that the best candidates would be submitted, and there would be no occasion to fear dissatisfaction amongst the governments, whose susceptibilities would have been soothed since they were entrusted with the nominations.

M. de Lapradelle fully understood the difficulties of the system he suggested, but he nevertheless thought that the advantages outweighed them. For this reason he recommended his amendment to the attention of the Committee, and he proposed that it should be considered as a further amendment to that of M. Loder.

Le PRESIDENT pense que le système préconisé par M. de Lapradelle éliminera les membres de la Cour Permanente d'Arbitrage et rendra inévitables des négociations et des intrigues diplomatiques.

The PRESIDENT thought that the system proposed by M. de Lapradelle would eliminate the members of the Permanent Court of Arbitration and render political bargains and diplomatic intrigues inevitable.

M. DE LAPRADELLE ne partage pas cet avis. Les gouvernements se borneront à consulter les corps compétents.

M. DE LAPRADELLE did not share this opinion. The Governments would limit themselves to consulting competent bodies.

Le PRESIDENT croit que M. de Lapradelle méconnaît l'influence des considérations

The PRESIDENT thought that M. de Lapradelle underestimated the effect of the poli-

politiques qui entreront en jeu, si le choix est confié aux gouvernements.

M. ADATCI a toujours été préoccupé quant à la possibilité de réaliser dans la pratique les projets Root—Phillimore et Descamps. Les membres du Japon à la Cour Permanente d'Arbitrage se trouvent dans leur pays, en Amérique et en Europe. Ceux qui sont au Japon ne pourront pas venir siéger à un collège électoral. Il serait presque impossible à ces membres, dispersés comme ils le sont, de se mettre d'accord sur une présentation. C'est pourquoi il n'a pas été tout à fait satisfait des dispositions du projet Root—Phillimore, au sujet des présentations. Son inquiétude a été dissipée par le sous-amendement de M. de Lapradelle, d'après lequel les candidats seront désignés par les gouvernements. Il n'a pas encore d'opinion arrêtée sur la deuxième partie du sous-amendement, c'est-à-dire sur la présentation de candidats non nationaux, mais il désire affirmer qu'il se rallie à la première partie de l'amendement.

Selon M. HAGERUP, on se trouve en présence de deux questions; celle du nombre des candidats et celle de la méthode de présentation. Pour la première, il n'est pas convaincu que le chiffre de 4 soit satisfaisant. Il faut donner aux corps chargés de la présentation l'occasion de présenter autant de candidats qu'il y a de vacances. Et s'il est possible qu'à un moment donné il n'y ait qu'une seule vacance, il se peut aussi qu'il y en ait plus de dix. C'est pourquoi il propose qu'on décide qu'il y aura autant de candidats par Etat qu'il y a de vacances à remplir.

Il y a une autre raison, d'ordre politique celle-là, qui s'oppose à l'adoption du nombre de 4. S'il est facile de désigner les candidats nationaux, on se heurte à de graves difficultés lorsqu'il s'agit de la présentation de candidats étrangers. Des considérations politiques entrent en jeu. Il est impossible de ne pas froisser les susceptibilités de certains Etats. Ce point de vue a une importance particulière si ce sont les gouvernements et non les membres de la Cour d'Arbitrage, qui font les présentations. Certes, la désignation doit se faire en dehors de toute influence politique, mais il faut tenir compte aussi des réalités.

M. Hagerup prie donc les membres de considérer sérieusement les objections qu'il a soulevées et qu'il exprime sous forme d'amendement, en proposant qu'on ajoute à l'article 6 du projet Root—Phillimore l'article 6 du projet

tical considerations which would come into play if governments were called upon to make the selections.

M. ADATCI had always had doubts regarding the possibility of the practical realisation of the Root—Phillimore and Descamps plans. The Japanese members of the Permanent Court of Arbitration were in their own country, or in America, or in Europe. Those who were in Japan would not be able to take part in a meeting of the electoral body. It would be almost impossible for the members, scattered as they were, to come to an agreement concerning the composition of a list. For this reason he had not been quite satisfied with the arrangements contained in the Root—Phillimore project concerning the nominations. His anxiety had been set at rest by the further amendment of M. de Lapradelle, according to which the candidates would be chosen by the governments. He had not yet formed a definite opinion concerning the second part of the amendment, that is to say, on the nomination of foreign candidates, but he wished to state that he supported the first part of the amendment.

M. HAGERUP said that they were faced with two problems: the number of the candidates, and the method of nomination. As to the first he was not convinced that the number 4 was satisfactory. The bodies entrusted with the nomination must be enabled to nominate as many candidates as there were vacancies. And though it might be that at a given moment there would be only one vacancy, it might also happen that there were more than ten. For this reason he proposed that each State should submit as many candidates as there were vacancies to be filled.

There was another reason against the adoption of the number 4; a reason of a political nature. Though it might be easy to select national candidates, serious difficulties would be encountered in the nomination of foreign candidates. Political considerations would come into play. It would be impossible to avoid hurting the feelings of certain countries. This point of view would have much more weight if the governments were the nominators, than if the groups of members of the Court of Arbitration selected the candidates. There is no doubt that the selection must be made independently of any political influence, but practical considerations must be taken into account.

For this reason M. Hagerup asked the members to give serious consideration to the objections he had put forward. He expressed these objections in the form of an amendment by pro-

des Cinq Puissances (pour les détails de l'amendement voir plus haut).

S'adressant à Mr. Root, M. Hagerup dit qu'il se peut qu'un groupe veuille se borner à ne présenter qu'un candidat national. Il se peut aussi qu'il n'y ait aucune présentation de faite. Mr. Root a dit que, dans ce cas, le Secrétaire-Général de la Société des Nations inviterait le corps présentateur à remplir son devoir. Mais les groupes des membres de la Cour d'Arbitrage n'ont pas de devoirs à cet égard. Par contre, on peut concevoir un devoir qui oblige des gouvernements. Sur ce point particulier, la proposition de M. de Lapradelle offre un avantage d'ordre formel.

Sur la question de fond, celle de savoir si la présentation doit se faire par les gouvernements ou par les membres de la Cour d'Arbitrage, M. Hagerup est d'accord avec le Président. Il faut éviter l'intervention des gouvernements avant la présentation afin d'assurer aux élections un maximum d'autorité. Les gouvernements auront tout loisir d'exprimer leur point de vue dans le Conseil et dans l'Assemblée. L'essentiel c'est de donner le droit de présentation à des personnes qui soient, autant que possible, indépendantes de leurs gouvernements et étrangères à des considérations politiques. Pour cette raison, tout en lui reconnaissant certains avantages, M. Hagerup ne peut pas se rallier à l'idée de M. de Lapradelle.

LORD PHILLIMORE dit que Mr. Root et lui sont disposés à accepter l'amendement de M. Loder sous sa forme originale (article 2 des amendements de M. Loder, abstraction faite du sous-amendement). L'addition que vient de proposer M. Loder paraît inacceptable à Lord Phillimore. En effet, si la Grande-Bretagne n'était autorisée à désigner qu'un candidat national, elle aurait des difficultés avec ses dominions. Elle n'a pour le moment qu'une place dans la Cour d'Arbitrage, mais elle en a six dans l'Assemblée de la Société des Nations. Il faut qu'elle soit à même de nommer au moins deux candidats nationaux.

Lord Phillimore rappelle que le nombre de 4 représente une solution transactionnelle. Lord Phillimore aurait préféré donner toute liberté aux corps présentateurs, mais il a cru devoir tenir compte de l'idée exprimée par le Président lorsqu'il a dit qu'il y aurait une cohue de candidats. Il trouve cependant le nombre de 4 satisfaisant, mais il rappelle que la pro-

posing that Article 6 of the project of the Five Powers should be added to Article 6 of the Root—Phillimore project (for the details of the amendment see above).

Addressing Mr. Root, M. Hagerup said that it was possible that a group might wish to limit itself to submitting one national candidate only. It was also possible that no nomination might be made. Mr. Root had said that under these circumstances the Secretary of the League of Nations would request the nominating bodies to carry out their duty. The groups of members of the Court of Arbitration, however, had no duty in this respect. On the other hand, it could be considered as a duty of the governments. In this particular respect M. de Lapradelle's proposal offered an advantage of a positive nature.

Upon the main question, the question whether the nomination should be carried out by the governments or by the members of the Court of Arbitration, M. Hagerup agreed with the President. The intervention of the Governments before the nominations must be avoided in order to make the elections as authoritative as possible. The governments would have every opportunity of expressing their views in the Council and the Assembly. The essential point was to give the right of nomination to persons who were independent of their governments and above political considerations. For this reason M. Hagerup could not support M. de Lapradelle's idea, although he recognised that it had certain advantages.

LORD PHILLIMORE said that Mr. Root and he were disposed to accept M. Loder's amendment in its original form (Article 2 of M. Loder's amendments, not including the additional amendment). The addition just proposed by M. Loder was inacceptable to Lord Phillimore because, if Great Britain were only authorised to nominate one national candidate, she would be put in a difficult position with regard to her dominions. She had, at the moment, only one place on the Court of Arbitration, but she had six in the Assembly of the League of Nations. She must be able to nominate at least two national candidates.

Lord Phillimore recalled the fact that the number 4 represented a compromise. He would have preferred to have given a free hand to the nominating bodies, but he had felt that he must take into account the view held by the President; namely that there would be an unwieldy number of candidates. He thought however that the number 4 was satisfactory

position de M. Hagerup aurait pour effet de donner un plus grand nombre de candidats.

Après les discours de M. de Lapradelle et du Président, Lord Phillimore croit devoir souligner le caractère transactionnel du projet Root—Phillimore. S'il accepte la présentation par la Cour d'Arbitrage, c'est pour se rapprocher du Président, car il semblait que l'accord était en train de se faire sur cette idée. Mais si l'on abandonne cette idée, à la suite de M. de Lapradelle, la nature transactionnelle du projet disparaît, et aussi l'accord.

Personnellement, Lord Phillimore croit que l'idée de M. de Lapradelle est juste, mais, dans un esprit de conciliation, il préfère s'en tenir à la transaction que représente le projet Root—Phillimore.

A cet égard, il désire cependant faire valoir que, lorsque le Président parle comme si ce n'était plus à chaque Etat de présenter une liste, lorsqu'il veut que l'on vote sur une liste double de candidats, alors il s'écarte du projet transactionnel et va à l'encontre de toutes les idées qui ont présidé à sa rédaction. Cela reviendrait en effet à donner un double avantage aux petits Etats, au détriment des grands. Si le Président veut abandonner cette idée pour se rallier à l'idée de la présentation par groupes, Lord Phillimore peut le suivre; sinon il devrait se ranger à l'opinion M. de Lapradelle.

Le PRESIDENT répond que les idées contenues dans son avant-projet peuvent se rapprocher d'autres idées suivant le cours de la discussion.

M. DE LAPRADELLE déclare qu'il se rend bien compte du caractère pratique du système Root—Phillimore, qui est le système de la désignation par les groupes nationaux de la Cour Permanente d'Arbitrage. Il remarque qu'on semble craindre l'influence politique lorsque la désignation est faite par les gouvernements, tandis que cette influence ne serait plus à craindre lorsqu'il s'agit d'une désignation faite par les groupes nationaux. C'est se payer de mots. Les membres de la Cour d'Arbitrage, étant nommés par les gouvernements, agiront sous leur influence.

Il vaut mieux créer des garanties telles que les gouvernements soient liés par les consulta-

but he reminded the Committee that M. Hagerup's proposal would result in a larger number of candidates.

After having heard the speeches of M. de Lapradelle and the President, Lord Phillimore felt that he must emphasise the fact that the Root—Phillimore project was in the nature of a compromise. The system of nomination by the Court of Arbitration had been adopted in order to reconcile the scheme to that of the President as far as possible, for it had seemed that an agreement was well on the way towards accomplishment on this basis. If, however, they were to abandon this idea, as M. de Lapradelle suggested, the compromise contained in the scheme would disappear, and they would be as far as ever from an agreement.

Personally, Lord Phillimore thought M. de Lapradelle's suggestion was well-founded, but, in order to conciliate opposing views, he preferred to continue his support of the compromise represented by the Root—Phillimore plan.

In this connection, however, he wished to point out that the President, speaking as if it were not a question of the submission of a list by each State, but of a vote to be taken upon a double list of candidates, was disregarding the compromise upon which the plan was based, and was going against all the ideas which gave it its present form. In fact, it amounted to giving a twofold advantage to the smaller States, as against the large States. If the President were prepared to abandon this idea and adopt nomination by groups, Lord Phillimore could support him; otherwise he felt that he must support M. de Lapradelle.

The PRESIDENT answered that the ideas contained in his draft-plan and the other ideas put forward might become reconciled in the course of the discussion.

M. DE LAPRADELLE said that he was quite prepared to take into consideration the practical nature of the Root—Phillimore system, in which candidates were to be nominated by the national groups of the Permanent Court of Arbitration. He remarked that a fear seemed to exist that political influence would make itself felt if governments made the nominations, and that there would be no such danger if the nominations were made by the national groups. The difference was superficial. As the members of the Court of Arbitration were appointed by the governments, they would be under governmental influence.

tions préalables auxquelles ils doivent procéder. Les groupements scientifiques ne seront guidés que par leur conscience professionnelle; les consultations constitueront ainsi une protection des hommes éminents contre l'arbitraire gouvernemental, et dont le besoin ne se fait d'ailleurs sentir qu'en ce qui concerne la désignation des candidats nationaux. Quant à la présentation des étrangers, la garantie se trouve déjà dans le fait que la désignation sera effectuée par le gouvernement d'un pays autre que le leur.

It would be better to establish guarantees to ensure that the governments would be bound to consult certain bodies and to abide by their advice. The various scientific and professional bodies would be guided only by their professional judgment, so that their advice would protect the claims of distinguished men from arbitrary decisions on the part of the governments. Further, the need for such protection only applies in the case of the nomination of national candidates. In the case of the nomination of foreigners, a sufficient guarantee already exists in the fact that the nomination is to be made by the government of another country.

Le PRESIDENT doute que les gouvernements, au milieu des influences multiples qui les assaillent, tiennent toujours compte du résultat de ces consultations.

The PRESIDENT doubted whether governments, surrounded as they are by many different influences, would always take into account the results of such consultations.

M. DE LAPRADELLE répond qu'on créera pour les gouvernements l'obligation de consulter certains corps, facultés, académies, groupements scientifiques internationaux, tels que l'Institut de Droit International; ces corps ne se laisseront guider que par des considérations techniques et on liera les gouvernements en publiant les opinions exprimées par ces corps: on aura pour cela l'appui puissant de la presse. Les gouvernements feront les présentations dans un esprit vraiment éclairé et international. En outre, ils sentiront tout le poids de leur responsabilité. M. de Lapradelle croit donc que le système qu'il a proposé est le plus pratique.

M. DE LAPRADELLE replied that it would be made binding upon the governments to consult certain bodies, such as academies and faculties, and also international scientific institutions such as the "Institut de Droit International"; such bodies would only be guided by professional considerations and the hands of the governments could be tied by the publication of the opinions given by these bodies; the powerful support of the Press would thus be obtained. Consequently, the governments would make the nominations in a really enlightened and international spirit. Further, they would feel the whole weight of their responsibility. M. de Lapradelle thought therefore, that the system he proposed was the most practical one.

M. ALTAMIRA, satisfait de voir que l'opinion qu'il avait déjà manifestée sur les qualités des juges et leur caractère international est partagée par ses collègues, les invite à se demander si les difficultés d'organiser une réunion du collège électoral n'ont pas été exagérées. Les objections seraient sans doute justifiées, s'il s'agissait de réunir tous les membres de la Cour d'Arbitrage; mais il ne sera nécessaire de faire venir qu'un seul membre de chaque pays. Il cite à l'appui l'exemple de l'Espagne: très probablement un seul membre espagnol de la Cour pourrait se déplacer.

M. Altamira ajoute que, d'autre part, il faut tenir compte du fait que la plupart des membres de la Cour sont des hommes politiques. On se retrouve donc en présence des mêmes difficultés. Dans ces conditions, il convient de considérer qu'il vaut mieux compter sur les garanties morales que sur des garanties extérieures. Que l'on

M. ALTAMIRA expressed his satisfaction that the members had agreed with the opinion he had previously manifested as to the qualifications and the international character of the judges, and asked them to consider, whether the difficulties of organising a meeting of the electoral body had not been exaggerated. The objection would be fully justified, if it were a question of assembling all the members of the Court of Arbitration, but it was only necessary that one member for each country should come. He quoted in support the case of Spain; it is most probable that one Spanish member of the Court only would be able to attend a meeting.

He added that it must be borne in mind that the greater number of the members of the Court, were politicians; the same difficulties therefore arose. Under these circumstances it would be better to rely upon moral rather than upon ex-

obtienne ces garanties morales, et la méthode de présentation devient à peu près indifférente.

La seule chose essentielle est de choisir des hommes possédant les plus hautes qualités morales, quelque soit le pays auquel ils appartiennent.

M. RICCI-BUSATTI déclare qu'il voit encore une foule d'objections aux différents systèmes qui ont été proposés. Il est d'accord avec M. Altamira pour reconnaître que la garantie essentielle consiste dans la conscience des électeurs: mais il ne croit pas, comme lui, que la méthode de présentation soit indifférente, puisqu'elle sert à mettre en jeu cette garantie fondamentale, et à la dégager autant que possible de toute influence étrangère. M. Altamira, comme le Président, voudrait réunir un collège électoral. M. Ricci-Busatti élève deux objections contre cette manière de procéder; d'abord il est difficile de réunir, pour la désignation des candidats, un grand nombre de personnes de tous les pays du monde, et en second lieu, le but de la réunion serait hors de proportion avec le dérangement qu'elle causerait. Le Conseil et l'Assemblée devront toujours avoir d'autres questions à régler en même temps que l'élection des juges.

M. Ricci-Busatti a également de graves objections à soulever contre le système qui veut confier la désignation aux gouvernements. Ceux-ci ne pourront pas se soustraire à l'influence des intérêts politiques, qu'il s'agisse de candidats étrangers ou nationaux. Il faut, afin d'éviter ces inconvénients, essayer d'obliger les gouvernements à effectuer leur choix conformément aux recommandations émises par les différents corps professionnels. C'est à cela que vise le système préconisé par M. de Lapradelle, moyennant une consultation obligatoire des corps professionnels; mais ce moyen est insuffisant et peu pratique: il faudrait, en effet, consulter une foule de personnes, d'opinions différentes, qui présenteraient un très grand nombre de candidats, parmi lesquels le gouvernement aurait toute liberté pour son choix. C'est retomber dans l'arbitraire; le meilleur moyen d'en sortir c'est, selon M. Ricci-Busatti, de confier la présentation aux groupes nationaux de trois ou quatre personnes que constituent les membres de la Cour d'Arbitrage; c'est la solution adoptée par le projet Root—Phillimore, et qu'on retrouve dans le sien. Les membres de la Cour d'Arbitrage sont en général des personnes trop haut placées pour ne pas être indépendantes.

M. Ricci-Busatti pense que le nombre de quatre candidats par groupe, proposé par Lord Phillimore comme une solution transaction-

ternal guarantees. The method of nomination was almost a matter of indifference, provided that these moral guarantees were obtained.

The only essential point was that men possessing the highest moral qualities should be chosen, regardless of the country from which they came.

M. RICCI-BUSATTI said that he could still see a host of objections to the various systems that had been proposed. He supported M. Altamira in recognising that the essential guarantee lay in the conscientious performance of their task by the electors, but he did not agree with him that the method of nomination was unimportant, since it allowed this fundamental guarantee to be brought to bear, and would serve to free it as much as possible from all outside influence. M. Altamira, like the President, wished for a meeting of the electoral body. M. Ricci-Busatti saw two objections to this: first of all it would be difficult to assemble a large number of persons from all the countries of the world for the nomination of the candidates; and secondly the object of the meeting would be out of proportion to the trouble involved. The Council and the Assembly should always have other questions to deal with at the same time as the election of judges.

M. Ricci-Busatti also had some serious objections to the system whereby the nominations were to be entrusted to the governments. The latter could not get away from political interests, whether in the choice of national or foreign candidates. To avoid these difficulties an attempt must be made to tie the hands of the governments in making their choice. M. de Lapradelle's system was intended to effect this by means of a compulsory consultation with professional bodies; but this means was not sufficient, and was hardly practical. A large number of individuals holding divergent opinions would have to be consulted, and they would put forward a very large number of candidates, from amongst whom the governments would be quite free to choose. The result would again be arbitrary selection. The best means of overcoming the difficulty, in M. Ricci-Busatti's opinion, would be to entrust nomination to the national groups of three or four persons who are members of the Court of Arbitration; this was the solution adopted in the Root—Phillimore plan and also to be found in his own. The members of the Court of Arbitration are, generally speaking, persons holding such high positions, that they cannot fail to be independent.

M. Ricci-Busatti thought that the num-

nelle, est un peu arbitraire. On aurait un nombre total d'environ cent candidats pour chaque élection, même s'il ne s'agissait que de nommer, deux ou trois juges, ce qui est peu pratique. Le système proposé par M. Hagerup (autant de candidats qu'il y a de vacances) se heurte à la même objection, au moins pour la première élection.

En ce qui concerne la nationalité des candidats, M. Ricci-Busatti est d'avis que les considérations présentées par Mr. Root sont très justes, lorsqu'il s'agit de groupes d'Etats présentant certaines affinités, comme c'est le cas pour l'Amérique du Sud, par exemple; mais le problème ne se présente pas de la même façon en Europe où l'on sera bien embarrassé quand il faudra choisir entre des personnes qualifiées appartenant à une douzaine de pays différents, deux ou trois candidats étrangers.

Il est d'ailleurs possible qu'un candidat désigné par un groupe étranger ne soit pas celui qui aurait eu la préférence dans son propre pays, étant donné que, d'après le projet que l'on discute, aucun Etat ne pourra avoir plus d'un de ses ressortissants parmi les membres de la Cour. N'est-il pas plus utile de s'en remettre au choix des co-nationaux qui seront toujours mieux en mesure d'apprécier les différentes qualités intellectuelles et morales de la personne à choisir?

M. Ricci-Busatti déclare qu'il ne saurait dire quel est le projet qu'il appuiera; il est encore indécis à ce sujet. Il croit cependant pouvoir recommander le système qui est contenu dans l'amendement qu'il a présenté, en adaptant à la désignation des *candidats* celui qu'il avait déjà proposé pour la désignation des *juges*: chaque groupe désigne seulement une personne, et les personnes ainsi désignées sont seules à figurer sur la liste. Si les arbitres qui forment le groupe ne peuvent se mettre d'accord, le gouvernement choisira parmi les noms qu'ils auront proposés.

La difficulté soulevée par le Président et par M. de Lapradelle, concernant la présentation éventuelle de personnes qui font partie du groupe lui-même, sera, à son avis, écartée par ce système.

Mr. ROOT remarque que la discussion a porté sur deux questions:

1. Le nombre des candidats à proposer par la Cour d'Arbitrage. Cette question est assez indifférente à Mr. Root; il est certain qu'il y aura un nombre suffisant de candidats, et

ber of four candidates for each country, proposed by Lord Phillimore as a compromise, was rather arbitrary. The result would be a total number of about a hundred candidates, for each election, even if it were only a question of electing two or three judges, and this was not at all practical. On the other hand the system proposed by M. Hagerup, that there should be as many candidates as there were vacancies, was subject to the same objections, at any rate for the first election.

Concerning the nationality of the candidates, M. Ricci-Busatti thought that the considerations put forward by Mr. Root on the subject of groups of States between whom certain affinities existed, were fully justified; as, for instance, in the case of South America. The problem, however, was not the same in Europe, where it would be most embarrassing to have to choose two or three candidates from amongst duly qualified persons belonging to a dozen different countries.

It was also possible that a candidate nominated by a foreign group would not have been chosen by his own country, seing that, according to the plan under discussion, no State could have more than one of its subjects amongst the members of the Court. Would it not be better to confine the right of selecting candidates to persons of the same nationality, who would invariably be better able to appreciate the various intellectual and moral qualities of the individual to be chosen?

M. Ricci-Busatti declared that he was uncertain which plan he would support; he had not yet quite made up his mind on this subject. He thought however that he could recommend the system contained in the amendment he was submitting, in which he had adapted the system that he had already proposed for the selection of *judges* to the selection of *candidates*: each group was to nominate one person only, and only the persons so nominated would be included on the list of candidates. If the arbitrators forming the group could not agree, the government would choose from amongst the names proposed by the group.

The difficulty raised by the President and M. de Lapradelle, concerning the nomination of persons who belong to the group itself, will be, in his opinion, avoided by this system.

Mr. ROOT said that the discussion concerned two questions:

1. The number of candidates to be submitted by the Court of Arbitration. This question was a matter of indifference to Mr. Root. It was quite certain that there would be a

il est certain que leurs qualités sont sauvegardées par le fait que le droit de présentation est conféré à la Cour d'Arbitrage. Cependant il croit devoir recommander la solution contenue dans l'article 6, alinéa 2 du projet des Cinq Puissances.

2. La question soulevée par M. de Lapradelle qui propose que la présentation des candidats soit faite par les gouvernements.

La disposition selon laquelle la présentation est confiée à la Cour d'Arbitrage a été insérée dans le projet Root—Phillimore par égard pour le Président.

La disposition représente le maximum de concessions possible envers les idées de celui-ci. La présentation par la collectivité des membres de la Cour d'Arbitrage ne pouvait pas être insérée parce qu'elle ne serait pas acceptée. L'idée d'une réunion à La Haye ne pouvait pas être adoptée parce que les membres ne viendraient pas.

On propose maintenant d'abandonner entièrement cette idée telle qu'elle se trouve exprimée dans le projet Root—Phillimore. Mr. Root n'est pas disposé à le faire. Il croit que le Comité a le devoir de proposer pour la nouvelle Cour un plan d'organisation qui oblige les gouvernements à tenir compte de la qualité des juges et non de leurs relations politiques. Ce résultat ne peut être assuré qu'en exigeant d'eux qu'ils présentent des hommes connus pour leur compétence, leur haut caractère, leur bon sens et pour être inaccessibles aux influences politiques; si cette exigence n'est pas introduite dans le plan, il échouera infailliblement.

Les gouvernements auront leur mot à dire lors de l'élection par le Conseil et par l'Assemblée: ils n'ont pas à s'occuper de la composition de la liste des candidats.

En outre, il vaut mieux que les gouvernements ne soient pas liés par rapport aux noms figurant sur cette liste. D'ailleurs aucun Ministre des Affaires Etrangères ne voudrait prononcer un jugement sur les mérites d'un homme de valeur appartenant à un autre pays, et rejeter ainsi sur son gouvernement la responsabilité de ce jugement: cela serait inadmissible.

En ce qui concerne la désignation de leurs propres nationaux, les gouvernements se prononceront au moment de l'élection. Comme il y aura beaucoup plus de candidats que de sièges à attribuer, les gouvernements devront faire un choix: il serait très imprudent, dans ces conditions, de lier officiellement les gouvernements à l'avance.

sufficient number of candidates, and that their suitability was ensured by the fact that the right of nomination was conferred upon the Court of Arbitration. Nevertheless he thought that he should recommend the solution contained in Article 6 Paragraph 2 of the Five Power plan.

2. The question raised by M. de Lapradelle, who had proposed that the nomination of candidates should be carried out by the governments.

The clause entrusting the nomination to the Court of Arbitration had been inserted in the Root—Phillimore plan in deference to the President.

It was the greatest concession possible to the ideas of the latter. Nomination by the whole body of the Court of Arbitration could not be put in the plan because it would not be accepted. It was no use adopting the idea of a meeting at the Hague because the members would not come.

It was now proposed entirely to abandon the idea contained in the Root—Phillimore plan. Mr. Root was not prepared to do this. He thought that the Committee's task was to submit a scheme of organisation for the new Court which would compel the governments to consider the quality of the judges and not their political relations. This result could only be ensured by requiring from the governments the nomination of men well known for their ability, high character, good common sense, and power of raising themselves above political influences; if no provision to this effect were contained in the plan, it was bound to fail.

The governments would have their opportunity at the time of the election by the Council and the Assembly; they must have no hand in the preparation of the list of candidates.

Further, it would be better if the governments did not commit themselves to the names on the list. Besides, no Foreign Minister would give an opinion upon the merits of a distinguished subject of another country, thus putting upon his government the responsability for this opinion: such a thing would be quite inadmissible.

As concerns the nomination of their own national candidates, governments could express their wishes at the elections. As there would be far more candidates than vacancies to be filled, the governments must choose. It would therefore be very bad policy to commit the governments officially beforehand. It would be far preferable that the nominations should be made by

Pour cette raison, il est bien préférable que la présentation vienne des juristes et savants qui composent la Cour d'Arbitrage et qui appuient leurs avis sur leur expérience, sans lier par là leurs gouvernements. L'idée de faire une désignation par les gouvernements est irréalisable.

Si l'on chargeait les gouvernements de composer la liste des candidats, puis de faire les élections sur cette liste, le caractère de la Cour ne serait guère différent de celui du Conseil de la Société des Nations. La Cour serait un corps politique basé sur des considérations politiques; un corps représentant les différents gouvernements, au lieu d'un corps composé d'une élite d'hommes compétents chargés d'administrer la justice sans regard à aucune considération nationale.

M. FERNANDES se déclare d'accord avec le projet Root—Phillimore, surtout si ses auteurs sont disposés à accepter les amendements de M. Hagerup.

Personnellement, M. Fernandes pourrait se rallier à l'amendement de M. Loder, mais Lord Phillimore s'est opposé à cet amendement pour des raisons particulières à son pays, et dont il est le meilleur juge. Cependant, il craint que Lord Phillimore n'arrive qu'à aggraver, en l'ajournant, la difficulté de politique intérieure qu'il veut prévenir.

Quant à l'idée suggérée par M. de Lapradelle, M. Fernandes pense que le discours de Mr. Root, qui a du reste devancé sa pensée, l'a définitivement écartée: avec le système de M. de Lapradelle les électeurs seraient trop liés par la position prise d'avance par leurs gouvernements, au préjudice de cet esprit de transaction et de conciliation qui est nécessaire pour aboutir.

Le PRESIDENT rappelle qu'il y aura une réunion officieuse pour l'examen des règles de procédure l'après-midi du même jour, à 4 heures.

La séance est levée à 12.30 heures de l'après-midi.

Le Président:
(signé) Brn. DESCAMPS.

Le Secrétaire-Général:
(signé) D. ANZILOTTI.

the jurists and experts composing the Court of Arbitration, who would rely on their experience in forming their opinions, without in this way committing their governments. The idea of nomination by governments was not practicable.

If the governments were entrusted with the preparation of the lists of candidates and also carried out the elections upon these lists, the Court would differ but little in character from the Council of the League of Nations. The Court would be a political body founded on political considerations; a body representing the various governments, instead of a body composed of picked and specially qualified men entrusted with the administration of justice regardless of any national considerations.

M. FERNANDES declared that he supported the Root—Phillimore plan especially if the authors of it were prepared to accept M. Hagerup's amendment.

M. Fernandes said that he personally was prepared to support M. Loder's amendment, but Lord Phillimore had opposed this amendment for reasons peculiar to his own country, of which he was the best judge. However, M. Fernandes feared that Lord Phillimore would only succeed in postponing and at the same time aggravating the internal political difficulty; which he wished to avoid.

Concerning M. de Lapradelle's suggestion, he thought that Mr. Root's speech, which had also expressed his own views, had definitely settled the matter. According to M. de Lapradelle's system, the electors would be too much bound by the positions taken up beforehand by their governments; this would be greatly to the detriment of that spirit of compromise and conciliation which was a necessary condition for success.

The PRESIDENT reminded the members that there would be an unofficial meeting to consider the rules of procedure at 4 o'clock in the afternoon.

The meeting closed at 12.30 p.m.

The President:
(signed) Brn. DESCAMPS.

The Secretary-General:
(signed) D. ANZILOTTI.

19IÈME SÉANCE (non-publique), tenue au Palais de la Paix, à La Haye, le 8 juillet 1920.

Présidence de M. le BARON DESCAMPS.

Sont présents: tous les membres du Comité (à l'exception de M. Bevilaqua); M. Fernandes; Mr. James Brown Scott; les secrétaires particuliers du Baron Descamps et de M. Adatci; les membres du Secrétariat.

La séance est ouverte à 9.40 heures du matin.

Le PRESIDENT rouvre la discussion sur l'article 6 du projet Root—Phillimore. Il mentionne les deux amendements qui s'y rapportent:

1. l'amendement de M. de Lapradelle, dont il donne lecture. (Voir procès-verbal du 7 juillet);
2. un amendement que vient de déposer M. Ricci-Busatti. (Voir annexe 1re).

Le Président donne la parole à M. Ricci-Busatti en le priant d'expliquer son amendement.

M. RICCI-BUSATTI commence par observer qu'on se trouve, pour la présentation des candidats, en présence de trois systèmes:

1. le système de l'article 6 du projet Root—Phillimore, amendé par M. Loder et par M. de Lapradelle;
2. le système de M. Hagerup, qui prévoit la présentation d'autant de candidats qu'il y a de vacances à remplir (quinze pour la première élection);
3. le sien, qu'il résume brièvement.

Ce dernier, qui prévoit la présentation d'un seul candidat par chaque groupe national de membres de la Cour d'Arbitrage, écarte, à son avis, les principaux inconvénients qu'on peut reprocher aux deux autres; il coïncide avec celui de M. Hagerup, pour le cas où il n,y aurait qu'une seule vacance à remplir.

M. FERNANDES approuve la seconde idée de M. Ricci-Busatti, c'est-à-dire celle d'ex-

19TH MEETING (Private), held at the Peace Palace, the Hague, on July 8th, 1920.

BARON DESCAMPS in the chair.

Present: all members of the Committee (with the exception of M. Bevilaqua); M. Fernandes; Mr. James Brown Scott; the private secretaries of Baron Descamps and of M. Adatci; the members of the Secretariat.

The meeting opened at 9.40 a.m.

The PRESIDENT reopened the discussion upon the 6th Article of the Root—Phillimore plan. He mentioned the two amendments dealing with this Article:

1. the amendment of M. de Lapradelle, which he read. (See procès-verbal of July 7th);
2. an amendment just submitted by M. Ricci-Busatti (See Annex 1).

The President called upon M. Ricci-Busatti to explain his amendment.

M. RICCI-BUSATTI began by pointing out that three systems for the nomination of candidates had been laid before the Committee:

1. the system contained in Article 6 of the Root—Phillimore plan, which system had been amended by M. Loder and M. de Lapradelle;
2. the system of M. Hagerup, according to which as many candidates as there were vacancies to be filled could be nominated; in the case of the first election, fifteen candidates;
3. his own amendment, which he described shortly.

This latter system, in his opinion, avoided the principal difficulties attaching to the other two, by providing for the nomination of one candidate by each national group of the members of the Court of Arbitration; this system coincided with that of M. Hagerup, when there was one vacancy only to be filled.

M. FERNANDES approved of the second idea put forward by M. Ricci-Busatti, that

clure du droit de présentation les Etats qui ont déjà dans la Cour des membres de leur nationalité. Mais, d'autre part, si l'on adopte l'idée contenue dans la première partie de l'amendement, la nomination des juges ne sera plus précédée de ce plébiscite qui semble si désirable; on perdra aussi l'avantage que présente la désignation faite par des étrangers.

LORD PHILLIMORE constate d'abord que les amendements de M. Ricci-Busatti ont trait à deux cas différents: la première élection, et celles qui seront faites pour remplir les vacances ultérieures. Lord Phillimore pense qu'il n'y a pas lieu d'aborder pour l'instant la seconde question.

Avant de s'occuper des différences entre le projet Root—Phillimore et l'amendement de M. Ricci-Busatti, Lord Phillimore tient à faire constater qu'à son avis, l'ordre entre les différents articles doit être celui qui a été adopté par M. Loder, et d'autre part que Mr. Root et lui-même sont d'accord pour accepter la modification à l'article 6 du projet Root—Phillimore proposée par M. Loder.

Quant à la première partie de l'amendement de M. Ricci-Busatti, elle ne vise que le cas où un groupe national parmi les membres de la Cour permanente d'Arbitrage n'a pu se mettre d'accord sur la présentation.

Lord Phillimore ne croit pas qu'il soit opportun de régler cette éventualité de la façon préconisée par M. Ricci-Busatti. Il croit, en effet, qu'il faut exclure les gouvernements de toute part dans la présentation. Pour cette raison Lord Phillimore doit déclarer qu'il ne peut accepter la proposition de M. Ricci-Busatti.

L'idée de faire désigner une seule personne par chaque groupe est nouvelle, mais elle n'est guère opportune. Elle aurait pour résultat cinquante présentations nationales, et le collège électoral n'aurait pas assez de liberté de choix sur une liste aussi restreinte. Il est d'ailleurs peu souhaitable de donner à la liste le caractère d'un corps de délégués des divers gouvernements. Lord Phillimore répète encore qu'un tel système ne saurait être accepté de la Grande-Bretagne, qui, à cause de ses dominions, doit pouvoir désigner au moins deux personnes. Il recommande donc à l'attention du Comité le projet Root—Phillimore avec l'amendement Loder.

Lord Phillimore fait encore observer qu'on se trouve en présence de deux autres problèmes:

is to say, the exclusion of those States, which already had members of their nationality upon the Court, from the right of nomination. But, on the other hand, if the idea expressed in the first portion of the amendment were adopted, the appointment of judges would not be preceded by the "plebiscite", which seemed so desirable; the advantage obtained by the nomination by foreigners would also be lost.

LORD PHILLIMORE began by stating that M. Ricci-Busatti's amendments dealt with two different cases: the first election, and bye-elections held to fill subsequent vacancies. Lord Phillimore thought that there was no need, at the moment, to deal with the second question.

Before considering the differences between the Root—Phillimore project and M. Ricci-Busatti's amendment, Lord Phillimore wished to state that, in his opinion, the order of the Articles should be that adopted by M. Loder, and also that Mr. Root and himself had agreed to accept the amendment proposed by M. Loder to Article 6 of the Root—Phillimore plan.

Dealing with the first part of M. Ricci-Busatti's amendment, he said that it only referred to a case in which a national group of the members of the Permanent Court of Arbitration could not come to an agreement upon the nomination.

He did not think it would be advisable to deal with this possibility in the way indicated by M. Ricci-Busatti. He thought, in fact, that the Governments must be excluded from taking any part in the nominations. For this reason, Lord Phillimore said that he could not accept M. Ricci-Busatti's proposal.

The nomination of a single individual by each group was a new idea, but it was hardly to be recommended; the result of it would be the nomination of fifty national candidates, and the electoral body would not have sufficient freedom of choice from such a limited list. Again, it was not desirable that the list should be of the nature of a body of delegates of different Governments. Lord Phillimore once more repeated that such a system would be inacceptable to Great Britain, which, by reason of its Dominions, must be able to nominate at least two persons. He therefore recommended to the Committee the Root—Phillimore plan as amended by M. Loder.

Lord Phillimore also pointed out that they were faced with two other problems:

1. la question soulevée par M. de Lapradelle à la séance de la veille. Lord Phillimore croit que les membres ne sont en général pas d'accord avec M. de Lapradelle pour les raisons déjà exposées hier par Mr. Root et le Président. Dans ces conditions il croit qu'on doit donner à M. de Lapradelle l'occasion de s'expliquer davantage et, après cette explication, procéder au vote sur la proposition;

2. la question du nombre des candidats. M. Loder proposait quatre présentations, dont deux au plus de candidats nationaux. Le Président a exprimé l'avis que ce système rendrait la liste trop nombreuse. D'autre part M. Hagerup a suggéré l'idée de présenter autant de candidats qu'il y a de vacances. A la suite de conversations avec Mr. Root, M. Loder et M. Hagerup, Lord Phillimore, s'inspirant d'une idée de M. Fernandes, désire proposer comme solution transactionnelle, le nombre de six candidats, dont un tiers de candidats nationaux.

Mais, Lord Phillimore propose qu'on examine d'abord l'amendement de M. Ricci-Busatti et que, si cet amendement n'est pas adopté, on prenne en considération la proposition de M. de Lapradelle.

Le PRESIDENT constate que le Comité est d'accord pour adopter cet ordre de procédure. Il prie M. Ricci-Busatti de bien vouloir réserver la seconde partie de son amendement.

M. RICCI-BUSATTI accepte, en ajoutant qu'il retire la première partie de son amendement qu'il considère comme rejetée. Il déclare cependant, en se référant aux remarques de Lord Phillimore, qu'il avait pensé que les dominions britanniques étaient représentés à la Cour d'Arbitrage par les membres britanniques de cette Cour.

M. DE LAPRADELLE aurait de nombreuses considérations à faire valoir au sujet de la question qu'on est en train de discuter. Il veut cependant se borner à demander des éclaircissements sur certains points du projet Root—Phillimore. Il rappelle qu'il s'est tout d'abord rallié à ce projet, et, aujourd'hui encore, loin de vouloir le détruire, il est persuadé qu'il traduit l'opinion de tout le Comité. Une difficulté a brusquement surgi au cours de la séance précédente: les listes seront-elles composées exclusivement

1. the question raised by M. de Lapradelle at the previous meeting. Lord Phillimore thought that the bulk of members did not agree with M. de Lapradelle, for the reasons already given yesterday by Mr. Root and the President. In these circumstances he thought that M. de Lapradelle ought to be given an opportunity of giving a further explanation of his views; after his explanations, a vote should be taken upon the proposal;

2. the question of the number of candidates. M. Loder had proposed four, of which two at most should be national candidates. The President had expressed the opinion that, if this system were adopted, the list would be too large. On the other hand, M. Hagerup had suggested that as many candidates should be submitted as there were vacancies to be filled. After conversations with Mr. Root, M. Loder and M. Hagerup, Lord Phillimore, adopting an idea of M. Fernandes, wished to propose as a compromise the number of six candidates, of which one third should be national candidates.

Lord Phillimore, however, proposed that they should first of all consider M. Ricci-Busatti's amendment; if this amendment were not adopted, they could then consider M. de Lapradelle's proposal.

The PRESIDENT stated that the Committee accepted this procedure. He requested M. Ricci-Busatti to reserve the second part of his amendment.

M. RICCI-BUSATTI agreed to do so, and added that he would also withdraw the first part of his amendment, which he considered as having been rejected. Referring to Lord Phillimore's remarks, however, he said that he had thought that the British Dominions were represented on the Court of Arbitration by the British members of that Court.

M. DE LAPRADELLE had a good many points to bring up relating to the question under discussion. He would, however, content himself with asking for explanations concerning certain points in the Root—Phillimore plan. He recalled the fact that he had, at first, supported this project, and that to-day still, far from wishing to destroy it, he felt sure that it represented the ideas of all members of the Committee. A difficulty had suddenly arisen during the previous meeting: were the lists to be composed entirely

de candidats nationaux, ou comprendront-elles aussi des candidats étrangers? M. Loder a présenté un amendement relatif à cette question; M. de Lapradelle demande à être exactement informé sur la portée de cet amendement.

M. LODER donne lecture de l'article 2 de son amendement avec les modifications qui y ont été introduites. (Voir procès-verbal du 7 juillet).

LORD PHILLIMORE ajoute que M. Loder est maintenant disposé à accepter le nombre de six candidats, dont un tiers de candidats nationaux. M. DE LAPRADELLE ayant remarqué que le nombre de six ne devrait être adopté que pour la première élection, LORD PHILLIMORE déclare qu'il est disposé à accepter une modification dans ce sens à l'article 6.

Le Comité est d'accord pour limiter la discussion aux présentations pour la première élection.

M. DE LAPRADELLE trouve très intéressante l'idée de présenter à la fois des nationaux et des étrangers. Si la présentation de nationaux doit être obligatoire, il envisage cependant certains inconvénients. Si un petit Etat, dont les jurisconsultes ne peuvent se mesurer avec les premiers jurisconsultes du monde, était obligé de présenter des candidats de sa nationalité, il aurait l'humiliation de voir toujours rejeter leurs noms. S'il a le droit de présenter six candidats et si la désignation de candidats nationaux n'est que facultative, il sera certainement heureux de désigner six étrangers: son choix serait un choix désintéressé, et, partant, probablement très judicieux. Comme il y a dans le monde beaucoup plus d'Etats dans cette situation, qu'on ne le pense, M. de Lapradelle désirerait que le droit de désigner des nationaux fût seulement facultatif.

LORD PHILLIMORE dit que telle est la pensée du projet Root—Phillimore.

M. DE LAPRADELLE déclare que, dans ces conditions, ce projet lui donne à cet égard pleine satisfaction.

Il examine ensuite la question de savoir par qui seront faites les présentations. Il avait d'abord pensé que les présentations seraient faites par les gouvernements qui devraient au préalable consulter les académies, les universités, les hauts magistrats, etc. Mais Mr. Root a fait valoir contre cette idée des considérations fondées sur son expérience d'homme d'Etat. M. de Lapradelle s'incline devant ces considérations et est prêt à retirer sa proposition, à condition qu'on lui donne satisfaction sur le point suivant, à sa-

of national candidates, or should they also contain foreign candidates? M. Loder had submitted an amendment on this subject. M. de Lapradelle asked to be informed of the exact scope of the amendment.

M. LODER read Article 2 of his amendments with the modifications which had been introduced into it. (See procès-verbal of July 7th).

LORD PHILLIMORE said that M. Loder was now disposed to accept the number of 6 candidates, of which one third should be national candidates. M. DE LAPRADELLE remarked that the number six ought only to be adopted for the first election and LORD PHILLIMORE said he was prepared to accept an amendment to Article 6 to this effect.

The Committee agreed to limit the discussion to the subject of the nominations for the first election.

M. DE LAPRADELLE thought that the idea of simultaneous nomination of national and foreign candidates was very interesting. If the nomination of national candidates was to be compulsory, however, he foresaw certain difficulties. If a little State, whose jurisconsults could not be compared with the leading jurisconsults of the world, were obliged to nominate candidates of its own nationality, it would be humiliated by always seeing their names rejected. If it had the right of nominating six candidates, and if the nomination of national candidates were optional, it would certainly be content to nominate six foreigners; as its choice would be disinterested, it would probably be very judicious. As there are in the world far more States in this position than might be thought, M. de Lapradelle would like the right of nominating national candidates to be optional only.

LORD PHILLIMORE said that such was the intention of the Root—Phillimore plan.

M. DE LAPRADELLE declared that, under these circumstances, the plan was entirely satisfactory to him in this respect.

He then went on to consider by whom the nominations should be made. He had, first of all, thought that the nominations should be made by the Governments, who should have previously consulted Academies, Universities and the principal judges. But Mr. Root had brought out objections to this idea, based on his experience as a practical statesman. M. de Lapradelle yielded to these objections and was prepared to withdraw his proposal, provided he received satisfaction upon the following point, namely: that

voir: que les membres nationaux de la Cour d'Arbitrage ne soient pas seuls à présenter les candidats, mais qu'on accorde la même prérogative et sur un pied d'égalité à d'autres corps. On a fait valoir contre la présentation des candidats par les gouvernements la possibilité d'intrigues et d'influences politiques. Mais M. de Lapradelle ne croit pas qu'il y ait une véritable différence entre les groupes nationaux des membres de la Cour d'Arbitrage et les gouvernements qui les nomment. Il prend comme exemple le groupe français; M. de Lapradelle a la plus grande confiance dans les hommes qui composent cette section; mais puisque ce sont tous des hommes politiques ou des juristes gouvernementaux, il ne croit pas qu'on puisse les distinguer du gouvernement français.

M. FERNANDES fait remarquer que si la désignation est faite par ces groupes, ni la responsabilité, ni le vote des Etats ne seront engagés.

Le PRESIDENT insiste sur l'entière indépendance des membres de la Cour d'Arbitrage.

M. DE LAPRADELLE, tout en reconnaissant l'indépendance d'esprit des arbitres, croit devoir maintenir son point de vue, d'après lequel il n'y a pas de distinction absolue entre eux et le gouvernement.

Il continue en disant qu'il faut tenir compte du facteur important qu'est l'opinion publique nationale et internationale. La Société des Nations est une grande institution démocratique, qui aura la mission de permettre aux peuples de donner une nouvelle impulsion à la politique extérieure des Etats en y exerçant leur influence; beaucoup de pays démocratiques sont encore aristocratiques à cet égard. En réglant la méthode de la présentation des candidats à la Cour Permanente de Justice Internationale, il faut tenir compte de ces considérations et par conséquent aussi de l'opinion publique internationale. Or cette opinion se trouvera-t-elle satisfaite si seule la section nationale de la Cour d'Arbitrage est consultée pour cette présentation? Elle jugera probablement utile que cette section soit consultée, mais elle n'approuverait pas qu'on ne consultât qu'elle.

M. de Lapradelle attire alors l'attention sur la proposition faite antérieurement par M. Altamira au sujet de la consultation des universités et des corps scientifiques. M. de Lapradelle mentionne à ce propos l'Institut de Droit International; il croit que les sections nationales de cet Institut devraient être placées sur le même

the national members of the Court of Arbitration should not carry out the nomination of candidates alone, but that other bodies should be granted the same right to be exercised on an equal footing. As an objection to the nomination of candidates by Governments, it had been pointed out that intrigues and political influences might intervene. But M. de Lapradelle did not think that there was any essential difference between the national groups of the members of the Court of Arbitration, and the Governments who appointed them. He quoted as an example the French group. M. de Lapradelle had the greatest confidence in the men composing this group, but, as they were all politicians, or jurists in Government service, he did not think that there was any real difference between them and the French Government.

M. FERNANDES said that if the selection were made by these groups, neither the responsibility nor the votes of the Governments would be pledged.

The PRESIDENT laid emphasis upon the complete independence of the members of the Court of Arbitration.

M. DE LAPRADELLE, whilst admitting the independence of the arbitrators, felt that he must maintain his point: that there was no definite distinction between them and the Government.

He went on to say that one must not lose sight of national and international public opinion, which was a very important factor. The League of Nations was a great democratic institution, whose task it was to enable the peoples to give a fresh impulse to the foreign policy of their countries by making their influence felt. Many democratic countries were still aristocratic in this respect. In settling the system of nomination of candidates for the Permanent Court of International Justice, these considerations and also, therefore, international public opinion must be taken into account. But would this opinion be satisfied if only the national section of the Court of Arbitration were consulted with respect to these nominations? It would probably consider it advisable that this section should be consulted, but it would not be content if it alone were consulted.

M. de Lapradelle then called attention to the proposal previously made by M. Altamira, concerning the consultation of Universities and scientific bodies. In this connection M. de Lapradelle mentioned the Institut de Droit International; he thought that the national sections of this Institute ought to be placed on the same

pied que les groupes nationaux des membres de la Cour d'Arbitrage. Les professeurs de droit international devraient également être consultés.

Dans cet ordre d'idées M. de Lapradelle retire l'amendement qu'il a déposé la veille et propose à sa place de permettre aux sections nationales de l'Institut de Droit International, à tous les Professeurs de droit international de chaque pays, et peut-être encore à d'autres groupes du même ordre, de présenter des listes de candidats au même titre que les groupes nationaux de la Cour d'Arbitrage. Si l'on décide que les listes comprendront de 4 à 6 noms, on aura une présentation vraiment complète et satisfaisante: les internationalistes de tous les pays se connaissent entre eux et ils sont ainsi les mieux renseignés sur les mérites et les dispositions de leurs collègues; on aura en même temps les avantages de la présentation d'étrangers. M. de Lapradelle propose comme un minimum l'assimilation des sections nationales de l'Institut de Droit International aux groupes nationaux de la Cour d'Arbitrage.

M. ADATCI a écouté avec beaucoup d'intérêt les explications de M. de Lapradelle sur son nouveau projet.

Bien que s'étant tout d'abord rallié au premier amendement de M. de Lapradelle, M. Adatci, réflexion faite, croit maintenant que le projet Root—Phillimore est le seul qui ait quelque chance d'aboutir parce qu'il est le seul à représenter le bon sens pratique. Il réserve cependant son opinion sur le nombre des candidats. Sur ce point il incline vers la proposition de M. Hagerup, dont les observations méritent d'être examinées attentivement.

M. Adatci déclare qu'il retire formellement son adhésion au premier amendement de M. de Lapradelle et qu'il adhère à l'article 6 du projet Root—Phillimore.

M. ALTAMIRA remarque que le nouvel amendement de M. de Lapradelle embrasse, non seulement l'article 6 du projet Root—Phillimore, mais aussi l'article 8.

M. Altamira peut se rallier à ce projet à condition qu'on y introduise la dernière modification proposée par M. Loder, c'est-à-dire qu'on stipule l'obligation, pour les groupes nationaux des membres de la Cour d'Arbitrage, de présenter des étrangers, tout en rendant facultative la désignation de candidats nationaux.

Il fait observer que M. de Lapradelle s'est inspiré de l'idée contenue dans les amendements proposés par M. Altamira lui-même à l'ar-

footing as the national groups of the members of the Court of Arbitration. The professors of International Law should also be consulted.

Acting on this idea, M. de Lapradelle withdrew the amendment that he had submitted on the previous day and substituted a proposal to allow the national sections of the Institut de Droit International, all the professors of International Law in each country and perhaps other bodies of the same kind, to submit lists of candidates on the same footing as the national groups of the Court of Arbitration. If it were decided that the lists should contain from four to six names, the nominations would be really complete and satisfactory; the international jurists of all countries are well known to each other, and are therefore best informed as to the merits and propensities of their colleagues. At the same time, the advantages offered by the nomination of foreigners would be obtained. M. de Lapradelle proposed that as a minimum measure the national sections of the Institut de Droit International should be assimilated to the national groups of the Court of Arbitration.

M. ADATCI had listened with great interest to M. de Lapradelle's explanation of his new plan.

Although he had begun by supporting M. de Lapradelle's first amendment, M. Adatci, after reflection, now thought, that the Root—Phillimore plan was the only one which had a real chance of success, because it was the only one based on practical common sense. He reserved his opinion, however, concerning the number of candidates. Upon this point, he was inclined to support the proposal of M. Hagerup, whose remarks were worthy of serious consideration.

M. Adatci stated that he formally withdrew his support from M. de Lapradelle's first amendment, and that he would support Article 6 of the Root—Phillimore plan.

M. ALTAMIRA pointed out that M. de Lapradelle's new amendment included not only Article 6 of the Root—Phillimore plan, but also Article 8.

M. Altamira would be able to support this plan, provided that the last modification proposed by M. Loder were introduced into it, that is to say: the national groups of the members of the Court of Arbitration must be bound by a definite obligation to nominate foreign candidates, while, at the same time, the nomination of national candidates should be made optional.

He pointed out that M. de Lapradelle had drawn his inspiration from the amendments pro-

ticle 8 du projet Root—Phillimore. Ces amendements seront considérés en détail lors de la discussion de l'article en question; pour le moment, il se borne à signaler certaines difficultés que présente cette idée, telle qu'elle a été exposée par M. de Lapradelle.

Dans certains pays, par exemple, il n'existe pas de section de l'Institut de Droit International; dans d'autres il n'y a qu'un membre de cet Institut, lequel exercerait alors une influence trop considérable. M. Altamira ne s'oppose pas à l'amendement, mais il voudrait voir ajouter d'autres corps au corps proposé par M. de Lapradelle.

M. FERNANDES croit qu'au fond M. de Lapradelle a raison; mais il faut tenir compte de la réalité. Si l'on se borne à consulter un certain nombre de corps scientifiques, il n'y a pas d'objection; mais si ces corps doivent présenter des listes, des difficultés surgiront.

On obtiendra d'abord un nombre beaucoup trop grand de candidats, et en outre le système créera une certaine inégalité entre les Etats, les corps dont il s'agit n'étant pas également nombreux et n'ayant pas la même importance dans tous les pays; par contre, le groupe national de la Cour d'Arbitrage est toujours composé de quatre membres nommés par les gouvernements.

M. HAGERUP a déposé la veille, comme amendement à l'article 6 du projet Root—Phillimore, l'article 6, alinéa 2 du projet des Cinq Puissances, qui a obtenu l'assentiment de Mr. Root. Cependant, comme il se rend compte que cet amendement ne serait pas accepté, il le retire dans un esprit de conciliation, pour se rallier également au projet Root—Phillimore.

Il demande à M. de Lapradelle de bien vouloir formuler l'amendement qu'il a proposé et dont M. Hagerup n'a pas bien saisi la portée.

M. DE LAPRADELLE croit pouvoir l'exprimer provisoirement ainsi:

„Aux présentations faites (aux termes de l'article 8 du projet Root—Phillimore) doivent être ajoutées les listes proposées par (tel ou tel corps)."

M. de Lapradelle ajoute qu'il considère comme essentiel de mettre les autres institutions qu'on pourrait ajouter aux groupes nationaux de la Cour d'Arbitrage, sur un pied d'égalité avec ces groupes.

posed by M. Altamira himself to Article 8 of the Root—Phillimore plan; these amendments would be considered in detail when this Article was brought up for discussion; for the moment, M. Altamira would content himself with pointing out certain difficulties arising out of the idea as put forward by M. de Lapradelle.

In some countries, for instance, no section of the Institut de Droit International exists; in other countries there is only one member of this institute; he would, therefore, have too great an influence. For this reason M. Altamira did not object to the amendment but wished other bodies to be added to that proposed by M. de Lapradelle.

M. FERNANDES thought that M. de Lapradelle was fundamentally right, but realities must be faced. If it were merely a question of consulting a number of scientific bodies, there would be no objection, but if these bodies were to have the duty of nominating candidates, difficulties would arise.

In the first place, much too large a number of candidates would be obtained; further, the system would create a certain inequality between States, because the bodies in question were not of the same number or importance in all countries; on the other hand, the national groups of the Court of Arbitration were always composed of four members appointed by the Governments.

M. HAGERUP had, on the previous day, submitted Article 6, Paragraph 2 of the Five Power plan as an amendment to Article 6 of the Root—Phillimore plan, and Mr. Root had expressed his approval. As, however, he felt sure that this amendment would not be accepted, he withdrew it from motives of a conciliatory nature and gave his support to the Root—Phillimore plan.

He asked M. de Lapradelle to be so good as to formulate the amendment which the latter had proposed, and which he had not quite grasped.

M. DE LAPRADELLE thought that he could, provisionally, word it as follows:

"To the nominations made (according to the provisions of Article 8 of the Root—Phillimore plan), are to be added the lists submitted by (such and such a body)."

M. de Lapradelle added that, in his opinion, it was essential to put the other institutions that might be added to the national groups of the Court of Arbitration upon the same footing as these groups.

M. HAGERUP croit qu'il est difficile de créer l'égalité entre les sections nationales de l'Institut de Droit International, qui est une corporation privée, et les groupes nationaux de la Cour d'Arbitrage, dont les membres sont nommés par les gouvernements.

M. DE LAPRADELLE déclare qu'après la discussion qui vient d'avoir lieu, il retire son amendement et se rallie à l'article 6 du projet Root—Phillimore, tel qu'il a été amendé par M. Loder.

M. LODER a composé un nouveau texte où il a tenu compte de toutes les modifications sur lesquelles on est tombé d'accord. Il donne lecture de ce texte qui est ainsi conçu: „Trois mois au moins avant la première élection, le Secrétaire-Général de la Société des Nations demande par écrit aux membres de la Cour Permanente d'Arbitrage de La Haye, de procéder par groupes — chaque groupe comprenant les membres nommés par un pays déterminé — à la présentation de six noms au plus de personnes remplissant à leur avis les conditions requises et qui sont disposées à accepter la dignité de juge, de sorte que chaque groupe ne pourra présenter plus de deux ressortissants du pays que représente ce groupe".

LORD PHILLIMORE et M. DE LAPRADELLE déclarent se rallier à ce texte.

Le PRESIDENT dit que l'idée de faire présenter simultanément des candidats nationaux et étrangers est très séduisante. Il craint cependant que cette idée, telle qu'elle se trouve exprimée dans le texte qu'on vient de soumettre, ne conduise à des désignations faites à l'aventure, à des coalitions et à des intrigues. Elle aurait été réalisée d'une façon plus simple par le système qu'il a proposé lui-même. Le principe peut être bon, mais la pratique risque d'être défectueuse.

Le Président ne votera pas contre le texte, mais il s'abstiendra.

Il n'a pas confiance dans la consultation, telle qu'elle a été proposée par M. de Lapradelle. Il aurait préféré le système développé dans son avant-projet et d'après lequel des hommes d'une compétence remarquable, tels que les membres de la Cour Permanente d'Arbitrage, nommés eux-mêmes par les gouvernements, auraient choisi les juges dans des conditions extraordinairement favorables.

M. HAGERUP thought that it would be difficult to put the national sections of the Institut de Droit International, which is a private corporation, and the national groups of the Court of Arbitration, of which the members are appointed by the Governments, upon a basis of equality.

M. DE LAPRADELLE declared that, in view of the discussion which had just taken place, he withdrew his amendment and supported Article 6 of the Root—Phillimore plan, as amended by M. Loder.

M. LODER had composed a new wording containing all the modifications that had been agreed upon. He read this wording, which was as follows: "Three months at least before the first election, the Secretary-General of the League of Nations shall address a written request to the members of the Permanent Court of Arbitration at the Hague, to undertake, by groups, — each group containing the members appointed by a particular State — the nomination of a maximum of six persons, fulfilling, in their opinion, the required conditions, and who are prepared to accept the appointment as judges, subject to the condition that each group shall not submit more than two candidates of the same nationality as the country which it represents."

LORD PHILLIMORE and M. DE LAPRADELLE said that they would accept this formula.

The PRESIDENT said that the idea of nominating national and foreign candidates simultaneously was very attractive. Nevertheless, he feared that the idea, as expressed in the wording just submitted, would lead to haphazard nominations, and to coalitions and intrigues. It would have been realised in a much simpler way by the system which he had himself proposed. The principle might be good; but this did not appear to be a satisfactory way of putting it into practice.

The President would not vote against this formula, but he would abstain from voting.

He had no confidence in the method of consultation, suggested by M. de Lapradelle. He would have preferred the system worked out in his own draft scheme, which provided for the selection of the judges, under extremely favourable conditions, by men of unusual ability, such as the members of the Permanent Court of Arbitration, who were themselves appointed by Governments.

M. RICCI-BUSATTI, tout en reconnaissant le bien fondé des considérations du Président, déclare qu'il se rallie à la proposition Root—Phillimore.

Le PRESIDENT passe à l'examen de ce projet, tel qu'il a été amendé par M. Loder. Il craint que le système proposé par M. de Lapradelle, avec l'appui de M. Altamira, ne fasse une impression peu favorable sur l'Assemblée, qui se verra obligée de voter sur une liste de candidats proposés par une foule très diverse de collèges. D'autre part le Président craint, il le répète, que le fait de proposer six candidats dont deux nationaux, ne donne lieu à des intrigues. Il aurait préféré quelque chose de plus net, par exemple une liste de candidats nationaux dressée par les quatre membres de la Cour d'Arbitrage pour chaque pays, et puis une discussion entre les membres de tous les pays. Donc, les Etats ayant ainsi participé à la désignation seraient tous représentés.

M. ALTAMIRA trouve que l'expression finale de l'article 6, tel qu'il se trouve maintenant formulé, n'est pas suffisamment claire. Il propose qu'on y ajoute une formule s'inspirant de celle adoptée par la Conférence de Bruxelles des associations pour la Société des Nations.

Chaque Etat aurait le droit de proposer un nombre maximum de candidats de sa nationalité et, afin qu'il fût indiqué clairement que le juge est exclusivement au service de la justice, un nombre plus élevé de candidats d'autres nationalités. Il suggère d'ajouter la formule suivante: „les autres étant des jurisconsultes étrangers".

On décide que l'idée de M. Altamira sera prise en considération par le Comité de rédaction.

Le PRESIDENT met au vote l'article 6 du projet Root—Phillimore tel qu'il est formulé dans le texte soumis par M. Loder.

A la suite du vote, fait par appel nominal, l'article est adopté, sauf rédaction, à l'unanimité; le Président s'est abstenu.

Le Président ouvre la discussion sur l'article 7 et invite Lord Phillimore à fournir des explications à son sujet.

M. LODER rappelle son amendement, se rapportant à cet article (voir article 3 des amendements soumis le 6 juillet par M. Loder).

M. RICCI-BUSATTI recognised the soundness of the President's arguments, but nevertheless declared that he would support the Root—Phillimore proposal.

The PRESIDENT went on to consider this project, as amended by M. Loder, in detail. He feared that the system proposed by M. de Lapradelle, and supported by M. Altamira, would create an unfavourable impression upon the Assembly, which would find itself obliged to vote upon a list of candidates proposed by a collection of bodies of very different kinds. On the other hand, the President feared — he emphasised this — that the submission of six candidates of whom two were national candidates, would give rise to intrigues. He would have preferred something simpler, for instance, a list of national candidates prepared by the four members of the Court of Arbitration for each country, followed by a discussion between the members of all countries. As all States would thus have taken part in the selection, they would all be represented.

M. ALTAMIRA thought that the final expression contained in Article 6 as now amended, was not sufficiently clear. He proposed that a formula based upon that adopted by the Conference of Associations for the League of Nations, held at Brussels, should be added.

Each State should have the right to submit a certain maximum number of candidates of its own nationality, and a larger number of candidates of other nationalities, in order to make it quite clear that the judge's sole duty is the administration of justice. He suggested that the following formula should be added: "the others being foreign jurisconsults."

It was agreed that M. Altamira's idea should be considered by the drafting Committee.

The PRESIDENT put Article 6 of the Root—Phillimore project, as drafted by M. Loder, to the vote.

The vote, which was taken by calling over the names, resulted in the adoption of the Article, subject to drafting amendments. The voting was unanimous except that the President abstained from voting.

The President opened the discussion upon the 7th Article, and requested Lord Phillimore to explain its contents.

M. LODER drew attention to his amendment dealing with this Article. (See Article 3 of the amendments submitted by M. Loder on the 6th July).

LORD PHILLIMORE remarque que cet amendement diffère de l'article 7 du projet Root—Phillimore principalement en ce qu'il charge le Secrétaire-Général de la Société des Nations d'ajouter, aux noms des candidats, le nombre de voix qu'ils ont obtenu. Lord Phillimore n'y voit pas d'inconvénient. Il poursuit en disant que l'article 7, dont il donne lecture, n'est que la continuation de l'article 6, et fait observer que la dernière partie de l'article renferme l'idée exprimée par Mr. Root, relativement à la Commission médiatrice. Lord Phillimore a consulté Mr. Root sur l'idée suggérée par l'amendement de M. Loder.

Mr. ROOT pense qu'il faut rechercher la procédure la plus simple; s'il n'y a pas d'objection à ce que le Secrétaire-Général ajoute aux noms des candidats le nombre des voix obtenues, il n'est pas non plus nécessaire de le stipuler expressément. Le Secrétaire-Général est naturellement libre de répondre à des questions qu'on pourrait lui poser à ce sujet.

LORD PHILLIMORE se range à cette opinion. Selon lui toute disposition inutile est une pierre d'achoppement.

Le PRESIDENT demande si l'on doit vraiment mentionner le nombre de voix, sans indiquer en même temps les pays qu'elles représentent. La voix de Haïti ne saurait avoir la même importance que celle de l'Angleterre.

M. LODER ne voit pas d'objection à ce qu'on mentionne également les nominateurs.

Le PRESIDENT, comme Lord Phillimore, pense qu'il vaut mieux ne point régler cette question dans le texte, et laisser au Secrétaire-Général le soin de la résoudre.

Il constate que la première phrase de l'article 7 est adoptée sans opposition.

Le Président donne lecture de la seconde phrase, et, à la demande de M. Altamira, il lit également les remarques que ce dernier a formulées au sujet de cette phrase.

M. ALTAMIRA a la parole pour exposer l'idée qui est au fond de ses remarques. Il veut éviter que la majorité des juges soit élue en dehors de la liste de candidats présentée au Conseil et à l'Assemblée. Dans cet ordre d'idées, il voudrait limiter le droit qu'a la Commission médiatrice de recommander la nomination de personnes non mentionnées sur cette liste.

LORD PHILLIMORE stated that the principal difference between this amendment and Article 7 of the Root—Phillimore plan, was that the former provided that the Secretary-General of the League of Nations should add to each name upon the list of candidates, the number of nominations obtained. Lord Phillimore saw no objection to this. He went on to say that Article 7, which he read, was only a continuation of Article 6. He pointed out that the last portion of the Article contained the idea expressed by Mr. Root, concerning the Joint Conference. Lord Phillimore consulted Mr. Root on the idea suggested in M. Loder's amendment.

Mr. ROOT thought that the most simple procedure must be sought. Though there was no objection to the addition by the Secretary-General of the number of nominations received to the names of the candidates, there was no necessity to insert a definite stipulation to this effect, The Secretary-General was naturally free to answer questions that might be put to him on this subject.

LORD PHILLIMORE agreed. In his opinion, every useless condition would be a possible stumbling block.

The PRESIDENT wondered whether the number of nominations should be mentioned without at the same time indicating which countries had made them. The nominations of Haiti could not have the same value as those of England.

M. LODER had no objection to the nominating States being mentioned.

The PRESIDENT agreed with Lord Phillimore, that it would be better not to deal with this question in the text, but to leave it to be settled by the Secretary-General.

He declared that the first sentence of Article 7 was adopted without opposition.

The President read the second sentence, and, at M. Altamira's request, also read the notes that the latter had drawn up concerning this sentence.

M. ALTAMIRA obtained permission to speak in order to develop the idea upon which his notes were based. He wished to avoid any possibility that the majority of judges might be elected from outside the list of candidates submitted to the Council and the Assembly. With this object, he wished to limit the right possessed by the Joint Conference, to recommend the appointment of persons not contained in the list.

M. LODER propose la solution suivante: substituer à la dernière phrase de l'article 7 une formule ainsi conçue: „Sont seuls éligibles les candidats qui figurent sur la liste mentionnée à l'alinéa précédent".

Mr. ROOT dit que la disposition qu'on est en train de discuter visait à deux fins. Elle devait d'abord écarter la difficulté que souleva la proposition de M. de Lapradelle, c'est-à-dire éviter de paraître enlever aux gouvernements un rôle qui doit leur revenir. En second lieu, on voulait assurer un projet réalisable; il ne fallait pas exagérer les garanties jusqu'à rendre irréalisable l'organisation qu'elles devaient sauvegarder.

Mr. Root fait remarquer que l'expérience démontre que, lorsque deux corps naturellement opposés doivent se mettre d'accord, il pourrait être impossible d'obtenir cet accord à moins que l'on n'y ait recours à des moyens de conciliation. Pour que cette conciliation puisse être obtenue, il est essentiel qu'on laisse toute liberté à ceux qui sont chargés de cette tâche. Si le Conseil s'oppose absolument à la nomination d'une personne désignée par l'Assemblée, ou réciproquement, il pourra devenir nécessaire de trouver une troisième personne, qui puisse satisfaire tout le monde. Mais il faut laisser toute liberté de choix à ceux qui doivent la trouver.

En exigeant que les listes soient composées par les membres de la Cour Permanente d'Arbitrage, on aura établi un niveau de compétence et de conduite si élevé qu'il est inconcevable que la personne désignée en dehors de la liste ne possède pas les mêmes qualités.

Le PRESIDENT demande si MM. Altamira et Loder maintiennent leurs amendements. Il exprime l'avis que, si la Commission de conciliation peut choisir en dehors de la liste dans tous les cas où il y aura désaccord, on court le danger que la Cour soit composée de trop de personnes ne figurant pas sur la liste: il faut que cette procédure soit limitée à des cas strictement exceptionnels.

MM. ALTAMIRA et LODER admettent la nécessité politique d'avoir recours à des personnes qui ne figurent pas sur la liste, mais ils pensent qu'il sera difficile de trouver d'autres personnes compétentes: d'autant plus que la liste, assez nombreuse en elle-même, renfermera des noms de personnes d'inégale compétence.

M. LODER suggested the following method: the substitution of the words "only those candidates contained in the list mentioned in the preceding Paragraph shall be eligible," for the last sentence of Article 7.

Mr. ROOT said that the clause under discussion had been intended to fulfil two purposes. Firstly, it was to overcome the difficulty raised by M. de Lapradelle's proposal; that is to say, to avoid appearing to take away from the Governments a rôle which ought, by right, to be theirs. Secondly, the intention was to ensure that the plan should be realisable; the nature of the guarantees must not be such as to render the organisation, which they were intended to protect, impracticable.

Mr. Root pointed out that experience showed that whenever two bodies, which are by nature opposed to each other, have to come to an agreement, such agreement might be impossible, unless some method of conciliation be used. If this process of conciliation is to be fruitful, it is essential that as much liberty as possible should be allowed to those who have to carry out the task. If the Council were absolutely opposed to the appointment of a person selected by the Assembly, or vice-versâ, it might be necessary to find a third person who would be satisfactory to everyone. But those who had to find this person, must be given complete freedom in their choice.

Such a high standard of competence and moral authority would be established by laying down that the lists should be drawn up by the members of the Permanent Court of Arbitration, that it would be inconceivable that the person selected from outside this list, would not conform to this standard.

The PRESIDENT asked whether M. Altamira and M. Loder wished to maintain their respective amendments. He expressed the opinion that, if the Joint Conference were able to choose from outside the list in every case of disagreement, there would be a danger that the Court would contain too many persons not included in the list. Such a procedure must be strictly limited to exceptional cases.

MM. ALTAMIRA and LODER admitted that it might be politically necessary to make use of persons not contained in the list, but they thought that it would be difficult to find competent persons elsewhere; more especially, as the list itself, being of considerable size, would probably exceed the total number of suitable persons.

M. DE LAPRADELLE propose au Comité de maintenir le texte original de la phrase sans l'amendement de M. Loder. Mr. Root a démontré avec beaucoup de force les raisons qui militent en faveur de son système. Les gouvernements conservent pleinement leur droit d'élection. Mais si au moment de l'élection il y a désaccord entre le Conseil et l'Assemblée, et s'il faut que la Commission de conciliation soit saisie de l'affaire, il faut lui laisser toute liberté pour que la conciliation aboutisse. On peut imposer des restrictions au droit d'user de ce moyen, mais on ne doit pas enlever la possibilité d'arriver à une conciliation. On peut fixer des propositions, ou poser des conditions, en un mot trouver une formule de transaction; mais il ne faut pas abandonner l'idée exprimée dans le projet Root—Phillimore, et que vient d'appuyer Mr. Root.

M. RICCI-BUSATTI croit avec MM. Loder et Altamira qu'on aurait peu de chances de trouver, en dehors de la liste, des personnes mieux qualifiées que celles qui y figurent. D'ailleurs, si des difficultés surgissent entre l'Assemblée et le Conseil, ce sera probablement au sujet de la nationalité du juge à élire, plutôt que de ses qualités personnelles. Dans ces conditions il préférerait que la Commission fût obligée de choisir sur la liste.

M. ALTAMIRA déclare que les paroles de M. de Lapradelle, qui a lui-même fait valoir que les membres de la Cour permanente représentent les gouvernements, l'étonnent. Si cela est vrai, les gouvernements auront toujours leur part dans la présentation des candidats, et il n'est pas besoin de leur donner encore la liberté d'en chercher de nouveaux en dehors de la liste. La Commission doit avoir toute liberté, mais dans les limites de la liste.

Mr. ROOT, répondant à MM. Altamira et Loder, dit que, lorsque la situation nécessite l'intervention de la Commission de conciliation, on n'a plus à choisir entre tous les noms de la liste, mais seulement entre deux ou trois. Il s'agira en effet de trouver un juge qui puisse représenter, en connaissance de cause, un groupe d'Etats déterminés, unis par la communauté de leurs systèmes juridiques ou de leur civilisation. C'est une difficulté qu'il est absolument nécessaire de surmonter, et il se peut très bien que des personnes pleinement compétentes et qui n'ont pas voulu accepter de figurer sur la liste des candidats,

M. DE LAPRADELLE proposed to the Committee that the original wording of the sentence should be maintained, without M. Loder's amendment. Mr. Root had shown very clearly the reasons militating in favour of his system. The Governments would retain all their electoral rights. But if, when it came to the election, the Council and the Assembly could not come to an agreement, and if the Joint Conference had to be called into play, it must be given complete freedom of action, or it would be unable to achieve success. Restrictions might be made governing the use of this means, but the possibility of arriving at a compromise must not be excluded. A proportion might be fixed or conditions laid down; in a word, a formula could be found in the nature of a compromise; but the idea contained in the Root—Phillimore plan, and which Mr. Root had just been supporting, must not be abandoned.

M. RICCI-BUSATTI thought, like MM. Loder and Altamira, that it would not be easy to find, outside the list, persons better qualified than those contained in it. Besides, if difficulties arose between the Council and the Assembly, they would probably be in connection with the nationality of the judge to be elected, rather than with his personal qualities. Under these circumstances, M. Ricci-Busatti would prefer that the Joint Conference should be obliged to choose from within the list.

M. ALTAMIRA was astonished at M. de Lapradelle's remarks; the latter had himself pointed out that the members of the Permanent Court of Arbitration represented the Governments. If that were true, the Governments would always have a share in the nominations of candidates, and there was no need to give them a subsequent right to choose from outside the list. The Joint Conference must be given complete liberty, but only within the limits of the list.

Mr. ROOT, in reply to MM. Altamira and Loder, said that when it became necessary for the Joint Conference to intervene, it would no longer be a question of choosing from all the names on the list, but only between two or three. It would really be a question of finding a judge who could represent, with an adequate understanding of the conditions, a certain group of States, between which a close relationship existed, arising out of a common legal system or civilisation. This was a difficulty which must be overcome, and it was quite likely that fully qualified persons, who had not been willing to

soient, devant la nécessité de sortir d'une situation difficile, disposés à accepter une nomination.

M. HAGERUP se rallie à l'idée de Mr. Root.

Le PRESIDENT suggère l'idée d'adopter une formule indiquant qu'on doit autant que possible se tenir aux noms figurant sur la liste.

LORD PHILLIMORE croit cette idée juste, mais il faut lui donner plus de précision. Il propose d'exiger pour le choix en dehors de la liste l'unanimité des membres de la Commission.

M. DE LAPRADELLE envisage le cas d'une personne de la plus haute compétence, ne figurant pas sur la liste, parce que, lorsque celle-ci a été composée, elle exerçait des fonctions incompatibles avec celle de juge. Cette personne peut être libre au moment de l'élection; il doit donc être possible de la nommer. Toutefois, s'il est désirable que la Commission puisse chercher en dehors de la liste, il faut cependant créer des garanties pour éviter que toute la Cour ne soit composée de personnes autres que les candidats officiels. Selon M. de Lapradelle, cette garantie ne saurait être trouvée dans l'unanimité de la Commission; ce serait dangereux. Il croit qu'il faut la chercher dans la limitation du nombre des juges qui peuvent être désignés par la procédure extraordinaire, à un cinquième, par exemple, du nombre total.

M. HAGERUP, le PRESIDENT et Mr. ROOT se rallient à l'idée de Lord Phillimore.

M. ALTAMIRA votera contre la proposition.

Le PRESIDENT soumet au vote à mains levées l'article 7 du projet Root—Phillimore, sauf rédaction, et avec une addition s'inspirant de l'idée de Lord Phillimore. L'article est adopté.

Le Président ouvre alors la discussion sur l'article 8 du projet Root—Phillimore.

LORD PHILLIMORE fait observer que M. Altamira a proposé des modifications de détail à cet article. Il le prie de bien vouloir les expliquer. Personnellement il n'a pas d'objection à ce qu'on ajoute à l'article toutes les institutions qu'on trouve utiles, pourvu que l'on n'exagère pas en mentionnant des institutions tout-à-fait

be included upon the list of candidates, would be prepared to accept an appointment, in order to provide a means of ending a difficult situation.

M. HAGERUP agreed with Mr. Root on this point.

The PRESIDENT suggested that a formula should be adopted indicating that the names upon the list should be used as far as possible.

LORD PHILLIMORE thought that this was a good idea but that it should be made a little more precise. He proposed that the choice of a person not contained on the list should require the unanimous consent of the members of the Conference.

M. DE LAPRADELLE pointed out that it was possible that a person with the highest qualifications might not be contained in the list, because, at the time it was drawn up, he held a position incompatible with the duties of a judge. This person might be available at the time of the election; it should therefore be possible to appoint him. Nevertheless, though it was desirable that the Committee should be free to choose from outside the list, guarantees should be created to avoid the possibility of the whole Court being composed of persons other than the official candidates. In M. de Lapradelle's opinion, the unanimity of the Joint Commission would not serve as such a guarantee; there was an element of danger. He thought it must be found in the limitation of the number of judges who could be appointed by this exceptional procedure, for instance, to one-fifth of the total number.

M. HAGERUP, the PRESIDENT and Mr. ROOT supported Lord Phillimore's idea.

M. ALTAMIRA said that he would vote against the proposal.

The PRESIDENT put Article 7 of the Root—Phillimore plan, subject to amendments of form, to the vote by a show of hands. The Article was adopted.

The President then opened the discussion upon the 8th Article of the Root—Phillimore plan.

LORD PHILLIMORE drew attention to the fact that M. Altamira had proposed amendments affecting the detail of this Article. He asked M. Altamira to be so good as to explain them. Personally, he had no objection to the addition of all institutions which it was thought advisable to include in the Article, provided that

insignifiantes. Il est vrai qu'il ne s'agit que d'une recommandation; mais ce n'est pas une raison pour aller trop loin.

M. ALTAMIRA explique la portée des remarques qu'il a faites au sujet de l'article 8. Il fait observer que dans certains pays les universités sont dirigées par des recteurs; ce titre devrait donc être mentionné. Il y a aussi des pays où il n'y a pas de facultés de droit, mais seulement des écoles de droit; on ne devrait pas les omettre. En outre, les recteurs peuvent être des savants sans être des jurisconsultes; il faut en tenir compte. Afin d'exclure les corps non qualifiés, et pour ne pas oublier les collèges compétents, il voudrait substituer à l'expression „sociétés scientifiques" les mots „académies nationales et royales".

Le PRESIDENT signale la formule qu'il avait adoptée dans son avant-projet (article 5, alinéa 3); il a mentionné les Hautes Cours de Justice, les facultés de droit des universités, les académies ou sections d'académies vouées à l'étude du droit, et enfin les autres grands organes de la vie juridique, estimés particulièrement compétents. Il croit que ces quatre catégories sont celles dont il faut tenir compte; il fait spécialement observer qu'elles comprennent les sections nationales de l'Institut de Droit International.

M. ALTAMIRA croit pouvoir accepter la formule du Président.

M. RICCI-BUSATTI déclare qu'il votera contre cet article qui lui paraît inutile, et qui peut être nuisible. Les membres de la Cour d'Arbitrage s'adresseront certainement aux personnes qu'ils estimeront pouvoir consulter avec le plus d'utilité. Si l'on adopte cet article, on crée pour eux une obligation morale de procéder à certaines consultations; s'ils n'en tenaient pas compte, des froissements et des difficultés en résulteraient. C'est une complication qui causera des démarches sans fin, la plupart absolument inutiles. En Italie cinq Cours Suprêmes, vingt universités, plusieurs académies et associations doivent être consultées. M. Ricci-Busatti n'est pas opposé à l'idée même, mais il voudrait que les membres de la Cour d'Arbitrage fussent libres de s'adresser à qui bon leur semble.

Après une courte discussion sur le terme à employer pour désigner le tribunal qui doit être consulté, on se met d'accord sur la formule proposée par M. DE LAPRADELLE „les plus hau-

this was not carried too far by the inclusion of quite insignificant institutions. It was true that it was only a question of a recommendation, but this was not a reason for exaggeration.

M. ALTAMIRA explained the bearing of the notes he had made upon Article 8. He pointed out that in certain countries, Universities were under the direction of Rectors; this title should therefore be mentioned. In some countries also there were no legal faculties, but only schools of law; these should not be omitted. Further, the Rectors might be learned men but not jurisconsults; this fact must be reckoned with. In order to exclude bodies which were not properly qualified, and to avoid the exclusion of competent bodies, he wished to substitute the words "national and royal academies" for the expres sion "scientific societies."

The PRESIDENT drew attention to the formula he had used in his scheme (Article 5, Paragraph 3): he had mentioned the high Courts of justice, the legal Faculties of Universities, the Academies or sections of Academies devoted to the study of law, and finally any other great legal bodies considered particularly competent to advise. He thought that these were the four categories which must be taken into account; he particularly pointed out that they included the national sections of the Institut de Droit International.

M. ALTAMIRA thought that he could accept the President's terminology.

M. RICCI-BUSATTI said that he would vote against this Article, as it seemed to him to be useless and even harmful. The members of the Court of Arbitration would certainly consult those persons whose advice they thought would be most useful. If this Article were adopted they would be under a moral obligation to consult certain bodies; if they did not take the advice offered, offence might be given, and difficulties would follow. It was a complication which would lead to endless negociations, which would mostly be quite useless. In Italy there were five Supreme Courts, twenty Universities, several Academies and associations which must be consulted. M. Ricci-Busatti was not opposed to the idea itself, but he wanted the members of the Court of Arbitration to be free to consult whomsoever they might wish.

After a short discussion as to the phrase to be used in the description of the tribunal which was to be consulted, the Committee, on the pro-

tes Cours de Justice", formule générale et qui s'adapte également bien aux pays où il n'y a qu'une juridiction judiciaire suprême, et à ceux où il y en a plusieurs. Quant à la formule employée pour distinguer les corps scientifiques, on se met d'accord, après un échange de vues, pour laisser aux membres de la Cour d'Arbitrage eux-mêmes le soin de l'interpréter; toutefois, on ajoutera au mot „académies" l'épithète „nationales" et à l'expression „facultés de droit" la phrase „ou, à leur défaut, les grandes écoles de droit".

Le PRESIDENT met au vote à mains levées l'article 8 du projet Root—Phillimore amendé par le Président et sous-amendé de la façon indiquée ci-dessus. L'article est adopté, sauf rédaction, à l'unanimité, moins le vote de M. Ricci-Busatti. L'article est ainsi conçu: „Les membres pour chaque pays de la Cour Permanente d'Arbitrage seront priés de consulter les plus hautes Cours de Justice, les facultés de droit des universités ou, à leur défaut, les grandes écoles de droit, les académies nationales ou sections d'académies internationales vouées à l'étude du droit, ainsi que les autres grands organes de la vie juridique estimés particulièrement compétents, afin d'assurer la présentation des personnes les plus compétentes, les plus expérimentées, et possédant la plus haute considération morale et juridique".

Après un échange de vues avec Lord Phillimore sur la procédure à suivre, on se met d'accord pour entreprendre la discussion de l'article 11 du projet Root—Phillimore, cet article se rapportant à la question de la nomination des juges: le Président en donne lecture.

Un court débat s'engage sur plusieurs points d'ordre rédactionnel. On se met d'accord sur les points suivants:

1. l'expression „dans la mesure du possible" doit être supprimée;
2. l'obligation morale s'applique seulement à la représentation des différentes civilisations et des différents systèmes juridiques;
3. le terme „chercher" doit être maintenu.

M. HAGERUP rappelle son amendement concernant la représentation des différentes formes de civilisation et des différents systèmes juridiques. Il maintient son point de vue, mais n'insiste pas devant l'opposition de plusieurs (surtout de M. Adatci) qui tiennent beaucoup à cette phrase. Mais il préfère la formule suggérée par

posal of M. DE LAPRADELLE, agreed upon the words "the highest Courts of Justice"; this expression, owing to the use of the plural, was equally adapted to countries in which there was only one supreme judicial jurisdiction and to countries in which there were several. After a discussion concerning the phraseology used in describing the scientific bodies, it was agreed to allow the members of the Court of Arbitration themselves to put their own interpretation upon it; however, to "Academies" the adjective "national" was added, and after the expression "legal Faculties" the words "or if none exist, the great schools of law" were inserted.

The PRESIDENT put to the vote, by a show of hands, Article 8 of the Root—Phillimore plan, as amended by the President, and as further amended in the way described above. Article 8 was adopted, subject to amendments of form, by all members except M. Ricci-Busatti. The article read as follows: "The Members of the Permanent Court of Arbitration of each Country shall be requested to consult the highest Courts of justice, the legal Faculties of Universities or, if none exist, the great Schools of law, the National Academies or sections of international Academies devoted to the study of law, also any other great legal bodies considered particularly competent to advise, in order to ensure that persons of the greatest ability and experience, and of the highest moral character and judicial reputation, may be nominated."

After exchanging views with Lord Phillimore concerning the procedure to be adopted, the Committee agreed to consider Article 11 of the Root—Phillimore plan next: this Article dealt with the question of the appointment of the judges. The President read it.

A short discussion ensued, upon several points connected with the phrasing. An agreement was reached on the following points:

1. the expression "so far as practicable" was to be deleted;
2. the moral obligation only applies to the representation of different civilisations and legal systems;
3. the word "seek" was to be maintained.

M. HAGERUP reminded the Committee of his amendment concerning the representation of the various forms of civilisation and legal systems. He still held to his opinion, but he would not press it in face of the opposition of several members (in particular M. Adatci) who attached much importance to this phrase. Neverthe-

le Président „les *grandes* formes de civilisation et les *principaux* systèmes juridiques".

Mr. ROOT a la parole pour s'expliquer sur la forme à donner à cette idée. Il trouve, dit-il, deux formules différentes; celle qu'il a employée dans ses instructions aux délégués américains à la deuxième Conférence de la Paix, et celle qui se trouve dans le projet Root—Phillimore. Toutes deux avaient pour but d'écarter, non pas par définition, mais par description, une difficulté pratique dont Mr. Root avait l'expérience, celle de s'expliquer les formes de procédure et les manières de penser d'autres nations. Mr. Root s'est trouvé dans la nécessité de suivre l'activité des Cours de l'Amérique Espagnole. Il a senti toute la difficulté de saisir l'esprit de la procédure de ces Cours, mais en même temps il l'a trouvée admirablement adaptée aux besoins des pays où elle était appliquée, bien qu'elle fût absolument inapplicable aux Etats-Unis. Dans le monde entier, le droit est le produit des habitudes et des coutumes des peuples. On a donc besoin d'une Cour où figurent les particularités de tous les peuples du monde civilisé. Il ne s'agit pas de faire représenter à la Cour tel ou tel pays, mais bien de créer une Cour qui comprenne tous les cas qui sont portés devant elle, et qui sympathise avec eux. On peut, à ce sujet, trouver un grand nombre de formules satisfaisantes; l'essentiel c'est, dans le plan pour l'établissement de la Cour, d'en insérer une qui indique, d'une façon générale, que la Cour doit comprendre tous les éléments nécessaires pour assurer l'étude sympathique de tous les conflits.

Le PRESIDENT, LORD PHILLIMORE et M. ALTAMIRA expriment leur adhésion aux idées exposées par Mr. Root.

M. ALTAMIRA remercie Mr. Root de ses explications ainsi que de l'appui qu'il vient de donner à la doctrine qu'il a toujours lui-même défendue.

M. LODER déclare au contraire que le discours de Mr. Root ne l'a pas converti, mais, se sentant seul, il s'abstient pourtant de présenter un amendement.

Il propose la suppression du mot „cependant" au début de la dernière phrase de l'article 11.

Le PRESIDENT constate que les modifications proposées par M. Hagerup, c'est-à-dire l'insertion dans l'article 11 du projet Root—

less, he preferred the wording suggested by the President: "the *great* forms of civilisation and the *principal* legal systems."

Mr. ROOT obtained permission to speak in order to give his views concerning the way in which this idea should be expressed. He said that he had found two different wordings for it: that which he had used in his instructions to the American Delegates at the second Peace Conference, and that contained in the Root—Phillimore plan. Both were intended, not by definition but by the descriptive method, to avoid a practical difficulty which Mr. Root had himself experienced, namely that of understanding the methods of procedure and modes of thought of other nations. Mr. Root had had to follow the proceedings of the Courts of Spanish America. He had found it extremely difficult to grasp the significance of the procedure of these Courts, but at the same time, he had found that it was admirably adopted to the needs of the countries in which it was used though quite unsuitable to the United States. All the world over, law is the product of the habits and customs of the peoples. For this reason, a Court was needed on which the special characteristics of all the nations of the civilised world were represented. It was not a question of the representation of any particular country upon the Court, but of creating a Court which would understand, and be in sympathy with, all the cases brought before it. There were a large number of satisfactory methods of expressing this; the essential point was to insert, in the plan for the establishment of the Court, a general indication that the Court must contain all the elements necessary to ensure that all disputes receive a sympathetic hearing.

The PRESIDENT, LORD PHILLIMORE and M. ALTAMIRA expressed their agreement with the views put forward by Mr. Root.

M. ALTAMIRA thanked Mr. Root for his explanations, and also for the support he had given to a doctrine which he himself had always upheld.

M. LODER, on the contrary, said that Mr. Root's speech had not converted him, but as he felt that he stood alone, he would refrain from putting forward an amendment.

He proposed the deletion of the word "nevertheless" at the commencement of the last sentence of Article 11.

The PRESIDENT declared that the amendment proposed by M. Hagerup, that is to say, the insertion of the expression concerning

Phillimore, de la formule de l'avant-projet du Président sur la présentation des systèmes juridiques, sont adoptées.

M. DE LAPRADELLE propose une série de modifications à la rédaction de l'article 11:

1. la suppression de la première proposition, qu'il trouve complètement inutile;
2. en vue de souligner le caractère mondial de la Cour, l'insertion, à la première phrase, des mots „du monde" au lieu „des Membres de la Société des Nations";
3. l'insertion de cette dernière expression à la fin de la deuxième phrase.

M. de Lapradelle trouve que la deuxième proposition de la première phrase, ainsi que la deuxième phrase, qui sont très importantes, doivent être soumises au vote.

Le PRESIDENT s'oppose à la suppression de la première proposition, qui contient une indication fort utile.

LORD PHILLIMORE insiste pour que la rédaction primitive de l'article 11, sauf la dernière phrase, soit soumise au vote.

M. RICCI-BUSATTI tient à faire une déclaration. Il n'aime pas l'insertion dans un texte tel que celui que l'on est en train de rédiger, de formules relatives à une „obligation morale" aux „formes de civilisation" et aux „différents systèmes juridiques"; tout cela est trop vague et prête à une foule de critiques, mais comme ses collègues apprécient les formules de ce genre, il est prêt à voter en faveur de l'article tel qu'il résulte des amendements adoptés, puisqu'il contient quelques garanties pour la composition de la Cour.

M. HAGERUP demande que le texte amendé de l'article 11 soit lu avant d'être mis au vote; ce texte est ainsi conçu: „Dans toute élection de juges ou de juges suppléants, les électeurs devront s'assurer que les juges élus soient en possession des conditions requises; ils auront l'obligation morale de chercher la représentation à la Cour des grandes formes de civilisation et des principaux systèmes juridiques du monde. Tous les juges doivent appartenir à des Etats différents."

M. DE LAPRADELLE demande la division après le mot „requises".

Le PRESIDENT met au vote la première partie de l'article jusqu'au mot indiqué. Cette partie est adoptée à mains levées.

the representation of legal systems, contained in the President's draft scheme, in Article 11 of the Root—Phillimore plan, was adopted.

M. DE LAPRADELLE proposed a series of amendments to the form of Article 11:

1. the deletion of the first proposition, which he thought entirely unnecessary;
2. the substitution at the end of the first part of the Article, of the words "of the world" for the words "of the Members of the League of Nations", in order to emphasise the universal character of the Court;
3. the insertion of the latter expression at the end of the Article.

M. de Lapradelle thought that the second proposition contained in the first part, and also the second part of the Article, which were very important, should be put to the vote.

The PRESIDENT opposed the deletion of the first proposition, as he thought it gave a very useful indication.

LORD PHILLIMORE insisted that the original form of Article 11, with the exception of the last part, should be put to the vote.

M. RICCI-BUSATTI wished to make a statement. He did not approve of the insertion of an expression, implying a "moral obligation" to assure the representation of "forms of civilisations" and "different legal systems", in a draft of this kind; such expressions were too vague and lent themselves to a host of criticisms. As, however, his colleagues seemed to like expressions of this kind, he declared that he was prepared to vote in favour of the Article as now amended, since it contained a number of guarantees for the composition of the Court.

M. HAGERUP asked that the amended draft of Article 11 should be read before being put to the vote. The draft was as follows: "In all elections of judges and supplementary judges the electors shall satisfy themselves that the judges elected are in possession of the necessary qualifications; they shall be under the moral obligation to seek to have represented in the Court the main forms of civilisation and the principal legal systems of the world; but there shall be but one member of the Court elected from any one State."

M. DE LAPRADELLE requested that the first part should be divided after the word "qualifications" for the purpose of voting.

The PRESIDENT put the first part of the Article, as thus divided, to the vote. This part was adopted by a show of hands.

Le Président met au vote la deuxième partie de la première phrase. Cette partie est également adoptée à mains levées.

Enfin, le Président met au vote la deuxième phrase de l'article. Cette phrase est adoptée à mains levées.

L'article 11 du projet Root—Phillimore est donc adopté par le Comité, sauf rédaction finale.

LORD PHILLIMORE déclare qu'on se trouve maintenant en présence du premier article, et de la première phrase du deuxième article du projet Root—Phillimore. Il fait remarquer que MM. Altamira et Loder ont proposé des modifications à ces articles; il demande à M. Loder s'il insiste sur ses amendements.

M. LODER répond affirmativement.

LORD PHILLIMORE propose alors que la discussion des dispositions en question soit différée jusqu'à la séance prochaine.

Le PRESIDENT propose la substitution des articles 1 et 2 de son avant-projet aux dispositions du projet Root—Phillimore que vient d'indiquer Lord Phillimore. Il est d'accord pour remettre au lendemain la discussion de ces questions.

Mr. ROOT propose qu'on utilise la fin de la séance pour voter sur la question du nombre des juges et des suppléants.

M. RICCI-BUSATTI rappelle qu'il y a encore des points concernant la nomination des juges, qui n'ont pas été soumis au vote, à savoir:

1. la co-optation par la Cour (article 6 des amendements Loder);
2. le nombre des scrutins (articles 4 et 6 des amendements Loder).

LORD PHILLIMORE fait observer qu'on a déjà pris des décisions sur ces deux points, sauf rédaction.

M. DE LAPRADELLE voudrait qu'on tranchât d'abord la question des suppléants.

Le PRESIDENT lui fait remarquer qu'on a déjà voté sur cette question et que le principe des suppléants a été adopté.

Le Président propose de soumettre au vote:

1. le nombre de juges;
2. la durée de leur mandat.

The President then put the remainder of the first part of the Article to the vote. This was also adopted by a show of hands.

Finally, the President put the second part of the Article to the vote. This part was adopted in the same way.

Article 11 of the Root—Phillimore plan was thus adopted by the Committee, subject to final drafting.

LORD PHILLIMORE said that they should now deal with the first Article and the first sentence of the 2nd Article of the Root—Phillimore plan. He said that MM. Altamira and Loder had proposed amendments to these Articles, and he asked M. Loder whether he maintained his amendments.

M. LODER replied in the affirmative.

LORD PHILLIMORE then proposed that the discussion of the clauses in question should be postponed until the next meeting.

The PRESIDENT proposed that Articles 1 and 2 of his scheme should be substituted for those clauses of the Root—Phillimore plan mentioned by Lord Phillimore. He agreed to postpone the discussion of these questions until the following day.

Mr. ROOT proposed that the time still remaining should be used for the purpose of voting upon the question of the number of judges and deputy judges.

M. RICCI-BUSATTI pointed out that there were still some points concerning the appointment of judges, which had not yet been voted upon. These were:

1. co-optation by the Court (Article 6 of the Loder amendments);
2. the number of ballots (Articles 4 and 6 of the Loder amendments).

LORD PHILLIMORE pointed out that these two points had already been decided; it only remained to draft them.

M. DE LAPRADELLE wished the question of deputy judges to be dealt with first.

The PRESIDENT called his attention to the fact that this question had already been voted upon, and that deputy judges had been accepted in principle.

The President proposed that the following points should be voted upon:

1. the number of judges;
2. the period of their appointment.

Sauf rédaction et l'addition éventuelle d'une disposition tirée de son avant-projet, il propose l'adoption de la première partie de l'article 2 du projet Root—Phillimore.

He proposed that the first part of the second Article of the Root—Phillimore plan should be adopted, subject to redrafting and to the possible addition of a clause taken from his draft plan.

LORD PHILLIMORE, à la demande de M. Hagerup, explique pourquoi ce projet propose le chiffre de onze juges et de quatre suppléants. Comme on l'a expliqué de façon plus détaillée au cours d'une séance précédente, on veut que la Cour soit finalement composée de quinze juges, mais ce nombre ne doit être atteint que progressivement, au fur et à mesure que s'élargira la juridiction de la Cour. Le quorum de 9 étant proposé, il faut toujours avoir onze juges nommés, pour l'assurer, en cas de maladie, ou en toute autre cause d'absence. Le chiffre 11 est le minimum auquel on doive s'arrêter si l'on veut assurer une Cour vraiment représentative.

LORD PHILLIMORE, at the request of M. Hagerup, explained why the number of 11 judges and 4 deputy judges had been proposed in this plan. The intention, as had already been more fully explained at a previous meeting, was that the Court should be finally composed of fifteen judges, but the increase up to this number was to be gradual, keeping pace with the extension of the Court's jurisdiction. As the number of 9 had been proposed as a quorum, at least eleven judges must be appointed in order to provide for cases of illness and other causes of absence. Eleven was the minimum number which would ensure a genuinely representative Court.

M. HAGERUP se déclare satisfait de l'explication fournie par Lord Phillimore. Il fait cependant remarquer que si le nombre des juges est limité à 9, il sera difficile de faire représenter d'une façon adéquate les différents systèmes juridiques.

M. HAGERUP declared himself satisfied with Lord Phillimore's explanation. He pointed out, however, that if the number of judges were limited to 9 it would be difficult to obtain the adequate representation of the different legal systems.

M. RICCI-BUSATTI, en remarquant que la discussion s'est maintenant transportée dans le domaine de l'organisation intérieure de la Cour, reprend l'idée qu'il a exposée à plusieurs reprises, à ce sujet, et qui tient à la façon dont il conçoit son fonctionnement et sa nature. Il voudrait une Cour composée d'un nombre plus considérable de juges prêts à siéger; le chiffre de vingt cinq serait pour lui le minimum. Si l'on adoptait ce chiffre, on se trouverait plus en accord avec l'esprit de l'article 11, qu'on vient d'approuver. Comme il sait, cependant, que ses idées ne sont pas partagées par la majorité de ses collègues, il se déclare disposé à accepter le nombre de 15.

M. RICCI-BUSATTI after pointing out that the discussion now bore upon the interior organisation of the Court, once more put forward an idea which he had already expressed on several occasions in this connection, and which arose out of his conception of the operation and nature of the Court. He wanted a Court composed of a larger number of judges, all available to sit; he took the number of 25 as a minimum. The number of 25 would be more in accordance with the spirit of Article 11 which had just been adopted. As, however, he knew that his opinion was not shared by the majority of the members, he said that he was prepared to accept the number of 15.

Mr. ROOT propose que la suggestion de M. Ricci-Busatti soit considérée comme une proposition et mise au vote.

Mr. ROOT proposed that M. Ricci-Busatti's suggestion should be considered as a motion and put to the vote.

M. RICCI-BUSATTI se rallie.

M. RICCI-BUSATTI agreed.

Le PRESIDENT met au vote la question de savoir si la Cour doit comprendre vingt cinq juges.

Le Comité, à mains levées, répond négativement.

The PRESIDENT put to the vote the question as to whether the Court should be composed of twenty five judges.

The motion was rejected by the Committee by a show of hands.

Le PRESIDENT met au vote la proposition de composer la Cour de onze juges et de quatre suppléants.

Cette proposition est adoptée à mains levées.

Le PRESIDENT met au vote la proposition de fixer à neuf ans la durée du mandat des juges.

Cette proposition est adoptée à mains levées.

La séance est levée à 12.30 heures de l'après-midi.

Le Président:
(signé) Brn. DESCAMPS.

Le Secrétaire-Général:
(signé) D. ANZILOTTI.

The PRESIDENT then put to the vote the proposal that the Court should be composed of eleven judges and four deputy judges.

This proposal was adopted by a show of hands.

The PRESIDENT put to the vote the proposal that the judges should be appointed for a period of nine years.

This proposal was also adopted by a show of hands.

The meeting closed at 12.30 p.m.

The President:
(signed) Brn. DESCAMPS.

The Secretary-General:
(signed) D. ANZILOTTI.

ANNEXE No. 1.

Amendement à l'article 6 du projet Root-Phillimore proposé par M. Ricci-Busatti.

Après les mots: „la liste sera composée de la manière suivante" substituer les alinéas suivants:

Chaque Membre de la Société des Nations pourra désigner une personne, choisie par ses délégués à la Cour Permanente d'Arbitrage, soit parmi ses nationaux, soit parmi les nationaux d'un pays différent. Si ces délégués ne sont pas d'accord sur la personne à choisir, le Gouvernement désignera la personne qu'il préfère, parmi celles dont ils lui auront proposé les noms.

Lorsqu'un juge cessera, pour quelque motif que ce soit, de faire partie de la Cour, les Membres de la Société, autres que ceux par lesquels ont été désignés les juges restant en charge, seront invités à faire une nouvelle désignation conformément à l'alinéa précédent et la nouvelle nomination sera faite conformément à l'article 2.

(Voir les articles 2 et 6 du projet déposé par moi le 30 juin).

(*signé*) RICCI-BUSATTI.

ANNEX No. 1.

Amendment by M. Ricci-Busatti to Article 6 of the Root-Phillimore plan.

The following paragraphs to be substituted after the words: "the list shall be composed in the following manner":

Each member of the League of Nations may nominate one person chosen by its delegates to the Permanent Court of Arbitration, either from amongst its subjects or from amongst the subjects of another country. If the delegates cannot agree upon the choice of a person, they shall submit a number of names from which the Government shall select one for nomination.

Whenever a judge ceases for any reason to belong to the Court, the Members of the League other than those who nominated the judges still holding office, shall be invited to submit a new nomination in accordance with the preceding paragraph and the new appointment shall be made in accordance with Article 2.

(See Articles 2 and 6 of the plan submitted by me on the 30th June).

(*signed*) RICCI-BUSATTI.

ANNEXE No. 2.

Texte présenté par Lord Phillimore (voir projet Root-Phillimore, Article 6).

Trois mois au moins avant la première élection, le Secrétaire Général de la Société demande par écrit aux membres de la Cour Permanente d'Arbitrage à La Haye de procéder par groupes, chaque groupe renfermant les membres nommés par un pays déterminé à la présentation d'au plus 6 noms de personnes remplissant à leur avis les conditions requises et qui sont disposées à accomplir la dignité de juge, de sorte que chaque groupe ne pourra présenter plus de deux ressortissants du pays présenté par le groupe.

ANNEX No. 2.

Text submitted by Lord Phillimore (compare Root-Phillimore plan, Article 6).

At least three months before the first election, the Secretary-General of the League shall request in writing the Members of the Permanent Court of Arbitration at the Hague to undertake by groups, each group consisting of the Members appointed by a particular country, the nomination of a maximum of six persons, who, in their opinion, fulfil the required conditions and are prepared to accept the position of judge, subject to the condition that no group may nominate more than two subjects of the country which it represents.

20IÈME SÉANCE (non-publique), tenue au Palais de la Paix, à La Haye, le 9 juillet 1920.

Présidence de M. le BARON DESCAMPS.

Sont présents: tous les membres du Comité (à l'exception de M. Bevilaqua); M. Fernandes; Mr. James Brown Scott; les secrétaires particuliers du Baron Descamps et de M. Adatci; les membres du Secrétariat.

La séance est ouverte à 9.40 heures du matin.

LORD PHILLIMORE rappelle que l'on a pris, la veille, la décision de commencer cette séance par la discussion du premier article et de la première partie du second article du projet Root—Phillimore. Il déclare que Mr. Root et lui-même sont d'accord pour accepter les articles 1 et 2 de l'avant-projet du Président, au lieu des dispositions sus-mentionnées, à condition que deux modifications soient introduites dans le texte Descamps:

a. les mots: „et en mesure d'assurer la continuité et le progrès de la jurisprudence internationale des arrêts" doivent être rayés du premier article de l'avant-projet Descamps;

b. ces mêmes mots doivent être introduits, avec les modifications nécessaires, à la fin du second alinéa de l'article 2.

Lord Phillimore continue en disant que M. Altamira a proposé d'ajouter au dernier alinéa de l'article 2 de l'avant-projet Descamps la formule: „ou des arbitres exercés dans des affaires d'un caractère international". Il se rallie à cette proposition et répète que, si le Président veut bien accepter les deux modifications qu'il vient de signaler, il pourra, ainsi que Mr. Root, adopter le texte du Président.

Le PRESIDENT, en remerciant Lord Phillimore de s'être rallié au texte de son avant-projet, déclare accepter la modification demandée.

En ce qui concerne l'amendement de M. Altamira, il fait valoir que les mots: „et posséder une expérience reconnue", à l'alinéa 2 de l'article 2 ont été insérés justement en vue des mêmes considérations qui ont dicté cet amendement.

20TH MEETING (Private), held at the Peace Palace, the Hague, on July 9th, 1920.

BARON DESCAMPS in the chair.

Present: all members of the Committee (with the exception of M. Bevilaqua); M. Fernandes, Mr. James Brown Scott; the private secretaries of Baron Descamps and of M. Adatci; the members of the Secretariat.

The meeting opened at 9.40 a.m.

LORD PHILLIMORE reminded the Committee that it had been decided, on the previous day, to commence this meeting by discussing the first Article and the first part of the second Article of the Root—Phillimore plan. He said that Mr. Root and he had agreed to accept Articles 1 and 2 of the President's plan instead of the above mentioned clauses, provided that the two following modifications were introduced into the Descamps text:

a. the words "and for the purpose of assuring the continuity and progress of international jurisprudence" to be struck out of the first Article of the Descamps plan;

b. these words to be inserted, with the necessary modifications, at the end of the second paragraph of Article 2.

Lord Phillimore went on to say that M. Altamira had proposed to add the expression, "or Arbitrators with experience in cases of an international character", to the last paragraph of the 2nd Article of the Descamps plan. He accepted this proposal and repeated that, if the President would agree to the two alterations that he had just mentioned, both he and Mr. Root would be in a position to adopt the President's version.

The PRESIDENT thanked Lord Phillimore for having accepted the text of his plan and stated that he agreed to the required alterations.

Concerning M. Altamira's proposal, he pointed out that the words "and be of recognised experience", contained in Paragraph 2 of the second Article had been inserted for

exactly the same purpose as that which had inspired M. Altamira's amendment.

Le Président donne lecture de l'article 1 de son avant-projet.

M. RICCI-BUSATTI propose que l'expression „le traité de Versailles du 28 juin 1919", qui figure à l'article 1 de l'avant-projet du Président, soit remplacée par les mots „le Pacte de la Société des Nations".

Après une courte discussion cette proposition est adoptée à l'unanimité.

M. DE LAPRADELLE voudrait supprimer, dans la dernière partie de l'article 1er le mot „directement" qui lui semble inadéquat.

Après un échange de vues, au cours duquel on fait valoir que le mot en question est utile pour marquer la différence entre la nouvelle Cour et la Cour d'Arbitrage, la proposition de M. de Lapradelle est mise au vote. Elle est rejetée, contre les voix de MM. Hagerup, de Lapradelle et Ricci-Busatti.

M. LODER demande des explications sur l'expression employée dans le premier article de l'avant-projet Descamps, indiquant que les États demeurent libres d'avoir recours à des tribunaux spéciaux d'arbitrage.

Le PRESIDENT déclare que cette expression indique que la nouvelle Cour n'est pas destinée à remplacer les tribunaux internationaux, dont l'existence et la constitution peuvent résulter de la simple volonté des parties. Il importe de maintenir cette disposition.

L'article venant d'ailleurs d'être adopté, le Président prie M. Loder de revenir lors de la seconde lecture, sur la question qu'il a soulevée.

Le Président donne lecture du second article de son avant-projet; il fait observer que l'amendement Altamira doit être pris en considération en même temps.

M. ALTAMIRA lit alors son amendement.

LORD PHILLIMORE appuie cet amendement.

M. DE LAPRADELLE fait valoir que le but visé par le Comité est d'assurer à la Cour les services de juges qui aient en même temps la compétence d'hommes pratiques et celle d'hommes d'étude: on veut des arbitres et des savants. Dans ces circonstances, il croit préférable d'insérer à l'alinéa 2 de l'article 2 de l'avant-projet Descamps le mot „compétence" au-lieu du mot „expérience".

The President read Article 1 of his draft scheme.

M. RICCI-BUSATTI proposed that the expression "the treaty of Versailles of June 28th, 1919" in Article 1 of the President's plan should be replaced by the words "the Covenant of the League of Nations".

After a short discussion this proposal was unanimously adopted.

M. DE LAPRADELLE wished to delete the word "directement" in the last part of Article 1 (French text), as it seemed to him to miss the point.

After a discussion, in which it was pointed out that the word in question served to bring out the difference between the new Court and the Court of Arbitration, M. de Lapradelle's proposal was put to the vote. It was rejected; MM. Hagerup, de Lapradelle and Ricci-Busatti voted in favour of it.

M. LODER asked for an explanation of the expression, used in the first Article of the Descamps plan, which provided that States retained the right to make use of special Courts of Arbitration.

The PRESIDENT said that this expression was meant to indicate that the new Court was not intended to replace international tribunals, whose existence and constitution were entirely dependent upon the will of the parties concerned. This provision must be maintained.

As the Article had just been adopted, the President asked M. Loder to bring this question up again at the second reading.

The President read the second Article of his draft scheme; he pointed out that M. Altamira's amendment must be considered at the same time.

M. ALTAMIRA then read this amendment.

LORD PHILLIMORE seconded it.

M. DE LAPRADELLE pointed out that the Committee's intention was to ensure the appointment of judges possessing both practical and theoretical ability. Men who were both arbitrators and learned were needed. Under these circumstances, he thought it preferable to insert the word "competence", instead of the word "experience" in Paragraph 2 of Article 2 of the Descamps plan.

Le PRESIDENT explique que le mot „expérience" a été inséré en vue de donner satisfaction à certains points de vue exposés par Lord Phillimore, qui craignait de voir exclure de la Cour les hommes pratiques.

D'après M. DE LAPRADELLE il y a entre les alinéas 2 et 3 de l'article 2 une certaine contradiction: à l'alinéa 2, on parle seulement de l'expérience pratique, tandis qu'à l'alinéa 3, on se sert, d'une façon générale, de l'expression compétence, qui comprend en même temps la compétence théorique et pratique. Il fait également observer que le mot „ou", à l'alinéa 3, semble ouvrir la Cour à des juges qui n'ont pas de compétence en matière de droit international.

Le PRESIDENT est disposé à insérer l'amendement de M. Altamira dans l'alinéa 2 du deuxième article de son avant-projet, bien que l'idée de M. Altamira se trouve, à son avis, déjà exprimée dans le texte de cet alinéa.

M. ALTAMIRA explique que nombre d'hommes d'Etat, ayant une haute compétence en matière de droit international, n'ont jamais publié de travaux scientifiques dans ce domaine: il faut éviter de les exclure de la Cour.

M. FERNANDES appuie ce point de vue.

M. HAGERUP, après avoir obtenu du Président une explication sur la question de savoir de quelle façon l'amendement Altamira sera inséré à l'article 2 du projet du Président, déclare qu'il ne s'oppose pas à cette insertion, à condition qu'on maintienne au troisième alinéa le mot „jurisconsultes". Les gouvernements ont, à plusieurs reprises, nommé à la Cour d'Arbitrage des personnes qui n'étaient pas des jurisconsultes; cette chose ne doit pas arriver en ce qui concerne la Cour de Justice.

Le PRESIDENT propose de supprimer au 2ème alinéa de l'article 2 les mots „et posséder une expérience reconnue" pour insérer au 3ième alinéa, après les mots „d'une compétence notoire", les mots „ou d'une expérience reconnue".

Plusieurs membres se rallient à cette proposition.

M. DE LAPRADELLE remarque que l'expérience n'est qu'une forme, ou peut-être qu'une source, de la compétence. Il craint que les critiques qui s'occuperont du projet ne disent que lorsque le projet présuppose la compétence sans l'expérience, il prévoit en même temps l'expérience sans la compétence.

The PRESIDENT explained that the word "experience" had been inserted to satisfy certain views expressed by Lord Phillimore who feared that practical men might be excluded from the Court.

In M. DE LAPRADELLE's opinion, Paragraphs 2 and 3 of Article 2 were, to some extent, contradictory. In Paragraph 2 practical experience only was mentioned, whereas, in Paragraph 3, the expression "repute" was used, in a general way, to include both theoretical and practical ability. He also pointed out that the word "or" in Paragraph 3, seemed to throw the Court open to judges of no special ability in international law.

The PRESIDENT was prepared to insert M. Altamira's amendment in Paragraph 2 of the second Article of his plan, though he thought that M. Altamira's idea was already expressed in that Paragraph.

M. ALTAMIRA explained that there were a number of statesmen of great ability in international law, who had never published scientific works upon the subject. These men must not be excluded from the Court.

M. FERNANDES supported this point of view.

M. HAGERUP, after obtaining an explanation from the President concerning the method of inserting the Altamira amendment in Article 2 of the President's plan, said that he would not oppose this insertion, provided that the word "jurisconsults", in the third paragraph, were retained. Governments had, on several occasions, appointed persons to the Court of Arbitration, who were not jurisconsults. This must not happen in the case of the Court of Justice.

The PRESIDENT proposed to delete the words "and be of recognised experience" in the second Paragraph of the 2nd Article, and to insert the words "or of recognised experience", in the third Paragraph, after the words "of established repute".

Several members supported this proposal.

M. DE LAPRADELLE said that experience was only one form, or perhaps one source, of competence. He feared that the critics who would discuss the plan would say that, as the plan presupposed ability without experience, it must also admit the possibility of experience without ability.

M. de Lapradelle rappelle également que les conditions requises pour être nommé aux hautes fonctions dans la magistrature ne sont pas les mêmes dans tous les pays, et qu'en France ces conditions sont si simples qu'elles ne constituent pas une garantie suffisante.

Mr. ROOT remarque que la question la plus importante lui paraît être celle des moyens qui permettront d'obtenir des juges d'une grande expérience judiciaire, des juges qui ont cette habitude de penser juridiquement et cette largeur d'esprit que seule l'expérience peut donner: l'expérience acquise dans des Cours telles que celles où siègent M. Loder et Lord Phillimore, par exemple, serait la meilleure compétence pour la tâche de juge international.

Le PRESIDENT croit que le texte qu'il a proposé tient suffisamment compte de cette observation.

M. DE LAPRADELLE demande si le Comité admet la possibilité de nommer comme juge un jurisconsulte qui n'a jamais fait fonction de juge ni d'arbitre.

Le PRESIDENT répond affirmativement.

M. RICCI-BUSATTI fait valoir que plus on élargit la formule, plus on crée de difficultés; c'est pourquoi il croit que la formule la plus brève serait la meilleure; et il propose de s'en tenir à celle qui a été adoptée par la Convention de 1907 pour la Cour d'Arbitrage.

Se référant aux observations de Mr. Root, il admet que l'expérience judiciaire est sans doute utile et que les qualités requises pour un grand magistrat sont peut-être aussi requises pour un bon juge international; mais il faut également posséder une expérience spécifique dans les questions internationales, qui seront l'objet des jugements de la Cour; sans cela, on risquerait d'y apporter un esprit qui ne serait pas exactement celui dans lequel ces jugements devront être rendus. Il s'oppose d'ailleurs à l'expression „d'une expérience reconnue", parce qu'on ne sait pas de quelle expérience il s'agit; cette allusion à l'expérience devrait viser un domaine déterminé pour être efficace. Il n'aime pas non plus l'expression „magistrats . . . . . constitués dans des conditions de réelle permanence": c'est la Cour qui est permanente et non pas les juges, et la manière dont elle le sera doit ressortir des dispositions qui la concernent.

M. de Lapradelle also recalled the fact that the qualifications required for appointment to high judicial office were not the same in all countries, and that in France these conditions were so simple as to be of no value as a guarantee.

Mr. ROOT said that, in his opinion, the most important question was that of the means by which it would be possible to obtain judges with great judicial experience who were in the habit of thinking judicially and who possessed that broadmindedness which experience alone can bring. The experience gained in Courts such as those, for instance, in which M. Loder and Lord Phillimore sat, would be a most admirable qualification for the position of an international judge.

The PRESIDENT thought that the wording proposed by him took sufficient account of this consideration.

M. DE LAPRADELLE asked whether the Committee would admit the possibility of appointing, as judge, a jurisconsult who had never performed the duties of either judge or arbitrator.

The PRESIDENT replied in the affirmative.

M. RICCI-BUSATTI pointed out that every addition to the clause would lead to corresponding difficulties; for this reason he thought that the shortest possible formula would be the best. He suggested that that adopted by the Convention of 1907 for the Court of Arbitration should be used.

Referring to Mr. Root's remarks, M. Ricci-Busatti said that judicial experience was doubtless useful, and that the qualities required in a great national judge are, perhaps, also required in a good international judge; but, for the latter, specific experience was also necessary in international questions of the kind which would come before the Court for decision; otherwise there would be a danger that the judgments of the Court would not be delivered in a true international spirit. Further he was opposed to the expression "of recognised experience", because it was not stated what experience was referred to. If this reference to experience were to serve a useful purpose, it should refer to experience in some definite sphere. Nor did he like the expression "judges . . . . . established under conditions of permanence": it was the Court that was permanent, not the judges; the nature of this permanence must be brought out in the clauses dealing with the Court.

Le PRESIDENT dit que les trois points mentionnés au 1er alinéa de l'article 2 de son avant-projet sont ceux qui caractérisent les juges de la Cour permanente de Justice. Même si l'on supprimait une partie de l'article, on devrait maintenir ces points. C'est le portique placé à l'entrée de l'édifice.

Personnellement, le Président préférerait supprimer la référence à la magistrature administrative qui se trouve à l'alinéa 3 de l'article 2, et il demande aux membres qui ont proposé cette formule s'ils y tiennent. Si l'on ouvre la Cour aux administrateurs, on l'ouvre en même temps aux politiciens, ce qu'il faut éviter.

The PRESIDENT said that the three points mentioned in the first Paragraph of Article 2 of his draft scheme were intended to characterise the judges of the Permanent Court of Justice. Even if the greater part of this Article were to be deleted, these points must be maintained. They constituted an introduction to the work of the Committee.

Personally the President would prefer to delete the reference to the administrative magistracy contained in the third Paragraph of Article 2, and he asked the members who had proposed it whether they insisted upon its retention. If the Court were thrown open to administrators it would at the same time be open to politicians; this must be avoided.

LORD PHILLIMORE propose d'accepter l'article 2 de l'avant-projet du Président, avec les modifications proposées par le Président lui-même au début de la séance. On maintiendrait ainsi la formule simple „d'une expérience reconnue"; pour satisfaire le Président, on devrait peut-être supprimer l'expression „magistrature administrative".

LORD PHILLIMORE proposed that Article 2 of the President's plan should be accepted with the modifications proposed by the President himself at the beginning of the meeting. The simple expression "of recognised experience" would thus be retained; perhaps the "administrative offices" should be deleted, to meet the wishes of the President.

Après un échange de vue général, M. DE LAPRADELLE propose de supprimer le 3ème alinéa de l'article 2 de l'avant-projet du Président.

After a general discussion, M. DE LAPRADELLE proposed that the third Paragraph of Article 2 of the President's scheme should be deleted.

M. HAGERUP insiste sur la nécessité de marquer, dans le texte, que les juges doivent posséder des connaissances juridiques.

M. HAGERUP insisted upon the necessity of a definite statement in the text to the effect that the judges must have a thorough knowledge of law.

M. DE LAPRADELLE fait valoir que tout l'article 2 est plutôt adressé à l'opinion publique qu'aux juges.

Le PRESIDENT rappelle que dans les textes jusqu'ici adoptés, il a toujours été fait mention des qualités morales que devront posséder les juges en même temps qu'une compétence notoire en droit international.

M. DE LAPRADELLE pointed out that the whole of Article 2 was addressed to public opinion rather than to the judges.

The PRESIDENT recalled that, in all texts adopted hitherto, the moral qualities required of judges, and also well known ability in international law, had always been mentioned.

M. DE LAPRADELLE propose l'adoption d'une rédaction aux termes de laquelle l'expérience de juge national serait un criterium suffisant de la compétence nécessaire aux juges de la Cour Permanente.

M. DE LAPRADELLE proposed that a wording should be adopted laying down that experience as a national judge would be a sufficient criterion of competence to perform the duties of a judge of the Permanent Court.

Le PRESIDENT s'oppose à cette formule: il ne suffit pas d'être un jurisconsulte éminent en droit civil pour être un bon juge international; il faut l'expérience des questions de droit international, afin d'éviter que les conflits internationaux ne soient traités comme de pures affaires civiles. Il est du reste impossible de faire abstraction

The PRESIDENT opposed this. An eminent jurisconsult in civil law would not necessarily be a good international judge; experience of questions of international law was needed, in order to prevent international disputes being treated as ordinary civil cases. Besides, it was impossible to disregard entirely conditions

des conditions qui ont toujours été exprimées dans les textes antérieurs.

Mr. ROOT donne lecture de la formule proposée par M. Renault lors de la 2ème Conférence de la Paix et adoptée par cette Conférence après de longues discussions: „...... se compose de juges et de juges suppléants choisis parmi les personnes jouissant de la plus haute considération morale et qui tous devront remplir les conditions requises, dans leur pays respectif, pour l'admission dans la Haute Magistrature, ou être des jurisconsultes d'une compétence notoire en matière de droit international".

La plupart des membres se rallient à ce texte, et M. Altamira déclare que la formule Renault lui donne pleine satisfaction, puisqu'elle tient compte en même temps de la compétence acquise par la science et de celle acquise par l'expérience.

Le PRESIDENT appuie la proposition de Mr. Root et, à la demande de Lord Phillimore, soumet au vote la formule de M. Renault.

La formule est adoptée à main levée. (En conséquence elle sera insérée comme alinéa 3 de l'article 2 de l'avant-projet Descamps).

M. HAGERUP veut faire ressortir que, d'après le texte adopté, des fonctions dans la magistrature administrative ne seraient pas considérées comme un titre de compétence pour le poste de juge international. A son avis, le point est capital, parce que les connaissances juridiques ne sont pas toujours requises pour l'entrée dans la magistrature administrative.

Le PRESIDENT constate que le Comité est d'accord avec M. Hagerup sur ce point.

Le Président ouvre la discussion sur l'article 9 du projet Root—Phillimore. Il en donne lecture.

LORD PHILLIMORE obtient la parole et explique qu'une disposition correspondante à celle de l'article 9 du projet Root—Phillimore se retrouve dans la plupart des projets antérieurs, et que son expérience lui fait considérer une telle disposition comme désirable. Il sait que M. de Lapradelle a des doutes à cet égard, mais il espère qu'on pourra néanmoins se mettre d'accord.

M. LODER n'est pas satisfait du mot „instruction" dans le texte du projet. Ce mot lui semble trop étroit.

Le PRESIDENT voudrait remplacer les derniers mots de l'article: „dont ils ont été appelés

which had always been included in previous plans.

Mr. ROOT read the formula which had been proposed by M. Renault, at the second Peace Conference, and adopted by that Conference after lenghty discussion: "...... is composed of judges and deputy judges chosen from persons of the highest moral reputation, and all fulfilling conditions qualifying them, in their respective countries, to occupy high legal posts, or jurists of recognised competence in matters of international law".

Most of the members accepted this wording and M. Altamira said that the Renault formula completely satisfied him, since it took into account both competence acquired by scientific research and that obtained by experience.

The PRESIDENT seconded Mr. Root's proposal and, at Lord Phillimore's request, put M. Renault's wording to the vote. It was adopted by a show of hands. (This formula was therefore inserted as Paragraph 3 in Article 2 of the Descamps plan).

M. HAGERUP wished to point out that, according to the wording adopted, the holding of an administrative post would not be considered as a qualification for the position of international judge. In his opinion, this point was most important because legal qualifications were not always required for administrative appointments.

The PRESIDENT stated that the Committee agreed with M. Hagerup on this point.

The President then laid Article 9 of the Root—Phillimore project before the Committee for its consideration. He read the Article in question.

LORD PHILLIMORE was given permission to speak. He explained that a clause corresponding to Article 9 of the Root—Phillimore plan was to be found in most of the preceding plans, and his experience convinced him that some such provision was desirable. He knew that M. de Lapradelle had doubts on this point, but nevertheless he hoped that an agreement could be reached.

M. LODER was not satisfied with the word "instruction" in the French text of the plan. It seemed to him that the meaning was too narrow.

The PRESIDENT wished to replace the last words of (the French text of) this Article by the

à connaître" par le mot „saisis". Il a également quelques objections à faire sur l'ordre des articles adopté dans le projet Root—Phillimore.

LORD PHILLIMORE répond qu'il se rallie à l'adoption du terme „saisis". L'ordre dans lequel les articles doivent se succéder est une question que le Comité de rédaction pourra examiner plus tard.

Le Comité se rallie à l'opinion de Lord Phillimore sur ces deux points.

M. DE LAPRADELLE pose la question suivante: un juge soumis à la réélection et qui n'a pas été réélu, doit-il pouvoir continuer à connaître d'une affaire dont il a été saisi? ne doit-on pas considérer qu'il a perdu la confiance de la Société des Nations et, dans ces conditions, ne serait-il pas nuisible à l'autorité de la Cour et de la justice de lui permettre de continuer l'exercice de ses fonctions de magistrat? Il est, quant à lui, enclin à répondre „oui" à cette dernière question et demande, en conséquence, le rejet de l'article 9 du projet Root—Phillimore.

Le PRESIDENT remarque que M. de Lapradelle se place à un point de vue de perfection en exigeant une règle applicable à tous les cas qu'on peut imaginer. Cependant il s'agit ici de tenir compte avant tout de l'expérience pratique et de faire la balance entre les inconvénients et les avantages d'un système. En realité l'article exprime un principe généralement admis: un juge doit liquider une affaire qu'il a commencée.

M. DE LAPRADELLE cite à l'appui de son opinion l'exemple de l'organisation judiciaire française.

M. LODER cite l'article 11 du projet des Cinq Puissances aux termes duquel les juges ayant atteint la limite d'âge, terminent les affaires dont ils ont été saisis. Il croit qu'il faut ou bien, comme le veut cet article, laisser les juges terminer les affaires dont ils sont saisis, ou bien, ainsi que l'a proposé M. de Lapradelle, laisser tomber l'article. Dans la première éventualité il faut en tout cas substituer au terme „instruction" une expression moins limitative.

LORD PHILLIMORE après s'être mis d'accord avec Mr. Root, déclare que toutes les solutions que l'on peut envisager présentent des inconvénients. L'inconvénient le plus sérieux est celui-ci: une partie à un litige est en justice de-

word "saisis". He also had some objections to raise concerning the order in which the Articles were placed in the Root—Phillimore plan.

LORD PHILLIMORE answered that he accepted the word "saisis". The relative position of the Articles could be considered later by the drafting Committee.

The Committee agreed with Lord Phillimore on these two points.

M. DE LAPRADELLE put the following questions: Supposing that a judge had been put up for re-election but had not been re-elected, would he be able to continue to sit in a case which he had begun? Should it not be considered that he had lost the confidence of the League of Nations and that, under these circumstances, it would be harmful to the authority of the Court and to the interests of justice, to allow him to continue in the exercise of his duties as a judge? In his opinion, the answer to the latter question should be in the affirmative, and he consequently asked for the rejection of the 9th Article of the Root—Phillimore plan.

The PRESIDENT said that M. de Lapradelle had adopted a counsel of perfection: he demanded a rule which could be applied under all conceivable circumstances. It was essential, however, to consider the matter in the light of practical experience, and to weigh the advantages of a system against its disadvantages. As a matter of fact, the Article expressed a generally admitted principle: a judge must complete a case which he has begun.

M. DE LAPRADELLE quoted the example of the French judicial organisation in support of his opinion.

M. LODER quoted Article 11 of the Five Power Plan, according to which judges who had attained the age limit would complete cases they had begun. He thought that either, as laid down in this Article, the judges should be allowed to complete cases which they have begun, or that, as M. de Lapradelle had proposed, the Article should be omitted. If the first alternative were adopted, the word "instruction" in the French text must, in any case, be replaced by a less restrictive expression.

LORD PHILLIMORE, after having come to an agreement with Mr. Root, stated that every possible solution would have some disadvantages. The most serious difficulty would be the following: A party to a suit, which has been proceeding

puis un certain temps et prévoit qu'elle va perdre sa cause. Si le mandat d'un ou de plusieurs des juges de la Cour est près d'expirer, la partie peut essayer, par des chicanes, de traîner la procédure en longueur de telle sorte que la procédure doit être reprise par le nouveau juge. Pour éviter cette éventualité fâcheuse, il faut permettre aux juges de terminer les affaires. Rien ne s'oppose à ce que le Comité leur donne cette faculté; puisqu'il a toute liberté pour déterminer la durée du mandat, il peut fixer cette durée, par ex., à neuf ans et le temps qui sera nécessaire pour terminer les affaires en cours de procédure.

M. DE LAPRADELLE ne croit pas que le danger signalé par Lord Phillimore soit réel: la Cour est suffisamment armée pour prévenir des chicanes. Elle peut, par ex., user de son droit de fixer des délais.

Après un échange de vues entre M. DE LAPRADELLE, LORD PHILLIMORE et M. LODER, l'on décide que le mot „saisis" sera substitué à „appelés à connaître" à la fin de l'article et que le mot „jugement" sera substitué au mot „instruction".

Le PRESIDENT met aux voix l'article ainsi modifié: „Les juges ou juges suppléants termineront même après l'expiration de la durée de leur mandat, le jugement des affaires dont ils ont été saisis".

L'article est adopté à main levée, sauf rédaction.

M. HAGERUP s'abstient de voter.

LE PRESIDENT ouvre la discussion sur l'article 10 du projet Root—Phillimore. Il en donne lecture.

Le texte orginal du projet est en anglais; en conséquence le Président soumet à l'assentiment du Comité la traduction suivante, en français, de l'article 10:

„Si un juge ou juge suppléant devient incapable ou inapte à faire fonction de juge, les autres membres de la Cour pourront notifier ce fait au Secrétaire Général de la Société des Nations". Cette formule est acceptée, à l'exclusion de la formule précédemment soumise au Comité, et qui était moins adéquate.

Le PRESIDENT donne lecture de l'article 8 de son avant-projet. Cet article fournit, selon lui, une meilleure expression des idées contenues dans l'article 10 du projet Root—Phillimore.

for some time, foresees that he is about to lose his case. If the tenure of office of one or more of the judges is about to come to an end, the party might try by means of legal quibbles to lengthen the proceedings so that the case would have to be started afresh by the new judge. To prevent this undesirable possibility judges must be allowed to complete cases. There was nothing to prevent the Committee giving them this right, since it had full power to determine the duration of appointment. For instance, it could fix a period of nine years *plus* the time necessary to complete cases actually before the Court.

M. DE LAPRADELLE did not think that the danger pointed out by Lord Phillimore was a real one. The Court was sufficiently equipped with means to prevent legal quibbles; it could, for instance, use its right to impose time limits.

After a discussion between M. DE LAPRADELLE, LORD PHILLIMORE and M. LODER, it was agreed that the word "saisis" should be substituted for the words "appelés à connaître" at the end of the Article (French text), and that the word "jugement" should be substituted for the word "instruction".

The PRESIDENT took a vote upon the Article, which, as thus amended, read as follows: "Les juges ou juges suppléants termineront, même après l'expiration de la durée de leur mandat, le jugement des affaires dont ils ont été saisis".

The Article was adopted by a show of hands, subject to amendments of form.

M. HAGERUP abstained from voting.

The PRESIDENT next laid Article 10 of the Root—Phillimore plan before the Committee. He read the Article in question.

The original wording of the plan being in English, the President submitted the following French translation of Article 10 for the approval of the Committee:

"Si un juge ou juge suppléant devient incapable ou inapte à faire fonction de juge, les autres membres de la Cour pourront notifier ce fait au Secrétaire Général de la Société des Nations". This wording was adopted instead of that previously submitted to the Committee, which was not entirely satisfactory.

The PRESIDENT read Article 8 of his draft scheme. In his opinion this gave better expression to the ideas contained in Article 10 of the Root—Phillimore plan.

Mr. ROOT déclare que Lord Phillimore et lui-même se rallient à la proposition faite par le Président.

M. LODER signale la formule adoptée par le projet des Cinq Puissances (voir article 10 de ce projet).

M. DE LAPRADELLE attire l'attention sur la nature délicate de la question.

Dans certains cas, on pourra sans difficulté obtenir la démission volontaire du juge; dans d'autres cas, il sera presque impossible d'obtenir cette démission ou, à son défaut, l'unanimité de la Cour. Il y aura des discussions qui mettront l'autorité de la Cour en danger; parce que quelque chose en transpirera toujours au dehors. Les collègues du juge devenu incapable de servir n'auront guère le courage moral de donner leur vote pour son exclusion. Le danger de son maintien ne serait pas d'ailleurs très grand, parce que la Cour contiendra assez de juges d'une intelligence pleine et vigoureuse pour que la présence d'un juge dont les facultés sont en déclin ne nuise point à la valeur de ses jugements.

Il s'agit d'une question purement morale de dignité personnelle et de dignité de la Cour, qu'il n'est pas possible de régler dans un article: c'est pourquoi M. de Lapradelle s'abstiendra de voter sur l'article qu'on est en train de discuter.

LORD PHILLIMORE fait remarquer qu'il est possible que l'occasion de se servir de l'article 10 ne se présente jamais. En Angleterre, les juges ont été inamovibles depuis le temps de George Ier, mais le Roi peut destituer un juge à la demande des deux Chambres du Parlement. Ceci n'est jamais arrivé, bien qu'on y ait pensé deux ou trois fois; mais cette disposition a été très utile comme une condition *in terrorem*. Lord Phillimore croit que l'article 10 aurait le même effet: c'est pourquoi il propose qu'on le maintienne. Toutefois, l'unanimité doit être conservée comme condition obligatoire de la destitution.

M. HAGERUP comprend parfaitement les hésitations de M. de Lapradelle. Il dit que les trois commissions scandinaves sont arrivées au même résultat que le projet Root—Phillimore, qui exprime cependant leur idée d'une façon plus adoucie, en instituant le recours au Secrétaire Général de la Société des Nations.

Mr. ROOT stated that Lord Phillimore and he accepted the proposal made by the President.

M. LODER drew attention to the wording used in the Five Power Plan. (See Article 10 of this plan).

M. DE LAPRADELLE pointed out the delicacy of the question.

In some cases the voluntary resignation of a judge could be obtained without difficulty; in other cases it would be almost impossible to obtain such resignation, or, failing it, the unanimous agreement of the Court. There would be discussions which would jeopardise the authority of the Court, since something was always bound to leak out. The colleagues of the judge who had become incapable of performing his duties, would hardly have the moral courage to vote for exclusion; besides, the danger involved in his retention would not be very great, because the Court would contain sufficient judges retaining the full use of their intellectual powers to prevent the presence of a judge, whose powers were on the wane, from detracting from the value of its judgments.

It was a purely moral question affecting the personal dignity of the judge and the dignity of the Court, which it was impossible to deal with in an Article. For this reason M. de Lapradelle would abstain from voting upon the Article under discussion.

LORD PHILLIMORE pointed out that it was quite possible that Article 10 would never be made use of. In England, judges have been appointed for life since the time of George I, but the King can remove a judge at the request of the two Houses of Parliament. This has in fact never happened but it has been contemplated two or three times. This possibility however, had had a very useful moral effect as a condition *in terrorem* Lord Phillimore thought that Article 10 would have the same effect; for this reason he proposed that it should be retained. Nevertheless it must be laid down that dismissal is dependent upon the unanimity of the remaining judges.

M. HAGERUP understood perfectly M. de Lapradelle's hesitation. He said that the three Scandinavian Commissions had arrived at the same result as the Root—Phillimore plan; the latter, however, expressed the same idea rather more tactfully by introducing the intervention of the Secretary-General of the League of Nations.

Le PRESIDENT met au vote le principe de l'article 10 du projet Root—Phillimore, tel qu'il a été exprimé dans l'article 8 de l'avant-projet du Président.

La disposition est adoptée à main levée.

Le Président, avant d'ouvrir la discussion sur l'article 12 du projet Root—Phillimore, signale l'article 6 de son avant-projet. Il explique les motifs qui sont à la base de cet article. L'Assemblée de la Société des Nations doit se réunir à des périodes fixes; mais il se peut qu'à un moment donné, l'Assemblée ne puisse se réunir à la date déterminée et que le mandat des juges expire. Dans ce cas fortuit et de force majeure la Cour doit pouvoir continuer à fonctionner.

Mr. ROOT attire l'attention sur la règle, courante aux Etats-Unis, selon laquelle tous les fonctionnaires qui sont nommés pour un terme fixe, obtiennent leur mandat pour ce terme, et en outre jusqu'à la nomination et l'entrée en fonction de leurs successeurs. Cette règle donne des résultats tout-à fait satisfaisants. Elle équivaut à celle qui est proposée par le Président dans l'article 6 de son avant-projet.

Le PRESIDENT se déclare heureux de l'appui que lui donne Mr. Root. L'idée qu'il préconise permettra de combler une lacune du texte de l'article 6 de son projet. Il donne lecture de ce texte.

M. RICCI-BUSATTI signale la différence qu'il y a entre la règle telle qu'elle a été exposée par Mr. Root, et celle qui est exposée dans le texte du Président. Selon ce dernier, il faudrait une décision de la Cour pour prolonger le mandat des juges; selon le premier, la prolongation se fait automatiquement.

Le PRESIDENT est disposé à modifier son texte dans le sens de la règle rappelée par Mr. Root. La dernière partie de l'article 6 serait ainsi conçue, après modification:

„Jusqu'à la réunion de cette Assemblée, les membres en fonction, dont le mandat serait expiré, continuent l'exercice de leurs attributions."

Le Président met aux voix l'article ainsi modifié. Il est adopté à main levée.

Le Président attire l'attention du Comité sur l'article 7 de son avant-projet, dont il donne lecture. Après un échange de vues avec Lord Phillimore, le Président consent à ce que cet article soit discuté en même temps que l'article 26 du projet Root—Phillimore, qui correspond au premier alinéa de l'article 7 de l'avant-projet du Président.

The PRESIDENT took a vote upon the principle contained in Article 10 of the Root—Phillimore plan as expressed in Article 8 of his own draft scheme.

The clause was adopted by a show of hands.

The President before commencing the discussion of the 12th Article of the Root—Phillimore plan, drew attention to Article 6 of his own plan. He explained the motives which gave rise to this Article. The Assembly of the League of Nations must meet at fixed intervals; but it might happen that the Assembly could not meet on the date fixed and that the period, for which the judges were appointed, had expired. The Court must be able to continue in operation, should such unavoidable circumstance arise.

Mr. ROOT called attention to the rule prevailing in the United States, according to which all officials, who were appointed for a fixed period, held their appointments for this period and further, until their successors had been appointed and had taken up their duties. This rule had given perfectly satisfactory results. It was equivalent to that proposed by the President in Article 6 of his plan.

The PRESIDENT was very glad to have the support of Mr. Root, whose suggestion also supplied an omission in Article 6 of the President's plan. He read this Article.

M. RICCI-BUSATTI drew attention to the difference existing between the rule, as explained by Mr. Root, and as contained in the President's plan. According to the latter a decision of the Court was required for the extention of the judges' mandate; according to the former the extention was automatic.

The PRESIDENT was prepared to modify his wording so as to adapt it to the rule mentioned by Mr. Root. The last part of Article 6 would, after such modifications, be worded as follows:

"Until such meeting of the Assembly, the members, whose term has expired, shall continue to perform their duties".

The President took a vote upon the Article as thus amended; it was adopted by a show of hands.

The President then called the attention of the Committee to the 7th Article of his plan, which he read. After a discussion with Lord Phillimore, the President agreed that this Article should be discussed together with the 26th Article of the Root—Phillimore plan,

Le Président ouvre la discussion sur l'article 12 du projet Root—Phillimore. Il en donne lecture.

which corresponded to the first Paragraph of the 7th Article of his draft scheme.

The President next laid before the Committee the 12th Article of the Root—Phillimore plan, which he read.

LORD PHILLIMORE dit que l'article 15 de l'avant-projet du Président comprend la même matière que les articles 12 et 13 du projet Root—Phillimore, et que la dernière phrase de cet article 12 se retrouve dans la proposition soumise par M. Ricci-Busatti.

Il se rallie à l'idée de faire du greffier de la Cour un lien entre la Cour de Justice et la Cour d'Arbitrage: on éviterait ainsi, d'ailleurs, des dépenses inutiles.

LORD PHILLIMORE said that the 15th Article of the President's plan dealt with the same subject as the 12th and 13th Articles of the Root—Phillimore plan, and that the last sentence of Article 12 was also found in the proposal submitted by M. Ricci-Busatti.

He supported the idea of making the Registrar of the Court a connecting link between the Court of Justice and the Court of Arbitration; also useless expenditure would thus be avoided.

M. HAGERUP attire l'attention sur le fait que le greffier de la Cour Permanente d'Arbitrage s'appelle en réalité Secrétaire Général. Ce titre doit lui être conservé.

M. HAGERUP drew attention to the fact that the Registrar of the Permanent Court of Arbitration was called Secretary-General. He must retain this title.

M. LODER propose la suppression de la dernière partie de l'article 12 du projet Root—Phillimore: si l'on stipule que la Cour nommera son greffier, on aura en même temps dit qu'elle peut nommer qui elle veut et, par conséquent, le greffier de la Cour d'Arbitrage.

M. LODER proposed that the last part of Article 12 of the Root—Phillimore plan should be deleted. If it were laid down that the Court would appoint its own Registrar, this would imply that it could appoint whomsoever it wished, and consequently, this would include the Registrar of the Court or Arbitration.

Mr. ROOT est d'avis que la question a peu d'importance; mais on rendrait la Cour impopulaire en la rendant trop coûteuse, et il serait inutile de payer deux greffiers et le personnel de deux greffes alors qu'un seul greffe et un seul greffier pourraient suffire.

Mr. ROOT thought that the question was of little importance; but the Court would be unpopular if it were too costly, and it was quite unnecessary to pay two Registrars and a double staff, when a single Registrar and Registry would suffice.

M. DE LAPRADELLE suggère l'idée de constater simplement qu'il n'y a pas d'incompatibilité entre les fonctions de Secrétaire Général de la Cour d'Arbitrage et celles de greffier de la Cour de Justice.

M. DE LAPRADELLE suggested that it should merely be stated that there was no incompatibility between the duties of the Secretary-General of the Court of Arbitration, and those of Registrar of the Court of Justice.

M. RICCI-BUSATTI trouve cette constatation inutile; si l'on ne stipule pas une incompatibilité, il n'y en a pas. Il pense qu'un seul greffier sera suffisant. Il rappelle la formule de la Convention de 1907 d'après laquelle le bureau international „sert de greffe à la Cour"; on pourrait employer une formule analogue pour la Cour de Justice, en donnant en outre à cette dernière le droit de nommer, le cas échéant, un greffier-adjoint conformément à l'article 14 de son projet. Tout cela répond à son idée de rapprocher, autant que possible, la Cour d'Arbitrage de la Cour de Justice.

M. RICCI-BUSATTI thought that this statement was unnecessary. If no incompatibility were mentioned, none would exist. He thought that one Registrar would suffice. He recalled the clause of the Convention of 1907, which laid down that the International Bureau is to act as Registry to the Court. A similar phrase might be used for the Court of Justice, giving it, in addition, the right to appoint, if necessary, an Assistant-Registrar, as indicated in Article 14 of his plan. This was in accordance with his idea of establishing as close a connection as possible between the Court of Arbitration and the Court of Justice.

Le PRESIDENT constate que Mr. Root et Lord Phillimore acceptent l'amendement de M. de Lapradelle.

L'article 12 du projet Root—Phillimore avec l'amendement de M. de Lapradelle est adopté à main levée.

MM. RICCI-BUSATTI et HAGERUP se sont abstenus de voter.

Sauf rédaction, l'article 12 serait à peu près le suivant: „La Cour élira son président et son vice-président; elle nommera son greffier. Il n'y a pas d'incompatibilité entre les fonctions de Secrétaire Général de la Cour Permanente d'Arbitrage et de greffier de la Cour Permanente de Justice".

Le PRESIDENT ouvre la discussion sur l'article 13 du projet Root—Phillimore et en donne lecture.

LORD PHILLIMORE constate avec plaisir qu'une disposition analogue se retrouve dans le premier alinéa de l'article 15 de l'avant-projet du Président et que par conséquent il y a accord entre lui et le Président, sur ce point. Mais, comme il ne connaît pas l'opinion de ses autres collègues au sujet de cet article, il désire l'expliquer.

A son avis, il serait dangereux de faire du président de la Cour un trop grand personnage. Dans le système anglo-américain, le président d'une cour n'est que le premier d'entre ses pairs. Lord Phillimore croit que le système continental n'est pas le même: c'est pourquoi il faut créer des garanties. Le meilleur moyen sera de stipuler un terme pour les fonctions de président. Ce terme ne doit cependant pas être trop court, puisque le président est soumis à l'obligation de résider à La Haye et peut être obligé d'y transporter son domicile. Pour plusieurs raisons Lord Phillimore croit qu'une période de trois ans sera satisfaisante; si l'on rend le président rééligible, on est presque certain qu'un bon président conservera son mandat de président pendant neuf ans, tandis qu'un mauvais président ne le conservera que pendant trois ans.

Lord Phillimore recommande l'adoption de l'article 13 du projet Root—Phillimore.

M. RICCI-BUSATTI se déclare d'accord avec Lord Phillimore et rappelle que le système proposé par lui prévoyait des présidents de section qui auraient nommé, tous les 6 mois, celui qui serait pour ce terme considéré comme „le premier" entre eux. Ce système a l'avantage de

The PRESIDENT said that Mr. Root and Lord Phillimore accepted M. de Lapradelle's amendment.

The 12th Article of the Root—Phillimore plan, as amended by M. de Lapradelle, was carried by a show of hands.

MM. RICCI-BUSATTI and HAGERUP did not vote.

Subject to amendments of form, the Article would read more or less as follows: "The Court shall elect its President and its Vice-President, and appoint its Registrar. No incompatibility shall be held to exist between the duties of Secretary-General of the Permanent Court of Arbitration and those of Registrar of the Permanent Court of Justice".

The PRESIDENT then laid the 13th Article of the Root—Phillimore plan before the Committee. He read the Article.

LORD PHILLIMORE was happy to say that there was a similar clause in the 1st Paragraph of the 15th Article of the President's plan, and that, consequently, he and the President were in agreement on this point; but, as he did not know the opinion of his other colleagues upon the contents of the Article, he would like to explain it.

In his opinion, it would be dangerous to make the Presidency of the Court too important a post. Under the Anglo-American system, the President of the Court was only *primus inter pares*. Lord Phillimore thought that the Continental system was not the same; for this reason precautions must be taken. The best way was to lay down a fixed duration for the appointment of the president. This period, however, must not be too short, because the president is obliged to be domiciled at the Hague, and might therefore have to change his residence. For various reasons Lord Phillimore thought that a period of 3 years would be satisfactory; if the president were made eligible for reelection, it was almost certain that a good president would keep his appointment for 9 years, whereas a bad president would only do so for 3 years.

Lord Phillimore recommended that Article 13 of the Root—Phillimore plan should be adopted.

M. RICCI-BUSATTI said that he agreed with Lord Phillimore, and recalled the fact, that the system proposed by him provided for presidents of sections, who would select one of their number every six months, who would be considered as *primus inter pares* for this

ne pas donner trop d'importance à la durée des fonctions présidentielles. Il demande encore si le président sera élu à la majorité relative ou absolue. D'une manière générale, il voudrait souligner la nécessité de régler la méthode d'élection.

LORD PHILLIMORE croit qu'on doit laisser à la Cour le soin de régler cette méthode.

M. DE LAPRADELLE voudrait savoir si les juges suppléants auront le droit de prendre part à l'élection du président.

LORD PHILLIMORE estime qu'il faut, en effet, trancher cette question.

Mr. ROOT pense que les juges suppléants ne doivent pas prendre part à l'élection puisqu'ils ne sont pas membres de la Cour. Pour cette raison, on doit insérer à l'article 13 l'expression „par les juges titulaires".

M. LODER et LORD PHILLIMORE se rallient à l'opinion de Mr. Root.

M. RICCI-BUSATTI pense qu'en excluant les juges suppléants de l'élection, on abaissera l'importance de leur rôle.

D'après M. DE LAPRADELLE les juges suppléants ont deux missions: 1. la mission pratique de pourvoir aux vacances; 2. la mission politique de donner satisfaction à des pays dont aucun ressortissant ne peut être juge titulaire à la Cour.

Cette seconde fonction des juges suppléants exige qu'il y ait entre eux et les juges titulaires une parfaite égalité, en ce qui concerne l'élection du président.

LORD PHILLIMORE croit qu'on doit se placer exclusivement au point de vue pratique. Est-il vraiment possible de faire venir à La Haye, tous les trois ans, les juges suppléants, exclusivement pour prendre part à l'élection du président, c'est-à-dire pour une pure question de dignité? Il appuie la proposition d'ajouter la formule „par les juges titulaires" au texte de l'article 13 du projet Root—Phillimore.

M. DE LAPRADELLE fait observer que si un juge suppléant se trouve empêché de venir à La Haye pour l'élection, il aura la faculté de s'abstenir. La seule différence entre les juges titulaires et les juges suppléants est que, tandis que le premier fonctionne de droit, le dernier fonctionne en cas d'empêchement des autres; il

period. This system had the advantage of not making the period of tenure of office as president a matter of great importance. He also raised the question as to whether the president should be elected by a simple or absolute majority. He wished, in a general way, to lay emphasis upon the necessity of regulating the method of election.

LORD PHILLIMORE thought that it ought to be left to the Court to decide the method.

M. DE LAPRADELLE wished to know whether the deputy-judges would have the right of taking part in the election of the president.

LORD PHILLIMORE thought that this question ought to be settled.

Mr. ROOT thought that the deputy-judges ought not to take part in the election, because they were not members of the Court. For this reason, the expression "by the ordinary judges" must be added to Article 13.

M. LODER and LORD PHILLIMORE agreed with Mr. Root.

M. RICCI-BUSATTI pointed out that by excluding deputy-judges from the election, the importance of their position would be lessened.

In M. DE LAPRADELLE's opinion, the deputy-judges served two purposes: 1. the practical purpose of filling vacancies; and 2. the political purpose of giving satisfaction to countries which could not have one of their subjects as an ordinary judge upon the Court.

This second purpose demanded that there should be complete equality between the deputy-judges and the ordinary judges in the matter of the election of the president.

LORD PHILLIMORE thought that the matter should be looked upon solely from the practical point of view. Was it really possible to make the deputy-judges come to the Hague every three years solely for the purpose of taking part in the election of the President, that is to say for a mere question of dignity? He supported the proposal that the expression "by the ordinary judges" be added to Article 13 of the Root—Phillimore plan.

M. DE LAPRADELLE pointed out that if a deputy-judge found himself unable to come to the Hague for the election, he would be entitled to abstain from doing so. The only difference between ordinary judges and deputy-judges was that, whereas the former would take their seats in their own right, the latter would do duty only

n'y a donc aucun motif pour qu'ils ne prennent pas part à l'élection du président.

Le PRESIDENT signale un inconvénient. Il pourra arriver que les juges suppléants rendent possible l'élection d'un président contre la volonté de la majorité des juges titulaires.

Mr. ROOT croit qu'on ne doit pas envisager la question comme une question de dignité. Il ne s'agit que d'assurer à la Cour la possibilité de fonctionner dans les meilleures conditions. Les juges titulaires devront collaborer tous les jours avec le président, et ce qui importe, c'est que cette collaboration soit agréable et féconde. Si l'on donnait aux suppléants le droit de prendre part à l'élection du président, il pourrait arriver que le président élu eût un caractère si difficile et si autoritaire que le travail en souffrît. Il ne faut donc pas que les juges suppléants aient le droit de décider de l'attribution d'une fonction qui peut avoir une influence si considérable sur le travail et le bien-être des juges titulaires.

M. DE LAPRADELLE a la parole pour répondre aux deux objections qui ont été exprimées par le Président et par Mr. Root. Contre celle du Président, M. de Lapradelle fait valoir que les suppléants ne pourraient déterminer le résultat de l'élection, contre la volonté des juges titulaires, que si le nombre des juges titulaires était beaucoup plus restreint qu'il ne le sera normalement.

Répondant à l'objection de Mr. Root, M. de Lapradelle se rallie d'abord à l'opinion que la charge de président doit être considérée comme une charge de travail plutôt que de dignité. Mais il n'en est pas moins vrai que le fait de participer ou non à l'élection est pour les juges suppléants une question de dignité. A l'appui de sa thèse M. de Lapradelle fait observer que les doyens des facultés sont élus par tous les membres de la faculté, quelle que soit leur fonction ou leur grade. Un président, qui sera *primus inter pares*, doit sortir de l'élection de tous. Il maintient la proposition qu'il a faite.

M. RICCI-BUSATTI admet que, si l'on fait des juges suppléants des juges de second ordre, qui ne viendront à La Haye que rarement, il ne sera pas raisonnable de leur faire entreprendre un voyage qui pourra être assez long, uniquement pour prendre part à l'élection du prési-

in the absence of the former. There was, therefore, no reason why they should not take part in the election of the president.

The PRESIDENT pointed out a drawback. It might happen that the deputy judges would make possible the election of a president against the wishes of the majority of the ordinary judges.

Mr. ROOT thought that this question should not be considered as one of dignity; it was only a question of enabling the Court to carry out its duties under the most favourable conditions. The ordinary judges would have to work with the president daily, and the important point was that their collaboration should be pleasant and profitable. If the deputy judges were given the right of taking part in the election of the president, it was quite conceivable that the president elected would be so authoritative and difficult to get on with, that the work of the Court would suffer in consequence. The deputy judges, therefore, ought not to have the right to take part in a proceeding which might have such an influence upon the work and wellbeing of the ordinary judges.

M. DE LAPRADELLE obtained permission to speak in order to answer the two objections put forward by the President and Mr. Root. In answer to the President's objection, M. de Lapradelle pointed out that the deputy judges could not decide the result of an election against the wishes of the ordinary judges, unless the number of ordinary judges were much smaller than it normally would be.

In answer to Mr. Root's objection, M. de Lapradelle began by stating that he agreed that the post of president should be considered as one entailing work rather than an additional dignity. Nevertheless the fact remained that, from the point of view of the deputy judges, the question of taking part or not in the election, was a question of dignity. In support of his argument M. de Lapradelle pointed out that Presidents of Faculties were elected by all the members of the Faculty, no matter what their position or rank was. A president who was to be *primus inter pares* must be elected by all. M. de Lapradelle maintained the proposal he had made.

M. RICCI-BUSATTI admitted that if deputy judges were to be made a species of second class judge, who would only come to the Hague occasionally, it would not be reasonable to make them undertake a journey, that might be of considerable length, simply to take part in the

dent. Si, au contraire, comme dans son système, les juges suppléants ne diffèrent que peu des juges effectifs, faisant partie de la Cour au même titre que ces derniers, il ne voit pas pourquoi on ne permettrait pas aux deux catégories de prendre part aux élections sur un pied d'égalité.

Le PRESIDENT fait remarquer à M. de Lapradelle que, quel que soit le nombre des juges titulaires, il pourra toujours arriver qu'il y ait partage de voix de telle sorte que les juges suppléants restent arbitres de la situation, ce qu'il faut tâcher d'éviter.

Le Président demande à M. de Lapradelle s'il maintient sa proposition.

M. DE LAPRADELLE la maintient et propose en conséquence l'insertion à l'article 13 de la formule: „par les juges titulaires et suppléants".

Le PRESIDENT met au vote cette proposition. Elle est rejetée à main levée.

M. DE LAPRADELLE constate que sa proposition a été rejetée par une seule voix.

Le PRESIDENT met aux voix le texte original de l'article 13 avec addition de l'expression „par les juges titulaires". Ce texte est adopté à main levée.

M. RICCI-BUSATTI propose qu'on ajoute au texte ainsi adopté l'expression suivante: „à la majorité absolue des voix".

Le PRESIDENT met au vote cette proposition. Elle est rejetée.

Le Président passe à l'article 14 du projet Root—Phillimore, dont il donne lecture. Il donne également lecture des articles 9 et 10 de son avant-projet, qui se rapportent au même point. Il fait remarquer que ces articles correspondent au résultat de la discussion qui eut lieu au sein du Comité au sujet des incompatibilités. Par conséquent il en propose l'adoption.

LORD PHILLIMORE fait observer que les deux premiers alinéas de l'article 10 de l'avant-projet du Président correspondent à l'article 14 du projet Root—Phillimore. Dans ces conditions on pourra procéder au vote indifféremment sur l'un ou sur l'autre des deux projets.

Le dernier alinéa de l'article 10 de l'avant-projet traite plutôt de la matière dont il est question à l'article 16 du projet Root—Phillimore.

election of the president. If, on the other hand, as in his own plan, the deputy judges differed but little from the ordinary judges and formed part of the Court upon a footing of equality with them, he saw no reason why both classes of judges should not be allowed to take part in the elections on equal terms.

The PRESIDENT pointed out against M. de Lapradelle's proposal that, whatever the number of judges might be, it was possible that their votes would be so divided that the deputy judges might be left in a position to decide the result: steps must be taken to avoid this.

The President asked M. de Lapradelle if he still maintained his proposal.

M. DE LAPRADELLE replied in the affirmative, and proposed that the phrase "by the ordinary and deputy judges" be inserted in Article 13.

The PRESIDENT took a vote upon this proposal. It was rejected by a show of hands.

M. DE LAPRADELLE pointed out that his proposal had been rejected by a majority of one vote only.

The PRESIDENT took a vote upon the original text of Article 13 with the addition of the expression "by the ordinary judges"; this was adopted by a show of hands.

M. RICCI-BUSATTI proposed that the expression "by an absolute majority", should be added to the wording which had been adopted.

The PRESIDENT put this proposal to the vote; it was rejected.

The President then passed to the consideration of Article 14 of the Root—Phillimore plan, which he read. He also read Articles 9 and 10 of his own draft scheme, which dealt with the same subject. He pointed out that these Articles were in accordance with the result of the discussion which had taken place in the Committee on the subject of incompatibilities. Consequently he proposed that they should be adopted.

LORD PHILLIMORE pointed out that the two first paragraphs of Article 10 of the President's plan were similar to the 14th Article of the Root—Phillimore plan. It was a matter of indifference, therefore, which of the two projects was voted upon.

The last paragraph of Article 10 of the President's plan, on the other hand, dealt with the subject contained in Article 16 of the Root—Phillimore plan.

M. FERNANDES signale une disposition qui se trouve dans le projet de M. Bevilaqua: un juge doit renoncer temporairement à siéger à la Cour, si un des plaideurs est de sa nationalité.

Le PRESIDENT explique les diverses mesures restrictives qu'il a insérées dans son avant-projet. Il faut d'abord se demander ce qu'un juge ne peut pas faire pendant la durée de son mandat. Il faut en outre se demander si, avant son entrée en fonctions, il ne s'est pas mis dans une situation telle qu'elle ne lui permette pas de siéger dans certaines affaires. Il ne faut pas confondre, d'autre part, certaines incapacités avec les incompatibilités.

Le Président fait observer à M. Fernandes que le point qu'il a soulevé sera examiné lors de la discussion sur l'article 27 du projet Root—Phillimore.

LORD PHILLIMORE propose la division: On voterait d'abord sur l'article 14 du projet Root—Phillimore, sauf rédaction.

M. RICCI-BUSATTI observe qu'il y a un point qui ne peut pas être laissé au Comité de rédaction. Il s'agit d'une petite divergence entre l'article 14 du projet Root—Phillimore et le deuxième alinéa de l'article 10 de l'avant-projet du Président. Dans la première disposition on retrouve la formule: „de n'importe quelle manière"; dans la deuxième, l'expression: „ou à tout autre titre"; mais, d'après la position de la première formule, les incompatibilités ne subsistent que dans le cadre des cas spéciaux qui sont énumérés à la suite, tandis que l'expression employée dans l'avant-projet du Président ouvre encore d'autres possibilités. Il se déclare plutôt en faveur de la solution adoptée dans le projet Root—Phillimore.

M. DE LAPRADELLE demande à M. Ricci-Busatti s'il trouve l'énumération dans l'article 14 de ce projet complète, comme doit l'être une énumération limitative. Quant à lui, il est partisan d'une formule élargie.

M. RICCI-BUSATTI demande, à son tour, si l'expression d'une opinion sur une certaine affaire, faite publiquement par un juge, antérieurement à son élection comme juge et alors qu'il exerçait des fonctions publiques, — par exemple des fonctions parlementaires — serait suffisante pour entraîner l'exclusion de ce juge, dans un procès devant la Cour ayant cette question pour objet.

M. FERNANDES drew attention to a clause contained in M. Bevilaqua's plan to the effect that a judge must give up his seat upon the Court if one of the contesting parties were of his nationality.

The PRESIDENT explained the various restrictive provisions which he had inserted in his plan. The first question was to decide those things which a judge could not do during his tenure of office. It was possible that before taking up his duties, his situation had been such that he would not be able to sit in certain cases: this question must also be considered. On the other hand, the question of disqualification must not be confused with that of incompatibility.

The President called M. Fernandes' attention to the fact that the point he had raised would be discussed when Article 27 of the Root—Phillimore plan was considered.

LORD PHILLIMORE proposed that the question under consideration should be divided; a vote should first be taken upon Article 14 of the Root—Phillimore plan, subject to final drafting.

M. RICCI-BUSATTI said that there was one point which could not be left to the drafting Committee. There was a slight divergence between Article 14 of the Root—Phillimore plan and the second Paragraph of Article 10 of the President's plan. The former contained the expression "in any way whatever"; the second the expression "or in any other capacity"; the position of the former expression implied that incompatibilities could only arise out of the special cases enumerated thereafter, whereas the expression used in the President's plan admitted of other possibilities. He said that he preferred the version of the Root—Phillimore plan.

M. DE LAPRADELLE asked M. Ricci-Busatti whether he thought the enumeration contained in Article 14 of this plan was as complete as an exclusive enumeration ought to be; for his part he would prefer a wider formula.

M. RICCI-BUSATTI, in return, asked whether a public expression of opinion, made by a judge before his election and during the performance of some public duty — such as the duty of a member of a House of Parliament — upon a particular question, would suffice to entail his exclusion from the Bench, in the event of a case being brought before the Court bearing upon this question.

Le PRESIDENT répond négativement; on pourrait envisager des cas où une personne serait intervenue dans un litige sans y avoir été mêlée de la façon visée dans les catégories énumérées. Il trouve que l'expression „intervenus" contient toute la limitation nécessaire et désirable.

Le Président met aux voix les deux premiers paragraphes de l'article 10 de son avant-projet; ils sont adoptés à main levée.

LORD PHILLIMORE prend alors la parole sur la question de l'incompatibilité des fonctions. Il déclare que, dans cette direction, Mr. Root et lui-même ne peuvent aller plus loin qu'ils ne l'ont fait dans l'article 14 de leur projet. Ils ne peuvent pas accepter l'article 9 de l'avant-projet du Président.

Il attire l'attention du Comité sur l'article 7 du projet de 1907:

„L'exercice des fonctions judiciaires est interdit au juge dans les affaires au sujet desquelles il aura, à un titre quelconque, concouru à la décision d'un tribunal national, d'un Tribunal d'arbitrage ou d'une Commission d'enquête, ou figuré dans l'instance comme conseil ou avocat d'une Partie.

Aucun juge ne peut intervenir comme agent ou comme avocat devant la Cour de Justice arbitrale ou la Cour Permanente d'Arbitrage, devant un tribunal spécial d'arbitrage ou une Commission d'enquête, ni y agir pour une partie en quelque qualité que ce soit, pendant toute la durée de son mandat."

Il croit qu'il faut laisser aux membres de la Cour d'Arbitrage et aux Etats toute liberté pour choisir les meilleurs juges, sans créer des incompatibilités légales. Les membres de la Cour d'Arbitrage, d'abord, et puis les Etats, doivent avoir le droit de se prononcer sur ce qu'ils entendent considérer comme des incompatibilités.

Le PRESIDENT fait valoir qu'en supprimant l'article 9 de son avant-projet, on perd de vue la distinction entre la justice et la politique. Tout en comprenant les motifs de Lord Phillimore, il ne peut qu'à regret se rallier à son opinion: il croit qu'il faut à tout prix éviter l'intervention de la politique dans le fonctionnement de la Cour.

M. LODER se rallie à l'opinion du Président à cet égard.

Mr. ROOT déclare qu'il n'a pas d'objection contre l'article 9 de l'avant-projet du Président; il croit qu'il y a malentendu. Lord Phil-

The PRESIDENT replied in the negative; it was quite possible that a person might be concerned in a case in ways other than those provided for under the classification given. He thought that the expression "connected" was as specific as was either necessary or desirable.

The President took a vote upon the first two Paragraphs of Article 10 of his plan. They were adopted by a show of hands.

LORD PHILLIMORE then spoke upon the question of incompatible duties. He stated that Mr. Root and he could not go further in this direction than they had done in Article 14 of their plan. They could not accept Article 9 of the President's plan.

He called the attention of the Committee to Article 7 of the Draft of the Conference of 1907:

"A judge may not exercise his judicial functions in any case in which he has, in any way whatever, taken part in the decision of a national tribunal, of a tribunal of arbitration, or of a Commission of inquiry, or has appeared in the suit as counsel or advocate for one of the parties.

A judge cannot act as agent or advocate before the Judicial Arbitration Court or the Permanent Court of Arbitration, before a special Tribunal of Arbitration or a Commission of inquiry, nor act for one of the parties in any capacity whatsoever so long as his appointment lasts".

He thought that the members of the Court of Arbitration and the various States ought to be left completely free to choose the best judges, without creating a number of legal incompatibilities. The members of the Court of Arbitration, in the first place, and, subsequently, the States, should have the right to express their opinion as to the duties which ought to be considered as incompatible.

The PRESIDENT pointed out that, by rejecting Article 9 of his plan, the distinction between justice and politics was lost sight of. Though he quite understood Lord Phillimore's motives, he could not, much to his regret, agree with him. He thought that the intervention of politics in the work of the Court must be avoided at any cost.

M. LODER agreed with the President on this subject.

Mr. ROOT declared that he had no objection to Article 9 of the President's plan; there must be a misunderstanding. Lord Philli-

limore a parlé seulement du dernier alinéa de l'article 10 de cet avant-projet, mais il est, comme lui, partisan de l'article 9.

Le PRESIDENT propose que l'on ne fasse point mention spéciale des fonctions parlementaires, en raison de la difficulté créée par le caractère spécial de la Chambre des Lords.

M. ALTAMIRA estime que si l'on ne mentionne pas les fonctions parlementaires, on les exclut absolument.

M. DE LAPRADELLE observe que dans l'article 9 la méthode de rédaction adoptée est positive pour une partie de l'article et négative pour l'autre partie, ce qui n'est pas admissible. Pour cette raison, il voudrait que l'on supprimât le dernier alinéa de l'article 9.

M. ALTAMIRA répète qu'il ne faut pas exclure tous les parlementaires.

Mr. ROOT est d'avis que la question est fort importante. Il s'agit d'exclure la politique de la Cour et de tenir la Cour en dehors de la politique. La fonction de juge à la Cour doit être la seule fonction du juge; il faut prendre les mesures nécessaires pour éviter que cette fonction ne soit considérée comme un simple accident au cours d'une carrière politique.

Le PRESIDENT partage la manière de voir de Mr. Root. Il déclare que la discussion reste ouverte et qu'elle sera continuée à la séance prochaine.

M. RICCI-BUSATTI déclare qu'il maintient l'article 5 de son second projet, qui est le suivant:

„La qualité de membre de la Cour de Justice internationale est incompatible avec toute autre charge se rattachant aux différents organes de la Société des Nations ou aux relations internationales des Etats, sauf la qualité de membre de la Cour Permanente d'Arbitrage ou d'un tribunal arbitral international.

Tout membre de la Cour de Justice qui se trouverait dans un des cas d'incompatibilité visés à l'alinéa précédent, sera considéré comme démissionnaire de ses fonctions de juge."

La séance est levée à 12.30 heures de l'après-midi.

Le Président:
(signé) Brn. DESCAMPS.

Le Secrétaire-Général:
(signé) D. ANZILOTTI.

more had only spoken of the last Paragraph of Article 10 of this plan, but he accepted Article 9, as did Mr. Root himself.

The PRESIDENT suggested that parliamentary duties should not be specially mentioned, on account of the difficulty created by the unique position of the House of Lords.

M. ALTAMIRA thought that if parliamentary duties were not specifically mentioned they would be inadmissible.

M. DE LAPRADELLE pointed out with reference to Article 9 that one part of the Article was positive in form, and another part was negative; this could not be allowed to stand. He therefore wished to have the last Paragraph of Article 9 deleted.

M. ALTAMIRA repeated that members of Houses of Parliament must not be excluded.

Mr. ROOT thought that the question was a very important one. The point was to exclude politics from the Court and to keep the Court out of politics. His duties as judge must be the only duties undertaken by a member of the Court; steps must be taken to prevent these duties from being considered as an incident in a political career.

The PRESIDENT agreed; the discussion would be adjourned and continued at the next meeting.

M. RICCI-BUSATTI stated that he still advocated the adoption of the 5th Article of his second plan, which was as follows:

"An appointment as member of the Court of International Justice is incompatible with any duty connected with the different organisations of the League of Nations, or with the international affairs of States, except that of a member of the Permanent Court of Arbitration or of an International Tribunal of Arbitration.

Any member of the Court of Justice who may hold a position involving an incompatibility arising out of the preceding Paragraph, shall be considered as having resigned his appointment as judge".

The meeting closed at 12.30 p.m.

The President:
(signed) Brn. DESCAMPS.

The Secretary-General:
(signed) D. ANZILOTTI.

21IÈME SÉANCE (non-publique), tenue au Palais de la Paix, à La Haye, le 10 juillet 1920.

Présidence de M. le BARON DESCAMPS.

Sont présents: tous les membres du Comité (à l'exception de M. Bevilaqua); M. Fernandes; Mr. James Brown Scott; les secrétaires particuliers de M. le Baron Descamps et de M. Adatci; les membres du Secrétariat.

La séance n'est ouverte qu'à 11 heures, en raison d'une réunion officieuse du Comité qui a pris place de 9.30 à 11 heures.

Le PRESIDENT rappelle qu'on va continuer la discussion ouverte la veille sur la question des incompatibilités.

La parole est à Mr. ROOT. Il dit que les conversations entre les membres ont amené un accord général sur la formule suivante, relative à la matière traitée dans l'article 9 de l'avant-projet du président, constituant une addition à l'article 14 du projet Root—Phillimore. Mr. Root donne lecture du texte anglais de la formule: il est ainsi conçu:

"The exercise of any function which belongs to the political direction, national or international, of States, by the members of the Court, during their terms of office, is declared incompatible with their judicial duties."

Le PRESIDENT déclare qu'il sera donné lecture à la séance prochaine de la traduction française du texte anglais adopté: le Secrétariat est chargé de la préparer.

Le Président constate que le Comité est d'accord pour adopter l'article 14 du projet Root—Phillimore.

M. DE LAPRADELLE demande qu'il soit constaté au procès-verbal qu'il y a deux interprétations du même texte — l'une française, l'autre anglaise: l'interprétation française sera communiquée au Comité seulement à la séance prochaine.

21ST MEETING (Private), held at the Peace Palace, the Hague, on July 10th, 1920.

BARON DESCAMPS in the chair.

Present: all the members of the Committee (with the exception of M. Bevilaqua); M. Fernandes; Mr. James Brown Scott; the private secretaries of Baron Descamps and M. Adatci; the members of the Secretariat.

The meeting opened at 11 o'clock; the time from 9.30 to 11 having been occupied by a private meeting of the Committee.

The PRESIDENT reminded the Committee that the discussion of the question of incompatibility, which had been commenced on the previous day, was to be continued.

Mr. ROOT was the first to speak. He said that informal discussion between the members had resulted in a general agreement upon a wording for the subject-matter of Article 9 of the President's plan, which would form an addition to Article 14 of the Root—Phillimore plan. Mr. Root read the English version of this formula, which was as follows:

"The exercise of any function which belongs to the political direction, national or international, of States, by the members of the Court, during their terms of office, is declared incompatible with their judicial duties."

The PRESIDENT stated that the French translation of the English version adopted would be read at the next meeting. The Secretariat was entrusted with the task of preparing it.

The President declared that the Committee was agreed on the adoption of article 14 of the Root—Phillimore plan.

M. DE LAPRADELLE requested that the procès-verbal should record the fact that there were two constructions of the same clause, one French and one English; the French one would not be communicated to the Committee until the next meeting.

Le PRESIDENT ouvre la discussion sur l'article 15 du projet Root—Phillimore. Il en donne lecture.

LORD PHILLIMORE, en remarquant que, dans l'avant-projet du Président, la matière se trouve traitée aux articles concernant la nomination des juges, exprime l'avis que, dans le texte final, l'article 15 doit prendre place avec les articles qui traitent de la nomination des juges. Il laisse de côté ce point qui est une question de rédaction. Pour ce qui est du fond de la question, Lord Phillimore croit qu'on doit adopter la même méthode pour les élections partielles que pour les élections générales, c'est à dire celle de la première élection des juges. Il voit dans l'article deux problèmes différents:

1. la manière dont sera élu un juge qui aura à prendre la place d'un juge décédé ou démissionnaire;

2. la durée du mandat de ce juge: doit-il viser une période entière de neuf ans, ou seulement le temps qui reste à courir du mandat du prédécesseur du juge?

Lord Phillimore préfère la première solution, mais ajoute que, pour lui, la question n'a pas beaucoup d'importance. Il propose qu'on considère d'abord la première phrase de l'article 15.

Le PRESIDENT est d'avis que cette phrase ne présente pas de difficultés.

M. RICCI-BUSATTI est d'un avis contraire. Si la phrase signifie que les nouveaux juges seront également nommés par le Conseil et l'Assemblée, il est certain qu'il n'y a pas d'objections. Mais il n'en est pas de même si elle se rapporte aussi à la présentation des candidats. On comprend que chaque groupe national présente six candidats pour la première élection. On ne le comprend plus dans le cas d'élections partielles, lorsqu'il ne s'agira peut-être que de la nomination d'un ou deux juges; d'autant plus que l'on a déjà admis que chaque Etat ne peut avoir plus d'un de ses ressortissants parmi les membres de la Cour. Il est fort probable que si le juge d'un grand Etat vient à manquer, son successeur sera de la même nationalité. Dans ces circonstances, il semble absolument inutile, peut être dangereux, de faire présenter un si grand nombre de candidats par toutes les nations.

M. LODER fait observer que tous les pays ont le même intérêt au bon fonctionnement de la Cour et, partant, à ce qu'un bon juge soit nommé.

The PRESIDENT next laid the 15th Article of the Root—Phillimore plan before the Committee. He read this article.

LORD PHILLIMORE pointed out that, in the President's plan, this subject was dealt with in the Articles concerning the appointment of the judges, and expressed the opinion, that, in the final draft, Article 15 should be placed with the Articles dealing with the appointment of judges. However he did not propose to deal with this point now, as it was a question for the drafting Committee. Lord Phillimore thought that substantially the same method should be adopted for by-elections as for general elections, that is to say, the same method as for the first election of the judges. In his opinion, the Article contained two different problems:

1. the method of electing a judge to replace a judge who had died or retired;

2. the period for which this judge should be appointed: should he be appointed for a complete period of nine years, or only for the unexpired portion of his predecessor's appointment?

Lord Phillimore preferred the former solution, but added that he did not attach much importance to the question. He proposed that the first sentence of Article 15 should be dealt with first.

The PRESIDENT thought that this sentence would not offer any difficulty.

M. RICCI-BUSATTI held the contrary opinion. If the sentence were intended to mean that the new judges would likewise be appointed by the Council and the Assembly, there would certainly be no objections. But it was quite a different matter if the sentence also referred to the nomination of candidates. It was comprehensible that each national group should submit six candidates for the first election; but this was not so in the case of by-elections, when perhaps only one or two judges were to be elected; especially as it had already been laid down that no State might have more than one of its subjects as a member of the Court. It was also extremely probable that if a judge belonging to an important State ceased to be a member of the Court, his successor would be of the same nationality. Under these circumstances, it seemed quite useless and possibly dangerous to have such a large number of candidates nominated by all nations.

M. LODER pointed out that all countries would have the same interest in the efficient working of the Court, and consequently in the appointment of good judges.

Le PRESIDENT s'oppose énergiquement à la proposition de Lord Phillimore. Sa règle briserait l'économie du système de l'élection en donnant à chaque juge, élu séparément, un mandat de neuf ans. Cette méthode est du reste en désaccord avec celle qui est universellement adoptée. La coutume est que lorsqu'un juge en remplace un autre, il ne reste en fonction que pour le temps qui reste à parfaire du mandat de son prédécesseur. Si l'on adoptait la règle préconisée par Lord Phillimore, on n'aurait, dans quelques années, que des élections partielles. En outre, le système que le Comité a déjà adopté pour les élections des juges serait complètement faussé et ne pourrait plus fonctionner. Le Président propose que le suppléant qui entre pour remplir une vacance, reste en fonction jusqu'à la prochaine élection générale.

LORD PHILLIMORE croit qu'il y a un malentendu. Il demande au Président si, à son avis, en cas de décès ou de démission d'un juge, c'est le premier suppléant qui doit prendre la place, sans qu'il y ait besoin d'une élection partielle.

Le PRESIDENT répond affirmativement.

LORD PHILLIMORE dit que pour sa part il a cru que le corps des juges titulaires devait toujours être complet. Dès qu'un juge titulaire aurait cessé de fonctionner, il faudrait par conséquent procéder à une élection pour le remplacer. Le suppléant n'exercerait les fonctions de juge qu'en attendant le résultat de l'élection. La question est alors de savoir, si l'élection doit viser une période complète de neuf ans ou seulement le temps qui reste du mandat du prédécesseur. Il remarque que, dans le système du Président, l'article 15 du projet Root—Phillimore serait superflu.

Mr. ROOT pense qu'on peut mettre fin à la discussion en retournant simplement à la première idée, qui est celle d'appliquer toujours la méthode adoptée pour la première élection.

Si un juge suppléant devait prendre la place d'un juge décédé ou démissionnaire, on arriverait facilement à priver de représentation certains Etats qui doivent être représentés à la Cour.

Si, par exemple, le membre japonais meurt, il peut aisément arriver qu'il soit remplacé par un juge norvégien, français, britannique, etc. Il n'y aurait plus dans la Cour un seul juge capable de comprendre les conditions et les coutumes des pays de l'Extrême Orient. Selon la méthode du

The PRESIDENT strenuously opposed Lord Phillimore's proposal. It would undermine the whole system of election if each judge elected at a by-election was to be appointed for nine years. Further, such a provision was contrary to the system universally adopted. The recognised custom was, that when one judge replaced another, he should only hold the post for the unexpired portion of his predecessor's appointment. If the rule proposed by Lord Phillimore were adopted, in the course of a few years there would be by-elections only. In addition, the system already adopted by the Committee for the election of judges would be completely thrown out of gear and would cease to operate. The President proposed that a deputy called upon to fill a vacancy, should continue in office until the next general election.

LORD PHILLIMORE thought that there was a misunderstanding. He asked the President whether in his opinion, in the event of the death or retirement of a judge, the senior deputy judge should take his place; without any need for a by-election.

The PRESIDENT replied in the affirmative.

LORD PHILLIMORE said that, as far as he was concerned, he thought that the body of judges ought always to be complete. Whenever, therefore, a judge ceased to perform his duties, an election should be held for the purpose of replacing him. The deputy judge would only do duty as judge pending the result of the election. The question therefore was whether the election should be for a complete period of nine years, or only for the unexpired portion of the predecessor's appointment. He remarked that, according to the President's system, Article 15 of the Root—Phillimore plan would be superfluous.

Mr. ROOT thought that the discussion might be ended by simply returning to the original idea; which was to make invariable use of the system adopted for the first election.

If a deputy judge were to take the place of a judge who had died or retired, it might easily come to pass, that certain States which ought to be represented on the Court would be deprived of such representation.

Suppose, for instance, that the Japanese member were to die, it was quite conceivable that he would be replaced by a Norwegian, French or British judge, etc. In that case the Court would no longer contain a judge capable of understanding the conditions and

projet Root—Phillimore, au contraire, le Secrétaire-Général de la Société des Nations inviterait les Etats à proposer des candidats pour remplacer le juge japonais décédé. Selon toute probabilité, le Japon répondrait seul à cette invitation, et si d'autres Etats le faisaient, ils proposeraient certainement des japonais éminents. Le système du Président pourrait aisément aboutir à priver de toute représentation, pour une période de sept à huit années, le Japon, l'Italie, la France etc., ce qui est inadmissible.

Si, au contraire, c'est un des dix représentants des quarante petites puissances qui meurt, tous ces pays voudront être consultés sur le choix du nouveau juge. Il est possible, qu'ils ne soient pas d'avis que l'état, dont le juge décédé était ressortissant, doive toujours être représenté à la Cour. Il faudra leur fournir l'occasion d'exprimer cet avis. Ils doivent être soustraits au hasard des juges suppléants. La seule méthode qui offre toutes les garanties, c'est d'appliquer uniformément le système adopté pour les élections générales.

M. DE LAPRADELLE avait demandé la parole pour exprimer à peu près les mêmes idées que celles qui viennent d'être exposées par Mr. Root. Il voudrait cependant ajouter qu'il ne faut pas oublier que ce ne sont pas les Etats qui sont représentés par les juges, et qu'en théorie les juges à la Cour n'ont pas de nationalité.

Le système du Président ne lui semble guère pratique. La Cour est nommé pour neuf ans, et elle sera renouvelée après l'expiration de cette période. Si un juge doit sortir, c'est un autre juge, élu en même temps que lui, qui le remplace automatiquement: le suppléant entre comme juge titulaire. Mais il n'y a que quatre juges suppléants et onze uges titulaires prévus par le texte adopté par le Comité. Si dans les deux premières années de cette période, quatre juges mouraient, ce qui est après tout possible, tous les suppléants seraient entrés dans la Cour, et pendant les sept dernières années du terme, il ne resterait plus aucun suppléant pour remplir les vacances qui pourraient éventuellement se produire, et la Cour devrait rester incomplète. C'est pour cette raison que le suppléant ne devrait prendre la place d'un juge titulaire que temporairement et jusqu'à ce qu'une nouvelle élection puisse avoir lieu, c'est à dire jusqu'à la prochaine réunion de l'Assemblée; or, ces réunions seront certainement assez fréquentes; probablement, il y en aura au moins une tous les deux ans. Le juge titulaire, qui sera nommé pour remplacer le juge décédé, devra prendre son siège

customs of countries of the Far East. According to the system of the Root—Phillimore plan, on the contrary, the Secretary-General of the League of Nations would request the States to submit candidates to replace the deceased Japanese judge. Very probably Japan only would respond to this request, and if other States did so, they would certainly propose distinguished Japanese candidates. The President's system might easily deprive Japan, Italy or France, etc. of any representation for a period of seven or eight years: such a possibility could not be allowed to exist.

If, on the other hand, one of the ten representatives of the forty small States were to die, all these States would wish to be consulted upon the choice of the new judge. Quite possibly they would not consider that the State, of which the deceased judge was a subject, should continue to be represented on the Court. The opportunity to give expression to this opinion must be given to them. They ought not to be left to casual representation by deputy-judges. The only method which would provide the necessary guarantees was the uniform application of the system adopted for general elections.

M. DE LAPRADELLE had asked permission to speak in order to put forward very much the same ideas as those just expounded by Mr. Root. He wished, however, to add that it must not be forgotten that the judges would not represent States and that, in theory, the judges of the Court would have no nationality.

He did not think that the system proposed by the President was a really practical one. The members of the Court would be appointed for nine years, and there would be a fresh election at the end of this period. If a judge had to relinquish his post, another judge, elected at the same time as him, would automatically replace him. A deputy judge would take his place as an ordinary judge. Not more than four deputy judges and eleven judges, however, were provided for by the plan adopted by the Committee. Supposing that in the first two years of this period of nine years, four judges were to die, which after all was quite possible, then all the four deputies would be absorbed into the Court and during the remaining seven years, there would be no deputy judges left to fill possible vacancies, and therefore the Court would have to remain incomplete. Deputy-judges, therefore, should only replace regular judges temporarily and until a new election could be held, that is to say, until the next meeting of the Assembly. These meetings would certainly be fairly frequent; probably there would be a meeting at least every two years. A judge who was appointed to replace a deceased

pour la totalité d'un mandat ordinaire, c'est-à-dire pour neuf ans. Ainsi, il n'y aura jamais de renouvellement intégral de la Cour.

M. de Lapradelle proteste contre l'idée du renouvellement intégral, qui irait à l'encontre de la nécessité impérative d'assurer la continuité de la jurisprudence de la Cour. Il faut qu'à tout moment il y ait des hommes qui, n'étant pas venus en même temps, maintiennent parmi les nouveaux venus l'esprit des anciens. C'est en somme ce que vient de proposer Mr. Root.

Ainsi des raisons de fond viennent s'ajouter aux raisons politiques exposées par Mr. Root en faveur du système adopté par le projet Root—Phillimore.

M. LODER se rallie à M. de Lapradelle. La Cour doit toujours être complète. Les juges suppléants ne seront appelés à siéger qu'occasionnellement. Il est probable, d'ailleurs, que les suppléants auront accepté leur charge en vue du fait qu'ils ne sont pas obligés d'entrer comme titulaires à la Cour et d'y siéger, par conséquent, pendant de longues périodes. En tous cas, les vacances qui pourront se produire devront être remplies par des titulaires. Le système du Président susciterait des difficultés.

M. Loder se rallie à Lord Phillimore au sujet de la durée du mandat des juges qui sont sortis d'une élection partielle. Dans cet ordre d'idées, il fait observer que la période de neuf ans n'a pas eu pour but de réaliser un système de roulement, mais d'empêcher qu'un juge ne continue à siéger après neuf ans, si sa présence à la Cour ne semble pas désirable.

M. ADATCI fait observer qu'on discute maintenant une question qui intéresse principalement son pays. Il se rallie en principe à l'article 15 du projet Root—Phillimore; cependant il est d'avis qu'il pourrait être utile de tenir compte de certaines objections faites par M. Ricci-Busatti. M. Adatci se trouve spécialement d'accord avec la disposition de l'article 15 du projet, qui fournit un moyen de remplir les vacances occasionnelles. Il croit que les suppléants sont élus seulement en vue de remplir temporairement les sièges laissés vacants jusqu'à ce qu'une élection ait eu lieu.

M. HAGERUP croit que, même si le système préconisé par le Président était adopté, il pourrait être nécessaire, pour les raisons expliquées par M. de Lapradelle, d'arranger des élections partielles. Par conséquent, il se rallie au projet Root—Phillimore; cependant il croit qu'il

judge, must take his seat for the whole period of an ordinary appointment, that is for nine years. In this way, there would never be a complete renewal of the membership of the Court.

M. de Lapradelle protested against the idea of a complete renewal; it was directly opposed to the pressing need for ensuring the continuity of the Court's jurisprudence. There must always be some judges, who have already been members of the Court for some time, and can imbue the newcomers with the spirit of their predecessors. This was practically what Mr. Root had just proposed.

Thus, intrinsic arguments combined with the reasons of policy set forth by Mr. Root, to support the system adopted in the Root—Phillimore plan.

M. LODER agreed with M. de Lapradelle. The Court must always be complete. The deputy judges should only be called upon to sit as occasion required. Further, it was probable that a deputy judge would have accepted his post in consideration of the fact that he would not be obliged to undertake duty as a regular judge on the Court and, consequently, would not have to sit for long periods. In any case, any vacancies that might occur, must be filled by the appointment of regular judges. The system of the President would lead to difficulties.

M. Loder agreed with Lord Phillimore concerning the period for which judges chosen at by-elections should hold their appointment. In this connection he pointed out that the period of nine years was not intended to create a system of rotation, but to prevent a judge from continuing to serve upon the Court for more than nine years, if his presence there seemed no longer desirable.

M. ADATCI pointed out that the question now under discussion would interest principally his own country. In principle he supported Article 15 of the Root—Phillimore plan; however, he thought that it might be advisable to consider the objections put forward by M. Ricci-Busatti. M. Adatci particularly approved of the method in which the question of the filling of casual vacancies was dealt with in Article 15 of the plan. He thought that the deputies were only elected for the purpose of filling vacant seats temporarily, pending an election.

M. HAGERUP thought that even if the system advocated by the President were adopted, it might be necessary, for the reasons given by M. de Lapradelle, to hold by-elections. Consequently, he supported the Root—Phillimore plan; but he thought that M. Ricci Busatti's

faut tenir compte des observations de M. Ricci-Busatti: Il est en effet peu pratique d'obliger les groupes nationaux de la Cour Permanente d'Arbitrage de proposer le nombre total de candidats lorsqu'il s'agit seulement de remplir une vacance accidentelle. Dans cet ordre d'idées il propose une addition à l'article 15 du projet Root—Phillimore. Cette addition, qu'il communique au Président, est ainsi conçue:

„Dans ce cas, le nombre des candidats à pro-„poser par les groupes nationaux de la Cour per-„manente d'arbitrage ne doit pas dépasser le „double du nombre des juges ou des juges sup-„pléants à élire".

Cette addition devrait être insérée avant la dernière phrase de l'article.

Le PRESIDENT désire répondre à certains critiques adressées à son système. Il a été accusé de méconnaître la nécessité d'assurer la continuité de la jurisprudence de la Cour.

Il croit qu'on a beaucoup exagéré; la question n'est pas aussi grave.

Il explique l'idée qui est à la base de son projet. Tous les mandats sont conférés pour une durée de 9 ans. Si l'un des juges quitte la Cour, le suppléant devra siéger à sa place jusqu'à la prochaine réunion de l'Assemblée.

L'élection d'un nouveau juge titulaire, qui sera faite lors de cette réunion, doit-elle viser une période entière de 9 ans, ou seulement le temps qui reste à courir jusqu'à la fin du mandat? Les deux solutions ont leurs avantages et leurs désavantages. Il croit cependant qu'en adoptant le système de l'élection pour l'achèvement d'un mandat, on évitera beaucoup d'inconvénients. Il craint qu'avec l'autre système, la méthode des élections générales, adoptée par le Comité, ne fonctionne qu'une fois, la première.

Le Président propose le texte suivant:

„En ce cas, le suppléant remplira les fonctions de juge jusqu'à la prochaine Assemblée."

LORD PHILLIMORE indique qu'il est parfaitement d'avis, ainsi qu'il l'a déjà expliqué, que le juge suppléant doit rester en fonction jusqu'à l'entrée en office du nouveau juge titulaire, et il croit qu'on est d'accord sur ce point.

Toutefois, il peut être impossible de faire élire le nouveau juge à la première réunion de l'Assemblée qui suivra l'ouverture d'une vacance à la Cour: il faut prendre en considération le temps nécessaire pour la présentation des candidats. Le suppléant devra siéger pendant toute cette période, mais le nouveau titulaire devra être nommé aussitôt que possible par l'Assemblée, pour une période de 9 ans.

observations should be taken into account. It was hardly practical to oblige the national groups of the Permanent Court of Arbitration to submit the full number of candidates when it was only a question of filling a casual vacancy. In this connection, he proposed an addition to Article 15 of the Root—Phillimore plan. This addition, which he handed to the President, was worded as follows:

"In such cases, the number of candidates to be submitted by the national groups of the Permanent Court of Arbitration shall not be more than twice the number of judges or deputy judges to be elected."

This addition was to be inserted as a new sentence, after the word "appointments" in the Article, the last part of which was to form a separate sentence.

The PRESIDENT wished to reply to some criticisms levelled at his system. He had been accused of failing to recognise the necessity of assuring the continuity of the Court's jurisprudence.

He thought that there had been much exaggeration; the question was not nearly so serious.

He explained the idea upon which his plan was based. All the appointments were to be made for a period of 9 years. If a judge left the Court, a deputy would sit in his stead until the next meeting of the Assembly.

The question was, whether the election of a new judge, which would take place at this meeting, should be for a complete period of 9 years, or only for the unexpired portion of the period. Both solutions had advantages and disadvantages. He thought, however, that by adopting the system of election for the outstanding period of an appointment only, many difficulties would be avoided. He was afraid that, if the other system were adopted, the system adopted by the Committee for general elections would only operate once, that is to say upon the first occasion.

The President proposed the following:

"In such cases the deputy judge shall do duty as judge until the next meeting of the Assembly."

LORD PHILLIMORE said that he quite thought, as he had already explained, that the deputy judge should do duty until the new judge had taken up his appointment; he thought that the Committee was agreed upon this point.

It might, however, be impossible to elect the new judge at the first meeting of the Assembly following the creation of a vacancy in the Court; the time necessary for the nomination of candidates must be allowed for. The deputy should sit for the whole of this period, but the new regular judge should be appointed as soon as possible by the Assembly, for a period of 9 years.

Se référant ensuite à la formule soumise par M. Hagerup, Lord Phillimore demande quel serait exactement l'effet de cette formule quant au rôle de la Cour d'Arbitrage dans la présentation des candidats.

M. HAGERUP répond que son amendement n'aurait d'autre effet que de limiter le nombre des candidats que cette Cour serait appelée à proposer.

Le PRESIDENT donne lecture de l'amendement proposé par M. Hagerup (voir ci-dessus).

Après une courte discussion les membres du comité se trouvent d'accord pour ajouter à l'article 15 du projet Root—Phillimore l'amendement de M. Hagerup, afin de bien marquer que le nombre de candidats ne pourra, même dans le cas visé par cet amendement, excéder le chiffre de six.

On est également d'accord pour remplacer le mot „pas" dans la phrase „ne doit pas dépasser", par le mot „jamais".

Le Président donne lecture de l'article ainsi amendé, qui, sauf rédaction, est conçu de la manière suivante:

„Il sera pourvu à la nomination aux sièges de juges ou de juges suppléants devenus vacants, selon la méthode adoptée pour la première élection.

Dans ce cas (le cas d'élection partielle) le nombre des candidats à proposer par les groupes nationaux de la Cour permanente d'arbitrage, ne doit jamais dépasser le double du nombre des juges ou juges suppléants à élire. Dans chaque cas spécial l'élection visera la période de neuf ans".

M. FERNANDES rappelle au Comité qu'il s'est parfois trouvé obligé d'écarter des considérations logiques pour des considérations politiques. Mr. Root a soulevé des difficultés très graves lorsqu'il a indiqué qu'avec le système du Président, certains pays représentés à la Cour pourraient facilement perdre leur représentation. On lui a donné raison, très sagement, et c'est là une première infraction à la logique; car, en principe, on devrait admettre que les juges suppléants, par définition, deviendraient titulaires en cas de vacance.

M. Fernandes demande maintenant à Lord Phillimore de faire à son tour une concession aux exigences pratiques, en admettant que les juges titulaires choisis dans les élections partielles, ne seront nommés que pour le temps qui reste à courir du mandat de leur prédécesseur. C'est, selon M. Fernandes, la seule façon possible de faire fonctionner le système qu'on a adopté pour la nomination des juges.

Referring to the formula proposed by M. Hagerup, Lord Phillimore asked what exactly its effect would be upon the rôle of the Court of Arbitration in the nomination of candidates.

M. HAGERUP answered that his amendment could only have the effect of limiting the number of candidates that that Court would be called upon to submit.

The PRESIDENT read the amendment proposed by M. Hagerup (see above).

After a short discussion the members of the Committee agreed to add M. Hagerup's amendment to the 15th Article of the Root—Phillimore plan, in order to emphasise that the number of candidates could not, even in the case contemplated by this amendment, exceed six in number.

It was also agreed to replace the word "not" in the phrase "shall not be more than" by the word "never".

The President read the Article as thus amended; subject to amendments of form, it was worded as follows:

"Vacancies in the office of judge or supplementary judge shall be filled as in the case of original appointments.

In such cases (bye-elections) the number of candidates to be submitted by the national groups of the Permanent Court of Arbitration shall never be more than twice the number of judges or deputy judges to be elected. In every case the appointment shall be for the full term of nine years."

M. FERNANDES reminded the Committee that it was sometimes necessary to put political considerations before logical considerations. The difficulties put forward by Mr. Root when he had pointed out that, under the President's system, certain countries represented on the Court might easily lose their representation, were very serious. The Committee had admitted that he was right, and this in itself amounted to a first breach of the rules of logic; for theoretically, the deputy judges should, as their title implies, become full rank judges in the event of a vacancy.

M. Fernandes now asked Lord Phillimore, in his turn, to make a concession to practical requirements, and to agree that regular judges elected at by-elections should only be appointed for the unexpired portion of their prodecessors' mandate. In M. Fernandes' opinion this was the only possible way in which the system adopted for the appointment of judges could be made to work.

M. Fernandes croit qu'il sera facile de mettre d'accord pour une élection générale trente pays qui sont représentés par dix juges, tandis qu'il serait très difficile d'obtenir un accord sur une élection isolée. Il remarque qu'en tout cas, les grandes Puissances sont à l'abri; elles n'ont rien à perdre sous le système Root—Phillimore, tandis que les autres Etats risquent de voir aggraver les difficultés qu'ils doivent éprouver pour arriver à l'entente nécessaire.

M. DE LAPRADELLE demande à M. Fernandes ce que devient dans son système la continuité de la jurisprudence.

M. FERNANDES répond que les juges qui ont servi d'une façon satisfaisante, seront réélus. Il ajoute que si un changement de jurisprudence peut être amené par un changement de personnes, aucun système au monde ne pourra l'empêcher; et, en tout cas, ce point de vue a été déjà délaissé par l'acceptation du mandat temporaire des juges au lieu du mandat à vie.

LORD PHILLIMORE rappelle l'idée, déjà suggérée par lui, de diviser l'article 15 après le mot „élection". Il croit pouvoir constater que la majorité des membres, y compris Mr. Root et lui même, sont d'accord pour ne point admettre l'idée du Président de prendre un suppléant comme juge titulaire, pendant le temps qui reste à courir du mandat d'un titulaire décédé. Il croit cependant que les membres sont d'accord sur la partie de l'article qu'il vient de signaler.

Si l'accord est ainsi établi sur la nécessité d'avoir de nouveaux titulaires, reste à résoudre la question de savoir pour combien de temps ceux-ci seront nommés. Il y a des considérations d'ordre pratique qui militent en faveur des deux solutions possibles.

Lord Phillimore n'a pas négligé les difficultés qui, ainsi que l'a fait valoir M. Fernandes, découleront pour les petites Puissances du système Root—Phillimore. Mais ces difficultés sont contrebalancées par l'avantage de l'enchevêtrement des mandats. Lord Phillimore croit que beaucoup de membres appuient le système qu'il préconise justement à cause de cet avantage.

Le PRESIDENT met aux voix la première phrase de l'article 15 du projet Root—Phillimore. Elle est adoptée par le Comité.

Il met aux voix la seconde phrase du même article (amendement de M. Hagerup). Elle est éga-

M. Fernandes thought that it would be easy for the thirty countries represented by ten judges, to come to an agreement at a general election; whereas this would be very difficult at a by election. He pointed out that, in any case, the great Powers were protected; they would have nothing to lose under the Root—Phillimore system whereas the other States are exposed to the danger of seeing the difficulties, which they have to encounter in order to reach the necessary agreement, become greater.

M. DE LAPRADELLE asked M. Fernandes how the continuity of jurisprudence would be assured under his system.

M. FERNANDES replied that those judges whose service had been satisfactory would be reelected. He added that if a change in personnel could bring about a change in jurisprudence, no system in the world could prevent it; in any case this point of view had already been abandoned by the acceptance of the principle of temporary appointment instead of appointment for life.

LORD PHILLIMORE called attention to the suggestion he had already made, that is to say, to divide Article 15 into two, after the word "appointments". He thought he could state that the majority of the members, including Mr. Root and himself, were agreed not to accept the President's idea, according to which a deputy judge would become a regular judge for the unexpired portion of the appointment of a deceased regular judge. He thought, however, that the whole Committee accepted that part of the Article which he had just mentioned.

Presuming therefore that they were agreed upon the necessity of having new regular judges, the question of the period for which these should be appointed remained to be settled. There were practical considerations which militated in favour of two possible solutions.

Lord Phillimore had not overlooked the difficulties which, as M. Fernandes had pointed out, would arise for the small Powers under the Root—Phillimore system. But, these difficulties were counterbalanced by this advantage: the appointments would overlap. Lord Phillimore thought that many members would support the system he advocated precisely for this reason.

The PRESIDENT took a vote upon the first part of Article 15 of the Root—Phillimore plan. It was adopted by the Committee.

He then put the second sentence, consisting of M. Hagerup's amendment to the same Article,

lement adoptée; le Président déclare s'abstenir.

Le Président demande aux membres s'ils ont des observations à faire au sujet de la troisième phrase de l'article.

M. FERNANDES proposè que cette phrase soit rédigée de la manière suivante: „Dans chaque cas spécial, l'élection visera la période qui reste à accomplir par le juge sortant."

M. DE LAPRADELLE fait valoir que lorsqu'il ne reste qu'une ou deux années à courir jusqu'à l'expiration du mandat du juge sortant, le nouveau titulaire serait élu pour une période si courte qu'il serait difficile de trouver une personne disposée à accepter le poste.

Mr. ROOT déclare que l'argument de M. de Lapradelle relatif à la nécessité d'assurer la continuité de la jurisprudence de la Cour, a fait sur lui une grande impression. Cette continuité est encore plus importante en matière de droit international que lorsqu'il s'agit de la juridiction interne, puisque dans ce dernier cas on peut toujours suivre le droit positif, tandis que le juge international doit souvent se laisser guider par ses conceptions juridiques. L'argument de M. de Lapradelle ne peut pas être réfuté, si l'on se place au point de vue de l'effectivité de la Cour.

Mr. Root signale également la difficulté de s'assurer le concours d'un juge compétent pour une période très courte. Il ne pense pas qu'il soit difficile d'obtenir un accord sur le choix d'un bon juge lorsqu'il n'y a qu'une seule place à remplir. Quand il s'agit de l'élection d'un plus grand nombre de juges, le danger d'un marchandage est beaucoup plus grand.

Le PRESIDENT remarque que la dernière observation de Mr. Root frappe tout le système pour la nomination des juges, adopté par le Comité.

Après quoi il met aux voix l'amendement proposé par M. Fernandes.

MM. HAGERUP et RICCI-BUSATTI s'abstiennent.

L'amendement est rejeté par 5 voix contre 2.

M. DE LAPRADELLE déclare que la discussion antérieure a été inspirée par le souci de la Cour plutôt que par celui des juges, par des considérations d'ordre juridique plutôt que par des considérations politiques. Il demande qu'il soit fait mention de sa déclaration au procès-verbal.

to the vote. This was also adopted; the President abstained from voting.

The President asked the members whether they had any remarks to make concerning the third sentence of the article.

M. FERNANDES proposed that this sentence should be as follows: "Every special election shall be for the unexpired portion of the appointment of the out-going judge."

M. DE LAPRADELLE pointed out that if only one or two years of the out-going judges' appointment remained outstanding, the new judge would be elected for such a short time that it would be difficult to find any one prepared to accept the post.

Mr. ROOT stated that M. de Lapradelle's remarks concerning the necessity of ensuring the continuity of the Court's jurisprudence, had greatly impressed him. This continuity was still more important in international law than in the case of a national jurisdiction, since, in the latter case, positive law could always be applied, whereas an international judge must often be guided by his own conceptions of law. M. de Lapradelle's argument was unanswerable if considered from the point of view of the efficiency of the Court.

Mr. Root also drew attention to the difficulty there would be in obtaining a competent judge for a very short period. He did not think it would be difficult to agree upon the selection of a good judge when there was only one vacancy to fill. In the case of the election of a larger number, the danger of bargaining was much greater.

The PRESIDENT stated that Mr. Root's last remark affected the whole system of appointment of judges adopted by the Committee.

He then took a vote upon the amendment proposed by M. Fernandes.

Messrs. HAGERUP and RICCI-BUSATTI abstained from voting.

The amendment was rejected by five votes to two.

M. DE LAPRADELLE declared that the preceding discussion had been inspired by anxiety for the welfare of the Court rather than by the interests of the judges — by judicial rather than political considerations. He requested that this statement should be recorded in the Procès-Verbal.

Le PRESIDENT ouvre la discussion sur l'article 16 du projet Root—Phillimore. Il remarque que l'article 10, alinéa 3, de son avant-projet s'y rapporte. Il donne lecture de ces deux dispositions. Le Président distingue trois cas:

1. Un juge déclare au président de la Cour de ne pouvoir siéger; si le président est d'accord avec lui, le juge s'abstient.

2. Le juge fait une déclaration au président de la Cour qui n'en reconnaît pas le bien-fondé; dans ce cas l'affaire doit être portée devant la Cour.

3. Le président de la Cour estime que le juge doit s'abstenir; s'il y a désaccord entre le président et le juge, la décision doit être prise par la Cour elle-même.

Il serait, en effet, dangereux de laisser au président le droit de décider s'il y a lieu ou non que le juge s'abstienne.

LORD PHILLIMORE ramène la question à deux points:

1. Si un juge ne voit pas quel est son devoir, le président doit le lui suggérer.

2. Si le juge est trop consciencieux.

Lord Phillimore explique qu'en Angleterre il n'y a pas de règle positive au sujet de ces deux cas. Toutefois, un arrêt rendu par un juge qui a, soit directement, soit par sa femme, un intérêt pécuniaire dans une affaire, est nul. La stipulation expresse qui a été insérée dans le projet avait pour but de donner satisfaction aux idées continentales sur ce point.

Le PRESIDENT insiste sur les raisons pour lesquelles on ne peut donner au président de la Cour le droit de décider, en cas de désaccord entre lui et un juge.

M. LODER propose la suppression de la première phrase de l'article 16 du projet Root—Phillimore.

LORD PHILLIMORE y consent: il n'insiste pas pour maintenir cette partie de l'article qui y avait été introduite dans un but de conciliation. La récusation est une institution continentale dont il ne comprend pas bien la nécessité.

M. LODER pense également que la phrase est superflue. Si une partie trouve qu'un juge a un interêt direct dans une affaire, elle pourra toujours le faire récuser; seulement elle ne pourra pas le faire dans les conditions posées dans l'article 16.

The PRESIDENT opened the discussion of the 16th Article of the Root—Phillimore plan, and stated that Article 10, Paragraph 3 of his own plan dealt with the same subject. He read both these clauses. He distinguished three possible cases:

1. A judge declares to the president of the Court that he cannot sit; if the president agrees, the judge withdraws.

2. The judge acts as in (1); if the President is not of the same opinion, the matter must be taken before the Court.

3. The president of the Court thinks that the judge ought not to sit. If the president and the judge do not agree, the point must be decided by the Court itself.

It would indeed be dangerous to allow the president to have the right of deciding whether or not the judge should sit.

LORD PHILLIMORE suggested two possible contingencies:

1. If a judge did not see his duty clearly, the president should suggest it to him.

2. A judge might be too conscientious.

Lord Phillimore explained that in England there was no definite rule for these two cases, but a decision, made by a judge who, either personally or through his wife, had a financial interest in the case, was void. The express stipulation inserted in the plan was intended to satisfy continental ideas on this point.

The PRESIDENT laid emphasis on the reasons against giving the president of the Court the power of decision in the event of a difference of opinion between him and a judge.

M. LODER proposed that the first sentence of Article 16 of the Root—Phillimore plan should be deleted.

LORD PHILLIMORE agreed; he attached no great importance to the retention of this part of the Article; it had been introduced in order to reconcile opposing views. The right of challenge was a continental institution, and he did not really see the necessity for it.

M. LODER also thought that the sentence was superfluous. If a party thought that a certain judge had a personal interest in the case, that party could always arrange for his exclusion from the case, but would not be able to do so under the provisions of Article 16.

M. RICCI-BUSATTI prie M. Loder de bien vouloir expliquer quelle sorte de récusation il accepte et quelle sorte il repousse.

M. LODER répond qu'il n'admet pas la récusation qui permet aux parties d'exclure des juges, jusqu'à ce que la cour soit réduite à un petit noyau. Le seule récusation qu'il admet est celle qui est fondée sur un intérêt personnel dans l'affaire.

M. FERNANDES se rallie à M. Loder; il ajoute que si le droit de récusation n'est pas formellement admis, il n'existe pas. Dans ces conditions, il est inutile de maintenir la première phrase de l'article 16.

Au sujet de la 2ème phrase, M. Fernandes attire l'attention sur l'article 12 du projet soumis par M. Bevilaqua. Selon le projet Root—Phillimore, un Etat qui est partie à un litige et qui n'est pas représenté à la Cour par un de ses ressortissants, doit envoyer un juge extraordinaire. M. Fernandes trouve que ce procédé est juste, si l'on n'exclut pas le juge ressortissant de l'autre partie. Cependant, il préfère la solution proposée par M. Bevilaqua, qui consistait à exclure tout ressortissant d'un des Etats en litige, du droit de siéger à la Cour. En effet, on se trouverait en face de l'une ou de l'autre de deux éventualités possibles: Ou le juge national est un homme capable d'impartialité vis-à-vis de son Etat, ou il ne l'est pas. Dans le deuxième cas, il est indésirable comme juge. Dans le premier, si sa conscience de juge l'obligeait à émettre un vote contraire à l'Etat dont il est ressortissant, on lui créerait une situation vraiment malheureuse. Très probablement, il se mettrait en opposition avec l'opinion publique nationale, dont la moralité moyenne ne serait pas à la hauteur de la sienne et qui, toujours influencée par des passions dans l'appréciation des questions internationales, le condamnerait sans le compendre.

LORD PHILLIMORE fait valoir que les observations de M. Fernandes se rapportent à l'article 27 du projet Root—Phillimore.

M. FERNANDES répond que si l'on adopte maintenant l'article 16 sans tenir compte de ces observations, il faudra y revenir dans la suite.

Le PRESIDENT dit qu'on pourrait adopter l'article sous réserve des observations de M. Fernandes.

M. RICCI-BUSATTI asked M. Loder to explain what forms of challenge he accepted, and what forms he rejected.

M. LODER replied that he could not accept a system of challenge which would allow the parties to exclude so many judges that only a small nucleus would remain. The only right of challenge that he could admit was that founded upon personal interest in the case.

M. FERNANDES agreed with M. Loder; he added that if the right of challenge were not formally mentioned, it would not exist. Under these circumstances it was unseless to retain the first sentence of Article 16.

Concerning the second sentence, M. Fernandes drew attention to Article 12 of the plan submitted by M. Bevilaqua. According to the Root—Phillimore plan, a State, which was a party in a case and which was not represented on the Court by one of its subjects, must send a special judge. M. Fernandes thought that this procedure was just, if the national judge of the other party were not excluded. He, however, preferred the solution submitted by M. Bevilaqua; that is to say, the exclusion of any subject of any of the States concerned in the case from sitting upon the Court. As a matter of fact there were only two possible alternatives: the judge would either be capable of impartiality towards his own Country, or he would not; in the latter case he would be an undesirable judge, in the former, if his conscience as a judge compelled him to vote against his own country, he would be put in a very unenviable position. Very likely he would become embroiled with national public opinion, as the average moral standard would not be as high as his own, and public opinion, always influenced by its feelings in international questions, would condemn without understanding him.

LORD PHILLIMORE pointed out that M. Fernandes' remarks referred to Art. 27 of the Root—Phillimore plan.

M. FERNANDES answered that if Article 16 were to be adopted now without considering these points, the subject must be returned to later on.

The PRESIDENT said that the Committee might adopt the Article, subject to further consideration of M. Fernandes' remarks.

M. DE LAPRADELLE propose la suppression de la première phrase de l'article 16. L'idée exprimée dans cette phrase peut être sousentendue. Il est difficile de transplanter ici des règles de droit interne. Si les parties ont des raisons spéciales pour désirer qu'un certain juge cède sa place, elles auront toujours le moyen de les faire valoir auprès du Président de la Cour ou auprès des juges.

Après un échange de vues, au cours duquel le PRESIDENT propose d'insérer après les mots „si pour des raisons déterminées" les mots „tenant au fonctionnement normal de la Cour", et M. RICCI-BUSATTI, l'insertion au même endroit des mots „que chaque partie pourra lui soumettre", les membres du Comité se mettent d'accord sur les points suivants:

1. La première phrase doit être supprimée.

2. La rédaction doit exprimer clairement que le président de la Cour ne pourra jamais décider, en cas de désaccord entre lui et un membre, au sujet du devoir de ce dernier de céder sa place, cette décision étant réservée à la Cour.

3. L'addition proposée par le Président doit être écartée, puisqu'elle forcerait la Cour à ouvrir toute procédure par un procès fait au juge.

Sur la remarque du Président qu'une partie aura toujours le moyen de faire connaître ses objections contre tel ou tel juge, sans qu'il soit nécessaire de formuler cette faculté dans le texte du statut, M. RICCI-BUSATTI retire sa proposition.

Le PRESIDENT met aux voix l'article 16 du projet Root—Phillimore. Cet article est adopté, sauf rédaction et sous bénéfice des points sur lesquels les membres viennent de se mettre d'accord, ainsi que de la remarque susdite.

LORD PHILLIMORE a la parole pour une motion d'ordre. Après mûre réflexion et après avoir consulté ses collègues il est arrivé à la conclusion que la première lecture pourra être achevée mardi, ou au plus tard mercredi prochain. Le reste de la semaine pourra être consacré aux travaux du Comité de rédaction, puis, pendant la semaine suivante jusqu'à vendredi le Comité pourra s'occuper de la seconde lecture. Ainsi il sera possible de présenter au Conseil de la Société des Nations, se réunissant à Saint Sébastien le 27, le projet et le rapport du Comité.

M. DE LAPRADELLE proposed that the first sentence of Article 16 should be deleted. The idea contained in this sentence could be taken for granted. It was difficult to transplant the rules of national law into international law. If the contesting parties had special reasons for wishing that a certain judge should give up his seat, they would always be able to state them to the President of the Court, or to the judges.

After a discussion, during which the PRESIDENT proposed that the words "concerning the normal operation of the Court" be inserted after the words "if for a specific reason", and M. RICCI-BUSATTI proposed that the words "which either party may submit to it" be inserted at the same place; the members of the Committee agreed upon the following points:

1. The first sentence to be deleted.

2. The wording must clearly state that in the event of disagreement between the President of the Court and a member concerning the question of the latter giving up his seat, the decision can never be made by the former; it is reserved for the Court.

3. The addition proposed by the President cannot be accepted, since it would force the Court to commence all proceedings by an enquiry concerning the judges.

M. RICCI-BUSATTI, following upon an observation made by the President, to the effect that a party would always be able to make known its objections to a particular judge, without its being necessary to make a definite provision to this effect in the statute, withdrew his proposal.

The PRESIDENT put Article 16 of the Root—Phillimore plan to the vote. It was adopted, subject to amendments of form and to the points which the members had just agreed upon, also to the remark just made by the President.

LORD PHILLIMORE obtained permission to speak upon a point of order. After much reflection, and after discussion with his colleagues, he had come to the conclusion that the first reading could be ready on Tuesday, or, at the latest, on Wednesday next. The rest of the week could be devoted to the work of the drafting Committee; then the Committee could employ the following week until Friday for the second reading. In this way it would be possible to submit the plan and the report to the Council of the League of Nations which was to meet at San Sebastian on the 27th of July.

Lord Phillimore ajoute que le rapporteur accepte, en ce qui le concerne, ces arrangements.

M. ADATCI demande à Lord Phillimore si ce sera le rapport définitif et le texte adopté en seconde lecture qui seront présentés au Conseil.

LORD PHILLIMORE répond affirmativement.

Le PRESIDENT pense que la proposition de Lord Phillimore est pratique; il tâchera d'en tenir compte, dans la mesure du possible. Il remarque cependant qu'il reste encore quelques points spéciaux à discuter. Lui-même a l'intention de soumettre au Comité une proposition relative à la création d'une Haute Cour de Justice qui aurait à juger, pour l'avenir, les crimes contre l'ordre public et le droit des gens universel.

Il invite les membres qui voudront de même soumettre des propositions, à les communiquer au Président lundi matin pour qu'elles puissent être prises en considération.

Le Comité continuera lundi la discussion du projet Root—Phillimore.

La séance est levée à 12.30 heures de l'après-midi.

Le Président :
(signé) Brn. DESCAMPS.

Le Secrétaire-Général :
(signé) D. ANZILOTTI.

Lord Phillimore added that the Reporter agreed with him concerning these proposed arrangements.

M. ADATCI asked Lord Phillimore, whether it was to be the final report and the text as adopted at the second reading which were to be submitted to the Council.

LORD PHILLIMORE replied in the affirmative.

THE PRESIDENT thought that Lord Phillimore's proposal was practical; he would try as far as possible to act upon it. He remarked, however, that some special points still remained to be discussed: thus he himself intended to submit to the Committee a proposal dealing with the creation of a High Court of Justice which was to try future crimes against public order and the universal law of nations.

He asked the members who also wished to submit proposals, to deliver them to the President on Monday morning, so that they might be considered.

The Committee was to continue the discussion of the Root—Phillimore plan on Monday.

The meeting closed at 12.30 p. m.

The President :
(signed) Brn. DESCAMPS.

The Secretary-General :
(signed) D. ANZILOTTI.

22IÈME SÉANCE (non-publique), tenue au Palais de la Paix à La Haye, le 12 juillet 1920.

Présidence de M. le BARON DESCAMPS.

Sont présents: tous les membres du Comité (à l'exception de M. Bevilaqua); M. Fernandes; Mr. James Brown Scott; le Secrétaire particulier de M. Adatci; les membres du Secrétariat.

La séance est ouverte à 9.40 heures du matin.

Le PRESIDENT, avant de reprendre la discussion des dispositions du projet Root—Phillimore concernant l'organisation de la Cour, désire faire une proposition relative à l'ordre du jour. Plusieurs membres ont exprimé le désir d'être fixés sur la distribution du temps qui reste encore au Comité pour achever ses travaux. A ce propos, le Président, se conformant à l'idée suggérée l'autre jour par Lord Phillimore, propose de continuer la discussion en première lecture pendant les séances d'aujourd'hui et de demain, pour consacrer le reste de la semaine aux travaux du Comité de rédaction et à la préparation du rapport. Les séances seraient reprises lundi prochain pour la seconde lecture. S'il était impossible d'achever demain la première lecture, les questions pendantes seraient renvoyées au Comité de rédaction, qui ferait sur ces questions un rapport sommaire, pour être soumis au Comité lundi prochain. Les membres qui auraient des propositions à faire pourraient les envoyer au Comité de rédaction.

La proposition du Président est adoptée.

Le Président donne lecture de l'article 17 du projet Root—Phillimore. Il fait remarquer que l'article 3 de son avant-projet a trait à la même question.

LORD PHILLIMORE se rallie à l'article 3 de l'avant-projet du Président.

Cet article est adopté sans discussion.

Le PRESIDENT donne alors lecture de l'article 18 du projet Root—Phillimore.

22ND MEETING (Private), held at the Peace Palace, the Hague, on July 12th, 1920.

BARON DESCAMPS in the chair.

Present: all the members of the Committee (except M. Bevilaqua); M. Fernandes; Mr. James Brown Scott; the private secretary of M. Adatci; the members of the Secretariat.

The meeting opened at 9.40 a.m.

The PRESIDENT, before recommencing the discussion of the Root—Phillimore plan, concerning the organisation of the Court, wished to make a proposal concerning the Agenda. Several members had expressed the wish that the distribution of the time still remaining for the completion of the work of the Committee should be settled. In this connection, and in conformity with the suggestion put forward at the last meeting by Lord Phillimore, the President proposed that the first reading should be continued during the present meeting and that of Tuesday, and that the rest of the week should be devoted to the work of the drafting Committee and to the preparation of the report. The meetings would be recommenced upon the following Monday for the second reading. If it were found impossible to finish the first reading on Tuesday, the questions left outstanding would be handed over to the drafting Committee, which would prepare a brief report on these questions, to be submitted to the Committee on Monday next. Those members who had proposals to make could send them to the drafting Committee.

The President's proposal was adopted.

The President read Article 17 of the Root—Phillimore plan. He pointed out that Article 3 of his own plan dealt with the same question.

LORD PHILLIMORE accepted Article 3 of the President's plan.

This Article was adopted without discussion.

THE PRESIDENT then read Article 18 of the Root—Phillimore plan.

LORD PHILLIMORE observe que tout le monde est d'accord sur la nécessité d'un serment à prêter ou d'une déclaration à faire par les juges: on peut cependant discuter sur la formule. Lord Phillimore croit que celle qu'il a proposée, d'accord avec Mr. Scott, peut être adoptée avec avantage.

M. HAGERUP trouve cette formule un peu trop étroite. Il voudrait lui donner un peu plus d'ampleur; par exemple, y ajouter une expression indiquant que les juges doivent juger selon leur conscience. Il demande à Lord Phillimore et à M. de Lapradelle quelles sont les formules en usage en Angleterre et en France.

Le PRESIDENT constate qu'il faut distinguer ici deux points différents:

1. doit-on exiger un serment ou simplement une déclaration?

2. quelle sera la formule à employer?

Quant au premier point, le Président préférerait le serment, mais il peut se rallier au système d'une déclaration; quant à la formule, il croit que le Comité pourrait utilement s'inspirer des considérations de M. Hagerup. Mais il se demande si l'on peut improviser une formule.

Mr. ROOT attire l'attention sur la formule adoptée dans le projet de 1907, qui lui semble bonne. Elle est ainsi conçue:

„Avant de prendre possession de leur siège, les juges et juges suppléants doivent.... prêter serment ou faire une affirmation solennelle d'exercer leurs fonctions avec impartialité et en toute conscience."

Après une courte discussion sur une question de rédaction, le PRESIDENT résume ainsi la conclusion obtenue: Les juges doivent faire une déclaration affirmant leur volonté d'exercer leurs fonctions dans les conditions exprimées par l'article 5 du projet de 1907, et de se conformer au droit international.

M. RICCI-BUSATTI voudrait éviter que l'on préjugeât, par cette dernière phrase, de la question de savoir si la Cour pourra, à la demande éventuelle des parties, statuer comme tribunal arbitral en s'écartant de l'application pure et simple des règles du droit international. L'appel à la conscience et à l'esprit de justice est, à son avis, suffisant.

LORD PHILLIMORE said that it was generally admitted that judges must take an oath or make a declaration. The wording, however, was a matter for discussion. He thought that the one which he had proposed, in agreement with Mr. Scott, might advantageously be adopted.

M. HAGERUP thought that this wording was rather too restricted. He wished to amplify it a little; for instance, by adding an expression indicating that the judges must deliver judgment according to the dictates of their conscience. He asked Lord Phillimore and M. de Lapradelle what were the forms of oath in use in England and France.

The PRESIDENT said that a distinction must be made between two different points:

1. Must an oath be taken, or would a declaration suffice?

2. What wording was to be adopted?

With reference to the first of these points, the President preferred an oath, but was prepared to accept a declaration. As to the wording, he thought that the Committee might profitably make use of M. Hagerup's ideas; but he doubted whether a suitable wording could be improvised.

Mr. ROOT called attention to the wording adopted in the 1907 project, which he thought was a good one. It was as follows:

"Before taking their seat the judges and deputy judges must swear or... make a solemn affirmation to exercise their fonctions impartially and conscientiously."

The PRESIDENT after a short discussion upon a question of drafting, summed up as follows: The judges must make a declaration affirming their intention to carry out their duties according to the conditions laid down in Article 5 of the project of 1907, and further, to conform to the rules of international law.

M. RICCI-BUSATTI thought that, by the inclusion of the last sentence, the question as to whether the Court could, if so requested by the parties, pronounce judgment as a tribunal of arbitration without confining itself to the strict application of rules of international law, would be prejudiced. He wished to avoid this. In his opinion, it would suffice to appeal to the conscience and to the sense of justice of the judges.

Après un échange de vues, LORD PHILLIMORE propose de mettre aux voix purement et simplement la formule de 1907.

Le PRESIDENT met au vote cette formule. Elle est adoptée.

Le Président donne lecture de l'article 19 du projet Root—Phillimore.

LORD PHILLIMORE ayant constaté l'accord existant sur cet article, et le PRESIDENT ayant déclaré que la question du domicile des juges sera discutée plus tard, l'article est adopté sans discussion.

Le PRESIDENT donne lecture de l'article 20 du projet Root—Phillimore. Cet article correspond à l'article 12 de l'avant-projet du Président.

LORD PHILLIMORE constate qu'une disposition du même ordre se retrouve dans tous les projets.

M. RICCI-BUSATTI désire qu'il soit bien entendu que les juges ne jouiront des privilèges diplomatiques que dans l'exercice effectif de leurs fonctions; il remarque que l'opinion publique n'est pas très favorable, en général, à l'élargissement de ces privilèges.

Après discussion, le Comité se trouve d'accord pour reconnaître que les juges doivent jouir des privilèges diplomatiques dans les mêmes conditions que les diplomates: ils doivent, par exemple, en jouir, non seulement pendant leur séjour en Hollande, mais aussi dans les pays qu'ils traversent pour se rendre à leur poste, ou à leur retour.

LORD PHILLIMORE attire l'attention sur la formule de l'article 5 du projet de 1907, qui a trait à cette question.

M. DE LAPRADELLE pense qu'il y a lieu d'améliorer cette formule qui, lorsqu'elle a été adoptée pour la première fois en 1899, était destinée à répondre à une situation différente de celle d'aujourd'hui. Il voudrait y insérer, par exemple, une expression disant que les juges jouiront des privilèges seulement „durant le terme de leurs fonctions" ou „pendant le temps de leurs fonctions."

On se met cependant d'accord sur l'adoption de la formule de 1907 qui est ainsi conçue: „Les juges jouissent des privilèges et des immunités diplomatiques dans l'exercice de leurs fonctions et en dehors de leur pays".

After an exchange of opinions, LORD PHILLIMORE proposed that the wording of 1907 alone should be voted upon.

The PRESIDENT took a vote upon this wording, and it was adopted.

The President read Article 19 of the Root—Phillimore plan.

LORD PHILLIMORE stated that the members of the Committee were in agreement concerning this Article, and the PRESIDENT said that the question of the domicile of judges would be discussed later; the Article was thereupon adopted without discussion.

The PRESIDENT then read Article 20 of the Root—Phillimore plan. This Article corresponds to Article 12 of the President's plan.

LORD PHILLIMORE said that a clause of the same kind was contained in all plans.

M. RICCI-BUSATTI wanted it to be clearly understood that diplomatic privileges would only be given to judges during the actual performance of their duties. He remarked that public opinion, generally speaking, did not favour the extension of these privileges.

After a discussion, the Committee agreed that the judges should enjoy diplomatic privileges under the same conditions as diplomats; for instance, they should enjoy these rights not only during their residence in Holland, but also in the countries through which they would have to travel on their way to and from their duties.

LORD PHILLIMORE called attention to the wording contained in Article 5 of the project of 1907, which dealt with this question.

M. DE LAPRADELLE thought that this wording could be improved; at the time of its adoption in 1899 it had been intended to meet different requirements from those now existing. He wished for instance to insert an expression to the effect that the judges would only enjoy such privileges during the period of their appointment or during the performance of their duties.

The Committee however agreed to adopt the wording of 1907, which was as follows: "The judges enjoy diplomatic privileges and immunities in the exercise of their functions and outside their own country."

Le PRESIDENT donne lecture des articles 21 et 22 du projet Root—Phillimore.

A la demande de LORD PHILLIMORE ces deux articles seront discutés en même temps.

Le PRESIDENT remarque que l'article 14 de son avant-projet traite du même sujet.

LORD PHILLIMORE déclare qu'il préfère le texte du Président, d'après lequel le traitement des juges serait fixé par l'Assemblée et non par le Conseil.

Le PRESIDENT préfère, de son côté, se rallier maintenant au texte du projet Root—Phillimore qui donne au Conseil le droit de fixer l'indemnité.

LORD PHILLIMORE rappelle que, lors d'une des premières discussions, le Comité, sur l'initiative de Mr. Root, s'est mis d'accord pour omettre, dans le projet qu'il doit présenter, de mentionner le montant du traitement des juges.

Si, cependant, le Comité désire indiquer, soit dans le texte même, soit dans le rapport — et de préférence dans celui-ci — une somme déterminée, Lord Phillimore suggère que l'on se base sur celui des plus hauts magistrats anglais, c'est-à-dire £ 6.000.—.

Le PRESIDENT déclare qu'il préfère l'article de Lord Phillimore et retire le sien.

M. LODER est d'avis que c'est le statut et non pas le Conseil qui doit fixer le traitement des juges. Il faut en tous cas que le traitement ne soit pas fixé annuellement. Si, après un certain temps, on désire le modifier, on peut le faire en modifiant le statut. Comme le Comité n'est chargé de faire qu'un projet, il n'y a pas de raison de ne pas proposer une somme; le Conseil aura la faculté de ne pas l'accepter. Si le montant ne devait pas être fixé par le statut, M. Loder préférerait, en général, l'idée du Président de conférer à l'Assemblée le droit de le fixer.

M. Loder remarque que les observations qu'il vient de faire au sujet de l'article 21, se rapportent également à l'article 22. A propos de cet article, il remarque encore que la disposition d'après laquelle le Conseil dressera un plan ne lui semble pas claire. Le Président a proposé que les juges aient droit à l'éméritat comme pension: à son avis le montant de la pension devrait être fixé dans le statut indépendamment de l'éméritat.

The PRESIDENT read Articles 21 and 22 of the Root—Phillimore plan.

At LORD PHILLIMORE'S request, these two Articles were to be discussed at the same time.

The PRESIDENT pointed out that Article 14 of his plan dealt with the same subject.

LORD PHILLIMORE said that he preferred the President's text, according to which the salary of the judges was to be fixed by the Assembly and not by the Council.

The PRESIDENT, on the other hand, now preferred the text of the Root—Phillimore plan which gave the right of fixing the salary to the Council.

LORD PHILLIMORE recalled that, at one of the first meetings, the Committee had agreed, at Mr. Root's suggestion, not to mention the amount of the judges' salaries in the plan to be submitted.

If, however, the Committee, wished to indicate a definite amount either in the plan itself, or in the report—preferably in the report—Lord Phillimore suggested the same sum as that paid to the highest English judges, that is to say, £ 6.000.

The PRESIDENT said that he withdrew his Article, as he thought that Lord Phillimore's was better.

M. LODER thought that the statute of the Court should fix the salaries of the judges, and not the Council. In any case the salary must not be fixed annually. If, after a certain time, it were desired to alter the salary, this might be done by amending the statute. As the Committee's task was only to prepare a draft-scheme, there was no reason why it should not propose a sum; the Council need not accept the suggestion made. If the amount were not to be fixed by the statute, M. Loder would, generally speaking, prefer the President's idea; namely to give the right of fixing the salary to the Assembly.

M. Loder said that the remarks he had just made concerning Article 21 applied equally to Article 22. With regard to the latter article, he said further that the clause providing for the preparation of a plan by the Council, did not seem to him to be clear. The President had proposed that the judges should be entitled to their salary as a pension on retirement. In his opinion the amount of the pension should be laid down in the statute, quite independently of any comparison with the salary.

Le PRESIDENT explique que l'article 22 du projet Root—Phillimore repose sur l'idée de donner aux juges une pension variant avec la durée effective de leurs fonctions.

M. FERNANDES se range à l'opinion de M. Loder, qui veut que le traitement soit fixé par l'Assemblée de la Société des Nations. Comme tous les Etats participeront au paiement de ces traitements, ils ont le droit de dire leur mot sur cette question.

Le projet présenté par le Comité ne doit pas mentionner une somme fixe, car le Comité n'est pas en possession des renseignements qui lui seraient nécessaires pour en déterminer le montant.

M. Fernandes insiste pour que les juges obtiennent la garantie qu'ils recevront pendant toute la durée de leur mandat le même traitement que celui qui leur est accordé au moment de leur entrée en fonctions. Il propose, dans cet ordre d'idées, l'amendement suivant: insérer après les mots „à fixer" dans l'article 21, les mots „pour la durée de leur mandat".

M. DE LAPRADELLE ajoute qu'il est désirable que le traitement soit le même pour tous les juges.

M. RICCI-BUSATTI rappelle les liens qui existent entre la question du traitement des juges et toute l'organisation de la Cour. Il reconnaît que ses idées sur ce dernier point n'ont pas été acceptées par la majorité du Comité. Toutefois, il croit devoir rappeler quelle serait la conséquence de son système pour le traitement des juges: il pourrait s'accorder, d'ailleurs, avec ce qui a été décidé concernant leur nomination: l'indemnité serait proportionnelle (sauf pour le Président) aux périodes de service effectif; il y aurait lieu en même temps d'accorder au juge un certain traitement annuel fixe. Il est convaincu que les juges n'auront pas beaucoup à faire; il vaudrait donc mieux les laisser résider dans leurs pays et s'occuper de leurs affaires; dans ce cas, le système qu'il vient de proposer, lui semble le meilleur. Mais il reconnaît que s'ils doivent résider à La Haye, et s'ils sont obligés de renoncer à toute autre occupation, la question du traitement se pose d'autre façon.

M. Ricci Busatti a entendu exprimer des idées bien différentes au sujet de la résidence des juges; selon M. Loder ils siégeront „au moins six mois par an", tandis que selon Lord Phillimore, ils ne le feraient probablement pas plus de deux ou trois mois, et seulement s'il y a des affaires à examiner. Tout dépend donc de la ques-

The PRESIDENT explained that Article 22 of the Root—Phillimore plan was based upon the idea of giving the judges a pension which would vary according to the actual duration of their appointments.

M. FERNANDES agreed with M. Loder in wishing the salary to be fixed by the Assembly of the League of Nations. As all the States would share in the payment of these salaries they have a right to express their opinions upon the subject.

The plan submitted by the Committee must not mention a definite amount because the Committee was not in possession of the necessary information to enable it to fix this sum.

M. Fernandes insisted that the salary which was paid to the judges when they first took up their appointment must be guaranteed to them for the whole length of their appointment. With this object he proposed the following amendment: the words "for the period of their appointment" to be inserted after the words "to be fixed" in Article 21.

M. DE LAPRADELLE added that it was desirable that the salaries of all the judges should be the same.

M. RICCI-BUSATTI pointed out the close connection which existed between the question of the salary of the judges and the whole organisation of the Court. He realised that his point of view upon this matter was not that of the majority of the Committee. Nevertheless, he felt that he must remind the Committee of the way in which his system for the payment of judges would work out; this system would also fit in with the decision taken with regard to the appointment of judges. Payments would be made in proportion to the periods of actual duty (except in the case of the President); a small fixed annual salary might also be granted to the judges. He was convinced that the judges would not have much to do; it would therefore be better to allow them to live in their own countries and to engage in their own work; under such circumstances, the system he had just proposed seemed to him to be the best. He admitted, however, that if the judges had to live at the Hague, and if they were obliged to give up all other work, the question of salary would be quite different.

M. Ricci-Busatti had heard very different ideas put forward concerning the residence of the judges; according to M. Loder the judges would sit for at least six months every year; while ac-

tion de savoir si la Cour devra fonctionner pour un temps plus ou moins long. Or, il ne croit pas qu'il y ait lieu de s'attendre à ce que les rapports des Etats changent radicalement avec la constitution de la Cour de Justice. Quelques auteurs du Pacte ont peut-être eu l'idée que la Société des Nations était quelque chose de tout à fait nouveau; cette idée n'est pas exacte; on se tromperait également si l'on pensait que la Cour de Justice va donner un nouvel aspect aux relations internationales: qu'on se borne à espérer que la justice et le droit seront mieux respectés. Pendant quinze ans — de 1899 à 1914 — il n'y a eu effectivement que onze arbitrages, devant la Cour de La Haye; la plupart des solutions ont été achevées, à peu près en deux semaines. Cette expérience semble justifier l'opinion que les juges ne seront pas très occupés.

Dans ces conditions, il ne croit pas qu'il y ait lieu de leur donner une rémunération fixe très élevée. Si le Comité est d'un autre avis, M. Ricci-Busatti s'abstiendra de voter, afin de ne pas appuyer une solution qui, à son avis, s'écarte de la réalité des choses.

cording to Lord Phillimore, they would probably not do so for more than two or three months, and only if there were cases to be dealt with. Thus the whole question depended upon the time during which the Court would sit.

He did not think that there was any reason to suppose that relations between States would radically alter with the formation of the Court of Justice. Some of the authors of the Covenant perhaps thought that the League of Nations was something quite new; but this was not so. It would also be a mistake to imagine that the Court of Justice would give a new aspect to international relations: all that could be hoped was that law and justice would be held in greater respect. During the fifteen years—from 1899 to 1914—there were only eleven effectual cases of arbitration before the Hague Court; the greater number of these cases were completed in about two weeks. This would appear to justify the opinion that the judges would not be very busy.

Under these circumstances, he did not think that there was any occasion to give them a high rate of fixed salary. If the Committee thought otherwise, M. Ricci-Busatti would abstain from voting, in order to refrain from giving his support to an arrangement which in his opinion lost sight of realities.

D'après M. HAGERUP, la question qu'on est en train de discuter est grave et délicate. Si l'indemnité n'est pas très considérable, il sera difficile dans certains pays de trouver une personne compétente disposée à accepter la dignité de juge. D'autre part, si on donne aux juges une rémunération par trop élevée en proportion de leur travail, on rendra la Cour impopulaire, et cela nuira à son prestige.

M. Hagerup se demande également quelle sera, sous le rapport des traitements, la situation faite aux juges suppléants. Doivent-ils être assimilés ou non aux juges titulaires? Personnellement M. Hagerup croit que pour les juges suppléants le système préconisé par M. Ricci-Busatti, c'est-à-dire un système de traitement proportionné à la durée effective des fonctions, peut être adopté.

Enfin, il faut prendre en considération la question du remboursement des frais de voyage.

La suggestion de M. Loder de faire proposer par le Comité lui-même le montant des traitements, ne paraît pas opportune à M. Hagerup. Le Comité risquerait de compromettre son travail. Il est, en effet, problématique que l'on obtienne l'unanimité du Conseil et de l'Assemblée sur une question de cette nature; la question des salaires est toujours une pierre d'achoppement. Mais il ne voit

In M. HAGERUP's opinion, the question under discussion was very important and delicate. If the salary were not very considerable it would, in certain countries, be difficult to find a competent person prepared to accept a post as judge. On the other hand, if the judges were remunerated upon a scale which was too high in proportion to their work, the Court would be made unpopular and its prestige would be damaged.

M. Hagerup also wondered what would be the position of deputy judges in the matter of salaries. Should they be treated in the same way as regular judges, or not? Personnally M. Hagerup thought that for the deputy-judges, the system advocated by M. Ricci-Busatti might be adopted; that is to say, a system of payment proportionate to the length of their tours of duty.

Lastly the question of the repayment of travelling expenses must be considered.

M. Loder's suggestion, that the Committee itself should propose the amount of the salaries, did not appear advisable to M. Hagerup. The Committee might thereby endanger the success of its work; it was very doubtful whether a unanimous decision would be reached in the Council and Assembly upon a question of this

pas d'inconvénient à insérer dans le rapport, les considérations qui doivent régir la fixation du traitement.

Qui, du Conseil ou de l'Assemblée, devra fixer le montant du traitement? M. Hagerup observe qu'en laissant cette détermination à l'Assemblée, on se heurte à une difficulté pratique qui découle du fait que l'Assemblée doit prendre ses décisions à l'unanimité. Il estime qu'il vaudrait mieux, pour cette raison, confier cette tâche au Conseil.

M. Hagerup se résume en formulant brièvement les 3 points à résoudre:

1. L'indemnité des suppléants sera-t-elle égale à celle des juges titulaires?

2. Comment les frais de voyage seront-ils remboursés?

3. Par quelle stipulation doit on garantir que le montant de l'indemnité ne sera pas changé pendant la période d'un mandat? A ce dernier égard M. Hagerup sa rallie à l'opinion de M. Fernandes.

kind; the question of salaries was always a stumbling block. But he saw no objection to inserting the considerations which should govern the assessment of salary in the report.

Concerning the question as to whether the Assembly or Council should fix the amount of the salary, M. Hagerup said that, if this point were left to the Assembly, a practical difficulty would be encountered, arising out of the fact that the decisions of the Assembly must be unanimous. For this reason M. Hagerup thought that it would be better to entrust this task to the Council.

M. Hagerup summarised his remarks by stating three questions to be solved:

1. Should the payment of the deputy judges be equal to that of the regular judges?

2. How should travelling expenses be repaid?

3. What stipulation should be inserted to guarantee that the rate of salary would not be changed during the period of an appointment? On this last point M. Hagerup agreed with M. Fernandes.

LORD PHILLIMORE dit que les articles 21 et 22 du projet Root—Phillimore sont inspirés des articles 13 et 14 du projet des Cinq Puissances; pour cette raison l'opposition de MM. Loder et Hagerup n'est pas sans l'étonner.

Lord Phillimore avait d'abord pensé que le Conseil, en tant qu'organe administratif de la Société des Nations, devait fixer le traitement. Il peut cependant se rallier à l'idée de confier la décision formelle à l'Assemblée: le Conseil pourra toujours faire des propositions.

Quant à la question du traitement des suppléants, Lord Phillimore est d'avis que le texte du projet des Cinq Puissances, qui fait une distinction entre le traitement annuel des juges titulaires et l'indemnité des juges suppléants, est préférable à celui du projet Root—Phillimore.

Répondant à M. Fernandes, Lord Phillimore dit qu'il n'a jamais eu l'idée que le montant du traitement puisse changer pendant la durée d'un mandat; il trouve qu'une stipulation expresse dans ce sens serait presque superflue, mais il n'a pas d'objection à ce qu'elle soit insérée.

En mentionnant le chiffre de £ 6000, Lord Phillimore a seulement voulu indiquer que le traitement des juges doit être large. Il s'oppose à l'idée de M. Loder de mentionner dans le projet un chiffre déterminé. Tout au plus devrait-on indiquer dans le rapport que la somme à fixer doit être importante.

Les idées exposées par M. Ricci-Busatti se basent sur une conception de la Cour, différente de celle qui a été adoptée; il est évident qu'elles ne peuvent pas entrer en ligne de compte.

LORD PHILLIMORE said that Articles 21 and 22 of the Root—Phillimore plan were based upon Articles 13 and 14 of the Five Power Plan; for this reason he was somewhat astonished at the opposition of MM. Loder and Hagerup.

Lord Phillimore had at first thought that the Council, as the administrative body of the League of Nations, ought to fix the salary. He was prepared, however, to fall in with the idea of entrusting the formal decision to the Assembly; the Council could always make proposals.

Concerning the payment of deputy judges, Lord Phillimore thought that the wording of the Five Power Plan, which makes a distinction between the annual salary of judges and the payment of grants to deputy judges, was preferable to that of the Root—Phillimore plan.

Answering M. Fernandes, Lord Phillimore said that it had never occurred to him that the amount of a salary could be changed during the period of an appointment. He thought that an express stipulation to this effect would be almost superfluous, but he had no objection to its insertion.

When he had mentioned the figure £ 6.000, Lord Phillimore had only wished to indicate that the salary of judges must be generous. He was opposed to M. Loder's idea of mentioning a fixed sum in the plan. The utmost that should be done was to indicate in the report that the amount should be generous.

M. Ricci-Busatti's ideas were based on a conception of the Court which differed from that adopted; it was obvious therefore that they could not be taken into consideration.

Répondant à M. Hagerup, Lord Phillimore dit que les frais de voyage doivent être pris en considération, lorsqu'on fixera les traitements. Il trouve que cette question se pose pour les juges suppléants d'une façon différente que pour les juges titulaires.

M. DE LAPRADELLE, en sa qualité de rapporteur, désire préciser les questions qu'on a discutées.

1. Il croit qu'on est d'accord pour reconnaître qu'aucun chiffre ne doit être mentionné dans le projet, mais que le rapport doit indiquer que le traitement des juges doit être large.

2. C'est à la Société des Nations, c'est à dire au Conseil et à l'Assemblée, qu'il revient de fixer la somme, en tenant compte du rapport du Comité. Par conséquent, le texte doit laisser le chiffre en blanc, et le rapport indiquera la signification de ce blanc.

3. On est aussi d'accord pour reconnaître la nécessité d'une formule qui indique que le traitement accordé originairement à un juge, doit être considéré comme le minimum pendant la durée de son mandat.

4. A son avis, le traitement des juges doit être fixé de façon à couvrir en même temps les frais de voyage. En principe les juges devront être domiciliés au siège de la Cour; même si la non-résidence est tolérée, elle ne doit pas être favorisée par la restitution des frais de voyage.

5. Reste à déterminer la situation des juges suppléants. A cet égard, M. de Lapradelle remarque d'abord que jusqu'ici le Comité ne s'est occupé des juges suppléants que d'une façon fragmentaire et épisodique. On a seulement décidé qu'ils seront au nombre de quatre. Ceci posé, il remarque que ce ne serait pas imposer une grande charge pécuniaire à la Société des Nations, que d'assimiler les juges suppléants aux juges titulaires au point de vue pécuniaire.

Mais il y a des raisons plus décisives en faveur de la même solution. Les juges suppléants doivent toujours être à la disposition de la Cour. Par conséquent, ils doivent être domiciliés à son siège, et ils doivent, tout comme les juges titulaires, suspendre leurs travaux professionnels. Pour cette raison, il serait extrêmement difficile de trouver de bons juges suppléants, si on ne leur donnait pas un traitement suffisant; d'autant plus qu'ils n'auront même pas la satisfaction morale, réservée aux juges titulaires, de juger des litiges importants entre des parties de premier ordre.

In answer to M. Hagerup, Lord Phillimore said that travelling expenses must be considered when the salaries were fixed. He thought that this question was rather different in the cases of the deputy judges and of the regular judges.

M. DE LAPRADELLE, as reporter, wished to summarise the questions under discussion:

1. He thought it was agreed that no figure should be mentioned in the plan, but that the report should indicate that the salary of the judges must be large.

2. It was to be left to the League of Nations, that is to say to the Council and to the Assembly, to fix the amount, giving due consideration to the report of the Committee. Consequently the plan should leave the amount blank, and the report should indicate the meaning of this blank.

3. It was agreed that a formula was necessary indicating that the original salary granted to a judge must be considered as a minimum during the period of his appointment.

4. In his opinion the salary of judges should be so calculated as to cover also travelling expenses. In principle the judges should be domiciled at the seat of the Court; even if non-residence were permitted, it must not be encouraged by the refund of travelling expenses.

5. The position of the deputy judges remained to be defined. In this connection, he began by remarking that the Committee had, up till now, only considered the question of the deputy judges partially and episodically. They had only decided that these deputies were to be four in number. M. de Lapradelle went on to say that it would not, consequently, constitute a heavy charge upon the League of Nations if the deputy judges were classed with the regular judges from the point of view of salary.

There were, however, more decisive reasons in favour of this solution. The deputy judges must always be at the disposal of the Court. Consequently they must reside at its seat and they must, just like the regular judges, give up their professional work. For this reason it would be extremely difficult to get good deputy judges, unless they were given a sufficient salary; especially as they would not even have the moral satisfaction of giving judgment upon important cases between contesting parties of the first rank; this would only be experienced by the regular judges.

Les juges suppléants doivent siéger à côté des juges titulaires: ils sont là pour élargir la Cour. C'est donc dans l'intérêt du prestige dont la Cour doit être environné que l'on doit éviter de donner l'impression que les juges suppléants ont une position inférieure à celle des juges titulaires; et pour cela il faut leur donner un traitement identique. Mais M. de Lapradelle insiste surtout sur le fait que les juges suppléants seront, tout comme les juges titulaires, privés de leurs occupations ordinaires. Ils ne le seront peut-être pas en raison d'un travail déterminé; mais ils le seront en raison de l'obligation où on les mettra de se tenir à la disposition de la Cour pour un travail possible.

6. M. de Lapradelle s'adresse à M. Ricci-Busatti. Il remarque que la proposition de celui-ci fait partie d'un système parfaitement logique; mais, comme on a écarté l'idée fondamentale de ce système, il faut également en écarter les conséquences. M. Ricci-Busatti avait dit qu'il serait inadmissible de payer largement des juges qui ne travailleraient que peu. Mais M. de Lapradelle fait observer que si les juges restent inoccupés, ce ne sera pas leur faute; mais bien celle des gouvernements, qui ne soumettront pas leurs litiges à la Cour. L'existence d'une Cour avec des juges recevant des salaires élevés ne fera que mieux sentir aux Etats l'obligation de s'en servir; et c'est ainsi que les traitements élevés des juges deviendront une garantie d'activité pour la Cour et les juges qui la composeront.

M. ADATCI préfère pour sa part le système de M. Loder, d'après lequel le montant du traitement sera fixé dans le statut de la Cour. Le Comité connaît à fond la question et peut en faire l'objet d'une considération consciencieuse, tandis que le Conseil n'aura le temps de la traiter que superficiellement. Dans ces circonstances, le Conseil s'attend à ce que le Comité lui soumette une proposition relative aux traitements, et le Comité manquerait à son devoir s'il ne le faisait pas.

Il se rallie au point de vue de M. de Lapradelle concernant la situation à faire aux juges suppléants: il croit qu'il faut assimiler les deux catégories de juges.

M. Adatci insiste sur la question des frais de voyage. Cette question est extrêmement sérieuse lorsqu'il s'agit d'obtenir de bons juges qui doivent venir de pays lointains, comme le Japon: elle ne doit pas être traitée comme une question indifférente.

Mr. ROOT pense que la discussion a bien fait ressortir les difficultés qui ont amené Lord Phillimore et lui-même à adopter, pour les indemnités,

The deputy judges must sit side by side with the regular judges: they would be appointed for the purpose of enlarging the Court. In the interests of the prestige which the Court must possess, steps must be taken to avoid giving the impression that the deputy judges held a position inferior to that of the regular judges; therefore they must be given an equal salary. M. de Lapradelle, however, laid most emphasis upon the fact that deputy judges would be deprived of their ordinary occupation just like the regular judges. This would perhaps be not so much on account of actual work, but in view of the obligation, under which they would be placed, to hold themselves at the disposal of the Court for possible work.

6. M. de Lapradelle then addressed M. Ricci-Busatti. He said that the latter's proposal was part of a perfectly logical system; but, as the fundamental idea of this system had been discarded, the results of the system must likewise be discarded. M. Ricci-Busatti had said that it would be inadmissible to pay large salaries to judges who worked but little; but M. de Lapradelle pointed out that if the judges were unoccupied it would not be their fault, but that of the Governments for not submitting their cases to the Court. The existence of a Court consisting of highly paid judges would tend to make the States feel an obligation to make use of it; thus the fact of giving the judges high salaries would become a guarantee for the employment of the Court and its judges.

M. ADATCI, for his part, preferred M. Loder's system, according to which the amount of the salary would be fixed in the statute of the Court. The Committee had thorough knowledge of the question and could devote conscientious consideration to it, whereas the Council would only have the time to consider it superficially. Under these circumstances the Council would expect the Committee to submit a proposal concerning the salaries, and the Committe would fail in its duty if it did not do so.

He agreed with M. de Lapradelle concerning the position of the deputy judges: the two classes of judges should be assimilated.

M. Adatci laid emphasis on the question of travelling expenses. This was very important in connection with obtaining good judges from distant countries, such as Japan, and must not be passed over lightly.

Mr. ROOT thought that the discussion had clearly brought out the difficulties which had led Lord Phillimore and himself to adopt the

la formule qui se retrouve aux articles 21 et 22 du projet Root—Phillimore.

Il fait observer que le chiffre de £ 6000 lui a été suggéré par Lord Phillimore dans des conversations privées. Le chiffre de 6000 florins, mentionné dans le projet de 1907, est naturellement inadmissible.

Il sera extrêmement difficile pour le Comité de se mettre d'accord sur un chiffre. Le Comité n'est pas en possession de toutes les informations nécessaires pour pouvoir soumettre au Conseil une proposition déterminée. Le résultat auquel on arrivera sera forcément de la nature d'un compromis; ce sera une conciliation entre deux forces, celle de ceux qui reçoivent et celle de ceux qui donnent. Cette transaction doit être faite par des représentants de ces deux forces, tandis que les membres du Comité n'en représentent aucune: il s'agit d'une affaire, et d'une affaire qui n'est pas très simple parce que les conditions à régler sont très différentes; les frais pour un juge hollandais et les dépenses que devrait faire un juge japonais sont toutes autres.

Mr. Root ajoute qu'indépendamment du résultat auquel on arriverait, on rencontrerait des objections. Il y aura, au sein du Conseil et de l'Assemblée, les mêmes divergences qu'au Comité; or ceux qui ne seraient pas favorables à la proposition du Comité concernant les traitements, deviendraient des ennemis du plan tout entier. C'est pourquoi Mr. Root préfère laisser la décision au Conseil ou à l'Assemblée de la Société des Nations; mais il ne veut pas choisir lui-même entre ces deux organes.

Mr. Root reconnaît que les observations de M. de Lapradelle l'invitent à penser qu'il faut augmenter l'importance des juges suppléants. Il est disposé à abandonner la position qu'il a prise précédemment en ce qui concerne le droit pour les juges suppléants, de prendre part à l'élection du Président de la Cour. Il est disposé à donner ce droit aux juges suppléants afin de donner aux pays dont ils sont les ressortissants, l'impression qu'ils sont représentés à la Cour par des personnes d'une dignité égale à celle des juges titulaires.

D'autre part, Mr. Root prie M. de Lapradelle de considérer s'il ne pourrait pas abandonner l'idée de laisser en blanc dans le texte du projet du Comité le montant du traitement des juges. Ce blanc donnerait l'impression fâcheuse que le Comité a tâché de se mettre d'accord sans y réussir, et rendrait aussi le document incomplet. Ne vaudrait-il pas mieux expliquer clairement que la somme doit être fixée par le Conseil ou par l'Assemblée? En tous cas on peut se décider pour l'un de ces deux organes, puisque le Pacte ne contient aucune disposition qui résolve ce point.

wording, dealing with salary and allowances, contained in Articles 21 and 22 of the Root—Phillimore plan.

He said that the amount £ 6.000 had been mentioned to him by Lord Phillimore in a private conversation. The sum of 6.000 florins, mentioned in the plan of 1907, was naturally quite out of the question.

It would be extremely difficult for the Committee to agree upon a figure. It was not in possession of all the information necessary to enable it to submit a definite proposal to the Council. The result eventually arrived at would necessarily be of the nature of a compromise between two opposing forces: those who received and those who paid. This bargain must be made between representatives of the two forces; but the members of the Committee represented neither. It was a matter of business and not a very simple one at that; as the conditions to be dealt with were very different. The expenses incurred by a Dutch judge and a Japanese judge respectively would be on an altogether different plan.

Mr. Root added that, no matter what result were arrived at, there would always be objections. The same differences of opinion would exist in the Council and Assembly as in the Committee, and those who objected to the Committee's proposal concerning salaries, would oppose the whole plan. For this reason Mr. Root preferred to leave the decision to the Council or the Assembly of the League of Nations; but he did not wish to choose between these two bodies himself.

Mr. Root said that M. de Lapradelle's remarks had led him to think that the importance of the position of the deputy judges should be increased. He was inclined to abandon his previous standpoint with regard to the question as to whether the deputy judges should have the right to take part in the election of the President of the Court. He was now disposed to give the deputy judges this right, in order to make their respective countries feel that they were represented upon the Court by Members holding a position equal to that of the regular judges.

On the other hand, Mr. Root asked M. de Lapradelle to reconsider his view that the amount of the salary to be given to judges should be left blank in the Committee's draft scheme. Such a blank would give the undesirable impression that the Committee had tried to come to an agreement and failed; further the document would appear incomplete. Would it not be better to explain clearly that the amount was to be fixed by the Council or the Assembly? In any case they could decide in favour of one of these two bodies, since the Covenant contained no provision which settled the point.

M. DE LAPRADELLE remercie Mr. Root de s'être rallié à son idée sur la situation qu'il convient de donner aux juges suppléants.

Le PRESIDENT communique au Comité une proposition émanant de M. Hagerup et relative au traitement des juges; cette proposition est ainsi conçue:

„Les juges toucheront un traitement annuel à fixer par la Société des Nations. Ce traitement ne peut pas changer pendant le terme du mandat d'un juge.

Les juges suppléants toucheront dans l'exercice de leurs fonctions une indemnité à fixer pour chaque affaire par le Conseil de la Société des Nations.

Les juges et juges suppléants qui ne résident pas au siège de la Cour auront droit à une indemnité pour frais de voyage nécessités par l'accomplissement de leurs fonctions."

M. HAGERUP explique son amendement. Il remarque qu'on est d'accord pour éviter de fixer, dans le statut de la Cour, le montant de l'indemnité. Il a cru devoir laisser ouverte dans son texte la question de savoir si la décision doit être prise par le Conseil ou par l'Assemblée: personnellement il serait satisfait que l'on donnât la décision au Conseil, à cause de la difficulté d'obtenir l'unanimité nécessaire dans l'Assemblée. Si, cependant, la décision du Conseil doit également être prise à l'unanimité, il peut se rallier à l'idée de donner la décision à l'Assemblée.

Le PRESIDENT suggère l'idée de donner la décision à la majorité de l'Assemblée sur la proposition du Conseil.

En réponse à une question de M. Ricci-Busatti, le Président constate que l'Assemblée ne pourra qu'accepter ou rejeter la proposition du Conseil. Elle pourra cependant jouer un rôle positif, en faisant entendre au Conseil que telle ou telle proposition lui semble agréable.

Le Président donne lecture d'un nouveau texte soumis par M. Hagerup. Ce texte est ainsi conçu:

„Les juges toucheront un traitement annuel à fixer par la majorité de l'Assemblée de la Société des Nations, sur la proposition du Conseil. Ce traitement ne peut être changé pendant le terme du mandat d'un juge.

Les juges suppléants toucheront, dans l'exercice de leurs fonctions, une indemnité à fixer pour chaque affaire par l'Assemblée de la Société des Nations statuant à la majorité des voix sur la proposition du Conseil.

M. DE LAPRADELLE thanked Mr. Root for having adopted his view of the position that should be given to deputy judges.

The PRESIDENT communicated to the Committee a proposal concerning the salary of judges, made by M. Hagerup, which was as follows:

"The judge shall receive an annual salary to be fixed by the League of Nations. This salary cannot be altered during the period of a judge's appointment.

The deputy judges, for the actual performance of their duties, shall receive an indemnity to be fixed in each case by the Council of the League of Nations.

Judges and deputy judges who do not reside at the seat of the Court shall be entitled to a refund of travelling expenses incurred in the performance of their duties."

M. HAGERUP explained his amendment. He said that it was agreed that the amount of salary should not be determined in the statute of the Court. He had thought it better to leave the question, as to whether the point was to be decided by the Council or the Assembly, open in his proposed wording. Personally he was in favour of allowing the Council to decide, on account of the difficulty of obtaining the necessary unanimity in the Assembly. If, however, the decision of the Council must also be unanimous, he was prepared to accept the idea of giving the right of decision to the Assembly.

The PRESIDENT suggested that the question should be decided by a majority in the Assembly upon a proposal submitted by the Council.

In answer to a question of M. Ricci-Busatti, the President said that the Assembly would only be able to accept or refuse the Council's proposal. It might however take a more active part, by informing the Council that such or such a proposal would be acceptable to it.

The President read another wording submitted by M. Hagerup. This amendment was as follows:

"The judges shall receive an annual salary to be fixed by a majority of the Assembly of the League of Nations upon a proposal made by the Council. This salary shall not be altered during the period of a judge's appointment.

The deputy judges shall, for the actual performance of their duties, receive an indemnity to be fixed in each case by the majority vote of the Assembly of the League of Nations, upon a proposal made by the Council.

Les juges ou juges suppléants qui ne résident pas au siège de la Cour auront droit à une indemnité pour frais de voyage nécessités par l'accomplissement de leurs fonctions."

M. RICCI-BUSATTI constate qu'en proposant que l'Assemblée statue à la majorité des voix, on propose en même temps un amendement à l'article 5 du Pacte; d'ailleurs il n'a pas d'objection à faire à cette proposition.

M. LODER attire l'attention sur la nécessité de donner le même traitement à tous les juges siégeant en même temps.

M. ALTAMIRA propose d'insérer dans l'amendement de M. Hagerup une formule qui indique que l'indemnité des juges est égale, tout comme leur situation.

Mr. ROOT s'oppose à cette idée. Il faut pouvoir tenir compte de la différence entre les dépenses que les divers membres auront à supporter, et aussi de la cherté de la vie; en général, Mr. Root ne voudrait pas imposer trop de restrictions à la Société des Nations relativement à la décision qu'elle doit prendre.

Le PRESIDENT observe que le texte de M. Hagerup distingue entre traitement et indemnité et donne aux juges titulaires un traitement fixe, tandis que les suppléants ne recevront qu'une indemnité. C'est la différence fondamentale entre l'idée de M. Hagerup et celle de M. de Lapradelle.

Le Président propose qu'on procède au vote sur le traitement à donner aux juges titulaires, réserve faite des frais de voyage. Quant aux autres parties de l'amendement de M. Hagerup, il y a plusieurs points sur lesquels il faut se mettre d'accord:

1. La décision doit-elle être prise par l'Assemblée statuant à la majorité des voix sur la proposition du Conseil?

2. Comment sera fixée l'indemnité des juges suppléants?

3. Comment faut-il exprimer que, le traitement une fois fixé pour un juge déterminé, le montant en doit être maintenu comme minimum pendant la durée du mandat de ce juge?

M. ALTAMIRA votera le texte à la condition que dans le rapport soit clairement exprimée l'importance que le Comité attribue aux traitements

Judges or deputy judges who do not reside at the seat of the Court shall be entitled to a refund of travelling expenses incurred in the performance of their duties."

M. RICCI-BUSATTI stated that a proposal that the Assembly should decide by a majority would amount to a proposal to amend Article 5 of the Covenant; however he had no objection to make to the proposal.

M. LODER called attention to the necessity of giving the same salary to all judges sitting at the same time.

M. ALTAMIRA proposed that a clause should be inserted in M. Hagerup's amendment, indicating that the emoluments and position of judges would alike be equal.

Mr. ROOT opposed this. It must be possible to take into consideration the difference between the expenses of the various members, and also the cost of living. Generally speaking, Mr. Root did not want to impose too many restrictions upon the freedom of the decision to be taken by the League of Nations.

The PRESIDENT pointed out that M. Hagerup's wording distinguished between salary and indemnities. It gave the regular judges a fixed salary, whereas the deputy judges would only receive an indemnity. That was the essential difference between M. Hagerup's idea and that of M. de Lapradelle.

The President proposed that a vote should be taken upon the salary to be given to regular judges, reserving the question of travelling expenses. Concerning the other parts of M. Hagerup's amendment there were several points upon which an agreement had yet to be reached:

1. Should the Assembly decide by a majority upon the proposal of the Council?

2. How should the payment of deputy judges be fixed?

3. How could it be best expressed that, once the salary of a certain judge has been fixed, the amount fixed must be considered as a minimum during the period of his appointment?

M. ALTAMIRA said that he would vote for the text of the proposal, provided that the importance attached by the Committee to the salary

des juges. La dignité et la considération sociale d'un fonctionnaire a été et sera toujours proportionnelle au traitement qu'il reçoit; c'est-à-dire à la situation économique. Il faut aussi considérer que, en général, les jurisconsultes ne sont pas riches. Il faut s'assurer, enfin, le concours des hommes les plus éminents en leur faisant connaître qu'ils jouiront d'une situation économique vraiment avantageuse, d'autant plus que les juges de la Cour future, tels que nous les désirons, seront tenus de quitter et peut-être de perdre pour toujours, les moyens d'existence qu'ils avaient dans leur pays.

Le PRESIDENT met au vote le premier alinéa de l'amendement de M. Hagerup. Cet amendement est adopté sauf rédaction et sauf la question des frais de voyage. Il est convenu que l'indication faite par M. Altamira sera prise en considération pour le texte du rapport.

M. RICCI-BUSATTI s'est abstenu.

Le PRESIDENT ouvre la discussion sur le second alinéa de l'amendement de M. Hagerup. Cet alinéa a trait à l'indemnité à donner aux juges suppléants.

M. HAGERUP apprécie les observations de M. de Lapradelle; il ne tient pas au mot indemnité. Mais, d'autre part, il ne croit pas que l'opinion publique comprenne pourquoi on donnerait aux suppléants, qui ne travaillent pas, le même traitement qu'aux juges titulaires. Les juges suppléants ne résideront pas nécessairement à La Haye: le projet Root—Phillimore prévoit, dans son article 26, qui fixe le quorum définitif à sept juges, l'absence de plusieurs juges titulaires avant qu'il soit nécessaire d'appeler des juges suppléants.

Le PRESIDENT fait remarquer que dans le système adopté, le premier, et peut-être le second des juges suppléants, pourront venir siéger quelquefois, tandis que les autres n'auront presque rien à faire. Dans ces conditions, le Président ne peut pas être favorable à l'idée de mettre tous les juges suppléants sur un pied d'égalité avec les juges titulaires.

M. DE LAPRADELLE admet que cette observation est très sérieuse. Il répond à celle de M. Hagerup en remarquant que la Cour doit toujours commencer à siéger avec neuf juges. D'ailleurs, les juges suppléants ne se trouveront pas

of the judges was clearly expressed in the report. The dignity and social position of an official were, and always would be, in proportion to the salary he received, that is, in proportion to his financial position. It must also be remembered that, as a rule, jurisconsults were not rich. In order to ensure that the most distinguished men would compete for these posts, they must know that they would have an advantageous financial position; especially as the judges of the future Court, according to the Committee's views, would be bound to give up, and perhaps lose altogether, their means of livelihood in their own country.

The PRESIDENT put the first Paragraph of M. Hagerup's amendment to the vote. It was adopted, subject to amendment in wording; the question of travelling expenses was left undecided. It was agreed that the suggestions made by M. Altamira would be taken into consideration in the report.

M. RICCI-BUSATTI abstained from voting.

The PRESIDENT opened the discussion of the second Paragraph of M. Hagerup's amendment. This Paragraph dealt with the indemnities to be paid to deputy judges.

M. HAGERUP appreciated M. de Lapradelle's remarks; he did not insist on the word "indemnité" (indemnity), but, on the other hand, he did not think that public opinion would understand why the same salary was given to deputy judges, who did not work, as to regular judges. The deputy judges would not necessarily live at the Hague. The Root—Phillimore plan, in Article 26, which fixed the quorum at seven judges, made allowance for the absence of several regular judges before it would become necessary to summon deputy judges.

The PRESIDENT pointed out that in the system adopted, the first, and possibly the second, deputy judges would sometimes take their seats, whereas the others would have practically nothing to do. Under these circumstances, the President could not look favourably upon the idea of putting all the deputy judges upon the same footing as the regular judges.

M. DE LAPRADELLE admitted that this was a very important point of view. In answer to M. Hagerup he said that the Court must always commence its sittings with nine judges. Besides, the deputy judges would not necessarily reside near the

nécessairement près de la Haye; ils seront dans des pays différents, peut-être très éloignés, d'où il serait difficile, parfois impossible, de les faire venir d'urgence, lorsqu'on en aurait besoin. Ils devront donc être disponibles à La Haye. Même s'il n'y avait pas d'autres raisons, leur présence serait hautement désirable, presque nécessaire, afin de leur donner l'opportunité de se pénétrer de l'esprit de justice internationale, dont le tribunal sera le promoteur.

Il est d'une importance extrême pour le recrutement de la Cour que le jeune magistrat ait l'occasion d'en suivre les travaux sans y siéger. Or, ces jeunes magistrats qui se formeront aux affaires, doivent être les meilleurs, tout comme les juges titulaires doivent être les meilleurs. Mais on ne peut assurer de bons juges suppléants sans leur donner un traitement égal à celui des juges titulaires.

M. RICCI-BUSATTI trouve les observations de M. de Lapradelle très justes et très sérieuses. Il croit aussi fort importante l'observation du Président. Il faut concilier les deux points de vue, et on pourra le faire en donnant à tous les juges un traitement proportionnel à leurs services.

Mr. ROOT fait valoir que le bon sens s'oppose à l'idée de donner le même traitement à ceux qui font un travail effectif et à ceux qui ne sont pas obligés de travailler ni de renoncer à leurs anciennes occupations, mais qui viennent seulement pour s'instruire. Il serait du reste impossible pour les juges titulaires d'être, même dans la chambre des délibérations, entourés de juges élèves. Il croit d'ailleurs qu'on doit donner une large indemnité aux juges suppléants pour les périodes où ils sont appelés à servir, même une indemnité qui, par jour, dépasse celle des juges titulaires. Avant tout, il ne faut pas restreindre la liberté du Conseil et de l'Assemblée dans la détermination des traitements et des indemnités.

M. HAGERUP désire préciser la divergence d'opinion qui existe entre lui et M. de Lapradelle. Dans le système de M. de Lapradelle, les juges suppléants se trouveront toujours à La Haye. Le système de M. Hagerup est tout autre. Il croit que, puisque le Président saura d'avance quels sont les cas qui devront être jugés par la Cour, lors d'une session déterminée, il pourra connaître, en temps utile, quels juges seront empêchés de siéger et prendre les dispositions nécessaires pour les remplacer. Les seuls cas imprévus sont ceux de maladie ou de décès qui

Hague, they would be in different countries, possibly very remote, whence it would be difficult and sometimes impossible for them to come at short notice, when needed. They must therefore be available at the Hague. Even if there were no other reasons for it, their presence there would be highly desirable, if not necessary, in order to give them the opportunity of saturating themselves with the spirit of international justice evolved by the Court.

It was extremely important, from the point of view of the recruiting of the Court, that young judges should have the opportunity of following the work of the Court without sitting on it. Further, these young judges, who were to train themselves up for the business of the Court, must be the best, just as the regular judges must be the best. Good deputy judges, however, could not be obtained, unless they were given a salary equal to that of the regular judges.

M. RICCI-BUSATTI thought that M. de Lapradelle's remarks were very true and very important. He thought that the remarks of the President were also of great importance. The two points of view must be reconciled by some means; this might be done by giving all the judges a salary in proportion to their services.

Mr. ROOT pointed out that it was contrary to common sense to give the same rate of pay to those who did the actual work and to those who were neither obliged to work, nor to give up their former occupations, but came simply to learn. It would also be an impossible situation for the regular judges to be continually surrounded by student judges, even when considering their judgments. He thought that a large indemnity should be given to the deputy judges for the periods during which they were called upon to do duty, possibly one which, in daily rate, would exceed the salary of regular judges. Above all, no restriction must be put upon the freedom of the Council and the Assembly to determine the salaries and indemnities.

M. HAGERUP wished to define the difference of opinion existing between him and M. de Lapradelle. According to M. de Lapradelle's system, the deputy judges would always be at the Hague. M. Hagerup's system was quite different. He thought, that, since the President would always know beforehand what cases were to be tried by the Court at a particular session, he would know in good time which judges would be unable to sit, and could take the necessary steps to replace them. The only unforeseen contingencies would be cases of illness or death occurring during the session;

pourraient se produire au cours de la session; mais pour ces cas l'article 26 du projet Root—Phillimore fournit une soupape de sûreté suffisante en stipulant, en cas de nécessité, un quorum minimum de sept juges.

but Article 26 of the Root—Phillimore plan, by providing, if need be, for a quorum of seven judges, allowed a sufficient margin for such cases.

M. DE LAPRADELLE se demande si la conséquence des objections qui ont été présentées ne serait pas la suppression des juges suppléants et l'élargissement du nombre des juges titulaires. La situation est difficile. Un juge titulaire vient à mourir et un juge suppléant est appelé à siéger en attendant l'élection d'un nouveau titulaire. Ce suppléant restera suppléant et n'aura pas la situation d'un titulaire. Quelle situation faut-il lui donner au point de vue économique? Le régime auquel on le soumettra sera, ou bien trop, ou bien trop peu avantageux, mais toujours injuste: trop avantageux si on lui donne plus par jour qu'aux autres juges, trop peu avantageux si on le maintient dans son régime d'exception.

M. de Lapradelle croit qu'il faut tenir compte non pas du travail que les juges auront à faire, mais des occupations qu'ils ont dû laisser.

On veut pour juges suppléants des hommes éminents; or ces hommes éminents doivent faire les mêmes renonciations que les autres puisqu'ils doivent toujours être préparés à abandonner les travaux qui leurs sont imposés par leur profession. Mais si l'on demande aux suppléants les mêmes renonciations qu'aux titulaires, et aussi les mêmes qualifications, il faut leur donner un traitement égal. Il faut se régler non pas d'après ce qu'on leur demandera, mais d'après ce qu'on pourra leur demander.

La décision, si elle était prise, de traiter les juges titulaires et les suppléants sur un pied d'égalité, n'entraînerait qu'une augmentation de dépense minime, en raison du petit nombre des suppléants, et elle aurait l'avantage de contribuer à maintenir la haute qualité et le prestige de la Cour.

M. DE LAPRADELLE wondered whether the objections, which had been put forward, would not result in the suppression of the deputy judges, and in an increased number of regular judges. It was a difficult position. A regular judge died, and a deputy judge was called upon to take his seat, pending the election of a new regular judge. This deputy judge would remain a deputy, and would not have the position of a regular judge. What should be his position from a financial point of view? The intended system would either be too advantageous, or not sufficiently so; in either case, it would be unfair; it would be too advantageous, in that he was receiving more per diem than the other judges, not sufficiently advantageous, in that he continued to be a deputy only.

M. de Lapradelle thought that the occupations which the judges had had to give up should be considered, and not the work that they would have to do.

Distinguished men were required, as deputy judges; these distinguished men would have to make the same sacrifices as the others, since they would always have to be prepared to abandon their professional work. But, if the deputies were called upon to make the same sacrifices as the regular judges, and also to have the same qualifications, they must be given an equal salary. The guiding principle must be, not that which was actually asked of them, but that which might be asked of them.

If it were decided to pay the judges and deputy judges alike, the increase in expenses thus involved would be very slight, since the deputy judges were very few in number, while such a decision would help to maintain the quality and the prestige of the Court.

LORD PHILLIMORE propose de laisser la décision à la Société des Nations en adoptant le texte proposé par M. Hagerup. Il trouve que l'idée suggérée par M. de Lapradelle ne tient pas suffisamment compte des exigences pratiques. En Angleterre, lorsqu'une vacance se produit dans la Cour d'Assises, on appelle un membre éminent du barreau à siéger sur un pied d'égalité avec les autres juges, sous le nom de Commissaire du Roi. Ce Commissaire du Roi reçoit une indemnité de £ 500.— par assise. Cette somme est considérée suffisamment large pour l'indemniser des pertes qu'il doit subir, en abandonnant temporairement

LORD PHILLIMORE proposed to leave the decision to the League of Nations, by adopting M. Hagerup's proposed wording. He thought that M. de Lapradelle's idea did not take sufficient account of practical requirements. In England, when a vacancy occurs in an Assize Court, a distinguished member of the Bar is called upon to sit in a position of equality with the other judges, and is called "Kings Commissioner". This Commissioner received the fixed payment of £ 500.— for the Assizes. This sum is considered sufficient to indemnify him for the losses which he must undergo by temporarily abandoning his

sa profession, pour siéger comme juge. La situation qu'il reçoit comme Commissaire est très honorable. Lord Phillimore pense que la Société des Nations, en prenant sa décision, doit s'inspirer des mêmes idées.

Le PRESIDENT met aux voix le second alinéa des amendements de M. Hagerup.

M. FERNANDES demande la parole. Il remarque qu'il y a dans l'alinéa une contradiction: la décision de laisser toute la détermination à la Société des Nations ne cadre pas avec l'emploi du terme „traitement", dans le premier alinéa, et le terme „indemnité" dans le second. Celui-ci, en outre, limite les honoraires des juges suppléants en les proportionnant aux affaires auxquelles ils prennent part. Ce sont des différences qui tracent un cadre d'avance et ne laissent pas la question entière à la décision de la Société des Nations, comme on en a généralement exprimé le désir.

M. HAGERUP est disposé à substituer au second alinéa le mot „traitement" au mot „indemnité". Il est également disposé à supprimer l'expression „pour chaque affaire".

M. DE LAPRADELLE demande au Président de donner lecture du texte du second alinéa tel qu'il se trouve amendé.

Le PRESIDENT lit le texte suivant: „les juges suppléants toucheront, dans l'exercice de leurs fonctions, une indemnité à fixer par l'Assemblée de la Société des Nations, statuant à la majorité des voix sur la proposition du Conseil."

M. DE LAPRADELLE déclare qu'il votera contre ce texte à cause du mot indemnité.

M. FERNANDES soulève la question de l'ordre dans lequel les suppléants seront appelés à siéger.

LORD PHILLIMORE renvoie à l'article 26 du projet Root—Phillimore.

Le PRESIDENT met aux voix l'alinéa 2 de l'amendement de M. Hagerup. Cet amendement est adopté. MM. de Lapradelle, Ricci-Busatti et Altamira se sont abstenus.

Le Président ouvre la discussion sur l'alinéa 3 de l'amendement de M. Hagerup.

profession to sit as a judge. His position as Commissioner is a very honourable one. Lord Phillimore thought that the League of Nations should base its decision upon the same idea.

The PRESIDENT put the second Paragraph of M. Hagerup's amendment to the vote.

M. FERNANDES asked permission to speak. He pointed out that there was a contradiction in the Paragraph; the decision to leave the questions to be settled by the League of Nations did not quite accord with the employment of the word "salary" in the first Paragraph and the word "indemnity" in the second. The latter, in addition, limits the emoluments of the deputy judges by making them proportionate to the cases in which they take part. These are differences which would give more than an indication of the line to be taken and would not leave the whole question to be decided by the League of Nations, as was generally desired.

M. HAGERUP felt inclined to substitute, in the second Paragraph, the word "salary" for the word "indemnity". He was equally willing to leave out the expression "in each case".

M. DE LAPRADELLE asked the President to be good enough to read the second Paragraph in its amended form.

The PRESIDENT read the French of the following: "The deputy-judges shall, for the actual performance of their duties, receive an indemnity to be fixed by a majority vote of the Assembly of the League of Nations, upon a proposal made by the Council."

M. DE LAPRADELLE stated, that he would vote against this on account of the word "indemnity".

M. FERNANDES raised the question as to the order in which the deputies would be called upon to do duty.

LORD PHILLIMORE referred him to the 26th Article of the Root—Phillimore plan.

The PRESIDENT put the second Paragraph of M. Hagerup's amendment to the vote. This amendment was adopted. MM. de Lapradelle, Ricci-Busatti and Altamira abstained from voting.

The President then commenced the discussion of the 3rd Paragraph of M. Hagerup's

Après une courte discussion sur les avantages respectifs du système d'un barème et de celui de l'envoi de notes concernant les frais de voyage, on se met d'accord pour laisser à la Société des Nations le choix entre ces deux systèmes.

M. ANZILOTTI fait observer que la Société des Nations a déjà adopté le système des notes de voyage.

L'alinéa 3 de l'amendement de M. Hagerup est adopté.

M. DE LAPRADELLE soulève la question de savoir si les mêmes incompatibilités seront applicables aux juges suppléants qu'aux juges titulaires.

Le PRESIDENT donne lecture de l'article 10 du projet Root—Phillimore qui traite de cette question. A son avis, d'après ce texte, le juge suppléant doit être considéré comme libre d'exercer certaines fonctions qui sont incompatibles avec la position d'un juge titulaire; il pourra, par exemple, servir comme avocat ou conseil dans des litiges internationaux. Le Président croit qu'il serait utile en tout cas d'indiquer dans le texte de l'article qu'il n'a trait qu'aux juges titulaires.

M. HAGERUP, au contraire, croit qu'il faut assimiler les juges suppléants aux juges titulaires, en ce qui regarde l'incompatibilité.

M. DE LAPRADELLE est du même avis. En ne soumettant pas les suppléants à certaines incompatibilités, on s'exposerait à avoir des juges suppléants qui pourraient compromettre la Cour. Lorsqu'on a l'honneur d'être appelé à La Haye, on doit laisser toute occupation qui puisse être considérée comme incompatible; par exemple on ne doit pas donner des consultations: c'est justement cette nécessité qui constitue une des difficultés du recrutement des juges suppléants.

M. LODER fait observer qu'aux Pays-Bas cette incompatibilité n'existe pas.

M. HAGERUP demande quelle sera la situation d'un diplomate.

LORD PHILLIMORE pense d'accord avec Mr. Root, que la question des incompatibilités concernant les suppléants est peu importante. Il trouve cependant préférable d'assimiler les juges suppléants aux juges titulaires.

amendment. After a short discussion upon the respective merits of a schedule system and that of submitting statements of travelling expenses, it was agreed to leave the choice between these two systems to be made by the League of Nations.

M. ANZILOTTI pointed out that the League of Nations had already adopted the latter system.

The third Paragraph of M. Hagerup's amendment was adopted.

M. DE LAPRADELLE raised the question as to whether the same rules concerning incompatible duties would be applicable to deputy judges and to regular judges.

The PRESIDENT read Article 10 of the Root—Phillimore plan, which dealt with this question. In his opinion, according to this clause, the deputy judges must be considered free to undertake certain duties which were incompatible with the position of a regular judge. They could for instance act as advocate or counsel in international disputes. The President thought that in any case it would be advisable to make it clear in the wording that the Article only referred to regular judges.

M. HAGERUP, on the contrary, thought that deputy judges should be subject to the same rules concerning incompatible duties as regular judges.

M. DE LAPRADELLE was of the same opinion. If the deputy judges were allowed to undertake any kind of duties without certain restrictions, there would be a danger that some of them might compromise the position of the Court. Anyone, who had the honour to be summoned to the Hague, must give up any occupation which could be considered as incompatible; for instance, advisory opinions must not be given: this necessity in particular formed one of the main difficulties of recruiting deputy judges.

M. LODER pointed out that this was not regarded as an incompatible function in Holland.

M. HAGERUP asked how a diplomat would be situated.

LORD PHILLIMOTE thought, as also did Mr. Root, that the question of incompatible functions was unimportant, with regard to the deputy judges. He thought, however, that it would be preferable to class the deputy and regular judges together.

Mr. ROOT croit qu'il n'y a pas de danger à laisser la question sans être réglée, parce que personne ne dépassera les limites de ce qui est convenable à cet égard. Il fait observer la ressemblance qu'il y a entre le problème devant lequel on se trouve maintenant placé, et celui qu'on a eu à résoudre en 1907, lorsqu'il s'agissait des membres de la Cour d'Arbitrage; ces membres peuvent en effet, à certains points de vue, être considérés comme des suppléants, puisqu'ils ne sont appelés à siéger que dans des cas particuliers. La solution adoptée en 1907 est exprimée dans l'article 62 de la Convention sur le règlement pacifique des conflits internationaux. La formule employée dans cet article est la suivante:

„Les membres de la Cour Permanente ne peuvent exercer les fonctions d'agents, conseils ou avocats, qu'en faveur de la Puissance qui les a nommés membres de la Cour."

Mr. Root trouve cette formule suffisante pour les besoins actuels.

Le PRESIDENT fait observer que le texte appuyé par Mr. Root a été introduit en 1907; il ne se trouve pas dans la Convention de 1899. Aussi le Président réserve-t-il son opinion à cet égard. En 1899 on a trouvé exagéré de restreindre de cette façon la liberté des membres de la Cour. Il rappelle que sur 200 membres de la Cour d'Arbitrage, seulement une vingtaine ont effectivement exercé une fonction d'arbitre.

Mr. ROOT déclare qu'il est disposé à adopter une formule qui assimilerait, au point de vue des incompatibilités, les juges suppléants aux juges titulaires.

Le PRESIDENT met aux voix la formule proposée par Mr. Root, c'est-à-dire la formule qui se trouve dans l'art. 62 de la Convention de 1907.

Cette formule est adoptée.

Le Président, rappelant la communication qu'il a faite à la séance précédente au sujet du texte français de la formule relative aux incompatibilités, sur laquelle les membres du Comité se sont mis d'accord, donne lecture d'une traduction française de cette formule, préparée par le Secrétariat; cette formule est ainsi conçue:

„L'exercice par les membres de la Cour, pendant la durée de leur mandat, de toute fonction qui relève de la direction politique, soit nationale, soit internationale, des divers Etats, est déclaré incompatible avec leur fonction de juge."

Elle est approuvée.

Le Président ouvre la discussion sur l'art. 23 du projet Root—Phillimore.

Mr. ROOT thought there would be no danger in leaving the question without a definite ruling, since nobody would transgress the generally accepted principles upon the subject. He drew attention to the resemblance which existed between the present problem and that which had to be solved in 1907, with reference to the members of the Court of Arbitration; these members could in some respects all be considered as deputies, since they were only called upon to sit in special cases. The solution adopted in 1907 was contained in Article 62 of the Convention for the peaceful settlement of international disputes. The wording used in this article was as follows:

"The members of the Permanent Court may not act as agents, counsel or advocates except on behalf of the Power which appointed them members of the Court."

Mr. Root thought this wording sufficient for the present needs.

The PRESIDENT pointed out that the wording advocated by Mr. Root had been introduced in 1907; it was not contained in the Convention of 1899. The President also reserved his opinion concerning it. In 1899 it had been thought unnecessary to limit in this way the freedom of action of members of the Court of Arbitration. He recalled the fact that, of the 200 members of the Court of Arbitration, only 20 have actually done duty as arbitrators.

Mr. ROOT said he was prepared to accept a wording which would class the deputy judges with the regular judges for the purpose of the rules governing incompatible functions.

The PRESIDENT took a vote upon the formula proposed by Mr. Root, that is to say, the formula contained in Article 62 of the Convention of 1907.

This wording was adopted.

The President recalled the announcement he had made at the last meeting concerning the French version of the formula upon which the members of the Committee had agreed, dealing with incompatible functions, and read a French translation of this formula prepared by the Secretariat, which was as follows:

"L'exercice par les membres de la Cour, pendant la durée de leur mandat, de toute fonction qui relève de la direction politique, soit nationale, soit internationale, des divers Etats, est déclaré incompatible avec leur fonction de juge."

It was approved.

The President then laid Article 23 of the Root—Phillimore plan before the Committee.

LORD PHILLIMORE remarque que l'article 17 de l'avant-projet du Président contient une disposition d'après laquelle les Etats Membres de la Société des Nations sont tenus de supporter les frais de la Cour par parts égales. La même disposition se trouve dans le projet des Cinq Puissances. Le projet Root—Phillimore n'a pas adopté cette formule, craignant qu'on n'imposât aux Etats vraiment petits un fardeau trop lourd.

M. LODER fait observer que la disposition du projet des Cinq Puissances avait été adoptée en vue de souligner l'égalité des Etats.

On est d'accord pour laisser à la Société des Nations le soin de distribuer les frais.

M. HAGERUP soulève la question de la situation des Etats qui ne sont pas Membres de la Société des Nations, mais qui ont pourtant signé la Convention établissant la Cour.

On est d'accord pour considérer que cette question doit être traitée lors de la discussion des règles de procédure.

Le PRESIDENT, ouvrant la discussion sur l'article 24 du projet Root—Phillimore, soulève la question de savoir s'il ne faut pas indiquer que la Cour aura la faculté de siéger ailleurs. Il attire l'attention sur la formule insérée dans l'article 13 de son avant-projet.

LORD PHILLIMORE pense qu'il est évident que, si les Parties se mettent d'accord pour le demander, la Cour pourra siéger ailleurs qu'à La Haye. Il ne trouve pas qu'il soit nécessaire de donner une indication spéciale à ce sujet.

M. DE LAPRADELLE est d'avis que, puisque c'est la Société des Nations qui fixe le siège de la Cour, c'est également elle qui doit décider si la Cour peut se transporter ailleurs dans un cas déterminé.

En réponse à une question posée par M. Ricci-Busatti, LORD PHILLIMORE déclare que lorsqu'il y a accord entre les parties et la Cour, celle-ci pourra sans aucun doute transférer son siège.

M. RICCI-BUSATTI déclare qu'il peut accepter le texte du projet Root—Phillimore sous le bénéfice de la déclaration de Lord Phillimore.

Mr. ROOT s'oppose formellement à donner aux Parties et à la Cour le droit de transférer le siège de la Cour dans un cas déterminé. Ce qui fait la

LORD PHILLIMORE said that Article 17 of the President's draft scheme contained a clause according to which the States Members of the League of Nations were bound to contribute to the expenses of the Court in equal shares. The same clause was to be found in the Five Power Plan. The Root—Phillimore plan had not adopted this provision, fearing that too heavy a burden would be thereby imposed upon the really small States.

M. LODER pointed out that the clause in the Five Power plan had been adopted in order to emphasise the equality of States.

It was agreed to leave the task of allotting shares in the expenses to the League of Nations.

M. HAGERUP raised the question of the position of States which were not Members of the League of Nations, but which had signed the Convention establishing the Court.

The Committee agreed that this question should be dealt with when the rules of procedure were considered.

The PRESIDENT, in laying Article 24 of the Root—Phillimore plan before the Committee, raised the question as to whether a provision should not be included giving the Court the right to sit elsewhere. He drew attention to the clause contained in Article 13 of his plan.

LORD PHILLIMORE thought that it was obvious that, if the parties mutually agreed to make a request to this effect, the Court could sit elsewhere than at the Hague. He did not think it necessary to insert any special provision to this effect.

M. DE LAPRADELLE thought that, as it was the League of Nations which would fix the seat of the Court, the League should also decide whether the Court could move elsewhere in any particular case.

In answer to a question put by M. Ricci-Busatti, LORD PHILLIMORE said that if the parties and the Court were agreed upon the point, the latter could undoubtly sit elsewhere.

M. RICCI-BUSATTI said that he could now accept the wording of the Root—Phillimore plan, thanks to Lord Phillimore's statement.

Mr. ROOT was definitely opposed to giving the parties and the Court the right to transfer the seat of the Court for a particular case. The

différence entre la Cour permanente de Justice et la Cour d'Arbitrage, c'est précisément que les membres, et avant tout le Président, de la première se trouveront toujours à La Haye, et que les parties sauront toujours où s'adresser. On doit se borner à dire que le siège de la Cour est établi à la Haye.

essential difference between the Permanent Court of Justice and the Court of Arbitration lay in the fact that the members, and in particular the President, of the former would always be present at the Hague, and that parties would always know where to make application. All that should be said was that the seat of the Court would be established at the Hague.

Le PRESIDENT relève la différence entre le transfert du siège de la Cour et certains déplacements momentanés qui peuvent être nécessaires. Il fait également observer qu'aux termes de l'article 7 du Pacte de la Société des Nations, celle-ci peut transférer son siège.

The PRESIDENT drew a distinction between the transfer of the seat of the Court and temporary removals which might be necessary. He also pointed out that, according to the terms of Article 7 of the Covenant of the League of Nations, the League could transfer its seat.

M. DE LAPRADELLE fait valoir que cet argument parle en faveur de l'adoption de la formule simple qui se trouve à l'article 24 du projet Root—Phillimore.

M. DE LAPRADELLE pointed out that this argument was in favour of the adoption of the simple wording contained in Article 24 of the Root—Phillimore plan.

Le PRESIDENT met aux voix cette formule. Elle est adoptée.

The PRESIDENT put this wording to the vote. It was adopted.

La séance est levée à 12.40 heures de l'après-midi.

The meeting closed at 12.40 p.m.

Le Président :
(signé) Brn. DESCAMPS.

Le Secrétaire-Général :
(signé) D. ANZILOTTI.

The President :
(signed) Brn. DESCAMPS

The Secretary-General :
(signed) D. ANZILOTTI.

23ième SÉANCE (non-publique), tenue au Palais de la Paix, à La Haye, le 13 juillet 1920.

Présidence de M. le BARON DESCAMPS.

Sont présents: tous les membres du Comité (à l'exception de M. Bevilaqua); M. Fernandes; Mr. James Brown Scott; les secrétaires particuliers du Baron Descamps et de M. Adatci, les membres du Secrétariat.

La séance est ouverte à 9.40 heures du matin.

Le PRESIDENT prend la parole. Il dit que les membres du Comité forment une famille de jurisconsultes associés pour la réalisation d'un grand but et unis par une sincère amitié. L'un d'eux va quitter le Comité pour quelques jours afin d'aller célébrer une fête qui rappelle pour lui de nombreuses années de bonheur familial.

Le Président demande la permission de devancer un peu l'heure qui va sonner pour offrir à ce membre, avant son départ, les plus cordiales félicitations de ses collègues et tous les voeux qu'ils forment en ce moment pour lui et pour les siens. Les membres du Comité sont heureux de trouver une occasion de lui exprimer les sentiments de haute estime et de vive affection qu'ils ont pour l'homme éminent qui a rendu, non seulement à son pays, mais au monde international les plus importants services. Le Président prie Lord Phillimore au nom des membres du Comité, de présenter à Lady Phillimore, avec leurs respectueux hommages, l'expression des sentiments qu'il vient d'exprimer.

LORD PHILLIMORE remercie le Président de ses aimables paroles.

Le PRESIDENT déclare qu'il a deux propositions à communiquer:

1. Une proposition signée par Mr. Root et par lui-même, concernant la convocation d'une conférence à la Haye pour l'avancement du droit international. Il en donne lecture (voir annexe 1).

23rd MEETING (Private), held at the Peace Palace, the Hague, on July 13th, 1920.

BARON DESCAMPS in the chair.

Present: all the members of the Committee (except M. Bevilaqua); M. Fernandes; Mr. James Brown Scott; the private secretaries of Baron Descamps and M. Adatci; the members of the Secretariat.

The meeting opened at 9.40 a.m.

The PRESIDENT opened the discussion. He said that the members of the Committee were a family party of jurisconsults met togethen to accomplish a great object and united by ties of true friendship. One of their number was about to leave the Committee for a few days to celebrate an anniversary which would remind him of many years of domestic happiness.

The President asked permission to offer this Member, before his departure, the somewhat premature but most cordial congratulations of his colleagues, and all good wishes for the happiness of him and his family. The members of the Committee were happy to have the opportunity of giving expression to the high esteem and real affection which they felt for the distinguished man who had rendered such important services, not only to his own country but to international society. The President on behalf of the members of the Committee asked Lord Phillimore to present their respects to Lady Phillimore, and to convey to her the congratulations and good wishes he had just expressed.

LORD PHILLIMORE thanked the President for his kindness.

The PRESIDENT said that he had two proposed amendments to bring to the notice of the Committee:

1. A proposal signed by Mr. Root and himself, concerning the calling of a Conference at The Hague for the advancement of international law. He read this proposal. (See Annex 1).

2. Une proposition faite par le Président relative à l'établissement d'une Haute Cour de Justice Internationale, chargée de juger les crimes contre le droit des gens universel. (Cette proposition est reproduite à l'annexe 2). En l'introduisant, le Président rappelle que dans la séance de la veille, il avait attiré l'attention sur le projet qu'il avait déposé au début des travaux du Comité, à la demande de Mr. Root, et où se trouve une disposition concernant l'institution d'une Haute Cour de Justice Internationale, appelée à juger les crimes contre l'ordre public international et contre le droit des gens universel. (Voir annexe au procès-verbal du 21 juin: projet d'organisation de la Justice Internationale, articles 3 et 4).

Il désire appeler l'attention du Comité sur cette disposition et indiquer brièvement pourquoi il la considère comme n'étant pas étrangère au but que poursuit le Comité, à titre de complément nécessaire de l'organisation de la justice internationale.

Et, d'abord, peut-il exister des crimes contre le droit des gens universel, c'est à dire tels que la sécurité de tous les Etats se trouve atteinte par de tels attentats?

Le droit international connaît de tels crimes, et l'expérience prouve, malheureusement, qu'ils ne sont pas un mythe dans l'histoire des rapports internationaux, spécialement en temps de guerre. La constitution même de la Société des Nations sur des bases positives fournit d'ailleurs un terrain nouveau, sur lequel on peut se représenter la perpétration de tels crimes; par exemple, des attentats contre des institutions d'un caractère essentiellement international, comme le Conseil de la Société des Nations. Ce n'est pas seulement un Etat, ce sont tous les Etats, Membres de cette Société, qui pourraient, dans certains cas, se trouver atteints par de tels attentats.

Et ici se pose une seconde question: faut-il attendre que de tels attentats soient commis pour organiser à leur égard une juridiction *ex post facto*? Au sens du Président, il est plus sage d'organiser une juridiction qui n'ait à aucun point de vue, le caractère d'une vindicte après coup, et dont l'existence seule puisse exercer une action préventive importante.

Troisième question: comment composer une telle juridiction?

Le meilleur moyen semble bien être que le groupe des délégués de la Cour Permanente d'Arbitrage nommé par chaque Etat, désigne un membre de la Haute Cour, car ici surtout il importe que tous les Etats soient représentés et que le but de justice internationale poursuivi demeure à l'abri des influences politiques diverses.

Quatrième question: quelles garanties donner

2. A proposal submitted by the President with reference to the establishment of a High Court of International Justice for the purpose of trying crimes against the universal law of nations. (This proposal is inserted in Annex 2). In introducing this plan, the President recalled the fact that at the last meeting he had drawn attention to the plan which he had handed in at the commencement of the Committee's sittings, at the request of Mr. Root, in which a clause was contained dealing with the establishment of a High Court of International Justice for the purpose of trying crimes against international public order and against the universal law of nations. (See Annex to the Proces-Verbal of 21st June; plan for the organisation of International Justice, Articles 3 and 4).

He wished to call the Committee's attention to this suggestion and to indicate shortly the reasons why he considered that it was not unconnected with the object which the Committee had in view, but a necessary complement to it in the organisation of international justice.

First of all the question arises: do crimes against the law of nations exist, that is to say, crimes of such a nature that the security of all States would be imperilled by them?

International Law recognises the existence of such crimes, and experience unfortunately shows that they are no mere myth in the history of international affairs, especially in war time. Further the formation of the League of Nations upon a definite basis opens up a new field in which the perpetration of such crimes is conceivable; e.g. outrages against the authority of institutions of an essentially international character, such as the Council of the League of Nations. In certain cases not merely one particular State, but all States which are Members of this League, might be affected by such acts.

A second question now arises: should one wait until such outrages are committed and then organise an *ex post facto* tribunal to deal with them? In the President's opinion it would be wiser so to organise a tribunal for this purpose that a prosecution could not in any way be considered as a revenge, and that the very existence of this tribunal might have a considerable preventative effect.

Thirdly, how should such a tribunal be composed?

The best way would seem to be for each group of Delegates appointed by a particular State to the Permanent Court of Arbitration to nominate one member of the High Court; because in this case it is particularly essential that all States should be represented, and that the aim in view—the administration of international justice—should be protected from all political influences.

oncernant le fonctionnement juste et opportun 'une telle juridiction? L'intervention nécessaire de Assemblée ou du Conseil de la Société des Nations.

Mise en mouvement sur leur initiative, la Haute Cour posséderait les pouvoirs appréciateurs nécesaires pour caractériser le délit, appliquer la peine t déterminer les moyens éventuellement appropriés l'exécution de la sentence. Et elle déterminerait ar un règlement d'ordre sa procédure.

Telle est, dit le Président, l'économie de la lisposition qu'il a soumise au Comité et dont il ollicite la prise en considération en priant les nembres d'y voir, non une proposition du Président qu'ils ont choisi et auquel ils ont donné ant de marques de cordiale déférence, mais la imple suggestion d'un membre qui appelle l'atention de ses collègues sur un point qui lui paraît nériter une particulière attention.

Aucun des membres n'ayant pris la parole, le Président demande si le Comité désire un change de vues au sujet de la proposition.

Fourthly, what guarantees should be imposed to ensure the just and timely operation of such a tribunal? The previous intervention of the Assembly or the Council of the League of Nations must be stipulated.

The High Court, if set in operation on the initiative of these bodies, would possess the necessary powers to define the crime, to impose the penalty and to determine the appropriate means for the execution of the sentence in each case. The Court would determine its procedure by rules of Court.

Such, said the President, was the operation of the provision which he had submitted to the Committee, and which he begged the Committee not to consider as a proposal made by the President whom they had chosen and to whom they had paid so many friendly marks of respect, but as a mere suggestion of a member who wished to call the attention of his colleagues to a subject which seemed to him to be worthy of special consideration.

As none of the Members made any remarks, the President asked whether the Committee wished to have a discussion upon this proposal.

M. RICCI-BUSATTI croit qu'on ne pourrait liscuter cette proposition sans en avoir le texte ous les yeux. Pour cette raison, il suggère l'idée le remettre la discussion à plus tard.

M. RICCI-BUSATTI thought that it was not possible to discuss the proposal without having the text before them. For this reason he suggested that the discussion should be postponed until later.

Le PRESIDENT ayant déclaré que le texte sera listribué au cours de la séance, M. RICCI-BUSATTI léclare qu'il préférerait que la discussion fût remise à la semaine prochaine.

The PRESIDENT stated that the text would be distributed during the meeting, and M. RICCI-BUSATTI said that he would prefer that the discussion should be postponed until the following week.

M. DE LAPRADELLE croit que l'institution proposée vise exclusivement l'avenir.

M. DE LAPRADELLE thought that the proposed institution was only intended to deal with future events.

Le PRESIDENT confirme cette opinion. Il ajoute que, comme les nations institueront tôt ou tard l'organisation qu'il vient de proposer, il vaut nieux que le Comité s'en occupe dès maintenant.

The PRESIDENT confirmed this opinion. He added that, as the nations would, sooner or later, establish the institution he had just proposed, it would be better for the Committee to consider the question now.

M. HAGERUP ne peut pas se prononcer sur e fond de la question. Son opinion personnelle a été exposée par lui, il y a déjà des années, lans ses cours à l'Université. Il tient a déclarer que la guerre n'a aucunement modifié cette opinion. Mais il trouve que la question est en dehors du nandat du Comité: l'invitation adressée par Sir Eric Drummond aux membres parle seulement l'une juridiction internationale qui doit être ouverte aux parties. Si le mandat avait compris la création l'une Haute Cour de Justice, M. Hagerup

M. HAGERUP felt that he could not commit himself upon the principle of the question. His personal opinion he had already expounded many years ago in his lectures at the University. He wished to state that the war had in no way modified his opinion. He thought, however, that the question was outside the scope of the Committee's mandate; the invitation sent by Sir Eric Drummond to the members mentioned only an international tribunal to which parties should have a free access. If the mandate had included the creation of a High Court

aurait refusé de l'accepter, et si le Comité entre dans la discussion du fond de la question, M. Hagerup s'abstiendra d'y prendre part; si nécessaire, il se retirera même du Comité. Bien que la proposition du Président ne vise que l'avenir, elle est incontestablement de nature politique; quelle que fût l'attitude prise par lui, lors d'une discussion éventuelle, sa responsabilité serait engagée; or il tient absolument à garder sa neutralité, moins pour des raisons personnelles, que parce que son attitude pourrait, dans une certaine mesure, engager son pays.

Le PRESIDENT respecte les scrupules de M. Hagerup, mais il se trouve, par rapport à lui, dans une position diamétralement opposée: s'il avait pu prévoir qu'on tâcherait d'empêcher la discussion de la question de l'établissement d'une Haute Cour de Justice, cette perspective eût été pour lui une raison de plus de participer aux discussions du Comité. La proposition du Président ne s'occupe pas du passé. Il s'agit de prévenir la perpétration de crimes contre le droit des gens universel: elle n'est que le complément indispensable de l'œuvre que le Comité est appelé à accomplir.

M. DE LAPRADELLE a été frappé de l'objection de conscience formulée par M. Hagerup. Lorsqu'on pose une question de conscience on pose en même temps une question de sentiment, et cela ne prête pas à discussion. Cependant, et afin d'éviter toute équivoque, M. de Lapradelle, en se plaçant à son tour au point de vue de la conscience, demande à M. Hagerup de retirer le mot de neutralité qu'il a prononcé, ce mot étant devenu impropre, puisqu'on se trouve maintenant dans la Société des Nations.

M. de Lapradelle a eu, à une certaine époque, l'esprit du belligérant, mais il l'a abandonné pour l'esprit du citoyen qui est entré dans la Société des Nations, et qui veut réaliser, dans le cadre de la Société, la Paix et la Justice.

Il s'agit maintenant de construire l'avenir et non d'évoquer le passé. On ne se trouve plus devant des crimes déterminés, on ne sait pas qui seront les auteurs des crimes à l'avenir; c'est pourquoi on peut construire une Cour *in abstracto.* La Société des Nations est née des souffrances des peuples et a pour but de prévenir la répétition des calamités qui lui ont donné naissance. Pour pouvoir réaliser ce but, il faut une organisation judiciaire stable qui puisse agir contre les coupables d'attentats à la justice internationale, de quelque nationalité qu'ils soient. On n'a pas encore assez de sang-froid pour pouvoir regarder le passé;

of Justice, M. Hagerup would have refused to accept it, and if the Committee undertook a discussion of the principle of the question, M. Hagerup would take no part in it. If necessary, he would even retire from the Committee. Though the President's proposal only referred to the future, it was indisputably of a political nature. Whatever attitude he might adopt if a discussion were to take place, he would be held responsible; he insisted upon maintaining his neutrality, less for personal reasons than because his attitude might, to some extent, be binding upon his country.

The PRESIDENT respected M. Hagerup's scruples but he took a view diametrically opposed to that of M. Hagerup. If he had been able to foresee that an attempt would be made to prevent discussion of the question of the establishment of the High Court of Justice, this circumstance would have been for him an additional reason for taking part in the Committee's meetings. The President's proposal did not concern the past. Its purpose was to prevent the perpetration of crimes against the law of nations: it was but the indispensable complement of the work that the Committee had been called upon to do.

M. DE LAPRADELLE had been struck by the conscientious objections expressed by M. Hagerup. Conscientious scruples also involved a question of feeling, and that did not lend itself to discussion. Nevertheless M. de Lapradelle, in order to avoid any misunderstanding, and in his turn raising a conscientious objection, asked M. Hagerup to withdraw the word "neutrality": this word was now unsuitable since they were all Members of the League of Nations.

M. de Lapradelle had at one time felt the belligerent spirit, but he had discarded it and now felt as a citizen of the League of Nations, who wished to see peace and justice established through the instrumentality of the League.

It was now a question of building up the future and not raking up the past. There was no longer any question of particular crimes; no one knew who would be the perpetrators of the crimes in the future, and therefore a Court could be constructed *in abstracto.* The League of Nations was born of the sufferings of the nations, and its object was to prevent a repetition of the calamities which gave rise to its creation. For the achievement of this end a stable judicial organisation was required which could take action against those guilty of crimes against international justice, no matter what nation they belonged to. The past could not yet be considered as coolly and impartially

mais on peut en avoir bien assez pour construire l'avenir, en assurant l'organisation de la justice internationale puisque cette justice elle-même existe. Il y a d'ailleurs d'autres crimes contre le droit international universel que des crimes de guerre. On peut donc procéder en regardant l'avenir sans rien évoquer du passé. M. de Lapradelle croit que, dans cet esprit, la conscience de M. Hagerup et la sienne peuvent se rencontrer.

Le PRESIDENT déclare qu'il fait sienne la déclaration de M. de Lapradelle.

M. HAGERUP demande la parole pour expliquer dans quel sens il s'est servi du mot „neutralité". Il dit qu'il n'a pas pensé à la neutralité entre deux belligérants, mais à celle entre deux opinions divergentes. Il apprécie les considérations de M. de Lapradelle; mais, en se plaçant à un point de vue théorique et pratique, il ne conçoit pas comment serait fait un code pénal international ni comment serait organisée l'application des peines. D'ailleurs, il n'a pas invoqué, comme l'a dit M. de Lapradelle, des raisons de sentiment. Il a dit que la question, par la force des choses, a assumé un caractère politique et qu'il ne peut pas, comme membre de cette commission, se mêler de la politique. C'est là une raison qui n'est pas sentimentale mais tout à fait pratique, qui s'ajoute pour lui à la raison de conscience, ou plutôt peut-être, de prudence, qu'il vient d'exposer: — de prudence, parce qu'elle engagerait non seulement sa propre attitude, mais, il le répète, celle de son pays.

M. Hagerup finit en rappelant que le mandat qu'il a reçu de la Société des Nations ne comprend que l'établissement d'une Cour de Justice; il demande au Comité de tenir compte de ce fait.

M. ALTAMIRA déclare qu'il se rallie complètement à la proposition du Président et au commentaire de M. de Lapradelle. Tel a été toujours son point de vue, celui qui l'a guidé en écrivant son livre sur la situation de l'Espagne pendant la guerre, et l'espoir le plus chéri de son esprit en ce qui concerne les conséquences possibles de la terrible leçon reçue par l'humanité. Il pense toutefois qu'il faudrait remplir une condition: les liens organiques qui à coup sûr existent entre la proposition du Président et le travail qui est visé dans le mandat des membres doivent être expliqués.

as necessary, but it was quite possible to be sufficiently impartial to build up the future by organising International Justice, since the latter was already in existence. There were also other crimes against International Law besides crimes against the rules of war. It was possible therefore to make provision for the future without stirring up memories of the past. M. de Lapradelle believed that if they worked in this spirit, M. Hagerup and he would be able to reconcile their respective consciences.

The PRESIDENT declared that he endorsed every word that M. de Lapradelle had said.

M. HAGERUP requested permission to speak, in order to explain his use of the word "neutrality". He said that he had not meant neutrality as between belligerent States, but as between two opposite opinions. He fully appreciated M. de Lapradelle's arguments, but looking upon the matter from a theoretical and practical point of view, he could not see how an international penal code could be drawn up, or how the enforcement of penalties was to be organised. Again, he had not, as M. de Lapradelle had affirmed, made any reference to a question of feeling. He had said that the question was, by force of circumstances, vested with a political character and that he could not, as a member of this Committee, become involved in politics. Herein lay a purely practical reason, with nothing sentimental about it, which supplemented the conscientious scruples—or perhaps he should rather say motives of prudence—which he had just explained. He used the word prudence because not only his own attitude but, he repeated, that of his country would be involved.

M. Hagerup ended by recalling the fact that the mandate given him by the League of Nations only referred to the establishment of a Court of Justice. He asked the Committee to bear this in mind.

M. ALTAMIRA stated that he completely agreed with the President's proposal and with M. de Lapradelle's remarks concerning it. He had always held the views which found expression in this proposal, and had been guided by them in writing his book on the situation of Spain during the war: it had been his most cherished hope, in connection with the possible results of the terrible lesson administered to mankind, that such a Court would be evolved. He thought, however, that there was one condition to be complied with: the organic connection undoubtedly existing between

Si l'on réussit à convaincre, non seulement les membres du Comité, mais aussi l'opinion du grand public, des relations étroites qui peuvent exister entre la Cour Permanente de Justice et la Haute Cour, telle qu'elle a été conçue par le Président; si de cette manière, on fait comprendre que la nouvelle organisation contemplée rentre dans le mandat du Comité, ou en est le complément nécessaire, alors la discussion sera plus facile parce qu'on verra la proposition sous un aspect différent, et on ne craindra plus de sortir des limites du mandat en la prenant sérieusement en considération.

M. ADATCI est favorable à la création d'une Haute Cour de Justice préalablement à la perpétration des crimes qu'elle aura à juger. Il rappelle que, lors de la Conférence de la Paix à Paris, on a beaucoup discuté la question d'établir un tribunal compétent pour juger les crimes de guerre. Mais cette idée l'a choqué parce que ce tribunal aurait eu à connaître des crimes *ex post facto*.

Le problème se pose autrement lorsqu'il s'agit d'établir une Cour avant la perpétration des actes punissables; c'est pourquoi la proposition du Président plaît beaucoup à M. Adatci. Seulement, le Comité est chargé, à son avis, de créer une Cour et non pas deux: il croit donc que le Comité dépasserait les limites de son mandat en s'occupant de la proposition soumise par le Président. Il pense que cette proposition doit être renvoyée à une nouvelle Conférence de droit international.

A ces considérations, viennent s'ajouter pour M. Adatci des considérations d'ordre pratique: le Comité n'a devant lui qu'un temps extrêmement limité pour achever les travaux dont il a été chargé.

M. RICCI-BUSATTI aurait préféré que la question ne fût pas discutée à la présente séance; mais la discussion s'étant engagée, il croit devoir déclarer quelle est son attitude vis à vis de cette question.

Tous les membres qui se sont prononcés jusqu'ici ont évoqué le cauchemar du passé, quoique tous désirent écarter ce souvenir des travaux du Comité. Cela démontre que le passé est nécessairement lié à la question et que la discussion ne peut pas éviter le terrain politique. Cette circonstance est pour M. Ricci-Busatti un motif suffisant pour écarter la proposition préjudiciellement.

A la raison qu'il vient d'exposer, viennent s'ajouter des considérations d'ordre juridique. Selon l'ar-

the President's proposal and the work covered by the mandate given to the members must be fully explained. If not only the members of the Committee, but also general public opinion could be convinced of the close ties which might exist between the Permanent Court of Justice and the High Court, as conceived by the President; if in this way it could be made generally understood that the proposed new organisation came within the mandate of the Committee or was its necessary complement, then its discussion would be easier because the proposal would be looked upon in a different light, and there need be no fear of overstepping the limits of the mandate by devoting serious consideration to it.

M. ADATCI was in favour of creating a High Court of Justice before the crimes which it would have to try had been committed. He recalled that, at the time of the Peace Conference at Paris, the question of establishing a tribunal with jurisdiction over crimes against the rules of war had been much discussed. But this notion had shocked him because this tribunal would have had to deal with crimes defined *ex post facto*.

It was quite a different matter, now that the intention was to establish a Court before the punishable acts had been committed; for this reason the President's proposal pleased M. Adatci very much. In his opinion, however, the Committee was entrusted with the task of creating one Court and not two: he thougt therefore that the Committee would exceed its mandate if it concerned itself with the proposal submitted by the President. He thought that this proposal ought to be submitted to a new Conference on international law.

In addition to these considerations, in M. Adatci's opinion, there were some practical reasons to be taken into account: the Committee had only an extremely limited time in which to complete the work with which it had been entrusted.

M. RICCI-BUSATTI would have preferred that the question should not be discussed at the present meeting; but as the discussion had been commenced, he felt that he must make his attitude clear.

All the members who had already spoken on the subject had referred to the nightmare of the past, though they all wished to exclude any remembrance of it from the work of the Committee. This showed that the past was necessarily bound up in the question and that the discussion was bound to have a political bearing. This fact was for M. Ricci-Busatti a sufficient reason for ruling the proposal out of order.

To the reason he had just given there were

ticle 3 du plan soumis par le Président au Comité, il serait créé une nouvelle Cour spéciale „la Haute Cour de Justice", constituée différemment de celle que nous sommes en train d'organiser pour les affaires contentieuses: voilà déjà une complication regrettable! La compétence de cette Cour est définie dans l'article 4. Mais cet article repose sur des idées que M. Ricci-Busatti croit pouvoir qualifier d'erronnées; il ne sait pas au juste ce que l'on entend par „délit contre le droit des gens universel": il ne croit pas possible, dans les rapports entre Etats, de distinguer entre un droit civil et un droit pénal, ainsi que cela se fait dans le droit national selon certains principes, dont l'application n'est pas d'ailleurs exempte de controverses et d'incertitudes même dans ce domaine, et ne saurait pas avoir lieu en droit international. Tout cela a été l'objet de longues discussions théoriques au sein de la Commission des Responsabilités et des Sanctions, à la Conférence de Paris; il ne croit pas utile ni désirable de les renouveler au sein du Comité.

Le PRESIDENT fait observer que les conditions de fait sont changées; la Société des Nations est maintenant en mesure de signaler les crimes contre le droit international.

M. RICCI-BUSATTI maintient son opinion; il demande si les criminels dont il s'agit seront des Etats ou des particuliers. Dans le premier cas, comment appliquer les règles du droit pénal? Quant aux individus, il ne croit pas qu'ils puissent violer le droit international qui est un droit entre Etats; aucun rapport juridique de cette nature n'est admissible, à son avis, entre des Etats et des particuliers. En tout cas il y a là une foule de questions à résoudre; c'est pourquoi il estime qu'il vaut mieux s'abstenir de discuter le problème et s'en tenir aux raisons de compétence qui nous autorisent à le laisser de côté.

M. LODER rend hommage à l'esprit qui a dicté la proposition du Président. Il comprend que celui-ci et M. de Lapradelle, ressortissants de pays qui ont subi les malheurs de la guerre, l'aient faite et supportée. M. Loder croit que le problème traité dans la proposition ne rentre pas dans le mandat du Comité, qui doit organiser la Cour prévue à l'article 14 du Pacte, mais ce n'est pas là, pour lui, un argument décisif pour refuser de prendre part à la discussion. En effet il se rallie complètement à la proposition d'un vœu concernant la convocation de nouvelles Conférences

others of a legal nature to be added. According to Article 3 of the plan submitted by the President on the 21st of June, a new special Court was to be created, "the High Court of Justice", constituted in a different way from the Court which the Committee was now organising for international lawsuits: this was a regrettable complication. The jurisdiction of this Court was defined in Article 4. This Article, however, was based on an idea that M. Ricci-Busatti thought was unsound; he did not quite know what was to be understood by "a crime against the universal law of nations." He did not think it was possible in international affairs to make a distinction between civil law and penal law as was done in national law in accordance with certain principles, the application of which is not, however, free from argument and uncertainty even in this sphere, and which could not be applied to International Law. All this was the subject of long theoretical discussion in the Commission for the Establishment of Responsabilities and Penalties during the Conference at Paris; he did not think it would be either useful or desirable for the Committee to renew the discussion.

The PRESIDENT pointed out that the conditions had changed; the League of Nations was now in a position to define crimes against International Law.

M. RICCI-BUSATTI held to his opinion; he asked whether the criminals in question would be States or private individuals: if the former, how were the rules of penal law to be applied? As to individuals, he did not think that they could commit infractions of International Law, as it was law between States; a legal relationship of this kind between States and individuals was, in his opinion, inadmissible. In any case there were a host of questions to be solved; he thought, therefore, that it would be better not to discuss the problem, but to abide by the interpretation of the Committee's mandate which justifies the omission of it.

M. LODER paid homage to the spirit which had inspired the President's proposal. He could understand that the President and M. de Lapradelle, being subjects of countries which had suffered the horrors of war, had, respectively, made and supported this proposal. M. Loder thought, however, that the question dealt with in the proposal did not come within the Committee's mandate; the Committee's task was to organise the Court provided for in Article 14 of the Covenant; but this fact was not, in his opinion, a decisive reason for refusing to take part in the

pour l'avancement du droit international: ce vœu ne rentre pas non plus dans le mandat du Comité, mais on ne saurait prétendre que le Comité ne puisse pas faire un vœu à ce sujet.

M. Loder se demande plutôt si, en voulant créer une Cour pour juger des crimes internationaux, le Président n'aborde pas le problème en commençant par la fin. Il rappelle la règle de Beccaria; „nulla poena sine praevia lege poenali", et demande quel est le droit qui doit être appliqué par la nouvelle Cour. Il admet que le droit pourra être formulé et il croit, avec M. Altamira, qu'il serait utile de le faire. Mais le plan du Président suggère l'établissement d'une Cour avant de définir le droit que cette Cour appliquera: on y parle de crimes qui ne sont pas encore déterminés. Dans ces circonstances, la Cour ne pourrait être qu'une Cour politique; d'autant plus que les Etats seraient représentes chacun par un juge.

Pour sa part, il est favorable à l'idée d'élargir graduellement le domaine de la juridiction de la Cour Permanente, dont on est en train de tracer l'organisation. Mais il est absolument opposé à l'idée de faire appliquer, par une Cour politique, des peines non définies à des crimes non déterminés. En résumé, il déclare qu'il trouve bonne l'idée du Président, mais qu'à son avis, elle n'est pas encore mûre pour être réalisée.

M. FERNANDES exprime l'opinion que la proposition du Président répond à un désir universel. Mais la discussion à démontré qu'il y a au sein du Comité des divergences profondes d'opinion qui revèlent les graves difficultés techniques et politiques de la question. Il rend hommage à la façon dont M. Loder a sagement rappelé le principe fondamental du droit pénal „nullum crimen sine lege". A la raison découlant de ce principe et qui est de nature à faire écarter la proposition du Président, au moins dans le texte sous lequel elle a été présentée, vient s'ajouter la considération qu'il s'agit de crimes politiques. L'Assemblée de la Societé des Nations hésiterait à accepter pour des crimes de cet ordre une Cour qui aurait à définir les crimes et à fixer les peines. Il ne faut pas oublier que les criminels seront les gouvernements eux-mêmes ou leurs agents autorisés. Dans ces circonstances, la juridiction de la Cour constituerait un danger pour la souveraineté même des Etats, peut-être une menace pour la paix. M. Fernandes croit qu'on pourrait parvenir à concilier les opinions divergentes au moyen d'un vœu demandant qu'il soit procédé à la définition des crimes et à la fixation des peines, de

discussion. In fact he was entirely in favour of a resolution recommending the calling of new Conferences to make further progress in international law. Such action was not authorised by the mandate of the Committee either, but it was impossible to contend that the Committee could not pass resolution on this subject.

M. Loder was inclined to think that, in wishing to establish a Court for the trial of international crimes, the President was beginning at the wrong end of the problem. He recalled Beccaria's rule " Nulla poena sine praevia lege poenali", and asked what system of law should be applied by the new Court. He acknowledged that law could be formulated and, like M. Altamira, thought that it would be useful to do so. The President's plan, however, suggested the establishment of a Court before defining the law to be applied by it. Crimes were mentioned in it which were not yet defined. Under such circumstances the Court could only be of a political nature; especially as each State would be represented by a judge.

M. Loder was in favour of the gradual extention of the jurisdiction of the permanent Court, the organisation of which they were now planning, but he was absolutely opposed to the idea of the application of undefined penalties to undefined crimes by a political Court. M. Loder, in summing up, said that he thought the President's idea was good, but that the time was not yet ripe for its realisation.

M. FERNANDES expressed the opinion that the President's proposal met a universal desire, but the discussion had shown that the opinions of the members of the Committee differed profoundly and that the question involved serious technical and political difficulties. He acknowledged the wisdom with which M. Loder had recalled the fundamental principle of penal law: " nullum crimen sine lege". To the reasons arising from this principle, which were sufficient to rule out the President's proposal, at any rate in the form in which it had been presented, must be added the fact that the crimes in question were of a political nature. The Assembly of the League of Nations would hesitate to accept a Court, to deal with crimes of this nature, which would have both to define the crime and to fix the punishment. It must not be forgotten that the criminals would be either Governments or the accredited agents of Governments. Under these circumstances the jurisdiction of the Court would be a danger to the sovereign rights of States, perhaps even a menace to peace. M. Fernandes thought that a resolution which would reconcile the divergent opinions, might be drawn up, to the effect that steps should be taken to

manière à rendre possible l'activité d'une Haute Cour. Ainsi le Comité éviterait de dépasser son mandat; ce qui arriverait, au contraire, si l'on adoptait la proposition du Président qui suggère l'établissement d'une Haute Cour, indépendante de la Cour Permanente de Justice. On donnerait également satisfaction aux scrupules de conscience de M. Hagerup et, enfin, on indiquerait à l'Assemblée la direction qui paraît la plus désirable en cette matière.

Mr. ROOT déclare qu'il prend un grand intérêt à la proposition du Président. Il a pensé qu'il était désirable d'établir entre les nations civilisées un accord sur la façon dont on devait traiter les crimes contre les principes universellement reconnus de l'humanité, de la justice et de la morale. La proposition du Président, si éloquemment supportée par M. de Lapradelle, a par conséquent toutes ses sympathies.

Il voudrait donc que le fait que le Comité n'est pas fermé aux idées dont s'inspire cette proposition fût clairement exprimé; mais il reconnaît que des difficultés sérieuses se présentent. D'abord il faut qu'il y ait une loi pour qu'il puisse y avoir une punition. Les Etats étant les seuls sujets de droit international, un particulier ne peut être puni que si l'acte qu'il a commis est punissable selon le droit national applicable en l'espèce, c'est à dire, si l'acte qui viole la loi des nations compromet en même temps la paix et la dignité du pays dont la loi est applicable.

Dans ces circonstances la question se transforme en une question de souveraineté. Il s'agit en effet de savoir dans quelle mesure un État déterminé est disposé à modifier les exigences de la souveraineté en vue de permettre aux représentants d'une autre souveraineté de punir des actes commis sur son territoire. Cette question implique celle d'un individu qui doit obéissance à deux autorités différentes. Un officier qui obéit à son gouvernement peut être considéré par la Société des Nations, dans un cas déterminé, comme commettant un crime contre le droit international. Si cette opinion prévaut, l'autorité de la Société des Nations prime la souveraineté de l'Etat. Ceci est inadmissible, tant que l'on ne peut s'autoriser que de principes généraux. Il faut que les cas soient nettement définis. Autrement on créerait le „sur-Etat:" une grande autorité centrale, exerçant son pouvoir sur les Etats, jusque-là indépendants.

Mr. Root croit qu'il faut faire une distinction. Il y a un domaine de justice punitive qui est entièrement séparé de celui qu'on est maintenant en train de discuter; c'est l'application des lois de

define the crimes and assess the penalties in order to make the operation of a High Court possible. In this way the Committee would not exceed its mandate, which would be the case if, on the other hand, the President's proposal, which contemplated the establishment of a High Court independent of the Permanent Court of Justice, were adopted. The conscientious scruples of M. Hagerup would also be satisfied, and lastly, an indication of the most desirable line to take in this connection would be given to the Assembly.

Mr. ROOT declared that he took a deep interest in the President's proposition. He had long felt that it would be desirable to establish an understanding between civilised nations as to how crimes against universally recognised principles of humanity, justice and morality should be dealt with. He consequently sympathised profoundly with the President's proposal, which had been so eloquently supported by M. de Lapradelle.

He would therefore like the fact that the Committee was not opposed to the ideas on which this proposition was based to be clearly recorded; but he recognised that some serious difficulties existed. In the first place, unless there is a law to be broken there can be no penalty for breaches of it. As only States are subjects of International Law, an individual can only be punished if the act which he has committed is punishable according to the national law which applies to the case, that is to say, if the act, which constitutes a breach of the law of nations, also affects the welfare and dignity of the country whose law is applicable.

Under these circumstances, the question transforms itself into one of sovereignty; it practically amounts to a question as to how far a given State is prepared to modify its sovereign rights, in order to allow representatives of another sovereign State to punish acts committed within the former's territory. This question involves another: the situation of an individual owing allegiance to two different authorities. An official who obeys his Government may, in a given case, be considered by the League of Nations as having committed an offence against International Law. If this opinion were upheld, the authority of the League of Nations would supersede the sovereignty of the State, and, so long as the only authorisation for this is based on general principles, it is inadmissible. Cases must be clearly defined, otherwise a " super-State" would be created —a great central authority exercising its power over States which, up to that time, had been independent.

Mr. Root thought it necessary to make a distinction. There is a sphere of penal justice, which

la guerre aux actes de guerre. L'échange de vues actuel porte sur la juridiction dont ressortissent les crimes internationaux en temps de paix. C'est dans ce domaine qu'une définition soigneuse est indispensable. Parmi les actes qui rentrent dans cette catégorie, Mr. Root distingue entre les actes dont les Etats assument la responsabilité et ceux qui sont désavoués pas les Etats. Pour ce qui est des premiers, ils créent une relation entre Etats; pour ce qui est des seconds, ils mettent leurs auteurs hors de la protection de leur gouvernement, c'est à dire hors de la loi. Mr. Root prend l'exemple de la traite des noirs.

Dans cet ordre d'idées Mr. Root préconise la création d'une catégorie spéciale de criminels qui ont été désavoués par leurs gouvernements et mis hors la loi. Si l'on créait ensuite une juridiction spéciale pour ces criminels, cette juridiction élargirait successivement sa sphère d'activité. C'est la méthode normale à employer pour assurer la collaboration de l'opinion publique à la réalisation du progrès.

Il faudrait d'abord créer pour tous les États l'obligation d'extrader les personnes accusées, parce qu'il est impossible de donner à la Cour ou à un gouvernement déterminé le droit de s'assurer, dans le territoire d'un Etat quelconque, de la personne du criminel: ce serait un acte de guerre.

En outre, selon Mr. Root, la juridiction devrait être mise en mouvement par les gouvernements souverains, qui devraient s'adresser à la Cour en disant que telle et telle personne a commis tel et tel acte qui a été désavoué par son gouvernement.

Mr. Root se demande quelle sera la nature de la procédure à suivre. Il croit qu'il est impossible de la confier à un "sur-Etat". Il pense qu'il sera nécessaire de se servir de l'autorité des différents Etats. Dans ces circonstances, la première question qui se pose est la suivante: les Etats du monde sont ils disposés à renoncer, dans la mesure nécessaire, à leur souveraineté individuelle? Ce n'est qu' après avoir obtenu une réponse à cette question, que l'on pourrait procéder à la création d'une Cour. Pour le moment, Mr. Root pense devoir se borner à suggérer l'idée de référer la question à la conférence visée par la proposition Root—Descamps, dont le Président a donné lecture, la conférence devant formuler une recommandation sur ce point. Il sera en effet nécessaire de donner à tous les Etats du monde le moyen de se prononcer sur ce problème.

LORD PHILLIMORE croit devoir exprimer son opinion sur la question puisque ses collègues ont jugé bon de le faire.

is quite distinct from that under discussion: that is, the application of laws of war to acts of war. The present exchange of views concerned jurisdiction over international crimes in time of peace. An exact definition of such offences is indispensable. Amongst acts included in this category, Mr. Root distinguished between acts for which States accept responsibility, and those disowned by States. The former give rise to relations between States; the persons responsible for the latter are deprived of the protection of their Governments, that is to say, they are outlawed. Mr. Root took the Slave Trade as an example.

In this connection, Mr. Root pointed out the advantages of the creation of a special classification for criminals who have been disowned by their Governments and outlawed. If, following upon this, a special tribunal for these crimes were created, the jurisdiction of this tribunal would be gradually extended. This was the normal method which should be employed to assure the collaboration of public opinion in the realisation of progress.

In the first place it would be necessary to create an obligation binding all States to extradite accused persons, because it would be impossible to give the Court, or a particular Government, the right to arrest the criminal within the territory of some other State: it would be an act of war.

Further, in Mr. Root's opinion, the tribunal should be set in operation by a communication from Governments of sovereign States, to the effect that such and such a person had committed such and such an act, which had been repudiated by his Government.

Mr. Root next considered the nature of the procedure to be followed. He thought that it would be impossible to entrust it to a "super-State"; the authority of the various States must be used. Under these circumstances, the first question which arises is the following: Are the Governments of the world prepared to give up their individual sovereign rights to the necessary extent? Only when an answer had been given to this question, would it be possible to proceed with the creation of a Court. For the moment, Mr. Root thought it better to limit himself to a suggestion that the question should be referred to the Conference contemplated by the Root—Descamps proposal which the President had read; the Conference should be called upon to make a recommendation on the subject. It would, in fact, be necessary to give all the Governments of the world an opportunity to express their views on the problem.

LORD PHILLIMORE thought that he should express his opinion on the question, since his colleagues had seen fit to do so. He thought that

Il est d'avis que la question ne rentre pas dans le mandat du Comité, et il a été un peu surpris de voir qu'elle avait été soulevée dans la proposition du Président. Toutefois il pense que le Comité pourra émettre un vœu, après avoir accompli sa tâche principale.

Mais la détermination du contenu de ce vœu, n'est pas sans présenter des difficultés. Il se demande quels sont les crimes à punir, les criminels à poursuivre? La proposition du Président ne dit rien de précis à ce sujet. Les criminels doivent-ils être des Etats ou des particuliers? On semble être d'accord pour considérer que les Etats ne peuvent pas entrer en ligne de compte: il cite le mot de Burke: „il est impossible de dresser un acte d' accusation contre un Etat": au surplus il n'y a pas de criterium pour distinguer entre un Etat criminel et un Etat qui ne l'est pas: un Etat qui se trouve lésé pense toujours que son adversaire est un criminel, et il arrive souvent qu'il va jusqu'à la guerre pour le punir.

Pour ce qui est des particuliers, il faut distinguer trois cas:

1. les actes commis en temps de paix;
2. les crimes de guerre;
3. le crime d'avoir fait la guerre.

Pour les crimes commis en temps de paix, il y a toujours une juridiction nationale compétente. Le coupable peut être puni par les tribunaux de son propre pays; ou bien par les tribunaux d'un Etat autre que le sien, sous la juridiction duquel il se trouve; ou bien l'Etat national peut demander l'extradition du coupable en se basant sur le principe qu'un acte violant la loi des nations est un acte contre la paix et la dignité de l'Etat national, qui pourrait être plongé dans une guerre par l'effet de cet acte. Si, par conséquent, on se demande s'il y a une punition effective contre les crimes de droit international en temps de paix, il faut répondre que, comme l'a remarqué M. Root, un acte commis par un particulier, ou est ratifié par son Gouvernement, ou désavoué: dans le premier cas il donne naissance à une affaire entre Etats; dans le deuxième cas, une juridiction nationale est toujours compétente, et cette punition est beaucoup plus effective que celle qui pourrait être infligée par une Cour internationale, qui manquerait de moyens d'exécution. Le tribunal international serait, dans l'opinion de Lord Phillimore, non seulement inutile, mais encombrant.

Pour ce qui est des crimes de guerre proprement dits, Lord Phillimore ne s'oppose pas à une juridiction internationale, pour cette raison qu'il y a une loi. En effet, le Réglement sur les

the question was not included in the Committee's mandate, and he was a little surprised to see it raised in the President's proposal. However, he thought that the Committee might pass a resolution after having discharged its principal duty.

There would however be certain difficulties to contend with, in settling the terms of the resolution. He raised the question of the nature of the crimes to be punished, and asked what class of offender was to be prosecuted. The proposal of the President made no specific statement on this subject. Were the offenders to be States or individuals? It seemed to be agreed that States could not be so dealt with. He quoted Burke's saying to the effect that it is impossible to draw up an indictment against a State: furthermore there is no criterion for distinguishing between a criminal State and one which is not. A State which considers itself wronged will always consider that its adversary is a criminal and, often, it will even go to war to punish it.

Concerning individuals, three cases must be differentiated:

1. Acts committed in time of peace.
2. Crimes of War.
3. The crime of having made war.

For crimes committed in time of peace, a competent national jurisdiction always exists. An offender can be punished by the Courts of his own country, or by the Courts of a State other than his own, under the jurisdiction of which he may happen to be; or his own State can request his extradition on the grounds that an act violating the law of nations is an offence against its own peace and dignity, since it might be plunged into war as a result of this act. Consequently, if the question is raised as to whether there is any effective means of punishing crimes against International Law, in time of peace, the answer must be, as Mr. Root had said, that an act committed by an individual is either approved by his Government, or disowned by it: in the first instance, the outcome is a question between Governments, in the second case, a national tribunal always has jurisdiction, and punishment by this means is much more effective than a penalty imposed by an international Court which would lack means of execution; an international tribunal would be, in Lord Phillimore's opinion, not only useless but a hindrance.

Concerning crimes of war in the true sense of the word, Lord Phillimore was not opposed to an international jurisdiction, because an applicable law does exist. The Regulations respecting the

Lois et Coutumes de la Guerre sur Terre, adopté en 1907, contient une série d'actes défendus et punissables. Dans ces circonstances, rien ne s'oppose à l'établissement d'un tribunal et d'une procédure. Cette loi pourrait être élargie par une nouvelle Convention qui, en même temps, élargirait la sphère d'activité de la juridiction.

L'objection de Lord Phillimore contre la proposition du Président est donc basée sur le fait que cette proposition ne dit pas si elle vise le temps de paix, le temps de guerre, ou les deux à la fois. Si elle tient compte seulement des crimes de guerre, Lord Phillimore peut se rallier à la proposition qu'un vœu soit émis.

Il arrive au crime d'avoir fait la guerre. Ce crime peut être conçu comme un crime contre le Pacte de la Société des Nations: on pourrait peut-être procéder contre les personnes responsables en invoquant l'autorité de Grotius; mais il est indispensable de préciser et de définir ce que c'est que ce crime. L'esquisse du Président est trop vague et trop peu développée. Lord Phillimore hésiterait à confier la compétence en matière criminelle à un tribunal sans procédure, sans lois fixes, composé de 40 à 50 personnes qui auraient un caractère plus ou moins politique.

M. Léon Bourgeois, dans le discours par lequel il proposait au Conseil de la Société des Nations la constitution de ce Comité, dit que le mandat du Comité est d'assurer l'établissement d'une juridiction civile dans des matières déterminées; et maintenant on propose au Comité de recommander la création d'un tribunal avec compétence criminelle. Lord Phillimore rappelle encore que M. Léon Bourgeois a qualifié de ridicule un tribunal composé de 40 à 50 juges.

Le maximum auquel Lord Phillimore peut consentir est le vœu que la Conférence de droit international soit saisie de la question de l'établissement d'un tribunal pour cet ordre de crimes. Ce vœu doit être conçu en termes généraux. Lord Phillimore ne peut prendre en considération une proposition détaillée, qui serait formulée d'une façon plus précise.

M. DE LAPRADELLE dit que la discussion antérieure appelle des observations et des conclusions.

La première question qui se pose est celle de savoir s'il y a lieu d'établir une autre Cour, soit pour le temps de paix, soit pour le temps de guerre. Pour ce qui est de la première éventualité, Lord Phillimore croit que non: il n'y a pas de crime international qui ne trouve un tribunal national

laws and customs of war on land, adopted in 1907, contains a series of forbidden and punishable acts: accordingly there is no reason against the establishment of a tribunal and a method of procedure. The scope of this law might be extended by a new Convention, which would at the same time extend the jurisdiction of the Court.

Lord Phillimore's objection to the President's proposition was therefore based on the fact that this proposition did not state whether it referred to a condition of peace, a condition of war, or to both. If it only referred to crimes committed in time of war, Lord Phillimore was prepared to agree to the adoption of a resolution.

He now turned to the crime of having made war. This may he considered as an offence against the Covenant of the League of Nations. It might be possible, acting on the authority of Grotius, to proceed against the persons responsible; it is however essential to specify and to define the nature of this crime. The President's outline was too vague and not sufficiently developed. Lord Phillimore would hesitate to entrust a jurisdiction over criminal cases to a tribunal, with no recognised procedure, without definite laws and composed of 40 to 50 persons who would have more or less political tendencies.

M. Léon Bourgeois, in the speech in which he proposed to the Council of the League of Nations that the present Committee should be formed, said that the task given to the Committee would be to provide for the establishment of a civil jurisdiction in certain defined classes of cases: now a proposal had been laid before the Committee to recommend the creation of a tribunal with criminal jurisdiction. Lord Phillimore recalled the fact that M. Leon Bourgeois derided the idea of a tribunal composed of from 40 to 50 judges.

The utmost to which Lord Phillimore would consent was a resolution to the effect that the Conference on International Law should be instructed to consider the question of the establishment of a tribunal for this class of offences. This resolution should be drawn up in general terms. Lord Phillimore was not prepared to consider a detailed proposal formulated in a more definite way.

M. DE LAPRADELLE said that the previous discussion called for certain observations and led to certain conclusions.

The first question which presented itself was whether there was a need for the establishment of another Court either for time of peace, or for time of war. Lord Phillimore thought that there was no need in the former of these two cases: there is no international crime which

pour le punir. M. de Lapradelle admet la justesse de cette observation. Si les tribunaux nationaux de l'Etat ne sont pas compétents, et si la juridiction de la nation où l'infraction s'est produite ne l'est pas non plus, les tribunaux de n'importe quel pays peuvent être saisis en vertu de la théorie de la dénaturalisation du criminel. Cette éventualité se produit par exemple dans le cas de piraterie.

Mais justement dans ce cas M. de Lapradelle trouverait plus naturel de rendre compétent un tribunal international au lieu de la juridiction d'un Etat tiers. C'est un des devoirs de la Société des Nations de veiller à la réalisation de la justice internationale. Il n'est pas nécessaire de créer dans ce but un tribunal spécial; la nouvelle Cour permanente serait certainement compétente. Et puisque les affaires de cet ordre ne se présentent que rarement, ce ne serait pas lui conférer une tâche bien lourde que de l'en charger. Ces affaires se trouveraient en outre mieux résolues par une juridiction internationale, en raison des incertitudes des juridictions nationales. La Cour internationale pourrait aussi créer une jurisprudence uniforme dans cette matière.

M. de Lapradelle réserve son opinion sur la manière d'organiser la justice internationale en matière pénale. Mais il constate la nécessité de cette justice et la possibilité de la faire entrer dans la compétence ordinaire de la nouvelle Cour.

D'après lui, les difficultés commencent lorsqu'on aborde les crimes de guerre; il rappelle à cet égard la distinction faite par Lord Phillimore entre crime de guerre proprement dit, et le crime d'avoir fait la guerre.

M. de Lapradelle fait observer que, même dans le système de la Société des Nations, la guerre est possible. Mais lorsque deux Etats, Membres de la Société des Nations, se font la guerre, ils doivent la conduire conformément aux principes de l'humanité et de la civilisation. Il est naturel que la Société des Nations soit chargée de surveiller l'observance du droit de la guerre par les belligérants, puisqu'ici les non-belligérants n'ont eu aucune influence sur la manière de conduire la guerre. Cette condition doit être considérée comme changée avec l'entrée en vigueur de la Société des Nations, qui pourrait demander l'extradition du criminel pour le juger; et selon M. de Lapradelle, une Cour compétente pour rendre le jugement existera dès que la nouvelle Cour permanente aura été créée. Il trouve inutile de développer en détail le fait que lorsqu'il y aura une juridiction de la Société des Nations, la Société pourra renvoyer devant elle les criminels de droit international.

M. de Lapradelle approuve sans réserve

cannot be punished by some national tribunal. M. de Lapradelle admitted the truth of this statement. If neither the national tribunals of a given State nor the Courts of the State in which the crime is committed have jurisdiction, an action may be brought before the tribunals of any other country, in virtue of the theory which deprives the criminal of his nationality. This applies for instance in the case of piracy.

In this very case, however, M. de Lapradelle thought that it would be more natural to give jurisdiction to an international tribunal, rather than to the Courts of a third State. It is one of the duties of the League of Nations to see that international justice is done. It is not necessary to create a special tribunal for this purpose; the new permanent Court would certainly have jurisdiction. Since cases of this kind only rarely occur, to entrust them to the Court would not be putting too heavy a burden upon it. Further it would be better if these cases were dealt with by an international tribunal, considering the uncertainties attaching to national jurisdictions. The international Court could also establish a uniform jurisprudence on this subject.

M. de Lapradelle deferred judgment on the method of organising an international jurisdiction for penal cases, but he recognised the necessity for this jurisdiction and the possibility of including it in the normal powers of the new Court.

According to him, the difficulties began to appear when the subject of crimes of war was broached; he recalled in this connection the distinction made by Lord Phillimore between crimes of war as such, and the crime of having made war.

M. de Lapradelle pointed out that, even under the régime of the League of Nations, war is possible; but when two States, Members of the League of Nations, wage war, they should do so in accordance with the principles of humanity and of civilisation. It is natural that it should fall to the League of Nations to watch the observance of the rules of war by the belligerents, since, up to this time, non-belligerents have had no influence on the method of conducting a war. This condition must be considered as having changed, now that the League of Nations has come into force, which could request the extradition of a criminal, for the purpose of his trial. According to M. de Lapradelle a Court competent to render a decision will exist as soon as the new Permanent Court has been created. He thought it useless to develop in detail the fact that when a tribunal of the League of Nations came into existence, the League would be able to bring before it offenders against International Law.

M. de Lapradelle approved wholeheartedly

l'esprit qui a inspiré le projet si intéressant et si beau du Président. Mais il croit qu'il ne faut pas trop insister sur l'esquisse du tribunal futur.

Si une distinction doit être faite entre deux juridictions différentes, c'est à la Société des Nations de la faire. Pour sa part, M. de Lapradelle croit que la distinction n'est pas nécessaire: la nouvelle Cour permanente peut avoir une compétence en même temps civile et pénale. Il faut espérer, en tout cas, que cette Cour sera apte à fonctionner si le malheur d'une guerre entre deux Membres de la Société des Nations se produisait.

M. de Lapradelle se rallie au vœu proposé par Mr. Root; il croit en effet qu'il faut se borner à un vœu à formule large, sans se lier à la conception d'un nouveau tribunal. Mais il croit que ce vœu doit faire partie du vœu sur la convocation des conférences de droit international. Ce qui importe le plus en matière de droit de guerre, ce sont des sanctions effectives, et non pas des peines pécuniaires dérisoires telles que celles stipulées dans la convention de 1907. Il faut qu'on puisse revenir à La Haye avec confiance pour reconsidérer les lois de la guerre. Et on le fera si dans le document qui prend l'initiative de la reprise de l'œuvre de La Haye dans cette matière, l'idée de la convocation est renouée à celle des sanctions.

M. Lapradelle demande donc que dans le vœu proposé par MM. Root et Descamps, il soit fait mention que les conférences ultérieures auront à chercher des sanctions aux lois de la guerre, et éventuellement à déterminer la procédure qui sera suivie devant la juridiction internationale. On pourra ensuite examiner si cette juridiction ne peut être la Cour permanente de Justice. M. de Lapradelle croit qu'ainsi les exigences de l'opinion publique pourront être conciliées avec les scrupules de certains membres du Comité.

Le PRESIDENT estime qu'il a le devoir de répondre à quelques objections formulées contre son projet et d'essayer de faire la lumière sur quelques points qui ont été signalés.

Et d'abord, la proposition d'établir une Haute Cour criminelle internationale, rentre-t-elle dans le mandat confié au Comité? Malgré certains doutes qui peuvent être émis, il semble qu'il faille répondre affirmativement; l'institution d'une telle Cour apparaît en effet, comme le complément nécessaire de l'organisation d'une justice internationale. Cependant, pour respecter les motifs de conscience allégués

of the spirit which had inspired the President's extremely interesting and able plan; but he thought that too much importance should not be attached to the outline of the future tribunal.

If a distinction must be drawn between two different jurisdictions, the League of Nations must do it. For his part, M. de Lapradelle thought that the distinction was not necessary: the new permanent Court could have at the same time both civil and penal jurisdiction. It must in any case be hoped that this Court would be capable of action in the unhappy event of war between two Members of the League of Nations.

M. de Lapradelle agreed with the resolution proposed by Mr. Root; he thought in fact that it was necessary to confine the resolution to general terms, and not to bind the Committee to the idea of a new tribunal, but he thought that this resolution should form part of the resolution concerning the convocation of Conferences on International Law. The most important thing in connection with the rules of war is the existence of effective sanctions, and not ludicrous pecuniary penalties, such as those stipulated in the Convention of 1907. The Conference should be able to assemble at the Hague with due confidence to reconsider the rules of war; this would be the case, if the document which suggested the resumption of the work already done at the Hague in this connection, linked the question of sanctions with the idea of convoking the new Conference.

M. de Lapradelle therefore requested that in the resolution proposed by MM. Root and Descamps, it should be mentioned that the future Conferences would be called upon to find sanctions to enforce the rules of war, and subsequently to determine the procedure to be followed before the international tribunal. It might then be considered whether this tribunal could not be the Permanent Court of Justice. M. de Lapradelle thought that the requirements of public opinion could thus be reconciled with the scruples of certain members of the Committee.

The PRESIDENT thought that it was his duty to answer some objections raised against his plan and to attempt to throw light on some points which had been brought out.

First of all, did the proposition to establish an international Criminal High Court, come within the scope of the mandate given to the Committee? Despite certain doubts which might be raised, the answer appeared to be in the affirmative, since the establishment of such a Court seemed necessary to complete the organisation of international justice. However, out of respect for the conscientious

par certains de ses collègues, le Président se déclare disposé, sans abandonner personnellement des idées qu'il croit justes, à rechercher ici une solution transactionnelle.

Le Président tient, d'ailleurs, à remercier ses Collègues qui ont reconnu l'importance et l'opportunité de la discussion actuelle.

Lord Phillimore a reconnu que l'établissement de la Haute Cour, en ce qui concerne certaines violations aux lois et coutumes de la guerre, pouvait se justifier. Mais pourquoi n'a-t-il pas rappellé, dans ses citations, les dispositions des paragraphes 6 et suivants, placés en tête des Conventions de 1899 et de 1907, où il est dit qu': „En attendant qu'un Code plus complet des lois de la guerre puisse être édicté les Hautes Parties Contractantes jugent opportun de constater, que dans les cas non compris dans les dispositions réglementaires, adoptées par Elles, les populations et les belligérants restent sous la sauvegarde et sous l'empire des principes du droit des gens, tels qu'ils résultent des usages établis entre nations civilisées, des lois de l'humanité et des exigences de la conscience publique"? Il y a là des bases suffisantes d'une action répressive, sans laquelle les populations et les belligérants ne demeureraient manifestement pas *sous la sauvegarde et sous l'empire des principes du droit des gens.*

Lord Phillimore a posé la question de savoir si le fait d'avoir déclaré la guerre constitue une violation du droit des gens. On peut regretter que le Pacte de la Société des Nations reconnaisse l'existence de guerres qui ne sont pas considérées comme illicites. Mais il ne résulte pas de là qu'il n'y ait pas de guerres qui puissent constituer de véritables crimes contre l'ordre public international et le droit des gens universel. Et il semble bien que personne ne conteste plus aujourd'hui qu'une guerre, caractérisée par la violation d'un territoire reconnu par tous comme perpétuellement neutre dans un intérêt général et permanent de la communauté internationale, ne présente ce caractère.

Le Président estime, au demeurant, que dans la présente discussion, on perd trop de vue la situation ancienne et la situation actuelle, telle qu'elle résulte de l'établissement, sur des bases moins précaires, de la Société des Nations.

Lord Phillimore croit que la solution proposée en ce qui concerne la Haute Cour, est „trop mince". Bien que le projet du Président renferme des règles fondamentales concernant l'organisation de la Haute Cour, sa compétence propre, son mode de mise en mouvement, son pouvoir de caractériser le délit, d'appliquer la peine, et de pourvoir, dans la limite possible, à l'exécution de

objections raised by some of his colleagues, the President said that he was prepared, though he still maintained his own ideas, to seek a compromise on this subject.

The President also wished to thank his colleagues, who had acknowledged the importance and the opportuneness of the present discussion.

Lord Phillimore had acknowledged that the establishment of a High Court, in so far as it concerned certain violations of rules and customs of war, was justifiable. But why had he not recalled, amongst his quotations, the provisions of paragraph six and the following paragraphs, placed at the beginning of the Conventions of 1899 and 1907, where it is stated that: "Until a more complete code of the rules of war has been issued, the High Contracting Parties deem it expedient to declare that in cases not included in the regulations adopted by them, the inhabitants and the belligerents remain under the protection and the rule of the principles of the law of nations, as they result from the usages established among civilised peoples, from the laws of humanity and from the dictates of the public conscience"? Therein lie sufficient grounds for repressive action, without which the civilian populations and the belligerents would manifestly not remain *under the protection and the rule of the law of nations.*

Lord Phillimore had raised the question whether the fact of having declared war constituted a violation of the law of nations. It may be regretted that the Covenant of the League ot Nations acknowledges the existence of wars which are not considered as illegal; but it does not follow from that that there cannot be wars which actually constitute crimes against international public order and the universal law of nations. It seems that no one now denies that a war characterised by the violation of a territory recognised by all as neutralised for all time in the general and permanent interests of international society, is of this character.

The President thought that the contrast between the former situation and the present situation which resulted from the establishment on less precarious foundations of the League of Nations, had been too much left out of consideration in the present discussion.

Lord Phillimore appeared to think that the proposed plan for the High Court was too indefinite. Although his plan included fundamental rules governing the organisation of the High Court, its special jurisdiction, the method of setting the procedure in motion, its powers of defining the offences, of fixing the penalty, and of providing as far as possible for the execution of the sentences

la sentence, le Président est le premier à reconnaître que son œuvre est perfectible et peut être complétée. Il estime, en tout cas, que l'imperfection et l'insuffisance de la solution qu'il a proposée, ne peuvent être alléguées comme une raison pour ne point faire un pas dans la voie du progrès.

MM. Root et Loder sont, il est vrai, d'avis, qu'avant de constituer une Haute Cour, il faudrait instituer un droit applicable par elle. La définition des délits contre le droit des gens universel est cependant assez nette en droit international: elle vise des délits en face desquels tous les Etats se trouvent atteints dans leur sécurité commune, et qui donnent ainsi à tous un titre autorisé à exiger justice. La faiblesse de l'organisation de la Société internationale jusqu'en ces derniers temps, a pu faire que chacun, sans s'inquiéter des autres, a procédé à la répression de tels délits, comme en matière de piraterie. Ce n'est pas une raison pour admettre, que sous un régime plus avancé d'organisation internationale, le fonctionnement d'une Haute Cour criminelle internationale n'ait aucune raison d'être.

Il ne faut d'ailleurs rien exagérer ici, ni exiger plus que l'on n'exige parfois, même dans l'ordre national, en des matières qui ne se prêtent pas à une énumération détaillée des délits rentrant dans un type général suffisamment déterminé. C'est le cas, par exemple, pour les délits qui, en droit national, mettent en cause la responsabilité ministérielle. La Constitution belge, si libérale, et si stricte en matière de pénalités, n'hésite pas à stipuler que la Chambre des Représentants peut mettre en accusation les Ministres, et les traduire devant la Cour de Cassation, à qui est expressément reconnu le pouvoir appréciateur de caractériser le délit et de déterminer la peine.

Il ne faut nullement voir, dans l'institution d'une Haute Cour, l'érection d'un Super-Etat, ni une abdication injustifiée d'attributs souverains. Il convient seulement d'y voir un usage commun et éclairé de la souveraineté, l'admission que dans un ordre de rapports, à certains égards nouveaux, des mesures parfaitement justifiées peuvent s'imposer à tous dans un intérêt général.

Mr. Root a mis le Comité en présence de certains cas. Sans les examiner en détail, et sans rechercher dans quelle mesure ils s'opposent à l'institution que le Président préconise, il désire mettre, à son tour, Mr. Root en présence d'un cas fort topique. Il suppose que dans un lieu où siège le Conseil de la Société des Nations, deux membres, un Brésilien et un Belge, qui viennent de soutenir certaines thèses en matière d'organisation du travail, sont mis à mal par des soviétistes.

—although his plan included all this—the President was the first to acknowledge that his work was open to improvement and could be made more complete. Nevertheless he considered that the fact that his proposal was imperfect and incomplete could not be advanced as a reason for not taking a step forward on the path of progress.

MM. Root and Loder, it was true, were of opinion that before establishing a High Court it would be necessary to provide laws to be applied by it. Offences against the universal law of nations are, however, defined with sufficient clearness in International Law: they are offences of such a nature as to affect the common safety of all States, and to entitle all to demand that justice should be done. The weakness of the organisation of international society up to recent times has been such that each nation, without troubling about the others, has undertaken to repress all such offences as, for instance, cases of piracy. It does not however follow that, under a more advanced régime of international organisation, an international Criminal High Court would not justify its existence.

Care must be taken, however, not to stipulate too much and not to insist upon a detailed enumeration which is not always insisted upon, even in national affairs, with reference to offences which do not lend themselves to such an enumeration and which are of a sufficiently definite general type. This applies for instance to offences which, in national law, involve ministerial responsibility. The Belgian Constitution, which is so liberal, and so scrupulous in its enforcement of penalties, does not hesitate to lay down that the House of Representatives may bring charges against the Ministers and bring them to trial before the Court of Cassation, which is expressly invested with power to define the offence and to determine the punishment.

There is no need whatever to imagine that the institution of a High Court would amount to the creation of a super-State, and would involve an unjustified abdication of sovereign powers. It is a mere question of the recognition of the fact that the new Court involves a joint and enlightened use of the attributes of sovereignty and that, under a set of conditions which are in some respects new, it may, in the common interest, be incumbent upon all to give their adherence to certain perfectly justifiable measures.

Mr. Root has suggested certain possible cases to the Committee. Without examining them in detail and without ascertaining to what extent they were opposed to the institution which he advocated, the President wished in turn to suggest to Mr. Root a case very much to the point. Suppose that in some place where the Council of the League

Mr. Root croit-il que la simple tentative de poursuivre les coupables faite par les Gouvernements brésilien et belge réponde à la gravité et à l'étendue de l'infraction, et que tous les Etats ne se trouvent pas atteints par la violence exercée sur leurs mandataires internationaux dans l'exercice de leurs fonctions? Il n'est nullement impossible ici, et il peut être nécessaire dans bien des cas, d'harmoniser les fonctions insuffisantes des juridictions nationales avec le fonctionnement adéquat d'une juridiction internationale.

Envisageons donc les questions, au moment où nous travaillons pour la Société des Nations, sous l'aspect nouveau qui peut leur convenir. Et au moment où nous organisons, sur des bases nouvelles, la justice internationale, ne craignons pas d'aborder les problèmes nouveaux qui s'offrent à nous, et de hâter leur solution d'une manière conforme aux exigences de l'avenir.

of Nations was assembled, two members—one Brazilian and one Belgian, who had just upheld certain theories dealing with labour organisation—were injured by Sovietists. Did Mr. Root think that ordinary steps taken by the Brazilian and Belgian Governments to prosecute the offenders would suffice, considering the gravity and the nature of the crime, and that all States would not be affected by the attack made upon their international agents whilst in the exercise of their duties? It is by no means impossible in this case, and might be necessary in many others, to reconcile the shortcomings in the operation of national jurisdictions and the adequate working of an international tribunal.

Therefore, as the Committee was working on behalf of the League of Nations, questions must be examined in a new light to suit the new conditions; now that international justice was being organised on a new basis, new problems must be tackled boldly as they arise and must be expeditiously solved in a way calculated to meet the requirements of the future.

Le PRESIDENT annonce qu'il a reçu deux propositions, l'une de M. Ricci-Busatti, l'autre de M. Hagerup.

The PRESIDENT announced that he had received two propositions, one from M. Ricci-Busatti and another from M. Hagerup.

M. RICCI-BUSATTI attire l'attention sur celle déposée par M. Hagerup.

M. RICCI-BUSATTI drew attention to M. Hagerup's proposal.

M. HAGERUP en donne lecture. Elle est ainsi conçue:

„Pendant les délibérations de la Commission, on a relevé l'avantage qu'il pourrait y avoir à l'établissement d'une juridiction internationale criminelle.

„La Commission recommande que les différents problèmes se rattachant à celui-ci soient pris en considération par une Conférence internationale future."

Il ajoute que cette formule a été proposée par lui, dans un esprit de conciliation. Il ne peut pas aller plus loin.

M. HAGERUP read his proposal which was as follows:

"During the deliberations of the Committee, reference was made to the advantages of the establishment of a tribunal with an international criminal jurisdiction.

The Commission recommends that the various problems connected with this question be considered by a future international Conference."

He added that he had proposed this in a conciliatory spirit: he could not go further.

M. DE LAPRADELLE exprime l'avis que le Comité pourrait se rallier à l'idée de Mr. Root, sauf rédaction.

M. DE LAPRADELLE expressed the opinion that the Committee could adopt M. Root's idea, which would however have to be put in writing.

M. HAGERUP remarque que la rédaction est essentielle; il faut faire ressortir d'une façon parfaitement claire qu'il s'agit seulement d'une recommandation et non pas d'une résolution.

M. HAGERUP remarked that the wording was an essential point: it must be stated quite clearly that only a recommendation and not a resolution was intended.

M. ADATCI déclare que la proposition de M. Hagerup est conforme à sa pensée pour le fond et pour les détails.

M. ADATCI declared that M. Hagerup's proposition was in accordance with his ideas both in principle and in detail.

Le PRESIDENT donne lecture de partie de la formule de M. Ricci-Busatti, qui diffère de celle de M. Hagerup. Elle est ainsi conçue:

„...que la Conférence prenne en considération les différents problèmes qui se rattachent à l'organisation éventuelle d'une juridiction criminelle internationale."

M. HAGERUP déclare pouvoir se rallier à cette formule, mais il croit qu'elle ne devra pas être rattachée au vœu proposé par Mr. Root.

LORD PHILLIMORE a la parole pour une question d'ordre. Il fait observer que toute la présente séance a été remplie par la discussion de la proposition du Président. Il ne s'en plaint pas; on reprendra demain le travail qui est plutôt le travail du Comité; mais il propose qu'on essaye maintenant d'arriver à formuler un vœu sur la matière traitée dans la proposition du Président, afin d'en finir.

M. LODER est d'avis qu'un vœu n'est pas suffisant, à moins que le Président ne veuille retirer sa proposition.

Le PRESIDENT pourrait le faire si l'on trouvait une formule transactionnelle satisfaisante; il donne lecture d'une formule tirée des deux propositions de M. Hagerup et de M. Ricci-Busatti, et qui, selon lui, pourrait concilier toutes les opinions. Elle est ainsi conçue:

„Pendant la délibération de la Commission, on a relevé l'avantage qu'il pourrait y avoir dans l'établissement d'une juridiction criminelle internationale.

Le Comité prie la Conférence de prendre en considération les différents problèmes qui se rattachent à l'établissement d'une telle juridiction."

M. LODER trouve cette formule trop vague.

Le PRESIDENT se rallie à l'opinion de M. Loder; il déclare qu'il préfère ne pas retirer sa proposition. Elle sera mise aux voix: ainsi la responsabilité du Président et celle de tout le monde sera dégagée.

M. LODER attire l'attention sur le passage suivant de la proposititon du Président:

„La Cour possédera un pouvoir appréciateur pour caractériser le délit, fixer la peine et déterminer les moyens appropriés à l'exécution de la sentence."

The PRESIDENT read a portion of the draft submitted by M. Ricci-Busatti, which differed from that of M. Hagerup and which was as follows:

"... that the Conference should consider the various problems in connection with the subsequent organisation of an international criminal jurisdiction."

M. HAGERUP stated that he could accept this, but he thought that it should not be attached to the resolution proposed by Mr. Root.

LORD PHILLIMORE spoke on a point of order. He observed that the whole of that meeting had been occupied by discussion of the President's proposition. He was not complaining of this; the work which was more especially the task of the Committee would be resumed on the following day; but he proposed that an attempt be made at once to decide upon the wording of a resolution on the subject dealt with in the President's proposition, so that the question might be closed.

M. LODER was of the opinion that a recommendation was not sufficient, unless the President were willing to withdraw his proposition.

The PRESIDENT was prepared to do this if a satisfactory formula for a compromise could be found: the President read a draft based on the two propositions of MM. Hagerup and Ricci-Busatti and which, in his opinion, would reconcile all the points of view. It was as follows:

"During the deliberations of the Committee, reference was made to the advantages of the establishment of a tribunal with an international criminal jurisdiction.

The Committee requests the Conference to take into consideration the different problems relating to this establishment of such jurisdiction."

M. LODER thought the wording too vague.

The PRESIDENT agreed with M. Loder. He declared that he would prefer not to withdraw his proposition; it would be the subject of a vote. In this way the President's and everybody's responsibility would be clear.

M. LODER drew attention to the following passage from the President's proposition:

"the Court shall have power to define the character of the offence, to fix the penalty and to determine the means by which the terms of the sentence are to be enforced."

LORD PHILLIMORE remarque que cette disposition est empruntée au droit anglais, mais le texte du Président va beaucoup plus loin: il donne l'autorité de juger sans qu'il y ait aucun droit sur lequel on puisse se baser.

M. DE LAPRADELLE constate qu'on est d'accord pour ne pas rattacher l'idée du Président au projet d'organisation de la nouvelle Cour permanente que le Comité est en train d'établir, et pour se borner à émettre un vœu. La rédaction de ce vœu doit être remise à plus tard. Il serait en effet impossible d'improviser maintenant une formule; si le Comité insiste pour le faire, M. de Lapradelle doit s'abstenir de voter comme membre de la Commission, mais suivra la discussion en sa qualité de rapporteur.

Le PRESIDENT exprime l'avis qu'il vaut mieux en finir maintenant. Il donne de nouveau lecture du texte transactionnel proposé tout à l'heure.

M. DE LAPRADELLE déclare qu'il ne peut pas se rallier à cette rédaction.

Au contraire, LORD PHILLIMORE s'y rallie.

Mr. ROOT déclare que, dans son opinion, la question est suffisamment importante et suffisamment différente de la question de la convocation d'une conférence de droit international pour qu'elle fasse l'objet d'une déclaration séparée. La formule de M. Hagerup semble tout à fait suffisante à Mr. Root, si elle recueille aussi l'approbation des autres membres. Le vœu doit avoir le caractère d'une recommandation faite à la Conférence et que celle-ci devra prendre en considération, si elle est convoquée.

Le PRESIDENT met aux voix le texte qu'il a lu et qui est basé sur la proposition de M. Hagerup et de M. Ricci-Busatti. Il ajoute qu'il est entendu que ce texte formera un vœu ou une déclaration séparée.

M. ALTAMIRA déclare qu'il s'abstiendra de voter, ne trouvant pas assez satisfaisante la formule mise aux voix, qui, à son avis, s'écarte trop de la proposition originaire du Président. Il est, à ce sujet, comme l'on dit en Espagne, plus papiste que le pape.

LORD PHILLIMORE remarked that this clause was borrowed from English Law, but that the President's text went much further: he gave the tribunal power to try cases in which there was no law on which to base its judgments.

M. DE LAPRADELLE stated that the Committee was agreed not to attach the President's suggestion to the draft plan for the organisation of the new permanent Court which the Committee was engaged in preparing, and to confine itself to the adoption of a new recommendation. The drafting of this recommendation should be postponed until later. It would be impossible at the moment to improvise a wording; if the Committee insisted upon doing so, M. de Lapradelle would abstain from voting as a member of the Committee, but would follow the discussion in his capacity as rapporteur.

The PRESIDENT expressed the opinion that it would be better to complete the matter now. He again read the compromise draft which he had just proposed.

M. DE LAPRADELLE declared that he could not agree to this drafting.

LORD PHILLIMORE on the contrary supported it.

Mr. ROOT declared that, in his opinion, the question was sufficiently important and sufficiently distinct from the question of the convocation of an International Law Conference, to be made the subject of a separate declaration. M. Hagerup's draft seemed to Mr. Root to be quite satisfactory, provided that it was approved by the other members. The resolution should have the character of a recommendation made to the Conference, to be considered by the latter if it were convoked.

The PRESIDENT took a vote upon the draft which he had read and which was based on the propositions of M. Hagerup and M. Ricci-Busatti. He added that it was to be understood that this draft would constitute a resolution or a separate declaration.

M. ALTAMIRA declared that he would not vote, as he was not quite satisfied with the draft voted upon, which, in his opinion, differed too much from the President's original proposal. On this subject he was, according to a Spanish saying, "more catholic than the Pope".

M. DE LAPRADELLE s'abstiendra également de voter.

La proposition est adoptée par cinq voix de majorité.

M. RICCI-BUSATTI a formulé une série d'amendements aux articles 25 à 28 du projet Root—Phillimore. Il déclare que ces amendements, ainsi que les autres qui ont été présentés par lui, ne sont que des épaves; son vaisseau a sombré, mais il essaye d'en sauver des débris en les adaptant à celui que l'on est en train de bâtir; ils pourront peut-être lui permettre de se rallier au résultat final des travaux du Comité. (Voir annexe 4).

Le PRESIDENT ouvre la discussion sur l'article 25 du projet Root—Phillimore.

A cet article se rattache le premier amendement de M. Ricci-Busatti.

LORD PHILLIMORE pense qu'il ne s'agit que de questions de formule, et le PRESIDENT déclare que le Comité de rédaction tiendra compte de cet amendement.

M. RICCI-BUSATTI appelle l'attention du Comité sur ce qu'il y aurait lieu de faire si, à l'ouverture de la session annuelle, il n'y avait aucune affaire à régler. Il pense qu'il y aurait lieu d'insérer dans l'article une disposition qui permette de suspendre la session en pareil cas.

M. LODER croit qu'il serait nécessaire que la Cour se réunît, même s'il n'y a pas d'affaires à juger.

LORD PHILLIMORE fait observer qu'en Angleterre la Cour se réunit même s'il n'y a pas d'affaires. Dans ce cas, elle se proroge; mais il est nécessaire que les membres de la Cour se réunissent au moins une fois par an.

Lord Phillimore ajoute que le passage suivant doit être ajouté à la fin de l'article 25 du projet Root—Phillimore:

„Le Président aura aussi le droit, à la requête des parties, de convoquer trois juges pour décider les affaires que les parties voudront voir déterminer de cette manière."

Le PRESIDENT est d'avis que la Cour devrait pouvoir se diviser en chambres afin de hâter la procédure. Il attire l'attention du Comité sur les dispositions de son projet original à cet égard (voir annexe au procès-verbal du 21 juin).

M. DE LAPRADELLE also did not vote.

The proposition was adopted by a majority of five votes.

M. RICCI-BUSATTI had drawn up a series of amendments on Articles 25 to 28 of the Root—Phillimore plan. He declared that these amendments, as also the others that he had submitted, were only wreckage; his ship had sunk but he was trying to save some of the pieces and to adapt them to the vessel now under construction; if they were accepted he might perhaps be able to accept the final results of the Committee's labours. (See Annex 4).

The PRESIDENT next laid Article 25 of the Root—Phillimore plan before the Committee.

M. Ricci-Busatti's first amendment referred to this Article.

LORD PHILLIMORE thought that this amendment was only a question of wording. The PRESIDENT stated that the drafting Committee would consider the amendment.

M. RICCI-BUSATTI called the Committee's attention to the possibility that, at the opening of the annual session, there would be no cases for decision. He thought that a provision should be inserted in the Article authorising the postponement of the session under such circumstances.

M. LODER thought that it would be necessary for the Court to meet even if there were no cases to be heard.

LORD PHILLIMORE observed that in England a Court would meet even if there were no cases. In such event it would adjourn; but the members of the Court must meet at least once a year.

Lord Phillimore went on to say that the following sentence should be added to the end of Article 25 of the Root—Phillimore plan:

"The President shall also have the right, when requested by the parties, to assemble three judges to try cases which the parties wish to settle in this way."

The PRESIDENT was of opinion that the Court should be able to divide itself into chambers in order to expedite the procedure. He drew attention to the provisions of his original plan relating to this. (See Annex of the Procès-Verbal of June 21).

LORD PHILLIMORE dit qu'il croit que les articles 25 et 26 peuvent êtres considérés séparément. Il y a dans le premier de ces articles, deux idées distinctes:

1. la Cour doit toujours siéger *in pleno*; Lord Phillimore s'oppose au système des chambres;

2. d'autre part il n'est pas opposé à l'idée d'avoir une Cour peu nombreuse. Il a pensé que pendant les vacances, un tribunal composé d'un nombre fort restreint de juges pourrait fonctionner. Mr. Root pense que cette Cour devrait être composée du président et de trois juges.

Le PRESIDENT met aux voix l'article 25 du projet Root-Phillimore, avec l'addition dont Lord Phillimore vient de donner lecture.

Avant le vote, le Président déclare, en réponse à une question de M. de Lapradelle, que, si les parties peuvent, en se mettant d'accord, soumettre leur différend au tribunal de trois juges, elles n'ont pas le droit de choisir ces juges.

M. DE LAPRADELLE déclare que dans ce cas il peut accepter l'article.

M. RICCI-BUSATTI se rallie à l'addition de Lord Phillimore, mais insiste pour que les parties aient le droit de choisir elles-mêmes les trois juges, ou un seul juge, si bon leur semble. Il renvoie d'ailleurs à l'article 26 *bis* de ses amendements, qui exprime toute sa pensée.

Le PRESIDENT attire l'attention sur l'article 6 du projet de Convention de 1907, aux termes duquel la Cour désigne annuellement trois juges qui forment une délégation spéciale, et trois autres juges, destinés à les remplacer en cas d'empêchement.

Il préfère une chambre de vacations nommée annuellement à une petite Cour nommée *ad hoc* par le Président, lequel assumerait une responsabilité formidable en faisant le choix des juges.

M. LODER se rallie à l'opinion que vient d'exprimer le Président.

Quelques explications sont alors fournies sur les conditions spéciales qui ont présidé à la rédaction de l'article cité par le Président, et sur le sens véritable du terme „chambre de vacations".

LORD PHILLIMORE déclare qu'à son avis la différence entre le point de vue du Président et le sien n'est pas bien grande. A son idée, les parties qui voudront avoir une affaire réglée pendant les vacances, s'adresseront au Président avec la prière de tâcher de composer une Cour pour en prendre connaissance.

LORD PHILLIMORE said that he thought Articles 25 and 26 could be considered separately. There were two distinct ideas in the first of these Articles:

1. The Court must always sit *in pleno*: Lord Phillimore was opposed to the system of chambers.

2. On the other hand, he was not opposed to the idea of having a small Court. He thought that, during vacations, a tribunal composed of a very limited number of judges might act. Mr. Root thought this Court should be composed of the President and three judges.

The PRESIDENT put Article 25 of the Root—Phillimore plan to the vote, including the addition just read by Lord Phillimore.

Before the vote the President declared, in answer to a question by M. de Lapradelle, that though the parties could by agreement submit their dispute to a tribunal of three judges, they would not have the right to choose them.

M. DE LAPRADELLE declared that under these conditions he could accept the Article.

M. RICCI-BUSATTI accepted Lord Phillimore's addition but insisted that the parties should have the right to choose the three judges themselves—or a single judge if they thought fit. He referred to Article 26 *bis* of his amendments, which expressed his views.

The PRESIDENT called attention to Article 6 of the draft Convention of 1907, according to the terms of which the Court would appoint annually three judges to form a special section and three other judges to replace them, if they were unable to sit.

He preferred a vacation chamber, appointed annually, to a small Court appointed *ad hoc* by the President, who would assume a heavy responsibility by choosing the judges.

M. LODER agreed with the opinion just expressed by the President.

Some explanations were then given concerning the special conditions which governed the drafting of the article quoted by the President, and concerning the real meaning of the term "vacation chamber".

LORD PHILLIMORE declared that, in his opinion, the difference between the President's point of view and his own was not great. In his opinion, parties who wished to have a case decided during vacation, should apply to the president, requesting him to try to form a Court to hear the case.

Le PRESIDENT craint, en se ralliant au projet Root—Phillimore, d'aller à l'encontre de la décision unanime de 1907.

Après une courte discussion, LORD PHILLIMORE se déclare disposé à rédiger un texte, qu'il soumettra demain, destiné à concilier le point de vue du Président avec le sien.

La séance est levée à 12.45 heures de l'après-midi.

Le Président :

(signé) Brn. DESCAMPS.

Le Secrétaire-Général :

(signé) D. ANZILOTTI.

The PRESIDENT feared that, in accepting the Root—Phillimore plan, he was going against the unanimous decision of 1907.

After a short discussion, LORD PHILLIMORE stated that he was ready to prepare a draft, which he would submit on the following day, intended to reconcile the President's point of view and his own.

The meeting closed at 12.45 p. m.

The President :

(signed) Brn. DESCAMPS.

The Secretary-General :

(signed) D. ANZILOTTI.

ANNEXE No. 1.

Projet de résolution, concernant la convocation de Conférences de droit international, présenté par Mr. Root et le baron Descamps.

Convaincus que la sécurité des Etats et le bien-être des peuples exigent impérieusement l'extension de l'empire du droit et le développement des juridictions internationales:

Animés du désir de promouvoir la réalisation de ces résultats dans le monde:

Les soussignés proposent au Comité international des jurisconsultes réunis à La Haye d'adopter, à titre de recommandations, les résolutions suivantes:

I. Que le Conseil ou l'Assemblée ou les Autorités qui en ont le moyen réunissent, dans le plus bref délai possible, une nouvelle Conférence des Etats, faisant suite aux deux premières Conférences de La Haye, dans le but de poursuivre les objectifs suivants:

1. de raffermir les règles existantes du droit des gens, spécialement et en première ligne dans les domaines affectés par les événements de la récente guerre;
2. de formuler et de sanctionner les modifications et additions dont la nécessité ou l'utilité s'est révélée à l'occasion de la guerre et à raison des changements dans les conditions de la vie et des rapports internationaux qui ont suivi ce conflit armé;
3. de s'efforcer de concilier les vues divergentes et de ménager une entente générale relativement aux règles qui ont donné lieu à controverse;
4. de prendre en particulière considération les points, qui, actuellement, ne sont pas réglés d'une manière adéquate et à l'égard desquels les exigences de la justice internationale réclament des déterminations précises et une entente commune.

II. Que „l'Institut de droit international," „l'American Institute of International Law", „l'Union juridique internationale" et „l'International Law Association" soient invités à instaurer tel mode de travail ou de collaboration qui leur paraîtra convenir afin de préparer, concernant l'œuvre à réaliser, des avant-projets qui puissent d'abord être soumis aux divers Gouvernements, puis être présentés à la Conférence et recevoir telle suite qu'il appartiendra.

ANNEX No. 1.

Draft Resolution concerning the convocation of Conferences on International Law, submitted by Mr. Root and Baron Descamps.

Convinced that the extension of the sway of justice and the development of international tribunals are urgently required to ensure the security of States and well-being of the nations:

Moved by an earnest desire to forward the achievement of these results in the world;

The undersigned propose to the International Committee of Jurists assembled at the Hague the adoption of the following resolutions to be regarded as recommendations:

I. That the Council or Assembly or some other authority, which has the necessary powers, should convoke as soon as possible, a new interstate Conference to carry on the work of the two first Conferences at the Hague, for the purpose of:

1. Reestablishing the existing rules of the Law of Nations, more especially, and in the first place, those affected by the events of the recent war;
2. Formulating and approving the modifications and additions rendered necessary or advisable by the war and by the changing of the conditions of life and of international relations following upon the armed conflict;
3. Endeavouring to reconcile divergent opinions, and bring about a general understanding concerning the rules which have been the subject of controversy;
4. Giving special consideration to those points, which are not at the present time adequately provided for, and of which a definite settlement by general agreement is required, in the interests of International Justice.

II. That the Institut de Droit International, the American Institute of International Law, the Union Juridique Internationale, the International Law Association should be invited to adopt any method, of working or of collaboration, that they may think fit, with a view to the preparation of Draft Plans to be submitted, first to the various Governments, and then to the Conference, for the accomplishment of this task.

III. Qu'en vue de mieux mettre en relief l'œuvre à entreprendre, la Conférence nouvelle prenne, si possible, le nom de Conférence pour l'avancement du droit international.

IV. Que cette Conférence soit suivie de Conférences périodiques semblables, assez rapprochées pour permettre de continuer, en toute opportunité et fécondité, l'œuvre entreprise, dans ce qu'elle aura d'inachevé.

Le projet actuel de Cour Permanente de Justice Internationale organise une juridiction générale compétente pour toutes les questions que lui soumettra l'accord volontaire des Parties, avec judicature obligatoire pour les questions spécifiées à l'article 13 du Pacte de la Société des Nations, en tant que leur solution dépend des traités ou de règles reçues en droit des gens.

Il y a lieu d'admettre que l'activité de la Conférence dont les réunions sont ici recommandées, en étendant incessamment le domaine du droit international, élargira incessamment aussi le cadre de la judicature obligatoire devant la Cour, sans abolir les limites qui constituent une sauvegarde contre tout excès de pouvoir.

Et l'on peut désormais envisager l'ensemble des institutions établies pour l' application du droit aux affaires internationales comme un vaste organisme, à la fois souple et intégral, où le fonctionnement des juridictions proprement arbitrales peut alterner avec un office permanent de justice internationale et sous l'égide duquel est appelée à se déployer, dans le respect effectif et progressif de l'ordre juridique, la vie des Nations.

(Signé) ROOT, DESCAMPS.

III. That in order to emphasise the character of the task to be undertaken, the new Conference should, if possible, be called the Conference for the advancement of International Law.

IV. That this Conference should be followed by periodical similar Conferences, at intervals sufficiently short to enable the work undertaken to be continued, in so far as it may be incomplete, with every prospect of success.

The present project for a permanent Court of International Justice organises a tribunal with a general jurisdiction over all questions submitted to it by voluntary agreement between the parties, and with a special compulsory jurisdiction in the questions specified in Article 13 of the Covenant of the League of Nations, in so far as their settlement depend upon the interpretation of treaties or of rules recognised by the Law of Nations.

It is most probable that the operations of the Conference herewith recommended, by continually extending the scope of International Law, will also continually develop the Court's compulsory jurisdiction, but without destroying the limits which form a protection against any abuse of power.

Thereafter the group of institutions, set up for the application of law to international affairs may be regarded as one vast organisation, flexible yet complete, in which Tribunals of Arbitration constitute an alternative to a Permanent Court of International Justice, and under the aegis of which international life will develop and law will be held in real and increasing respect.

(Signed) ROOT, DESCAMPS.

ANNEXE No. 2.

Proposition du Baron Descamps.

Article 1. Il est institué une Haute Cour de Justice Internationale.

Article 2. Cette Cour se compose d'un membre par Etat respectivement choisi par le groupe des délégués de chaque Etat à la Cour d'Arbitrage.

Article 3. La Haute Cour de Justice Internationale sera compétente pour juger les crimes contre l'ordre public international et le droit des gens universel, qui lui seront déférés par l'Assemblée plénière de la Société des Nations ou par le Conseil de cette Société.

Article 4. La Cour possédera un pouvoir appréciateur pour caractériser le délit, fixer la peine et déterminer les moyens appropriés à l'exécution de la sentence.

Elle déterminera la procédure à suivre dans ce cas, par son règlement d'ordre intérieur.

ANNEX No. 2.

Proposal submitted by Baron Descamps.

Article 1. A High Court of International Justice is hereby established.

Article 2. This Court shall be composed of one member for each State chosen by the group of delegates of each State upon the Court of Arbitration.

Article 3. The High Court of International Justice shall be competent to try crimes against international public order and the universal law of Nations, referred to it by a public full meeting of the Assembly of the League of Nations, or by the Council of the said League.

Article 4. The Court shall have power to define the character of the offence, to fix the penalty and to decide the means by which the terms of the sentence are to be enforced.

The Court shall lay down the procedure to be used in this case in its internal regulations.

ANNEXE No. 3.

Tirage à part des Articles 25 et suivants du projet Root—Phillimore.

(Texte revisé, d'après les décisions du 13 juillet).

Article 25.

La Cour aura une session chaque année. Sauf disposition contraire dans le règlement d'ordre de la Cour, cette session commencera le 15 juin et continuera tant que l'ordre du jour de la Cour n'aura pas été épuisé. Le Président aura le droit de convoquer la Cour en session extraordinaire quand cela lui paraîtra nécessaire.

Le Président aura aussi le droit, à la requête des parties, de convoquer trois juges pour décider les affaires que les parties voudront voir déterminer de cette manière.

Article 26.

A la première audition d'un cas, au moins neuf juges devront être présents. Si neuf juges ne sont pas disponibles, les juges suppléants entreront en fonction jusqu'à concurrence de ce nombre. Les juges suppléants seront appelés à siéger d'après un système de rotation suivant leur ancienneté d'âge.

Si, pour une raison quelconque, un ou plusieurs des juges se trouvent hors d'état de continuer à siéger pendant toute l'audition du cas, l'audition pourra néanmoins être poursuivie, à condition qu'il y ait un quorum de sept juges présents.

Article 27.

Si, lors de l'instruction d'un cas déterminé, la Cour ne renferme pas de juge de la nationalité d'un des Etats parties au litige, cet Etat nommera, en vue de l'instruction, un juge qui prendra part à la décision du litige sur un pied de parfaite égalité avec les autres juges, membres de la Cour.

Si la Cour ne renferme pas de juge de la nationalité d'aucune des parties au litige, chacune d'elles nommera un juge qui prendra part à la procédure concernant le litige et à la décision à son sujet.

S'il y a plus de deux parties et que deux ou plusieurs des parties fassent cause commune, elles seront représentées à la Cour par un juge seulement. Ce juge sera nommé de commun accord par les parties.

ANNEX No. 3.

Separate copy of Articles 25 to 28 of the Root—Phillimore plan.

(Revised version, embodying the decisions of July 13th).

Article 25.

The Court shall have one session every year, which, unless otherwise provided by rule of Court, shall begin on the 15th of June and continue until the business before the Court is disposed of. The President shall have the power to convoke an extraordinary session of the Court when he deems it necessary.

The President shall also have the right, when requested by the parties, to assemble three judges to try cases that the parties wish to settle in this way.

Article 26.

There shall be present at the first hearing of a case not less than nine judges and, if there be less than this number available, their places shall be filled by supplementary judges called in rotation in the order of age.

If, for any reason, any of the judges are unable to continue during the hearing, the remaining judges, provided there is a quorum of seven, can continue the case.

Article 27.

If, on the trial of a case, there is no judge upon the Court belonging to one of the litigating States, that State shall, for the purpose of the trial, appoint a judge who shall take part in the disposition of the case with equal rank with the other judges on the bench.

If neither of the parties in litigation before the Court has a judge, each shall appoint a judge to take part in the proceedings and the disposition of the case.

If two or more of the parties are in the same interest, they shall have but one judge, to be agreed upon between them.

Article 28.

La Cour est accessible à tous les Etats qui sont Membres de la Société des Nations et aux Etats qui ne sont pas Membres de la Société, mais qui acceptent les conditions posées par le Conseil de la Société, en conformité avec l'article 17 du Pacte. La Cour connaîtra seulement des litiges entre Etats, mais un Etat pourra soumettre à la Cour les droits qu'il fait valoir au nom de ses ressortissants ou au nom de ressortissants d'un autre Etat que le premier Etat a le droit de représenter en vertu d'un traité.

Article 28.

The Court is open to all States who are Members of the League of Nations and to States not Members of the League of Nations who comply with the conditions laid down by the Council under Article 17 of the Covenant. The Court shall take cognisance only of suits between States, but the State may put forward rights which it claims on behalf of any of its citizens or for the nationals of another State on whose behalf it is entitled by treaty to appear.

ANNEXE No. 4.

Amendements proposés par M. Ricci-Busatti aux Articles 25—28 du projet Root—Phillimore.

Article 25. Supprimer la phrase: „Sauf disposition contraire dans le règlement d'ordre de la Cour" et rédiger la première partie de l'article de telle façon qu'il soit établi que la session n'aura pas lieu s'il n'y a pas d'affaires à régler.

Article 26. Ajouter, au début de l'article, les mots: „Lorsque, soit sur la demande des parties, soit par décision du Président, la Cour siégera en séance plénière.": sauf rédaction pour ce qui reste.

Ajouter l'article suivant (26 *bis*):

„Dans chaque affaire, les parties en cause pourront demander, de commun accord, que le tribunal soit composé de trois juges ou d'un seul juge, à désigner soit par elles-mêmes soit par le Président, parmi les membres de la Cour.

„Sous réserve des dispositions de l'article 26 et de l'alinéa précédent, le tribunal serait composé, dans chaque affaire, de cinq juges et deux juges suppléants: le règlement de la Cour établira l'ordre dans lequel les juges seront appelés à siéger."

Article 27. Alinéa premier: substituer aux mots: „cet Etat nommera, en vue de l'instruction.....", les suivants: „cette partie pourra, soit nommer parmi les personnes qui figurent sur la liste visée à l'article . . . un juge . . ., soit demander que les ressortissants des deux Parties adverses, s'ils figurent parmi les juges, soient exclus du tribunal."

2me alinéa: Substituer les mots: „nommera" par les mots: „pourra nommer".

Article 28. Substituer aux mots: „mais un Etat etc." jusqu'à la fin, les mots suivants: „soit que le différend porte exclusivement sur les droits de l'Etat lui même, soit qu'il ait indirectement pour objet les droits et intérêts de ses ressortissants, ou des ressortissants d'un pays dont l'Etat partie en cause a la protection."

ANNEX No. 4.

Amendments proposed by M. Ricci-Busatti to Articles 25 to 28 of the Root—Phillimore plan.

Article 25. The words "unless otherwise provided by rule of Court" to be deleted, and the first portion of the Article to be so worded that it shall be laid down that the session shall not take place if there should be no cases to be tried.

Article 26. Add at the beginning of the Article the words: "Whenever, either at the request of the parties, or upon the decision of the President, the full Court sits" the remainder of the Article approved, subject to amendments in wording.

The following Article to be added (26 *bis*):

"In any case the contesting parties may by mutual agreement request that the tribunal should be composed of three judges or of a single judge, to be appointed either by themselves or by the President from amongst the members of the Court.

"Subject to the provisions of Article 26 and the preceding paragraph, the Court shall be composed in each case of five judges and two deputy judges. The rules of Court shall lay down the order in which the judges shall be called upon to take their seats."

Article 27. In the first paragraph substitute the words "this party may either nominate a judge from amongst persons included on the list mentioned in Article . . . . . . or claim that the subjects of the two contesting parties, if any are included amongst the judges, shall be excluded from the Court", for the words "that State shall for the purpose of the trial appoint . . ."

In the second paragraph substitute the words "may appoint" for the words "shall appoint".

Article 28. Substitute the words "whether the dispute concerns rights of the State itself exclusively, or whether it indirectly concerns the rights and interests of its subjects or of subjects of a country which the State concerned in the case has under its protection", for the words "but the State etc." to the end of the paragraph.

24IÈME SÉANCE (non-publique), tenue au Palais de la Paix, à La Haye, le 14 juillet 1920.

Présidence de M. le BARON DESCAMPS.

Sont présents : tous les membres du Comité (à l'exception de M. Bevilaqua) ; M. Fernandes; Mr. James Brown Scott; les secrétaires particuliers du Baron Descamps et de M. Adatci ; les membres du Secrétariat.

La séance est ouverte à 9.50 heures du matin.

Le PRESIDENT rouvre la discussion sur les articles 25 et 26 du projet Root—Phillimore. Il appelle l'attention du Comité sur l'amendement déposé par Lord Phillimore en vue de se rapprocher du point de vue du Président, et comme suite à sa déclaration de la veille.

Cet amendement est ainsi conçu :

Ajouter à la fin de l'article 25 :

„La Cour désigne annuellement trois juges qui, avec le président, forment une section spéciale. Les parties peuvent, de consentement mutuel, s'adresser au président pour que leurs affaires soient décidées par cette section.

Si un juge faisant partie de la section est empêché, le président a le droit de désigner un des autres juges à sa place."

Ajouter au commencement de l'article 26 :

„Sauf dans les cas visés dans l'article précédent."

Le Président constate, en réponse à des questions qui lui sont posées, que l'article 25 n'a pas encore été adopté. Il explique que la proposition de Lord Phillimore se rapproche du Projet de Convention de 1907, qui également prévoit une section spéciale de trois juges. Ce rapprochement constitue un gage pour que l'amendement soit trouvé acceptable. Personnellement, le Président aurait préféré plusieurs chambres dont une composée de cinq juges, et l'institution d'un ou de plusieurs juges uniques; mais il constate le pas fait par la proposition de Lord Phillimore.

Il donne lecture d'un texte qui exprime toute sa pensée au sujet de l'organisation de la section spéciale. Ce texte est inséré à l'annexe 2.

Une discussion s'engage au sujet de l'amendement proposé par Lord Phillimore. Le mode

24TH MEETING (Private), held at the Peace Palace, the Hague, on July 14th, 1920.

BARON DESCAMPS in the chair.

Present : all the members of the Committee (except M. Bevilaqua); M. Fernandes; Mr. James Brown Scott; the private secretaries of Baron Descamps and M. Adatci ; the Members of the Secretariat.

The meeting opened at 9.50 a.m.

The PRESIDENT re-opened the discussion on Articles 25 and 26 of the Root—Phillimore plan, and drew the Committee's attention to the amendment presented by Lord Phillimore, in accordance with his statement on the previous day, with a view to reconciling the President's point of view and his own. This amendment was worded as follows :

Add at the end of article 25 :

" The Court shall designate, annually, three judges who, with the President, shall form a special section. Parties may, by mutual consent, apply to the President for the purpose of having their case decided by this section.

If a judge included in the Section is unable to sit, the President may appoint one of the other judges to take his place."

Add at the beginning of article 26 :

" Except in the case mentioned in the preceding article."

The President stated, in answer to a question put to him, that Article 25 had not yet been adopted. He explained that the proposal of Lord Phillimore resembled the plan of the 1907 Convention, which also made provision for a special section of three judges. This similarity gave promise that the amendment would be found acceptable. Personally, the President would have preferred several chambers of which one should be composed of five judges, and the institution of one or more chambers with a single judge, but he admitted that Lord Phillimore's proposal was a step in the right direction.

He read a statement which expressed his ideas on the organisation of a special section ; this statement is included in Annex 2.

de désignation des juges qui feront partie de la section spéciale, est particulièrement étudié. Les juges seront-ils désignés par le président ou par les parties, ou bien pourront-ils siéger d'office?

M. RICCI-BUSATTI fait valoir qu'il est désirable de laisser aux parties directement, ou par l'intermédiaire du président, une certaine influence sur la composition de la section, tandis que M. Loder et le Président font valoir que cette méthode rappellerait trop celle propre à l'arbitrage.

Au cours de la discussion, la question suivante est également soulevée: la Cour peut-elle utilement juger avec un nombre pair de juges?

M. FERNANDES dépose l'amendement suivant: „La Cour statuera au complet, les juges suppléants étant appelés à remplacer les juges titulaires absents ou empêchés. Si toutefois onze juges ne sont pas disponibles, neuf juges suffiront comme quorum minimum pour l'audience."

Cet amendement se rapporte à l'article 26 du projet Root—Phillimore.

Le PRESIDENT en donne lecture, mais déclare qu'il ne peut pas s'y rallier.

LORD PHILLIMORE explique l'idée du projet Root—Phillimore. Le chiffre 11 ne serait que nominal; des cas inévitables de maladie et d'absence ramèneraient presque toujours ce chiffre à 9; c'est le chiffre qu'il trouve préférable.

Mr. ROOT donne son approbation à l'amendement de M. Fernandes. Il croit qu'on doit pouvoir compléter la Cour en faisant appel à autant de suppléants qu'il faut pour faire le nombre de 11; mais d'autre part, ce chiffre ne doit pas être obligatoire. La Cour doit pouvoir siéger avec neuf juges.

Le PRESIDENT donne lecture de sa proposition et déclare qu'il lui est impossible d'accepter le chiffre de 11 juges proposé par M. Fernandes et appuyé par Mr. Root. Son système comprenait cinq juges; dans un esprit de conciliation il est allé jusqu'à neuf, mais ce chiffre représente le maximum des concessions qu'il peut faire. Dans ces conditions il reprend sa proposition.

M. RICCI-BUSATTI se rallie au texte du Président, sauf rédaction.

A discussion took place on the subject of the amendment proposed by Lord Phillimore. The method of appointing the judges who were to form the special section was especially considered: should they be named by the President or by the parties, or could they sit *ex officio*?

M. RICCI-BUSATTI pointed out that it was desirable to allow the Parties, either directly or through the President, to have a certain influence on the composition of the section, while M. Loder and the President pointed out that this method would too much resemble that proper to arbitration.

In the course of the discussion, the question was also raised whether the Court could successfully perform its duties with an even number of judges.

M. FERNANDES proposed the following amendment: "The full Court shall sit, deputy judges being called upon to replace regular judges who are absent or unable to sit. If at any time eleven judges are not available, nine judges shall suffice to constitute a quorum for the hearing of a case."

This amendment related to Art. 26 of the Root—Phillimore plan.

The PRESIDENT read it but stated that he could not accept it.

LORD PHILLIMORE explained the idea of the Root—Phillimore plan. The number 11 would be merely nominal; cases of illness and absence would always reduce the number to 9, which number he thought preferable.

Mr. ROOT expressed his approval of M. Fernandes' amendment. He thought that it should be possible to make up the number of the Court to 11 by calling upon as many deputy judges as might be necessary for this purpose. On the other hand, however, this number should not be compulsory. The Court should be able to sit with nine judges.

The PRESIDENT read his proposition and said that it was impossible for him to accept the number of eleven judges, proposed by M. Fernandes and supported by Mr. Root. His system involved five judges; in an attempt to effect a compromise he had consented to nine judges, but this number represented the utmost concession which he could make. Under these circumstances he reverted to his proposal.

M. RICCI-BUSATTI agreed to the President's proposition, subject to alterations in wording.

Le PRESIDENT met aux voix sa proposition.

Elle est adoptée à main levée, à une voix de majorité, et avec deux réserves.

En conséquence il n'y a pas lieu de procéder à un vote sur l'amendement de M. Fernandes.

The PRESIDENT took a vote upon his proposition. It was adopted by a majority of one vote, on a show of hands; two members made reservations.

Consequently, there was no need to vote upon M. Fernandes' amendment.

MM. ALTAMIRA et DE LAPRADELLE demandent des explications sur le vote.

En réponse à une question de LORD PHILLIMORE, le PRÉSIDENT déclare que la question de l'ordre dans lequel les suppléants seront appelés à siéger a été déjà décidée dans un autre sens que celui qui est proposé à la fin de l'article 26 du projet Root-Phillimore.

MM. ALTAMIRA and DE LAPRADELLE asked for an explanation concerning the vote.

In answer to a question of LORD PHILLIMORE, the PRESIDENT stated that the question of the order in which the deputy judges should be called to the Bench had been already decided in a way different from that proposed at the end of Art. 26 of the Root—Phillimore plan.

Mr. ROOT demande au Président quelle est exactement la portée du texte qui a été adopté. Il a l'impression qu'on a adopté d'abord l'amendement de Lord Phillimore, puis celui du Président. Il y a cependant contradiction entre ces deux amendements; pour sa part, Mr. Root n'a pas de préférences, mais il croit qu'il faut choisir l'un ou l'autre de ces amendements.

Mr. ROOT asked the President what was the exact scope of the text which had been adopted; he was under the impression that first of all Lord Phillimore's amendment had been adopted and then that of the President. There was, however, a contradiction between these two amendments. Mr. Root personally had no preference, but he thought that it would be necessary to select one or the other of these amendments.

Le PRESIDENT explique qu' té suffisamment discuté. L'amendement qu'il a proposé a un caractère nettement transactionnel. Il a adopté le principe que la Cour siégera normalement *in pleno*, sauf la division de la Cour en chambres. Il lui a été impossible d'accepter le nombre de onze juges. En tout cas, la question est maintenant tranchée par le vote qu'on vient de prendre. Si l'on veut y revenir, on pourra le faire en seconde lecture.

The PRESIDENT explained that, in his opinion, the whole question had been sufficiently discussed. The amendment which he had proposed was clearly in the nature of a compromise. He had adopted the principle that the Court should normally sit *in pleno*, subject to the division of the Court into Chambers; he had found it impossible to accept the number of eleven judges. At all events, the question had now been settled by the vote just taken. If it were desired to reconsider it, it might be done at the second reading.

LORD PHILLIMORE donne lecture de l'article 25 du projet Root—Phillimore et de l'amendement qu'il a déposé. Il demande si ce dernier texte a été adopté à la place du texte correspondant de l'article 25 et quelle est, dans ce cas, la relation entre ce texte et celui soumis par le Président — texte qui a été également adopté. Il croit qu'on est d'accord sur le premier alinéa de l'article 25; mais entre le 2ème alinéa et l'amendement du Président il y a contradiction.

LORD PHILLIMORE read article 25 of the Root—Phillimore plan and the amendment which he had proposed. He asked if the latter had been adopted instead of the corresponding text of Art. 25, and if so, what the relation was between this amendment and the one presented by the President, which had also been adopted. He thought that the first paragraph of Article 25 had been agreed upon, but that Paragraph 2 and the President's amendment were contradictory.

Le PRESIDENT déclare que le texte de l'article 25 du projet Root—Phillimore a été adopté jusqu'aux mots „lui paraîtra nécessaire", inclusivement; puis on a adopté le texte du Président jusqu'à l'expression „à la demande des parties" inclusivement.

The PRESIDENT stated that the text of Article 25 of the Root—Phillimore plan had been adopted up to and including the words "when he deems it necessary;" then the President's text had been adopted up to and including the expression "at the request of the parties."

Cette dernière partie tiendra lieu du 2ème alinéa de l'article 25 et de l'article 26 du projet Root—Phillimore.

LORD PHILLIMORE se déclare satisfait de cette réponse.

M. DE LAPRADELLE constate que la proposition du Président a été adoptée à une voix de majorité, qu'elle a été adoptée contre deux réserves et que certains d'entre ceux qui ont voté pour la proposition ont déclaré avoir des doutes au sujet de la question de savoir quel texte ils ont voté, et quelle est la fonction de ce texte.

M. LODER demande la parole pour une motion d'ordre. Il constate que l'on se trouve dans une impasse, et qu'il faut tâcher d'en sortir maintenant, afin d'éviter de s'y retrouver en seconde lecture.

Il fait observer qu'on a voté la proposition du Président, sans en avoir le texte sous les yeux; c'est la première fois qu'il arrive qu'un texte ait été voté de cette manière; il propose que le texte soit multigraphié et distribué, et qu'on procède à un nouveau vote, lorsque les membres auront eu le temps d'en prendre connaissance.

Le PRESIDENT fait observer que le texte de sa proposition a déjà été lu plusieurs fois. Il regrette de ne pouvoir accepter la proposition de M. Loder; il veut bien faire multiplier et distribuer le texte, mais dans l'intérêt de la bonne marche des travaux, il ne peut admettre qu'on revienne sur un vote acquis, à moins qu'on ne le fasse en seconde lecture.

Le Président ouvre la discussion sur l'article 27 du projet Root—Phillimore; il en donne lecture.

LORD PHILLIMORE a la parole pour expliquer cet article. A son avis, il a été reconnu, lors d'une des discussions antérieures, qu'il serait nécessaire de donner aux parties la possibilité d'être représentées dans la Cour par un membre de leur nationalité; ou du moins qu'il faut empêcher que l'une des parties soit représentée tandis que l'autre ne l'est pas. Il y a plusieurs manières d'arriver à ce but. Ou bien on peut exclure le juge ressortissant de l'une des parties, ou bien on peut adjoindre un juge ressortissant de l'autre. Mais, dans son opinion, il est préférable de donner aux parties une représentation nationale, non seulement pour défendre leurs intérêts, mais pour permettre à la Cour de comprendre certaines questions qui demandent des connaissances tout à fait spéciales,

This last part replaced paragraph 2 of Article 25 and article 26 of the Root—Phillimore plan.

LORD PHILLLIMORE said that the answer satisfied him.

M. DE LAPRADELLE stated that the President's proposal had been adopted by a majority of one vote, and subject to two reservations; further, that certain members amongst those who had voted for the proposal had expressed doubts as to the identity and purport of the clause which they had voted for.

M. LODER raised a point of order. He stated that they had come to a deadlock and that an attempt must be made to find a way out of it at once, so as to avoid meeting the same difficulty at the second reading.

He observed that the President's proposition had been voted upon without having the text of it at hand. This was the first time that a vote had been taken in this way. He proposed that the text be duplicated and distributed, and that a new vote be taken when the members had had time to consider it.

The PRESIDENT pointed out that the text of his proposal had already been read several times; he regretted that he could not accede to M. Loder's suggestion. He would be pleased to have the text duplicated and distributed, but he could not in the interest of the progress of their work consent to reconsider a vote already taken, except at the second reading.

The President laid Art. 27 of the Root—Phillimore plan before the Committee; he read it.

LORD PHILLIMORE explained the purport of this article. In his opinion, it had been acknowledged, in the course of a previous discussion, that it would be necessary to make it possible for parties to be represented on the Court by a member of their nationality; or that at any rate it would be necessary to prevent one party being represented if the other party were not. There were several ways of obtaining this end; the judge of the nationality of one party might be excluded, or a judge of the nationality of the other might be added; but, in his opinion, it would be preferable to give a national representative to both parties, not only to protect their interests, but to enable the Court to understand certain questions which require highly specialised knowledge and relate to

et qui tiennent à la différence entre les divers systèmes juridiques. Lord Phillimore mentionne le système fidei-commissaire en Angleterre et en Amérique, qui présente des difficultés toutes particulières.

Après mûre réflection, Lord Phillimore croit que le système du projet Root—Phillimore est le meilleur, et il exprime l'espoir que les membres du Comité voudront bien s'y rallier.

M. ADATCI considère que l'article 27 est très important. Au début des délibérations du Comité, il a lui-même formulé une proposition fragmentaire dans la matière. Il a vu, avec une vive satisfaction, comment l'idée contenue dans cette proposition avait été perfectionnée dans le projet Root—Phillimore, et, en abandonnant les scrupules formalistes que lui avait inspiré le fait que le système adopté se trouve en désaccord avec le droit interne et les principes théoriques du droit international, il s'est rallié au projet.

Il rappelle que la Cour de justice qu'il s'agit d'instituer embrassera toutes les nations, toutes les races, toutes les religions. Il évoque le souvenir de M. Louis Renault, qui a dit qu'en matière d'arbitrage, des éléments nationaux doivent être compris dans la Cour même; des assesseurs ne suffisent pas. Le juge représentant une partie doit être admis à prendre part aux délibérations et aux votes. Il sera un collaborateur précieux, surtout pour la rédaction de la sentence, question délicate déjà en matière de droit national, et plus encore en matière internationale, où il s'agit de formuler des sentences auxquelles des Etats, parfois même des grands Etats, devront se soumettre. Il faut que l'exposé des motifs de la sentence explique celle-ci, de façon à écarter les obstacles que la susceptibilité nationale sera disposée à dresser contre l'exécution du verdict.

Pour bien formuler cet exposé de motifs, il faut connaître la psychologie des peuples. Ceci est important, surtout lorsqu'il s'agit d'un jugement rendu en Europe ou en Amérique, mais concernant des Etats de races différentes.

M. Adatci prend l'exemple du Japon. Il dit que l'Europe et l'Amérique ont une psychologie basée sur le fond du christianisme, tandis que la psychologie de l'Extrême Orient est basée sur le bouddhisme, le shintoisme ou le confucionisme. A des peuples obéissant aux lois de cette psychologie, il faudrait expliquer les sentences d'une façon très minutieuse pour les leur faire accepter. Ses compatriotes, par exemple, accepteraient difficilement des décisions qui ne leur seraient pas raisonnablement expliquées. Il en est de même

the differences between the various legal systems. Lord Phillimore mentioned the trustee system in England and America, which presents very special difficulties.

After mature reflection, Lord Phillimore thought that the system of the Root—Phillimore plan was the best, and he expressed the hope that the members of the Committee would see fit to accept it.

M. ADATCI considered that Art. 27 was very important. At the beginning of the Committee's deliberations he had himself prepared a rough, incomplete proposal on this subject. He had observed with great satisfaction that the idea contained in this proposal had been perfected in the Root—Phillimore plan, and, after abandoning certain formal scruples aroused by the fact that the system adopted was at variance with municipal law and the theoretical principles of international law, he had accepted the plan.

He recalled the fact that the sphere of action of the Court of Justice which was to be established would include all nations, races and religions. He referred to M. Louis Renault, who said that, in cases of arbitration, national representatives should be included in the Court itself; assessors did not suffice. A judge representing a party should be admitted to take part in the deliberations and the vote. He would be of great assistance, especially in the drafting of the sentence, a sufficiently delicate question in cases of national law and even more so in international cases, where sentences have to be drawn up, which must be complied with by States, sometimes by powerful States. It is essential that the explanatory statement accompanying the sentence should be so drawn up as to remove the possibility of obstacles which national susceptibilities would be inclined to put in the way of the execution of the sentence.

In order to prepare this statement of reasons satisfactorily, the psychology of the various peoples must be understood: this is important, especially in the case of a judgment given in Europe or America, but affecting States of different races.

M. Adatci took Japan as an example: he said that Europe and America have a psychology based on Christianity, while the psychology of the Far East is based on Buddhism, Shintoism and Confucianism. Peoples subject to the laws of the latter psychology require a very detailed explanation of the sentence in order to make it acceptable to them. His fellow countrymen, for instance, would find it difficult to accept decisions which were not explained to them in a clear and satisfactory manner.

ıns tout l'Orient. Il est nécessaire de tenir compte ɜ ces circonstances.

S'il est donc nécessaire que les pays soient re-résentés à la Cour par un membre de leur natio-alité, la question se pose de savoir si, de cette ıanière, celui qui viendrait siéger serait revêtu de ›ute la dignité nécessaire. M. Adatci n'en est as sûr: il croit qu'il faut établir des garanties érieuses à cet égard. On pourra, par exemple, ipuler que les juges *ad hoc* soient choisis sur . liste des candidats présentée au Conseil et à Assemblée.

En finissant, M. Adatci déclare qu'il donne ɔn appui au projet Root-Phillimore qui, ıalgré la souplesse et les autres qualités du projet .icci-Busatti, correspond le plus à ses idées.

En réponse à des questions formulées par M. .LTAMIRA, LORD PHILLIMORE constate ue dans les cas visés par l'article 27 du projet .oot-Phillimore, le nombre des juges à la 'our s'élèvera à dix ou à onze; il déclare que les ifficultés qui en découleront pour obtenir une ıajorité pourront facilement être surmontées.

M. FERNANDES rappelle qu'à une des séances ntérieures il a attiré l'attention sur la disposition ɔntenue dans l'article 12 du projet de M. Bevi-ıqua, et qu'on avait décidé que l'idée ainsi ɔulevée serait discutée lors des débats sur l'ar-cle 27. Il pense que le moment de reprendre la uestion est maintenant venu. Mais, tandis que idée de M. Bevilaqua cadrait parfaitement vec le système tel qu'il s'esquissait au moment ù M. Fernandes y attira, pour la première ›is, l'attention, elle ne se trouve plus en harmonie vec le système modifié par les amendements doptés. Dans ces circonstances, et se ralliant au ɜxte du projet Root-Phillimore, M. Fernan-es préfère retirer sa proposition.

M. HAGERUP propose l'addition suivante à article 27 du projet Root—Phillimore:

„Le juge nommé par les parties en vertu du présent rticle, doit, si possible, être choisi parmi les candi-ats proposés à la Société des Nations conformément l'article 6 (du projet Root—Phillimore)."

M. Hagerup explique cet amendement: il .it valoir qu'il pourrait être impossible de se con-ırmer à cette règle dans certains cas; c'est pourquoi a inséré l'expression „si possible".

M. ADATCI et LORD PHILLIMORE se ıllient en principe à l'addition.

It is the same throughout the whole of the East; these facts must be borne in mind.

If therefore it is necessary that countries be represented on the Court by a member of their nationality, the question arises whether, by this method, the person taking his seat would be of the required standing. M. Adatci was not sure of this; he thought it would be necessary to create real guarantees in this respect. For instance it might be stipulated that judges *ad hoc* should be chosen from the list of nominations submitted to the Council and to the Assembly.

In concluding, M. Adatci stated that he gave his support to the Root—Phillimore plan, which, in spite of the elasticity and other qualities of the Ricci-Busatti plan, corresponded most nearly to his ideas.

In answer to questions raised by M. ALTAMIRA, LORD PHILLIMORE stated that in the circum-stances dealt with by Article 27 of the Root—Phillimore plan, the number of judges on the Court would increase to ten or eleven; he asserted that any difficulties in securing a majority, which arose from this increase, could easily be overcome.

M. FERNANDES recalled the fact that at a pre-vious meeting he drew attention to the provision con-tained in Article 12 of the plan of M. Bevilaqua, and that it had been decided to discuss the idea therein contained at the time of the discussion of Article 27. He thought that the time had now come to take up the question again. While, however, M. Bevilaqua's idea harmonised perfectly with the system as outlined at the time when M. Fer-nandes first drew attention to it, it was no longer in harmony with the system as modified by the amendments adopted. In these circumstances M. Fernandes preferred to withdraw his proposal and to support the text of the Root—Phillimore plan.

M. HAGERUP proposed the following addition to Article 27 of the Root—Phillimore plan:

"Judges appointed by the parties in accordance with this Article, should, if possible, be chosen from amongst the candidates proposed to the League of Nations in conformity with Article 6 (of the Root—Phillimore plan)."

M. Hagerup explained this amendment: he pointed out that it might be impossible to comply with this rule in some cases; that was the reason for inserting the expression "if possible."

M. ADATCI and LORD PHILLIMORE agreed in principle to the addition.

M. DE LAPRADELLE admet la proposition Root—Phillimore, mais désirerait préciser certains points. Il se demande, par exemple, si le juge *ad hoc* aura le droit de marquer son dissentiment.

LORD PHILLIMORE dit que oui.

M. DE LAPRADELLE continue alors en disant que c'est un point extrêmement délicat, parce qu'un juge national marquera toujours son dissentiment contre une sentence qui est défavorable à son pays. C'est pourquoi on ne doit recourir aux juges *ad hoc* qu'en dernier lieu. La méthode à employer serait de prendre d'abord le juge ressortissant d'une des parties en litige dans la Cour, et de donner aux parties le droit de choisir chacune un juge *ad hoc* parmi les suppléants. Ainsi on arriverait en même temps à donner un peu de vie à l'institution des juges suppléants.

M. LODER, bien que se sachant en minorité, tient à faire une déclaration. Il est hostile à l'article 27 du projet Root—Phillimore parce que cet article évoque encore l'idée de l'arbitrage au lieu de celle de la justice. Il pense que l'idée de donner aux parties un représentant à la Cour est erronée. Si l'on donne aux parties le droit de choisir ce juge, on se trouve en pleine procédure d'arbitrage. Si l'on stipule que les systèmes juridiques seront représentés, on a encore adopté une idée fausse. Il y a du reste contradiction entre les efforts qu'on a faits pour instituer une Cour composée des meilleurs juges, et la proposition d'y introduire des juges occasionnels.

M. Loder voudrait que l'on supprimât tout l'article 27, mais si l'on ne trouve pas cela possible, il ne peut en tout cas aller plus loin que d'accepter des assesseurs avec voix consultative nommés par les parties. Dans cet ordre d'idées il propose la rédaction suivante de l'article 27:

„Si, lors de l'instruction d'un cas déterminé, la Cour ne renferme pas de juge de la nationalité d'un des Etats partie au litige, cet Etat nommera, en vue de l'instruction, un juge qui aura une voix consultative dans la Chambre du Conseil.

„Si la Cour ne renferme pas de juge de la nationalité d'aucune des parties au litige, chacune d'elles nommera un juge qui prendra part à la procédure avec voix consultative".

En réponse à une question de M. de Lapradelle, M. Loder déclare que, dans son système, un juge ressortissant d'une des parties doit sortir de la Cour.

M. DE LAPRADELLE accepted the Root—Phillimore proposal, but desired to make certain points clear. He wished to know, for instance, whether a judge *ad hoc* would have the right to have his dissent recorded.

LORD PHILLIMORE answered in the affirmative.

M. DE LAPRADELLE then went on to say that this was an extremely delicate point, because a national judge would always record his disapproval of a sentence unfavourable to his country. For this reason, judges *ad hoc* should not be used except as a last resort. The method to be employed would be, first of all to remove from the Court the judges representing one of the parties in the case, and then to confer on each of the parties the right to choose a judge *ad hoc* from amongst the deputy judges. Thus, at the same time, a little life would be put into the institution of deputy judges.

M. LODER, although he realised he was in the minority, wished to make a statement. He was opposed to Article 27 of the Root—Phillimore plan, because this Article still involved the idea of arbitration instead of justice. He believed that the idea of giving the parties representatives upon the Court was wrong. If the right to choose such judges were given to the parties, this would give the proceedings a characteristic essentially belonging to arbitration. Again, by stipulating that the various legal systems should be represented, a mistaken idea would be introduced. Furthermore, there was a contradiction between the attempts which had been made to ensure the establishment of a Court composed of the best judges, and the proposal to bring temporary judges into the Court.

M. Loder desired to suppress the whole of Article 27 but if that was found impossible, he was prepared to agree to assessors with advisory powers appointed by the parties, but he could not in any case go further. He consequently proposed the following wording for Article 27:

"If at the time of the preliminary examination of a given case, the Court does not include a judge of the nationality of one of the States parties in the case, this State shall appoint, for the preliminary examination, a judge who shall take part with an advisory capacity in the deliberations preceding the judgment.

"If the Court does not contain a judge of the nationality of either of the parties in the case, each State shall appoint a judge who shall participate in the proceedings, in an advisory capacity."

In answer to a question by M. de Lapradelle,

LORD PHILLIMORE exprime l'avis que si l'on adopte une idée, il faut en accepter les conséquences jusqu'au bout. Il apprécie beaucoup l'idée de M. Loder, et il la trouve très belle, puisqu'elle est entièrement conforme aux exigences du droit strict, mais elle n'est pas pratique: c'est pourquoi il croit devoir se rallier plutôt à l'idée de M. Adatci; il peut accepter aussi l'amendement de M. Hagerup qui s'en inspire.

M. RICCI-BUSATTI déclare que les mêmes raisons pour lesquelles M. Loder est hostile à l'article 27 lui semblent militer en faveur de cet article. Il admet cependant que les objections de M. Loder sont très graves, et il relève surtout la difficulté qui ressortirait de la différence d'origine entre les juges — les juges ordinaires, élus par le Conseil et par l'Assemblée, tenant leur mandat de la Société des Nations, tandis que les juges adjoints seraient nommés par leurs gouvernements: pour la cohérence du système, il lui paraît plus raisonnable de donner aux représentants des parties le caractère d'assesseurs. D'autre part, afin que la disposition dont il s'agit puisse satisfaire aux différentes circonstances qui peuvent se présenter, il propose un amendement portant que, si l'une des parties en cause est représentée dans la Cour, et non l'autre, celle-ci pourra, soit nommer un juge parmi les personnes qui figurent sur la liste des présentations, soit demander que le ressortissant de la partie adverse soit exclu du tribunal.

Mr. ROOT est d'avis que tout ce qui a été dit par M. Loder, s'applique parfaitement à la juridiction nationale. Pour ce qui est de la juridiction internationale, il faut tenir compte des observations de M. Adatci. Les nations doivent aller à la Cour avec l'assurance d'y rencontrer une pleine compréhension: dans ce but il est nécessaire, au moins pour les pays qui diffèrent le plus de l'ordinaire, d'avoir à la Cour un juge de leur nationalité et un juge qui y siège sur un pied de parfaite égalité avec les autres. C'est pourquoi Mr. Root appuie la proposition du projet Root-Phillimore, tout en voulant y ajouter l'amendement de M. Hagerup.

Le PRESIDENT déclare qu'à son avis M. Loder confond l'organisation juridique nationale et

M. Loder stated that, according to this system, a judge of the nationality of one of the parties would give up his seat.

LORD PHILLIMORE expressed the opinion that, if a theory were adopted, all the consequences must also be accepted. He appreciated M. Loder's idea highly and found it admirable in that it was entirely in conformity with the requirements of strict law, but it was not practicable. Lord Phillimore felt therefore that he would be better able to support M. Adatci's view; he could also accept M. Hagerup's amendment which was based upon it.

M. RICCI-BUSATTI stated that, as far as he was concerned, the reasons for which M. Loder was opposed to Article 27 appeared to be in its favour. He admitted, however, that M. Loder's objections were very serious, and he mentioned in particular the difficulty which would result from the fact that the judges would derive their positions from different sources—the ordinary judges elected by the Council and the Assembly, holding their position under the League of Nations, and the judges *ad hoc* being appointed by their Governments. It would therefore seem more consistent with the system adopted to give the representatives of the parties the character of assessors. On the other hand, in order that the provision in question should meet the various circumstances which might arise, he presented an amendment to the effect that, if one of the parties were represented on the Court but not the other, the latter should be able, either to appoint a judge from amongst the persons who appear on the list of nominations, or to request that the representative of the opposing party be excluded from the tribunal.

Mr. ROOT was of opinion that all that M. Loder had said applied perfectly to national tribunals; but in relation to an international tribunal, M. Adatci's observations must be taken into consideration. Nations should be able to go before the Court with the certainty that their case will be fully understood. For this purpose there must be, at any rate in the case of those countries which differ most widely from the normal type, a judge of their nationality on the Court, who must sit on a footing of complete equality with the others. For this reason Mr. Root supported the provisions of the Root—Phillimore plan, and, at the same time, wished to have M. Hagerup's amendment added to it.

The PRESIDENT said that, in his opinion, M. Loder had confused national and international

l'organisation juridique internationale. Une assimilation complète, entre ces deux organisations est impossible. Le but de la justice internationale est de remplacer la violence par la procédure devant le juge. Pour arriver à ce but il faut inspirer aux parties la confiance; il faut leur donner la garantie qu'elles seront défendues comme elles entendent être défendues. Dans cet ordre d'idées il paraît nécessaire de leur assurer qu'un des leurs soit présent au tribunal.

L'observation de M. de Lapradelle sur le droit des juges nationaux de motiver leur dissentiment dans la sentence, doit être réservée pour la séance où l'on s'occupera de la motivation des jugements.

Reste à examiner l'idée de mettre les assesseurs nationaux sur un pied d'égalité avec les juges. Le Président croit que donner suite à cette idée serait dépasser le but: il suffit de mettre les assesseurs dans une situation qui leur permette de remplir leur mission, et à ce point de vue il n'est pas nécessaire de leur accorder autre chose qu'une voix consultative. Les assesseurs eux-mêmes préféreront du reste souvent n'être pas obligés de se prononcer sur la solution du litige. Pour ces raisons, le Président qui avait auparavant eu une opinion différente, croit pouvoir se rallier maintenant à la proposition de M. Loder. Il suffit d'avoir des assesseurs, mais d'autre part il est nécessaire d'en avoir.

LORD PHILLIMORE observe d'abord qu'un juge national ne donnera pas nécessairement toujours son vote en faveur de son pays: il cite l'exemple de Sir Robert Webster, qui dans l'affaire de l'Alaska s'est prononcé contre la Grande-Bretagne.

Lord Phillimore signale une difficulté du système préconisé par le Président; si deux Etats sont en litige, et que l'un d'eux soit représenté à la Cour, celui-ci devra-t-il dégrader son juge au rang d'assesseur pour assurer l'égalité entre le juge de sa nationalité et l'assesseur envoyé par l'autre partie? Lord Phillimore croit que cette solution est inadmissible: il vaudrait certainement mieux donner à l'autre partie le droit de nommer un juge.

M. HAGERUP se rallie à Lord Phillimore. Comme lui, il pense qu'il est inadmissible de dégrader un juge au rang d'assesseur.

Le PRESIDENT fait observer que, dans le système Loder, un juge ressortissant d'une des parties doit se retirer pour être remplacé par un assesseur, nommé par cette partie.

legal organisations; a complete analogy between these two organisations could not be established. The object of international justice is to substitute procedure before a judge for methods of violence. To attain this end, the parties must feel confident—they must be given a guarantee that their case will be defended as they would wish it to be done. For this purpose it would seem necessary to assure them of the presence of one of their subjects upon the tribunal.

M. de Lapradelle's remark concerning the right of national judges to have the reasons of their dissent recorded in the judgment, should be brought up for discussion at the meeting at which the question of including a statement of reasons in the judgment would be considered.

It remained to consider the idea of placing assessors on an equal footing with the judges. The President thought that by adopting this suggestion they would overshoot the mark. All that was required was to give the assessors a position which would enable them to fulfil their duties; for this purpose it would suffice to give them advisory powers. The assessors, furthermore, would themselves prefer not to be forced to commit themselves to an opinion upon the solution of cases. For these reasons, the President, who had previously held a different opinion, now felt that he could agree to M. Loder's proposal: assessors would suffice, but on the other hand, they were absolutely essential.

LORD PHILLIMORE observed, in the first place, that a national judge would not necessarily always vote in favour of his own country. He quoted the example of Sir Robert Webster, who pronounced against Great Britain in the Alaska affair.

Lord Phillimore drew attention to a difficulty involved in the system contemplated by the President. If two States were concerned in a dispute, one of which was represented on the Court, would the latter have to reduce its judge to the status of assessor in order to assure complete equality between the judge of its nationality and the assessor sent by the other party? Lord Phillimore thought that such a solution was inadmissible; it would certainly be better to give the other party the right to appoint a judge.

M. HAGERUP agreed with Lord Phillimore: like him he thought that it was inadmissible to degrade a judge to the rank of assessor.

The PRESIDENT observed that in M. Loder's system a judge who was of the nationality of one of the parties would retire and be replaced by an assessor appointed by that party.

Mr. ROOT est convaincu que la présence des assesseurs ne donnerait satisfaction ni aux grandes ni aux petites puissances, parce qu'un assesseur aura toujours une position d'infériorité. Ils ne peuvent que donner des renseignements, et la Cour n'est pas obligée de tenir compte de ce qu'ils disent. C'est seulement le droit de prendre part aux délibérations et aux décisions qui donnerait à la présence d'un représentant des parties une importance réelle. Tout autre arrangement ne pourrait donner satisfaction ni aux grandes puissances, qui pourraient occasionnellement ne pas être représentées à la Cour, ni aux petites puissances, qui ne le seraient que rarement.

M. LODER prie Mr. Root, qui croit que le système préconisé par M. Loder est inacceptable, de proposer une solution qui soit à la fois équitable et possible.

L'idée exprimée par Mr. Root, dans l'opinion de M. Loder, n'est pas pratique. Mr. Root voudrait qu'il y eût toujours à la Cour un juge représentant chacune des parties; mais cela sera difficile, lorsqu'il y aura plus de deux parties.

Le projet Root—Phillimore a bien proposé une solution à cette difficulté, mais cette solution, dans la pensée de M. Loder, n'en est pas une.

Il prend un exemple: il y a un litige entre deux Etats, un qui est représenté à la Cour et un autre qui ne l'est pas. Ce dernier envoie un juge *ad hoc*, qui siège à la Cour sur le même pied que les autres juges, bien que nommé par un gouvernement. Quoique opposé à cette idée, M. Loder l'admet pour le moment, mais il fait observer que de cette façon on arrivera à un nombre pair de juges, ce qui rendra impossible le fonctionnement du tribunal.

M. DE LAPRADELLE fait ressortir la difficulté de la question en présence de laquelle on se trouve. Il considère que si la justice internationale était arrivée à un haut degré de perfection, il ne serait pas nécessaire de toucher à la composition de la Cour. Le serment ou la déclaration qui devra être prononcée par les juges, doit déjà exprimer l'idée de leur parfaite impartialité qui induira les Etats à soumettre tout naturellement leurs différends à la Cour, sans penser à sa composition: les juges seront, non pas dénationalisés, mais supra-nationalisés.

M. de Lapradelle admet cependant que la justice internationale n'a pas encore atteint ce degré de perfection. La solution qui s'impose, pour le degré immédiatement inférieur, est que le juge ressortissant d'une des parties laisse sa place. Le fait d'avoir la nationalité d'une des parties

Mr. ROOT was convinced that the presence of assessors would satisfy neither the great nor the small Powers, because an assessor would always be in a position of inferiority. He would only be able to give information, and the Court would not be obliged to take account of what he said. The presence of representatives of the parties would only be of real value if they were given the right to take part in the deliberations and in the decision. Any other arrangement would give satisfaction neither to the great Powers, who might perhaps at times not be represented on the Court, nor to the small Powers who would but rarely be represented upon it.

M. LODER asked Mr. Root, who thought that the system suggested by M. Loder was unacceptable, to propose a solution which would be both equitable and possible.

Mr. Root's idea, in M. Loder's opinion, was not practical. Mr. Root desired that there should always be a judge upon the Court representing each of the parties; but this would be difficult when there were more than two parties.

The Root—Phillimore plan included a proposed solution for this difficulty, but this solution, in M. Loder's opinion, did not dispose of the difficulty.

He took an example: a case arises between a Country represented on the Court and another which is not. The latter sends a judge *ad hoc* who sits on the Court with the same status as the other judges, although appointed by a Government. Though opposed to this idea, M. Loder admitted it for the sake of argument; he wished to point out that the result would be an even number of judges, which would render it impossible for the Court to proceed.

M. DE LAPRADELLE underlined the difficult character of the question now before the Committee. He considered that, if international justice reached a high degree of perfection, it would not be necessary to meddle with the composition of the Court. The oath to be taken or the declaration to be made by the judges should of itself suffice to convey the notion of that complete impartiality on their part, which would induce the States to submit their disputes to the Court as a matter of course, without considering its composition. The judges would be not denationalised but super-nationalised.

M. de Lapradelle admitted, however, that international justice had not yet reached this pitch of perfection. The solution applicable to the next lower stage of development would be to cause a judge of the nationality of one of the parties to give up his seat. The fact that a judge was of the

peut être considéré comme une juste cause de récusation: dans la pratique le juge offrira probablement lui-même de se retirer.

Il admet toutefois qu'il y a contre ce système une grave objection tirée de l'expérience arbitrale: on a besoin des lumières des représentants nationaux dans la chambre des délibérations, on a besoin de quelqu'un qui puisse éclairer le tribunal, même sur les préjugés nationaux, et apprécier l'effet que produira, dans son pays, la forme sous laquelle la sentence aura été rédigée.

M. de Lapradelle, qui est très sensible à l'évocation par M. Adatci du souvenir de M. Renault, se rappelle avoir entendu ce dernier dire que les objections contre l'exécution des sentences arbitrales venaient, le plus souvent, non pas de leur contenu, mais de leur forme, qui blessait les préjugés nationaux, dont il faut tenir compte si l'on veut assurer le but de la juridiction internationale qui est de garantir la paix: la sentence doit produire le minimum de froissement; pour arriver à ce résultat, il faut que les parties aient un de leurs nationaux, ou un autre homme de leur confiance, à la Cour. De l'avis de M. de Lapradelle, cet homme peut parfaitement se contenter du rôle d'assesseur: un assesseur peut être aussi écouté qu'un juge; la seule différence est que sa voix ne compte pas dans la majorité.

Donc la vraie solution semble être que le juge ressortissant d'une des parties se retire et soit remplacé par un assesseur. Si on adopte la solution contraire, si l'on permet à la partie non représentée d'envoyer un juge *ad hoc*, on peut arriver à l'égalité, mais jamais à la réciprocité de situation. Cette réciprocité peut être obtenue seulement par le système des assesseurs.

Ce système doit donc être adopté, mais il ne doit être mis en exercice que si, parmi les juges suppléants, il n'y a pas de national de la partie ou des parties non représentées.

M. de Lapradelle désire très vivement donner de la vie à l'institution des juges suppléants. Si l'on nomme des juges *ad hoc*, ils motiveront toujours leurs opinions; et comme ils seront, dans la plupart des cas, d'opinions divergentes, leurs votes n'auront pas de valeur; mais l'exposé des motifs de leurs opinions reprendra tous les arguments qui seront de nature à froisser les parties; leur présence à la Cour pourra ainsi, parfois, rendre difficile l'exécution des sentences.

nationality of one of the parties might be considered as a sufficient ground for challenging his right to sit. In practice, a judge would, in all probability, offer to withdraw.

M. de Lapradelle nevertheless admitted that there was a grave objection to this system: experience gained in proceedings by arbitration shows that there is a need for the special knowledge of national representatives during the deliberations; someone is needed who can enlighten the Court even on such matters as national prejudices and estimate the effect which the form given to the sentence would produce in his country.

M. de Lapradelle, who appreciated highly the reference made by M. Adatci to M. Renault, remembered that he had heard him say that objections raised with reference to the execution of sentences of arbitration more often arose, not from their substance, but from their form, which wounded such national prejudices as must be taken into account, if the object of an international jurisdiction—to guarantee peace—were to be attained. The sentence should cause a minimum amount of offence; to attain this result both parties must have one of their own citizens, or someone else in whom they have confidence, upon the Court. M. de Lapradelle's opinion was that this man would find the rôle of assessor quite sufficient: just as much attention might be paid to an assessor as to a judge; the only difference would be that he would not be able to affect the decision by his vote.

The true solution, therefore, would seem to be that a judge of the nationality of one of the parties should withdraw and be replaced by an assessor. If the contrary solution were adopted, if the unrepresented party were allowed to send a judge *ad hoc*, theoretical equality might be attained, but not an exactly similar situation for both parties. The latter could be obtained only by the system of assessors.

This method should, therefore, be adopted; but it should not be used unless there were no deputy judge of the nationality of the party or parties represented.

M. de Lapradelle was very anxious to put life into the constitution of deputy judges. If judges *ad hoc* were appointed, they would always give the reasons for their opinions, and as they would generally dissent from the majority, their votes would have no value; but the statement of the reasons for their opinions would restate all the arguments likely to hurt the parties' feelings; the presence of such judges on the Court might sometimes therefore render the enforcement of sentences difficult.

M. LODER demande une réponse aux objections qu'il a soulevées contre le projet Root-Phillimore.

M. FERNANDES constate qu'un certain nombre des membres du Comité se sont maintenant ralliés autour de l'amendement qu'il a déposé l'autre jour, mais qu'il vient de retirer.

Il croit que le système Root-Phillimore est le plus sage. La plupart des Etats ne seront pas représentés à la Cour; il faut leur donner la satisfaction légitime, d'être représentés par un juge qui prend sa place sur un pied de parfaite égalité avec les autres juges, lorsqu'une affaire qui les concerne est soumise à la Cour.

M. Fernandes croit que ces considérations doivent l'emporter sur celles que lui-même avait jusqu'ici fait valoir en se plaçant à un point de vue théorique.

S'adressant à M. Loder, M. Fernandes dit que dans tous les systèmes, et non seulement dans celui qui prévoit la nomination d'un juge *ad hoc*, il peut arriver qu'on aboutisse à un partage des voix.

LORD PHILLIMORE est surpris de l'objection de M. Loder concernant la parité du nombre des juges de la Cour, parité à laquelle on arrivera nécessairement par l'adjonction d'un juge *ad hoc*. Cette conséquence de l'institution des juges *ad hoc*, aux yeux de M. Loder, rend ce point spécial du système Root—Phillimore peu pratique. A ceci, Lord Phillimore répond que le nombre des juges composant les cours en Angleterre est très souvent un nombre pair. Il ne croit pas que l'éventualité du partage des juges puisse se produire souvent. Elle pourrait du reste se produire même dans le système préconisé par M. Loder.

Lord Phillimore est d'avis que ce système soit dès maintenant mis aux voix.

Pour ce qui est des arguments si habiles de M. de Lapradelle, Lord Phillimore les apprécie certainement, mais il croit qu'il y a une considération pratique qui doit l'emporter sur ces arguments, et c'est la nécessité d'arriver à un système qui garantisse que les sentences de la Cour seront acceptées. Elles le seraient difficilement dans les pays de l'Amérique du Sud et de l'Asie, si elles étaient rendues par une Cour composée exclusivement d'Européens ou d'Américains, et où les pays intéressés n'auraient que des assesseurs sans voix délibérative.

Le PRESIDENT fait observer qu'il n'est pas certain que même les grandes puissances soient toujours représentées.

M. LODER requested an answer to the objections he had raised against the Root—Phillimore plan.

M. FERNANDES stated that a certain number of the members of the Committee were now in favour of the amendment which he had submitted on a previous day, but which he had just withdrawn.

He thought that the Root—Phillimore plan was the wiser. The great majority of States would not be represented on the Court. Their dignity must be satisfied by allowing them to be represented by a judge who would take his seat on an equal footing with the other judges, when a case which affected them was brought before the Court.

M. Fernandes thought that these considerations should outweigh those which he himself had until now put forward, looking at the matter from a theoretical point of view.

Speaking to M. Loder, M. Fernandes said that a split vote might occur under any system and was by no means confined to that which provided for the appointment of judges *ad hoc*.

LORD PHILLIMORE expressed his surprise at M. Loder's objection to a Court of an even number of judges, which would follow automatically upon the addition of a judge *ad hoc*. The consequence of the employment of judges *ad hoc* appeared to lead M. Loder to consider that this particular part of the Root—Phillimore plan was not practical. Lord Phillimore's answer to this was that the Courts in England were very often composed of an even number of judges. He did not believe that it would often happen that the judges would be equally divided: besides, the same thing might happen even in the system advocated by M. Loder.

Lord Phillimore thought that this system should be voted upon at once.

Concerning M. de Lapradelle's very able arguments, Lord Phillimore certainly recognised their value, but he thought that there was a practical consideration which should out-weigh them, and that was the necessity of finding a system which would guarantee the acceptance of the sentences of the Court. It would be very difficult to induce South-American and Asiatic countries to accept them, if they were pronounced by a Court composed exclusively of Europeans and Americans, and on which the interested countries were only represented by assessors without the right to vote.

The PRESIDENT observed that it was not certain that even the great Powers would always be represented.

LORD PHILLIMORE admet la justesse de cette remarque, mais fait valoir qu'il est encore moins probable que les Etats asiatiques et sud-américains aient un représentant.

Le PRESIDENT continue en disant que les petits Etats n'auront tous ensemble que cinq ou six juges à la Cour, tandis que les grandes puissances y seront pour la plupart représentées. On cherche à réaliser la justice impartiale. Dans ce but il est nécessaire de laisser aux parties le droit de défendre leurs intérêts, et d'exercer une juste influence sur la sentence, mais, d'autre part, il faut se souvenir du principe que personne ne peut être en même temps partie et juge.

M. LODER admet la justesse de l'observation de Lord Phillimore qu'une Cour peut très bien juger avec un nombre pair de juges. Aussi ses objections ne se sont-elles pas adressées contre ce point. Il a seulement voulu souligner que le nombre des juges doit être fixé d'avance. Si une partie non représentée à la Cour a le droit d'y envoyer un juge *ad hoc* et d'augmenter ainsi le nombre des juges, la Cour sera dénaturée. Il se peut que la méfiance entre les nations soit si grande qu'on ne puisse faire accepter une Cour telle qu'elle devrait être; mais ceci n'est pas une raison pour former une Cour qui n'en est pas une: le projet Root—Phillimore semble impossible à M. Loder.

M. HAGERUP s'adresse au Président. Il ne veut pas parler de grandes et petites puissances; il veut distinguer seulement entre les pays qui sont représentés à la Cour et ceux qui ne le sont pas. Il pense que ces derniers seront représentés d'une façon plus adéquate selon le système Root—Phillimore. Il n'a pas eu l'occasion d'étudier pratiquement, dans son fonctionnement, le système d'assesseurs. Mais il ne croit guère que ce système soit pratique; il pense en effet qu'une puissance ne remplacera pas volontiers son représentant à la Cour par un assesseur, dans un cas qui l'intéresse particulièrement. C'est pourquoi il se rallie à l'article 27 du projet Root-Phillimore avec l'addition que lui-même a proposée.

M. DE LAPRADELLE croit que le système des assesseurs servira mieux les intérêts des petits Etats. Un petit Etat qui n'est pas représenté à la Cour n'obtient pas une situation d'égalité avec une grande Puissance en envoyant un juge *ad hoc:* beaucoup de raisons contribueraient à accentuer

LORD PHILLIMORE admitted the accuracy of this statement, but submitted that it was even less probable that the Asiatic and South-American States would have a representative.

The PRESIDENT went on to say that the small States would not have more than five or six judges altogether on the Court, while the great Powers would for the most part be represented. Their aim was to secure an impartial administration of justice. To achieve this, the parties must retain the right to defend their interests and to exert a reasonable influence upon the sentences; but on the other hand the principle that no one can be a judge in his own case must be borne in mind.

M. LODER admitted the accuracy of Lord Phillimore's remark to the effect that a Court could very well deliver judgment with an even number of judges. His objections were not directed against this point. He had only wished to emphasise that the number of judges must be fixed beforehand. If a party not represented on the Court had the right to send a judge *ad hoc* and thus to increase the number of judges, the nature of the Court would be changed. It might well be that there was such a degree of distrust between the Nations, that it would be impossible to get them to accept a Court composed as it really should be; but this was no reason for forming a Court which was not a true Court. The Root—Phillimore plan seemed impossible to M. Loder.

M. HAGERUP addressed the President. He did not wish to distinguish between great and small Powers; he only wished to distinguish between the countries which were represented on the Court and those which were not. He thought that the latter would be represented in a more satisfactory way under the Root—Phillimore system. He was not conversant with the workings of the system of assessors, but he hardly believed that it was a practical one. He thought that as a matter of fact a Power would not willingly replace its representative on the Court by an assessor in a case which was of especial interest to it. For that reason he supported article 27 of the Root—Phillimore plan, with the addition which he had himself proposed.

M. DE LAPRADELLE believed that the system of assessors was better calculated to serve the interests of the small States. A small State which was not represented on the Court would not attain a footing of equality with a great Power by sending a judge *ad hoc:* many reasons would combine to

la différence entre le juge *ad hoc* et le juge titulaire. L'envoi d'un juge pourrait donner une satisfaction d'amour-propre au petit Etat, mais ses intérêts véritables seraient mieux servis si lui et son adversaire nommaient des assesseurs. Ce système seul peut assurer l'égalité.

Mr. ROOT croit que c'est une erreur de considérer la question comme une question isolée. On demande à tous les pays du monde de consentir à être assignés devant une Cour, même contre leur volonté, dans une affaire dans laquelle ils sont intéressés. C'est une chose qu'on n'a jamais demandé aux nations auparavant, et à moins qu'elles ne soient unanimes à y consentir, tout le travail du Comité sera sans aucune utilité. La grande difficulté qui s'oppose à ce consentement vient de l'antipathie instinctive des peuples pour une Cour composée de juges étrangers, aux décisions de laquelle ils devraient se soumettre: si on ne peut pas leur dire qu'ils seront représentés à la Cour, il sera impossible d'obtenir leur consentement.

Ce consentement sera encore plus difficile à obtenir si on leur dit que les représentants qu'ils auront à la Cour devront céder leur place quand il s'agira de juger un litige auquel ils sont parties. Il faut s'assurer le consentement des masses, avant d'obtenir celui des Ministères des Affaires Etrangères; mais dans ce but, il faut pouvoir dire aux masses qu'il y a dans la Cour au moins une personne qui peut les comprendre. Les petites questions, telles que la question de savoir si le nombre des juges devrait être pair ou impair, n'ont pas d'importance; ce qui importe, c'est de rédiger le projet de sorte qu'il soit facile aux peuples d'accepter l'idée de la juridiction obligatoire.

Le PRESIDENT déclare que si la question se pose sur ce terrain, elle devient très délicate. Si à la situation déjà très inégale, on ajoute encore un élément d'inégalité, le système devient inacceptable.

Le Président rappelle ce qu'il a dit auparavant au sujet de la tâche du Comité, qui est de créer une juridiction impartiale: il remarque que dans le système qu'il préconise, il y aurait toujours quelqu'un pour défendre les intérêts des petits Etats.

Le Président voudrait donner à l'assesseur une voix délibérative, mais il peut se rallier à l'amendement de M. Loder, d'après lequel le juge ressortissant d'une des parties se retirerait, et les parties seraient représentées chacune par un assesseur avec voix consultative. Il mettra tout d'abord aux voix cet amendement.

Avant le vote, un court échange de vues s'engage; il en ressort que:

accentuate the difference between a judge *ad hoc* and a regular judge. The dignity of a small State might be satisfied by sending a judge, but its real interest would be better served if it and its opponent each appointed assessors. Only this system could guarantee equality.

Mr. ROOT believed that it was wrong to consider this as an isolated question; every country in the world was invited to consent to be summoned before a Court, even against its will, with reference to questions in which it was interested; that was a thing which had never been asked of nations before, and unless they all gave their consent, the entire work of the Committee would be useless. The main difficulty in obtaining this consent arises from the instinctive mistrust felt by nations for a Court composed of foreign judges and from their reluctance to submit to its decisions. If they cannot be assured of representation on the Court it will prove impossible to obtain their assent.

This assent will be still more difficult to obtain if a State is informed that any representative which it may have on the Court must give up his place when a case in which it is concerned is brought up for trial. The support of the masses must be assured before obtaining that of the Foreign Offices; but for this purpose it must be possible to tell the masses that there will be at least one person upon the Court who is able to understand them. The minor questions, such as whether the number of judges should be odd or even, are not important. The important point is to frame the plan in such a way that it will be easy for the people to accept the idea of compulsory submission to jurisdiction.

The PRESIDENT declared that the question, regarded from this point of view, was an extremely delicate one. If an already unequal situation were rendered still more unequal the system would be unacceptable.

The President reminded the Committee of what he had said previously with reference to the Committee's task, which was to create an impartial tribunal. He remarked that, in the system which he advocated, someone would always be present to protect the interests of the small States.

The President wished to give the assessors the right to vote, but was prepared to accept M. Loder's amendment which eliminated the judge of the nationality of one party and introduced assessors with advisory powers only. He would first take a vote upon this amendment.

Before the vote a brief exchange of views took place, in which the following points were brought out:

1. L'amendement de M. Loder vise aussi le cas où aucune des parties n'est représenté à la Cour.

2. L'amendement de M. Hagerup est rattaché au texte de l'article 27 du projet Root—Phillimore, tel qu'il a été amendé par M. Loder.

Ce texte est soumis au vote. Il est adopté.
L'amendement de M. Hagerup est mis aux voix séparément; il est également adopté.

Le PRESIDENT ouvre la discussion sur l'article 28 du projet Root—Phillimore.

LORD PHILLIMORE exprime l'avis que les articles 28—30 (voir annexe 3 au procès-verbal de la séance précédente) du projet Root—Phillimore ont été déjà adoptés par le Comité après de longues discussions.

M. RICCI-BUSATTI rappelle qu'il a proposé des modifications à ces articles. (Voir annexe 4.)

M. ADATCI annonce également qu'il proposera un amendement à l'article 28. Il s'y voit obligé surtout parce que l'article 27 a été adopté seulement avec l'amendement de M. Loder.

Le PRESIDENT distingue dans l'article 28 deux points déterminés:

1. La Cour a-t-elle le droit de connaître seulement de litiges entre Etats, ou aussi de litiges auxquels des particuliers sont parties? Le Président constate que le Comité est d'accord pour reconnaître que la Cour sera compétente seulement pour des litiges entre Etats.

2. Quels sont les Etats qui peuvent être parties devant la Cour?

LORD PHILLIMORE est d'avis que cet article a été, en principe, adopté dans les discussions antérieures. Il croit que les remarques que M. Ricci-Busatti a formulées relativement à la dernière partie de l'article sont plutôt d'ordre rédactionnel, et qu'elles peuvent être renvoyées au Comité de rédaction. Pour son compte, il persiste à croire que la rédaction adoptée dans le projet est la meilleure.

M. RICCI-BUSATTI demande s'il pourrait être admis à défendre sa proposition devant le Comité de rédaction. Il déclare que la formule qu'il a proposée est, à un certain point de vue, rédactionnelle, mais la rédaction a, dans ce cas, beaucoup d'importance au point de vue théorique et

1. M. Loder's amendment also covered the case in which none of the parties were represented on the Court.

2. M. Hagerup's amendment related to the text of Article 27 of the Root—Phillimore plan, as amended by M. Loder.

This text was voted upon and adopted.
M. Hagerup's amendment was voted upon separately; and was also adopted.

The PRESIDENT laid Article 28 of the Root—Phillimore plan before the Committee.

LORD PHILLIMORE expressed the opinion that Articles 28 to 30 incl. (see Annex 3 to the preceding Procès-Verbal) of the Root—Phillimore plan had already been adopted by the Committee after long discussions.

M. RICCI-BUSATTI announced that he had modifications to propose to these articles. (See Annex 4.)

M. ADATCI also announced that he intended to propose an amendment to Article 28. He felt obliged to do this mainly because Article 27 had only been adopted with M. Loder's amendment.

The PRESIDENT drew attention to two distinct points in Article 28:

1. Should jurisdiction of the Court be limited to cases between States, or should the Court also have jurisdiction over cases in which private individuals are parties? The President stated that the Committee was agreed that the Court should only have jurisdiction over cases between States.

2. What States may be parties to cases brought before the Court?

LORD PHILLIMORE was of opinion that this Article had in principle been adopted in the preceding discussions. He thought that the observations which M. Ricci-Busatti had made with reference to the last part of the Article, only affected the phraseology of the Article and that they might be left to the Drafting Committee. Personally, he still thought that the wording adopted in the project was the better.

M. RICCI-BUSATTI asked if he would be allowed to defend his proposal before the Drafting Committee. He admitted that the formula which he had proposed, from one point of view, affected only the wording, but the wording, in this case, was of great importance, both from the practical and theoretical point

pratique; il pourra accepter l'article si la rédaction en est faite conformément à sa proposition, tandis qu'il ne l'accepterait pas sous sa forme actuelle.

Le PRESIDENT fait observer que le Comité de rédaction est un comité strictement restreint et que pour lui conserver ce caractère, il est préférable que les membres du Comité ne participent pas à ses travaux.

M. HAGERUP se demande si l'article 17 du Pacte, auquel on s'est référé dans l'article 28 du projet Root-Phillimore, couvre la question des frais. Les opinions des membres sont divisées sur ce point.

Le PRESIDENT constate que le point peut être différé jusqu'à la discussion des règles de procédure.

M. RICCI-BUSATTI fait observer qu'il y a des cas où il serait impossible de soumettre à des conditions spéciales, aux termes de l'article 17 du Pacte, l'accès à la Cour des Etats qui ne sont pas Membres de la Société des Nations. Ces cas sont, par exemple, ceux dans lesquels l'appel à la Cour est directement visé par les traités de paix pour toutes les parties contractantes, sans distinction.

Les membres du Comité reconnaissent la justesse de l'observation de M. Ricci-Busatti; il en sera tenu compte lors de la rédaction.

Les membres du Comité, à l'exception de M. Ricci-Busatti, reconnaissent également que par Etats Membres de la Société des Nations, on doit comprendre tous les Etats mentionnés à l'annexe au Pacte.

Après un échange de vues avec M. Ricci-Busatti, LORD PHILLIMORE déclare que la dernière phrase de l'article 28 dans la rédaction du projet Root-Phillimore, vise les minorités dont certains Etats ont accepté la protection.

M. RICCI-BUSATTI avait compris la phrase autrement: la dernière partie de son amendement doit être, par conséquent, modifiée.

Le PRESIDENT met aux voix l'article 28 du projet Root—Phillimore, sauf les observations de M. Ricci-Busatti.

L'article est adopté par le Comité avec cette réserve.

Le Président ouvre la discussion sur l'article 29 du projet Root—Phillimore.

of view. He could accept the article if it were formulated in accordance with his proposition, while he could not do so if it retained its present form.

The PRESIDENT pointed out that the Drafting Committee was a body with a strictly limited sphere of action and that, in order to preserve this character, it would be preferable that members of the Committee should not take part in its work.

M. HAGERUP asked if Article 17 of the Covenant, to which reference was made in Article 28 of the Root—Phillimore plan, covered the question of expenses. The opinion of the members was divided on this point.

The PRESIDENT stated that the point could be postponed until the discussion of the Rules of procedure.

M. RICCI-BUSATTI observed that there were cases in which it would be impossible to make access to the Court, in the case of States which were not Members of the League of Nations, subject to special conditions as laid down in Article 17 of the Covenant. Such cases were, for instance, those in which recourse to the Court on the part of all the contracting parties, without distinction, was directly provided for by the Treaties of Peace.

The members of the Committee acknowledged the accuracy of M. Ricci-Busatti's observation, which would be duly considered in the drafting of the Article.

The members of the Committee—except M. Ricci-Busatti—recognised also that the phrase "States, Members of the League of Nations" should be understood to mean all the States mentioned in the Annex to the Covenant.

After an exchange of views with M. Ricci-Busatti, LORD PHILLIMORE declared that the last sentence of Article 28 in the Root—Phillimore plan referred to the minorities which certain States had undertaken to protect.

M. RICCI-BUSATTI had understood the sentence in a different way; the last part of his amendment would therefore have to be altered.

The PRESIDENT took a vote upon Article 28 of the Root—Phillimore plan subject to M. Ricci-Busatti's comments.

The Article was adopted by the Committee with this reservation.

The President laid Article 29 of the Root—Phillimore plan before the Committee.

M. ADATCI demande la parole. Il confesse d'abord qu'il hésite en face de la déclaration qu'il va faire, parce qu'il sent que l'atmosphère y est hostile. Toutefois, il espère pouvoir convaincre ses collègues. Il rappelle que le 26 juin déjà, il a déclaré avoir des opinions très arrêtées sur la question de la compétence de la Cour. Il a même, dès le 18 juin, déposé une proposition à cet égard. Il maintient cette proposition en vue de l'importance de la question. Il divisera ses remarques en quatre parties:

1. La question du mandat du Comité. Il sait que sur ce point il se trouve en désaccord avec quelques-uns de ses collègues. Mais il est convaincu que la formule adoptée par le projet Root—Phillimore dépasse le mandat du Comité. Le Conseil est tenu de ne point dépasser les limites qui lui ont été tracées par le Pacte de la Société des Nations, et plus particulièrement par l'article 14. Il en donne lecture. Le Pacte charge clairement le Conseil d'élaborer le plan de la nouvelle Cour. Si le Conseil délègue ce travail au Comité, il ne peut évidemment pas déléguer d'autres pouvoirs que ceux dont il est investi lui-même: cela serait contraire à la théorie du mandat. Pour répondre au mandat qui lui a été confié, le Comité doit garder une attitude parfaitement correcte, en se conformant aux stipulations de l'article 14, qui sont très claires.

2. L'interprétation de l'article 14 du Pacte. A cet égard, M. Adatci est d'avis que le Pacte a délibérément voulu limiter la compétence aux affaires que les parties lui soumettront. A l'appui de cette thèse M. Adatci cite les preuves suivantes:

a. l'opinion de la Section Juridique du Secrétariat Permanent exprimée sous I (a) de son mémoire: „il est vrai que la compétence de la Cour dépend d'un accord entre les Parties";

b. les réserves danoise et norvégienne à l'article 21 du projet dit des Cinq Puissances;

c. la note de Lord Phillimore annexée au procès-verbal du 29 juin;

d. la déclaration du Président au procès-verbal du 25 juin;

e. les procès-verbaux de la Commission de la Société des Nations à la Conférence de Paris: ces procès-verbaux démontrent que c'est après mûres délibérations qu'on est arrivé à la décision de ne pas étendre la compétence de la Cour au

M. ADATCI asked permission to speak. He began by confessing that in view of the statement he was about to make, he hesitated to speak because he felt that the atmosphere was hostile to him. Notwithstanding, he hoped to be able to convince his colleagues. He recalled the fact that, as long ago as June 26, he had declared that he had very definite opinions on the question of the jurisdiction of the Court. He had even submitted a proposition in this connection on 18th June. He now maintained this proposition in view of the importance of the question. He would divide his remarks into four parts:

1. The question of the Committee's mandate. He was aware that on this point he was not in agreement with some of his colleagues, but he was convinced that the clause adopted in the Root—Phillimore plan exceeded the Committee's mandate. The Council was bound not to go an inch beyond the limits marked out for it by the Covenant of the League of Nations, and in particular by Article 14. He then read this Article. The Covenant clearly instructs the Council to work out the plan for the new Court. If the Council delegated this work to the Committee, it obviously could not delegate powers other than those which were granted to it: to do so would be contrary to the mandatory theory. The Committee, to comply with the terms of the mandate given to it, must preserve a strictly correct attitude and conform to the provisions of Article 14, which are very definite.

2. The interpretation of Article 14 of the Covenant. In this connection, M. Adatci was of opinion that the Covenant deliberately intended to limit the competence of the Court to cases submitted to it by the parties. In support of this theory M. Adatci quoted the following.

a. The opinion of the Legal Section of the Permanent Secretariat set out under I (a) of its memorandum: "It is true that the competence of the Court is dependent upon an agreement between the Parties."

b. The Danish and Norwegian reservations to Article 21 of the plan known as that of the Five Powers.

c. Lord Phillimore's note annexed to the Procès-verbal of June 29th;

d. The President's statement in the Procès-verbal of June 25th;

e. The Procès-verbaux of the League of Nations' Commission at the Paris Conference: these Procès-verbaux show that it was decided, after mature deliberation, not to extend the jurisdiction of the Court beyond disputes submitted by the parties.

delà des différends qui lui sont soumis par les parties. Dans ces circonstances, M. Adatci trouve qu'il n'y a pas l'ombre d'un doute sur l'interprétation qu'il faut donner à l'article 14.

3. Parvenu à ce point de son raisonnement, la question que M. Adatci se pose, est celle de savoir si le Comité a obtenu le rôle d'un législateur international et s'il est par conséquent compétent pour envisager des questions générales; si, en particulier, il peut proposer des modifications au Pacte de la Société des Nations.

A cette dernière question M. Adatci donne une réponse affirmative dans ce sens, que le Comité peut proposer des amendements au Pacte au même titre que des individus quelconques; en effet, tout le monde, même „the man in the street", le premier passant venu, peut le faire. Mais les gouvernements seuls ont le droit de le faire officiellement, et le Comité ne doit donc pas supposer qu'il a mandat pour cela. Pour M. Adatci, il est parfaitement clair que le Comité doit se tenir dans les limites du Pacte, telles qu'elles ont été définies par certains documents qu'il énumère: article 23 du projet Bevilaqua: „Les parties fixeront les points sur lesquels la Cour est appelée à se prononcer"; — réserve à l'article 21 des Cinq Puissances; — procès-verbaux de l'Hôtel Crillon, déjà cités. Il ajoute que même en ce qui concerne l'arbitrage, on a qualifié la compétence en ajoutant au texte le mot „généralement".

4. M. Adatci a été en correspondance dans ces derniers temps avec beaucoup de personnes compétentes dans les pays voisins, principalement avec des compatriotes, et toutes ont été unanimes à reconnaître la nécessité d'éviter de débuter en franchissant les limites tracées par le Pacte. Le Comité a accompli déjà un miracle social en réussissant à créer une Cour permanente, une véritable Cour de justice internationale, toujours immédiatement accessible et composée de juges élus, résidant à son siège. Personne n'a parlé jusqu'ici des difficultés qui avaient fait douter de la possibilité même de l'œuvre à accomplir, et dont la réalisation est dûe principalement au génie créateur de Mr. Root, qui a été si admirablement secondé par Lord Phillimore.

Lui-même, ainsi que beaucoup d'amis étrangers, était certain, en arrivant à La Haye, que le Comité n'aboutirait pas. Maintenant il faut laisser travailler le temps. Il faut assurer les moyens par lesquels on pourra faire accepter l'œuvre du Comité, ou lui faire passer avec succès les différentes épreuves auxquelles elle doit être soumise. Avant tout, il importe d'éviter de créer des difficultés, en étendant la compétence de la Cour. M. Adatci cite

Under these conditions, M. Adatci felt that there was not a shadow of doubt as to the interpretation to be put upon Article 14.

3. Having reached this stage in his argument, M. Adatci raised the question as to whether the Committee had been assigned the duty of international legislation and if, consequently, it was competent to deal with general questions; in particular, if it might propose modifications in the Covenant of the League of Nations.

To this last question M. Adatci gave an affirmative answer in the sense that the Committee might propose amendments to the Covenant, just as other private individuals might do so; indeed everybody, even the man in the street, could do so. Governments alone, however, have the right to do it officially; the Committee, therefore, should not imagine that its mandate covered this. It appeared quite clear to M. Adatci that the Committee must keep within the limits of the Covenant, as defined by certain documents which he enumerated: Article 23 of the Bevilaqua plan: "the parties shall determine the points which the Court shall be called upon to decide;" the reservation to Article 21 of the Five Powers' plan; and the Procès-verbaux of the Hotel Crillon, mentioned above. He added that, even with regard to arbitration, the jurisdiction was qualified by the addition of the word "generally."

4. M. Adatci had been in correspondence lately with many able persons in adjoining countries, mainly with compatriots, and all had unanimously recognised how necessary it was not to start by transgressing the limits set by the Covenant. The Committee had already accomplished a social miracle in succeeding in the creation of a permanent Court, a true Court of international Justice, at all times accessible and available, and composed of elected judges residing at its seat. No one had till this moment spoken of the difficulties which had made the task to be performed appear virtually impossible; the accomplishment of this task was principally due to the creative genius of Mr. Root, who had been so admirably seconded by Lord Phillimore.

He himself, like many friends of other nationalities, was certain on his arrival at the Hague, that the Committee would not succeed. Now time must be allowed to do its work; measures must be taken to ensure that the product of the Committee's labour would be accepted, and to enable it to undergo successfully the various tests to which it would be put. Above all, difficulties arising from an extension of the Court's jurisdiction must not be created.

l'adage français „qui trop embrasse, mal étreint". Il croit que le Comité doit être satisfait d'avoir créé la Cour et qu'on ne doit pas essayer d'aller plus loin. Il a la conviction que la Cour se développera normalement, si elle est suffisamment alimentée, mais il conseille au Comité d'agir prudemment envers ce nouveau-né, de l'observer pendant quelque temps et d'éprouver la force de ses fonctions vitales avant de lui donner plus d'aliments. Il sent que l'atmosphère du Comité est hostile à cette exhortation, néanmoins il répète: soyons modestes et pratiques.

Pendant son discours, M. Adatci a fait distribuer l'amendement suivant: „La Cour est compétente pour statuer sur les différends entre Etats, conformément à l'article 14 du Pacte de la Société des Nations".

LORD PHILLIMORE est d'avis que la déclaration de M. Adatci mérite la plus grande attention. Il en est d'autant plus convaincu que le texte modifié de l'article 27 a été adopté seulement à une voix de majorité. Cependant, il veut demander à M. Adatci si ses remarques ne se rapportent pas à l'alinéa 2 de l'article 30 du projet Root-Phillimore, plutôt qu'à l'article 29 de ce projet.

M. ADATCI répond que d'après lui, les deux articles doivent être considérés en bloc. Il peut cependant consentir à ce que son amendement soit considéré comme se rapportant à l'article 30.

M. HAGERUP fait remarquer avec insistance que l'amendement de M. Adatci doit être considéré comme se rapportant seulement à l'article 29 du projet.

LORD PHILLIMORE fait une motion d'ordre. Comme ses collègues ne se trouvent pas d'accord avec lui sur le fond de la question, il est probable qu'une discussion assez approfondie sera nécessaire. En tout cas, il n'est pas possible d'arriver à une conclusion en une demi-heure: les considérations de M. Adatci sont beaucoup trop sérieuses pour que cela puisse se faire. Dans ces circonstances, Lord Phillimore croit que le Comité de rédaction peut se mettre au travail sur les articles 1—28 du projet. Pendant ce temps, les membres pourront réfléchir sur la suite qu'il convient de donner aux déclarations de M. Adatci.

M. RICCI-BUSATTI appuie cette motion d'ordre.

Après une courte discussion sur la portée de l'amendement de M. ADATCI, celui-ci déclare

M. Adatci quoted the French proverb: "qui trop embrasse mal étreint"—"Who attempts too much does nothing well." He thought that the Committee should be satisfied with the fact that it had created the Court, and should not try to go further. He was convinced that the Court would develop on normal lines if it were given sufficient material, but he advised the Committee to go gently with the infant, to watch it for some time and to test the strength of its vitality before giving it more nourishment. He felt that the atmosphere of the Committee was opposed to this advice, but he repeated "let us be modest and practical."

During his speech, M. Adatci had the following amendment distributed: "The Court is competent to hear and determine disputes between States in accordance with Article 14 of the Covenant of the League of Nations."

LORD PHILLIMORE said that M. Adatci's statement, in his opinion, was worthy of earnest attention. He was still more convinced of this, since the modified text of Article 27 had only been adopted by a majority of one vote. Nevertheless, he wished to ask M. Adatci whether his remarks did not relate to Paragraph 2 of Article 30 of the Root—Phillimore plan rather than to Article 29 of this plan.

M. ADATCI answered that he thought the two Articles should be considered together. He would consent, however, to have his amendment considered as relating to Article 30.

M. HAGERUP insisted that M. Adatci's amendment should be considered as relating solely to Article 29 of the plan.

LORD PHILLIMORE moved a point of order; as his colleagues did not agree with him on the principle involved in the question, it was probable that a fairly thorough discussion would be necessary. In any case, it would not be possible to arrive at a conclusion in half an hour. M. Adatci's arguments were much too weighty for this to be possible. Under these conditions Lord Phillimore thought that the drafting Committee could commence work on Articles 1 to 28 of the plan. In the meantime, the members would be able to consider what action should be taken with regard to M. Adatci's pronouncement.

M. RICCI-BUSATTI seconded this motion.

After a short discussion concerning the scope of M. ADATCI's amendment, the latter formally

formellement qu'il accepte l'article 29 du projet Root—Phillimore, et que son amendement se rapporte à l'article 30, alinéa 2 de ce projet; par conséquent il présente son amendement comme un projet de rédaction nouvelle de cette partie de l'article 30, basée sur les idées qu'il vient d'exprimer.

M. RICCI-BUSATTI déclare alors que, dans ces conditions, il demande que l'amendement de M. Adatci fasse l'objet d'une discussion séparée, en tant qu'il concerne l'article 29 du projet Root—Phillimore.

M. DE LAPRADELLE reprend la motion d'ordre de Lord Phillimore: le Comité de rédaction s'arrêtera devant l'article 29 pour donner satisfaction à M. Ricci-Busatti. D'autre part, ce Comité prendra en considération les règles de procédure adoptées par le Comité *in pleno*, en séance officieuse. Il présentera son texte lundi prochain. A cette époque la discussion sur l'amendement de M. Adatci pourra être ouverte.

LORD PHILLIMORE appuie la proposition de M. de Lapradelle.

M. RICCI-BUSATTI fait observer qu'il y a encore plusieurs points d'une grande importance, relatifs à la procédure, qui n'ont pas encore reçu de solution.

Le PRESIDENT déclare que la prochaine réunion du Comité aura lieu le lundi 19 juillet.

La seance est levée à 12.50 heures de l'après-midi.

Le Président :
(signé) Brn. DESCAMPS.

Le Secrétaire-Général :
(signé) D. ANZILOTTI.

declared that he accepted Article 29 of the Root—Phillimore plan and that his amendment related to Article 30, paragraph 2 of that plan; consequently he submitted the amendment as a proposed new draft for that portion of Article 30, based on the ideas he had just expressed.

M. RICCI-BUSATTI then declared that, under these conditions, he would request that M. Adatci's amendment should form the subject of a separate discussion in so far as it related to Article 29 of the Root—Phillimore plan.

M. DE LAPRADELLE again moved the point of order raised by Lord Phillimore: the drafting Committee would cease work, on reaching Article 29, in order to satisfy M. Ricci-Busatti. On the other hand, the Drafting Committee would consider the rules of procedure adopted by the full Committee at an unofficial meeting. The drafting Committee would present its text on the following Monday. The discussion upon M. Adatci's amendment might then be commenced.

LORD PHILLIMORE supported M. de Lapradelle's proposal.

M. RICCI-BUSATTI observed that several points of great importance relating to procedure remained to be dealt with.

The PRESIDENT stated that the next meeting of the Committee would take place on Monday, July 19th.

The meeting closed at 12.50. p. m.

The President :
(signed) Brn. DESCAMPS.

The Secretary-General :
(signed) D. ANZILOTTI.

ANNEXE No. 1.

Amendements proposés par Lord Phillimore en vue d'un accord avec le Président.

Ajouter à l'article 25 à la fin:

„La Cour désigne annuellement trois juges qui, avec le président, forment une section spéciale. Les parties peuvent, de consentement mutuel, s'adresser au président pour que leurs affaires soient décidées par cette section. Si un juge faisant partie de la section est empêché, le président a le droit de désigner un des autres juges à sa place."

A l'article 26, au commencement:

„Sauf dans les cas visés dans l'article précédent."

ANNEX No. 1.

Amendments proposed by Lord Phillimore with a view to an agreement with the President.

To be added at the end of Article 25:

"The Court shall appoint annually three judges who, with the President, shall form a special section. Parties may by mutual consent apply to the President for the purpose of having their case decided by this section. If a judge included in the section is unable to sit, the President may appoint one of the other judges to take his place."

To be added at the beginning of Article 26:

"Except in the case mentioned in the preceding Article."

ANNEXE No. 2.

Proposition du Baron Descamps.

La Cour exerce ses attributions en séance plénière. Si la présence de neuf juges titulaires n'est pas assurée, ce nombre sera parfait par l'entrée en fonction des suppléants.

En vue de l'expédition des affaires suivant les convenances éventuelles des parties, la Cour compose annuellement une chambre ordinaire de cinq juges ainsi qu'une chambre de trois juges spécialement consacrée au jugement des affaires en procédure sommaire. Elle peut, de même, désigner un ou plusieurs juges pour statuer comme juges uniques à la demande des parties.

ANNEX No. 2.

Proposal by Baron Descamps.

The Court shall exercise its powers in full session. If it is not certain that nine regular judges will be present, the number shall be made up by calling upon deputy judges.

With a view to disposing of cases in conformity with the possible requirements of parties, the Court shall form, annually, an ordinary chamber of five judges, and a special chamber of three judges devoted to the trial of cases by a summary procedure. The Court may also appoint one or more judges to sit singly at the request of the parties.

ANNEXE No. 3.

Articles 29—32 du projet Root—Phillimore.

(Voir annexe 3 au procès-verbal de la séance précédente.)

29. — La Cour Permanente de Justice Internationale est compétente pour statuer sur les contestations entre Etats concernant les différends qui sont d'ordre juridique, c'est-à-dire ceux qui concernent :

a. l'interprétation d'un traité ;

b. tout point de droit international ;

c. la réalité de tout fait qui, s'il était établi, constituerait la rupture d'un engagement international ;

d. l'étendue ou la nature de la réparation dûe pour la rupture d'un engagement international ;

e. l'interprétation d'une sentence rendue par la Cour.

Sont assimilés aux différends d'ordre juridique, au point de vue juridictionnel, les différends qui, bien que ne pouvant être formulés et résolus juridiquement, sont l'objet d'un accord intervenu entre les parties quant à leur solution par voie judiciaire.

En cas de contestation sur le point de savoir si tel différend rentre, oui ou non, dans les catégories visées à cet article, la Cour Permanente décide cette question en ordre préjudiciel.

30. Lorsqu'un différend, tel qu'il est prévu dans l'article 29, s'élève entre deux États, que toutes les voies diplomatiques pour arranger ce différend ont été épuisées et que l'on n'est pas convenu de choisir une Cour d'Arbitrage dans le sens de l'article XIII du Pacte, la partie qui se prétend lésée peut en saisir la Cour Permanente.

Si l'autre partie refuse de soumettre le différend à la Cour, celle-ci décide en premier lieu s'il y a, oui ou non, engagement de soumettre le différend en conformité avec les exigences de l'article XIV du Pacte, à la Cour Permanente.

Tout Etat signataire du présent acte est considéré comme acceptant de soumettre à la Cour Permanente tout différend caractérisé par l'article 24 qui s'élève entre cet Etat et un autre Etat signataire, si on n'est pas déjà convenu de choisir une Cour d'Arbitrage comme il est indiqué ci-dessus.

ANNEX No. 3.

Articles 29 to 32 of the Root—Phillimore plan.

(See annex 3 to the preceding procès-verbal.)

29. The Permanent Court of International Justice shall be competent to hear and determine cases between States concerning questions of a legal nature, that is to say which affect:

a. the interpretation of a treaty;

b. any question of international law;

c. the existence of any fact which, if established, would constitute a breach of an international obligation ;

d. the extent or nature of reparation due for the breach of an international obligation ;

e. the interpretation of a sentence passed by the Court.

Disputes which, though they cannot be expressed in legal terms and are not suited to legal settlement, form the subject of an agreement between the parties with reference to a judicial settlement, shall be classed with disputes of a legal nature for the purposes of jurisdiction.

In the event of a dispute as to whether a case does or does not come within one of the categories mentioned in this article, the Permanent Court shall decide the point as an interlocutory question.

30. When a dispute coming under the provisions of Article 29 arises between two States, and when all diplomatic means for settlement of the dispute have been exhausted, and provided that it has not been agreed to choose a Court of Arbitration, within the meaning of Article 13 of the Covenant, the party which claims to have been wronged may bring the case before the Permanent Court.

If the other party refuses to submit the case to the Court, the latter shall, in the first place, decide whether an engagement to submit the case to the Permanent Court, in accordance with the terms of Article 14 of the Covenant, does or does not exist.

Every State signing the present act shall be considered as having agreed to submit to the Permanent Court all disputes, provided for under Article 29, which arises between the said State and another signatory State, provided that it has not already been agreed to choose a Court of Arbitration as indicated above.

31. Les règles à appliquer par la Cour, dans les limites de la compétence ci-dessus prévues, pour la solution des différends internationaux, sont les suivantes dans l'ordre successif où elles s'imposent à son examen:

1. Le droit international conventionnel, soit général, soit spécial, comme constituant des règles expressément adoptées par les États parties au litige;
2. La coutume internationale comme attestation d'une pratique commune des nations acceptée par elles comme loi;
3. Les principes généraux de droit reconnus par les peuples civilisés;
4. L'autorité des décisions judiciaires et les opinions des publicistes comme organes d'application et de développement du droit.

32. La Cour aura le droit de donner une opinion consultative sur toute provision ou question qui lui sera soumise à cette fin par le Conseil ou l'Assemblée de la Société des Nations.

31. The rules to be applied by the Court, within the limits of its jurisdiction as defined above, in the settlement of international disputes, are the following, and are to be applied in the order in which they appear below:

1. Conventional international law, whether of a general or special nature, forming the rules expressly adopted by the States which are parties to the case;
2. International custom, as evidence of a common practice in use between nations and accepted by them as law;
3. The general principles of law recognised by civilised nations;
4. The precedent of judicial decisions and the opinions of the publicists as means for the application and development of law.

32. The Court shall have the right to give an advisory opinion upon any subject or question submitted to it for this purpose by the Council or the Assembly of the League of Nations.

ANNEXE No. 4.

Amendements aux Articles 29—31 du projet Root—Phillimore par M. Ricci-Busatti.

Article 29 par. 1. (Voir les amendements qui résultent de la rédaction déposée le 30 juin.)

Article 29 par. 2. Ajouter, soit comme dernier alinéa, soit comme article à part, la disposition suivante: „Toutefois, sur la demande des Parties, la Cour pourra toujours régler selon les convenances et l'équité les différends dont elle aura été saisie."

Articles 30 et 31. Remplacer ces articles par les suivants:

1. „La Cour donnera son avis sur toute question de droit qui lui serait soumise à cet effet par le Conseil ou par l'Assemblée de la Société des Nations. Elle ne sera pas liée par les avis qu'elle aura ainsi formulés, dans le cas où la même question ou une question pareille serait soumise à son jugement par les Etats intéressés.

2. Le Cour pourra également, soit sur demande de l'Assemblée ou du Conseil, soit de sa propre initiative, rédiger des projets de règles ou formuler des propositions sur toute matière ou question de droit international.

L'Assemblée, le Conseil et la Cour elle-même pourront dans ce cas désigner des membres adjoints, particulièrement compétents pour prendre part aux travaux dont il s'agit."

ANNEX No. 4.

Amendments to Articles 29 to 31 of the Root—Phillimore plan proposed by M. Ricci-Busatti.

Article 29. Paragraph 1. (See the amendments arising out of the draft submitted on the 30th June).

Article 29. Paragraph 2. The following clause to be added either as a last paragraph or as a separate Article: "Nevertheless, at the request of the parties, the Court may always decide cases submitted to it in arcordance with established principles and equity.

Articles 30 and 31. These Articles to be replaced by the following:

1. The Court shall give its opinion upon any questions of law submitted to it for this purpose by the Council or by the Assembly of the League of Nations. It shall not be bound by the opinions thus formulated in the event of the same question or a similar question being submitted for its decision by the States concerned.

2. The Court may also, either at the request of the Assembly or of the Council, or acting on its own initiative, prepare codes of rules or formulate proposals concerning any point of international law.

The Assembly, the Council and the Court itself may, in these circumstances, appoint additional members possessing outstanding ability to take part in the work in question.

ANNEXE No. 5.

Amendement proposé par M. Adatci.

Art. . La Cour est compétente pour statuer sur les différends entre Etats, conformément à l'article 14 du Pacte de la Société des Nations.

ANNEX No. 5.

Amendment proposed by M. Adatci.

Article . The Court shall be competent to hear and determine disputes between States in accordance with Article 14 of the Covenant of the League of Nations.

25ième SÉANCE (non-publique), tenue au Palais de la Paix, à La Haye, le 19 juillet 1920.

Présidence de M. le BARON DESCAMPS.

Sont présents: tous les membres du Comité (à l'exception de M. Bevilaqua); M. Fernandes; Mr. James Brown Scott; les secrétaires particuliers de M. le Baron Descamps et de M. Adatci; les membres du Secrétariat *).

La séance est ouverte à 9.30 heures du matin.

Le PRESIDENT constate qu'on commencera pendant cette séance la discussion du texte préparé par le Comité de rédaction. (Annex 2.) On procédera article par article. Les articles qui ne provoqueront pas d'objections de la part des membres du Comité, seront immédiatement adoptés. Tous les articles sur lesquels un membre désirera faire des observations de fond seront réservés provisoirement. Les simples observations de forme, au contraire, seront discutées de suite.

M. ALTAMIRA exprime le désir que les membres aient l'occasion de voir les épreuves des procès-verbaux.

M. DE LAPRADELLE appuie cette proposition: aucun membre ne peut être lié par les opinions énoncées comme siennes au procès-verbal, s'il n'a pas donné lui-même le bon à tirer. Mais ce bon ne peut être donné qu'après examen des épreuves, certains membres ayant apporté à leurs discours des modifications, qui pourraient nécessiter quelques remaniements dans ceux des autres.

*) Le membre du Comité, M. Bevilaqua, empêché de prendre part aux travaux du Comité, lui avait fait parvenir un projet détaillé expliquant son point de vue. M. Raoul Fernandes fut désigné pour suivre, comme conseiller de M. Bevilaqua, les travaux du Comité et pour défendre sa thèse. Lorsqu'il devint évident que M. Bevilaqua ne pourrait pas se rendre à la Haye même pour prendre part aux votes du Comité, le président du Conseil de la Société des Nations informa le Secrétaire-Général de la Société, que M. Fernandes pouvait, sauf confirmation ultérieure par le Conseil, prendre part aux votes, sur un pied de parfaite égalité avec les membres du Comité.

25TH MEETING (Private), held at the Peace Palace, the Hague, on July 19th, 1920.

BARON DESCAMPS in the chair.

Present: all the Members of the Committee (except M. Bevilaqua); M. Fernandes; Mr. James Brown Scott; the private secretaries of Baron Descamps and M. Adatci; the Members of the Secretariat *).

The meeting opened at 9.30 a.m.

The PRESIDENT stated that, at this meeting, the discussion of the text prepared by the drafting Committee would be begun. (Annex 2.) Each article would be considered in turn. Those articles to which no objections were made by members of the Committee would be adopted at once. All articles concerning which any members wished to raise a question of principle would be provisionally put on one side. On the other hand, simple questions of wording would be dealt with at once.

M. ALTAMIRA expressed the hope that the members would have an opportunity to see the proofs of the procès-verbaux.

M. DE LAPRADELLE supported this proposal. No member could be bound by opinions purporting to be his in the procès-verbal, unless he had himself approved them. Such approval could not be given until after examination of the proofs, as some members had made modifications in their speeches, which might call for certain alterations in the speeches of others.

*) M. Bevilaqua, a member of the Committee, was unable to take part in the work of the Committee, but sent in a detailed plan setting out his opinions. M. Raoul Fernandes was appointed to follow the work of the Committee as M. Bevilaqua's Counsel, and to uphold his views. When it became evident that M. Bevilaqua would not be able to come to The Hague even to take part in the votings of the Committee, the President of the Council of the League of Nations informed the Secretary-General of the League that M. Fernandes could, subject to subsequent confirmation by the Council, take part in the votings upon an equal footing with the members of the Committee.

Le PRESIDENT, après avoir entendu le Secrétaire Général, dit qu'il sera tenu compte des observations de M. Altamira et de M. de Lapradelle. Les épreuves des procès-verbaux seront remises aux membres, qui pourront encore y apporter des retouches et qui les renverront au Secrétariat dans les 24 heures. Ensuite, le Président et le Secrétaire-Général revêtiront les procès-verbaux des signatures qui les rendront définitifs.

Après un échange de vues entre M. HAGERUP, M. LODER, LORD PHILLIMORE et le PRESIDENT, ce dernier déclare qu'il y aura deux lectures du texte, après quoi un vote sera émis sur l'ensemble du projet.

Le PRESIDENT dit qu'il y a lieu d'examiner la question de la langue dans laquelle le projet et les procès-verbaux seront rédigés. Il demande si pour ces documents il y aura deux textes ayant le même caractère authentique, ou bien un texte officiel dans une des deux langues, avec traduction dans l'autre certifiée conforme par le Secrétaire-Général.

Il suggère l'idée que le texte français des procès-verbaux soit authentique pour les membres qui ont fait leurs discours en français, tandis que le texte anglais sera authentique pour les discours de Mr. Root.

M. ANZILOTTI répond que c'est une règle du Secrétariat de la Société des Nations, que tout document soit rédigé dans les deux langues. Il confirme que le texte français des discours prononcés en français doit être considéré comme authentique, tandis que c'est le texte anglais qui doit l'être pour les discours de Mr. Root.

M. Anzilotti ajoute que c'est au Comité de décider dans quelle langue le rapport doit être rédigé: en tout cas il en sera immédiatement fait une traduction officielle.

Le PRESIDENT donne au nom du Comité son approbation à la méthode exposée par M. Anzilotti et résume comme suit la décision prise sans opposition par le Conseil. Il n'y aura qu'une seule langue officielle pour le projet, et il sera fait une traduction certifiée conforme par le Secrétariat. Le texte authentique du rapport sera celui qui aura été approuvé par les membres.

Le Président ouvre la discussion sur les articles du projet du Comité de rédaction.

Article 1er.

M. RICCI-BUSATTI demande que le mot „directement" soit expliqué dans le rapport.

The PRESIDENT, after obtaining the opinion of the Secretary-General, said that the remarks of M. Altamira and M. de Lapradelle would be acted upon. The proofs of the procès-verbaux would be sent to the members, who could then make further slight alterations in them, and return them to the Secretariat within 24 hours. Afterwards the President and the Secretary-General would finally approve them and attach their signatures.

After a discussion between M. HAGERUP, M. LODER, LORD PHILLIMORE and the PRESIDENT, the latter stated that there would be two readings of the text, after which a vote would be taken upon the plan as a whole.

The PRESIDENT said that the question of the language in which the plan and the procès-verbaux should be drafted must be considered. He asked whether there should be two versions of these documents of equal authenticity, or an official version in one of the two languages and a translation in the other certified correct by the Secretary-General.

He suggested that the French version of the procès-verbaux should be the official version for those members who had made their speeches in French, while the English version should be official for the speeches of Mr. Root.

M. ANZILOTTI answered that it was a rule of the Secretariat of the League of Nations that every document should be prepared in both languages. He agreed that the French version of speeches given in French should be considered as the original, and the English version in the case of Mr. Root's speeches.

Concerning the report, M. Anzilotti added that it was for the Committee to decide in which language it should be prepared. In any case an official translation would be made immediately.

The PRESIDENT in the name of the Committee approved the method explained by M. Anzilotti. He went on to give a recapitulation of the decision arrived at by the Council without opposition. There would only be one official language for the Project, and a translation would be made, certified correct, by the Secretariat. The official text of the Report would be that approved by the members.

The President then proceeded to lay the Articles of the drafting Committee's plan before the committee.

Article 1.

M. RICCI-BUSATTI asked that an explanation of the word "direct" should be given in the report.

Le PRESIDENT estime qu'il pourra facilement être donné satisfaction à ce désir.

L'article est adopté.

Article 2.

M. ALTAMIRA fait observer que l'expression „expérience reconnue" est vague. En quoi cette „expérience reconnue" doit-elle consister?

M. DE LAPRADELLE déclare que le Comité de rédaction tiendra compte de l'observation de M. Altamira et trouvera une formule plus précise.

Mr. ROOT demande aux membres du Comité de rédaction pour quelle raison la rédaction de 1907, adoptée par le Comité *in pleno*, a été écartée.

M. DE LAPRADELLE explique la manière de procéder du Comité de rédaction et ajoute, quant à la question de fond, que ce Comité a essayé de concilier dans la formule les deux opinions continentale et anglo-américaine, dont la première préfère, comme juges internationaux, les jurisconsultes qui ne sont pas des magistrats, tandis que la dernière donne sa préférence aux magistrats nationaux. Le Comité a voulu exclure de la fonction de juge international les magistrats nationaux qui n'ont pas fait de travaux spéciaux en matière de droit international.

Après un échange de vues sur le procédé suivi par le Comité de rédaction, M. HAGERUP ramène la discussion sur la question de fond, en expliquant les motifs pour lesquels il croit qu'il n'y aurait pas de danger à se rallier à la formule du Comité. L'essentiel est de fixer comme condition que les juges doivent être des jurisconsultes.

M. FERNANDES appuie cette opinion en prenant l'exemple de l'organisation de la haute magistrature du Brésil. La constitution brésilienne ne pose, comme condition pour être nommé juge à la Haute Cour, qu'un „savoir notoire". Cette formule n'a pas eu d'inconvénients puisque, dans la pratique, elle a toujours été comprise comme exigeant un savoir spécial en matière de droit.

Sur la proposition de M. de LAPRADELLE, l'article 2 est réservé.

Mr. ROOT proposera de nouveau, lorsque la discussion de l'article sera reprise, l'adoption de la rédaction de 1907.

The PRESIDENT thought that this request could easily be satisfied.

The Article was adopted.

Article 2.

M. ALTAMIRA pointed out that the expression " well known experience" was vague—of what should it consist?

M. DE LAPRADELLE said that the drafting Committee would bear M. Altamira's remarks in mind and would find a more definite expression.

Mr. ROOT asked the members of the drafting Committee why the wording of 1907, which had been adopted by the Committee *in pleno*, had been set aside.

M. DE LAPRADELLE explained the procedure adopted by the drafting Committee and added that, with regard to the principle involved, the drafting Committee had tried, in the wording adopted, to reconcile the continental and Anglo-American points of view, the former of which preferred to have as international judges jurisconsults who were not judges by profession, whereas the latter preferred national magistrates. The Committee had wished to exclude national judges who had not specialised in International Law from appointment as international judges.

After an exchange of views on the procedure of the drafting Committee, M. HAGERUP again brought the discussion to bear on the principal question, and explained the reasons which led him to believe that there would be no danger in accepting the wording of the Committee. The essential thing was to lay down that the judges must be jurisconsults.

M. FERNANDES supported this opinion, and took as an example the organisation of the Brazilian Bench. In the Brazilian Constitution the only condition required for appointment as judge of the High Court was "an outstanding knowledge". No difficulties had arisen from this provision, as, in practice, it had been always understood to imply a special legal knowledge.

On M. DE LAPRADELLE's proposal, Article 2 was reserved.

Mr. ROOT said that he would again propose the adoption of the wording of 1907 when the Article was once more brought up for discussion.

Article 3.

M. HAGERUP soulève la question de savoir si la résolution de l'Assemblée et du Conseil doit être prise à l'unanimité, ainsi que le Comité avait tout d'abord été d'accord pour le proposer.

Après un court échange de vues, on reconnaît qu'on doit laisser à ces organes le soin de résoudre eux-mêmes cette question.

L'article est adopté avec de légères modifications rédactionnelles.

Article 4.

M. FERNANDES soulève la question de la durée du mandat du juge élu pour remplacer un juge sorti ou décédé.

A son avis le remplaçant ne devrait siéger que pour le reste du temps du mandat de son prédécesseur, pour les raisons déjà données par lui à ce sujet dans une des séances précédentes.

Sur la proposition du Président, cette question est réservée.

M. ALTAMIRA demande s'il ne serait pas utile de consigner dans cet article la faculté pour les juges de démissionner; mais on est d'accord pour reconnaître qu'une stipulation expresse à cet effet n'est pas nécessaire.

M. RICCI-BUSATTI demande des explications sur le sens du terme „remplacement effectif". Il désire qu'il soit fixé à partir de quel moment le nouveau juge est à considérer comme membre de la Cour.

Plusieurs membres ayant exprimé leurs opinions à cet égard, M. DE LAPRADELLE précise ainsi la question: à quel moment commence à courir le délai de neuf ans, qui est la durée du mandat ordinaire des juges? Il constate que les membres du Comité sont d'accord pour reconnaître la nécessité qu'un juge reste en fonction jusqu'à la nomination de son remplaçant.

Dans ces circonstances on convient de supprimer le mot „effectif".

Article 5.

M. ALTAMIRA met en doute la nécessité de cet article. Il pense qu'il fera double emploi avec un autre article subséquent.

Mr. ROOT demande au contraire que l'article soit maintenu.

M. HAGERUP a proposé une addition, renvoyant aux articles 6 et suivants (présentation etc.)

Article 3.

M. HAGERUP raised the question whether the decision of the Assembly and the Council must be unanimous, as the Committee had, at the outset, agreed to propose.

After a short discussion it was agreed that this question should be left for those bodies to decide.

The Article was adopted with some slight alterations in the wording.

Article 4.

M. FERNANDES raised the question of the period for which judges, elected to replace judges who had retired or died, should be appointed. In his opinion the successor should only take his seat for the unexpired portion of his predecessor's appointment, for the reasons he had already given at a previous meeting.

On the President's proposal this question was reserved.

M. ALTAMIRA asked whether it would not be advisable to mention in this Article that judges would have the right to resign: however, it was agreed that an explicit stipulation to this effect was unnecessary.

M. RICCI-BUSATTI asked for an explanation of the meaning of the phrase "their places have been actually filled." He wished the exact time at which the new judge would become a member of the Court to be laid down.

After several members had given their opinions on this point, M. DE LAPRADELLE summarised the question as follows: when should the period of nine years, which was the normal length of the appointment of judges, actually commence? He stated that the members of the Committee were agreed upon the necessity of a judge continuing to do duty until his successor had been appointed.

In these circumstances it was agreed to delete the word "actually".

Article 5.

M. ALTAMIRA raised a doubt as to whether this Article was really necessary. He thought that it was duplicated by a subsequent Article.

Mr. ROOT on the other hand wished it to be maintained.

M. HAGERUP proposed an addition referring to Article 6 and the following articles (nomination etc.).

M. DE LAPRADELLE voudrait que l'article 4, alinéa 1, et l'article 5, fussent combinés dans la rédaction suivante:

„Les membres de la Cour sont élus pour neuf ans par l'Assemblée et par le Conseil."

LORD PHILLIMORE se rallie aux idées de M. Hagerup et de M. de Lapradelle, et propose une formule ainsi conçue:

„Les membres de la Cour sont élus par l'Assemblée et par le Conseil de la manière suivante."

Le PRESIDENT suggère la rédaction suivante:

„Les membres de la Cour sont élus par l'Assemblée et par le Conseil sur une liste de personnes présentée par les groupes nationaux de la Cour d'Arbitrage."

M. DE LAPRADELLE offre alors une rédaction transactionelle conçue en ces termes:

„Les membres de la Cour sont élus pour neuf ans de la manière suivante."

L'article est réservé.

Article 6.

M. HAGERUP s'élève contre le changement apporté par le Comité de rédaction à la décision, prise par le Comité *in pleno*, de fixer le nombre des présentations à 6.

Il est appuyé par Mr. ROOT.

Le PRESIDENT explique que le nombre de 6 aurait pour résultat un nombre trop élevé de présentations.

M. RICCI-BUSATTI désire savoir si les membres de la Cour Permanente d'Arbitrage nommés par un certain pays parmi les ressortissants d'un autre pays sont visés par le texte.

Mr. ROOT est d'avis que la formule par laquelle sont désignés les Etats qui sont autorisés à faire la présentation n'est pas assez large, d'autres Etats que ceux mentionnés à l'Annexe au Pacte devant être invités.

LORD PHILLIMORE propose, d'accord avec Mr. Root, la rédaction suivante: „tous ceux qui, à l'avenir, entreront dans la Société des Nations."

M. RICCI-BUSATTI préférerait: „chacun des Etats faisant partie de la Société des Nations ou mentionnés à l'Annexe au Pacte."

Pour les raisons qu'il vient d'indiquer, Mr. ROOT demande que l'alinéa 1er soit réservé.

M. DE LAPRADELLE wished Article 4, Paragraph 1, to be combined with Article 5, as follows:

"The members of the Court shall be elected for nine years by the Assembly and by the Council."

LORD PHILLIMORE agreed with the suggestions of M. Hagerup and M. de Lapradelle and proposed the following:

"The members of the Court shall be elected by the Assembly and by the Council according to the following system."

The PRESIDENT proposed the following:

"The members of the Court shall be elected by the Assembly and by the Council from a list of nominations submitted by the national groups of the Court of Arbitration."

M. DE LAPRADELLE then proposed as a compromise:

"The members of the Court shall be elected for nine years according to the following system."

The Article was reserved.

Article 6.

M. HAGERUP objected to the change made by the drafting Committee affecting the decision, arrived at by the Committee in full session, to fix the number of nominations at 6.

He was supported by Mr. ROOT.

The PRESIDENT explained that if the number 6 were adopted, the result would be that too large a number of nominations would be obtained.

M. RICCI-BUSATTI wished to know whether the wording of the Article covered members of the Permanent Court of Arbitration appointed by certain countries from amongst the subjects of another country.

Mr. ROOT thought that the phrase, which indicated the States authorised to make nominations, was too limited in its scope; States other than those mentioned in the Annex to the Covenant must be invited to do so.

LORD PHILLIMORE, in agreement with Mr. ROOT, proposed the following wording: "all those which shall subsequently join the League of Nations."

M. RICCI-BUSATTI preferred the following: "each of the States belonging to the League of Nations, or mentioned in the Annex to the Covenant."

Mr. ROOT, for the reasons he had just given, asked that the first Paragraph should be reserved.

Le PRESIDENT déclare que l'alinéa 2 est également réservé.

Article 7.

Sur la proposition de LORD PHILLIMORE, les membres du Comité conviennent de supprimer l'expression „à la majorité des voix." L'expression „groupe national" doit être modifiée pour s'accorder avec la rédaction future de l'article 6, réservé.

L'article est adopté; M. RICCI-BUSATTI s'abstient de voter.

Article 8.

Mr. ROOT préfère la rédaction de l'article 7 du projet Root—Phillimore.

M. RICCI-BUSATTI voudrait que la matière traitée dans cet article fût renvoyée au règlement de la Cour.

Le PRESIDENT, appuyé par M. HAGERUP, fait valoir que le but de l'article est de caractériser le système, qui fait appel à trois organes, le Conseil, l'Assemblée et le corps présentateur.

Sur la proposition de M. HAGERUP, les membres du Comité conviennent d'ajouter au premier alinéa de l'article un renvoi à l'article 11, alinéa 2.

A cet égard, M. DE LAPRADELLE propose la rédaction suivante: „.... éligibles sauf l'exception prévue à l'article 11, al. 2."

A la demande de Mr. ROOT, l'article est réservé.

Article 9.

Après une discussion sur la rédaction de l'alinéa 1er, on se met d'accord sur la rédaction suivante, proposée par M. de Lapradelle:

„L'Assemblée et le Conseil procèdent, indépendamment l'une de l'autre, à l'élection d'abord des juges titulaires et ensuite des juges suppléants."

Cet alinéa formera un nouvel article 9; l'alinéa 2 est adopté comme article 9 bis.

L'alinéa 3 est adopté comme article 9 ter, 1er alinéa. L'alinéa 4 est adopté, avec des modifications de rédaction, comme article 9 ter, 2e alinéa.

Article 10.

Sur la proposition de LORD PHILLIMORE, le mot „élection" est substitué au mot „scrutin". Lord Phillimore fait valoir que, puisqu'il y aura deux sortes de scrutins, le mot „scrutin" serait équivoque.

The PRESIDENT stated that Para. 2 would also be reserved.

Article 7.

On LORD PHILLIMORE's proposal, the Committee agreed to delete the expression "by a majority of votes." The phrase "national group" was to be modified to make it tally with the future wording of Article 6, which had been reserved.

The Article was adopted; M. RICCI-BUSATTI abstained from voting.

Article 8.

Mr. ROOT preferred the wording of Article 7 of the Root—Phillimore plan.

M. RICCI-BUSATTI wished the subject dealt with in this Article to be left to the rules of Court.

The PRESIDENT, supported by M. HAGERUP, pointed out that the object of this Article was to describe the system, in which three bodies took part: the Council, the Assembly and the nominating body.

On M. HAGERUP's proposal, the Committee agreed to add a reference to Article 11, Para. 2, to the first Paragraph of this Article.

For this, M. DE LAPRADELLE proposed the following wording: "... eligible for appointment, except as provided in Article 11, para. 2."

At Mr. ROOT's request.this Article was reserved.

Article 9.

After a discussion concerning the wording of the first Paragraph, the following wording, proposed by M. de Lapradelle, was adopted:

"The Assembly and the Council shall proceed to elect, by independent voting, first the judges and then the deputy judges."

This Paragraph would form a new 9th Article; Paragraph 2 was adopted as Article 9 bis.

Parapraph 3 was adopted as Article 9 ter para. 1; the 4th paragraph, with an amended wording, as Article 9 ter para. 2.

Article 10.

At LORD PHILLIMORE's proposal the word "voting" (scrutin) was replaced by the word "election." Lord Phillimore pointed out that, as there would be two kinds of votings (scrutin), the word might lead to misunderstanding.

Article 11.

M. HAGERUP, appuyé par LORD PHILLIMORE, propose l'addition à l'alinéa 1er d'un renvoi au principe exprimé dans l'article 17 des règles de procédure, afin d'assurer une solution en cas de partage des voix.

M. ADATCI s'oppose à l'adoption, dans cet alinéa, d'un nombre limité d'élections; il fait valoir que le Comité a déjà provisoirement discuté le système contraire.

M. DE LAPRADELLE répond, se référant aux dispositions du projet, que le cas se trouve organiquement résolu par celui-ci.

Sur la proposition de LORD PHILLIMORE on se met d'accord pour adopter un moyen artificiel à trouver, qui permette le départage des voix.

M. FERNANDES demande si, au sens du texte, le Conseil et l'Assemblée auront à choisir dans une liste plus ou moins large proposée par la commission médiatrice, ou s'ils devront adopter ou rejeter la proposition faite par cette commission.

En vue de donner satisfaction à cette observation, M. DE LAPRADELLE propose de rédiger les deux dernières lignes du premier alinéa de la manière suivante:

„en vue de choisir pour chaque siège non pourvu un nom à présenter à l'adoption séparée de l'Assemblée et du Conseil".

Pour donner satisfaction à l'opposition de M. ADATCI, qui voudrait retourner au texte de l'article 3 du projet Root—Phillimore, M. FERNANDES propose de laisser aux deux corps le choix du moment où la médiation doit prendre place. L'article est réservé. Contre le vote de M. ALTAMIRA, qui renvoie aux déclarations faites par lui lors de la discussion de l'article correspondant du projet Root—Phillimore, l'alinéa 2 est adopté, avec une modification rédactionnelle.

Mr. ROOT fait valoir que le délai (de trois jours) ne peut être fixé par le Comité.

Sur la proposition de M. HAGERUP, et avant que les objections de Mr. Root aient été formulées, le Comité se met d'accord pour reconnaître

Article 11.

M. HAGERUP, supported by LORD PHILLIMORE, proposed that a reference to the principle laid down in Article 17 of the rules of procedure be added to the first Paragraph in order to ensure a result in the event of an equality of votes.

M. ADATCI opposed the adoption of a limited number of votings in this Paragraph; he pointed out that the Committee had already provisionally discussed the alternative system.

M. DE LAPRADELLE answered by referring to the provisions of the plan and said that the problem was implicitly solved therein.

On the proposal of LORD PHILLIMORE, it was agreed to adopt an artificial means for attaining a result in the event of an equal division of votes.

M. FERNANDES asked whether the meaning of the text was that the Council and the Assembly would have to choose from a more or less extensive list proposed by the Joint Conference, or whether they would have to adopt or reject the proposal made by the Joint Conference.

In order to make this point clear, M. DE LAPRADELLE proposed that the last two lines of the first Paragraph should be worded as follows:

"for the purpose of choosing one name for each seat still vacant, to submit to the Assembly and to the Council for their respective acceptance."

In order to meet the wishes of M. ADATCI, who desired to return to the wording of Article 3 of the Root—Phillimore plan, M. FERNANDES proposed that the choice of the time when the joint Conference should take place, should be left to the two bodies concerned. The Article was reserved. Paragraph 2 was adopted with a modified wording; M. ALTAMIRA voted against it and referred to the views expressed by him at the time of the discussion of the corresponding Article of the Root—Phillimore plan.

Mr. ROOT pointed out that the time limit (three days) could not be laid down by the Committee.

On M. HAGERUP's proposal and before Mr. Root's objections had been stated, the Committee agreed that a provision should be added to the

qu'il faut ajouter à l'alinéa une disposition destinée à départager les voix en cas de partage au sein de la Cour.

L'alinéa est réservé.

La séance est levée à 12.45 heures de l'après-midi.

Le Président :
(signé) Brn. DESCAMPS.

Le Secrétaire-Général :
(signé) D. ANZILOTTI.

paragraph, providing for a decision in case of an equal division of votes upon the Court.

The paragraph was reserved.

The meeting closed at 12.45 p. m.

The President :
(signed) Brn. DESCAMPS.

The Secretary-General :
(signed) D. ANZILOTTI.

ANNEXE No. 1.

APERÇU des questions relatives à l'établissement d'une Cour Permanente de Justice Internationale qui n'ont pas encore été discutées à fond par le Comité, le 15 juillet.

1. La Cour pourra-t-elle avoir des fonctions arbitrales? (interprétation du mot „arbitrage" dans le Pacte de la Société des Nations: ce mot a-t-il seulement le sens étroit et technique ou équivaut-il au terme: règlement judiciaire?)

2. Il est reconnu par le Comité que les traités de paix rendent la nouvelle Cour compétente dans un certain nombre de cas déterminés, indépendamment des limites générales qui pourront être tracées pour l'activité de la Cour. Dans les traités de paix ces cas ne sont pas définis d'une manière absolument certaine: parfois la juridiction est désignée seulement par l'expression „juridiction instituée par la Société des Nations". Le Comité doit-il se prononcer, éventuellement sous forme d'un vœu, sur l'interprétation des expressions de cet ordre?

3. Les conditions sous lesquelles la Cour doit pouvoir donner des avis consultatifs. Ces conditions doivent viser à éviter à la Cour de se lier les mains par des opinions dans des cas qui pourront être soumis à sa juridiction.

4. La Cour comme cour d'appel en matière de droit international, comme cour internationale des prises, comme tribunal pour certaines questions de travail, etc.

5. Conditions à remplir par les juges au point de vue de leur compétence, si la Cour doit connaître des questions visées sous no. 4 ci-dessus.

6. L'élection d'un juge pourra-t-elle être invalidée s'il est démontré que la personne élue ne remplit pas les conditions requises par le statut de la Cour?

7. Les juges auront-ils le droit de recevoir des appointements, allocations ou honoraires d'autres sources que la Société des Nations?

ANNEX No. 1.

SUMMARY of the questions relating to the establishment of a Permanent Court of International Justice which have not yet been fully discussed by the Committee; July 15th.

1. Will the Court be competent to act as a Court of arbitration? (interpretation of the word "arbitration" in the Covenant of the League of Nations: is this word to be understood in the narrow and technical sense only, or is it equivalent to the term: "judicial settlement"?)

2. The Committee recognises that the Treaties of Peace give the new Court competence in a certain number of specified cases, independently of any general limits which might be set to the activities of the Court. In the Treaties of Peace these cases are not defined with absolute accuracy: sometimes the jurisdiction is described by the term "tribunal instituted by the League of Nations." Shall the Committee ultimately give its decision, possibly in the form of a recommendation, with regard to the interpretation of terms of this kind?

3. The conditions in which the Court should be able to give advisory opinions. The aim of these conditions must be to prevent the Court from binding itself by giving such opinions in cases which might eventually be submitted to its jurisdiction.

4. The Court as a Court of Appeal in questions of international law, as an international Prize Court, as a tribunal for certain labour-questions etc.

5. Conditions to be fulfilled by the judges from the point of view of their competence, if the Court is to deal with the questions referred to in Paragraph 4.

6. Can the election of a judge be invalidated if it can be proved that the person chosen does not fulfil the conditions required by the Statute of the Court?

7. Will the judges be allowed to accept salaries, allowances or emoluments from sources other than the League of Nations?

8. Doit-il y avoir des chambres spéciales à la Cour pour les questions visées dans no. 4 ci-dessus?

9. De la force de la sentence: seulement pour le litige spécial et pour les parties à ce litige? (sauf sous forme de précédent).

10. Droit d'intervention.

11. Révision ou appel.

12. *Locus standi* spécial pour la Société des Nations, pour le Bureau du Travail, pour les autres organisations du même ordre, relevant de la Société des Nations.

13. Délais et sanctions pour l'exécution des sentences (le dernier alinéa de l'article 13 du Pacte est-il applicable?)

14. Les signataires du Statut de la Cour doivent-ils assumer l'obligation de modifier leur législation intérieure en cas de conflit entre cette législation et une sentence rendue par la Cour?

15. Plusieurs questions de détail concernant la procédure.

8. Should there be special branches of the Court for the questions referred to in Paragraph 4?

9. The legal force of the sentence: for the suit only which it terminated, and for the parties to this suit? (except in the form of a precedent).

10. Right of intervention.

11. Revision or appeal.

12. A special *locus standi* to be given to the League of Nations, to the Labour Bureau, and to other similar organisations dependent on the League of Nations.

13. Times and sanctions for the proper carrying out of sentences (is the last Paragraph of Article 13 of the Covenant applicable?)

14. Shall the signatories of the Statute of the Court take upon themselves the duty of modifying their internal legislation in cases where this legislation and a sentence pronounced by that Court do not agree?

15. Several questions of detail relative to procedure.

ANNEXE No. 2.

Texte préparé par le Comité de rédaction, d'un avant-projet pour l'institution d'une Cour Permanente de Justice Internationale.

Article 1er.

Indépendamment de la Cour d'Arbitrage, organisée par les Conventions de La Haye de 1899 et de 1907, et des Tribunaux spéciaux d'Arbitres, auxquels les Etats demeurent toujours libres de confier la solution de leurs différends, il est institué, conformément à l'Article 14 du Pacte de la Société des Nations, une Cour Permanente de Justice Internationale, directement accessible aux parties.

CHAPITRE 1.

Organisation de la Cour.

Article 2.

La Cour Permanente de Justice Internationale est un corps de magistrats indépendants, choisis sans égard à leur nationalité parmi les personnes d'une expérience reconnue, jouissant de la plus haute considération morale, et possédant une compétence notoire en matière de droit international.

Article 3.

La Cour se compose de quinze membres: onze juges et quatre suppléants. Le nombre des juges et suppléants peut être éventuellement augmenté par l'Assemblée, sur la proposition du Conseil de la Société des Nations, à concurrence de quinze juges et six suppléants.

Article 4.

Les membres de la Cour sont élus pour neuf ans. Ils sont rééligibles.

Ils restent en fonction jusqu'à leur remplacement effectif. Même après ce remplacement, ils continuent de connaître des affaires dont ils sont déjà saisis.

Article 5.

Les membres de la Cour sont élus par l'Assemblée et par le Conseil.

Article 6.

Trois mois au moins avant la date de l'élection, le Secrétaire-Général invite par écrit les membres de la Cour d'Arbitrage appartenant à chacun des Etats mentionnés à l'Annexe au Pacte de la Société

ANNEX No. 2.

Text prepared by the drafting Committee, of a Draft Scheme for the establishment of a Permanent Court of International Justice.

(Translation).

Article 1.

A Permanent Court of International Justice, to which Parties shall have direct access, is hereby established, in accordance with Article 14 of the Covenant of the League of Nations. This Court shall be in addition to the Court of Arbitration organised by the Hague Conventions of 1899 and 1907, and to the special Tribunals of Arbitration to which States are always at liberty to submit their disputes for settlement.

CHAPTER 1.

Organisation of the Court.

Article 2.

The Permanent Court of International Justice shall be composed of a body of independent judges, chosen regardless of their nationality, from amongst persons of wellknown experience and high moral character, who possess a recognised competence in international law.

Article 3.

The Court shall consist of fifteen members: eleven judges and four deputy-judges. The number of judges and deputy-judges may be hereafter increased by the Assembly, upon the proposal of the Council of the League of Nations, to a total of fifteen judges and six deputy-judges.

Article 4.

The members of the Court shall be elected for nine years. They may be re-elected.

They shall continue to discharge their duties until their places have actually been filled. Though replaced, they shall complete any cases which they may have begun.

Article 5.

The members of the Court shall be elected by the Assembly and by the Council.

Article 6.

At least three months before the date of the election, the Secretary General of the League of Nations shall address a written request to the members of the Court of Arbitration, belonging

des Nations, à procéder par groupes nationaux à la présentation des personnes en situation de remplir les fonctions de membre de la Cour.

Chaque groupe ne peut en aucun cas présenter plus de deux personnes, sans distinction de nationalité.

Article 7.

Avant de procéder à cette désignation à la majorité des voix, il est recommandé à chaque groupe national de consulter la plus Haute Cour de Justice, les Facultés de Droit des Universités, ou les Académies ou sections d'Académies nationales ou internationales, vouées à l'étude du droit.

Article 8.

Le Secrétaire-Général dresse, par ordre alphabétique, une liste de toutes les personnes ainsi désignées; seules ces personnes sont éligibles.

Le Secrétaire-Général communique cette liste à l'Assemblée et au Conseil.

Article 9.

L'Assemblée et le Conseil procèdent indépendamment l'une de l'autre à l'élection des juges titulaires.

Dans toute élection, les électeurs veilleront à ce que les personnes appelées à faire partie de la Cour, non seulement réunissent individuellement les conditions requises, mais assurent dans l'ensemble la représentation des grandes formes de civilisation et des principaux systèmes juridiques du monde.

Sont élus ceux qui ont réuni la majorité absolue des voix dans l'Assemblée et dans le Conseil.

Au cas où le scrutin de l'Assemblée et du Conseil appellerait à la Cour deux membres de la même nationalité, le plus âgé est seul élu.

Article 10.

Si après le premier scrutin il reste encore des sièges à pourvoir, il est procédé de la même manière à un second scrutin, puis à un troisième.

Article 11.

Si, après un troisième tour de scrutin, il reste encore des sièges à pourvoir, il est formé une Commission médiatrice de six membres, nommés, trois par l'Assemblée, trois par le Conseil, en vue d'obtenir la formation d'une liste commune, à présenter à l'adoption de l'Assemblée et du Conseil.

Peuvent être portées sur cette liste, à l'unanimité, toutes personnes satisfaisant aux conditions requises, alors même qu'elles n'auraient pas figuré sur la liste de présentation de la Cour d'Arbitrage.

to each of the States mentioned in the Annex to the Covenant, inviting them to undertake, by national groups, the nomination of persons in a position to accept the duties of a member of the Court.

No group may nominate more than two persons; the nominees may be of any nationality.

Article 7.

Before making these nominations, which will be decided by a majority of votes, each national group is hereby recommended to consult its Highest Court of Justice, its Legal Faculties and Schools of Law, and its National Academies and national sections of International Academies devoted to the study of Law.

Article 8.

The Secretary-General shall prepare a list, in alphabetical order, of all the persons thus nominated. These persons only shall be eligible for appointment.

The Secretary-General shall submit this list to the Assembly and to the Council.

Article 9.

The Assembly and the Council shall proceed to elect the judges by independent votings.

At every election, the electors shall bear in mind that not only should all the persons appointed as members of the Court possess the qualifications required, but the whole body also should represent the main forms of civilisation and the principal legal systems of the world.

Those candidates who obtain an absolute majority of votes in the Assembly and the Council shall be considered as elected.

In the event of two candidates of the same nationality being elected by the votes of both the Assembly and the Council, the eldest of these shall be considered as elected.

Article 10.

If, after the first voting, one or more seats remain to be filled, a second, and if necessary a third voting shall take place.

Article 11.

If, after the third voting, one or more seats still remain unfilled, a Joint Conference shall be formed consisting of six members, three appointed by the Assembly and three by the Council, for the purpose of composing one list to submit to the Assembly and Council for their acceptance.

If the Conference is unanimously agreed upon any person who fulfils the required conditions he may be included in its list, even though he was not included in the list of nominations made by the Court of Arbitration.

Si trois jours après la réunion de la Commission médiatrice l'entente n'est pas obtenue, les membres de la Cour déjà nommés pourvoient par cooptation aux sièges vacants, en choisissant parmi les personnes qui auront eu des voix, soit à l'Assemblée, soit au Conseil.

Article 12.

Quand la désignation des juges titulaires est terminée, il est procédé de la même manière à celle des juges suppléants.

Article 13.

Les juges titulaires reçoivent un traitement annuel, déterminé d'une manière égale, et pour neuf ans, par l'Assemblée, sur la proposition du Conseil.

Le Président reçoit une indemnité spéciale, et déterminée pour la même période de temps.

Les juges suppléants reçoivent une indemnité égale au tiers du traitement des juges titulaires.

Un règlement spécial détermine les pensions auxquelles ont droit les juges.

Article 14.

L'exercice de toute fonction qui relève de la direction politique, soit nationale, soit internationale, des Etats, est incompatible avec la qualité de membre de la Cour.

Article 15.

Les membres de la Cour ne peuvent exercer les fonctions d'agents ou de conseils dans aucune affaire d'ordre international.

Ils ne peuvent participer au règlement d'aucune affaire dans laquelle ils sont antérieurement intervenus comme agents ou conseils de l'une des parties membres d'un Tribunal national ou international, d'un Tribunal d'Arbitrage, d'une Commission d'enquête, ou à tout autre titre.

En cas de doute, la Cour décide.

Article 16.

Les membres de la Cour ne peuvent être relevés de leurs fonctions que si, au jugement unanime des autres membres, ils ont cessé de répondre aux conditions requises.

Le Secrétaire-Général en est officiellement informé.

Cette communication emporte vacance de siège.

Article 17.

En dehors de leurs propres pays, les membres de la Cour jouissent des mêmes privilèges et immunités que les agents diplomatiques.

If an agreement is not reached within three days of the assembly of the Joint Conference, those members of the Court who have already been appointed shall proceed to fill the vacant seats by co-optation, making their selection from amongst those candidates who have obtained votes either in the Assembly or in the Council.

Article 12.

When all the judges have been appointed, the election of the deputy judges shall take place in the same way.

Article 13.

The judges shall receive an equal annual salary, fixed for a period of nine years, to be determined by the Assembly upon the proposal of the Council.

The President shall receive a special grant to be fixed for the same period.

Deputy-judges shall receive a grant equal to one third of the salary of the judges.

Special provision shall be made for the pensions to which judges shall be entitled.

Article 14.

The exercise of any function which belongs to the political direction, national or international, of States, by the members of the Court, during their term of office, is declared incompatible with their judicial duties.

Article 15.

No member of the Court can act as agent or Counsel in any case of an international nature.

No member may participate in the decision of any case in which he has previously taken an active part as agent or counsel for one of the contesting parties, or as a member of a national or international Court, or of a Commission of Inquiry, or in any other capacity.

Any doubt upon this point is settled by the decision of the Court.

Article 16.

A member of the Court cannot be dismissed unless, in the unanimous opinion of the other members, he has ceased to fulfil the required conditions.

When this happens a formal notification shall be given to the Secretary-General.

This notification makes the seat vacant.

Article 17.

The members of the Court, when outside their own country, shall enjoy the privileges and immunities of diplomatic representatives.

Article 18.

Tout membre de la Cour doit, avant d'entrer en fonctions, donner, en séance publique, une déclaration solennelle de sa volonté d'exercer ses attributions avec impartialité et en toute conscience.

Article 19.

La Cour élit, pour trois ans, son Président et son Vice-Président: ils sont rééligibles.

Elle nomme son Greffier.

La fonction de Greffier de la Cour n'est pas incompatible avec celle de Greffier de la Cour permanente d'Arbitrage.

Le traitement du Greffier est fixé par le Conseil sur la proposition de la Cour.

Article 20.

Le siège de la Cour est fixé à La Haye.

Le Président et le Greffier résident au siège de la Cour.

Article 21.

La Cour tient une session chaque année.

Sauf disposition contraire du règlement d'ordre de la Cour, cette session commence le 15 juin et continue tant que le rôle n'est pas épuisé.

Le Président convoque la Cour en session extraordinaire quand il lui paraît que les circonstances l'exigent.

Article 22.

La Cour exerce ses attributions en séance plénière.

Si, pour une raison spéciale, l'un des membres de la Cour estime ne pouvoir participer au jugement d'une affaire déterminée, il en fait part au Président.

Si le Président estime qu'un des membres de la Cour ne peut siéger pour une raison spéciale dans une affaire déterminée, il en avertit le membre intéressé.

Si l'un et l'autre ne sont pas d'accord dans chacun de ces cas sur l'attitude à prendre, la Cour décide.

Si la présence de neuf juges titulaires n'est pas assurée, ce nombre est parfait par l'entrée en fonction de suppléants.

Article 23.

Les suppléants sont appelés dans l'ordre du tableau.

Le tableau est dressé par la Cour, en tenant compte, d'abord de la priorité d'élection; ensuite,

Article 18.

Every member of the Court shall, before taking up his duties, make a solemn declaration in open Court that he will exercise his powers impartially and conscientiously.

Article 19.

The Court shall elect its President and Vice-President for three years: they may be re-elected.

It shall appoint its Registrar.

The duties of the Registrar of the Court shall not be considered incompatible with those of Registrar of the Permanent Court of Arbitration.

The salary of the Registrar shall be decided by the Council upon the proposal of the Court.

Article 20.

The seat of the Court shall be established at The Hague.

The President and the Registrar shall reside at the seat of the Court.

Article 21.

A session shall be held every year.

Unless otherwise provided by rules of Court, this session shall begin on the 15th June and shall continue for so long as may be necessary to complete the cases on the list.

The President may summon an extraordinary meeting of the Court whenever he considers that necessary.

Article 22.

The full Court shall sit.

If, for some special reason, a member of the Court considers that he cannot take part in the decision of a particular case, he shall so inform the President.

If, for some special reason, the President considers that one of the members of the Court should not sit on a particular case, he shall give notice to the member concerned.

In the event of the President and the member not agreeing as to the course to be adopted in any such case, the matter shall be settled by the decision of the Court.

If nine judges cannot be present, deputy-judges shall be called upon to sit, in order to make up this number.

Article 23.

Deputy-judges shall be called upon to sit in the order laid down in the list.

This list shall be prepared by the Court, having regard first to the order in time of each election,

du nombre de voix obtenues au dernier scrutin; enfin, à l'égalité de voix, par l'ancienneté d'âge.

secondly to the number of votes obtained at the last voting and lastly, in the event of an equality of votes, to age.

Article 24.

En vue de la prompte expédition des affaires, la Cour compose annuellement une chambre de trois juges, spécialement consacrée au jugement des affaires en procédure sommaire.

Article 24.

With a view to the speedy despatch of business the Court shall form, annually, a chamber composed of three judges; this chamber shall be devoted to the trial of cases by summary procedure.

Article 25.

Si la Cour renferme un juge titulaire de la nationalité d'un seul des Etats en litige, et qu'elle compte un juge suppléant de la nationalité de l'autre partie, il est procedé par voie de tirage au sort à la détermination d'un juge titulaire qui lui cède son siège.

Lorsqu'une des parties n'a pas de ressortissants parmi les membres de la Cour, elle désigne un juge de sa nationalité, en le choisissant autant que possible parmi les personnes qui ont été l'objet d'une présentation de la part des groupes nationaux de la Cour d'Arbitrage.

Le juge ainsi nommé devient temporairement membre de la Cour sur un pied de parfaite égalité avec ses collègues.

Si, parmi les membres de la Cour il n'existe aucun juge, ni titulaire ni suppléant, de la nationalité d'aucune des parties en cause, chacune peut désigner (sur la liste de présentation de la Cour d'Arbitrage) un juge qui prendra part, à titre consultatif, au jugement du litige.

Au cas où l'une des deux parties seulement aurait, soit un juge titulaire, soit un juge suppléant dans la Cour, l'autre partie peut demander que le juge se retire, pour être remplacé par un autre juge, nommé dans les mêmes conditions que le sien.

S'il ne fait pas usage de ce droit, le juge national ne se retire pas, mais il n'a plus, lors du délibéré, qu'une voix consultative.

Article 25.

If the Court includes a judge of the nationality of one only of the contesting States, but contains a deputy-judge of the nationality of the other State, the judges shall draw lots in order to decide which of them shall give up his seat to the deputy-judge.

Should one of the parties have no judge of its nationality amongst the members of the Court, this party shall appoint a judge of its nationality, if possible making its selection from amongst the persons who have been nominated by the national groups of the Court of Arbitration.

A judge, thus appointed, temporarily becomes a member of the Court upon a footing of absolute equality with his colleagues.

If there is no judge or deputy-judge of the nationality of either of the contesting parties upon the Court, each party may appoint (making its selection from the list of nominations made by the Court of Arbitration) a judge who will take part in the trial in an advisory capacity.

Should only one of the parties have a judge or deputy-judge upon the Court, the other may request that this judge be called upon to withdraw from the Court and be replaced by another judge appointed under the same conditions as its own.

If the said party does not exercise this right, the national judge will not withdraw, but will only take part in the deliberations in an advisory capacity.

Article 26.

Les frais de la Cour sont supportés par la Société des Nations.

Article 26.

The expenses of the Court shall be borne by the League of Nations.

CHAPITRE 2.

La compétence de la Cour.

Article 27.

La Cour connaît des litiges entre Etats.

La réclamation d'un particulier contre un Etat étranger ne peut venir devant la Cour que si l'Etat du réclamant la présente en son nom.

Un Etat peut présenter non seulement la réclamation d'un de ses ressortissants, mais aussi celles des membres d'une minorité nationale, à la protection de laquelle il est habilité par traité.

Article 28.

La Cour est accessible aux Etats mentionnés à l'annexe au Pacte de la Société des Nations.

Elle l'est également aux Etats qui se soumettent aux conditions fixées par le Conseil de la Société des Nations, conformément à l'Article 17 du Pacte.

Article 29.

Entre Etats, Membres de la Société des Nations, la Cour statue, sans convention spéciale, sur:

a. l'interprétation d'un traité;

b. tout point de droit international;

c. la réalité de tout fait, qui, s'il était établi, constituerait la violation d'un engagement international;

d. la nature ou l'étendue de la réparation due pour la rupture d'un engagement international;

e. l'interprétation d'une sentence rendue par la Cour.

Peut être soumis à la Cour, par la convention des parties, soit générale, soit spéciale, tout différend de quelque nature qu'il puisse être.

En cas de contestation sur le point de savoir si un différend rentre, ou non, dans les catégories ci-dessus visées, la Cour décide.

Article 30.

Lorsqu'une partie dénie compétence à la Cour, il appartient à celle-ci de statuer sur le point de savoir si, par une convention antérieure, la partie n'a pas accepté cette compétence.

CHAPTER 2.

Competence of the Court.

Article 27.

The Court shall have jurisdiction to hear and determine suits between States.

The claim of a private individual against a foreign State can only be taken into consideration by the Court if the State to which the applicant belongs has submitted it in its own name.

A State can submit, not only the claim of one of its own nationals, but also those of the members of a national minority, when it has been entrusted with their protection by treaty.

Article 28.

The Court shall be open to the States mentioned in the Annex to the Covenant of the League of Nations.

It is also open to States which accept the conditions laid down by the Council of the League of Nations, in accordance with Article 17 of the Covenant.

Article 29.

Between States which are Members of the League of Nations, the Court shall have jurisdiction (and this without any special convention giving it jurisdiction) to hear and determine cases concerning:

a. the interpretation of a treaty;

b. any question of international law;

c. the existence of any fact which, if established, would constitute a breach of an international obligation;

d. the nature or extent of reparation to be made for the breach of an international obligation;

e. the interpretation of a sentence passed by the Court.

A dispute of any kind may be submitted to the Court by a general or particular convention between the parties.

In the event of a dispute as to whether a certain case comes within any of the categories above mentioned, the matter shall be settled by the decision of the Court.

Article 30.

Wherever a party refuses to recognise the jurisdiction of the Court, it will be for the Court to decide whether the party has agreed to submit to its jurisdiction by virtue of some previous convention.

Article 31.

Dans les limites de sa compétence, telle qu'elle est déterminée par l'article 29, la Cour applique successivement:

1. les conventions internationales, soit générales, soit spéciales, posant des règles expressément reconnues par les Etats en litige;
2. la coutume internationale, attestation d'une pratique commune, acceptée comme loi;
3. les principes généraux de droit reconnus par les nations civilisées;
4. les règles de droit qui se dégagent des décisions judiciaires et de la doctrine des publicistes les plus qualifiés des différentes nations.

Article 32.

La Cour donne son avis sur tout point ou tout différend d'ordre international qui lui est soumis par le Conseil ou par l'Assemblée.

Lorsque la Cour donne son avis sur un point d'ordre international, indépendamment de tout différend actuellement né, elle constitue une Commission spéciale de trois à cinq membres.

Lorsqu'elle donne son avis sur une question qui fait l'objet d'un différend actuellement né, elle statue dans les mêmes conditions, que s'il s'agissait d'un litige porté devant elle.

CHAPITRE 3.

Procédure.

Article 1.

La langue de la Cour est le français.

La Cour peut, à la demande des parties, autoriser l'emploi d'une autre langue devant elle.

Article 2.

La Cour est saisie par une requête adressée au Greffe.

La requête indique l'objet du différend et désigne les parties en cause.

Le Greffe fait immédiatement notification de la requête aux intéressés.

Il en informe également les Membres de la Société des Nations, par l'entremise du Secrétaire-Général.

Article 2bis.

Dans le cas où la cause du différend consiste en un acte effectué ou sur le point de l'être, la Cour

Article 31.

The Court shall, within the limits of its jurisdiction, as defined in Article 29, apply in the order following:

1. international conventions, whether general or particular, establishing rules expressly recognised by the contesting States;
2. international custom, as evidence of a general practice, which is accepted as law;
3. the general principles of law recognised by civilised nations;
4. rules of law derived from judicial decisions and the teachings of the most highly qualified publicists of the various nations.

Article 32.

The Court shall give an advisory opinion upon any question or dispute of an international nature referred to it by the Council or Assembly.

When the Court shall give an opinion on a question of an international nature which does not refer to any dispute that may have arisen, it shall appoint a special Commission of from three to five members.

When it shall give an opinion upon a question which forms the subject of an existing dispute, it shall do so under the same conditions as if the case had been actually submitted to it for decision.

CHAPTER 3.

Procedure.

Article 1.

The official language of the Court shall be French.

The Court may, at the request of the contesting parties, authorise another language to be used before it.

Article 2.

A State desiring to have recourse to the Court shall lodge a written application addressed to the Registrar.

The application shall indicate the subject of the dispute, and name the contesting parties.

The Registrar shall forthwith communicate the application to all concerned.

He shall also notify the Members of the League of Nations through the Secretary-General.

Article 2bis.

If the dispute arises out of an act which has already taken place or which is imminent, the

a le pouvoir d'indiquer, si elle estime que les circonstances l'exigent, quelles mesures conservatoires du droit de chacun doivent être prises à titre provisoire.

En attendant son arrêt, cette suggestion de la Cour est immédiatement transmise aux parties et au Conseil.

Article 3.

Les parties sont réprésentées par des agents.

Elles peuvent charger des conseils ou avocats d'assister les agents devant la Cour.

Article 4.

La procédure a deux phases: l'une écrite, l'autre orale.

Article 5.

La procédure écrite comprend la communication à juge et à partie des mémoires, contre-mémoires, et, éventuellement, répliques, ainsi que de toute pièce et document à l'appui.

La communication se fait par l'entremise du Greffe dans l'ordre et les délais déterminés par la Cour.

Toute pièce produite par l'une des parties doit être communiquée à l'autre en copie certifiée conforme.

Article 6.

La procédure orale consiste dans l'audition par la Cour des témoins, experts, agents et avocats.

Pour toute notification à faire en dehors du pays où elle siège, la Cour s'adresse directement au Gouvernement de la Puissance sur le territoire de laquelle la notification doit produire effet.

Il en est de même s'il s'agit de faire procéder sur place à l'établissement de tous moyens de preuve.

Article 7.

Les débats sont dirigés par le Président, et à défaut par le Vice-Président; en cas d'empêchement par le plus ancien des juges présents.

Article 8.

L'audience est publique, à moins qu'il n'en soit autrement décidé par la Cour, à la demande de l'une des parties.

Article 9.

Il est tenu de chaque audience un procès-verbal, signé par le Greffier et le Président.

Ce procès-verbal a seul caractère authentique.

Court shall have the power to suggest, if it considers that circumstances so require, the provisional measures that should be taken to preserve the respective rights of either party.

Pending the final decision, notice of the measures suggested shall forthwith be given to the parties and the Council.

Article 3.

The parties shall be represented by agents.

They may have Counsel or advocates to assist the agents in Court.

Article 4.

The procedure shall consist of two parts: written and oral.

Article 5.

The written proceedings shall consist of the communication to the judges and to the parties of cases, counter-cases and, if necessary, replies; also all papers and documents in support.

These communications shall be made through the Registrar, in the order and within the time fixed by the Court.

A certified copy of every document produced by one party shall be communicated to the other party.

Article 6.

The oral proceedings shall consist of the hearing by the Court of witnesses, experts, agents and advocates.

For the service of all notices outside the country in which the seat of the Court is situated, the Court shall apply direct to the Government of the State upon whose territory the notice has to be served.

The same provision shall apply whenever steps are to be taken to procure evidence on the spot.

Article 7.

The Proceedings shall be under the direction of the President, or, in his absence, of the Vice-President; if both are absent, the senior judge shall preside.

Article 8.

The hearing in Court shall be public, unless the Court, at the written request of one of the parties, shall otherwise decide.

Article 9.

Minutes shall be made at each hearing and signed by the Registrar and the President.

These minutes shall be the only authentic record.

Article 10.

La Cour peut, même avant tout débat, demander aux agents de lui produire tous actes, et de fournir toutes explications.

En cas de refus, elle en prend acte.

Article 11.

A tout moment, la Cour peut confier une requête ou expertise à une ou plusieurs personnes de son choix.

Article 12.

Au cours des débats, les juges posent aux témoins, agents, experts, avocats ou conseils, toutes questions qu'ils estiment utiles; les agents, avocats et conseils ont le droit de poser, par l'entremise du Président, toute question que la Cour juge utile.

Article 13.

La Cour rend des ordonnances pour la direction du procès, la détermination des formes et délais dans lesquels chaque partie doit finalement conclure, et prend toutes les mesures que comporte l'administration des preuves.

Article 14.

Après avoir reçu les preuves et témoignages dans les délais déterminés par elle, la Cour peut écarter toutes dépositions ou documents nouveaux qu'une des parties voudrait lui présenter sans l'assentiment de l'autre.

Article 15.

Lorsqu'une des parties ne se présente pas, ou s'abstient de faire valoir ses moyens, l'autre partie peut demander à la Cour de lui adjuger ses conclusions.

La Cour y fait droit, après s'être assurée que ces conclusions:

1. sont conformes à la matérialité des faits;

2. reposent sur des preuves sérieuses;

3. sont fondées en droit.

Article 16.

Quand les agents, avocats et conseils ont fait valoir, sous le contrôle de la Cour, tous les moyens qu'ils jugent utiles, le Président prononce la clôture des débats.

La Cour se retire en chambre de conseil pour délibérer.

Les délibérations de la Cour sont et restent secrètes.

Article 10.

The Court may, even before the hearing begins, call upon the agents to produce any document or to supply to the Court any explanations.

Any refusal shall be recorded.

Article 11.

The Court may, at any time, entrust one or more persons whom it may select, with the task of carrying out an inquiry or giving an expert opinion.

Article 12.

During the hearing in Court, the judges may put any questions, considered by them to be necessary, to the witnesses, agents, experts, advocates or Counsels. The agents, advocates and Counsels shall have the right to ask, through the President, any questions that the Court considers useful.

Article 13.

The Court shall make orders for the conduct of the case, shall decide the form and time in which each party must conclude its arguments, and make all arrangements connected with the taking of evidence.

Article 14.

After the Court has received the proofs and evidence within the time specified for the purpose, it may refuse to accept any further oral or written evidence that one party may desire to present, unless the other agrees.

Article 15.

Whenever one of the parties shall not appear before the Court or shall fail to defend his case, the other party may call upon the Court to decide in favour of his claim.

The Court shall do so provided that it is satisfied that the claim is:

1. in conformity with the actual facts;

2. supported by substantial evidence;

3. well founded in law.

Article 16.

When the agents, advocates and Counsel, subject to the control of the Court, have presented all the evidence and taken all other steps that they consider advisable, the President shall declare the case closed.

The Court shall withdraw to consider the judgment.

The deliberations of the Court shall take place in private and remain secret.

Article 17.

Les décisions de la Cour sont prises à la majorité des juges présents.

En cas de partage de voix, le moins ancien des juges est considéré comme s'abstenant.

Article 17.

All questions shall be decided by a majority of the judges present at the hearing.

In the event of an equality of votes, the vote of the junior judge shall not count.

Article 18.

L'arrêt est motivé.

Il mentionne les noms des juges qui y ont pris part.

Article 18.

The judgment shall state the reasons on which it is based.

It shall contain the names of the judges who have taken part in the decision.

Article 19.

Si l'arrêt n'exprime pas, en tout ou en partie, l'opinion unanime des juges, les dissidents ont la faculté de demander l'insertion de leur opinion motivée, à la suite de l'exposé des motifs qui précède la décision de la majorité.

Cette faculté n'est pas ouverte aux juges de la nationalité des parties.

Article 19.

If the judgment given does not represent, wholly or in part, the unanimous opinion of the judges, the dissenting judges shall be entitled to have their opinions and the reasons on which they are based inserted after the statement of reasons which precede the decision of the majority.

Judges of the nationality of parties in dispute shall not have this right.

Article 20.

L'arrêt est signé par le Président et par le Greffier.

Il est lu en séance publique, les agents dûment prévenus.

Article 20.

The judgment shall be signed by the President and by the Registrar.

It shall be read in open Court, due notice having been given to the agents.

Article 21.

L'arrêt est définitif et sans recours.

En cas de doute sur le sens et la portée de l'arrêt, il appartient à la Cour de l'interprêter à la demande de toute partie.

Article 21.

The judgment is final and without appeal.

In the event of uncertainty as to the meaning and scope of the judgment, the Court shall construe it upon the request of any party.

Article 22.

La révision de l'arrêt ne peut être éventuellement demandée à la Cour qu'à raison de la découverte d'un fait nouveau, de nature à exercer une influence décisive, et qui, avant le prononcé de l'arrêt était inconnu de la Cour et de la partie demanderesse.

La procédure de révision s'ouvre par un arrêt de la Cour, constatant expressément l'existence du fait nouveau, et lui reconnaissant les caractères qui donnent ouverture à la révision, déclarant à cet égard la demande recevable.

La Cour peut subordonner l'ouverture de la procédure en révision à l'exécution préalable de l'arrêt.

Aucune demande de révision ne peut être formée après l'expiration d'un délai de cinq ans.

Article 22.

An application for revision of a judgment can be made only when it is based upon the discovery of some new fact, of such a nature as to be a decisive factor, which fact was, when the judgment was given, unknown to the Court and also to the party claiming revision.

The proceedings in revision will be opened by a judgment of the Court expressly recording the existence of the new fact, recognising that it has such a character as to lay the case open to revision, and declaring the application admissible on this ground.

The Court may require previous compliance with the terms of the judgment before it admits proceedings in revision.

No application for revision may be made after the lapse of five years from the date of the sentence.

Article 23.

Lorsqu'il s'agit de l'interprétation d'une convention à laquelle ont participé d'autres Etats que les parties en litige, le Greffe, au vu de la requête introductive d'instance, avertit sans délai toute puissance signataire.

Chacun des Etats a la faculté d'intervenir au procès, et, s'il l'exerce, devient partie en litige au point de vue de la chose jugée.

Article 24.

S'il n'en est autrement décidé par la Cour, chaque partie supporte ses frais de procédure.

Article 23.

Whenever the construction of a convention, in which States other than those concerned in the case are parties, is in question, the Registrar, upon receipt of the application opening the proceedings, shall notify all such States forthwith.

Every State so notified has the right to intervene in the proceedings, but if it uses this right, the judgment will have the force of *res judicata* also concerning the intervening party.

Article 24.

Unless otherwise decided by the Court, each party shall bear its own costs.

26ième SÉANCE (non-publique), tenue au Palais de la Paix, à La Haye, le 19 juillet 1920.

Présidence de M. le BARON DESCAMPS.

Sont présents: tous les membres du Comité (à l'exception de M. Bevilaqua); M. Fernandes; Mr. James Brown Scott; les secrétaires particuliers du Baron Descamps et de M. Adatci; les membres du Secrétariat.

La séance est ouverte à 2.15 heures de l'apres-midi.

Sur la proposition du PRESIDENT le Comité décide de se réunir de nouveau, ce même jour, à 8.30 du soir.

Le PRESIDENT ouvre la discussion sur les articles 12 et suivants du texte du Comité de rédaction.

Article 12.

Sur la proposition du PRESIDENT, les membres du Comité se trouvent d'accord pour reconnaître que l'article n'est pas nécessaire; il est par conséquent supprimé.

Article 13.

Sur la proposition du PRESIDENT on décide de transférer l'article 13 après l'article 25.

Article 14.

Sur la proposition de M. HAGERUP, qui constate que le 3ième alinéa de l'article 15 ne vise pas tous les points envisagés dans l'article 14, et que, par conséquent, cet article doit contenir une stipulation analogue, on se met d'accord pour ajouter à l'article 14 un nouvel alinéa ainsi conçu:

„En cas de doute, la Cour décide."

La proposition de M. DE LAPRADELLE, d'ajouter l'alinéa suivant:

„Quiconque exerce une fonction incompatible avec la qualité de membre de la Cour est considéré comme démissionnaire", est rejetée.

On reconnaît la nécessité d'expliquer en détail les considérations qui ont abouti à l'adoption de

26TH MEETING (Private), held at the Peace Palace, the Hague, on July 19th, 1920.

BARON DESCAMPS in the chair.

Present: all the Members of the Committee (except M. Bevilaqua); M. Fernandes; Mr. James Brown Scott; the private secretaries of Baron Descamps and M. Adatci; the members of the Secretariat.

The meeting opened at 2.15 p. m.

On the proposal of the PRESIDENT the Committee decided to meet again at 8.30 in the evening.

The PRESIDENT opened the debate upon Article 12 and the following Articles of the drafting Committee's text.

Article 12.

In consequence of a proposal made by the PRESIDENT the members of the Committee agreed that the Article was not necessary; consequently it was deleted.

Article 13.

On the PRESIDENT'S proposal, it was decided to transfer Article 13 to follow Article 25.

Article 14.

On the proposal of M. HAGERUP, who pointed out that the third Paragraph of Article 15 did not cover all the points dealt with in Article 14, and that, consequently, this Article should contain an analogous provision, it was agreed to add to article 14 a new Paragraph as follows:

"Any doubt upon this point is settled by the decision of the Court."

A proposal made by M. DE LAPRADELLE to add the following Paragraph was rejected: "Any judge who undertakes a duty incompatible with his position as a member of the Court shall be considered as having resigned."

The Committee recognised the necessity of explaining in detail the considerations which led to

l'article 14, ce texte ayant été formulé pendant une des séances secrètes, pour lesquelles il n'y pas eu de procès-verbal.

M. RICCI-BUSATTI propose que l'explication soit fournie dans le rapport, LORD PHILLIMORE qu'elle soit donnée sous forme d'une annexe au procès-verbal.

L'article est adopté.

Article 15.

Cet article est adopté sans discussion, sauf une modification rédactionnelle.

Article 16.

Cet article est adopté après une explication sur la portée du fait de cesser de répondre aux conditions requises.

Article 17.

Cet article est adopté sans discussion.

Article 18.

Cet article est adopté sans discussion.

Article 19.

On se met d'accord pour reconnaître que le dernier alinéa doit être transféré immédiatement après l'article 13, à sa nouvelle place (voir ci-dessus). Le reste de l'article est adopté, sauf une modification rédactionnelle.

Article 20.

Cet article est adopté sans discussion.

Article 21.

Cet article est adopté. Sur une question posée par M. RICCI-BUSATTI, on décide que la Cour devra se réunir chaque année. Elle devrait se réunir même dans le cas où il n'y aurait pas d'affaires à traiter.

Article 22.

Les alinéas *1* et 5 sont adoptés.

Sur la proposition de LORD PHILLIMORE, le Comité décide de faire de ces deux alinéas un nouvel article 22.

Les alinéas 2, 3, 4 sont réservés.

A cette occasion, M. FERNANDES reprend son amendement aux articles 25 et 26 du projet Root—Phillimore, visant l'élargissement du rôle des juges suppléants, amendement qui, lors de la discussion de ces textes, avait été renvoyé à la seconde lecture.

M. RICCI-BUSATTI s'abstient de voter.

the adoption of Article 14, as it had been drawn up at a secret session, of which no procès-verbal was taken.

M. RICCI-BUSATTI proposed that the explanation should be given in the report; LORD PHILLIMORE, that it should be given as an annex to the procès-verbal.

The Article was adopted.

Article 15.

This Article was adopted without discussion, with a slight alteration in the wording.

Article 16.

After an explanation concerning the scope of the expression „cease to fulfil the required conditions", the Article was adopted.

Article 17.

This Article was adopted without discussion.

Article 18.

This Article was adopted without discussion.

Article 19.

The Committee agreed that the last Paragraph should be transferred to follow immediately after Article 13 in its new position (see above). The rest of the Article was adopted with a modification in the wording.

Article 20.

This Article was adopted without discussion.

Article 21.

This Article was adopted. In consequence of a question asked by M. RICCI-BUSATTI, it was decided that the Court should meet every year; it should meet even though there might be no cases to deal with.

Article 22.

Paragraphs 1 and 5 were adopted.

The Committee, on LORD PHILLIMORE's proposal, decided to make these two Paragraphs into a new Article 22.

Paragraphs 2, 3 and 4 were reserved.

At this point, M. FERNANDES again put forward his amendment to Articles 25 and 26 of the Root—Phillimore plan, which was intended to increase the part played by the deputy-judges; this amendment was, at the time of the discussion of these clauses, postponed to the second reading.

M. RICCI-BUSATTI abstained from voting.

Article 23.

Mr. ROOT n'accepte pas le principe de la distinction entre les juges titulaires et les juges suppléants.

Les mots: „du nombre d'ordre des voix obtenues au dernier scrutin; enfin à égalité de voix par" sont biffés. L'article est adopté contre l'abstention de M. RICCI-BUSATTI.

Article 24.

M. HAGERUP demande si la chambre composée de trois juges ne sera compétente que par le consentement des parties.

LORD PHILLIMORE et M. DE LAPRADELLE croient que l'article doit être compris ainsi. Sur leur proposition, il est décidé d'y ajouter la phrase „si les parties le demandent".

Le PRESIDENT, en rappelant que, lors de la discussion de l'article 4, on a réservé la question de la durée du mandat des juges appelés pour combler les vacances survenues par la sortie ou le décès d'autres juges, propose que cette question soit tranchée avant la discussion de l'article 25.

Le Président propose le texte suivant:

„Il est pourvu aux sièges devenus vacants par expiration du terme des fonctions, par décès, par retraite ou par toute autre cause, selon la méthode suivie pour la première élection de l'ensemble des juges".

Le Président propose en même temps de revenir sur le système antérieurement adopté de l'enchevêtrement des mandats, fût-ce en confiant au juge suppléant l'achèvement du mandat de son prédécesseur. Il faut assurer la possibilité de nouvelles élections tous les neuf ans.

LORD PHILLIMORE explique ainsi le système sur lequel on s'est en principe mis d'accord:

L'élection du nouveau juge est faite selon la méthode adoptée pour l'élection de l'ensemble des juges.

Un juge suppléant est élu de la même manière. Le nouveau juge prend la place du juge sortant pour le reste du mandat de celui-ci; le nouveau juge suppléant remplace de la même manière un juge suppléant sortant. Il y aurait donc de nouvelles élections tous les neuf ans.

Cette méthode est acceptée, sauf rédaction.

Article 25.

Le PRESIDENT soumet, à titre transactionnel, une rédaction nouvelle de cet article.

Article 23.

Mr. ROOT did not accept the principle of making a distinction between judges and deputy-judges.

The words: "to the number of votes obtained at the last voting and lastly in case of an equality of votes" were struck out. The article was adopted; M. RICCI-BUSATTI abstained from voting.

Article 24.

M. HAGERUP asked whether the jurisdiction of the section of three judges would be dependent upon the consent of the parties.

LORD PHILLIMORE and M. DE LAPRADELLE thought that the article should be read in this way. On their proposal it was decided to add the words: "at the request of the contesting parties."

The PRESIDENT recalled the fact that, when Article 4 was discussed, the question of the period for which judges, appointed to fill vacancies caused by retirement or death, should be appointed, had been reserved; he now proposed that this question should be dealt with before discussing Article 25.

The President proposed the following wording:

"Vacancies which may occur owing to the expiration of an appointment, death or retirement or any other reason, shall be filled by the same method as that laid down for the first election of the whole-body of judges."

The President proposed, at the same time, that the system of overlapping appointments previously adopted should be changed and that deputy judges should be allowed to complete the unexpired portion of their predecessor's appointments. The possibility of new elections every nine years must be assured.

LORD PHILLIMORE explained the system which had, in principle, been agreed upon, as follows:

The election of a new judge is carried out according to the method adopted for the election of the whole body of judges.

A deputy-judge is elected in the same way. The new judge replaces the retiring judge for the remainder of the latter's appointment; the same applies to a deputy-judge replacing a retired deputy judge. There would therefore be fresh elections every nine years.

This method was adopted, subject to amendments in wording.

Article 25.

The PRESIDENT submitted a new wording for this Article with a view to a compromise.

LORD PHILLIMORE, en rappelant qu'il a été absent lors de la séance secrète au cours de laquelle la question a été discutée, fait quelques remarques.

Il pose d'abord ce principe que le juge doit avoir le caractère d'un vrai juge, quelle que soit son origine. Mais, d'autre part, il faut tenir compte de l'opinion publique qui exige que chaque pays, partie au litige, puisse introduire à la Cour un juge de sa nationalité: c'est une condition absolue pour que le projet soit adopté.

Lord Phillimore répond aux critiques qui ont été soulevées contre cette opinion. Il s'élève d'abord contre ceux qui prétendent que les juges *ad hoc* ne seraient pas sur un pied d'égalité avec les juges ordinaires. Il admet la justesse de cette observation, mais fait valoir d'autre part que dans le texte soumis par le Président il est donné tant de garanties que le danger peut être considéré comme écarté.

Il reprend ensuite les objections de M. Loder concernant les conséquences de l'addition d'un juge *ad hoc*, addition qui aurait pour effet, doublement fâcheux, de rendre le nombre des juges pair et variable. Lord Phillimore ne pense pas qu'il y ait lieu d'attribuer beaucoup d'importance à ces objections. En effet, des circonstances semblables se présentent tous les jours en Angleterre sans inconvénient appréciable.

En achevant, Lord Phillimore déclare que l'institution de juges *ad hoc* sera précieuse surtout pour les petits Etats.

M. LODER remercie Lord Phillimore de ses explications. Il croit cependant devoir maintenir son opposition contre l'article qui, dans son opinion, crée une Cour qui n'en est pas une, en instituant des juges qui n'ont pas le caractère de véritables juges.

M. ALTAMIRA donnera un vote contraire, bien que quelques-unes des objections qu'il a soulevées contre l'article soient disparues.

M. DE LAPRADELLE pense qu'il est évident que l'article doit être réservé. Il propose cependant la suppression de l'alinéa 1er.

Mr. ROOT appuyé par M. Adatci, s'oppose à ce que l'article soit réservé.

M. LODER se rallie à eux, en remarquant qu'il n'a pas demandé la réserve.

LORD PHILLIMORE, after recalling the fact that he had been absent at the time of the secret session at which the question had been discussed, went on to make some further observations.

First of all he laid down the principle that a judge must have the characteristics of a real judge, no matter how he came to be chosen. But, on the other hand, public opinion, which required that every country concerned in a case should have the right to introduce a judge of its own nationality into the Court, must be duly considered. This was a condition upon which the acceptance of the plan depended.

Lord Phillimore then proceeded to answer the criticism which had been directed against this view. He first of all dealt with those who thought that judges *ad hoc* would not be on an equal footing with the ordinary judges. He admitted the justice of this, but pointed out, on the other hand, that the text submitted by the President contained so many guarantees that the danger might be considered as disposed of.

He then turned to consider M. Loder's objections with reference to the consequences which would ensue from the addition of a judge *ad hoc*; these consequences would be that the number of judges composing the Court would be made even and would vary, which was very regrettable in M. Loder's opinion. He did not think there was any need to attach much importance to these considerations. Indeed this was a matter of daily occurrence in England and involved no real difficulty there.

Finally, Lord Phillimore said that the provision for judges *ad hoc* would be especially valuable to the smaller States.

M. LODER thanked Lord Phillimore for his explanations. He felt, however, that he must continue to oppose the Article, as, in his opinion, it would establish a Court that was not a true Court, since it would create judges not possessing the characteristics of true judges.

M. ALTAMIRA opposed the adoption of the Article, although some of the objections he had raised against it had now disappeared.

M. DE LAPRADELLE thought that it was evident that the Article would have to be reserved. However, he proposed that Paragraph 1 should be deleted.

Mr. ROOT, supported by M. Adatci, opposed the reservation of this Article.

M. LODER agreed with them, stating that he had not asked for it to be reserved.

M. DE LAPRADELLE maintient son point de vue, se référant à la méthode de procédure adoptée pour les séances.

Sur la proposition du PRESIDENT, le texte présenté par lui doit être considéré comme une partie intégrante du texte soumis par le Comité de rédaction.

L'accord sur ce point est constaté par un vote.

Article 13.

(Transféré après l'article 25; voir ci-dessus).

La rédaction définitive de l'article est laissée, sauf approbation par le Comité, à MM. Hagerup, de Lapradelle et Fernandes.

M. HAGERUP propose l'amendement suivant:

„Les juges toucheront un traitement annuel à fixer par l'Assemblée de la Société des Nations sur la proposition du Conseil. Ce traitement ne peut être changé pendant le terme du mandat d'un juge.

Les juges suppléants toucheront, pendant l'exercice de leurs fonctions, une indemnité à fixer de la même manière.

Les juges titulaires et les juges suppléants qui ne résident pas au siège de la Cour auront droit à une indemnité pour frais de voyages nécessités par l'exercice de leurs fonctions."

Sur la proposition de LORD PHILLIMORE le Comité décide de reconnaître que le salaire du Président ne doit être déterminé que pour trois ans, ce qui nécessite une modification à l'alinéa 2.

MM. ROOT et HAGERUP s'opposent à la fixation du traitement des suppléants à un tiers de celui des titulaires.

Mr. ROOT et LORD PHILLIMORE voudraient que l'on laissât à la Société des Nations le soin de prendre une décision au sujet de la matière visée dans l'alinéa 3.

M. LODER constate que le règlement visé à l'alinéa 4 doit être fait par la Société des Nations.

On passe alors à la question du traitement qu'il convient de donner aux juges nationaux *ad hoc*.

Le transfert de l'alinéa 4 de l'article 19, immédiatement après l'article 13, est décidé.

Article 26.

M. HAGERUP soulève la question de la situation des Etats qui ne sont pas Membres de la Société des Nations et qui n'ont pas adhéré à la Convention établissant la Cour. Le texte du Comité de rédaction ne vise ces Etats que pour les cas qui rentrent dans l'article 17 du Pacte. M. Hagerup voudrait, cependant, que les frais de la Cour fussent

M. DE LAPRADELLE maintained his opinion, and referred to the method of procedure adopted for the meetings.

On the PRESIDENT's proposal, the text submitted by him was considered as an integral part of the text submitted by the drafting Committee.

This decision was recorded by a vote.

Article 13.

(Transferred to follow Article 25; see above).

The final draft of the Article was left to MM. Hagerup, de Lapradelle and Fernandes, subject to the Committee's approval.

M. HAGERUP proposed the following amendment:

"The judges shall receive an annual salary to be determined by the Assembly of the League of Nations upon the proposal of the Council. This salary must not be altered during the period of a judge's appointment.

The deputy-judges shall receive a grant, to be fixed in the same way, for the actual performance of their duties.

Travelling expenses incurred in the performance of their duties shall be refunded to judges and deputy-judges who do not reside at the seat of the Court."

On LORD PHILLIMORE's proposal, the Committee decided that the President's salary should only be fixed for three years; this decision rendered a modification in Paragraph 2 necessary.

Mr. ROOT and M. HAGERUP were opposed to the idea of fixing the salary of the deputy-judges at one third of that of the judges.

Mr. ROOT and LORD PHILLIMORE preferred to leave the contents of Paragraph 3 to be decided by the League of Nations.

M. LODER expressed the opinion that the conditions laid down in Paragraph 4 should be decided by the League of Nations.

The question of the salary to be given to national judges *ad hoc* was then raised.

It was decided to transfer Paragraph 4 of Article 19 to follow immediately after Article 13.

Article 26.

M. HAGERUP raised the question of the position of States which were not Members of the League of Nations, and which had not given their adherence to the Convention establishing the Court. The text of the drafting Committee only provided for such States in connection with cases coming within the provisions of Article 17 of the Covenant. M.

supportés par tous les Etats qui participent à l'activité ordinaire de la Cour.

M. RICCI-BUSATTI, appuyé par M. HAGERUP, propose la suppression de l'article; M. Hagerup attire l'attention sur le projet des commissions des trois pays du Nord.

Mr. ROOT pense que l'article 17 couvre tous les cas.

M. DE LAPRADELLE propose le nouveau texte suivant:

„Les frais de la Cour sont supportés par la Société des Nations de la manière que l'Assemblée décide sur la proposition du Conseil."

L'article est adopté contre le vote de M. Ricci-Busatti.

Article 27.

La discussion s'engage sur la portée du terme „protectorat" et „protégés".

Selon M. DE LAPRADELLE, les ressortissants des protectorats sont assimilés aux ressortissants de la métropole.

M. ALTAMIRA s'oppose, au point de vue de la langue espagnole, à cette interprétation.

M. RICCI-BUSATTI déclare que l'amendement à cet article qu'il a antérieurement déposé, n'avait en vue ni les protectorats, ni les minorités; mais des hypothèses différentes. N'ayant pas le temps nécessaire pour examiner la formule sous le nouvel aspect qu'elle affecte, il s'abstiendra de voter. Pour lui la question principale concerne la première partie de l'article; il s'agit d'expliquer bien nettement que la partie en cause est toujours l'Etat pour la défense d'un droit qui lui appartient, même si le litige a indirectement pour objet les droits ou intérêts d'un particulier.

Mr. ROOT signale le danger pour le Comité de s'engager dans la voie de la législation internationale.

La discussion de l'article est ajournée à la réunion du soir.

La séance est levée à 4.45 heures de l'après-midi.

Le Président:

(signé) Brn. DESCAMPS.

Le Secrétaire-Général:

(signé) D. ANZILOTTI.

Hagerup, however, wanted the expenses of the Court to be borne by all States who participated in the normal activity of the Court.

M. RICCI-BUSATTI, supported by M. HAGERUP, proposed that the Article should be deleted. M. Hagerup called attention to the plan drown up by the commissions of the three Scandinavian countries.

Mr. ROOT thought that Article 17 covered all contingencies.

M. DE LAPRADELLE proposed the following new wording:

"The expenses of the Court shall be borne by the League of Nations, in such a manner as shall by decided by the Assembly upon the proposal of the Council."

The Article was adopted.

M. Ricci-Busatti voted against it.

Article 27.

A discussion took place as to the meaning of the terms "Protectorate" and "Protégés".

According to M. DE LAPRADELLE, the inhabitants of protectorates are classified with subjects of the protecting State.

M. ALTAMIRA was opposed to this interpretation, in view of the meaning conveyed by the corresponding Spanish phrase.

M. RICCI BUSATTI declared that the amendment he had previously submitted with reference to this Article did not contemplate the inclusion of protectorates or minorities, but different cases. As he had not time to study the question in its new aspect, he would not vote. In his mind, the important point concerns the first part of the Article; it is necessary to make it quite clear that contesting parties are always States: these claim their own right also when the case is indirectly concerned with the rights and interests of a private individual.

Mr. ROOT pointed out the danger of the Committee's becoming involved in international legislation.

The discussion of the Article was adjourned to the evening meeting.

The meeting closed at 4.45 p. m.

The President:

(signed) Brn. DESCAMPS.

The Secretary-General:

(signed) D. ANZILOTTI.

27ième SÉANCE (non-publique), tenue au Palais de la Paix, à La Haye, le 19 juillet 1920.

Présidence de M. le BARON DESCAMPS.

Sont présents: tous les membres du Comité (à l'exception de M. Bevilaqua); M. Fernandes; Mr. James Brown Scott; les secrétaires particuliers de M. le Baron Descamps et de M. Adatci; les membres du Secrétariat.

La séance est ouverte à 8.30 heures du soir.

Article 27.

La discussion porte sur la détermination de la situation respective des particuliers et de l'Etat qui prend fait et cause pour eux devant la Cour de Justice.

Le PRESIDENT a tout d'abord communiqué au Comité le texte suivant:

„La Cour ne connaît que de litiges entre Etats. Mais un Etat peut saisir la Cour de demandes concernant des droits qu'il fait valoir en faveur de ses ressortissants ou des ressortissants d'un protectorat ou même d'un autre Etat à la protection duquel il est habilité par traité."

Comme suite à la discussion de cette formule, le Président propose ce texte:

„La Cour connaît de litiges entre Etats. Nulle réclamation d'un particulier contre un Etat étranger ne peut venir devant la Cour à moins qu'un Etat ne prenne fait et cause pour ses nationaux ou pour d'autres personnes dont la protection lui appartient en droit."

Le Président soulève la question d'un *locus standi* spécial pour la Société des Nations et ses organes.

Il propose ensuite une formule aux termes de laquelle l'Etat serait toujours le *dominus litis.*

M. DE LAPRADELLE suggère l'idée de baser la rédaction sur la conception de la protection diplomatique.

Mr. ROOT s'oppose à cette formule qui lui semble trop large.

27TH MEETING (Private), held at the Peace Palace, the Hague, on July 19th, 1920.

BARON DESCAMPS in the chair.

Present: all the members of the Committee (except M. Bevilaqua); M. Fernandes; Mr. James Brown Scott; the private secretaries of Baron Descamps and M. Adatci; the members of the Secretariat.

The meeting opened at 8.30 p.m.

Article 27.

The debate bore upon the definition of the respective positions of private individuals and States which took up cases on their behalf before the Court of Justice.

The PRESIDENT first of all read the following text to the Committee:

"The Court shall only have jurisdiction to hear and determine suits between States. A State may, however, bring before the Court a suit which it has taken up on behalf of its subjects or of the subjects of a Protectorate or even of the subjects of another State, which it has been empowered to protect by treaty."

In consequence of the discussion upon this wording, the President proposed the following.

"The Court shall hear and determine cases between States. No claims made by an individual against a foreign State may be brought before the Court, unless taken up by a State on behalf of its subjects or of other persons whom it has a right to protect."

The President raised the question of a special *locus standi* for the League of Nations and its organisations.

He then proposed a formula according to which a State must always be the *dominus litis.*

M. DE LAPRADELLE suggested that the wording should be based on the conception of diplomatic protection.

Mr. ROOT opposed this wording, as he considered that it was too vague.

LORD PHILLIMORE propose de procéder par énumération. L'accord ne s'établissant pas, le Comité décide, par un vote formel, de ne point compléter l'article 27, alinéa 1.

L'alinéa 1er est adopté.

M. ALTAMIRA vote contre, le texte ainsi réduit ne donnant pas assez de garanties que les Etats appuyeront impartialement les réclamations des particuliers.

Article 28.

M. HAGERUP propose l'amendement suivant (addition au texte originaire):

„Les conditions sous lesquelles la Cour est accessible aux Etats qui ne sont pas Membres de la Société des Nations, sont fixées par le Conseil de cette Société."

A l'appui de cet amendement, M. Hagerup fait valoir, d'abord, qu'il appartient à la Société des Nations plutôt qu'au Comité de poser des conditions d'admission à la Cour. Puis il fait remarquer que le premier alinéa de l'article semble enlever à la Société des Nations le droit de poser des conditions d'admission pour les Etats mentionnés à l'Annexe au Pacte, mais qui ne sont pas encore Membres de la Société des Nations. Il lui enlève aussi, par conséquent, le droit d'établir que des Etats de cet ordre doivent participer aux frais de la Cour. Enfin, M. Hagerup remarque que le second alinéa couvre seulement les cas où des conflits ont été portés devant le Conseil de la Société des Nations. Dans cet ordre d'idées M. Hagerup attire l'attention sur la disposition de l'article 20 du projet des Cinq Puissances qui a tenu compte de la nécessité d'élargir la compétence et l'activité de la Cour.

En réponse à une objection du Président, M. Hagerup dit qu'il désire seulement éviter toute distinction entre les Etats mentionnés à l'Annexe au Pacte et les autres Etats qui ne sont pas Membres de la Société des Nations. Il laisse donc de côté l'article 17 du Pacte.

Le PRESIDENT émet la contre-proposition suivante:

„La Cour est accessible aux Membres de la Société des Nations et aux Etats mentionnés à l'Annexe au Pacte de cette Société. Les conditions sous lesquelles la Cour est accessible aux Etats qui ne sont pas Membres de la Société des Nations sont fixées par le Conseil de cette Société en conformité avec l'article 17 du Pacte."

LORD PHILLIMORE proposed that the method of enumeration should be used. As no agreement could be reached, the Committee, by a formal vote, decided not to add anything to Article 27, Para. 1.

Paragraph 1 was adopted.

M. ALTAMIRA voted against this Article, as the text, thus reduced, did not afford a sufficient guarantee that States would impartially support claims of private individuals.

Article 28.

M. HAGERUP proposed the following amendment (an addition to the original text):

"The conditions under which States which are not Members of the League of Nations shall have access to the Court shall be determined by the Council of the League of Nations."

In support of this amendment, M. Hagerup pointed out, firstly, that it was the task of the League of Nations, rather than of the Committee, to lay down conditions for admission to the Court. He went on to say that the first Paragraph of the Article seemed to take away from the League of Nations the right of fixing the conditions under which those States, mentioned in the Annex of the Covenant, but not yet Members of the League of Nations, should be admitted. Consequently, also, it deprives the League of the right of stipulating that States in this category must share in the expenses of the Court. Lastly, M. Hagerup said that the second Paragraph referred only to cases in which disputes had been taken to the Council of the League of Nations. In this connection, M. Hagerup called attention to the provisions of Article 20 of the Five Powers' Plan. which recognised the necessity for extending the jurisdiction and sphere of action of the Court.

In reply to an objection raised by the President, M. Hagerup said that he only wished to avoid any distinction between the States mentioned in the Annex to the Covenant and the other States which are not Members of the League of Nations. He therefore left Article 17 of the Covenant out of consideration.

The PRESIDENT made the following counter-proposal:

"The Court shall be open to the Members of the League of Nations, and to the States mentioned in the Annex to the Covenant of the League. The conditions under which the Court shall be accessible to States which are not Members of the League of Nations, shall be fixed by the Council of the League, in accordance with Article 17 of the Covenant."

M. de LAPRADELLE propose, d'accord avec Lord Phillimore, la nouvelle rédaction suivante:

„La Cour est ouverte aux Membres de la Société des Nations et aux Etats mentionnés à l'Annexe. Elle est accessible aux autres Etats aux conditions, fixées par le Conseil."

Le PRESIDENT distingue entre trois différentes catégories d'Etats:

1. les Membres de la Société des Nations;

2. les Etats mentionnés à l'Annexe au Pacte, qui ne sont pas encore Membres de la Société des Nations, mais qui peuvent le devenir à tout moment;

3. les autres Etats.

Il s'oppose formellement à l'omission de tout renvoi à l'article 17 du Pacte, dans le texte de l'article 28 du projet du Comité.

LORD PHILLIMORE, d'accord avec le Président, distingue deux classes, parmi les Etats qui ne sont pas Membres de la Société des Nations. La Cour est ouverte aux Membres de la Société sans aucune condition; elle est ouverte aux Etats qui ne sont pas Membres de la Société, mais qui sont mentionnés à l'Annexe au Pacte, ainsi qu'à tout autre Etat conditionnellement; mais les conditions ne doivent cependant pas être nécessairement les mêmes pour les Etats mentionnés à l'Annexe et pour les Etats qui n'y sont pas mentionnés. Pour les Etats appartenant à la première catégorie, la condition peut être limitée, par exemple, à la participation aux frais.

Lord Phillimore constate qu'il y a accord sur les principes qu'il vient d'exposer, c'est à dire:

1. La Cour est ouverte de droit aux Etats Membres de la Société des Nations;

2. La Cour est ouverte, sous conditions, aux Etats non Membres, cités à l'Annexe;

3. La Cour est accessible aux autres Etats, qui acceptent de se soumettre aux conditions fixées par la Société des Nations. Il propose qu'une rédaction soit préparée pour la séance prochaine.

M. ADATCI appelle l'attention sur la différence de traitement, prévue par le Traité de Versailles, entre diverses catégories d'Etats.

Après une discussion sur la question de savoir si le renvoi à l'article 17, proposé par le Président, doit être maintenu, ou s'il peut être omis, ainsi que cela a été proposé dans la formule de Lord

M. DE LAPRADELLE, in agreement with Lord Phillimore, proposed the following new wording:

"The Court shall be open to Members of the League of Nations, and to States mentioned in the Annex to the Covenant. Other States shall have access to it under the conditions laid down by the Council."

The PRESIDENT drew a distinction between three different classes of States:

1. Members of the League of Nations;

2. States mentioned in the Annex to the Covenant, who are not yet Members of the League of Nations, but which may become so at any time;

3. Other States.

He formally opposed the omission of any reference to Article 17 of the Covenant in the text of Article 28 of the Committee's project.

LORD PHILLIMORE, in agreement with the President, wished to distinguish between two classes of States not Members of the League of Nations. The Court would be open to Members of the League unconditionally, and it would be open to States, not Members of the League but mentioned in the Annex to the Covenant, and to all other States, on certain conditions. The conditions, however, would not necessarily be the same for States mentioned in the Annex and for those that were not. For States belonging to the former class, the conditions might, for instance, be limited to a share of the expenses.

Lord Phillimore stated that the Committee was agreed upon the principles he had just put forward, namely:

1. The Court shall be open of right to States which are Members of the League of Nations;

2. The Court shall be open of right, but subject to conditions, to States, not Members, but mentioned in the Annex;

3. The Court shall be accessible to other States, which agree to submit to conditions to be fixed by the League of Nations.

He proposed that a draft should be prepared for the next meeting.

M. ADATCI called attention to the different treatment accorded by the Treaty of Versailles to States in various categories.

After a discussion as to whether the reference to Article 17, proposed by the President, should be maintained, or could be omitted, as proposed by Lord Phillimore and M. de

Phillimore et de M. de Lapradelle, le PRESIDENT propose la formule transactionnelle suivante:

„.... tenant compte de l'article 17 du Pacte de la Société des Nations."

L'article, rédigé d'après le texte proposé par Lord Phillimore et M. de Lapradelle, avec l'addition que vient de proposer le Président, est adopté.

M. ADATCI se basant sur sa conception de l'interprétation qu'il faut donner à l'article 14 du Pacte, s'oppose à l'institution d'une juridiction obligatoire avec droit d'assignation unilatérale.

LORD PHILLIMORE et M. DE LAPRADELLE contestent ce point de vue.

M. RICCI-BUSATTI le partage dans une certaine mesure. En principe, il est partisan de la juridiction obligatoire, qui a été acceptée déjà par l'Italie dans certains traités d'arbitrage, mais il croit qu'il ne serait pas utile d'en parler dans le projet d'organisation de la Cour puisqu'elle ne ressort pas des dispositions du Pacte. Si l'on veut faire des propositions à ce sujet, il vaut mieux les faire séparément, pour ne pas mettre en danger le projet tout entier. Il maintient la proposition qu'il a soumise au Comité le 30 juin.

M. ADATCI propose l'amendement suivant:

„La Cour est compétente pour connaître des différends entre Etats, conformément à l'article 14 du Pacte de la Société des Nations."

Il ajoute qu'il défendra autant que possible cet amendement; mais qu'il se rallierait à l'idée exprimée par M. Ricci-Busatti, si l'amendement n'était pas accepté.

Le PRESIDENT propose l'addition suivante à l'alinéa 1: „et sauf acceptation par les parties d'une autre juridiction."

Cet amendement n'est pas adopté parce qu'il est considéré comme faisant double emploi avec l'article 1 qui exprime la même idée.

Le PRESIDENT propose la rédaction suivante de l'alinéa 1er:

„Entre Etats Membres de la Société des Nations, la Cour statue sans convention spéciale sur les différends d'ordre juridique, c'est à dire ceux qui ont pour objet...."

Cette formule est adoptée sauf suppression des mots „c'est à dire ceux".

Lapradelle in their wording, the PRESIDENT proposed the following draft as a compromise:

".... In accordance with Article 17 of the Covenant of the League of Nations."

The Article was adopted in the form proposed by Lord Phillimore and M. de Lapradelle, with the addition just proposed by the President.

M. ADATCI, in view of the interpretation which he put upon Article 14 of the Covenant, opposed the institution of a compulsory jurisdiction and the right of unilateral arraignment.

LORD PHILLIMORE and M. DE LAPRADELLE opposed this view.

M. RICCI-BUSATTI agreed with it to some extent. He was, as a rule, in favour of a compulsory jurisdiction; this had already been accepted by Italy in certain treaties of Arbitration; but he thought that it would not be advisable to mention it in the plan for the organisation of the Court, since it was included in the provisions of the Covenant. If it were desired to put forward proposals on this subject, it would be better to make them separately, so as not to endanger the whole plan. He still held to the proposal he had submitted on the 30th June.

M. ADATCI proposed the following amendment:

"The Court shall be competent to hear and determine disputes between States in accordance with the terms of Article 14 of the Covenant of the League of Nations."

He added that he would press for the acceptance of the amendment, but that he would support M. Ricci-Busatti's suggestion if the amendment were not accepted.

The PRESIDENT proposed the following addition to Paragraph 1: "and unless the parties agree to accept another jurisdiction."

This amendment was not adopted as this was thought to duplicate Article 1, which contained the same idea.

The PRESIDENT proposed the following wording for Paragraph 1:

"Between States which are Members of the League of Nations, the Court shall have jurisdiction (and this without any special convention giving it jurisdiction) to hear and determine cases of a legal nature, that is to say, cases concerning...."

This wording was adopted, except that the words: „that is to say, cases" were deleted.

M. RICCI-BUSATTI propose un amendement au premier alinéa:

„La Cour connaît également de tous différends, de quelque nature qu'ils soient, qui lui sont soumis par la convention, soit générale, soit spéciale, des parties."

Cet amendement est adopté.

Après l'adoption de l'article, M. ADATCI, dont l'amendement principal est rejeté, reprend la proposition de M. Ricci-Busatti concernant la disjonction du statut de la Cour de toute la question de la compétence de celle-ci.

Cette proposition est mise aux voix et rejetée.

M. DE LAPRADELLE propose de substituer dans le numéro 2 de l'article 29 les mots „dans les catégories ci-dessus visées" par les mots „dans sa compétence."

La proposition est rejetée. Il est expressément entendu que le no. 2 (alinéa 4) de l'article 29, doit rester tel qu'il est.

L'article est adopté avec les amendements signalés ci-dessus.

M. RICCI-BUSATTI vote contre; M. ALTAMIRA s'abstient considérant que le texte n'exprime pas assez nettement le concept juridique de justice obligatoire.

Article 30.

Le PRESIDENT a proposé la substitution du mot „engagement" au mot „convention" en adoptant la formule suivante:

„Si par un engagement les parties ont accepté cette compétence".

LORD PHILLIMORE, qui ne partage pas l'avis du Président, mais reconnaît le besoin d'une rédaction plus claire, propose un nouveau texte:

„Lorsqu'une partie dénie compétence à la Cour, il appartient à celle-ci de statuer sur ce point en ordre préjudiciel".

Ce texte n'est cependant pas adopté.

M. RICCI-BUSATTI fait valoir que la disposition de l'article 30 ne diffère pas, au fond, de celle du no. 2 de l'article 29.

Mr. ROOT s'oppose formellement à ce qu'une modification quelconque soit apportée au no. 2 de l'article 29.

M. DE LAPRADELLE, dans ces circonstances, retire l'article 30, et LORD PHILLIMORE en propose la suppression.

M. RICCI-BUSATTI proposed the following amendment to the first Paragraph:

"The Court shall also have jurisdiction to hear and determine all disputes of any kind, which may be submitted to it by a general or particular convention between the parties."

This amendment was adopted.

After the adoption of the Article, M. ADATCI, whose principal amendment had been rejected, again took up the proposal made by M. Ricci-Busatti, to omit the whole question of competence from the Statute of the Court.

This proposal was put to a vote, and rejected.

M. DE LAPRADELLE proposed to substitute the words: "within its competence" for the words: "within any of the categories above mentioned," in Paragraph 2 of Article 29.

The proposal was rejected. It was expressly agreed that Number 2 (Paragraph 4) of Article 29 should remain as it was.

The Article was adopted with the amendments mentioned above.

M. RICCI-BUSATTI voted against this Article. M. ALTAMIRA abstained from voting, as he considered that the text did not express the legal conception of compulsory jurisdiction with sufficient clearness.

Article 30.

The PRESIDENT proposed the substitution of the word "obligation" for the word "convention" by the adoption of the following formula:

"Whether the parties have bound themselves by an obligation to accept its jurisdiction."

LORD PHILLIMORE did not share the President's opinion, but recognising the need for a clearer wording, proposed the following:

"Should a party dispute the jurisdiction of the Court, the latter shall determine this point before proceeding with the case."

This wording, however, was not adopted.

M. RICCI-BUSATTI pointed out that Article 30 did not fundamentally differ from No. 2 of Article 29.

Mr. ROOT formally opposed any alteration of No. 2 of Article 29.

M. DE LAPRADELLE, in these circumstances, withdrew Article 30, and LORD PHILLIMORE proposed that it should be deleted.

Sur la proposition du PRESIDENT, et dans l'intention expresse de permettre aux membres de se rendre compte si l'article est vraiment inutile, il est réservé.

On the proposal of the President, and with the object of allowing members to consider whether the Article was really useless, it was reserved.

Article 31.

Le PRESIDENT propose l'addition suivante au no. 4:

„Comme moyens auxiliaires de la détermination des règles de droit".

LORD PHILLIMORE présente quelques objections à la rédaction actuelle du numéro. Il fait valoir que les décisions judiciaires constatent, mais ne créent pas le droit.

M. RICCI-BUSATTI s'oppose à la différence d'expression qu'il note entre les numéros 1 et 2 en ce qui concerne la portée de la règle; la coutume, comme toute convention, qu'il s'agit d'appliquer, doit être en vigueur entre les parties en cause; il maintient les autres objections qu'il a déjà formulées contre la rédaction originaire de l'article.

M. DE LAPRADELLE déclare qu'il est opposé à toute modification des numéros 1—3, tandis qu'il désire la suppression totale du numéro 4. On ne peut pas fixer la source de droit visée sous ce numéro, d'une manière distincte: il n'est pas possible d'appliquer les lois, la coutume, les principes généraux du droit sans avoir recours à la jurisprudence et à la doctrine.

L'article est adopté.

M. DE LAPRADELLE vote contre le numéro 4.

Article 31.

The PRESIDENT proposed the following addition to Number 4:

"As subsidiary means for the determination of rules of law."

LORD PHILLIMORE put forward some objections to the present wording of this item. He pointed out that judicial decisions state, but do not create, law.

M. RICCI-BUSATTI opposed the different methods of expression used in Numbers 1 and 2; with reference to the scope of the application of the rules. Custom, like any convention applicable to a case, must be in force between the parties in dispute. He also maintained the other objections, which he had already expressed, to the original draft of the article.

M. DE LAPRADELLE stated that he was opposed to any modification of Numbers 1 to 3, but that he wished Number 4 to be deleted. The source of law referred to under this heading could not be clearly defined. Laws, customs, and general principles of law could not be applied without reference to jurisprudence and teaching.

The Article was adopted.

M. DE LAPRADELLE voted against the fourth heading.

Article 32.

M. DE LAPRADELLE explique la différence entre un différend et un point soumis à la Cour pour avis; tandis qu'un différend est un conflit actuel, un point est plutôt une question théorique. Cette différence entraîne la nécessité d'une solution différente dans les deux cas. Un point peut être examiné par un nombre restreint de juges, tandis qu'un différend doit être examiné selon une procédure qui se rapproche de celle qui doit être suivie pour un jugement.

Mr. ROOT s'élève contre le droit qu'aurait la Cour de donner des avis consultatifs à l'occasion d'un conflit actuellement né, ce qui lui paraît être une violation de toute convenance juridique.

Article 32.

M. DE LAPRADELLE explained the difference between a dispute and a point submitted to the Court for an advisory opinion; whereas the former was a practical case, the latter was more in the nature of a theoretical question. This difference made it necessary to adopt a different method of solution in the two cases. A point of law might be considered by a limited number of judges, whereas a dispute must be dealt with by a procedure more nearly resembling a trial.

Mr. ROOT was opposed to the Court's having the right to give an advisory opinion with reference to an existing dispute. In his opinion this was a violation of all juridical principles.

M. DE LAPRADELLE attire son attention sur les dispositions de l'article 13 du Pacte et sur le droit qu'a le Conseil de renvoyer à la Cour un conflit qui lui a été soumis, mais qui aurait dû être tranché judiciairement, et sur la nécessité pour la Cour de procéder, dans ces circonstances, comme s'il s'agissait d'un véritable jugement.

Mr. ROOT se déclare convaincu par ces arguments.

La séance est levée à 11 heures du soir.

Le Président:
(signé) Brn. DESCAMPS.

Le Secrétaire-Général:
(signé) D. ANZILOTTI.

M. DE LAPRADELLE called his attention to the provisions of Article 13 of the Covenant and to the right of the Council to send to the Court any case which had been submitted to it but which ought to have been settled by judicial means; in such circumstances the Court must adopt a procedure similar to that of an actual trial.

Mr. ROOT stated that he was convinced by these arguments.

The meeting closed at 11 p. m.

The President:
(signed) Brn. DESCAMPS.

The Secretary-General:
(signed) D. ANZILOTTI.

28IÈME SÉANCE (non-publique), tenue au Palais de la Paix, à La Haye, le 20 juillet 1920.

Présidence de M. le BARON DESCAMPS.

Sont présents: tous les membres du Comité (à l'exception de M. Bevilaqua); M. Fernandes; Mr. James Brown Scott; les secrétaires particuliers de M. le Baron Descamps et de M. Adatci; les membres du Secrétariat.

La séance est ouverte à 9.40 heures du matin.

Le PRESIDENT, constatant que le Secrétariat a déjà fait distribuer les trois compte-rendus des séances de la veille, lui adresse les remerciements du Comité (Annexe No. 1); il déclare que, ce faisant, le Secrétariat a accompli un véritable tour de force. (Applaudissements).

On passe à la discussion du Chapitre III (procédure) du texte soumis par le Comité de Rédaction.

Article 1er.

Cet article est adopté sans discussion.

Article 2.

LORD PHILLIMORE attire l'attention sur l'article 23 du chapitre III et soulève la question du droit d'intervention. Il croit que l'alinéa 4 est inutile si ce droit n'est pas admis dans une mesure plus large que cela n'a été fait dans l'article 23, qui parle seulement de traités généraux.

Le PRESIDENT et M. DE LAPRADELLE font valoir que l'alinéa a deux autres buts:

1. notification pour autres fins que l'intervention;

2. tenir lieu de stipulation concernant la publicité.

M. FERNANDES propose la formule suivante:

„Le droit d'intervention est reconnu aux Etats ayant un intérêt légitime, soit d'assister une des parties en cause, en raison d'un droit conjoint,

28TH MEETING (Private), held at the Peace Palace, the Hague, on July 20th, 1920.

BARON DESCAMPS in the chair.

Present: all the members of the Committee (except M. Bevilaqua); M. Fernandes; Mr. James Brown Scott; the private secretaries of Baron Descamps and M. Adatci; the members of the Secretariat.

The meeting opened at 9.40 a.m.

The PRESIDENT stated that the Secretariat had already distributed the three summaries of the meetings of the previous day, and expressed the thanks of the Committee (Annex No. 1). He said that the Secretariat had really achieved the impossible. (Applause).

The Committee then proceeded to discuss Chapter III (Procedure) of the text submitted by the Drafting Committee.

Article 1.

This Article was adopted without discussion.

Article 2.

LORD PHILLIMORE called attention to Article 23 of Chapter III, and raised the question of the right of intervention. He thought that Paragraph 4 would be useless if this right were not conceded to a wider extent than had been done in Article 23, which only mentioned general treaties.

The PRESIDENT and M. DE LAPRADELLE pointed out that the Paragraph had two other objects:

1. Notification for purposes other than intervention;

2. To take the place of a provision regulating publicity.

M. FERNANDES proposed the following wording:

"The right of intervention is granted to States having a legitimate interest, either to assist one of

soit d'exclure le demandeur ou le défendeur. Dans le premier cas, l'intervenant agira dans les mêmes délais accordés à la partie assistée. Dans le second cas, l'opposition sera formée dans les délais et selon les formes déterminées par la Cour."

M. HAGERUP de son côté a proposé la formule de l'article 21 du projet des trois pays Scandinaves, qui ne limite pas le droit d'être notifié et le droit d'intervention aux Membres de la Société des Nations.

L'article est adopté.

Article 2 bis.

M. FERNANDES voudrait voir appuyer les mesures conservatoires par des sanctions efficaces, tout en laissant à la Cour l'appréciation des limites imposées par les circonstances à la portée de ces sanctions, selon le texte de l'amendement qu'il a présenté et qui a été distribué aux membres du Comité. (Voir annexe 2).

MM. ROOT, ADATCI, DE LAPRADELLE et LORD PHILLIMORE s'opposent à cette idée qui leur semble imprudente.

Sur la proposition de M. de LAPRADELLE la rédaction suivante du second alinéa est adoptée.

„En attendant l'arrêt, l'indication de ces mesures est immédiatement transmise aux parties et au Conseil".

L'article est adopté, avec des modifications rédactionnelles.

Article 3.

Cet article est adopté avec des modifications de rédaction.

Article 4.

Cet article est adopté sans discussion.

Article 5.

Cet article est adopté avec des modifications de rédaction.

Article 6.

Il est décidé que le premier alinéa formera seul l'article 6. Les deux autres alinéas seront insérés à un endroit à déterminer.

M. FERNANDES signale que le projet adopte un système différent pour les notifications qui devront être faites dans le pays où est établi le siège de la

the contesting parties, by reason of a joint right, or to debar the plaintiff or the defendant. In the former case, the intervening party shall conform to the same time-limits as those fixed for the party which it is assisting. In the latter case, the opposition shall be formulated within the times and according to the forms laid down by the Court."

M. HAGERUP, for his part, proposed the wording of Article 21 of the plan of the three Scandinavian countries, according to which the right to receive notification and the right of intervention were not limited to Members of the League of Nations.

The Article was adopted.

Article 2 bis.

M. FERNANDES wished the provisional measures to be supported by effective penalties, though it should be left to the Court to decide the extent to which the penalties should be imposed in the particular instances, as provided in the amendment which he had submitted and which had been distributed to the members of the Committee. (See annex 2).

MM. ROOT, ADATCI, DE LAPRADELLE and LORD PHILLIMORE were opposed to this, as they thought it would be unwise.

At M. DE LAPRADELLE's proposal, the following wording for the second Paragraph was adopted:

"Pending the final decision, notice of these measures shall forthwith be given to the parties and to the Council."

The Article was adopted with some modifications in the wording.

Article 3.

This Article was adopted with modifications in the wording.

Article 4.

This Article was adopted without discussion.

Article 5.

This Article was adopted with modifications in the wording.

Article 6.

It was decided that the first Paragraph alone should form Article 6. The other two Paragraphs would be inserted in a position to be settled later.

M. FERNANDES pointed out that the project adopted a different system for the service of notices in the country in which the seat of the

Cour, et pour celles qui devront être faites dans d'autres pays; cela lui paraît être inadmissible dans plusieurs cas.

Il est reconnu que tous les Etats doivent être placés sur un pied d'égalité à cet égard. Dans cet ordre d'idées on suggère de biffer les mots „en dehors du pays où est le siège", tandis que Mr. ROOT attire l'attention sur l'article 25 de la Convention de 1907, et M. HAGERUP sur les dispositions du projet des trois pays Scandinaves et de celui des cinq Puissances neutres.

M. DE LAPRADELLE, fait valoir que le cas ne peut présenter d'intérêt actuel que s'il s'agit de notifications à faire à des personnes qui ne sont pas directement ou indirectement en contact avec la Cour; il propose la rédaction suivante:

„Pour toute notification à faire aux témoins et aux experts, la Cour s'adresse directement au Gouvernement de l'Etat sur le territoire duquel la notification doit produire effet."

L'amendement est adopté, mais après avoir été légèrement modifié: les mots „à d'autres personnes que les agents, conseils et avocats" sont substitués aux mots „aux témoins et aux experts".

L'article est adopté avec cet amendement.

Article 7.

Cet article est adopté avec des modifications de rédaction.

Article 8.

Cet article est adopté avec des modifications de rédaction.

Article 9.

Cet article est adopté sans discussion.

Article 10.

Cet article est adopté avec des modifications de rédaction.

Article 11.

M. ADATCI propose d'ajouter à l'article la phrase suivante:

„Elle peut également requérir l'avis des comités techniques constitués par le Conseil de la Société des Nations, lorsqu'il s'agit de questions qui rentrent par leur nature dans le ressort de leur compétence spéciale."

Cet amendement est rejeté, mais, en s'en inspirant, le PRESIDENT propose l'insertion après le mot „personnes" des mots „corps ou organes".

Court was established, and in other countries; in his opinion, this was inadmissible in many cases.

It was admitted that all States must be treated alike in this respect. In this connection, it was proposed to delete the words "outside the country in which the Court has its seat", while Mr. ROOT called attention to Article 25 of the Convention of 1907, and M. HAGERUP to the provisions of the plan of the three Scandinavian countries, and of that of the five Neutral Powers.

M. DE LAPRADELLE pointed out that the question would only be of importance in connection with the service of notices upon persons, who were not, either directly or indirectly, in permanent contact with the Court, and proposed the following wording:

"For the service of all notices upon witnesses and experts, the Court shall apply directly to the Government of the State upon whose territory the notice has to be served."

The amendment was adopted, except that the words "upon witnesses and experts" were replaced by the words: "upon persons other than the agents, counsel, and advocates."

The Article was adopted with this amendment.

Article 7.

This Article was adopted with modifications in wording.

Article 8.

This Article was adopted with modifications in wording.

Article 9.

This Article was adopted without discussion.

Article 10.

This Article was adopted with modifications in wording.

Article 11.

M. ADATCI proposed the addition of the following sentence:

"It may also consult the technical bodies constituted by the Council of the League of Nations, upon questions of such a nature as to come within their special competence."

This amendment was rejected, but, borrowing an idea contained in it, the PRESIDENT proposed that the words: "bodies or organisations" should be inserted after the word "individuals".

LORD PHILLIMORE veut ajouter le mot „bureaux".

Sur la proposition de M. DE LAPRADELLE l'insertion de la formule „corps, bureaux, commissions ou organes" est adoptée.

L'article ainsi modifié est adopté.

Article 12.

Cet article est adopté avec des modifications de rédaction.

Article 13.

Cet article est adopté sans discussion.

Article 14.

Cet article est adopté sans discussion.

Article 15.

M. HAGERUP fait valoir que l'hypothèse du no. 1 est l'une de celles qui sont visées par le no. 2; le no. 1 devrait par conséquent, être supprimé.

On reconnaît le bien-fondé de cette observation.

Le PRESIDENT propose la formule suivante, destinée à remplacer l'alinéa 2:

„La Cour a toute liberté pour les accueillir après s'être assurée que ces conclusions sont suffisamment fondées en fait et en droit."

M. DE LAPRADELLE appuie la suppression du no. 1.

LORD PHILLIMORE propose une formule de transaction qui est amendée par M. de Lapradelle de la façon suivante: „La Cour fait droit à la condition de s'être assurée que ces conclusions, reposant sur des preuves sérieuses, sont fondées en fait et en droit."

M. RICCI-BUSATTI fait valoir que l'article est parfaitement inutile si les pouvoirs de la Cour restent absolument les mêmes lorsqu'il s'agit de rendre un jugement par défaut. Une disposition expresse à ce sujet ne se justifierait que si l'on avait l'intention de limiter ces pouvoirs dans l'intérêt du demandeur et pour punir la partie adverse de sa négligence. Mais une telle prétention n'étant pas admise dans les rapports entre Etats, il propose la suppression de l'article.

Mr. ROOT maintient, premièrement, la nécessité des jugements par contumace, et, deuxièmement, la nécessité que ces jugements soient bien motivés.

LORD PHILLIMORE wished to add the word "bureaux."

On M. DE LAPRADELLE's proposal, the expression "bodies, bureaux, commissions or organisations" was adopted.

The Article was adopted with this modification.

Article 12.

This Article was adopted with modifications in wording.

Article 13.

This Article was adopted without discussion.

Article 14.

This Article was adopted without discussion.

Article 15.

M. HAGERUP pointed out that the hypothesis contained in number 1, was covered by number 2; therefore, number 1 should be eliminated. The justice of this contention was admitted.

The PRESIDENT proposed the following wording, to replace Paragraph 2:

"The Court shall be free to decide accordingly, provided that it has satisfied itself, that the claim is well-founded in fact and law."

M. DE LAPRADELLE supported the deletion of Number 1.

LORD PHILLIMORE proposed a compromises which was amended by M. de Lapradelle at follows: "The Court shall do so provided tha- it is satisfied that the claim is supported by con, clusive evidence and well-founded in fact and law."

M. RICCI-BUSATTI pointed out that the Article was quite useless if the powers of the Court were to be exactly the same even in case of judgment by default. The inclusion of a special provision on this point would be justified only if the intention were to limit these powers in the interests of the plaintiff and in order to punish the other party for its negligence. But, as such a provision does not apply to international affairs, he proposed the suppression of the Article.

Mr. ROOT maintained, firstly, that judgments by default were necessary, and secondly, that such judgments must contain a full statement of reasons.

M. DE LAPRADELLE soumet la nouvelle formule suivante:

„La Cour, avant d'y faire droit, doit s'assurer que ses conclusions, reposant sur des preuves sérieuses, sont fondées en fait et en droit.".

Le PRESIDENT veut ajouter à cette formule, entre les mots „sont" et „fondées", le mot „suffisamment".

Cette proposition est mise aux voix et rejetée.

La formule de M. de Lapradelle est adoptée.

M. RICCI-BUSATTI vote contre.

Article 16.

Cet article est adopté avec des modifications de rédaction.

Article 17.

Cet article est adopté avec des modifications de rédaction.

Article 18.

Cet article est adopté sans discussion.

Article 19.

Le PRESIDENT propose la formule suivante destinée à remplacer la dernière partie du premier alinéa:

„Les dissidents ont la faculté de demander que leurs oppositions ou leurs réserves soient constatées."

Sur la proposition de M. DE LAPRADELLE un vote préalable est pris sur les deux questions suivantes:

1. Le juge peut-il marquer son dissentiment sur le dispositif seulement? Le résultat du vote sur cette question est affirmatif.

2. Le juge peut-il marquer son dissentiment sur les motifs? Le résultat du vote sur cette question est négatif.

Le PRESIDENT propose l'addition suivante: „sans pouvoir être motivées" à la formule qu'il a soumise.

Avec cette formule l'alinéa 1 de l'article 19 est adopté, malgré l'abstention de M. DE LAPRADELLE; celui-ci déclare que, n'ayant pas pu saisir la proposition, il doit s'abstenir.

Au sujet de l'alinéa 2, M. DE LAPRADELLE appuyé par M. Fernandes exprime le désir

M. DE LAPRADELLE submitted the following wording:

"The Court must, before doing so, satisfy itself that the claim is supported by conclusive evidence and well-founded in fact and law."

The PRESIDENT wished to add the word "sufficiently" to the expression "well-founded".

This proposal was rejected by a vote.

The Article was adopted with M. de Lapradelle's wording.

M. RICCI-BUSATTI voted against it.

Article 16.

This Article was adopted with amendments in wording.

Article 17.

This Article was adopted with amendments in wording.

Article 18.

This Article was adopted without discussion.

Article 19.

The PRESIDENT proposed the following wording, to replace the last part of the first Paragraph:

"Dissenting judges shall be entitled to have the fact of their dissent or reservations mentioned."

On M. DE LAPRADELLE's proposal, a preliminary vote was taken upon the following questions:

1. Should the judge have the right to record the fact of his dissent only? This question was decided in the affirmative.

2. Should the judge be entitled to give his reasons for dissent? This question was decided in the negative.

The PRESIDENT proposed the following addition to the wording proposed by him: "The reasons for dissent or reservations shall not be expressed."

With this wording Paragraph 1 of Article 19 was adopted. M. DE LAPRADELLE abstained from voting, saying that, as he had not understood the proposal, he was bound to do so.

In connection with Paragraph 2., M. DE LAPRADELLE, supported by M. Fernandes, wished to

que l'on n'étende pas aux juges nationaux le droit de marquer leur dissentiment, afin de leur garantir une plus grande indépendance envers leur pays.

LORD PHILLIMORE et Mr. ROOT s'opposent à cette idée. La question de savoir si les juges nationaux doivent pouvoir marquer leur dissidence est mise aux voix. En conséquence du résultat du vote, l'alinéa 2 est supprimé.

L'alinéa 1er de l'article est adopté.

Article 20.

Cet article est adopté sans modifications.

Article 21.

Cet article est approuvé sans discussion.

Article 22.

M. FERNANDES demande s'il n'y aurait pas lieu de déterminer la nature du fait nouveau en indiquant qu'il ne pouvait pas être connu par la partie en question. Le bien-fondé de cette observation est entièrement admis.

Dans cet ordre d'idées, LORD PHILLIMORE propose l'insertion d'une formule qui réponde à l'expression anglaise „due diligence".

M. DE LAPRADELLE propose la formule suivante:

„Et que, même en faisant toute diligence, la partie ne pouvait connaître..."

La rédaction de l'alinéa est réservée.

Les alinéas 2, 3 et 4 sont mis au vote et adoptés. L'alinéa 1er est adopté en principe.

Article 23.

LORD PHILLIMORE expose l'institution de l'intervention dans le droit anglais. Il souligne particulièrement le fait qu'en Angleterre un intervenant peut s'associer seulement à la partie défenderesse.

M. LODER donne des explications sur la même institution telle qu'elle existe dans le droit néerlandais: ce droit reconnaît l'intervention à côté du demandeur aussi bien que l'intervention à côté du défendeur.

Le PRESIDENT explique comment le droit d'intervention au cas où il s'agit d'une Convention

debar national judges from the right of recording their dissent; the object of this was to afford them a greater measure of independence with regard to their own country.

LORD PHILLIMORE and Mr. ROOT opposed this. The question as to whether national judges should have the right to record their dissent was put to the vote. As a result of this vote, Paragraph 2 was eliminated.

The first Paragraph 2 of the Article was adopted.

Article 20.

This Article was adopted without alteration.

Article 21.

This Article was adopted without discussion.

Article 22.

M. FERNANDES thought that it should be tated that the new fact must be of such a nature hat the party in question could not have knowedge of it. The justice of this was fully recognised.

In this connection, LORD PHILLIMORE proposed the insertion of an expression corresponding to the English expression "due diligence."

M. DE LAPRADELLE proposed the following wording:

"And that, even by the use of due diligence, the party could not have knowledge of..."

The wording of the Paragraph was reserved.

Paragraphs 2, 3 and 4 were put to the vote and adopted. Paragraph 1 was adopted in principle.

Article 23.

LORD PHILLIMORE explained the right of intervention as existing in English Law. He emphasised, in particular, the fact, that in England, an intervening party could only associate itself with the defendant.

M. LODER gave an explanation of the same institution as it existed in Dutch Law. This admits of intervention both on the side of the plaintiff and of the defendant.

The PRESIDENT explained that the right of intervention in a case concerning a general Con-

générale constitue une extension de la notion de chose jugée. En effet, il est nécessaire de distinguer entre l'intervention du chef d'un intérêt né et l'intervention en raison d'un intérêt exclusivement virtuel.

M. HAGERUP déclare qu'il trouve le texte de l'art. 23 acceptable mais incomplet. Il faudrait y faire une addition qui pourrait être formulée en ces termes:

„Chacun des Etats signataires a la faculté d'intervenir au procès et, s'il exerce cette faculté, il devient partie au litige au point de vue de la chose jugée. Il en est de même de tout Etat dont les intérêts sont touchés par le procès."

M. LODER propose, dans le même ordre d'idées, l'article 48 du projet des Cinq Puissances.

LORD PHILLIMORE suggère la formule suivante:

„Lorsqu'un Etat tiers pense qu'un différend soumis à la Cour touche ses intérêts, cet Etat peut former une requête aux fins d'admission à l'intervention; et la Cour, si bon lui semble, y fera droit."

M. FERNANDES se trouve quant au fond d'accord avec Lord Phillimore, mais il voudrait qu'on fît dépendre le droit d'intervention de certaines conditions: par exemple, il faudrait indiquer que les intérêts en jeu doivent être des intérêts légitimes.

Le PRESIDENT croit que la solution de la question de l'intervention doit être empruntée au droit commun; il propose un texte basé sur cette thèse:

„Lorsqu'un Etat estime que, dans un différend, il peut être porté atteinte à ses droits, cet Etat peut adresser à la Cour une requête aux fins d'intervention, et la Cour peut y donner satisfaction ..."

M. ADATCI propose d'amender le texte proposé par M. Loder en y remplaçant le mot „droit" par le mot „intérêt".

M. DE LAPRADELLE demande si la Cour, dans sa composition normale, sera compétente pour connaître du cas des tiers intervenants, bien que ceux-ci ne soient pas représentés à la Cour par un de leurs nationaux.

On est d'accord pour laisser cette question ouverte.

Le PRESIDENT propose la nouvelle formule suivante:

vention amounted to an extension of the principle of *res judicata.* A distinction must be drawn between intervention based upon an existing interest, and intervention for a purely potential reason.

M. HAGERUP said he thought the wording of Article 23 was satisfactory as far as it went, but that it was incomplete. An addition was necessary, which might be worded as follows:

"Every signatory State shall have the right to intervene in the proceedings. If it exercises this right, it shall become a party to the case in so far as the *res judicata* is concerned. The same shall apply to any State whose interests are affected by the case."

M. LODER suggested Article 48 of the Five Powers' plan in the same connection.

LORD PHILLIMORE suggested the following wording:

"Should a third State consider that a dispute submitted to the Court affects its interests, it may request to be allowed to intervene; the Court shall grant permission if it thinks fit."

M. FERNANDES agreed with Lord Phillimore on principle, but wished to make the right of intervention dependent upon certain conditions; for instance, it should be stated that the interests affected must be legitimate interests.

The PRESIDENT thought that the solution of the question of intervention should be drawn from common law. He proposed a wording based on this idea:

"Should a State consider that its rights may be affected by a dispute, it may request the Court to grant it permission to intervene, and the Court shall accord such permission ..."

M. ADATCI suggested to amend the wording proposed by M. Loder, by replacing the word "right" by the word "interest."

M. DE LAPRADELLE wished to know whether the Court, with its normal composition, would be competent to hear the suits of third parties, supposing that the latter were not represented on the Court by a judge of their nationality.

It was agreed to leave this question open.

The PRESIDENT proposed to following new wording:

„Lorsqu'un Etat estime que dans un différend un intérêt d'ordre juridique le concernant est en cause, il peut adresser à la Cour une requête, à fin d'intervention. La Cour décide."

La formule du Président est adoptée sauf rédaction. Elle formera un article à part à insérer avant l'art. 23 originaire.

Ce dernier article est adopté sous la forme suivante empruntée à M. Asser et inspirée par l'article 84, de la Convention de 1907:

„Lorsqu'il s'agit de l'interprétation d'une Convention à laquelle ont participé d'autres Etats que les parties en litige, le greffe avertit sans délai tous les signataires.

Chacun d'eux a le droit d'intervenir au procès et s'il exerce cette faculté, l'interprétation contenue dans la sentence est également obligatoire à son égard."

M. HAGERUP s'est opposé à l'expression „au point de vue de la chose jugée" dans la rédaction originaire de l'article 23.

Article 24.

Cet article est adopté sans discussion.

M. LODER attire l'attention sur l'aperçu des questions laissées encore ouvertes par le Comité et qui ont été soumises par le Secrétariat; (voir annexe au procès-verbal du 19 juillet, matin; 25e séance).

Il croit que le Comité doit discuter au moins le point qui traite de l'établissement pour la Cour d'une compétence en matière de droit international privé.

Le PRESIDENT fait valoir les grandes difficultés de ce problème et recommande qu'on s'abstienne de l'aborder. Les membres du Comité se rangent à l'avis du Président.

La séance est levée à 12.40 heures de l'après-midi.

Le Président:
(signé) Brn. DESCAMPS.

Le Secrétaire-Général:
(signé) D. ANZILOTTI.

"Should a State consider that it has an interest of a legal nature, which may be affected by the decision in the case, it may submit a request to the Court to be permitted to intervene. It will be for the Court to decide upon this request."

The President's formula was adopted, subject to amendments in wording. It would be a separate article to be inserted before the original Article 23.

The latter Article was adopted in the following terms, borrowed from M. Asser and based on Article 84 of the Convention of 1907:

"Whenever the construction of a Convention to which States other than those concerned in the case are parties is in question, the Registrar shall notify all such States forthwith."

Every State so notified has the right to intervene in the proceedings; but if it uses this right, the construction given by the judgment shall be as binding upon it as upon the original parties to the dispute."

M. HAGERUP objected to the expression "will take force of *res judicata*" (au point de vue de la chose jugée) in the original wording of Article 23.

Article 24.

This article was adopted without discussion.

M. LODER called attention to the summary of questions still left open by the Committee, submitted by the Secretariat; (see Annex to the Procès-Verbal of the morning of July 19th; 25th meeting).

He thought that the Committee should, at any rate, discuss the question of granting the Court a Jurisdiction in private International Law.

The PRESIDENT pointed out the great difficulty of this problem and recommended that they should not deal with it. The members of the Committee agreed with the President.

The meeting closed at 12.40 p. m.

The President:
(signed) Brn. DESCAMPS.

The Secretary-General:
(signed) D. ANZILOTTI.

ANNEXE No. 1.

LA COUR PERMANENTE DE JUSTICE INTERNATIONALE.*)

(Texte revisé du Comité de Rédaction, avec, en regard, compte-rendu des délibérations du Comité du 19 juillet.)

Article 1er.

Adopté.

M. RICCI-BUSATTI demande que le mot „directement" soit expliqué dans le rapport.

Indépendamment de la Cour d'Arbitrage, organisée par les Conventions de la Haye de 1899 et 1907, et des Tribunaux spéciaux d'Arbitres, auxquels les Etats demeurent toujours libres de confier la solution de leurs différends, il est institué, conformément à l'Article 14 du Pacte de la Société des Nations, une Cour Permanente de Justice Internationale, directement accessible aux parties.

CHAPITRE I.

Organisation de la Cour.

Article 2.

Réservé.

Mr. ROOT proposera de nouveau, lorsque la discussion de l'article sera reprise, l'adoption de la rédaction Renault.

Article 3.

Adopté (avec des additions rédactionnelles).

La Cour se compose de quinze membres: onze juges titulaires et quatre juges suppléants. Le nombre des juges titulaires et des juges suppléants peut être éventuellement augmenté par l'Assemblée, sur la proposition du Conseil de Société des Nations, à concurrence de quinze juges titulaires et six juges suppléants.

Article 4.

Adopté (avec des modifications rédactionnelles.)

Toutefois les deux questions suivantes sont réservées:

1. La question des juges élus pour remplacer un juge sorti, décédé, etc.

2. La question de savoir à quel moment commence à courir la période pour laquelle un juge est élu.

Il a été proposé de transférer l'article 4, alinéas 2 et 3, après l'article 12.

Les membres de la Cour sont élus pour neuf ans.

Ils sont rééligibles.

Ils restent en fonction jusqu'à leur remplacement. Après ce remplacement, ils continuent de connaître des affaires dont ils sont déjà saisis.

*) Le présent document a été distribué seulement en français; il en est de même pour les documents altérieurs du même ordre.

Article 5.

Réservé.

M. HAGERUP a proposé une addition, renvoyant aux articles 6 et suivants. (Présentation, etc.)

M. DE LAPRADELLE a proposé la combination de l'article 4, alinéa 1, avec l'article 5, dans la rédaction suivante:

„Les membres de la Cour sont élus pour neuf ans par l'Assemblée et par le Conseil".

LORD PHILLIMORE se rallie aux idées de M. Hagerup et de M. de Lapradelle, et propose la rédaction suivante:

„Les membres de la Cour sont élus par l'Assemblée et par le Conseil de la manière suivante."

Le PRESIDENT a proposé la rédaction suivante:

„Les membres de la Cour sont élus par l'Assemblée et par le Conseil sur une liste de personnes présentée par les groupes nationaux de la Cour d'Arbitrage."

M. DE LAPRADELLE propose encore cette rédaction transactionnelle:

„Les membres de la Cour sont élus pour neuf ans de la manière suivante."

Article 6.

Réservé, sauf l'alinéa 1er qui est adopté.

M. RICCI-BUSATTI pose la question de savoir si les membres non-nationaux pour un certain pays de la Cour Permanente d'Arbitrage sont visés par le texte.

Mr. ROOT est d'avis que la manière de désigner les Etats qui sont autorisés à faire la présentation n'est pas assez large, d'autres Etats que ceux mentionnés à l'Annexe du Pacte devant être invités. LORD PHILLIMORE propose, d'accord avec Mr. ROOT, la rédaction suivante:

"all who shall hereafter join the League."

M. RICCI BUSATTI propose la formule suivante:

„Chacun des Etats faisant partie de la Société des Nations, ou mentionnés à l'Annexe du Pacte."

Article 7.

Adopté.

L'expression „à la majorité des voix" doit être biffée.

L'expression „Groupes nationaux" doit être rem-

Avant de procéder à cette désignation il est recommandé à chaque groupe national de consulter la plus Haute Cour de Justice, les Facultés de Droit des Universités, et les Académies ou sections

:e pour s'accorder avec la rédaction future de cle 6, réservé.

d'Académies nationales ou internationales, vouées à l'étude du droit.

Article 8.

éservé.

Ir. ROOT préfère la rédaction de l'article 7 projet Root-Phillimore.

. RICCI-BUSATTI voudrait renvoyer la ma- traitée dans cet article au règlement de la Cour. n est d'accord, sur la proposition de HAGERUP, d'ajouter au premier alinéa de icle un renvoi à l'article 11, alinéa 2.

A cet égard, M. DE LAPRADELLE propose la rédaction suivante:

...éligible „sauf l'exception prévue à l'article 11, paragraphe 2".

Article 9.

L'alinéa 1 est adopté dans la rédaction suivante, proposée par M. DE LAPRADELLE:

„L'assemblée et le Conseil procèdent, indépendamment l'une de l'autre, à l'élection, d'abord des „juges titulaires, ensuite des juges suppléants."

Cet alinéa formera un nouvel article 9.

Alinéa 2 adopté comme article 9 bis.

Alinéa 3 adopté comme article 9 ter, 1er alinéa.

Alinéa 4 adopté avec des modifications de rédaction, comme article 9 ter, 2e alinéa.

L'Assemblée et le Conseil procèdent, indépendamment l'une de l'autre, à l'élection, d'abord des juges titulaires, ensuite des juges suppléants.

Article 9 bis.

Dans toute élection, les électeurs veillent à ce que les personnes appelées à faire partie de la Cour, non seulement réunissent individuellement les conditions requises, mais assurent dans l'ensemble la représentation des grandes formes de civilisation et des principaux systèmes juridiques du monde.

Article 9 ter.

Sont élus ceux qui ont réuni la majorité absolue des voix dans l'Assemblée et dans le Conseil.

Au cas où le double scrutin de l'Assemblée et du Conseil se porterait sur plus d'un membre de la même nationalité, le plus âgé est seul élu.

Article 10.

Adopté.

Sur la proposition de LORD PHILLIMORE le mot „scrutin" est substitué par le mot „élection".

Si après la première élection il reste encore des sièges à pourvoir, il est procédé de la même manière à une seconde élection, puis à une troisième.

Article 11.

Alinéa 1er réservé.

M. ADATCI s'oppose à l'adoption dans l'alinéa d'un nombre limité d'élections.

M. FERNANDES fait valoir que le Conseil et l'Assemblée n'auront pas à choisir dans une liste proposée par le comité de médiation, mais à adopter ou rejeter une proposition faite par le comité.

Alinéa 2. Peuvent être portées sur cette liste, à l'unanimité, toutes personnes satisfaisant aux conditions requises, alors même qu'elles n'auraient pas figuré sur la liste de présentation de la Cour d'Arbitrage.

En vue de donner satisfaction à cette observation, M. DE LAPRADELLE propose de rédiger les deux dernières lignes du premier alinéa de la manière suivante:

„ou de choisir pour chaque siège non pourvu „un nom à présenter à l'adoption séparée de l'As- „semblée et du Conseil".

Pour donner satisfaction à l'opposition de M. ADATCI, qui voudrait retourner au texte de l'article 3 du projet Root—Phillimore, M. FERNANDES propose de laisser aux deux corps le choix du moment où la médiation doit prendre place.

Alinéa 2 adopté; contre le vote de M. ALTAMIRA qui renvoie aux déclarations faites par lui lors de la discussion de l'article correspondant du projet Root—Phillimore.

Alinéa 3 réservé.

Mr. ROOT fait valoir que le délai (de 3 jours) ne peut pas être fixé par le comité.

Sur la proposition de M. HAGERUP, et avant que les objections de Mr. ROOT aient été formulées, le Comité se met d'accord qu'il faut ajouter à l'alinéa une disposition tendant à départager les voix en cas de partage au sein de la Cour.

Article 12.

Supprimé.

Article 13.

Transféré après l'article 25.

La rédaction de l'article est laissée, sauf approbation par le Comité, à MM. HAGERUP, DE LAPRADELLE et FERNANDES.

M. HAGERUP propose l'amendement suivant:

„Les juges toucheront un traitement annuel à fixer par l'Assemblée de la Société des Nations sur la proposition du Conseil. Ce traitement ne peut être changé pendant le terme du mandat d'un juge.

Les juges suppléants toucheront pendant l'exercice de leurs fonctions, une indemnité à fixer de la même manière.

Les juges titulaires et les juges suppléants qui ne résident pas au siège de la Cour auront droit à une indemnité pour frais de voyages nécessités par l'exercice de leurs fonctions."

Sur la proposition de LORD PHILLIMORE le Comité se met d'accord pour reconnaître que le salaire du président ne doit être déterminé que pour 3 ans.

MM. ROOT et HAGERUP s'opposent contre la fixation du traitement des suppléants à un tiers de celui des titulaires.

Mr. ROOT et LORD PHILLIMORE sont en faveur de laisser la décision dans la matière visée dans l'alinéa 3 à la Société des Nations.

Il est constaté par M. LODER que le règlement visé à l'alinéa 4 doit être fait par la Société des Nations.

La question du traitement à donner aux juges nationaux *ad hoc* est soulevée.

Article 19, alinéa 4, doit être transféré immédiatement après l'article 13.

Article 14.

Adopté avec l'addition d'un nouvel alinéa ainsi conçu:

„En cas de doute, la Cour décide."

La proposition de M. DE LAPRADELLE, d'ajouter l'alinéa suivant:

„Quiconque exerce une fonction incompatible „avec la qualité de membre de la Cour est con„sidéré comme démissionnaire",
est rejetée.

La nécessité d'expliquer en détails les considérations qui ont abouti à l'adoption de cet article est reconnue, à cause du fait que la formule a été acceptée en séance secrète où il n'y avait pas de procès-verbal. L'explication peut être fournie dans le rapport (M. Ricci-Busatti) ou sous forme d'un annexe au procès-verbal (Lord Phillimore).

L'exercice de toute fonction qui relève de la direction politique, soit nationale, soit internationale, des Etats, est incompatible avec la qualité de membre de la Cour.

En cas de doute la Cour décide.

Article 15.

Adopté (avec une modification rédactionnelle).

Les membres de la Cour ne peuvent exercer les fonctions d'agents, de conseils ou d'avocats dans aucune affaire d'ordre international.

Ils ne peuvent participer au règlement d'aucune affaire dans laquelle ils sont antérieurement intervenus comme agents, conseils ou avocats de l'une des parties, membres d'un Tribunal national ou international, d'un Tribunal d'arbitrage, d'une Commission d'enquête, ou à tout autre titre.

En cas de doute la Cour décide.

Article 16.

Adopté.

Les membres de la Cour ne peuvent être relevés de leurs fonctions que si, au jugement unanime des autres membres, ils ont cessé de répondre aux conditions requises.

Le Secrétaire-Général en est officiellement informé.

Cette communication importe vacance de siège.

Article 17.

Adopté.

En dehors de leurs propres pays, les membres de la Cour jouissent des mêmes privilèges et immunités que les Agents diplomatiques.

Article 18.

Adopté (avec une modification rédactionnelle).

Tout membre de la Cour doit, avant d'entrer en fonctions, faire, en séance publique, une déclaration solennelle de sa volonté d'exercer ses attributions avec impartialité et en toute conscience.

Article 19.

Adopté (avec une modification rédactionnelle). Le dernier alinéa doit être transféré immédiatement après l'article 13, à sa nouvelle place (voir ci-dessus).

La Cour élit, pour trois ans, son Président et son Vice-Président: ils sont rééligibles.

Elle nomme son Greffier.

La fonction de Greffier de la Cour n'est pas incompatible avec celle de Secrétaire-Général de la Cour Permanente d'Arbitrage.

Article 20.

Adopté.

Le siège de la Cour est fixé à la Haye.

Le Président et le Greffier résident au siège de la Cour.

Article 21.

Adopté.

Il est entendu que la Cour doit se réunir chaque année quand même il n'y aurait pas d'affaires à traiter.

La Cour tient une session chaque année.

Sauf disposition contraire du règlement d'ordre de la Cour, cette session commence le 15 juin, et continue tant que le rôle n'est pas épuisé.

Le Président convoque la Cour en session extraordinaire quand les circonstances l'exigent.

Article 22.

Les alinéas 1 et 5 sont adoptés. Sur la proposition de LORD PHILLIMORE, le comité se met d'accord pour faire de ces deux alinéas un nouvel article (22).

Les alinéas 2, 3, 4 sont réservés. A propos de ces alinéas M. FERNANDES a repris son amendement aux articles 25 et 26 du projet Root—Phillimore.

Cet amendement fut, lors de la discussion de ces textes, renvoyé à la seconde lecture. Il vise l'élargissement du rôle des juges suppléants.

La Cour exerce ses attributions en séance plénière.

Si la présence de neuf juges titulaires n'est pas assurée, ce nombre est parfait par l'entrée en fonction des juges suppléants.

Article 23.

Adopté (contre l'abstention de M. Ricci-Busatti).

Les suppléants sont appelés dans l'ordre du tableau.

Les mots : „du nombre d'ordre des voix obtenues au dernier scrutin ; enfin, à égalité de voix, par" sont biffés.

Le tableau est dressé par la Cour, en tenant compte, d'abord de la priorité d'élection et ensuite de l'ancienneté d'âge.

Article 24.

Adopté.

La phrase „si les parties le demandent" est ajoutée.

En vue de la prompte expédition des affaires, la Cour compose annuellement une chambre de trois juges, spécialement consacrée au jugement des affaires en procédure sommaire, si les parties le demandent.

La question visée ci-dessus au point 2 de l'art 4 est reprise.

Le PRESIDENT propose le texte suivant:

„Il est pourvu aux sièges devenus vacants du terme des fonctions, de décès, de retraite ou pour toute autre cause, selon la méthode suivie pour la première élection de l'ensemble des juges.

Le juge suppléant qui prend la place d'un juge titulaire devenue vacante, achève son mandat. Le mandat de 9 ans commence à courir à la date de cet achèvement."

LORD PHILLIMORE explique ainsi le système proposé :

L'élection du nouveau juge est faite selon la méthode adoptée pour l'élection de l'ensemble des juges.

Un juge suppléant est élu de la même manière. Le nouveau juge prend la place du juge sorti pour le reste du mandat de celui-ci ; de même pour le juge suppléant remplaçant un juge suppléant sorti. Il y aurait donc de nouvelles élections tous les neuf ans.

Cette méthode est acceptée sauf rédaction.

Article 25.

Le PRESIDENT propose le texte suivant:

1. Lorsque la Cour renferme un juge titulaire de la nationalité de chacune des parties en cause, ces juges conservent le droit de siéger dans l'affaire dont la Cour est saisie.

2. Si la Cour ne renferme qu'un juge titulaire de la nationalité d'une seule des parties en cause, l'autre partie désigne pour siéger, parmi les juges suppléants, un juge de sa nationalité, s'il en existe. S'il n'en existe pas, elle choisit un juge, de préférence parmi les personnes qui ont été l'objet d'une présentation de la part des groupes nationaux de la Cour d'Arbitrage.

3. Si la Cour ne renferme aucun juge titulaire de la nationalité des parties en cause, chacune de ces parties procède à la désignation ou au choix d'un juge de la même manière que dans le cas précédent.

4. Lorsque plusieurs parties font cause commune, elles ne peuvent désigner ou choisir qu'un seul juge de commun accord.

5. Les juges désignés ou choisis comme il est dit ci-dessus, doivent satisfaire aux prescriptions des articles, 2, 14, 15, 18, 22 du présent statut. Ils statuent sur un pied d'égalité avec leurs collègues.

Ce texte est adopté comme partie du texte préparé par le comité de rédaction, et puis réservé.

Ici entrent l'article 13 et l'article 19, alinéa 4; voir ci-dessus.

Article 26.

Les frais de la Cour sont supportés par la Société des Nations.

Adopté (contre le vote de M. Ricci-Busatti).

M. HAGERUP soulève la question de la situation des Etats qui ne sont pas Membres de la Société des Nations et qui n'ont pas adhéré à la convention établissant la Cour. Ces Etats sont visés par le projet de rédaction seulement dans les cas qui rentrent sous l'article 17 du Pacte.

M. RICCI-BUSATTI, supporté par M. HAGERUP, propose la suppression de l'article.

Mr. ROOT pense que l'article 17 couvre tous les cas.

M. DE LAPRADELLE propose le nouveau texte suivant:

„Les frais de la Cour seront supportés par la Société des Nations de la manière que l'Assemblée décidera sur la proposition du Conseil".

Chapitre II.

La compétence de la Cour.

Article 27.

La Cour connaît des litiges entre Etats.

Alinéa 1er est adopté. Les alinéas suivants sont supprimés.

La discussion a porté sur la définition de l'idée de la représentation de particuliers par un Etat.

Le PRESIDENT a proposé le texte suivant:

„La Cour ne connaît que de litiges entre Etats. Mais un Etat peut saisir la Cour de demandes concernant des droits qu'il fait valoir en faveur de ses ressortissants, ou des ressortissants d'un protectorat ou même d'un autre Etat à la protection duquel il est habilité par traité."

Après discussion le président propose la formule suivante:

„Mais un Etat peut saisir la Cour des demandes „en faveur de personnes dont la protection lui „incombe ou à la protection desquelles il est „habilité par traité."

Après le Président propose encore le texte suivant:

„La Cour connaît de litiges entre Etats. Nulle réclamation d'un particulier contre un Etat étranger ne peut venir devant la Cour que si un Etat prend fait et cause pour ses nationaux ou pour d'autres personnes dont la protection lui appartient en droit."

Le Président soulève la question d'un *locus standi* spécial pour la Société des Nations et ses organes.

Il propose une formule aux termes de laquelle l'Etat sera toujours le *dominus litis*.

M. DE LAPRADELLE suggère l'idée de baser la rédaction sur la conception de la protection diplomatique.

Mr. ROOT s'oppose contre cette formule qui lui semble trop large.

LORD PHILLIMORE propose de procéder par énumération.

Le Comité décide par un vote formel de ne point compléter l'article 17, alinéa 1er, dans le sens proposé par le Président.

Article 28.

Adopté (contre le vote de M. de Lapradelle).

M. HAGERUP avait proposé l'amendement suivant (addition au texte originaire):

„Les conditions sous lesquelles la Cour est accessible aux Etats qui ne sont pas Membres de la Société des Nations, sont fixées par le Conseil de cette Société."

Le PRESIDENT a proposé la formule suivante:

„La Cour est accessible aux „Membres de la Société des Nations et aux Etats mentionnés à l'Annexe du Pacte de cette Société. Les conditions sous lesquelles la Cour est accessible aux Etats qui ne sont pas Membres de la Société des Nations sont fixées par le Conseil de cette Société en conformité avec l'article 17 du Pacte."

M. DE LAPRADELLE, d'accord avec LORD PHILLIMORE, a proposé la formule suivante:

„La Cour est ouverte aux Membres de la Société des Nations et aux Etats mentionnés à l'Annexe. Elle est accessible aux autres Etats aux conditions sous lesquelles la Cour est ouverte aux Etats qui ne sont pas Membres de la Société des Nations fixées par le Conseil."

La Cour est ouverte aux Etats Membres de la Société des Nations.

Elle l'est de même aux Etats mentionnés à l'Annexe au Pacte de la Société des Nations.

Elle est aussi accessible aux autres Etats.

Les conditions auxquelles elle est ouverte ou accessible aux Etats qui ne sont pas Membres de la Société des Nations sont réglées par le Conseil, en tenant compte de l'article 17 du Pacte.

Lord Phillimore a proposé le même texte sauf le mot „réglées" au lieu de „fixées" dans la première partie.

Le PRESIDENT propose l'addition suivante au texte proposé par Lord Phillimore: „en tenant compte de l'article 17 du Pacte de la Société des Nations."

Adopté (avec certaines modifications et contre le vote de M. Ricci-Busatti et l'abstention de M. Altamira.)

M. ADATCI propose l'amendement suivant:

„La Cour est compétente pour connaître des différends entre Etats, conformément à l'article 14 du Pacte de la Société des Nations".

Cet amendement est rejeté en vertu de l'adoption de l'article.

Le PRESIDENT propose l'addition suivante à l'alinéa 1er: „et sauf acception par les parties d'une autre juridiction."

Cet amendement n'est pas adopté à cause de l'expression déjà donnée à l'article 1er de la même idée.

Le PRESIDENT propose la rédaction suivante de l'alinéa 1er:

„Entre Etats Membres de la Société des Nations, la Cour statue sans convention spéciale sur les différends d'ordre juridique, c'est à dire ceux qui ont pour objet."

Cette formule est adoptée, sauf suppression des des mots „c'est à dire ceux".

M. RICCI-BUSATTI propose l'amendement suivant au dernier alinéa du no. 1er:

„La Cour connaît également de tous différends de quelque nature qu'ils soient, qui lui sont soumis par la convention, soit générale, soit spéciale, des parties."

Cet amendement est adopté.

Sur une proposition de M. RICCI-BUSATTI, reprise par M. ADATCI, après le rejet de son amendement principal, la disjonction du statut de la Cour de toute la question de sa compétence est mise aux voix.

Cette proposition est rejetée.

M. DE LAPRADELLE propose de substituer dans le numéro 2 de l'article 29 les mots „dans les catégories ci-dessus visées" par les mots „dans sa compétence".

La proposition est rejetée. Il est expressément entendue que le no. 2 (alinéa 4) de l'article 29 doit rester tel quel.

Article 29.

Entre Etats Membres de la Société des Nations la Cour statue sans convention spéciale sur les différends d'ordre juridique, qui ont pour objet:

a. L'interprétation d'un traité;

b. Tout point de droit international;

c. La réalité de tout fait, qui, s'il était établi, constituerait la violation d'un engagement international;

d. La nature ou l'étendue de la réparation dûe pour la rupture d'un engagement international;

e. L'interprétation d'une sentence rendue par la Cour.

La Cour connaît également de tous différends de quelque nature qu'ils soient, qui lui sont soumis par la convention, soit générale, soit spéciale, des parties.

2. En cas de contestation sur le point de savoir si un différend rentre, oui ou non, dans les catégories ci-dessus visées, la Cour décide.

Article 30.

Réservé.

LORD PHILLIMORE a proposé de substituer aux deux derniers membres de phrase la formule suivante:

„Si par un engagement les parties ont accepté cette compétence".

Cet amendement n'est pas adopté.

LORD PHILLIMORE propose une nouvelle rédaction:

„Lorsqu'une partie dénie compétence à la Cour, il appartient à celle-ci de statuer sur ce point en ordre préjudiciel."

Cet amendement n'est pas non plus adopté. M. RICCI-BUSATTI a fait valoir que l'article 30 rentre dans le no. 2 de l'article 29. M. DE LAPRADELLE a, dans ces circonstances, retiré l'article 30 et LORD PHILLIMORE et M. LODER en ont proposé la suppression.

La réserve est faite sur la proposition du Président dans l'intention expresse de permettre aux membres de se rendre compte si l'article est vraiment inutile.

Article 31.

Dans les limites de sa compétence, telle qu'elle est déterminée par l'article 29, la Cour applique successivement:

1. Les conventions internationales, soit générales, soit spéciales, établissant des règles expressément reconnues par les Etats en litige;

2. La coutume internationale, attestation d'une pratique commune, acceptée comme loi;

3. Les principes généraux de droit reconnu par les nations civilisées;

4. Les règles de droit qui se dégagent des décisions judiciaires et de la doctrine des publicistes les plus qualifiés des différentes Nations, comme moyens auxiliaires de la détermination des règles de droit.

Adopté.

M. RICCI-BUSATTI s'oppose contre la différence d'expression entre les nos. 1 et 2 dont le dernier dit „acceptée comme loi" tandis que le premier dit que les règles doivent être expressément reconnues par les parties.

Il vote contre le no. 2.

Le PRESIDENT propose l'addition suivante au no. 4:

„Comme moyens auxiliaires de la détermination des règles de droit."

L'alinéa étant mis aux voix avec cette addition, M. DE LAPRADELLE vote contre.

Il déclare qu'il considère qu'il n'est pas possible de fixer la source de droit visée sous no. 4, d'une manière distincte des conventions internationales, de la coutume, des principes généraux du droit.

Article 32.

La Cour donne son avis sur tout point ou tout différend, d'ordre international qui lui est soumis par le Conseil ou par l'Assemblée.

Lorsque la Cour donne son avis sur un point d'ordre international, indépendamment de tout différend actuellement né, elle constitue une Commission spéciale de trois à cinq membres.

Lorsqu'elle donne son avis sur une question qui fait l'objet d'un différend actuellement né, elle statue dans les mêmes conditions, que s'il s'agissait d'un litige porté devant elle.

Adopté.

Des objections soulevées par Mr. ROOT contre le droit pour la Cour de donner des avis consultatifs dans des différends actuellement nés, ont été écartées par des arguments tirés de l'article 13 du Pacte.

ANNEXE No. 2.

Mémoire de M. Hagerup concernant la question visée à l'art. 43 du projet des Cinq Puissances neutres.

Lorsque la partie assignée devant une Cour ne se présente pas à la Cour, les législations différentes ont adopté des différents systèmes dont les principaux sont les suivants. Pour mieux élucider ces différences prenons un exemple.

Supposez que le demandeur prétend d'avoir livré des marchandises à la partie adverse. D'après l'un système, la Cour n'a pas à demander des preuves pour le fait de la livraison des marchandises, mais seulement à rechercher si, en droit et en justice, le fait est une base suffisante pour les conclusions du demandeur. D'après l'autre système le demandeur a — même dans l'absence de la partie adverse — à prouver la livraison des marchandises. Ce dernier système est le système anglais. Le premier système est le système continental adopté — avec quelques modifications légères — dans les codes de procédure civile les plus récents. C'est aussi le système adopté par l'article 43 du projet des Cinq Puissances Neutres. Le texte de ce projet se trouve aussi dans le projet des commissions premières des trois pays du Nord. Il a été proposé par moi au sein de ces commissions et sur le sens de ce texte il ne peut pas y avoir de doute.

Ce système est en général recommandé par la science contemporaine, parce que l'autre système soumet le demandeur au désavantage de devoir prouver même des faits que la Partie adverse ne pourrait pas en bonne foi contester si elle s'était présentée devant la Cour. Cependant, on a fait valoir que ce système ne donne pas satisfaction aux exigences des rapports internationaux. Ce n'est pas, dit-on, conforme à la dignité des Etats souverains qu'un Etat puisse unilatéralement assigner un autre Etat et dans l'absence de la Partie adverse puisse demander que la Cour admette sans preuve tout fait allégué par lui.

Je m'incline devant cette considération. Seulement, je ne peux pas me rallier à un texte qui oblige la Cour de demander en tout cas des preuves pour les faits invoqués par le demandeur. Il peut y avoir des faits notoires (c. à. d. des faits que chaque personne dans la situation de juges connaît) et il se peut aussi que pour d'autres raisons, dans l'espèce, la Cour trouve une preuve superflue. Je crois qu'on doit laisser à la Cour une libre appréciation des circonstances. Pour cette raison je préfère — après mûre reflection — la formule proposée en premier lieu par M. le Rapporteur avec la modification de la rédaction adoptée par lui.

ANNEX No. 2.

Memorandum of M. Hagerup concerning the question raised in article 43 of the Scheme of the Five Neutral Powers.

To meet the case which arises from the non-appearance of the defendant before a Court, different methods, of which the following are the principal, have been adopted in different systems of law.

As an example to make these differences clearer, let us suppose that the plaintiff claims to have delivered goods to the other party. According to one system, the Court must not demand proofs of the fact that the goods were delivered, but only to consider whether in law and justice the fact is a sufficient basis for the conclusions of the plaintiff. According to the other system the plaintiff is called upon — even in the absence of the other party — to prove that the goods were delivered. The latter is the English system. The former is the continental system, adopted—with some slight modifications—in the most recent codes of civil procedure. It is also the system formulated in Article 43 of the Scheme of the Five Neutral Powers. The text of this Scheme is also embodied in the scheme of the first Commissions of the three Northern Countries. It was proposed by me at the sittings of these Commissions and there can be no doubt as to the meaning of this text.

This system is generally recommended by modern expert opinion, because the other system places the plaintiff under the disadvantage of having to prove even such facts as the other party could not in good faith dispute if he had presented himself before the Court. Nevertheless, it is claimed that this method does not satisfy the demands of international relations. The claim is put forward that it is not in conformity with the dignity of sovereign States that a State should unilaterally be able to summon another State and should, in the absence of the other party, be in a position to demand that the Court should admit without proof any allegation made against that other party.

I admit the force of this consideration. But I cannot agree to a text which makes it necessary for the Court in every case to demand proofs of the facts brought forward by the plaintiff. There may be well-known facts (i. e. facts known to every person in the position of a judge); and also for other reasons the Court may possibly consider proof superfluous. I hold that the Court should be given free powers to appraise the circumstances. For this reason, after careful consideration, I prefer the formula first proposed by your Rapporteur, but with his modification of the drafting.

ANNEXE No. 3.

Amendement concernant une procédure pour suppléer à celle des interdits, par M. Raoul Fernandes.

On ne saurait prétendre que la procédure ordinaire, telle que le projet l'institue, peut convenir à tous les différends éventuels entre des Etats.

L'action judiciaire, selon la pénétrante analyse de Savigny, est une réaction du droit violé, qui, étant spécifique, doit assumer, pour atteindre son but, la nature et la forme commandées par le caractère du droit lui-même.

Les Etats, dans leurs rapports avec les choses, soit dans le domaine patrimonial à titre public ou à titre privé, soit dans le domaine de la souveraineté territoriale, exercent *de jure* ou *de facto* la possession, dont l'objet est tantôt une chose, tantôt la jouissance d'une servitude et souvent, en dehors de toute idée de propriété, l'ensemble des pouvoirs politiques constitutifs de la souveraineté.

Ce rapport juridique est réglé en droit international d'après les principes empruntés au droit romain.

Or, dans le droit romain la protection possessoire, comprenant la possession des choses et la quasi-possession des servitudes, était assurée par les interdits, dont la procédure a été adoptée par le droit judiciaire des nations modernes comme une nécessité *sine qua non* du régime économique basé sur la propriété, telle que nous l'avons héritée des Romains.

Dans les rapports internationaux aussi bien que dans les relations nationales, la défense judiciaire de la possession en dehors du rite des actions possessoires est une impossibilité logique, tout au moins en ce qui concerne la possession ou *quasi-possessio retinenda*, avec son double caractère de répression immédiate du trouble de la possession et d'exclusion de toute controverse basée sur la propriété.

Cependant, quoique convaincus que la juridiction internationale sera très imparfaite tant qu'elle n'admettra pas l'action possessoire dans le cadre infranchissable tracé par la fonction juridique de l'institut de la possession, nous nous rendons compte qu'il y a des étapes à franchir et qu'il serait peut-être impolitique de placer la Cour dès à présent dans l'obligation de s'engager dans des procédures comportant une voie exécutoire immédiate et dépourvue de souplesse.

Mais, d'autre part, il nous semble possible de

ANNEX No. 3.

Amendments regarding a procedure to take the place of the procedure of interdicts, by M. Raoul Fernandes.

The ordinary procedure established by the scheme can hardly be considered applicable to all disputes which might arise between States.

Legal action is, according to Savigny's profound analysis, a reaction of the law that has been violated, a reaction which, being of a specific nature, must, in order to attain its end, assume the character and form prescribed by the nature of the law itself.

In their relations with things, States, whether as subjects of private or public property, or in the sphere of territorial sovereignty, exercise *de jure* or *de facto* possession, sometimes over things, sometimes over servitudes and often—outside any conception of property—with regard to the complex of political powers which constitute sovereignty.

In international law, these legal relations are based on principles borrowed from Roman Law.

In Roman Law, possessory protection, including the possession of things and the quasi-possession of servitudes, was assured by interdicts, and the interdict procedure was adopted by the laws of modern nations as a *sine qua non* of an economic system based on property, such as we have inherited from the Romans.

In international, as well as national, relations, any legal defence of possession—apart from the procedure of possessory actions—is a logical impossibility, at least in the matter of the possession or *quasi-possessio retinenda* in its double character as immediately repressing interference with possession and as excluding all controversy based on rights of ownership.

Although we are aware that international jurisdiction will be far from perfect as long as it does not admit possessory action within the strictly-defined limits formed by the legal characteristics of possession, we realise that this can only be done by degrees, and that it would, perhaps, be inexpedient to burden the Court at the outset with the duty of undertaking procedures which would entail a course of direct executory action, devoid of elasticity.

On the other hand, it would seem possible to meet the need in question, to some extent at least, by adopting a compromise which already exists in Article 4 of the Treaty of October 13th 1914, between the United States of America and Sweden,

parer dans une certaine mesure au besoin dont il est question en nous inspirant d'un expédient déjà adopté par l'article 4 du Traité du 13 Octobre 1914, passé entre les Etats-Unis d'Amérique et la Suède pour le règlement pacifique des litiges, et dont le texte est le suivant:

„Dans le cas où la cause du différend consisterait en actes déterminés déjà effectués ou sur le point de l'être, la Commission indiquera, dans le plus bref délai possible, quelles mesures conservatoires du droit de chacun, devraient, selon son avis, être prises à titre provisoire et en attendant le dépôt de son rapport."

En l'adaptant à la jurisdiction de la Cour, nous suggérons le texte suivant, comme amendement au chapitre de la procédure.

Article: „Dans le cas où la cause du différend consiste en actes déterminés déjà effectués ou sur le point de l'être, la Cour pourra ordonner, dans le plus bref délai, à titre provisoire, des mesures conservatoires adéquates, en attendant le jugement définitif".

(signé) R. FERNANDES.

regarding the peaceful settlement of disputes. The text of the Article reads as follows:

" In case the cause of the dispute should consist of certain acts already committed, or about to be committed, the Commission shall, as soon as possible, indicate what measures to preserve the rights of each party ought, in its opinion, to be taken provisionally, and pending the delivery of the report."

In order to adapt this text to the jurisdiction of the Court, we would suggest the following, as an amendment to the Chapter on Procedure.

Article: " In case the cause of the dispute should consist of certain acts already committed or about to be committed, the Court may, provisionally and with the least possible delay, order adequate protective measures to be taken, pending the final judgment of the Court."

(signed) R. FERNANDES.

29IÈME SÉANCE (non-publique), tenue au Palais de la Paix, à La Haye, le 20 juillet 1920.

Présidence de M. le BARON DESCAMPS.

Sont présents: tous les membres du Comité (à l'exception de M. Bevilaqua); M. Fernandes; Mr. James Brown Scott; les secrétaires particuliers de M. le Baron Descamps et de M. Adatci; les membres du Secrétariat.

La séance est ouverte à 3.30 heures de l'après-midi.

Le PRESIDENT ouvre la discussion sur les articles qui ont été réservés lors des séances du 19 et de la séance du matin du 20 juillet.

Article 2.

Mr. ROOT retire la réserve qu'il a faite le jour précédent au sujet de cet article, mais propose l'insertion après le mot „morale" de la formule suivante:

„qui tous devront remplir les conditions requises dans leurs pays respectifs pour l'admission dans la haute magistrature ou possédant...."

M. DE LAPRADELLE rappelle l'article 44 de la Convention de 1907. Il dit qu'il se serait contenté de la formule suivante:

„La Cour Permanente de Justice Internationale est un corps de magistrats indépendants, choisis sans égard à leur nationalité, parmi les personnes d'une science et d'une expérience juridique reconnues".

Mr. ROOT, appuyé par Lord Phillimore, fait valoir la nécessité de laisser ouverte la possibilité pour certains pays de choisir leurs juges internationaux dans leur haute magistrature.

M. ALTAMIRA attire l'attention de ses collègues sur le fait que les juges des différents Etats ne possèdent pas tous, d'une manière égale, la préparation juridique indispensable à un bon juge international. Il n'est pas douteux, par exemple, que, tandis que le juge anglais ou américain pos-

29TH MEETING (Private), held at the Peace Palace, the Hague, on July 20th, 1920.

BARON DESCAMPS in the chair.

Present: all the members of the Committee (except M. Bevilaqua); M. Fernandes; Mr. James Brown Scott; the private secretaries of Baron Descamps and M. Adatci; the members of the Secretariat.

The meeting opened at 3.30 p. m.

The PRESIDENT opened the debate upon the Articles which had been reserved at the meetings of the 19th and the morning of the 20th July.

Article 2.

Mr. ROOT withdrew the reservation he had made on the previous day, concerning this article, but proposed that the following formula should be inserted after the word "character":

"who must all possess the qualifications required in their respective countries for appointment to high judicial office, or be of..."

M. DE LAPRADELLE called attention to Article 44 of the Convention of 1907. He said that he would be satisfied with the following wording:

"The Permanent Court of International Justice shall be composed of a body of independent judges, chosen regardless of their nationality from amongst persons of recognised legal knowledge and experience."

Mr. ROOT, supported by LORD PHILLIMORE, pointed out the necessity of allowing certain countries to choose their international judges from among persons holding high judicial office.

M. ALTAMIRA called his colleague's attention to the fact that judges in different countries do not possess, in an equal degree, the legal training essential for a good international judge. There is no doubt, for instance, that whereas an English or American judge has been prepared by such a

sède cette préparation à un degré supérieur, d'autres juges nationaux n'ont que rarement l'opportunité de s'occuper de questions internationales.

Le PRESIDENT suggère l'adoption de la formule „les conditions requises pour l'exercice de la plus haute magistrature".

Mr. ROOT demande un vote sur la formule qu'il a proposée.

M. DE LAPRADELLE en propose une autre ainsi conçue:

„...plus haute magistrature de leurs pays, ou „des jurisconsultes possédant...."

L'article est adopté avec des modifications s'inspirant des propositions qui viennent d'être faites.

Article 4.

M. ALTAMIRA soulève la question du droit que devraient avoir les juges de donner leur démission.

LORD PHILLIMORE répond que cette faculté résulte du droit commun.

Article 5.

Une nouvelle formule est proposée par le PRESIDENT. Il explique que l'expression „groupes nationaux", qui avait, la veille, soulevé quelques objections, peut être maintenue puisqu'elle ne signifie pas „groupes de nationaux".

L'article est adopté dans les termes proposés par le Président.

Article 6.

Le PRESIDENT propose pour le premier alinéa une nouvelle formule qui est adoptée.

Au sujet du second alinéa M. HAGERUP s'oppose à la fixation du nombre des candidats à deux; il rappelle qu'on a, dans une séance précédente, adopté le nombre de six.

Une suggestion du Président tendant à insérer dans l'alinéa 2 l'expression „pour chaque place" n'est pas admise.

Article 8.

Un nouveau texte proposé par le PRESIDENT, est adopté par le Comité sans discussion.

Article 11.

Après une discussion prolongée, au cours de laquelle un nombre considérable de rédactions ont été proposées par MM. FERNANDES, ADATCI,

training to a very high degree, other national judges rarely have the opportunity of dealing with international questions.

The PRESIDENT suggested that the expression "the qualifications required for appointment to high judicial office" should be adopted.

Mr. ROOT asked for a vote to be taken upon the wording that he had proposed.

M. DE LAPRADELLE proposed another:

"the highest judicial offices in their country, or jurisconsults of..."

The Article was adopted with modifications based on the proposals just made.

Article 4.

M. ALTAMIRA raised the question of the right of the judges to resign.

LORD PHILLIMORE answered that this was a natural right.

Article 5.

A new wording was proposed by the PRESIDENT. He explained that the expression "national groups", which had given rise to some objections on the previous day, could be maintained, as it did not mean "groups of persons of a particular nationality" (groupe de nationaux).

The Article was adopted with the wording proposed by the President.

Article 6.

The PRESIDENT proposed a new wording for the first Paragraph, which was adopted.

Concerning the second paragraph, M. HAGERUP was opposed to the limitation of the number of candidates to two. He recalled the fact that, at a previous meeting, the number six had been adopted.

A suggestion made by the President to insert the words "for each seat" in Paragraph 2 was rejected.

Article 8.

A new wording proposed by the PRESIDENT, was unanimously adopted without discussion.

Article 11.

After a prolonged discussion, in the course of which a large number of suggested wordings were put forward by MM. FERNANDES, ADATCI,

ROOT, DE LAPRADELLE, LORD PHILLIMORE, M. HAGERUP, et le PRESIDENT, on se met d'accord sur le fond de la question à résoudre. Cet accord est consigné par M. DE LAPRADELLE dans la formule suivante, qu'il propose pour l'alinéa 1er de cet article:

„Si, après la troisième élection, il reste encore des sièges à pourvoir, il est à tout moment formé, sur la seule demande, soit de l'Assemblée, soit du Conseil, une Commission médiatrice..."

Sur la proposition du PRESIDENT il est décidé que la rédaction finale de l'alinéa sera laissée à M. de Lapradelle qui la présentera demain.

En ce qui concerne l'alinéa 3, l'alinéa 2 ayant été déjà adopté la veille, M. HAGERUP propose la formule suivante:

„Si après la réunion de la Commission médiatrice l'entente n'est pas obtenue, les membres de la Cour déjà nommés pourvoient, dans un délai à fixer par le Conseil, par cooptation aux sièges vacants."

M. DE LAPRADELLE en propose une autre ainsi conçue: „Si, par le moyen de la Commission médiatrice, l'élection n'a pu être faite ou l'entente ne peut être obtenue, les membres de la Cour déjà nommés pourvoient par cooptation aux sièges vacants en choisissant parmi les personnes..."

La rédaction finalement adoptée est fondée sur ces deux propositions.

Article 15.

Cet Article est adopté avec une légère modification de rédaction.

Article 22.

Le Comité se met d'accord pour former des alinéas 2 à 4 de l'ancien article 22 un nouvel article qui portera le no. 22.

D'autre part, les alinéas 1 et 5 doivent former un nouvel article 22 bis.

A ce dernier article M. FERNANDES propose un amendement portant augmentation du nombre des juges réguliers à onze; le quorum serait de neuf juges. L'article est adopté sous cette forme amendée.

Article 24 bis.

Le PRESIDENT soumet une nouvelle rédaction destinée à remplacer celle qu'il a indiquée la veille. Cette nouvelle rédaction est adoptée sans discussion.

ROOT, DE LAPRADELLE, LORD PHILLIMORE, HAGERUP and the PRESIDENT, agreement was reached upon the principle of the question under discussion. This agreement was expressed by M. DE LAPRADELLE in the following provision, which he proposed should be adopted as paragraph 1 of the Article:

"If, after the third sitting, one or more seats still remain unfilled, a joint Conference may be formed at any time, at the request of either the Assembly or the Council."

On the PRESIDENT's suggestion, it was decided that the final wording of the paragraph should be left to M. de Lapradelle, who would submit it on the following day.

Paragraph 2 having been already adopted on the previous day, M. HAGERUP proposed the following formula for para. 3:

"If, after the joint Conference has met, an agreement is still impossible, the members of the Court, who have already been appointed, shall, within a time-limit to be laid down by the Council, proceed to fill the vacant seats by a system of co-optation."

M. DE LAPRADELLE proposed the following:

"If the Joint Conference is not successful in procuring an election or coming to an agreement, those members of the Court who have already been appointed, shall proceed to fill the vacant seats by co-optation, making their selection from amongst those persons..."

The wording finally adopted was based on these two proposals.

Article 15.

This Article was adopted with a slight modification in the wording.

Article 22.

The Committee agreed to form a new 22nd Article out of paragraphs 2 and 4 of the old Article 22.

Paragraphs 1 and 5 were to form a new Article 22 bis.

M. FERNANDES proposed an amendment to the latter Article, intended to increase the number of judges to eleven; the quorum would be nine.

The Article was adopted as thus amended.

Article 24 bis.

The PRESIDENT submitted a new wording intended to replace that which he had proposed on the previous day. This new wording was adopted without discussion.

Article 25.

M. DE LAPRADELLE propose la suppression du 1er alinéa qu'il trouve superflu. Cette proposition, mise aux voix, est rejetée.

M. RICCI-BUSATTI déclare que la rapidité des travaux du Comité l'empêche de faire une série de remarques sur cet article, ainsi que sur certains autres. On ne dispose pas du temps qu'il faudrait pour approfondir d'une façon suffisante les dispositions dont il s'agit, et les amendements que l'on voudrait y introduire.

L'article est adopté sans modifications.

Article 25 bis (anciens 13 et 19, alinéa 2).

M. DE LAPRADELLE soumet, d'accord avec M. Fernandes et M. Hagerup, une nouvelle rédaction.

M. RICCI-BUSATTI propose que l'allocation des juges *ad hoc* soit définie de la même manière que l'allocation des juges suppléants.

Le texte de M. de Lapradelle est d'abord soumis au vote et approuvé.

Puis le PRESIDENT propose une formule qui exprime l'idée de M. Ricci-Busatti.

Cette formule, mise aux voix, est adoptée, de même que l'avant, dernier alinéa de l'article.

Il est decidé que les appointements du greffier seront réglés dans le même article.

Article 26.

Le PRESIDENT donne lecture d'une rédaction nouvelle.

On reprend alors le texte proposé par M. de Lapradelle la veille.

La rédaction du Président, avec une modification résultant du texte de M. de Lapradelle, est adoptée.

M. RICCI-BUSATTI appelle l'attention du Comité sur les cas sporadiques visés dans les grands traités de paix, où la Cour est compétente pour juger de conflits auxquels une des parties est un Etat qui n'est pas Membre de la Société des Nations.

On reconnaît qu'il est inutile de faire une exception pour ces cas, puisque le Conseil, en posant ses conditions, s'inspirera du Traité de Versailles.

M. DE LAPRADELLE maintient son vote contraire à cet article. L'article est adopté.

Article 25.

M. DE LAPRADELLE proposed that the first Paragraph should be deleted, as he thought it superfluous. This proposal was put to a vote and rejected.

M. RICCI-BUSATTI said that the rapidity with which the work of the Committee had to be done prevented him from making various comments concerning this Article, as also concerning certain others; there was not sufficient time for satisfactory consideration of the provisions in question and the amendments which it was desired to introduce into them.

The Article was adopted without alteration.

Article 25 bis (old numbers 13 and 19, para. 2).

M. DE LAPRADELLE, in agreement with M. Fernandes and M. Hagerup, submitted a new wording.

M. RICCI-BUSATTI proposed that the grants made to judges *ad hoc* should be fixed in the same way as those made to the deputy-judges.

First of all, the wording proposed by M. de Lapradelle was voted upon and adopted.

The PRESIDENT then proposed a wording intended to express M. Ricci-Busatti's idea.

This wording was voted upon and adopted, as was also the last Paragraph but one in the Article.

It was decided that the salary of the Registrar should be dealt with in the same Article.

Article 26.

The PRESIDENT read a new wording.

The wording proposed by M. de Lapradelle on the previous day was then considered.

The President's draft, with an alteration drawn from M. de Lapradelle's version, was adopted.

M. RICCI-BUSATTI called the attention of the Committee to the various cases, mentioned in the principal treaties of Peace, in which the Court would have jurisdiction to hear and determine disputes in which one of the parties was a State not a Member of the League of Nations.

It was agreed that it was unnecessary to make an exception for such cases, since the Council, when formulating its conditions, would base them upon the Treaty of Versailles.

M. DE LAPRADELLE voted against this Article. The Article was adopted.

Article 29.

Mr. ROOT remarque l'omission de la disposition contenue dans l'article 30 du projet Root—Phillimore, aux termes de laquelle les moyens diplomatiques doivent être épuisés avant que soit formé le recours à la juridiction internationale.

En soulignant l'importance de la disposition en question, il en demande l'insertion dans le projet du Comité.

M. FERNANDES rappelle que, sur sa proposition, le Comité avait déjà décidé de modifier la formule du projet Root—Phillimore, de manière à écarter l'obligation de recourir préalablement à *toutes* les voies diplomatiques. Il appuie sur les inconvénients pratiques d'une telle condition, et propose à nouveau qu'on se borne à exiger en termes généraux la tentative d'arrangement amiable par la voie diplomatique.

LORD PHILLIMORE, dans cet ordre d'idées, propose la formule suivante:

„Lorsqu'un différend tel qu'il est prévu dans . . . s'élève entre Etats, et que le différend n'a pu être réglé par voie diplomatique et que l'on n'est pas convenu pour une autre juridiction dans le sens de l'article 13 du Pacte, la partie qui se prétend lésée peut en saisir la Cour permanente".

On admet qu'il est désirable d'insérer une disposition à cet effet. Une rédaction sera préparée pour mercredi. La place que la nouvelle disposition devra occuper dans le texte est réservée.

M. ALTAMIRA se félicite de voir adopter de nouveau l'article 30 du projet Root—Phillimore, qui a ses préférences, étant une expression la plus claire possible de la justice obligatoire.

Article 30.

M. FERNANDES propose l'amendement suivant:

„Lorsque la partie assignée allègue de ne pas avoir accepté la juridiction de la Cour, celle-ci décide sur le point de savoir s'il y a un engagement de sa part."

LORD PHILLIMORE demande des renseignements sur la portée du mot „engagement". Il voudrait savoir si ce terme comprend également les obligations involontaires.

Article 29.

Mr. ROOT noticed that the provision contained in Article 30 of the Root—Phillimore plan, according to which diplomatic means must be exhausted before recourse to the International Jurisdiction, had been omitted.

He emphasised the importance of this provision, and asked that it should be inserted in the Committee's plan.

M. FERNANDES recalled the fact that the Committee, on his proposal, had already decided to modify the wording of the Root—Phillimore plan, in such a way as to eliminate the stipulation that *all* diplomatic methods must be attempted before recourse is made to the Court. He laid emphasis on the practical difficulties entailed by such a condition, and again proposed that a provision, laying down in general terms only that an attempt must be made to settle the dispute by diplomatic means, should be inserted.

LORD PHILLIMORE proposed the following wording in this connection:

"When a dispute, of the nature provided for in . . . has arisen between States, and it has been found impossible to settle it by diplomatic means, and no agreement has been made to choose another jurisdiction, as provided in article 13 of the Covenant, the party complaining may bring the case before the Permanent Court."

It was admitted that it was desirable to insert a provision to this effect. A draft was to be prepared for Wednesday; the place in which the new provision was to be inserted was left open.

M. ALTAMIRA was very glad that Art. 30 of the Root—Phillimore plan had once more been adopted. This provision appealed to him as being the clearest possible way of expressing the adoption of a compulsory jurisdiction.

Article 30.

M. FERNANDES proposed the following amendment:

"When the defendant party alleges that it has not accepted the jurisdiction of the Court, the latter shall decide whether an agreement exists."

LORD PHILLIMORE asked to be informed as to the meaning of the word "engagement" (agreement). He wished to know whether it also included involuntary obligations.

Mr. ROOT soulève des objections contre une formule qui lierait les Etats également dans des cas où ils ne sont pas liés par le Pacte de la Société des Nations ou par des traités ou conventions.

En réponse à une proposition de M. LODER, appuyée par Mr. Root, de supprimer l'article, le PRESIDENT explique la différence entre l'obligation générale de soumettre les litiges à un règlement judiciaire et l'obligation de porter un cas déterminé devant une certaine Cour.

Le President dit qu'il importe de couvrir les deux alternatives.

LORD PHILLIMORE fait valoir que la rédaction actuelle a été interprétée de deux façons diamétralement opposées par M. Hagerup et par M. de Lapradelle; le texte est donc équivoque.

D'accord avec M. Root il propose de nouveau la suppression de l'article.

M. HAGERUP propose la formule suivante:

„Lorsqu'une partie dénie la compétence de la Cour, il appartient à celle ci de statuer sur le point de savoir si la partie n'a pas accepté cette compétence, soit par son adhésion au Pacte de la Société des Nations, soit par une autre convention."

M. FERNANDES propose une autre formule:

„Si la compétence de la Cour est contestée par l'Etat défendeur, soit en raison de l'objet du litige, soit parce que le dit Etat ne se croit pas obligé à la juridiction de la Cour, celle-ci statue sur la question en ordre préjudiciel."

La suppression de l'article est finalement décidée, sur la proposition de M. DE LAPRADELLE.

La séance est levée à 6.35 heures de l'après-midi.

Le Président:
(signé) Brn. DESCAMPS.

Le Secrétaire-Général:
(signé) D. ANZILOTTI.

Mr. ROOT objected to a wording which would be equally binding upon States in cases in which they were not bound by the Covenant or by Treaties or Conventions.

In answer to a proposal by M. LODER, supported by Mr. Root, to eliminate the article, the PRESIDENT explained the difference between a general obligation to submit cases for judicial settlement, and an obligation to submit a certain case to a particular Court.

The President said that both alternatives must be mentioned.

LORD PHILLIMORE pointed out that the present wording had been interpreted in two diametrically opposite ways by M. Hagerup and M. de Lapradelle: it was therefore ambiguous.

In agreement with Mr. Root, he again proposed that the Article be deleted.

M. HAGERUP proposed the following wording:

"When a party refuses to recognise the jurisdiction of the Court, the latter shall decide whether the party has accepted this jurisdiction by virtue, either of its adherence to the Covenant of the League of Nations, or of some other Convention."

M. FERNANDES proposed another wording:

"If the jurisdiction of the Court is disputed by the defendant State, either by reason of the subject matter of the case, or because it does not consider itself bound to submit to the jurisdiction of the Court, the latter shall decide the point as an interlocutory question."

The Article was finally deleted, on M. DE LAPRADELLE's proposal.

The meeting closed at 6.35 p. m.

The President:
(signed) Brn. DESCAMPS.

The Secretary-General:
(signed) D. ANZILOTTI.

30IÈME SÉANCE (non-publique), tenue au Palais de la Paix, à La Haye, le 21 juillet 1920.

Présidence de M. le BARON DESCAMPS.

Sont présents: tous les membres du Comité (à l'exception de M. Bevilaqua); M. Fernandes; Mr. James Brown Scott; les secrétaires particuliers de M. le Baron Descamps et de M. Adatci; les membres du Secrétariat.

La séance est ouverte à 9.50 heures du matin.

Le PRESIDENT ouvre la discussion sur les articles du texte du Comité de rédaction qui restent réservés après les séances du 19 et du 20 juillet.

Article 11 (alinea 1er.)

Le PRESIDENT propose le texte suivant de l'alinéa 1er:

„Si après la troisième élection il reste encore un ou plusieurs sièges à pourvoir, l'Assemblée ou le Conseil peut à tout moment demander la formation d'une Commission médiatrice de six membres, nommés trois par l'Assemblée et trois par le Conseil, en vue de choisir pour chaque siège non pourvu un nom à présenter à l'adoption séparée de l'Assemblée et du Conseil."

M. DE LAPRADELLE attire l'attention sur le texte proposé par lui la veille (voir procès-verbal de la (28e.) séance du matin du 20 juillet).

Cette formule est adoptée avec une légère modification.

Article 28 bis.

Le PRESIDENT propose le texte suivant pour le nouvel article sur l'insertion duquel on s'est mis d'accord lors de la discussion sur l'article 29 (voir procès-verbal de la (29e.) séance de l'après-midi du 20 juillet.)

„Lorsqu'un différend surgit entre Etats, qu'il n'a pu être réglé par la voie diplomatique et que l'on n'est pas convenu de choisir une autre juridiction, la partie qui se prétend lésée peut en

30TH MEETING (Private), held at the Peace Palace, The Hague, on July 21st, 1920.

BARON DESCAMPS in the chair.

Present: all the members of the Committee (except M. Bevilaqua); M. Fernandes; M. James Brown Scott; the private secretaries of Baron Descamps and M. Adatci; the members of the Secretariat.

The meeting opened at 9.50 a. m.

The PRESIDENT opened the debate upon the articles of the text of the Drafting Committee which had been reserved and had not been dealt with at the meetings of July 19th and 20th.

Article 11 (Paragraph 1.)

The PRESIDENT proposed the following wording for Paragraph 1.:

"If, after the third sitting, one or more seats still remain unfilled, the Assembly or the Council may, at any time, call for the formation of a Joint Conference of six members, three appointed by the Assembly and three by the Council, for the purpose of choosing one name for each seat still vacant, to submit to the Assembly and Council for their respective acceptance."

M. DE LAPRADELLE called attention to the text proposed by him on the previous day, (See Proces-Verbal of the (28th) meeting on the morning of July 20th).

The wording was adopted with a slight modification.

Article 28 bis.

The PRESIDENT proposed the following text for the new Article which it had been agreed to insert at the time of the debate upon Article 29. (See Proces-Verbal of the (29th) meeting on the afternoon of July 20th).

"When a dispute has arisen between States, and it has been found impossible to settle it by diplomatic means, and no agreement has been made to choose another jurisdiction, the party

saisir la Cour qui statue sous les conditions et limitations déterminées par l'article 29 ci-après."

Ce texte est d'abord adopté.

On soulève ensuite la question de savoir si c'est la Cour qui décide si une partie s'est engagée à recourir à une juridiction. La question est résolue affirmativement.

Lors de la discussion de l'article 29, no. 2, on propose d'ajouter à l'article 28bis la formule:

„En cas de contestation la Cour statue sur sa compétence."

Après une discussion sur des formules de transaction soumises par M. DE LAPRADELLE et par le PRESIDENT, celui-ci propose finalement la rédaction suivante qui est adoptée:

„La Cour, après avoir décidé s'il est satisfait aux prescriptions précédentes, statue...."

Article 29.

M. HAGERUP propose la suppression de l'article 29, no. 2, qui, après l'adoption de l'article 28bis, lui semble inutile, et qui du reste lui paraît incomplet, la Cour devant statuer sur sa compétence non seulement en cas de contestation, mais aussi d'office.

M. FERNANDES reprend l'amendement qu'il a déposé la veille (voir procès-verbal de l'après-midi du 20 juillet).

LORD PHILLIMORE propose d'introduire un nouvel article qui se réfèrerait en même temps à l'article 28bis et à l'article 29, et qui contiendrait, en ce qui concerne ces deux articles, des stipulations analogues à celles du no. 2 de l'article 29. Il propose, comme alternative, d'introduire dans les règles de procédure une stipulation constatant le devoir de la Cour de statuer sur sa propre compétence en cas de jugement par contumace; dans ce cas le no. 2 de l'article 29 pourrait être maintenu.

M. HAGERUP propose la formule suivante pour le nouvel article dont l'insertion a été suggérée par Lord Phillimore:

„En cas de contestation sur le point de savoir si un différend rentre, oui ou non, dans les catégories visées à l'article..., ou si les conditions visées à l'article... sont remplies, la Cour décide en ordre préjudiciel."

complaining may bring the case before the Court: the Court shall hear and determine the case in accordance with the provisions and within the limits laid down in Article 29 below."

This wording was first adopted.

The question was then raised as to whether it should be for the Court to decide whether a party had agreed to have recourse to a tribunal. The question was decided in the affirmative.

During the discussion of Article 29, No. 2, it was proposed to add the following to Article 28 bis:

"In the event of a dispute regarding its jurisdiction the matter shall be settled by the decision of the Court."

After a discussion concerning the compromises proposed by M. DE LAPRADELLE and the PRESIDENT, the latter finally proposed the following wording, which was adopted:

"The Court shall first of all decide whether the preceding conditions have been complied with; if so, it shall hear and determine..."

Article 29.

M. HAGERUP proposed that Article 29, Paragraph 2, should be deleted, as it seemed to him to be useless, now that Article 28 bis had been adopted. Further, it seemed to him to be incomplete, as the Court must decide the question of its jurisdiction, not merely in the event of a dispute, but of its own accord.

M. FERNANDES again put forward the amendment that he had submitted on the previous day. (See Procès-Verbal of July 20th, afternoon).

LORD PHILLIMORE proposed the introduction of a new Article, referring both to Article 28 bis, and to 29, containing provisions similar to those of No. 2 of Article 29 to be read in conjunction with these two Articles. As an alternative, he proposed the introduction in the rules of procedure of a provision, laying down that it is the duty of the Court to decide whether it has jurisdiction in cases of judgment by default: under these circumstances No. 2 of Article 29 could be maintained.

M. HAGERUP proposed the following wording for the new Article which Lord Phillimore had suggested:

"In the case of a dispute as to whether a case does or does not come within any of the categories mentioned in the Article, or as to whether the conditions laid down in the Article are complied with, the matter shall be decided by the Court as an interlocutory question."

M. RICCI-BUSATTI propose, dans le même ordre d'idées, la formule suivante:

„La Cour statue sur sa propre compétence en ordre préjudiciel, en ce qui concerne soit l'objet en litige, soit tout autre motif qui pourrait exclure sa juridiction."

LORD PHILLIMORE, qui n'est pas satisfait de cette formule, en propose une autre qui est ainsi amendée par M. DE LAPRADELLE:

„Si la compétence de la Cour est déniée parce qu'il n'est pas satisfait aux conditions ou limitations prévues dans les articles 28 bis et 29, la Cour statue sur sa compétence. L'examen de cette question est préjudiciel par rapport à tout autre."

Mr. ROOT s'oppose formellement à la suppression de l'article 29, no. 2. Il dit que son consentement à l'article 29 a été basé sur l'existence du no. 2 de cet article. Il fait valoir que le consentement des nations au grand progrès que constitue l'institution d'une juridiction obligatoire dépendra de l'adoption d'une règle conférant à la Cour le droit de statuer sur sa compétence seulement d'après des normes fixées d'avance; en tout cas, la Cour ne doit pouvoir établir d'abord ces normes et puis juger si, en vertu de ces mêmes normes, elle est compétente.

LE PRESIDENT rappelle que déjà en 1907 on a consacré la règle de la juridiction obligatoire pour certains conflits internationaux.

A la suite de la discussion, l'article 29 est adopté sans modifications. Une addition est faite à l'article 28 bis (voir ci-dessus).

Article 24.

M. LODER fait valoir la nécessité d'arrêter des règles pour la procédure sommaire. Il attire l'attention sur l'article 51 du projet des Cinq Puissances.

Le PRESIDENT se réfère aux règles adoptées en 1907.

LORD PHILLIMORE propose la suppression des mots „en procédure sommaire" à l'article 24.

Mr. ROOT suggère l'idée de laisser à la Cour le soin d'établir un règlement pour la procédure sommaire.

M. RICCI-BUSATTI in the same connection proposed the following wording:

" Any question as to the jurisdiction of the Court arising out of the subject matter of the case, or from any other reason which might preclude its jurisdiction, shall be decided by the Court as an interlocutory question."

As LORD PHILLIMORE was not satisfied with this, he proposed another wording which was amended by M. DE LAPRADELLE as follows:

" If a party refuses to acknowledge the jurisdiction of the Court, on the ground that the provisions and limitations contained in Article 28 bis and 29 have not been complied with, the matter shall be decided by the Court. This question shall take precedence of all others."

Mr. ROOT formally opposed the deletion of Article 29 No. 2. He said that his consent to Article 29 depended upon the existence of No. 2 of this article. He pointed out that the consent of the nations to the great progressive measure represented by the institution of a compulsory jurisdiction would be dependent upon the adoption of a provision, limiting the Court's right to decide the question of its own jurisdiction, in accordance with rules laid down beforehand. In any case, the Court must not have the power, both to establish these rules, and also to decide whether it has jurisdiction, in accordance with the same rules.

The PRESIDENT pointed out that the rules of compulsory jurisdiction for certain international disputes had already been recognised in 1907.

Following upon this discussion, Article 29 was adopted without alteration. One addition was made to Article 28 bis (See above).

Article 24.

M. LODER pointed out the necessity of laying down rules for the summary procedure. He called attention to Article 51 of the Five Powers' plan.

The PRESIDENT referred to the rules adopted in 1907.

LORD PHILLIMORE proposed that the words "by summary procedure" in Article 24 should be deleted.

Mr. ROOT suggested that the regulation of the summary procedure should be left to the Court.

Dans cet ordre d'idées, le PRESIDENT propose le texte suivant qui est adopté comme un nouvel article:

„La Cour détermine par un règlement d'ordre le mode suivant lequel elle exerce ses attributions. Elle règle spécialement ce qui concerne la procédure sommaire."

En raison de la décision prise lors de la discussion de l'article 24, M. RICCI-BUSATTI propose de formuler ainsi le premier alinéa de l'article 22bis:

„La Cour exerce normalement ses attributions...."

Comme alternative M. Ricci-Busatti propose d'ajouter au commencement de cet alinéa:

„Sauf le cas prévu à l'article 24, la Cour exerce...."

Sur la proposition de M. DE LAPRADELLE on se met d'accord pour ajouter au commencement de l'alinéa la formule suivante:

„Sauf exception expressément prévue...."

Cette formule, mise au vote, est adoptée.

Le PRESIDENT déclare ne pouvoir pas prendre part à un vote portant sur des dispositions qu'il regrette au point de vue du bon fonctionnement de la Cour.

Article 31.

Le Président propose de substituer au mot „successivement" l'expression „en ordre successif". On se met d'accord sur cette modification.

Le Président suggère la rédaction suivante du no. 4 à titre de transaction:

„La Cour tient compte des décisions judiciaires et de la doctrine des publicistes les plus qualifiés des différentes nations comme moyens auxiliaires de la détermination des règles de droit".

M. RICCI-BUSATTI voudrait substituer à l'expression „de la détermination des règles de droit" l'expression „d'interprétation juridique".

Cette proposition est rejetée.

LORD PHILLIMORE propose la suppression des mots „règles de droit qui se dégagent des".

Le texte original est adopté avec les modifications indiquées ci-dessus.

M. RICCI-BUSATTI vote contre.

Afin de donner satisfaction aux objections soulevées par M. Hagerup lors de la discussion

In this connection, the PRESIDENT proposed the following clause, which was adopted as a new Article:

"The Court shall frame rules for regulating its procedure. In particular, it shall lay down rules for summary procedure."

In virtue of the decision arrived at during the debate upon Article 24, M. RICCI-BUSATTI proposed to word the first Paragraph of Article 22 bis thus:

"The Court shall normally exercise its powers..."

As an alternative, he suggested the following addition at the commencement of the Paragraph:

"Except as provided in Article 24, the Court shall exercise..."

At the suggestion of M. DE LAPRADELLE, the Committee agreed to add the following words to the Paragraph:

"Except when it is expressly provided otherwise..."

This wording was put to the vote and adopted.

The PRESIDENT declared that he could not take part in a vote on the subject of provisions which he thought would be detrimental to the performance of the Court's functions.

Article 31.

The President (with reference to the French version) proposed to substitute the expression: "en ordre successif" for the word "successivement". This modification was agreed to.

The President, as a compromise, suggested the following wording for heading No. 4:

"The Court shall take into consideration judicial decisions and the teachings of the most highly qualified publicists of the various nations as subsidiary means for the determination of rules of law."

M. RICCI-BUSATTI wished to substitute the expression "juridical interpretation" for the expression "determination of rules of law".

This proposal was rejected.

LORD PHILLIMORE proposed that the words "rules of law derived from" should be deleted.

The original wording was adopted with the modifications indicated above.

M. RICCI-BUSATTI voted against the Article.

In order to meet the objections raised by M. Hagerup, during the discussion of Article 29 no. 2,

de l'article 29 no. 2, on se met d'accord pour insérer à l'alinéa 2 de l'article 15 les mots:

„non seulement qu'elle a compétence mais...." entre les mots „s'assurer" et „que ces conclusions".

M. HAGERUP formule des objections contre la disposition d'après laquelle „l'autre partie peut demander à la Cour... etc." Il va de soi que cette faculté appartient à la partie en question.

Cette observation, qui ne paraît pas fondée, n'est pas prise en considération.

Article 22.

La rédaction de l'alinéa 1er, qui avait été réservée, est complétée par l'addition des mots „et que la partie, sans faute de sa part, pouvait ne pas connaître."

L'article sous cette nouvelle forme est adopté.

Article 22 bis.

Des objections sont soulevées contre l'expression „intérêts d'ordre juridique". Ces objections ne donnent pas lieu à des modifications.

Le PRESIDENT prie le Secrétariat de préparer et de distribuer avant 4 heures de l'après-midi du même jour une édition complète du texte des articles qu'on a adoptés pendant les 6 dernières séances. Les articles doivent être numérotés dans un ordre consécutif et logique.

Sur la proposition de M. DE LAPRADELLE, la réunion pour la seconde lecture est fixée, non pas à 4 heures du même jour, mais à 9 heures 30 du jour suivant

Mr. ROOT attire l'attention sur les vœux provisoirement adoptés par le Comité et qui attendent un vote définitif.

Le PRESIDENT met aux voix le premier vœu, proposé par M. Root et le Baron Descamps et relatif à la convocation de conférences périodiques pour le progrès du droit international.

Ce vœu est adopté, avec l'addition, dans l'énumération des grandes académies internationales, de la „International Law Association", et sauf rédaction.

Le second vœu concernant l'établissement d'une juridiction internationale en matière criminelle, proposé par le Président, est maintenant présenté par lui dans une nouvelle rédaction qui est adoptée à l'unanimité.

the Committee agreed to insert the following words in Paragraph 2 of Article 15:

"Not only that it has jurisdiction but also..." between the words "satisfy itself" and "that the claim".

M. HAGERUP objected to the provision, by which "the other party may call upon the Court... etc." The party in question would naturally have this right.

This proposal was not taken into consideration, as it did not appear to be justified.

Article 22.

The wording of the first Paragraph, which had been reserved, was completed by the addition of the words: "and of which the said party might be ignorant, through no fault of its own."

The Article was adopted with this new wording.

Article 22 bis.

Some objections were raised to the expression "interests of a legal nature", but did not give rise to any alterations.

The PRESIDENT requested the Secretariat to prepare and distribute before 4 p. m. of the same day a complete edition of the text of the Articles adopted during the last 6 meetings. The Articles were to be numbered in a consecutive and logical order.

At M. DE LAPRADELLE's proposal, the meeting for the second reading was fixed for 9.30 a. m. on the following day, instead of 4 p. m. the same day.

Mr. ROOT drew attention to the resolutions, which had been provisionally adopted by the Committee, but had yet to be put to a final vote.

The PRESIDENT took a vote upon the first resolution which he and Mr. Root had proposed, concerning the convocation of periodical conferences for the development of international Law.

This resolution was adopted subject to amendment in wording. In the enumeration of great international academies, the International Law Association was added.

The second resolution concerning the establishment of an international jurisdiction for criminal cases, proposed by the President, was then presented by him in a new form, which was unanimously adopted.

M. LODER donne lecture d'un troisième projet de vœu, relatif à l'établissement d'une Académie de droit international à La Haye.

Dans la discussion qui s'en suit, M. DE LAPRADELLE attire l'attention sur le fait qu'une Académie de droit international existe déjà, du moins virtuellement, depuis 1913, bien que la guerre l'ait empêchée d'entrer en activité.

Il fait en outre valoir que le siège de la Cour n'est pas nécessairement la meilleure place pour l'établissement de l'Académie. Pour ces raisons, il se voit, à regret, dans l'impossibilité d'appuyer la proposition, sous sa forme actuelle.

M. HAGERUP, de sa part, dit que l'Académie de 1913 non seulement existe, mais est munie d'un curatorium, dont il est membre. Dans ces circonstances, on devra se borner à recommander que l'Académie soit mise en activité.

M. DE LAPRADELLE fait encore valoir la différence qui existe entre les deux premiers et le dernier vœu, ceux-là devant être présentés à la Société des Nations, tandis que celui-ci est indépendant de la Société.

Une nouvelle rédaction du vœu de M. Loder, tenant compte des observations qui viennent d'être indiquées, est adoptée à l'unanimité.

La séance est levée à 12.45 heures de l'après-midi.

Le Président :
(signé) Brn. DESCAMPS.

Le Secrétaire-Général :
(signé) D. ANZILOTTI.

M. LODER read a third draft resolution, concerning the establishment of an Academy of International Law at The Hague.

During the discussion which followed, M. DE LAPRADELLE pointed out that an Academy of International Law had already existed, at any rate on paper, since 1913, though the war had prevented it from coming into operation.

Further, he pointed out that the seat of the Court was not necessarily the best place in which to establish the Academy. For these reasons, and much to his regret, he could not support the proposal in its present form.

M. HAGERUP, for his part, said that the Academy of 1913 not only existed, but possessed a Governing Body of which he was a member. Under these circumstances they should confine themselves to a recommendation to the effect that the existing Academy should be set in operation.

M. DE LAPRADELLE also pointed out the difference between the two first and the last resolutions. The former had to be presented to the League of Nations, whereas the latter did not concern the League.

A new wording of M. Loder's resolution, drawn up in accordance with the observations mentioned above, was unanimously adopted.

The meeting closed at 12.45 p. m.

The President :
(signed) Brn. DESCAMPS.

The Secretary-General :
(signed) D. ANZILOTTI.

ANNEX No. 1.

(Texte revisé des Articles réservés le 19 juillet, avec, en regard, compte-rendu des délibérations du Comité, du 20 juillet.)

Article 2.

Mr. ROOT retire la réserve qu'il avait fait le jour auparavant au sujet de cet article, mais propose l'insertion après le mot „morale" de la formule suivante:

„qui tous devront remplir les conditions requises dans leurs pays respectifs pour l'admission dans la haute magistrature ou possédant..."

M. DE LAPRADELLE rappelle l'article 44 de la convention de 1907.

Il dit qu'il se serait contenté de la formule suivante:

„La Cour Permanente de Justice Internationale est un corps de magistrats indépendants, choisis sans égard à leur nationalité parmi les personnes d'une science et d'une expérience juridique reconnues."

Le PRESIDENT suggère l'adoption de la formule „la *plus* haute magistrature."

Mr. ROOT demande un vote sur la formule qu'il a proposée.

M. DE LAPRADELLE en propose une autre: „...plus haute magistrature de leurs pays ou des jurisconsultes possédant..."

La Cour Permanente de Justice Internationale est un corps de magistrats indépendants, choisis sans égard à leur nationalité parmi les personnes jouissant de la plus haute considération morale, et réunissant les conditions requises pour l'exercice dans leurs pays respectifs de la plus haute magistrature, ou étant des jurisconsultes possédant une compétence notoire en matière de droit international.

Article 4.

M. ALTAMIRA soulève la question du droit de démission.

LORD PHILLIMORE lui répond que ce droit résulte du droit commun.

Les membres de la Cour sont élus pour 9 ans.

Ils sont rééligibles.

Ils restent en fonction jusqu'à leur remplacement.

Après ce remplacement, ils continuent de connaître des affaires dont ils sont déjà saisis.

Article 5.

La nouvelle formule est proposée par le PRESIDENT. Il explique que l'expression „groupes nationaux" peut être maintenue puisqu'elle ne signifie pas „groupes de nationaux".

Les membres de la Cour sont élus par l'Assemblée et par le Conseil sur une liste de personnes présentées par les groupes nationaux de la Cour d'Arbitrage, conformément aux dispositions suivantes.

Article 6.

La formule adoptée pour le premier alinéa est proposée par le Président.

Trois mois au moins avant la date de l'élection, le Secrétaire-Général invite par écrit les membres

Au sujet du second alinéa M. HAGERUP s'oppose contre le nombre de deux candidats; il rappelle qu'on avait d'abord adopté le nombre de six.

Une proposition du PRESIDENT d'insérer dans l'alinéa 2 l'expression „pour chaque place" est rejetée.

de la Cour d'Arbitrage appartenant à des Etats faisant partie de la Société des Nations ou mentionnés à l'Annexe au Pacte de la Société des Nations, à procéder par groupes nationaux à la présentation des personnes en situation de remplir les fonctions de membre de la Cour.

Chaque groupe ne peut en aucun cas présenter plus de 2 personnes, sans distinction de nationalité.

Article 8.

Le nouveau texte est proposé par le PRESIDENT.

Le Secrétaire-Général dresse, par ordre alphabéthique, une liste de toutes les personnes ainsi désignées: seules ces personnes sont éligibles, sauf le cas prévu à l'article 11, paragraphe 2.

Le Secrétaire-Général communique cette liste à l'Assemblée et au Conseil.

Article 11.

Un très grand nombre de formules sont proposées par MM. FERNANDES, ADATCI, ROOT, DE LAPRADELLE, LORD PHILLIMORE, HAGERUP et le PRESIDENT.

Le PRESIDENT propose la formule suivante: „Si après la troisième élection il reste encore un ou plusieurs sièges à pourvoir, il peut être formé sur l'initiative, soit de l'Assemblée, soit du Conseil, une Commission médiatrice . . ."

LORD PHILLIMORE propose la formule suivante:

„A tout moment après la troisième élection l'Assemblée ou le Conseil pourra demander une commission médiatrice et il sera formé . . . ."

M. DE LAPRADELLE propose la formule suivante:

„Si après la troisième élection, il reste encore des sièges à pourvoir, il est à tout moment formé sur la seule demande soit de l'Assemblée, soit du Conseil, une Commission médiatrice . . . ."

Sur la proposition du PRESIDENT il est décidé que la rédaction finale de l'alinéa soit laissée à M. de Lapradelle.

L'alinéa 2 a été adopté déjà la veille.

Peuvent être portées sur cette liste, à l'unanimité, toutes personnes satisfaisant aux conditions requises, alors même qu'elles n'auraient pas figuré sur la liste de présentation de la Cour d'Arbitrage.

Alinéa 3. M. HAGERUP propose la formule suivante:

„Si après la réunion de la Commission médiatrice l'entente n'est pas obtenue, les membres de

Si par le moyen de la Commission médiatrice l'élection n'a pu être faite, les membres de la Cour déjà nommés pourvoient, dans un délai à fixer par le Conseil de la Société des Nations, par coopta-

la Cour déjà nommés pourvoient, dans un délai à fixer par le Conseil, par cooptation aux sièges vacants."

M. DE LAPRADELLE propose cette formule: „Si, par le moyen de la commission médiatrice, l'élection n'a pu être faite, ou l'entente ne peut être obtenue, les membres de la Cour déjà nommés pourvoient par cooptation aux sièges vacants en choisissant parmi les personnes ...."

La rédaction finale est basée sur ces deux propositions.

tion aux sièges vacants, en choisissant parmi les personnes qui ont eu des voix, soit à l'Assemblée, soit au Conseil.

Si, parmi les juges, il y a partage égal de voix, la voix du juge le plus âgé l'emporte.

Article 22.

Formé par les alinéas 2, 3, et 4 de l'article 22 du texte du comité de rédaction.

Si, pour une raison spéciale, l'un des membres de la Cour estime ne pouvoir participer au jugement d'une affaire déterminée, il en fait part au Président.

Si le Président estime qu'un des membres de la Cour ne peut siéger pour une raison spéciale dans une affaire déterminée, il en avertit le membre intéressé.

Si l'un et l'autre ne sont pas d'accord dans chacun de ces cas sur l'attitude à prendre, la Cour décide.

Article 22bis.

Correspond aux alinéas 1 et 5 du texte originaire du Comité de rédaction, avec un amendement de M. Fernandes.

Le troisième alinéa a été proposé par M. Fernandes.

La Cour exerce ses attributions en séance plénière.

Si la présence d'onze juges titulaires n'est pas assurée, ce nombre est parfait par l'entrée en fonction des juges suppléants.

Toutefois, si onze juges ne sont pas disponibles, le quorum de neuf sera suffisant pour constituer la Cour.

Article 24bis.

Le texte adopté a été proposé par le Président en remplacement du texte proposé par lui la veille.

Il est pourvu aux sièges devenus vacants selon la méthode suivie pour la première élection.

Le membre de la Cour élu en remplacement d'un membre dont le mandat n'est pas expiré, achève le terme du mandat de son prédécesseur.

Article 25.

M. DE LAPRADELLE propose la suppression du premier alinéa. Cette proposition, mise aux voix, est rejetée.

M. RICCI-BUSATTI déclare que la hâte des travaux du Comité l'empêche de faire une série de remarques sur cet article, ainsi que sur certains autres, étant donné qu'il manque le temps nécessaire pour pénétrer d'une façon suffisante les dispositions en question.

1. Lorsque la Cour renferme un juge titulaire de la nationalité de chacune des parties en cause, ces juges conservent le droit de siéger dans l'affaire dont la Cour est saisie.

2. Si la Cour ne renferme qu'un juge titulaire de la nationalité d'une seule des parties en cause, l'autre partie désigne pour siéger, parmi les juges suppléants, un juge de sa nationalité, s'il en existe. S'il n'en existe pas, elle choisit un juge; de préférence parmi les personnes qui ont été l'objet d'une

Le texte est adopté comme partie du texte préparé par le Comité de rédaction, et puis réservé.

présentation de la part des groupes nationaux de la Cour d'Arbitrage.

3. Si la Cour ne renferme aucun juge titulaire de la nationalité des parties en cause, chacune de ces parties procède à la désignation ou au choix d'un juge de la même manière que dans le cas précédent.

4. Lorsque plusieurs parties font cause commune, elles ne peuvent désigner ou choisir qu'un seul juge de commun accord.

5. Les juges désignés ou choisis comme il est dit ci-dessus, doivent satisfaire aux prescriptions des articles 2, 14, 15, 18, 22, du présent statut. Ils statuent sur un pied d'égalité avec leurs collègues.

Article 25bis (anciens 13 et 19 alinéa 2.)

Le texte adopté est proposé par M. DE LAPRADELLE, d'accord avec MM. FERNANDES et HAGERUP.

L'avant dernier alinéa est proposé par M. RICCI-BUSATTI, qui est appuyé par LORD PHILLIMORE et par le PRESIDENT.

Les juges titulaires reçoivent un traitement annuel à fixer par l'Assemblée de la Société des Nations sur la proposition du Conseil. Ce traitement ne peut être diminué pendant la durée des fonctions du juge.

Le Président reçoit une indemnité spéciale déterminée de la même manière pour la durée de ses fonctions.

Les juges suppléants reçoivent dans l'exercice de leurs fonctions une indemnité à fixer de la même manière.

Un règlement spécial détermine les pensions auxquelles ont droit les juges.

Les juges titulaires et suppléants qui ne résident pas au siège de la Cour auront droit au remboursement des frais de voyages nécessités par l'accomplissement de leurs fonctions.

L'indemnité due aux juges désignés ou choisis conformément à l'article 25 est réglée de la même manière.

Le traitement du greffier est fixé par le Conseil sur la proposition de la Cour.

Article 26.

Le texte adopté est celui proposé la veille par M. DE LAPRADELLE.

Les frais de la Cour sont supportés par la Société des Nations de la manière que l'Assemblée décide sur la proposition du Conseil.

Article 28.

M. RICCI-BUSATTI soulève la question des cas sporadiques où la Cour est compétente pour juger de conflits auxquels une des parties est un Etat qui n'est pas Membre de la Société des Nations.

On se met d'accord pour reconnaître qu'il est inutile de faire une exception pour ces cas, puisque

La Cour est ouverte aux Etats Membres de la Société des Nations. Elle l'est de même aux Etats mentionnés à l'Annexe au Pacte de la Société des Nations.

Elle est aussi accessible aux autres Etats.

Les conditions, auxquelles elle est ouverte ou

le Conseil s'inspirera du Traité de Versailles en posant ses conditions.

M. DE LAPRADELLE maintient son vote contraire à cet article.

accessible aux Etats qui ne sont pas Membres de la Société des Nations sont réglées par le Conseil, en tenant compte de l'article 17 du Pacte.

Article 29.

Mr. ROOT remarque l'omission de la stipulation à l'article 30 du plan Root—Phillimore, aux termes de laquelle les moyens diplomatiques doivent être épuisés avant le recours à la juridiction internationale.

Il en demande l'insertion dans le projet du Comité.

LORD PHILLIMORE propose la formule suivante:

„Lorsqu'un différend tel qu'il est prévu dans... s'élève entre Etats et que le différend n'a pu être réglé par voie diplomatique et que l'on n'est pas convenu pour une autre juridiction dans le sens de l'article 13 du Pacte, la partie qui se prétend lésée, peut en saisir la Cour Permanente."

On est d'accord pour reconnaître la désirabilité de l'insertion d'une stipulation à cet effet. Une rédaction sera préparée pour mercredi. La place de la nouvelle disposition est réservée.

Entre Etats Membres de la Société des Nations la Cour statue sans convention spéciale sur les différends d'ordre juridique, qui ont pour objet:

a. L'interprétation d'un traité;

b. Tout point de droit international;

c. La réalité de tout fait, qui, s'il était établi, constituerait la violation d'un engagement international;

d. La nature ou l'étendue de la réparation due pour la rupture d'un engagement international;

e. L'interprétation d'une sentence rendue par la Cour.

La Cour connaît également de tous différends, de quelque nature qu'ils soient, qui lui sont soumis par la convention, soit générale, soit spéciale, des parties.

En cas de contestation sur le point de savoir si un différend rentre, oui ou non, dans les catégories ci-dessus visées, la Cour décide.

Article 30.

M. FERNANDES propose l'amendement suivant:

„Lorsque la partie assignée allègue ne pas avoir accepté la juridiction de la Cour, celle-ci décide sur le point de savoir s'il y a un engagement de sa part."

Mr. ROOT soulève des objections contre une formule qui lierait les Etats également dans des cas où ils ne sont pas liés par le Pacte de la Société des Nations ou par des traités ou conventions.

LORD PHILLIMORE fait valoir que la rédaction actuelle a été interprétée de deux façons diamétralement opposées par M. Hagerup et par M. de Lapradelle; le texte est donc équivoque.

D'accord avec Mr. ROOT, il propose la suppression de l'article.

M. HAGERUP propose la formule suivante:

„Lorsqu'une partie dénie la compétence de la Cour, il appartient à celle-ci de statuer sur le point de savoir, si la partie n'a pas ,accepté

Supprimé.

cette compétence, soit par son adhésion au Pacte de la Société des Nations, soit par une autre convention".

M. FERNANDES propose une autre formule: „Si la compétence de la Cour est contestée par l'Etat défendeur, soit en raison de l'objet du litige, soit parce que le dit Etat ne se croit pas obligé à la juridiction de la Cour, celle-ci statue sur la question en ordre préjudiciel."

La suppression de l'article est finalement décidée sur la proposition de M. de Lapradelle.

ANNEXE No. 2.

(Texte des Chapitres I et II de l'Avant-projet, avec les modifications adoptées les 19 et 20 juillet.)

Article 1er.

Indépendamment de la Cour d'Arbitrage, organisée par les Conventions de La Haye de 1899 et 1907, et des Tribunaux spéciaux d'Arbitres, auxquels les Etats demeurent toujours libres de confier la solution de leurs différends, il est institué, conformément à l'article 14 du Pacte de la Société des Nations, une Cour Permanente de Justice Internationale, directement accessible aux parties.

Chapitre I.

Organisation de la Cour.

Article 2.

La Cour Permanente de Justice Internationale est un corps de magistrats indépendants, choisis sans égard à leur nationalité parmi les personnes, jouissant de la plus haute considération morale, et réunissant les conditions requises pour l'exercice dans leurs pays respectifs de la plus haute magistrature, ou étant des jurisconsultes possédant une compétence notoire en matière de droit international.

Article 3.

La Cour se compose de quinze membres : onze juges titulaires et quatre juges suppléants. Le nombre des juges titulaires et des juges suppléants peut être éventuellement augmenté par l'Assemblée, sur la proposition du Conseil de la Société des Nations, à concurrence de quinze juges titulaires et six juges suppléants.

Article 4.

Les membres de la Cour sont élus pour 9 ans.
Ils sont rééligibles.

Ils restent en fonction jusqu'à leur remplacement. Après ce remplacement, ils continuent de connaître des affaires dont ils sont déjà saisis.

Article 5.

Les membres de la Cour sont élus par l'Assemblée et par le Conseil sur une liste de personnes présentées par les groupes nationaux de la Cour d'Arbitrage, conformément aux dispositions suivantes.

ANNEX No. 2.

(Text of Chapters I and II of the Draft Scheme, as amended on July 19th and 20th.)

Article 1.

A Permanent Court of International Justice, to which Parties shall have direct access, is hereby established, in accordance with Article 14 of the Covenant of the League of Nations. This Court shall be in addition to the Court of Arbitration organised by the Hague Conventions of 1899 and 1907, and to the special Tribunals of Arbitration to which States are always at liberty to submit their disputes for settlement.

Chapter I.

Organisation of the Court.

Article 2.

The Permanent Court of International Justice shall be composed of a body of independent judges, chosen regardless of their nationality, from amongst persons of high moral character, who possess the qualifications required, in their respective countries, for appointment to the highest judicial offices, or are jurisconsults of recognised competence in international law.

Article 3.

The Court shall consist of fifteen members : eleven judges and four deputy-judges. The number of judges and deputy-judges may be hereafter increased by the Assembly, upon the proposal of the Council of the League of Nations, to a total of fifteen judges and six deputy-judges.

Article 4.

The members of the Court shall be elected for nine years.

They may be re-elected.

They shall continue to discharge their duties until their places have been filled. Though replaced, they shall complete any cases which they may have begun.

Article 5.

The members of the Court shall be elected by the Assembly and the Council from a list of persons nominated by the national groups in the Court of Arbitration, in accordance with the following provisions.

Article 6.

Trois mois au moins avant la date de l'élection, le Secrétaire-Général invite par écrit les membres de la Cour d'Arbitrage appartenant à des Etats faisant partie de la Société des Nations ou mentionnés à l'Annexe au Pacte de la Société des Nations à procéder par groupes nationaux à la présentation de personnes en situation de remplir les fonctions de membre de la Cour.

Chaque groupe ne peut en aucun cas présenter plus de 2 personnes, sans distinction de nationalité.

Article 7.

Avant de procéder à cette désignation il est recommandé à chaque groupe national de consulter la plus Haute Cour de Justice, les Facultés de Droit des Universités, et les Académies ou sections d'Académies nationales ou internationales, vouées à l'étude du droit.

Article 8.

Le Secrétaire-Général de la Société des Nations dresse, par ordre alphabétique, une liste de toutes les personnes ainsi désignées: seules ces personnes sont éligibles, sauf le cas prévu à l'article 11 paragraphe 2.

Le Secrétaire-Général communique cette liste à l'Assemblée et au Conseil.

Article 9.

L'Assemblée et le Conseil procèdent, indépendamment l'une de l'autre, à l'élection, d'abord des juges titulaires, ensuite des juges suppléants.

Article 9 bis.

Dans toute élection, les électeurs veillent à ce que les personnes appelées à faire partie de la Cour, non seulement réunissent individuellement les conditions requises, mais assurent dans l'ensemble la représentation des grandes formes de civilisation et des principaux systèmes juridiques du monde.

Article 9 ter.

Sont élus ceux qui ont réuni la majorité absolue des voix dans l'Assemblée et dans le Conseil.

Au cas où le double scrutin de l'Assemblée et du Conseil se porterait sur plus d'un membre de la même nationalité le plus âgé est seul élu.

Article 6.

At least three months before the date of the election, the Secretary-General of the League of Nations shall address a written request to the members of the Court of Arbitration, belonging to the States which are Members of the League of Nations or mentioned in the Annex to the Covenant of the League of Nations, to undertake, by national groups, the nomination of persons in a position to accept the duties of a member of the Court.

No group may nominate more than two persons; the nominees may be of any nationality.

Article 7.

Before making these nominations, each national group is hereby recommended to consult its Highest Court of Justice, the legal faculties of its universities and its national or international Academies or sections of Academies, devoted to the study of law.

Article 8.

The Secretary-General of the League of Nations shall prepare a list, in alphabetical order, of all the persons thus nominated. These persons only shall be eligible for appointment except as provided in Article 12 Paragraph 2.

The Secretary-General shall submit this list to the Assembly and to the Council.

Article 9.

The Assembly and the Council shall proceed to elect by independent voting first the judges and then the deputy-judges.

Article 9 bis.

At every election, the electors shall bear in mind that not only should all the persons appointed as members of the Court possess the qualifications required, but the whole body also should represent the main forms of civilisation and the principal legal systems of the world.

Article 9 ter.

Those candidates who obtain an absolute majority of votes in the Assembly and the Council shall be considered as elected.

In the event of more than one candidate of the same nationality being elected by the votes of both the Assembly and the Council, the eldest of these shall be considered as elected.

Article 10.

Si après la première élection il reste encore des sièges à pourvoir, il est procédé de la même manière à une seconde élection, puis à une troisième.

Article 11.

Le texte du premier alinéa doit être préparé par M. de Lapradelle et Lord Phillimore. Au cours de la séance, M. DE LAPRADELLE a proposé la rédaction suivante:

„Si après la troisième élection il reste encore des sièges à pourvoir, il est à tout moment formé sur la seule demande, soit de l'Assemblée, soit du Conseil, une Commission médiatrice de six membres, nommés trois par l'Assemblé, trois par le Conseil, en vue de choisir pour chaque siège non pourvu un nom à présenter à l'adoption séparée de l'Assemblée et du Conseil.

Peuvent être portées sur cette liste, à l'unanimité, toutes personnes satisfaisant aux conditions requises, alors même qu'elle n'auraient pas figuré sur la liste de présentation de la Cour d'Arbitrage.

Si par le moyen de la Commission médiatrice l'élection n'a pu être faite, les membres de la Cour déjà nommés pourvoient, dans un délai à fixer par le Conseil de la Société des Nations, par cooptation aux sièges vacants, en choisissant parmi les personnes qui ont eu des voix, soit à l'Assemblée, soit au Conseil.

Si parmi les juges, il y a partage égal de voix, la voix du juge le plus âgé l'emporte."

Article 12.

Supprimé.

Article 13.

Transféré.

Article 14.

L'exercice de toute fonction qui relève de la direction politique, soit nationale, soit internationale, des Etats, est incompatible avec la qualité de membre de la Cour.

En cas de doute la Cour décide.

Article 15.

Les membres de la Cour ne peuvent exercer les fonctions d'agents, de conseil ou d'avocat dans aucune affaire d'ordre international.

Article 10.

If, after the first election, one or more seats remain to be filled, a second, and if necessary, a third election shall take place in the same way.

Article 11.

The text for the first Paragraph is to be prepared by M. de Lapradelle and Lord Phillimore. During the sitting M. DE LAPRADELLE proposed the following text:

"If after the third election one or more seats still remain unfilled, a joint Conference consisting of six members, three appointed by the Assembly and three by the Council, may be formed, at any time, at the request of either the Assembly or the Council, for the purpose of choosing one name for each seat still vacant, to submit to the Assembly and the Council for their respective acceptance.

If the Committee is unanimously agreed upon any person who fulfils the required conditions, he may be included in its list, even though he was not included in the list of nominations made by the Court of Arbitration.

If the Joint Conference is not successful in procuring an election, those members of the Court who have already been appointed shall, within a time limit to be fixed by the Council of the League of Nations and by cooptation proceed to fill the vacant seats by election from amongst those candidates who have obtained votes either in the Assembly or in the Council.

In the event of an equality of votes amongst the judges, the eldest judge shall have a casting vote."

Article 12.

Struck out.

Article 13.

Transferred.

Article 14.

The exercise of any function which belongs to the political direction, national or international, of States by the members of the Court, is declared incompatible with their judicial duties.

Any doubt upon this point is settled by the decision of the Court.

Article 15.

No member of the Court can act as agent, counsel or advocate in any case of an international nature.

Ils ne peuvent participer au règlement d'aucune affaire dans laquelle ils sont antérieurement intervenus comme agents, conseils ou avocats de l'une des parties, membres d'un Tribunal national ou international, d'une Commission d'enquête, ou à tout autre titre.

En cas de doute la Cour décide.

No member may participate in the decision of any case in which he has previously taken an active part, as agent, counsel or advocate for one of the contesting parties, or as a member of a national or international Court, or of a Commission of Inquiry, or in any other capacity.

Any doubt upon this point is settled by the decision of the Court.

Article 16.

Les membres de la Cour ne peuvent être relevés de leurs fonctions que si, au jugement unanime des autres membres, ils ont cessé de répondre aux conditions requises.

Le Secrétaire-Général en est officiellement informé.

Cette communication emporte vacance de siège.

Article 16.

A member of the Court cannot be dismissed unless, in the unanimous opinion of the other members, he has ceased to fulfil the required conditions.

When this happens, a formal notification shall be given to the Secretary-General.

This notification makes the place vacant.

Article 17.

En dehors de leurs propres pays, les membres de la Cour jouissent des mêmes privilèges et immunités que les Agents diplomatiques.

Article 17.

The members of the Court, when outside their own country, shall enjoy the privileges and immunities of diplomatic representatives.

Article 18.

Tout membre de la Cour doit, avant d'entrer en fonctions, faire, en séance publique, une déclaration solennelle de sa volonté d'exercer ses attributions avec impartialité et en toute conscience.

Article 18.

Every member of the Court shall, before taking up his duties, make a solemn declaration in open Court that he will exercise his powers impartially and conscientiously.

Article 19.

La Cour élit, pour trois ans, son Président et son Vice-Président: ils sont rééligibles.

Elle nomme son Greffier.

La fonction de Greffier de la Cour n'est pas incompatible avec celle de Secrétaire-Général de la Cour Permanente d'Arbitrage.

Article 19.

The Court shall elect its President and Vice-President for three years: they may be re-elected.

It shall appoint its Registrar.

The duties of the Registrar of the Court shall not be considered incompatible with those of the Secretary-General of the Permanent Court of Arbitration.

Article 20.

Le siège de la Cour est fixé à La Haye.

Le Président et le Greffier résident au siège de la Cour.

Article 20.

The seat of the Court shall be established at The Hague.

The President and Registrar shall reside at the seat of the Court.

Article 21.

La Cour tient une session chaque année.

Sauf disposition contraire du règlement d'ordre de la Cour, cette session commence le 15 juin, et continue tant que le rôle n'est pas épuisé.

Le Président convoque la Cour en session extraordinaire quand les circonstances l'exigent.

Article 21.

A session shall be held every year.

Unless otherwise provided by rules of Court, this session shall begin on the 15th June, and shall continue for as long as may be necessary to complete the cases on the list.

The President may summon an extraordinary meeting of the Court whenever necessary.

Article 22.

Si, pour une raison spéciale, l'un des membres de la Cour estime ne pouvoir participer au jugement d'une affaire déterminée, il en fait part au Président.

Si le Président estime qu'un des membres de la Cour ne peut siéger, pour une raison spéciale, dans une affaire déterminée, il en avertit le membre intéressé.

Si l'un et l'autre ne sont pas d'accord dans chacun de ces cas sur l'attitude à prendre, la Cour décide.

Article 22.

If, for some special reason, a member of the Court considers that he cannot take part in the decision of a particular case, he shall so inform the President.

If, for some special reason, the President considers that one of the members of the Court should not sit on a particular case, he shall give notice to the member concerned.

In the event of the President and the member not agreeing as to the course to be adopted in any such case, the matter shall be settled by the decision of the Court.

Article 22 bis.

La Cour exerce ses attributions en séance plénière.

Si la présence de onze juges titulaires n'est pas assurée, ce nombre est parfait par l'entrée en fonction des juges suppléants.

Toutefois, si onze juges ne sont pas disponibles, le quorum de neuf sera suffisant pour constituer la Cour.

Article 22 bis.

The full Court shall sit.

If eleven judges cannot be present, deputy-judges shall be called upon to sit, in order to make up this number.

If, however, eleven judges are not available, a quorum of nine judges shall suffice to constitute the Court.

Article 23.

Les suppléants sont appelés dans l'ordre du tableau.

Le tableau est dressé par la Cour, en tenant compte, d'abord de la priorité d'élection et ensuite de l'ancienneté d'âge.

Article 23.

Deputy-judges shall be called upon to sit in the order laid down in a list.

The list shall be prepared by the Court, having regard first to the order in time of each election and secondly to age.

Article 24.

En vue de la prompte expédition des affaires, la Cour compose annuellement une chambre de trois juges, spécialement consacrée au jugement des affaires en procédure sommaire, lorsque les parties le demandent.

Article 24.

With a view to the speedy despatch of business the Court shall form, annually, a chamber composed of three judges especially devoted to the hearing of cases by summary procedure, at the request of the contesting parties.

Article 24 bis.

Il est pourvu aux sièges devenus vacants selon la méthode suivie pour la première élection.

Le membre de la Cour élu en remplacement d'un membre dont le mandat n'est pas expiré, achève le terme du mandat de son prédécesseur.

Article 24 bis.

Vacancies which may occur shall be filled by the same method as that laid down for the first election.

A member of the Court elected to replace a member, the period of whose appointment has not expired, will hold the appointment for the remainder of his predecessor's term.

Article 25.

1. Lorsque la Cour renferme un juge titulaire de la nationalité de chacune des parties en cause, ces juges conservent le droit de siéger dans l'affaire dont la Cour est saisie.

2. Si la Cour ne renferme qu'un juge titulaire de la nationalité d'une seule des parties en cause,

Article 25.

1. If the Court includes upon the bench a judge of the nationality of each contesting party, they shall retain their right to sit in the case before the Court.

2. If the Court includes upon the bench a judge of the nationality of one of the parties only, the

l'autre partie désigne pour siéger, parmi les juges suppléants, un juge de sa nationalité, s'il en existe. S'il n'en existe pas, elle choisit un juge, de préférence parmi les personnes qui ont été l'objet d'une présentation de la part des groupes nationaux de la Cour d'Arbitrage.

3. Si la Cour ne renferme aucun juge titulaire de la nationalité des parties en cause, chacune de ces parties procède à la désignation ou au choix d'un juge de la même manière que dans le cas précédent.

4. Lorsque plusieurs parties font cause commune, elles ne peuvent désigner ou choisir qu'un seul juge de commun accord.

5. Les juges désignés ou choisis comme il est dit ci-dessus, doivent satisfaire aux prescriptions des articles 2, 14, 15, 18, 22 du présent statut. Ils statuent sur un pied d'égalité avec leurs collègues.

Article 25 bis (ancien 13).

Les juges titulaires reçoivent un traitement annuel à fixer par l'Assemblée de la Société des Nations sur la proposition du Conseil. Ce traitement ne peut être diminué pendant la durée des fonctions du juge.

Le Président reçoit une indemnité spéciale déterminée de la même manière pour la durée de ses fonctions.

Les juges suppléants reçoivent dans l'exercice de leurs fonctions une indemnité à fixer de la même manière.

Un règlement spécial détermine les pensions auxquelles ont droit les juges.

Les juges titulaires et suppléants qui ne résident pas au siège de la Cour auront droit au remboursement des frais de voyages nécessités par l'accomplissement de leurs fonctions.

L'indemnité dûe aux juges désignés ou choisis conformément à l'article 25 est réglée de la même manière.

Le traitement du greffier est fixé par le Conseil sur la proposition de la Cour.

Article 26.

Les frais de la Cour sont supportés par la Société des Nations de la manière que l'Assemblée décide sur la proposition du Conseil.

CHAPITRE II.

Compétence de la Cour.

Article 27.

La Cour connaît des litiges entre Etats.

other party may select, from among the deputy-judges, a judge of its nationality, if there be one. If there should not be one, the party may choose a judge, preferably from among those persons who have been nominated as candidates by some national group in the Court of Arbitration.

3. If the Court includes upon the Bench no judge of the nationality of the contesting parties, each of these may proceed to select or choose a judge as in the case mentioned above.

4. Should there be several parties in the same interest, they can nominate or choose, after having agreed together, one judge only.

5. Judges selected or chosen as laid down above, shall fulfil the conditions required by Articles 2, 14, 15, 18, 22 of this Statute. They shall take part in the decision on an equal footing with their colleagues.

Article 25 bis (old 13).

The judges shall receive an annual salary to be determined by the Assembly of the League of Nations upon the proposal of the Council. This salary must not be decreased during the period of a judge's appointment.

The President shall receive a special grant for his period of office, to be fixed in the same way.

Deputy-judges shall receive a grant, for the period of performance of their duties, to be fixed in the same way.

Special regulations will determine the pensions to which the judges shall be entitled.

Travelling expenses incurred in the performance of their duties shall be refunded to judges and deputy-judges who do not reside at the seat of the Court.

The indemnity due to judges selected or chosen as provided in Article 25 shall be determined in the same way.

The salary of the Registrar shall be decided by the Council upon the proposal of the Court.

Article 26.

The expenses of the Court shall be borne by the League of Nations in such a manner as shall be decided by the Assembly upon the proposal of the Council.

CHAPTER II.

Competence of the Court.

Article 27.

The Court shall have jurisdiction to hear and determine suits between States.

Article 28.

La Cour est ouverte aux Etats Membres de la Société des Nations.

Elle l'est de même aux Etats mentionnés à l'annexe au Pacte de la Société des Nations.

Elle est aussi accessible aux autres Etats.

Les conditions, auxquelles elle est ouverte ou accessible aux Etats qui ne sont pas Membres de la Société des Nations sont réglées par le Conseil, en tenant compte de l'article 17 du Pacte.

Article 28.

The Court shall be open to the States Members of the League of Nations.

It shall also be open to the States mentioned in the Annex to the Covenant of the League of Nations.

Other States may also have access to it.

The conditions under which the Court shall be open of right or accessible to States which are not Members of the League of Nations, shall be determined by the Council, in accordance with article 17 of the Covenant.

Article 29.

Entre Etats Membres de la Société des Nations la Cour statue sans convention spéciale sur les différends d'ordre juridique, qui ont pour objet:

a. l'interprétation d'un traité;

b. tout point de droit international;

c. la réalité de tout fait, qui, s'il était établi, constituerait la violation d'un engagement international;

d. la nature ou l'étendue de la réparation dûe pour la rupture d'un engagement international;

e. l'interprétation d'une sentence rendue par la Cour.

La Cour connaît également de tous différends, de quelque nature qu'ils soient, qui lui sont soumis par la convention, soit générale, soit spéciale, des parties.

En cas de contestation sur le point de savoir si un différend rentre, oui ou non, dans les catégories ci-dessus visées, la Cour décide."

Article 29.

Between States which are Members of the League of Nations, the Court shall have jurisdiction (and this without any special convention giving it jurisdiction) to hear and determine cases of a legal nature, concerning:

a. the interpretation of a treaty;

b. any question of international law;

c. the existence of any fact which, if established, would constitute a breach of an international obligation;

d. the nature or extent of reparation to be made for the breach of an international obligation;

e. the interpretation of a sentence passed by the Court.

The Court shall also take cognisance of all disputes of any kind which may be submitted to it by a general or particular convention between the Parties.

In the event of a dispute as to whether a certain case comes or does not come within any of the categories above mentioned, the matter shall be settled by the decision of the Court.

Article 29 bis.

(Nouvel article basé sur l'article 30 du projet Root—Phillimore).

Article 30.

Supprimé.

Article 31.

Dans les limites de sa compétence, telle qu'elle est déterminée par l'article 29, la Cour applique successivement:

1. les conventions internationales, soit générales, soit spéciales, établissant des règles expressément reconnues par les Etats en litige;

Article 29 bis.

(New Article based upon Article 30 of the Root—Phillimore plan).

Article 30.

Deleted.

Article 31.

The Court shall, within the limits of its jurisdiction as defined in Article 29, apply in the order following:

1. international conventions, whether general or particular, establishing rules expressly recognised by the contesting States;

2. la coutume internationale, attestation d'une pratique commune, acceptée comme loi;

3. les principes généraux de droit reconnus par les nations civilisées;

4. les règles de droit qui se dégagent des décisions judiciaires et de la doctrine des publicistes les plus qualifiés des différentes Nations, comme moyens auxiliaires de la détermination des règles de droit.

Article 32.

Le Cour donne son avis sur tout point ou tout différend d'ordre international qui lui est soumis par le Conseil ou par l'Assemblée.

Lorsque la Cour donne son avis sur un point d'ordre international, indépendamment de tout différend actuellement né, elle constitue une Commission spéciale de trois à cinq membres.

Lorsqu'elle donne son avis sur une question qui fait l'objet d'un différend actuellement né, elle statue dans les mêmes conditions, que s'il s'agissait d'un litige porté devant elle.

2. international custom, as evidence of a general practice, which is accepted as law;

3. the general principles of law recognised by civilised nations;

4. rules of law arising from judicial decisions and teachings of the most highly qualified publicists of the various nations, as subsidiary means for the determination of rules of law.

Article 32.

The Court shall give an advisory opinion upon any question or dispute of an international nature referred to it by the Council or Assembly.

When the Court shall give an opinion on a question of an international nature which does not refer to any dispute that may have arisen, it shall appoint a special commission of from three to five members.

When it shall give an opinion upon a question which forms the subject of an existing dispute, it shall do so under the same conditions as if the case had been actually submitted to it for decision.

ANNEXE No. 3.

Chapitre III.

Procédure.

(Texte revisé du Comité de rédaction, avec, en regard, compte-rendu des délibérations du Comité, du 20 juillet.)

Article 1er.

Adopté.

La langue de la Cour est le français.

La Cour peut, à la demande des parties, autoriser l'emploi d'une autre langue devant elle.

Article 2.

Adopté.

LORD PHILLIMORE attire l'attention sur l'article 23 du chapitre III et soulève la question du droit d'intervention.

Il croit que l'alinéa 4 est inutile si ce droit n'est pas admis dans une mesure plus large que cela n'a été fait dans l'article 23, qui parle seulement de traités généraux.

Le PRESIDENT et le Rapporteur font valoir que l'alinéa a deux autres buts:

1. notification pour autre fin qu'intervention;

2. tenir lieu de stipulation concernant la publicité des procès.

M. FERNANDES a proposé la formule suivante: „Le droit d'intervention est reconnu aux Etats ayant un intérêt légitime, soit d'assister une des parties en cause, en raison d'un droit conjoint, soit pour exclure le demandeur ou le défendeur. Dans le premier cas, l'intervenant agira dans les mêmes délais accordés à la partie assistée. Dans le second cas, l'opposition sera formée dans les délais et selon les formes déterminées par la Cour."

M. HAGERUP a proposé la formule de l'article 31 du projet des 3 pays scandinaves qui ne limite pas la notification et l'intervention aux Membres de la Société des Nations.

La Cour est saisie par une requête adressée au Greffe.

La requête indique l'objet du différend et désigne les parties en cause.

Le Greffe fait immédiatement notification de la requête aux intéressés.

Il en informe également les Membres de la Société des Nations par l'entremise du Secrétaire-Général.

Article 2 bis.

Adopté (avec modifications rédactionnelles).

M. FERNANDES voudrait voir appuyer les mesures conservatoires par des sanctions efficaces.

MM. ROOT, LORD PHILLIMORE, MM. ADATCI et DE LAPRADELLE s'opposent à cette idée qui leur semble imprudente.

Dans le cas où la cause du différend consiste en un acte effectué ou sur le point de l'être, la Cour a le pouvoir d'indiquer, si elle estime que les circonstances l'exigent, quelles mesures conservatoires du droit de chacun doivent être prises à titre provisoire.

En attendant l'arrêt, cette indication de ces mesures est immédiatement transmise aux parties et au Conseil.

Sur la proposition de M. DE LAPRADELLE la rédaction suivante du second alinéa est adoptée:

„En attendant l'arrêt, l'indication de ces mesures est immédiatement transmise aux parties et au Conseil."

Article 3.

Adopté (avec des modifications rédactionnelles).

Les parties sont représentées par des Agents.

Elles peuvent se faire assister devant la Cour par des conseils ou des avocats.

Article 4.

Adopté.

La procédure a deux phases: l'une écrite, l'autre orale.

Article 5.

Adopté (avec des modifications rédactionnelles).

La procédure écrite comprend la communication à juge et à partie des mémoires, des contre-mémoires et,. éventuellement, des répliques, ainsi que de toute pièce et document à l'appui.

La communication se fait par l'entremise du Greffe dans l'ordre et les délais déterminés par la Cour.

Toute pièce produite par l'une des parties doit être communiquée à l'autre en copie certifiée conforme.

Article 6.

Adopté (avec des modifications rédactionnelles). Le premier alinéa formera seul l'article 6. Les deux autres alinéas seront insérés à un endroit à déterminer.

M. FERNANDES soulève la question de savoir s'il y a lieu de stipuler un système différent pour les notifications dans le pays où est établi le siège de la Cour, et dans d'autres pays. Il est reconnu que tous les Etats doivent être sur un pied égal à cet égard. Dans cet ordre d'idées il est proposé de biffer les mots „en dehors du pays où est le siège." Dans le même ordre d'idées, Mr. ROOT attire l'attention sur l'article 25 de la Convention de 1907, et M. HAGERUP sur les dispositions du projet des trois Pays Scandinaves et de celui des cinq Puissances Neutres.

M. DE LAPRADELLE, qui fait valoir que le cas peut devenir actuel seulement en ce qui concerne les notifications à donner à des personnes qui ne sont pas en contact avec la Cour, propose la rédaction suivante:

„Pour toute notification à faire aux témoins et aux experts, la Cour s'adresse directement au Gouvernement de l'Etat sur le territoire duquel la notification doit produire effet."

La procédure orale consiste dans l'audition par la Cour des témoins, experts, agents, conseils et avocats.

Pour toute notification à faire en dehors du pays où elle siège, la Cour s'adresse directement au Gouvernement de l'Etat sur le territoire duquel la notification doit produire effet. Il en est de même s'il s'agit de faire procéder sur place à l'établissement de tous moyens de preuve.

Cet amendement est adopté avec cette modification, que les mots „aux témoins et aux experts" sont substitués par les mots „à d'autres personnes que les agents, conseils et avocats."

Article 7.

Adopté (avec des modifications rédactionelles).

Les débats sont dirigés par le Président, et à défaut de celui-ci par le Vice-Président; en cas d'empêchement par le plus ancien des juges présents.

Article 8.

Adopté avec des modifications rédactionelles (le mot „motivée" est inséré).

L'audience est publique, à moins qu'il n'en soit autrement décidé par la Cour à la demande motivée de l'une des parties.

Article 9.

Adopté.

Il est tenu de chaque audience un procès-verbal, signé par le Greffier et le Président.

Ce procès-verbal a seul caractère authentique.

Article 10.

Adopté (avec des modifications rédactionelles).

La Cour peut, même avant tout débat, demander aux agents de lui produire tout document et de lui fournir toutes explications. En cas de refus, elle en prend acte.

Article 11.

Adopté.

M. ADATCI propose l'addition suivante:

„Elle peut également requérir l'avis des comités techniques constitués par le Conseil de la Société des Nations, lorsqu'il s'agit de questions qui rentrent par leur nature dans le ressort de leur compétence spéciale."

Cet amendement est rejeté, mais en s'en inspirant le PRESIDENT propose l'insertion après le mot „personnes" des mots „corps ou organes".

LORD PHILLIMORE veut ajouter le mot „bureaux".

Sur la proposition de M. DE LAPRADELLE l'insertion de la formule „corps, bureaux, commissions ou organes" est adoptée.

A tout moment, la Cour peut confier une enquête ou une expertise à une ou plusieurs personnes (voir remarques) de son choix.

Article 12.

Adopté (avec des modifications rédactionelles).

Au cours des débats, les juges posent aux témoins, agents, experts, avocats et conseils, toutes questions qu'ils jugent utiles; les agents, avocats et conseils ont le droit de poser, par l'entremise du Président, toute question que la Cour juge utile.

Article 13.

La Cour rend des ordonnances pour la direction du procès, la détermination des formes et délais dans lesquels chaque partie doit finalement conclure, et prend toutes les mesures que comporte l'administration des preuves.

Adopté.

Article 14.

Après avoir reçu les preuves et témoignages dans les délais déterminés par elle, la Cour peut écarter toutes dépositions ou documents nouveaux qu'une des parties voudrait lui présenter sans l'assentiment de l'autre.

Adopté.

Article 15.

Lorsqu'une des parties ne se présente pas, ou s'abstient de faire valoir ses moyens, l'autre partie peut demander à la Cour de lui adjuger ses conclusions.

La Cour, avant d'y faire droit, doit s'assurer que ces conclusions, reposant sur des preuves sérieuses sont fondées en fait et en droit.

Adopté (avec des modifications) contre la voix de M. Ricci-Busatti.

M. HAGERUP fait valoir que l'hypothèse du no. 1 est couverte par le no. 2.

On reconnaît le bien-fondé de cette observation.

Le PRESIDENT propose la formule suivante, destinée à remplacer l'alinea 2:

„La Cour a toute liberté pour les accueillir après s'être assurée que ces conclusions sont suffisamment fondées en fait et en droit."

M. DE LAPRADELLE propose la suppression du no. 1.

LORD PHILLIMORE propose une formule transactionnelle:

„La Cour fait droit à condition de s'être assurée que ces conclusions reposent sur des preuves sérieuses, qui sont fondées en droit."

M. DE LAPRADELLE propose cette rédaction amend e de la formule de Lord Phillimore:

„La Cour fait droit à la condition de s'être assurée que ces conclusions, reposant sur des preuves sérieuses, sont fondées en fait et en droit."

M. RICCI-BUSATTI fait valoir que l'article est parfaitement inutile si les mêmes preuves doivent être exigées lorsqu'il s'agit d'un jugement par contumace qu'ailleurs; il propose la suppression de l'article.

Mr. ROOT maintient premièrement la nécessité des jugements par contumace, et deuxièmement la nécessité que ces jugements soient bien motivés.

M. DE LAPRADELLE soumet la formule suivante:

„La Cour, avant d'y faire droit, doit s'assurer que ces conclusions, reposant sur des preuves sérieuses, sont fondées en fait et en droit".

LE PRESIDENT veut ajouter à cette formule entre les mots „sont" et „fondées" le mot „suffisamment".

Cette proposition, mise aux voix, est rejetée.

La formule de M. de Lapradelle est adoptée.

Article 16.

Quand les agents, avocats et conseils ont fait valoir, sous le contrôle de la Cour, tous les moyens qu'ils jugent utiles, le Président prononce la clôture des débats.

La Cour se retire en chambre du Conseil pour délibérer.

Les délibérations de la Cour sont et restent secrètes.

Adopté.

Article 17.

Les décisions de la Cour sont prises à la majorité des juges présents.

En cas de partage de voix, la voix du Président ou de celui qui le remplace est prépondérante.

Adopté (avec des modifications rédactionnelles).

La dernière partie du second alinéa est formulée comme suit: „La voix du président ou de celui qui le remplace est prépondérante."

Article 18.

L'arrêt est motivé.

Il mentionne les noms des juges qui y ont pris part.

Adopté.

Article 19.

Si l'arrêt n'exprime pas, en tout ou en partie, l'opinion unanime des juges, les dissidents ont la faculté de demander l'insertion de leur opinion motivée, à la suite de l'exposé des motifs qui précède la décision de la majorité.

Cette faculté n'est pas ouverte aux juges de la nationalité des parties.

Adopté (avec modifications).

Le président propose la formule suivante à remplacer la première partie du dernier alinéa:

„Les dissidents ont la faculté de demander que leurs oppositions ou leurs réserves soient constatées."

Sur la proposition de M. DE LAPRADELLE un vote préalable est pris sur les deux questions suivantes:

1. Le juge peut-il marquer son dissentiment sur le dispositif seulement?

Cette question est répondue dans l'affirmative.

2. Le juge peut-il marquer son dissentiment sur les motifs?

Cette question est répondue dans la négative.

Le PRESIDENT lit de nouveau la formule qu'il a proposée avec une légère modification:

„Les dissidents ont la faculté de demander que leurs oppositions ou leurs réserves soient marquées",

et avec l'addition suivante:
„sans pouvoir être motivées."

Cette formule est adoptée comme alinéa 1 de l'article 19, contre l'abstention de M. DE LAPRADELLE; celui-ci s'abstient parce qu'il n'a pas pu saisir la proposition.

Au sujet de l'alinéa 2, M. de Lapradelle désire que les juges nationaux soient exclus du droit de marquer leur dissentiment, afin de leur garantir une plus grande liberté envers leur pays.

LORD PHILLIMORE et Mr. ROOT s'opposent à cette idée.

La question de savoir si les juges nationaux doivent pouvoir marquer la dissidence est mise aux voix.

En conséquence du résultat du vote, l'alinéa 2 est supprimé.

Article 20.

Adopté.

L'arrêt est signé par le Président et par le Greffier. Il est lu en séance publique, les Agents dûment prévenus.

Article 21.

Adopté.

L'arrêt est définitif et sans recours. En cas de doute sur le sens et la portée de l'arrêt, il appartient à la Cour de l'interprêter à la demande de toute partie.

Article 22.

Adopté (avec modifications).

Sur la proposition de M. HAGERUP les mots „de la partie demanderesse" sont substitués par les mots „de la partie qui demande la révision", (fin du premier alinéa).

M. FERNANDES soulève la question de savoir si le fait nouveau ne doit pas être de telle nature qu'il ne pouvait pas être connu par la partie en question. Le bien fondé de cette observation est entièrement reconnu.

LORD PHILLIMORE propose l'insertion d'une formule qui réponde à l'expression anglaise „due diligence". M. DE LAPRADELLE propose la formule suivante: „et que même en faisant toute diligence la partie ne pouvait connaître . . ."

La rédaction de l'alinéa est réservée.

La révision de l'arrêt ne peut être éventuellement demandée à la Cour qu'à raison de la découverte d'un fait nouveau de nature à exercer une influence décisive, et qui, avant le prononcé de l'arrêt, était inconnu de la Cour et pouvait l'être de la partie qui demande la révision. La procédure de révision s'ouvre par un arrêt de la Cour constatant expressément l'existence du fait nouveau, et lui reconnaissant les caractères qui donnent ouverture à la révision et déclarant de ce chef la demande recevable. La Cour peut subordonner l'ouverture de la procédure en révision à l'exécution préalable de l'arrêt. Ancune demande de révision ne peut être formée après l'expiration d'un délai de 5 ans.

Article 23.

Adopté (avec une addition à insérer avant l'article).

Lorsqu'il s'agit de l'interprétation d'une convention à laquelle ont participé d'autres Etats que

Pour cette addition M. HAGERUP propose la formule suivante:

„Chacun des Etats signataires a la faculté d'intervenir au procès, et s'il l'exerce, il devient partie au litige au point de vue de la chose jugée.

Il en est de même de tout Etat dont les intérêts sont touchés par le procès."

M. LODER propose l'article 48 du projet des Cinq Puissances.

LORD PHILLIMORE propose la formule suivante:

„Lorsqu'un Etat tiers pense qu'un différend soumis à la Cour touche ses intérêts, cet Etat peut former une requête d'être admis à l'intervention et la Cour, si bon lui semble, l'accordera."

Le PRESIDENT propose une rédaction basée sur l'idée que la solution de la question de l'intervention doit être laissée au droit commun:

„Lorsqu'un Etat estime que dans un différend il peut être porté atteinte à ses droits, cet Etat peut adresser à la Cour une requête à fin d'intervention, et la Cour peut y donner satisfaction..."

M. ADATCI veut amender le texte proposé par M. Loder en y remplaçant le mot „droit" par le mot „intérêt".

M. DE LAPRADELLE soulève la question de savoir si la Cour, dans sa composition normale, sera compétente pour juger des intervénients bien que ceux-ci ne soient pas représentés à la Cour par un de leurs nationaux.

On est d'accord pour laisser cette question ouverte.

Le PRESIDENT propose la nouvelle formule suivante:

„Lorsqu'un Etat estime que dans un différend un intérêt d'ordre juridique est pour lui en cause, il peut adresser à la Cour une requête, afin d'intervention. La Cour décide".

M. DE LAPRADELLE propose l'amendement suivant à cette formule:

„Lorsqu'un Etat estime que ses intérêts légitimes sont mis en péril par..."

La formule du Président est adoptée sauf rédaction et sans amendement.

L'article 23 originaire est adopté dans la rédaction suivante inspirée par l'article 84 de la Convention de 1907:

„Lorsqu'il s'agit de l'interprétation d'une convention à laquelle ont participé d'autres Etats que les parties en litige, le Greffe, en vue de la requête introductive d'instance, avertit sans délai toute puissance signataire.

Chacun des Etats a la faculté d'intervenir au procès, et s'il exerce cette faculté il devient partie en litige au point de vue de la chose jugée.

les parties en litige, le greffe avertit sans délai tous les signataires. Chacun d'eux a le droit d'intervenir au procès et s'il l'exerce l'interprétation contenue dans la sentence est également obligatoire à son égard".

M. HAGERUP s'est opposé contre l'expression „au point de vue de la chose jugée" dans le rédaction originaire de l'article 23.

Les modifications à la rédaction de l'article 84 de 1907 sont introduites sur la proposition de Lord Phillimore.

Article 24.

S'il n'en est autrement décidé par la Cour, chaque partie supporte ses frais de procédure.

Adopté.

31IÈME SÉANCE (non-publique), tenue au Palais de la Paix, à La Haye, le 22 juillet 1920.

Présidence de M. le BARON DESCAMPS.

Sont présents : tous les membres du Comité (à l'exception de M. Bevilaqua); M. Fernandes; Mr. James Brown Scott; les secrétaires particuliers du Baron Descamps et de M. Adatci; les membres du Secrétariat.

La séance est ouverte à 9.45 heures du matin.

LE PRESIDENT déclare que le Comité va consacrer cette séance à la seconde lecture du texte approuvé provisoirement pendant les séances des 19, 20 et 21 juillet, et qui a été distribué aux membres la veille. (Voir Annexe 1re).

Le Président procédera article par article; il invite les membres à communiquer leurs objections ou amendements éventuels lorsque les articles auxquels ces propositions se réfèrent seront évoqués. Il propose que le procès-verbal de la séance — de même que les procès-verbaux des autres séances de la semaine — soit sommaire et qu'il se borne à indiquer les résultats obtenus.

Les propositions du Président sont approuvées.

Article 1.

Approuvé sans discussion.

Article 2.

M. HAGERUP propose de substituer le mot „élus" au mot „choisis" pour éviter une contradiction avec l'article 28. L'article est adopté avec cette modification.

M. ALTAMIRA demande qu'il soit fait mention au procès-verbal des objections qu'il a formulées antérieurement au sujet de l'effet que l'article peut avoir dans certains pays sur l'élection de magistrats comme membres de la Cour.

Article 3.

Approuvé sans discussion.

31ST MEETING (Private), held at the Peace Palace, the Hague, on July 22nd, 1920.

BARON DESCAMPS in the chair.

Present: all the members of the Committee (except M. Bevilaqua); M. Fernandes; Mr. James Brown Scott; the private secretaries of Baron Descamps and M. Adatci; the members of the Secretariat.

The meeting opened at 9.45 a. m.

The PRESIDENT stated that the Committee was to devote this meeting to the second reading of the text provisionally adopted at the meetings of the 19th, 20th and 21st July, which had been distributed on the previous day. (See Annex 1).

The President intended to deal with each article in turn. He requested the members to submit possible objections or amendments as and when the Articles to which these applied were mentioned. He proposed that the Procès-Verbal of the meeting—as those of the previous meetings of the week— should be short, and confined to an indication of the results obtained.

The proposals of the President were agreed to.

Article 1.

Approved without discussion.

Article 2.

M. HAGERUP proposed that the word "elected" should be substituted for the word "chosen" in order to avoid a contradiction with Article 28. The Article was adopted with this modification.

M. ALTAMIRA asked that the objections which he had previously raised with reference to this Article and its possible effect in some countries upon the election of magistrates as members of the Court, should be recorded in the Procès-Verbal.

Article 3.

Adopted without discussion.

Article 4.

Cet article prend le numéro 13.

Les anciens articles 5—13 prennent les numéros 4—12.

Article 5.

Approuvé sans discussion.

Article 6.

Approuvé sans discussion.

Article 7.

Approuvé avec une modification suggérée par M. ALTAMIRA.

Articles 8—11.

Approuvés sans discussion.

Article 12.

Approuvé avec une modification de rédaction proposée par M. DE LAPRADELLE.

M. ALTAMIRA demande qu'il soit constaté au procès-verbal qu'il a voté contre l'alinéa 2 de cet article.

Article 13.

Approuvé sans discussion.

Article 14.

M. ALTAMIRA déclare que si l'on n'explique pas dans le rapport la portée de l'article 14, les juges internationaux seront tous choisis parmi les juges nationaux, qui sont seuls indépendants.

LE PRESIDENT déclare qu'il sera expliqué dans le rapport que l'article a pour objet d'exclure les membres des gouvernements et les personnes qui occupent des situations présentant un caractère politique.

Articles 15—17.

Approuvés sans discussion.

Article 18.

Approuvé avec une modification de rédaction suggérée par M. FERNANDES.

Articles 19—21.

Approuvés sans discussion.

Article 4.

This Article was now numbered 13.

The Articles formerly numbered 5 to 13 were now numbered 4 to 12.

Article 5.

Adopted without discussion.

Article 6.

Adopted without discussion.

Article 7.

Adopted with a modification suggested by M. ALTAMIRA.

Articles 8 to 11.

Adopted without discussion.

Article 12.

Adopted with a modification in wording suggested by M. DE LAPRADELLE.

M. ALTAMIRA requested that the fact that he had voted against Paragraph 2 of this Article should be recorded in the Procès-Verbal.

Article 13.

Adopted without discussion.

Article 14.

M. ALTAMIRA said that if the import of Article 14 were not explained in the report, international judges would all be chosen from amongst national judges, who alone were truly independent.

The PRESIDENT said that it would be explained in the report that the object of the Article was to exclude members of Governments and persons holding positions of a political nature.

Articles 15 to 17.

Approved without discussion.

Article 18.

Approved with a slight alteration in wording suggested by M. FERNANDES.

Articles 19 to 21.

Adopted without discussion.

Article 22.

Le PRESIDENT propose l'insertion des mots: „ou dont l'expérience démontrera la nécessité".

Cette proposition ayant été rejetée, le Président exprime le désir que l'on mentionne au procès-verbal qu'il a voté contre cet article.

L'article est adopté.

Article 23.

Approuvé sans discussion.

Article 24.

Cet article prend la place du numéro 15.

Article 25.

Cet article prend la place du numéro 14. En conséquence les anciens numéros 14—23 deviennent les numéros 16—25.

Article 26.

Sur la proposition de M. DE LAPRADELLE la question de savoir si la chambre de trois juges doit servir seulement comme chambre de procédure sommaire, est mise aux voix.

Le vote donne à cette question une réponse affirmative.

Le PRESIDENT demande que soit consigné au procès-verbal son vote contraire.

Article 27.

M. HAGERUP voudrait ajouter à cet article une phrase qui donnerait à la Cour la faculté de combler, par la voie de règlements d'ordre, toutes les lacunes éventuelles du projet.

Le PRESIDENT ayant déclaré que la première phrase de l'article a déjà ce caractère, M. HAGERUP retire son amendement sous bénéfice de la déclaration du Président.

L'article est approuvé sans discussion ultérieure.

Article 28.

Les alinéas 1 et 2 de l'article ayant subi, en conséquence d'une discussion prolongée, des modifications considérables, Mr. ROOT déclare que si cet article, qui est le fruit mûr de longs débats et dont la rédaction est due au Président, est remanié, Mr. Root, se verra obligé de retirer son consentement à l'article.

Article 22.

The PRESIDENT proposed to insert the words: " or for a reason based on experience."

This proposal was rejected. The President therefore expressed a wish that the fact that he had voted against the Article should be recorded in the Procès-Verbal.

The Article was adopted.

Article 23.

Adopted without discussion.

Article 24.

This Article was now numbered 15.

Article 25.

This Article was now numbered 14; consequently, the former numbers 14 to 23 now became numbers 16 to 25.

Article 26.

At M. DE LAPRADELLE's proposal a vote was taken upon the question as to whether the chamber of three judges should only be used as a section for summary procedure.

The result of the vote was in the affirmative.

The PRESIDENT requested that his opposition should be recorded in the Procès-Verbal.

Article 27.

M. HAGERUP wished to make an addition to this Article, giving the Court the power to make good any omissions which might be found to exist in the plan by means of rules of Court.

The PRESIDENT said that the first sentence of the Article already had this effect. M. HAGERUP, therefore, withdrew his amendment in view of the President's statement.

This Article was approved without further discussion.

Article 28.

Paragraphs 1 and 2 of this Article, as a result of a prolonged discussion, were considerably altered. Mr. ROOT declared that, if this Article, which was the outcome of long discussion and had been drafted by the President, were reconstructed, he would be obliged to withdraw his consent to it.

Les autres alinéas ayant été légèrement retouchés au point de vue de la rédaction, l'article est mis aux voix, alinéa par alinéa.

Les deux premiers alinéas sont adoptés.

Cependant, M. ALTAMIRA vote contre le second alinéa à cause de l'expression „de préférence" qui y est contenue.

Les alinéas 3—5 sont adoptés sans discussion ultérieure.

Article 29—31.

Sont adoptés sans discussion.

Article 32.

Est soumis à un vote formel et adopté.

Article 33.

M. RICCI-BUSATTI constate au procès-verbal qu'il vote contre cet article; il maintient ses préférences pour le système qu'il a préconisé.

M. ADATCI, rappelant son amendement, qui ne donnait compétence à la Cour qu'au cas d'accord entre les parties, fait toutes ses réserves sur le présent article, et demande que le fait soit mentionné au procès-verbal.

Article 34.

Une discussion s'engage sur la question de savoir si l'article est applicable seulement aux Etats qui sont à présent Membres de la Société des Nations ou s'il est applicable aussi aux Membres futurs. La situation des Etats-Unis d'Amérique est tout spécialement visée.

De la discussion semble se dégager la solution que le Statut de la Cour, qui doit être accepté par le Conseil et l'Assemblée de la Société des Nations, peut conférer des droits ou privilèges à des Etats qui ne sont pas Membres de la Société, mais qu'il peut imposer des obligations exclusivement aux Etats qui sont membres. Il est reconnu qu'un Etat qui entre dans la Société des Nations accepte par ce fait même les obligations relatives à la juridiction obligatoire qui résulte du Statut, mais il est également reconnu que les obligations du Statut peuvent être imposées aux Etats qui ne sont pas membres, exclusivement en vertu d'une convention spéciale, conclue à cet effet entre l'Etat en question et tous les Membres de la Société des Nations.

The wording of the other Paragraphs having been slightly altered, the Article was voted upon, Paragraph by Paragraph.

The two first Paragraphs were adopted.

M. ALTAMIRA voted against Paragraph 2 on account of the expression "preferably" contained in it.

Paragraphs 3 to 5 were adopted without further discussion.

Article 29—31.

Adopted without discussion.

Article 32.

Adopted by a formal vote.

Article 33.

M. RICCI-BUSATTI formally stated, for record in the Procès-Verbal, that he voted against this Article. He still maintained his views with regard to the system he had advocated.

M. ADATCI reminded the Committee of his amendment, according to which the Court's jurisdiction would be dependent upon an agreement between the parties, and put a reservation on this article. He wished the Procès-Verbal to record his opposition.

Article 34.

A discussion took place as to whether the Article applied only to States which were already Members of the League of Nations, or whether it was also applicable to future Members. The situation of the United States was especially considered.

The outcome of the discussion was that the Statute of the Court, which was subject to the approval of the Council and the Assembly of the League of Nations, could confer rights and privileges upon States which were not Members of the League, but could impose obligations only upon States which were Members. It was recognised that a State entering the League of Nations, by so doing, accepted the obligations concerning compulsory submission to jurisdiction contained in the Statute; but it was also recognised that the obligations contained in the Statute could only be made binding upon States, which were not members of the League, by virtue of a special Convention, concluded, for this purpose, between the State in question and the whole body of Members of the League.

A ce propos M. DE LAPRADELLE, tout en déclarant qu'à son avis le texte de l'article 34 doit être maintenu et qu'il peut se rallier à l'opinion que Lord Phillimore vient d'exprimer, déclare que, en sa qualité de jurisconsulte, il doit s'élever contre l'idée qu'on puisse, en faisant le Statut de la Cour, préparer une combinaison par laquelle on permette à certains Etats de jouir des privilèges de la juridiction, sans accepter les obligations qui en découlent. Il demande que sa déclaration soit mentionnée au procès-verbal. Il estime que l'existence d'Etats qui ne sont pas Membres de la Société des Nations, mais qui, en ce qui concerne la Cour, ont les mêmes droits que s'ils étaient Membres, peut être fatale pour la Société.

Article 35.

M. DE LAPRADELLE donne lecture de la rédaction suivante du numéro 3: „les principes généraux du droit reconnus par les nations civilisées à la lumière des décisions judiciaires et de la doctrine des publicistes les plus qualifiés des différents pays."

Sachant que cette rédaction, qui a ses préférences, n'obtiendra pas l'approbation de ses collègues, il s'abstient de voter.

M. HAGERUP se rallie à M. de Lapradelle et s'abstient également de voter.

M. RICCI-BUSATTI constate au procès-verbal qu'il vote contre les articles 34—35.

L'article 35 est adopté.

Article 36.

Après une courte discussion cet article est adopté contre l'abstention de M. RICCI-BUSATTI, qui déclare que, n'ayant pas eu le temps nécessaire pour réfléchir sur les dispositions de l'article, qui n'ont jamais été discutées à fond, il ne croit pas pouvoir prendre part au vote.

Articles 37 et 38.

Sont adoptés sans discussion.

Article 39.

M. RICCI-BUSATTI propose la suppression de la première partie de la phrase, afin que la disposition dont il s'agit puisse s'appliquer aussi à des hypothèses différentes.

Cette proposition est rejetée, et l'article est adopté avec une légère modification rédactionnelle.

In this connection, M. DE LAPRADELLE, whilst declaring that, in his opinion, the text of Article 34 should be maintained and that he agreed with the view just expressed by Lord Phillimore, stated, that as a jurisconsult, he felt that he must protest against the notion that, in drawing up the Statute of the Court, an opportunity could be afforded to certain States to enjoy the privileges of the jurisdiction without accepting the accompanying obligations. He thought that the existence of States which were not Members of the League of Nations but which had the same rights, with regard to the Court, as if they were Members, might have fatal results for the League.

Article 35.

M. DE LAPRADELLE read the following wording for No. 3: "The general principles of Law recognised by civilised Nations as interpreted by judicial decisions and by the teaching of the most highly qualified publicists of the various countries."

As he knew that his preference for this formula would not be shared by his Colleagues, he would not take part in the vote.

M. HAGERUP was of the same opinion and also abstained from voting.

M. RICCI-BUSATTI stated for record in the Procès-Verbal that he voted against Articles 34 and 35.

Article 35 was adopted.

Article 36.

After a short discussion, this Article was adopted. M. RICCI-BUSATTI did not vote; since he had not had sufficient time to consider the provisions of the Article, which he felt had never been discussed thoroughly.

Articles 37 and 38.

Adopted without discussion.

Article 39.

M. RICCI-BUSATTI proposed that the first portion of the sentence be deleted, so that the provision in question could also be applied under other circumstances.

This proposal was rejected, and the Article was adopted with a slight modification in wording.

Articles 40—46.

Sont adoptés sans discussion.

Articles 47—49.

Prennent les numéros 48—50.

Article 50.

Prend le numéro 47.

Article 51.

Adopté sans discussion.

Article 52.

M. HAGERUP propose un renvoi aux articles 33 et 34. Cette proposition est adoptée.

L'article est approuvé sans autre modification.

Articles 53—55.

Sont adoptés sans modifications.

Article 56.

Est adopté avec des modifications de rédaction.

Article 57.

Est adopté sans modification.

Article 58.

M. HAGERUP propose d'y ajouter un renvoi à l'article suivant. Cette proposition est rejetée, et l'article est adopté sans modifications.

Article 59.

La question de la durée du délai est soulevée par M. HAGERUP. Toutefois les dispositions du texte ne sont pas modifiées.

MM. RICCI-BUSATTI et HAGERUP s'abstiennent de voter sur l'alinéa 3 de l'article, et demandent que leur abstention soit constatée au procès-verbal.

Articles 60 et 61.

Ces articles sont adoptés sans modifications.

M. DE LAPRADELLE suggère l'idée d'introduire des modifications visant à réunir le premier membre de phrase dans le second alinéa de l'article 61 au 1er alinéa, et à rendre le second alinéa applicable en même temps à l'article 60 et au premier alinéa de l'article 61.

Cette proposition est rejetée.

Articles 40 to 46.

Adopted without discussion.

Articles 47 to 49.

Were renumbered 48 to 50.

Article 50.

Renumbered 47.

Article 51.

Adopted without discussion.

Article 52.

M. HAGERUP proposed that a reference be made to Articles 33 and 34. This was adopted.

The Article was approved without further alteration.

Articles 53 to 55.

Adopted without alteration.

Article 56.

Adopted with some alterations in the wording.

Article 57.

Adopted without alteration.

Article 58.

M. HAGERUP proposed to add a reference to the following Article. This was rejected; the Article was adopted as it stood.

Article 59.

The question of the time limit was raised by M. HAGERUP, but no amendment was made.

M. RICCI-BUSATTI and M. HAGERUP abstained from voting upon Paragraph 3 of the Article and requested that this fact might be recorded in the Procès-verbal.

Articles 60 and 61.

Adopted without alteration.

M. DE LAPRADELLE suggested an amendment intended to bring the first portion of the second Paragraph of Article 61 into Paragraph 1, and to make the second Paragraph applicable both to Article 60 and to the first Paragraph of Article 61.

This proposal was rejected.

Article 62.

Cet article est adopté sans discussion.

LE PRESIDENT passe au vote d'ensemble. Il procède à l'appel nominal, par ordre alphabétique.

Avant qu'il soit procédé à l'appel, M. ADATCI fait la déclaration suivante:

„En vertu du No. 7 des règles de procédure, que nous avons arrêtées nous-mêmes au début de notre Conférence, je présente respectueusement au Président une requête de faire mention dans le protocole final de mon opinion divergente au sujet des articles 33 et 34 qui traitent la question de judicature internationale obligatoire par citation unilatérale.

J'apprécie hautement et admire infiniment le génie créateur, l'esprit juridique et pratique, la grande âme de conciliation de mon voisin de droite, Mr. Elihu Root, que la postérité considérera probablement comme père de notre Cour. Venu ici presque désespéré, j'ai aperçu bientôt une lueur dans le chemin indiqué par notre collègue américain. Sans lui, je n'aurais probablement pas pu continuer à participer aux travaux de cette conférence. Je tiens donc ici à témoigner publiquement tout mon respect reconnaissant et affectueux au grand jurisconsulte du nouveau monde, et à dire toute ma peine de me séparer de lui sur une question qui lui tient à coeur.

L'édifice de notre Cour, grâce à notre bonne volonté mutuelle, est déjà si beau dans ses grandes lignes.

Nous sommes assurés de sa vie, de sa croissance et de sa prospérité. Je la vois déjà chargée de nombreuses affaires importantes. Ma seule inquiétude est pourtant de voir poindre à l'horizon un écueil dans la passe dangereuse de la judicature internationale obligatoire par citation unilatérale.

J'ai la plus claire vision que la judicature qui nous est si chère, sera un fait accompli dans un avenir rapproché.

Toutefois, en présence de l'article 14 du Pacte, dont la clarté est aveuglante, et vu l'historique de la rédaction dudit article, je me sens lié dans mon mandat.

D'ailleurs, malgré tout mon plus vif désir de voir immédiatement s'établir la judicature en question, j'estime qu'il serait prématuré de la réaliser dès le début de la Société des Nations, vu les relations internationales de nos jours, prises dans leur ensemble. Il faudrait à mon sens faire débuter notre Cour dans le cadre esquissé par le Pacte,

Article 62.

Adopted without discussion.

The PRESIDENT then proceeded to take a vote upon the plan as a whole. He called upon the members by name, in alphabetical order.

Before the vote, M. ADATCI made the following statement:

"By virtue of No. 7 of the rules of Procedure, drawn up by us at the commencement of the Conference, I most respectfully beg the President to record, in the final protocol, my dissent from the provisions of Articles 33 and 34, which deal with the question of compulsory submission to an International Jurisdiction following upon the institution of proceedings by one party only.

I greatly appreciate and admire the creative genius, the juridical and practical mind, and the conciliatory spirit of my neighbour, Mr. Elihu Root; posterity will probably look upon him as the founder of the Court. I came here almost without hope, but I soon saw a possibility of success in the direction indicated by our American Colleague. Without his aid, I should probably not have been able to continue to take part in the work of the Committee. I therefore wish to record publicly my gratitude and the affectionate respect which I feel for the great Jurisconsult of the New World, and to state how much it grieves me to have to disassociate myself from him upon a question so dear to his heart.

Thanks to our mutual goodwill, the main features of the structure of our Court already represent a very remarkable achievement.

We can rest assured that it will endure, grow and prosper. I can already picture it entrusted with many important cases. On one point however I feel anxious, and that is that the inclusion of the provision stipulating compulsory submission to international adjudication, following upon unilateral proceedings, may prove a serious danger.

I firmly believe that the jurisdiction which we so earnestly desire will be an accomplished fact in the near future.

However, in view of Article 14 of the Covenant, the meaning of which is absolutely clear, and in view of the history of the preparation of this Article, I feel that I am strictly bound by the limits of my mandate.

Further, though I desire most keenly to see such a jurisdiction set up as soon as possible, I am of opinion that it would be premature to give effect to this wish at the outset of the career of the League of Nations, considering the present

et observer pendant quelque temps son développement afin de former une saine opinion basée sur les expériences (voir partie finale du Procès-verbal du 14 juillet).

En pleine reconnaissance de l'immense importance de l'établissement immédiat de la Cour, je vote cependant volontiers pour l'ensemble du Projet. Pour un seul point, les deux articles dont il s'agit, je vous demande la permission de maintenir ma réserve".

M. RICCI-BUSATTI manifeste son désir de faire une déclaration, dont le but n'est que de résumer sa manière de voir vis-à-vis du résultat des travaux du Comité, en confirmant ses points de vue et en expliquant son vote. A cet effet il donne lecture de la déclaration suivante:

„Profondément convaincu des avantages que notre œuvre a le but de réaliser dans les rapports des Etats, ainsi que de l'utilité de ne pas entraver par un dissentiment final l'effort commun que notre Commission vient de faire dans ce but, je donne mon vote au projet, malgré la divergence des points de vue que j'ai eu l'occasion de soutenir au cours de nos débats, concernant ses grandes lignes ainsi que certaines de ses dispositions".

Tous les membres, en réponse à l'appel nominal du PRESIDENT constatent leur approbation du projet.

Le PRESIDENT déclare que celui-ci a été unanimement adopté en seconde lecture. Il ajoute que les réserves formulées par MM. Adatci et Ricci-Busatti seront insérées textuellement dans le rapport du Comité, mais ne seront pas autrement mentionnées.

Sur la proposition de M. DE LAPRADELLE, il est décidé que le vote définitif sur les trois voeux qui ont été préalablement adopté par le Comité par un vote provisoire, sera remis à la séance suivante qui aura lieu à 9.30 heures le lendemain.

L'exemplaire du texte auquel les membres doivent apposer leur signature, sera préparé sans délai et présenté à cette séance.

La séance est levée à 1 heure de l'après-midi.

Le Président:
(signé) Brn. DESCAMPS.

Le Secrétaire-Général:
(signé) D. ANZILOTTI.

condition of international relations, taken as a whole. In my opinion our Court should be launched within the limits set by the Covenant, and its development should be watched for some time, in order to form a sane judgment, based on experience. (See end of Procès-verbal of July 14th).

However, fully recognizing the immense importance of the immediate establishment of the Court, I gladly vote for the plan as a whole. I only ask permision to make one reservation in respect of the two Articles in question."

M. RICCI-BUSATTI expressed a wish to make a statement summarising his views with regard to the result achieved by the Committee's labours, and at the same time reaffirming his opinions and explaining the reasons for his vote. With these intentions, he read the following declaration:

„Fully convinced of the improvements which our work is intended to produce in relations between States, and of the advisability of not detracting from the value of the united effort made by our Committee to this end by a dissentient vote, and in spite of the divergent opinions, expressed by me during our debates, both with reference to the main features of the plan and to some of its provisions, I give my vote for the plan."

All the members in turn, as the PRESIDENT called their names, recorded their votes in favour of the plan.

The PRESIDENT stated that the plan had been unanimously approved at the second reading. He added that the reservations expressed by MM. Adatci and Ricci-Busatti would be included verbatim in the Committee's report, but would not be otherwise mentioned.

On M. DE LAPRADELLE's proposal, it was decided that the final vote upon the three Resolutions, which had previously been provisionally adopted by the Committee, would be postponed till the next meeting, to be held at 9.30 on the following day.

The copy of the plan to be signed by the members would be prepared forthwith and presented at the meeting arranged above.

The meeting closed at 1 p.m.

The President:
(signed) Brn. DESCAMPS.

The Secretary-General:
(signed) D. ANZILOTTI.

ANNEXE No. 1.

(Questions laissées ouvertes le 19 et 20, discutées le 21 juillet.)
(Textes révisés, avec, en regard, compte-rendu des délibérations.)

Article 11.

Alinéa 1er.

Le PRESIDENT propose le texte suivant:
„Si après la troisième élection il reste encore un ou plusieurs sièges à pourvoir l'Assemblée ou le Conseil peut à tout moment demander la formation d'une Commission médiatrice de six membres, nommés trois par l'Assemblée et trois par le Conseil, en vue de choisir pour chaque siège non pourvu un nom à présenter à l'adoption séparée de l'Assemblée et du Conseil."

M. DE LAPRADELLE attire l'attention sur le texte proposé par lui la veille (voir Annexe Ire au premier Procès-verbal du 20 juillet; 28e séance).
Cette formule est adoptée avec une légère modification.

Si après la troisième élection il reste encore des sièges à pourvoir, il peut être à tout moment formé, sur la seule demande, soit de l'Assemblée, soit du Conseil, une Commission médiatrice de six membres, nommés trois par l'Assemblée, trois par le Conseil, en vue de choisir pour chaque siège non pourvu un nom à présenter à l'adoption séparée de l'Assemblée et du Conseil.

Article 28 bis.

(Article visé *sub* art. 29 à l'Annexe Ire au premier Procès-verbal du 20 juillet; 28e séance).

Le PRESIDENT propose le texte suivant:
„Lorsqu'un différend surgit entre Etats, qu'il n'a pu être réglé par la voie diplomatique et que l'on n'est pas convenu de choisir une autre juridiction, la partie qui se prétend lésée peut en saisir la Cour qui statue sous les conditions et limitations déterminées par l'article 29 ci-après."
Ce texte est d'abord adopté.
La question est soulevée de savoir si c'est la Cour qui décide si une partie a eu recours à une juridiction. La question est résolue affirmativement.
Lors de la discussion de l'article 29, no. 2, il est proposé d'ajouter à l'article 28 bis la formule:
„En cas de contestation la Cour statue sur sa compétence."
Le Président soumet un autre texte:
„. . . la partie qui se prétend lésée peut saisir la Cour.
Celle-ci, après avoir décidé les conditions préalables de compétence, statue sous les conditions . . ."

Lorsqu'un différend surgit entre Etats, qu'il n'a pu être réglé par la voie diplomatique et que l'on n'est pas convenu de choisir une autre juridiction, la partie qui se prétend lésée peut en saisir la Cour. La Cour, après avoir décidé s'il est satisfait aux prescriptions précédentes, statue sous les conditions et limitations déterminées par l'article suivant.

M. DE LAPRADELLE propose la rédaction suivante de la formule à ajouter:

„La Cour, après avoir constaté qu'il est satisfait aux prescriptions précédentes, statue . . ."

Le PRESIDENT propose la formule suivante à titre transactionnel:

„La Cour, après avoir décidé s'il est satisfait aux prescriptions précédentes, statue . . ."

La formule finalement adoptée est soumise par le Président.

Article 29.

M. HAGERUP propose la suppression de l'article 29, No. 2, qui lui semble inutile après l'adoption de l'article 28 bis et qui du reste lui paraît incomplet parce que la Cour doit statuer sur sa compétence non seulement en cas de contestation mais aussi d'office.

M. FERNANDES reprend l'amendement qu'il a déposé la veille (voir compte-rendu du 20 juillet).

LORD PHILLIMORE propose d'introduire un nouvel article qui se référerait en même temps à l'article 28 bis et à l'article 29, et qui donnerait, pour ce qui concerne ces deux articles, des stipulations analogues à celles du No. 2 de l'article 29. Il propose *alternativement* d'introduire dans les règles de procédure une stipulation constatant le devoir de la Cour de statuer sur sa propre compétence en cas de jugement par contumace; dans ce cas le No. 2 de l'article 29 pourrait être maintenu.

M. HAGERUP propose la formule suivante pour le nouvel article dont l'insertion a été suggérée par Lord Phillimore:

„En cas de contestation sur le point de savoir si un différend rentre, oui ou non, dans les catégories visées à l'article . . . ., ou si les conditions visées à l'article . . . . sont remplies, la Cour décide en ordre préjudiciel."

M. RICCI-BUSATTI propose, dans le même ordre d'idées, la formule suivante:

„La Cour statue sur sa propre compétence en ordre préjudiciel, soit en raison de l'objet en litige, soit pour tout autre motif qui pourrait exclure sa juridiction."

LORD PHILLIMORE, ne s'en trouvant pas satisfait, en propose une autre:

„Si la compétence de la Cour est contestée par l'Etat défendeur et en raison que les conditions de l'article 28 bis ou en raison que les limitations de l'article 28 ne sont pas satisfaites . . . ."

Entre Etats Membres de la Société des Nations la Cour statue sans convention spéciale sur les différends d'ordre juridique, qui ont pour objet:

a. l'interprétation d'un traité;

b. tout point de droit international;

c. la réalité de tout fait, qui, s'il était établi, constituerait la violation d'un engagement international;

d. la nature ou l'étendue de la réparation due pour la rupture d'un engagement international;

e. l'interprétation d'une sentence rendue par la Cour.

La Cour connaît également de tous différends, de quelque nature qu'ils soient, qui lui sont soumis par la convention, soit générale, soit spéciale, des parties.

2. En cas de contestation sur le point de savoir si un différend rentre, oui ou non, dans les catégories ci-dessus visées, la Cour décide.

M. DE LAPRADELLE propose un amendement à la formule de Lord Phillimore:

„Si la compétence de la Cour est déniée parce qu'il n'est pas satisfait aux conditions ou limitations prévues dans les articles 28 bis et 29, la Cour statue sur sa compétence. L'examen de cette question est préjudiciel à tout autre."

Mr. ROOT s'oppose formellement à la suppression de l'article 29, no. 2.

A la suite de la discussion, l'article 29 est adopté sans modifications. Une addition est faite à l'article 28 bis (voir ci-dessus).

Article 31.

Sur la proposition du PRESIDENT on est d'accord pour échanger le mot „successivement" pour l'expression „en ordre successif".

No. 4. Le Président propose la rédaction suivante, à titre transactionnel.

„La Cour tient compte des décisions judiciaires et de la doctrine des publicistes les plus qualifiés des différentes nations, comme moyens auxiliaires de la détermination des règles de droit."

M. RICCI-BUSATTI voudrait substituer à l'expression „de la détermination des règles de droit" l'expression „d'interprétation juridique".

Cette proposition est rejetée.

LORD PHILLIMORE propose la suppression des mots „règles de droit qui se dégagent des."

Le texte original est adopté (avec modifications).

M. RICCI-BUSATTI vote contre.

Dans les limites de sa compétence, telle qu'elle est déterminée par l'article 29, la Cour applique en ordre successif:

1. les conventions internationales, soit générales, soit spéciales, établissant des règles expressément reconnues par les Etats en litige;

2. la coutume internationale, attestation d'une pratique commune, acceptée comme loi;

3. les principes généraux de droit reconnus par les nations civilisées;

4. les décisions judiciaires et la doctrine des publicistes les plus qualifiés des différentes Nations, comme moyens auxiliaires de la détermination des règles de droit.

Article 24.

M. DE LAPRADELLE fait valoir la nécessité d'arrêter des règles pour la procédure sommaire. Il attire l'attention sur l'article 51 du projet des Cinq Puissances.

Le PRESIDENT se réfère aux règles adoptés en 1907.

LORD PHILLIMORE propose la suppression des mots „en procédure sommaire" à l'article 24.

Mr. ROOT suggère l'idée de laisser à la Cour d'établir un règlement pour la procédure sommaire.

Dans cette ordre d'idées, le PRESIDENT propose le texte suivant, qui est adopté comme un nouvel article:

„La Cour détermine par un règlement d'ordre le mode suivant lequel elle exerce ses attributions. Elle règle spécialement ce qui concerne la procédure sommaire".

En vue de la prompte expédition des affaires, la Cour compose annuellement une chambre de trois juges, spécialement consacrée au jugement des affaires en procédure sommaire, lorsque les parties le demandent.

La Cour détermine par un réglement d'ordre le mode suivant lequel elle exerce ses attributions. Elle règle spécialement ce qui concerne la procédure sommaire.

Article 22 bis.

En raison de la décision prise lors de la discussion de l'article 24 (voir ci-dessus), M. RICCI-BUSATTI propose de formuler ainsi le premier alinéa de l'article 22 bis:

„La Cour exerce *normalement* ses attributions..."

Alternativement M. RICCI-BUSATTI propose d'ajouter au commencement de cet alinéa:

„Sauf le cas prévu à l'article 24, la Cour exerce..."

Sur la proposition de M. DE LAPRADELLE on se met d'accord pour ajouter au commencement de l'alinéa la formule suivante:

„Sauf exception expressément prévue..."

Cette formule, mise au vote, est adoptée.

Le PRESIDENT ne prend pas part au vote.

Sauf exception expressément prévue, la Cour exerce ses attributions en séance plénière.

Si la présence de onze juges titulaires n'est pas assurée, ce nombre est parfait par l'entrée en fonction des juges suppléants.

Toutefois, si onze juges ne sont pas disponibles, le quorum de neuf sera suffisant pour constituer la Cour.

Chapitre III.

Procédure.

Article 15.

Afin de donner satisfaction aux objections soulevées par M. HAGERUP lors de la discussion de l'article 29 No. 2, on se met d'accord pour insérer à l'alinéa 2 de l'article 15 les mots:

„non seulement que la compétence, mais..." entre les mots „s'assurer" et „que ces conclusions."

M. Hagerup a des objections contre la stipulation que „l'autre partie peut demander à la Cour... etc.". Il faudrait stipuler que la Cour a le devoir de prendre une décision.

Il n'est pas donné satisfaction à cette observation.

Lorsqu'une des parties ne se présente pas, ou s'abstient de faire valoir ses moyens, l'autre partie peut demander à la Cour de lui adjuger ses conclusions.

La Cour, avant d'y faire droit, doit s'assurer non seulement qu'elle a compétence, mais que ces conclusions, reposant sur des preuves sérieuses, sont fondées en fait et en droit.

Article 22.

La rédaction de l'alinéa Ier, laquelle avait été réservée, est complétée par l'addition des mots „et que la partie sans faute de sa part pouvait ne pas connaître."

La révision de l'arrêt ne peut être éventuellement demandée à la Cour qu'à raison de la découverte d'un fait nouveau de nature à exercer une influence décisive et qui, avant le prononcé de l'arrêt, était inconnu de la Cour et de la partie qui demande la révision et que la partie, sans faute de sa part, pouvait ne pas connaître. La procédure de révision s'ouvre par un arrêt de la Cour constatant expressément l'existence du fait nouveau, et lui reconnaissant les caractères qui donnent ouverture à la révision et déclarant de ce chef la demande recevable.

La Cour peut subordonner l'ouverture de la procédure en révision à l'exécution préalable de l'arrêt.

Aucune demande de révision ne peut être formée après l'expiration d'un délai de cinq ans.

Article 22 bis.

Des objections sont soulevées contre l'expression „intérêts d'ordre juridique". Ces objections n'ont pas donné lieu à des modifications.

Lorsqu'un Etat estime que dans un différend un intérêt d'ordre juridique est pour lui en cause, il peut adresser à la Cour une requête, afin d'intervention.

La Cour décide.

ANNEXE No. 2.

TEXTE ADOPTE EN PREMIERE LECTURE.

Article 1.

Indépendamment de la Cour d'Arbitrage, organisée par les Conventions de la Haye de 1899 et 1907, et des Tribunaux spéciaux d'Arbitres, auxquels les Etats demeurent toujours libres de confier la solution de leurs différends, il est institué, conformément à l'Article 14 du Pacte de la Société des Nations, une Cour Permanente de Justice Internationale, directement accessible aux parties.

CHAPITRE I.

Organisation de la Cour.

Article 2.

La Cour Permanente de Justice Internationale est un corps de magistrats indépendants, choisis sans égard à leur nationalité parmi les personnes, jouissant de la plus haute considération morale, et réunissant les conditions requises pour l'exercice dans leurs pays respectifs de la plus haute magistrature, ou étant des jurisconsultes possédant une compétence notoire en matière de droit international.

Article 3.

La Cour se compose de quinze membres: onze juges titulaires et quatre juges suppléants. Le nombre des juges titulaires et des juges suppléants peut être éventuellement augmenté par l'Assemblée, sur la proposition du Conseil de la Société des Nations, à concurrence de quinze juges titulaires et six juges suppléants.

Article 4.

Les membres de la Cour sont élus pour neuf ans.

Ils sont rééligibles.

Ils restent en fonction jusqu'à leur remplacement.

Après ce remplacement, ils continuent de connaître des affaires dont ils sont déjà saisis.

Article 5.

Les membres de la Cour sont élus par l'Assemblée et par le Conseil sur une liste de personnes

ANNEX No. 2.

TRANSLATION OF THE TEXT ADOPTED IN FIRST READING.

Article 1.

A Permanent Court of International Justice, to which Contesting Parties shall have direct access, is hereby established in accordance with Article 14 of the Covenant of the League of Nations. This Court shall be in addition to the Court of Arbitration organised by the Hague Conventions of 1899 and 1907, and to the special Tribunals of Arbitration to which States are always at liberty to submit their disputes for settlement.

CHAPTER I.

Organisation of the Court.

Article 2.

The Permanent Court of International Justice shall be composed of a body of independent judges, elected regardless of their nationality, from amongst persons of high moral character, who possess the qualifications required, in their respective countries, for appointment to the highest magistracy or are jurisconsults of recognised ability in international law.

Article 3.

The Court shall consist of fifteen members: eleven judges and four deputy-judges. The number of judges and deputy-judges may be increased by the Assembly, upon the proposal of the Council of the League of Nations, to a total of fifteen judges and six deputy-judges.

Article 4.

The members of the Court shall be elected for nine years.

They may be re-elected.

They shall continue in office until the vacancy has been filled.

Though replaced, they shall complete cases which they may have commenced.

Article 5.

The members of the Court shall be elected by the Assembly and the Council from a list of nomi-

présentées par les groupes nationaux de la Cour d'Arbitrage, conformément aux dispositions suivantes.

Article 6.

Trois mois au moins avant la date de l'élection, le Secrétaire-Général invite par écrit les membres de la Cour d'Arbitrage appartenant à des Etats faisant partie de la Société des Nations ou mentionnés à l'Annexe au Pacte de la Société des Nations à procéder par groupes nationaux à la présentation des personnes en situation de remplir les fonctions de membre de la Cour.

Chaque groupe ne peut en aucun cas présenter plus de deux personnes, sans distinction de nationalité.

Article 7.

Avant de procéder à cette désignation il est recommandé à chaque groupe national de consulter la plus Haute Cour de Justice, les Facultés de Droit des Universités, les Académies ou sections d'Académies nationales ou internationales, vouées à l'étude du droit.

Article 8.

Le Secrétaire Général dresse, par ordre alphabétique, une liste de toutes les personnes ainsi désignées: seules ces personnes sont éligibles, sauf le cas prévu à l'article 13, paragraphe 2.

Le Secrétaire Général communique cette liste à l'Assemblée et au Conseil.

Article 9.

L'Assemblée et le Conseil procèdent, indépendamment l'une de l'autre, à l'élection, d'abord des juges titulaires, ensuite des juges suppléants.

Article 10.

Dans toute élection, les électeurs veillent à ce que les personnes appelées à faire partie de la Cour, non seulement réunissent individuellement les conditions requises, mais assurent dans l'ensemble la représentation des grandes formes de civilisation et des principaux systèmes juridiques du monde.

Article 11.

Sont élus ceux qui ont réuni la majorité absolue des voix dans l'Assemblée et dans le Conseil.

Au cas où le double scrutin de l'Assemblée et du Conseil se porterait sur plus d'un membre de la même nationalité le plus âgé est seul élu.

nations made by the national groups of the Court of Arbitration, in accordance with the following provisions.

Article 6.

At least three months before the date of the election, the Secretary-General shall address a written request to the members of the Court of Arbitration, belonging to the League of Nations or mentioned in the Annex to the Covenant of the League of Nations inviting them to undertake, by national groups, the nominations of persons able to accept the duties of a member of the Court.

In no case may any group nominate more than two persons; these nominations shall be regardless of their nationality.

Article 7.

Before making these nominations, each national group is hereby requested to consult the Highest Court of Justice, the Legal Faculties of the Universities, the National or International Academies and sections of such Academies devoted to the study of law.

Article 8.

The Secretary-General shall prepare a list, in alphabetical order, of all the persons thus nominated. These persons only shall be eligible for appointment, except as provided in Article 13, Paragraph 2.

The Secretary-General shall submit this list to the Assembly and to the Council.

Article 9.

The Assembly and the Council shall concurrently carry out the election, first of the judges and then of the deputy-judges.

Article 10.

At every election the electors shall bear in mind, not only that all the persons appointed as members of the Court should possess the qualifications required, but also that the whole body should represent the main forms of civilisation and the principal legal systems of the world.

Article 11.

Those candidates who obtain an absolute majority of votes in the Assembly and in the Council shall be considered as elected.

In the event of more than one candidate of the same nationality being selected by the votes of both the Assembly and the Council, the eldest of these only shall be considered as elected.

Article 12.

Si après la première élection il reste encore des sièges à pourvoir, il est procédé de la même manière à une seconde élection puis à une troisième.

Article 13.

Si après la troisième élection il reste encore des sièges à pourvoir, il peut être à tout moment formé sur la seule demande, soit de l'Assemblée, soit du Conseil, une Commission médiatrice de six membres, nommés trois par l'Assemblée, trois par le Conseil, en vue de choisir pour chaque siège non pourvu un nom à présenter à l'adoption séparée de l'Assemblée et du Conseil.

Peuvent être portées sur cette liste, à l'unanimité, toutes personnes satisfaisant aux conditions requises, alors même qu'elles n'auraient pas figuré sur la liste de présentation de la Cour d'Arbitrage.

Si par le moyen de la Commission médiatrice l'élection n'a pu être faite, les membres de la Cour déjà nommés pourvoient, dans un délai à fixer par le Conseil de la Société des Nations, par cooptation aux sièges vacants, en choisissant parmi les personnes qui ont eu des voix, soit à l'Assemblée, soit au Conseil.

Si, parmi les juges, il y a partage égal de voix, la voix du juge le plus âgé l'emporte.

Article 14.

L'exercice de toute fonction qui relève de la direction politique, soit nationale, soit internationale, des Etats, est incompatible avec la qualité de membre de la Cour.

En cas de doute, la Cour décide.

Article 15.

Les membres de la Cour ne peuvent exercer les fonctions d'agent de conseil ou d'avocat dans aucune affaire d'ordre international.

Ils ne peuvent participer au règlement d'aucune affaire dans laquelle ils sont antérieurement intervenus comme agents, conseils ou avocats de l'une des parties, membres d'un Tribunal national ou international, d'une Commission d'enquête, ou à tout autre titre.

En cas de doute, la Cour décide.

Article 16.

Les membres de la Cour ne peuvent être relevés de leurs fonctions que si, au jugement unanime

Article 12.

If, after the first election, one or more seats remain to be filled, a second, and if necessary, a third election shall take place.

Article 13.

If, after the third election, one or more seats still remain unfilled, a joint Conference consisting of six members, three appointed by the Assembly and three by the Council, may be formed, at any time, at the request of either the Assembly or the Council, for the purpose of choosing one name for each seat still vacant, to submit to the Assembly and to the Council for their respective acceptance.

Provided that the Committee is unanimously agreed, any person fulfilling the required conditions may be included in this list, even though not contained in the list of nominations made by the Court of Arbitration.

If the election cannot be completed by means of the Joint Conference, those members of the Court who have already been appointed, shall, within a time limit to be arranged by the Council of the League of Nations, proceed by cooptation to fill the vacant seats by selection from amongst those candidates who have obtained votes either in the Assembly or in the Council.

In the event of an equality of votes amongst the judges, the eldest judge shall have a casting vote.

Article 14.

The exercise of any function which belongs to the political direction, national or international, of States by the members of the Court, during their terms of office, is declared incompatible with their judicial duties.

In doubtful cases, the Court shall decide.

Article 15.

The members of the Court may not act as agent, counsel or advocate in any case of an international nature.

They may not participate in the decision of any case in which they have previously taken an active part, as agent, counsel or advocate for one of the contesting parties, or as members of a National or International Court, or of a Commission of Inquiry, or in any other capacity.

In doubtful cases, the Court shall decide.

Article 16.

A member of the Court cannot be dismissed unless, in the unanimous opinion of the other mem-

des autres membres, ils ont cessé de répondre aux conditions requises.

Le Secrétaire Général en est officiellement informé.

Cette communication importe vacance de siège.

Article 17.

En dehors de leurs propres pays, les membres de la Cour jouissent des mêmes privilèges et immunités que les Agents diplomatiques.

Article 18.

Tout membre de la Cour doit, avant d'entrer en fonctions, faire, en séance publique, une déclaration solennelle de sa volonté d'exercer ses attributions avec impartialité et en toute conscience.

Article 19.

La Cour élit, pour trois ans, son Président et son Vice-Président: ils sont rééligibles.

Elle nomme son Greffier.

La fonction de Greffier de la Cour n'est pas incompatible avec celle de Secrétaire Général de la Cour Permanente d'Arbitrage.

Article 20.

Le siège de la Cour est fixé à la Haye.

Le Président et le Greffier résident au siège de la Cour.

Article 21.

La Cour tient une session chaque année.

Sauf disposition contraire du règlement d'ordre de la Cour, cette session commence le 15 juin et continue tant que le rôle n'est pas épuisé.

Le Président convoque la Cour en session extraordinaire quand les circonstances l'exigent.

Article 22.

Si, pour une raison spéciale, l'un des membres de la Cour estime ne pouvoir participer au jugement d'une affaire déterminée, il en fait part au Président.

Si le Président estime qu'un des membres de la Cour ne peut siéger pour une raison spéciale dans une affaire déterminée, il en avertit le membre intéressé.

Si l'un et l'autre ne sont pas d'accord dans chacun de ces cas sur l'attitude à prendre, la Cour décide.

bers, he has ceased to fulfil the required conditions.

The Secretary-General shall be officially informed.

Such communication shall imply that the seat is vacant.

Article 17.

The members of the Court shall, outside their own countries, enjoy the privileges and immunities of diplomatic representatives.

Article 18.

Every member of the Court shall, before taking up his duties, make a solemn declaration in open session of his will to exercise his powers impartially and conscientiously.

Article 19.

The Court shall elect its President and Vice-President for three years: they may be re-elected.

It shall appoint its Registrar.

The duties of Registrar of the Court shall not be considered incompatible with those of Secretary-General of the Permanent Court of Arbitration.

Article 20.

The seat of the Court shall be established at the Hague.

The President and Registrar shall reside at the seat of the Court.

Article 21.

A session shall be held every year.

Unless otherwise provided in the Court's rules of procedure, this session shall commence on the 15th June, and shall continue for so long as may be necessary to complete the cases on the list.

The President may summon an extraordinary meeting of the Court whenever necessary.

Article 22.

If, for some special reason, a member of the Court considers that he cannot take part in the decision of a particular case, he shall so inform the President.

If, for some special reason, the President considers that one of the members of the Court should not sit for a particular case, he shall give notice to the member concerned.

In the event of the President and the member not agreeing as to the course to be adopted in any such case, the Court shall decide.

Article 23.

Sauf exception expressément prévue, la Cour exerce ses attributions en séance plénière.

Si la présence de onze juges titulaires n'est pas assurée, ce nombre est parfait par l'entrée en fonction des juges suppléants.

Toutefois, si onze juges ne sont pas disponibles, le quorum de neuf sera suffisant pour constituer la Cour.

Article 23.

The Court shall exercise its powers in full session except as expressly provided otherwise.

If eleven judges cannot be present, deputy judges shall be called upon to sit, in order to make up this number.

Nevertheless if, including deputy judges, eleven judges are not available, a quorum of nine judges shall suffice to constitute the Court.

Article 24.

Les suppléants sont appelés dans l'ordre du tableau.

Le tableau est dressé par la Cour, en tenant compte, d'abord de la priorité d'élection et ensuite de l'ancienneté d'âge.

Article 24.

Deputy-judges shall be called upon to sit in the order laid down in a list.

This list shall be prepared by the Court, having regard, firstly, to the order of election and, secondly, to age.

Article 25.

Il est pourvu aux sièges devenus vacants selon la méthode suivie pour la première élection.

Le membre de la Cour élu en remplacement d'un membre dont le mandat n'est pas expiré, achève le terme du mandat de son prédécesseur.

Article 25.

Vacancies which may occur shall be filled by the same method as that laid down for the first election.

A member of the Court elected to replace a member, the period of whose appointment has not expired, shall complete this period.

Article 26.

En vue de la prompte expédition des affaires, la Cour compose annuellement une chambre de trois juges, spécialement consacrée au jugement des affaires en procédure sommaire, lorsque les parties le demandent.

Article 26.

With a view to avoiding unnecessary delays, the Court shall form, annually, a chamber composed of three judges specially affected to the decision of cases by summary procedure, at the request of the contesting parties.

Article 27.

La Cour détermine par un règlement d'ordre le mode suivant lequel elle exerce ses attributions. Elle règle spécialement ce qui concerne la procédure sommaire.

Article 27.

The Court shall draw up rules of procedure, in order to detail the method in which it shall exercise its powers. In particular it shall lay down rules for the summary procedure.

Article 28.

1. Lorsque la Cour renferme un juge titulaire de la nationalité de chacune des parties en cause, ces juges conservent le droit de siéger dans l'affaire dont la Cour est saisie.

2. Si la Cour ne renferme qu'un juge titulaire de la nationalité d'une seule des parties en cause, l'autre partie désigne pour siéger, parmi les juges suppléants, un juge de sa nationalité, s'il en existe. S'il n'en existe pas, elle choisit un juge, de préférence parmi les personnes qui ont été l'objet d'une présentation de la part des groupes nationaux de la Cour d'Arbitrage.

Article 28.

1. If the Court includes a judge of the nationality of each contesting party, these judges shall retain their rights to sit in the case before the Court.

2. If the Court includes an ordinary judge of the nationality of one of the contesting Parties only, the other Party selects from among the deputy judges, the judge of its nationality, if there be one. If there should not be one, the party chooses a judge, preferably from among those persons who have been nominated as candidates by the national groups of the Court of Arbitration.

3. If the Court includes no ordinary judge of the

3. Si la Cour ne renferme aucun juge titulaire de la nationalité des parties en cause, chacune de ces parties procède à la désignation ou au choix d'un juge de la même manière que dans le cas précédent.

4. Lorsque plusieurs parties font cause commune, elles ne peuvent désigner ou choisir qu'un seul juge de commun accord.

5. Les juges désignés ou choisis comme il est dit ci-dessus, doivent satisfaire aux prescriptions des articles 2, 14, 15, 18, 22 du présent statut. Ils statuent sur un pied d'égalité avec leurs collègues.

nationality of the contesting parties, each of these proceeds to select or choose a judge as provided for in the case already dealt with.

4. Should several parties take joint action, they must agree on the nomination or election of one judge only.

5. Judges selected or chosen as laid down above, shall fulfil the conditions required by Articles 2, 14, 15, 18, 22 of this Act. They shall take part in the decision on an equal footing with their colleagues.

Article 29.

Les juges titulaires reçoivent un traitement annuel à fixer par l'Assemblée de la Société des Nations sur la proposition du Conseil. Ce traitement ne peut être diminué pendant la durée des fonctions du juge.

Le Président reçoit un indemnité spéciale déterminée de la même manière pour la durée de ses fonctions.

Les juges suppléants reçoivent dans l'exercice de leurs fonctions une indemnité à fixer de la même manière.

Un règlement spécial détermine les pensions auxquelles ont droit les juges.

Les juges titulaires et suppléants qui ne résident pas au siège de la Cour auront droit au remboursement des frais de voyages nécessités par l'accomplissement de leurs fonctions.

L'indemnité due aux juges désignés ou choisis conformément à l'article 25 est réglée de la même manière.

Le traitement du greffier est fixé par le Conseil sur la proposition de la Cour.

Article 29.

Judges shall receive an annual salary to be determined by the Assembly of the League of Nations upon the proposal of the Council. This salary must not be decreased during the period of a judge's appointment.

The President shall receive a special allowance, to be fixed in the same way, for the period of his functions.

Deputy-judges shall receive an allowance, to be fixed in the same way, for the actual performance of these duties.

A special regulation shall provide for the pensions to which the judges shall be entitled.

Travelling expenses incurred in the performance of their duties shall be refunded to judges and deputy-judges who do not reside at the seat of the Court.

Allowances due to judges selected or chosen as provided in Article 28 shall be assessed in the same way.

The salary of the Registrar shall be decided by the Council upon the proposal of the Court.

Article 30.

Les frais de la Cour sont supportés par la Société des Nations de la manière que l'Assemblée décide sur la proposition du Conseil.

Article 30.

The expenses of the Court shall be borne by the League of Nations, according to rules laid down by the Assembly upon the proposal of the Council.

CHAPITRE II.

Compétence de la Cour.

Article 31.

La Cour connaît des litiges entre Etats.

Article 32.

La Cour est ouverte aux Etats Membres de la Société des Nations.

CHAPTER II.

Competence of the Court.

Article 31.

The Court shall be competent to hear and determine suits between States.

Article 32.

The Court shall be open of right to States Members of the League of Nations.

Elle l'est de même aux Etats mentionnés à l'annexe au Pacte de la Société des Nations.

Elle est aussi accessible aux autres Etats.

Les conditions, auxquelles elle est ouverte ou accessible aux Etats qui ne sont pas Membres de la Société des Nations, sont réglées par le Conseil, en tenant compte de l'article 17 du Pacte.

It is likewise open to States mentioned in the Annex to the Covenant of the League of Nations.

Other States may have access to it.

The conditions under which the Court shall be open of right or accessible to States which are not Members of the League of Nations shall be determined by the Council, in accordance with Article 17 of the Covenant.

Article 33.

Lorsqu'un différend surgit entre Etats, qu'il n'a pu être réglé par la voie diplomatique et que l'on n'est pas convenu de choisir une autre jurisdiction, la partie qui se prétend lésée peut en saisir la Cour. La Cour, après avoir décidé s'il est satisfait aux prescriptions précédentes, statue sous les conditions et limitations déterminées par l'article suivant.

Article 33.

When, a dispute having arisen between States, it has been found impossible to settle it by diplomatic means, and no agreement has been made to choose another jurisdiction, the party claiming to have been wronged may bring the case before the Court. The Court shall, first of all, decide whether the preceding conditions have been complied with ; if so, it shall deliver judgment according to the terms and within the limits of the Article which follows.

Article 34.

Entre Etats Membres de la Société des Nations la Cour statue sans convention spéciale sur les différends d'ordre juridique, qui ont pour objet :

a. l'interprétation d'un traité ;

b. tout point de droit international ;

c. la réalité de tout fait, qui, s'il était établi, constituerait la violation d'un engagement international ;

d. la nature ou l'étendue de la réparation due pour la rupture d'un engagement international ;

e. l'interprétation d'une sentence rendue par la Cour.

La Cour connaît également de tous différends, de quelque nature qu'ils soient, qui lui sont soumis par la convention, soit générale, soits péciale, des parties.

En cas de contestation sur le point de savoir si un différend rentre, oui ou non, dans les catégories ci-dessus visées, la Cour décide.

Article 34.

In the absence of any special convention, the Court shall be competent to hear and determine cases of a legal nature, between States which are Members of the League of Nations, concerning :

a. the interpretation of a Treaty ;

b. any question of international law ;

c. the existence of any fact which, if established, would constitute a breach of an international obligation ;

d. the nature or extent of reparation to be made for the breach of an international obligation ;

e. the interpretation of a sentence passed by the Court.

The Court shall also take cognisance of all disputes of any kind which are submitted to its jurisdiction by a general or special convention between the parties.

In the event of a dispute as to whether a certain case comes within the categories defined above, the Court shall decide.

Article 35.

Dans les limites de sa compétence, telle qu'elle est déterminée par l'article 34, la Cour applique en ordre successif :

1. les conventions internationales, soit générales, soit spéciales, établissant des règles expressément reconnues par les Etats en litige ;

Article 35.

The Court shall, within the limits of its competence as defined in Article 34, apply in the following order :

1. international conventions, general and special, establishing rules expressly recognised by the contesting States ;

2. la coutume internationale, attestation d'une pratique commune, acceptée comme loi;

3. les principes généraux de droit reconnus par les nations civilisées;

4. les décisions judiciaires et la doctrine des publicistes les plus qualifiés des différentes Nations, comme moyens auxiliaires de la détermination des règles de droit.

Article 36.

La Cour donne son avis sur tout point ou tout différend d'ordre international qui lui est soumis par le Conseil ou par l'Assemblée.

Lorsque la Cour donne son avis sur un point d'ordre international, indépendamment de tout différend actuellement né, elle constitue une Commission spéciale de trois à cinq membres.

Lorsqu'elle donne son avis sur une question qui fait l'objet d'un différend actuellement né, elle statue dans les mêmes conditions, que s'il s'agissait d'un litige porté devant elle.

CHAPITRE III.

Procédure.

Article 37.

La langue de la Cour est le français.

La Cour peut, à la demande des parties, autoriser l'emploi d'une autre langue devant elle.

Article 38.

La Cour est saisie par une requête adressée au Greffe.

La requête indique l'objet du différend et désigne les parties en cause.

Le Greffe fait immédiatement notification de la requête aux intéressées.

Il en informe également les Membres de la Société des Nations par l'entremise du Secrétaire Général.

Article 39.

Dans le cas où la cause du différend consiste en un acte effectué, ou sur le point de l'être, la Cour a le pouvoir d'indiquer, si elle estime que les circonstances l'exigent, quelles mesures conservatoires du droit de chacun doivent être prises à titre provisoire.

En attendant l'arrêt, l'indication de ces mesures est immédiatement transmise aux parties et au Conseil.

2. international custom, being the recognition of a general practice, accepted as law;

3. the general principles of law recognised in civilised nations;

4. judicial decisions and the teachings of the most highly qualified publicists of the various nations, being subsidiary means for the definition of rules of law.

Article 36.

The Court shall give an advisory opinion upon any question or dispute of an international nature, referred to it by the Council or the Assembly.

When the Court shall give an opinion on a question of an international nature which does not refer to any dispute that may have arisen, it shall appoint a special Committee of from three to five Members.

When it shall give an opinion upon a question which forms the subject of an existing dispute, it shall do so under the same conditions as if the case had been actually submitted to it for decision.

CHAPTER III.

Procedure.

Article 37.

The official language of the Court shall be French.

The Court may, at the request of the contesting parties, authorise another language to be used before it.

Article 38.

Appeal to the Court shall be made by means of an application addressed to the Registry.

The application shall indicate the subject of the dispute, and name the contesting parties.

The Registry shall forthwith notify all concerned of the application.

It shall also notify the Members of the League of Nations through the Secretary-General.

Article 39.

If the dispute arises out of acts which have already taken place or which are imminent, the Court shall have the power to suggest, if it considers that circumstances require it, the measures that must be taken provisionally to ensure that the respective rights be not prejudiced.

Pending the decision, notice of the measures suggested shall forthwith be given to the parties and the Council.

Article 40.

Les parties sont représentées par des Agents.
Elles peuvent se faire assister devant la Cour par des Conseils ou des Avocats.

Article 41.

La procédure a deux phases: l'une écrite, l'autre orale.

Article 42.

La procédure écrite comprend la communication à juge et à partie des mémoires, des contremémoires et, éventuellement, des répliques, ainsi que de toute pièce et document à l'appui.

La communication se fait par l'entremise du Greffe dans l'ordre et les délais déterminés par la Cour.

Toute pièce produite par l'une des parties doit être communiquée à l'autre en copie certifiée conforme.

Article 43.

La procédure orale consiste dans l'audition par la Cour des témoins, experts, agents, conseils et avocats.

Pour toute notification à faire à d'autres personnes que les agents, conseils et avocats, la Cour s'adresse directement au Gouvernement de l'Etat sur le territoire duquel la notification doit produire effet.

Il en est de même s'il s'agit de faire procéder sur place à l'établissement de tous moyens de preuve.

Article 44.

Les débats sont dirigés par le Président, et à défaut de celui-ci, par le Vice-Président; en cas d'empêchement, par le plus ancien des juges présents.

Article 45.

L'audience est publique, à moins qu'il n'en soit autrement décide par la Cour à la demande motivée de l'une des parties.

Article 46.

Il est tenu de chaque audience un procès-verbal signé par le Greffier et le Président.

Ce procès-verbal a seul caractère authentique.

Article 47.

La Cour rend des ordonnances pour la direction du procès, la détermination des formes et

Article 40.

The parties shall be represented by agents.
They may make use of counsel or advocates before the Court.

Article 41.

The procedure shall consist of two phases: written and oral.

Article 42.

The written proceedings shall consist of the communication to the judges and to the parties, of statements of cases, counter-cases and, if necessary, rejoinders; also all proofs and documents in support.

These communications shall be made through the Registry, in the order and within the times fixed by the Court.

A certified copy of every document produced by one party shall be communicated to the other party.

Article 43.

The oral proceedings shall consist in the hearing of witnesses, experts, agents, counsel and advocates before the Court.

For the service of all notices upon persons other than the agents, counsel and advocates, the Court shall apply direct to the Government of the State upon whose territory the notice has to be served.

The same shall apply whenever steps are to be taken to procure evidence on the spot.

Article 44.

The proceedings shall be under the direction of the President, or in his absence, of the Vice-President; if both are absent, the senior judge shall preside.

Article 45.

The hearing in Court shall be public, unless otherwise decided by the Court, at the request, accompanied by a statement of the reasons, of one of the parties.

Article 46.

A procès-verbal shall be made for each hearing, to be signed by the Registrar and the President.

This procès-verbal shall be the only authentic record.

Article 47.

The Court shall make rules for the conduct of the case, shall decide the form and time in which each

délais dans lesquels chaque partie doit finalement conclure, et prend toutes les mesures que comporte l'administration des preuves.

Article 48.

La Cour peut, même avant tout débat, demander aux agents de lui produire tout document et de lui fournir toutes explications. En cas de refus, elle en prend acte.

Article 49.

A tout moment, la Cour peut confier une enquête ou une expertise à une ou plusieurs personnes (corps, bureaux, commissions ou organes) de son choix.

Article 50.

Au cours des débats, les juges posent aux témoins, agents, experts, avocats et conseils, toutes questions qu'ils jugent utiles ; les agents, avocats et conseils ont le droit de poser, par l'entremise du Président, toute question que la Cour juge utile.

Article 51.

Après avoir reçu les preuves et témoignages dans les délais déterminés par elle, la Cour peut écarter toutes dépositions ou documents nouveaux qu'une des parties voudrait lui présenter sans l'assentiment de l'autre.

Article 52.

Lorsqu'une des parties ne se présente pas, ou s'abstient de faire valoir ses moyens, l'autre partie peut demander à la Cour de lui adjuger ses conclusions.

La Cour, avant d'y faire droit, doit s'assurer non seulement qu'elle a compétence, mais que ces conclusions, reposant sur des preuves sérieuses, sont fondées en fait et en droit.

Article 53.

Quand les agents, avocats et conseils ont fait valoir, sous le contrôle de la Cour, tous les moyens qu'ils jugent utiles, le Président prononce la clôture des débats.

La Cour se retire on chambre du Conseil pour délibérer.

Les délibérations de la Cour sont et restent secrètes.

party must conclude its arguments, and make all arrangements connected with the taking of evidence.

Article 48.

The Court may, even before the commencement of the hearing, call upon the representatives to produce any document, or to supply to the Court any explanations. It shall put on record any refusal.

Article 49.

The Court may, at any time, entrust one or more individuals, corps, bureaux, commissions or other bodies that it may select, with the task of carrying out an enquiry or giving an expert opinion.

Article 50.

During the hearing in Court, the judges may put any questions considered by them to be necessary, to the witnesses, agents, experts, advocates or counsels. The agents, advocates and counsels shall have the right to ask, through the President, any questions that the Court considers useful.

Article 51.

After the expiration of the times laid down by the Court, it may refuse to accept any further written or oral evidence that any party may desire to submit without the consent of the other.

Article 52.

Whenever one of the parties shall not appear before the Court, or shall refrain from presenting its case and the evidence in support, the other party may call upon the Court to pronounce that the case submitted by it is justified.

The Court must, before doing so, ascertain not only that it is competent, but also that the demands are based upon sound proof, and are well founded in fact and law.

Article 53.

When the agents, advocates and counsels have, under the Court's supervision, submitted all evidence, and taken all other steps that they consider advisable, the President shall declare the Court closed.

The Court shall withdraw to consider the finding.

The deliberations of the Court shall take place in private and remain secret.

Article 54.

Les décisions de la Cour sont prises à la majorité des juges présents.

En cas de partage de voix, la voix du Président ou de celui qui le remplace est prépondérante.

Article 55.

L'arrêt est motivé.

Il mentionne les noms des juges qui y ont pris part.

Article 56.

Si l'arrêt n'exprime pas, en tout ou en partie, l'opinion unanime des juges, les dissidents ont la faculté de demander que leurs oppositions ou leurs réserves soient constatées, sans pouvoir être motivées.

Article 57.

L'arrêt est signé par le Président et par le Greffier. Il est lu en séance publique, les agents dûment prévenus.

Article 58.

L'arrêt est définitif et sans recours. En cas de doute sur le sens et la portée de l'arrêt, il appartient à la Cour de l'interprêter à la demande de toute partie.

Article 59.

La révision de l'arrêt ne peut être éventuellement demandée à la Cour qu'à raison de la découverte d'un fait nouveau de nature à exercer une influence décisive et qui, avant le prononcé de l'arrêt, était inconnu de la Cour et de la partie qui demande la révision, et que la partie, sans faute de sa part, pouvait ne pas connaître.

La procédure de révision s'ouvre par un arrêt de la Cour constatant expressément l'existence du fait nouveau, lui reconnaissant les caractères qui donnent ouverture à la révision et déclarant de ce chef la demande recevable.

La Cour peut subordonner l'ouverture de la procédure en révision à l'exécution préalable de l'arrêt.

Aucune demande de révision ne peut être formée après l'expiration d'un délai de cinq ans.

Article 60.

Lorsqu'un Etat estime que dans un différend un intérêt d'ordre juridique est pour lui en cause,

Article 54.

Decisions of the Court shall be taken by a majority of the judges present.

In the event of an equality of votes, the President or his deputy shall have a casting vote.

Article 55.

The sentence shall state the reasons on which it is based.

It shall contain the names of the judges who have taken part.

Article 56.

If the sentence given does not represent, wholly or in part, the unanimous opinion of the judges, the dissenting judges shall be entitled to claim that their dissent or reservations shall be mentioned. No reasons for the dissent or reservations may be given.

Article 57.

The sentence shall be signed by the President and by the Registrar. It shall be read in open Court, due notice having been given to the agents.

Article 58.

The sentence is final and without appeal. In the event of uncertainty as to the meaning and scope of the sentence, the Court shall interpret it at the request of any party.

Article 59.

An appeal for revision of a sentence may only be made when based upon the discovery of a new fact, of such a nature as to be a decisive factor, and which was, before pronouncement of sentence, unknown to the Court and to the party claiming revision, always provided that the party could ignore the fact without lack of due diligence.

The procedure of revision shall be opened with a declaration by the Court explicitly stating the existence of the new fact, and the features inherent in it which make revision admissible, and declaring, on these grounds, that a case for revision is made out.

The Court may make the commencement of the procedure in revision depend upon previous compliance with the terms of the sentence.

No appeal for revision may be made after the lapse of five years from the date of the sentence.

Article 60.

Should a State consider that it has an interest of a legal nature in a certain case, it may submit

il peut adresser à la Cour une requête, afin d'intervention.

La Cour décide.

Article 61.

Lorsqu'il s'agit de l'interprétation d'une convention à laquelle ont participé d'autres Etats que les parties en litige, le Greffe avertit sans délai tous les signataires.

Chacun d'eux a le droit d'intervenir au procès et s'il exerce cette faculté, l'interprétation contenue dans la sentence est également obligatoire à son égard.

Article 62.

S'il n'en est autrement décidé par la Cour, chaque partie supporte ses frais de procédure.

a request to the Court to be permitted to appear as a third party.

The Court shall decide.

Article 61.

Whenever the interpretation of a convention in which States, other than those concerned in the case, are parties, is in question, the Registry shall notify all such States forthwith.

They shall each have the right to intervene in the proceedings; if they use this right, the interpretation given by the sentence shall be equally binding upon them.

Article 62.

Unless otherwise decided by the Court, each party shall pay its own costs.

32IÈME SÉANCE (non-publique), tenue au Palais de la Paix, à La Haye, le 23 juillet 1920.

Présidence de M. le BARON DESCAMPS.

Sont présents: tous les membres du Comité (à l'exception de M. Bevilaqua); M. Fernandes; Mr. James Brown Scott; les secrétaires particuliers du Baron Descamps et de M. Adatci; les membres du Secrétariat.

La séance est ouverte à 10 heures du matin.

Sur l'invitation du PRESIDENT tous les membres du Comité, y compris M. Fernandes, apposent leur signature à l'exemplaire préparé par le Secrétariat pour cette fin, du texte voté la veille en seconde lecture. (Annexe No. 1).

Le Président met aux voix les trois vœux qui ont été provisoirement adoptés à la séance du 21 juillet.

Ces vœux sont adoptés en principe, en seconde lecture.

Toutefois le rapporteur, d'accord avec le Président, pourra apporter des modifications de style au texte des vœux.

Le Président invite le rapporteur, M. de Lapradelle, à commencer la lecture de son rapport.

M. DE LAPRADELLE, avant de commencer la lecture, s'excuse des imperfections de son œuvre et dit que, s'il lui a été possible de l'achever et de la présenter dans sa forme actuelle, c'est grâce au dévouement, sans exemple dans l'histoire des conférences internationales, dont a fait preuve le Secrétariat du Comité. *(Applaudissements).*

M. de Lapradelle commence la lecture de son rapport.

Au cours de cette lecture, certains passages du travail sont, après discussion, amendés.

A 12.45 heures cette lecture est ajournée jusqu'à 3.30 heures de l'après-midi.

La séance est levée à 12.45 heures de l'après-midi.

Le Président:
(signé) Bm. DESCAMPS.

Le Secrétaire-Général:
(signé) D. ANZILOTTI.

32ND MEETING (Private), held at the Peace Palace, the Hague, on July 23rd 1920.

BARON DESCAMPS in the chair.

Present: all members of the Committee (with the exception of M. Bevilaqua); M. Fernandes; Mr. James Brown Scott; the private secretaries of Baron Descamps and of M. Adatci; the members of the Secretariat.

The meeting opened at 10 a.m.

At the request of the PRESIDENT, all the members of the Committee, among whom M. Fernandes, signed the copy of the text adopted in second reading on the previous day (Annex No. 1), which had been prepared by the Secretariat for this purpose.

The President took a vote upon the three Recommendations, provisionally adopted at the meeting of 21st July.

These Recommendations were adopted, in principle, in second reading; the Reporter however, subject to the President's approval, was to be permitted to improve the style and phraseology of the texts of the Recommendations.

The President called on M. de Lapradelle, the Reporter, to commence the reading of his report.

M. DE LAPRADELLE, before complying, apologised for the imperfections of his work and said that only a devotion to duty, without parallel in any International Conference on the part of the Secretariat of the Committee, had enabled him to finish it and to submit it in its present form. *(Applause).*

M. de Lapradelle began to read his report.

During this reading, certain passages were amended after discussion.

The reading was adjourned at 12.45 until 3.30 in the afternoon.

The meeting closed at 12.45 p.m.

The President:
(signed) Bm. DESCAMPS.

The Secretary-General:
(signed) D. ANZILOTTI.

ANNEXE No. 1.

AVANT-PROJET.

Article 1.

Indépendamment de la Cour d'Arbitrage, organisée par les Conventions de La Haye de 1899 et 1907, et des Tribunaux spéciaux d'Arbitres, auxquels les Etats demeurent toujours libres de confier la solution de leurs différends, il est institué, conformément à l'article 14 du Pacte de la Société des Nations, une Cour Permanente de Justice Internationale, directement accessible aux parties.

CHAPITRE I.

Organisation de la Cour.

Article 2.

La Cour Permanente de Justice Internationale est un corps de magistrats indépendants, élus, sans égard à leur nationalité, parmi les personnes jouissant de la plus haute considération morale, et qui réunissent les conditions requises pour l'exercice, dans leurs pays respectifs, des plus hautes fonctions judiciaires, ou qui sont des jurisconsultes possédant une compétence notoire en matière de droit international.

Article 3.

La Cour se compose de 15 membres: 11 juges titulaires et 4 juges suppléants. Le nombre des juges titulaires et des juges suppléants peut être éventuellement augmenté par l'Assemblée, sur la proposition du Conseil de la Société des Nations, à concurrence de 15 juges titulaires et de 6 juges suppléants.

Article 4.

Les membres de la Cour sont élus par l'Assemblée et par le Conseil sur une liste de personnes présentées par les groupes nationaux de la Cour d'Arbitrage, conformément aux dispositions suivantes.

Article 5.

Trois mois au moins avant la date de l'élection, le Secrétaire Général de la Société des Nations invite par écrit les membres de la Cour d'Arbitrage appartenant à des Etats mentionnés à

ANNEX No. 1.

DRAFT-SCHEME.

Article 1.

A Permanent Court of International Justice, to which Parties shall have direct access, is hereby established, in accordance with Article 14 of the Covenant of the League of Nations. This Court shall be in addition to the Court of Arbitration organised by the Hague Conventions of 1899 and 1907, and to the special Tribunals of Arbitration to which States are always at liberty to submit their disputes for settlement.

CHAPTER I.

Organisation of the Court.

Article 2.

The Permanent Court of International Justice shall be composed of a body of independent judges, elected regardless of their nationality, from amongst persons of high moral character. who possess the qualifications required, in their respective countries, for appointment to the highest judicial offices, or are jurisconsults of recognised competence in international law.

Article 3.

The Court shall consist of 15 members: 11 judges and 4 deputy-judges. The number of judges and deputy-judges may be hereafter increased by the Assembly, upon the proposal of the Council of the League of Nations, to a total of 15 judges and 6 deputy-judges.

Article 4.

The members of the Court shall be elected by the Assembly and the Council from a list of persons nominated by the national groups in the Court of Arbitration, in accordance with the following provisions.

Article 5.

At least three months before the date of the election, the Secretary-General of the League of Nations shall address a written request to the members of the Court of Arbitration,

l'Annexe au Pacte ou entrés ultérieurement dans la Société des Nations, à procéder par groupes nationaux à la présentation de personnes en situation de remplir les fonctions de membres de la Cour.

Chaque groupe ne peut en aucun cas présenter plus de deux personnes, sans distinction de nationalité.

Article 6.

Avant de procéder à cette désignation il est recommandé à chaque groupe national de consulter la plus Haute Cour de Justice, les Facultés et Ecoles de Droit, les Académies nationales et les sections nationales d'Académies internationales, vouées à l'étude du droit.

Article 7.

Le Secrétaire Général de la Société des Nations dresse, par ordre alphabétique, une liste de toutes les personnes ainsi désignées: seules ces personnes sont éligibles, sauf le cas prévu à l'article 12 paragraphe 2.

Le Secrétaire Général communique cette liste à l'Assemblée et au Conseil.

Article 8.

L'Assemblée et le Conseil procèdent, indépendamment l'une de l'autre, à l'élection, d'abord des juges titulaires, ensuite des juges suppléants.

Article 9.

Dans toute élection, les électeurs veillent à ce que les personnes appelées à faire partie de la Cour, non seulement réunissent individuellement les conditions requises, mais assurent dans l'ensemble la représentation des grandes formes de civilisation et des principaux systèmes juridiques du monde.

Article 10.

Sont élus ceux qui ont réuni la majorité absolue des voix dans l'Assemblée et dans le Conseil.

Au cas où le double scrutin de l'Assemblée et du Conseil se porterait sur plus d'un membre de la même nationalité, le plus âgé est seul élu.

belonging to the States mentioned in the Annex to the Covenant or to the States which shall have joined the League subsequently, inviting them to undertake, by national groups, the nomination of persons in a position to accept the duties of a member of the Court.

No group may nominate more than two persons; the nominees may be of any nationality.

Article 6.

Before making these nominations, each national group is hereby recommended to consult its Highest Court of Justice, its Legal Faculties and Schools of Law, and its National Academies and national sections of International Academies devoted to the study of Law.

Article 7.

The Secretary-General of the League of Nations shall prepare a list, in alphabetical order, of all the persons thus nominated. These persons only shall be eligible for appointment, except as provided in Article 12 Paragraph 2.

The Secretary-General shall submit this list to the Assembly and to the Council.

Article 8.

The Assembly and the Council shall proceed to elect by independent voting first the judges and then the deputy-judges.

Article 9.

At every election, the electors shall bear in mind that not only should all the persons appointed as members of the Court possess the qualifications required, but the whole body also should represent the main forms of civilisation and the principal legal systems of the world.

Article 10.

Those candidates who obtain an absolute majority of votes in the Assembly and the Council shall be considered as elected.

In the event of more than one candidate of the same nationality being elected by the votes of both the Assembly and the Council, the eldest of these only shall be considered as elected.

Article 11.

Si, après la première séance d'élection, il reste encore des sièges à pourvoir, il est procédé de la même manière à une seconde, puis à une troisième.

Article 11.

If, after the first sitting held for the purpose of the election, one or more seats remain to be filled, a second and if necessary, a third sitting shall take place.

Article 12.

Si après la troisième séance d'élection il reste encore des sièges à pourvoir, il peut être à tout moment formé sur la seule demande, soit de l'Assemblée, soit du Conseil, une Commission médiatrice de six membres, nommés trois par l'Assemblée, trois par le Conseil, en vue de choisir pour chaque siège non pourvu un nom à présenter à l'adoption séparée de l'Assemblée et du Conseil.

Peuvent être portées sur cette liste, à l'unanimité, toutes personnes satisfaisant aux conditions requises, alors même qu'elles n'auraient pas figuré sur la liste de présentation de la Cour d'Arbitrage.

Si par le moyen de la Commission médiatrice l'élection n'a pu être faite, les membres de la Cour déjà nommés pourvoient dans un délai à fixer par le Conseil aux sièges vacants, en choisissant parmi les personnes qui ont eu des voix, soit à l'Assemblée soit au Conseil.

Si parmi les juges il y a partage égal des voix, la voix du juge le plus âgé l'emporte.

Article 12.

If after the third sitting one or more seats still remain unfilled, a Joint Conference consisting of six members, three appointed by the Assembly and three by the Council, may be formed, at any time, at the request of either the Assembly or the Council, for the purpose of choosing one name for each seat still vacant, to submit to the Assembly and the Council for their respective acceptance.

If the Committee is unanimously agreed upon any person who fulfils the required conditions, he may be included in its list, even though he was not included in the list of nominations made by the Court of Arbitration.

If the Joint Conference, is not successful in procuring an election, those members of the Court who have already been appointed, shall, within a time limit to be arranged by the Council, proceed to fill the vacant seats by selection from amongst those candidates who have obtained votes either in the Assembly or in the Council.

In the event of an equality of votes amongst the judges, the eldest judge shall have a casting vote.

Article 13.

Les membres de la Cour sont élus pour neuf ans.

Ils sont rééligibles.

Ils restent en fonction jusqu'à leur remplacement. Après ce remplacement, ils continuent de connaître des affaires dont ils sont déjà saisis.

Article 13.

The members of the Court shall be elected for nine years.

They may be re-elected.

They shall continue to discharge their duties until their places have been filled. Though replaced, they shall complete any cases which they may have begun.

Article 14.

Il est pourvu aux sièges devenus vacants selon la méthode suivie pour la première élection. Le membre de la Cour élu en remplacement d'un membre dont le mandat n'est pas expiré achève le terme du mandat de son prédécesseur.

Article 14.

Vacancies which may occur shall be filled by the same method as that laid down for the first election. A member of the Court elected to replace a member the period of whose appointment has not expired will hold the appointment for the remainder of his predecessor's term.

Article 15.

Les juges suppléants sont appelés dans l'ordre du tableau.

Article 15.

Deputy-judges shall be called upon to sit in the order laid down in a list.

Le tableau est dressé par la Cour, en tenant compte, d'abord de la priorité d'élection et ensuite de l'ancienneté d'âge.

Article 16.

L'exercice de toute fonction qui relève de la direction politique, soit nationale, soit internationale, des Etats, est incompatible avec la qualité de membre de la Cour.

En cas de doute, la Cour décide.

Article 17.

Les membres de la Cour ne peuvent excercer les fonctions d'agent, de conseil ou d'avocat dans aucune affaire d'ordre international.

Ils ne peuvent participer au règlement d'aucune affaire dans laquelle ils sont antérieurement intervenus comme agents, conseils ou avocats de l'une des parties, membres d'un tribunal national ou international, d'une commission d'enquête, ou à tout autre titre.

En cas de doute la Cour décide.

Article 18.

Les membres de la Cour ne peuvent être relevés de leurs fonctions que si, au jugement unanime des autres membres, ils ont cessé de répondre aux conditions requises.

Le Secrétaire Général de la Société des Nations en est officiellement informé.

Cette communication emporte vacance de siège.

Article 19.

En dehors de leur propre pays, les membres de la Cour jouissent des mêmes privilèges et immunités que les agents diplomatiques.

Article 20.

Tout membre de la Cour doit, avant d'entrer en fonction, en séance publique prendre engagement solennel d'exercer ses attributions en pleine impartialité et en toute conscience.

Article 21.

La Cour élit, pour trois ans, son Président et son Vice-Président; ils sont rééligibles.

Elle nomme son Greffier.

La fonction de Greffier de la Cour n'est pas

This list shall be prepared by the Court, having regard first to the order in time of each election and secondly to age.

Article 16.

The exercise of any function which belongs to the political direction, national or international, of States, by the Members of the Court, during their terms of office is declared incompatible with their judicial duties.

Any doubt upon this point is settled by the decision of the Court.

Article 17.

No member of the Court can act as agent, counsel or advocate in any case of an international nature.

No member may participate in the decision of any case in which he has previously taken an active part, as agent, counsel or advocate for one of the contesting parties, or as a member of a national or international Court, or of a Commission of Inquiry, or in any other capacity.

Any doubt upon this point is settled by the decision of the Court.

Article 18.

A member of the Court cannot be dismissed unless, in the unanimous opinion of the other Members, he has ceased to fulfil the required conditions.

When this happens a formal notification shall be given to the Secretary-General.

This notification makes the place vacant.

Article 19.

The members of the Court when outside their own country, shall enjoy the privileges and immunities of diplomatic representatives.

Article 20.

Every member of the Court shall, before taking up his duties, make a solemn declaration in open Court that he will exercise his powers impartially and conscientiously.

Article 21.

The Court shall elect its President and Vice-President for three years: they may be re-elected.

It shall appoint its Registrar.

The duties of Registrar of the Court shall

incompatible avec celle de Secrétaire Général de la Cour Permanente d'Arbitrage.

not be considered incompatible with those of Secretary-General of the Permanent Court of Arbitration.

Article 22.

Le siège de la Cour est fixé à la Haye.

Le Président et le Greffier résident au siège de la Cour.

Article 22.

The seat of the Court shall be established at the Hague.

The President and Registrar shall reside at the seat of the Court.

Article 23.

La Cour tient une session chaque année.

Sauf disposition contraire du règlement d'ordre de la Cour, cette session commence le 15 juin, et continue tant que le rôle n'est pas épuisé.

Le Président convoque la Cour en session extraordinaire quand les circonstances l'exigent.

Article 23.

A session shall be held every year.

Unless otherwise provided by rules of Court this session shall begin on the 15th June, and shall continue for so long as may be necessary to complete the cases on the list.

The President may summon an extraordinary meeting of the Court whenever necessary.

Article 24.

Si, pour une raison spéciale, l'un des membres de la Cour estime ne pouvoir participer au jugement d'une affaire déterminée, il en fait part au Président.

Si le Président estime qu'un des membres de la Cour ne peut siéger, pour une raison spéciale, dans une affaire déterminée, il en avertit le membre intéressé.

Si l'un et l'autre ne sont pas d'accord dans chacun de ces cas sur l'attitude à prendre, la Cour décide.

Article 24.

If, for some special reason, a member of the Court considers that he cannot take part in the decision of a particular case, he shall so inform the President.

If, for some special reason, the President considers that one of the members of the Court should not sit on a particular case, he shall give notice to the member concerned.

In the event of the President and the member not agreeing as to the course to be adopted in any such case, the matter shall be settled by the decision of the Court.

Article 25.

Sauf exception expressément prévue, la Cour exerce ses attributions en séance plénière.

Si la présence de 11 juges titulaires n'est pas assurée, ce nombre est parfait par l'entrée en fonction des juges suppléants.

Toutefois, si 11 juges ne sont pas disponibles, le quorum de 9 est suffisant pour constituer la Cour.

Article 25.

The full Court shall sit except when it is expressly provided otherwise.

If 11 judges cannot be present, deputy-judges shall be called upon to sit, in order to make up this number.

If, however, 11 judges are not available, a quorum of 9 judges shall suffice to constitute the Court.

Article 26.

En vue de la prompte expédition des affaires, la Cour compose annuellement une chambre de trois juges, appelée à statuer en procédure sommaire, lorsque les parties le demandent.

Article 26.

With a view to the speedy despatch of business the Court shall form, annually, a chamber composed of three judges who, at the request of the contesting parties, may hear and determine cases by summary procedure.

Article 27.

La Cour détermine par un règlement d'ordre le mode suivant lequel elle exerce ses attributions. Elle règle spécialement la procédure sommaire.

Article 27.

The Court shall frame rules for regulating its procedure. In particular, it shall lay down rules for summary procedure.

Article 28.

Les juges de la nationalité de chacune des parties en cause conservent le droit de siéger dans l'affaire dont la Cour est saisie.

Si la Cour compte sur le siège un juge de la nationalité d'une seule des parties, l'autre partie peut désigner pour siéger un juge suppléant, s'il s'en trouve un de sa nationalité. S'il n'en existe pas, elle peut choisir un juge, pris de préférence parmi les personnes qui ont été l'objet d'une présentation de la part des groupes nationaux de la Cour d'Arbitrage.

Si la Cour ne compte sur le siège aucun juge de la nationalité des parties, chacune de ces parties peut procéder à la désignation ou au choix d'un juge de la même manière qu'au paragraphe précédent.

Lorsque plusieurs parties font cause commune, elles ne comptent pour l'application des dispositions qui précèdent que pour une seule.

Les juges désignés ou choisis comme il est dit aux §§ 2 et 3 du présent article, doivent satisfaire aux prescriptions des articles 2, 16, 17, 20, 24 du présent Acte. Ils statuent sur un pied d'égalité avec leurs collègues.

Article 28.

Judges of the nationality of each contesting party shall retain their right to sit in the case before the Court.

If the Court includes upon the Bench a judge of the nationality of one of the parties only, the other party may select from among the deputy-judges, a judge of its nationality, if there be one. If there should not be one, the party may choose a judge, preferably from among those persons who have been nominated as candidates by some national group in the Court of Arbitration.

If the Court includes upon the Bench no judge of the nationality of the contesting parties, each of these may proceed to select or choose a judge as provided in the preceding paragraph.

Should there be several parties in the same interest, they shall, for the purpose of the preceding provisions, be reckoned as one party only.

Judges selected or chosen as laid down in Paragraphs 2 and 3 of this Article shall fulfil the conditions required by Articles 2, 16, 17, 20, 24 of this Statute. They shall take part in the decision on an equal footing with their colleagues.

Article 29.

Les juges titulaires reçoivent un traitement annuel à fixer par l'Assemblée de la Société des Nations sur la proposition du Conseil. Ce traitement ne peut être diminué pendant la durée des fonctions du juge.

Le Président reçoit une indemnité spéciale déterminée de la même manière pour la durée de ses fonctions.

Les juges suppléants reçoivent dans l'exercice de leurs fonctions une indemnité à fixer de la même manière.

Les juges titulaires et suppléants qui ne résident pas au siège de la Cour reçoivent le remboursement des frais de voyages nécessités par l'accomplissement de leurs fonctions.

Les indemnités dues aux juges désignés ou choisis conformément à l'article 28 sont réglées de la même manière.

Article 29.

The judges shall receive an annual salary to be determined by the Assembly of the League of Nations upon the proposal of the Council. This salary must not be decreased during the period of a judge's appointment.

The President shall receive a special grant for his period of office, to be fixed in the same way.

Deputy-judges shall receive a grant, for the actual performance of their duties, to be fixed in the same way.

Travelling expenses incurred in the performance of their duties shall be refunded to judges and deputy-judges who do not reside at the seat of the Court.

Grants due to judges selected or chosen as provided in Article 28 shall be determined in the same way.

Le traitement du Greffier est fixé par le Conseil sur la proposition de la Cour.

Un règlement spécial détermine les pensions auxquelles ont droit les juges et le Greffier.

The salary of the Registrar shall be decided by the Council upon the proposal of the Court.

A special regulation shall provide for the pensions to which the judges and Registrar shall be entitled.

Article 30.

Les frais de la Cour sont supportés par la Société des Nations de la manière que l'Assemblée décide sur la proposition du Conseil.

Article 30.

The expenses of the Court shall be borne by the League of Nations, in such a manner as shall be decided by the Assembly upon the proposal of the Council.

Chapitre II.

Compétence de la Cour.

Article 31.

La Cour connaît des litiges entre Etats.

Article 32.

La Cour est ouverte aux Etats mentionnés à l'Annexe au Pacte et à ceux qui seront ultérieurement entrés dans la Société des Nations.

Elle est accessible aux autres Etats.

Les conditions auxquelles elle est ouverte ou accessible aux Etats qui ne sont pas Membres de la Société des Nations, sont réglées par le Conseil, en tenant compte de l'article 17 du Pacte.

Article 33.

Lorsqu'un différend surgit entre Etats, qu'il n'a pu être réglé par la voie diplomatique, et que l'on n'est pas convenu de choisir une autre juridiction, la partie qui se prétend lésée peut en saisir la Cour. La Cour, après avoir décidé s'il est satisfait aux prescriptions précédentes, statue sous les conditions et limitations déterminées par l'article suivant.

Article 34.

Entre Etats Membres de la Société des Nations la Cour statue sans convention spéciale sur les différends d'ordre juridique, qui ont pour objet:

a. l'interprétation d'un traité;

Chapter II.

Competence of the Court.

Article 31.

The Court shall have jurisdiction to hear and determine suits between States.

Article 32.

The Court shall be open of right to the States mentioned in the Annex to the Covenant, and to such others as shall subsequently enter the League of Nations.

Other States may have access to it.

The conditions under which the Court shall be open of right or accessible to States which are not Members of the League of Nations shall be determined by the Council, in accordance with Article 17 of the Covenant.

Article 33.

When a dispute has arisen between States, and it has been found impossible to settle it by diplomatic means, and no agreement has been made to choose another jurisdiction, the party complaining may bring the case before the Court. The Court shall, first of all, decide whether the preceding conditions have been complied with; if so, it shall hear and determine the dispute according to the terms and within the limits of the next Article.

Article 34.

Between States which are Members of the League of Nations, the Court shall have jurisdiction (and this without any special convention giving it jurisdiction) to hear and determine cases of a legal nature, concerning:

a. the interpretation of a treaty;

b. tout point de droit international;

c. la réalité de tout fait, qui, s'il était établi, constituerait la violation d'un engagement international;

d. la nature ou l'étendue de la réparation due pour la rupture d'un engagement international;

e. l'interprétation d'une sentence rendue par la Cour.

La Cour connait également de tous différends, de quelque nature qu'ils soient, qui lui sont soumis par la convention, soit générale, soit spéciale, des parties.

En cas de contestation sur le point de savoir si un différend rentre dans les catégories cidessus visées, la Cour décide.

Article 35.

Dans les limites de sa compétence, telle qu'elle est déterminée par l'article 34, la Cour applique en ordre successif:

1°. les conventions internationales, soit générales, soit spéciales, établissant des règles expressément reconnues par les Etats en litige;

2°. la coutume internationale, attestation d'une pratique commune acceptée comme loi;

3°. les principes généraux de droit reconnus par les nations civilisées;

4°. les décisions judiciaires et la doctrine des publicistes les plus qualifiés des différentes nations, comme moyens auxiliaires de détermination des règles de droit.

Article 36.

La Cour donne son avis sur tout point ou tout différend d'ordre international qui lui est soumis par le Conseil ou par l'Assemblée.

Lorsque la Cour donne son avis sur un point d'ordre international indépendamment de tout différend actuellement né, elle constitue une Commission spéciale de trois à cinq membres.

Lorsqu'elle donne son avis sur une question qui fait l'objet d'un différend actuellement né, elle statue dans les mêmes conditions que s'il s'agissait d'un litige porté devant elle.

b. any question of international law;

c. the existence of any fact which, if established, would constitute a breach of an international obligation;

d. the nature or extent of reparation to be made for the breach of an international obligation;

e. the interpretation of a sentence passed by the Court.

The Court shall also take cognisance of all disputes of any kind which may be submitted to it by a general or particular convention between the parties.

In the event of a dispute as to whether a certain case comes within any of the categories above mentioned, the matter shall be settled by the decision of the Court.

Article 35.

The Court shall, within the limits of its jurisdiction as defined in Article 34, apply in the order following:

1. international conventions, whether general or particular, establishing rules expressly recognised by the contesting States;
2. international custom, as evidence of a general practice, which is accepted as law;
3. the general principles of law recognised by civilised nations;
4. judicial decisions and the teachings of the most highly qualified publicists of the various nations, as subsidiary means for the determination of rules of law.

Article 36.

The Court shall give an advisory opinion upon any question or dispute of an international nature referred to it by the Council or Assembly.

When the Court shall give an opinion on a question of an international nature which does not refer to any dispute that may have arisen, it shall appoint a special Commission of from three to five members.

When it shall give an opinion upon a question which forms the subject of an existing dispute, it shall do so under the same conditions as if the case had been actually submitted to it for decision.

CHAPITRE III.

Procédure.

Article 37.

La langue de la Cour est le français.

La Cour peut, à la demande des parties, autoriser l'emploi d'une autre langue devant elle

Article 38.

La Cour est saisie par une requête adressée au Greffe.

La requête indique l'objet du différend et désigne les parties en cause.

Le Greffe fait immédiatement notification de la requête aux intéressés.

Il en informe également les Membres de la Société des Nations par l'entremise du Secrétaire Général.

Article 39.

Dans le cas où la cause du différend consiste en un acte effectué ou sur le point de l'être, la Cour a le pouvoir d'indiquer, si elle estime que les circonstances l'exigent, quelles mesures conservatoires du droit de chacun doivent être prises à titre provisoire.

En attendant l'arrêt définitif l'indication de ces mesures est immédiatement transmis aux parties et au Conseil.

Article 40.

Les parties sont représentées par des agents.

Elles peuvent se faire assister devant la Cour par des conseils ou des avocats.

Article 41.

La procédure a deux phases: l'une écrite, l'autre orale.

Article 42.

La procédure écrite comprend la communication à juge et à partie des mémoires, des contremémoires, et, éventuellement, des répliques, ainsi que de toute pièce et document à l'appui.

La communication se fait par l'entremise du Greffe dans l'ordre et les délais déterminés par la Cour.

CHAPTER III.

Procedure.

Article 37.

The official language of the Court shall be French.

The Court may, at the request of the contesting parties, authorise another language to be used before it.

Article 38.

A State desiring to have recourse to the Court shall lodge a written application addressed to the Registrar.

The application shall indicate the subject of the dispute, and name the contesting parties.

The Registrar shall forthwith communicate the application to all concerned.

He shall also notify the Members of the League of Nations through the Secretary-General.

Article 39.

If the dispute arises out of an act which has already taken place or which is imminent, the Court shall have the power to suggest if it considers that circumstances so require, the provisional measures that should be taken to preserve the respective rights of either party.

Pending the final decision, notice of the measures suggested shall forthwith be given to the parties and the Council.

Article 40.

The parties shall be represented by agents.

They may have counsel or advocates to plead before the Court.

Article 41.

The procedure shall consist of two parts: written and oral.

Article 42.

The written proceedings shall consist of the communication to the judges and to the parties of cases, counter-cases and, if necessary, replies; also all papers and documents in support.

These communications shall be made through the Registrar, in the order and within the time fixed by the Court.

Toute pièce produite par l'une des parties doit être communiquée à l'autre en copie certifiée conforme.

A certified copy of every document produced by one party shall be communicated to the other party.

Article 43.

La procédure orale consiste dans l'audition par la Cour des témoins, experts, agents, conseils et avocats.

Pour toute notification à faire à d'autres personnes que les agents, conseils et avocats, la Cour s'adresse directement au Gouvernement de l'Etat sur le territoire duquel la notification doit produire effet.

Il en est de même s'il s'agit de faire procéder sur place à l'établissement de tous moyens de preuve.

Article 43.

The oral proceedings shall consist of the hearing by the Court of witnesses, experts, agents, counsel and advocates.

For the service of all notices upon persons other than the agents, counsel and advocates, the Court shall apply direct to the Government of the State upon whose territory the notice has to be served.

The same provision shall apply whenever steps are to be taken to procure evidence on the spot.

Article 44.

Les débats sont dirigés par le Président et à défaut de celui-ci par le Vice-Président; en cas d'empêchement, par le plus ancien des juges présents.

Article 44.

The proceedings shall be under the direction of the President, or in his absence, of the Vice-President; if both are absent, the senior judge shall preside.

Article 45.

L'audience est publique, à moins qu'il n'en soit autrement décidé par la Cour à la demande motivée de l'une des parties.

Article 45.

The hearing in Court shall be public, unless the Court, at the written request of one of the parties, accompanied by a statement of his reasons, shall otherwise decide.

Article 46.

Il est tenu de chaque audience un procès-verbal signé par le Greffier et le Président.

Ce procès-verbal a seul caractère authentique.

Article 46.

Minutes shall be made at each hearing, and signed by the Registrar and the President.

These minutes shall be the only authentic record.

Article 47.

La Cour rend des ordonnances pour la direction du procès, la détermination des formes et délais dans lesquels chaque partie doit finalement conclure; elle prend toutes les mesures que comporte l'administration des preuves.

Article 47.

The Court shall make orders for the conduct of the case, shall decide the form and time in which each party must conclude its arguments, and make all arrangements connected with the taking of evidence.

Article 48.

La Cour peut, même avant tout débat, demander aux agents de lui produire tout document et de lui fournir toutes explications. En cas de refus, elle en prend acte.

Article 48.

The Court may, even before the hearing begins, call upon the agents to produce any document, or to supply to the Court any explanations. Any refusal shall be recorded.

Article 49.

A tout moment, la Cour peut confier une

Article 49.

The Court may, at any time, entrust any

enquête ou une expertise à toute personne, corps, bureau, commission ou organe de son choix.

individual, bureau, commission or other body that it may select, with the task of carrying out an inquiry or giving an expert opinion.

Article 50.

Au cours des débats, les juges posent aux témoins, agents, experts, avocats et conseils toutes questions qu'ils estiment utiles; les agents, avocats et conseils ont le droit de poser, par l'entremise du Président, toute question que la Cour juge utile.

Article 50.

During the hearing in Court, the judges may put any questions considered by them to be necessary, to the witnesses, agents, experts, advocates or counsel. The agents, advocates and counsel shall have the right to ask, through the President, any questions that the Court considers useful.

Article 51.

Après avoir reçu les preuves et témoignages dans les délais déterminés par elle, la Cour peut écarter toutes dépositions ou documents nouveaux qu'une des parties voudrait lui présenter sans l'assentiment de l'autre.

Article 51.

After the Court has received the proofs and evidence within the time specified for the purpose, it may refuse to accept any further oral or written evidence that one party may desire to present unless the other side consents.

Article 52.

Lorsqu'une des parties ne se présente pas, ou s'abstient de faire valoir ses moyens, l'autre partie peut demander à la Cour de lui adjuger ses conclusions.

La Cour, avant d'y faire droit, doit s'assurer non seulement qu'elle a compétence aux termes des articles 33 et 34, mais que les conclusions, reposant sur des preuves sérieuses, sont fondées en fait et en droit.

Article 52.

Whenever one of the parties shall not appear before the Court, or shall fail to defend his case, the other party may call upon the Court to decide in favour of his claim.

The Court must, before doing so, satisfy itself, not only that it has jurisdiction in accordance with Articles 33 and 34, but also that the claim is supported by substantial evidence and well founded in fact and law.

Article 53.

Quand les agents, avocats et conseils ont fait valoir, sous le contrôle de la Cour, tous les moyens qu'ils jugent utiles, le Président prononce la clôture des débats.

La Cour se retire en chambre du conseil pour délibérer.

Les délibérations de la Cour sont et restent secrètes.

Article 53.

When the agents, advocates and counsel have, subject to the control of the Court, presented all the evidence, and taken all other steps that they consider advisable, the President shall declare the case closed.

The Court shall withdraw to consider the judgment.

The deliberations of the Court shall take place in private and remain secret.

Article 54.

Les décisions de la Cour sont prises à la majorité des juges présents.

En cas de partage de voix, la voix du Président ou de celui qui le remplace est prépondérante.

Article 54.

All questions shall be decided by a majority of the judges present at the hearing.

In the event of an equality of votes, the President or his deputy shall have a casting vote.

Article 55.

L'arrêt est motivé.

Il mentionne les noms des juges qui y ont pris part.

Article 56.

Si l'arrêt n'exprime pas, en tout ou en partie, l'opinion unanime des juges, les dissidents ont la faculté de demander que leur opposition ou leurs réserves soient constatées, mais sans indication des motifs.

Article 57.

L'arrêt est signé par le Président et par le Greffier. Il est lu en séance publique, les agents dûment prévenus.

Article 58.

L arrêt est définitif et sans recours. En cas de dispute sur le sens et la portée de l'arrêt, il appartient à la Cour de l'interpréter, à la demande de toute partie.

Article 59.

La révision de l'arrêt ne peut être éventuellement demandée à la Cour qu'à raison de la découverte d'un fait nouveau de nature à exercer une influence décisive et qui, avant le prononcé de l'arrêt, était inconnu de la Cour et de la partie qui demande la révision, sans qu'il y ait, de sa part, faute à l'ignorer.

La procédure de révision s'ouvre par un arrêt de la Cour constatant expressément l'existence du fait nouveau, lui reconnaissant les caractères qui donnent ouverture à la révision, et déclarant de ce chef la demande recevable.

La Cour peut subordonner l'ouverture de la procédure en révision à l'exécution préalable de l'arrêt.

Aucune demande de révision ne peut être formée après l'expiration d'un délai de cinq ans.

Article 60.

Lorsqu'un Etat estime que dans un différend un intérêt d'ordre juridique est pour lui en

Article 55.

The judgment shall state the reasons on which it is based.

It shall contain the names of the judges who have taken part in the decision.

Article 56.

If the judgment given does not represent, wholly or in part, the unanimous opinion of the judges, the dissenting judges shall be entitled to have the fact of their dissent or reservations mentioned in it. But their reasons for their dissent or reservations shall not be expressed in the judgment.

Article 57.

The judgment shall be signed by the President and by the Registrar. It shall be read in open Court, due notice having been given to the agents.

Article 58.

The judgment is final and without appeal. In the event of uncertainty as to the meaning or scope of the judgment, the Court shall construe it upon the request of any party.

Article 59.

An application for revision of a judgment can be made only when it is based upon the discovery of some new fact, of such a nature as to be a decisive factor, which fact was, when the judgment was given, unknown to the Court and also to the party claiming revision, always provided that such ignorance was not due to negligence.

The proceedings for revision will be opened by a judgment of the Court expressly recording the existence of the new fact, recognising that it has such a character as to lay the case open to revision, and declaring the application admissible on this ground.

The Court may require previous compliance with the terms of the judgment before it admits proceedings in revision.

No application for revision may be made after the lapse of five years from the date of the sentence.

Article 60.

Should a State consider that it has an interest of a legal nature which may be affected by the

cause, il peut adresser à la Cour une requête, à fin d'intervention.

La Cour décide.

Article 61.

Lorsqu'il s'agit de l'interprétation d'une convention à laquelle ont participé d'autres Etats que les parties en litige, le Greffe avertit sans délai tous les signataires.

Chacun d'eux à le droit d'intervenir au procès, et s'il exerce cette faculté, l'interprétation contenue dans la sentence est également obligatoire à son égard.

Article 62.

S'il n'en est autrement décidé par la Cour, chaque partie supporte ses frais de procédure.

decision in the case, it may submit a request to the Court to be permitted to intervene as a third party.

It will be for the Court to decide upon this request.

Article 61.

Whenever the construction of a convention in which States, other than those concerned in the case, are parties, is in question, the Registrar shall notify all such States forthwith.

Every State so notified has the right to intervene in the proceedings: but if it uses this right, the construction given by the judgment will be as binding upon it as upon the original parties to the dispute.

Article 62.

Unless otherwise decided by the Court, each party shall bear its own costs.

33IÈME SÉANCE (non-publique), tenue au Palais de la Paix, à La Haye, le 23 juillet 1920.

Présidence de M. le BARON DESCAMPS.

Sont présents: tous les membres du Comité (à l'exception de M. Bevilaqua); M. Fernandes; Mr. James Brown Scott; les secrétaires particuliers du Baron Descamps et de M. Adatci; les membres du Secrétariat.

La séance est ouverte à 3.30 heures de l'après-midi.

Le PRESIDENT invite M. de Lapradelle à continuer la lecture de son rapport.

M. DE LAPRADELLE se rend à cette invitation. La lecture a lieu dans les mêmes conditions que lors de la séance du matin.

Cette lecture a été interrompue à 7 heures du soir, pour être continuée à 9 heures le matin suivant.

La séance est levée à 7 heures du soir.

Le Président:
(signé) Brn. DESCAMPS.

Le Secrétaire-Général:
(signé) D. ANZILOTTI.

33RD MEETING (Private), held at the Peace Palace, the Hague, on July 23rd, 1920.

BARON DESCAMPS in the chair.

Present: all members of the Committee (with the exception of M. Bevilaqua); M. Fernandes, Mr. James Brown Scott; the private secretaries of Baron Descamps and of M. Adatci; the members of the Secretariat.

The meeting opened at 3.30 p.m.

The PRESIDENT asked M. de Lapradelle to continue the reading of his report.

M. DE LAPRADELLE complied. The reading took place as at the morning meeting.

The reading was adjourned at 7 p.m. until 9 a.m. on the following morning.

The meeting closed at 7 p.m.

The President:
(signed) Brn. DESCAMPS.

The Secretary-General:
(signed) D. ANZILOTTI.

34ième SÉANCE (non-publique), tenue au Palais de la Paix, à La Haye, le 24 juillet 1920.

Présidence de M. le BARON DESCAMPS.

Sont présents: tous les membres du Comité (à l'exception de M. Bevilaqua); M. Fernandes; Mr. James Brown Scott; les secrétaires particuliers du Baron Descamps et de M. Adatci; les membres du Secrétariat.

La séance est ouverte à 9 heures du matin.

Sur l'invitation du PRESIDENT, M. DE LAPRADELLE continue et achève la lecture de son rapport, dont quelques points donnent lieu à des discussions et à des amendements.

La lecture finie, le Président remercie M. de Lapradelle pour son travail si remarquable, qui procurera une aide précieuse à tous ceux qu'intéresse le problème de l'établissement d'une Cour Permanente de Justice Internationale.

M. ALTAMIRA demande que la gratitude du Comité envers M. de Lapradelle soit consignée au procès-verbal, ainsi que sa reconnaissance envers le Secrétariat.

Mr. ROOT demande qu'un vote ait lieu sur le rapport.

Le rapport est mis aux voix et adopté à l'unanimité. (Annexe No. 1).

Le PRESIDENT prend la parole pour exprimer la haute appréciation et la vive reconnaissance du Comité à l'égard du Secrétariat, qui non seulement a accompli un travail énorme, mais a, en même temps, su prêter une collaboration précieuse à l'œuvre du Comité. Le Président signalera dans une lettre, qu'il adressera au Conseil de la Société des Nations, les excellents services du Secrétariat.

M. LODER prend la parole pour exprimer au Président la gratitude du Comité pour les éminentes qualités et la grande patience dont il a fait preuve, dans la direction des travaux du Comité.

M. Loder ajoute que c'est, dans une large mesure, grâce aux efforts du Baron Descamps, que les travaux du Comité ont abouti.

34th MEETING (Private), held at the Peace Palace, the Hague, on July 24th, 1920.

BARON DESCAMPS in the chair.

Present: all members of the Committee (with the exception of M. Bevilaqua); M. Fernandes; Mr. James Brown Scott; the private secretaries of Baron Descamps and of M. Adatci; the members of the Secretariat.

The meeting opened at 9 a.m.

At the request of the PRESIDENT, M. DE LAPRADELLE continued and completed the reading of his report; several points in it gave rise to discussion and were amended.

After the reading, the President thanked M. de Lapradelle for his valuable work, which would be of very great assistance to all who were interested in the problem of the establishment of a Permanent Court of International Justice.

M. ALTAMIRA requested that the Committee's gratitude to M. de Lapradelle should be recorded in the procès-verbal, as also their gratitude to the Secretariat.

Mr. ROOT asked that a vote should be taken upon the report.

The report was accordingly submitted to a vote and adopted unanimously. (Annex No. 1).

The PRESIDENT expressed the Committee's appreciation of services rendered by the Secretariat and sincere gratitude towards it; it had not only accomplished an enormous amount of work, but had also seen its way to assist the Committee in the accomplishment of its task. The President would record in a letter to the Council of the League of Nations the excellent work done by the Secretariat.

M. LODER then expressed the gratitude of the Committee for the great qualities and unwearied patience, which the President had shown in his direction of the Committee's labours.

M. Loder added, that it was largely due to Baron Descamps' efforts that the work of the Committee had been crowned with success.

Le PRESIDENT remercie M. Loder de ses aimables paroles. Il exprime le vœu que les liens de confraternité qui se sont formés entre les membres du Comité, persistent et que les membres se sentent toujours à l'avenir associés à l'œuvre qu'ils ont commencée.

Le Président adresse au nom du Comité tous ses remerciements à M. Loder pour les attentions cordiales dont il a entouré ses collègues et pour le concours qu'il a prêté aux travaux du Comité.

Sur la proposition de M. ADATCI et de M. DE LAPRADELLE, on se met d'accord pour consigner au procès-verbal l'expression de la gratitude du Comité envers les fonctionnaires de la bibliothèque du Palais de la Paix, qui ont su contribuer au résultat obtenu en facilitant aux membres les recherches qu'ils avaient besoin de faire.

Mr. ROOT prend la parole et exprime ses remerciements personnels aux membres du Comité pour leur aimable courtoisie qui a si grandement atténué les difficultés qu'il a dû surmonter pour se faire comprendre de ses collègues et pour suivre les délibérations du Comité.

Le PRESIDENT est heureux de saisir cette occasion pour remercier Mr. Root de sa précieuse collaboration.

M. RICCI-BUSATTI soulève la question de savoir de quelle façon le résultat des travaux du Comité doit être porté à la connaissance du Conseil. Il dit que l'on doit choisir entre le Président et le Secrétariat. Il se demande s'il ne serait pas opportun que le President voulût bien se rendre à Saint Sébastien.

LORD PHILLIMORE croit que le Secrétariat doit servir d'intermédiaire en l'occurrence.

Mr. ROOT fait une proposition en trois points:

1. Aux termes de l'invitation adressée aux membres du Comité, il paraît évident que le Comité doit communiquer au Secrétariat de la Société des Nations le résultat de ses travaux;
2. Le Comité doit demander à son Secrétaire Général de porter à la connaissance du Conseil que toutes informations et explications ultérieures que pourra désirer le Conseil, lui seront fournies par le Président ou par le Rapporteur;

The PRESIDENT thanked M. Loder for his kind words. He hoped that the ties established between the members of the Committee would endure, and that in the future the members would always feel their mutual association in the great work of which they had laid the foundations.

The President, in the name of the Committee, thanked M. Loder very heartily for the kindness he had shown to his colleagues and for his valuable assistance in the work of the Committee.

At M. ADATCI's and M. DE LAPRADELLE's proposal, it was agreed to record, in the procès-verbal, the Committee's gratitude to the Officials of the Library of the Peace Palace who had contributed to the result achieved, by facilitating the research work that members had found it necessary to do.

Mr. ROOT expressed his personal thanks for the courtesy which the members of the Committee had shown him and which had greatly reduced his difficulties in making himself understood and in following the Committee's discussions.

The PRESIDENT gladly took the opportunity of thanking Mr. Root for his valuable collaboration.

M. RICCI-BUSATTI asked how the result of the Committee's work was to be laid before the Council. He said that the choice lay between the President and the Secretariat. He asked whether it would not be advisable for the President to undertake the task of going to San Sebastian.

LORD PHILLIMORE thought that the Secretariat ought to represent the Committee at the Council meeting.

Mr. ROOT submitted the three following propositions:

1. that it is clear from the terms of the invitation sent to members of the Committee, that the Committee must place the result of its labours in the hands of the Secretariat of the League of Nations;
2. that the Committee should ask its Secretary-General to inform the Council, that any further information or explanation that the Council might wish for, would be supplied by the President or by the Reporter;

3. Il doit être consigné au procès-verbal que le Comité ne veut, dans aucune mesure, se faire l'avocat du résultat de ses travaux. Ayant été sollicité de donner son avis, le Comité ne pourrait pas presser l'adoption de cet avis, sans que sa dignité en soit diminuée.

Ces trois propositions sont mises aux voix et adoptées.

Sur la proposition de Mr. Root, les vœux adoptés par le Comité en première et deuxième lectures sont soumis à un vote final, avec des modifications de rédaction.

Les vœux sont adoptés définitivement et signés par les membres du Comité. (Voir les trois dernières pages de l'annexe 1re).

La séance est levée à midi.

Le Président:
(signé) Brn. DESCAMPS.

Le Secrétaire-Général:
(signé) D. ANZILOTTI.

3. that it must be stated in the procès-verbal that the Committee have no wish to advocate or argue its conclusions. Having been asked to advice the Committee could not press for the adoption of this advice without detracting from its dignity.

These three propositions were voted upon and adopted.

At the proposal of Mr. Root, the Resolutions adopted by the Committee in both first and second readings, the wording of which had been modified, were submitted to a final vote.

The Resolutions were finally approved and signed by the members of the Committee. (See last three pages of Annex 1).

The meeting closed at noon.

The President:
(signed) Brn. DESCAMPS.

The Secretary-General:
(signed) D. ANZILOTTI.

ANNEXE No. 1.

RAPPORT.

MESSIEURS,

L'article 14 du Pacte de la Société des Nations est ainsi conçu:

> Le Conseil est chargé de préparer un projet de Cour Permanente de Justice Internationale et de le soumettre aux Membres de la Société. Cette Cour connaîtra de tous différends d'un caractère international que les Parties lui soumettront. Elle donnera aussi des avis consultatifs sur tout différend ou tout point dont la saisira le Conseil ou l'Assemblée.

Chargé de préparer ce projet de Cour de Justice Internationale, le Conseil de la Société des Nations a, le 13 février dernier, décidé d'en confier l'examen à une Commission de Jurisconsultes. Cette Commission s'est réunie à la Haye le 16 juin 1920. Elle était ainsi composée:

MM. Adatci (Japon), Altamira (Espagne), Bevilaqua (Brésil), remplacé par M. Fernandes, Baron Descamps (Belgique), Hagerup (Norvège), de Lapradelle (France), Loder (Pays-Bas), Lord Phillimore (Grande-Bretagne), MM. Ricci Busatti (Italie), et Elihu Root (Etats-Unis).

Le premier devoir du Comité était de considérer, d'après le Pacte, quelle était, de sa nature, cette Cour Permanente de Justice Internationale, dont elle avait à déterminer l'organisation, la compétence et la procédure.

Si sobres de renseignements que soient à cet égard les travaux préparatoires du Pacte, quelques indications peuvent cependant être recueillies sur l'origine de l'article 14. Aucune trace de Cour Permanente de Justice Internationale ne se trouve dans les projets de Lord Robert Cecil ou du Général Smuts; aucune trace, non plus, dans les deux premiers projets américains. Pénétré de la nécessité d'un tribunal international, qui fût vraiment en mesure d'introduire dans la justice internationale les pro-

ANNEX No. 1.

REPORT.

GENTLEMEN,

Article 14 of the Covenant of the League of Nations is worded as follows:

> The Council shall formulate and submit to the Members of the League for adoption plans for the establishment of a Permanent Court of International Justice. The Court shall be competent to hear and determine any dispute of an international character which the parties thereto submit to it. The Court may also give an advisory opinion upon any dispute or question referred to it by the Council or the Assembly.

Having been given the task of preparing this plan for a Court of International Justice, the Council of the League of Nations, on the 13th February last, decided to entrust the examination of the question to a Committee of Jurisconsults. This Committee met at the Hague on the 16th June, 1920. It was composed as follows:

Messrs. Adatci (Japan), Altamira (Spain), Bevilaqua (Brazil) replaced by M Fernandes, Baron Descamps (Belgium), Hagerup (Norway), de Lapradelle (France), Loder (Netherlands), Lord Phillimore (Great Britain), Messrs. Ricci Busatti (Italy), and Elihu Root (United States).

The first duty of the Committee was to consider what, according to the terms of the Covenant, was the nature of this Permanent Court of International Justice, the organisation, competence and procedure of which it had to define.

Some indications can be traced concerning the origin of Article 14, though the work carried out preparatory to the Covenant contains very limited information on the subject. No trace of the Permanent Court of International Justice is to be found in the plans of Lord Robert Cecil or General Smuts, nor in the two first American plans. The authors of the first Anglo-American plan for a League of Nations, convinced of the necessity for an international tribunal which should really in-

cédés, les formes et les sûretés du droit interne, le premier projet anglo-américain d'une Société des Nations, chapitre II, art. 2, 4 et 7, prévoit une Cour de droit international.

Qu'on l'appelle „Cour de droit international", ou, comme dans une rédaction ultérieure, (Bases de discussion, 3 février 1919, art. 11 et 12) „Cour Permanente de Justice Internationale" par une dénomination qui lui est restée, cette Cour naît dans des conditions telles qu'elle forme, à côté de la Cour d'Arbitrage de la Haye, une institution judiciaire, qui prend vis-à-vis d'elle une physionomie distincte et une valeur complémentaire.

Quels qu'aient été les services rendus à la Justice et à la Paix par l'institution en 1899, à La Haye, d'une Cour Permanente d'Arbitrage international, il n'en est pas moins incontestable qu'en vertu même des dispositions fondamentales de sa constitution, elle n'est guère plus qu'un cadre permanent, un vaste collège d'arbitres, où passent d'une manière intermittente des tribunaux internationaux éphémères; les arbitres parfois inclinent à se considérer en médiateurs plutôt qu'en interprètes fidèles du droit, en diplomates plutôt qu'en juges, en conciliateurs appelés à prononcer entre Etats de la manière la moins pénible pour chacun d'eux plutôt qu'en magistrats appelés à tenir rigoureusement égales les balances de la justice, „Il y a là", disait Mr. Root dans ses instructions aux délégués américains à la Conférence de la Haye en 1907, „deux méthodes radicalement différentes, qui correspondent à des conceptions très distinctes, qui conduisent à des conséquences très différentes. Il arrive souvent qu'un Etat, qui serait disposé à soumettre son litige à une décision judiciaire impartiale, ne soit pas disposé à le soumettre à cette manière de procédure diplomatique. S'il pouvait exister un tribunal prononçant sur les litiges entre Etats avec autant d'impartialité et d'objectivité que la Cour suprême des Etats-Unis dans les procès qui se déroulent entre citoyens des divers Etats de l'Union, ou entre étrangers et citoyens américains, il n'y a pas de doute que les Etats seraient beaucoup plus prêts à soumettre leurs difficultés à la décision de ce tribunal qu'ils ne le sont maintenant à recourir aux chances d'un arbitrage".

Une loi d'évolution constante des institutions juridictionnelles indique que toujours une justice facultative n'est pas restée longtemps sans être

troduce the procedure, forms and guarantees of national law into international Justice, provided in its second Chapter, Articles 2, 4 and 7, for a Court of International Law.

Whether it is called „a Court of International Law" or, as in a subsequent wording, (Bases de discussion, February 3rd, 1919, Articles 11 and 12) „a Permanent Court of International Justice", which latter title has remained, the circumstances under which this Court comes into existence are such that it forms, side by side with the Court of Arbitration at the Hague, a judicial institution, which assumes, in relation to that Court, a quite distinct character and a complementary position.

However great were the services rendered to the cause of Justice and Peace by the creation, in 1899, at the Hague, of a Permanent Court of International Arbitration, it is nevertheless indisputable that, by reason of the fundamental provisions in its constitution, that Court was hardly more than a permanent framework, a vast body of arbitrators, from which a number of international tribunals were composed from time to time, only to disappear. There was at times a tendency for the arbitrators to consider themselves as mediators rather than as faithful interpreters of Law, as diplomats rather than as judges, as conciliators called upon to decide between States in the way least painful to each of them, rather than as judges, whose duty it is to administer impartial justice. „The two methods", said Mr. Root in his instructions to the American Delegates to the Hague Conference of 1907, „are radically different, proceed upon different standards of honorable obligation and frequently lead to widely differing results. It very frequently happens that a nation, which would be very willing to submit its differences to an impartial judicial determination is unwilling to subject them to this kind of diplomatic process. If there could be a tribunal which would pass between nations upon questions with the same impartial and impersonal judgment that the Supreme Court of the United States gives to questions arising between citizens of the different States, or between foreign citizens and the citizens of the United States, there can be no doubt that nations would be much more ready to submit their controversies to its decision than they are now to take the chances of Arbitration."

There is an immutable law, in the evolution of legal institutions, which shows that an optional jurisdiction has always sooner or later been fol-

suivie d'une justice fixe obligatoire. „Les décisions d'un litige par une Cour Permanente composée de juges de profession seraient judiciaires", disait M. Asser à la Conférence de 1907; „elles constitueraient un précédent, tendraient à faire progresser le droit international; elles seraient obligatoires non seulement pour les parties en litige, mais encore pour tous les Etats participant à la création de la Cour, elles seraient rapides, elles seraient, enfin, *last but not least*, peu coûteuses, et la justice, pour être populaire, doit être bon marché. Au lieu d'une Cour Permanente, la Convention de 1899 ne donna que le fantôme d'une Cour, un spectre impalpable, ou, pour parler plus nettement, elle donna un Greffe avec une liste." (*Actes et documents*, II, p. 235).

M. de Martens, après avoir été un des champions de la Cour Permanente d'Arbitrage à la première Conférence, croyait, lors de la seconde, devoir se poser cette question: „Quelle est donc cette Cour, dont les membres ne se connaissent même pas?" et il y répondait: „La Cour de 1899 n'est qu'une idée qui, quelquefois, prend corps et âme, puis disparaît de nouveau."

Avec la Cour d'Arbitrage, ce sont les parties qui choisissent leurs juges, après que le litige est né; avec la Cour Permanente de Justice Internationale, les plaideurs ne doivent plus avoir le choix du juge. Avec la Cour d'Arbitrage, il n'y a pas chez ceux qui jugent un lien permanent, et dès lors pas d'esprit de corps, ni de continuité progressive de jurisprudence; avec la Cour de Justice Internationale, composée de magistrats, associés d'une manière constante à la même œuvre et, sauf exception, toujours maintenus, d'affaire en affaire, sur leur siège, la persistance d'une tradition est obtenue, le développement harmonieux et logique du droit international est assuré. Dans la Cour d'Arbitrage, il est à craindre que les juges, enclins à considérer l'affaire du point de vue politique, ne donnent pas à la règle de droit assez d'importance. Dans la Cour Permanente de Justice Internationale, le droit prendra, nécessairement, plus d'autorité, et même de rigueur. A la Cour d'Arbitrage il y a place, à côté de jurisconsultes, pour des hommes politiques. A la Cour de Justice, il y aura place, à côté de jurisconsultes, pour de grands magistrats, n'eussent-ils, durant toute leur carrière, rencontré que d'une manière indirecte et rare les problèmes du droit international.

lowed by a definite compulsory jurisdiction. M. Asser, at the Conference of 1907 said: „The sentences of a Court composed of professional judges would have a judicial character, they would create precedent and make for progress in International Law. They would be binding, not only upon the contesting parties, but also upon all States taking part in the creation of the Court; they would also be speedy, and, last but not least, they would be inexpensive, and justice, if it is to be popular, must be cheap. Instead of a Permanent Court, the Convention of 1899 created only a phantom, an impalpable ghost, or, in plain words, it consisted of a Registry and a list." (*Actes et Documents*, II, p. 235).

M. de Martens, who had been one of the champions of the Permanent Court of Arbitration at the First Conference, felt, at the Second Conference, the need to consider the real nature of this Court, the members of which did not even know each other. His answer to this question was as follows: „The Court of 1899 is only a shadow which, from time to time, materialises, only to fade away once again."

In the Court of Arbitration, it falls to the parties to choose their judges, after the commencement of the dispute; whereas in the case of the Permanent Court of International Justice, the contesting parties no longer have the choice of the judges. In the Court of Arbitration there is no permanent tie between the sitting judges, and consequently, no "esprit de corps" nor progressive continuity in jurisprudence; on the other hand, the Court of International Justice, being composed of judges, permanently associated with each other in the same work, and, except in rare cases, retaining their seats from one case to another, can develop a continuous tradition, and assure the harmonious and logical development of International Law. It is to be feared that the judges of the Court of Arbitration, being inclined to regard the case from a political standpoint, may not give sufficient weight to the rules of Law. In the Permanent Court of International Justice, Law necessarily becomes more authoritative and also, possibly, more severe. The Court of Arbitration may include politicians in addition to Jurisconsults. In the Court of Justice, there will be, besides Jurisconsults, great judges, who may have only encountered questions of International Law indirectly or rarely during their careers.

Comme le disait M. Léon Bourgeois, en ouvrant, le 16 juin, les travaux du Comité: „Cette Cour permanente ne sera pas une Cour d'arbitrage, mais une Cour de justice."

L'arbitrage peut tenir compte de mille éléments de fait, de mille contingences, souvent de certaines nécessités d'ordre politique. L'arrêt de justice ne tient compte que de la règle définie et fixée par la loi.

Mais, si la Cour Permanente de Justice Internationale n'est pas une Cour d'Arbitrage, au sens strict du mot, il n'en demeure pas moins que, si l'on prend le mot arbitrage comme synonyme de jugement entre Etats souverains, la Cour de Justice Internationale est, à côté des autres tribunaux internationaux, un des organes par lesquels s'exerce le fonctionnement de l'arbitrage international. Sans doute elle n'est pas le seul; d'autres tribunaux arbitraux peuvent exister en dehors d'elle, et parmi eux, la Cour Permanente d'Arbitrage de la Haye, telle que l'a créée la Convention de 1899 et développée celle de 1907. Mais elle n'en est pas moins, non seulement de sa nature, mais aux termes du Pacte (art. 13) une Cour éventuellement appelée à statuer toutes les fois qu'il est stipulé que les parties peuvent, ou doivent, recourir à l'arbitrage. Non seulement les dispositions du Pacte, relatives à l'arbitrage, doivent être considérées comme dominant aussi bien l'organisation d'une procédure arbitrale, au sens strict du mot, qu'une procédure devant la Cour, mais, aux articles 12, 13, 15 du Pacte, l'expression „arbitrage" doit être interprétée comme signifiant „règlement judiciaire international".

Le 16 juin, en ouvrant les séances du Comité, M Léon Bourgeois demandait: „Quelles seront les limites de la compétence? Sur ce dernier point, le Pacte lui-même et les divers traités qui viennent d'être signés ne donnent pas seulement un certain nombre d'indications, mais apportent des décisions précises, et, si quelques dispositions de ces traités et du Pacte semblent indiquer des restrictions regrettables, il ne faut pas oublier que, sans même envisager aucun amendement au Pacte, le Conseil et l'Assemblée, inspirés par vos travaux, peuvent, en vertu des art. 12 et 15, accroître considérablement le champ d'action de la Cour."

Dans la disposition de l'article 14, nul commentaire ne pouvait être plus autorisé que celui de l'homme d'Etat qui, appelé à organiser à la Haye, en 1899 et 1907, sous sa première

As M. Léon Bourgeois said in his opening speech at the commencement of the Committee's labours, on the 16th June: This Permanent Court will not be a Court of arbitration, but a Court of justice.

Arbitration can take account of a thousand elements of fact and a thousand contingencies and, often, of certain necessities of a political kind. The decrees of justice take account only of a rule defined and fixed by law.

But, though the Permanent Court of International Justice is not a Court of Arbitration, in the strict sense of the word, it is none the less true that, if the word "Arbitration" be considered as signifying the administration of Justice between sovereign States, it is, like the other International Tribunals, one of the institutions whose functions are international Arbitration. Doubtless it is not the only such body; other tribunals of Arbitration may exist in addition, amongst others the Permanent Court of Arbitration of the Hague, as created by the Convention of 1899 and developed by that of 1907. Nevertheless, it is to be a real Court, not only by definition, but by the express terms of the Covenant (Art. 13), and must, if called upon, hear and determine all cases, which it is laid down that the contesting parties may or shall submit to arbitration. Not only must the provisions of the Covenant, concerning arbitration, be considered as governing both the organisation of procedure by arbitration, in the strict sense of the term, and proceedings before this Court, but also, in Articles 12, 13 and 15 of the Covenant, the word „Arbitration" must be interpreted as implying „Judicial Settlement of International Disputes."

On the 16th June, when opening the session of the Committee, M. Léon Bourgeois asked: „What are to be the limits of the competence of the Court? On this point, the Covenant itself and the different treaties which have been lately signed not only give a certain number of indications, but also definite decisions; and if some of the dispositions of these treaties and of the Covenant appear to imply regrettable restrictions, it must not be forgotten that, without necessarily contemplating any amendment of the Covenant, the Council and the Assembly, inspired by your labours and in virtue of Articles 12 and 15, can considerably increase the field of activity of the Court."

No one is more entitled to interpret the dispositions of Article 14 than the statesman, who was first called upon to take part at the Hague in 1899 and 1907, in the organisation,

forme, ce qu'il appelait déjà la „Société juridique des nations", a pris part, à Paris, à la rédaction du Pacte, dont il est maintenant, au Conseil, chargé d'assurer le fonctionnement.

De cet historique de l'article 14 du Pacte, de ce commentaire si autorisé de M. Léon Bourgeois, sortaient pour le Comité des indications précieuses, qui déjà lui montraient la direction dans laquelle il devait s'engager, en examinant tour à tour

1. l'organisation,
2. la compétence,
3. la procédure

de la Cour de Justice Internationale.

Dans l'étude de ces trois points, le Comité rencontrait des difficultés graves et nombreuses.

Heureusement, il pouvait s'appuyer non seulement sur les travaux des deux Conférences de la Haye, de 1899 et surtout de 1907, mais sur les projets émanés des Gouvernements, des Conférences intergouvernementales, des Associations scientifiques internationales, et des jurisconsultes de toutes nationalités, qui, depuis la publication du Pacte, s'étaient empressés d'étudier les différents problèmes de la création de la Cour prévue à l'Article 14.

A cet égard, le Comité devait trouver une source d'information précieuse dans le projet des Cinq Puissances, (Danemark, Norvège, Pays-Bas, Suède, Suisse) qui s'étaient réunies à la Haye, sous la présidence de M. Loder, du 16 au 27 février 1920.

Après avoir tenu, au début de ses travaux, à rendre, par une résolution spéciale, hommage à l'œuvre si autorisée de ses devanciers, Gouvernements, Associations scientifiques internationales, jurisconsultes de toutes nationalités, dont les études avaient précédé la sienne, le Comité se mit au travail avec la conviction qu'il pouvait, grâce à leur aide, aborder en toute confiance, malgré leur réelle difficulté, les trois grands problèmes qui se posaient à lui.

in its primitive form, of „the Legal Society of Nations" (Société Juridique des Nations), as he already called it, and subsequently took part, at Paris, in the drafting of the Covenant, the operation of which it is now his duty to ensure in the deliberations of the Council.

Some very valuable guidance was given to the Committee by this outline of the origin of Article 14 of the Covenant and by the authoritative comments made by M. Léon Bourgeois, showing it already the direction that its work must take in the successive examination of the questions of:

1. Organisation;
2. Competence;
3. Procedure

of the Court of International Justice.

In the study of these three problems, the Committee met with many serious difficulties.

Happily, it was aided not only by the work of the two Hague Conferences of 1899 and more particularly of 1907, but also by the plans prepared by Governments, by Conferences between representatives of Governments, by international scientific bodies, and by jurisconsults of all nations, all of whom had, since the publication of the Covenant, not failed to study the various problems connected with the creation of the Court provided for in Article 14.

In particular, the Committee was to find a very valuable source of information in the plan of the Five Powers (Denmark, Norway, the Netherlands, Sweden and Switzerland), who met at the Hague under the presidency of M. Loder from the 16—27th February, 1920.

The Committee, at the outset of its work, felt called upon to pay homage, in a special resolution, to the labours of its predecessors, whether Governments, international scientific bodies, or jurisconsults of all nations; it then faced its task with the conviction that, thanks to their aid, it could undertake the solution of the three great problems before it, in spite of their real difficulty, with complete confidence.

I.

ORGANISATION.

Il était facile de s'entendre sur un certain nombre de principes.

La Cour Permanente de Justice Internationale a pour trait caractéristique d'être directement accessible aux parties.

La Cour Permanente d'Arbitrage de la Haye n'est pas immédiatement prête à juger; collège d'arbitres, elle est essentiellement une liste sur laquelle les parties font elles-mêmes le choix des juges — 3 à 5 — appelés à composer leur tribunal.

Même après avoir accepté la compétence de la Cour d'Arbitrage de la Haye, il est nécessaire de déterminer par un compromis spécial ceux des arbitres inscrits sur la liste de la Cour qui siégeront dans l'affaire.

Le titre de Cour Permanente ne convient pas complètement à la Cour Permanente d'Arbitrage de la Haye, formée d'une liste de plus de cent noms d'où les parties au litige extraient dans chaque affaire les arbitres qui formeront leur tribunal: elle est moins un tribunal permanent d'arbitrage qu'une série de tribunaux éphémères dans un cadre constant.

Par opposition à la Cour d'Arbitrage, la Cour Permanente de Justice internationale méritera vraiment son nom parce qu'elle sera composée de juges qui siégeront d'affaire en affaire, sans que les parties aient à les désigner pour ce rôle et, sauf une exception dont il sera parlé plus loin en matière de procédure sommaire, sans qu'il soit permis aux parties de déterminer le nombre des juges. De plus, si les magistrats de la Cour Permanente de Justice internationale ont, comme ceux de la Cour d'Arbitrage, à jouir de la plus haute considération morale, ils doivent de plus remplir les conditions requises pour l'exercice, dans leurs pays respectifs, des plus hautes fonctions judiciaires. De cette manière, à côté des jurisconsultes qui possèdent une autorité reconnue en matière de droit international, il sera possible d'obtenir la présence au siège d'hommes qui, sans avoir fait une étude spéciale du droit international, n'en porteront pas moins à la Cour l'expérience des grands magistrats. Si dans le Comité un léger doute s'est élevé sur le point de savoir si, dans certains pays de l'Europe continentale, les hauts magistrats auraient toujours l'ouverture d'esprit nécessaire à la connaissance des litiges inter-

I.

ORGANISATION.

It was easy to come to an understanding upon a certain number of principles.

A characteristic feature of the Permanent Court of International Justice is that parties shall have direct access to it.

The Permanent Court of Arbitration of the Hague is not immediately available to try cases; being a body of arbitrators, it is essentially a list from which the parties themselves choose the judges — 3 to 5 — called upon to form their tribunal.

Even when the jurisdiction of the Court of Arbitration of the Hague has been accepted, it still remains to arrange, by a special agreement — a "compromis" — which of the arbitrators, contained in the list of the Court, are to sit in the particular case.

The name Permanent Court is not quite fitted to the Permanent Court of Arbitration at the Hague; formed as it is, of a list of more than one hundred names, from which the contesting parties in each case choose the arbitrators who are to form the tribunal, it is rather a series of temporary tribunals drawn from a permanent corps of members, than a Permanent Court of Arbitration.

In contradistinction to the Court of Arbitration, the Permanent Court of International Justice will really deserve its name, as it will consist of judges, who will continue to sit from one case to another; the parties will not have to choose them for this purpose, and with one exception, which will be dealt with later in connection with summary procedure, the parties may not fix the number of judges. Further, though the judges of the Permanent Court of International Justice, like those of the Court of Arbitration, must be of the highest moral character, they must, in addition, possess the qualifications required in their respective countries for appointment to the highest judicial offices. Thus, in addition to jurisconsults of well-known authority in International Law, the Bench can include men who though they may not have made a special study of International Law, will none the less strengthen the Court by their experience as judges. Though a slight doubt arose in the Committee as to whether the most important judges, in certain European countries, would always possess the openmindedness necessary in international law suits, there is no doubt that the great judges of Federal States are

nationaux, nul doute que les grands juges des Etats fédéraux ne soient particulièrement qualifiés pour rendre les plus grands services en apportant à des jurisconsultes, voués à l'étude théorique du droit international, le lumineux concours d'une expérience mûrie dans la décision de problèmes où le droit international, et, dans certains cas, le droit constitutionnel, prennent une grande place. Le Comité s'est mis promptement d'accord sur ces règles essentielles.

Article 1.

Indépendamment de la Cour d'Arbitrage, organisée par les Conventions de La Haye de 1899 et 1907, et des Tribunaux spéciaux d'Arbitres, auxquels les Etats demeurent toujours libres de confier la solution de leurs différends, il est institué, conformément à l'article 14 du Pacte de la Société des Nations, une Cour Permanente de Justice Internationale, directement accessible aux parties.

Article 2.

La Cour Permanente de Justice Internationale est un corps de magistrats indépendants, élus sans égard à leur nationalité parmi les personnes jouissant de la plus haute considération morale, et qui réunissent les conditions requises pour l'exercice dans leurs pays respectifs des plus hautes fonctions judiciaires, ou qui sont des jurisconsultes possédant une compétence notoire en matière de droit international.

Pour rendre les services qu'on attend d'elle, une Cour véritablement permanente doit être composée d'un petit nombre de juges. Mais, d'autre part, pour remplir sa fonction de justice internationale, elle doit s'ouvrir à tous les Etats du monde; or, pour appeler tous les Etats du monde, elle doit leur donner confiance en leur offrant des juges au choix desquels ils aient participé. En 1907, le projet offrait aux grandes Puissances un juge à demeure dans la Cour, aux autres un juge par roulement: cette disposition avait fait échouer le système, repoussé, à la demande instante du Brésil, par toutes les nations qui n'étaient pas de grandes Puissances, au nom du principe de l'égalité des Etats.

L'égalité des Etats est-elle véritablement en cause lorsqu'il s'agit de participer à l'organisation d'une justice internationale? L'égalité

particularly well qualified to render very great services; the illuminating experience, gathered from the decision of questions in which International Law, and in some cases Constitutional Law, play an important part, would be combined with the knowledge of Jurisconsults devoted to the study of the theory of International Law. The Committee came to an immediate agreement on the subject of these essential principles.

Article 1.

A Permanent Court of International Justice, to which contesting parties shall have direct access, is hereby established in accordance with Article 14 of the Covenant of the League of Nations. This Court shall be in addition to the Court of Arbitration organised by the Hague Convention of 1899 and 1907, and to the special Tribunals of Arbitration to which States are always at liberty to submit their disputes for settlement.

Article 2.

The Permanent Court of International Justice shall be composed of a body of independent judges, elected regardless of their nationality, from amongst persons of high moral character, who possess the qualifications required, in their respective countries, for appointment to the highest judicial offices, or are jurisconsults of recognised ability in international law.

In order to perform the duties required of it, a really permanent Court must be composed of a small number of judges; on the other hand, in order to be a really international Tribunal, it must be open to all States in the world. If it is to be accepted by all the States in the world, it must inspire their confidence by offering them judges whom they have helped to select. In 1907 the plan afforded the great Powers a permanent judge upon the Court, whereas the other Powers were to be represented in rotation: this provision caused the failure of the scheme; it was rejected, at the urgent instance of Brazil, by all States which were not great Powers, as being contrary to the principle of equality of States

Is the equality of States really at issue when determining who is to have a share in the composition of an international Jurisdic-

des Etats n'implique-t-elle pas uniquement qu'aucun Etat ne saurait intervenir dans les affaires intérieures des autres, en restreignant leur souveraineté? Et, du moment que tous les Etats sont souverains, ne sont-ils pas par cela même égaux, quelle que soit l'influence qu'ils exercent, en fait, au point de vue politique, sur la question des intérêts communs de l'humanité? Il se peut que ce point de vue, développé par un des membres du Comité, fût en droit rigoureusement exact; mais, du point de vue psychologique, dans l'opinion publique des différents Etats, le fait pour un certain nombre d'entre eux de réclamer un juge à demeure, en leur qualité de grande Puissance, était contraire à l'égalité.

Dès lors, il était nécessaire de trouver une combinaison qui permît aux grandes Puissances d'obtenir presque certainement, de la libre adhésion des autres, le juge que leur méritait la puissance de leur action civilisatrice et de leur progrès juridique, alors même qu'on eût refusé de tenir compte de l'intérêt de la Cour à le compter sur le siège pour le respect de décisions, qui ne pouvaient devenir exécutoires qu'avec le concours prééminent de leur puissance militaire, économique et financière. Le système de l'élection des juges était le seul pratique. Avant l'organisation de la Société des Nations, le collège électoral eût été composé de l'ensemble des Nations, de telle manière que les grandes fussent placées sur un pied d'égalité complète avec les autres. La formation d'une Société des Nations avec un double corps politique, le Conseil, où les grandes Puissances étaient assurées d'être spécialement représentées, et l'Assemblée, leur permettait de se mettre à l'abri des dangers d'un vote de coalition qui pourrait se former contre elles dans l'Assemblée.

Si, dans le Conseil, les grands Etats risquent de faire la loi aux petits, dans l'Assemblée les petits Etats risquent de faire la loi aux grands. Pour égaliser la situation entre les uns et les autres il n'y a dès lors qu'un moyen. Au lieu de préférer, comme les uns le demandaient, le Conseil à l'Assemblée, ou, comme les autres le réclamaient, l'Assemblée au Conseil, il n'y a qu'à faire sortir la Cour d'une désignation égale, simultanée, du Conseil et de l'Assemblée.

Assemblée et Conseil, placés sur le même plan, doivent élire les juges, de telle manière qu'aucun ne puisse entrer à la Cour s'il n'a la

tion? Does not the equality of States simply mean that no State may interfere in the internal affairs of another, thereby infringing its sovereign rights? Granted that all States are sovereign States, are they not made equal by this very fact, no matter what the extent of their influence may actually be, from a political point of view, upon the common interests of mankind? It may well be that this standpoint, which was taken up by one member of the Committee, is legally, strictly correct; however, from a psychological point of view, in the public opinion of the various countries, the fact that a certain number of States claimed a permanent judge, on the ground of their position as great Powers, would be opposed to the principle of equality.

It therefore became necessary to find a system which would almost certainly ensure that the great Powers would be represented by judges, with the free consent of the other Powers, as their great civilising influence and juridical progress entitle them to be, even though no weight were attached to the fact that it would be greatly to the interest of the Court to include them on the Bench, to increase respect for its sentences, which could not be put into execution without the all-important support of their military, economic and financial powers. The system of election of the judges was the only practical one. Before the organisation of the League of Nations, the electoral body would have been the whole body of nations, and the great States would have been on the same footing as the others. The formation of the League of Nations, with two political bodies — the Council in which the special representation of the great Powers was assured, and the Assembly, — enabled the Great Powers to obtain protection from the dangers of a possible coalition vote against them in the Assembly.

If there is a danger that the great Powers may dictate to the small States, in the Council, the converse applies in the Assembly. There is therefore but one way of adjusting the balance between them. Instead of preferring the Council to the Assembly, as some would have wished, or the Assembly to the Council, as others advocated, the only possible system for the formation of the Court was that of equal and simultaneous election by the Council and the Assembly.

Both the Assembly and the Council, on an equal footing, must elect the judges, so as to ensure that no person can be appointed to the Court

confiance de l'Assemblée, et qu'aucun ne puisse entrer à la Cour s'il n'a la confiance du Conseil.

Dès lors, plus de danger de coalition, ni des grands Etats contre les autres, ni des autres Etats contre les grands, nulle inquiétude, nulle surprise possible, qui infligeât à une grande Puissance l'humiliation de se trouver privée, seule ou presque seule entre les autres, du juge national sur lequel elle avait compté.

En même temps, l'égalité des Etats, selon le Pacte, se trouvait respectée.

Cette solution était d'autant plus juste qu'aux termes de l'article 14 du Pacte, la Cour, non seulement connaît de tout différend d'un caractère international que les parties lui soumettent, mais encore donne des avis consultatifs sur tout différend ou tout point dont la saisit le Conseil ou l'Assemblée. Il y a le plus grand intérêt à ce que, non seulement l'Assemblée, mais le Conseil puissent ramener à la procédure judiciaire, recommandée par ses qualités spéciales, une affaire que les parties revêtent inexactement d'un caractère politique. Et, pour que ce renvoi soit possible, il importe que la Cour ait la confiance non seulement de l'Assemblée, mais du Conseil; comme l'Assemblée, le Conseil doit, au même titre, intervenir dans l'élection des juges.

Certains projets, celui de M. Bevilaqua, celui de l'Union Juridique Internationale, celui des Cinq Puissances de la Haye, prévoyaient l'élection des juges par les membres de l'Assemblée. Un certain nombre de voix dans le Comité se prononçaient aussi de préférence dans ce même sens. Mais, devant l'opposition de ceux qui prétendaient donner aux grandes Puissances des garanties contre une coalition hostile de la part des autres États, il parut difficile de laisser à l'Assemblée seule l'élection des juges.

Restait à mettre en œuvre les détails du système. Unanimement, le Comité exprima le désir que le choix des juges, répondant aux conditions techniques prévues par l'article 2, fût, non pas laissé complètement à la discrétion des Gouvernements, mais largement influencé par l'opinion publique ou du moins l'opinion de l'élite éclairée, compétente à cet égard pour discerner le mérite des hommes.

Dans cet ordre d'idées, certains membres du Comité avaient eu tout d'abord l'idée de laisser la détermination des juges à la Cour Permanente d'Arbitrage de La Haye.

who does not possess the confidence both of the Assembly and the Council.

Hence there is no danger of a coalition either on the part of the great States against the others, or of the other States against the great. There is therefore no cause for anxiety, and no possibility of a surprise occurring which might inflict upon a great Power the humiliation of finding itself, contrary to its anticipations, alone, or almost alone amongst the other great Powers, without a judge of its nationality.

In addition, the principle of equality of States, as contained in the Covenant, is respected.

This solution would be still further justified in that, according to Article 14 of the Covenant, the Court is not only to hear and determine all disputes of an international nature submitted to it by the contesting parties, but also to give advisory opinions upon any dispute or question presented to it by the Council or the Assembly. It is highly desirable that not only the Assembly, but also the Council should be able to cause a judicial procedure, with the special advantages which it offers, to apply to a case wrongly given a political aspect by the parties. To make this possible the Court must possess the confidence not only of the Assembly but of the Council; therefore the Council must take part in the election of judges upon the same footing as the Assembly.

Some plans, including that of M. Bevilaqua, that of the "Union Juridique Internationale" and that of the Five Powers at the Hague, arranged for the election of the judges by the members of the Assembly. Some of the members of the Committee also favoured this idea. However, in face of the opposition of those members who wished to guarantee the great Powers against a hostile coalition on the part of the other Powers, it was difficult to leave the election of judges to the Assembly alone.

It remained to work out the details of the system. The Committee unanimously agreed that the choice of the judges, who must of course fulfil the technical conditions mentioned in Article 2, should not be left entirely to the discretion of Governments, but that public opinion, or at any rate the opinions of the enlightened few who are qualified to gauge the merits of persons to be selected for nomination, should have a great influence.

In this connection, some members of the Committee at first thought of leaving the selection of judges to the Permanent Court of Arbitration at the Hague.

Pour procéder à la détermination des juges, chaque groupe de membres, nommés par un même Etat, de la Cour d'Arbitrage de La Haye, eût choisi un délégué, puis tous les délégués se seraient réunis à La Haye pour procéder à l'élection des juges. Ce système eût offert des avantages multiples; il eût rattaché la nouvelle institution arbitrale aux institutions antérieures, maintenu l'ancienne Cour dans le même moment que se créait la nouvelle, uni l'une à l'autre par un intime rapport de filiation, fait disparaître le fâcheux antagonisme et la superficielle antithèse qu'un déplorable esprit d'opposition avait un moment tenté de marquer entre l'œuvre du Pacte et celle des Conférences de La Haye; enfin, il eût respecté les susceptibilités égalitaires des Etats, puisque tous, également aptes à nommer des juges à la Cour d'Arbitrage de La Haye, fussent venus également au grand collège électoral où les arbitres procèdent, à égalité, à la détermination des juges, en en vérifiant la compétence technique: choisis à raison de leur haute moralité, de leur science, et de leur expérience des affaires internationales, réunissant, dès lors, en eux toutes les qualités qui doivent, en matière internationale, constituer le bon juge, les membres de la Cour actuelle d'Arbitrage les auraient, de la manière la plus sûre, reconnues chez les autres. Rétablissement, dans l'œuvre du progrès juridique et pacifique, d'une continuité, momentanément rompue, mais non irrévocablement brisée par la guerre; élimination des influences politiques et, par suite, nomination des juges indépendante de toute influence particulière d'Etats; choix technique de techniciens par des techniciens; désignation des meilleurs par les meilleurs: ces multiples qualités recommandaient un système, dont le développement, présenté à deux reprises avec une très grande force, retint, ainsi qu'il convenait, l'attention du Comité.

Mais ce système, en dépit de ses grands avantages, n'était pas sans présenter de graves inconvénients. Pour rattacher l'institution nouvelle, née du Pacte, aux institutions antérieures, issues des Conférences de La Haye, il ne craignait pas de placer la Cour nouvelle dans la dépendance de l'ancienne. Il appelait en qualité d'électeurs, à La Haye, de toutes les régions du monde, des jurisconsultes et des hommes politiques, en vue d'une simple opération électorale; il donnait à des hommes, qui pour la plupart

According to this scheme, the appointment of judges would have taken place as follows: each group of judges of the Court of Arbitration appointed by a particular State, would choose one delegate; all the delegates would assemble at the Hague to carry out the election of the judges. This system offered many advantages; it would have established a connection between the new institution and previous institutions of Arbitration; it would have maintained the old Court, whilst creating the new, and, by uniting the two, by the affiliation of the new to the old, would have put an end to the regrettable antagonism and seeming contrasts, which a lamentable spirit of opposition at one time endeavoured to create between the Covenant and the two Hague Conferences. Finally, it would have respected the susceptibilities of States regarding their equality, since all, having equal rights in the appointment of judges to the Court of Arbitration at the Hague, would have been equally represented in the great electoral body in which the arbitrators, again on a footing of equality, would have carried out the election of the judges and satisfied themselves as their scientific ability and qualifications.' The arbitrators themselves, chosen for their high moral character, their scientific knowledge, and their experience in international affairs, and therefore possessing all the qualities required for good international judges, would have been eminently able to recognise these qualities in others. The manifold advantages of this system: the re-establishment of continuity in the progress of law and peace, which had been broken for the moment, but not irrevocably shattered by the War; the elimination of political influences, and the consequent appointment of judges independent of the influence of particular States; the choice of experts by experts; the appointment of the best by the best; all these weighed in favour of a system which was twice expounded with very great ability, and which, as was only right, received the earnest consideration of the Committee.

This system, however, in spite of its great advantages, entailed some very great difficulties. In order to link the new institution, arising out of the Covenant, with the previous institutions, founded by the Hague Conferences, it did not hesitate to put the new Court in a position of dependence upon the existing one. Further, it entailed the assembly at the Hague of jurisconsults and politicians from all over the world, simply to act as an electoral body. It gave the rôle of elector to men who, for the most part,

n'étaient jamais venus et ne viendraient jamais à La Haye pour juger, un rôle d'électeur qui, dans ces conditions, devenait principal, alors que celui de juge n'était plus, pour eux, que subsidiaire. Afin de soustraire la désignation du juge à toute influence d'ordre gouvernemental, par crainte des combinaisons et tractations politiques, sur la base du *do ut des*, il éloignait par trop le juge du justiciable, le magistrat, appelé à statuer entre les Etats, de ces Etats eux-mêmes. Sans doute, les membres de la Cour d'Arbitrage de La Haye, nommés par leurs Gouvernements respectifs, tenaient leur titre, indirectement, d'Etats souvérains; mais c'était au second degré que ces Etats choisiraient ainsi leurs juges, tandis que, dans l'arbitrage, le choix s'exerçait au premier degré: la distance devenait trop grande pour que les Etats eussent toujours pleine confiance dans leurs juges. D'autre part, puisque les membres de la Cour d'Arbitrage étaient sortis d'une désignation gouvernementale, comment espérer que les préoccupations du Gouvernement, dont ils tenaient leurs pouvoirs, ne fussent pas dans une certaine mesure les leurs? Comment dès lors ne pas craindre qu'il n'y eût entre eux cette possibilité d'entente et de coalition contre laquelle certains Etats entendaient rigoureusement se prémunir? Enfin et surtout, il était inexact de marquer, entre l'ancienne et la nouvelle Cour, un rapport de filiation. Jamais il n'était entré, en 1907, dans la pensée de la seconde Conférence de la Paix, d'établir un tel rapport entre la Cour de Justice arbitrale, vraiment permanente, et la Cour d'Arbitrage; pourquoi dès lors nouer entre une Cour qui visiblement devait réaliser la pensée de 1907, et la Cour d'Arbitrage, un lien que la Conférence de 1907 n'avait jamais entendu établir? S'il convenait, pour la continuité de l'évolution juridique et la justice de l'histoire, que la nouvelle Cour ne se créât pas sans se retourner vers La Haye comme vers son origine première, n'était-il pas excessif de vouloir qu'elle fût, par une filiation directe de la Cour d'Arbitrage, placée dans la dépendance de celle-ci? Ne suffisait-il pas d'un droit de présentation de la Cour d'Arbitrage, organisé sur place, dans des conditions pratiques, par chaque Nation, sans une réunion, de tous les points du monde, à La Haye, de juges qui, ne venant pas pour juger, viendraient pour élire? La Cour de Justice arbitrale de 1907, dont procédait la Cour Permanente de Justice Internationale, avait été conçue d'une manière nettement distincte de la Cour d'Arbitrage de 1899. Pour marquer, entre l'une et l'autre Cour, une absolue com-

had never come and would never come to the Hague to act as judges; this rôle therefore assumed the greater importance, and their potential duties as judges became secondary. In order to safeguard the appointment of judges from any influence of Governments, and through a fear of political combinations and intrigues based on the principle of "*do ut des*", this system would have set too wide a gulf between the judge and those subject to his authority, between the magistrate called upon to administer justice between States, and the States themselves. Of course the members of the Court of Arbitration of the Hague, being appointed by their respective Governments, held their positions indirectly from sovereign States; but, by this system, the States would only choose their judges indirectly, whereas in arbitration, the selection was direct. The connection was not sufficiently close to ensure that States would invariably have complete confidence in their judges. On the other hand, as the members of the Court of Arbitration were appointed by Governments, how could it be hoped that the ideas of the Government, from which they received their powers, would not also to some extent affect them? It would seem therefore impossible to avoid the fear that, intrigues and combinations amongst the electors would be possible against which certain States had firmly made up their minds to protect themselves. Last but not least, it would not be correct to establish an affiliating relationship between the new Court and the old. The Second Peace Conference of 1907 never entertained the idea of establishing such a connection between the really permanent Court of Arbitral Justice, and the Court of Arbitration. Why therefore create a link between a Court which obviously fulfils the intentions of the Conference of 1907, and the Court of Arbitration, which link it was never the intention of that Conference to establish? Even though it might seem desirable, for the sake of maintaining the continuity of the evolution of law, and for reasons of historical justice, that the new Court should not be formed entirely without any link connecting it with the Hague as its original source, surely it would be too much to place it in a position of dependence by affiliating it directly to the Court of Arbitration. Would it not suffice to give the Court of Arbitration the right of making the nominations, this right to be exercised under practical conditions, by each national group in its own country, without the necessity of assembling

patibilité, n'était-il pas exagéré de les faire procéder l'une de l'autre, alors que l'esprit, et par suite, la composition, les méthodes, de l'une et de l'autre devenaient profondément différents? La Cour d'Arbitrage de La Haye de 1899 est une institution extérieure à la Société des Nations fondée par le Pacte. Pour la faire procéder, maintenant, à l'élection des juges de la Cour de Justice Internationale, il fallait en rompre le cadre en retranchant de la liste des arbitres actuels les noms de ceux dont la désignation provenait des Etats qui n'étaient pas encore admis à faire partie de la Société des Nations. La difficulté de trouver, dans cette Cour, des représentants d'Etats nouveaux, la Pologne, la Tchéco-Slovaquie, ne s'opposait pas sans doute à l'utilisation de la Cour d'Arbitrage de 1899 à titre de collège électoral des membres de la Cour de Justice Internationale; ce n'était là qu'une difficulté de détail, facile à résoudre par l'accession des Etats nouveaux à la Convention relative à la solution pacifique des conflits internationaux, de 1899, renouvelée en 1907. Mais comment dire que la Cour de Justice Internationale sortirait de la Cour d'Arbitrage de La Haye, prise dans son unité globale, alors que ni l'Allemagne, ni l'Autriche, ni la Hongrie, ni la Turquie, ni la Russie, toutes Puissances représentées par des juges dans la Cour d'Arbitrage, ne pouvaient participer à l'élection des membres d'une Cour chargée de l'Administration de la Justice dans une Société des Nations dont, pour des raisons diverses, ces Etats se trouvaient exclus? Là se trouvait, pour la solution du problème, l'idée directrice: organe judiciaire de la Société des Nations, la nouvelle Cour ne pouvait naître qu'au sein de la Société des Nations. Sa filiation dans la Société des Nations ne pouvait procéder d'un organe extérieur, mais d'un organe intérieur à cette Société.

Où trouver cet organe?

Ici, la comparaison de la justice nationale et de la justice internationale donnait la solution. Dans presque tous les Etats du monde civilisé, le juge est nommé par le pouvoir exécutif ou le pouvoir législatif ou par l'un et par l'autre. Agent de la souveraineté manifestée par le glaive et la balance, le pouvoir judiciaire,

judges, from all parts of the world, at the Hague, who would come, not to act as judges, but merely as electors? The Court of Arbitral Justice of 1907, from which the Permanent Court of International Justice derives its origin, was founded on ideas quite distinct from those upon which the Court of Arbitration of 1899 was based. It would seem excessive to make one dependent upon the other, merely in order to show that there is no incompatibility in the co-existence of the two Courts, especially as the spirit, and consequently, the composition and the methods of each differ profoundly. The Court of Arbitration of the Hague of 1899 is an institution outside the League of Nations founded by the Covenant. Therefore, in order to carry out the election of the judges of the Court of International Justice by means of it, its composition must be altered, for the purpose of the election, by withdrawing from the list the names of those arbitrators appointed by States not yet admitted into the League of Nations. The difficulty of finding representatives from new States, such as Poland and Czecho-Slovakia, for this Court would not be an objection to its use as an electoral college for the members of the Court of International Justice; this would be a mere question of detail, easily solved by the accession of new States to the Convention for the Pacific Settlement of International Disputes of 1899, renewed in 1907. But how could it be said that the Court of International Justice derived its origin from the Court of Arbitration of the Hague in its entirety, since Germany, Austria, Hungary, Turkey and Russia, all of which are represented by judges on the Court of Arbitration, could not participate in the election of the members of a Court entrusted with the administration of Justice in a League of Nations from which, for various reasons, they are excluded? The principle governing the solution of the problem is brought out by the above: the new Court, being the judicial organ of the League of Nations, can only be created within this League. As it is to be a component part of the League, it must originate from an organisation within the League and not from a body outside it.

Where is such an organisation to be found?

At this point a comparison between national jurisdictions and international jurisdictions gave the clue to the problem. In nearly every civilised country in the world, judges are appointed by the Executive or by the Legislature, or by both together. The Judicial Power, though representing that aspect of sovereignty which is sym-

constitué comme indépendant, n'en tire pas moins sa source, à défaut de l'élection directe par les justiciables, de l'un ou de l'autre de ces pouvoirs. Tantôt il est désigné par le législatif, tantôt par l'exécutif, tantôt par le législatif sur la proposition de l'exécutif ou par l'exécutif avec l'assentiment du législatif: de toute manière c'est de la souveraineté générale de l'Etat que le juge, membre de l'organe judiciaire de l'Etat, tire son pouvoir. A qui, dans la Société des Nations, appartient l'autorité? Manifestement aux Membres de la Société des Nations.

C'est donc aux Membres de la Société des Nations, justiciables du haut tribunal, qu'il appartient, normalement, d'en déterminer les juges, non par une désignation indirecte, par l'entremise de leurs réprésentants à la Cour d'Arbitrage, mais par une désignation directe, faite, au moment même, en pleine connaissance de cause. Et comme, dans la Société des Nations, deux organes existent, l'Assemblée où toutes les Nations de la Société sont représentées, le Conseil où, tantôt d'une manière constante, pour les grandes Puissances, tantôt d'une manière occasionnelle, pour les autres, certaines nations, seules, sont, par privilège, appelées, c'est à l'Assemblée et au Conseil qu'il doit simultanément appartenir de procéder à cette élection.

Les juges sont ainsi déterminés par la Société des Nations; mais, de la proposition faite en vue de leur désignation par la Cour d'Arbitrage de La Haye, réunie en collège électoral chargé de désigner les membres de la Cour de Justice Internationale, il devait rester que, si la Cour d'Arbitrage ne peut exercer, par rapport à l'autre, le droit d'élection qui, normalement, revient aux organes investis des pouvoirs de la Société des Nations, du moins la Cour d'Arbitrage peut se voir attribuer un rôle important: celui de dresser la liste des personnes, entre lesquelles l'Assemblée et le Conseil exerceront leur choix.

Mais pouvait-on demander aux différents Etats, appelés à procéder à l'élection au sein de la Société des Nations, de faire venir, parfois de très loin, avec une grande perte de temps et à grands frais, des membres de la Cour Permanente d'Arbitrage à seule fin de se réunir à La Haye, non pour juger, ni simplement pour

bolised by the sword and balance, and though constituted as an independent power, nevertheless is derived from one or other of these bodies, unless it is directly elected by those under its jurisdiction. Appointments to it are made, sometimes by the Legislature, in some cases by the Executive, sometimes by the Executive with the consent of the Legislature or sometimes by the Legislature on the proposal of the Executive; however this may be, a judge, being a member of the judicial organisation of the State, derives his powers from the sovereignty of the State as a whole. In whom is the ultimate authority in the League of Nations vested? Obviously in the Members of the League.

It must therefore fall to the Members of the League of Nations, who alone are subject to the jurisdiction of this high Court, to appoint the judges in normal circumstances; and this not indirectly, through their representatives on the Court of Arbitration, but by direct selection, made at the time and in possession of all relevant information. Since there are two bodies in the League of Nations, the Assembly and the Council, in the former of which all nations within the League are represented, and in the latter certain nations only by a special privilege, which is permanent in the case of the great Powers and occasional and temporary in the case of others, the duty of carrying out the elections must fall to these two bodies simultaneously.

In this way, the judges are appointed by the League of Nations; but the proposal that they should be appointed by the Court of Arbitration of the Hague, assembled as an electoral college entrusted with the selection of the members of the Court of International Justice, should to some extent be taken into account: if it is inadmissible that the Court of Arbitration should exercise electoral rights in connection with the other Court, because these rights belong normally to those bodies, in which the powers of the League of Nations are vested, at any rate an important part in the election can be given to the Court of Arbitration, namely: the task of preparing the list of persons from whom the Assembly and the Council shall make their selection.

But the various nations, called upon to take part in the election within the organisation of the League of Nations, can hardly be asked to send their members of the Permanent Court of Arbitration, from long distances, at great expense and with great loss of time, for the simple purpose of assembling at the Hague,

élire, mais, plus simplement encore, pour présenter? Entre le procédé, la convocation d'un membre par Etat de la Cour d'Arbitrage à la Haye même, et le résultat, la présentation d'une liste de personnes entre lesquelles la Société des Nations devrait choisir, la disproportion était trop grande pour qu'il pût être question d'employer une telle méthode. Les arbitres électeurs ne viendront donc pas à La Haye; ils resteront sur place. Mais chaque Etat, qui, appelé à prendre part à l'élection de la Cour Permanente de Justice Internationale, aura déjà désigné des arbitres à la Cour d'Arbitrage de La Haye, les réunira, chacun appelant les arbitres, nommés par lui, à former, au lieu d'un grand collège électoral, un collège particulier, ou groupe national, en vue de la présentation des personnes entre lesquelles Assemblée et Conseil exercent leur choix.

Ce n'est pas aux Etats eux-mêmes, mais au corps des arbitres nommés par eux dans la Cour Permanente d'Arbitrage de La Haye qu'il appartient de déterminer les hommes qui, dans leur opinion, sont parmi les plus qualifiés pour être appelés par la Société des Nations à la Cour Permanente de Justice Internationale. Grâce à ce procédé, les Gouvernements ne sont pas totalement écartés, puisqu'ils ont eux-mêmes nommé les membres de la Cour d'Arbitrage qui prennent part en leur nom à cette présentation ; mais, d'autre part, ils laissent à des arbitres de leur choix, hommes d'une compétence éprouvée dans les questions d'ordre international, le soin de désigner ceux dont la présence au siège de la Cour leur inspire, en raison de leurs qualités morales et techniques, la confiance la plus grande.

Article 4.

Les membres de la Cour sont élus par l'Assemblée et par le Conseil sur une liste de personnes présentées par les groupes nationaux de de la Cour d'Arbitrage, conformément aux dispositions suivantes.

Dans cette présentation ils seront, suivant une heureuse proposition, aidés par les suggestions qu'ils auront, non seulement à recevoir, mais encore à provoquer, de la part des personnes particulièrement compétentes pour recommander les noms des meilleurs.

not to act as judges, not even to carry out an election, but merely to make nominations. If one member of the Court of Arbitration for each State were to meet at the Hague, and if the Assembly thus formed were merely to submit a list of names from which the League of Nations would make its selection, such a method would present too great a disparity between the procedure involved and the result obtained to make it admissible. The Arbitrators, therefore, are not to come to the Hague in their capacity as electors: they will remain where they are. Each State, however, called upon to take part in the election of members of the Permanent Court of International Justice, will have already appointed arbitrators on the Court of Arbitration of the Hague, and will assemble them, not as one great electoral college, but as separate electoral colleges or national groups for the purpose of nominating persons from whom Assembly and Council are to make their selection.

It will fall to the body of arbitrators, appointed to the Permanent Court of Arbitration of the Hague by the States, and not to the States themselves, to select the men who, in their opinion, are best qualified to be summoned by the League of Nations to sit upon the Permanent Court of International Justice. In this way, the Governments will not be entirely excluded, as they will have appointed, the members of the Court of Arbitration taking part in the nominations on their behalf, but, on the other hand, it will be to these arbitrators, men of proved ability in international affairs and chosen by the Governments, that the task will be left of selecting those candidates in whose moral and scientific qualifications for the Bench they have most confidence.

Article 4.

The members of the Court shall be elected by the Assembly and the Council from a list of persons nominated by the national groups in the Court of Arbitration, in accordance with the following provisions.

By the adoption of a very opportune proposal, they will be assisted in these nominations by suggestions, which they must not only receive but invite, made by persons particularly well fitted to recommend the best candidates.

Cette recommandation viendra d'abord des plus hautes Cours de Justice. Elles sont spécialement aptes à proposer les magistrats les plus capables de s'élever de la justice interne à la justice internationale, dans les pays anglo-saxons, où le droit international fait partie du *Common Law*, et dans les pays fédératifs, où le juge, par suite de sa compétence politique au regard des Etats particuliers, est prêt à passer d'un jugement entre Etats non souverains au jugement entre Etats souverains. Il n'en est pas de même dans les pays du Continent, où l'exercice normal de la magistrature interne ne comporte pas de semblables ouvertures sur des questions de droit public, soit fédéral soit international. Mais, puisque les juges peuvent être choisis parmi de hauts magistrats (art. 2), il importe que de hauts magistrats signalent les hommes qu'ils connaissent bien, à l'attention du corps qui fait la présentation.

Après cette consultation de la plus haute magistrature vient celle des corps particulièrement qualifiés pour indiquer, parmi les hommes les plus aptes à l'application du droit international, le nom des spécialistes qui enseignent dans les Universités, étudient dans les Académies nationales et dans les sections nationales des grandes Académies internationales, telles que l'Institut de Droit international, l'Institut Américain de Droit international, l'Union Juridique Internationale, l'International Law Association, l'Institut Ibérique de Droit Comparé.

Mais, alors que nulle élection ne peut être faite par l'Assemblée et le Conseil (sauf en un cas exceptionnel auquel on reviendra plus loin) que sur présentation de la Cour d'Arbitrage, les désignations par les corps scientifiques nationaux, ou les sections nationales des grands corps internationaux voués à l'étude du droit, n'ont que le caractère d'une simple recommandation : la consultation, moralement imposée, n'est pas juridiquement obligatoire ; pas de nullité si l'on omet de consulter l'un de ces corps ; et, fussent-ils tous consultés, aucune obligation stricte de faire porter le choix sur le nom qui eût, de leur part, obtenu le plus de suffrages ; au contraire toute liberté de se prononcer pour un autre, si le groupe national de la Cour d'Arbitrage décide pour chaque Etat de procéder autrement.

Grâce à ce procédé, le choix d'hommes très qualifiés, parce qu'ils sont eux-mêmes appelés aux

Such recommendations will, in the first place, be made by the highest Courts of Justice. The members of these Courts may be in the best position to recommend the names of those judges most capable of rising above the level of national justice to international affairs; this is so in Anglo-Saxon countries where International Law forms part of Common Law, and in Federal countries where a judge, by reason of his competence in political matters between individual States, is well able to pass from the settlement of cases between States without sovereign rights, to the judgement of disputes between sovereign States. It is not the same in continental countries; there the normal functions of national judges do not include such opportunities for dealing with questions of public law, either of a federal or of an international nature. However, since the judges may be selected from amongst the holders of high national judicial office (Art. 2.), these must recommend men, whom they are in a position to know well, to the notice of the nominating body.

Next after the advice of the judges of the highest Courts follows that of bodies particularly well qualified to suggest the names of men of the highest ability in International Law: experts, who teach in Universities, or who study in national Academies or national sections of the great international Academies, such as the Institute of International Law, the American Institute of International Law, the Union Juridique Internationale, the International Law Association, and the Iberian Institute of Comparative Law.

As, however, no election can be carried out by the Assembly and the Council (save under particular circumstances dealt with later), except from the list of nominations of the Court of Arbitration, these recommendations, made by national scientific bodies, or by national sections of great international bodies devoted to the study of Law, are only in the nature of suggestions: only a moral obligation to take this advice exists, there is no legal obligation; the nomination is not rendered void if one of these bodies is not consulted; and even if they are all consulted there is no definite obligation to choose the name of the person who has received most support from them; if any State's national group of the Court of Arbitration should decide upon another name, it is quite free to do so.

Thanks to the foregoing provisions men who are themselves very highly qualified, since they

fonctions d'arbitre par un Etat déterminé, sera hautement éclairé. L'opinion publique, au vrai sens du mot, c'est-à-dire non pas l'opinion ignorante, mais celle des milieux bien informés, pourra se prononcer: la compétence, alors même que sa voix n'est pas nécessairement suivie d'une adhésion commandée, n'en a pas moins le plus souvent une influence persuasive.

Nul doute qu'elle ne l'exerce de la manière la plus heureuse en donnant à chaque section nationale de la Cour Permanente d'Arbitrage l'occasion de procéder à la désignation des meilleurs, en lui offrant, le cas échéant, un point d'appui contre l'arbitraire du pouvoir.

D'autre part, comme les membres de la Cour permanente nommés par un Etat ont sa confiance, le Gouvernement ne saurait se plaindre, en aucun cas, du choix qu'ils font. Faite par des hommes qui ont la confiance du Gouvernement, en s'aidant du jugement professionnel de corps d'une réelle impartialité et d'une haute indépendance, la présentation, par chaque Etat, des éligibles ne peut manquer de donner les meilleurs hommes.

Article 6.

Avant de procéder à cette désignation il est recommandé à chaque groupe national de consulter la plus Haute Cour de Justice, les Facultés et Ecoles de Droit, les Académies nationales et les sections nationales d'Académies internationales, vouées à l'étude du droit.

Pour inviter les électeurs à mûre réflexion, en réduisant le nombre des candidats qu'ils peuvent proposer, le Comité a pensé qu'une garantie supplémentaire consisterait dans le petit nombre des candidats que chaque groupe de la Cour d'Arbitrage aurait à présenter: bien qu'une proposition eût un moment tenté de permettre à chaque Etat de proposer, pour quelque nombre de sièges que ce fût, 6 candidats, dont 2 nationaux au maximum, le Comité s'est arrêté au chiffre de 2 candidats quel que fût le nombre des sièges à pourvoir, mais, en même temps, elle a tenu formellement à déclarer que le choix est indépendant de la nationalité.

Un Etat qui, pour une raison ou pour une autre, ne compte pas parmi ses nationaux de personnes en situation d'être juge, doit cependant être en mesure de s'intéresser à l'élection, même dans la première phase, celle de la présentation, en

have been called upon by some State to perform the duties of Arbitrators, should be able to make a very enlightened choice. Public opinion in the true sense of the word, i. e. not the opinion of the masses, but that of well-informed circles, can thus obtain expression: it will, more often than not, prevail, in spite of the fact that its views need not necessarily be adopted.

There is no doubt that the best use that can be made of public opinion is to enable each national group of the Court of Arbitration to nominate the very best candidates, and should it be necessary, to afford them moral support against the arbitrary use of power.

On the other hand, as each State has appointed its own members of the Permanent Court, it must have confidence in them, and the Governments can never justifiably complain of the selections made by them. The nomination of duly qualified candidates by each State cannot fail to produce the best men, as it is carried out by persons, in the confidence of the Government and aided by the professional opinions of really impartial and independent organisations.

Article 6.

Before making these nominations, each national group is hereby recommended to consult its Highest Court of Justice, its Legal Faculties and Schools of Law, and its National Academies and national sections of International Academies devoted to the study of Law.

The Committee thought that the small number of candidates to be nominated by each group would constitute an additional guarantee, in that it would induce the electors to weigh every consideration, because the number of candidates they could propose was reduced. At one time, a proposal was made to allow each State to nominate six candidates, of whom two at most might be its subjects, no matter how many vacancies were to be filled; but the Committee decided upon the number of two candidates, regardless of the number of vacancies to be filled, and, at the same time, formally stated that the choice was to be made without regard to nationality.

A State, which, for any reason, does not possess amongst its subjects persons suitable for appointment as judges, must nevertheless be enabled to take an active interest in the election, even in the first phase, that of nomination, and

offrant des noms dignes d'être retenus. Si, par modestie ou toute autre cause, cet Etat ne peut en trouver parmi ses nationaux, il demeure libre d'en choisir parmi les étrangers. Tel Etat qui aurait pu présenter un de ses nationaux pour être juge sera dès lors heureux de faire présentation d'un étranger. La Cour lui paraîtra d'autant mieux constituée qu'il sentira ainsi qu'il y a, sur le siège, non pas seulement des hommes à l'élection desquels il aura participé, mais des hommes en qui il aura d'autant plus confiance qu'ils auront été, dès le début, de sa part l'objet spontané d'une marque directe de préférence.

Telles sont les raisons pour lesquelles le Comité a cru devoir, après mûr examen, adopter cette formule:

Article 5, paragraphe 2.

Chaque groupe ne peut en aucun cas présenter plus de deux personnes sans distinction de nationalité.

Si chaque Etat présente ainsi des candidats de son choix, on peut s'attendre à ce que la liste résume toutes les grandes formes de civilisation et les principaux systèmes juridiques du monde. Mais, en faisant leur choix parmi les personnes ainsi présentées, dont le Secrétaire Général de la Société des Nations dresse alphabétiquement la liste, l'Assemblée et le Conseil auront à veiller, non seulement à ce que les conditions de moralité, de compétence et d'expérience requises soient effectivement remplies, mais encore à ce que les différentes formes de civilisation et les grands systèmes juridiques du monde soient représentés. Alors qu'à la Conférence de La Haye de 1907 il n'était question que des divers systèmes juridiques du monde, il a semblé que les différentes formes de civilisation devaient être également indiquées.

Par ces mots „principaux systèmes juridiques" il ne pouvait entrer dans l'esprit du Comité de désigner les différents systèmes de droit international. Sans doute, sur certains points, en matière de prises maritimes par exemple, il existe, ou du moins il existait avant la guerre, deux systèmes de jurisprudence européenne, et peut-être existe-t-il encore, sur certains points, des divergences dans la manière dont tantôt les Européens, tantôt les Américains ou les Asiatiques abordent les questions de droit interna-

must therefore be able to submit names worthy of consideration. Should a State, whether from modesty or for any other reason, be unable to find suitable persons amongst its subjects, it is at liberty to choose from the subjects of other States. The same State, which might otherwise have nominated one of its subjects as a candidate, would, under these circumstances, gladly nominate a foreigner. The composition of the Court would be the more satisfactory to it, since it would feel that not only men in whose election it had taken part were on the Bench, but also men whom it had, from the outset, directly supported, and in whom, therefore, it had a fuller degree of confidence.

For the above reasons, the Committee, after mature consideration, adopted this formula:

Article 5, par. 2.

No group may nominate more than two persons; the nominees may be of any nationality.

If every State nominates its chosen candidates, it may be confidently anticipated that the list will contain representatives of all the main forms of civilisation and the principal legal systems of the world. Further, however, the Assembly and the Council, in selecting from the alphabetical list of the nominations as prepared by the Secretary-General of the League of Nations, must, independently, endeavour to assure not only that the moral qualifications and those of ability and experience required are actually possessed, but also, that the elections should result in the representation of the different forms of civilisation and main legal systems of the world. At the time of the Hague Conference of 1907, only the various legal systems of the world were considered, but it would now seem that the various forms of civilisation should also be mentioned.

The Committee in using these words "the principal legal systems" had no intention of referring to the various systems of International Law. Doubtless, on certain matters, for instance in Naval Prize Law, two systems of European jurisprudence exist, or at any rate did exist before the War; perhaps, on some points, differences still exist between the respective methods used by Europeans, Americans or Asiatics, in dealing with questions of International Law; but no matter what the main national ten-

tional; mais, quels que puissent être les grands courants nationaux de droit international, l'esprit de la formule arrêtée par le Comité ne pouvait pas être de retenir les différences de conception juridique d'ordre international, car cela eût été contraire à la grande idée sur laquelle repose l'établissement d'une Cour de Justice unique pour toutes les Nations: l'idée de l'unité et de l'universalité du droit international. Ce que le Comité a pensé en recommandant de la manière la plus formelle la représentation des principaux systèmes juridiques, c'est qu'il y avait, non pas des systèmes distincts de droit international dont on eût à tenir compte dans leur antagonisme, national ou continental, mais, ce qui est très différent, des éducations juridiques distinctes: le juge d'Angleterre et des Etats Unis ne procède pas de la même manière que le juge des autres pays, l'un s'attachant davantage aux précédents, l'autre à la déduction logique, à l'enchaînement en syllogisme des conséquences des textes ou des principes Ce qu'on a voulu, c'est que, dans chaque cas, et quelle que fût la nature des points de droit interne liés à la position du problème de droit international, tous fussent également compris; ce qu'on a voulu, car il est toujours possible de faire monter sur le siège un juge expressément choisi dans la circonstance par l'une des parties, si elle n'en a déjà pas un de sa nationalité, c'est qu'au moment où un système de droit est engagé dans un litige, les autres systèmes de droit puissent en être immédiatement rapprochés, de manière que ce soit vraiment l'esprit juridique de toutes les nations qui se tienne en permanence au siège.

Et, dès lors, ce n'était pas assez de demander une représentation des grands systèmes juridiques du monde, il fallait également une représentation des différentes formes de civilisation. C'est à cette condition seulement que, dans la Société universelle des Nations, la Cour permanente de Justice internationale sera vraiment une Cour du Monde.

En procédant à l'élection des juges, l'Assemblée et le Conseil auront donc à veiller à ce que les grandes formes de civilisation et les principaux systèmes juridiques du monde soient représentés.

Article 9.

Dans toute élection, les électeurs veillent à ce que les personnes appelées à faire partie de la Cour, non seulement réunissent individuellement les conditions requises, mais assurent, dans l'en-

dencies in International Law may be, the meaning of the expression adopted by the Committee is not and cannot be to maintain existing distinctions between various conceptions of International Law, for such an intention would be opposed to the guiding principle upon which the establishment of a single Court of Justice for all nations is based: that is to say, the principle of the unity and universality of International Law. The Committee, in expressly recommending that the principal legal systems should be represented, had in mind, not that there were distinct systems of International Law, the national or continental tendencies of which must be considered, but that there were distinct systems of legal education, which is a very different consideration. Judges in England and the United States do not act in the same way as judges in other countries: the former attach more importance to precedent, the latter to logical deduction and to the logical sequence of inferences from authorities and principles. The intention is to try and ensure that, no matter what points of national law may be involved in an international suit, all shall be equally comprehended; and further, since it is always possible to appoint a judge *ad hoc*, chosen by any party which does not already possess one of its nationality, whenever a particular legal system is involved in a case, to enable the other systems of law to be brought into line with it, so that the Bench may really and permanently represent the legal conceptions of all nations.

It was not enough therefore, to recommend the representation of the great legal systems of the world; the various forms of civilisation must also be represented. This is an essential condition, if the Permanent Court of International Justice is to be a real World Court for the Society of all Nations.

The Assembly and the Council therefore, in the election of the judges, must take care that the great forms of civilisation and the principal legal systems of the world are represented.

Article 9.

At every election, the electors shall bear in mind that not only should all the persons appointed as members of the Court possess the qualifications required, but the whole body also

semble, la représentation des grandes formes de civilisation et des principaux systèmes juridiques du monde.

Cette représentation détermine indirectement le nombre des juges: la Cour se composera de 15 membres, 11 juges titulaires et 4 juges suppléants. Ce n'est qu'un commencement. Plus tard, les Etats, momentanément écartés de la Société des Nations, prendront leur place: alors, le nombre des justiciables augmentant, l'Assemblée pourra, sur la proposition du Conseil, accroître le nombre des juges.

Mais comme on ne saurait trouver justice auprès d'un collège trop nombreux, en aucun cas la Cour ne pourra compter plus de 15 titulaires et 6 suppléants; c'est seulement jusqu'à concurrence de ce chiffre que le nombre des juges titulaires et des juges suppléants pourra être éventuellement augmenté par l'Assemblée sur la proposition du Conseil.

Article 3.

La Cour se compose de 15 membres: 11 juges titulaires et 4 juges suppléants. Le nombre des juges titulaires et des juges suppléants peut être éventuellement augmenté par l'Assemblée, sur la proposition du Conseil de la Société des Nations, à concurrence de 15 juges titulaires et de 6 juges suppléants.

COMMENT ÉLIRE LES JUGES?

Grâce à la liste de présentation dressée par chaque section nationale de la Cour d'Arbitrage de La Haye, les membres de l'Assemblée et du Conseil ont devant eux une liste de candidats qui n'excède pas le double des Etats appelés à participer à l'élection, c'est à dire, au maximum, théoriquement, près d'une centaine de membres et pratiquement guère plus d'une cinquantaine.

Dans ces conditions il peut y avoir, malgré le caractère relativement restreint de la liste, à raison du petit nombre des hommes vraiment dignes, en position d'accepter, certaines hésitations, quelques tâtonnements. Le plus souvent, pour un certain nombre de juges, il n'y aura guère de difficulté — les uns seront élus, les autres réélus, au premier tour d'élection, dans chacun des deux grands corps appelés à y procéder, Assemblée et Conseil. Mais, les premiers juges élus, il se peut qu'un certain nombre de sièges restent à pourvoir. La difficulté est

should represent the main forms of civilisation and the principal legal systems of the world.

This representation indirectly fixes the number of the judges. The Court is to be composed of 15 members: 11 judges and 4 deputy-judges; but this is only a beginning. Later on those States which are, for the time being, outside the League of Nations, will enter it: as and when this takes place, the Assembly, acting on the proposal of the Council, may increase the number of judges.

As, however, too large a body cannot administer justice satisfactorily, the composition of the Court must not exceed 15 judges and 6 deputies; this is the maximum to which the Assembly, acting on the Council's proposal, may increase the number of judges and deputy-judges.

Article 3.

The Court shall consist of 15 members: 11 judges and 4 deputy-judges. The number of judges and of deputy-judges may be hereafter increased by the Assembly, upon the proposal of the Council of the League of Nations, to a total of 15 judges and 6 deputy-judges.

THE METHOD OF ELECTING THE JUDGES.

The members of the Assembly and of the Council will have before them the list of nominations prepared by the national Sections of the Court of Arbitration of the Hague, which list will not exceed twice the number of the States taking part in the election, that is to say, in theory, about one hundred members, but actually hardly more than fifty.

Under these circumstances, in spite of the comparative shortness of the list, there may be a certain amount of hesitation and uncertainty owing to the very limited number of men really worthy of appointment and in a position to accept it. There will probably be no difficulty as a rule in the election of a certain number of judges — some will be elected and others re-elected at the first vote, by both the Council and the Assembly. But after the first judges have been elected, there may still be a certain number of vacancies. The difficulty is that a

qu'il ne suffit pas d'avoir la majorité, soit dans l'Assemblée, soit dans le Conseil, mais qu'il faut les obtenir à la fois dans l'un et l'autre corps.

Le Conseil et l'Assemblée, votant chacun séparément, pour assurer leur indépendance et leur égalité, il est possible que les noms des hommes qui, de part et d'autre, sont préférés, ne coincident pas.

D'abord, il se peut que plusieurs tours de scrutin se succèdent avant que chaque organe ait formé sa liste. Puis, il se peut que plusieurs séances electorales se succèdent sans que l'un et l'autre organe, Assemblée et Conseil, parvienne à former, chacun de son côté, une liste identique. Pour sortir du *deadlock*, il est donc nécessaire qu'à un moment donné ce procédé s'arrête. A quel moment? Après deux séances électorales? Après un plus grand nombre? D'abord fixée à deux séances, puis étendue à trois, la limite paraissait encore trop rapprochée à un certain nombre de membres du Comité, qui eussent préféré voir le Conseil et l'Assemblée décider simultanément du moment où l'on passerait de ce procédé à un autre. Alors se fit accepter une proposition transactionnelle qui, pour empêcher le conflit de s'éterniser, ouvre à l'un des deux corps, Assemblée ou Conseil, la faculté d'arrêter les séances électorales séparées. Immédiatement s'engage la procédure d'entente : Assemblée et Conseil désignent, chacun de son côté, parmi eux, trois membres, qui forment une Commission médiatrice.

Les six pourront d'autant plus aisément s'entendre qu'ils auront la possibilité de choisir en toute liberté leur candidat, pourvu que ce soit à l'unanimité. Règle très sage. Il se peut qu'un homme tout à fait désirable à la Cour ne soit pas en mesure, en raison d'imcompatibilités sur lesquelles on reviendra plus loin, d'accepter les fonctions de juge au temps de la présentation, mais qu'au moment de l'élection il soit libre : il faut que le choix puisse se porter sur lui. Ou encore il s'agit d'un homme qui, désiré, préférerait ne pas accepter les fonctions, et, dès lors, ne se laisserait porter sur aucune liste de présentation, mais qui, cependant, apparaît, au moment de procéder à la constitution de la Cour, comme l'homme nécessaire; il faut qu'on puisse tenter de le faire revenir sur un refus qu'en présence de cette nécessité, il hésitera peut-être à maintenir. Enfin il faut qu'un homme qui n'a pas voulu livrer son nom au hasard d'une élection puisse être sollicité d'entrer à

majority in either the Assembly or the Council is not sufficient by itself; it must be obtained in both bodies.

As, in order to ensure their independence and equality, the Council and the Assembly vote separately, it may well be that the names obtaining most support in each body are not the same.

In the first place it may happen that several votes have to be taken before either body has completed its list. Further it may happen that, even after several sittings, the two bodies, the Council and the Assembly, will not have succeeded in preparing an identical list. In order to prevent a deadlock, it must be laid down that this procedure terminates at a given moment. When is this to be? After two sittings, or after a larger number? The number of sittings was at first limited to two, and later to three, but some members of the Committee thought that this was too restrictive, and they would have preferred that the Council and the Assembly should decide simultaneously at what point this procedure should be superseded by another. A compromise was therefore adopted which gives both to the Assembly and to the Council the power of ending the separate electoral sessions, in order to avoid an indefinite continuance of the deadlock. The conclusion of the electoral sessions is immediately followed by a procedure intended to reconcile the opposing views : the Assembly and the Council each appoint, from amongst their members, three representatives to form a Joint Conference.

Agreement between the six members is made easier by the fact that they have a completely free hand in choosing candidates, provided that such choice is unanimous. This is a very sensible provision. It may well happen that a man, whom it is most desirable to have on the Court, is not in a position to accept an appointment as judge when the nominations are made, on account of some disqualification (a subject which is dealt with later on) but that at the time of the election he is free to accept. It is highly desirable that it should be possible to choose him. Or again, it may be that a man whom it is desirable to appoint, prefers not to accept an appointment, and therefore, does not suffer himself to be nominated; later, when the constitution of the Court is in progress, he seems to be the very man required; it should therefore be possible to try and induce him to withdraw his refusal, in consideration of the special circumstances.

la Cour, en toute certitude, à l'unanimité.

S'il convenait d'élargir le cercle des éligibles en cessant d'exiger la condition d'une présentation directe par les différentes sections de la Cour d'Arbitrage, il fallait prendre une garantie contre le choix arbitraire, à ce moment, sous des influences politiques, de deux corps d'un caractère éminemment politique, Assemblée et Conseil. Aussi, pour avoir la possibilité d'élire, dans ces conditions, sans présentation par un groupe national de la Cour d'Arbitrage, il est nécessaire que les six membres de la Commission médiatrice s'accordent sur le même nom.

La Commission médiatrice ayant, en elle, réalisé l'entente, propose autant de noms qu'il y a de sièges à pourvoir à l'Assemblée d'une part, au Conseil de l'autre, et chacun de ces corps, au rapport de ceux de ses membres qui se trouvent dans la majorité du Conseil et de l'Assemblée, vote pour le nom recommandé par cette majorité, ou, dans les cas exceptionnels auquel on faisait allusion tout à l'heure, accepté à l'unanimité.

Y a-t-il lieu de prévoir que, dans la Commission médiatrice, aucune entente ne se forme? Hypothèse sans doute bien problématique, mais un système électoral doit être conçu de manière à ce qu'aucune éventualité ne soit omise.

Dans le cas où la Commission médiatrice ne pourrait aboutir, à l'expiration d'un temps qu'il n'appartient qu'à elle et au Conseil et à l'Assemblée, sous l'autorité desquels elle procède, de déterminer, c'est aux élus déjà nommés qu'est laissé le soin de procéder par cooptation à la détermination des autres.

La Cour se trouve ainsi constituée, d'abord pour neuf ans, puis pour autant de périodes de neuf ans, qu'il s'en présentera.

L'élection, d'abord faite pour les juges titulaires, se fait ensuite, de la même manière, pour les juges suppléants.

En aucun cas, la Cour ne peut compter sur le siège plus d'un juge de la même nationalité. La règle n'était pas aussi stricte dans le projet des cinq Puissances (qui acceptait deux juges de la même nationalité), mais elle résulte nécessairement des deux considérations suivantes: assurer la représentation des grandes formes de civilisation et des principaux systèmes juridiques du monde; permettre aux Etats de participer

Lastly, it should be possible by a unanimous decision to request a man, who was unwilling to submit his name to the uncertainties of an election, to accept an assured appointment upon the Court.

Though it seemed desirable to give more scope for choice by the removal of the condition stipulating direct nomination by the various sections of the Court of Arbitration, at the same time a guarantee had to be created to prevent an arbitrary choice made under the political influences of two such essentially political bodies as the Assembly and the Council. It is therefore stipulated that before a name which has not been submitted by one of the national groups of the Court of Arbitration can be chosen, the six members of the Joint Conference must be unanimous.

When the Joint Conference has come to an agreement, it is to propose to the Council on the one hand and to the Assembly on the other, as many names as there are vacancies to be filled; each of these bodies after hearing the majority report of the members of the Joint Conference, will vote for the name which is recommended by this majority, or in the exceptional case mentioned above, accepted unanimously by the Conference.

The question then arises whether there is any need to provide for the possibility of a deadlock in the Joint Conference. This is no doubt extremely unlikely, but an electoral system must provide for every conceivable eventuality.

Should the Joint Conference not find a solution within a time limit to be fixed by itself, and by the Council and the Assembly, by whose authority it is formed, the judges already elected are entrusted with the election of the remainder by co-optation.

The Court is thus constituted; in the first place for a period of nine years, and for equal periods thereafter.

The election of the judges is first carried out; that of the deputy-judges follows, and is carried out in the same manner.

The Court can never include more than one judge of the same nationality. This rule was not so strict in the plan of the Five Powers (which allowed two judges of the same nationality), but it is necessary for the two following reasons: to ensure the representation of the main forms of civilisation and the principal legal systems of the world; and to enable as many States as possible to have a share in the composition of

le plus largement possible à la constitution d'une Cour par laquelle ils doivent être jûgés, ce qui, même si l'on établit un mode spécial de juges de la nationalité des parties, n'en a pas moins l'utilité de rendre ce mécanisme complémentaire aussi rare que possible.

Article 11.

Si après la première séance d'élection il reste encore des sièges à pourvoir, il est procédé de la même manière à une seconde, puis à une troisième.

Dans la pensée du Comité, les juges étant élus pour neuf ans, tous les neuf ans les Etats ont à choisir d'abord 15 membres de la Cour (11 juges titulaires et 4 juges suppléants) et plus tard, au maximum, 21 membres (15 juges titulaires et 6 juges suppléants.)

Non seulement il y aura lieu de procéder ainsi la première fois, mais il conviendra de procéder de même à l'expiration du délai de neuf ans, choisi pour garantir une certaine continuité de jurisprudence en même temps que pour assurer aux Etats la possibilité d'écarter les juges qui, sans être véritablement hors d'état de continuer leur tâche, ne répondraient cependant plus à la confiance que, tout d'abord, les Etats auraient mise en eux.

Il est indispensable que les juges soient rééligibles. Ainsi ceux qui ont rendu de véritables services, et bien mérité de la Société des Nations par une administration de la justice aussi éclairée qu'impartiale, resteront en fonctions. Dès lors, on peut, tous les neuf ans, procéder au renouvellement de la Cour. Si l'un des juges vient à laisser son siège par mort, démission ou toute autre cause avant le terme des neuf ans, son successeur doit-il être nommé pour un même terme de neuf ans, ou seulement jusqu'à l'expiration des neuf ans commencés? Dans le premier cas, le terme des fonctions des juges venant à des époques très différentes, on assurerait, par l'enchevêtrement des mandats, une plus grande suite de traditions de jurisprudence.

Mais, pour obtenir cet avantage, on peut croire qu'il suffira de la sage réélection des juges dont les services à la Cour mériteront une nouvelle marque de confiance, sans qu'il leur manque aucune des forces nécessaires à l'accomplissement de leurs fonctions. Avant tout, il convient de laisser plus de jeu, au moment de l'élection, à la liberté des Etats, en faisant procéder tous les neuf ans à une redistribution générale des sièges.

the Court by which they are to be judged; though a special provision is made for the inclusion of judges of the nationality of contesting parties, this rule serves the purpose of making the use of this exceptional procedure as rare as possible.

Article 11.

If, after the first sitting held for the purpose of election, one or more seats remain to be filled, a second, and if necessary, a third sitting shall take place.

The Committee was of opinion that, as the judges were to be elected for nine years, every nine years the States must choose, at first 15 members for the Court (11 judges and 4 deputy-judges), and later, a maximum of 21 members (15 judges and 6 deputy-judges).

This would have to be carried out not only at the first election but at the expiration of each nine year period. This period was chosen in order to ensure to some extent the continuity of jurisprudence, and also to make it possible for States to eliminate judges who, though not actually unfit for their duties, no longer justify the confidence that the States at one time reposed in them.

The judges must be eligible for re-election. This will ensure that those who have done good service and have deserved well of the League of Nations by their enlightened and impartial administration of justice retain their positions. The Court can thus be reconstituted every nine years. If a judge dies, resigns, or vacates his seat for any other reason before the expiration of nine years, the question arises whether his successor should be appointed for a fresh period of nine years, or only for the unexpired portion of the period. If the former alternative were adopted, the mandates of the judges would expire at varying times, and a greater continuity in the traditions of jurisprudence would thus be assured.

But this advantage should be sufficiently assured by the judicious re-election of those judges whose services merit a renewal of the trust committed to them, provided that they retain the powers needed in the performance of their functions. Above all, the free play afforded to States at the time of election, by a general redistribution of seats every nine years, is very desirable.

Article 14.

Il est pourvu aux sièges devenus vacants selon la méthode suivie pour la première élection. Le membre de la Cour élu en remplacement d'un membre dont le mandat n'est pas expiré achève le terme du mandat de son prédécesseur.

Toutes les dispositions qui s'appliquent à l'élection des juges titulaires, s'appliquent également à celle, qui suit immédiatement, des juges suppléants.

Article 15.

Les juges suppléants sont appelés dans l'ordre du tableau.

Le tableau est dressé par la Cour, en tenant compte, d'abord de la priorité d'élection et ensuite de l'ancienneté d'âge.

Il ne suffit pas d'assurer le recrutement de la Cour par une élection entourée de toutes les garanties de réflexion, de connaissance et de liberté. Il faut encore ne pas éloigner l'homme de la fonction par des incompatibilités trop nombreuses.

La permanence de la Cour implique, de la part des juges, qu'ils soient toujours prêts à venir siéger. En outre l'importance de leurs fonctions, d'ailleurs largement rémunérées, en permet difficilement le cumul avec d'autres. Cependant la Cour doit pouvoir se recruter parmi les meilleurs; or, les meilleurs sont précisément ceux que réclament, dans leur pays, des fonctions d'où leurs nations, à raison des services qu'ils y rendent, ne les laisseraient pas volontiers se dégager.

D'autre part, il se peut qu'à l'origine l'activité de la Cour ne soit pas très intense. Des hommes de grande compétence, hautement désireux de se rendre utiles, ne se laisseraient pas retenir exclusivement par des occupations d'un caractère trop intermittent. Pour toutes ces raisons les incompatibilités ne pouvaient être fixées par le Comité d'une manière très stricte. Un haut magistrat, un grand professeur, que la confiance des nations appelle à la Cour, doit pouvoir continuer, le magistrat à juger dans son pays, le professeur à donner son enseignement: pour eux, aucune espèce d'incompatibilité.

Article 14.

Vacancies which may occur shall be filled by the same method as that laid down for the first election. A member of the Court elected to replace a member, the period of whose appointment has not expired, will hold the appointment for the remainder of his predecessor's term.

All clauses which apply to the election of judges apply equally to that of deputy judges, which follows immediately afterwards.

Article 15.

Deputy-judges shall be called upon to sit in the order laid down in a list.

This list shall be prepared by the Court, having regard first to the order in time of each election and secondly to age.

It is not enough to ensure that the election of members of the Court is carried out with mature consideration, full knowledge and complete freedom. In addition care must be taken not to erect a barrier between the man and the Bench by creating too great a number of grounds of disqualification.

The permanence of the Court implies that the judges should always be ready to take their seats upon it. Besides, the importance of their duties, which are, incidentally, very highly paid, does not readily permit them to be exercised in conjunction with others. The Court, however, must be recruited from the very best men, and it is the best men who, in their countries, are needed for positions which by reason of their valuable services they will not readily be allowed to leave.

On the other hand, it may well happen that, at the outset, the amount of work before the Court will not be very great. Men of great ability, and intensely anxious to do useful work, will not suffer themselves to be limited to the performance of duties of too intermittent a nature. For the above reasons, the Committee felt that it could not formulate the provisions dealing with incompatibility very strictly. A great judge or a great professor, in whom the nations have sufficient confidence to call him to the Court, must be allowed to continue in his present functions — the judge to administer justice in his country, and the professor to give his lectures —: no incompatibility exists in their cases.

De même, un parlementaire éminent pourra garder son mandat législatif. Mais un membre du Gouvernement, Ministre ou sous-secrétaire d'Etat, un représentant diplomatique, un directeur de Ministère, ou l'un de ses subordonnés, le jurisconsulte d'un Ministère des Affaires étrangères, bien qu'il puisse être investi des fonctions d'arbitre à la Cour de 1899, ne saurait l'être des fonctions de juge à notre Cour. D'une part, il n'aurait pas de vacances suffisantes pour concilier ces deux fonctions. D'autre part, il n'aurait pas l'indépendance nécessaire pour siéger à la Cour, parce que, engagé à fond dans la politique active, il n'aura pas la sérénité d'esprit nécessaire à l'exercice de cette haute fonction. Si, au moment d'une élection à la Cour, l'élu est dans cette situation, son élection n'est pas nulle: il s'agit ici d'une incompatibilité, non d'une incapacité; mais il doit opter dans le délai fixé par le règlement intérieur de la Cour. Si, postérieurement à son entrée à la Cour, un juge accepte des fonctions, dont le caractère d'activité politique ne lui permet pas de garder son siège, il peut être mis en demeure d'opter dès l'instant qu'il est constaté qu'il les a effectivement acceptées.

L'incompatibilité des fonctions de juge avec la participation active à la direction politique d'un pays déterminé s'étend également au cas d'une activité internationale, telle que celle qui résulterait de la qualité de représentant d'une nation Membre de la Société soit au Conseil, soit à l'Assemblée, de Secrétaire-Général, ou, à un titre quelconque, de membre du Secrétariat de la Société des Nations. Mais, de même que la qualité de membre de la Cour n'est pas incompatible avec celle de membre d'un tribunal national, elle ne l'est pas davantage avec celle de membre d'un tribunal international, notamment, de membre de la Cour d'Arbitrage de La Haye: solution déjà admise pour la Cour de Justice arbitrale de 1907, dont les membres peuvent faire partie de la Cour Permanente d'Arbitrage; ainsi se soudent, une fois de plus, les liens des deux Cours.

Mais, à partir du jour où le juge entre en fonctions, il ne peut plus exercer comme agent, conseil, ou avocat dans aucune affaire d'ordre international, fût-ce même de son propre pays: incompatibilité que ne connaissait pas la Cour d'Arbitrage, mais qu'il n'est pas permis d'oublier dans une Cour de Justice.

Similarly, an eminent member of Parliament may retain his legislative function. On the other hand, a member of a Government, a Minister or Under-Secretary of State, a diplomatic representative, a director of a Ministry, or one of his subordinates, or the legal adviser to a Foreign Office, though they would be eligible for appointment as Arbitrators to the Court of 1899, are certainly not eligible for appointment as judges upon our Court. On the one hand, the vacations would not be sufficiently long to admit of the two duties being combined, and on the other hand such persons would not possess the independent spirit required in judges of the Court, because, being deeply engaged in active politics, they would not have the serenity of mind which is so essential in the performance of such duties. If the person elected holds such an office at the time of the election, his election is not void; the question is one of incompatibility, not of disqualification. He must however, decide which of the two posts he will occupy, within a time limit to be laid down in the Court's rules of procedure. If, after taking his seat, a judge accepts a post involving active political work which is incompatible with the retention of his seat on the Court, he may be called upon to make his choice directly it is known that he has actually accepted the post.

The incompatibility between the duties of a judge and an active part in the political control of a particular country, also applies in the case of international political duties, such as those of the representative of a State, which is a Member of the League of Nations, either in the Council or in the Assembly, or of Secretary-General, or of member, in any capacity, of the Secretariat of the League of Nations; but just as membership of the Court is not incompatible with that of a national tribunal, neither is it with that of membership of an international tribunal, in particular, membership of the Court of Arbitration of the Hague: this view was taken in 1907 in the case of the Court of Arbitral Justice, the members of which were also to be permitted to belong to the Permanent Court of Arbitration. Thus yet another link between the two Courts is created.

But once the judge has taken up his duties, he may no longer act as representative, counsel or advocate in any case of an international nature, even on behalf of his own country. This incompatibility, though not recognised by the Court of Arbitration, must be taken into account by a Court of Justice.

Article 16.

L'exercice de toute fonction qui relève de la direction politique, soit nationale, soit internationale, des Etats est incompatible avec la qualité de membre de la Cour.

En cas de doute la Cour décide.

Article 16.

The exercise of any function which belongs to the political direction, national or international, of States by the members of the Court during their terms of office, is declared incompatible with their judicial duties.

Any doubt upon this point is settled by the decision of the Court.

Article 17.

Les membres de la Cour ne peuvent exercer les fonctions d'agent, de conseil ou d'avocat dans aucune affaire d'ordre international.

Ils ne peuvent participer au règlement d'aucune affaire dans laquelle ils sont antérieurement intervenus comme agents, conseils ou avocats de l'une des parties, membres d'un Tribunal national ou international, d'une Commission d'enquête, ou à tout autre titre.

En cas de doute la Cour décide.

Article 17.

No member of the Court can act as agent, counsel or advocate in any case of an international nature.

No member may participate in the decision of any case in which he has previously taken an active part, as agent, counsel or advocate for one of the contesting parties, or as a member of a national or international Court, or of a Commission of Inquiry, or in any other capacity.

Any doubt upon this point is settled by the decision of the Court.

Il ne suffit pas, pour la Cour, de s'assurer les meilleurs hommes, il faut encore prendre garde qu'ils restent les meilleurs: l'âge, la maladie, peuvent faire fléchir la vigueur physique, l'intégrité intellectuelle. Dans ce cas, c'est à la Cour qu'il appartiendra, au jugement unanime de ses membres, de décider s'ils seront relévés de leurs fonctions.

The Court must not only ensure that it obtains the best men, it must also take care that they remain the best. Age or sickness may affect their physical vigour and their intellectual powers. In such cases, it is for the Court to decide whether they are to be relieved of their duties; its decision must be unanimous.

Article 18.

Les membres de la Cour ne peuvent être relevés de leurs fonctions que si, au jugement unanime des autres membres, ils ont cessé de répondre aux conditions requises.

Le Secrétaire-Général de la Société des Nations en est officiellement informé.

Cette communication emporte vacance de siège.

Article 18.

A member of the Court cannot be dismissed unless, in the unanimous opinion of the other members, he has ceased to fulfil the required conditions.

When this happens a formal notification shall be given to the Secretary-General.

This notification makes the place vacant.

En rehaussant, par une assimilation des plus honorables, le prestige inhérent à leur haute valeur personnelle, le projet donne, en dehors de leurs propres pays, aux membres de la Cour, les mêmes privilèges et immunités qu'aux agents diplomatiques.

The members of the Court are given by this plan the same rights and immunities as diplomatic agents, outside their own country; the grant of these privileges will increase the prestige due to their great personal merits.

Article 19.

En dehors de leur propre pays, les membres de la Cour jouissent des mêmes privilèges et immunités que les Agents diplomatiques.

Article 19.

The members of the Court, when outside their own country, shall enjoy the privileges and immunities of diplomatic representatives.

Tout, dans la Cour, étant ainsi préparé pour qu'elle soit et reste composée des meilleurs, il n'y a plus, l'élection finie ou renouvelée, qu'à déterminer comment le juge, ainsi appelé au siège, exercera ses fonctions parmi ses collègues.

After every precaution has thus been taken to ensure that the Court shall consist, and shall continue to consist of the best men, and after the question of election or re-election, it only remains to decide in what manner the judges, thus appointed, shall carry out their duties.

FONCTIONNEMENT DE LA COUR.

Pour assurer le bon fonctionnement de la Cour de Justice Internationale, convenait-il de lui donner le même siège qu'aux autres organes de la Société des Nations? Aux termes de l'article 7 du Pacte, le siège de la Société des Nations est établi à Genève; mais il n'est pas dit que tous les organes de la Société doivent s'y fixer. De si grands souvenirs d'espérance pacifique et de progrès juridique s'attachent à La Haye, surtout depuis la construction, peu de temps avant la guerre, du Palais de la Paix, qu'afin de renouer les traditions anciennes, en rendant un légitime hommage à l'œuvre des grands devanciers, la Cour de Justice de la Société des Nations ne saurait manquer de venir se fixer au point, où, depuis 1899, la Cour d'Arbitrage est elle-même établie. A l'unanimité, le Comité a pensé que le siège de la Cour devait être fixé à La Haye.

THE OPERATION OF THE COURT.

Should the seat of the Court of International Justice be established in the same town as the other organisations of the League of Nations, in order to assure its efficient operation? According to Article 7 of the Covenant, the seat of the League of Nations is established at Geneva; but it was not stated that all the organisations of the League should be established there. Such a high tradition of pacific hopes and legal progress surrounds The Hague, especially since the construction of the Peace Palace shortly before the War, that the Court of Justice of the League of Nations should undoubtedly be established at the place which, since 1899, has been the seat of the Court of Arbitration, in order to create a link with this tradition and as an act of well merited homage to the work of its great predecessors. The Committee unanimously decided that the seat of the Court ought to be at The Hague.

Article 22.

Le siège de la Cour est fixé à La Haye.

Le Président et le Greffier résident au siège de la Cour.

Les membres de la Cour ne sont pas astreints, hors le Président et le Greffier, à résidence permanente. Il leur suffit de venir au moment des sessions. Le petit nombre des affaires, qui, au début, pourraient être soumises à la Cour, le désir d'occuper effectivement hors du pays du siège des fonctions, qui demandent au moins 5 à 6 mois de résidence, tendaient naturellement à limiter la permanence de la Cour à une session semestrielle.

Article 22.

The seat of the Court shall be established at the Hague.

The President and the Registrar shall reside at the seat of the Court.

The members of the Court, apart from the President and the Registrar, are not bound to reside there permanently. They need only attend the sessions. The small number of cases which at the outset would probably be submitted to the Court, combined with the fact that the judges will probably wish to perform duties requiring at least 5 or 6 months residence outside the country in which the Court has its seat, will naturally tend to limit the permanence of the Court to a half-yearly session.

Article 23.

La Cour tient une session chaque année.

Sauf disposition contraire du règlement d'ordre de la Cour, cette session commence te 15 juin, et continue tant que le rôle n'est pas épuisé.

Article 23.

A session shall be held every year.

Unless otherwise provided by rules of Court, this session shall begin on the 15th June, and shall continue for so long as may be necessary to complete the cases on the list.

Le Président convoque la Cour en session extra-ordinaire quand les circonstances l'exigent.

The President may summon an extraordinary meeting of the Court whenever necessary.

Des 11 juges et 4 suppléants, qui, pendant un certain temps, composeront seuls la Cour, les 11 titulaires doivent, soit au 15 juin, en session ordinaire, soit, sur convocation spéciale du Président en session extraordinaire, se rendre à La Haye. Leur réunion forme le plenum de la Cour. On s'était demandé s'il n'y avait pas lieu, dans l'intérêt d'une bonne justice, de permettre à la Cour, par son règlement d'ordre intérieur, de se diviser en chambres de 5 juges et même de permettre aux parties, pour obtenir une justice plus rapide, et surtout plus économique, de réduire, par leur accord, le nombre des juges de 11 à 5. Mais cette disposition eût rompu l'unité de la Cour. C'est dans la justice arbitrale qu'il appartient aux parties de restreindre ou d'augmenter à leur gré le nombre des juges. C'est seulement en vue de la prompte expédition des affaires qu'à la demande des parties la Cour pourrait les diriger vers une chambre de 3 juges appelés à statuer en procédure sommaire, d'après un règlement d'ordre intérieur qui, s'inspirant de la Convention de 1907, dira qu'en pareil cas la procédure n'est pas orale, mais écrite.

Of the 11 judges and 4 deputy-judges of which the Court will at first consist, the 11 judges are bound to come to The Hague, on the 15th June for the ordinary session, or whenever an extraordinary session is summoned by the President. A meeting of these judges constitutes the full Court. The question was raised as to whether it would not be in the interests of the administration of Justice to allow the Court, in its rules of procedure, to divide itself into Chambers consisting of 5 judges, and further to allow the contesting parties, by mutual agreement, to reduce the number of judges from 11 to 5, in order to obtain an earlier decision and to save expense. But such a provision would have destroyed the unity of the Court. It is only in arbitration that the parties have the right to limit or increase the number of judges at their will. The only exception is that the Court may, at the request of the parties and in order to obtain a speedy decision, recommend the use of a section of 3 judges formed to hear cases by a summary procedure based on rules of Court, which, being derived from the Convention of 1907, will expressly state that in such cases the procedure will not be oral but written.

Article 26.

En vue de la prompte expédition des affaires, la Cour compose annuellement une chambre de trois juges, appelée à statuer en procédure sommaire, lorsque les parties le demandent.

Article 26.

With a view to the speedy despatch of business the Court shall form, annually, a chamber composed of three judges who, at the request of the contesting parties, may hear and determine cases by summary procedure.

Article 27.

La Cour détermine, par un règlement d'ordre, le mode suivant lequel elle exerce ses attributions. Elle règle spécialement la procédure sommaire.

Article 27.

The Court shall frame rules for regulating its procedure. In particular, it shall lay down rules for summary procedure.

Sauf cette exception de la procédure sommaire, la Cour exerce ses attributions en séance plénière. Si 11 juges ne sont pas présents, il est pourvu à leur remplacement, jusqu'à concurrence de ce nombre, en faisant appel aux juges suppléants dans l'ordre de leur inscription au tableau, c'est

Except in this case of the summary procedure, the full Court shall sit. If 11 judges are not present, this number shall be completed by calling upon the deputy-judges in the order in which they are contained on a list, drawn up in accordance with the order of their election

à dire en tenant compte, d'abord de la priorité de l'élection, et ensuite de l'ancienneté d'âge. Par cette disposition, la situation du juge suppléant se relève; ses chances d'entrer en fonction augmentent. Ce résultat présente de nombreux avantages: il intéresse les Etats qui, n'espérant pas, à raison de leur importance, un juge titulaire, voient s'ouvrir devant eux la possibilité d'exercer, par un juge suppléant, une participation à la Cour. D'autre part, en donnant une réelle activité aux juges suppléants, on favorise le recrutement d'une magistrature capable parmi des hommes qui, d'affaire en affaire, auront pris, avec l'expérience judiciaire, l'esprit de suite indispensable à la continuité des traditions de la Cour. Elus de la même manière que les juges titulaires, quoiqu'après eux, devant présenter les mêmes conditions de capacité, frappés des mêmes incompatibilités, tenus à la même déclaration solennelle avant d'entrer en fonction, les juges suppléants ne se séparent des juges titulaires que par l'intermittence de leur activité. Un juge titulaire a-t-il un empêchement momentané? Le suppléant le remplace. Un juge titulaire est-il atteint d'une incapacité absolue de continuer ses fonctions et son siège est-il déclaré vacant? Le juge suppléant prend ce siège jusqu'à la prochaine élection. Ainsi, le rôle du suppléant n'est pas seulement honorifique, mais actif. Il est membre de la Cour au même titre que le juge titulaire. On peut prévoir que ces fonctions ne manqueront pas d'être effectives: l'article 25 y contribuera.

and their age. This provision improves the position of deputy-judges; their chances of sitting are increased. This has various advantages; it is made possible for States which are not sufficiently important to hope to obtain a judge of their nationality, to take a share in the operations of the Court, in the person of a deputy-judge. On the other hand, the active employment of the deputy-judges, makes possible a supply of capable judges, drawn from men who have, in case after case, gained judicial experience and that sequence of ideas which is essential for the continuity of the Court's traditions The deputy-judges are elected in the same way as the judges, though after them, must possess the same qualifications, are subject to the same incompatibilities, and must make the same solemn declaration before entering upon their duties; they only differ in that their employment is intermittent. If a judge is temporarily prevented from sitting, a deputy takes his place. If a judge is permanently incapacitated from carrying out his duties, and his seat therefore becomes vacant, a deputy takes his place until the next election. So that the appointment of a deputy judge is not a mere sinecure, but involves active employment. He is a member of the Court, just as much as a regular judge. It is easy to foresee that the deputy-judges will be actively employed. Article 25 tends to this effect.

Art. 25.

Sauf exception expressément prévue, la Cour exerce ses attributions en séance plénière.

Si la présence de onze juges titulaires n'est pas assurée, ce nombre est parfait par l'entrée en fonction des juges suppléants.

Toutefois, si onze juges ne sont pas disponibles, le quorum de neuf est suffisant pour constituer la Cour.

Article 25.

The full Court shall sit except when it is expressly provided otherwise.

If eleven judges cannot be present, deputy-judges shall be called upon to sit, in order to make up this number.

If, however, eleven judges are not available, a quorum of nine judges shall suffice to constitute the Court.

L'une des plus difficiles questions était celle de la présence au siège du juge de la nationalité des parties.

Aux termes de l'Art. 2 du projet, la Cour Permanente de Justice Internationale est une Cour de magistrats indépendants, élus sans égard à leur nationalité. Mais, si les juges sont élus sans aucune considération de nationalité, il n'en demeure pas moins qu'une fois au siège ils gardent cette nationalité. Ayant fait

One of the most difficult questions was that of the inclusion on the Court of judges of the nationality of the contesting parties.

According to Article 2 of the plan, the Court is a body of independent judges elected regardless of their nationality. If, however, the judges are elected without regard to their nationality, the fact still remains that they retain their nationality after appointment to the Court. As they have given a solemn undertaking to ad-

la déclaration solennelle de juger en toute conscience, en pleine impartialité, il n'est pas à craindre qu'ils manquent à leur devoir en ayant pour l'Etat dont ils sont les ressortissants une préférence quelconque. Choisis parmi des hommes jouissant de la plus haute considération morale, on peut être sûr que leurs scrupules de justice seront plus grands encore quand ils auront en face d'eux, comme plaideur, l'Etat dont ils ont la nationalité; mais il ne suffit pas que la justice soit juste, il faut encore qu'elle le paraisse; non seulement le juge doit être impartial, mais son impartialité ne saurait être suspectée par personne.

Dès lors, deux hypothèses, bientôt suivies d'une troisième, se présentent:

Première hypothèse. Si les deux parties ont chacune un juge sur le siège, on comprendrait que chacun de ces juges s'abstînt. Mais il se pourrait que le quorum des juges descendît ainsi dans des proportions trop fortes, alors surtout que plusieurs Etats viendraient ensemble comme parties jointes dans un même procès. Les différentes formes de civilisation et les principaux systèmes juridiques du monde, qui doivent donner à notre Cour son caractère universel, risqueraient de ne plus trouver une représentation nécessaire à la bonne administration de la justice.

Il est d'autre part éminemment désirable que les juges puissent, dans les délibérations, faire entendre jusqu'au dernier moment les arguments et moyens de l'Etat et veiller à ce que les termes de la sentence, si pénible puisse-t-elle être au fond, soient conçus de manière à ne froisser, à aucun degré, les susceptibilités nationales. Enfin, les deux points de vue opposés se trouvant représentés au siège se font équilibre.

Il ne saurait donc être question, quand deux parties ont un juge de leur nationalité au siège, de le faire s'abstenir.

La Cour composée de juges choisis sans égard à leur nationalité doit rester la même dans sa composition, alors que les deux plaideurs, ou groupes de plaideurs, sont chacun représentés sur le siège.

Deuxième hypothèse. Si l'une des parties est représentée sur le siège, l'autre non, il n'y a pas de raison pour que le juge déjà nommé se retire — par là notre Cour ressemble à un tribunal interne; mais, d'autre part, si la composition de la Cour ne subissait aucune modification et bien qu'avec des hommes de la moralité de nos juges il n'y ait à craindre aucune partialité, l'opinion publique de l'Etat

minister justice impartially and conscientiously, there is no danger that they will fail in their duty by showing any partiality towards the State whose subjects they are. Chosen as they are from amongst men of the highest moral character, one may rest assured that their scruples in the administration of justice will be increased in the event of their having before them as a party the State whose subjects they are. Justice, however, must not only be just, but appear so. A judge must not only be impartial, but there must be no possibility of suspecting his impartiality.

Therefore there are two possibilities, to which a third may be added.

First possibility. If both parties have a judge upon the Bench, it would be logical if both of these judges abstained from sitting. But it might well happen that the number of judges would in this way be too much diminished, especially if several States had a joint interest in the same proceedings. There would be a risk that the various forms of civilisation and the principal legal systems of the world, which are to give our Court its character as a World Court, would not be sufficiently represented for the satisfactory administration of Justice.

Further it is highly desirable that the judges should be able up to the last minute during the deliberations, to put forward and explain the statements and arguments of the States, and to ensure that the sentence, however painful it may be in substance, should be drawn up so as to avoid ruffling national susceptibilities in any way. Lastly, if the opposing views are both represented on the Bench, they counterbalance one another.

When each of the two parties has a judge of its nationality upon the Bench, there will therefore be no question of their abstention from sitting.

When each of the two parties or groups of parties is represented on the Bench, the composition of the Court of judges selected regardless of their nationality must not be changed.

Second possibility. If one of the parties is represented on the Bench and not the other, this is no reason for the judge already appointed to withdraw — in this respect our Court resembles a national tribunal; but on the other hand, if the composition of the Court underwent no change, although with men of the high moral character of our judges there would be no occasion to fear any lapse from impartiality, public opinion

sans juge au siège pourrait s'inquiéter d'une inégalité qui frapperait cet Etat, non comme Etat, mais comme plaideur.

Ne pouvant, pour les raisons déjà données, faire retirer le juge de la nationalité de l'une des parties, il faut, pour rétablir l'égalité, faire monter sur le siège le juge suppléant de la nationalité de l'autre partie ou, à son défaut, un juge exceptionnellement nommé pour la circonstance par elle, en le choisissant de préférence parmi les personnes qui ont été l'objet d'une présentation de la part des groupes nationaux de la Cour d'Arbitrage.

Troisième hypothèse. Aucun des juges du siège n'a la nationalité d'un des Etats en cause. Dans ce cas encore il n'est pas inutile qu'ils puissent, chacun, désigner, pour siéger, un juge suppléant de sa nationalité, ou, à défaut, choisir un juge pris de préférence parmi les personnes qui ont été l'objet d'une présentation de la part des groupes nationaux de la Cour d'Arbitrage.

Sous ce rapport, notre Cour s'écarte du type de la Cour de Justice interne pour se rapprocher de la Cour d'Arbitrage. Mais cet écart est nécessaire. Si notre Cour est une Cour, il ne faut pas oublier que c'est une Cour entre Etats. Et les Etats tiennent à faire monter, quand ils viennent devant la justice, pour les raisons déjà données, un des leurs sur le siège.

in the State without a judge on the Bench might consider that this inequality would affect it adversely, not as a State, but in its position as a contesting party.

It follows therefore that, as we cannot exclude the judge of the same nationality as one of the parties, a deputy-judge of the nationality of the other party must be summoned to take his seat on the Bench in order to re-establish equality; failing a deputy-judge, a judge must be specially appointed for the particular case by that party, preferably chosen from amongst those persons who have been nominated by the national groups of the Court of Arbitration.

Third possibility. There may be no judge on the Bench of the nationality of any of the States concerned. In this eventuality also it is advisable that each party should be entitled to appoint a deputy-judge of its nationality to take his seat; failing a deputy-judge, they should choose a judge preferably selected from those persons who have been nominated by the national groups of the Court of Arbitration.

In this particular, our Court more nearly resembles a Court of Arbitration than a national Court of Justice. But this variation is necessary. Though our Court is a true Court, we must not forget that it is a Court between States. For the reasons already given, States attach much importance to having one of their subjects on the Bench when they appear before a Court of Justice.

II.

COMPETENCE.

A quels plaideurs la Cour est-elle ouverte? Aux particuliers contre des Etats ou seulement à des Etats contre des Etats?

Un particulier traite avec un Etat étranger, dans l'exercice, non de sa souveraineté politique, mais de son activité économique, de la même manière qu'il le ferait avec un autre étranger, sur le pied de l'égalité. Sachant toute la difficulté de trouver justice devant les tribunaux internes, soit de cet Etat, soit de tout autre, à raison, à l'intérieur, de l'irresponsabilité, à l'extérieur, de l'indépendance de l'Etat, certaines propositions doctrinales demandent qu'ici l'individu puisse citer directement l'Etat devant une haute juridiction internationale:

II.

COMPETENCE.

To whom shall the Court be open? May private persons appear against States or only States against States?

Suppose that a private person has dealings with a foreign State, not in its character as a sovereign State, but in economic matters upon a footing of equality, exactly as he would with another foreigner. In view of the great difficulty of obtaining justice before national tribunals, whether of the State in question or of any other, arising out of a State's internal irresponsibility and external independence, certain theoretical proposals have been put forward to the effect that an individual should be able to bring an action directly against States before some high inter-

cette juridiction pourrait-elle être notre Cour ?

Pour prendre un cas, moins cité mais plus délicat encore, un particulier, que deux Etats se disputeraient comme national, ne pourrait-il assigner l'un d'entre eux, ou même les deux, pour faire juger quelle est, vis-à-vis d'eux, sa véritable nationalité? Ces problèmes peuvent être intéressants mais, pour l'instant, ils sont prématurés parce qu'ils tendent à mettre en question la souveraineté, l'indépendance, et même l'existence des Etats.

Le Comité a été unanime à penser que, sans rien préjuger du développement ultérieur de la Cour Permanente de Justice Internationale, il convenait pour le moment de lui donner une base d'autant plus solide et plus ferme qu'elle serait étroite.

La Cour prévue par l'article 14 du Pacte „connaîtra de tous différends d'un caractère international que les parties lui soumettront." Les „parties", d'après le Comité, ne sauraient être de simples particuliers. Cette solution, déjà donnée en 1899 et en 1907, non seulement, ce qui est d'évidence, pour la Cour d'Arbitrage, mais aussi pour la Cour de Justice arbitrale, était expressément formulée par le projet des Cinq Puissances: „La Cour ne connaît que des conflits entre Etats". Mais le texte (art. 20 par. 2) continue ainsi: „Cependant un Etat peut saisir la Cour de demandes fondées sur des droits qu'il fait valoir en faveur d'un de ses ressortissants contre un autre Etat." Si le texte de la Commission ne reproduit pas cette mention, on ne saurait en induire qu'un Etat ne peut soumettre à la Cour des droits qu'il ferait valoir, aux termes du droit des gens, en faveur des particuliers.

Il est certain qu'un Etat ne peut prendre fait et cause que pour ceux au regard desquels il a, dans les relations internationales, droit de protection: en cas de doute la Cour décide.

Les dispositions spéciales de récents traités prévoient un régime spécial de protection des droits des minorités. Ces droits sont placés sous la protection de la Société des Nations. En cas de différend sur leur application, un Etat Membre de la Société des Nations peut, aux termes de ces traités, exercer un recours juridictionnel devant la Cour de Justice de l'article 14 du Pacte.

Notre Cour a donc compétence.

national jurisdiction. Should this jurisdiction be our Court?

To take a case less quoted but of a still more delicate nature, could an individual, who is claimed by two States as a subject, bring an action against one or both of them in order to obtain a decision as to his real nationality with regard to them? These problems may be interesting, but at the moment they are premature, because they tend to affect the sovereignty, independence and even existence of States.

The Committee was unanimously of opinion that, without prejudice to any subsequent development of the Permanent Court of International Justice, for the moment it must be given a basis which, though restricted, would, for that very reason, be firmer and more substantial.

The Court projected by Article 14 of the Covenant ,,shall be competent to hear and determine any dispute of an international character which the parties thereto submit to it". In the opinion of the Committee, the „parties" cannot be private individuals. This answer, which was given in 1899 and 1907, and which was evidently intended to apply not only to the Court of Arbitration, but also to the Court of Arbitral Justice, was expressly laid down in the Five-Power-Plan: „The Court shall take cognisance only of inter-state litigation". But the clause (art. 20 par. 2) continues as follows: „Nevertheless a State may lay before the Court a suit based upon rights which it claims to put forward on behalf of one of its citizens against another State". Though the present text does not definitely mention this, it must not be deduced therefore, that the law of nations does not authorise a State to bring an action before the Court on behalf of private individuals.

It is certain that a State can only act on behalf of those over whom it has a right of protection in international relations: in doubtful cases the Court shall decide.

Special provisions in recent treaties introduce a special method of protecting the rights of minorities. These rights are put under the protection of the League of Nations. In the event of disputes as to their application, a State which is a Member of the League of Nations may, according to the terms of these treaties, appeal to the jurisdiction of the Court of Justice mentioned in Article 14 of the Covenant.

Our Court therefore is competent to deal with these cases.

Elle a compétence également dans les cas où les traités lui donnent l'appel des décisions rendues par les commissions fluviales internationales, compétence également dans les cas prévùs par les dispositions relatives à la constitution d'une organisation internationale du travail. Il eût été facile au Comité d'énumérer tous ces cas, mais elle a pensé qu'il était inutile de les indiquer en détail.

Article 31.

La Cour connaît des litiges entre Etats.

Si la Cour est ouverte à des Etats contre des Etats, est-ce seulement à ceux qui sont actuellement Membres de la Société des Nations? Par une exception, qui ne peut être, dans la pensée de tous, que temporaire, les Etats-Unis d'Amérique, mentionnés au Traité de Versailles parmi les Membres originaires de la Société des Nations, ne sont pas encore entrés dans cette Société. Signataires du Pacte sans l'avoir encore ratifié, ils sont dans une situation spéciale. Une semblable situation appelait un régime particulier: la Cour leur est ouverte sans autres conditions que de satisfaire aux prescriptions de l'article 17, qui, pour eux, se réduiront certainement à prendre une part aux frais généraux de son administration.

Mais la situation est plus délicate pour des Etats, qui, non mentionnés à l'Annexe au Pacte de la Société des Nations, n'ont pas encore donné les garanties nécessaires pour y être admis: Etats qui ne sauraient rester indéfiniment en dehors d'une Société où, d'avance, leur place est marquée, mais qui, cependant n'y ont pas encore accès. Comme on ne saurait les citer eux-mêmes, devant la Cour, il est clair qu'ils ne sauraient citer, sans son assentiment, un autre Etat, mentionné à l'Annexe au Pacte, devant cette Cour.

Mais s'ils sont d'accord avec cet Etat pour venir devant la Cour, on ne saisit pas pourquoi celle-ci ne serait pas compétente. De même, si deux Etats non-mentionnés au Pacte ont un litige entre eux, on ne voit pas pourquoi, s'ils s'entendaient pour porter leur litige devant la Cour, celle-ci ne serait pas aussi compétente.

La seule réserve que les circonstances commandent est qu'en pareil cas il doit appartenir

It is also competent in those cases in which treaties make it the Court of Appeal against the decisions of the International River Commissions; it is also competent to deal with the cases mentioned in the provisions dealing with the formation of an International Labour Organisation. It would have been easy for the Committee to enumerate all these cases, but it was thought unnecessary to indicate them in detail.

Article 31.

The Court shall have jurisdiction to hear and determine suits between States.

Suits may be brought to the Court by States against States; does this mean only those who are actually Members of the League of Nations? Owing to exceptional circumstances, which every one believes to be only temporary, the United States of America which are mentioned in the Treaty of Versailles among the original Members of the League of Nations, have not yet joined the League; they have signed the Covenant, but have not yet ratified it, and are therefore in an exceptional position. Such a situation calls for special treatment: the Court is to be open to them subject only to the condition that the provisions of art. 17 are complied with, but in their case this condition will certainly be confined to taking a share in the general expenses of administration.

The situation is much more difficult in the case of those States which are not mentioned in the Annex to the Covenant of the League of Nations and have not yet given the guarantees required of them before admission. These States cannot remain indefinitely outside a League, in which a place has already been allotted to them, but nevertheless they do not as yet possess the right of access. As an action cannot be brought against them before the Court, it is obvious that they cannot bring an action against another State, mentioned in the Annex to the Covenant, without its consent.

But, supposing that they have agreed with such a State to submit to the Court, it is not clear why the latter should not have jurisdiction. Similarly, if two States not mentioned in the Covenant have a dispute, there appears to be no reason why the Court should not be competent to deal with the case, provided that they mutually agree to submit it to the Court.

The only condition necessary in such cases is that it must be left to the Council to decide

au Conseil de déterminer à quelles conditions les Etats qui, en dehors des Etats-Unis, ne seraient pas Membres de la Société des Nations, pourraient venir devant la Cour. Cette solution se déduit à la fois des principes et des textes: des principes, parce qu'il est de l'intérêt général de la paix du monde de favoriser le développement de la justice internationale et d'élargir le cercle d'action de la Cour; des textes, parce que l'article 17 du Pacte indique lui-même que les modes de solution des différends créés par le Pacte sont susceptibles d'extension à des Etats qui ne sont pas Membres de la Société des Nations. Mais leur situation ne saurait être ici la même que celle des autres Etats: le Conseil pourra mettre entre eux des différences.

Pour mieux marquer la différence entre le cas de l'Etat signataire du Pacte sans l'avoir ratifié, et celui des Etats qui doivent, pour entrer dans la Société des Nations, présenter une demande d'admission formelle, au premier la Cour est ouverte, aux autres la Cour est accessible; cette nuance de mots indique que la situation des seconds n'est pas aussi favorable que celle du premier.

Article 32.

La Cour est ouverte aux Etats mentionnés à l'Annexe du Pacte et à ceux qui seront ultérieurement entrés dans la Société des Nations.

Elle est accessible aux autres Etats.

Les conditions auxquelles elle est ouverte ou accessible aux Etats qui ne sont pas Membres de la Société des Nations, sont réglées par le Conseil, en tenant compte de l'Article 17 du Pacte.

Tandis qu'un particulier peut, *de plano*, citer son adversaire devant une Cour de Justice interne, un Etat ne le peut, devant la Cour de Justice internationale, sans que le différend ait été l'objet d'une tentative de solution amiable par la voie diplomatique. Le droit de La Haye reprend ici le dessus sur le droit interne. Il serait inadmissible qu'un Etat cite devant la Cour, directement, un autre Etat, sans avoir au préalable essayé de résoudre, à l'amiable, l'affaire.

Aux termes de la Convention de 1899: „La justice arbitrale internationale n'aspire pas à

under what conditions those States, with the exception of the United States, which are not Members of the League of Nations, may come before the Court. This solution is based both on principles and existing provisions: on principles because it is to the general interest of the peace of the world to extend the development of the international jurisdiction, and to enlarge the Court's sphere of action; on existing provisions, because Article 17 of the Covenant itself indicates that the methods created by the Covenant for the settlement of disputes may be extended to apply to States which are not Members of the League. But their position cannot be quite the same as that of other States. The Council must be able to make a distinction between them.

In order to distinguish more clearly between those States which have signed the Covenant but have not ratified it, and those States which must, before admission to the League of Nations submit a formal request, the wording used in the plan states that the Court is open of right to the former and is accessible to the latter. These shades of meaning are intended to indicate that the latter are not in such a favorable position as the former.

Article 32.

The Court shall be open of right to the States mentioned in the Annex to the Covenant and to such others as shall subsequently enter the League of Nations.

Other States may have access to it.

The conditions under which the Court shall be open of right or accessible to States which are not Members of the League of Nations shall be determined by the Council in accordance with Article 17 of the Covenant.

Whereas in national law a private citizen may *de plano* bring an action before a Court of Justice, a State cannot bring an action before the Court of International Justice, until an attempt has been made to settle the dispute by diplomatic means. In this respect, the Convention of the Hague is here followed rather than the system of national law. It would be inadmissible for a State to bring a direct action against another State before the Court without having previously attempted to settle the case by friendly means.

In the words of the Convention of 1899: „the International Jurisdiction of Arbitration

supplanter les négotiations directes; elle s'applique aux litiges qui n'ont pas été résolus par les voies diplomatiques" (article 16), „aux différends internationaux, qui n'ont pas été réglés par la voie diplomatique." (Article 20. Les textes correspondants de 1907 sont articles 18 et 41.)

Cette disposition, qui commande toute l'organisation de la justice arbitrale, doit dominer de même l'organisation de la Cour Permanente de Justice Internationale. Il est de toute sagesse qu'un Etat ne puisse être, même en vertu d'une convention d'arbitrage antérieure, brusquement cité devant la Cour Permanente de Justice Internationale. Ce serait manquer aux égards que mutuellement les Etats se doivent. Le recours au juge ne doit intervenir que lorsque tous les moyens de réglement amiables ont été tentés. Mais il ne saurait entrer dans la pensée du Comité de donner à une partie le droit d'éluder la juridiction de notre Cour en alléguant que toute espérance de règlement par la voie diplomatique n'est pas encore perdue. En pareil cas, c'est à la Cour qu'il appartiendrait de statuer sur une telle exception d'incompétence. Si, d'autre part, il advient que les parties, tout en acceptant de confier leur litige à la juridiction internationale, aient désigné, dans une convention antérieure, une autre Cour, ou toute autre juridiction d'ordre arbitral, il appartient encore à la partie défenderesse de contester la compétence de la Cour; mais, alors, c'est également à la Cour qu'il appartient de décider si l'exception est fondée.

Après s'être assuré que le litige a été l'objet d'une tentative de règlement par la voie diplomatique et qu'il n'y a pas d'autre juridiction, qui, d'après la convention des parties, soit applicable à la circonstance, la Cour, cette vérification faite *in limine litis,* statue, sous un certain nombre de conditions, auxquelles le Comité attache une toute particulière importance.

Article 33.

Lorsqu'un différend surgit entre Etats, qu'il n'a pu être réglé par la voie diplomatique et que l'on n'est pas convenu de choisir une autre juridiction, la partie qui se prétend lésée peut en saisir la Cour. La Cour, après avoir décidé s'il est satisfait aux prescriptions précédentes, statue sous les conditions et limitations déterminées par l'article suivant.

La Conférence de La Haye de 1907, après avoir constaté l'adhésion de plus des trois quarts

is not intended to replace direct negotiation; it is to deal with disputes which diplomacy has failed to settle," (Art. 16), — with „international differences which it has not been possible to settle by diplomacy." (Art. 20. The corresponding texts of the 1907 convention are to be found in Articles 18 and 41.)

This provision which is a dominating factor in the organisation of Jurisdiction by Arbitration must also be the main factor in the organisation of the Permanent Court of International Justice. It would not be wise that a State should be subject to an unforeseen summons before the Permanent Court of International Justice, even in virtue of a previous Convention of Arbitration. Such a proceeding would fail in the respect which States owe to each other. Appeal to the Court should not be made until all means of friendly settlement have been tried. But the Committee did not intend to enable a party to avoid the jurisdiction of the Court by alleging that there was still some hope of settlement by diplomatic means. In such a case it is for the Court to decide whether it has jurisdiction. On the other hand, supposing that the parties, though they have agreed to submit their case to an international jurisdiction, have in a previous convention selected another Court or any other jurisdiction of the nature of a tribunal of arbitration, it also falls to the defendant party to dispute the competence of the Court; in this case also it is for the Court to decide whether the objection is to be upheld.

The Court, after satisfying itself *in limine litis* that an attempt has been made to settle the case by diplomatic means, and that no agreement exists between the parties, in virtue of which the case should be submitted to another jurisdiction, shall deliver judgment under certain conditions to which the Committee attach special importance.

Article 33.

When a dispute has arisen between States, and it has been found impossible to settle it by diplomatic means, and no agreement has been made to choose another jurisdiction, the party complaining may bring the case before the Court. The Court shall, first of all, decide whether the preceding conditions have been complied with; if so, it shall hear and determine the dispute according to the terms and within the limits of the next Article.

The Conference of the Hague of 1907, after recording the fact that more than three quarters

des Etats représentés à un projet de traité d'arbitrage universel, avait adopté la résolution suivante :

„La Conférence est unanime :

1° à reconnaître le principe de l'arbitrage obligatoire ;

2° à déclarer que certains différends, et notamment ceux relatifs à l'interprétation et à l'application des stipulations et conventions internationales, sont susceptibles d'être soumis à l'arbitrage obligatoire, sans aucune restriction."

Au moment où tous les Etats vont constituer une Cour Permanente de Justice Internationale, il est nécessaire qu'ils fassent un pas important dans la voie si remarquablement tracée par la Conférence de 1907.

L'article 34 déclare en conséquence qu'entre Etats, Membres de la Société des Nations, la Cour statue sans convention spéciale sur les différends d'ordre juridique, qu'il définit en reproduisant les spécifications de l'article 13 du Pacte. Il n'est pas question de lier les Etats par l'arbitrage obligatoire sans leur assentiment. La compétence arbitrale ne peut naître que d'une convention. La convention qui établit ici l'arbitrage obligatoire est le statut qui organise la Cour.

Indépendamment des litiges d'ordre juridique, qui relèvent ainsi de l'arbitrage obligatoire, tous différends, de quelque nature qu'il soient, peuvent être portés à la Cour en vertu d'une convention, soit générale, soit spéciale, des parties.

En cas de contestation sur le point de savoir si la question rentre dans l'une des catégories ci-dessus visées, la Cour décide. Telle est la solution de l'article 34.

Un membre du Comité a exprimé ici une réserve formelle. Pour lui le Comité ne tient pas de son mandat le droit de proposer des modifications au Pacte, mais doit simplement renvoyer aux termes de l'article 14 qui lui paraît parfaitement clair. D'autre part, à son avis, le moment n'est pas venu de réaliser une telle réforme, qu'il juge prématurée.

Un autre membre du Comité déclara qu'il eût préféré, pour un motif d'opportunité, la disjonction des dispositions concernant la compétence de celles qui ont trait à l'organisation de la Cour.

Le Comité n'a pas cru devoir partager ni l'une, ni l'autre de ces deux opinions. Non seulement il est clair que le statut organique de la Cour peut attribuer à la Cour telle com-

of the States represented had given their adherence to a draft of a treaty of universal arbitration, adopted the following resolution :

„The Conference is unanimous :

1. In admitting the principle of obligatory arbitration ;
2. In declaring that certain disputes, in particular those relating to the interpretation and application of the provisions of international agreements, be submitted to obligatory arbitration without any restriction."

In constituting a Permanent Court of International Justice the States must take an important step in the direction so well indicated by the Conference of 1907.

Article 34 consequently lays down that the Court may hear and determine, without any special convention, disputes between States which are Members of the League of Nations if such disputes are of a legal nature ; this Article defines them in the terms of Article 13 of the Covenant. There is no question of binding States to submit to arbitration without their consent. The competence of arbitral jurisdiction is dependent upon the existence of a convention. In this case the convention establishing compulsory arbitration is the constituent Statute of the Court.

Apart from cases of a legal nature to which compulsory arbitration is applicable in this way, all disputes of any kind may be brought before the Court by virtue of a general or special convention between the parties.

In the event of a dispute as to whether the question falls under one of the categories referred to above, the Court decides. This is the solution given by Article 34.

One member of the Committee made an explicit reservation on this subject. In his opinion, the Committee's mandate did not give it the right to propose alterations in the Covenant ; it should simply refer to Article 14, which he thought was perfectly clear. Further, he thought that the time had not yet come for the realisation of such a reform, which he considered premature.

Another member of the Committee stated that, on the ground of expediency, he would have preferred that the provisions affecting competence should be separated from those dealing with the organisation of the Court.

The Committee did not share either of these opinions. Not only is it obvious that the constituent Statute of the Court can confer upon it the degree of competence, which the States

pétence que les Etats, auteurs de ce statut, entendent lui donner, mais, de l'avis de la majorité du Comité, une telle attribution de compétence, bien qu'elle ne soit peut-être pas rigoureusement conforme aux termes du Pacte, est dans un tel accord avec son esprit qu'on ne comprendrait pas qu'au moment d'organiser définitivement la Cour on n'achevât pas, par ce dernier trait, le progrès qu'elle apporte.

Une opinion s'est fait jour au sein du Comité, d'après laquelle, conformément à l'article 14 du Pacte, la Cour pouvait être saisie, non par les „parties", mais par une seule „partie", le mot „parties" étant pris ici dans son sens le plus général, comme exprimant non seulement toutes les parties, mais chacune d'elles. Et, si cette interprétation, restreinte à l'un des membres du Comité, put sembler aux autres excessive, la majorité reconnut cependant qu'à son avis les Etats qui forment la Société des Nations, doivent, en constituant la Cour, lui donner compétence dans le cas de litiges d'ordre juridique, sans autre convention que le statut qui organise la Cour.

Non seulement une telle réforme est au pouvoir des Etats qui créent la Cour, mais elle n'est pas étrangère à l'article 13 du Pacte. De cet article il suit qu'il y a des cas où les Etats sont tenus à se soumettre à l'arbitrage:

> „Les Membres de la Société conviennent que s'il s'élève entre eux un différend susceptible, à leur avis, d'une solution arbitrale et si ce différend ne peut se régler de façon satisfaisante par la voie diplomatique, la question sera soumise intégralement à l'arbitrage.
>
> „Parmi ceux qui sont généralement susceptibles de solution arbitrale, on déclare tels les différends relatifs à l'interprétation d'un traité, à tout point de droit international, à la réalité de tout fait qui, s'il était établi, constituerait la rupture d'un engagement international, ou à l'étendue ou à la nature de la réparation dûe pour une telle rupture."

Les mots „à leur avis" semblent affaiblir ces termes. Mais on doit supposer la bonne foi des Etats en cause. Le mot „généralement" atténue encore la force de l'idée. Mais il n'en demeure pas moins qu'en vertu de l'article 13 les Etats sont convenus de se soumettre à l'arbitrage obligatoire, dans un certain nombre de cas. Comme ces dispositions ne sont pas nouvelles, mais trouvent dans la résolution de 1907 une base, ce n'est pas de la part du Comité dépasser son mandat, c'est au contraire l'accomplir, en conformité de l'intention du Pacte et de l'esprit

drawing up the Statute, wish to give it, but also, in the opinion of the majority of the Committee, the grant of such powers, though perhaps not strictly in accordance with the letter of the Covenant, follows its spirit so exactly that it would seem a great pity, now that the Court is being definitely organised, not to complete the progress made by this last provision.

Within the Committee the opinion was expressed that, according to Article 14 of the Covenant, a case could be submitted to the Court, by one "party" only and not necessarily by the "parties"; this idea was based on the notion that the word "parties" was used in its general sense and included not only "all the parties" but also "each party". Though this interpretation which was limited to one member of the Committee, seemed too drastic to the others, the majority recognised that the States forming the League of Nations, in constituting the Court, must give it a competence in cases of a legal nature, without any convention other than the constituent Statute of the Court.

Not only is such a reform within the powers of the States creating the Court, but it is implied in Art. 13 of the Covenant. It follows from that Article that there are cases in which States are bound to submit to Arbitration.

> "The members of the League agree that whenever any dispute shall arise between them which they recognise to be suitable for submission to arbitration and which cannot be satisfactorily settled by diplomacy, they will submit the whole subject-matter to arbitration.
>
> "Disputes as to the interpretation of a treaty, as to any question of international law, as to the existence of any fact which if established would constitute a breach of any international obligation, or as to the extent and nature of the reparation to be made for any such breach, are declared to be among those which are generally suitable for submission to arbitration".

The words "in their opinion" seem to weaken these provisions, but the good faith of States concerned must be presumed. The word "generally" still further diminishes the force of the expression, but nevertheless the fact remains that, according to the terms of Article 13, the States have agreed to submit to compulsory arbitration in a certain number of cases. As these dispositions are not new, but are founded upon the resolution adopted in 1907, the Committee is not going beyond its mandate; on the contrary, it is fulfilling it as intended by

de La Haye, que de donner à la Cour une compétence qui relève du consentement préalable des Etats, auteurs du Statut d'organisation de la Cour.

Article 34.

Entre Etats Membres de la Société des Nations la Cour statue sans convention spéciale sur les différends d'ordre juridique, qui ont pour objet:

a. l'interprétation d'un traité;

b. tout point de droit international;

c. la réalité de tout fait, qui, s'il était établi, constituerait la violation d'un engagement international;

d. la nature ou l'étendue de la réparation dûe pour la rupture d'un engagement international;

e. l'interprétation d'une sentence rendue par la Cour.

La Cour connaît également de tous différends, de quelque nature qu'ils soient, qui lui sont soumis par la convention soit générale, soit spéciale des parties.

En cas de contestation sur le point de savoir si un différend rentre dans les catégories ci-dessus visées, la Cour décide.

Dans les limites de cette compétence, comment la Cour de justice procédera-t-elle?

La Convention de La Haye relative à la Cour Internationale des Prises (18 Octobre 1907) avait pris soin d'établir en son article 7:

„A défaut de stipulations expresses, la Cour applique les règles de droit international. Si des règles généralement reconnues n'existent pas, la Cour statue d'après les principes généraux de la justice et de l'équité."

Il ne pouvait être question de donner une base aussi large aux décisions de la Cour. S'inspirant de l'article 7 de la Convention de La Haye, pour fixer en ordre successif les règles de droit applicables, le texte indique que la Cour doit appliquer d'abord les règles conventionnelles, ensuite, à défaut de conventions, soit générales, soit spéciales, la coutume internationale dont la continuité atteste une pratique commune, ultérieurement les principes généraux du droit reconnus par les nations civilisées, enfin les décisions judiciaires et la doctrine des publicistes les plus qualifiés des différentes nations, en tant que moyens auxiliaires de la détermination des règles de droit.

the Covenant, and in the spirit of the Conferences of the Hague, by giving the Court a competence based on the previous consent of the States responsible for the constituent Statute of the Court.

Article 34.

Between States which are Members of the League of Nations, the Court shall have jurisdiction (and this without any special convention giving it jurisdiction) to hear and determine cases of a legal nature, concerning:

a. the interpretation of a treaty;

b. any question of international law;

c. the existence of any fact which, if established, would constitute a breach of an international obligation;

d. the nature or extent of reparation to be made for the breach of an international obligation;

e. the interpretation of a sentence passed by the Court.

The Court shall also take cognisance of all disputes of any kind which may be submitted to it by a general or particular convention between the parties.

In the event of a dispute as to whether a certain case comes within any of the categories above mentioned, the matter shall be settled by the decision of the Court.

What rules are to be applied by the Court of Justice within the limits of this competence?

The Hague Convention relative to the creation of an International Prize Court (18 October 1907), explicitly laid down in Article 7 that:

„In the absence of such provisions, the Court shall apply the rules of International Law. If no generally recognised rule exists, the Court shall give judgment in accordance with the general principles of justice and equity."

There can be no question of giving such an unrestricted field to the decisions of the Court. The wording adopted, which is based on Article 7 of the Hague Convention and lays down an order in which the rules of law are to be applied, states that the Court is to apply, firstly, the rules embodied in conventions; secondly, in the absence of general or special conventions, international custom in so far as its continuity proves a common usage; thirdly, the general principles of law recognized by civilised nations; fourthly, judicial decisions and the teachings of the most highly qualified publicists of the various nations, as subsidiary means of determining the rules of law.

Article 35.

Dans les limites de sa compétence, telle qu'elle est déterminée par l'article 34, la Cour applique en ordre successif:

1⁰. les conventions internationales soit générales, soit spéciales, établissant des règles expressément reconnues par les Etats en litige;

2⁰. la coutume internationale, attestation d'une pratique commune acceptée comme loi;

3⁰. les principes généraux de droit reconnus par les nations civilisées;

4⁰. les décisions judiciaires et la doctrine des publicistes les plus qualifiés des différentes nations, comme moyens auxiliaires de détermination des règles de droit.

Compétente pour statuer à la demande des Etats entre lesquels il existe un différend, la Cour l'est encore, hors du cadre de sa compétence judiciaire, pour „donner des avis consultatifs sur tout point, ou tout différend, dont la saisit le Conseil et l'Assemblée". Il est clair que ce différend, ne peut être que d'ordre international: c'est la disposition formelle de l'article 14 du Pacte.

Dans les deux cas, la Cour, saisie, soit par le Conseil, soit par l'Assemblée, ne donne qu'un avis consultatif dont ensuite il appartient, soit au Conseil, soit à l'Assemblée, de s'approprier les termes et de déduire les conséquences. Tandis que la décision de la Cour, dûment saisie par la partie, a caractère obligatoire et force de chose jugée, il n'en est pas de même de la décision qu'elle donne sur renvoi du Conseil ou de l'Assemblée: ici elle ne juge plus, elle consulte.

Cette consultation se présente-t-elle en dehors de tout différend actuellement né? Alors, comme la question est ensuite susceptible d'être judiciairement posée devant la Cour, soit à raison de sa nature, soit à raison de l'assentiment spécial des parties, il importe que la Cour se forme de telle manière que la solution donnée *in abstracto* sur la question théorique ne restreigne pas son libre pouvoir de statuer, lorsque le problème reviendra devant elle, non plus en théorie, mais en pratique, non plus d'une manière abstraite, mais dans une espèce concrète. Par cela même que l'avis de la Cour aura été *in abstracto* purement consultatif, il importe qu'au moment où l'affaire vient devant elle *in concreto*, la Cour ne soit pas liée par l'opinion précédemment

Article 35.

The Court shall, within the limits of its jurisdiction as defined in Article 34, apply in the order following:

1⁰. international conventions, whether general or particular, establishing rules expressly recognised by the contesting States;

2⁰. international custom, as evidence of a general practice, which is accepted as law;

3⁰. the general principles of law recognised by civilised nations;

4⁰. judicial decisions and the teachings of the most highly qualified publicists of the various nations, as subsidiary means for the determination of rules of law.

The Court is not only competent to hear and determine cases at the request of States between whom a dispute exists, but also, and apart from its judicial competence, to "give an advisory opinion upon any dispute or question referred to it by the Council or by the Assembly." It is obvious that such a dispute can only be of an international nature. This is expressly laid down in Article 14 of the Covenant.

In both cases, the Court, acting on the request of the Council or the Assembly, only gives an advisory opinion which it is for the Council or the Assembly to adopt and of which they must deduce the consequences. Whereas a judgment of the Court, following upon an action brought by a party, is binding and has the force of *res judicata*, this is not so in the case of a decision given upon a point referred to it by the Council or by the Assembly. In this case the Court does not pass judgment, it merely advises.

If an advisory opinion is to be given which does not refer to any actually existing dispute, as the question may subsequently be brought before the Court in its judicial capacity, either on account of its character, or because the parties make a special agreement to that effect, the Court must be so constituted that the opinion given in the abstract upon the theoretical question, does not restrict the freedom of its decision, should the question come before it later in practice and no longer as a theoretical problem, as a concrete case and not merely in the abstract. As the opinion by the Court *in abstracto* is simply advisory, the Court must not be bound by this opinion, should the question come before it as a concrete case; otherwise the

exprimée par elle: sans quoi l'avis ne serait plus consultatif. Pour éviter de mettre la Cour dans l'obligation ou de se contredire ou de se répéter, il importe de la constituer d'une manière différente, et, pour cela, de la réduire, pour l'exercice de cette attribution, à quelques-uns seulement de ses membres, 3 à 5, suivant l'estimation de son règlement intérieur.

Mais il peut arriver que le différend renvoyé, soit par le Conseil, soit par l'Assemblée, ait le caractère d'un véritable litige, parce qu'il s'agit d'un différend actuellement né. Ce différend n'est pas soumis par les parties à l'arbitrage, soit de la Cour, soit de tout autre mode de justice internationale, mais, cependant, il présente un caractère tel que sa solution par la voie judiciaire internationale est, incontestablement, la meilleure. Il se peut même qu'il s'agisse d'une affaire qui présente, de sa nature, le caractère d'ordre juridique qui détermine le recours à l'arbitrage, mais que les parties, d'un commun accord, s'entendent pour le transférer de la procédure judiciaire qui, naturellement, lui convient, à la procédure conciliatrice qui, à des combinaisons plus souples, joint l'avantage, pour les parties, de substituer l'exigence d'une décision à l'unanimité dans le Conseil ou à la majorité spéciale de l'article 15 du Pacte dans l'Assemblée, à la majorité de l'article 54 du projet dans la Cour. Pour éviter ce résultat, les parties peuvent être tentées d'altérer, d'un commun accord, le véritable caractère de leur différend. Dans ce cas, il importe que le Conseil puisse lui restituer sa véritable nature, en le renvoyant à la Cour. Sans doute celle-ci ne peut être judiciairement saisie que par les parties, non par le Conseil ni l'Assemblée. Mais, si les parties ont décidé de saisir le Conseil ou l'Assemblée, elles n'ont pas à s'étonner que la Cour puisse connaître de l'affaire sur renvoi du Conseil ou de l'Assemblée. Cela ne donnera pas à l'avis de la Cour force de chose jugée obligatoire entre les deux parties. Mais la décision de la Cour n'en aura pas moins la valeur morale qui s'attache à tous ses arrêts et, si le Conseil ou l'Assemblée se l'approprient, elle aura sur l'opinion publique le même heureux effet. Dès l'instant qu'il s'agit d'un différend actuellement né, la Cour devra donc statuer de la même manière que s'il s'agissait d'un litige porté devant elle, c'est-à-dire en laissant monter, à la demande des parties, un juge de leur nationalité sur le siège, et en permettant aux parties de faire valoir les preuves et moyens de la même manière que dans une affaire portée directement devant elle par les plaideurs.

opinion ceases to be advisory. In order to avoid the possibility of the Court being forced to contradict or repeat itself, it must be differently constituted, and consequently reduced, for the performance of this function, to a smaller number, say from 3 to 5 of its members, as may be decided in the rules of Court.

It may, however, happen that the dispute referred to the Court by the Council or by the Assembly is of the nature of an actual case, since it concerns a dispute wich actually exists. This dispute has not been submitted by the parties to arbitration either by the Court or by any other international tribunal, but, nevertheless, it is of such a nature that the best method of solving it is, undoubtedly, by an international judicial procedure. It may even happen that the case in question is of a legal nature and should therefore be submitted to arbitration, but that the parties mutually agree to transfer it from the judicial procedure which ought normally to be applied to it, to a procedure of conciliation which, in addition to its greater adaptability, offers to the parties the advantage of requiring a unanimous decision in the Council or a decision by the majority in the Assembly, as provided in Article 15 of the Covenant, instead of a decision by the majority in the Court, as laid down in Article 54 of the Scheme. To avoid the possibility of the latter, the parties may be tempted to alter the real character of their dispute, by mutual agreement. Under such circumstances the Council should be able to re-establish the true character of the case and send it to the Court. Of course the Court can only take judicial cognisance of a case brought by the contesting parties, and not by the Council or Assembly; but if the parties have decided to bring it before the Council or Assembly, they must not be surprised if the Council or Assembly refer the case to the Court. The advisory opinion given by the Court, under such circumstances, would not have the force of a sentence binding upon the two parties. But the Court's decision would nevertheless have the moral force attaching to all its decisions; and, if the Council or Assembly adopt it, it would have the same wholesome effect on public opinion. Whenever therefore, an existing dispute is in question, the Court must take its decision in the same manner as if an action had actually been brought before it, that is to say a judge of the nationality of each of the contesting parties must be allowed to take his place on the Bench, if the parties request it, and the parties must be allowed to present all arguments and proofs just as in a case brought directly before the Court by them.

Article 36.

La Cour donne son avis sur tout point ou tout différend d'ordre international qui lui est soumis par le Conseil ou par l'Assemblée.

Lorsque la Cour donne son avis sur un point d'ordre international indépendamment de tout différend actuellement né, elle constitue une Commission spéciale de 3 à 5 membres.

Lorsqu'elle donne son avis sur une question qui fait l'objet d'un différend actuellement né, elle statue dans les mêmes conditions que s'il s'agissait d'un litige porté devant elle.

III.

PROCÉDURE.

La première question à résoudre était celle de la langue. Cette langue ne pouvait varier d'espèce en espèce au gré des circonstances; elle devait rester fixe, identique à elle-même. La permanence de la Cour devait s'affirmer dans cette permanence de la langue. Comment donner aux 15 à 20 juges de la Cour la possibilité, pour chacun, de s'exprimer dans une langue différente? Comment admettre que les parties puissent venir devant le juge en se servant d'une langue qu'il ne comprendrait pas? Une Cour de tous les peuples du monde fût ainsi devenue une Cour de toutes les langues. Il était nécessaire de faire un choix entre les langues, d'en désigner une qui fût officiellement la langue de la Cour.

Le français, langue des Conférences de La Haye de 1899 et 1907, langue, sauf quand les deux parties furent toutes deux de langue anglaise, de la Cour Permanente d'Arbitrage de La Haye, devenait naturellement la langue de la Cour. S'il était ainsi de la Cour Permanente d'Arbitrage, formée de tribunaux temporaires dans un cadre permanent, à plus forte raison devait-il en être de même d'une Cour véritablement permanente, c'est-à-dire composée d'une manière qui doit la rendre, d'une façon constante, identique à elle-même.

„Dans les amendements à la Convention de 1899" (1907 art. 61), écrivait en son rapport sur la Cour de Justice Arbitrale M. James Brown Scott, „il est prévu que les parties en litige détermineront la langue ou les langues, dont il sera fait usage dans la Cour

Article 36.

The Court shall give an advisory opinion upon any question or dispute of an international nature referred to it by the Council or Assembly.

When the Court shall give an opinion on a question of an international nature which does not refer to any dispute that may have arisen, it shall appoint a special Commission of from three to five members.

When it shall give an opinion upon a question which forms the subject of an existing dispute, it shall do so under the same conditions as if the case had been actually submitted to it for decision.

III.

PROCEDURE.

The first question to be settled was that of the language. This language cannot vary from case to case according to circumstances, it must be fixed and invariable. The permanence of the language must be an outward sign of the permanence of the Court. It would be absurd to allow each of 15 to 20 judges to express himself in a different language. It would be impossible to allow parties to come before the judges and use a language that they, the judges, did not understand. A Court composed of all the nations of the World would thus become a Court of all tongues. It was imperative therefore, to choose one language, to be the official language of the Court.

French, which was the language used by the Hague Conferences of 1899 and 1907, and, except when both parties were of English speaking nationality, that of the Permanent Court of Arbitration of the Hague, naturally became the official language of the Court. If this were so in the case of the Permanent Court of Arbitration, which consists of temporary tribunals drawn from a permanent list of members, there is much stronger reason for it to be so in the case of a really permanent Court, composed in such a way that it is bound to remain invariable.

"In the amendments to the Convention of 1899" (1907 Art. 61), Mr. James Brown Scott wrote in his report on the Court of Arbitral Justice, "it is provided that the parties litigant shall determine the language or languages to be used in the Court of

d'Arbitrage. Dans une Cour Internationale, composée d'un grand nombre de juges, il est évident que l'obligation d'une langue particulière pourrait être fort gênante, même pénible pour les juges. Les parties au litige devront donc accepter la langue ou les langues prescrites par la Cour."

Mais, de manière à ne pas donner à cette règle un caractère trop rigoureux, qui nuisît à la bonne administration de la justice, en empêchant deux parties de même langage d'employer devant la Cour une langue qui eût été, par ses membres, également comprise, il fallait que la règle générale, qui fait du français la langue de la Cour, pût fléchir quand les circonstances l'exigent. C'est à la Cour qu'il appartient souverainement d'en décider. Deux conditions sont seules posées: les parties doivent en faire la demande; la Cour doit y acquiescer. Il suffit, ou que la demande des parties manque, ou que la Cour refuse, pour que l'emploi, toujours exceptionnel, d'une autre langue ne soit pas admis. Cette double condition était posée dans le projet des Cinq Puissances. Elle se trouvait de même au projet antérieur des trois Puissances du Nord.

Article 37.

La langue de la Cour est le français.

La Cour peut, à la demande des parties, autoriser l'emploi d'une autre langue devant elle.

Cette question générale réglée, la Commission devait déterminer de quelle manière la Cour est saisie. Ni dans la Convention de 1899, ni dans celle de 1907 ne se trouvent à cet égard de dispositions expresses.

Dans une Cour Permanente d'Arbitrage, simple cadre de tribunaux temporaires, tirés par le compromis d'une liste d'arbitres, toute précision à cet égard pouvait sembler inutile. Préoccupé du grand problème, alors non résolu, de la désignation des juges, le projet de Cour de Justice Arbitrale de 1907 n'avait attaché qu'une intention réduite à un point aussi particulier.

Mais, dès l'instant que la constitution de la Société des Nations permettait la création d'une Cour vraiment permanente, de tels détails devaient être directement abordés.

Arbitration. In an International Court, composed of a large number of judges, it is evident that the imposition of any one language might greatly embarrass or even work a hardship on the judges. The parties litigant must therefore accept the language or languages prescribed by the Court."

In order, however, not to make this rule too rigid, thereby possibly affecting adversely the administration of Justice by preventing two parties, both speaking the same language, from using before the Court a language, which might be equally well understood by the members of the Court, the general rule, which makes French the official language, must be subject to exception when circumstances require it. It is for the Court alone to give a decision on this point. Two conditions only are laid down: the parties must make a request, and the Court must sanction it. The employment of another language, which must always be regarded as exceptional, will not be admitted, unless the parties request it and the Court gives its sanction. This twofold condition was included in the Five Powers Plan. It was also contained in the previous plan of the three Scandinavian Powers in exactly the same terms.

Article 37.

The official language of the Court shall be French.

The Court may, at the request of the contesting parties, authorise another language to be used before it.

Having settled the general principles, the Committee had to determine the method of bringing an action before the Court. There is no explicit provision dealing with this point in either the Convention of 1899 or that of 1907.

In a Permanent Court of Arbitration, which is simply a framework for temporary tribunals, chosen by a special agreement (compromis) from a list of arbitrators, any definite rule on this point might seem unnecessary. The project for the Court of Arbitral Justice of 1907, owing to the great problem of the method of appointing judges, which was not at that time solved, only gave a cursory attention to a question of such detail.

Directly, however, the constitution of the League of Nations made the creation of a really permanent Court possible, such details had to be dealt with.

Le projet des trois Puissances du Nord (Art. 32) se bornait à renvoyer d'une manière générale au règlement de procédure de la Convention de La Haye de 1907 et du projet d'une Cour de Justice Arbitrale, pourvu qu'il n'en fût pas autrement statué dans les dispositions qui devaient suivre; mais, comme rien ne s'y trouve sur la manière dont est saisie la Cour, le projet des Cinq Puissances ne manqua pas d'en fixer la manière (Art. 30).

C'est de ce texte que s'inspire le projet du Comité.

La Cour est saisie par une déclaration ou une requête faite au Greffe.

Cette requête détermine l'objet du différend. „L'objet", terme juridique, a paru plus précis et plus utile, au point de vue de l'effet de la chose jugée, que la „nature", dont parlait l'article 30 du texte des Cinq Puissances.

Les parties doivent être désignées. Mais les conclusions ne sont pas encore prises dans leur forme définitive. Il ne s'agit que d'une indication d'ordre général, suffisante pour préciser le litige et permettre à l'instance de s'ouvrir. Le Greffe, qui reçoit une pareille requête, la fait connaître aux intéressés, c'est-à-dire aux parties, et, éventuellement, à toute personne, qui pouvait avoir, au vu de cette requête, occasion d'intervenir, suivant une précision qui sera faite plus tard à l'article 60. Mais tandis qu'on s'était demandé, au sein du Comité, s'il y aurait lieu, pour le Greffe, de donner immédiatement la plus large publicité, fût-ce par voie de la Presse, à la requête, il apparut, à la réflexion, qu'il serait imprudent de procéder ainsi. Mais, comme la Cour Permanente de Justice Internationale est une institution de la Société des Nations, que cette Société, suivant la lettre même du Pacte, en son préambule, recommande „d'entretenir au grand jour des relations internationales fondées sur la justice et l'honneur", et par l'enrégistrement des traités, d'assurer une publicité parfaite entre Membres de la Société des Nations, de tous les grands actes internationaux, il apparut qu'il appartenait au Greffe d'informer de la requête les Membres de la Société des Nations par l'intermédiaire naturel de ses différents organes, Assemblée, Conseil ou Cour, c'est-à-dire par les soins du Secrétaire-Général de la Société des Nations.

The project of the three Scandinavian Powers (Art. 32) merely made a general reference to the rules of procedure of the Hague Convention of 1907, and to the draft convention for a Court of Arbitral Justice, subject to the provisions following in the project; as, however, there was no mention of the method of bringing an action before the Court, the plan of the Five Powers was careful to deal with this point in Article 30.

The Committee's solution is based on this article.

Appeal to the Court shall be made by means of an application addressed to the Registry.

This application shall state the point at issue. It was thought that a juridical term should be used as being more exact and more suitable from the point of view of the *res judicata*, than the term "nature" used in Article 30 of the Five Power's plan.

The contesting parties shall be named. The demands, however are not yet set out in their final form; a general indication is all that is required, sufficient to define the case and to allow the proceedings to be commenced. The Registrar, to whom this application is made, informs all concerned, that is to say, the contesting parties and also any others who might conceivably feel called upon to intervene in the case on receipt of this information; a provision dealing more fully with this question is contained in Article 60. The question was raised in the Committee as to whether the Registrar should immediately publish full information concerning the application, and whether the agency of the Press should be used; after due consideration it appeared unwise to do this. Nevertheless, as the Permanent Court of International Justice is a component part of the League of Nations, and as the League, according to the preamble to the Covenant, considers desirable "the prescription of open, just and honourable relations between nations", and that complete publicity should be given to all important international documents between Members of the League, by the registration of treaties, it is clear that it is the duty of the Registrar to inform the Members of the League of the application through the Secretary-General of the League, who is the natural channel of communication between the Members and the various organisations, the Assembly, Council or Court of the League of Nations.

Article 38.

La Cour est saisie par une requête adressée au Greffe.

La requête indique l'objet du différend et désigne les parties en cause.

Le Greffe fait immédiatement notification de la requête aux intéressés.

Il en informe également les Membres de la Société des Nations par l'entremise du Secrétaire-Général.

Article 38.

A State desiring to have recourse to the Court shall lodge a written application addressed to the Registrar.

The application shall indicate the subject of the dispute, and name the contesting parties.

The Registry shall forthwith communicate the application to all concerned.

He shall also notify the Members of the League of Nations through the Secretary-General.

Dès le début de l'instance les circonstances peuvent exiger qu'il soit pris, à titre provisoire, des mesures conservatoires du droit de chacun. Il en est ainsi quand le différend naît d'un acte qui vient d'être effectué, par exemple de la saisie d'un objet, de l'invasion d'un territoire. Lorsqu'un tel acte est ainsi effectué, ou sur le point de l'être, il peut être extrêmement opportun, ou d'en effacer, momentanément, des conséquences, ou d'en empêcher, s'il en est encore temps, l'accomplissement.

S'inspirant d'une mesure qui figure aux traités, signés pour les Etats-Unis par le Secrétaire d'Etat Bryan avec un certain nombre d'Etats (la France, la Chine, la Suède) en 1914, le Comité donne à la Cour le pouvoir de suggérer les mesures à prendre, à titre provisoire, pour assurer la conservation du droit de chacun.

Mais il ne s'agit pas ici d'un arrêt, même interlocutoire, immédiatement exécutoire, par provision. Quand il s'agit de limiter la souveraineté des Etats, il convient d'être circonspect. Déjà il est difficile d'obtenir l'exécution d'une décision définitive; à plus forte raison sera-t-il difficile d'obtenir l'exécution d'une décision purement provisoire. Les décisions de ce genre prises en cas de transit, suivant les vues de la Commission du Transit, sont ici, par la prudence de leurs termes, d'une indication précieuse. Les traités Bryan, auxquels est empruntée l'idée d'un tel pouvoir de la Cour, s'expriment avec une grande prudence, en ne donnant à la Cour d'autre droit que d'indic[illegible] les mesures à prendre à titre provisoire, [illegible]endant

At the very outset of the case, circumstances may exist requiring that provisional measures be taken to ensure that the rights of each party are not prejudiced. This is the case in the event of a dispute arising out of an act just performed, for instance, the seizure of an object or the invasion of a territory. If such an act has just been, or is on the point of being, put in into execution, it may be highly desirable to undo the consequences for the time being, or to prevent it from taking place if there is still time.

The Committee, drawing its inspiration from a provision contained in the treaties between the United States and certain other States, (France, China, Sweden) which were signed in 1914 on behalf of the former by Mr. Bryan, the then Secretary of State, gives the Court the power of suggesting the measures to be taken provisionally, to ensure that the respective rights are not prejudiced.

There is no question here of a definite order, even of a temporary nature, which must be carried out at once. Great care must be exercised in any matter entailing the limitation of sovereign powers. It is sufficiently difficult to ensure compliance with a definite decision; it would be much more difficult to ensure the putting into effect of a purely temporary decision. The decisions of this kind taken in transit cases, in accordance with the views of the Communications and Transit Committee, are a valuable guide in this connection owing to the prudence shown in them; the Bryan treaties, from which the idea of giving such a power to the Court is borrowed, were also very prudent in their expressions, and only gave the Court the right

le rapport d'une Commission internationale d'enquête. (1)

Mais tandis que, par les traités Bryan, l'indication des mesures à prendre à titre conservatoire était simplement transmise par la Cour aux parties, elle l'est naturellement, une fois donnée par une Cour de la Société des Nations, au Conseil, organe particulièrement compétent de cette Société pour proposer au regard des sentences arbitrales les mesures qui doivent en assurer l'effect.

Article 39.

Dans le cas, où la cause du différend consiste en un acte effectué ou sur le point de l'être, la Cour a le pouvoir d'indiquer, si elle estime que les circonstances l'exigent, quelles mesures conservatoires du droit de chacun doivent être prises à titre provisoire.

En attendant l'arrêt définitif, l'indication de ces mesures est immédiatement transmise aux parties et au Conseil.

Dans la détermination de la procédure, après avoir décidé que les parties seraient, suivant les règles de la procédure arbitrale, représentées par des agents, et assistées par des conseils ou des avocats, le Comité a entendu marquer avec netteté que la procédure comprenait deux phases.

Déjà l'article 39 de la Convention de 1899 (le texte correspondant de 1907 est l'art. 63), pour le règlement pacifique des conflits internationaux, divise la procédure arbitrale en deux phases distinctes: l'instruction écrite, et les débats. En renvoyant à cette règle, le projet des trois Puissances du Nord donnait une indication générale que le projet des Cinq Puissances devait reprendre, en incorporant à son texte les détails des dispositions, dont il avait déjà cependant modifié les termes. L'article 39 distingue l'instruction et les débats. L'article 32 du projet des Cinq Puissances dis-

(1) Article 4 du traité du 15 septembre 1914.

„Dans le cas où la cause du différend consisterait en actes déterminés déjà effectués ou sur le point de l'être, la Commission indiquera dans le plus bref délai possible quelle mesure conservatoire du droit de chacun devrait à son avis être prise à titre provisoire en attendant le dépôt de son rapport."

of suggesting the measures to be taken provisionally, pending the report of the international commission of inquiry, entrusted with the task of reporting on the dispute. 1)

Whereas, however, in the Bryan treaties, the suggested measures to be taken to preserve existing rights, were simply communicated by the Court to the parties, in the present case, these measures are, once they have been suggested by a Court of the League of Nations, indicated to the Council of the League as the body most competent to take such action, in order that it may suggest that the measures calculated to ensure the effect of sentences of Arbitration be carried out.

Article 39.

If the dispute arises out of an act which has already taken place or which is imminent, the Court shall have the power to suggest if it considers that circumstances require it, the provisional measures that should be taken to preserve the respective rights of either party.

Pending the final decision, notice of the measures suggested shall forthwith be given to the parties and the Council.

The Committee, in defining the procedure, decided that the parties should be represented by Agents, and assisted by Counsel or Advocates, in accordance with the rules of procedure in arbitration, and further that it should be clearly stated that the procedure included two phases.

Article 39 of the Convention of 1899 (corresponding text of the 1907 Convention: Art. 63), for the Pacific Settlement of International Disputes divided arbitral procedure into two distinct phases: written pleadings, and hearings in Court. The project of the three Scandinavian Countries, by referring to this article, gave a general line, which was followed in the Five-Power-Plan, in which the details of the provisions were adopted in a somewhat modified form. Article 39 draws a distinction between pleadings and oral discussions; Article 32 of the Five-Power-Plan distinguished between

1) Article 4 of the Treaty of 15 September 1914:

„In case the cause of the dispute should consist of certain acts already committed, or about to be committed, the Commission shall as soon as possible indicate what measures to preserve the rights of each party, ought in its opinion to be taken provisionally, and pending the delivery of the report."

tingue entre „l'instruction écrite et les débats". Il a semblé plus net au Comité de distinguer deux phases: l'une écrite, l'autre orale. Il se peut, en effet, que dans la phase orale, se poursuive l'instruction.

"written pleadings and oral discussions". The Committee thought it clearer to draw the line between two phases, the one written, the other oral. It may happen that the pleadings continue in the oral phase.

Article 41.

La procédure a deux phases: l'une écrite, l'autre orale.

Article 41.

The procedure shall consist of two parts: written and oral.

Les deux parties de la procédure sont toutes les deux aussi nécessaires l'une que l'autre. Tandis qu'à la Cour Permanente d'Arbitrage de La Haye, on peut se contenter uniquement de la première, seule indispensable, à la Cour Permanente de Justice Internationale les deux phases, écrite et orale, sont également requises.

Tel était le sens général du projet des Cinq Puissances; tel est de même celui du Comité qui ne s'écarte de celui des Cinq Puissances que pour des précisions d'idées ou des simplifications de rédaction.

De là les articles, votés sans difficulté, qui suivent:

Both parts of the procedure are equally necessary. Whereas in the case of the Permanent Court of Arbitration of the Hague the former only need be used, as it alone is essential, both phases, written and oral, are equally necessary in the case of the Permanent Court of International Justice.

Such was the general bearing of the Five-Power-Plan, and such is also that of the Committee's project, as the latter only varies from the former in being more definite and in simplification of wording.

Therefore the following articles were voted upon and accepted without difficulty.

Article 42.

La procédure écrite comprend la communication à juge et à partie des mémoires, des contremémoires, et, éventuellement, des répliques, ainsi que de toute pièce et document à l'appui.

La communication se fait par l'entremise du Greffe dans l'ordre et les délais déterminés par la Cour.

Toute pièce produite par l'une des parties doit être communiquée à l'autre en copie certifiée conforme.

Article 42.

The written proceedings shall consist of the communication to the judges and to the parties of statements of cases, counter-cases, and, if necessary, replies; also all papers and documents in support.

These communications shall be made through the Registrar, in the order and within the time fixed by the Court.

A certified copy of every document produced by one party shall be communicated to the other party.

Article 43.

La procédure orale consiste dans l'audition par la Cour des témoins, experts, agent, conseils et avocats.

Pour toute notification à faire à d'autres personnes que les agents, conseils et avocats, la Cour s'adresse directement au Gouvernement de l'Etat sur le territoire duquel la notification doit produire effet.

Il en est de même s'il s'agit de faire procéder sur place à l'établissement de tous moyens de preuve.

Article 43.

The oral proceedings shall consist in the hearing by the Court of witnesses, experts, agents, counsel and advocates.

For the service of all notices upon persons other than the agents, counsel and advocates, the Court shall apply direct to the Government of the State upon whose territory the notice has to be served.

The same provision shall apply whenever steps are to be taken to procure evidence on the spot.

Article 44.

Les débats sont dirigés par le Président, et à défaut de celui-ci par le Vice-Président; en cas d'empêchement, par le plus ancien des juges présents.

Adoucissant la règle un peu trop stricte du projet des cinq Puissances (Art. 34 par. 2) prévoyant que les débats auraient lieu en séance publique, le projet du Comité se borne à poser cette règle sous la condition qu'il n'en serait pas autrement décidé par la Cour, mais celle-ci ne peut le faire qu'à la demande motivée de l'une des parties.

Aux termes de la Convention de 1899 sur le règlement pacifique des conflits internationaux (Article 41 ; texte correspondant de 1907 : Art. 66): „les débats ne sont publics qu'en vertu d'une décision du Tribunal prise avec l'assentiment des parties."

C'est à raison du double caractère de franchise de la Société des Nations et de publicité d'une Cour de Justice que la règle diplomatique du secret, inhérente à la Cour d'Arbitrage, juridiction plus diplomatique que juridique, se trouve ici renversée.

C'est seulement si les parties le demandent que la Cour peut prononcer le huis-clos.

Encore le Comité a-t-il tenu à marquer le caractère exceptionnel d'une telle décision en imposant à la demande de l'une des parties d'être motivée. Au cas où les deux parties seraient d'accord pour la non-publicité, le fait serait, sans doute, de nature à impressionner la Cour ; elle n'en garde pas moins, comme il convient à une Cour de Justice, le droit de refuser le huis-clos, même lorsqu'il est demandé par les deux parties, si elle juge que leurs susceptibilités et craintes de publicité sont excessives. Une précision spéciale a été faite en vue de permettre à la Cour de confier une enquête ou une expertise, non seulement à toute personne, mais à tout corps, bureau, commission et, d'une façon plus générale, organe de son choix.

Un certain nombre de dispositions qui ne pouvaient faire difficulté ont été de la part du Comité l'objet d'une tentative de groupement simple et logique dans les textes qui suivent:

Article 45.

L'audience est publique, à moins qu'il n'en soit autrement décidé par la Cour à la demande motivée de l'une des parties.

Article 44.

The proceedings shall be under the direction of the President, or in his absence, of the Vice-President; if both are absent, the senior judge shall preside.

The provision of the Five-Power-Plan (Art. 34, par. 2), laying down that the sessions of the Court shall be public, is somewhat less strict in the Committee's project, in which it may be set aside by the decision of the Court, but only at the request of one of the parties, accompanied by a statement of reasons.

According to Article 41 of the Convention of 1899 (corresponding text in the 1907 Convention: Art. 66) for the Pacific Settlement of International Disputes: "the discussions are only public, if it be so decided by the tribunal with the assent of the parties."

The diplomatic custom of secrecy inherent in the jurisdiction of the Court of Arbitration, which is more diplomatic than legal, is now reversed, since both the frankness required between members of the League of Nations and the publicity of a Court of Justice demand it.

Only at the request of the parties can the Court sit in secret.

The Committee thought it desirable to emphasise the fact that such a decision was to be exceptional, by stipulating that the request made by a party should be accompanied by a statement of reasons. If both parties agree in desiring secrecy, the fact would no doubt have weight with the Court; but nevertheless the Court retains the right, as a Court of Justice should, to refuse to sit in secret, even supposing that both parties request it, if it considers that their susceptibilities and fears of publicity are excessive. A special provision has been included, giving the Court the right to entrust an inquiry to, or to take an expert opinion from, not only any person, but any organisation, bureau or commission, or, in general, any body that it may choose.

The Committee endeavours to group together in a simple and logical manner, a certain number of provisions, giving rise to no difficulty, in the following Articles:

Article 45.

The hearing in Court shall be public, unless the Court, at the written request of one of the parties accompanied by a statement of his reasons, shall otherwise decide.

Article 46.

Il est tenu de chaque audience un procès-verbal signé par le Greffier et le Président.

Ce procès-verbal a seul caractère authentique.

Article 47.

La Cour rend des ordonnances pour la direction du procès, la détermination des formes et délais dans lesquels chaque partie doit finalement conclure; elle prend toutes les mesures que comporte l'administration des preuves.

Article 48.

La Cour peut, même avant tout débat, demander aux agents de lui produire tout document et de lui fournir toutes explications. En cas de refus, elle en prend acte.

Article 49.

A tout moment, la Cour peut confier une enquête ou une expertise à toute personne, corps, bureau, commission ou organe de son choix.

Article 50.

Au cours des débats, les juges posent aux témoins, agents, experts, avocats et conseils, toutes questions qu'ils estiment utiles; les agents, avocats et conseils ont le droit de poser, par l'entremise du Président, toute question que la Cour juge utile.

Une question délicate appelait l'attention du Comité. Il se peut que l'une des parties, dûment citée devant la Cour, refuse de comparaître; déniant compétence à la Cour, elle ne se présente que pour faire valoir cette exception, ou même ne se présente pas. Si la Cour estime que c'est un cas de sa compétence, elle retient l'affaire; mais la défenderesse, persistant en son attitude, ne se présente pas, ou, si elle s'est déjà présentée pour faire valoir l'exception d'incompétence, se retire de l'instance à partir de ce moment; de cette manière, ou d'une autre, elle s'abstient de faire valoir ses moyens. On peut se demander, si, alors, il n'y a pas lieu d'adjuger au demandeur ses conclusions sans

Article 46.

Minutes shall be made at each hearing, and signed by the Registrar and the President.

These minutes shall be the only authentic record.

Article 47.

The Court shall make orders for the conduct of the case, shall decide the form and time in which each party must conclude its arguments, and make all arrangements connected with the taking of evidence.

Article 48.

The Court may, even before the hearing begins, call upon the agents to produce any document, or to supply to the Court any explanations. Any refusal shall be recorded.

Article 49.

The Court may, at any time, entrust any individual, bureau, commission or other body that it may select, with the task of carrying out an inquiry or giving an expert opinion.

Article 50.

During the hearing in Court, the judges may put any questions considered by them to be necessary, to the witnesses, agents, experts, advocates or counsel; the agents, advocates and counsel shall have the right to ask, through the President, any questions that the Court considers useful.

The Committee's attention was called to a delicate question. It might happen that one of the parties, although duly summoned, would refuse to enter an appearance. Since it denied the competence of the Court, it would only appear to register this denial, or might not appear at all. If the Court considered that the case fell within its jurisdiction, it would continue to deal with it; but the defendant party, persisting in the attitude taken up, either would not appear, or if it had already appeared for the purpose of entering a demurrer against the Court's competence, would withdraw immediately afterwards; anyhow, in this or some other way, it would abstain from presenting

exiger de preuves. Certains systèmes de procédure interne l'admettent; mais il ne faut pas oublier qu'ici les plaideurs sont des Etats, et qu'il est particulièrement grave de prononcer une condamnation contre eux, lorsqu'ils dénient à la Cour le droit de les juger. Pour rendre acceptable aux susceptibilités de la souveraineté le jugement par la Cour, même au refus de comparaître, il était nécessaire d'entourer la condamnation qui frapperait l'État défaillant, de toutes les garanties désirables pour lui donner l'autorité morale et, par suite, en assurer le respect en attendant d'en faciliter l'exécution.

Au sein du Comité un membre ne manqua pas d'observer que l'Angleterre était le pays qui demandait, en cas de défaut du défendeur, le plus de développement de preuves et de démonstration des conclusions de la part du demandeur. Du côté de l'Amérique, il fut également rappelé que, devant la Cour Suprême des Etats-Unis, un Etat peut être assigné sans l'assentiment de l'autre, et que, dans ce cas, s'ouvre une procédure *ex parte*, dans laquelle on exige du demandeur qu'il établisse le bien-fondé de sa demande, en fait et en droit, avec le même soin que s'il avait en face de lui un contradicteur.

C'est en s'inspirant de ces exemples de la jurisprudence anglaise interne et de la jurisprudence américaine de la Cour Suprême en matière d'action d'Etat à Etat, en vertu de la Constitution des Etats-Unis, que le Comité a formulé cette règle :

Article 52.

Lorsqu'une des parties ne se présente pas, ou s'abstient de faire valoir ses moyens, l'autre partie peut demander à la Cour de lui adjuger ses conclusions.

La Cour avant d'y faire droit, doit s'assurer non seulement qu'elle a compétence aux termes des articles 33 et 34, mais que les conclusions, reposant sur les preuves sérieuses, sont fondées en fait et en droit.

Maintenant les débats sont terminés.

Article 53.

Quand les agents, avocats et conseils ont fait valoir sous le contrôle de la Cour, tous les mo-

its case. It may be asked if, under such circumstances, the demands of the plaintiff should not be accepted without calling for proofs. Some systems of national procedure adopt this principle, but it must not be forgotten that in the present case the contesting parties are States, and that it is a particularly serious matter to pronounce sentence against them, in the event of their denying the Court's right to try them. To make the Court's judgments, even in the event of a refusal to appear, acceptable to the sensitiveness of sovereign States, the sentence pronounced on the State at fault, must rest upon all desirable guarantees to give it moral force, and consequently to ensure that it is respected and more easily put into execution.

One member of the Committee did not fail to point out that England was the country in which the plaintiff was called upon to produce most proofs and to establish his case most completely, in the event of the defendant's non-appearance. As concerns America the fact was recalled that an action may be brought against a State without its consent before the Supreme Court, and that in these circumstances, a procedure *ex parte* is opened in which the plaintiff is called upon to show that his demands are well founded both in fact and law, with the same care as if his opponent were present in Court.

The Committee, in formulating the following article, drew its inspiration from the example set by English national legal practice, and the legal practice of the American Supreme Court in interstate litigation, arising out of the constitution of the United States.

Article 52.

Whenever one of the parties shall not appear before the Court, or shall fail to defend his case, the other party may call upon the Court to decide in favour of his claim.

The Court must, before doing so, satisfy itself, not only that it has jurisdiction in accordance with Articles 33 and 34, but also that the claim is supported by substantial evidence and well founded in fact and law.

We have now reached the point at which the hearing in Court terminates.

Article 53.

When the agents, advocates and counsel, subject to the control of the Court, have presented

yens qu'ils jugent utiles, le Président prononce la clôture des débats.

La Cour se retire en chambre du conseil pour délibérer.

Les délibérations de la Cour sont et restent secrètes.

Les dispositions de l'article qui précède sont empruntées à la Convention de 1899 sur le règlement pacifique des conflits internationaux (art. 51), à la Convention de 1907 (art. 78) et au projet de Convention pour une Cour de Justice Arbitrale (art. 27). L'art. 51 prévoit une délibération à huis clos ; l'art. 27, de même que l'art. 78, ajoute que la délibération reste secrète. Les deux dispositions sont fondues ensemble dans le dernier alinéa de l'article qui précède. Ces dispositions ne sauraient souffrir de difficulté, mais, une fois la Cour entrée dans la chambre du conseil pour rendre son arrêt, de nombreuses questions se présentent. Les décisions de la Cour seront-elles prises à la majorité des juges tant présents qu'absents, (art. 51, 1899, et art. 78, 1907), ou des juges présents (art. 27, projet de 1907)? Entre ces deux solutions, le grand nombre des juges de la Cour, plus étendu que ceux des juges d'un tribunal temporaire au sein du cadre permanent de la Cour d'Arbitrage, permettait de statuer à la majorité des juges présents.

Si la Cour siège en nombre pair, et qu'il y ait partage de voix, comment obtenir une solution ?

D'après l'article 27 du projet de 1907, la voix du dernier des juges ne serait pas comptée. On avait d'abord pensé à dire en conséquence, qu'ici „le moins ancien des juges serait considéré comme s'abstenant". Mais, à raison de la possibilité pour la Cour de comprendre des juges entrés simultanément sur le siège comme représentants des parties, le même jour, sans qu'on puisse faire de classement entre eux, on a pensé préférable de faire procéder au partage par le Président, auquel est reconnu voix prépondérante.

Article 54.

Les décisions de la Cour sont prises à la majorité des juges présents.

En cas de partage de voix, la voix du Président ou de celui qui le remplace est prépondérante.

all the evidence, and taken all other steps that they consider advisable, the President shall declare the case closed.

The Court shall withdraw to consider the judgment.

The deliberations of the Court shall take place in private and remain secret.

The provisions of the preceding article are taken from the Convention of 1899 for the Pacific Settlement of International Disputes (Art. 51), from the 1907 Convention (Art. 78) and from the draft convention for a Court of Arbitral Justice (Art. 27). Article 51 provides for private deliberations; Article 27, and also Article 78, adds that the proceedings are secret; both provisions are embodied in the last paragraph of the preceding article. These provisions can give rise to no difficulty, but numerous problems arise after the Court has withdrawn to consider the finding. The decisions of the Court are to be taken by a majority of the judges both present and absent (according to Article 51 of 1899, and Article 78 of 1907) or present only (Article 27 of the 1907 draft)? The large number of judges on the Court, which is greater than that of the judges on a temporary tribunal formed out of the permanent list of the Court of Arbitration, allows the latter solution, whereby decisions are taken by a majority of the judges present, to be adopted.

If the Court contains an even number of judges, and the vote is split, how is a result to be obtained?

According to Article 27 of the draft of 1907, the vote of the junior judge would not be counted. It was therefore at first suggested that in this case the „junior judge should be considered as having abstained from exercising his vote". However, as the Court might include judges who had taken their seats simultaneously on the same day as representatives of the parties, so that no distinction could be drawn between them in seniority, it was thought better to overcome the difficulty by giving the President a casting vote.

Article 54.

All questions shall be decided by a majority of the judges present at the hearing.

In the event of an equality of votes, the President or his deputy shall have a casting vote.

S'il est hors de doute que des arrêts de justice doivent être motivés, on pouvait se demander si les juges qui y ont pris part et dont les noms doivent être nécessairement mentionnés ne doivent pas avoir le droit d'exprimer leur dissentiment. Ce droit, qui leur était reconnu à la Cour d'Arbitrage par l'article 52 de la Convention de 1899, leur était refusé à la Cour de Justice par l'article 28 du projet de convention d'une Cour de Justice arbitrale de 1907.

Fallait-il leur donner le droit de mentionner leur dissentiment?

Et dans ce cas, leur donner celui de motiver ce dissentiment?

En 1899 la Convention pour le règlement pacifique des conflits internationaux leur accordait le droit de marquer leur dissentiment, mais sans leur permettre d'exprimer leurs motifs, parce qu'autrement on se serait exposé à avoir, dans chaque affaire, deux jugements et à porter le dissentiment des auteurs de la décision devant l'opinion publique. Mais, en 1907, cette faculté a été supprimée. D'autre part, en 1907, au projet de convention pour une Cour de Justice arbitrale, on a refusé de permettre au juge de marquer son dissentiment, en paraissant croire que, s'il l'indiquait, il aurait, comme dans un jugement interne, le droit de le motiver; le Comité s'est contenté d'accorder au juge le droit d'exprimer son dissentiment, faculté qui lui était refusée par le projet de la Cour de Justice arbitrale de 1907, pour lui donner le même droit qu'aux membres d'un tribunal international créé dans le cadre de la Cour d'Arbitrage de La Haye (art. 52 de la Convention relative au règlement pacifique des conflits internationaux, d'ailleurs retiré; art. 78 et 79 de la Convention de 1907.)

Vainement une opinion s'est-elle fait jour, demandant que le juge ait le droit de donner les motifs de son dissentiment, selon une coutume qui s'est développée, depuis un certain temps, dans la jurisprudence arbitrale; cette proposition n'a pas été accueillie. Il a semblé difficile de permettre aux juges de la nationalité des parties d'entamer de longs plaidoyers en faveur de l'Etat de cette nationalité, alors qu'il avait été débouté. Et, puisqu'on refusait aux juges nationaux le droit de motiver leur dissentiment, on n'a pas voulu que les juges tiers eussent un droit qui manquât aux juges nationaux. La proposition faite par certains

Though there is no doubt that the sentences of a Court must include a statement of reasons, it might be asked whether the judges taking part, whose names must necessarily be mentioned, should not have the right to record their dissent. This right was granted to them in the Court of Arbitration by Article 52 of the Convention of 1899, but was withheld in the case of the Court of Arbitral Justice, by Article 28 of the Draft Convention of 1907 for that Court.

Should they be given the right of recording their dissent?

If so, should they be permitted to state their reasons?

In 1899 the Convention for the Pacific Settlement of International Disputes granted judges the right to record their dissent, but not to explain their reasons, since otherwise there would be a risk in every case of having two verdicts, and the dissent amongst those responsible for the decision would be brought to the notice of the public; this right was withdrawn in 1907. On the other hand, however, in 1907, in the Draft Convention for a Court of Arbitral Justice, the judges were not to be allowed to record their dissent; this was apparently because it was thought that, if the fact of the dissent were recorded, it would follow, as in the case of a decision of national law, that a right to explain the reasons for such dissent would ensue. The Committee contented itself with granting the judge a right to record his dissent; a right which was refused by the draft plan of the Court of Arbitral Justice of 1907, and which is the same as that accorded to the members of an international tribunal formed from the list of the Court of Arbitration of the Hague (Art. 52 of the Convention for the Pacific Settlement of International Disputes of 1899, which Article was withdrawn, Articles 78 and 79 of the 1907 Convention.)

An opinion was vainly put forward, according to which a judge should have the right to give the reasons for his dissent, in accordance with a custom which has grown up lately in the jurisprudence of arbitration; however this proposal was not favorably received. It seemed inadvisable to allow a judge of the same nationality as one of the parties to write long statements in favour of that State after it had lost its case. It followed that, as national judges were not to be given the right to give the reasons for their dissent, it was not thought desirable that other judges should have a right not possessed by national judges. A proposal made by certain

membres du Comité de fermer aux juges de la nationalité des parties la faculté de marquer leur dissentiment afin de leur faciliter l'accomplissement de leur devoir de juge, n'a pas été accueillie, bien qu'elle fût de nature à donner plus de garanties de bonne justice en mettant le juge à l'abri des reproches de son opinion nationale. Une raison pratique a été déterminante: il se peut que, par suite des déclarations de dissentiment des juges, on sache en effet, au simple calcul de la majorité, de quel côté se trouve un juge de la nationalité; il n'y a donc pas, dans ce cas, de raison de ne pas lui permettre de dire franchement, s'il le désire, de quel côté il se trouve; et, s'il le peut en ce cas, pourquoi le lui interdire dans les autres? Le juge de la nationalité des parties ne peut être inégal aux autres.

Article 55.

L'arrêt est motivé.

Il mentionne les noms des juges qui y ont pris part.

Article 56.

Si l'arrêt n'exprime pas, en tout ou en partie, l'opinion unanime des juges, les dissidents ont la faculté de demander que leur opposition ou leurs réserves soient constatées, mais sans indication des motifs.

Ce sont seulement des remaniements de détail au texte de 1899 (art. 53; 1907: art. 80) et au projet des Cinq Puissances (art. 46) qui ont inspiré les variations des dispositions qui suivent:

Article 57.

L'arrêt est signé par le Président et par le Greffier. Il est lu en séance publique, les agents dûment prévenus.

members of the Committee, to the effect that the right of recording their dissent should not be given to national judges, in order to make the performance of their duty as judges easier for them, was not favourably received, though it was calculated to give better security for a just sentence, by shielding the judge from the reproaches of national public opinion.

The deciding factor was a practical reason: it might happen that, as a result of the declaration of dissent recorded by the judges, it would be easy to find out on which side a national judge voted, by a simple calculation of the majority: there is therefore no reason why he should not be allowed, if he so desires, to say frankly on which side he has voted. If he can do so in this case, why should he be forbidden to do so in others? Judges of the nationality of a contesting party cannot be put in a position unequal to that of the other judges

Article 55.

The judgment shall state the reasons on which it is based.

It shall contain the names of the judges who have taken part in the decision.

Article 56.

If the judgment given does not represent, wholly or in part, the unanimous opinion of the judges, the dissenting judges shall be entitled to have the fact of their dissent or reservations mentioned in it. But the reasons in it for their dissent or reservations shall not be expressed in the judgment.

The following articles vary only from the scheme of 1899 (Art. 53; Art. 80 of 1907) and from the Five-Powers-plan (Art. 46) upon points of detail:

Article 57.

The judgment shall be signed by the President and by the Registrar. It shall be read in open Court, due notice having been given to the agents.

Article 58.

L'arrêt est définitif et sans recours. En cas de doute sur le sens et la portée de l'arrêt, il appartient à la Cour de l'interpréter à la demande de toute partie.

La question de la révision figurait dans la Convention pour le règlement pacifique des conflits internationaux de 1899 (art. 55; 1907, art. 83): elle peut être réservée dans le compromis, auquel il appartient de déterminer le délai dans lequel la demande de révision doit être formée. Aucune disposition de ce genre ne se trouve dans le projet d'une Cour de Justice arbitrale. Il faut se prononcer indépendamment de toute décision des parties. Le droit de révision est un droit très grave, qui heurte, avec l'autorité des sentences rendues, ce qui, pour la paix des nations, doit être considérée comme acquis ; mais la justice a cependant ses légitimes revendications. Tout bien pesé, le Comité a estimé que la révision devait être de droit. Ses conditions demeurent les mêmes qu'au cas où (d'après la Convention relative au règlement pacifique des conflits internationaux de 1899, art. 55; 1907, art. 83) le compromis l'autorise; il faut un fait nouveau de nature à exercer une influence décisive et qui, au moment du jugement, était inconnu du tribunal.

Par une amélioration, on ne se contente pas, comme dans l'art. 55 de 1899; (1907, art. 83), d'une non-connaissance de ce fait par la partie que demande la révision, mais on exige que cette ignorance du fait n'engage à aucun degré sa responsabilité, par ce qu'elle n'aura pas manqué, à cette occasion, de faire toute diligence („due diligence''): on a fini, d'ailleurs, par se contenter ici du mot „l'absence de faute".

Aucune indication ne se trouvait, pour les délais de la révision, au texte de 1907: c'est aux parties qu'il appartenait d'en fixer le temps. Dans la nécessité d'en indiquer, abstraction faite de la volonté des parties, le Comité, considérant comme trop courts les délais de 3 et 6 mois mentionnés en 1907, comme trop vague le délai mentionné par l'art. 13 du traité d'arbitrage italo-argentin de 1907, (avant que la sentence soit exécutée) s'est arrêté au terme fixe de cinq ans.

Craignant qu'une partie ne retardât jusqu'à

Article 58.

The judgment is final and without appeal. In the event of uncertainty as to the meaning and scope of the judgment, the Court shall construe it upon the request of any party.

The question of revision was dealt with in the Convention for the Pacific Settlement of International Disputes in 1899 (Art. 55; 1907: Art. 83): it may be reserved in the special agreement (compromis) in which also the period, within which a request for revision must be made, would be fixed. No provision of this kind is to be found in the draft plan for a Court of Arbitral Justice. Decisions must be made regardless of any arrangement made by the parties concerned. The right of revision is a very important right, and affects adversely in the matter of *res judicata*, a point which for the sake of international peace should be considered as finally settled. Justice, however, has certain legitimate requirements; the Committee, after due consideration, decided that there must be a right of revision. The conditions would be the same as in the case in which it was authorised by the "compromis" (according to the Convention for the Pacific Settlement of International Disputes of 1899, Art. 55; Art. 83 of the 1907 Convention); a new fact is required which is of a nature to exercise a decisive influence, and which, before pronouncement of sentence, was unknown to the Court.

An improvement is introduced whereby the Committee, not content as in Art. 55 of 1899 (Art. 83 of 1907), with ignorance of the fact on the part of the party requesting revision, stipulates that such ignorance must not be due to a failure on the part of the party to use due diligence in the conduct of the case. Eventually the words: "not due to negligence" were considered sufficient.

No time limit for revision was given in the provisions of 1907; it was for the parties to fix this time limit. As it was necessary to lay down a limit, since the matter should not to be left to the free will of the parties, the Committee decided upon a limit of five years; it considered the three to six months' limit mentioned in 1907 to be too short, and the period mentioned in Art. 13 of the Arbitration Treaty between Italy and the Argentine in 1907, in which revision may be applied for at any time before the execution of the sentence, as too vague.

Fearing that a party might delay compli-

ce moment l'exécution d'un arrêt de la Cour sous prétexte que dans ce délai un fait nouveau pouvait être découvert qui en entrainât le retrait, le Comité a jugé utile de donner à la Cour le pouvoir, non prévu en 1907, de refuser de statuer sur la demande de révision, tant que l'exécution préalable de l'arrêt de la Cour n'aurait pas été obtenue.

Article 59.

La révision de l'arrêt ne peut être éventuellement demandée à la Cour qu'à raison de la découverte d'un fait nouveau de nature à exercer une influence décisive et qui, avant le prononcé de l'arrêt, était inconnue de la Cour et de la partie qui demande la révision, sans qu'il y ait, de sa part, faute à l'ignorer.

La procédure de révision s'ouvre par un arrêt de la Cour constatant expressément l'existence du fait nouveau, lui reconnaissant les caractères qui donnent ouverture à la révision et déclarant de ce chef la demande recevable.

La Cour peut subordonner l'ouverture de la procédure en révision à l'exécution préalable de l'arrêt.

Aucune demande de révision ne peut être formée après l'expiration d'un délai de cinq ans.

Enfin une question qui dans le projet de Cour de Justice Arbitrale de 1907, projet nécessairement très court pour des raisons déjà dites, n'était pas même mentionnée, et qui, dans la Convention relative au règlement pacifique des Conflits de 1899 n'était qu'accessoirement envisagée à propos de l'effet de chose jugée et du caractère obligatoire des sentences arbitrales (art. 56; 1907, art. 84) vient ici d'une manière directe: c'est celle du droit d'intervention.

Trois cas peuvent se présenter: une partie peut vouloir se ranger, soit près du demandeur, soit près du défendeur. Une partie peut faire valoir certains droits qui lui sont propres. Une partie peut demander que l'un des deux Etats en cause disparaisse parce qu'il n'est pas le véritable *dominus* du droit qu'il revendique. Dans ce cas l'intervention tend à l'exclusion, mais le plus souvent un Etat se borne à joindre son assistance à celle de l'une des parties: doit-on le lui permettre? Oui, répond le Comité,

ance with a sentence until the expiration of this period, on the ground that during this period some new fact might be discovered which would lead to a reversal of the sentence, the Committee considered it advisable to give the Court the power, not provided for in 1907, of refusing to grant the request for revision, until the sentence of the Court has been carried out.

Article 59.

An application for revision of a judgment can be made only when it is based upon the discovery of some new fact, of such a nature as to be a decisive factor, which fact was, when the judgment was given, unknown to the Court and also to the party claiming revision, always provided that such ignorance was not due to negligence.

The proceedings for revision will be opened by a judgment of the Court expressly recording the existence of the new fact, recognising that it has such a character as to lay the case open to revision, and declaring the application admissible on this ground.

The Court may require previous compliance with the terms of the judgment before it admits proceedings in revision.

No application for revision may be made after the lapse of five years from the date of the sentence.

Lastly, the question of the right of intervention, a question which was not even mentioned in the project of the Court of Arbitral Justice of 1907, which was necessarily very short for reasons already given, and which question was only incidentally dealt with by the Convention for the Pacific Settlement of International Disputes of 1899 in connection with the force of the *res judicata* and the compulsory character of sentences by arbitration (Art. 56; Art. 84 of the 1907 Convention), is dealt with explicitly in this plan.

There are three possibilities: a party may wish to take sides with the plaintiff or the defendant; a party may claim certain exclusive rights; or a party may request that one of the two contesting States should withdraw on the ground that it is not the real *dominus* of the right which it claims. In this latter case intervention tends to become exclusion, but as a rule a State is content to take joint action with one of the parties: should this be allowed? The Committee replies in the affirma-

mais à la condition qu'il s'agisse d'un intérêt d'ordre juridique. La Cour statue sur la légitimité de cet intérêt, et, par suite, sur la recevabilité de l'intervention. Dénier absolument l'intervention pourrait avoir des conséquences fâcheuses. L'essentiel est de la limiter aux cas d'intérêt d'ordre juridique, pour exclure l'intervention politique, et d'en faire juge la Cour.

Il y a de plus un cas où la Cour ne saurait refuser la demande d'intervention ; c'est lorsqu'il s'agit l'interprétation d'une Convention à laquelle ont participé d'autres Etats que les parties en litige; chacun d'eux a le droit d'intervenir au procès. S'il exerce ce droit, l'interprétation contenue dans l'arrêt devient obligatoire entre lui et les autres parties en cause.

Lorsqu'il s'agit de traités collectifs, on peut obtenir ainsi très promptement des interprétations générales, en harmonie avec le caractère de la Convention.

Article 61.

Lorsqu'il s'agit de l'interprétation d'une Convention à laquelle ont participé d'autres Etats que les parties en litige, le Greffe avertit sans délai tous les signataires.

Chacun d'eux a le droit d'intervenir au procès, et, s'il exerce cette faculté, l'interprétation contenue dans la sentence est également obligatoire à son égard.

Reste la question des frais par laquelle se termine toute la série des dispositions relatives à la procédure Elle est prévue par l'article 29 du projet de Cour de Justice arbitrale de 1907 en ces termes: „Chaque partie supporte ses propres frais et une part égale des frais spéciaux de l'instance".

Elle se trouve résolue par le Comité d'une manière légèrement différente.

Article 62.

S'il n'en est autrement décidé par la Cour, chaque partie supporte ses frais de procédure.

tive, but on condition that an interest of a legal nature is involved. The Court is to decide whether the interest is legitimate and consequently whether the intervention is admissible. To refuse all right of intervention, might have unfortunate results. The essential point is to limit it to cases in which an interest of a legal nature can be shown, so that political intervention will be excluded, and to give the Court the right of decision.

Further there is one case in which the Court cannot refuse a request to be allowed to intervene; that is in questions concerning the interpretation of a Convention in which States, other than the contesting parties, have taken part; each of these is to have the right to intervene in the case. If such a State uses this right, the interpretation contained in the sentence becomes binding between it and the other parties to the case.

Where collective treaties are concerned, general interpretations can thus be obtained very quickly, which harmonise with the character of the Convention.

Article 61.

Whenever the construction of a convention in which States, other than those concerned in the case, are parties, is in question, the Registrar shall notify all such States forthwith.

Every State so notified has the right to intervene in the proceedings: but if it uses this right, the construction given by the judgment will be as binding upon it as upon the original parties to the dispute.

There remains the question of expenses which ends the series of provisions dealing with procedure. The question was dealt with in Art. 29 of the Draft for the Court of Arbitral Justice as follows: "Each party pays its own costs and an equal share of the costs of the trial".

The Committee dealt with the question in a slightly different way.

Article 62.

Unless otherwise decided by the Court, each party shall bear its own costs.

VOEUX.

Au moment de se séparer, le Comité a, à l'unanimité, adopté les trois Voeux qui suivent, tous en connexion étroite avec l'objet direct de ses travaux, et dont les deux premiers s'adressent au Conseil de la Société des Nations.

PREMIER VOEU.

Le Comité Consultatif de Juristes, réuni à la Haye pour élaborer le statut d'une Cour Permanente de Justice Internationale;

Convaincu que la sécurité des Etats et le bien-être des peuples exigent impérieusement l'extention de l'empire du droit et le développement des jurisdictions internationales;

Recommande:

I. Qu'une nouvelle Conférence des Etats faisant suite aux deux premières Conférences de la Haye, soit réunie dans le plus bref délai possible, en vue:

1. *de raffermir les règles existantes du droit des gens, spécialement et d'abord dans les domaines affectés par les évènements de la récente guerre;*
2. *de formuler et sanctionner les modifications et additions dont la nécessité ou l'utilité s'est révélée à l'occasion de la guerre et à raison des changements des conditions de la vie internationale qui ont suivi ce grand conflit;*
3. *de concilier les vues divergentes et de ménager une entente générale relativement aux règles qui ont donné lieu à controverse;*
4. *de prendre en considération toute spéciale les points qui, actuellement, ne sont pas réglés d'une manière adéquate et dont la justice internationale réclame la détermination précise dans une entente commune.*

II. Que l'Institut de Droit international, l'American Institute of International Law, l'Union juridique internationale, l'International Law Association et l'Institut ibérique de droit comparé, soient invités à instituer tel mode de travail ou de collaboration qui leur paraîtra convenable afin de préparer pour la réalisation de cette œuvre,

RESOLUTIONS.

Before breaking up, the Committee unanimously adopted the three following Resolutions, all of which are closely associated with the object of its labours, and of which the two first are addressed to the Council of the League of Nations.

FIRST RESOLUTION.

The Advisory Committee of Jurists, assembled at the Hague, to prepare the constituent Statute of a Permanent Court of International Justice;

Convinced that the extention of the sway of Justice and the development of international jurisdictions are urgently required to ensure the security of States and well-being of the Nations;

Recommend that:

I. A new interstate Conference, to carry on the work of the two first Conferences at the Hague, should be called as soon as possible for the purpose of:

1. *Re-establishing the existing rules of the Law of Nations, more especially and in the first place, those affected by the events of the recent War;*
2. *Formulating and approving the modifications and additions rendered necessary or advisable by the War, and by the changes in the conditions of international life following upon this great struggle;*
3. *Reconciling divergent opinions, and bringing about a general understanding concerning the rules which have been the subject of controversy;*
4. *Giving special consideration to those points, which are not at the present time adequately provided for, and of which a definite settlement by general agreement is required in the interests of international justice.*

II. That the Institute of International Law, the American Institute of International Law, the Union juridique internationale, the International Law Association and the Iberian Institute of Comparative Law should be invited to adopt any method, or use any system of collaboration that they may think fit, with a view to

des avant-projets qui, d'abord soumis aux divers Gouvernements, seraient ensuite présentés à la Conférence.

III. Que la Conférence nouvelle prenne le nom de Conférence pour l'avancement du droit international.

IV. Que cette Conférence soit suivi de Conférences périodiques semblables, assez rapprochées pour permettre de continuer, en toute opportunité et fécondité, l'œuvre entreprise, dans ce qu'elle aura d'inachevé.

DEUXIEME VOEU.

Le Comité Consultatif de Juristes, réuni à la Haye pour élaborer le statut d'une Cour Permanente de Justice Internationale,

Saisi par son président d'une proposition concernant, pour l'avenir, l'établissement d'une Haute Cour de Justice Internationale, formulée en ces termes:

„Article 1.

Il est institué une Haute Cour de Justice Internationale.

Article 2.

Cette Cour se compose d'un membre par Etat respectivement, choisi par le groupe des délégués de chaque Etat à la Cour d'Arbitrage.

Article 3.

La Haute Cour de Justice Internationale sera compétente pour juger les crimes contre l'ordre public international et le droit des gens universel, qui lui seront déférés par l'Assemblée plénière de la Société des Nations ou par le Conseil de cette Société.

Article 4.

La Cour possédera un pouvoir appréciateur pour caractériser le délit, fixer la peine et déterminer les moyens appropriés à l'exécution de la sentence. Elle détermine la procédure à suivre dans ce cas, par son règlement d'ordre intérieur."

Reconnaissant toute l'importance de cette proposition,

the preparation of draft plans to be submitted, first to the various Governments, and then to the Conference, for the realisation of this work.

III. That the new Conference should be called the Conference for the advancement of international Law.

IV. That this Conference should be followed by periodical similar Conferences, at intervals sufficiently short to enable the work undertaken to be continued, in so far as it may be incomplete, with every prospect of success.

SECOND RESOLUTION.

The Advisory Committee of Jurists assembled at the Hague to prepare the constituent Statute of a Permanent Court of International Justice;

Having had laid before it by its President a proposition for the establishment for the future, of a High Court of International Justice;

Recognising the great importance of this proposition;

Recommends it to the consideration of the Nations.

This proposition is conceived as follows:

„Article 1.

A High Court of International Justice is hereby established.

Article 2.

This Court shall be composed of one Member for each State, to be chosen by the group of Delegates of each State on the Court of Arbitration.

Article 3.

The High Court of International Justice shall be competent to try crimes constituting a breach of International public order or against the universal law of nations, referred to it by the Assembly or by the Council of the League of Nations.

Article 4.

The Court shall have the power to define the nature of the crime, to fix the penalty and to decide the appropriate means of carrying out the sentence. It shall formulate its own rules of procedure."

En recommande l'examen au Conseil et à l'Assemblée de la Société des Nations.

TROISIEME VOEU.

Le Comité Consultatif de Juristes, réuni à la Haye pour élaborer le statut d'une Cour Permanente de Justice Internationale,

Saisit, avec satisfaction, cette occasion d'exprimer le vœu que l'Académie de Droit International fondée à la Haye en 1913, et dont le fonctionnement a été arrêté par les circonstances, entre aussi prochainement que possible en activité, à côté de la Cour Permanente d'Arbitrage et de la Cour Permanente de Justice Internationale, au Palais de la Paix, à la Haye.

THIRD RESOLUTION.

The Advisory Committee of Jurists assembled at the Hague to prepare the constituent Statute of a Permanent Court of International Justice;

Gladly takes this opportunity of recording a wish that the Academy of International Law, founded at the Hague in 1913, and of which the work has been suspended owing to circumstances, may be set in operation in as near a future as possible, side by side with the Permanent Court of International Justice and the Permanent Court of Arbitration, at the Peace Palace at the Hague.

35IÈME SÉANCE (publique), tenue au Palais de la Paix, à La Haye, le 24 juillet 1920.

Présidence de M. le BARON DESCAMPS.

Sont présents: M. le Jonkheer van Karnebeek, Ministre des Affaires Etrangères des Pays-Bas; tous les membres du Comité (à l'exception de M. Bevilaqua); M. Fernandes et les membres du Secrétariat.

La séance est ouverte à 3 heures de l'après-midi.

Le PRESIDENT donne lecture du télégramme suivant qui lui a été adressé par M. LÉON BOURGEOIS:

Paris, le 23 juillet 1920.

„De la part de M. Léon Bourgeois, pour le Baron Descamps, Président du Comité des Juristes. Très urgent.

Retenu au Sénat par discussion quotidienne du budget, je regrette profondément de ne pouvoir répondre à l'invitation du Comité des Juristes, assister demain à la séance officielle de clôture de ses travaux, et lui apporter moi-même l'expression de tous les remerciements du Conseil. Je n'ai pas encore reçu connaissance des projets adoptés par le Comité, mais l'autorité incontestée des membres qui le composent nous assure que ses résolutions apporteront au Conseil de la Société des Nations tous les éléments nécessaires à la constitution prochaine de la grande institution qui doit contribuer si puissamment à assurer l'empire du droit dans le monde."

Le Président prononce ensuite le discours qui se trouve reproduit à l'annexe 1ère.

M. VAN KARNEBEEK répond au nom du Gouvernement de Sa Majesté la Reine des Pays-Bas. (Voir annexe 2).

La séance est levée à 3.20 heures de l'après-midi.

Le Président:
(signé) Brn. DESCAMPS.

Le Secrétaire-Général:
(signé) D. ANZILOTTI.

35TH MEETING (Public), held at the Peace Palace, the Hague, on July 24th, 1920.

BARON DESCAMPS in the chair.

Present: M. the Jonkheer van Karnebeek, Minister of Foreign Affairs of the Netherlands; all the members of the Committee (with the exception of M. Bevilaqua); M. Fernandes, and the members of the Secretariat.

The meeting opened at 3 p.m.

The PRESIDENT read the following telegram, which he had received from M. LÉON BOURGEOIS:

Paris, July 23rd, 1920.

"From M. Léon Bourgeois to Baron Descamps, President of the Jurists Committee. Very urgent.

Detained in the Senate by the continued discussion of the budget, I deeply regret not to be able to accept the invitation of the Jurists' Committee to be present to-morrow at the official session terminating their labours, and not to be able to convey to them personally the thanks of the Council. I have not yet been informed of the plan adopted by the Committee, but the unquestioned authority of its members is an assurance that its resolutions will lay before the Council of the League of Nations all the points necessary for the establishment in the near future of the great institution which will do so much to assure the sway of justice throughout the world".

The President then read the speech contained in the Annex 1.

M. VAN KARNEBEEK replied on behalf of the Government of Her Majesty the Queen of the Netherlands. (See Annex 2).

The meeting closed at 3.20 p.m.

The President:
(signed) Brn. DESCAMPS.

The Secretary-General:
(signed) D. ANZILOTTI.

ANNEXE No. 1.

Discours du Baron Descamps.

Lorsque le Comité international des Jurisconsultes nommé par le Conseil de la Société des Nations pour élaborer un projet d'organisation d'une Cour Permanente de Justice International, se réunit pour la première fois en séance publique dans ce palais, l'impression dominante de tous ses membres était celle de la rédoutable responsabilité qu'ils avaient assumée.

A coup sûr, nous avions la bonne volonté d'aboutir, mais nous savions que les meilleures intentions et les efforts les plus soutenus, ne sont pas toujours suffisants pour arriver à des résultats désirés.

Nous avions la claire-vue du but à atteindre, mais le chemin à parcourir pour y arriver était long, et il nous apparaissait comme semé de tant d'obstacles que nous pouvions nous demander s'il nous serait donné de les surmonter.

Les efforts tentés en 1907 par l'Assemblée mondiale des Puissances, dans l'ordre de l'organisation d'une Cour Permanente de Justice Arbitrale et dans l'ordre de la juridiction obligatoire, étaient là d'ailleurs pour augmenter nos appréhensions.

Tenant compte de la grandeur de la tâche à accomplir et du progrès qu'il s'agissait de réaliser pour le bien de toutes les nations, nous nous sommes mis à l'œuvre, nous gardant de ce scepticisme *à priori* qui est de mise chez d'aucuns, mais appliquant à l'étude des problèmes qui se posaient devant nous le doute méthodique de Descartes, qui, bien appliqué, est un puissant instrument de lumière et le plus sûr garant de positifs résultats.

Nous avons commencé par de longs échanges de vue, nous avons passé au crible du plus sévère examen nos opinions, parfois divergentes. Et c'est dans une atmosphère de vivante et libre critique que sont nées et qu'ont grandi chez nous les espérances d'une entente commune.

Nous ne pouvons certes nous flatter d'avoir réalisé une œuvre parfaite. La matière ne paraît pas le comporter, et sans doute, il convient de nous rappeler ici cette topique parole de Portalis dans le discours préliminaire du Code civil: „Il est absurde de se livrer à des idées absolues de perfection dans des choses qui ne sont susceptibles que d'une bonté relative". Mais nous avons

ANNEX No. 1

Address of Baron Descamps.

When the International Committee of Jurisconsults, appointed by the Council of the League of Nations to prepare a plan for the organisation of a Permanent Court of International Justice, met for the first time in public session in this palace, the dominating impression of all the members was that of the enormous responsibility which they had assumed.

Assuredly, we were animated by a keen desire to succeed, but nevertheless, we knew that the best intentions and the most earnest efforts are not always sufficient to bring about the desired results.

We had a very clear idea of the end in view, but the road which had to be followed in order to reach it was a long one, and it appeared to us to be sewn with so many obstacles, that we might well ask ourselves if it would be given to us to surmount them.

The efforts made in 1907 by an Assembly of the Powers of the world with a view to the organisation of a Permanent Court of Arbitral Justice and to the creation of obligatory jurisdiction were also calculated to increase our apprehensions.

Bearing in mind the grandeur of our task and the progress which we were called upon to achieve for the benefit of all nations, we devoted ourselves to our work, taking care to avoid a certain *a priori* scepticism which some affect, but applying to the study of the problems which lay before us Descartes' methodical caution which, when properly applied, is a very efficient means of throwing light upon doubtful points and the surest guarantee of attaining tangible results.

We commenced by a lengthy interchange of ideas and subjected our opinions, which sometimes differed widely, to severe cross-examination. In this atmosphere of free and active criticism our hope of obtaining general agreement gradually materialised and took definite shape.

We cannot certainly flatter ourselves that we have achieved a faultless piece of work. The subject — matter does not indeed permit of that, and doubtless at this juncture it is fitting to recall that very apt remark made by Portalis in the introductory speech of the Code civil: "It is absurd to indulge in ideas of absolute

la conscience de pouvoir proposer aux Etats un système général de justice internationale, dont la projection sur l'avenir nous semble devoir être heureuse et largement féconde.

Dans l'élaboration à laquelle nous nous sommes livrés, nous avons estimé ne pas devoir nous enfermer dans une tour d'ivoire inaccessible aux simples mortels. Nous nous félicitons d'avoir tenu le grand public au courant de nos discussions. Aujourd'hui que ces discussions sont terminées, tout en réservant à nos mandants, comme il convient, la primeur des 62 articles qui forment le statut composé par nous, nous croyons pouvoir répondre à l'attention mondiale en résumant d'ensemble ce que la presse a déjà publié et en esquissant d'une manière générale le système de nos travaux.

Trois grands problèmes ont surtout été examinés par nous.

Le premier est celui de l'organisation de la Cour de justice internationale. Il nous a paru nécessaire de marquer d'abord nettement la place occupée par l'institution nouvelle parmi les offices qui composent la juridiction internationale. Il s'agit de constituer une Cour de justice vraiment permanente, directement accessible aux parties, et formant un corps de magistrats indépendants, choisis sans égard à leur nationalité parmi les personnes jouissant de la plus haute considération morale et qui réunissent les conditions exigées dans leurs pays respectifs pour l'exercice de plus hautes fonctions judiciaires, ou sont des jurisconsultes possédant une compétence notoire en matière de droit international.

C'est une institution existante et qui a fait ses preuves, la Cour actuelle d'Arbitrage de La Haye, que nous avons pris pour base de l'édifice nouveau à construire, en ce sens que nous avons estimé qu'il y avait lieu de confier aux membres de cette Cour, la tâche de procéder, par groupes nationaux, à la présentation limitée de personnes en situation de remplir les fonctions de membres de la Cour. Et nous avons demandé à chaque groupe national, afin qu'il s'éclaire dans ses choix, de consulter, dans chaque pays, la plus haute Cour de justice, les facultés et écoles de droit, les académies nationales, et les sections nationales d'Académies internationales vouées à l'étude du droit.

Deux noms doivent être choisis par chacun de ces groupes nationaux sans distinction de nationalité.

Quant au choix définitif, il est attribué à l'Assemblée et au Conseil de la Société des Nations, de telle manière que l'élection des membres de

perfection when considering problems which are only capable of a relatively satisfactory solution". But nevertheless we feel that we can propose to the nations a general system of international justice which should, in our opinion, prosper and bear very fruitful results in the future.

In setting ourselves to the working out of this plan, we decided that we should not lock ourselves up in a secret chamber inaccessible to the ordinary man. We are glad indeed to have kept the general public in touch with our discussions. Now that these discussions are terminated and whilst reserving, as is only right, the 62 Articles forming the project drawn up by us to be communicated in the first place to the authority from which we derive our powers, we believe that nevertheless we can respond to the universal interest shown by giving a summary of that which the Press has already published and by outlining in a general way the system of our work.

Three great problems particularly called for our consideration.

The first was that of the organisation of the Court of International Justice. It appeared to us necessary, at the outset, to indicate clearly the position to be taken by the new institution amongst the various bodies which together go to make up international jurisdiction. It was a question of creating a really permanent Court of Justice, directly accessible to the parties and composed of magistrates who should be independent, chosen without regard to their nationality amongst persons of high moral character and fulfilling the conditions required in their respective countries for appointment to the highest judicial offices, or being jurisconsults of recognised competence in International Law.

We have taken an existing institution which has proved its worth — the present Court of Arbitration of the Hague —, as a foundation for the new organisation in the sense that we have thought fit to entrust to the members of this Court the task of undertaking, by national groups, the nomination of a limited number of candidates in a position to undertake the duties of members of the Court. And we have asked the national groups, in order to secure the best advice in its choice, to consult, in their respective countries the Highest Court of Justice, the Faculties and Schools of law, the national Academies and the national sections of international Academies devoted to the study of law.

Two names are to be chosen by each of these national groups regardless of nationality.

The final choice, however, is left to the As-

la Cour ne puisse résulter que de l'action concordante de l'une et de l'autre.

Nous avons ensuite adopté un ensemble de dispositions, qui, d'une part, orientent les choix vers la réprésentation des grandes formes de civilisation et des principaux systèmes juridiques du monde, de manière à conserver à la Cour une physionomie vraiment mondiale, et qui, d'autre part, pourvoient au cas ou l'accord ne s'établirait pas d'emblée entre le Conseil et l'Assemblée.

En ce qui concerne le fonctionnement de la Cour, nous avons prévu la formation annuelle d'une chambre de trois juges appelée à statuer en procédure sommaire, lorsque les parties le demanderont.

La seconde question capitale sur laquelle devait naturellement se porter notre attention, c'était la compétence de la Cour. Notre effort principal a porté sur deux points: d'abord la réalisation d'un système de juridiction obligatoire concernant les différends d'ordre juridique, et par extension, tous autres différends en tant qu'ils peuvent faire l'objet de conventions soit générales, soit spéciales entre les parties. Les déclarations faites et les engagements pris par la seconde Conférence de la Paix en 1907 ont été dans cet ordre le point de départ de nos travaux.

Nous avons ensuite essayé de déterminer les règles d'interprétation juridique dont le juge doit faire application dans l'examen des causes qui lui sont soumises.

Un troisième point a été de notre part l'objet d'une attention particulière: la procédure devant la Cour. Nous croyons avoir résolu dans cet ordre, d'une manière satisfaisante, d'assez nombreuses questions, notamment quant aux mesures conservatoires à indiquer au début de certaines contestations, quant à l'intervention des tiers dans les litiges entre parties contendantes, quant aux conditions dans lesquelles peuvent être rendus les jugements par défaut.

Si nous ajoutons à ces dispositions contenues dans le statut organique, deux recommandations concernant d'une part, la continuation méthodique de l'œuvre entreprise par les premières conférences de La Haye pour l'avancement du droit international, d'autre part, l'institution d'une Haute Cour de justice internationale chargée de juger les crimes contre l'ordre public international et contre le droit des gens universel, et le vœu formulé par nous concernant le prochain fonctionnement de l'académie de Droit international fondée à La Haye, nous aurons donné un aperçu du cadre dans lequel s'est développée notre activité.

L'accueil qui nous a été fait dans la capi-

sembly and the Council of the League of Nations and is carried out in such a way that the election of the members of the Court is dependent on the joint action of both of these bodies.

Moreover we have adopted a series of provisions which, on the one hand, tend to influence the selection so that the main forms of civilisation and the principal legal systems of the world will be represented, in order to make the Court a really representative world-tribunal and, on the other hand, provide for the contingency of possible failure on the part of the Council and the Assembly to come to a complete understanding.

As regards the working of the Court, we have provided for the annual formation of a chamber of three judges for the purpose of hearing cases by summary procedure when the parties so request.

The second main question, to which our attention was naturally called, was the jurisdiction of the Court.

Our main efforts were directed towards the achievement of two objects: first, the introduction of a system of compulsory jurisdiction in disputes of a legal nature which should also be applicable to all other cases in so far as they may be covered by general or particular conventions between the parties. The declarations made and the engagements entered into by the second Peace Conference in 1907 served as a starting point for our efforts in this direction.

Next we attempted to lay down the rules of juridical interpretation to be applied by the judges in the examination of cases submitted to them.

The third point to which we devoted particular attention, was the procedure before the Court. We believe that we have satisfactorily solved a considerable number of problems in this connection, especially with regard to the provisional measures to be suggested at the outset of certain cases, with regard to the intervention of third parties in disputes, and with regard to the conditions under which judgment may be passed by default.

Add to the provisions, contained in the project itself, two recommendations, the first advocating the methodical continuation of the work commenced by the first Hague Conferences for the advancement of international law, and the second, the creation of a High Court of International Justice to try future crimes against international welfare and the universal law of nations, and finally, the recommendation which we drew up advocating that of the Academy of

tale des Pays-Bas par Sa Majesté la Reine, les multiples et cordiales attentions dont nous avons été l'objet de la part de Monsieur le Ministre des Affaires Etrangères et du Vice-Président de notre Comité, comme de tant d'autres personnes et institutions dont les noms se pressent en ce moment sur mes lèvres, nous imposent l'agréable devoir d'exprimer ici des sentiments de profonde gratitude. Nous ne doutons pas que le Conseil de la Société des Nations ne se joigne à nous pour exprimer à son tour toute sa reconnaissance pour l'accueil fait à ses mandataires. Nous formons le vœu que notre séjour sur le sol néerlandais demeure fécond pour le bien-être du pays qui nous a si aimablement accueillis, pour le rapprochement des peuples dans l'ordre de la justice internationale, et pour le bien-être de l'humanité.

international law at the Hague should be set in operation as soon as possible, — and we shall then have a general idea of the scope of our efforts. The welcome given to us in the capital of the Netherlands by Her Majesty the Queen, the many friendly attentions paid us by the Foreign Minister and the Vice-President of our Committee, as well as by a large number of other persons and institutions, whose names I could mention, impose upon us the pleasant duty of taking this opportunity of expressing our deep sense of gratitude. We do not doubt that the Council of the League of Nations will join with us, and give expression, in its turn, to its gratitude for the reception accorded to its representatives. We earnestly hope that our stay upon Dutch soil may bear fruit which will benefit the Country which has given us such a welcome, and will tend to a better understanding between peoples based on the conception of international justice, and to the good of humanity.

ANNEXE No. 2.

Discours de M. van Karnebeek.

Messieurs,

Avant que cette séance soit levée, je tiens à vous adresser, Messieurs, quelques paroles pour vous traduire les sentiments qui animent le Gouvernement de la Reine à l'heure de la séparation.

Le peuple néerlandais, heureux et fier de votre présence en ces lieux, a suivi vos travaux avec un vif intérêt. Les communiqués intéressants qui en indiquaient régulièrement le progrès, en signalant à la fois la nature et la portée de vos délibérations, ont permis au public de se faire une idée de votre tâche et d'apprécier le succès qui a couronné vos efforts assidus. Permettez-moi de vous féliciter d'avoir abouti en élaborant d'un commun accord un projet auquel, j'espère, la Société des Nations donnera son adhésion et assurera une réalisation prochaine.

Il ne m'appartient pas à l'heure présente de m'étendre sur les mérites de votre œuvre. Permettez-moi, cependant, de vous dire que l'honneur que vous avez fait à mon pays en désignant dans votre projet la ville où vous vous êtes réunis, comme le siège futur de la Cour de Justice, a été vivement apprécié. Votre résolution unanime à cet égard, a ému mes compatriotes, et je me fais l'interprête de leur désir sincère d'entourer la grande institution de Justice mondiale, dont vous avez élaboré le statut, de toutes les marques de respect et d'attachement qu'un peuple, heureux de servir la cause du droit international de toutes ses forces, est capable de donner en obéissant à des traditions respectables et vivantes. Le vœu, que vous avez formulé, relatif à la convocation régulière de conférences internationales, appelées à faire suite aux deux premières conférences de La Haye, et celui qui a trait à la mise en activité de l'Académie de Droit International, fondée à La Haye en 1913, évoquent de précieux souvenirs qui nous sont chers. Si ces vœux se réalisent, Votre Conférence, Messieurs, aura contribué largement à entourer la Cour de Justice d'un système de lois internationales et de notions juridiques, dont l'ensemble est indispensable à l'établissement du règne du droit dans les rapports internationaux. Je tiens à vous assurer, que le Gouvernement de la Reine se fera un devoir de répondre à l'appel que vous avez fait à son concours et à sa collaboration.

ANNEX No. 2.

Speech of M. van Karnebeek.

Gentlemen,

Before this meeting ends, I wish to address to you on your departure a few words on behalf of the Government of H. M. the Queen.

The Dutch people, glad and proud that you should have honoured the Hague with your presence, has followed the course of your work with keen interest. The interesting communiqués, which have indicated regularly the progress made and the nature and scope of your deliberations, have enabled the public to form an idea of your task and to appreciate the success which has crowned your concentrated efforts. Allow me to congratulate you upon having succeeded in preparing a plan based on a unanimous agreement, which, I hope, the League of Nations will accept and put into execution in the near future.

It is not for me, at this time, to discourse upon the merits of your work. Allow me, however, to say that the honour you have done to my country by naming the city, in which you have met, as the future seat of the Court of Justice has been highly appreciated. Your unanimous resolution to this effect has moved my fellow-countrymen deeply, and I wish to say, on their behalf, that they are sincerely desirous of surrounding the great institution for the administration of Justice throughout the world, the Statute for which you have prepared, with all the marks of respect and affection which a Nation, glad to serve the interests of International Justice to the utmost of its power, and inspired by worthy and living traditions, can show.

The resolution you have drawn up concerning the periodical convocation of International Conferences to carry on the work of the two first Conferences at the Hague, and that referring to the setting in motion of the Academy of International Law, founded at the Hague in 1913, awakes memories which are very dear to us.

If these resolutions produce the desired results, your Conference, Gentlemen, will have contributed largely towards supplying the Court of Justice with a system of international rules of law and juridical conceptions which is indispensable to the establishment of Justice as governing international affairs. I can assure you, that the

En vous remerciant, Monsieur le Président, des aimables paroles que vous avez eues à l'égard du pays que je représente, je voudrais exprimer, en terminant, de mon côté, le vœu, que vous voudrez bien, en quittant, réserver parmi vos souvenirs une place modeste au pays qui a été heureux de mettre ses ressources et son hospitalité à la disposition de Votre Conférence. Vous y avez été les bienvenus, et c'est avec regret que nous vous voyons partir.

Soyez-en convaincus, Messieurs, Sa Majesté la Reine sera touchée par l'hommage de reconnaissance que vous lui avez adressé, Monsieur le Président, et dont je ne manquerai pas d'être l'interprête au près d'Elle.

Queen's Government will make it its duty to respond to your call for assistance and collaboration.

I thank you, Monsieur le President, for your kind references to my country and, before closing my remarks, I venture to express the hope that you will, on your departure, keep in remembrance the Country which has been glad to put its resources and hospitality at the disposal of your Conference. You have been most welcome and we much regret your departure.

Rest assured, Gentlemen, that Her Majesty the Queen will be deeply touched by the homage and thanks to which you have given expression, Monsieur le President, and which I shall not fail to communicate to Her.

LISTE DES ANNEXES.

(Les chiffres romains indiquent le numéro de la Séance au Procès-verbal de laquelle les annexes respectives sont attachées. Les chiffres arabes indiquent le numéro de l'annexe parmi les annexes attachées au Procès-verbal d'une certaine Séance.)

LIST OF ANNEXES.

(Roman figures indicate the number of the Meeting to the Procès-verbal of which the respective annexes are attached. Arabic figures indicate the number of the annex among the annexes attached to the Procès-verbal of a given Meeting.)

INDEX ANALYTIQUE.

A.

B.

C.

D.

E.

F.

G.

H.

I.

J.

K.

L.

M.

N.

O.

P.

Q.

R.

S.

T.

U.

V.

W.

ANALYTICAL INDEX.

A.

B.

C.

Q.

R.

S.

T.

U.

V.

W.

Table des Matières.

Contents.

www.ingramcontent.com/pod-product-compliance
Lightning Source LLC
LaVergne TN
LVHW080751300926
849162LV00008BA/1794